Psychology

Danae L. Hudson
Missouri State University

Brooke L. Whisenhunt
Missouri State University

 Pearson

Executive Courseware Portfolio Manager: Erin Mitchell
Content Producer: Lisa Mafrici
Content Developer: Julie Kelly
Portfolio Manager Assistant: Louis Fierro
Content Producer Manager: Amber Mackey
Senior Executive Product Marketing Manager:
   Chris Brown
Associate Director of Design: Blair Brown
Design Lead: Kathryn Foot

Technical Manager: Caroline Fenton
Digital Producer: Lindsay Verge
Full-Service Project Management/Composition:
   Gina Linko/Integra
Compositor: Integra
Printer/Binder: Menasha/Sharon Bower
Cover Printer: Phoenix/Mark Jordan
Cover Design: Noma Bar, Pentagram

Credits and acknowledgments borrowed from other sources and reproduced, with permission, in this textbook appear on appropriate page within text (or on pages).

Copyright © 2019 by Pearson Education, Inc. All rights reserved. Printed in the United States of America. This publication is protected by copyright, and permission should be obtained from the publisher prior to any prohibited reproduction, storage in a retrieval system, or transmission in any form or by any means, electronic, mechanical, photocopying, recording, or otherwise. For information regarding permissions, request forms and the appropriate contacts within the Pearson Education Global Rights & Permissions department, please visit **www.pearsoned.com/permissions/**.

This work is solely for the use of instructors and administrators for the purpose of teaching courses and assessing student learning. Unauthorized dissemination or publication of the work in whole or in part (including selling or otherwise providing to unauthorized users access to the work or to your user credentials) will destroy the integrity of the work and is strictly prohibited.

PEARSON, ALWAYS LEARNING, and REVEL are exclusive trademarks in the U.S. and/or other countries owned by Pearson Education, Inc. or its affiliates.

Unless otherwise indicated herein, any third-party trademarks that may appear in this work are the property of their respective owners and any references to third-party trademarks, logos or other trade dress are for demonstrative or descriptive purposes only. Such references are not intended to imply any sponsorship, endorsement, authorization, or promotion of Pearson's products by the owners of such marks, or any relationship between the owner and Pearson Education, Inc. or its affiliates, authors, licensees or distributors.

Library of Congress Cataloging-in-Publication Data

Cataloging-in-Publication Data is available on file at the Library of Congress.

1   18

Student Loose Leaf Edition:
ISBN: 0-13-396936-3
ISBN: 978-0-13-396936-8

Annotated Instructor's Edition:
ISBN: 0-13-397271-2
ISBN: 978-0-13-397271-9

Revel:
ISBN: 0-13-397275-5
ISBN: 978-0-13-397275-7

Brief Contents

Contents

Preface

Why We Wrote this Book

Whether or not a digital learning program can change reading behavior and course performance is an empirical question. We, authors Danae Hudson and Brooke Whisenhunt, are both teachers and researchers at heart, and the idea that we could create a digital program based on empirically supported teaching and learning strategies *and* conduct efficacy testing throughout the development of the program was a dream come true for us. As a result, we ensured this first edition of *Psychology* was empirically-derived and empirically-tested at every stage of development. It evolved from our experiences in course redesign, more than 30 years of combined experience in the classroom, and a friendship few people are lucky enough to experience.

In this Revel *Psychology* digital learning program, we provide engaging, evidence-based materials to transform learning both *outside* and *inside* the classroom by offering a combination of (1) Adaptive Pathways, which are personalized assessment and instructional content that identify and correct student misconceptions in real-time and prepare them for deeper-level class interactions and (2) feedback for instructors to be able to tailor the classroom environment to meet the needs of their students.

This journey began in 2010 when we experienced what we refer to as our "existential teaching crisis." We had grown disillusioned with the less than optimal student learning outcomes and retention rates in Introductory Psychology. An opportunity arose to participate in a Missouri state-wide initiative in course redesign, and we embarked on a journey that completely transformed our course at Missouri State University.

One of the biggest challenges in our course redesign involved restructuring how we thought about our own role as instructors. Rather than "primary content deliverers," we began to see ourselves as "designers of the learning environment." Technology afforded us the opportunity to digitally deliver content utilizing learning science principles (e.g., the testing effect, spaced practice, timely feedback), which in return allowed us to focus more time on students' needs. With sections of more than 300 students, creating a classroom environment that would benefit all students was a challenge. After several years of using evaluating performance data to identify where students struggled the most in each chapter, we discovered predictable topics that emerged semester after semester (we call them Most Difficult Concepts or MDCs). Our redesigned Introductory Psychology course was extremely successful and has served as a model for many institutions across the country, and our hope is that this digital learning program will further expand on those successes for even more students and instructors.

Some people might wonder why we chose to deliver this content digitally. We are well aware of some students' (and instructors') stated preference for printed textbooks. We are also familiar with some research lab studies demonstrating better comprehension from printed texts compared to electronic texts (e.g., Ackerman & Goldsmith, 2011; Chen et al., 2014; Mangen et al., 2013; Singer & Alexander, 2016) when students are brought into a lab and randomly assigned to read in print versus electronic formats. However, outside of the lab, the reality is that the majority of students in college courses aren't engaging in much reading at all. Instructors around the country routinely say that getting students to read their textbook is one of the biggest course challenges they face, and research since the 1970s has shown that less than 30 percent of students come to class having completed the assigned readings. This leads us to strongly believe that technology can play an important role for students in ensuring access for everyone, engaging them in a mobile world, and motivating their continuous involvement throughout the term. Interactive, digital learning programs, like this one, that contain assignable and gradable activities provide the opportunity to encourage the reading behavior we all wish to see. In fact, we recently conducted a "real world classroom" study with 219 students using *Psychology*, First Edition and found that the students spent an average of 40 minutes interacting with the learning materials in one chapter and demonstrated a 45 percent improvement in learning from pretest to posttest. When students receive personalized assistance on the spot while engaging with interactive learning materials based on learning science, in the "real world" they choose to spend time with the materials and ultimately made significant learning gains.

We hope you and your students find this learning experience as compelling and effective as we have.

Approach of the Program

Psychology is based on the science of learning with an emphasis on providing solutions to the challenges students and instructors face in Introductory Psychology. Through our years of teaching and recent research, we know students struggle with predictable misconceptions on most difficult concepts specific to each topic in the course. While most assessment or feedback solutions available today simply indicate "what" the student got wrong, or even where to re-read information on the topic, they don't go far enough to identify "why" the student is struggling. For example, in the Social Psychology chapter, students routinely struggle with the most difficult concept of attribution. But are they confusing situational with dispositional attributions? Or is it actor observer bias versus fundamental attribution error that's throwing them for a loop? To really help struggling students, this program is built around specific personalized assessments of these difficult concepts and misconceptions and the provision of brief, targeted instruction via short whiteboard animation videos, which we call *Adaptive Pathways*.

Adaptive Pathway 13.1 Attribution Bias

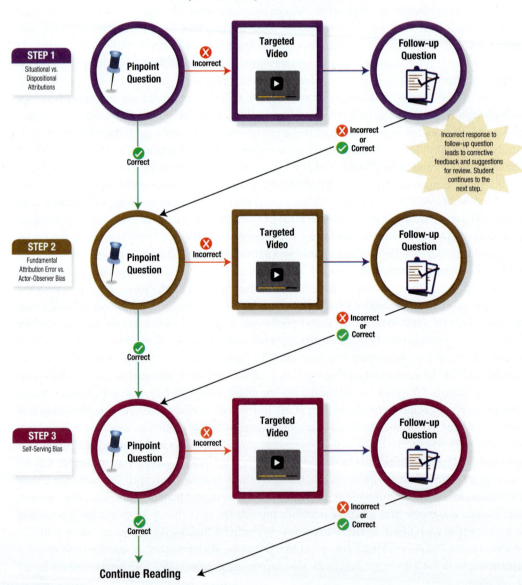

Each chapter contains 2–3 Adaptive Pathways on the top most difficult concepts (MDCs) identified by our research. For example, in the Learning chapter, data from both students and instructors suggests that operant conditioning is one of the most difficult concepts. Therefore, one of the three Adaptive Pathways in the learning chapter focuses on operant conditioning.

But, we know the answer to *"Why do students struggle with this concept?"* is often multi-faceted, which is why each Adaptive Pathway addresses between one and three specific misconceptions related to the MDC. Each Adaptive Pathway begins with a *pinpoint question*—a multiple-choice question we wrote to specifically target a common misconception. Distractor items were written to fit the misconception, so we know if a student answers the multiple-choice question incorrectly, they could benefit from targeted instruction that focuses on that specific misconception of the difficult concept, and they are provided with a short targeted video that addresses that specific misconception. If, however, a student answers the pinpoint question correctly, they automatically proceed to the pinpoint question for the next misconception (i.e., Step 2), keeping them on pace to move through the chapter.

In the operant conditioning example, we know students often have difficulty understanding that positive reinforcement involves adding something to increase a behavior, whereas negative reinforcement involves removing something aversive to increase behavior (Chapter 5 Learning: Adaptive Pathway 5.2.1). Students also tend to confuse the concepts of negative reinforcement and punishment (Chapter 5 Learning: Adaptive Pathway 5.2.2) and have trouble distinguishing positive punishment from negative punishment (Chapter 5 Learning: Adaptive Pathway 5.2.3).

Adaptive Pathway 5.2.1: Pinpoint Question

In this Adaptive Pathway, this pinpoint question will determine if a student is having trouble distinguishing between positive and negative reinforcement. If answered correctly, the student will immediately be presented with the next pinpoint question assessing the next misconception/difficult concept from the Adaptive Pathway. If, however, the question is answered incorrectly, the student will be immediately presented with a short (i.e., generally less than 2 minute) targeted video that specifically attempts to correct the misconception and deliver an accurate explanation of the concept, in a novel way not previously presented in Revel.

Short, informative videos are an important part of Adaptive Pathways. The emphasis on brief videos emerged as an attempt to hold students' attention throughout the video and the need to have the student maintain a reasonable pace along the learning pathway.

Adaptive Pathway 5.2.1: Targeted Video

After the student has watched the targeted video, a follow-up question will be presented. The follow-up questions are different from the pinpoint question but assess the same content and are similar in level of difficulty.

Adaptive Pathway 5.2.1: Follow-Up Question

INTRODUCTION	ADAPTIVE PATHWAY	RESULTS

A negative reinforcer is a stimulus that _____, and a positive reinforcer is a stimulus that _____.

- ○ adds something positive; adds something negative
- ○ adds something negative; adds something positive
- ○ removes something negative; removes something positive
- ○ removes something negative; adds something positive

CHECK ANSWER   BACK TO VIDEO

PREVIOUS   STEP 1 OF 3   NEXT

We, the authors, carefully wrote each pinpoint question, follow-up question, and script for the targeted video. We also formulated the concept for each targeted video and consulted with the animators throughout the development process. Adaptive Pathways are central to the purpose of this program, and it was important to us that we drew on our own teaching experiences to know how to best deliver this content.

 The Adaptive Pathways are mapped to the learning objectives at the beginning of each chapter in the *Annotated Instructor's Edition* and are designated in the chapter by this logo.

Other Revel Features

REVEL INTERACTIVES   Revel was designed to help every student come to class ready to learn. To keep students engaged as they read through each chapter, Revel integrates videos, interactives, and assessments directly into the author-created narrative. Thanks to this media-rich presentation of content, students are more likely to complete their assigned reading and retain what they've read. So, they'll show up to class better prepared to participate and learn.

END-OF-MODULE AND END-OF-CHAPTER QUIZZES   Embedded assessments such as quizzes and concept checks afford students opportunities to check their understanding at regular intervals before moving on. Assessments in Revel let instructors gauge student comprehension frequently, provide timely feedback, and address learning gaps along the way.

PIECING IT TOGETHER (PIT)   One applied topic relevant to the chapter content will be explored in-depth using a puzzle graphic. Each piece of the puzzle will represent one of the "cross-cutting themes" identified by an APA working group on introductory psychology (Gurung et al., 2016). These cross-cutting themes include cultural and social diversity, ethics, variations in human functioning, and research methods. For example, the PIT topic for Chapter 1 is vaccines and autism, and this topic is considered from the perspective of each of the four cross-cutting themes. Each PIT feature will include written text, interactive activities, and writing prompts to help students integrate these themes with the specific content of each chapter. This feature will be a unique learning objective in each chapter, and instructors can decide how many to assign for the course.

SHARED WRITING: Assignable Shared Writing activities foster collaboration and critical thinking skills by providing students the opportunity to write brief responses to chapter-specific questions and engage in peer-to-peer feedback on a discussion board.

JOURNAL PROMPTS: Journal Prompts allow students to write short critical-thinking based journal entries about the chapter content, and allow students an opportunity to apply key concepts and new knowledge to their own experiences.

Cultural and Social Diversity

Ethics

Vaccines and Autism

Variations in Human Functioning

Research Methods

Features for Instructors

INSTRUCTOR DASHBOARD   Revel empowers educators to monitor class assignment completion as well as individual student achievement. Actionable information, such as points earned on quizzes and tests and time on task, helps educators intersect with their students in meaningful ways. For example, the trending column reveals whether students' grades are improving or declining, helping educators to identify students who might need help to stay on track.

ADAPTIVE PATHWAY GLOBAL RESULTS   Instructors often want to gauge their students' learning inside and outside of the classroom so they can know how to best spend their limited contact time with students. Instructors will be able to access global student data for each of the Adaptive Pathways questions. For each misconception of an Adaptive Pathway, instructors can see the total percent of students who answered the pinpoint question correctly, the total percent of students who answered the follow up question correctly, and the percent of students who answered both questions incorrectly. This data will provide instructors with a quick snapshot of student performance on difficult concepts, allowing them to tailor their class time to address student needs. You will also be able to easily access all 93 Adaptive Pathway targeted videos from the Adaptive Pathway dashboard located under the Resources tab in Revel.

Adaptive Pathway: Global Results

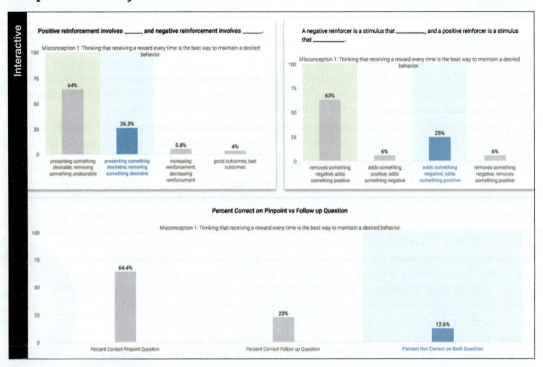

IN-CLASS ACTIVITIES TARGETING MDCS   For each difficult concept addressed in an Adaptive Pathway, a set of classroom activities/demonstrations/discussions will be provided for instructors. The annotated instructor's edition chapter opener will include a description of one classroom activity associated with an Adaptive Pathway. All of these activities have accompanying videos featuring expert instructors conducting the activity with students. The full *Instructor's Manual* will include a variety of activities for each Adaptive Pathway concept that are suited for different classroom modalities (e.g., small class, large class, online class).

ANNOTATED INSTRUCTOR'S EDITION (AIE)   The AIE was authored by a teaching expert, Dr. Melissa Beers, from The Ohio State University. Each chapter includes a variety of Teaching Tips that are noted within the margins of the content. These Teaching Tips will include a variety of "themes" such as lecture ideas, teaching traps, assessment strategies, options for different class modalities, opportunities for active learning, and teaching tips based on scholarship of teaching and learning research. The preface of the AIE includes a full description of each type of Teaching Tip and strategies for using the AIE.

Teaching and Learning Resources

Psychology is accompanied by a robust suite of instructor resources to help instructors have the ideal teaching experience. We have made every effort to recruit excellent psychology teachers and provide high-quality resources that will save you preparation time and will enhance the time you spend in the classroom.

The supplements can be accessed from the Resources tab in the Revel course as well as downloaded from the Instructor's Resource Center website (www.pearsonhighered.com/irc).

Instructor's Resource Manual (ISBN 0133972771), prepared by Garth Neufeld from Cascadia College and Manda Williamson from the University of Nebraska-Lincoln, offers a variety of teaching demonstrations and activities based on the Adaptive Pathways within each chapter. We were careful to include activities relevant to all class modalities, including small classes, large classes, and online classes. On the Instructor's Resources tab in Revel, you will find links to all of these activities and the 17 original video clips of expert instructors demonstrating a class activity focusing on a difficult concept from the chapter.

Test Bank (ISBN 0133972690) prepared by Regina M. Hughes, Collin College-Frisco Campus; Linda Lockwood, Ph.D, Metropolitan State University of Denver; and Alan Swinkels, Ph.D, St. Edward's University, and reviewed by authors, Danae Hudson and Brooke Whisenhunt, the test bank contains a vast selection of multiple choice, short answer, and essay questions for each chapter, categorized by learning objective, topic, difficulty and skill level, and APA Learning Objectives. The test bank will include questions specifically written to assess the content addressed in the Adaptive Pathways for each chapter. Rationales for each correct answer and the key distracter in the multiple-choice questions help instructors evaluate questions and provide more feedback to students. Each chapter of the Test Bank contains a Total Assessment Guide, an easy-to-reference grid that organizes all test items by learning objective and question type.

Pearson MyTest (ISBN 0133972763), a powerful assessment generation program, helps instructors easily create and print quizzes and exams. Questions and tests can be authored online, allowing instructors ultimate flexibility. For more information, go to www.PearsonMyTest.com.

Standard ADA Compliant Lecture PowerPoint Slides (ISBN 0134003950) These ADA PowerPoint slides provide an active format for presenting concepts from each chapter and feature relevant figures and tables from the text. Thank you to Julie Lazarra, Paradise Valley Community College, for preparing the PowerPoint slides.

Art PowerPoint Slides (ISBN 013489622X) These slides contain only the photos, figures, and line art from the text.

Interactive PowerPoint Slides (ISBN 0134003942) offer an enhanced experience for the classroom, drawing students into the lecture and providing additional visuals and links to videos. The slides are built around the text's learning objectives and offer many direct links to interactive animations and videos.

Student Print Reference Edition Within Revel, students have the option to purchase a Print Reference Edition, which is a convenient, three-hole punched, loose-leaf text. This print edition is designed to be a helpful supplement for students; it contains the entire narrative, figures, images, and photographs. However, due to the fact that *Psychology* was built from the ground up as a digital experience, a print edition cannot contain all of the elements of the program. To experience all of the interactive and assessment components of the program, students must access the Revel program.

About the Authors

The story of this program began long ago when we (Danae and Brooke) met as clinical psychology graduate students in 1998. We came from different cultural backgrounds with Brooke growing up in Arkansas and Danae in Vancouver, Canada. However, fate brought us together at Louisiana State University, and we have been best friends since that time. We never imagined we would work together, but by 2003 we had both accepted academic jobs in the Psychology Department of Missouri State University. Since then, we have had offices side-by-side, teach many of the same classes, and co-direct a research lab together. We both know how incredibly lucky we are to be able to work every day with our best friend in careers that we love.

DANAE L. HUDSON, PH.D. Danae Hudson is a Professor in the Department of Psychology at Missouri State University (MSU). She obtained her bachelor's degree from Simon Fraser University in Burnaby, British Columbia, and she received her Ph.D. in clinical psychology from Louisiana State University. Her program of research initially focused on eating disorders and body image, but now, the majority of her work involves the scholarship of teaching and learning (SoTL). Since 2003, Dr. Hudson has taught large sections of Introductory Psychology in addition to other clinical psychology undergraduate and graduate courses. From 2010–2013, Dr. Hudson served as the team leader for a large-scale redesign of MSU's Introductory Psychology course. MSU participated in a state-wide initiative in course redesign where each public four-year institution in the state redesigned one large enrollment course. Since Fall 2012, all introductory psychology courses have been taught in the redesigned, blended format. Dr. Hudson and her colleagues have published peer-reviewed articles, case studies, and presented at national and international venues on the successful outcomes of the redesigned course. She has been interviewed by various educational consultants, and Introductory Psychology's success story has been documented in *Campus Technology* and on Michael Feldstein's blog *e-Literate*. Dr. Hudson served two years as a Provost Fellow for Teaching and Learning at MSU, is currently a Missouri Learning Commons Scholar, and a National Center for Academic Transformation (NCAT) Redesign Scholar. She is also actively involved in APA's Division 2: Society for the Teaching of Psychology (STP) as the Director of Teaching Resources in Psychology.

BROOKE LESLIE WHISENHUNT, PH.D. Brooke Whisenhunt is a Professor of psychology at Missouri State University where she has been a faculty member since 2002. She received her bachelor's degree from the University of Arkansas in 1997 and her Ph.D. in clinical psychology from Louisiana State University in 2002. Her research has focused on body image, obesity, and eating disorders, in addition to the scholarship of teaching and learning.

She teaches undergraduate courses, including Introductory Psychology, Abnormal Psychology, and Teaching of Psychology in addition to graduate-level courses in psychological assessment. In addition to her academic position, she is also a licensed clinical psychologist. She was a member of the introductory psychology redesign team at Missouri State University as part of a statewide mission in course redesign through the National Center for Academic Transformation (NCAT). The redesign team transformed introductory psychology at Missouri State University into a blended course and demonstrated significant improvements in learning outcomes. The results of this project have been published in *Psychology Learning and Teaching* and *Scholarship of Teaching and Learning in Psychology*. Since the completion of the redesign project, Dr. Whisenhunt has been serving as a Missouri Learning Commons Scholar to assist other institutions in the state implement redesign projects. She is also a National Center for Academic Transformation (NCAT) Redesign Scholar. She has presented across the country about pedagogical strategies to improve learning, decrease institutional costs, and improve retention in introductory psychology.

Acknowledgments

I would like to personally thank my husband, Geoff, and three children, Sophie, Sylvie, and Noah. It's hard to believe our kids were only 6, 5, and 2 years old when we started down this path. And to Geoff, who has been extremely patient, understanding, and willing to pick up the slack at home while I was writing or traveling: I love you with all my heart and can't image doing something like this without you by my side. Thank you for your encouragement when I needed it and your ear when I needed that—you definitely deserve an honorary doctorate in psychology! There probably aren't many babysitters who receive an acknowledgment in a textbook, but Jessie Curtis, you have been a godsend and have helped make this journey possible.

I have been so fortunate to have amazing mentors in the teaching of psychology world, who I am lucky to also call friends. Sue Frantz, Noland White, Eric Landrum, Stephen Chew, Missy Beers, Regan Gurung, and Barney Beins, just to name a few—you are all so talented and have inspired me to continue to be a better teacher, semester after semester.

My extended family has been particularly important during the development of this program. My Mom, Donna Barina was so excited we had this opportunity and was extremely proud of the work Brooke and I were doing. Sadly, she did not have the opportunity to see the finished project as she passed away in 2016. I am extremely grateful for the support of my family, especially my sister, Deserae Kataro, and her family, and my "Pearson family" during that very difficult year.

And finally, to my co-author, colleague, and very best friend Brooke, I can't imagine taking on a project of this magnitude with anyone else. Thank you for always listening to my (sometimes crazy) ideas that came to me in the shower, humoring my flair for the dramatic, taking care of me and my family when I couldn't do it, and for bringing your creative ideas and talented writing to this project. I love you and know my Mom was as proud of you as she was of me.

Danae L. Hudson
Missouri State University
Springfield, Missouri
danaehudson@missouristate.edu

First and foremost, I would like to thank my husband, Blaine Whisenhunt, and our two daughters, Riley and Brynn. This book has been a family endeavor from the start, and I would not have completed this project without my biggest supporters at home. Thank you for tolerating the late nights at work, the occasional distracted "mom" moments with my laptop in my lap, and the FaceTime tuck-ins while frequently traveling. Blaine, in particular, has been my rock, and my biggest cheerleader. I also want to thank my mother, Brenda Leslie, for a lifetime of support and love, which was once again on display throughout this project.

To Danae Hudson, my co-author, colleague, and best friend, I could never have imagined working on this project with anyone else. The hundreds of late night phone calls, meetings at coffee bars, and working side-by-side on cramped flights across the country were all made tolerable by the knowledge that I was never in it alone. Our friendship is the kind that has endured everything life can throw at us—weddings, births, deaths, and crises—and this book is a tangible representation of how lucky I am to call you my best friend.

Brooke Whisenhunt
Missouri State University
Springfield, Missouri
bwhisenhunt@missouristate.edu

To our friends and colleagues in the Department of Psychology at Missouri State University, we are forever grateful for your support, encouragement, and feedback. To the original Introductory Psychology redesign team (Carol Shoptaugh, Ann Rost, Rachel Happel), we will never forget the colleagues who started on this journey with us and helped make our introductory psychology course at MSU one that we are all proud of today. To Christie Cathey, who coordinates our Introductory Psychology program at MSU and our colleagues who are a part of our Introductory Psychology teaching team (Michelle Visio, Tanya Whipple, Charlie Hoogland, Sarah McNew), we are grateful to be a part of such an inspirational team of educators. We also want to say a special thank you to colleagues who have helped provide feedback on the book along the way, including Carly Yadon, Erin Buchanan, Tanya Whipple, and Bogdan Kostic.

We have also been fortunate to have incredible clinical psychology graduate students who have been willing to work with us as research assistants at various stages of this project: Shannon Nicholson, Jennifer Battles, and Brooke Bennett, thank you for always embracing short deadlines and going above and beyond what was expected.

To the thousands of Introductory Psychology students in our classes—you have always been on the front lines, willing to listen to new ideas or participate in research so we could be sure to get the Adaptive Pathways just right. We want to thank you for inspiring and motivating us to think outside the box when it comes to learning materials. Every class of 330 new faces reminds us that our job and our passion boils down to the people sitting in that classroom.

We are so grateful to have worked with such an incredible editorial team at Pearson. Erin Mitchell has been phenomenal from start to finish and has worked tirelessly to bring our vision for this product to light. Thank you for always believing in us and for keeping student learning at the forefront of this project. You are so much more than our acquisitions editor, you are a true friend. To our two development editors, Julie Swasey and Julie Kelly, we thank you both for your invaluable insights, tireless efforts, and genuine personalities. We have always been amazed at your ability to balance content, technological capabilities, and market needs. And, to Lou Fierro, editorial assistant extraordinaire, thanks for your organization and fulfillment of many last-minute requests! We also want to say a special thank you to all the people at, or working with Pearson who have been instrumental in helping bring this project to completion: Dickson Musslewhite, Paul Corey, Beth Shepard, Jeanette Koskinas, Caroline Fenton, Lindsay Verge, Lisa Mafrici, Amy Smith, Gina Linko, Jen Stevenson, Liz Kincaid, Ben Ferrini, Karen Mullane, Nicole Kunzman, Pamela Weldin, Wendy Gordon, Kate Stewart, Chris Brown, Debi Doyle, Noel Siebert, and Julie Lindstrom. To our first Pearson representative, Megan Lozano, we are so grateful you came to Missouri State University all those years ago to demo Pearson products. You have been our cheerleader, encourager, and friend — thank you.

Having high quality assessments was a top priority for us and we were fortunate to have the assistance of Kelly Miller from Ozarks Technical Community College. Thank you for your help in writing all of the in-Revel assessment items. We are so thankful to Regina M. Hughes, Linda Lockwood, and Alan Swinkels, who spent many hours writing, reviewing, and revising questions to make sure we provided a top-notch test bank. We are also extremely grateful for Garth Neufeld and Manda Williamson who embraced the task of developing the Instructor's Resource Manual.

And to Missy Beers, the day you agreed to work with us on the Annotated Instructor's Edition was one of the most exciting days because we knew you were the perfect person to help us develop this amazing resource for instructors. Thank you for "getting it" and for always being so encouraging and willing to help.

We took great care in assembling this collaborative resources team and we could not have asked for better "teammates" who are incredible teachers, creative thinkers, and devoted colleagues.

To the hundreds of instructors and students who served as reviewers, class testers, and focus-group participants, we are incredibly grateful for your helpful feedback and perceptive suggestions. A special thank you to our student, Sam Love, who provided excellent feedback for the Human Sexuality and Gender chapter.

Adam Austin, *Columbia Basin College*
Adam Crighton, *Kent State University*
Alisha Francis, *Northwest Missouri State University*
Alisha Janowsky, *University of Central Florida*
Allison Burton-Chase, *Albany College of Pharmacy and Health Sciences*
Amy Buckingham, *Red Rocks Community College*
Amy Carrigan, *University of Saint Francis*
Amy Skinner, *Troy State University*
Amy Spilkin, *San Diego State University*
Andrea Cartwright, *Jefferson Community and Technical College*
Andrea Clements, *East Tennessee State University*
Andrea Ericksen, *San Juan College*
Andrew Johnson, *Park University*
Angelina S. MacKewn, *University of Tennessee – Martin*
Angie Dahl, *Ferrum College*
Ann Cramer, *Technical College of the Lowcountry*
Anna-Marie, *Spinos Rudek Aurora University*
Anne Wilson, *The Ohio State University*
Anthony Adamopoulos, *Missouri Southern State University*
Anthony Eldridge, *Arkansas State University*
Antonio Zamoralez, *Brazosport College*
April Fugett, *Marshall University*
Ashley Gill, *Duquesne University*
Ashley Hall, *University of Southern Indiana*
Ava Santos, *Fort Lewis College*
Azadeh Aalai, *Queensboro Community College*
Baine Craft, *Seattle Pacific University*
Barb Hughson, *San Juan College*
Barbara Beaver, *University of Wisconsin - Whitewater*
Becky Meacham, *West Liberty University*
Belinda Blevins-Knabe, *University of Arkansas at Little Rock*
Belinda Marable, *Auburn University at Montgomery*
Benetha Jackson, *Angelina College*
Bernice Carson, *Virginia State University*
Bethany Fleck Dillen, *Metropolitan State University of Denver*
Bradley Mitchell, *Michigan State University*
Brandy Young, *Cypress College*
Brian Johnson, *The University of Tennessee at Martin*
Brian Parry, *Colorado Mesa University*
Brianna McCoy, *Marshall University*
Bruce LeBlanc, *Black Hawk College*
Bruce Reinauer, *Ventura College*
Bryan Fantie, *American University*
Carmen Culotta, *Wright State University*
Carolyn Cavanaugh, *Arizona State University-Tempe*
Cassandra Grey, *Auburn University at Montgomery*
Catherine Phillips, *Northwest Vista College*
Celeste Favela, *El Paso Community College*
Celine Ko Roberson, *University of Redlands*
Charlene Chester, *Morgan State University*
Charles Epstein, *CUNY/John Jay College of Criminal Justice*
Chase O'Gwin, *Northwest Missouri State*
Cheri Kittrell, *State College of Florida, Manatee–Sarasota*
Chris Creecy, *Freed Hardeman University*
Chris De La Ronde, *Austin Community College*
Christa Christ, *Hamilton College*
Christine Baerga, *John Jay College of Criminal Justice*
Christine Ford, *Bucks County Community College*
Christopher Anderson, *Schenectady County Community College*
Christopher Cronin, *Saint Leo University*
Christopher K. Randall, *Kennesaw State University*
Christopher Redker, *Ferris State University*
Christopher Stanzione, *Georgia Institute of Technology*
Christyn Dolbier, *East Carolina University*
Clarissa Chavez, *Auburn University at Montgomery*

Colin Key, *University of Tennessee Martin*
Colleen Sullivan (McMullin), *Muskingum University*
Conna Bral, *Kirkwood Community College*
Cynthia Bane, *Wartburg College*
Cynthia Rickert, *Ivy Tech*
Dan Fawaz, *Georgia Perimeter College*
Dan Mossler, *Hampden Sydney College*
Dan Segrist, *Southern Illinois University Edwardsville*
Dana Wallace, *University of Jamestown*
Daneen Deptula, *Fitchburg State College*
Daniel Graham, *Hobart & William Smith Colleges*
Danielle Richards, *College of Southern Nevada*
Darin LaMar Baskin, *Houston Community College*
David Baskind, *Delta College*
David Berg, *Community College of Philadelphia*
David Biek, *Middle Georgia State University*
David Devonis, *Graceland University*
David Sanchez, *College of Southern Nevada*
David Yells, *Utah Valley University*
Davido Dupree, *Community College of Philadelphia*
Dawn Eaton, *San Jacinto College*
Dawn Harvey, *Ivy Tech Community College*
Deborah Garfin, *Georgia State University*
Deborah Harding, *Amarillo College*
Debra Bacon, *Bristol Community College*
DeErica Barber, *Randolph Community College*
Dennis K. Miller, *University of Missouri*
Deborah Barrett, *Santiago Canyon College*
Des Robinson, *Tarrant County College*
Destinee Chambers, *American International College*
Diana Ciesko, *Valencia College*
Diane Ashe, *Valencia College*
Diane Dodge, *Columbus State Community College*
Donnell Griffin, *Davidson County Community College*
Donnye Ross, *Imperial Valley College*
Edward Cascio, *Palm Beach State College*
Edward Keane, *Housatonic Community College*
Elaine Augustine, *University of South Florida*
Elaine Cassel, *Lord Fairfax Community College*
Elisabeth Sherwin, *University of Arkansas at Little Rock*
Elizabeth Babcock, *Augustana College*
Elizabeth Coccia, *Austin Community College*
Elizabeth Maloney, *San Joaquin Delta College*
Elizabeth Melles, *Northeastern State University*
Elizabeth Sherwin, *University of Arkansas – Little Rock*
Elsa Mason, *College of Southern Nevada*
Emily Cohen-Shikora, *Washington University in St. Louis*
Eric Bruns, *Campbellsville University*
Eric Miller, *Kent State University*
Erikson Neilans, *Erie Community College North*
Erin Ambrose, *William Jessup University*
Estelle Campenni, *Marywood University*
Eva Lawrence, *Guilford College*
Eva Szeli, *Arizona State University*
Evelyn Blanch-Payne, *Middle Tennessee State University*
Fawn Caplandies, *University of Toledo*
Frank Igou, *Louisiana Tech University*
Garrett Berman, *Roger Williams University*
Gaye Hughes, *Austin Community College*
Georgann Wilis, *Umpqua Community College*
Gerry Braasch, *McHenry County College*
Gordon Hammerle, *Adrian College*
Gregg Bromgard, *Southern University at New Orleans*
Haili Marotti, *Florida Southwestern State College*
Heather Collins, *Trident Technical College*
Helana Girgis, *Hartwick College*
Herb Coleman, *Austin Community College*
Herbert Coleman, *Austin Community College*
Hilario Garcia, *St. Philip's College*

Ian Cheng, *Austin Community College*
Ilona Pitkanen, *Bellevue College*
Isabelle Chang, *Temple University*
Jacob Glazier, *University of West Georgia*
Jacquelyn Fargano, *Fresno City College*
James Cortright, *University of Wisconsin – River Falls*
James Hammond, *Aiken Technical College*
Jamie Hughes, *University of Texas of the Permian Basin*
Jamie Simpson, *Midland University*
Janelle McDaniel, *University of Louisiana at Monroe*
Jarrod Calloway, *Northwest Mississippi Community College*
Jason McCoy, *Cape Fear Community College*
Jay Warden, *Cape Cod Community College*
Jean Egan, *Asnuntuck Community College*
Jean Marie Bianchi, *Wilson College*
Jeffrey Cassisi, *University of Central Florida*
Jeffrey Helms, *Kennesaw State University*
Jennifer Bowler, *East Carolina University*
Jennifer Breneiser, *Valdosta State University*
Jennifer Brennom, *Kirkwood Community College*
Jennifer Engler, *York College of Pennsylvania*
Jennifer Fayard, *Ouachita Baptist Church*
Jennifer Gonder, *Farmingdale State College*
Jennifer Howell, *Ohio University*
Jennifer Silva Brown, *Drury University*
Jennifer Vendemia, *University of South Carolina*
Jessica Carpenter, *Elgin Community College*
Jessica Oladapo, *Rock Valley College*
Jessica Park, *Northern Kentucky University*
Jill Cooper, *Rutgers Prep High School*
Jill Ramet, *Metro Community College*
Jillene Seiver, *Bellevue College*
Jim Archer, *South Plains College*
Jo-Ann Tsang, *Baylor University*
Jodi Grace, *St. Thomas University*
John Bickford, *University of Massachusetts*
John Billimek, *University California Irvine*
John Gulledge, *Dalton State College*
John Haworth, *Chattanooga State Community College*
John Mavromatis, *Retired as of August 31, 2017*
John Updegraff, *Kent State University*
Johnathan Forbey, *Ball State University*
Jon Skalski, *Unviertsity of Southern Nevada*
Joni Caldwell, *Union College*
Jordan Alexander, *Columbia College*
Joseph Ferrari, *DePaul University*
Joyce Vogel, *Lewis and Clark Community College*
Judith Easton, *Texas State University*
Julia Heberle, *Albright College*
Julie Lazzara, *Paradise Valley Community College*
Julie Luker, *Concordia University, Saint Paul*
Julie Stanwood, *Lesley University*
Justin Couchman, *Albright College*
Karen Amesbury, *Luzerne County Community College*
Karen Beck, *Rio Hondo College*
Karen Markowitz, *University of San Diego*
Karen Thompson, *Columbia College*
Karen Yanowitz, *Arkansas State University*
Katherine Darling, *Kent State University*
Kathy Martin, *Johnson County Community College*
Kelly Charlton, *University of North Carolina at Pembroke*
Ken Sobel, *University of Central Arkansas*
Kerry Burd, *Rock Valley College*
Kerry Evans, *Onondaga Community College*
Kerry McCoy, *Mira Costa College*
Kevin O'Neil, *Florida Gulf Coast University*
Kevin Walters, *Colorado State University*
Khara Williams, *University of Southern Indiana*
Kimberli Freilinger, *Western Oregon University*

Kimberly Hima, *Gateway Community and Technical College*
Kirsten Li-Barber, *High Point University*
Kirsten Treadwell, *Columbus State Community College*
Krista Carter, *Colby Community College*
Kristen Diliberto-Macaluso, *Berry College*
Kristen Leraas, *Columbus State Community College*
Kristi Bitz, *University of Mary Washington*
Kristi Cordell-McNulty, *Angelo State University*
Kristie Harris, *The Ohio State University*
Kristin Anderson, *Houston Community College*
Kristin Bonnie, *Beloit College*
Kristin Larson, *Monmouth College*
Kristina Klassen, *North Idaho College*
Kristina Taylor, *Triton College*
Kylie Classey, *Cape Fear Community College*
Larolyn Zylicz, *Cape Fear Community College*
Lauren Bates, *Colorado State University*
Lauren Wissing, *Tidewater Community College*
Lawrence Eisenberg, *Guilford College*
Leslie Price, *Hartnell College*
Lillian Russell, *Alabama State University*
Linda Weldon, *Community College of Beaver County*
Lindsey Beck, *Emerson College*
Lisa Manriquez, *University of Arkansas – Fort Smith*
Lisa Murphy, *York County Community College*
Lisa Thomassen, *Indiana University Bloomington*
Lisamarie Bensman, *University of Hawaii*
Lonnie Yandell, *Belmont University*
Lucia Torchia-Thompson, *Reading Area Community College*
Lynda Mae, *Arizona State University – Tempe*
Maeve O'Donnell, *Colorado State University*
Malaika Brown, *Citrus College*
Manda Williamson, *The University of Nebraksa-Lincoln*
Margaret Ingate, *Rutgers University*
Margot Underwood, *Joliet Junior College*
Marie-Joelle Estrada, *University of Rochester*
Marina Baratian, *Eastern Florida State College*
Marion Mason, *Bloomsburg University*
Marion Perlmutter, *University of Michigan*
Marti Bonne DeMuth, *Joliet Junior College*
Martin Dennis, *University of South Dakota*
Mary Lewis, *Columbus State Community College*
Mary Shuttlesworth, *Mount Aloysius College*
Mary Strobbe, *San Diego Miramar College*
Mary Utley, *Drury University*
Marylou Robins, *San Jacinto College South*
Matt Diggs, *Collin County Community College*
Matthew Bell, *Santa Clara University*
Maya Aloni, *Western Connecticut State University*
Megan St Peters, *Ferrum College*
Meghan Novy, *Palomar College*
Melinda Ciccocioppo, *University of Pittsburgh*
Melissa Acevedo, *Westchester Community College*
Melissa Patton, *Eastern Florida State College*
Melissa Terlecki, *Cabrini University*
Melissa Wright, *Northwest Vista College*
Melodee Alexander, *Cleveland State Community College*
Michael Ainette, *Dominican College*
Michael Figuccio, *Farmingdale State College*
Michelle Fellows, *College of Western Idaho*
Mimi Phan, *Rutgers University*
Myra Bundy, *Eastern Kentucky University*
Nadja Compo, *Florida International University*
Nancy Gup, *Georgia Perimeter College*
Nancy Simpson, *Trident Technical College*
Naomi Ekas, *Texas Christian University*
Nic Bencaz, *University of Central Florida*
Nicholas Fernandez, *El Paso Community College*
Nicholas Greco, *College of Lake County*
Nicholas Herrera, *Long Beach City College*
Nicki Favero, *Lynchburg College*
Nickolas Dominello, *Penn State Abington*
Nicole Bragg Scott, *Mt. Hood Community College*
Nicole Brandt, *Columbus State Community College*

Pam Bradley, *Sandhills Community College*
Pam Garverick, *Wright State University*
Patricia Costello, *Walden University*
Patricia Crowe-Rubino, *Hawkeye Community College*
Paul Bartoli, *East Stroudsburg University*
Paul Herrie, *College of Southern Nevada*
Paul Johnson, *Oakton Community College*
Perry Fuchs, *UT Arlington*
Phyllis Freeman, *SUNY New Paltz*
Rachel Annunziato, *Fordham University*
Rachel Farr, *University of Kentucky*
Rachel Howard, *East Central College*
Randi Cramer, *Columbia College*
Raquel Henry, *Lone Star College*
Rebecca Langley, *Henderson State University*
Renee Engeln, *Northwestern University*
Renée L. Babcock, *University of Central Michigan*
Rick Buckwalter, *Quincy University*
Rita Barrett, *University of Arkansas – Fort Smith*
Robert Ferguson, *Buena Vista University*
Robert Hale, *Shippensburg University*
Robert Hensley, *The College of Saint Scholastica*
Robert Martinez, *University of the Incarnate Word*
Robert Rex, *Johnson Delaware County Community College*
Robert Short, *Arizona State University*
Robin Anderson, *St. Ambrose University*
Robin Campbell, *Eastern Florida State College*
Ron Faulk, *Saint Gregory's University*
Rosalyn King, *Northern Virginia Community College-Loudoun Campus*
Ryan Darrow, *Johnson County Community College*
Sandra Carpenter, *University of Alabama in Huntsville*
Sara Finley, *Pacific Lutheran University*
Sarah Wood, *University of Wisconsin – Stout*
Scott Freng, *University of Wyoming*
Scott Keiller, *Kent State University*
Seth Surgan, *Worcester State University*
Shai Tabib, *Kean University*
Shelda Borders, *Anderson University*
Sherece Fields, *Texas A&M University*
Sherry Ash, *San Jacinto College-Central*
Sheryl Civjan, *Holyoke Community College*
Stacy Walker, *Lone Star College Kingwood*
Stephanie DenHartog, *Anoka Ramsey Community College*
Stephanie Ding, *Del Mar College*
Stephen Burgess, *Southwestern Oklahoma State University*
Steven Dworkin, *Western Illinois University*
Steven Gomez, *William Rainey Harper College*
Steven Hall, *Butte College*
Steven McCloud, *BMCC/CUNY*
Steven Mewaldt, *Marshall University*
Susan Antaramian, *Christopher Newport University*
Susanne Auer, *Oglala Lakota College*
Suzanne Gibson, *Meridian Community College*
Sylvia Beyer, *University of Wisconsin – Parkside*
Tammy McClain, *West Liberty University*
Tawnda Bickford, *Hennepin Technical College*
Terry Stone, *University of Nebraska at Omaha*
Terry Trepper, *Purdue University Northwest*
Theresa DiDonato, *Loyola University Maryland*
Thomas Brothen, *University of Minnesota*
Thomas Vessey, *Corban University*
Tim Bono, *Washington University at St. Louis*
Tim VanderGast, *William Paterson University*
Todd Wilkinson, *University of Wisconsin – River Falls*
Toni Blake, *San Diego Mesa College*
Valerie Eastman, *Drury University*
Valerie Gutierrez, *Northeast Lakeview College*
Vias Nicolaides, *George Mason University*
Vicki Sheafer, *LeTourneau University*
Victor Karandashev, *Aquinas College*
Victoria DeSensi, *Wilmington College*
Victoria Van Wie, *Lone star. College*
Virginia Bare, *University of Montevallo*

Virginia Diehl, *Western Illinois University*
Wade Lueck, *Pima Community College*
Wanda Clark, *South Plains College*
Warren Fass, *University of Pittsburgh at Bradford*
Will Crescioni, *South Plains College*
William Dragon, *Cornell College*
William Fry, *Youngstown State University*
Wyndolyn Ludwikowski, *Xavier University of Louisiana*
Yasmine Kalkstein, *Mount Saint Mary College*
Yi Shao, *Oklahoma City University*
Yuthika Kim, *Oklahoma City Community College*
Zane Ferguson, *Hunter College (former)*
Zehra Peynircioglu, *American University*

Learning Outcomes and Assessment

Learning Objectives

Based on APA recommendations, each chapter is structured around detailed learning objectives. All of the instructor and student resources are also organized around these objectives, making the text and resources a fully integrated system of study. The flexibility of these resources allows instructors to choose which learning objectives are important in their courses, as well as which content they want their students to focus on.

Goals and Standards

In recent years, many psychology departments have been focusing on core competencies and how methods of assessment can better enhance students' learning. In response, the American Psychological Association (APA) established recommended goals for the undergraduate psychology major beginning in 2008 with a set of ten goals, and revised again in 2013 with a new set of five goals. Specific learning outcomes were established for each of the goals, and suggestions were made on how best to tie assessment practices to these goals. In writing this text, we have used the APA goals and assessment recommendations as guidelines for structuring content and integrating the teaching and homework materials.

For details on the APA learning goals and assessment guidelines, please see www.apa.org/.

APA Correlation Guide for Hudson/Whisenhunt *Psychology*

The APA Guidelines for the Undergraduate Psychology Major, Version 2.0

APA Learning Outcomes and Objectives	Text Learning Objectives and Features

Goal 1: Knowledge Base in Psychology

Demonstrate fundamental knowledge and comprehension of major concepts, theoretical perspectives, historical trends, and empirical findings to discuss how psychological principles apply to behavioral problems.

1.1 Describe key concepts, principles, and overarching themes in psychology.	*Learning Objectives:* 1.1, 1.2, 1.4, 1.5, 1.12, 1.13, 2.1, 2.2, 2.3, 2.5, 2.6, 2.7, 2.8, 2.9, 2.10, 2.13, 3.1, 3.4, 3.5, 3.6, 3.7, 3.9, 3.10, 3.11, 3.12, 3.13, 3.16, 4.1, 4.2, 4.4, 4.5, 4.7, 4.8, 4.11, 5.1, 5.2, 5.3, 5.4, 5.5, 5.6, 5.7, 5.8, 5.9, 5.10, 5.11, 5.13, 5.14, 6.1, 6.2, 6.3, 6.4, 6.5, 6.6, 6.7, 6.9, 6.10, 6.12, 6.13, 6.14, 7.1, 7.2, 7.3, 7.4, 7.5, 7.8, 7.9, 7.10, 7.11, 7.13, 7.14, 7.15, 8.1, 8.2, 8.3, 8.4, 8.5, 8.8, 8.9, 8.10, 8.11, 8.12, 8.13, 9.1, 9.2, 9.3, 9.5, 9.7, 9.8, 9.9, 9.11, 9.12, 9.13, 9.15, 10.1, 10.2, 10.3, 10.4, 10.5, 10.6, 10.7, 10.9, 10.10, 10.11, 10.12, 10.13, 10.14, 10.15, 11.1, 11.2, 11.3, 11.4, 11.5, 11.6, 11.7, 11.8, 11.9, 11.10, 11.11, 11.12, 11.13, 12.1, 12.2, 12.3, 12.4, 12.5, 12.6, 12.7, 12.8, 12.9, 12.10, 13.1, 13.2, 13.3, 13.4, 13.5, 13.6, 13.7, 13.8, 13.9, 13.10, 13.11, 13.12, 13.13, 13.14, 14.1, 14.3, 14.4, 14.5, 14.6, 14.8, 14.9, 14.10, 14.11, 14.12, 14.13, 15.1, 15.2, 15.3, 15.4, 15.5, 15.6, 15.7, 15.8, 15.9, 15.10, 15.11, 15.12, 15.13, 15.14, 16.1, 16.2, 16.3, 16.4, 16.5, 16.6, 16.7, 16.8, 16.9, 16.10, 16.11
1.2 Develop a working knowledge of the content domains of psychology	*Learning Objectives:* 1.1, 1.2, 1.3, 1.6, 1.7, 1.8, 1.9, 1.10, 1.11, 1.12, 2.1, 2.2, 2.3, 2.4, 2.5, 2.6, 2.7, 2.9, 2.10, 2.12, 3.1, 3.2, 3.3, 3.12, 3.13, 3.15, 4.1, 4.2, 4.5, 4.7, 4.8, 4.11, 5.1, 5.2, 5.3, 5.4, 5.5, 5.6, 5.7, 5.8, 5.11, 5.12, 5.13, 6.1, 6.2, 6.3, 6.4, 6.6, 6.7, 6.8, 6.10, 6.11, 6.12, 6.13, 6.14, 7.1, 7.2, 7.3, 7.4, 7.5, 7.7, 7.8, 7.10, 7.12, 7.14, 7.15, 8.1, 8.2, 8.3, 8.4, 8.5, 8.6, 8.7, 8.8, 8.9, 8.11, 8.13, 9.1, 9.2, 9.4, 9.5, 9.6, 9.7, 9.8, 9.9, 9.11, 9.12, 9.15, 10.3, 10.6, 10.7, 10.10, 10.11, 10.13, 10.14, 10.15, 11.1, 11.2, 11.3, 11.4, 11.5, 11.6, 11.7, 11.8, 11.9, 11.13, 12.1, 12.3, 12.4, 12.5, 12.10, 12.11, 13.2, 13.3, 13.4, 13.6, 13.7, 13.8, 13.9, 13.10, 13.11, 13.13, 13.14, 14.1, 14.2, 14.3, 14.4, 14.6, 14.7, 14.8, 14.9, 14.10, 14.12, 14.13, 14.14, 15.1, 15.2, 15.3, 15.4, 15.6, 15.8, 15.9, 15.10, 15.12, 16.2, 16.3, 16.4, 16.5, 16.6, 16.7, 16.8, 16.9, 16.10, 16.11, 16.12
1.3 Describe applications that employ discipline-based problem solving	*Learning Objectives:* 1.5, 1.13, 2.3, 2.9, 2.11, 2.12, 2.13, 3.1, 3.3, 3.8, 3.10, 3.15, 3.16, 4.4, 4.6, 4.8, 4.9, 4.10, 4.11, 5.1, 5.2, 5.4, 5.5, 5.6, 5.9, 5.10, 5.11, 5.14, 6.5, 6.7, 6.9, 6.10, 6.11, 7.2, 7.3, 7.4, 7.5, 7.6, 7.7, 7.11, 7.12, 7.13, 8.1, 8.5, 8.8, 8.9, 8.10, 8.11, 8.12, 8.13, 9.2, 9.3, 9.4, 9.5, 9.6, 9.8, 9.9, 9.10, 9.12, 9.13, 9.14, 9.15, 10.3, 10.4, 10.5, 10.6, 10.7, 10.8, 10.9, 10.12, 10.13, 10.14, 11.1, 11.2, 11.3, 11.6, 11.7, 11.8, 11.9, 11.10, 11.11, 11.12, 12.1, 12.2, 12.3, 12.4, 12.5, 12.6, 12.7, 12.8, 12.9, 12.10, 12.11, 13.5, 13.6, 13.7, 13.8, 13.9, 13.10, 13.11, 13.12, 13.13, 13.14, 13.15, 14.7, 14.8, 14.9, 14.10, 14.12, 15.2, 15.3, 15.5, 15.7, 15.8, 15.11, 15.13, 16.2, 16.7, 16.10, 16.11, 16.12, 16.13

Major concepts are reinforced with learning tools: Adaptive Pathways, Journal Prompts, Shared Writing, Essays to Assign, Experiment Simulations, and Video Quizzes.

Goal 2: Scientific Inquiry and Critical Thinking

Understand scientific reasoning and problem solving, including effective research methods.

2.1 Use scientific reasoning to interpret behavior	*Learning Objectives:* 1.4, 1.5, 1.12, 1.13, 2.2, 2.3, 2.8, 2.9, 2.11, 3.3, 3.11, 4.3, 4.5, 4.7, 4.8, 4.11, 5.1, 5.5, 5.10, 6.11, 6.12, 6.13, 6.14, 7.4, 7.6, 7.7, 7.13, 7.14, 7.15, 8.8, 8.9, 8.10, 9.2, 9.8, 9.15, 10.1, 10.2, 10.3, 10.4, 10.6, 10.7, 10.10, 10.12, 11.1, 11.2, 11.3, 11.7, 11.9, 11.11, 11.13, 12.2, 12.3, 12.5, 12.10, 13.2, 13.3, 13.6, 13.7, 13.8, 13.9, 13.10, 13.12, 13.13, 13.14, 14.1, 14.2, 14.6, 14.8, 14.10, 14.11, 14.12, 14.13, 15.2, 15.3, 15.14, 16.1, 16.2
2.2 Demonstrate psychology information literacy	*Learning Objectives:* 1.5, 1.9, 1.13, 10.15, 12.11, 14.14
2.3 Engage in innovative and integrative thinking and problem-solving	*Learning Objectives:* 1.13, 2.13, 3.16, 4.11, 5.1, 5.9, 5.14, 6.5, 6.14, 7.3, 7.4, 7.5, 7.6, 7.15, 8.13, 9.15, 10.3, 10.7, 10.15, 11.13, 12.11, 13.1, 13.11, 13.15, 14.11, 14.14, 15.1, 15.14, 16.2, 16.13
2.4 Interpret, design and conduct basic psychological research	*Learning Objectives:* 1.4, 1.6, 1.7, 1.8, 1.9, 1.10, 1.11, 1.12, 2.7, 2.10, 2.13, 3.16, 4.5, 4.11, 5.3, 5.5, 5.7, 5.8, 5.9, 5.14, 6.14, 8.4, 8.5, 8.6, 8.7, 8.13, 9.1, 13.15, 14.12, 14.13, 15.14
2.5 Incorporate sociocultural factors in scientific inquiry	*Learning Objectives:* 1.12, 1.13, 2.13, 3.16, 4.8, 4.11, 5.4, 5.14, 6.14, 7.13, 7.15, 8.2, 8.3, 8.4, 8.5, 8.10, 8.11, 8.12, 8.13, 9.5, 9.9, 9.15, 10.6, 10.13, 10.14, 10.15, 11.3, 11.4, 11.5, 11.6, 11.7, 11.9, 11.13, 12.3, 12.10, 12.11, 13.8, 13.9, 13.15, 14.1, 14.2, 14.3, 14.4, 14.14, 15.2, 15.3, 15.14, 16.1, 16.3, 16.4, 16.8, 16.10, 16.11, 16.12, 16.13

Scientific inquiry and Critical Thinking are reinforced with learning tools: Adaptive Pathways, Journal Prompts, Shared Writing, Essays to Assign, Experiment Simulations, and Video Quizzes.

APA Learning Outcomes and Objectives	Text Learning Objectives and Features
Goal 3: Ethical and Social Responsibility	
Develop ethically and socially responsible behaviors for professional and personal settings.	
3.1 Apply ethical standards to psychological science and practice	*Learning Objectives: 1.13, 2.13, 3.16, 4.11, 5.14, 6.14, 7.15, 8.13, 9.15, 10.15, 11.13, 12.11, 13.15, 14.14, 15.14, 16.13*
3.2 Promote values that build trust and enhance interpersonal relationships	*Learning Objectives: 11.3, 11.5, 11.6, 11.7, 16.11*
3.3 Adopt values that build community at local, national, and global levels	*Learning Objectives: 1.13, 4.8, 5.9, 5.14, 6.14, 8.10, 8.11, 8.12, 8.13, 9.15, 10.5, 10.15, 11.3, 11.4, 11.5, 11.6, 11.7, 11.12, 11.13, 12.5, 12.8, 12.9, 12.11, 13.11, 13.12, 13.14, 13.15, 15.1, 15.2, 15.3, 16.2, 16.10, 16.12, 16.13*

Ethical and Social Responsibility are reinforced with learning tools: Adaptive Pathways, Journal Prompts, Shared Writing, Essays to Assign, Experiment Simulations, and Video Quizzes.

APA Learning Outcomes and Objectives	Text Learning Objectives and Features
Goal 4: Communication	
Demonstrate competence in written, oral, and interpersonal communication skills and be able to develop and present a scientific argument.	
4.1 Demonstrate effective writing in multiple formats	*Learning Objectives: 1.9*
4.2 Exhibit effective presentation skills in multiple formats	
4.3 Interact Effectively with Others	*Learning Objectives: 10.11, 13.6*

Communication skills are reinforced with learning tools: Adaptive Pathways, Journal Prompts, Shared Writing, Essays to Assign, Experiment Simulations, and Video Quizzes.

APA Learning Outcomes and Objectives	Text Learning Objectives and Features
Goal 5: Professional Development	
Apply psychology-specific content and skills, effective self-reflection, project management skills, teamwork skills and career preparation to support occupational planning and pursuit.	
5.1 Apply psychological content and skills to professional work	*Learning Objectives: 1.13, 2.13, 3.16, 4.8, 4.9, 4.10, 5.9, 5.14, 6.5, 6.7, 6.9, 7.5, 7.6, 7.9, 8.11, 8.12, 8.13, 9.15, 10.5, 10.7, 10.8, 10.9, 11.6, 12.4, 12.5, 12.6, 12.7, 12.8, 12.9, 13.1, 13.11, 13.15, 14.1, 14.2, 15.1, 15.2, 15.3, 16.11*
5.2 Exhibit self-efficacy and self-regulation	*Learning Objectives: 8.9, 10.3, 10.7, 10.8, 10.9*
5.3 Refine project management skills	*Learning Objectives: 7.4, 7.6, 7.7, 13.10*
5.4 Enhance teamwork capacity	*Learning Objectives: 7.3, 7.4, 13.10*
5.5 Develop meaningful professional direction for life after graduation	

Professional development goals are reinforced with learning tools: Adaptive Pathways, Journal Prompts, Shared Writing, Essays to Assign, Experiment Simulations, and Video Quizzes.

Learning How to Learn

LO P.1 Distinguish between effective and ineffective study strategies based on the science of learning.

Welcome to *Psychology, First Edition*! As we begin, let's take a few minutes to consider your expectations and goals for this course. You may be fulfilling a course requirement, beginning a new college major, or you might even be interested in making a career change. An introductory course typically provides a broad overview of all areas of psychology—sort of an "around the world in 80 days" approach. This journey will likely both confirm and challenge some of your own beliefs and intuitions about human behavior. Regardless of what brought you to this course, hopefully one of your goals is related to learning. This introductory psychology program has been designed first and foremost with learning in mind. There is a wealth of scholarly evidence about the most effective (and ineffective) ways to learn, and these materials have been carefully designed to take advantage of what cognitive scientists currently know about learning. This digital learning program has implemented what is called an "evidence-based approach." Evidence-based means the development and creation of these materials have been guided by the scientific literature and evaluated according to principles of scientific investigation. With respect to this program, evidence-based means that (1) many of the features you encounter represent "best practices" for learning, and

(2) the effectiveness of the program features has been tested to demonstrate that they do lead to significant improvements in learning among students like you.

Ideally, taking a psychology course should help you in all of your other coursework. If you learn to apply what psychologists have discovered about how the mind works, you will be able to improve your own learning, studying, and memory skills in a variety of ways. In essence, one of your major tasks is to learn *how* to best learn. After all, there are entire chapters of this book devoted to helping you understand how human learning and memory work. You might be thinking that you've already spent years in a classroom at this point and you've developed some pretty good learning strategies. Take a moment to look at the different study techniques listed below and select the one you tend to rely on the most when preparing for an exam:

How Do You Study?

Survey: How Do You Study?

Interactive

○ Rereading the chapter

○ Highlighting

○ Reviewing notes

○ Writing your own exam questions

○ Drawing concept maps

○ Taking practice tests

○ Studying flashcards

Did you select rereading the chapter, highlighting, or reviewing your notes as the study strategies you depend on the most? If so, you are not alone. These strategies are often among the most popular choices for people when studying (Baier et al., 2011; Bell & Limber, 2009). For example, 84 percent of students surveyed in one study reported that rereading was their top study strategy (Karpicke et al., 2009). However, these very popular strategies (highlighting, rereading the text/notes) also appear to be generally ineffective and, as a result, give you the least "bang for your buck" in terms of time spent studying (Callendar & McDaniel, 2009; Dunlosky et al., 2013). For instance, experiments testing the effectiveness of rereading showed that exam scores did not significantly improve after students read a textbook chapter a second time (Callender & McDaniel, 2009). Another study showed that reviewing notes, highlighting, and rereading were actually not even related to students' exam scores; in fact, the total number of hours studying was only weakly related to exam scores (Gurung, 2005). For some reason, we seem to be drawn to study strategies that end up being fairly ineffective. Because our natural instincts don't appear to be leading us in the right direction, one of the goals of this Revel Psychology program is to provide you with information about how learning works best and to give you appropriate and effective tools to put this knowledge into practice.

What about Learning Styles?

How many times have you heard someone say, "I'm a visual learner, so I need to see diagrams" or "I record my lectures because I'm an auditory learner"? You may have even characterized yourself as a particular type of learner and come to see this as a part of your personality.

The idea that individuals differ with respect to the mode of instruction, or method of studying that is most effective for them, is referred to as *learning styles* (Pashler et al., 2008). In education, the implication of learning styles is the notion that matching your preferred method of learning to a similar mode of instruction will produce improved learning. Belief in learning styles is extraordinarily popular, with more than 90 percent of undergraduate psychology students acknowledging a belief in their own particular learning style (Riener & Willingham, 2010). The problem with this belief is there is *no scientific evidence* that matching an individual's learning style to a particular mode of instruction improves learning (Morse, 2014; Pashler et al., 2008; Riener & Willingham, 2010; Rohrer & Pashler, 2012). While it is true that each of us may have *preferences* about how we learn, there is no evidence that aligning your preferences and your instruction and/or studying will produce better results in learning.

The bottom line is effective instruction and learning has much more to do with designing a learning environment that uses strategies that promote learning in *all* people. Many of those strategies have been intentionally embedded throughout this digital learning program. So rather than focusing on your preferred "learning style," take advantage of all of the strategies built into this program, and you will likely see much better results.

Adopting the Right Frame of Mind for Learning

Think about a time when someone tried to teach you something you weren't particularly interested in learning. Perhaps a friend or someone you were dating wanted to teach you all the rules to his/her favorite sport—a sport you happen to find tedious and uninteresting. How well did you learn the rules of the game? How much attention and effort did you put into the task? You may have listened politely (with an internal eyeroll) and proceeded to let the information flow in one ear and out the other. Contrast this example with a time in your life when you've been very motivated to learn something new such as a time-saving app on your phone or the music to a new song you love. As these examples illustrate, there's no doubt that effective learning requires a particular frame of mind.

GROWTH VERSUS FIXED MINDSET   As you'll discover in the chapter on Motivation and Emotion, Carol Dweck's research on the importance of mindset when approaching a new task suggests that there are two types of people. The first kind of person views intelligence or learning as an ability that can be cultivated, and these people tend to flourish when challenged and see learning in a positive light. This is called a growth mindset. On the other hand, some people believe that learning ability or intelligence is something you either have or don't have and therefore effort is not important—in fact, having to put in extra effort only serves as evidence that you are lacking this in-born characteristic. This view of intelligence is called a fixed mindset. As you can see from the following image, people with a growth versus fixed mindset respond very differently to challenges, obstacles, and negative feedback. In the end, a person with a growth mindset is likely to achieve more than someone with a fixed mindset—even if they are equally talented.

So, how do you adopt a growth mindset? First, Dweck argues that your mindset is a choice—we can actively choose how to think about our own abilities and efforts. Start by rethinking the way you approach challenging or difficult topics. There will definitely be difficult topics in introductory psychology and different students will find certain topics more or less challenging. If you successfully adopt a growth mindset, you will view challenges as a true opportunity for learning. When you struggle or even fail at times, you are engaging in the hard work of learning. Consider an exercise analogy. If your exercise goal is to become more physically fit, you will never accomplish it by sticking with only easy and painless activities. The times when you push your limits physically and feel a little pain—whether it's lifting a little more weight than last time or running a little faster or a little longer—those are the moments when you are actually making progress. The same is true of learning. However, if we slip into a fixed mindset, we actually become afraid that a challenge or a little mental "pain" signifies a lack of ability or failure. In reality, those are the moments when you are building up your brain "muscle." So, the next time you catch yourself saying, "I just can't do the biology stuff" or "I'm just not good at _____," stop

Figure P.1 Two Mindsets

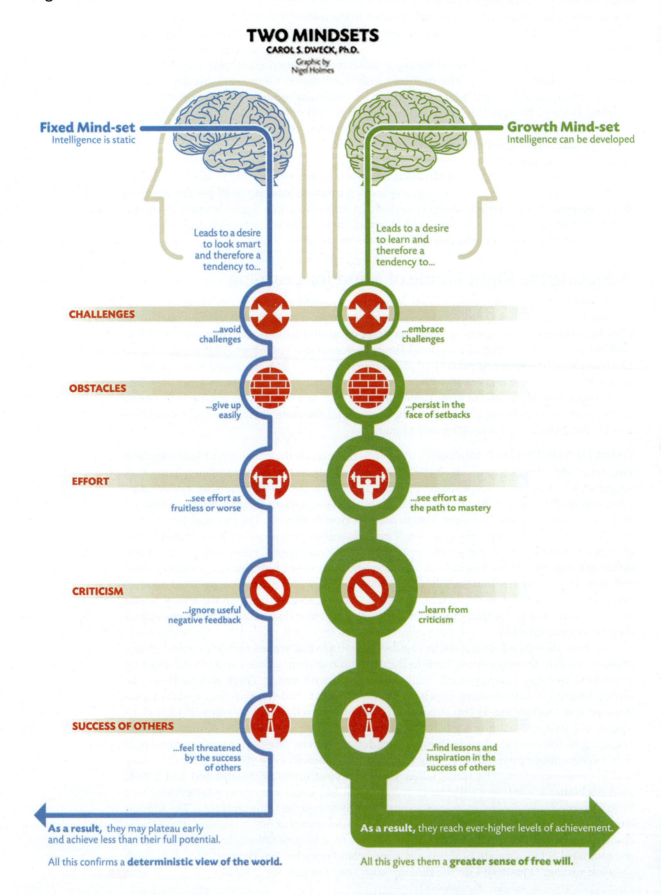

What Kind of Mindset Do You Have?

WHAT KIND OF MINDSET DO YOU HAVE?

GROWTH MINDSET

- Tell me I try hard.
- When I fail, I learn.
- I want to challenge myself.
- When I'm frustrated, I persevere.
- I can learn anything I want to.
- If you succeed, I'm inspired.
- My effort and attitude determine everything.

FIXED MINDSET

- Tell me I'm smart.
- When I fail, I'm no good.
- I don't want to be challenged.
- When I'm frustrated, I give up.
- I'm either good at it, or I'm not.
- If you succeed, I feel threatened.
- My abilities determine everything.

and remind yourself that this fixed mindset will only get in your way of learning something you are truly capable of grasping with effort and hard work.

THE DANGERS OF DISTRACTED READING   As more and more of our reading material becomes digital, some research has highlighted that people sometimes retain more information when reading a printed text compared to a digital text, in part because they have fewer distractions and engage in less multitasking when reading (Subrahmanyam et al., 2013; van der Schuur et al., 2015). This is not a problem inherent in digital reading, but it is a problem in the way that we think about reading digitally. We have a schema, or a mental framework (you'll learn all about this in the coming chapters), for reading a printed text. For example, the schema includes sitting in a quiet environment, having the book open on a desk or on our laps, and using a pen or highlighter to take notes or draw in the margins. Think about our schema for working on a computer or tablet screen. Even the home screen covered with apps is a "multitasking" schema. We see ourselves quickly hopping from one task to another—checking your bank account balance quickly, reading a text or email, opening up a story linked in your social media app, and clicking back over to the window with your digital text. Unfortunately, without some active effort to rethink this schema, learning will be more challenging than necessary. You've probably heard about the latest research on the dangers of distracted driving. Drivers who are talking on cell phones or texting are actually more impaired than drunk drivers (Strayer, Drews, & Crouch, 2006)! Study after study demonstrates that most people think they are good at multitasking—and most people are wrong!

In order to truly adopt a frame of mind for optimal learning, make sure you consider the time you spend working on course materials within the same schema you have for reading a printed text. Be sure to practice the following guidelines for getting the most out of your study time:

1. Turn off your phone (or put it in another room if the temptation is just too much).

2. Close all other windows/apps on your device.

3. Focus only on the course materials for a specified amount of time. It doesn't have to be a marathon session. In fact, smaller goals are often more manageable and achievable. For example, set aside 30 minutes or an hour of "distraction-free" time when you make a pact with yourself to tune out other things that clamor for your attention and dedicate that time to learning.

Despite what many people believe, multitasking is an ineffective strategy and leads to poorer learning.

Adaptive Pathway Example

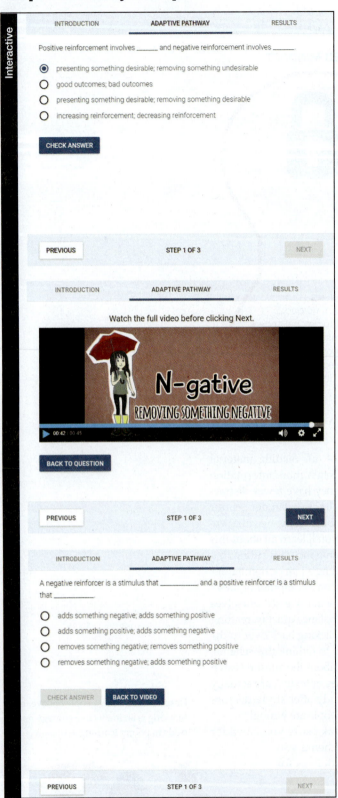

Five Effective Tools for Learning

There are many evidence-based learning strategies, but the following five categories represent those that (1) have significant evidence of effectiveness and (2) have been intentionally built into the current materials in a meaningful way. First, we'll give you a brief overview of the concept or strategy itself and then show you the specific features of these materials that use each strategy.

TOOL #1: ADDRESSING COMMON MISCONCEPTIONS AND DIFFICULT CONCEPTS Most of you will start this course with some preexisting knowledge about psychology. Much of this knowledge may be accurate, but you are also likely to have some misconceptions related to the field of psychology. For example, many people endorse the belief that "opposites attract" when it comes to romantic attraction, but there is ample evidence in psychology that this simply isn't true (Lilienfeld et al., 2010). As demonstrated by the initial discussion of ineffective but popular study strategies, students also hold misconceptions about the process of learning and effective study strategies (Chew, 2010). Therefore, because of your experience in the world, you will bring your own prior knowledge to the course, and this knowledge will also include some misconceptions. Addressing and combating misconceptions is critical to promote learning.

Students tend to find certain topics in psychology to be particularly challenging, and often need more assistance in grasping these concepts than can be found in a typical textbook. In order to provide additional support for these topics, experienced introductory psychology instructors were surveyed and asked to identify the most challenging concepts in each chapter. Some of these concepts are challenging for students because of common misconceptions and other concepts are challenging for other reasons. To help address these misconceptions or difficult concepts "on the spot," adaptive pathways have been built into each chapter. After coverage of a difficult concept, you will be asked to answer a multiple-choice pinpoint question. These questions have been carefully designed to clearly differentiate between a student's accurate understanding of a concept and any potential confusion or misconceptions. When a misconception is detected, you will be provided with immediate feedback and additional instruction and examples, in the form of a short targeted video, to help clarify the concept. After the targeted video, you will complete a follow-up question to determine if the misconception has been corrected. Your instructor will also be able to see how all students are performing on the questions before and after the video to determine what type of additional instructional assistance might be most helpful.

When you encounter these adaptive pathways, make sure you take the time to answer the questions carefully and watch the animations. The animations are brief (i.e., less than 2 minutes long), and previous students have shown significant improvements in their understanding of the concepts after watching them. Therefore, to maximize your own learning, make sure you complete each adaptive pathway as you work your way through a chapter.

TOOL #2: PRACTICE TESTING We tend to think of practice tests as a tool we can use to assess our current level of knowledge or comprehension related to a particular topic. We often think about academic learning in stages that progress from the "study phase" to the "testing phase." However, research on the effect of answering practice questions suggests that testing can actually be a critical part of the learning process itself. Researchers examining the impact of practice tests have found that "testing is a powerful means of improving learning, not just assessing it" (Roediger & Karpicke, 2006b). This phenomenon is known as the *testing effect*, and it has been repeatedly demonstrated that long-term memory of information can be significantly enhanced when retrieval practice (what happens when taking a practice test) is included in the "study phase" of learning (Eisenkraemer et al., 2013). In fact, using practice tests has been shown to improve later test performance more than additional study time (Roediger & Karpicke, 2006a). As Figure P.2 illustrates, retention of information is greatest when studying is paired with practice testing rather than spending time only studying. However, the group that studied and then studied some more performed better immediately, demonstrating why it's so tempting to believe this strategy is the best. In the real world, though, your ability to remember information days or weeks later is evaluated the most often, and the group that paired studying with practice testing did much better after a delay in time.

Figure P.2 The Effectiveness of Testing During the Learning Phase

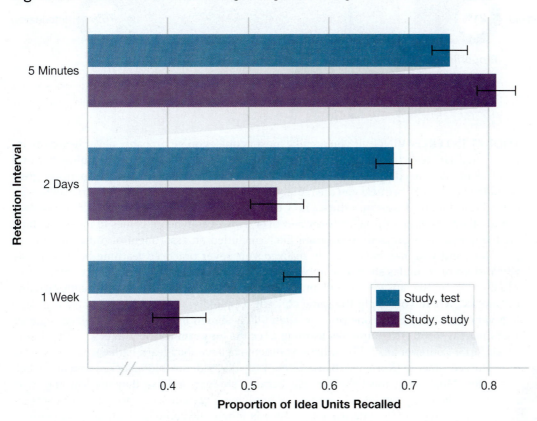

In order to enhance learning and take advantage of the testing effect, practice tests have been intentionally incorporated in a variety of ways within the chapters. Each module in the chapter will include a brief (less than 7 items) practice quiz. This end-of-module quiz will focus on the specific concepts addressed in the module. You will also encounter a variety of opportunities to capitalize on the testing effect by completing assessments in formats other than multiple choice. Every chapter will include various opportunities for writing. There will also be a variety of interactive assessments incorporated into each chapter. Every time you encounter a quiz, resist the urge to think of it as something you do "at the end of studying." Instead, keep in mind these activities are allowing you to engage in the effective learning strategy of combining studying and testing during the "study phase." In addition to the end-of-module quizzes, each chapter will conclude with a 30-item end-of-chapter quiz. This chapter quiz will offer an opportunity to assess your understanding of the material.

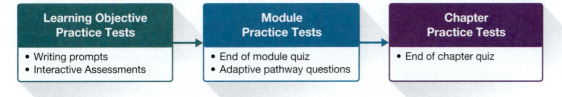

Figure P.3 Blocked versus Interleaved Practice

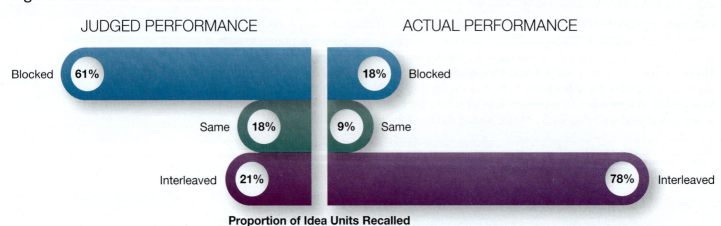

JUDGED PERFORMANCE   ACTUAL PERFORMANCE

Blocked   61%   18% Blocked

Same 18%   9% Same

Interleaved 21%   78% Interleaved

Proportion of Idea Units Recalled

This is an example of the image you will encounter with each Piecing It Together feature at the end of the chapter. The topic of cyberbullying will be discussed in Chapter 13.

TOOL #3: INTERLEAVING   If you are like most people, you've probably never heard of "interleaving." However, chances are good that you've encountered learning difficulties because of a lack of interleaved practice. Have you ever taken a math class where you perform great on all the homework because you are required to apply only one set of steps/formula repeatedly? Typical math classes introduce a new concept and then assign homework that involves solving the same type of problem over and over. However, when it comes to the exam, how are the questions organized? Your exam likely included an assortment of different types of problems, and you may have quickly realized you never practiced learning how to decide which steps or formulas should be applied to different problems. If you've encountered this situation before, the answer to your problem is interleaved practice. Rather than practicing in "blocks" where you apply the same concept repeatedly, interleaving provides exposure to a variety of concepts in one practice attempt. As shown in Figure P.3, evidence suggests that interleaved practice improves learning over the long run (Birnbaum et al., 2013; Lin et al., 2013; Rohrer et al., 2015), although students believe they learn better when they used blocked practice (Kornell & Bjork, 2008). Why do students think blocked practice is better? Most likely, this belief persists because students *feel* like they are learning more when they get into a "groove" of applying a certain set of principles or concepts repeatedly. Interleaved practice is inherently more difficult and demanding, but ultimately the rewards in terms of learning are much greater.

There are several ways interleaved practice opportunities have been embedded within this course material. Concepts from one chapter to the next are interleaved within the last module of each chapter in a feature called "Piecing It Together." This module addresses one current and/or controversial topic related to the content discussed in that chapter. Each issue is then examined from four different, interconnected perspectives: cultural and social diversity, variations in human functioning, ethics, and research methods. These themes are based on the American Psychological Association's recommendations that introductory psychology courses apply these "cross-cutting themes" using an interleaving approach rather than a "blocked" approach (Gurung et al., 2016).

Interleaving has also been incorporated through interactives that bring material together from different learning objectives throughout the chapter. This approach helps you practice learning a concept and then later applying that concept again in a different context. For example, in Chapter 2, after you learn about the anatomy of the brain, you will be asked to apply what you learned about the anatomy and functioning of the brain to determine the type and/or extent of brain damage suffered by a patient.

Cultural and Social Diversity

Ethics   Cyberbullying   Variations in Human Functioning

Research Methods

The Effects of Brain Damage

Interactive

In this activity, your job is to use what you have learned so far about the anatomy and functioning of the brain to determine the type and/or extent of brain damage suffered by a patient. Your task is to examine all of the available evidence and come to a reasoned conculsion based on the symptoms reported.

TOOL #4: DEEP PROCESSING OF INFORMATION   The Memory chapter will discuss how information can be processed at different levels (from shallow to deep). Our memory is best for information processed at a deeper level. In other words, we remember information that is meaningful to us more easily than information that is not as meaningful. For example, when trying to learn a new vocabulary word such as "interleaving," a shallow way to process the information would be to simply copy down the word and the definition in your notes. This is considered a shallow strategy because the information has not been processed in a meaningful way. Examples of deep processing approaches to learning a new vocabulary word might include (1) rewriting the definition in your own words with an example of how the term applies in your own life and (2) using the word to create a graphic of related concepts (Murtiana, 2012).

These types of strategies are often called "elaborative rehearsal" because you are not simply rehearsing the information in a repetitive, shallow way. Instead, you are elaborating on the information...which makes it more meaningful...which leads to better memory later.

This digital learning program has incorporated several tools to assist you in using deep processing strategies while studying and learning. Each of the adaptive videos provides a new example of a concept or a tip on how to process the information at a deeper level. In addition, there are reflective questions throughout each chapter prompting you to think at a deeper level about a particular concept, so make sure you answer the questions when you encounter them—they are there for a reason! The "Piecing it Together" features also provide excellent opportunities for deep processing of the content.

In addition to these built-in features, here are some additional study tips for you to consider while you work through the materials in your class:

1. Create your own "concept maps" which allow you to see the connections between concepts.

2. When taking notes, avoid writing down exactly what it is stated in the text or exactly what your instructor says. Take the time to write your notes in your own words and use your own examples wherever possible. Ask yourself, "How can I apply this to my own life?"

3. Create your own exam questions after working through the material in one learning objective. Try to write a multiple-choice question, a fill-in-the-blank question, and a short-answer question. Come back to your questions later and answer them. Various online programs/websites can help you in writing and saving these questions.

4. After learning a new concept, try explaining it or teaching it to someone else. Psychology is an exciting and interesting topic to many people. So, start a conversation with someone by saying "Hey, do you know what I learned in psychology today?" Having that conversation is a great way to promote the consolidation of information and your learning about the topic.

This is an example of concept map for the material covered in the current Learning How to Learn chapter.

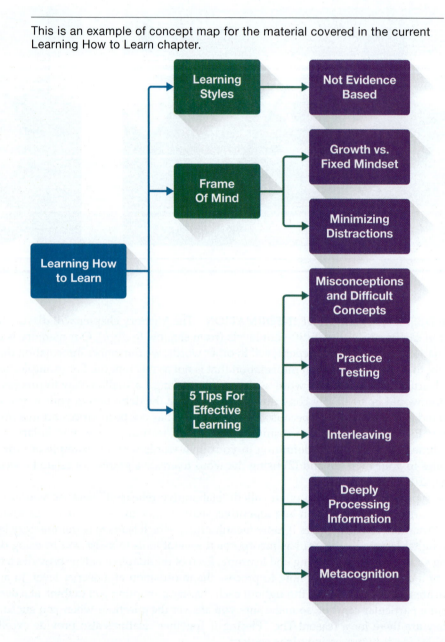

TOOL #5: METACOGNITIVE SKILLS Metacognition means "thinking about thinking," and it includes the ability to accurately assess your own knowledge and skills and to self-regulate your learning. Metacognition involves several different skills and abilities, but one of the most important is the ability to accurately assess and monitor your progress as a learner. For example, prior to taking an exam, you probably ask yourself the question, "Am I prepared?" Based on the answer to that question, you either continue to study or you stop. One of the key problems students face is the fact that many are not particularly good at accurately answering the question, "Am I prepared?" One of the most common complaints we hear after an exam is from the student who says, "I thought I was prepared, but then I got to the test and the questions seemed confusing and I totally bombed the exam." This scenario is an example of poor metacognition—this student stopped studying because he/she felt adequately prepared due to an inaccurate perception of their own understanding/knowledge level. As you can see, metacognitive skills are very important, not just for psychology, but for life.

Research studies have shown there is a relationship between poor performance on an exam or in a course and poor metacognitive skills (Dunlosky & Rawson, 2012; Foster et al., 2017). Most students tend to be overconfident about their performance—if you ask them to predict their exam score prior to taking the exam, they will make predictions that are higher than their actual score (Miller & Geraci, 2011). Overpredictions of exam performance are particularly common among students who are the weakest performers, and there is some evidence to suggest that having poor metacognitive skills can actually *cause* poor exam performance to some degree (Metcalfe & Finn, 2008) because students don't choose appropriate study methods or study long enough based on their misperception that they know enough already. However, research has also shown that two strategies can lead to improvements in metacognitive skills: (1) improving accuracy of metacognitive judgments and (2) encouraging selection of appropriate study strategies (Hartwig et al., 2012; Metcalfe, 2009). Therefore, this digital learning program focuses on both of these strategies.

In order to assist you in improving the accuracy of your own metacognition, feedback will be provided in several ways. Each end-of-module practice quiz will provide feedback, which will help you immediately recognize whether or not you have an adequate understanding of a particular topic or concept. The adaptive pathways will also help you judge your mastery of the content. Try thinking about how confident you are in your knowledge about that topic before submitting your answer. The more practice and feedback you get, the more accurate you will become in your metacognitive skills.

Summary

Now it is time to put all of the information about how learning works to good use. As you begin reading and interacting with the content in the chapters to come, keep the five tools for effective learning in mind: (1) addressing misconceptions and difficult concepts, (2) practice testing, (3) interleaving, (4) deeply processing information, and (5) metacognitive skills. Feel free to leave behind any of your past erroneous beliefs such as the importance of learning styles or the effectiveness of more shallow learning strategies like effortless highlighting and re-reading. In addition, make sure you approach your digital reading the same way you would approach reading a print textbook—put all distractions aside (e.g., turn off your phone and close all other windows or apps on your device) and focus only on reading. With this approach, you will maximize your "bang for your buck" in terms of time spent studying, and you will likely be successful in your course.

End-of-Chapter Quiz

1. Which of the following study strategies are relatively ineffective yet are very popular among students?

   a. Highlighting
   b. Making concept maps
   c. Writing your own quiz questions
   d. Teaching the concepts to another person

2. What does the scientific evidence suggest about learning styles, or the idea that individuals differ with respect to the mode of instruction, or method of studying that is most effective for them?

   a. There is no scientific evidence that matching an individual's learning style to a particular mode of instruction improves learning.

   b. Evidence for learning styles is mixed; some studies support the fact that matching an individual's learning style to a particular mode of instruction improves learning, and other studies do not support it.

   c. There is significant evidence supporting the fact that matching an individual's learning style to a particular mode of instruction improves learning.

   d. This issue has not yet been studied.

3. Which of the following statements was made by a person who has adopted a growth mindset?

   a. "I'm either good at it, or I'm not."

   b. "I can learn anything I want to."

   c. "I don't like to be challenged."

   d. "My abilities determine everything."

4. Imagine your roommate is reading online and you notice her cell phone is going off constantly, she keeps stopping her reading to respond to text messages, and she even does a quick Google search for movie times that evening. Which of the following responses indicates you understand the research on multitasking?

   a. "I guess you are just better at multitasking than I am."

   b. "It's great that your reading is online so that you can take care of lots of things at one time."

   c. "The research suggests that reading while distracted is really not going to be very effective—you might want to turn off your phone and close down your other apps."

   d. "Research shows that we get better at multitasking with practice so I guess you are definitely practicing!"

5. Bogdan studied the chapter for 1 hour, took a break, and then studied the chapter again for 30 minutes. Raquel studied the chapter for an hour, took a break, and then completed practice tests for 30 minutes. Who will likely perform better on the chapter exam a week later?

   a. Bodgan

   b. Raquel

   c. They will likely perform the same.

   d. There is no way to predict who will perform better.

6. Interleaved practice is practicing _____.

   a. different skills or concepts during the same study session

   b. one type of skill or concept at a time

   c. without breaks

   d. in short bursts followed by breaks

7. Which of the following is *not* an example of a strategy that leads to deep processing of information?

   a. Re-writing a definition in your own words with an example of how the term has applied in your own life

   b. Making a concept map

   c. Copying flashcards

   d. Writing your own practice quiz questions

8. The ability to accurately assess your own knowledge and skills and to self-regulate your learning is known as _____.

   a. interleaving

   b. blocked practice

   c. metacognition

   d. growth mindset

9. If you find yourself surprised by a poor exam score, it is possible you are struggling with metacognition. One strategy to improve your metacognition includes _____.

   a. trying to predict your score before taking practice quizzes and then comparing your prediction to your actual score

   b. avoiding looking at your score on practice quizzes

   c. waiting until after an exam to read the feedback on your practice quizzes

   d. skipping adaptive pathway animations

Chapter 1
Psychology As a Science

Chapter Outline and Learning Objectives

Module 1.1–1.3: The Discipline of Psychology

LO 1.1 Describe the major historical perspectives in psychology.

LO 1.2 Summarize the seven modern perspectives in psychology.

LO 1.3 Identify various career options available to those with a degree in psychology.

Module 1.4–1.5: Psychology and The Scientific Method

LO 1.4 List the steps of the scientific method, and apply them to the field of psychology.

LO 1.5 Recall some of the skills needed to be a critical thinker.

Module 1.6–1.8: Descriptive Research Methods

LO 1.6 Summarize the potential advantages and disadvantages of using naturalistic observation.

LO 1.7 Recall some uses and limitations of case studies.

LO 1.8 Explain the methods used by researchers when designing a survey.

Module 1.9–1.10: Correlational Studies

LO 1.9 Describe how correlations measure relationships between variables.

LO 1.10 Distinguish between correlation and causation.

Module 1.11–1.12: Experimental Research

LO 1.11 Recall the components of experimental research.

LO 1.12 Explain how researchers try to control for potential bias, and consider ethical standards when conducting research.

Module 1.13: Piecing It Together: Vaccines and Autism

LO 1.13 Analyze how the cross-cutting themes of psychology relate to the topic of vaccine research in autism.

What is Psychology?

psychology

the scientific study of behavior and mental processes

You are enrolled in an Introduction to Psychology course and have purchased the materials for the class. You likely believe you have some intuitive sense of what the class will be about. But, if your roommate, parent, or partner asked you to give them the definition of psychology, could you do it? Briefly stated, **psychology** is the scientific study of behavior and mental processes. This definition really includes two vital components. First, psychology is a science. While philosophers might speculate on why people act as they do, psychologists use scientific methods to accurately describe, explain, predict, or control human and animal behavior. Until approximately 130 years ago, psychology was considered a branch of philosophy. However, as the scientific method has been applied to psychology over the past century, psychology has developed into its own scientific field. Throughout this chapter, we will examine the development of psychology as a formal discipline in its own right and the ways in which the scientific method has been applied.

The second component of the definition of psychology pertains to the subject matter being studied. While botany is the scientific study of plants, psychology focuses on the study of human behavior and mental processes. *Behavior* includes any action that can be directly observed, while *mental processes* include internal activities in the mind that are not directly observable. For example, imagine you would like to know how another individual feels about you. You could examine the person's observable behaviors (e.g., Does he/she seek you out for conversations? Does he/she smile when talking to you? Does he/she return your calls or texts?), but you would also need to have some insight into their mental processes (e.g., What types of thoughts and emotions does he/she experience when thinking of you?) to really know whether the person has a positive, negative, or neutral opinion of you.

You may have encountered some skepticism from people who do not believe psychology is a science. This is a common misconception, born out of the fact that much of what psychologists study may be personally experienced. For example, you may believe that people often experience a "midlife crisis" because you have an uncle who, at age 45, bought a sports car and left his wife for a younger woman. Your individual experience has given you a false sense of actual scientific data that may or may not be true of the population as a whole. In fact, the concept of a "midlife crisis" is not supported by research, and middle-aged people often report that it's the happiest time in their lives (Freund & Ritter, 2009; Lachman et al., 2015).

This type of misconception is less common in the physical sciences. Few people would claim to have personal insight about the behavior of accelerated electrons or the results of a chemical reaction between hydrogen and nitrogen. Before they state their theories as facts,

Take the Poll

Interactive

Survey: Take the Poll

Rate the following statements as "true" or "false":

1. Birds of a feather flock together.

  ○ True

  ○ False

2. The pen is mightier than the sword.

  ○ True

  ○ False

3. Opposites attract.

  ○ True

  ○ False

4. Actions speak louder than words.

  ○ True

  ○ False

physicists and chemists undergo careful scientific processes to test their ideas. Although many people don't realize it, scientific processes are equally important in psychology. For example, the fact that you have personally encountered individuals who appear to experience a midlife crisis does not necessarily indicate that everyone has had the same experiences. There are limits to the use of intuition and "common sense" in terms of understanding our own behavior and the behavior of others. Not only are we limited by the boundaries of our own experiences, we are also limited by the reliability of our memories and the dangers of our personal biases. In order to make generalized, objective, and well-supported statements about human nature, psychologists need to act as scientists rather than as casual observers.

Of course, casual observers are often on the right track: Many times, theories that seem like "common knowledge" are in fact supported by rigorous psychological research. For example, the saying "birds of a feather flock together" has ample research support showing that we tend to be attracted to people who are similar to us (Byrne, 1971; Montoya & Horton, 2013). However, the opposing common saying that "opposites attract" is not supported by evidence. Scientific psychological research frequently does not support many of our culture's commonly held assumptions, highlighting the importance of critical, objective inquiry to the study of the human mind. This chapter includes information about the history of psychology and a review of the research methods that psychologists use to study human behavior and mental processes.

Module 1.1–1.3: The Discipline of Psychology

The field of psychology has a rich history dating back to the ancient philosophers. Over many centuries, the discipline has evolved to include a diverse array of perspectives on the scientific study of human behavior and mental processes. These days, you could encounter a psychologist in a school setting helping children better learn, in a business office assisting in employee selection, at a university conducting research in the neurosciences, or in a substance abuse treatment clinic counseling those with addictions.

A Brief History of Psychology

LO 1.1   Describe the major historical perspectives in psychology.

A basic understanding of how the field of psychology developed is vital to appreciating the present state of the discipline. Imagine if you were asked to provide information about yourself so that others could get to know you. You would inevitably provide your own personal history, discussing where you were raised, describing your family, and recounting significant past accomplishments or challenges. In so doing, the people around you would develop an understanding of you through hearing about your past. In other words, your history is what makes you the person you are today. The same is true for the field of psychology, and the following will provide you with your first "introduction" to the discipline with the hope that you will develop a greater understanding of psychology today by an awareness of its past.

PRESCIENTIFIC PSYCHOLOGY   Psychology has its roots in ancient philosophy. In the fifth century BCE, Greek philosophers began to speculate about how the mind works and how it might affect behavior. Socrates (470–399 BCE) and Plato (428–347 BCE) believed that the mind did not cease to exist when the body died and that thoughts and ideas could exist separately from the body—a concept known as **dualism**. They theorized that knowledge is built within us and that we gain access to it through logical reasoning.

Although Socrates and Plato's beliefs were developed nearly 2,500 years ago, it was not until the Scientific Revolution of the late Renaissance period that French philosopher René Descartes (1596–1650), a believer of Socrates' idea that mind is distinct from body, began to investigate how the two might be connected. By dissecting the brains of animals, Descartes concluded that the pineal gland at the base of the brain was the principle seat of the soul, where all thoughts were formed. He believed the soul flowed through the body via hollow tubes and controlled muscle movement. Although anyone who still subscribes to Descartes' beliefs about the soul would probably fail a biology exam, the hollow tubes that Descartes noted were, among other things, important for controlling reflexes: We now know them as nerves, and we will examine how the nervous system really works in future chapters.

dualism

the belief that the mind does not cease to exist when the body dies and that thoughts and ideas can exist separately from the body

Wilhelm Wundt (shown seated), in the first laboratory for psychological research.

empiricism

the view that knowledge originates through experience

structuralism

a school of psychology concerned with studying the individual elements of consciousness

introspection

an examination of one's own conscious thoughts and feelings

functionalism

a school of psychology focused on how organisms use their learning and perceptual abilities to function in their environment

natural selection

a theory that organisms best adapted to their environment tend to survive and transmit their genetic characteristics to succeeding generations

Not all 17th-century philosophers agreed with the theories of Socrates and Plato. British philosopher John Locke (1632–1704) believed that at birth, the human mind was a *tabula rasa*, or a "blank slate," containing no innate knowledge. Locke proposed that people gain knowledge through their experiences by means of observation, laying the foundations for later studies in sensation and perception and social learning theory. His theory that knowledge is gained through careful external and internal observation planted the early seeds of **empiricism** and contributed to the development of the scientific method.

SCIENTIFIC PSYCHOLOGY: HISTORICAL PERSPECTIVES
Most psychologists agree that the birth of modern psychology occurred in a laboratory in Germany in 1879. The founder of the laboratory, Wilhelm Wundt (1832–1920), argued that the mind could be examined both scientifically and objectively, and he invited students from around the world to learn how to study the structure of the human mind. This was the first time anyone had attempted to incorporate objectivity and measurement into the field of psychology, earning Wundt the title of "father of psychology." His lectures gained popularity throughout the 1880s and, before long, the new science of psychology had evolved into two early schools of thought: *structuralism* and *functionalism*.

One of Wundt's students, Edward Titchener (1867–1927), believed experiences could be broken down into individual emotions and sensations, much as a chemist or a physician might analyze matter in terms of molecules and atoms. His school of thought, which focused on identifying individual elements of consciousness and showing how they could be combined and integrated, became known as **structuralism**. Titchener was primarily interested in the *structure* of the mind and his approach was to engage people in **introspection**, or "looking inward," training them to report various elements of their experiences as they patted a dog, thought about the color blue, or smelled a flower. Introspection and structuralism were short-lived concepts, dying out in the early 1900s. This decline was due primarily to the limitations of introspection as a means of scientific discovery. After all, can we ever really accurately and reliably report on our own internal mental activities? Although they had little long-term effect on psychological science, the study of sensation and perception was highly influenced by structuralism and introspection and remains an important part of contemporary psychology.

Unlike Wundt and Titchener, American academic William James (1842–1910) believed it was impossible to break consciousness into individual elements. He saw consciousness as a continuing stream of ever-changing thoughts that could not be separated. Instead, James focused on how organisms use their learning and perceptual abilities to *function* in their environment—an approach that came to be known as **functionalism**. James speculated that thinking developed because it was adaptive, and he believed that useful behavioral traits (in addition to physical traits) could be passed from generation to generation. These views were influenced strongly by Darwin's theory of evolution and the principle of **natural selection**, which stated that characteristics that provide a survival advantage are more likely to be passed along to subsequent generations and "selected" over time.

To contrast the movements of structuralism and functionalism, consider the topic of pain. A structuralist would analyze the intensity, duration, or sensations of the pain, while a functionalist would be more interested in how pain functions to communicate to the individual that something is wrong so that they will not do further damage.

Although functionalism is no longer a major perspective in psychology, elements of functionalist thought paved the way for the emergence of the school of thought called *behaviorism* and can still be seen in educational psychology and organizational psychology. For example, by emphasizing individual differences, functionalism influenced the theory that children should be taught at the level for which they, as individuals, are developmentally prepared.

In Germany, psychologists were also objecting to structuralism, albeit for different reasons. Max Wertheimer (1880–1943) believed the acts of sensing and perceiving could not be broken into smaller elements and still be understood. When people look at a house, Wertheimer reasoned, they see a house, not a collection of doors, walls, and windows. Wertheimer and his colleagues believed the act of perception entails more than just the sum of its parts. Their ideas developed into a school of thought known as **Gestalt psychology**. Roughly translated, *gestalt* means "whole" or "form." Gestalt psychologists believed people naturally seek out patterns, or wholes, in the sensory information available to them.

Women also made valuable contributions to the emerging field of psychology, although many early female pioneers faced challenges and discrimination based on gender. The first female president of the American Psychological Association (APA) in 1905, Mary Whiton Calkins (1893–1930), trained under William James at Harvard University and completed the requirements for a PhD at Harvard in 1894. However, Harvard University refused to grant the degree because she was a woman. William James actually described Calkins' doctoral work by stating that her performance was "the most brilliant examination for the PhD that we have had at Harvard" (Hilgard, 1987). Margaret Floy Washburn (1871–1939) became the first woman in America to obtain her PhD in psychology in 1894 and later became the second female president of the APA in 1921. She is most known for her book *The Animal Mind* (Washburn, 1908), which became a leading publication in the area of animal cognition.

See Figure 1.1 for a timeline of some of the important early events in the field of psychology.

Gestalt psychology

a perspective in psychology that focuses on the study of how people integrate and organize perceptual information into meaningful wholes

Figure 1.1 Timeline of the Early History of Psychology

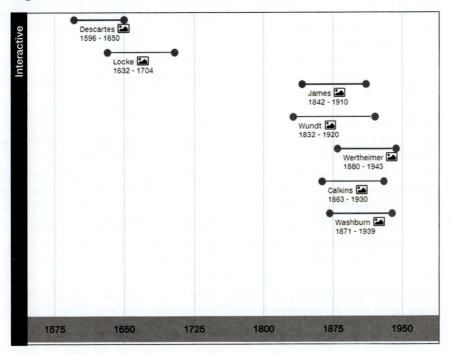

Contemporary Perspectives In Psychology

LO 1.2 Summarize the seven modern perspectives in psychology.

How do modern psychologists explain human behavior and mental processes? Seven predominant models or perspectives in contemporary psychology focus on a variety of factors in an attempt to best understand human behavior and mental processes. These perspectives differ in terms of how much influence is ascribed to qualities such as past experiences, inborn characteristics, environment, and culture.

PSYCHODYNAMIC APPROACH If a hallmark of fame is to have one's favorite terms and catchphrases become part of our everyday lexicon, then Sigmund Freud (1856–1939) has achieved the height of posthumous celebrity in the world of psychology. Have you ever described someone as *anal*, discussed the *Oedipus complex*, or accused someone of using humor as a *defense mechanism*? If so, you can thank Freud for these terms and the psychological theories behind them.

An Austrian medical doctor who specialized in disorders of the nervous system, Freud believed human beings were motivated by primitive sexual drives, forbidden desires, and traumatic

psychodynamic approach

an approach to psychology based on the belief that behaviors are motivated by internal factors unavailable to the conscious mind

Sigmund Freud (1856–1939) is considered the father of psychoanalysis.

psychoanalysis

a type of therapy that utilizes Freudian concepts with an emphasis on the influence of the unconscious

behavioral approach

an approach to psychology that concentrates on observable behavior that can be directly measured and recorded

John B. Watson (1878–1958) was an American psychologist who founded the field of behaviorism.

childhood memories unavailable to the conscious mind. According to Freud, these repressed urges constantly intrude on the conscious mind, expressing themselves through dreams and slips of the tongue (now known as "Freudian slips") or as symptoms of psychological disorders.

Freud's theories, which formed the foundation of the psychodynamic approach to psychology, were highly controversial. Many of his Victorian contemporaries were shocked, both by his focus on sexuality and by the implication that people are not always in control of their actions. However, Freud's theories were held in high regard and inspired many well-known researchers, including Swiss psychologist Carl Jung and Freud's daughter, Anna Freud, to continue his work. Freud's ideas formed the basis of **psychoanalysis**, a type of therapy that utilizes Freudian concepts with an emphasis on the influence of the unconscious.

While not the predominant approach to psychotherapy in the United States today, many therapists have been influenced by psychodynamic principles. Contemporary psychodynamic theories focus less on unconscious sexual drives and more on other unconscious processes related to social experiences and unresolved conflicts related to past relationships and experiences (Basham et al., 2016).

BEHAVIORAL APPROACH One disadvantage of the psychodynamic approach is that it is difficult to test scientifically. For example, it would be very difficult to prove that a grown woman has relationship problems because she unconsciously resents her father for not being around when she was a child. The theories of structuralism and functionalism faced similar challenges because both involved the study of consciousness—internal processes that, at the time, could not be measured or validated.

John B. Watson (1878–1958), however, wanted to make scientific inquiry a primary focus in psychology. In the 1900s, he developed the **behavioral approach** to psychology, which concentrates only on observable behavior that can be directly measured and recorded.

Watson conducted research using his new behavioral framework on a variety of topics, including child rearing, animal behavior, and advertising. Perhaps most famously, Watson and his colleague, Rosalie Rayner, conducted a study known thereafter as "Little Albert." They demonstrated that fear could be conditioned by teaching an 11-month-old child to fear a white rat (see LO 5.2). By repeatedly pairing the appearance of the rat with a loud, scary noise, the child eventually associated the rat with the noise and cried whenever he saw the creature (Watson & Rayner, 1920). Watson's radical views on child-rearing and his strong emphasis on environment in the nature/nurture debate are represented in the following famous quote:

> Give me a dozen healthy infants, well-formed, and my own specified world to bring them up in and I'll guarantee to take any one at random and train him to become any type of specialist I might select—doctor, lawyer, artist, merchant-chief, and, yes, even beggarman and thief, regardless of his talents, penchants, tendencies, abilities, vocations, and race of his ancestors. I am going beyond my facts and I admit it, but so have the advocates of the contrary and they have been doing it for many thousands of years. —John B. Watson, *Behaviorism*, 1930

Journal Prompt: What Do You Think?

Do you agree with Watson's assertion that he could take any infant and turn him/her into any type of specialist? Why or why not?

Behaviorism gained momentum through the work of B.F. Skinner, who supported Watson's idea of learning through conditioning. Skinner believed behavior could be altered through reinforcement—rewarding or punishing an individual for engaging in a particular behavior. Contemporary behavioral approaches have continued to focus on the use of rigorous scientific principles to study observable behaviors. Applied behavior analysis is a growing subfield of the behaviorist movement concerned with the application of learning principles to solve problems and issues of social importance such as *autism-spectrum disorders (ASD)* (see LO 5.9).

Throughout the first half of the 20th century, psychoanalysis and behaviorism were the two primary approaches to psychology. However, neither of them emphasized the notion that individuals have significant control over their own destinies. Behaviorists maintained that people's actions were learned responses to various stimuli, while psychoanalysts claimed that people were influenced by their unconscious desires.

HUMANISTIC APPROACH   In the 1950s, a new psychological perspective emerged that was in many ways a reaction to the psychodynamic and behavioral models. This new perspective emphasized the importance of self-esteem, self-expression, and reaching one's potential. Supporters of the **humanistic approach**, as it came to be known, believed people have free will and are able to control their own destinies.

Two founding theorists of the humanistic approach were Abraham Maslow (1908–1970), who studied motivation and emotion, and Carl Rogers (1902–1987), who made significant contributions to the study of personality and the practice of psychotherapy. Maslow believed people should strive for **self-actualization**—the achievement of one's full potential. Although the humanistic approach has contributed significantly to many disciplines, critics argue that it can come across as vague and naively optimistic.

COGNITIVE APPROACH   By the 1960s, developments in linguistics, neurobiology, and computer science were providing new insight into the workings of the human mind. The development of computers, in particular, stimulated an interest in studying thought processes. Pioneers in the field of **cognitive psychology** focused on the workings of the human brain and sought to understand how we process information we collect from our environments.

Focusing on memory, perception, learning, intelligence, language, and problem solving, cognitive psychologists expanded the definition of psychology to incorporate the study of specific mental processes into the more general concept of behavior. Developments in brain-imaging techniques have enabled cognitive psychologists to examine neurological processes that previously mystified scientists, such as how we store memories or how damage to particular areas of the brain increases the likelihood of specific mental disorders. In a relatively short period of time, the cognitive perspective has become one of the most rapidly advancing perspectives in modern psychology.

BIOLOGICAL APPROACH   The **biological approach** to psychology has a long history, but recent advances in knowledge about the nervous system have contributed to rising interest in this perspective. Biopsychology includes the study of biological bases of behavior and focuses on the structure of the nervous system as well as the function of the nervous system. Within this perspective, behavior is viewed as the direct result of biological events in the body, and biopsychologists often study brain structures, neurotransmitters, hormones, genetics, and disease processes. While a behavioral psychologist might examine how reinforcement can increase a behavior, a biopsychologist might study the neurotransmitters and brain structures involved in the process of learning to perform that behavior.

EVOLUTIONARY APPROACH   Based on Darwin's theory of natural selection, the **evolutionary approach** to psychology explores how human behavior has evolved because of its beneficial effects on survival. Just as certain physical traits that aid in survival were passed down at a higher rate than traits that hindered survival or reproduction, evolutionary psychologists investigate human behavior using the same lens. That is, certain human behaviors or psychological traits are more likely to be passed on from one generation to another because those characteristics were beneficial for survival or reproduction (Confer et al., 2010). Evolutionary psychologists study issues such as parenting, sexual attraction, and violence among different species and cultures to explain how these traits or behaviors might have been influenced by the process of evolution. For example, studies have shown that humans are generally fearful of snakes and spiders, and we have a finely-honed ability to detect these animals in our environment (Öhman & Mineka, 2003). Snakes and spiders were more threatening to survival in the past but continue to top the lists of fears and phobias in modern times. In fact, people are much more likely to experience fear of snakes or spiders than guns or cars, despite the fact that the latter are much more threatening to survival in modern times (Confer et al., 2010; Mineka & Öhman, 2002; Soares et al., 2014).

SOCIOCULTURAL PERSPECTIVE   More recently, psychologists have examined the influence of social and cultural factors on human behavior and mental processes—an approach known as the **sociocultural perspective**. Some factors important to consider from a sociocultural perspective include race, ethnicity, gender, culture, socioeconomic class, and religion. This approach to

Abraham Maslow (1908–1970), seen in the top image, and Carl Rogers (1902–1987), seen in the bottom image, are two of the founders of the humanistic approach to psychology.

humanistic approach

an approach to psychology based on the belief that people are innately good and that mental and social problems result from deviations from this natural tendency

self-actualization

the achievement of one's full potential

cognitive psychology

a field of psychology concerned with mental processes such as perception, thinking, learning, and memory that seeks to understand how people process information they collect from their environment

biological approach

perspective in psychology that includes the study of biological bases of behavior and focuses on the structure of the nervous system as well as the function of the nervous system

evolutionary approach

an approach to psychology that explores ways in which patterns of human behavior may be beneficial to people's survival

sociocultural perspective

an approach in which psychologists examine the influence of social and cultural factors on human behavior and mental processes

eclectic approach

an approach in which psychologists draw on multiple different perspectives and theories to gain an understanding of human behavior or mental processes

psychology focuses on the context in which humans function to better understand and explain human behavior, emotions, and attitudes. Think for a moment about your own race, religion, or gender. Do you believe these characteristics have an impact on how you interact with and interpret the world? For example, a child raised in rural China may interpret the same situation very differently than a child raised in Europe or a child raised in urban America. There have been findings suggesting that some psychological phenomena are universal. For example, studies have demonstrated that facial expressions of emotion can be identified universally across cultures (Ekman et al., 1987). However, research has also identified differences in how emotions are experienced, expressed, and perceived as a function of culture (Jack et al., 2009; Jack et al., 2012).

Over the years, the field of psychology has grown as scientists discover new and valuable ways of examining thoughts, actions, and behaviors. Today, psychologists use all of the approaches mentioned here—and more—to study the workings of the human mind. In fact, some psychologists have adopted what is called an **eclectic approach** by drawing on multiple different perspectives and theories to gain an understanding of human behavior or mental processes. For example, when treating a patient, a psychologist might consider the patient's genetic risk factors (biological approach), family/cultural factors (sociocultural approach), and aspects of the environment that may be reinforcing the problem (behavioral approach).

Some psychological perspectives may seem to contradict each other, and there's no consensus in the psychological community about which approach is the "right" approach. Rather, each of the many diverse approaches to psychology sheds new light on the fundamental questions of the field: Why do we act the way we do? What really goes on in our minds? Each perspective offers its own answers to questions like these, and each perspective in turn raises new questions of its own.

Identify the Perspectives

Interactive

Imagine that each of the following statements is made by a scientist interested in studying aggression. Read each statement, and then identify the perspective of the scientist using the list of options in the word bank. You can either type or drag your answer. Once all of the blanks have been filled in, click on the Check Answers button.

1. I am interested in how people learn to behave aggressively through environmental influences.

2. I am studying the advantages of aggressive behavior in the survival of humans over time.

3. My study examines how the brain processes information about threats and the decision-making process in engaging in aggressive behavior.

4. I am interested in studying the unconscious childhood conflicts that might lead to later aggressive behavior.

5. I am studying how socioeconomic status impacts aggressive behavior.

6. My study focuses on the negative impact of aggression on self-actualization.

7. I am studying the neuroanatomy of the brain to pinpoint the specific areas of the brain most associated with aggressive behavior.

WORD BANK

- Cognitive
- Humanistic
- Psychodynamic
- Sociocultural
- Biological
- Behavioral
- Evolutionary

Start Over   Check Answers

Careers in Psychology

LO 1.3 **Identify various career options available to those with a degree in psychology.**

With an increasing demand for psychological services in schools, hospitals, social service agencies, mental health centers, and private companies, the employment prospects for a psychology graduate are high. According to the Bureau of Labor Statistics, 173,900 psychologists were employed in 2014, and this employment rate is expected to rise 19 percent by 2024—much faster than the average for all occupations (Bureau of Labor Statistics, 2015). Job prospects are highest for people with a graduate degree in an applied specialty, such as counseling or health, and for people with a specialist or graduate degree in school psychology. The median salary of a doctoral-level psychologist in 2014 was $75,230; and, if you relish the thought of making your own hours, there is even better news—about one-third of all psychologists are self-employed.

Although the American Psychological Association (APA) has 54 professional divisions, careers in psychology can be broadly divided into three main categories: clinical psychology, academic psychology, and applied psychology.

WHERE DO PSYCHOLOGISTS WORK?

Psychologists held about 173,900 jobs in 2014. The largest employers of psychologists were as follows:

25%	**10%**	**9%**	**6%**	**5%**
Elementary and secondary schools; state, local, and private	Government	Offices of mental health practitioners (except physicians)	Hospitals; state, local, and private	Individuals and family services

HOW MUCH DO PSYCHOLOGISTS GET PAID?

In May 2016, the median annual wages for psychologists in the top industries in which they worked were as follows:

$92,880
$81,740
$75,670
$72,910
$66,220

WHAT IS THE JOB OUTLOOK FOR PSYCHOLOGISTS?

Percent change in employment, projected 2014-24

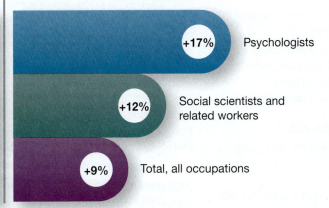

+17% Psychologists

+12% Social scientists and related workers

+9% Total, all occupations

CLINICAL PSYCHOLOGY **Clinical psychologists** diagnose and treat people with specific mental or behavioral problems, and the field of clinical psychology covers a wide variety of professions, ranging from mental health experts to family therapists. Clinical psychologists interview patients, give diagnostic tests, provide psychotherapy, and design and implement behavioral modification programs. Unlike psychiatrists, clinical psychologists are not medical doctors, and most do not have the ability to prescribe drugs. However, this is changing in some states. As of 2014, specially trained and licensed psychologists in New Mexico, Louisiana, and Illinois were

clinical psychology

a field of psychology that deals with the diagnosis and treatment of people with specific mental or behavioral problems

neuropsychology

a specialty in psychology that focuses on understanding brain-behavior relationships and the application of such knowledge to human problems

counseling psychologists

professionals who focus on how people function both personally and in their relationships across the lifespan

clinical social workers

professionals who apply social work theory and methods to help individuals deal with a variety of mental health and daily living problems

psychiatric nurses

a branch of nursing concerned with assessing mental health needs or treating people with mental disorders within a medical setting

school psychologists

professionals who engage in the science and practice of psychology within the context of schools

applied psychology

refers to the use of psychological theory and practice to tackle real-world problems

industrial and organizational (I/O) psychology

an area of applied psychology in which psychologists scientifically study human behavior in organizations and the workplace

sports psychologists

professionals who use psychological knowledge and skills to address optimal performance and well-being of athletes and sports organizations

academic psychologists

psychologists who usually divide their time between supervising and teaching students, completing administrative tasks, and carrying out psychological research

granted the right to prescribe prescription medications. Clinical psychologists typically have a doctoral degree—either a PhD (Doctor of Philosophy degree focusing equally on research and clinical practice) or a PsyD (Doctor of Psychology degree focusing primarily on clinical practice).

Along with clinical psychologists, other practitioners in this field include **neuropsychologists** (who study the relationship between the brain and behavior), **counseling psychologists** (who advise people on how to deal with problems of everyday living, such as school or career-related stress), **clinical social workers** (who help individuals deal with a variety of mental health and daily living problems), **psychiatric nurses** (who typically assess mental health needs or treat people with mental disorders within a medical setting; Advanced Practice Registered Nurses, or APRNs, also prescribe medications), and **school psychologists** (who address students' learning and behavioral problems). More psychology graduates gain employment in the field of clinical psychology than in any other subdiscipline.

APPLIED PSYCHOLOGY The term **applied psychology** refers to the use of psychological theory and practice to tackle real-world problems. For example, rather than simply examining whether a link exists between high stress levels and coronary heart disease, a health psychologist may work with patients at risk of coronary heart disease to reduce their stress levels. The field of applied psychology is not limited to any particular psychological discipline; it encompasses many different areas that share a common goal of using psychology in a practical form.

Imagine you are an employer looking to select the best possible candidate for a position in your company. How can you guarantee that your interviewing strategies determine a person's true character? Once you have hired your new employee, how can you ensure that he or she thrives in a productive, enjoyable working environment? **Industrial and organizational (I/O) psychology** is a form of applied psychology in which psychologists study behavior in the workplace and advise business owners based on their findings. An industrial/organizational (I/O) psychologist may conduct job analyses to determine candidates' suitability for a position, analyze fairness in employee compensation, use psychometric testing to assess employees' attitudes and morale, and train people to work more effectively in teams.

Many businesses encourage their employees to participate in annual team-building exercises to encourage bonding and teamwork in the office. Similar techniques are used in the rapidly growing field of sports psychology. If you were asked to name a film in which a new coach guides a poorly performing team to a seemingly impossible victory via a series of team-bonding exercises, you could probably easily rattle off several titles. **Sports psychologists** believe it is not enough for athletes to train their bodies; athletes also need to have a healthy mindset in order to succeed. Techniques to help athletes achieve this mindset include setting clear short-term goals, holding positive thoughts, using relaxation techniques, and visualizing desired outcomes—whether it be sinking a free throw or winning a race. Famous athletes, including three-time Olympic volleyball gold medalist Kerri Walsh, have consulted with sports psychologists for years.

Although I/O psychology and sports psychology provide excellent examples of "real-world" psychology, applied psychology is useful in areas other than athletics and business, too. In fact, any subfield of psychology mentioned in this chapter can be applied to real-world situations in some way. A personality or forensic psychologist may be consulted on the selection of a jury, for example, or an environmental psychologist might advise a town planning board. Contrary to the popular stereotype of a psychologist analyzing a patient on a couch, psychologists can contribute their knowledge and insight to numerous industries.

ACADEMIC PSYCHOLOGY Not all psychologists work directly with people to solve real-world problems or treat individuals with psychological disorders. If you talk to your psychology professors, you will probably learn that outside of the classroom, some professors have specialty areas of interest in which they conduct research. **Academic psychologists** usually divide their time between supervising and teaching students, completing administrative tasks, and carrying out psychological research. The proportion of time that each psychologist devotes to each of these tasks depends on the nature of his or her academic institution; some academic psychologists spend the majority of their time teaching, while others, particularly at larger schools, devote more time to research. Teaching positions at universities are generally very competitive. According to a 2011 report by the American Psychological Association, only 25.9 percent of individuals with new doctorates were employed at a university, although a much higher percentage planned on an academic career (American Psychological Association, 2011).

Some areas of academic expertise include **developmental psychology** (the study of the social and mental development of human beings), cognitive psychology (the study of internal mental processes), **abnormal psychology** (the study of mental disorders and other abnormal thoughts and behaviors), **personality psychology** (the study of patterns of thought, feeling, and behavior that make a person unique), and **social psychology** (the study of group behavior and the influence of social factors on the individual). Academic psychologists who specialize in these and other areas often aim to publish their research in approved journals related to their field of study. As you progress through the chapters, you'll become aware of how vast the field of psychology has become. You will likely find yourself very interested in some topics in this course and less interested in other topics. That doesn't mean psychology is not the right field for you—many successful and happy psychologists spend the majority of their education and career focused on the content of only one paragraph of the material in this course.

developmental psychology
branch of psychology that studies the physical, cognitive, and social changes of humans throughout the lifespan

abnormal psychology
the study of mental disorders and other abnormal thoughts and behaviors

personality psychology
a subfield of psychology that focuses on the study of patterns of thoughts, feelings, and behaviors that make a person unique

social psychology
the scientific study of how people's thoughts, feelings, and behaviors are influenced by the actual, imagined, or implied presence of others

Careers in Psychology

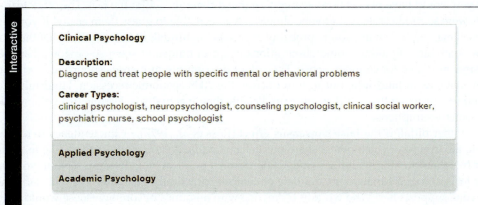

Interactive

Clinical Psychology

Description:
Diagnose and treat people with specific mental or behavioral problems

Career Types:
clinical psychologist, neuropsychologist, counseling psychologist, clinical social worker, psychiatric nurse, school psychologist

Applied Psychology

Academic Psychology

Quiz for Module 1.1–1.3

1. The school of psychology called *structuralism* used a technique called _____, which involved "looking inward" and reporting the contents of consciousness to study a person's experiences.

   a. induction
   b. intervention
   c. insight inventory
   d. introspection

2. _____ established the first psychological laboratory in 1879.

   a. Sigmund Freud
   b. John Locke
   c. Wilhelm Wundt
   d. William James

3. Professor Thomas approaches questions about human behavior from a perspective that emphasizes unconscious processes within the individual, such as inner forces or conflicts. It is most likely that she accepts which of the following psychological approaches?

   a. Sociocultural approach
   b. Humanistic approach
   c. Psychodynamic approach
   d. Behavioral approach

4. The _____ perspective is a psychological approach that emphasizes the mental processes in perception, memory, language, and problem solving.

   a. cognitive
   b. biological
   c. learning
   d. sociocultural

5. Which of the following professionals is NOT a mental health practitioner?

   a. Clinical psychologist
   b. Neuropsychologist
   c. Industrial organizational psychologist
   d. Psychiatric nurse

6. _____ usually divide their time between supervising and teaching students, completing administrative tasks, and carrying out psychological research.

   a. Sports psychologists
   b. Academic psychologists
   c. Counseling psychologists
   d. Psychiatric social workers

Module 1.4–1.5: Psychology and the Scientific Method

If you spend time online or on social media, you are probably exposed to constant tweets and Facebook links about the latest scientific research findings. Many of these studies are related to psychology. For example, you might have encountered a headline discussing a new research finding such as "Our brain's response to others' good news depends on empathy" (University College London, 2015). To be able to truly understand how psychological research is conducted, it is important to have a good grasp of how the scientific method applies to the field of psychology.

The Steps of the Scientific Method

LO 1.4   **List the steps of the scientific method, and apply them to the field of psychology.**

Have you ever been described as a "Monday morning quarterback"? It's easy to boast about how you would have played Sunday night's game differently—after the fact. The other team's plays were so predictable that anyone should have been able to guess them easily! If you find yourself making this claim, you're probably experiencing **hindsight bias**, or the belief that you knew something all along. Some observations made in hindsight seem so obvious that they are often mistaken for common sense. The risk of distributing numerous subprime mortgages seems obvious in hindsight, but it didn't before the 2008 economic recession. Hindsight bias encourages us to see the world as more predictable than it actually is, leading us to often make erroneous assumptions.

Another pitfall is the **false consensus effect** (Ross et al., 1977), or the tendency to overestimate the extent to which others share our beliefs and behaviors. Let's say you like to spend your free time chatting with like-minded friends on a political blog. It might seem to you and your fellow bloggers that your candidate of choice is practically guaranteed to win—after all, everyone supports her! Who wouldn't? Anyone with an ounce of common sense would agree with you that she's the best politician for the job. Or so it seems to you. However, it probably doesn't seem that way to your candidate's opponent or her supporters. In this case, your participation in the blogosphere, which in truth samples only a small portion of a self-selected population, has contributed to an occurrence of the false consensus effect.

Problems such as the hindsight bias and the false consensus effect may lead people to erroneously assume psychology is an unnecessary field that can be replaced by good old common sense. However, good researchers do not blindly accept theories, no matter how obvious they might seem—they use scientific methods to question and examine those theories. It's essential to think critically when carrying out scientific research. In other words, we need to examine our assumptions and challenge our gut instincts rather than rely solely on intuition and common sense, which are sometimes proved to be wrong.

Luckily, psychologists who perform experiments have a very valuable tool known as the **scientific method**, a process for conducting an objective inquiry through data collection and analysis. The following provides a summary of the scientific method as it is applied in the field of psychology.

1. *Identify the problem.* The first step in a scientific inquiry is to notice something you would like to explain or investigate. It is important to choose a problem you can study empirically, by *gaining knowledge through experience*. For example, there is no point in asking tempting philosophical or religious questions such as "Why are we here?" or "Does God exist?" Although the answers to these types of questions would provide valuable and fascinating insight into human behavior and the human experience, they cannot be answered using the scientific method and thus do not fall into the psychological realm. An example of a topic that *can* be investigated empirically using the scientific method is the relationship between media consumption and body image (thoughts and feelings about your own physical appearance). We know that body image has become increasingly negative for both men and women over the past decades, and some researchers

hindsight bias

a person's erroneous belief that he or she knew something all along after an event has occurred

false consensus effect

a person's tendency to overestimate the extent to which others share his or her beliefs and behaviors

scientific method

a process for conducting an objective inquiry through data collection and analysis

have examined whether or not the media plays some role in making people less satisfied with their own appearance.

2. *Conduct background research.* Has your question been studied before? If you are investigating a popular topic such as the media and body image, a great deal of research is probably already available that will provide further information about your topic of study. You can consult library and Internet resources to discover what research has already been done on your topic, how that research might be improved, and what areas might warrant further study.

3. *Formulate a hypothesis.* Based on your initial observations and your background research, you can make a **hypothesis**, or an educated guess, about an explanation for your observations. We use specific hypotheses to test **theories**, or general explanations about behavior and events.

   Your hypothesis should be written as a statement that can either be supported or unsupported by evidence. For example, you may have read several articles indicating that exposure to idealized images of thinness in magazines is associated with body dissatisfaction in women. Additionally, you discovered studies showing that social media has been associated with depression because of negative social comparisons. Considering both sets of findings, you might hypothesize, "Women who view images of thin and attractive friends on Instagram are more likely to experience negative body image than women who view images of average weight friends." This specific hypothesis provides a test of one theory related to social comparisons: People feel worse when making upward social comparisons or when they compare themselves to others who are better than them on some attribute.

4. *Test the hypothesis.* Psychologists use a variety of research methods, including surveys, case studies, and observations in laboratories or natural environments. However, the most conclusive way to test a hypothesis is to conduct an experiment. By manipulating a single characteristic, a researcher can study how this particular characteristic affects a specific outcome. Depending on the experiment, this outcome may involve the behavior of a person, the behavior of a group, or even the behavior of the human brain. While undertaking the proposed body image study, you would manipulate a particular situation and then examine the thoughts and feelings of several individuals within that situation. For example, you might select a group of women who are of similar age, education level, and cultural background. You would randomly divide the women into two groups, and have one group view images on Instagram of thin and attractive women (as rated by others) while the second group views images on Instagram of average weight women. You would then find some way of measuring body image in both groups.

5. *Analyze your results.* Once you have completed your experiment, you can analyze your results to determine whether they support your hypothesis. Psychologists use statistical analyses to help them summarize their data and determine how likely it is that the results they found were due to chance. One strategy researchers use to increase the confidence in their findings is to repeat an experiment several times (hopefully finding the same results each time) to demonstrate that the first set of results was not just a fluke. This process, called **replication**, is critical to the scientific process. The ability to replicate findings among different researchers, different settings, and different participants is important to establish the validity and generalizability of the original results. In recent years, a group of researchers failed to replicate a number of classic psychology research findings (Open Science Collaboration, 2015), leading the American Psychological Association and the Association for Psychological Science to develop major initiatives encouraging researchers to focus on replication studies.

   If your results do not support your hypothesis, you should consider another possible explanation for your observations and construct a new hypothesis. Maybe you didn't find any difference in body image between the groups. One explanation for this finding might be that the exposure to the images wasn't long enough to really impact body image. Or, perhaps your hypothesis might be that seeing images of strangers on Instagram does not have the same impact that viewing your own friends might have.

hypothesis
a testable prediction about new facts, based on existing theories

replication
the process of repeating a study using the same methods with different participants

In that case, you would need to conduct another experiment using images of the participants' actual friends in order to test the new hypothesis. Scientists continually refine their hypotheses until they are satisfied that their results have informed their theories and understanding of a phenomenon.

6. *Report your results.* Whether or not the results of your experiment support your hypothesis, it is important to share your results by making them available to others. Other researchers may be able to use your findings to learn from your mistakes, refine your hypothesis, or attempt to replicate your experiment to add support to your research. Once a research paper has been established as credible, researchers may use it to predict behavior based on the findings or use the results of the findings to modify or control behavior. Published research also becomes the background information read by others who are formulating and refining their own hypotheses, as described in step 2. In the past, publishing scholarly results in peer-reviewed journals was the primary means of communicating research findings. Currently, thanks to the Internet and social media, there are many more ways to communicate information. The advantage of this change in information transmission is that many more people, not just academics, can quickly access and use the information discovered through research than in the past. The downside, however, is that as the number of outlets have increased, the amount of peer review (or checks and balances regarding quality and accuracy) has decreased, making information literacy—which includes critical thinking—an extremely important skill for all to learn.

Steps of the Scientific Method

Identify the Problem
- must be capable of being investigated empirically

Conduct Background Research
- develop an understanding about what is already known about the problem

Formulate a Hypothesis
- a statement that can either be supported or not supported by the evidence

Test the Hypothesis
- experiments are the most conclusive tests of hypotheses

Analyze the Results
- using statistical analyses

Results Support Hypothesis

Report Your Results

Results Do Not Support Hypothesis

Formulate a New Hypothesis

Journal Prompt: Why Hypothesize?

Why is it important to formulate a hypothesis?

The Importance of Critical Thinking

LO 1.5   Recall some of the skills needed to be a critical thinker.

It's important to approach scientific claims with an open but skeptical mind. "Where's the evidence?" is often the first question on the lips of someone adept at **critical thinking**—a way of processing information in which we examine assumptions, evaluate evidence, look for hidden agendas, and assess conclusions.

    Critical thinking skills are some of the most, well, *critical* abilities for people to develop in order to participate in the scientific process and evaluate the outcomes of scientific efforts. While you may never conduct your own scientific research, you are constantly exposed to information that requires critical thinking skills. For example, have you ever had a symptom (e.g., a minor ache or pain) and looked up information online to see if you can determine the cause of your problem? If so, you're not alone. In 2012, 72 percent of Americans reported that they used the Internet to look for health information (Pew Research Center, 2013). If you conduct a simple Google search of "shoulder pain," you will get more than 89 million results. While the Internet is an amazing information-gathering tool, it can be very difficult to determine the accuracy or credibility of that information. To successfully navigate through the information world we live in today, people must develop the ability to think critically about information. Otherwise, you might end up considering an article about the need to attach leeches to your shoulder with the same level of interest as an article written by the American Academy of Orthopaedic Surgeons. The use of critical inquiry has convincingly discredited more recent assumptions, including the idea that opposites attract (Rosenbaum, 1986; Alford et al., 2011) and the notion that people who talk in their sleep are verbalizing their dreams (Brown, 2010; Mahowald & Ettinger, 1990).

    To become a better critical thinker, consider applying the following four steps when evaluating information or a particular claim made by a company or individual.

1. *Consider any underlying motives for making a particular claim.* Is the person or company impartial or unbiased with respect to the claim being made? Or, is there a reason that your belief in the claim would be advantageous to the person or company? For example, if someone is trying to sell a product, there is clearly an underlying motive that might justify an extra level of skepticism when evaluating the claim.

2. *Evaluate the quality of the evidence used to support the claim.* A thorough examination of the author's use of the scientific process is required to determine whether the claim is reliable. Consider if the research was conducted using the steps of the scientific method or if support for the claim is not based on sound scientific principles.

3. *Generate alternative explanations for the results.* Look just as hard for disconfirming information as confirmatory information. Is there a different explanation that might explain the results just as well (or even better) than the reason provided? If someone shows you research findings demonstrating that taking a certain pill was associated with weight loss, try to think of alternative explanations for the results. For example, were people eating the same and exercising the same amount before and after taking the pill? Perhaps dietary and activity changes—rather than the pill itself—led to weight loss.

4. *Avoid using emotions or personal experiences when evaluating the claim.* You may have personally experienced the same findings as the author of a particular paper (e.g., a study claiming that the middle child in a family is more sociable than the eldest child may accurately reflect your own family), but it is important to not allow your personal experiences to increase the legitimacy of the results. Also, keep in mind that not all popular claims are accurate—if they were, we'd be living on a flat planet surrounded by vicious sea monsters. It is important to try to disprove theories, including your own. As Aristotle once said, "It is the mark of an educated mind to be able to entertain a thought without accepting it."

    Critical thinking also requires a degree of humility. Scientists need to be able to reject their own theories and open their minds to unlikely findings. Imagine if fellow scientists had persistently rejected Copernicus's heliocentric theory because it was common knowledge that the Earth was the center of the universe, and the mere suggestion that things could be any other way was preposterous.

critical thinking

a way of processing information in which a person examines assumptions, evaluates evidence, looks for hidden agendas, and assesses conclusions

Four Steps to Critically Evaluate a Claim

CONSIDER...

any underlying motives for making a particular claim.

- Is the person or company impartial or unbiased with respect to the claim being made?
- Is there a reason that your belief in the claim would be advantageous to the person or company?

EVALUATE...

the quality of the evidence used to support the claim.

- Are the results based on sound scientific principles?
- How rigorously was the scientific method applied?

GENERATE...

alternative explanations for the results.

- Are there other ways to interpret the findings?
- Can you find any disconfirming evidence?

AVOID...

using emotions or personal experiences when evaluating the claim.

- Are you allowing your personal experiences to increase the legitimacy of the results?
- Are your emotions playing a role in how you interpret the findings?

Shared Writing: Using Critical Thinking

You are in a health food store and notice a presentation about a new dietary supplement that is supposed to improve energy levels. The presenter shows a graph demonstrating that people report having much higher energy levels after four weeks of taking the supplement compared to the four weeks prior to taking the supplement. You have recently been complaining about feeling groggy in the afternoons and begin to consider purchasing the supplement. Apply the four steps of critical thinking to evaluate the claims of this company.

Quiz for Module 1.4–1.5

1. The first step in any scientific investigation is
_____.
   a. forming a hypothesis
   b. coming to a conclusion
   c. identifying the question
   d. developing an argument

2. "Children who watch violent cartoons will become more aggressive." According to the scientific method, this statement is most likely a _____.
   a. conclusion
   b. result
   c. fact
   d. hypothesis

3. After you have identified a problem you want to study, the next step in the scientific method is to_____.

   a. conduct background research

   b. develop a hypothesis

   c. test the hypothesis

   d. report your results

4. A way of processing information in which we examine assumptions, evaluate evidence, look for hidden agendas, and assess conclusions is called _____.

   a. critical thinking   **c.** scientific evidence

   b. hindsight bias   **d.** false consensus

5. If you are reading a review of a product and discover that the person writing the review is a part owner of the product's company, you might question the reviewer's claims based on which of the following?

   a. The quality of the evidence

   b. The underlying motive of the writer

   c. The emotional appeal

   d. Alternative explanations for the results

Module 1.6–1.8: Descriptive Research Methods

Psychologists use a variety of research methods to answer questions about human behavior and mental processes. These methods differ in terms of what kind of data is collected, how the data is collected, and how well they identify cause-and-effect relationships. Each method has both advantages and disadvantages, and one of the first steps in conducting a study is determining the most effective method for answering the type of question being asked.

A **descriptive study** enables researchers to observe and describe behaviors without investigating the relationship between specific variables. Some descriptive studies have a narrow focus, such as observing how children react to a new environment or studying how people respond to confrontation. Other studies have a broader focus, such as observing the habits of animals in the wild. Descriptive studies may involve observing subjects (in either a natural habitat or a laboratory), using case studies, or conducting surveys. While the following research methodologies are not exclusively utilized in descriptive studies, they are the most common methods associated with descriptive studies.

Naturalistic Observations

LO 1.6 **Summarize the potential advantages and disadvantages of using naturalistic observation.**

We use **naturalistic observation** every day when we watch busy shoppers hurrying around the mall or observe children playing in the park. Naturalistic observation is the study of people or animals in their own environment. It enables researchers to obtain a realistic picture of how their subjects behave. Jane Goodall's 45-year study of the interactions of chimpanzees living in the wild in Tanzania is one of the most notable uses of naturalistic observational research methods. On a more contemporary note, the reality television show *Undercover Boss* contains many elements of a naturalistic observation. Executives go undercover to work in entry-level positions in their own company to evaluate how their business operates on a day-to-day basis and how their employees are functioning.

One disadvantage of naturalistic observation is the possibility of reactivity. **Reactivity** occurs in situations where a research participant's behavior is different than normal because the participant is being observed. Take the example of hand washing in one hospital. In an effort to improve the rates of hand washing upon entering and exiting patient rooms, one hospital secretly videotaped the rooms and then sent someone to secretly observe rates of hand washing. The rate of hand washing was only 6.5 percent when captured on the secret video cameras, whereas the secret observers recorded a 60 percent rate of hand washing.

descriptive study

a study that enables researchers to observe and describe behaviors without investigating the relationship between specific variables

naturalistic observation

the study of people or animals in their own environment

reactivity

a phenomenon that occurs in situations where a research participant's behavior is different than normal because the participant is being observed

Researchers conducting a naturalistic observation of lemur behavior.

Most likely, the hand washing increased in the secret observer condition because at least some of the people being monitored by the secret observer discovered they were being watched (Rosenberg, 2011). Reactivity likely plays a significant role in most reality television shows because it's very likely that people change their behavior when they know they are being filmed. In an attempt to reduce reactivity and produce more valid observations, *Undercover Boss* uses a fake cover story that the camera crew is following the entry-level worker as part of a documentary. However, most workers will still be influenced by the presence of the camera, regardless of the cover story. In order to reduce the impact of reactivity on the results of a naturalistic observation, setting up a study so the participants don't know they are being observed is ideal.

Another potential problem with naturalistic observation is **observer bias**. This occurs when the observer expects to see a particular behavior and notices only actions that support that theory. One way to avoid observer bias is to use **blind observers**, or people who do not know what the research is about. It is also advisable to use more than one observer, to enable them to compare notes. Another disadvantage to naturalistic observation is that because it takes place in real life, there is no possibility of repeating individual scenarios. This makes it difficult for psychologists to make generalizations based entirely on information from natural observations.

observer bias

a situation in which an observer expects to see a particular behavior and notices only actions that support that expectation

blind observers

observers who do not know what the research is about and are thus not subject to observer bias

---

Journal Prompt: Naturalistic Observations

Describe how to conduct a naturalistic observation of children on a playground that minimizes reactivity and observer bias.

---

laboratory study

a study conducted in a location specifically set up to facilitate collection of data and allow control over environmental conditions

case study

an in-depth study of one individual or a few individuals

In a **laboratory study**, participants are taken to a location specifically set up to facilitate collection of data and allow control over environmental conditions. The advantage of a laboratory study compared to a naturalistic observation is the degree of control the researcher can have over the environment. On the other hand, laboratory environments are so controlled that it is sometimes difficult to generalize the findings to behavior in the "real" world. To overcome the disadvantages of both laboratory and naturalistic studies, researchers sometimes conduct both a laboratory study and a naturalistic study to investigate the same question. If researchers arrive at the same conclusion using both methods, they can be more confident about the reliability of their findings. For example, in 2008, researchers at Auburn University asked participants to wear either sneakers or flip-flops as they walked on a special platform in a laboratory setting. After observing the flip-flop wearers' gaits, the researchers concluded that wearing flip-flops can cause injuries, specifically sore feet, ankles, and legs (Shroyer & Weimar, 2010). But are flip-flops in the lab the same as flip-flops in the "real world"? If the researchers had performed a field study by observing flip-flop wearers in their natural environment, they would have been able to collect further data to determine whether flip-flops are less supportive than other shoes on everyday surfaces like grass and asphalt.

Laboratory studies allow researchers to examine behavior in highly controlled environments.

Case Studies

LO 1.7 Recall some uses and limitations of case studies.

During a **case study**, researchers study one individual or a few individuals in depth. They may use real-life observations, interviews, or tests to obtain information about their subjects. Developmental psychologist Jean Piaget (1896–1980) famously studied his own children as they grew. He was able to make powerful discoveries about cognitive development as a result of his observations.

Case studies are useful for providing information that would otherwise not be possible—or ethical—to obtain. For example, no one is likely to conduct—or line up to participate in—an experiment that requires participants to undergo severe brain damage. Enter the famous case study of Phineas Gage. Gage was a railway foreman who suffered severe

Observations of child behavior can be conducted in school settings or home settings.

brain trauma when an explosion propelled a metal spike through his skull—and the frontal lobes of his brain—in 1848. Amazingly, Gage recovered from his injuries, but he experienced drastic personality changes as a result of the accident. The case of Phineas Gage provided evidence that the frontal lobes play a critical role in personality and behavior (Bechara et al., 1994).

Case studies can reveal fascinating information that we might not otherwise be able to obtain, but they do have their drawbacks. For example, since a case study provides only a single example of a phenomenon, that example may be atypical. It can be dangerous to make generalizations based on a case study without conducting further research.

Surveys

LO 1.8   Explain the methods used by researchers when designing a survey.

Have you ever received a phone call from a stranger who inquires, eagerly and persistently, about your opinion of everything from politics to zero-emission engines? If so, you may have participated in a **survey**. To conduct a survey, a researcher will ask a series of questions about people's behavior or opinions. Surveys can be useful because they have the potential to access private information from a large number of people relatively easily. Researchers commonly use surveys in both descriptive and correlational studies.

Surveys are usually conducted in the form of **self-report questionnaires** or **interviews**. Questionnaires include a standard set of items that all participants answer in the same format while interviews are often more open-ended. You may have recently evaluated your emotional neediness or your ideal celebrity match. Psychological surveys are similar in some ways to surveys on Facebook or Twitter, but they have a well-defined purpose and use careful controls such as precise wording and carefully constructed questions, and they are ideally administered to a large and random sample of people.

In an interview, people provide oral descriptions of themselves to the interviewer. Interviews can be either strictly structured, with a set list of questions, or loosely structured and more conversational. In some structured interviews, interviewers use numerical methods to score people's responses to questions. This technique allows researchers to make precise generalizations from their results. Researchers have to think long and hard about how they word their questions when they create a survey. Take a look at the following examples:

- Do you approve of guest workers being given permission to remain in the country?

- Do you believe illegal immigrants are entitled to stay in the country?

Both of these questions have a similar meaning, yet using one instead of the other is likely to alter the outcome of the survey. The words *guest workers* and *permission* have more positive connotations than the words *illegal*

survey
a series of questions about people's behavior or opinions, in the form of a questionnaire or interview

self-report questionnaire
a form of data collection in which people are asked to rate or describe their own behavior or mental state

interview
a form of data collection in which people provide oral descriptions of themselves that can either be strictly structured, with a set list of questions, or loosely structured and more conversational

Surveys provide a way for researchers to collect large amounts of data relatively easily.

immigrants and *entitled*, and this difference in wording could impact the survey's results in an uncontrolled way. Researchers also need to be aware that people do not always answer surveys honestly, either through fear of being judged or by misremembering things.

Random sampling can help researchers ensure that their sample is **representative** of the general population. For a sample to be truly random, every member of the population of interest has to have an equal chance of being included in the study. If you wanted to find out what people thought about the legalization of marijuana in Washington, you would likely get very different results if you interviewed only people who report regular use of marijuana than if you surveyed people who reported having never used marijuana. In this example, a truly random sample would mean that every person living in the state of Washington would need to have an equal chance of being included in the survey. Perhaps census records could be accessed and people's names could be randomly selected from the census data. If a large enough group was surveyed, it would ensure that the final sample would be representative of all the people living in the state of Washington. In any survey, it is important to question a cross section of the entire group you are interested in studying.

Surveys or polls about political issues or elections have become increasingly common, given the ease of participating online or through texting. Every news station and every political campaign conducts its own polls or surveys, and many of the results of these surveys suffer from problems related to random sampling. These types of surveys have been called "self-selected listener opinion polls," or SLOP (a term coined by Norman Bradburn from the University of Chicago), to indicate how inaccurate such polling data can be due to the type of biases in sampling that typically occur. Growing up an avid fan of the Arkansas Razorbacks, it was a family tradition for one of the authors (BW) to listen to the statewide sports radio talk show, *Drivetime Sports*. During football season, the hosts would instigate a "call-in" survey to get people to predict the score of the upcoming game. If those polls were an accurate estimate of the general public's view, then apparently no one in the United States ever believed the Razorbacks would lose a game. This example demonstrates the results of sampling bias in a harmless poll, but many times the stakes are much higher and the need for rigorous sampling methods much more important. For a recent high-stakes example, the surprise results of the U.S. presidential election in 2016 highlighted the inaccuracies of polling data.

random sampling

a technique in which the participants in a survey are chosen randomly in an attempt to get an accurate representation of a population

representative sample

a sample that has demographics and characteristics that match those of the population as a whole

Distinguish Descriptive Methods

Interactive

Use the word bank to identify the correct descriptive research method that goes with each example.

1. Frank is a full professor who is interested in the factors that affect the performance of rats who are learning to find their way through a complex maze. Every afternoon, he gives each of his 50 rats ten trials in the maze, counting the number of wrong turns each rat makes on its way through the maze. _____

2. Ben, a graduate student in clinical psychology, is counseling Eli in a small room in the neuropsychiatric hospital. Eli was admitted to the hospital after complaining that he hears voices shouting obscenities at him, and confiding that he thinks he is going through a spontaneous sex change. After each session with Eli, Ben writes a report describing Eli's verbal and nonverbal behavior and his interpretations of the behavior. _____

3. Dee is an assistant professor who will teach introductory psychology for the first time next term. She has chosen some videos to show to her class of more than 200 students and is now preparing a questionnaire to administer to her students after each video clip. She thinks getting student reactions to the films will be helpful for the next time she teaches the class. _____

4. Ed is an undergraduate psychology major. For his senior thesis, he is investigating the nature of the audience for pornography. This afternoon, he is sitting in his car across the street from one of the pornographic bookstores in the area. He is taking notes on the sex, approximate age, and ethnicity of the patrons as they enter and leave the store. _____

WORD BANK
- survey
- case study
- naturalistic observation
- laboratory observation

Start Over   Check Answers

Quiz for Module 1.6–1.8

1. Joaquin went to McDonald's to observe people eating in fast-food restaurants. He brought a camera crew and bright lights, and they all wore yellow jump suits. Joaquin said he wanted to do a naturalistic observation but may have had some problems because of _____.

   a. room crowding   **b.** participant observation

   c. reactivity   **d.** eating McDonald's food

2. When you watch dogs play in the park, or watch how your professors conduct their classes, you are engaging in a form of _____.

   a. naturalistic observation   **b.** survey research

   c. psychometric study   **d.** case study research

3. A case study would be the most appropriate method to investigate which of these topics?

   a. The development of a male baby raised as a female after a surgical error destroyed his penis

   b. The ways in which the games of boys differ from the games of girls

   c. The math skills of students in Japan as compared to those of U.S. students

   d. Physiological changes that occur when people watch violent movies

4. A detailed description of a particular individual being studied or treated is called a _____.

   a. case study   **b.** representative sample

   c. single-blind study   **d.** naturalistic observation

5. Which of the following questions could be answered best by using the survey method?

   a. What is the relationship between number of hours of study per week and grade point average?

   b. Does wall color affect the frequency of violence in prison populations?

   c. Do students prefer a grading system with or without pluses and minuses?

   d. What is the effect of ingesting alcohol on problem-solving ability?

6. A group of randomly selected participants for a study that matches the population on important characteristics such as age and sex is called _____.

   a. volunteer bias   **b.** an experimental group

   c. a control group   **d.** a representative sample

Module 1.9–1.10: Correlational Studies

To overcome some of the limitations of descriptive methods, **correlational studies** allow researchers to measure the degree to which two variables are related. A **variable** is a characteristic that can vary, such as age, weight, or height. In a correlational study, a researcher does not manipulate variables but instead observes whether a relationship exists between variables. Correlational studies allow us to make predictions about one variable based on the knowledge of another.

Correlational Coefficients

LO 1.9   Describe how correlations measure relationships between variables.

To quantify the relationship between variables, a statistic called a **correlation coefficient** is calculated. This coefficient is a number (represented by the lowercase letter "r") between +1.00 and −1.00 that

correlational studies

a type of study that allows researchers to measure the degree to which two variables are related

variable

a characteristic that can vary, such as age, weight, or height

correlation coefficient

describes the strength and direction of the relationship between two variables

Figure 1.2 Correlation Coefficients: from Weak to Strong

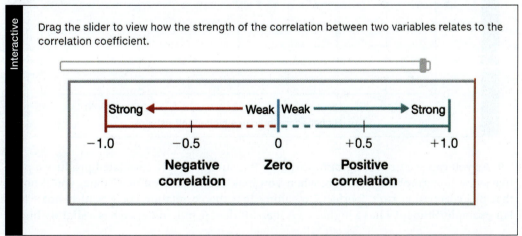

Interactive

Drag the slider to view how the strength of the correlation between two variables relates to the correlation coefficient.

provides two important pieces of information. As you can see, if you move the slider along Figure 1.2, the closer the correlation gets to either −1.00 or +1.00, the stronger the correlation between the two variables; and the closer the correlation is to zero, the weaker the relationship.

First, the correlation coefficient tells us how strongly the two variables are related. The strength of the relationship is signified by how close the coefficient is to the absolute value of 1.00 (the + or − of the number doesn't matter here). A correlation coefficient of (+/−)**.90** suggests a very strong correlation between two variables, while a correlation coefficient of (+/−)**.10** suggests that the two variables are very weakly related. The second piece of information provided by the correlation coefficient is the direction of the relationship. Now, the sign of the number is important. A **positive correlation** is indicated by a positive number between 0 and +1.00. Positive correlations indicate that the two factors vary in the same direction. Consider the example of academic success and high self-esteem. These two variables are positively correlated because they increase or decrease together; that is, as one variable increases (academic success), the other variable also increases (self-esteem). Take a moment to view the graph for the correlation between academic success and self-esteem by first using a **scatterplot** (a graph with two axes where each dot represents an individual data point) and then examining the best-fit line for the data points.

positive correlation

a relationship between two variables signifying that as one variable increases, the other variable also increases

scatterplot

a graph with two axes where each dot represents an individual data point

Graph a Positive Correlation

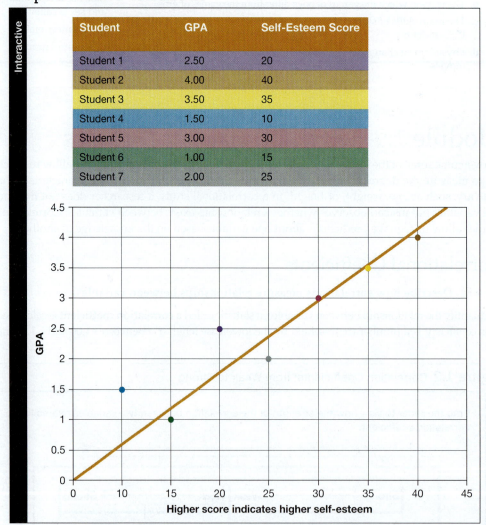

Student	GPA	Self-Esteem Score
Student 1	2.50	20
Student 2	4.00	40
Student 3	3.50	35
Student 4	1.50	10
Student 5	3.00	30
Student 6	1.00	15
Student 7	2.00	25

Higher score indicates higher self-esteem

As you can see from the graph, variables that are positively correlated produce a positive slope line graph. In addition, when you look back at the graphed data, you'll notice that this correlation isn't "perfect," meaning that the correlation coefficient is not +1.00. For example, Student 4 has a higher GPA than Student 6, but Student 6 has a slightly higher self-esteem score than Student 4. Perfect correlations are very unlikely with variables that are measured in psychological research.

Next, let's consider **negative correlations**. A negative correlation is indicated by a negative number between -1.00 and 0. Variables that are negatively correlated vary in the opposite direction; that is, as one variable increases, the other variable decreases. For example, there is likely a negative correlation between the amount of time spent on social media and exam scores. This means the more time a student spends on social media, the lower their exam scores are likely to be. To illustrate a negative correlation, take a moment to examine the correlation between time spent on social media and exam scores using the data provided.

negative correlations

a relationship between two variables signifying that as one variable increases, the other variable decreases

Graph a Negative Correlation

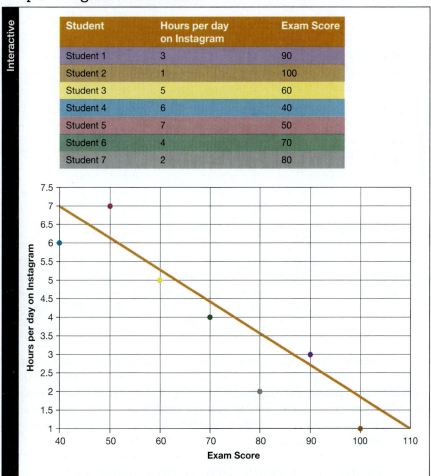

Student	Hours per day on Instagram	Exam Score
Student 1	3	90
Student 2	1	100
Student 3	5	60
Student 4	6	40
Student 5	7	50
Student 6	4	70
Student 7	2	80

As you can now see from the graph, variables that are negatively correlated have a negative slope line graph. In addition, when you look back at the graphed data, you'll again notice that this correlation isn't "perfect" either, meaning that the correlation coefficient is not -1.00. Another important point about negative and positive correlations is that the $(+/-)$ sign does not tell you anything about the strength of the relationship—it only tells you the direction of the relationship. This means that a correlation of $+.75$ and $-.75$ are both equally strong.

It is also important to realize that not all variables are related. The closer the correlation coefficient is to 0.00, the less likely it is that the two variables have any relationship to one another. One example of two variables that are not correlated is intelligence and shoe size. To illustrate variables that are not correlated, take a moment to view the correlation between IQ and shoe size based on the provided scatterplot.

Graph a Weak Correlation

Student	Shoe Size	IQ
Student 1	10	90
Student 2	12	115
Student 3	11	110
Student 4	13	100
Student 5	7	95
Student 6	8	120
Student 7	9	105

As you can see from the graph, variables that are not correlated have a zero slope line graph. In other words, the scatterplot of the data looks random, and the average of all of the data points is just a horizontal line. Just as perfect correlations of $(+/-)$ 1.00 rarely exist in the real world, we also rarely see variables that have a 0.00 correlation coefficient. We are much more likely to see variables that are not significantly related but still have a correlation coefficient between 0.00 and $(+/-)$ .10–.20.

Separating Correlation from Causation

LO 1.10 **Distinguish between correlation and causation.**

Correlational studies allow us to predict relationships between variables, but they do not provide us with information about cause and effect. Knowing a correlation exists between two variables does not tell us whether or not one variable caused the other. In other words, correlation does not equal causation. There are several possibilities when trying to understand a correlation. It's possible that variable A caused variable B, but it is also possible that variable B caused variable A. In the previous example of the correlation between academic success (variable A) and self-esteem (variable B), it's possible that experiencing academic success (e.g., making all As for a semester) might cause someone to experience an increase in self-esteem. On the other hand, it's also plausible that feeling really good about yourself, or having high self-esteem, might lead you to perform better in school.

Understanding the relationship between variables that are correlated is more than simply trying to figure out which came first—like the classic chicken/egg

"I hope we're not going to have the same old argument."

question. It's also possible that neither of the variables played a causal role at all and that some "third variable" is actually responsible for the relationship between the variables that are correlated. For example, you might observe that increased child mortality rates are related to increased ice cream consumption. So, is ice cream deadly? Or, do people resort to eating more ice cream because of the high number of deaths they are exposed to? Before you put down your ice cream cone, notice that both of these variables are also related to another factor—summer. In the summer, children eat more ice cream than during the rest of the year, and they are also more likely to get into accidents. Although both ice cream consumption and child mortality rise during the summer, neither of these variables causes the other to change. The third variable is, in fact, the actual cause of both events.

Adaptive Pathway 1.1: Correlations

Quiz for Module 1.9–1.10

1. Paul records data that indicate that the number of hot chocolates sold at the concession stand increases as temperature outside decreases (for example, more hot chocolates are purchased during late fall than late spring). Which of the following statements is the most accurate depiction of this finding?

   a. There is no correlation between the two variables.

   b. There is a negative correlation between the two variables.

   c. There is a strong, positive correlation between the two variables.

   d. There is a weak, positive correlation between the two variables.

2. All of the following variables, except for _____, would likely show a positive correlation.

   a. height and weight

   b. men's educational level and their income

   c. school grades and IQ scores

   d. alcohol consumption and scores on a driving test

3. A study shows that the correlation between shoe size and intelligence is .05. This means that _____.

   a. there is no relationship between shoe size and intelligence score.

   b. the larger your foot size, the higher your intelligence score.

   c. the smaller your shoe size, the lower your intelligence score.

   d. being highly intelligent causes people to have larger feet.

4. Golf skill is negatively correlated with golf scores. Based on this information, which of the following statements is true?

   a. The more skilled you are at golf, the lower your golf score.

   b. The more skilled you are at golf, the higher your golf score.

   c. The less skilled you are at golf, the lower your golf score.

   d. Being highly skilled at golf causes people to have low golf scores.

5. Which of the following correlation coefficients represents the weakest relationship between two variables?

   a. −.10   b. +.05

   c. +.50   d. −.70

6. The variables of stress and depression are positively correlated. This means _____.

   a. stress causes depression

   b. we cannot determine causality with a correlation

   c. depression causes stress

   d. there is a third variable that causes both stress and depression

Module 1.11–1.12: Experimental Research

Why do some people commit crimes? Why are teenagers often moody? Why do people sometimes become aggressive when they drink alcohol? Under what circumstances are we likely to help a stranger? The most conclusive way to test a hypothesis about human behavior is to conduct an **experiment**. Unlike correlational studies, experiments enable researchers to determine causality. In an experiment, a researcher can manipulate one variable while all other variables remain constant. This makes it possible to see how the variable that is manipulated affects an aspect of behavior. Watch the video *Research Methods* for an example of an experimental study being conducted.

experiments

a type of study that enables researchers to determine causality by manipulation of one or more independent variables and observing the effect on some outcome

bystander effect

when the presence of other people hinders a particular individual from helping a victim

confederate

a person who takes part in an experiment who is seemingly a subject but is really working with the researcher

Catherine Susan "Kitty" Genovese was stabbed to death outside her New York City apartment in 1964. The newspaper's report that no one responded to her calls for help triggered psychological research about what has been called the "bystander effect."

Research Methods

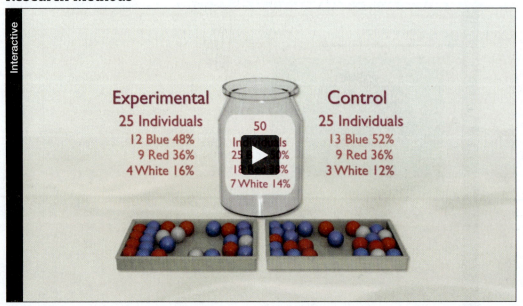

Components of an Experiment

LO 1.11   **Recall the components of experimental research.**

In 1964, Kitty Genovese was brutally murdered outside her apartment complex in Queens, New York City. She was stabbed repeatedly in an attack that spanned a total of 30 minutes. At the time, the *New York Times* reported that 38 people witnessed the attack but did nothing. Although evidence actually suggests that significantly fewer (approximately a dozen) individuals witnessed some part of the attack, you may still wonder why no one intervened or called the police. One person was famously quoted as saying "I didn't want to get involved" (Cook, 2014). More recent revelations about the case suggest that the original report of the event contained many errors, including the number of people who saw the attack and remained inactive (Manning et al., 2007). However, the news coverage of Kitty Genovese's murder and the portrayal of the people of New York as callous led psychologists to research the phenomenon known as the **bystander effect** (when the presence of other people hinders an individual from intervening). Several famous studies examined the bystander effect in a variety of situations. One such experiment conducted by Latane and Rodin (1969) evaluated whether or not the presence of others would affect people's actions in a seeming emergency situation. They recruited male participants who were sitting in a waiting room. The participants either (1) waited alone, (2) waited with a friend who was also participating, (3) waited with another unfamiliar participant, or (4) waited with an unfamiliar person who was a **confederate** (an actor who is part of the experiment and knows the aim of the study). In the room next door, the participants overheard a woman fall and cry out. The investigators were interested in whether or not the participants provided any help and, if so, how long it took them to help. For the participants who were waiting with a confederate, the confederate was instructed to act passively and simply shrug and continue working on the paperwork.

When designing or evaluating experiments, first try to identify what variable was manipulated, or what changed from one group of participants to another. The variable that is manipulated is called the **independent variable**. In the Latane and Rodin study, the independent variable was the number and type of people in the waiting room with the participant. The **dependent variable**, on the other hand, is the measurable response to the independent variable. To identify the dependent variable in a study, ask what the independent variable is expected to affect. In the bystander effect study, the researchers thought the number and type of people (the independent variable) would affect helping behavior (dependent variable). It is important to make sure the dependent variable is defined in a way that can be measured, such as the amount of time (or number of minutes) it took people to intervene and help the woman.

Identify the IV/DV

Interactive

Read the following description of different experiments, and identify the independent variable (IV) and the dependent variable (DV). Remember to ask yourself the following questions:
- IV: What variable is being manipulated? What is different between the groups?
- DV: What is the IV expected to affect? What is being measured as an outcome?

Does drinking caffeinated beverages versus decaffeinated beverages impact exam scores?
☐ exam scores
☐ drinking caffeinated beverages versus decaffeinated beverages

Are stress levels reduced by engaging in different types of exercise?
☐ engaging in different types of exercise
☐ stress levels

Does amount of sleep impact driving ability?
☐ amount of sleep
☐ driving ability

Is relaxation level impacted by listening to different types of music?
☐ relaxation level
☐ listening to different types of music

[Start Over] [Check Answers]

It is very important for researchers to develop an **operational definition** of the variables in their study. An operational definition provides a precise definition of each variable and specifies how the variables will be measured. For example, Latane and Rodin had to provide an operational definition of "helping behavior." They specifically defined their dependent variable as any intervention on the part of the participant, including opening the screen dividing the participant from the "injured" woman, leaving the waiting room to enter the room in another way, finding another individual to help, or simply verbally asking if the woman needed help. Operational definitions are critical so that the data can be interpreted appropriately. In this example, if the participant had simply looked to the other person in the waiting room and stated "do you think she needs help?" it would not have officially "counted" as an intervention.

Latane and Rodin discovered that when the participants were waiting alone, 70 percent of them attempted to help the woman. When waiting with a confederate, only 7 percent of participants intervened! You might find it hard to imagine that you could sit in a room and hear someone calling out for help and do nothing; however, this study demonstrates just how powerful the bystander effect can be in certain situations. The researchers also found that waiting with a friend increased helping behavior compared to waiting with an unfamiliar second participant.

In order to be as confident as possible that any differences between groups are due to the independent variable, researchers try to control any other factors that might have an impact on the experiment. A **confounding variable** is a variable other than the independent variable that could have an impact on the dependent variable. Let's imagine that the participants in the confederate condition were mostly male, but the participants in the friend condition were mostly female. It would be difficult to know if the relationship between the participants (being strangers or friends) caused the people in the confederate condition to wait passively (the independent variable) or if gender was actually the variable that caused the people in the two conditions to act differently.

One way to avoid having any systematic differences between groups is to use **random assignment**. When participants are randomly assigned to the **experimental group** (which is

---

independent variable
a variable that a researcher manipulates or changes in an experiment

dependent variable
the variable that is being measured in an experiment to determine the impact of changes in the independent variable

operational definition
a precise definition of each variable, including a specification of how the variables will be measured in the context of research

confounding variable
a variable other than the independent variable that could have an impact on the dependent variable

random assignment
the process by which participants in an experiment are randomly placed into experimental and control groups

experimental group
a group of participants in an experiment who receive the variable being tested

control group

a group of participants in an experiment who are either given no treatment or who are given treatment that should have no effect

subject to the independent variable) or the **control group** (which either gets no treatment or is given treatment that should have no effect), it means that any participant has an equal chance of being in either group. In the Latane and Rodin experiment, participants were randomly assigned to one of the four different groups. Participants who waited alone were in the control group, while the participants who waited with another individual were in the experimental group. When participants are assigned randomly to groups, it is likely that, given enough people, the groups will be roughly equivalent in terms of the ages, genders, and other characteristics of their members. Any differences between groups are the result of chance, and researchers use statistics to take chance into account when they analyze the resulting data.

Adaptive Pathway 1.2: Experiments

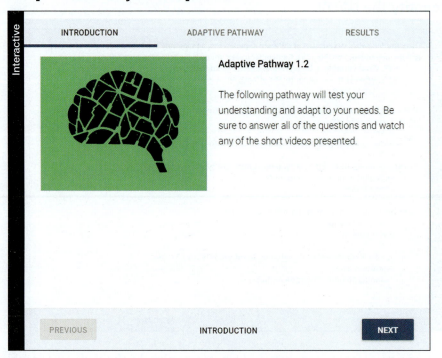

Cautions with Experimental Research

LO 1.12 **Explain how researchers try to control for potential bias, and consider ethical standards when conducting research.**

When designing and implementing an experiment, researchers have several important considerations. First, researchers try to eliminate or control for any potential biases in their studies. Additionally, research must also be conducted according to ethical principles.

placebo effect

phenomenon in which participants taking a placebo react as if they were receiving treatment simply because they believe they are actually receiving treatment

CONTROLLING FOR BIAS To have high confidence that any changes in the dependent variable were due to the independent variable, any potential biases must be addressed. The expectations of the participant are one source of potential bias in an experiment. Imagine a drug study in which participants are randomly assigned to either (1) receive a medication designed to improve mood or (2) receive no treatment. The group that receives the medication knows they are receiving a treatment. In a powerful psychological effect known as the **placebo effect**, research participants react as if they were receiving treatment simply because they believe they *are* receiving treatment. In other words, if people expect to experience improvement in their mood because of a pill, they will often report feeling better—even if the pill only contained sugar! Examples of the placebo effect abound, demonstrating the power of expectations and beliefs. One of the more notorious examples from research includes studies examining the placebo effect in consumption of alcohol. Researchers have demonstrated that giving participants beverages they thought contained vodka (but were actually only tonic water) affected not only behavior (e.g, the participants behaved as if they were intoxicated) but also other measurable factors such as memory and judgment (Assefi & Garry, 2003). Because of placebo effects, researchers must design studies to demonstrate that the independent variable has an impact on the dependent variable above and beyond what you might see from a placebo effect. That is why drug studies must compare the actual drug being tested to a control group receiving a placebo medication such as a sugar pill so that both groups of participants will experience the expectation of treatment. By using a placebo control group, the researcher is essentially setting up a single-blind experiment. **Single-blind experiments** occur when the research participants do not know whether they have been assigned to the experimental or control group. When participants don't know what group they are in, their expectations can no longer bias the results.

Another source of bias can actually come from the researcher. As you can imagine, many researchers spend significant time and energy devoted to their research, and they sometimes have a vested interest in the outcome of a study. For example, if you've developed a new medication that you hope will cure a certain disease, your own hopes and expectations may make it difficult for you to maintain an impartial stance. In cases such as this, a **double-blind** research design would be most effective at reducing bias. In this type of design, both the participants and the researchers do not know which participants are receiving the actual treatment and which are receiving a placebo treatment.

ETHICS IN RESEARCH   In addition to designing studies that have minimal potential for bias, researchers have to carefully consider the ethics of their research (American Psychological Association, 2002). **Ethics** refers to the moral principles that guide a person or group's behavior. When psychologists conduct research using human participants, several important ethical considerations are evaluated by an **Institutional Review Board** comprised of independent reviewers.

1. *Obtain informed consent:* Researchers must provide a complete and accurate description of the research so that participants can provide voluntary consent to participate based on being fully informed about the procedures and any potential risks associated with the study.

2. *Minimize harm to participants:* Researchers must ensure that any harm or discomfort participants might experience during a study is minimal, or no greater than the person would expect to encounter in everyday life. When studies do involve greater risk, researchers have an obligation to demonstrate that the benefits of the research significantly outweigh the risks involved.

single-blind experiments

an experiment in which research participants do not know whether they have been assigned to the experimental or control group

double-blind experiment

an experiment in which neither the participants nor the experimenters know who is receiving a particular treatment

ethics

refers to the moral principles that guide a person's or group's behavior

Institutional Review Board (IRB)

an ethics review panel established by a publicly funded research institution to evaluate all proposed research by that institution

Figure 1.3 Research Ethics

3. *Avoid deception when possible:* Researchers should avoid misleading participants about the purpose or procedures of the research study. Sometimes, the true aims of a study can't be revealed without impacting the outcome. In cases where deception is necessary, it must be minimized and not cause distress to the participants. Researchers must also **debrief** participants fully after the study is complete by providing them with a thorough and accurate description of the purpose and procedures of the study.

debrief

to provide participants with a verbal description of the true nature and purpose of a study after the study occurs

4. *Voluntary withdrawal from research:* Participants must be allowed to withdraw from participation in research at any point without experiencing any negative consequences.

5. *Protect the confidentiality of participants:* Identifying information about research participants must be kept confidential.

Journal Prompt: Minimizing Harm From Deception

Imagine you want to study the effectiveness of different memory aids on recall of information, but you don't want to tell participants you are studying memory. You decide to tell your participants that you are studying the impact of distraction on learning. What would you need to do to minimize the harm that comes from deception?

Quiz for Module 1.11–1.12

1. The administration of Midwest State University wants to know if the arrangement of chairs affects student participation in classrooms. They arrange the chairs in two different ways (theater style and circular) and then measure participation. In this study, _____ is the independent variable, and _____ is the dependent variable.

   a. arrangement of chairs; student participation
   b. arrangement of chairs: theater style or circular
   c. student participation; arrangement of chairs
   d. theater style or circular; arrangement of chairs

2. Experiments are more valuable than other research methods because they _____.

   a. are always double-blind
   b. can determine correlations
   c. require informed consent
   d. allow a determination of cause-effect relationships

3. In a laboratory, children are given either a beverage with sugar or one without sugar. The experimenter measures the level of hyperactivity in the children following consumption of the beverage. The experimental group in this scenario consists of children who _____.

   a. drink the beverage with sugar
   b. do not drink anything
   c. are in the waiting room
   d. drink the beverage without sugar

4. Isabella is planning on studying the influence of intelligence on the ability to recall events from the 1960s. If Isabella does not account for variables such as age, which could also influence one's ability to recall these events, age could be considered a(n) _____ variable.

   a. independent   b. random
   c. dependent   d. confounding

5. Which of the following is CORRECT concerning random assignment?

   a. In random assignment, each participant has an equal chance of being assigned to each condition.
   b. In random assignment, each participant is assigned alphabetically to each condition.
   c. Random assignment can only be determined after an experiment is over.
   d. The best formula for random assignment is birth dates.

Module 1.13: Piecing It Together: Vaccines and Autism

LO 1.13 **Analyze how the cross-cutting themes of psychology relate to the topic of vaccine research in autism.**

The question of whether or not childhood vaccines play a role in the development of autism has been a hotly contested issue over the past 15–20 years. Because autism is a condition that often manifests in early childhood around the same time that children receive immunizations, it's not surprising that the question of a possible connection between these two variables would arise.

What is surprising is that the findings from one fraudulent study in 1998 have continued to fuel rumors and emotions, while the findings from dozens of high-quality research studies do not seem to be able to overcome the stigma of vaccines.

To provide some history on this topic, here is a brief summary of the research findings in this area. Andrew Wakefield and several colleagues published an article in *The Lancet* in 1998 (which has since been retracted) that linked the measles, mumps, and rubella (MMR) vaccine to autism. Wakefield was later the focus of a long investigation and eventually had his medical license revoked due to his actions related to publishing the 1998 paper on autism and the MMR vaccine. However, after the publication of Wakefield's paper, many other researchers began to conduct studies examining the link between vaccines and autism. Since that time, dozens of research studies have been published and none have found any link between autism and MMR vaccines (e.g., Godlee et al., 2011; Jain et al., 2015; Mrozek-Budzyn et al., 2010). The Immunization Safety Review Committee of the Institute of Medicine published a review of all the literature in 2004 and stated that "The committee concludes that the body of epidemiological evidence favors rejection of a causal relationship between the MMR vaccine and autism" (Immunization Safety Review Committee, 2004). A more recent review of research published in 2014 examined the results of 67 studies and found no evidence of a link between MMR and autism (Maglione et al., 2014). While it may have seemed likely that the debate would end, a new outcropping of controversy occurred in 2014 with a re-analysis of data from a 2004 study conducted by researchers at the U.S. Centers for Disease Control and Prevention (CDC). The new study, published in 2014 by Brian Hooker, asserts that CDC researchers intentionally withheld findings suggesting a link between autism and Black males. CDC researchers have refuted this claim and argue that

Cultural and Social Diversity

Ethics

Vaccines and Autism

Variations in Human Functioning

Research Methods

The Science Facts About Autism and Vaccines

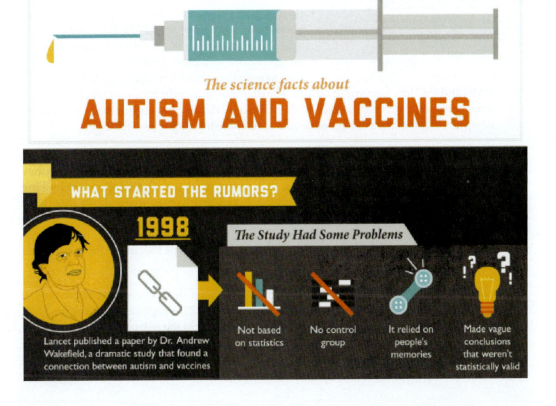

Wakefield's 1998 study was retracted in 2010 from the Lancet after being proven to be ethically and scientifically fraudulent.

EARLY REPORT

Early report

Ileal-lymphoid-nodular hyperplasia, non-specific colitis, and pervasive developmental disorder in children

A J Wakefield, S H Murch, A Anthony, J Linnell, D M Casson, M Malik, M Berelowitz, A P Dhillon, M A Thomson, P Harvey, A Valentine, S E Davies, J A Walker-Smith

Summary

Background We investigated a consecutive series of children with chronic enterocolitis and regressive developmental disorder.

Methods 12 children (mean age 6 years [range 3–10], 11 boys) were referred to a paediatric gastroenterology unit with a history of normal development followed by loss of acquired skills, including language, together with diarrhoea and abdominal pain. Children underwent gastroenterological, neurological, and developmental assessment and review of developmental records. Ileocolonoscopy and biopsy sampling, magnetic-resonance imaging (MRI), electroencephalography (EEG), and lumbar puncture were done under sedation. Barium follow-through radiography was done where possible. Biochemical, haematological, and immunological profiles were examined.

Findings Onset of behavioural symptoms was associated, by the parents, with measles, mumps, and rubella vaccination in eight of the 12 children, with measles infection in one child, and otitis media in another. All 12 children had intestinal abnormalities, ranging from lymphoid nodular hyperplasia to aphthoid ulceration. Histology showed patchy chronic inflammation in the colon in 11 children and reactive ileal lymphoid hyperplasia in seven, but no granulomas. Behavioural disorders included autism (nine), disintegrative psychosis (one), and possible postviral or vaccinal encephalitis (two). There were no focal neurological abnormalities and MRI and EEG tests were normal. Abnormal laboratory results were significantly raised urinary methylmalonic acid compared with age-matched controls (p=0.003), low haemoglobin in four children, and a low serum IgA in four children.

Interpretation We identified associated gastrointestinal disease and developmental regression in a group of previously normal children, which was generally associated in time with possible environmental triggers.

Lancet 1998; **351**: 637–41

See Commentary page

Inflammatory Bowel Disease Study Group, University Departments of Medicine and Histopathology (A J Wakefield FRCS, A Anthony MB, J Linnell PhD, A P Dhillon MRCPath, S E Davies MRCPath) **and the University Departments of Paediatric Gastroenterology** (S H Murch MB, D M Casson MRCP, M Malik MRCP, M A Thomson FRCP, J A Walker-Smith FRCP,), **Child and Adolescent Psychiatry** (M Berelowitz FRCPsych), **Neurology** (P Harvey FRCP), **and Radiology** (A Valentine FRCR), **Royal Free Hospital and School of Medicine, London NW3 2QG, UK**

Correspondence to: Dr A J Wakefield

Introduction

We saw several children who, after a period of apparent normality, lost acquired skills, including communication. They all had gastrointestinal symptoms, including abdominal pain, diarrhoea, and bloating and, in some cases, food intolerance. We describe the clinical findings, and gastrointestinal features of these children.

Patients and methods

12 children, consecutively referred to the department of paediatric gastroenterology with a history of a pervasive developmental disorder with loss of acquired skills and intestinal symptoms (diarrhoea, abdominal pain, bloating and food intolerance), were investigated. All children were admitted to the ward for 1 week, accompanied by their parents.

Clinical investigations

We took histories, including details of immunisations and exposure to infectious diseases, and assessed the children. In 11 cases the history was obtained by the senior clinician (JW-S). Neurological and psychiatric assessments were done by consultant staff (PH, MB) with HMS-4 criteria.[1] Developmental histories included a review of prospective developmental records from parents, health visitors, and general practitioners. Four children did not undergo psychiatric assessment in hospital; all had been assessed professionally elsewhere, so these assessments were used as the basis for their behavioural diagnosis.

After bowel preparation, ileocolonoscopy was performed by SHM or MAT under sedation with midazolam and pethidine. Paired frozen and formalin-fixed mucosal biopsy samples were taken from the terminal ileum; ascending, transverse, descending, and sigmoid colons, and from the rectum. The procedure was recorded by video or still images, and were compared with images of the previous seven consecutive paediatric colonoscopies (four normal colonoscopies and three on children with ulcerative colitis), in which the physician reported normal appearances in the terminal ileum. Barium follow-through radiography was possible in some cases.

Also under sedation, cerebral magnetic-resonance imaging (MRI), electroencephalography (EEG) including visual, brain stem auditory, and sensory evoked potentials (where compliance made these possible), and lumbar puncture were done.

Laboratory investigations

Thyroid function, serum long-chain fatty acids, and cerebrospinal-fluid lactate were measured to exclude known causes of childhood neurodegenerative disease. Urinary methylmalonic acid was measured in random urine samples from eight of the 12 children and 14 age-matched and sex-matched normal controls, by a modification of a technique described previously.[2] Chromatograms were scanned digitally on computer, to analyse the methylmalonic-acid zones from cases and controls. Urinary methylmalonic-acid concentrations in patients and controls were compared by a two-sample *t* test. Urinary creatinine was estimated by routine spectrophotometric assay.

Children were screened for antiendomyseal antibodies and boys were screened for fragile-X if this had not been done

the 2014 re-analysis was published based on invalid methodology and statistics. This 2014 study has now been removed from the public domain due to questions about the accuracy of the findings.

From this brief overview of the controversy, you are likely left with lots of questions. We will try to address these in the following sections.

Research Methods

- What was wrong with the Wakefield study?
- Why was the study by Hooker in 2014 removed from the public domain?

Wakefield et al.'s 1998 study reported that the MMR vaccine caused a variety of intestinal problems that led to the development of autism in his study participants. After the original publication by Wakefield et al., (1998), the following methodological concerns were raised about his study:

1. Small sample size
   - In the original publication, only 12 children with neurodevelopmental concerns were included as participants. Of those 12, eight were reported to have been diagnosed with autism.
   - In order to generalize to the population as a whole, a much larger sample size would be necessary.

2. Lack of a control group
   - In the original publication, all 12 children with neurodevelopmental concerns were given the MMR vaccine. All 12 of the children reportedly complained of intestinal problems and development of autism within one month of receiving the MMR vaccine.
   - Because autism is known to develop in early childhood (often before age 3) and MMR vaccines are also administered in early childhood, a control group of nonvaccinated children would be necessary to establish a causal relationship between MMR and the development of autism. For example, if a study showed that children who were vaccinated had a much higher chance of developing autism than children who were not vaccinated, a possible causal relationship might be established.

3. Nonblind researchers
   - When the surgeons interpreted the findings from evaluating the children, they were not blind to the study. That is, they knew what the researchers were looking for and since there was no control group, they knew each of the children they were evaluating were the ones considered "at risk." Ideally, those surgeons would have conducted procedures on a much larger sample of children who had received the MMR vaccine and children who did not receive the MMR vaccine without knowing to which group each child belonged.

In the 2004 study by DeStefano et al. at the CDC, no relationship between age at the time of MMR vaccination and autism was found. However, Hooker's 2014 paper argued that the CDC authors intentionally omitted data showing a dramatic increase in the risk of the development of autism in Black males who were vaccinated between the ages of 2 and 3. Hooker's paper was published in the *Journal of Translational Neurodegeneration* but has since been removed from the public domain. Concerns about the accuracy of Hooker's re-analysis center on the following issues:

1. The CDC paper used a *case-control* methodology. In case-controlled studies, researchers identify a group of individuals with the condition being studied (the "cases") and a group of individuals without the condition (the "controls"). These groups are matched as closely as possible on all other variables except for the factor of interest in a particular study. In this case, the age at which the MMR vaccine occurred was the factor of interest. The CDC researchers wanted to see if there was any difference between the "case" group (children with autism) and the "control" group (children who did not have autism) in the age at which they received their MMR vaccine.

   Hooker's 2014 re-analysis, however, took data collected for analyses based on case-control methodology and applied a different methodology. Hooker used a *cohort model* in his re-analysis. A cohort model looks at groups of people who are differentially exposed to a particular variable (e.g., receive vaccines at different times) and follows them over time to see if they have a different risk for developing a condition of interest. Both models are certainly acceptable, but it's a problem to analyze a set of data collected using a case-control design with statistics appropriate for a cohort model. Every statistic has a potential for error, and the choice of a particular statistic depends on the methodology used.

2. Hooker's findings focused on Black males between the ages of 2 and 3. However, a closer look at his results shows that he had to reduce the age of the 36-month Black male group to 31 months because he had fewer than 5 males in the group with the 36-month cut-off. This means that his findings were based on a very small group. When conclusions are based on very small sample sizes, there's an increased chance of statistical error.

Ethics

- What really happened in the Wakefield study?
- Why did he lose his medical license?

Wakefield's 1998 study was the focus of an investigative report conducted by Brian Deer from the *Sunday Times* in London. From 2003 to 2011, Deer uncovered multiple layers of fraud, dishonesty, and unethical behavior on behalf of Wakefield regarding his 1998 publication. The following is a summary of Wakefield's ethical misconduct with regard to his 1998 publication:

- Wakefield did not disclose a significant conflict of interest. He was actually paid the equivalent of 780,000 U.S. dollars by lawyers planning to file lawsuits against the manufacturers of the MMR vaccine months before he conducted his study. He also filed a patent for a single measles vaccine months before he held a press conference to review his study results and make a call for elimination of vaccines that included all three components (for measles, mumps, and rubella).

- Wakefield misrepresented his study participants as incidental patients seeking care in a London hospital. In fact, all 12 of the participants were recruited through negative MMR campaign events, and most of them were contacts of the lawyer who paid Wakefield to develop a case for a class action lawsuit. It was discovered that none of the 12 children even lived in London, and all were recruited specifically for the study.

- Not only were the children actively recruited because their parents believed the MMR vaccine contributed to their development problems, Deer's investigation also revealed that Wakefield falsified much of the data. Several of the participants who had allegedly reported an onset of autism within days of receiving the MMR vaccine had later records suggesting an onset of symptoms prior to vaccination. Other participants had normal records for months following the MMR vaccine, and still other participants did not actually have autism. Additionally, medical tests presented in the paper as evidence of intestinal problems were actually shown to be normal when participants' records were accessed during the investigation.

- Wakefield first reported that he received approval from the hospital's ethics committee to conduct the study, which required the children to undergo 5 days of invasive medical tests; however, it was revealed the hospital ethics board never gave approval for the study.

Wakefield's Ethics

Interactive

The following table includes a brief description of the 5 General Principles of the American Psychological Association's Code of Ethics. Assume that Wakefield was a psychologist and was brought before an APA ethics board, use the right column in the table to identify Wakefield's violation of each of the principles.

5 General Principles of the APA Code of Ethics	Wakefield's Behavior
1. **Beneficence and Non-Malfeasance**: "Psychologists strive to benefit those with whom they work and take care to do no harm."	As a result of Wakefield's falsified study, many people stopped vaccinating children and the incidence of measles and mumps increased.
2. **Fidelity and Responsibility**: "Psychologists establish relationships of trust with those with whom they work."	Wakefield did not get approval from an ethic's committee to conduct the study which was irresponsible and unethical.
3. **Integrity**: "Psychologists seek to promote accuracy, honesty and truthfulness in the science, teaching and practice of psychology."	Wakefield did not disclose that he was paid by attorneys wishing to bring a lawsuit against the MMR manufacturers, and he falsified the data.
4. **Justice**: "Psychologists recognize that fairness and justice entitle all persons to access to and benefit from the contributions of psychology and to equal quality in the processes, procedures and services being conducted by psychologists."	Wakefield unfairly recruited his research subjects.
5. **Respect for People's Rights and Dignity**: "Psychologists respect the dignity and worth of all people, and the rights of individuals to privacy, confidentiality, and self-determination."	Wakefield misrepresented his patients and did them a disservice by falsifying the data and concluding that they were injured by the MMR vaccine.

Start Over

Informed consent

when a study participant has agreed to participate after being provided with full knowledge of the potential benefits and risks of participating in the research

Between 1932 and 1972, hundreds of Black men with syphilis were studied by the U.S. Public Health Service. These men were never told they had syphilis and were never provided treatment for the condition in order to study the effects of untreated syphilis. The horrendous outcomes and subsequent outrage led to reforms in research ethics.

Cultural and Social Diversity

- What about the data showing an increased risk in Black males?
- Should parents of Black males be concerned about vaccines?

One of the particularly disturbing issues brought up in Hooker's re-analysis of the CDC data in 2014 is the notion that Black males are somehow especially at risk for the development of autism due to vaccines. His accusation that the CDC tried to cover up the link between autism and vaccines in this group triggered memories of past unethical research behavior targeting Blacks. From 1932 until 1972, the Tuskegee syphilis experiment was conducted by the U.S. government to examine the natural progression of untreated syphilis. Study participants included Black men who were unaware they were the subject of a research study. In fact, they were never told they had syphilis, and they never received any treatment for the condition despite the knowledge by 1940 that penicillin could cure the disease. Instead, these men believed they were receiving free health care. The results of the study were horrific. Many of the men in the study died from syphilis that could have been treated,

and their wives and even children contracted the disease. The outrage that followed the discovery of this study led to ethical reforms in medical research so that participants had to provide **informed consent** to participate in future research. Informed consent occurs when a study participant has agreed to participate after being provided with full knowledge of the potential benefits and risks of participating in the research.

The Tuskegee experiment left many Black citizens distrustful and wary of the medical establishment. The treatment of HIV/AIDS has been difficult at times due to a reluctance to use experimental drugs among the Black community. The findings that Hooker published are particularly alarming because it could lead to a lower level of vaccinations among Black children, which could lead to an increased incidence of disease in this population. The stakes are clearly very high, underscoring the need to closely evaluate the validity of findings like Hooker's with questionable methodology and very small sample sizes.

Variations in Human Functioning

- Imagine you have a new infant. How do you navigate through the research and make decisions about your child when it comes to vaccines?

Following Wakefield's 1998 publication, MMR vaccination rates dropped sharply and have only recently recovered from their pre-1998 levels. As a result, the incidence of measles and mumps increased significantly since 1998, resulting in severe injuries and in some cases, deaths (Smith et al., 2008).

Vaccine Vilification Survives

Journal Prompt: Parent Recommendations

Given the review of the research findings along with a summary of the problems in both the Wakefield and Hooker papers, what would you recommend to parents who are considering whether or not to vaccinate their newborn?

Quiz for Module 1.13

1. What does the evidence show about the link between autism and vaccines?
   a. There have been no scientifically sound studies showing a link between autism and vaccines.
   b. The evidence is mixed with some studies showing a link between autism and vaccines and other studies showing that no link exists.
   c. There is significant evidence of a link between autism and vaccines.
   d. Conclusions cannot be made because very few research studies have examined this question.

2. How were the research methods flawed in Wakefield et al's. 1998 study that linked MMR to the development of autism?
   a. Nonrandom assignment; too many variables; nonblind researchers
   b. Small sample size; too many variables; nonrandom assignment
   c. Small sample size; lack of control group; nonblind researchers
   d. Lack of control group; nonrandom assignment; nonblind researchers

3. Numerous ethical concerns were raised in Wakefield's study linking MMR to autism. Which concern was related to a conflict of interest?

   a. He falsified much of the data in the study.

   b. He actively recruited participants into his study out of a pool of parents who already held a belief that the MMR vaccine caused autism.

   c. He never received approval from the ethics review board at the hospital.

   d. He was paid $780,000 by lawyers planning to sue makers of the MMR vaccine months before he conducted his study.

4. Many Black citizens are distrustful and wary of the medical establishment based on what study conducted by the U.S Public Health Service between 1932 and 1972?

   a. Tuskegee syphilis experiment

   b. Tuskegee LSD experiment

   c. Autism experiment

   d. Marijuana experiment

Summary: Psychology as a Science

Module 1.1–1.3: The Discipline of Psychology

Psychology is the scientific study of behavior and mental processes and the field of psychology has roots in the ancient Greek philosophers. Socrates and Plato proposed the notion of dualism (that the mind exists separately from the body), and later philosophers such as Descartes and Locke expanded these theories, which led to interest in studying how the mind influences behavior. The official "birth" of psychology occurred in a German laboratory led by Wundt in 1879. Wundt's work led to divisions within the field of **structuralism** (focused on identifying individual elements of consciousness) and **functionalism** (focused on how organisms use their learning and perceptual abilities to function in their environment). The field of **Gestalt psychology** arose in objection to structuralism, focusing instead on the fact that perception entails more than just the sum of its parts.

Contemporary psychology is generally influenced by seven different perspectives, or approaches, including psychodynamic, behavioral, humanistic, cognitive, biological, evolutionary, and sociocultural. Freud developed the **psychodymanic approach** to psychology, which focuses on the role of the unconscious in influencing behavior. In diametric opposition to the psychodynamic approach, the **behavioral approach** arose with a focus on observable behavior and theories of learning. After many decades of dominance of the psychodynamic and behavioral models, a new approach emerged in the 1950s: the **humanistic approach**. This model focused on the notion that people have free will and are able to control their own destinies by striving toward **self-actualization** (the achievement of one's full potential). The **cognitive approach** developed in the 1960s continues to be very important today with a focus on memory, perception, learning, intelligence, language, and problem solving. The **biological approach** views behavior as the direct result of biological events in the body, while the **evolutionary approach** explores ways in which patterns of human behavior may be beneficial to our survival. Finally, the **sociocultural approach** emphasizes the context in which humans function to better understand and explain human behavior, emotions, and attitudes. Careers in psychology can be categorized into three main areas—clinical psychology, applied psychology, and academic psychology—and this chapter provided an overview of different career options within each area.

Module 1.4–1.5: Psychology and the Scientific Method

Psychology depends on the **scientific method** due to problems with relying on intuition or errors in thinking such as the **hindsight bias** (the belief that you knew something all along) or the **false consensus effect** (the tendency to overestimate the extent to which others share our beliefs and behaviors). The scientific method includes six steps: (1) identify the problem, (2) conduct background research, (3) formulate a hypothesis, (4) test the hypothesis, (5) analyze your results, and (6) report your results. Throughout the scientific process, **critical thinking skills** (a way of processing information in which we examine assumptions, evaluate evidence, look for hidden agendas, and assess conclusions) are imperative.

Module 1.6–1.8: Descriptive Research Methods

Descriptive methods of research in psychology include **naturalistic observations** (the study of people or animals in their own environment), **laboratory studies** (when participants are taken to a location specifically set up to facilitate collection of data and allow control over environmental conditions), **case studies** (studying one individual or a few individuals in depth), or **surveys** (when a researcher asks a series of questions about people's behavior or opinions in the form of a questionnaire or interview). Descriptive research methods can be useful in obtaining a picture of how people think or behave in certain situations. However, descriptive methods are limited in their generalizability and cannot provide information about cause-and-effect relationships between variables.

Module 1.9–1.10: Correlational Studies

Correlational methods allow researchers to measure the degree to which two variables are related. A **correlation coefficient** provides two pieces of information: (1) the strength of the relationship (signified by how close the coefficient is to the absolute value of 1.00) and (2) the direction of the relationship (either positive or negative). **Positive correlations** indicate that the two factors vary in the same direction, while **negative correlations** indicate that the two factors vary in the opposite direction. Correlations can only tell us whether or not two variables are related—they cannot tell us whether or not one variable caused the effect in the other variable. Correlation does not equal causation.

Module 1.11–1.12:   Experimental Research

The only research methodology that can establish causal relationships is the **experimental method.** In an experiment, a researcher manipulates an **independent variable** to see if it has an effect on the **dependent variable** (the measurable response to the independent variable). **Operationally defining** your variables is crucial in an experiment, and researchers must also be on the watch for any potential **confounds** (variables other than the independent variable that could have an impact on the dependent variable). To protect against confounding variables, researchers use **random assignment** to the **experimental versus control groups** and **blind** or **double-blind designs** whenever possible. When psychologists conduct research using human participants, there are several important **ethical** (moral principles that guide a person or group's behavior) considerations, including obtaining informed consent, minimizing harm to participants, avoiding deception when possible, **debriefing** participants (providing a complete and accurate description of the purpose and procedures of the study), providing for voluntary withdrawal from research, and protecting the confidentiality of participants.

Chapter 1 Quiz

1. Independent variable is to dependent variable as

   _____

   a. measure is to manipulate
   b. manipulate is to measure
   c. experimental is to correlation
   d. effect is to confound

2. Sam conducted a naturalistic observation as a project for a psychology class. He observed the interactions of parents and children at a restaurant. He believes many parents spoil their children in today's society. He observed many parents allowing children to get away with bad behavior such as being rude to the wait staff. When Sam described his work to his teacher, she suggested he find out more about the _____

   a. butterfly effect   b. observer effect
   c. parent effect   d. restaurant effect

3. Evolutionary psychology might suggest that certain cognitive strategies and goals are built into the brain because

   _____.

   a. they help humans adapt to their natural environment
   b. human brains are similar to the brains of the higher primates
   c. they are the result of learning that has taken place over many centuries
   d. they are the result of memories we have inherited from our ancestors

4. You attend a lecture by a psychologist who uses terms such as *free will* and *self-actualization*. Which psychological perspective is most consistent with the points the psychologist presented?

   a. Humanism   b. Behaviorism
   c. Functionalism   d. Psychodynamic

5. Correlations do not show

   a. causal relationships.
   b. the strength of a relationship between two variables.
   c. the direction of a relationship between two variables.
   d. the degree to which two variables are related.

6. Which of the following is NOT an example of applied psychology?

   a. A personality psychologist assists a prosecutor with the jury selection process for a trial.
   b. An I/O psychologist performs individual assessments to determine whether candidates are suitable for a position.
   c. A health psychologist researches a potential link between depression and brain tumors.
   d. A clinical psychologist teaches a patient to use breathing exercises to calm his anxiety.

7. Which of the following is a limitation of a case study?

   a. Case studies provide information that would otherwise be difficult to obtain.
   b. It is difficult to obtain detailed information using a case study.
   c. Case studies focus on too many people at one time.
   d. It is difficult to generalize to other people or situations based on a case study.

8. A psychology student had to use the steps of the scientific method for a class project. He first decided to study the effect of age on clothing choices. He then formulated a hypothesis that older people would prefer more conservative clothing than younger people. Where did he go wrong?

   a. He did not conduct background research before developing his hypothesis.
   b. His hypothesis was not a testable statement.
   c. He did not first test his hypothesis.
   d. He did not analyze his results first.

9. Ashley is using the scientific method to test whether male children are more violent than female children. What will she most likely do first?

    a. Research previous scientific studies about children, gender roles, and violence.

    b. Formulate a hypothesis stating that young males are more violent than young females.

    c. Select five male children and five female children and monitor their reaction to a violent video game.

    d. Perform statistical analysis to determine whether male children are more violent than female children.

10. Researchers designed an experiment that tested the impact of drinking alcohol on test taking abilities. They gave one group a drink with vodka and the other group a drink with tonic water. Neither group knew which drink they received. One interesting result of the experiment was that several members of the group who received the drink with the tonic water acted as if they were impaired. This result is called the

    _____

    a. bystander effect   b. placebo effect

    c. drunk effect   d. variable effect

11. Which of the following is an example of critical thinking?

    a. Accurately measuring and recording results

    b. Copying a previous experiment

    c. Considering alternative explanations for a study's results

    d. Researching facts about a topic

12. A large automobile company says the cars the company makes are the safest in the world. You have driven one of these vehicles for a week and have not had any accidents or problems. Therefore, you believe the company's claim about safety. This error in critical thinking is related to which of the following steps?

    a. Failing to do follow-up research

    b. Evaluate the quality of the evidence for the claim

    c. Consider any alternative explanations for the results

    d. Avoid using emotions or personal experiences when evaluating the claim

13. _____ occurs in situations where a research participant's behavior is different than normal because the participant is being observed.

    a. Reactivity   b. Hindsight bias

    c. Confounding   d. False consensus effect

14. Dr. Littman-Smith is conducting research in Kenya into the ways that mothers and their toddlers interact throughout the day. Given the purpose of her study, she most likely is engaged in _____.

    a. naturalistic observation

    b. laboratory observation

    c. correlational research

    d. experimental research

15. What advice might John B. Watson have offered to psychologists of his time?

    a. "Life is an effort to overcome inferiority."

    b. "We cannot know others until we know ourselves."

    c. "Remember that what we accomplish is due to the composition of our genes."

    d. "Focus on observable behavior."

16. Dr. Sardonicus wants to know whether or not the first three years of life are critical for acquiring language. She decides to study a child who was tragically deprived of human language by her parents. This type of research is called a(n):

    a. experiment

    b. survey

    c. case study

    d. correlational study

17. Julie finds that the more she sleeps on the eve of an exam, the higher the score she gets on the exam. There is _____ correlation between the amount Julie sleeps and her exam scores.

    a. a negative   b. a positive

    c. a perfect   d. no

18. Jana conducts a study in which she calls participants and asks them questions about their opinions. She is conducting a:

    a. survey   b. case study

    c. biased study   d. laboratory observation

19. Dr. Wiseman wants to know about the alcohol consumption patterns among college juniors in the United States. He should _____ .

    a. draw a representative sample among college juniors

    b. require students' names on each survey to avoid the tendency to lie

    c. remember that sample size is the most critical factor in survey research

    d. give the survey to every college junior in the country

20. _____ psychologists interview patients, give diagnostic tests, provide psychotherapy, and design and implement behavioral modification programs.

    a. Industrial organizational   b. Academic

    c. Developmental   d. Clinical

21. Which of the following correlation coefficients represents the strongest relationship between two variables?

    a. .25   **b.** –.25

    c. –.75   **d.** .50

22. Which early movement of psychology investigated how our minds help us adapt to the world around us?

    a. Behaviorism   **b.** Cognitivism

    c. Functionalism   **d.** Structuralism

23. If you are interested in how patterns, beliefs, and customs influence behavior, you are interested in the _____ perspective.

    a. sociocultural   **b.** behavioral

    c. cognitive   **d.** psychodynamic

24. You read online that people who make more money are also healthier. Your friends says, "I guess money can even buy good health now." You respond with:

    a. "Just because those variables are correlated doesn't mean that one caused the other."

    b. "Money and health can't possibly be related."

    c. "Actually, people who are healthier are able to make more money."

    d. "It looks like that is true!"

25. All of the following variables would likely be negatively correlated EXCEPT _____.

    a. average income and the incidence of dental disease

    b. the value of a car and the age of a car

    c. hours spent watching TV and grade point average

    d. calories consumed and weight gain

26. A researcher wants to know whether eating chocolate makes people nervous. Some participants are given two bars of chocolate to eat, and some are given no chocolate at all, and then all of the participants are tested for nervousness an hour later. In this experiment, the participants who eat the chocolate are in the _____ group, while the people who did not eat any chocolate are in the _____ group.

    a. control; experimental

    b. independent variable; dependent variable

    c. experimental; control

    d. dependent variable; independent variable

27. A research hypothesis proposes that consuming a low carbohydrate diet results in increased weight loss. One group of participants follows a low-carb diet for 3 weeks, whereas a second group follows a high-carb diet containing the same number of calories for 3 weeks. The average number of pounds lost for each group is then is compared. What is the dependent variable?

    a. Length of time on the diet

    b. Amount of carbs in each diet

    c. Number of calories in each diet

    d. Number of pounds lost

28. _____ is an experiment in which neither the participants nor the individuals running the experiment know if participants are in the experimental or the control group until after the results are tallied.

    a. The double-blind study   **b.** Field research

    c. The single-blind study   **d.** Correlational research

29. Which of the following is NOT an ethical principle for psychological research?

    a. Avoid any deception

    b. Voluntary withdrawal from research

    c. Minimize harm to participants

    d. Obtain informed consent

30. Testing a hypothesis is the _____ step in a scientific investigation.

    a. first   **b.** second

    c. third   **d.** fourth

Chapter 2
Neuroscience and the Biology of Behavior

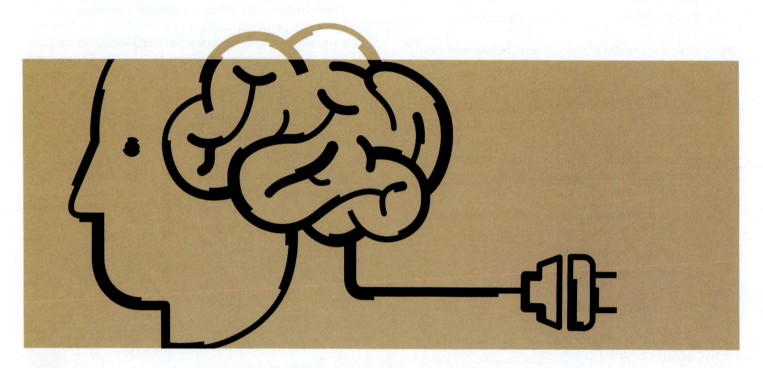

What Does Neuroscience Have to Do with Psychology?

Your Brain

Interactive

Survey: Your Brain

You are born with all the brain cells you will ever have in life. While the connections strengthen with age, you are not able to grow more brain cells.

○ True

○ False

It wasn't that long ago that scientists would have answered "true" to the above statement. Conventional wisdom has suggested the importance of taking care of and using our brain because if you lose it—you lose it forever. Thanks to modern-day technology and tenacious scientists, we now know that the most amazing organ of our body, our brain, has parts of it that can grow new brain cells. This process, known as *neurogenesis,* will be discussed in more detail later in this chapter. Why is this important? And, what does it have to do with psychology? To put it simply, the brain enables thinking, feeling, and behavior. If psychology is the study of behavior and mental processes, then understanding how the human brain works is a crucial first step to understanding why we do what we do. Exactly how the brain works, however, remains somewhat of a mystery to scientists. At present, we aren't able to draw many simple cause-and-effect conclusions between brain events and human behavior, but we can establish a number of consistent and predictable relationships between brain regions, neural networks, and categories of behavior. By the end of this chapter, you should gain a basic understanding of how our brain works and why it is the most important organ in the human body.

Module 2.1–2.4: The Anatomy and Functioning of Neurons

Have you ever considered how many times you have a thought, move a muscle, or feel an emotion in any given day? Probably not . . . . . . but if you have, then have you ever thought about how many parts of your brain, number of muscles, and variety of chemicals in your body are required for each one of those events to happen? This math very quickly becomes mind-boggling. The interaction between our brain and body is truly amazing and something we tend not to think about—unless something goes wrong. **Neuroscience** is a multidisciplinary field devoted to the study of the nervous system and the brain. It includes fields such as biology, chemistry, computer science, medicine, mathematics, genetics, and of course, psychology. **Biological psychology** is a field similar to neuroscience, but it is more narrowly focused on the scientific study of the biological basis of behavior and mental processes. In this chapter, we'll discuss important concepts from both fields. To understand how our brain plays a role in everything we think, feel, and do, we need to start at the beginning: with a single nerve cell.

neuroscience

multidisciplinary field devoted to the study of the nervous system and the brain

biological psychology

a specific field within neuroscience that focuses on the scientific study of the biological basis of behavior and mental processes

The Structure and Function of a Neuron

LO 2.1   **Identify the anatomy and function of a neuron.**

Neurons are the building blocks of the nervous system. Everything we experience starts with a neuron. A **neuron** is a tiny, excitable cell that receives stimulation and transmits information to other neurons throughout the body. While neurons are relatively simple

neuron

a tiny, excitable cell that receives stimulation and transmits information to other neurons throughout the body

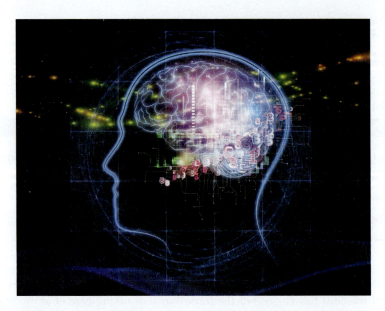

Our brain is constantly working and involved in everything we think, feel, and do. Psychologists study brain structure and brain function in an effort to better understand human behavior.

dendrites

the bushy end of the neuron responsible for receiving the incoming signal from the previous neuron

soma

cell body of the neuron; contains the nucleus, which houses the cell's genetic information

axon

part of a neuron; a long, thin fiber responsible for carrying information to the end of the neuron

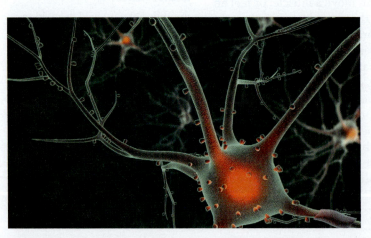

While neurons are fairly simple in structure, they play a vital role in the functioning of the nervous system.

in structure, each part of the neuron has a specialized function when it comes to communicating information. Before we can understand how neurons "talk" to each other, it is necessary to examine the anatomy of the neuron and understand the important role each component plays.

A typical neuron has a bushy end, a sleek body, and another end with "finger-type" branches. The bushy end of the neuron has what are called the **dendrites**, which actually means "branch," as they look like the branches of a tree. The dendrites have the important job of catching the signal, or information, from the previous neuron. Imagine a bucket of money was placed in front of you, and you were told you could use one hand to grab as much as you wanted. How would you place your hand into the bucket? If you were trying to get the most money, you would likely stretch out your fingers as much as possible to grab the widest area. In this example, your fingers are like the dendrites of the neuron: They stretch out over a large area to increase their chances of "grabbing onto" the incoming signal. Just like your own hands and arms are connected to the middle of your body, the dendrites are connected to the **soma**, or cell body. The word soma means "body," and it contains the cell's nucleus, which houses the cell's genetic information. The **axon** is a long, thin fiber responsible for carrying information down to the end of the neuron. Continuing with our own body as an example, the axon would be our spine. Just as ligaments protect our own spine, a layer of fatty tissue, called the **myelin sheath**, covers the axon. In addition to protection, the myelin sheath serves another important function. This fatty layer speeds up the transmission of information down the axon (think of it like a slip and slide). The end of the axon is responsible for then sending the information out to be caught by the dendrites or soma of the next neuron. The end of the axon also branches out, although less so than the dendrites, and each branch contains a swollen part at the end, which is called the **terminal button** (or sometimes referred to as the *axon terminal*). The terminal button contains the chemicals that will be used to enable neurons to "talk" to each other. Watch the following video, *Anatomy of the Neuron,* to review the important parts of a neuron and how they work together to communicate information throughout our body.

Anatomy of the Neuron

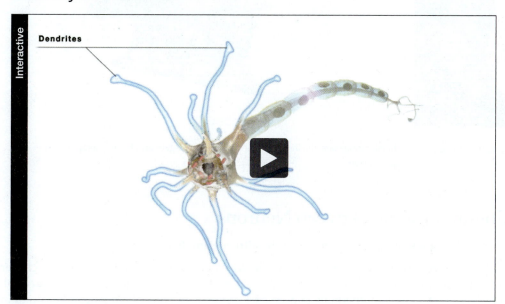

Now, test yourself to see that you can remember the important parts of the neuron and its respective functions.

Identify the Anatomy of the Neuron

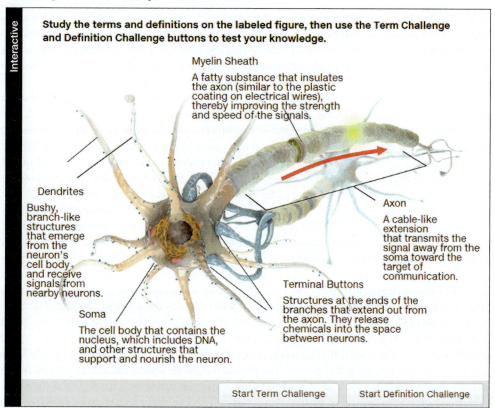

myelin sheath

fatty layer that covers the axon; serves as protection and speeds up the transmission of information down the axon

terminal button

located at the end of each neuron; contains vesicles holding the neurotransmitter, which is released into the synapse during an action potential

A neuron in its resting state is primed and ready to fire, much like preparing to shoot an arrow with a bow.

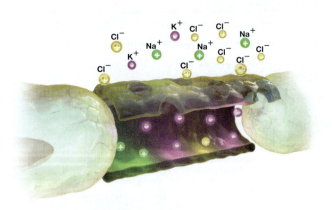

In its resting state, the inside of a neuron is more negatively charged compared to the outside.

Communication Between Neurons

LO 2.2 Explain how neurons communicate with one another.

Neurons are very social creatures. They live in large communities called *networks* and cluster in tight groupings called *nerves*. Neurons depend on contact with one another for survival, and they work both as individuals and as part of larger groups. Neurons communicate in much the same way people do when they have a bit of interesting gossip. Imagine an eighth grade student tearing down the hallway of her middle school to tell her closest friend the "latest news." Upon reaching her friend, she whispers in his ear; the friend laughs and is off to tell the next student. Of course, neurons transmit information via energy and chemicals rather than whispers, but their basic pattern of communication is similar to a teenage social butterfly.

action potential

a brief electrical charge that travels down the neuron; a neural impulse

THE NEURAL IMPULSE The activity within and between neurons are both *electrical* and *chemical* events. An **action potential** is a brief electrical charge that travels down the neuron. At first, the neural impulse is an electrical event. When the impulse reaches the end of the neuron, it becomes a chemical event in order to "pass on" the information to the next neuron. Neurons don't touch, which means ongoing electricity between neurons is impossible.

Most of the time, neurons are primed and prepared to send signals to one another. Neurons are both surrounded by, and filled with, fluid. This fluid contains ions, which are electrically charged atoms. Ions can be either positively charged or negatively charged. When a neuron is at rest, the inside of the neuron is more negatively charged compared to the outside of the neuron. This difference in charge across the neuron's membrane is what prepares the neuron to respond quickly to incoming messages from previous neurons. Think of it like preparing to shoot with a bow and arrow. When the arrow is drawn back, it pulls the string out creating tension that, when released, sends the arrow flying. The negative charge inside the cell, relative to the outside of the cell, is like the arrow being drawn back. This state of tension is referred to as the cell's **resting potential**.

resting potential

state of tension between the negative charge inside the cell relative to the outside of the cell; prepares the neuron for an action potential

all-or-none law

a principle regrading action potentials; states if the electrical impulse reaches its threshold, the neuron will fire and, if the impulse does not reach its threshold, the neuron will not fire

Some positively charged ions can permeate the cell membrane and when enough positive ions move into the cell, the cell becomes *depolarized*, or less negative. Once the cell becomes positive enough, the cell reaches its *threshold* and an action potential occurs. Neurons have a binary action: They either fire or they don't. So, once the threshold has been reached, nothing can happen to stop the action potential. This principle is referred to as the **all-or-none law**. The action potential begins near the soma and travels down the axon toward the terminal buttons. Not all of the cell membrane becomes permeable at once; the electrical charges "jump" or propagate down the axon. To understand this concept, it might help to imagine a number of people sitting on an axon playing a game of hot potato (the potato would represent the action potential moving down the axon.) There is a short period of time after an action potential, called the **refractory period**, where the neuron is "resting" and not able to fire again. Watch the following video on *The Action Potential* to review the entire process and then test yourself afterward.

refractory period

short period of time after an action potential where the neuron is not able to fire again

SYNAPTIC TRANSMISSION Neurons are either *excitatory* or *inhibitory*. This means in response to a signal, a neuron can "fire" by passing the signal along to the next neuron (excitatory), or it

The Action Potential

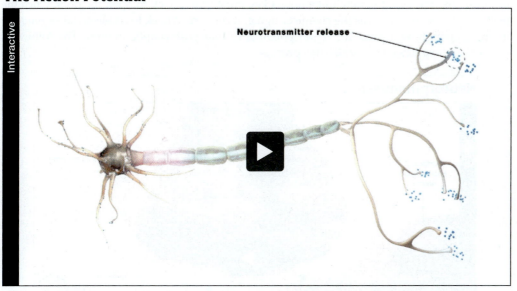

Interactive

Neurotransmitter release

Key Components of an Action Potential

Interactive

The following is a list of key terms. Match each term with its definition.

Terms	Definitions
All or None Law	Once the electrical impulse reaches its threshold, the neuron will fire. If the impulse does not reach its threshold, the neuron will not fire.
Action Potential	A brief electrical impulse that travels down the axon of the neuron.
Resting Potential	The slightly negative charge of a neuron while it is inactive, or "at rest."
Refractory Period	A brief period after an action potential occurs where the neuron is unable to fire again.

Start Over

can also hold its fire (inhibitory) by not transmitting the signal. The passing of information on to the neighboring neurons is the *chemical* part of a neural impulse.

As mentioned earlier, neurons are not actually connected to one another. There is a very small space between the neuron's terminal buttons and the next neuron's dendrites called the **synapse** or the *synaptic cleft*. The neuron that delivers the signal to the synapse is called the *presynaptic neuron,* and the neuron that receives the signal from the synapse is called the *postsynaptic neuron.*

When the electrical impulse reaches the terminal buttons at the end of a neuron, the electrical event becomes a chemical event. The terminal buttons contain small, fluid-filled sacs called **vesicles**. These vesicles contain **neurotransmitters** (the chemical messengers of the nervous system) and, when stimulated by the action potential, they burst and the neurotransmitter fills the synapse. Picture a number of water balloons that all pop at the same time; the balloons are the vesicles and the water inside is the neurotransmitter. Without neurotransmitters, neurons wouldn't be able to communicate and we wouldn't be able to experience life. After the vesicles burst, some of those neurotransmitters then travel across the synapse and chemically stimulate the dendrites of the neighboring neuron. Dendrites of neurons have specialized receptors ready to "catch" the incoming neurotransmitters. The various neurotransmitters have their

synapse

small space between the presynaptic neuron and the postsynaptic neuron; filled with the neurotransmitter after an action potential

vesicles

small, fluid-filled sacs located in the terminal buttons; typically hold the neurotransmitter

neurotransmitters

chemical messengers of the nervous system

own specific receptor proteins. In order to receive the incoming message, the neurotransmitter must "fit" the receptor, much like how a key must fit in a lock to open the door. Once the postsynaptic neuron receives the chemical signal, it converts it back to an electrical signal and, if strong enough, will cause an action potential in that postsynaptic neuron. The following video *Neurotransmission* illustrates this process.

Neurotransmission

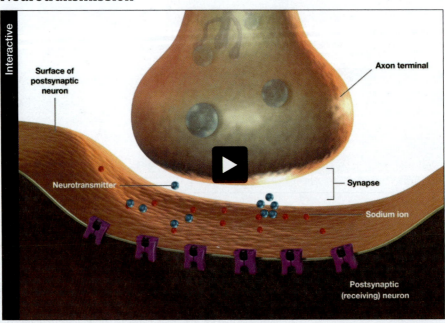

reuptake

a process that transports many of the released neurotransmitters back into the presynaptic neuron

Neurotransmitters don't stay in the synapse for long: A process called **reuptake** moves many of the released neurotransmitters back into the presynaptic neuron. Think of it as a recycling process. If a neurotransmitter doesn't quickly attach to a receptor on a neighboring neuron, it will fall victim to the reuptake process. Not all neurotransmitters are recycled; some neurotransmitters left behind in the synapse will be broken down, or degraded, by enzymes. Many psychotropic drugs interfere with this process in an attempt to positively affect mood and behavior.

Adaptive Pathway 2.1: The Action Potential

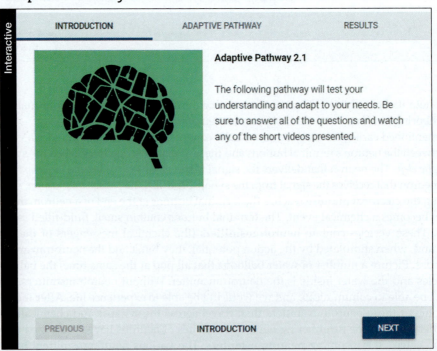

Types of Neurotransmitters

LO 2.3 **Recognize the effects of neurotransmitters on behavior.**

Each neuron typically has only one type of neurotransmitter, but many different neurons secrete their neurotransmitters into the synapse at the same time. Whether the postsynaptic neuron fires or not is determined by the balance of excitatory and inhibitory messages—it is somewhat like counting votes. The postsynaptic neuron simply goes with the majority. To complicate things further, while neurotransmitters tend to be either excitatory or inhibitory, their function is determined by the actual receptors on the dendrites of the postsynaptic neuron. That is, the same neurotransmitter can have an inhibitory effect on one neuron while it has an excitatory effect on another. Let's look at some of the major neurotransmitters that have the biggest effects on our thoughts, feelings, and behaviors.

Properties of Neurotransmitters

Neurotransmitters	Excitatory, Inhibitory, or Both?	Primary Function	Possible Outcomes of Malfunction
Acetylcholine (ACh)	Both	Arousal; attention and memory; muscle contractions	Low levels: Alzheimer's disease
Dopamine (DA)	Excitatory	Feelings of pleasure; learning and memory; movement	Low levels: Parkinson's disease, depression High levels: Schizophrenia
Serotonin (5-HT)	Both	Arousal and sleep; mood; appetite	Low levels: Depression, anxiety (OCD) High levels: Serotonin syndrome (symptoms may include agitation, rapid heart rate/high blood pressure, muscle rigidity, sweating, high fever, seizures; can be life threatening)
Norepinephrine (NE)	Excitatory	Alertness and arousal; mood	Low levels: Depression, bipolar disorder High levels: Agitation
Gamma-aminobutyric acid (GABA)	Inhibitory	Sleep; inhibits movement	Low levels: Insomnia, seizures, tremors, depression, anxiety
Glutamate	Excitatory	Learning and memory; synaptic plasticity	High levels: Migraines (often from MSG), seizures, anxiety, depression, schizophrenia, Parkinson's disease
Endorphins	Inhibitory	Blocks pain signals; produces feelings of pleasure; regulates immune system dysfunction	Low levels: Depression High levels: Runners high (although this is more likely due to anandamide in the brain since endorphins can't cross the blood-brain barrier)

Interactive

Check Your Understanding

Receptors can be activated by chemicals that originate from within the body (e.g., neurotransmitter, hormones) or from ingesting chemicals that originate outside of the body (e.g., alcohol, illicit drugs, prescription drugs). An **agonist** is a neurotransmitter or drug that binds to cell receptors and produces a biological response. That is, in the case of individual neurons, an agonist could be the actual neurotransmitter or a "look alike" that exerts either an excitatory or inhibitory effect on the postsynaptic neuron. Nicotine is an agonist, and many people who have tried to quit smoking have used a nicotinic agonist, such as *Nicorette* gum or the prescription *Chantix*. Nicorette gum actually contains nicotine, whereas Chantix contains another drug that acts as a nicotinic agonist.

agonist

a neurotransmitter or drug that binds to cell receptors and produces a biological response

antagonist

a neurotransmitter or drug that binds to cell receptors and blocks the effects of another substance

Chantix stimulates nicotinic receptors (i.e., still makes the receptors think they are getting nicotine) but produces less of an effect than pure nicotine.

An **antagonist** also binds to the receptors but, in this case, an antagonist *blocks* the effects of a particular chemical or neurotransmitter. *Botulism* is a serious and possibly fatal disease that arises from improperly preserved food. Botulinum toxin is an ACh antagonist, meaning that it attaches to ACh receptors thereby blocking the neurotransmitter's effects. The result of botulism is often paralysis that can eventually lead to death. Interestingly, small amounts of botulinum toxin are used for various medical problems and cosmetic issues. People who have a neuromuscular disorder called *spasmodic torticollis* receive botulinum toxin injections to calm muscle spasms. One of the most popular cosmetic procedures to eliminate or prevent wrinkles is *Botox,* which is merely the injection of botulinum toxin into the body (typically the face or neck). The wrinkles disappear by paralyzing the muscles underneath the skin.

Synaptic Plasticity and Neurogenesis

LO 2.4 **Distinguish the concepts of synaptic plasticity and neurogenesis.**

synaptic plasticity

the ability of the brain to adapt and change over time

One impressive characteristic of the brain is its **synaptic plasticity**, or its ability to adapt and change over time. The video *Neuroplasticity* shows how the brain can recover some functioning after a head injury or stroke. Synaptic plasticity is evident not only in the brain as a whole but also at the cellular level. Certain experiences and accompanied neural activity can modify brain function by changing what happens at the synapse (Citri & Malenka, 2007). Synapses can strengthen or weaken over time based on either increases or decreases in synaptic activity. Also, the number of neurotransmitter receptors at a synapse can change as a function of the amount of neurotransmitter available. One example of this involves individuals who abuse substances. Heroin is a drug synthesized from the opium poppy that binds to specialized, opioid receptors. With repeated use, the receptors begin to *downregulate* or decrease in number—it is like the cell has the realization that it doesn't need so many "hands on deck" (i.e., receptors) available to bind to scarce amounts of opioids because the drug is readily available (through the use of heroin).

Neuroplasticity

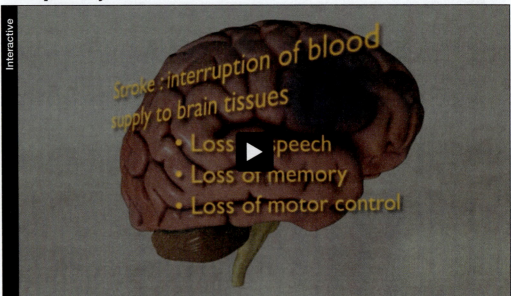

One of the best examples of the brain's ability to change in response to experience is the impact that playing a musical instrument can have on both structural and functional plasticity. Creating music involves a variety of sensory, motor, and cognitive processes, and research has shown various cognitive improvements, such as verbal, mathematical, and spatial skills, in both children and adults as a result of playing a musical instrument (Wan & Schlaug, 2010). Overall, synaptic plasticity has been an important concept in neuroscience because of its involvement in learning, memory (Caroni et al., 2012; Takeuchi et al., 2013) and mood regulation (Eisch & Petrik, 2012; Mahar et al., 2014).

In 1949, Donald Hebb first proposed the idea of synaptic plasticity as a theoretical model to account for how the brain learns and retains memories. Hebb theorized that the more cells

Figure 2.1 The Hippocampus

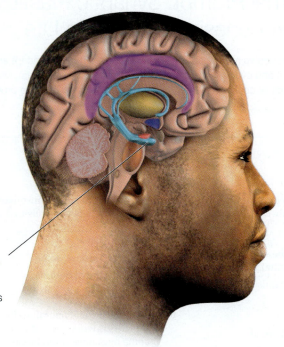

Hippocampus
plays a role in our learning, memory, and ability to compare sensory information to expectations

"talk" to one another, the more plentiful their synaptic connections become. In addition to providing a compelling model for learning and memory, this phenomenon helps us understand how individuals recover from damage to areas of the brain. Two main theories have been proposed to explain how synaptic plasticity works. The first theory is based on the assumption that the brain cannot make new functional neurons and therefore recruits and fortifies smaller, previously underutilized connections. Innovative studies with London taxi cab and bus drivers have provided support for Hebb's theory of synaptic plasticity. In one study, London taxi drivers exhibited increased hippocampus volume compared to similarly aged adults who were not taxi drivers. (The hippocampus, as shown in Figure 2.1, is a structure critical to spatial memory that will be discussed in more detail later in this chapter.)

Scientists believe that the drivers' increased hippocampus volume resulted from an increase in the number of synapses in that particular brain area, which was stimulated by learning numerous complicated driving routes (Maguire et al., 2000). Some researchers argued that the changes in the brain could merely be a result of self-motion, driving experience, and/or stress. Therefore, Maguire et al. (2006) conducted an additional study comparing London taxi cab drivers to London bus drivers (who still drove daily and experienced stress but had predetermined routes). Can you guess which group had the largest hippocampi? Yes, the taxi cab drivers still had more volume in a particular area of their hippocampus compared to the bus drivers.

The second theory regarding neural plasticity involves the concept of **neurogenesis**, or the birth of new neurons, particularly in the hippocampus and olfactory bulb (Eriksson et al., 1998). While neurogenesis is most prevalent during prenatal development, a few areas of the brain continue to "grow" new neurons throughout the lifespan. These new neurons have been found to be functional (van Praag et al., 2002) and to play an important role in the development and treatment of depression (Petrik et al., 2012). Depressed patients have been found to have a smaller hippocampus, and antidepressant medications appear to increase the volume of the hippocampus, which corresponds to a reduction in depressive symptoms (Eisch & Petrik, 2012). Evidence suggests that environmental interventions such as increased learning, enriched surroundings, and exercise can support and increase the amount of neurogenesis that occurs in the hippocampus (Sahay et al., 2011; van Praag et al., 1999). It was recently discovered that a particular protein secreted by muscles during exercise (cathepsin B) promotes neurogenesis in the hippocampus and is associated with improved memory (Moon et al., 2016). Therefore, it is not true that neuronal loss due to age, accidents, and unhealthy living are irreversible in all cases. In fact, research in neuroscience tells us to keep learning, exercising, and treating our bodies well in order to keep our brains healthy and strong.

neurogenesis

the birth of new neurons

Journal Prompt: Synaptic Plasticity and Neurogenesis in Your Own Life

Now that you've read about the ability of our brain cells to adapt and change over time (synaptic plasticity) and even regenerate in certain places (neurogenesis), what is something you have done in the past or could do in the future to take advantage of these processes?

Quiz for Module 2.1–2.4

1. Which part of the neuron improves the speed of the neural impulse?
   a. Soma
   b. Myelin sheath
   c. Axon
   d. Dendrite

2. What is the brief electrical impulse that travels down the axon called?
   a. Refractory period
   b. Resting potential
   c. Action potential
   d. Synaptic transmission

3. At its resting state, the outside of a neuron is more _____ than the inside of the neuron.
   a. negatively charged
   b. chemically charged
   c. electrically charged
   d. positively charged

4. An action potential occurs when the inside of a cell becomes more _____ charged and the _____ charge moves down the axon.
   a. negatively; electrical
   b. positively; electrical
   c. negatively; chemical
   d. positively; chemical

5. In the process of neurotransmission, the action potential causes neurotransmitters to be released from the _____ into the _____.
   a. soma; synapse
   b. synaptic vesicles; soma
   c. soma; terminal buttons
   d. synaptic vesicles; synapse

6. Danny has terrible migraines that interfere with his ability to complete his work. He just learned from his psychology class that the migraines could be caused by an overabundance of which neurotransmitter?
   a. Glutamate
   b. Dopamine
   c. Serotonin
   d. Norepinephrine

Our nervous system works interdependently much like an assembly line at a factory.

Module 2.5–2.6: The Nervous System and the Endocrine System

We have trillions of neurons throughout our body. These neurons function independently in some ways but must work in organized groups to produce the results we see in our daily lives. You can think of this similar to how an automotive factory works. Almost all modern cars and trucks are produced in factories that utilize assembly lines—where one person (or machine) is responsible for making the same part of the car day after day. All of the individual parts are made and eventually put together to make the car. Even though each person in the factory works independently, all of the different stages are *interdependent* on the other to make a complete car. If a change is made at one stage, it affects all of the other stages and ultimately slows down what was previously a very efficient system. Your nervous system is very much like this: Neurons fire individually but work together in a system to produce a desired outcome. If something interferes with the neurons or the organized groups (e.g., illnesses/diseases, substances), the entire system is affected and becomes less efficient.

The Nervous System: Structure and Function

LO 2.5 **Identify each division of the nervous system.**

The nervous system is divided into two parts: the central nervous system and the peripheral nervous system. The **central nervous system (CNS)** is the largest part of the nervous system

central nervous system (CNS)

the largest part of the nervous system, which includes the brain and spinal cord

and includes the brain and spinal cord. The **peripheral nervous system (PNS)** resides outside of the central nervous system but is connected with it since it carries information from the CNS to various organs and parts of the body. The word *peripheral* actually means *external to*; so, when trying to distinguish the CNS from the PNS, remember that the *peripheral* nervous system is *external to* the central nervous system, or *external to* the brain and spinal cord.

Three different types of neurons are responsible for communicating information throughout the body. While neurons are generally similar in structure, they come in a variety of shapes and sizes. All neurons, however, fall into one of three categories, depending on their location and function in the nervous system:

- **Sensory (afferent) neurons** carry information *toward* the central nervous system from the sensory organs (eyes, ears, nose, tongue, and skin). Just think "Sensory Neurons" are those that carry info from the Senses to the Nervous system.

- **Motor (efferent) neurons** carry information *away from* the central nervous system in order to operate muscles and glands. For this one, you can think about how Motor neurons Move information away from your central nervous system and toward your Muscles.

- **Interneurons** send information between sensory neurons and motor neurons. An interneuron gets its name from the fact that the cell's dendrites and axon are contained entirely within a single structure—the cell is *internal* to that structure.

There are millions of sensory and motor neurons, but there are about 100 *billion* interneurons. Located exclusively in the central nervous system, interneurons are capable of receiving and combining information from a variety of sources. As the workforce of the central nervous system, these cells are responsible for generating perception from sensation, creating our internal mental worlds, and organizing and initiating behaviors.

Glial cells, also known simply as **glia**, (from the Greek word for *glue*) are the other kind of cell in the central nervous system. There are about 10 glial cells for every neuron in the human brain. Glia support neurons in many ways: They keep neurons in place, clean up the neurons that die, create myelin, and provide nutrition and insulation. Recently, glial cells have been elevated to more than a "support role" and are thought to be a factor in the development of Alzheimer's disease (Heppner et al., 2015; Verkhratsky et al., 2016). Specialized forms of glial cells surround the brain's blood vessels and create what is known as the *blood-brain barrier,* a fatty envelope that filters substances trying to leave the bloodstream and reach the brain. Since many toxins and poisons are not soluble (i.e., dissolvable) in fat, they cannot penetrate the blood-brain barrier and harm the brain, which is a very good thing!

THE CENTRAL NERVOUS SYSTEM   Remember, the CNS consists of the brain and the spinal cord. The brain itself will be discussed in more detail in an upcoming module. The *spinal cord* connects the spinal nerves to the brain and organizes simple reflexes and rhythmic movements.

Specifically designed to keep you alive, **reflexes** are rapid and automatic neuromuscular actions generated in response to a specific stimulus. Most often, the spinal cord organizes these automatic actions without the conscious participation of the brain. To produce a reflex, a sensory neuron must carry the stimulus to the spinal cord, where an interneuron enables connection to a motor neuron that produces a specific motor pattern. Consider the following example of the *withdrawal reflex*: You reach over to pick something up off of a table and inadvertently touch the end of your finger to a burning candle. The sensory neurons in your finger are immediately activated by the painful stimulus and send a signal to the interneurons in the spinal cord. Interneurons answer this call by exciting the motor neurons leading to your finger. As a result, before you have time to consciously register pain, your finger has jerked up off the table, and you have avoided serious injury (see Figure 2.2).

Reflexes are not under conscious control. It would be very inefficient for a signal to travel all the way to the brain and back when only a simple movement is required. When there's the potential for harm, elaborate decision making becomes less important than getting away from the stimulus as fast as possible. Of course, if you step on something sharp, the pain signal will eventually reach your brain, although the pain signal travels more slowly than the spinal reflex signal. When the signal reaches the brain, you will consciously experience pain, followed by the awareness of your own rapidly moved foot. That is, you notice the pain and that your foot moved, *after* the fact. As this example illustrates, reflexes and conscious awareness aren't really connected, which explains why people with spinal cord injuries exhibit spinal reflexes, but they have no conscious or sensory awareness of the stimuli or the movement.

---

peripheral nervous system (PNS)

branch of the nervous system outside of the central nervous system (CNS) responsible for carrying information from the CNS to various organs and parts of the body

sensory (afferent) neurons

neurons that carry information toward the central nervous system from the sensory organs (eyes, ears, nose, tongue, and skin)

motor (efferent) neurons

neurons that carry information *away from* the central nervous system to the muscles and glands

interneurons

neurons that send information between sensory neurons and motor neurons

glial cells (glia)

abundant and versatile cells in the central nervous system that play an important role in supporting neurons; also thought to be potentially related to the development of Alzheimer's disease

reflexes

rapid and automatic neuromuscular actions generated in response to a specific stimulus

Figure 2.2 The Withdrawal Reflex

The withdrawal reflex is a simple reflex involving a sensory neuron, interneuron, and motor neuron and can take place outside of conscious awareness.

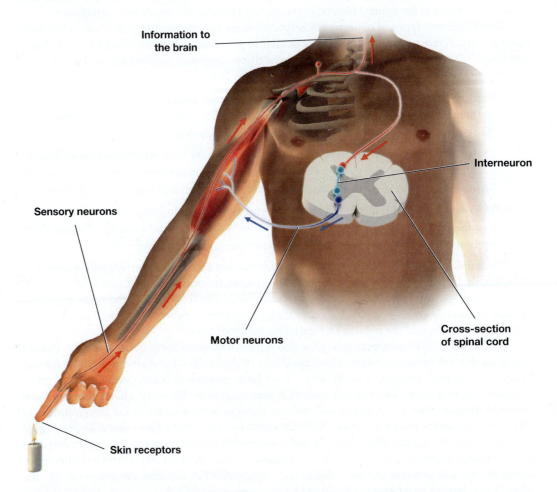

Spinal cord injuries typically occur when damage to the bones of the spinal column severs or chokes the spine. A person who suffers a spinal cord injury may lose some or all of the functions controlled by the area of the spine *below* the injury. For example, damage to the cervical vertebrae (those immediately below the skull) can cause the brain to be out of touch with the body. This injury would paralyze the chest and lungs (requiring patients to rely on a machine to breathe) as well as the trunk and both arms and legs. In contrast, injury to the lumbar, or lower spine area, may result in hip and leg paralysis. The spinal cord is rarely completely severed, so some patients manage to recover certain aspects of function; however, complete recovery is unlikely.

According to the National Spinal Cord Injury Statistical Center (2012), the overwhelming majority of spinal cord injuries result from motor vehicle accidents (39 percent), followed by accidental falls (29 percent), acts of violence (15 percent), and sports and recreation accidents (8 percent). Since 2005, the average age of injury is 41 years, and 80.6 percent of the injuries occur to males (National Spinal Cord Injury Statistical Center, 2016). Until very recently, it was assumed that the spinal cord was not able to repair itself following injury. However, recent stem cell research has shown promising evidence of the ability to repair damaged spinal cord cells. **Stem cells** are unspecified cells that have a very special talent. Stem cells can divide over and over again. With each division, the resulting cells can either remain stem cells or become another type of specialized cell in the body (e.g., brain cell, red blood cell). These new cells don't just mimic other specialized cells, they *become* those cells (see Figure 2.3).

In the case of spinal cord injury, research has demonstrated that stem cells can migrate to injury sites, differentiate into neurons and glial cells, and in turn form new myelin sheaths around the damaged nerve axons (Sabelström et al., 2013; Young, 2014). In addition to stem

stem cells

unspecified cells with the capability to evolve into other types of specialized cells in the body (e.g., brain cells, red blood cells)

Figure 2.3 The Capability of Stem Cells

Stem cells have the unique ability to change into other cells in the body, which could help heal injuries and cure diseases.

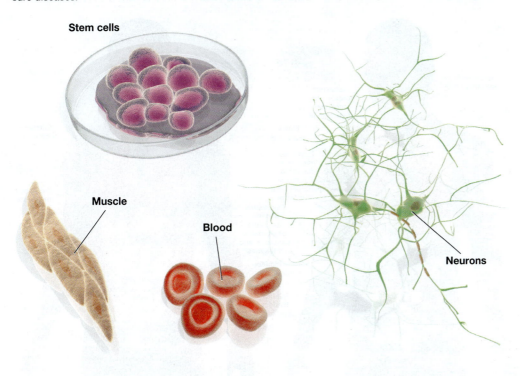

cells, olfactory cells (the specialized cells that form part of the sense of smell) have also been transplanted into patients' damaged spinal cords (Yazdani et al., 2012). You might wonder what smell cells have to do with the spinal cord, but the neurons responsible for our sense of smell are the only part of the nervous system that regenerates throughout adult life. Therefore, these specialized cells have been used to bridge the gap in the spinal cord that results from injury. A BBC report detailed the story of Darek Fidyka, a Polish man who was the first person ever to undergo surgery to transplant his own olfactory cells into his damaged spinal cord. Prior to the surgery, he had been paralyzed for two years with no signs of recovery. Two years after the surgery, Mr. Fidyka was walking with a walker (Walsh, 2014). While this research is still in its early stages, there is now hope for those who suffer from a spinal cord injury.

THE PERIPHERAL NERVOUS SYSTEM   The peripheral nervous system exists outside of the central nervous system and is further divided into the somatic nervous system and the autonomic nervous system (that's auto*nomic*, not auto*matic*). The **somatic nervous system** picks up stimuli from the outside world, coordinates our movements, and performs other tasks that we control consciously. The **autonomic nervous system** is responsible for the various involuntary functions of the internal organs of our bodies and consists of the sympathetic nervous system and the parasympathetic nervous system. In most situations, the **sympathetic nervous system** acts as an accelerator for the organs, while the **parasympathetic nervous system** acts as a brake. The sympathetic and parasympathetic nervous systems act in opposition to each other and therefore affect the same organs. The sympathetic system is always active and becomes significantly more active during periods of stress. The parasympathetic system, in contrast, is responsible for functions that do not require immediate action. While the two systems act oppositely to each other, this doesn't mean they are in conflict. In fact, the two systems are complementary: The sympathetic system does the quick intense work (like firemen working to put out a fire), and the parasympathetic system is responsible for returning the body to its natural resting state (like the people who come to clean up all of the debris after the fire has been extinguished). The two systems have rhyming job descriptions: While the sympathetic system's job is "fight or flight," the parasympathetic system's

somatic nervous system

part of the peripheral nervous system; receives stimuli from the outside world, coordinates movements, and performs other tasks under conscious control

autonomic nervous system

part of the peripheral nervous system responsible for the involuntary functions of the internal organs of our bodies

sympathetic nervous system

branch of the autonomic nervous system responsible for the involuntary functions of the body's internal organs; particularly active during times of stress

parasympathetic nervous system

a division of the autonomic nervous system responsible for returning the body to its natural resting state

Figure 2.4 The Actions of the Sympathetic and Parasympathetic Nervous Systems

The sympathetic and parasympathetic nervous systems work together to produce physiological arousal when under threat, and then return the body to its natural resting state, once the threat is removed or resolved.

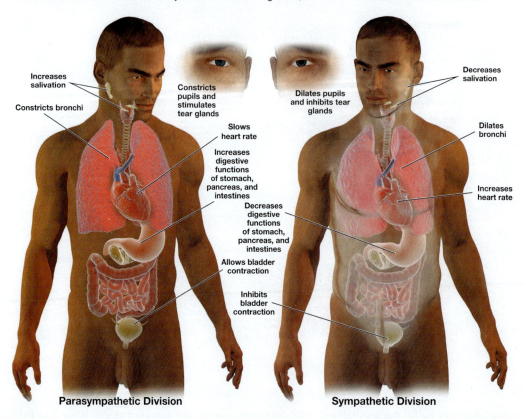

Parasympathetic Division

- Increases salivation
- Constricts bronchi
- Constricts pupils and stimulates tear glands
- Slows heart rate
- Increases digestive functions of stomach, pancreas, and intestines
- Allows bladder contraction

Sympathetic Division

- Decreases salivation
- Dilates pupils and inhibits tear glands
- Dilates bronchi
- Increases heart rate
- Decreases digestive functions of stomach, pancreas, and intestines
- Inhibits bladder contraction

priorities are "rest and digest." See Figure 2.4 for the different bodily functions controlled by the two autonomic systems.

One study strategy involves organizing information into a hierarchy. A hierarchy is a ranking of information and can be helpful when learning about the relationship between different concepts or systems. Use the following flow chart as a way of quizzing yourself on the divisions of the nervous system.

Branches of the Nervous System

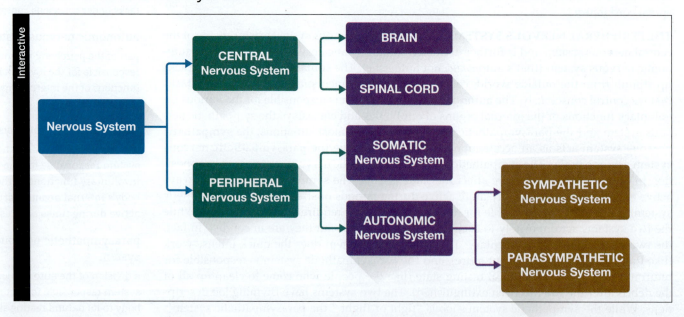

Interactive

- Nervous System
  - CENTRAL Nervous System
    - BRAIN
    - SPINAL CORD
  - PERIPHERAL Nervous System
    - SOMATIC Nervous System
    - AUTONOMIC Nervous System
      - SYMPATHETIC Nervous System
      - PARASYMPATHETIC Nervous System

The Endocrine System

LO 2.6 **Recognize the purpose of the endocrine system and how some hormones influence health and behavior.**

The electrochemical system, in the form of action potentials and neurotransmission, is a quick and efficient system for communicating information throughout the body, especially in stressful or dangerous situations. Another important system, but one that functions differently from the electrochemical system, is called the endocrine system. The **endocrine system** is a secondary and slower communication system in the body that involves hormones, which control most major bodily functions (e.g., immune system, growth, fertility, metabolism). **Hormones** are chemical messengers secreted by the glands into the bloodstream and regulate the activity of cells or organs. Imagine you have ordered something from Amazon. If you need it quickly, you might choose the one-day shipping option. If you aren't in a hurry, then you might choose the (free) standard shipping option where your package will arrive in four to five days. The communication that occurs in our nervous system is like the one-day shipping, whereas the standard shipping is our endocrine system. The package will arrive either way; one way is just a little faster than the other.

The endocrine system gets its name from the Greek words *endo* meaning within, and *crinis,* meaning to secrete. The endocrine system consists of glands that produce and secrete more than 50 hormones (Cachofeiro & Lahera, 2014). In addition to glands, adipose tissue (fat) is also considered an endocrine organ that influences various metabolic and hormonal responses (McGown et al., 2014). For example, you may have heard of *leptin*—an important hormone that helps to regulate food intake and body weight. Leptin is produced by fat cells, so typically the more adipose tissue, the more leptin is circulating in the blood. In general, higher levels of leptin should help control weight gain, but many obese people have become "leptin resistant," meaning their brain doesn't recognize the leptin anymore; therefore, they continue to eat more and gain weight over time (Galic et al., 2010).

It might also be surprising to learn that Vitamin D is not actually a vitamin but a hormone similar to the classic steroid hormones, like cortisol (Norman, 2008). Vitamin D is produced by the kidneys and regulates calcium levels in the blood, which helps us to develop strong bones. Taken together, all of the hormones in our body regulate much of our metabolism, growth and development, blood pressure, sexual function and reproduction, sleep, hunger, and mood.

Several important glands in our body secrete different hormones. You might wonder how these different glands know when to secrete hormones. The *hypothalamus* is a structure in the brain (that you will learn more about in an upcoming module) that is the ultimate director of glandular activity. The hypothalamus is the link between the endocrine system and the nervous system. The hypothalamus regulates hormone release by communicating directly with the pituitary gland through the secretion of *releasing hormones.* The **pituitary gland** is often referred to as the *master gland* because it sits in the brain and directly communicates with and influences (through its own hormones) all other glands in the body. The relationship between the hypothalamus and pituitary gland is similar to what you might see at a large company in the relationship between the Chief Executive Officer (CEO) and the Chief Operations Officer (COO). The CEO (hypothalamus) has little to do with the employees. He or she communicates directly with the COO (pituitary gland), who then takes the directives to the individual employees (other glands in the body). The pituitary gland has a diverse set of capabilities, which is why someone with a pituitary tumor often has a wide variety of sometimes bizarre symptoms, including weight loss or weight gain, sexual dysfunction, high blood pressure, bruising, excessive sweating, increased body hair, and/or breast growth in men. The pituitary gland releases a number of different hormones responsible for growth, sexual development and reproduction, and blood pressure. *Prolactin* is the hormone that initiates breast milk production, and *oxytocin* is the hormone that stimulates contractions during childbirth and the letdown of breast milk after birth.

endocrine system

secondary and slower communication system in the body that involves hormones, which control most major bodily functions (e.g., immune system, growth, fertility, metabolism)

hormones

chemical messengers secreted by the glands into the bloodstream that regulate the activity of cells or organs

pituitary gland

referred to as the *master gland*; releases hormones to influence all other glands and hormones in the body

pineal gland

a gland located deep in the center of the brain; plays an important role in the sleep-wake cycle

thyroid gland

one of the largest endocrine glands located at the base of the neck that plays an important role in metabolism and controls how sensitive the body is to the effects of other hormones

hyperthyroidism

condition resulting from an *overactive* thyroid; can produce symptoms of heart palpitations, sweating, diarrhea, increased appetite with weight loss, heat sensitivity, and bulging eyes

hypothyroidism

a condition that results from an *underactive* thyroid; can produce symptoms of tiredness, weight gain, cold intolerance, and slowed heart rate

adrenal glands

glands located at the top of each kidney that play an important role in the stress response by secreting predominantly epinephrine and some norepinephrine

pancreas

organ of the endocrine and digestive systems that produces hormones, including *insulin* and *glucagon*, which are important for regulating the concentration of glucose in the bloodstream

gonads

glands involved in sexual development, which include the *ovaries* in females and the *testes* in males

The **pineal gland** is located deep in the center of the brain and plays an important role in our sleep-wake cycle. In the evening, when it gets dark, the pineal gland secretes the hormone *melatonin*. Melatonin helps monitor our biological rhythms, including sleepiness and the lowering of body temperature. You have likely seen melatonin sold in health food stores or online. Melatonin is actually the only hormone available in the United States without a prescription. It can be sold as a dietary supplement and does not have to be approved by the Food and Drug Administration because it is contained naturally in some foods.

The **thyroid gland** is one of the largest endocrine glands and is located at the base of the neck. The thyroid plays an important role in metabolism (how quickly the body uses energy), and it controls how sensitive the body is to the effects of other hormones. Two of the most typical thyroid disorders include:

- **Hyperthyroidism** is an *overactive* thyroid that can produce symptoms of heart palpitations, sweating, diarrhea, increased appetite with weight loss, heat sensitivity, and bulging eyes. A number of these symptoms can be interpreted as signs of anxiety, so patients who complain of anxiety are often also tested for hyperthyroidism.

- **Hypothyroidism** is an *underactive* thyroid that can produce symptoms of tiredness, weight gain, cold intolerance, and slowed heart rate. Some of these symptoms overlap with depression, so patients who complain of depressed mood will also often be tested for hypothyroidism.

The **pancreas** is located behind the stomach and is part of both the endocrine system and the digestive system. As an endocrine gland, it produces hormones, including *insulin* and *glucagon,* which are both important for regulating the concentration of glucose in the bloodstream. The pancreas can become inflamed (known as pancreatitis), often due to recurrent gallstones or chronic alcohol use, and is associated with intense abdomen pain and digestive problems. The most common medical problem involving the pancreas is diabetes, where the pancreas does not produce enough insulin to keep blood sugar levels within the normal range.

The **adrenal glands** are located at the top of each kidney and play an important role in the stress response. The adrenal glands secrete predominantly epinephrine (also known as adrenaline) and some norepinephrine (also known as noradrenaline). Epinephrine and norepinephrine are somewhat unusual because they are both neurotransmitters (when they are used in the nervous system) and hormones (when they are used in the endocrine system). Because they act more quickly than most hormones, they are helpful in dangerous or stressful situations. The adrenal glands communicate with the sympathetic nervous system (via epinephrine) to initiate the "fight or flight" response in a stressful situation. The adrenal glands also produce corticosteroids (steroid hormones involved in stress and immune system responses, inflammation, and carbohydrate metabolism). *Cortisol* is one such hormone that you likely know of as the "stress hormone." Cortisol is secreted in response to physical or psychological stress and functions to increase blood sugar, increase metabolism of fat, protein, and carbohydrates and suppresses the immune system in an effort to manage stress. These functions related to cortisol have led to the increased attention to the role of stress in illness and weight gain (Cohen et al., 2012; Epel et al., 2001; Foss et al., 2014). Some people tend to gain weight when they are under significant stress, and cortisol likely has a role to play in this outcome. Research has shown that people who are stressed have increased cortisol secretion which leads them to eat more food, especially foods high in carbohydrates and saturated fat (Roberts et al., 2014). It appears that "comfort food" really does exist, but the long-term consequences of weight gain can actually lead to more stress.

The **gonads** are the glands involved in sexual development and include the *ovaries* in females and the *testes* in males. The ovaries produce the ovum (egg) and secrete the hormones estrogen, progesterone, and testosterone, while the testes produce sperm and secrete testosterone. Study Figure 2.5 and see if you can recall the important structures associated with the endocrine system.

Figure 2.5 The Endocrine System

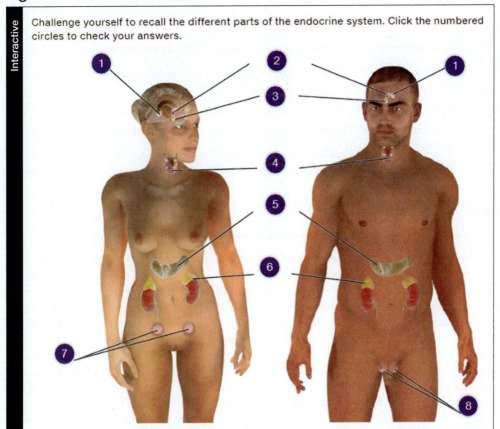

Challenge yourself to recall the different parts of the endocrine system. Click the numbered circles to check your answers.

Quiz for Module 2.5–2.6

1. A drug like nicotine that produces a biological response in the brain is called a(n) _____.

   a. antagonist
   b. agonist
   c. benzodiazepine
   d. GABA

2. Tomas has been playing the piano since age 5. Throughout his adolescence, he also taught himself to play guitar, bass, and the drums. Due to his practice with musical instruments, Tomas's brain would show improved _____.

   a. neurotransmitter release
   b. receptor sites
   c. synaptic plasticity
   d. synaptic pruning

3. When you touch a hot stove and immediately withdraw your hand, it is called a _____ and is the result of inter-neurons within the _____.

   a. reflex; brain
   b. reflex; spinal cord
   c. descending tract; brain
   d. ascending tract; spinal cord

4. Clayton incurred a spinal cord injury, and the doctors wanted to enroll him in a clinical trial that used stem cells in the treatment. Stem cells are special because they can _____.

   a. turn into other specialized cells in the body
   b. act like other cells in the body
   c. divide more quickly than other cells
   d. live only in the spinal cord

5. Chemical substances in the body that regulate bodily activities such as growth, metabolism, and sexual reproduction are called _____.

   a. pituitary proteins
   b. enzymes
   c. neurotransmitters
   d. hormones

6. The endocrine system consists of many glands that release hormones for different functions. Which gland is considered the master gland that communicates with all the other glands?

   a. Pituitary gland
   b. Adrenal gland
   c. Thyroid gland
   d. Pancreas

7. Javier has been complaining of being fatigued, cold, and depressed lately. His doctor decides to run some tests on his endocrine system. What condition might the doctor test for given his symptoms?

   a. Hypothyroidism
   b. Hyperthyroidism
   c. Diabetes
   d. Adrenal burnout syndrome

Module 2.7–2.8: The Structure and Function of the Brain

Generally speaking, the human brain has three major characteristics:

- **Sophistication.** Even the most high-tech computers can't match the human brain in complexity of thought and behavior.
- **Integration.** The brain's structures are constantly competing and cooperating.
- **Adaptability.** The human brain is always working and constantly changing.

The evolution of technology has afforded scientists an opportunity to examine the brain through a variety of methods to gain knowledge about its structure and functioning.

Methods of Studying the Brain

The human brain is a highly evolved and sophisticated organ. Researchers are fascinated by its ability to integrate information and adapt to new situations.

computed tomography (CT scan)

a machine that takes a series of x-rays from many different perspectives, which is sent to a computer that interprets the data and displays a two-dimensional image of the structure

magnetic resonance imaging (MRI)

an imaging procedure that utilizes a large magnet to examine the structural aspects of the brain, an organ, or tissue

LO 2.7   Differentiate structural and functional methods of studying the brain.

Since neuroscience is a multidisciplinary field that studies a variety of different questions, several approaches to studying the brain have emerged. In general, these methods vary in terms of whether they examine the *structure* versus the *function* of the brain. Structural questions tend to focus on anatomical structures and answer "what" or "where" questions, whereas functional questions focus more on "how" the brain works by examining the functioning within and between parts of the brain. One way to examine functioning is to *lesion,* or destroy, the neurons in a particular area of the brain, and then deduce what the function of that part of the brain was by observing what the patient or animal can no longer do. Thankfully, there are less permanent, and generally less invasive techniques used in modern medicine. Electrical brain stimulation can achieve a similar result to lesioning but only temporarily disturbs behavior (see the feature *Piecing It Together: Deep Brain Stimulation* for more about the topic of deep brain stimulation.) In this module, we'll introduce the most popular structural and functional brain imaging techniques and include some examples of the output or data produced from these assessments.

STRUCTURAL METHODS   Prior to the 1970s, the only definitive way to examine the structure of a person's brain was through a postmortem analysis (removing the brain and examining it after death). Postmortem studies are still conducted in neuroscience but thankfully, other methods of investigation have also emerged.

Computed tomography (CT scan) involves a machine that takes a series of x-rays from many different perspectives. The information from these x-rays is sent to a computer that interprets the data and then displays a two-dimensional image of the structure. CT scans can be performed on any body part and can be performed with or without contrast. Ingesting a contrast substance allows certain tissues or organs to be observed more clearly. CT scan usage in emergency rooms has increased significantly to the point where 7.5 percent of patients (97.1 million people) received at least one CT scan over a 12-year study period (Kocher et al., 2011). The most common complaints that led to CT scans in emergency rooms included abdominal pain, chest pain, and shortness of breath. CT scans are popular choices in emergency rooms because the scans can take fewer than five minutes (as opposed to 30 minutes for an MRI) and tend to be less expensive than other scans. In 2012, the husband of one of your authors fell from 15 feet and broke his back. He was unable to move his legs. He incurred what is technically called a "burst fracture" at L3 (the third lumbar vertebrae). The photo on the left is the actual CT scan from when he was in the hospital. You can see the chunks of bone fragments in his spinal column. After surgery and 10 days of rehabilitation, he miraculously walked out of the hospital and has only minor residual problems today.

A **magnetic resonance imaging (MRI)** scanner can be "open" or "closed." The machine itself is basically a large magnet that "excites" and aligns hydrogen atoms in the area of interest in the body. Our bodies are made up of water molecules, which contain hydrogen and oxygen atoms. Protons lie at the center of each atom and are sensitive to magnetic fields. The magnet in the MRI scanner "pulls" all of the body's water molecules so they line up in the same direction. Then, another magnetic field is turned on and off repeatedly (which is that clicking sound you hear if you've ever had an MRI), which causes the water molecules to move toward the new magnetic field and then return to their natural resting position. The MRI measures and compares the rate at which the atoms return to a state of equilibrium. This data is then converted

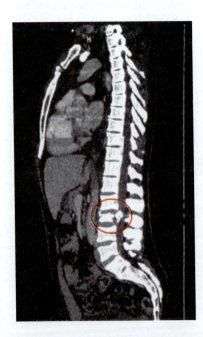

A CT scan of Dr. Hudson's husband's L3 burst fracture in 2012.

in a detailed picture of the brain, organ, or tissue. MRIs can provide a finer level of detail and analysis than CT scans and are viewed as safer because they don't use any radiation during the procedure. An MRI in conjunction with a mammogram is now considered the most effective method for screening for breast cancer in women identified as high risk (Lord et al., 2007).

MRIs are also helping to answer important questions about mental illness. For example, a team of researchers in England and Australia used MRI to scan the brains of individuals deemed "ultrahigh risk" for developing psychosis in the future. They were interested if they could detect any differences in the brains between those who did and didn't develop psychotic symptoms. Furthermore, they were interested in determining if there were any predictable differences between those with generic psychotic symptoms versus schizophrenia. All of the people who developed psychotic symptoms showed characteristic reductions in their frontal cortex, and those who were eventually diagnosed with schizophrenia also revealed reductions of brain volume in the parietal cortex (Dazzan et al., 2012). Researchers have long wondered if changes in the brain *result in* or *result from* mental illness; studies such as these provide preliminary answers to these important questions.

FUNCTIONAL METHODS   Different questions or problems require different types of assessments. For example, if someone has been in a motor vehicle accident and is suspected to have incurred a head injury, a CT or MRI scan may be performed initially to assess the overall structure of the brain (in terms of swelling and/or damage). However, in many other cases, doctors and researchers are interested in understanding how the brain functions in an effort to isolate a particular problem area and develop a treatment plan to reduce symptoms.

An **electroencephalogram (EEG)** is a noninvasive technique that measures electric activity of the brain (Woodman, 2010). The patient may wear a cap covered with electrodes or have electrodes placed directly on their scalp. The EEG produces output based on a series of electrical signals from neurons and, because EEG's timing is very precise (referred to as *temporal resolution*), it has been a useful tool in diagnosing sleep disorders, epilepsy, and brain death (Burle et al., 2015). The EEG continues to be used, often in conjunction with other measures, to assess various tasks such as reading comprehension (Yuan et al., 2014) and psychological disorders such as attention deficit disorder (Sangal & Sangal, 2014), depression (Jin & Phillips, 2014), and schizophrenia (Farmaki et al., 2015; Light et al., 2000, 2015).

electroencephalogram (EEG)
noninvasive technique to studying brain activity that measures electrical activity of the brain

magnetoencephalography (MEG)
procedure that measures faint *magnetic fields* generated by brain activity and provides precise information about brain activation and spatial localization

positron emission tomography (PET)
brain imaging technique that produces a three-dimensional image of the functioning of the brain

EEG Electrodes / EEG Output

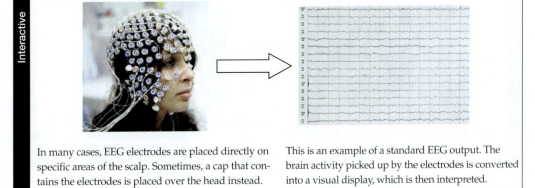

In many cases, EEG electrodes are placed directly on specific areas of the scalp. Sometimes, a cap that contains the electrodes is placed over the head instead.

This is an example of a standard EEG output. The brain activity picked up by the electrodes is converted into a visual display, which is then interpreted.

A related, but more expensive procedure, is **magnetoencephalography (MEG)**, which measures faint *magnetic fields* generated by brain activity rather than the electrical activity per se. The name of this assessment includes the word "magnet," which should help you differentiate this technique from its close cousin, the EEG. MEG provides precise information about brain activation (within milliseconds, which is much faster that other methods) as well as spatial localization (i.e., where the neural activities occur in the brain). A magnetic field map is produced and can be overlaid on an MRI to provide context for the functional map. MEG is particularly useful for surgical planning because of its high temporal (time) and spatial (location) resolution. However, it has also been used to study various developmental and disease processes such as language development, epilepsy, and schizophrenia (Elisevich et al., 2011; Kadis et al., 2011; Kato et al., 2011).

Another functional technique that has been used is referred to as **positron emission tomography (PET)**. A PET scan produces a three-dimensional image of the functioning of the brain. A type of radioactive glucose is injected into the body and, as it decays, it releases a *positron* (a particle with

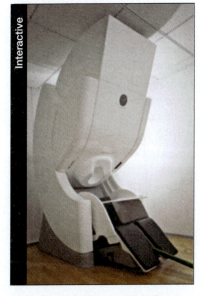

Magnetoencephalography (MEG) captures brain activity by measuring faint magnetic fields generated from the activity of the brain.

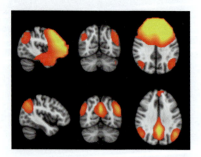

MEG output can be visually displayed in a number of ways. This scan shows localized activity in different brain areas.

the same mass as an electron, but with an opposite charge), which is picked up by the scanner. Areas with high glucose radioactivity are assumed to be associated with high brain activity. A computer interprets this data and organizes the output as a color-coded image of the brain, where brighter colors indicate more activity. Some of the original findings that psychopaths, or individuals with antisocial personality disorder, exhibited reduced brain activity in the fronto-temporal regions of the brain were credited to PET scans (Raine, 2001). Additionally, PET scans are useful because certain radioactive compounds can be used that bind to specific neurotransmitters, which can provide important information about the role of neurotransmitters in thinking, feeling, and certain behaviors. However, the equipment is very expensive, and the resolution of the images themselves are not as good as some of the other methods of assessing brain function (Bunge & Kahn, 2009).

PET Scanner / PET Scan output

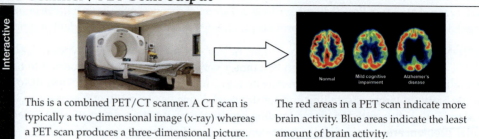

This is a combined PET/CT scanner. A CT scan is typically a two-dimensional image (x-ray) whereas a PET scan produces a three-dimensional picture.

The red areas in a PET scan indicate more brain activity. Blue areas indicate the least amount of brain activity.

Functional magnetic resonance imaging (fMRI) is a procedure that uses MRI technology to get a picture of the brain in addition to measurement of brain activity. The fMRI measures changes in blood flow, which is related to energy use by brain cells. The fMRI can produce *activation maps* that highlight which areas of the brain are most active during specific mental tasks. In essence, the fMRI blends techniques focused on structure *and* function. Like traditional MRI, fMRI doesn't use radiation and is seen as safe for patients. These benefits, in addition to the decreasing costs of scans and improved resolution, have currently made fMRI the most widely used brain imaging technique (Bunge & Kahn, 2009).

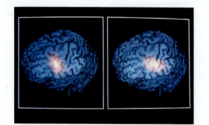

These pictures from MEG show the brain just before a patient starts moving their right index finger (left) and then just after the finger starts moving (right).

functional magnetic resonance imaging (fMRI)

a procedure that uses MRI technology to capture a picture of the brain in addition to measurement of brain activity

fMRI Scanner / fMRI Brain Scan

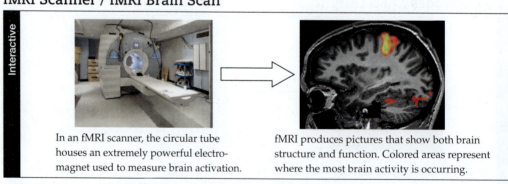

In an fMRI scanner, the circular tube houses an extremely powerful electromagnet used to measure brain activation.

fMRI produces pictures that show both brain structure and function. Colored areas represent where the most brain activity is occurring.

Assessing Structure and Function of the Brain

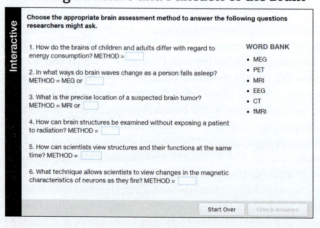

Choose the appropriate brain assessment method to answer the following questions researchers might ask.

1. How do the brains of children and adults differ with regard to energy consumption? METHOD = [ ]

2. In what ways do brain waves change as a person falls asleep? METHOD = MEG or [ ]

3. What is the precise location of a suspected brain tumor? METHOD = MRI or [ ]

4. How can brain structures be examined without exposing a patient to radiation? METHOD = [ ]

5. How can scientists view structures and their functions at the same time? METHOD = [ ]

6. What technique allows scientists to view changes in the magnetic characteristics of neurons as they fire? METHOD = [ ]

WORD BANK
- MEG
- PET
- MRI
- EEG
- CT
- fMRI

Start Over   Check Answers

The Anatomy of the Brain

LO 2.8 **Distinguish important anatomical areas of the brain and their functions.**

In 1909, German neurologist Korbinian Brodmann identified 52 distinct areas of the human and primate brain. This roadmap of the brain has been discussed for more than a century and has been the most widely used system of organization of the brain. However, in 2016, a team of neuroscientists published a paper that will likely change everything. Glasser and colleagues (2016) claimed to have identified a total of 180 distinct areas of the brain (which includes Brodmann's and other areas previously reported). By using advanced brain imaging technology and a sophisticated computerized classification system, the team was able to distinguish the 180 areas of the brain based on a number of different structural and functional features.

As we begin our tour of the anatomy of the brain, let's start with a short video overview. As you watch this video, don't be overwhelmed by the number of names and different structures; instead, just watch it as a preview of information to come. After all of the structures are introduced in the text, you can go back and watch the video again as a way to review. There is good evidence from the science of learning that people have the best chance of learning new information if it is presented at least three times (Nuthall, 2007). So, when it comes to learning about the brain in this module, you will likely improve your understanding and retention after watching the video, *Anatomy of the Brain,* reading the content that follows, and actively engaging in the interactive activities.

Anatomy of the Brain

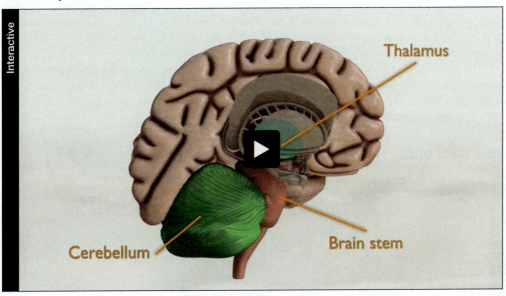

THE HINDBRAIN   There are three major developmental divisions of the brain: the hindbrain, the midbrain, and the forebrain. We will begin at the bottom of the brain (the part closest to your neck) and work our way up toward the most forward part of the skull. The **hindbrain**, which is the evolutionarily oldest part of the brain, is located at the top of the spinal cord. As it is the part of the brain shared with ancestors and animals from long ago, it makes sense that the hindbrain controls the majority of the basic functions required for survival. Furthermore, it was recently discovered that hindbrain neurons also control the body's autonomic, endocrine, and behavioral responses that regulate energy balance (Grill & Hayes, 2012). The hindbrain consists of the following important structures: the medulla, pons, and cerebellum.

The **medulla** is the place where the spinal cord and brain meet. Anatomically, it is represented by a "swelling" at the top of the spinal column. The medulla controls a number of important autonomic (involuntary) life-sustaining responses such as breathing and heartbeat and reflexes such as vomiting, coughing, and swallowing.

The **pons** is represented by a larger "swelling" above the medulla. The word pons means "bridge," so if you pair this term with an image of a "PONd" with a bridge connecting one side to the other, it should help you remember that the pons acts as a bridge connecting the lower

hindbrain

the evolutionarily oldest part of the brain located at the top of the spinal cord; responsible for the majority of the basic functions required for survival

medulla

structure in the hindbrain where the spinal cord and brain meet; responsible for several autonomic life-sustaining responses (i.e. breathing, heartbeat, and reflexes such as vomiting, coughing, and swallowing)

pons

structure in the hindbrain, above the medulla; connects the lower and upper parts of the brain

and upper parts of the brain. It is within this structure that the axons from each half of the brain cross to the opposite side of the spinal cord, which is why the left side of the body is controlled by the right side of the brain and vice versa. The pons also helps relay messages from the upper brain (the cortex) to the cerebellum which, as we will see, is an important area that directs movement. Finally, the pons plays a crucial role in arousal, sleep, and dreaming.

The **cerebellum**, which means "little brain," in many ways resembles a smaller version of the cerebral cortex (e.g., it contains two distinct hemispheres). It is located in the hindbrain, behind the pons and medulla. The cerebellum works to control and process perceptions and motor movements. Many neural pathways link the cerebellum with both the cerebral motor cortex and the spinal cord. The cerebellum smoothly integrates these pathways, receiving feedback about the body's position and using this information to direct our movements. Because the cerebellum *modifies* motor movement rather than producing it, damage to the cerebellum causes movement-related difficulties (e.g., lack of balance and coordination) rather than paralysis. These difficulties tend to be most obvious during rapid, well-timed sequences of movements such as walking and texting at the same time, playing sports, or playing a musical instrument. While alcohol affects numerous areas within the brain, its effects on the cerebellum are often quick to appear and very noticeable. Sobriety tests often involve walking a straight line and touching a finger to your nose with your eyes closed. Since the cerebellum controls balance, coordination, and fine muscle movements, a sobriety test can quickly and reliably assess whether or not cerebellar function appears to be impaired (Rubenzer, 2008).

In addition to alcohol's motor effects, chronic alcoholism has been found to produce *cerebellar degeneration,* including deficits in visuospatial and language skills, new learning and memory, executive functioning, and emotion regulation (Fitzpatrick & Crowe, 2013). These findings, in addition to other research, have highlighted the cerebellum's influential role on many nonmovement related tasks such as attention, executive function, language, working memory, learning, and emotion (Paulin, 1993; Strick et al., 2009). The cerebellum's wide range of functions makes the name "little brain" seem even more appropriate.

The **brainstem** is exactly what it sounds like: the "stem" or core of the brain that extends from the hindbrain through the midbrain to certain structures in the forebrain. Connected to the spinal cord, the brainstem houses the structures that control basic survival functions, including the medulla and pons. The brainstem has two main functions. First, it's a conduit

cerebellum

a structure in the hindbrain located behind the pons and medulla, which works to control and process perceptions and motor movements

brainstem

the "stem" or core of the brain that extends from the spinal cord through the brain and plays an important role in consciousness, pain, and other life-sustaining functions

Structures of the Hindbrain

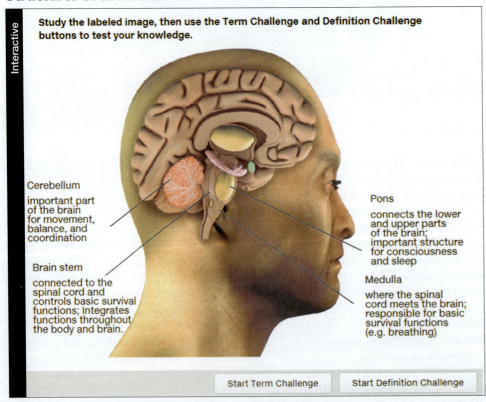

Interactive

Study the labeled image, then use the Term Challenge and Definition Challenge buttons to test your knowledge.

Cerebellum

important part of the brain for movement, balance, and coordination

Brain stem

connected to the spinal cord and controls basic survival functions; Integrates functions throughout the body and brain.

Pons

connects the lower and upper parts of the brain; important structure for consciousness and sleep

Medulla

where the spinal cord meets the brain; responsible for basic survival functions (e.g. breathing)

Start Term Challenge   Start Definition Challenge

for incoming sensory information and outgoing motor commands, much like the spinal cord. Second, it possesses integrative functions critical for cardiovascular system control, respiratory control, pain sensitivity control, alertness, and consciousness. Considering the functions associated with the brainstem, it's easy to understand why damage to the brainstem is often life-threatening.

THE MIDBRAIN The **midbrain**, as its name suggests, is the part of the brain between the hindbrain and the forebrain. In many ways, the midbrain serves as a relay station for visual and auditory information and is the center of the auditory and visual reflexes. That is, information from your eyes and ears is processed by your midbrain, which then either initiates movements (often in the form of reflexes) or sends the information for further processing (in the forebrain). The midbrain houses the majority of the **reticular formation**, or what is sometimes called the *reticular activating system.* The reticular formation includes a collection of neurons that play an important role in consciousness and arousal such as selective attention, habituation to repetitive stimuli (e.g., being able to block out the sound of a dishwasher running in the background), and sleep. Because its neurons are connected to diverse areas of the brain, the reticular formation is also involved in motor control and the perception and blockage of pain signals (Manzhulo et al., 2013).

Another important midbrain structure includes the *substantia nigra,* which is Latin for "black substance." This structure got its name because of its dark color, which is a consequence of being composed of numerous dopaminergic neurons (neurons containing dopamine have large amounts of *melanin,* which has a dark pigment). If you recall, dopamine is a neurotransmitter involved in movement and the experience of reward/pleasure. The *substantia nigra* provides both inputs and outputs to other structures, which are involved in both movement and the experience of reward. People with Parkinson's disease experience a progressive death of dopaminergic neurons in the *substantia nigra.* This lack of dopamine ultimately leads to less stimulation of the motor cortex and therefore slower onset of movements. It also explains the feelings of sadness or inability to experience pleasure that often accompanies the motor symptoms of Parkinson's disease (Lemke et al., 2005). Many years have been devoted to attempting to find a cure for Parkinson's disease. While the answer has not been found yet, clinical neuroscience has provided evidence that fetal dopamine midbrain cells can be successfully implanted into patients with Parkinson's disease and remain healthy, despite the progression of the disease, for at least 14 years (Mendez et al., 2008).

THE FOREBRAIN The forebrain is the largest, most forward and evolved part of the brain. It is also the part of the human brain that distinguishes us the most from other mammals. The forebrain structures can be split into two categories: the structures deep within the brain and the structures that form the outermost covering around the forebrain. Since we have been working our way up from the bottom, let's introduce the important structures deep within the forebrain and follow that with a discussion of the cerebral cortex, the area closest to our skull.

The **limbic system**, which has rich reciprocal connections with both the brainstem and the neocortex, is a series of structures responsible for a number of survival-related behaviors. The limbic system is critical for human emotion, motivation, memory, and some forms of emotional and social learning. There is, however, some disagreement with regard to which specific structures are included in the limbic system (Allen, 2009). Given the purpose of the present discussion, description of the limbic system will be limited to structures involved in emotionally driven behavior, including the thalamus, hypothalamus, basal ganglia, amygdala, and hippocampus (see Figure 2.6).

The **thalamus**, located just above the brainstem, has several critically important functions. It acts as a translator, receiving sensory information directly from most of the sense organs and processing that information into a form that the *cerebral cortex,* or the outer part of the brain, can understand. The thalamus then sends that information to various parts of the cerebral cortex. Imagine an old-fashioned telephone operator whose job was to "receive" all of the incoming calls and then "send" the calls to the correct people.

The thalamus is the telephone operator of the brain. All sensory information except olfaction (smell) is routed through the thalamus before being "sent" to another area of the brain for processing. Additionally, the thalamus helps to regulate our states of arousal, sleep and wakefulness, and consciousness.

midbrain

part of the brain between the hindbrain and the forebrain, which serves as a relay station for visual and auditory information and is the center of the auditory and visual reflexes

reticular formation

collection of neurons, primarily in the midbrain, involved in consciousness and arousal; also related to motor control and perception and blockage of pain

limbic system

a set of brain structures responsible for a number of survival-related and emotionally-driven behavior; includes the thalamus, hypothalamus, basal ganglia, amygdala, and hippocampus

thalamus

structure located just above the brainstem that processes incoming sensory information and directs the messages to the appropriate areas of the cerebral cortex

The job of the thalamus has often been equated to an original telephone operator.

Figure 2.6 Limbic System Structures

The limbic system includes a diverse set of brain structures involved in emotion, internal drives, and memory.

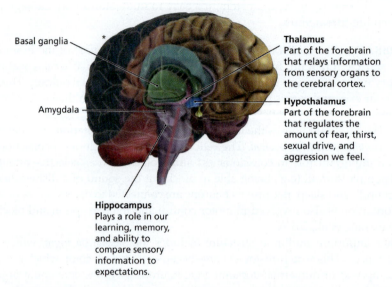

Basal ganglia

Amygdala

Thalamus
Part of the forebrain that relays information from sensory organs to the cerebral cortex.

Hypothalamus
Part of the forebrain that regulates the amount of fear, thirst, sexual drive, and aggression we feel.

Hippocampus
Plays a role in our learning, memory, and ability to compare sensory information to expectations.

*for illustration purposes, the right hemisphere is transparent in this image

hypothalamus

part of the limbic system; a structure that links the nervous system to the endocrine system and plays an important role in the regulation of biological drives

The **hypothalamus** is a relatively small but critically important structure that links the nervous system to the endocrine system. It can be thought of as the body's thermostat in that it regulates body temperature, hunger, thirst, sex drive, fatigue, anger, and circadian cycles. Located underneath the thalamus (*hypo* from the Greek meaning "under"), the hypothalamus is situated directly above the pituitary gland. It is through these connections that the hypothalamus is able to regulate a vast number of body processes.

The hypothalamus was made "famous" in 1954 when James Olds and Peter Milner published a study that identified what has become known as the reward center of the brain. The researchers were attempting to implant an electrode into a rat's reticular formation but missed that area and instead implanted it into the *septal area* of the brain, which is very close to the hypothalamus. They expected the rats to find the stimulation from the electrodes punishing but instead the rats seemed to find it pleasurable (Olds & Milner, 1954). Rather than avoiding that area of their box, the rats stayed there and even pressed the bar themselves to obtain more electrical stimulation—a behavior that has been described as self-stimulation (Hoebel & Teitelbaum, 1962). This early research helped pave the way for a greater understanding of the role of the brain in various addictive behaviors.

basal ganglia

a set of interconnected structures next to the thalamus that are an essential participant in motor control, cognition, different forms of learning (particularly motor learning), and emotional processing

The **basal ganglia** are a set of interconnected structures next to the thalamus. The human basal ganglia are richly connected to the brainstem, thalamus, and cerebral cortex and are an essential participant in motor control, cognition, different forms of learning (particularly motor learning), and emotional processing. Illnesses that affect the basal ganglia, such as Huntington's disease, often cause patients to experience writhing muscle spasms (called *chorea*) in the arms, legs, or face.

amygdala

part of the limbic system; a structure involved in fear detection, aggression, and reward

The **amygdala** (from the Greek word for "almond," which describes its shape) is a distinct group of nuclei involved in fear detection, aggression, and reward (Davis, 1992; Holland & Gallagher, 2004; LeDoux, 2007). This structure is viewed to have evolved to detect danger and promote life-saving responses. One of the most interesting aspects of the amygdala is that it can detect danger, even when we are not consciously aware that danger exists! For example, many researchers have demonstrated that the body produces physical responses consistent with fear when presented with fear-provoking stimuli (e.g., spiders, snakes, fearful faces), even though the stimuli is presented at a level below conscious awareness (Carlson et al., 2009; Öhman, 2005). Imagine you awake in the middle of the night to hear banging against your window. Before you can understand what you are seeing or hearing, the amygdala has received a "rough copy" of this sensory information. If the amygdala appraises the information it receives as threatening, then it will activate the sympathetic nervous system, which will initiate the physiological or *fight or flight* response that prepares your body for action. You may notice that your heart is racing and that you suddenly feel wide awake. Meanwhile, a second, more detailed, message travels from your eyes and ears to the appropriate sensory cortex for more extensive processing and conscious perception. The banging sound you heard is analyzed in detail, using information from many parts of the brain. Once your brain has decided whether the threat is real or imagined, a message to this effect is sent back to the amygdala. If a burglar is entering your bedroom, your amygdala has prepared your body to react. If the sound you heard was a branch tapping against your window, the fear circuit is switched off and you are able to go back to sleep (although it may take you a while because your parasympathetic nervous system works more slowly than your sympathetic nervous system).

The **hippocampus**, which means "seahorse" in Greek, is named for its curved shape when viewed in cross-section. It is essential for creating and consolidating information to make new memories. The hippocampus can be thought of as a top-notch administrative assistant in a very busy office. It is responsible for creating and logically organizing memory "files," knowing where those files are and retrieving them when necessary. Like a good administrative assistant, the hippocampus knows where everything is, meaning that it plays a critical role in a variety of memory processes, including spatial memory (remember the London taxi drivers described earlier). Individuals with hippocampus damage are able to hold new information for a short time but are unable to make enduring memories. For example, people who have used the illicit drug, ecstasy (MDMA), have been found to display significant memory impairments, even after their drug use has stopped (Becker et al., 2012). It is now assumed that the memory impairment stems from damage to the hippocampus due to the drug use. One study utilized MRI scans to determine that men with a history of ecstasy use (who were drug-free for two months at the time of the study) had a hippocampus that was 10.5 percent smaller in volume compared to an age and gender matched control group (den Hollander et al., 2012).

THE CEREBRAL CORTEX The cerebral cortex is, evolutionarily speaking, the newest part of the human brain. Translated from Latin, *cerebral cortex* means "brain bark." This is an appropriate name, as the cortex itself is actually made up of a thin layer of cells called *grey matter,* which covers the cerebrum and cerebellum like bark covers a tree. Like bark too, the cerebral cortex has ridges and grooves. These folds are what give the brain that wrinkled appearance, but they aren't merely aesthetic: The wrinkles increase the cortex's total surface area, which increases its processing power. If you flattened out the entire cortex, it would cover approximately 2.5 square feet and would be much too large to fit in a human skull.

The cerebral cortex is divided into the right and left hemispheres. Each hemisphere is further divided into four lobes that have relatively specialized functions, and our lobes often work together to produce complex thoughts and behaviors (see Figure 2.7). The boundaries of the four lobes are created by particularly deep sulci on the brain surface. Each lobe contains an area of primary cortex (motor or sensory) that serves basic sensory and motor functions. Each lobe also contains an area of association cortex that helps basic sensory and motor information from a specific lobe integrate with information from the rest of the brain. So, the primary visual cortex may perceive a series of dots and lines from a text message, but it is the visual association cortex that interprets those dots and lines as a smiley face.

The **occipital lobes** are located at the rearmost part of the skull, and are the smallest of the four lobes in the human brain (refer to Figure 2.7). The occipital lobe is known for its visual processing abilities. It receives input from the eyes and is able to translate that input into things we see. The occipital lobe's association cortex integrates the color, size, and movement of our visual perceptions so that visual stimuli become recognizable to us.

Optical illusions are often a result of the brain's attempt to organize incoming sensations into meaningful information. As you look at the following picture, your eyes convert the visual stimuli into neural impulses that travel from your eyes to your occipital lobes; first, to the primary visual cortex and then to its association cortex to "make sense" of what you are seeing. As you look at this picture, do you see a man looking straight at you, or do you see his profile? Stare at the picture for a minute or so and see if the face "turns" or "switches" while you are looking at it.

So why does the face appear to change directions? There are visual features in this picture that are typical of a forward view (e.g., the pupil looking straight ahead), but also features that are typical of a profile view (e.g., the blurred part of the end of the nose that forces into more of a point). As you look at this picture, it is as if the association area of your brain is saying "forward view, no profile, no forward view......I'm so confused!"

The **temporal lobes** are located in front of the occipital lobes, above the ears and are primarily involved in auditory processing (refer back to Figure 2.7). The association cortex within the temporal lobe is devoted to the complicated task of understanding language. In 1874, German neurologist Carl Wernicke noticed that patients who incurred damage to a particular area in

hippocampus

part of the limbic system; a structure essential for creating and consolidating information to make new memories

occipital lobes

structures located at the rearmost part of the skull and known for their visual processing abilities

temporal lobes

section of the brain located in front of the occipital lobes and above the ears, involved primarily in auditory processing, including understanding language

Do you see this man looking straight at you or do you see his profile? Can you see both?

Figure 2.7 The Cerebral Cortex and the Lobes of the Brain

Our brain is divided into two hemispheres, with each half containing four lobes, or areas. Each lobe is responsible for different but important parts of functioning.

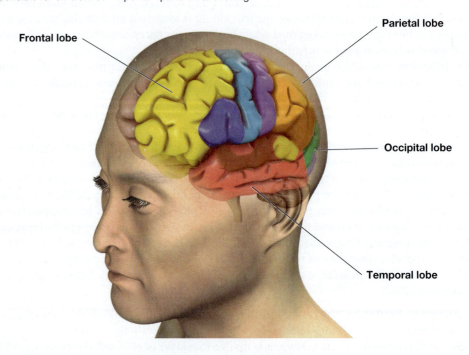

the left hemisphere of the temporal lobe had great difficulty in understanding language. This area of the brain is now referred to as *Wernicke's area* and is associated with receptive language deficits. Patients with brain damage to this area have difficulty understanding what was said to them. They can typically respond with lengthy sentences; however, the sentences themselves often don't make sense.

The **parietal lobes** are located in front of the occipital lobes, just above the temporal lobes (see Figure 2.8). The parietal lobes play an important role in the processing and integrating sensory information related to taste, temperature, and touch, which includes pain. The **somatosensory cortex**, which receives and interprets information about all of our bodily sensations, is located within the parietal lobe. Strange as it may seem, we can think of this area of the cortex as a homunculus, or "little man." The homunculus is a distorted body map, with each part of the body sized according to how much space the brain gives to processing information about that body part (see Figure 2.8).

For example, because so many neurons process information from the hands and lips, the homunculus's hands and lips are remarkably oversized. The primary somatosensory cortex doesn't literally look like a cartoon person, but its regions correspond to the regions of the homunculus: A lot of space in the cortex is devoted to the hands, while the area devoted to the hips doesn't take up much room. If you have ever had acupuncture, then you know this is true. While all of the needles are the same size, there are some places on your body where you can barely feel the insertion of the needle (e.g., your back) while there are other places where you are well aware of the needles because they are much more sensitive (e.g., your fingertips, feet, and lips). The amount or strength of the sensation you feel is directly related to the amount of your somatosensory cortex devoted to that specific body part.

The **frontal lobes** are the part of your brain that lies behind your forehead (refer back to Figure 2.7). Often referred to as the "executive" or "conductor" of the brain, the frontal lobe performs a variety of integration and management functions. At the very back of the frontal lobes lies the **motor cortex**, which is responsible for generating the neural impulses that control the execution of movements. This is an extremely important function, as no movement can "get out" of the human brain without some sort of action from the primary motor cortex. The related association cortex is devoted to helping integrate and orchestrate movement. For example, the frontal lobe must work closely with the parietal lobe to make sure that movements are performed correctly within space and that visual information is

parietal lobes

structures located in front of the occipital lobes, just above the temporal lobes, responsible for processing and integrating sensory information related to taste, temperature, and touch

somatosensory cortex

structure located at the front of the parietal lobe that receives and interprets information about bodily sensations

frontal lobes

part of that brain that lies behind the forehead that performs a variety of integration and management functions

motor cortex

structure at the back of the frontal lobes responsible for generating the neural impulses that control the execution of movements

Figure 2.8 Somatosensory Cortex Homunculus

The somatosensory cortex is part of the parietal lobe and interprets sensory information from the body.

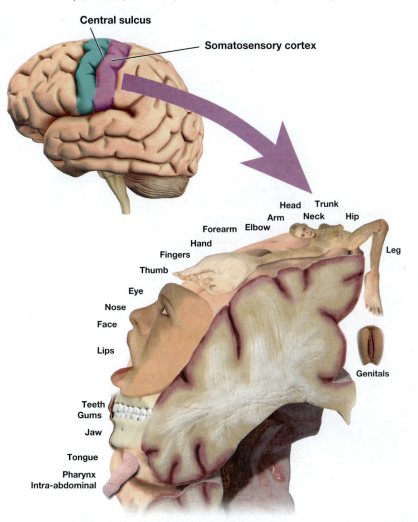

translated into the appropriate movements. The portion of the cortex that controls motor movements is right beside the somatosensory cortex and has a nearly identical homunculus (see Figure 2.9).

This connection between the primary motor cortex and somatosensory cortex makes sense because all movements require immediate sensory feedback in order to confirm their proper execution. One of the most important examples of the interaction between motion and sensory feedback is the process of human speech. A region within the frontal lobe, *Broca's area* (named after surgeon Paul Broca), initiates the movements needed to produce speech, and it is the careful interplay of the motor and sensory cortices that keeps you from mispronouncing words. Individuals who suffer an injury to this area of their brain have a very difficult time speaking or making the words come out correctly. Their comprehension is typically intact, but they have great difficulty expressing themselves.

The foremost portion of the frontal lobe is referred to as the **prefrontal cortex**. This small area of the brain is involved in a vast array of complex processes that are ultimately responsible for the expression of personality and many other thoughts and behaviors. The prefrontal cortex has also been found to play a role in various aspects of memory (Euston et al., 2012). This particular area of the brain is interesting because it sends and receives information from almost all sensory and motor systems and from many of the deeper brain structures discussed earlier (Miller & Cohen, 2001). These abundant connections result in the prefrontal cortex being responsible for what is known as **executive function**. Executive function is a collective term referring to the ability to plan and assess complex tasks, make decisions, engage in socially appropriate behavior, and create and work toward goals.

prefrontal cortex

a small area of the brain located in the foremost portion of the frontal lobe responsible for the complex processes referred to as executive function (e.g., planning, decision making, expression of personality)

executive function

the ability to plan and assess complex tasks, make decisions, engage in socially appropriate behavior, and create and work toward goals; associated with the prefrontal cortex

Figure 2.9 Motor Cortex Homunculus

The motor cortex resides in the frontal lobe and controls all movement.

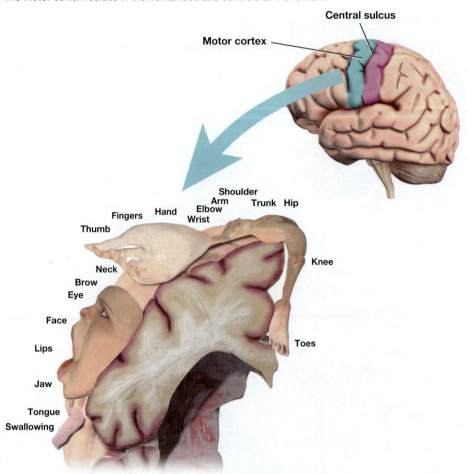

Adaptive Pathway 2.2: Neuroanatomy and Brain Functioning

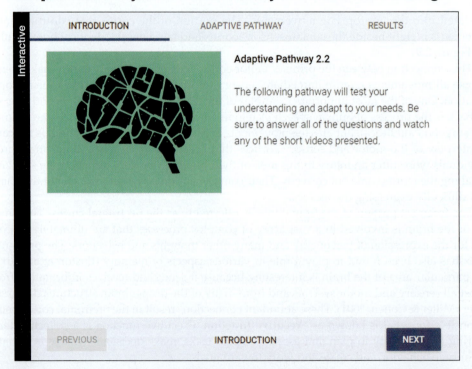

Quiz for Module 2.7–2.8

1. A doctor wants detailed pictures of the structures in a patient's brain but doesn't want to expose the patient to any radiation. What would be the best method of assessment for the doctor to use?
   a. Computed tomography (CT)
   b. Magnetic resonance imaging (MRI)
   c. Positron emission tomography (PET)
   d. Electroencephalogram (EEG)

2. Samson is a client in a sleep lab and is going to have his brain wave activity measured while sleeping. He will have electrodes placed all over his skull so that the test can measure his brain activity. This type of test is called _____.
   a. electroencephalogram (EEG)
   b. magnetic resonance imaging (MRI)
   c. positron emission tomography (PET)
   d. magnetoencephalography (MEG)

3. What part of the brain allows us to detect danger even below the level of conscious awareness?
   a. Amygdala
   b. Hippocampus
   c. Basal ganglia
   d. Reticular formation

4. The cerebral cortex is divided into _____ lobes with the _____ lobe at the back of the head.
   a. three; occipital
   b. four; parietal
   c. three; parietal
   d. four; occipital

5. Sophie has entered her first spelling bee. In addition to studying from a long list of words, she spends time planning how to psyche out her competitors on the big day. Which lobe of her brain would she primarily be using during these activities?
   a. Parietal
   b. Temporal
   c. Academic
   d. Frontal

6. Which structure in the limbic system is responsible for voluntary movement and coordination?
   a. Hippocampus
   b. Thalamus
   c. Hypothalamus
   d. Basal ganglia

Module 2.9–2.10: Concepts in Neuropsychology

As discussed in this chapter so far, the field of *neuroscience* is a multidisciplinary field that combines biology, chemistry, genetics, and psychology (just to name a few). **Neuropsychology** is a specialty within the field of psychology that focuses on how the structure and function of the brain affects psychological processes and behavior (see Figure 2.10). Simply put, neuropsychology studies brain-behavior relationships and the implications of them (Pennington, 2009; Rourke, 2008).

neuropsychology

specialty within the field of psychology that focuses on how the structure and function of the brain impacts psychological processes and behavior

---

Figure 2.10 The Relationship between Brain and Behavior

Our brain plays a role in everything we do when we are awake and even when we sleep. Neuropsychologists are interested in this relationship between the brain and behavior.

The Effects of Brain Damage

LO 2.9   Analyze how damage to the brain affects behavior.

Broadly speaking, **brain damage** refers to the destruction or degeneration of brain cells. Damage to the brain can be either widespread or localized, and the subsequent disability is dependent on the location and extent of the brain damage. Brain damage can result from a wide range of situations, including neurological illnesses and injuries.

In the 19th century, Phineas Gage became a case study for doctors interested in brain damage and the "poster child" for the role of the prefrontal cortex in shaping personality and behavior. Gage, a 25-year-old railroad worker in Vermont, experienced a horrific accident where an iron rod shot through his left cheek and came out the top of his skull. Not only did he lose his left eye, but Gage experienced significant damage to his brain's left frontal lobe (as you can probably imagine).

Despite the damage to Gage's left side of his brain, he was still able to speak and move. In fact, he was able to speak calmly to his doctor immediately after the accident. Shortly after his accident, it was reported that Gage was physically able to do some work and appeared well to others. The greatest change, however, was observed in his personality. After the accident, he was described as "fitful, irreverent, indulging in the grossest profanity, impatient, and obstinate" (Macmillan, 2000; O'Driscoll & Leach, 1998). In many ways, the iron bar had ripped through and destroyed his previous personality.

Physical trauma or a head injury from an outside source, as was the case with Phineas Gage, is now often referred to as a **traumatic brain injury (TBI)**. Violence and accidents are responsible for the majority of TBIs, but TBIs resulting from sports injuries have been receiving more attention in recent years. While most of the literature points to sports that have an increased risk of concussions (i.e., cycling, football), a recent study suggested that "heading" the ball in soccer, as part of regular play, can lead to abnormalities in the white matter of the brain and poorer neurocognitive performance, particularity in the area of memory (Lipton et al., 2013). These findings were unique in that they were independent of the brain damage that can result from soccer concussions (Maher et al., 2014).

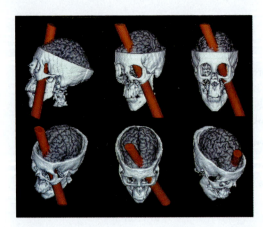

Phineas Gage has become a famous case study about how damage to the frontal lobe of the brain can affect personality.

brain damage

the destruction or degeneration of brain cells

traumatic brain injury (TBI)

physical trauma or a head injury from an outside source

The Effects of Brain Damage

Interactive

In this activity, your job is to use what you have learned so far about the anatomy and functioning of the brain to determine the type and/or extent of brain damage suffered by a patient. Your task is to examine all of the available evidence and come to a reasoned conculsion based on the symptoms reported.

The Divided Brain

LO 2.10 **Recognize the functional impairments that occur in a split brain patient.**

The brain is divided into two hemispheres (or halves) connected by an enormous band of axons called the **corpus callosum**. The corpus callosum acts as a "bridge" that enables the right hemisphere to "talk to" the left hemisphere of the brain. It is necessary for the hemispheres to communicate with each other for our brain to function as an integrated whole.

CONTRALATERAL CONTROL What is interesting about the way the two hemispheres operate, however, is the fact that the brain and body are crisscrossed: For example, the motor cortex in the *right* hemisphere controls the movement of the *left* side of the body, and sensory cortex in our *left* hemisphere is what registers pain if we burn our *right* hand. This crisscrossed connectivity is referred to as **contralateral**, which describes the vast majority of our brain-body connections (taste and smell are not crossed, so your right hemisphere gets smell information from your right nostril and the left side of your tongue sends taste information to the left side of your brain). It is this principle of contralateral control that explains why many people who suffer a stroke experience paralysis on the *opposite* side of the body from where the stroke occurred in their brain.

corpus callosum

band of axons that enables communication between the right and left hemispheres of the brain

contralateral

a neurological principle stating that each side of the brain controls the opposite side of the body

A Demonstration of Contralateral Control

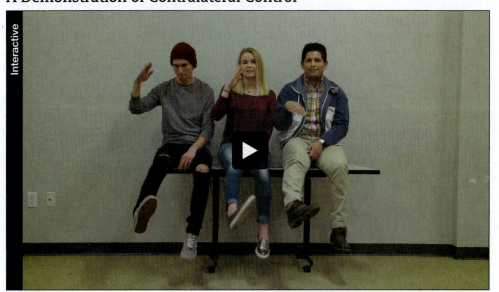

HEMISPHERIC SPECIALIZATION The fact that the two halves of the brain look identical does not mean that they have identical abilities. In some ways, you can think about it like a doubles tennis team, for example, Venus and Serena Williams. Both sisters are excellent tennis players. As a successful team, they capitalize on the fact that each player has slightly different strengths or areas of specialization. Individually, they are very good; together, they are a powerhouse. Your brain is the same way. As we will soon see, you can survive and manage life quite well if the left side and the right side of your brain were disconnected, but you function at a much higher level when both sides are connected and working as one integrated "team."

For the vast majority of right-handed people (approximately 95 percent), language appears to be dominant in the left side of the brain. This well-known statistic is what makes it easy for people to generalize and make a statement such as, "I'm a left-brain person because I'm very verbal and like to talk." Unfortunately, hemispheric specialization is not so simple. If it was, it would be logical to expect that 95 percent of left-handed people should have language dominant in the right side of the brain. In fact, only approximately 27 percent of strongly left-handed individuals are found to have their right hemisphere dominant for language (Knecht et al., 2000). This percentage drops to 15 percent when ambidextrous individuals are examined. Some researchers have suggested that a genetic factor is involved in the inheritance of both handedness and language lateralization (Szaflarski et al., 2002). Research with children has found similar patterns as adults but has also revealed that left-hemispheric specialization for language increases with age regardless of whether the children are right- or left-handed (Szaflarski et al., 2012).

The right hemisphere is often referred to as the "creative" side of the brain. While it is the case that nonverbal abilities (e.g., perceptual tasks, visual-spatial awareness, attention, and audio-spatial perception) are lateralized primarily in the right side of the brain (Dietz et al., 2014; Roser et al., 2011), certain aspects of language, including rhythm, intonation, and accentuation, are also dominant in the right hemisphere (Ross & Monnot, 2008; Wildgruber et al., 2004). Even the recognition of vocal emotion expressions (nonsense syllables spoken with an emotional tone) are encoded in the right frontal and temporal areas of the brain (Kotz et al., 2012). The right hemisphere is also given credit for the majority of the work in recognizing and interpreting both conscious and unconscious emotions in others (Indersmitten & Gur, 2003; Megreya & Havard, 2011; Perry et al., 2001; Sato & Aoki, 2006).

Work in hemispheric specialization or *lateralization* has been of interest to neuroscientists for years. Much of what we know today can be attributed to the work of Roger Sperry, Joseph Bogen, and Michael Gazzaniga, which began in the 1970s. However, even they credit neurosurgeons Van Wagenen and Herren who performed the first known callosotomy (severing of the fibers of the corpus callosum in an effort to control seizures of patients with severe epilepsy) with the beginning of the era of *split-brain research* (Gazzaniga, 2005).

During the 1960s and 1970s, Sperry and Gazzaniga studied patients who had undergone split-brain surgery as a method of treatment for intractable epilepsy. This surgery gave patients great relief from their epilepsy and did not appear to have much of an impact on their day-to-day living. Gazzaniga, however, was able to devise a series of tests that demonstrated two different minds, each with different abilities, in these split-brain patients. When common objects were presented in the right visual field and therefore received by the left hemisphere of split-brain patients (remember the concept of contralateral control), the patients had no trouble telling the experimenter what they saw. This was not the case when objects were presented in the left visual field and received by the right hemisphere. Patients claimed they had not seen anything, or they guessed randomly. It was as if their eyes saw it, but their brain did not. Then, patients were asked to use either their right or left hand to identify the object. The startling result was that when patients were unable to use speech to identify the object they were seeing, they were able to select the same object using their left hand (which is controlled by the right hemisphere, which is where the object was presented). This concept can be confusing, so take a look at this short video, *The Split-Brain Experiment* and see if you can predict how this patient will answer the questions posed to him during the activity.

The Split-Brain Experiment

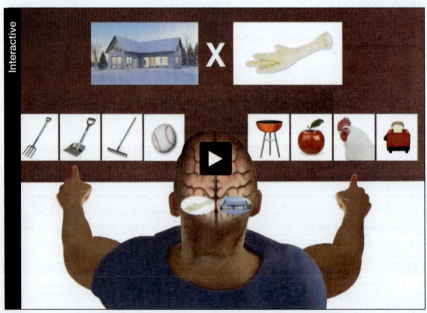

Quiz for Module 2.9–2.10

1. Andre suffered brain damage from an accident at work. Since his accident, he seems to be unaware of his own body parts and at times unable to feel pain. Which lobe of his brain is likely to have incurred damage?

   a. Parietal **b.** Frontal

   c. Temporal **d.** Somatosensory

2. Yuna loves to play soccer and is an aggressive player who will head the ball as often as she can. Her parents have noticed that she has been forgetting to turn in assignments and forgetting when she is supposed to hang out with friends. They are concerned because _____.

   a. she might be doing drugs.

   b. recent research has suggested that teenagers are very forgetful.

   c. recent research has suggested that heading the ball can lead to memory problems.

   d. recent research has suggested that specializing in only one sport can lead to cognitive impairment.

3. What is the name for the band of axons that connects the right hemisphere of the brain to the left hemisphere?

   a. Amygdala

   b. Thalamus

   c. Contralateral

   d. Corpus callosum

4. For most people, language is processed in which hemisphere of the brain?

   a. Left

   b. Right

   c. Split equally between the right and left sides of the brain

   d. Language is handled in the prefrontal cortex.

Module 2.11–2.12: Behavioral Genetics

It would be a mistake to conclude a chapter on neuroscience and the biology of behavior without discussing the role of genetics. The field of **behavioral genetics** recognizes that genes work in conjunction with the environment to build or change the biological structures that then interact with the environment to produce behavior. While we know that genes are necessary, they are not sufficient to fully account for all traits and behaviors of individuals. Genes may influence us,

behavioral genetics

field of study recognizing the interaction of genes and environment and how they influence each other to produce behavior

Genetics play an important role in how we look, think, feel, and behave. However, your genes are only one piece of the puzzle that unlocks who you are. The field of behavioral genetics examines the relationships between genetics, the environment, and behavior.

DNA (deoxyribonucleic acid)

molecules that constitute the building blocks of chromosomes; genes are contained within DNA

genes

sections of DNA that contain specific instructions to make thousands of different proteins in the body

alleles

genes located in the same position on a pair of chromosomes

homozygous

identical pairs of alleles (genes located in the same position on the pair of chromosomes)

heterozygous

nonidentical pairs of alleles (genes located in the same position on the pair of chromosomes)

dominant genes

genes that will always be expressed, even when paired with a recessive gene

recessive

genes that will not present themselves when paired with another gene that is dominant

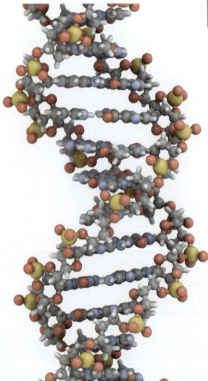

but they are not able to dictate precisely who we become because, ultimately, humans can and do control their own behavior. Hopefully, you can already see that the question of nature versus nurture is the wrong question to ask. The reality is nature and nurture are inextricably woven together and that genes and environment often have a reciprocal relationship.

The Basics of Genetics and Behavior

LO 2.11 **Recall the role of chromosomes, genes, and DNA in determining the expression of traits and behaviors.**

In organisms that reproduce sexually, the egg and sperm cells contain only half the number of chromosomes of all the other cells. During fertilization, the chromosomes of the mother pair up with those of the father to create a full set. As the fertilized egg divides, the DNA is replicated so that all cells contain the complete genetic information of that organism. Think about that—every cell in your entire body contains your complete and unique genetic code. Normal human cells have 23 pairs of chromosomes, 46 in total. Generally, chromosomes are spread throughout the nucleus and cannot be seen, but they become visible just before cell division. Take a closer look at these building blocks of our bodies in the following video *Genes and Chromosomes*.

Genes and Chromosomes

DOMINANT AND RECESSIVE GENES   Have you ever wondered how traits pass from parents to children? Why do some people resemble their blood relatives more than others? In the mid-19th century, an Austrian monk named Gregor Mendel cross-bred strains of round-seeded garden peas with wrinkled-seeded ones. When the offspring had round seeds, he concluded that inherited traits came from two factors and that the round-seeded factor dominated the wrinkled-seeded one. According to the idea of *Mendelian heredity,* a unit of heredity comes in pairs, and one pair can dominate another. Today, we know that these factors are chromosomes. The building blocks of chromosomes are **DNA (deoxyribonucleic acid)**. Molecules of DNA have a double helix form. As you can see from the figure to the left, they look like long, twisted ladders.

Genes are sections of the DNA that contain specific recipes to make thousands of different proteins in the body. Genes located in the same position on the pair of chromosomes are called **alleles**. Identical pairs of alleles are referred to as **homozygous** and nonidentical pairs are **heterozygous**. In heterozygous pairs, how does the body choose which gene to express? Like the round seeds of Mendel's pea plants, some genes are **dominant** and will always present themselves when paired with another gene that is **recessive**. For example, the widow's peak hairline gene dominates other genes to produce a certain observable trait, or *phenotype*.

If an individual's hairline has a widow's peak, he or she has at least one allele for the widow's peak. If paired heterozygously with a gene for a straight hairline, the widow's peak allele will ensure that the individual has a widow's peak. You may have heard

Figure 2.11 Dominant and Recessive Genes

This figure illustrates how dominant and recessive alleles combine to produce eye color. Blue eyes are less common due to relying solely on recessive genes.

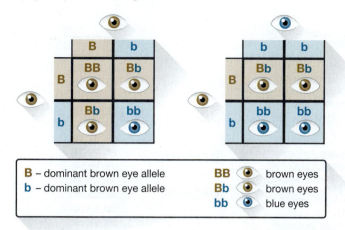

B – dominant brown eye allele	**BB**	brown eyes
b – dominant brown eye allele	**Bb**	brown eyes
	bb	blue eyes

If a person has the dominant "widow's peak" gene, their hairline will have a very distinct look.

"blue eyes come from recessive genes." What this means is individuals carry a number of recessive genes, which aren't expressed because they are recessive. That is, many people with brown eyes carry a recessive blue eye allele (see Figure 2.11). If an offspring inherits two blue eye alleles, then they will grow up with blue eyes (even though both parents may have brown eyes).

THE HUMAN GENOME   Let's briefly review some genetic terminology. Figure 2.12 illustrates the human genome from the largest unit (the cell) to the smallest unit (the gene).

Figure 2.12 The Human Genome

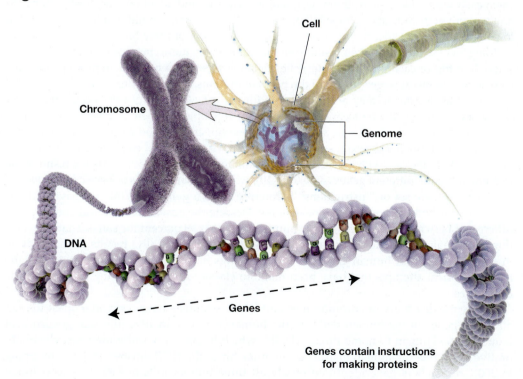

Genes contain instructions for making proteins

Figure 2.13 DNA Molecules

The strands of DNA are held together by nitrogenous base pairs that include: Adenine (A), Guanine (G), Cytosine (C), and Thymine (T).

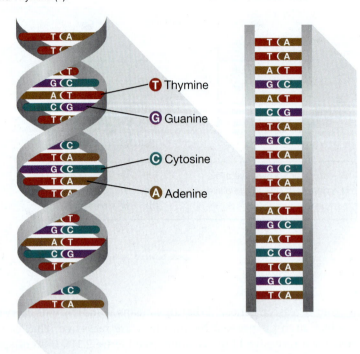

DNA can be thought of as an "instruction manual" for your body's 100 trillion cells. To understand how this instruction manual works, you have to envision unwinding one DNA molecule (see Figure 2.13).

Here you can see the "rungs of the ladder." Each rung is made from a combination of chemical building blocks (i.e., thymine, guanine, cytosine, and adenine). The "instructions" to build a human include about three billion pairs of these chemical building blocks. To put that in perspective, every sperm and every egg contains a copy of three billion pairs of chemical building blocks. Our genes then result from the unique way these chemicals are combined and stacked on top of each other, and our genes tell our cells which proteins to produce to make us who we are. Because genes control the types of proteins in the nervous, sensory, and motor systems of an organism, they are responsible for the development of our specific traits and behaviors. Therefore, it isn't technically correct when people say there is a gene that causes a particular behavior or disease. In actuality, the gene directs the production of particular proteins that then influence the expression of certain behaviors, physical characteristics, or disease processes. As in the case with personality, most human traits and behaviors are the result of the influence of many different genes (see LO 14.10), which is referred to as *polygenic inheritance*.

Our complete set of "instructions" is referred to as a **genome**. While we have trillions of cells in our body, we only have one genome. Despite the observable cultural and physical differences between human beings, our human genome is 99 percent the same! That is, everything that makes humans different (physically and psychologically) results from variation in one percent of our human genome. These findings have fascinating implications for the many historical attempts that have been made to classify groups according to their genetic differences.

Since the discovery of chromosomes and DNA, scientists have been on a quest to map all of the genes in the human body, or the human genome. In 1990, the U.S. government launched the Human Genome Project (HGP), which became a world-wide research collaborative to decode the human instruction manual. Since the HGP finished its basic mapping in 2003, researchers have identified nearly all three billion units of DNA and concluded that the human genome contains 20,500 genes (significantly fewer than expected). Research

genome

complete set of "instructions" or genetic material for an organism

now is focused on identifying specific genes linked to various diseases and conditions (and the reality is most diseases involve a complex interplay of many genes). The goal however, is that one day, when you are sick or diagnosed with an illness, your doctor can use your unique genetic information to prescribe the perfect type and dose of medication that will be the most effective for your condition. For more information on the Human Genome Project, visit http://www.genome.gov/10001772.

Behavioral Genetics and Epigenetics

LO 2.12 **Describe how the field of behavioral genetics contributes to the understanding of human behavior and disease.**

The entire genetic makeup of an organism is referred to as its **genotype**, whereas, the observable properties that come from these genetics are referred to as the **phenotype**. For example, the genotype of a particular flower may be "Rr" but its phenotype is "red." **Heritability** refers to the degree to which genetics (genotype) explains the individual variations in observable traits (phenotypes). In similar environments, heritability is important in influencing individual differences. If environments vary or influence certain traits, heritability would explain individual differences to a lesser degree. A trait like eye color has a high heritability because differing genetics cause variations in eye color without any environmental influence. In contrast, intelligence has a much lower heritability because environmental factors also influence differences in intelligence among individuals. Heritability does not tell us the degree to which a trait is caused by genetics but rather the extent to which, or percentage of, variation among individuals that can be attributed to genetic influence. This concept is also discussed in more detail in the chapter on personality and the heritability of personality traits.

Researchers in behavioral genetics try to determine the relative effects of genes and environment on behavior and mental processes. Do you know any sets of identical twins? If so, are they exactly the same in every way? If genetics were the only important factor in growth and development, then we would expect identical twins to be, well, identical, because they share 100 percent of their genes. However, their environments are different and how their environments interact with their genes affects which characteristics are expressed. That is, even people who have the same genotype can display different phenotypic characteristics or behaviors, depending on the environmental conditions they experience. This situation is most easily observed in identical twins who were separated at birth and raised in independent environments. For example, imagine a situation where identical twin brothers are born and both adopted, at birth, into different families. The brothers may have a particular gene, within their genotype, for being tall, yet they are raised in vastly different environments. One brother is raised with good nutrition and drinking water and grows to be 6' 1" while the other brother does not have access to nutritious food or unlimited, clean water and grows to be only 5' 7." Despite having the same genotype (because they are identical twins), their phenotype (actual height) is different due to the influence of their respective environments. Although real-life cases of identical twins raised separately are limited, behavioral genetics relies on twin studies to compare twins raised together with twins raised separately. When twins raised separately show similar traits, researchers infer that these traits probably have genetic origins. When twins raised together show different traits, researchers infer that environmental factors may have affected these differences.

TWIN AND ADOPTION STUDIES When Elyse Schein went looking for her birth mother, she had no idea that she had a

Heritability estimates account for the role of genetics in explaining individual differences in traits among a group of people.

genotype
the entire genetic makeup of an organism

phenotype
the observable characteristics that come from the genetic makeup of the organism

heritability
the degree to which genetics (genotype) explains the individual variations in observable traits (phenotypes)

Elyse Schein and Paula Bernstein are identical twins, separated at birth, and reunited three decades later.

twin sister. The first time they met, Elyse and her sister Paula Bernstein noticed that they had many similarities. They shared similar speech rhythms, facial expressions, gestures, and medical conditions. Both Elyse and Paula had been the editors of their high school newspapers, and both had taken trips to Italy at the same age. They had both even studied film in New York. Like Elyse and Paula, identical twins raised apart have shown remarkable similarities in many areas such as career choice, food preferences, and gestures (Wolff, 2007). But, identical twins raised apart have more dissimilar personalities than those raised in the same family (Pedersen et al., 1988).

In addition to twin studies, behavioral geneticists also use adoption studies to distinguish the degree of influence of nature and nurture. To calculate how particular traits are inherited, researchers compare the degree to which an individual's traits resemble those of biological parents as opposed to adoptive parents. Interestingly, adoptees have been found to resemble their biological parents more than their adoptive ones in certain personality traits, behaviors, and disorders of alcohol and substance abuse (Kendler et al., 2015; Verhulst et al., 2015). Watch the following video, *Genetic Mechanisms and Behavioral Genetics,* to learn more about the different research methods used in behavioral genetics.

Genetic Mechanisms and Behavioral Genetics

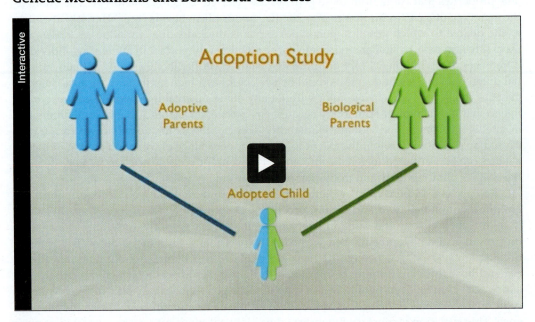

EPIGENETICS   In recent years, researchers have been working to identify the genetic roots of conditions as diverse as schizophrenia and obesity. This has proven to be difficult work because genes are not constant and unchanging; they work with the environment, self-regulate, and react by switching on and off, depending on the individual's environment. Environment includes everything around the organism and its surroundings, including an individual's life in utero. The following video, *Epigenetics,* provides a brief overview to a complicated field of study.

epigenetics

the study of heritable changes in gene function that cannot be explained by any changes in the DNA but likely involve environmental effects

Epigenetics is the study of heritable changes in gene function that cannot be explained by any changes in the DNA (Feil & Fraga, 2012; Mazzio & Soliman, 2012). That is, epigenetics involves changes in the expression of genes that do not result from underlying changes in the DNA sequence. To use the genetic terms introduced earlier: Epigenetics refers to a change in *phenotype* without a change in *genotype*. Most often, it is events and conditions in the individual's environment that exert an epigenetic effect on genes, which create the proteins that affect the individual's traits and behavior. The external environment includes what happens in the individual's outside world—the wealth or poverty of a nation, a loving or unloving family, a calm or stressful life. The chemical environment is made up of what happens inside the organism. An example of epigenetics at work involves the role

Epigenetics

Interactive

of genetics in obesity (Xia & Grant, 2013). Of course, it isn't as simple as you either have a gene for obesity or you don't. Research highlights the interplay between the predisposition for obesity and the environment (e.g., family eating habits, stress eating, food always present in work setting) in which the individual becomes obese (Loos, 2012). For example, there is evidence from research with animals (rats) and humans that becoming overweight alters the body's metabolism, thereby making it more difficult to lose weight and maintain a lower weight status in the future (MacLean et al., 2011; Tremblay & Chaput, 2009). In 2016, this discovery spread from the research labs to the world after the *New York Times* published a story showcasing research conducted with previous contestants from the reality television show "The Biggest Loser." The sobering results of this study highlighted that the vast majority of successful contestants experienced a significantly decreased resting metabolic rate (meaning they naturally burned hundreds of calories *less* per day compared to an average person) and subsequently regained a majority of the weight after the end of the show (Fothergill et al., 2016).

In an effort to understand the interaction between genes and environment in obesity, scientists developed a reversible genetic mouse model of obesity. That is, by selectively blocking the expression of a particular gene, a young mouse quickly became obese. By turning the gene back on, the mouse quickly lost weight and improved its overall health (Bumaschny et al., 2012). However, the effectiveness of reversing the obesity diminished significantly with the age of the mouse. These results suggest that the interaction between genetics and the environment can play an important role in the expression and possible treatment of disease. The findings also point to the importance of early prevention efforts and interventions to capitalize on the potential to reverse the damaging effects of physical and psychological conditions.

Shared Writing: Genetic Testing

Genetic tests can be performed on children and adults to test for a specific genetic condition or to see if the individual is a carrier (has only one copy of a mutated gene) for a genetic disorder. If you could obtain a genetic test that would tell you what (if any) diseases you would develop later in life, would you get the test? Why or why not?

Quiz for Module 2.11–2.12

1. Jaselyn has a pair of heterozygous genes for a "widow's peak" hairline. What kind of hairline will she inherit?

   a. A widow's peak hairline

   b. No widow's peak hairline

   c. One side of her hairline will follow a widow's peak shape and the other won't.

   d. This information doesn't tell us anything about the kind of hairline she will have when she is older.

2. The complete set of instructions for our physical and psychological characteristics is called our _____.

   a. phenotype

   b. recessive genes

   c. genome

   d. DNA

3. A person's genetic makeup is referred to as _____, whereas the observable traits that are expressed from genes is referred to as _____.

   a. DNA; heritability

   b. heritability; genotype

   c. phenotype; genotype

   d. genotype; phenotype

4. Twin sisters Leah and Lily know they have the genetics for heart disease. Both sisters like to exercise, but Lily also has a high-stress job and only sleeps four hours a night. Leah is a yoga instructor and eats a mostly vegetarian diet. The field of epigenetics would suggest

   a. the stress in Lily's life will increase her cortisol levels and therefore decrease her chance of heart disease.

   b. the environment has the ability to change gene expression, so both women can change their risk of developing heart disease.

   c. Leah will not get heart disease because she eats healthy and practices yoga.

   d. the genetic predisposition will outweigh any lifestyle change, so they are both likely to develop heart disease.

5. Grady was adopted shortly after birth into a loving home. Neither of his adopted parents drank alcohol or did any drugs. Throughout his adolescence and into adulthood, Grady struggled with substance abuse. He eventually found out that his biological mother was an alcoholic for her entire life. What does this scenario suggest?

   a. There is likely a strong genetic explanation for Grady's substance abuse.

   b. There is likely a strong environmental explanation for Grady's substance abuse.

   c. Both genetics and environment have equally contributed to Grady's substance abuse.

   d. Adoption is a significant environmental stressor and increases the probability a person will develop a substance use disorder.

Piecing It Together: Deep Brain Stimulation

LO 2.13   Analyze how the cross-cutting themes of psychology apply to the use of deep brain stimulation in the treatment of medical and psychological disorders.

Now that you've reached the end of this chapter, we hope you've developed some appreciation of the amazing capabilities of the brain. The brain is responsible for all of our thoughts, feelings, and behaviors. When we are physically and psychologically healthy, we may not give much thought to the fact that our brain is working 24/7 in the background of our lives. However, for those people who suffer from various neurological and/or psychological conditions, questions concerning the structure and function of the brain become much more relevant. The foundation of this chapter has been based on the fact that your brain works through a combination of electrical and chemical stimulation. The body's chemicals (i.e., neurotransmitters and hormones) were introduced, and the basics of how medicines interact with these chemicals in the brain were discussed.

When it comes to treating neurological (e.g., Parkinson's disease, epilepsy) or psychological (e.g., depression, obsessive-compulsive disorder) conditions, medications and/or therapy are the first-choice treatments. However, there are always a percentage of patients who do not respond well to medicines or therapies and are left struggling with a reduced quality of life. As technology has advanced and we have learned more about how the brain functions, treatments have emerged that directly identify and target the source of the symptoms in the brain itself.

Deep brain stimulation (DBS) involves the use of a small medical device, called a neurostimulator. Some people have referred to this equipment as a "brain pacemaker." The stimulator, which is surgically placed in the patient's chest, sends electrical signals through electrodes precisely implanted into the patient's brain.

If you are familiar with the history of psychology and psychiatry, you may recognize that the field has a long history of directly targeting the brain through lobotomies, psychosurgery, and even lesioning that was discussed earlier in the chapter. The difference between these methods and DBS is that DBS does not create any permanent changes in the brain. The stimulator interferes with the electrical signals of the brain when it is turned on and doesn't affect the brain at all when it is turned off. DBS was initially used in an attempt to treat chronic pain but quickly became known as a successful treatment option for some people with movement disorders (e.g., Parkinson's disease) and was initially approved by the FDA in 1997 (Sironi, 2011). Let's examine DBS from various psychological aspects, including variations in human functioning, research methods, social and cultural diversity, and ethics.

Variations in Human Functioning

- What conditions is DBS used to treat?

DBS has been used for decades to treat the motor symptoms (e.g., tremors, muscle rigidity) of Parkinson's disease, and there is ample evidence to suggest that when the electrodes are placed correctly in the brain, DBS can effectively reduce the abnormal movements associated with the disease (Alamri et al., 2015; Bang Henriksen et al., 2016; Hickey & Stacy, 2016). While the exact mechanism is still unclear, electrodes placed in a very specific location of the *basal ganglia* of the brain use electricity to disrupt the abnormal communication that occurs between neurons and throughout multiple brain regions (Shen, 2014). See if you can locate the basal ganglia in the brain below.

In deep brain stimulation (DBS), electrodes are implanted into an individual's brain and electrical stimulation is sent from a neurostimulator placed in the person's chest.

deep brain stimulation (DBS)

a treatment for medical and psychological disorders that involves direct electrical stimulation of the brain

Locate the Basal Ganglia

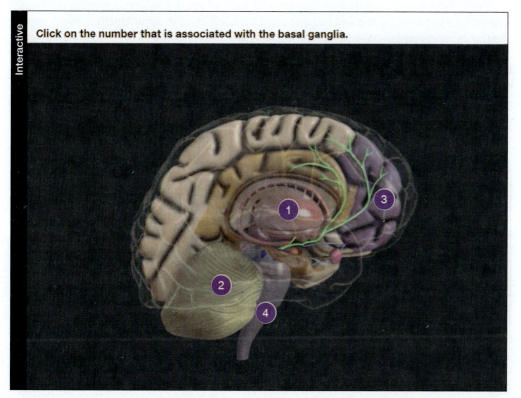

Interactive

Click on the number that is associated with the basal ganglia.

Figure 2.14 Neurological Dysfunction in OCD

Deep brain stimulation has been used to treat individuals with severe obsessive-compulsive disorder, which is thought to involve dysfunction between the nucleus accumbens and the prefrontal cortex.

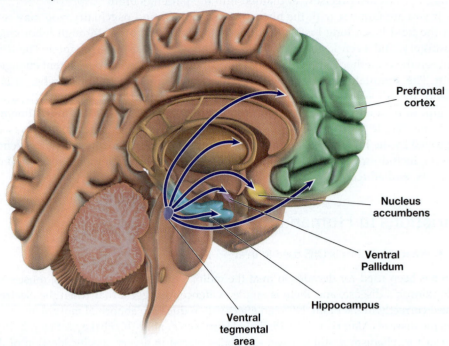

In 2008, the FDA also approved DBS for the treatment of obsessive-compulsive disorder (OCD). At this point, DBS is primarily reserved for the 10 percent of individuals who have severe OCD and have not responded to other treatments such as medication and/or cognitive-behavioral therapy (Denys et al., 2010). The symptoms of OCD are thought to arise from a dysfunction between the *nucleus accumbens* and its connection to the frontal cortex (see Figure 2.14) (Grant et al., 2016).

While DBS is not currently FDA-approved to treat severe depression, a number of research studies have been conducted and suggest that DBS is effective in approximately 60–65 percent of patients considered to have treatment-resistant depression (Fenoy et al., 2016; Kennedy et al., 2011; Mayberg et al., 2016; Moreines et al., 2014; Puigdemont et al., 2015). With the success of DBS in relation to these medical and psychological disorders, there has been some exploration of using DBS in various other conditions such as Alzheimer's disease, substance dependence, anorexia nervosa, Tourette syndrome, posttraumatic stress disorder, bipolar disorder, aggressive behavior, and even obesity (Cleary et al., 2015; Halpern et al., 2008; Holtzheimer et al., 2012; Kuhn et al., 2014).

Journal Prompt: Deep Brain Stimulation as a Treatment Option

In most cases, deep brain stimulation (DBS) is chosen as a "last resort" for patients who have not responded to other, more traditional treatments. However, as you just read, it is currently being tested in in a variety of conditions. If DBS is found to be effective in the majority of people, do you think patients should have the choice to pursue DBS as a first approach to treatment? Why, or why not?

Research Methods

- Does the research conclude that DBS is an effective treatment for the various conditions it is being used to treat?

- What are some of the challenges when conducting neuroscience research with people?

While DBS is currently being evaluated in various conditions, much of the research involves case studies (i.e., one person) or a very small sample size, which naturally limits the generalizability of the results. Since the procedure itself requires brain surgery, it is easy to see why some research studies involve only a small number of participants.

However, not all small sample size research involves case studies. In fact, a number of methodologically impressive research studies have been conducted, which adds to the confidence in the efficacy of this treatment. For example, a research team in Spain conducted a rigorous study of DBS in patients with treatment-resistant depression (Puigdemont et al., 2015). See if you can recall some of the important components of experimental research and design.

Research Design in Practice

Interactive

In the study conducted by Puigdemont and colleagues, five patients with severe, treatment-resistant depression received deep brain stimulation (DBS) and subsequently experienced a full remission. After three months of having no significant symptoms of depression, patients were randomly assigned to one of two conditions: (1) ON-OFF = three months of active electrode stimulation (DBS) or (2) OFF-ON = three months of sham stimulation, which means there is no active stimulation, but the patient doesn't know the DBS is off. After three months, each group switched to the other condition and their depression symptoms continued to be monitored. Neither the researchers nor the participants knew which group they were in throughout the study.

1. What is the dependent variable? [＿＿＿＿]
2. What is the independent variable? [＿＿＿＿]
3. This study is considered [＿＿＿＿], since the researchers and participants were unaware of whether or not they were receiving an active treatment.
4. In this study, the sham deep brain stimulation is considered a [＿＿＿＿].
5. Since participants experienced both conditions (ON and OFF), each patient served as their own [＿＿＿＿].

WORD BANK
- control group
- active or sham DBS
- placebo
- double-blind
- severity of depression symptoms

Start Over   Check Answers

The results of the study showed that four out of five patients maintained their low levels of depression (after receiving DBS for three months) when they were in the ON condition, but three out of five patients experienced a worsening of depression symptoms during the three months in the OFF condition.

Explore the Results

In this figure, each person is represented by a different color. The figure shows the severity of their symptoms before and after DBS. Each participant spent three months with DBS turned on and three months with DBS turned off. The participants were blind to whether they were in the "on" or "off" condition, which allowed researchers to compare the severity of the symptoms with and without the treatment.

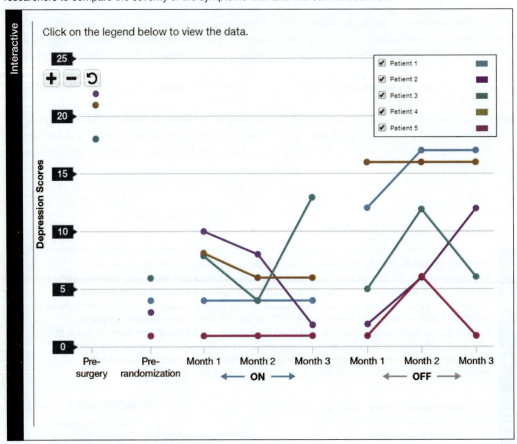

Cultural and Social Diversity

- What are some of the sociocultural factors that influence the access, selection, and success rates of DBS?

The conditions for which DBS is currently being used (i.e., Parkinson's disease, OCD, depression) affect both genders and all races. Yet, with respect to Parkinson's disease, research has highlighted gender and racial discrepancies, particularly involving access to care.

Gender differences in the prevalence of Parkinson's disease do exist, with men being 1.5–2 times more likely to develop the condition and have the symptoms emerge earlier in life compared to women (Chandran et al., 2014). However, even when controlling for these factors, research studies have provided evidence that women are less likely than men to receive DBS as a treatment option for Parkinson's disease (Chan et al., 2014; Willis et al., 2014). Given this data, it might be easy to conclude that a general bias exists against women receiving DBS as a treatment option. However, other possibilities may account for the difference. Hamberg and Hariz (2014) conducted an interview study with patients who eventually received DBS. The majority of patients were almost equally split between the "taking their own initiative" in seeking out DBS as a treatment option and the "agreeing when offered" by a doctor option. A smaller "hesitating and waiting" group included proportionally more women than men, suggesting that part of the reason why fewer women receive DBS is because they are choosing to wait longer before making a decision. It was also found that more than half of the men in the sample held a leadership position at work, compared to none of the women. Therefore, it is likely that life circumstances (e.g., the ability to be able to function at work) increase the immediacy of the treatment options for those men diagnosed with Parkinson's disease.

With respect to race, in a nationwide study of 657,000 individuals diagnosed with Parkinson's disease and receiving Medicare, Black and Asian patients were significantly less likely to receive

RACIAL DISPARITIES IN HEALTH CARE

There is unequal access to healthcare in the United States, with minorities reporting the most barriers to receiving quality care.

Blacks are at a 40% greater risk than Whites of having high blood pressure leading to heart disease.

Over **95%**

of American Indians have untreated asthma.

Non-White Hispanics are more than twice as likely to develop diabetes compared to Whites.

Minority groups often lack access to clinics and specialists because of income and housing areas.

Hispanics are 3 times less likely to have a regular health care provider than Whites.

DBS compared to White patients (Willis et al., 2014). In fact, it was found that all people who were treated in minority-serving practices (defined as practices where 67 percent or greater of the patients were minorities) were less likely to receive DBS, regardless of their race. Patients who lived in more affluent neighborhoods were the most likely to receive DBS to manage the symptoms of Parkinson's disease. All of these results suggest that various demographic and racial barriers limit the access to established treatment for a disease that can severely impair quality of life.

Ethics

- What are some of the ethical concerns relevant to the practice and research of DBS?
- Can DBS be used in children?

When interviewed in 2016, Dr. Michael Okun, a neurologist and leading researcher in DBS made the statement, "Your brain controls everything, and we can control your brain. This statement should make you a little bit uncomfortable." Well, does it? Statements such as this point to why we have guiding ethical principles in medicine. However, just because something is possible and seems effective sometimes for some people doesn't necessarily mean it should be regularly practiced. Some researchers suggest because we don't truly understand how DBS works that we shouldn't be quick to use it with other conditions/disorders. However, others would argue, as Dr. Benjamin Greenberg, a psychiatrist at

Brown University, did during a lecture where he stated, "As a clinician, that's not really the important question. The real questions are: Do these treatments help people? Are they safe?"

What about the situation where DBS *could* possibly help someone but that person is unable to give their expressed consent to the procedure? Deep brain stimulation has been used in an exploratory way with severely brain-injured patients who are in a wakeful, but unconscious state, which is often referred to as a persistent vegetative state (Patuzzo & Manganotti, 2014). The idea is that brain stimulation may help maintain activity among neurons in the brain that would otherwise remain disconnected due to the brain injury.

Journal Prompt: Deep Brain Stimulation and Consent

If a person is unable to give consent for an experimental (nonlifesaving) treatment, should the doctors or family members be allowed to consent for that person? Explain your answer.

While the answer is not an easy one, Patuzzo and Manganotti (2014) concluded that it was not necessary to obtain explicit consent from a patient in a persistent vegetative state because DBS could be construed as an *ordinary medical intervention* because it would not interrupt any ongoing treatment or entail significant risks relative to the patient's already bleak situation. They did, however, caution that this implied consent would not carry over to the use of DBS solely for research studies. As with all treatments, particularly invasive procedures that have capabilities to change brain function, ethical guiding principles should always be at the forefront of decisions.

Quiz for Module 2.13

1. The use of a neurostimulator to send electrical signals to electrodes implanted in the brain to help with physical and psychological disorders is called _____.
   a. transcranial magnetic stimulation
   b. electric shock therapy
   c. deep vagus nerve stimulation
   d. deep brain stimulation

2. Deep brain stimulation (DBS) has been used for decades to treat _____ and in 2008 was approved by the FDA to also treat _____.
   a. Alzheimer's disease; obsessive compulsive disorder
   b. Parkinson's disease; obsessive compulsive disorder
   c. addiction; Parkinson's disease
   d. psychosis; addiction

3. In addition to Parkinson's disease, deep brain stimulation (DBS) has also been approved for the treatment of _____.
   a. depression
   b. obsessive compulsive disorder

   c. schizophrenia
   d. substance use disorders

4. Cultural factors have been shown to play a role in determining who receives deep brain stimulation (DBS). Which group is the most likely to receive DBS as treatment for Parkinson's disease?
   a. White females
   b. Hispanic females
   c. Black males
   d. White males

5. Most research studies conducted on the efficacy of deep brain stimulation (DBS) have been conducted with a small number of participants. Researchers follow the participant's symptoms over time and note whether the symptoms are better or worse when using DBS. This type of research design is called a(n) _____.
   a. experiment
   b. correlation
   c. pilot study
   d. case study

Summary: Neuroscience and the Biology of Behavior

Module 2.1–2.4: **The Anatomy and Functioning of Neurons**

Neuroscience is a multidisciplinary field focused on studying the brain and nervous system. **Biological psychology** has a narrower focus involving the study of the biological basis of behavior and

mental processes. Both fields view the **neuron**, a tiny, excitable nerve cell, as the building block of the nervous system. A neuron consists of **dendrites**, which are branch-like extensions that receive incoming messages from previous neurons; a **soma**, or cell body; and an **axon**, which is a long, thin fiber that carries the message to the **terminal button** at the end of the neuron. Axons are covered with a fatty tissue, called the **myelin sheath**, which protects the axon and speeds up conduction.

The communication between neurons is both electrical and chemical. Neurons maintain a **resting potential**, which means the inside of the cell is more negatively charged than the outside of the cell. This difference in charge prepares the neuron for an **action potential**, which is a brief electrical charge that travels down the axon of the neuron causing the release of **neurotransmitters**, the chemical messengers of the nervous system. Action potentials operate on the **all-or-none law**, meaning that once the charge inside the cell becomes positive enough, the action potential will occur and neurotransmitters will be released into the **synapse**, the small space between two neurons. Neurotransmitters are contained in the terminal button of the neuron, in fluid-filled sacs call **vesicles.** Neurotransmitters communicate with the next or *postsynaptic neuron,* and then succumb to a process of **reuptake** where the majority of the neurotransmitter is reabsorbed into the previous or *presynaptic neuron.* Neurotransmitters and other chemicals can either be an **agonist**, where they bind to cell receptors and produce a biological response, or they can be an **antagonist** and bind to the receptors and block any possible response. After an action potential has occurred, there is a short period of time, called the **refractory period**, where the neuron is "resting" and not able to fire again.

The brain can adapt and change over time, a concept known as **synaptic plasticity**. There is evidence that the brain can grow new neurons, a concept known as **neurogenesis**, in the hippocampus and olfactory bulb and that healthy living can affect the rate of neurogenesis.

Module 2.5–2.6:   The Nervous System and the Endocrine System

The nervous system is divided into the **central nervous system**, which contains the brain and spinal cord, and the **peripheral nervous system**, which includes all other parts outside of the brain and spinal cord. **Sensory neurons** carry information toward the central nervous system, whereas **motor neurons** carry information away from the central nervous system, toward the muscles and glands. **Interneurons** are in the "middle" and send information between the sensory and motor neurons.

Reflexes, automatic neuromuscular actions in response to a specific stimulus, originate in the spinal cord and do not require the conscious participation of the brain. The automaticity of reflexes explains why some spinal cord injury patients still experience reflexes but have no conscious awareness of them. **Stem cells** are specialized cells that have the ability to evolve into other types of specialized cells in the body and hold promise for helping to repair the damaged spinal cord in some patients. The peripheral nervous system is subdivided into the **somatic nervous system**, which coordinates consciously controlled movements, and the **autonomic nervous system**, which controls the internal organs of the body. The autonomic nervous system is further divided into the **sympathetic nervous system**, known for *fight or flight,* which accelerates all of the internal bodily processes when confronted with danger, and the **parasympathetic nervous system**, known for *rest and digest,* which relaxes and calms the body down after a period of stress.

The **endocrine system** is a secondary and slower communication system that uses **hormones**, or internal chemical substances, to affect bodily changes. The **pituitary gland** is considered the master gland because, through the release of various hormones, it influences all other glands (and hormone release) in the body. The **pineal gland** is located deep in the brain and plays an important role in sleep through its secretion of melatonin. The **thyroid gland** is located in the neck and is intricately involved in the body's metabolism and sensitivity to other hormones. An overactive thyroid produces symptoms of **hyperthyroidism,** and an underactive thyroid often results in **hypothyroidism**. The **pancreas** is located behind the stomach and plays an important role in the regulation of glucose in the bloodstream. The **adrenal glands** are located on each kidney and produce corticosteroids, which are involved in a wide variety of responses, including stress, immune system, inflammation, and carbohydrate metabolism. The **gonads** include the ovaries and testes and secrete hormones related to sexual reproduction.

Module 2.7–2.8:   The Structure and Function of the Brain

A variety of methods are used to study the brain. Structural methods focus on anatomical structures and include **computed tomography (CT)** and **magnetic resonance imaging (MRI)**. Functional methods examine how the brain works and include **electroencephalogram (EEG), magnetoencephalography (MEG), positron emission tomography (PET),** and **functional magnetic resonance imaging (fMRI).**

There are three major divisions of the brain: the **hindbrain**, which is the evolutionarily oldest part of the brain; the **midbrain**, which contains many of the brain's deeper structures; and the **forebrain**, the most forward and evolved part of the human brain. The major structures in the hindbrain include the **medulla**, which controls a number of life-sustaining responses; the **pons**, a "bridge" connecting the lower to upper parts of the brain; and the **cerebellum**, which is involved in the perception of movement, coordination, and balance in addition to a variety of other processes related to language, learning, memory, and emotion. The **brainstem** extends from the top of the spinal cord to various forebrain structures and plays an important role in consciousness, pain, and other life-sustaining functions. The midbrain is considered a relay station for visual and auditory information and includes the **reticular formation**, which is involved in consciousness and arousal. The forebrain includes the **limbic system**, a group of structures critical for human emotion, motivation, memory, and some learning. The **thalamus** translates all incoming senses (except smell) and directs the information to different parts of the brain, much like a telephone operator. The **hypothalamus** is considered the body's thermostat and helps regulate various processes involved in hunger, thirst, temperature, sex, fatigue/sleep, and anger. The **basal ganglia** are a set of structures involved in movement, cognition, emotional processing, and some learning. The **amygdala** is a small but important structure involved in fear detection, aggression, and reward. The **hippocampus** plays an integral role in the creation and consolidation of new memories.

The **occipital lobes** are located at the back of the skull and are involved in processing visual information. The **temporal lobes** are located above the ears and are primarily involved in auditory processing. The **parietal lobes** are above the temporal lobes and contain the **somatosensory cortex**, which receives and interprets information about bodily sensations. The **frontal lobes** lie behind the forehead and contain the **motor cortex**, which is responsible for purposeful movement. The foremost portion of the frontal lobe is referred to as the **prefrontal cortex**, an area responsible for a variety of complex processes, including the expression of personality. Other sophisticated prefrontal cortex tasks include the ability to plan, make decisions, set and work toward goals, and engage in socially appropriate behavior, which is collectively known as **executive function**.

Module 2.9–2.10:   Concepts in Neuropsychology

Neuropsychology is a specialty within the field of psychology that focuses on how the structure and function of the brain impacts psychological processes and behavior. Neuropsychologists often conduct tests to measure **brain damage**, which refers to the destruction or degeneration of brain cells. Physical trauma or a head injury from an outside source is referred to as a **traumatic brain injury** and has become a popular area of study particularly with respect to contact sports.

The two hemispheres of the brain are connected by a large band of fibers called the **corpus callosum**. Information is communicated from one side of the brain to the other via the corpus callosum. Much of the brain and body's connectivity is **contralateral**, meaning brain activity in one side of the brain is expressed on the opposite side of the body.

Module 2.11–2.12:   Behavioral Genetics

Behavioral genetics is a field of study that examines genetic and environmental factors in explaining biological and behavioral changes. **Genes** are located on **DNA**, which is contained in chromosomes, which are contained in human cells. Genes located on the same position on the pair of chromosomes are called **alleles**. Identical pairs of alleles are referred to as **homozygous** and nonidentical pairs are **heterozygous**. **Dominant** genes will always be expressed, whereas **recessive** genes will only be expressed when both genes are recessive. The complete set of instructions for a human being is referred to as a **genome**. The genetic makeup for an individual is referred to as a **genotype**, whereas the observable properties that result from the genotype are referred to as the **phenotype**. **Heritability** refers to the degree to which genetics explains the individual variations in observable traits. **Epigenetics** is a field that studies the interaction of external and internal environments on genetic functioning. The field of behavioral genetics, including epigenetics, may eventually lead to better prevention and treatment of disease.

Chapter 2 Quiz

1. Sayla has had to monitor her blood sugar levels since she was a child to make sure she doesn't get sick. Although she would like to be able to eat sweets, she understands she can't because her _____ does not produce enough _____.

    a. pancreas; insulin

    b. adrenal glands; cortisol

    c. adrenal glands; insulin

    d. pancreas; sugar

2. This type of brain scan provides a functional assessment of the brain.

    a. Positron emission tomography (PET)

    b. Cranial ultrasound

    c. Computed tomography (CT)

    d. Magnetic resonance imaging (MRI)

3. The neuron that secretes neurotransmitters into the synapse is called the _____, and the neuron that receives the signal is called the _____.

    a. preneurotransmitter; postneurotransmitter

    b. postsynaptic neuron; presynaptic neuron

    c. presynaptic neuron; postsynaptic neuron

    d. postneurotransmitter; preneurotransmitter

4. Which structure is considered part of the endocrine system and the nervous system?

    a. Adrenal glands   b. Thalamus

    c. Pituitary gland   d. Hypothalamus

5. An action potential occurs when: the inside of the cell becomes _____ and reaches its threshold, which causes a(n) _____ reaction.

    a. depolarized; electrical   b. depolarized; chemical

    c. hyperpolarized;   d. hyperpolarized;
       electrical   chemical

6. An action potential becomes a(n) _____ event once the _____ is/are released into the synapse.

    a. electrical; enzymes

    b. electrical; neurotransmitter

    c. chemical; neurotransmitter

    d. chemical; enzymes

7. Muhammad Ali had trouble controlling his motor movements in the last decades of his life. He had tremors in his muscles, which made it difficult for him to walk and talk. He was diagnosed with Parkinson's

disease, which means he had low levels of which neurotransmitter?

a. Acetylcholine   b. Dopamine

c. Serotonin   d. Norepinephrine

8. An antagonist can be described as a:

a. chemical that increases the effect of a substance already in the body.

b. neurotransmitter that irritates the nervous system.

c. chemical that increases the likelihood of another action potential to occur.

d. chemical that blocks the effects of a substance or neurotransmitter.

9. A study with London taxi cab drivers found that the hippocampus of their brains had greater volume, which was presumed to mean more neural connections, as a result of learning and driving new routes around the city. This finding demonstrates the concept of _____.

a. neurotransmission

b. synaptic plasticity

c. downregulation

d. synaptic generativity

10. The study of how the external environment can influence and change gene functions is called _____.

a. epigenetics

b. genetic restructuring

c. heritability studies

d. epidemiology

11. Rayna considers herself to be a creative person. She creates sculptures out of recycled materials and loves to paint. She also seems to be skilled at reading people's emotional expressions. Which hemisphere of Rayna's brain would be the most active in these situations?

a. Predominantly the left hemisphere and some of the right hemisphere

b. A combination of both the left and the right hemispheres

c. Left hemisphere

d. Right hemisphere

12. As Makelah does squats and lunges to warm her body up to play basketball, she realizes she is using which part of her peripheral nervous system?

a. Parasympathetic nervous system

b. Somatic nervous system

c. Autonomic nervous system

d. Sympathetic nervous system

13. Brad is a 45-year-old man who was in a car accident and injured his lower spine area. As a result of the damage, he has lost feeling and movement in what parts of his body?

a. Arms and legs

b. Chest and lungs

c. Hips and legs

d. Chest and hips

14. At its resting state, the inside of a neuron is more _____ than the outside.

a. positively charged   b. negatively charged

c. electrically charged   d. chemically charged

15. Behavioral geneticists use twin and adoption studies to examine the role of genetics. In general, adopted individuals have traits that _____.

a. come from a mixture of genes from both biological and adopted parents

b. resemble their biological parents

c. resemble their adoptive parents

d. don't resemble either their biological or adoptive parents

16. Epinephrine and norepinephrine are secreted by the adrenal glands and are both _____ when used in the nervous system and _____ when used in the endocrine system.

a. neurotransmitters; hormones

b. hormones; neurotransmitters

c. stress regulators; calming agents

d. calming agents; stress regulators

17. Sensory neurons carry information _____ the central nervous system, and motor neurons carry information _____ the central nervous system.

a. within; outside   b. outside; within

c. away from; toward   d. toward; away from

18. The structures that extend out from the axon and release chemicals into the space between neurons are called _____.

a. dendrites   b. terminal buttons

c. myelin sheath   d. soma

19. Brett was up to bat and the pitcher threw a wild pitch hitting Brett in the back of the head. Luckily, Brett's batting helmet covered his neck protecting his _____, which controls breathing and heartbeat.

a. midbrain

b. cerebellum

c. pons

d. medulla

20. The only lobe of the brain that touches all other lobes is the _____ lobe.

    a. parietal   **b.** temporal

    c. frontal   **d.** occipital

21. We hear with our ears, but which lobe of our brain is used to understand language?

    a. Temporal lobe   **b.** Parietal lobe

    c. Frontal lobe   **d.** Occipital lobe

22. Which structure of the limbic system is considered the center of our emotions?

    a. Hippocampus   **b.** Amygdala

    c. Hypothalamus   **d.** Thalamus

23. Manny is a 15-year-old boy who has been begging his parents to let him try out for his high school football team. Manny's parents are concerned about the risk of a _____ if he plays football.

    a. broken leg

    b. concussion

    c. coma

    d. decrease in his grades

24. Phineas Gage became a famous case study demonstrating how damage to the _____ can lead to significant personality changes.

    a. prefrontal cortex

    b. parietal lobe

    c. somatosensory cortex

    d. prefrontal lobe

25. Keisha was brought to the ER with a bump on her head. The doctor ordered a test that consists of a series of x-rays from many different perspectives that will display a two-dimensional image of her brain. This test is called _____.

    a. positron emission tomography (PET)

    b. computed tomography (CT)

    c. magnetic resonance imaging (MRI)

    d. magnetoencephalography (MEG)

26. Ava has had her corpus callosum severed and is referred to as a "split brain patient." When her doctor presents an apple in her left visual field she claims she doesn't see anything. Why is this?

    a. The left visual field is processed by both sides of the brain, but because her corpus callosum has been cut, the hemispheres of her brain can't talk to each other.

    b. The severing of the corpus callosum decreases language ability.

    c. The left visual field is processed by the right side of the brain, which is not associated with language.

    d. The left visual field is processed by the left side of the brain, which is not associated with language.

27. Ricky has blue eyes. Both of his parents have brown eyes. How is this possible?

    a. Homozygous alleles were inherited from his grandparents.

    b. His parents both had recessive genes for blue eyes.

    c. His father had a dominant gene for blue eyes, and his mother had a dominant gene for brown eyes.

    d. His parents both had dominant genes for blue eyes.

28. The results of the Human Genome Project concluded that the human genome has approximately _____ genes.

    a. 5,000   **b.** 10,000

    c. 20,000   **d.** 50,000

29. Chen has felt depressed for the last six months and is on an antidepressant. He still struggles with depressed mood and difficulty with his memory. His psychologist suggested getting more _____ because that may increase the volume of the _____ in his brain.

    a. vitamin D; blood

    b. protein; neurotransmitters

    c. rest; hippocampus

    d. exercise; hippocampus

30. The cell body that contains the nucleus, which includes DNA and other structures that support the neuron, is called the _____.

    a. soma   **b.** axon

    c. dendrites   **d.** terminal buttons

Chapter 3
Sensation and Perception

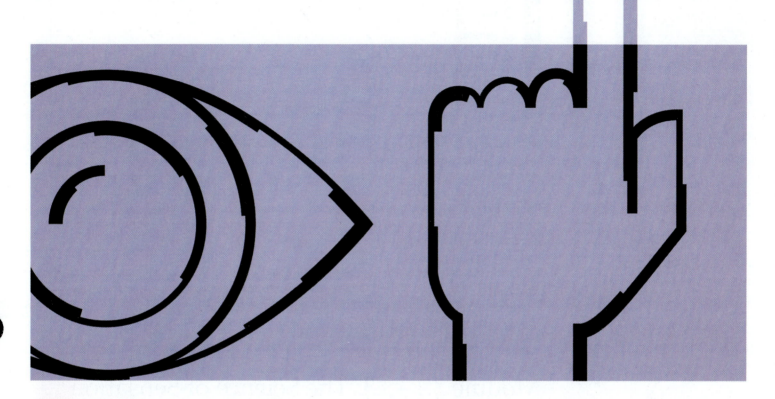

Chapter Outline and Learning Objectives

The Strength of the Senses and Power of Perception

Your Senses

Interactive

Which of your senses do you think you rely on the most?

○ Vision

○ Hearing

○ Smell

○ Touch

Did you know that the sense of smell can save lives? More than 10 years after a bloody civil war, the South African country of Mozambique still faced a serious issue—land mines were still hidden in densely populated areas, posing a grave threat to millions of residents. The solution? Indigenous rats, known for their highly developed sense of smell, were trained to sniff out the land mines. Easy to train and cheap to maintain, the mine-sniffing rats proved successful in protecting the safety of Mozambique's citizens. Smell is just one of the many senses we have that are vital to our survival.

Similarly, our ability to gather sensory information and make a meaningful interpretation, the process of *perception*, has been highlighted in many movies, crime-solving television shows, and real-life mysteries. The fictional private detective Sherlock Holmes has been a model of someone with excellent perceptual skills. In this chapter, we'll explore the relationship between sensation and perception and how together they are responsible for our experience in this world.

Module 3.1–3.3: The Science of Sensation

Sensory systems, or the parts of the nervous system responsible for processing sensory information, allow people and animals to interpret stimuli from the outside world. These systems are essential for survival and reproduction. Imagine if our ancestors were unable to hear the snap of a twig to warn them of approaching danger, smell the smoke from a fire, or see the signs of either predator or prey—the human race would not have lasted long! Sensory systems are need-specific. In other words, each species has a unique sensory system that fits its own behavior patterns and environment. For example, bats hunt in the dark of night, so they cannot rely on their eyesight. Instead their hearing is so finely attuned that they can use *echolocation*, echoes that determine the direction and distance of objects, to track down prey the size of a mosquito.

Defining Sensation

LO 3.1 Distinguish sensation from perception.

Sensation is the process through which we detect physical energy from the environment and code that energy into specific neural signals. Therefore, sensation begins with energy from the environment. That energy is picked up by one (or more) of our senses and sent to our brain for interpretation. The way our

Many animals, including rats, have a highly developed sense of smell and have been used to help people in various ways.

brain selects, organizes, and interprets this sensory information is the process of **perception**. We "perceive" what we "sense." Right now, you are likely experiencing many sensory inputs in the form of energy, such as the light energy from whatever device you are using to read this module, which is allowing you to see various black marks on a screen. Luckily, you don't see random black lines for long. Your brain is converting that light energy into neural signals that are interpreted by your brain. Think of sensing as the "raw data", or for anyone who has ever done any computer programming, sensation is like written code. The code itself doesn't make much sense, but the computer interprets it and turns it into something meaningful. In the case of reading, the light energy is converted into neural impulses that your brain, like the computer, interprets as meaningful words. Not only do you see the individual words, but you quickly string them together and gather the meaning of entire sentences. This interpretation, or making sense of the sensations, is perception. Sensation and perception are important processes on their own, but must work together to enable us to receive and interpret stimuli from the outside world.

Sensation occurs when a **receptor cell** in one of the sense organs is stimulated by energy. *Sensory neurons* carry information from the sensory receptors to the brain as a coded signal. The process through which physical energy such as light or sound is converted into an electrical charge is known as **transduction**. To transduce means to convert from one form of energy to another. The strength of the stimuli, or energy, will affect how rapidly the sensory neurons fire. For example, a bright light may cause a set of sensory neurons to rapidly fire, while a faint glow would set off a slower rate of neuronal firing. Each receptor cell is sensitive to a specific form of energy. Thus, receptor cells in the eye will respond only to light waves, while receptor cells in the ear will respond only to sound waves. Watch the following video *What Is Sensation* for a brief overview of this important aspect of human experience.

Bats, since they are active during the night, do not rely on their eyesight. Their hearing, however, is very sensitive and they use echolocation to move around and catch prey.

sensation

process where physical energy from the environment is converted into neural signals to be interpreted by the brain

perception

process in which the brain selects, organizes, and interprets sensory information

receptor cell

a cell in a sensory organ stimulated by energy, leading to sensation

transduction

the process through which physical energy, such as light or sound, is converted into an electrical (neural) charge

What is Sensation?

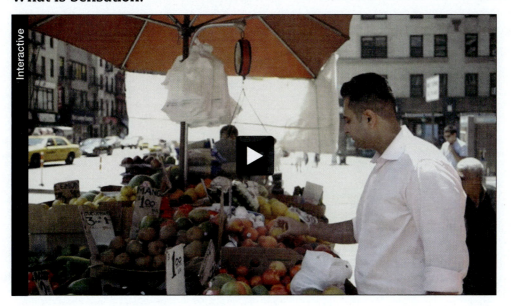

Sensory Thresholds

LO 3.2   Identify sensory threshold theories in applied examples.

We are unable to detect much of the physical energy around us. For example, sound waves that have very low or very high frequencies are out of the human range of hearing. However, every species has a different sensory threshold. That is why blowing a dog whistle has little effect on a human, but produces an instant response from any dog in the area. **Psychophysics** is the study of the relationship between physical characteristics of stimuli and the sensory experiences that accompany them. It helps us know how much sensory stimulation is needed to see a candle in the distance, or to hear a mouse scamper across a kitchen floor.

psychophysics

the study of the relationship between physical characteristics of stimuli and the sensory experiences that accompany them

absolute threshold

the smallest amount of energy needed to detect a stimulus (light, sound, pressure, taste, or odor) at least 50 percent of the time

An **absolute threshold** is the smallest amount of energy needed for a person to detect a stimulus (light, sound, pressure, taste, or odor) 50 percent of the time. Imagine if someone is whispering a word to you from across the room. Let's say they repeat the word 10 times and after each time, you have to tell them if you heard the word or not. If you couldn't correctly identify the word at least 50 percent of the time (i.e., at least five out of the 10 times), then your friend would take one giant step closer to you and start over. The point at which you could correctly hear what was whispered at least 50 percent of the time would become your absolute threshold for sound. Adults generally have a higher absolute threshold than children, particularly with hearing and smell, but all of us are remarkably sensitive to changes in the world around us (Doty & Kamath, 2014). For example, a human being can smell a single drop of perfume in a three-room apartment (Galanter, 1962). However, your authors can testify to the fact that not everyone has the same sensory thresholds. We have travelled together for years and shared many, many hotel rooms. While one of us can hear the ticking of a clock from the room next door (and not be able to get to sleep) the other would never hear any such clock and can sleep in any situation!

difference threshold
just noticeable difference (jnd)

the minimum difference between two stimuli needed to detect the difference at least 50 percent of the time

The **difference threshold**, or what is also known as the **just noticeable difference (jnd)**, is the minimum difference between two stimuli needed to detect a difference at least 50 percent of the time. Again, you don't have to be able to detect the difference between "Thing A" and "Thing B" every time; just at least 50 percent of the time. The interesting part about this threshold is, it is *relative*. That is, the difference threshold increases with the size of one of the stimuli. For example, if you add a spoonful of sugar to a glass of tea, you will probably notice that it tastes sweeter. However, if you add a spoonful of sugar to a gallon of tea, you probably won't be able to tell the difference at all (see Figure 3.1).

Figure 3.1 Difference Thresholds

Difference thresholds are relative to the size of the initial stimulus. Adding one teaspoon of sugar to a glass of tea would likely produce a noticeable difference in taste. However, adding that same teaspoon of sugar to an entire pitcher is much less likely to be noticed.

So, the bigger the container of tea, the more sugar you would have to add to be able to detect a difference. The point at which you could correctly notice the difference in sweetness at least 50 percent of the time would be considered the difference threshold.

Ernst Weber (1795–1878) noticed something else interesting about difference thresholds. He discovered that regardless of size, the two stimuli must differ by a constant proportion for the difference to be noticeable. That is, detectable differences are determined by ratios, not absolute numbers. Another way to look at this is to think of it in terms of percentages. A detectable difference exists when one object is at least x percent brighter, heavier, louder, or smellier than the other. The size of each "object" doesn't matter. What matters is the percentage by which they differ. Consider this demonstration we have often conducted in our own classes. Imagine there are two envelopes: one envelope is empty and the other contains three quarters. We ask for a volunteer wearing tennis shoes to come up to the front of the class. We ask them to take off their shoes (which is risky at times!) and then place one envelope in each shoe. Without watching us do this, our student volunteer then holds each shoe, one in each hand, and tells us if they can detect which shoe is heavier. That is, they have to choose which shoe has the

Your Difference Threshold

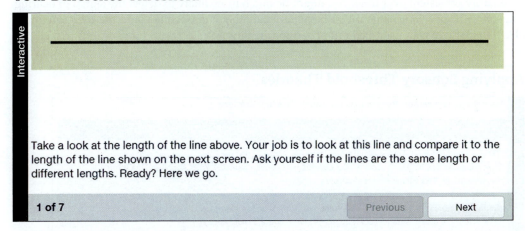

Take a look at the length of the line above. Your job is to look at this line and compare it to the length of the line shown on the next screen. Ask yourself if the lines are the same length or different lengths. Ready? Here we go.

1 of 7   Previous   Next

envelope with the 3 quarters inside. The vast majority of the time the student has no clue. Then, we take the envelopes out of the shoes and place the envelopes into the palms of the student's hands. As you can imagine, they can quickly tell which envelope is heavier. Why? By removing the weight of the shoe itself, we have increased the percentage of difference in weight between the two envelopes, surpassing the threshold of where a difference in weight can be detected.

This discovery has been consistently replicated with various senses (see Table 3.1), and became known as **Weber's Law** (Dawood et al., 2014; Heath et al., 2011; Möhring et al., 2012; Solomon & Hartmann, 2011). To experience Weber's Law for yourself, participate in the *Weber's Law Experiment* in the Appendix in Revel.

We've already established that there is variability in sensory capabilities between people. It turns out, there is also variability within people in that individuals are not always consistently able to detect stimuli. Awareness can depend on whether the individual is feeling tired or alert, whether the stimulus is expected, or if there are potential consequences associated with the detection of the stimulus. If you were told that your failure to detect the sound of a footstep would cause an explosion, you would probably be considerably more alert than usual. Psychologists using **signal detection theory** attempt to understand the differences between people's responses to different stimuli and how they vary depending on the circumstances. Signal detection theorists attempt to understand how decisions are made in the presence of uncertainty (Macmillan, 2002). Let's use a Transportation Security Administration (TSA) agent conducting baggage screens at the airport as an example. When faced with a decision, the agent must be able to separate the signal (e.g., is the item in this bag potentially dangerous?) from the "noise", or all the other internal and external factors that could influence their decision (e.g., all the other items showing up on the x-ray screen). One of the best examples of signal detection involves the cry of a newborn baby. Your authors can both attest to the fact that they could hear their own newborns' cry, within the first few seconds, from incredibly far distances and usually before anyone else. You might be at a place full of kids and commotion, say the circus, but a parent (mother or father) will be able to pick their child's cry out of a large group of children, every time (Gustafsson et al., 2013).

Weber's Law

law in psychophysics; the difference between two objects (i.e., difference threshold) varies proportionally to the initial size of the stimulus

signal detection theory

theory explaining differences in people's responses to stimuli based on varying circumstances

Table 3.1 Examples of Weber's Constants

According to Weber's Law, each of our senses have a different percentage required to detect a change in a stimulus. Notice how much variation there is between the various senses and even specific aspects within each sense (e.g., loudness vs. pitch.)

Sensation	Weber's Constant (Approximate)
Saltiness of food	20%
Pressure on Skin	14.2%
Loudness of sounds	10%
Odor	5%
Heaviness of weights	2%
Brightness of lights	1.6%
Pitch of sounds	0.3%

Signal detection theory makes it clear that our absolute thresholds and responses are not necessarily consistent over time. You might be much more likely to detect the signal of hearing someone whisper your name if you have just had a big cup of coffee (and are therefore more alert), than if you had just rolled out of bed for the day.

Applying Sensory Threshold Theories

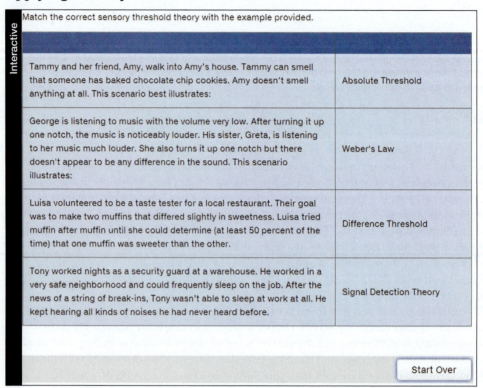

Match the correct sensory threshold theory with the example provided.

Tammy and her friend, Amy, walk into Amy's house. Tammy can smell that someone has baked chocolate chip cookies. Amy doesn't smell anything at all. This scenario best illustrates:	Absolute Threshold
George is listening to music with the volume very low. After turning it up one notch, the music is noticeably louder. His sister, Greta, is listening to her music much louder. She also turns it up one notch but there doesn't appear to be any difference in the sound. This scenario illustrates:	Weber's Law
Luisa volunteered to be a taste tester for a local restaurant. Their goal was to make two muffins that differed slightly in sweetness. Luisa tried muffin after muffin until she could determine (at least 50 percent of the time) that one muffin was sweeter than the other.	Difference Threshold
Tony worked nights as a security guard at a warehouse. He worked in a very safe neighborhood and could frequently sleep on the job. After the news of a string of break-ins, Tony wasn't able to sleep at work at all. He kept hearing all kinds of noises he had never heard before.	Signal Detection Theory

Start Over

Adaptive Pathway 3.1: Psychophysics

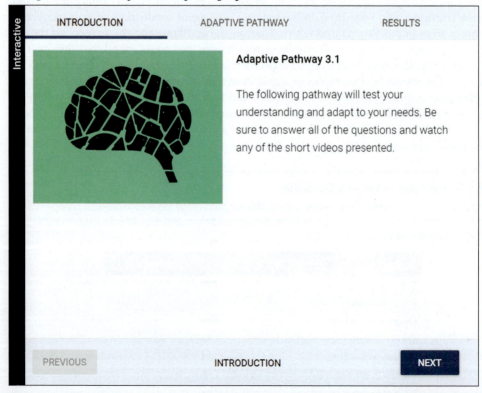

INTRODUCTION   ADAPTIVE PATHWAY   RESULTS

Adaptive Pathway 3.1

The following pathway will test your understanding and adapt to your needs. Be sure to answer all of the questions and watch any of the short videos presented.

PREVIOUS   INTRODUCTION   NEXT

If I Didn't Sense It, Was It Really There?

LO 3.3 **Differentiate subliminal perception from subliminal persuasion.**

It should be clear by now that we don't sense all of the stimuli around us at all times. There may be times where we aren't aware of any stimuli, but our brain is interpreting it anyway. Then, there are other times where our brain fatigues and stops perceiving even though the stimuli remain in the environment. Our body's interplay between sensation and perception has been intriguing psychologists for hundreds of years.

SUBLIMINAL PERCEPTION AND SUBLIMINAL PERSUASION What about the times where we do sense the stimuli, but we are not consciously aware that we have done so? When sensation falls below our absolute threshold, we say the stimulus is *subliminal*, meaning "below the threshold." There is a lot of scientific evidence to suggest that we are capable of **subliminal perception** (Bernat et al., 2001; Smith & McCulloch, 2012; Wiens, 2006). Some of this research is discussed in other chapters in the context of person perception (see LO 13.1) and emotion (particularly fear) detection (see LO 2.8). Advances in technology have afforded researchers the opportunity to determine exactly how long it takes the brain to sense a stimulus, even before that stimulus is perceived. Researchers have determined that the brain can detect images presented for just 250 *micro*seconds; that's 1/4000th of a second (Sperdin et al., 2015)! You, of course, are not consciously aware of what you saw. In fact, if asked, you would say you didn't see anything at all. But, the research tells us that your brain knows.

Because the brain can sense stimuli that are outside conscious awareness the question becomes, can subliminal stimuli influence behavior? **Subliminal persuasion** is generally defined as using subliminal techniques to cause people to engage in behaviors they would not typically do (Smith & McCulloch, 2012). Market researchers, James Vicary and Francis Thayer, are credited with inventing the concept of *subliminal advertising*. In 1957, they claimed to increase movie theater popcorn sales by 57.5 percent and Coca-Cola sales by 18 percent by subliminally flashing the words "EAT POPCORN" and "DRINK COCA-COLA" during the movies. For those in advertising, the results of this study seemed too good to be true, and in fact they were. Vicary later admitted to never having conducted any study at all and had made up the findings in an effort to save his failing marketing business.

Despite Vicary and Thayer's fraudulent study and results, more than half of a century later, researchers are still asking similar questions and conducting studies to determine exactly how much we can be influenced by subliminally-presented stimuli. Here are some key takeaway points regarding the power and effects of subliminal persuasion:

- Subliminally *priming* individuals, meaning presenting them with subliminally relevant information immediately prior to engaging in a behavior or making a choice, *can* lead to predictable behavior change (Karremans et al., 2006; Légal et al., 2012; Shimizu et al., 2013).

- However, the effects are the strongest when the priming includes goal-relevant cognitions. That is, a person's goals and motives need to be consistent with the desired outcome for subliminal persuasion to work. For example, Karremans et al. (2006) made subjects very thirsty prior to participating in a study where they were primed with the words "Lipton Ice." Those participants who were primed with the name of the beverage *and* who were very thirsty to begin with, reported stronger intentions to drink Lipton Ice compared to the other beverage, and compared to those participants who weren't thirsty.

- Despite the ability to influence behavior subliminally, researchers have noted that these effects tend to be very short-lived (Verwijmeren et al., 2011), and are less likely to occur in real-world situations (Smarandescu & Shimp, 2014).

- Finally, research has also demonstrated that it is possible to protect yourself from the effects of subliminal persuasion. Warning people that they were about to be primed with subliminal ads, either before or after the ads, eliminated any behavioral effect of the subliminal stimulus (Verwijmeren et al., 2013).

subliminal perception
when sensation falls below the absolute threshold

subliminal persuasion
using subliminal techniques to influence people's behaviors

Even the cover image of this digital program utilizes the principles of figure-ground to influence your perception. You likely recognize it as a brain, and maybe even the "pathways" through the brain. But, did you notice all the faces? Each dot is an eye and each face is unique.

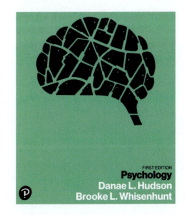

sensory adaptation

occurs when a sense is exposed to an unchanging stimulus and eventually stops registering the existence of that stimulus

SENSORY ADAPTATION   We have been discussing situations where you are not aware that you have sensed something. How about the situation where you are aware initially, but over time, "lose" your awareness? **Sensory adaptation** occurs when your senses are exposed to an unchanging stimulus and eventually stop registering the existence of that stimulus. One of the best examples of this is the smell of your own house or room. You might think, "My house doesn't smell!" But, every home has a distinct smell. You may have experienced this if you borrow a piece of clothing from a friend and recognize that the jacket smells like their house. You live in your house every day, so your olfactory (smell) receptors have adapted to its particular smell. It is as if your receptors are saying, "Hey, we know this smell and have registered it a thousand times, so we don't need to do that again." Now, go away on vacation for a week or two and then walk back into your home. Guess what? You are going to smell what everyone else smells when they walk into your house! Being away from the constant stimuli briefly lifts the sensory adaptation; however, it typically doesn't take long for it to resume (Wark et al., 2007).

In a unique, month-long study, Japanese researchers (Sekiyama et al., 2000) asked four students to wear prism glasses that reversed their left-right vision. While they were initially disoriented, within a few weeks the students were able to carry out tasks requiring complex coordination skills, such as riding a bicycle. At the end of the experiment, the students quickly readapted to normal vision.

Sensory adaptation enables us to focus on changes in our environment. Without it, we would be constantly aware of too many unnecessary things (e.g., the pressure of the ground under our feet), which would distract us from paying attention to changing information in our environments (Lan et al., 2012).

Adaptive Pathway 3.2: Subliminal Perception and Persuasion

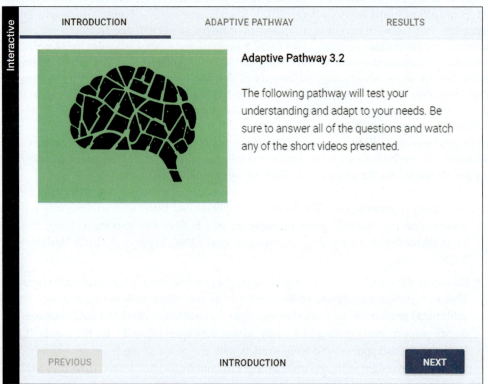

Shared Writing: Subliminal Marketing

Since human behavior can be influenced subliminally, should companies be allowed to use subliminal persuasion in marketing campaigns? Provide reasons for your answer.

Quiz for Module 3.1–3.3

1. The process by which we detect physical energy from our environment and send the information to our brain is called _____.

   a. sensation

   b. perception

   c. transduction

   d. neuron impulses

2. Julius gets up in the middle of the night and turns on the bathroom light to get a drink of water. The process by which his receptor cells take the light from the environment and convert it into electrical signals is referred to as: _____.

   a. photoreduction   b. transduction

   c. sensation   d. perception

3. What is the term for the minimum amount of energy needed for a person to detect a stimulus 50 percent of the time?

   a. Signal detection theory   b. Absolute threshold

   c. Just noticeable difference d. Difference threshold

4. Most parents can pick up their own baby's cry out of a large, noisy group such as a room full of children. This is an example of _____.

   a. absolute threshold

   b. difference threshold

   c. Weber's law

   d. signal detection theory

5. Kenai goes to the grocery store with a list to buy only milk and eggs, but she is also hungry. What Kenai does not know is that the grocery store is flooding the store with a very faint smell of cookies. Kenai doesn't register the smell consciously, but she does end up buying cookies from the bakery section. This is an example of _____.

   a. subliminal persuasion

   b. subliminal perception

   c. signal detection theory

   d. sensory adaptation

6. A person may not detect the smell of their house because their olfactory receptors have adapted to the stimuli. This is called _____.

   a. absolute threshold

   b. just noticeable difference

   c. subliminal perception

   d. sensory adaptation

Module 3.4–3.6: The Visual System

Living Without a Sense

If you were faced with losing one of your senses, and you could choose the sense to lose, which one would it be?

○ Vision

○ Hearing

○ Smell

○ Touch

○ Taste

So, which sense did you choose to lose? The majority of people pick smell. Another way of asking this question is "which of your senses do you value the most?" When faced with this question, many people choose vision. Although we could eventually adapt to navigating in a sightless world, most of us would find this adjustment a challenge. Vision is a key sense—but how does it work?

Visual Stimuli and the Eye

LO 3.4   Describe how light travels through various parts of the eye.

Focus your attention on an object within reach. Now focus on something slightly off in the distance. How is it possible that you can see both objects equally well? How is it that you enter a completely dark room only to be able to see things around you in a matter of minutes? The eyes are a truly remarkable part of the human body. There are so many processes that must occur in just the right way for us to be able to see accurately—and it all starts with light.

IT ALL BEGINS WITH LIGHT   When it comes to understanding how vision works, it is best to start at the very beginning. Vision is based on the availability of light—you probably already intuitively know this if you have ever walked through a haunted house in the dark! In this situation, you desperately want to see and probably squint your eyes in various ways to try to focus any available light. Light is energy that is contained within the electromagnetic spectrum, which is a continuum of waves of electromagnetic radiation. A simple description of the electromagnetic spectrum is that it contains a variety of waves of energy that interact with matter (Allison, 2013). The different energies within the spectrum can be described in terms of **wavelengths**—the distance between the peak of each wave of energy. Wavelengths are measured in nanometers and can range from very short wavelengths called gamma rays to long wavelength radio waves (see Figure 3.2). There is only a very small slice of the entire electromagnetic spectrum that contains visible light. The wavelength of the light that reaches our eyes creates a particular color, or **hue**. Humans can typically see wavelengths ranging from 400-700 nanometers and color is perceived at the different wavelengths within the visible part of the electromagnetic spectrum. Shorter wavelengths are seen as purple/blue, with the longest wavelengths appearing red. The *amplitude* or height of the wavelengths indicates the **brightness** of the color, with greater amplitude leading to increased brightness. The color's purity, which refers to how much white light has been added to the color, gives rise to its **saturation**, or richness of the color. The video *The Visible Spectrum* will provide more information about the components of the electromagnetic spectrum.

wavelengths

the distance between the peak of each wave of energy; measured in nanometers

hue

color, which is derived from the wavelength of light that hits the eye

brightness

a characteristic of color derived from the amplitude, or height, of wavelengths

saturation

refers to the richness of a color

Figure 3.2 The Electromagnetic Spectrum

Visible light is only a small portion of the entire electromagnetic spectrum.

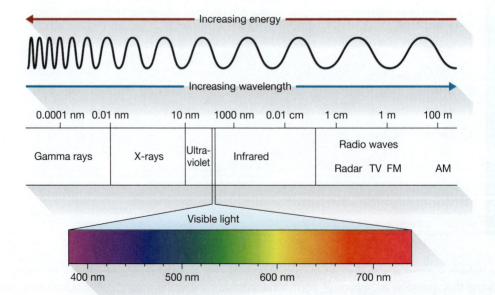

The Visible Spectrum

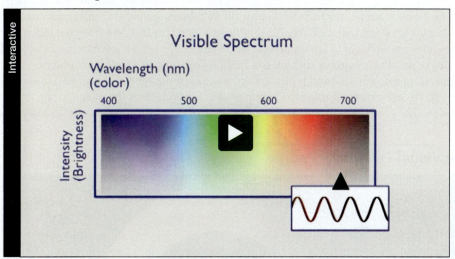

THE EYE: TURNING LIGHT INTO SIGHT   Light first makes contact with the eye through the **cornea**, which is the eye's protective cover (see Figure 3.3). The process of vision begins when the cornea refracts, or bends the light to focus on an object. LASIK is a corrective surgery that uses a laser to reshape the cornea to improve visual acuity. After making contact with the cornea, light enters the eye through the **pupil**, a small hole in the middle of the eye. The pupil is like a door that opens to varying degrees to allow light to enter the eye in order to eventually reach the back of the eye for processing. The pupil is black because its surrounding tissues absorb all of the light energy from the environment (i.e., think of black as the absence of color). The pupil is controlled by the **iris**, a colored muscle that dilates (gets bigger) or constricts (gets smaller) the pupil in response to light. The dilation of pupils is also associated with physiological arousal and is often used as in indictor of an emotional response (Kret et al., 2013). When people refer to the color of their eyes, they are really talking about the color of their irises. Each of our irises is unique, like our fingerprints, and similar to fingerprints, iris scanning is becoming a popular way of the verification of identity. In fact, a number of schools are replacing student ID cards with iris scanners (Segall & Fink, 2011).

cornea

the protective cover over the eye; refracts light to focus on objects

pupil

small hole in the middle of the eye that allows light to enter

iris

a colored muscle that dilates (gets bigger) or constricts (gets smaller) the pupil in response to light

Figure 3.3 Anatomy of the Eye

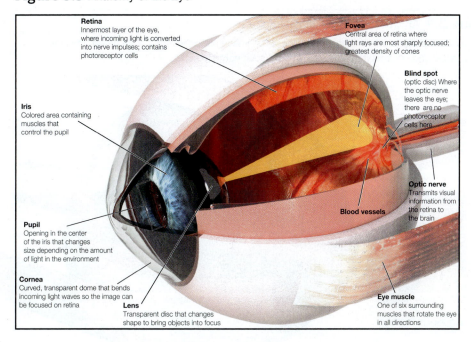

lens

a flexible structure in the eye that changes shape to refract and focus light on the retina

visual accommodation

a process that involves the lens of the eye changing shape to best refract and focus light on the retina

presbyopia

a hardening of the lens of the eye that leads to blurred near vision; typically occurs between the ages of 35 and 60

Behind the pupil lies the **lens**, which is a flexible structure that changes its shape to best refract and focus light on the retina, a process is called **visual accommodation**. Ask an elderly relative to first look at something in the distance and then immediately change their focus to something nearby. He or she will probably have difficulty with this task. As we grow older, the lens hardens and we are unable to accommodate for distance, a process known as presbyopia, which means "old eye." **Presbyopia** is characterized by blurred near vision (e.g., reading on the computer, threading a needle etc.) and typically occurs between the ages of 35 and 60 (He et al., 2014). The lens serves an important role as it is responsible for projecting the image to the retina. The video below, *The Visual Pathway—Part 1*, will demonstrate how this first stage of vision works.

The Visual Pathway – Part 1

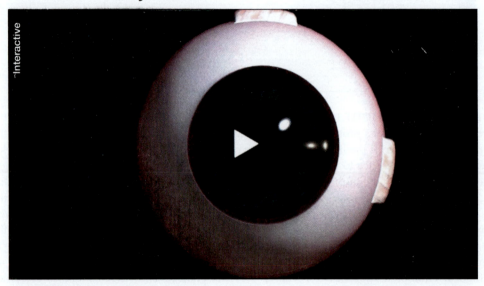

↑Interactive

retina

multilayered tissue at the back of the eye responsible for visual transduction, or the conversion of the light stimuli into neural communication leading to vision

The **retina** is the multilayered tissue at the back of the eye that is responsible for *visual transduction*, or the conversion of the light stimuli into neural communication. Due to the size and structure of the eye's lens, images are projected onto the retina upside-down, which could lead to much confusion (see Figure 3.4). Fortunately, receptor cells in the retina convert light

Figure 3.4 An Upside-Down Retinal Image

The eye's lens projects an inverted and upside-down image on to the retina. Fortunately, the brain compensates and corrects for this so the world is seen right-side up.

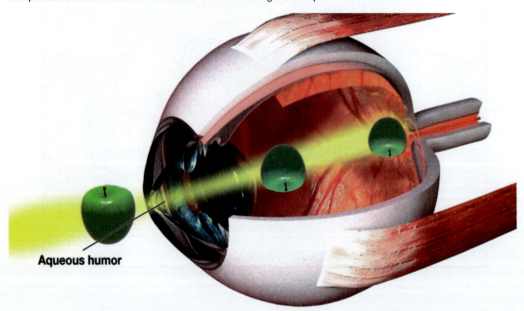

Aqueous humor

energy into neural impulses, which are sent to the brain for processing. Here, they are constructed into an upright image, enabling us to see the world the right way around.

Anatomy of the Eye: Quiz Yourself

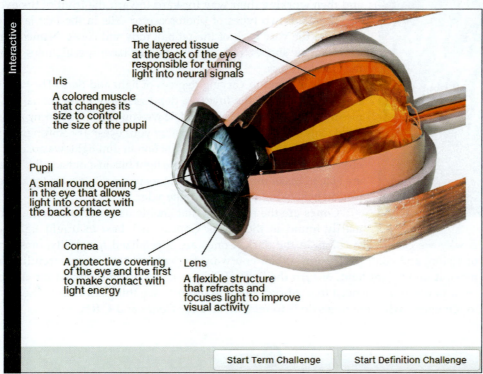

Retina
The layered tissue at the back of the eye responsible for turning light into neural signals

Iris
A colored muscle that changes its size to control the size of the pupil

Pupil
A small round opening in the eye that allows light into contact with the back of the eye

Cornea
A protective covering of the eye and the first to make contact with light energy

Lens
A flexible structure that refracts and focuses light to improve visual activity

Start Term Challenge   Start Definition Challenge

The Functioning of the Eye

LO 3.5   Recall the stages involved in visual processing.

Light must pass through a number of structures before it reaches the retina at the back of the eye. The retina is actually an extension of the brain—during fetal development, it moves from the brain to the eye. The retina has several layers of cells, each of which play an important role as light energy is transduced into neural energy. Once the light energy hits the back of the retina, it begins a process of moving toward the front of the eye by stimulating different layers of cells. Imagine a relay race where there are four people in a line (see Figure 3.5). You are in the front and have to throw the ball to the person farthest

---

Figure 3.5 An Example of the Process of Sight

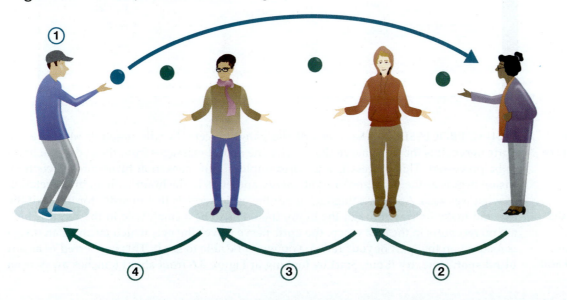

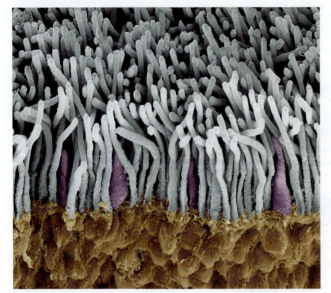

The first layer of cells in the back of the retina includes rods and cones. Cones gathered near the center of the retina help with visual acuity and color vision. Rods are found in the periphery of the retina and work best in dimly-lit conditions.

from you. Then, that person tosses the ball to the person closest to them and so on until the ball comes back to you. Now imagine that you are at the front of the eye, and instead of a ball, these are action potentials (see LO 2.2) starting from the front, to the back of the retina and then working their way forward toward the front of the eye.

There are two types of photoreceptor cells in the first layer of the retina (at the very back of the retina): rods and cones. Named for their characteristic shapes, rods and cones each have specific roles to play in the visual process.

Rods respond to varying degrees of light and dark. They are found everywhere outside the **fovea**—a depressed spot in the retina that occupies the center of your visual field. Have you ever tried staring at a star at night, only to have it disappear before your eyes? Try shifting your gaze to the side. Since rods are able to function in dim light, we are able to see objects in dim light clearer when the light hits just outside the fovea. We are able to make this happen by not focusing directly on the object, but instead by looking slightly off to the side.

Cones are the receptors that enable us to see color. They are primarily found in the fovea. Cones work best in bright light, which is why we cannot see colors in the dark. Cones are specialized for clarity, or sharpness of vision, and color perception. When you want to examine something carefully, do you move it into bright light, or turn the light off? Since cones are specialized for clarity and color perception, we need to use bright light in order to see things in detail. The best way to remember what the cones do is to remember **C** for **C**ones and **C** for:

C olor

C larity

C enter (of the retina)

rods

retinal receptors that respond to varying degrees of light and dark; work best in dimly lit conditions

fovea

a depressed spot in the retina that occupies the center of the visual field

cones

visual receptors specializing in the perception of color; found primarily in the fovea

Three Layers of Cells in the Retina

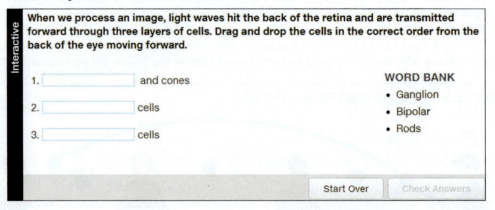

When we process an image, light waves hit the back of the retina and are transmitted forward through three layers of cells. Drag and drop the cells in the correct order from the back of the eye moving forward.

1. [_____] and cones

2. [_____] cells

3. [_____] cells

WORD BANK
- Ganglion
- Bipolar
- Rods

Start Over   Check Answers

optic nerve

nerve that carries the neural messages from the eye to the brain to be processed

blind spot

receptorless area at the back of the eye where the optic nerve exits; images focused on this part of the retina are not seen in the visual field

VISUAL PROCESSING The axons of the ganglion cells bundle together to create the **optic nerve**. It is the optic nerve that carries the neural messages from the eye to the brain to be processed. This process is a good example of how sensation turns into perception. Vision begins as the sensation of light energy and ends in the brain with an interpretation of what was seen. An interesting fact about the optic nerve is that in order for it to exit the eye and make its way through the brain, there has to be a small hole in the retina. There are no receptors in the area where the optic nerve leaves the eye, which means if an image is focused on that part of your retina, you won't be able to see it. This is referred to as our **blind spot**. Here, try it out. Start by looking at Figure 3.6 from about 6 inches away from

Figure 3.6 Find Your Blind Spot

    I   H   G   F   E   D   B   A

your screen. Close your right eye and stare at the letter "A" with your left eye. You should be able to see the thumbs up in your field of vision (if you can't, move closer.) Now, slowly start moving further away from the screen, while continuing to stare at the "A." At about an arm's distance away, you should notice that you can no longer see the thumbs up. Go back a little further and it will reappear! The point where you can no longer see the thumbs up, is your blind spot.

The following video, *The Visual Pathway—Part 2*, will review how the different cells of the retina work together to create neural signals to send to the brain for visual processing.

The Visual Pathway - Part 2

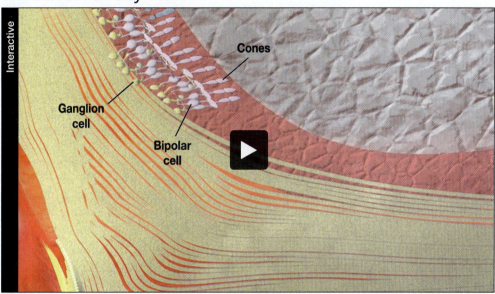

How the information travels from the retina to the brain can be a little confusing. It will help to first understand the concept of the visual field. When you look straight ahead, your entire receptive field can be split into two halves: the right visual field and the left visual field. One eye doesn't just see one visual field, which is a good thing if you ever lost functioning in one eye. As shown in Figure 3.7, *each* eye sees a portion of *each* visual field.

Because of the principle of contralateral control (see LO 2.10), the *right* half of each retina processes information from the *left* visual field and the *left* half of each retina processes information from the *right* visual field. The halves of the retina are referred to by their location, the *temporal retina* is the outside half of each retina (close to your temple) and the *nasal retina* refers to the inside half (close to your nose) of each retina.

Therefore, it is the *right temporal retina* and the *left nasal retina* that process information from the *left visual field*. We are still referring to the *right* half of each eye but introducing the description of temporal and nasal retina helps for understanding how the visual information moves from the retina to the brain. When looking at something straight ahead, we effectively have four parts of the retinas that receive information:

1. Right eye: temporal retina
2. Right eye: nasal retina
3. Left eye: temporal retina
4. Left eye: nasal retina

Figure 3.7 The Visual Fields

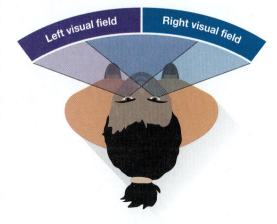

How the Eyes Process Stimuli from the Visual Field

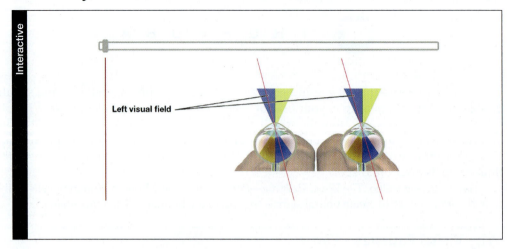

Imagine that each of part of the retina leads to a road (axons) carrying information from point A (eye) to point B (brain). The roads from each eye converge (and become the optic nerve) and exit the eye through a tunnel (the blind spot). Outside the tunnel of each eye, there is a two-lane highway where the roads from each half of the retina continue to travel with information. Shortly after entering the brain there is a junction where the two-lane highways from each eye meet (see Figure 3.8). At this junction, which is referred to as the **optic chiasm**, the roads from the *nasal retina* from each eye cross. In our example, these nasal roads are exiting one highway and merging onto the other highway at the junction. The roads from the *temporal retina* stay on the same highway the entire way through the brain. The crossover of impulses is important because it allows the brain to process two sets of images, which helps us to perceive in three dimensions.

After half of the axons cross over to the other side of the brain at the optic chiasm, the visual information travels to a special area of the thalamus, for further processing. Axons continue to spread out from the thalamus with the majority of them ending in the primary visual

optic chiasm

an area in the brain where a portion of both optic nerves cross over and continue to the visual cortex

Figure 3.8 The Visual System

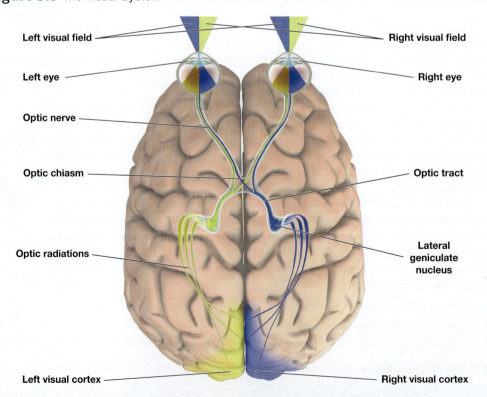

cortex of the occipital lobe of the brain. Neuroscience research has confirmed that there are many areas of the brain that are highly specialized to receive specific, incoming visual information (Goodale, 2013; Milner & Goodale, 1995).

Steps of Visual Processing

Imagine you are walking down the street and see someone waving at you. As you get closer, you recognize this person as a friend you have not seen in years. Arrange the following processes in order from beginning to end to explain the process of you seeing and recognizing your friend.

1	Light enters the eye through the pupil
2	Axons converge and form the optic nerve
3	The primary visual cortex receives visual information
4	Light activates the rods and cones
5	Ganglion cells receive information from nearby cells
6	Bipolar cells receive information from nearby cells
7	Optic nerve leaves the eye and half of the axons cross at the optic chiasm
8	The lens accommodates the image and projects it on to the retina
9	The thalamus receives visual information
10	Various areas of the brain work together to interpret what was seen

Check Answers

FEATURE DETECTION   Nobel Prize winners David Hubel and Torsten Wiesel demonstrated that the primary visual cortex has **feature detector** neurons that respond to specific types of features in the visual field. They found that *simple cells* respond to a single feature, such as a vertical line, while *complex cells* respond to two features of a stimulus, such as a vertical line that moves in a horizontal direction. *Hypercomplex cells* respond to multiple features of a stimulus (e.g., a vertical line moving in a horizontal direction that is a particular length). When many neuron systems work together, we are able to perceive whole objects. Some areas of the brain are very good at perceiving specific types of objects. For example, one area of the visual cortex, just behind the right and left ears, specifically responds to and recognizes faces. This brain area is significantly more active on fMRI scans when pictures of faces are viewed (Nasr & Tootell, 2012). Other specific areas within the temporal lobe have also been found to be important for facial recognition (Busigny et al., 2014; Collins & Olson, 2014; Ku et al., 2011).

feature detector

neurons that respond to specific types of features in the visual field

PARALLEL PROCESSING   Unlike a machine that works using a step-by-step process, our brains are able to do several things at once. In other words, the brain has a talent for **parallel processing**. When we view a painting, different areas of the brain process its color, depth, motion, and form (Livingstone & Hubel, 1988). Amazingly, we are able to reconstruct the image in our minds by pulling all of this information together in a fraction of a second. It's like putting together a jigsaw puzzle at record-breaking speed (see Figure 3.9).

parallel processing

the ability of the brain to simultaneously perceive many aspects of an object at one time

When you stop to think about how many different processes need to be simultaneously occurring in order to function in life, it is amazing that we don't have more malfunctions than we actually do. Damage to various areas of the brain important for vision can cause a variety of symptoms, some of which may seem bizarre. Damage to the primary visual cortex can cause people to experience blindness in part of their field of vision, a concept known as **blindsight**.

blindsight

blindness in part of the visual field due to damage to the primary visual cortex; despite not being able to consciously see, individuals are often still aware of the characteristics of objects in the blind spot

Figure 3.9 Parallel Processing

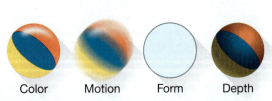

Color   Motion   Form   Depth

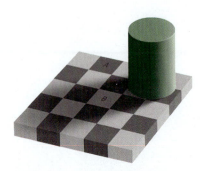

Our perception of color is highly dependent on the environment or context around it. Our brain can intervene and lead to incorrect perceptions as is the case in this example with the chessboard.

It was a picture of a dress that went viral in 2015 and ignited a debate about its color. People tended to see the dress as either blue and black (left picture) or as white and gold (right picture). It was the same dress but the perception of its color was very different. How can the same dress produce such differences in the perception of its color?

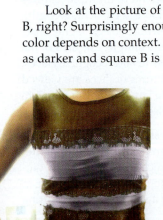

Despite having blind spots in which no stimuli can be consciously seen, patients are still able to maintain a high degree of accuracy when asked to guess about features of stimuli shown in their blind spots (Leopold, 2012). For example, patients may not be able to see an object such as a pencil in their blind field, but when asked about whether the pencil is vertical or horizontal, these patients will nearly always make the correct determination. It appears that there are certain areas of the brain, outside of the primary visual cortex that independently process some visual information, such as movement and emotional expressions, in an unconscious manner (Schmid & Maier, 2015).

Color Vision

LO 3.6 **Distinguish the major theories of color vision.**

Why is the sky blue? In a technical sense, the sky is every color but blue, because it reflects blue wavelengths. Light rays themselves are not colored; we create the experience of color in our brains. It can be a bit mind-blowing to realize that nothing in our world inherently has color. Our brain transduces the *sensations* from light into the *perception* of color. It is truly a phenomenal gift and one that contributes to our appreciation of the beauty around us. There are wide estimates in exactly how many colors the human brain can distinguish, but it is fair to say that it is at least one million (Roth, 2006).

Look at the picture of the green cylinder on a chessboard. Square A is darker than square B, right? Surprisingly enough, squares A and B are actually the same color. Our experience of color depends on context. Square A is surrounded by light squares, which make you *perceive* it as darker and square B is surrounded by dark squares making you *perceive* it as lighter (even though it isn't). Your brain also interprets the darker middle section as a shadow from the cylinder, which then suggests that square B is actually lighter than it appears (again, which isn't true). As the chessboard example shows, our perception of an object's color is not absolute; it depends, in part, on the color of surrounding objects. Every so often, an example of how the perception of color is in the eye of the beholder, makes its way through social media channels. In 2015, the "Blue Dress" picture, which was originally posted by Caitlin McNeil, ignited a controversy about its color.

Millions of people from all over the world engaged in a debate as to whether this dress was blue and black or white and gold. The dress is basically an optical illusion because of the confusing background light around the dress that distorts its color (the dress really is blue and black, by the way). This phenomenon became a mainstream lesson about how color is *perceived* and *influenced* by the environment around it. But, how exactly is color perceived by our brain?

COLOR MIXING   An important point to understand prior to learning about theories of color vision is the difference between the color of *light* versus the color of *objects*. Most of the colors we see in objects result from *reflected* light (this is why we would technically say a banana is everything *but* yellow—the banana has absorbed all colors, or wavelengths, of the spectrum except yellow).

When it comes to mixing colors, it is important, once again, to distinguish whether we are talking about mixing objects (e.g., paint) or light (e.g., spotlights). Mixing paints is referred to as **subtractive color mixture** because as paint is mixed some wavelengths of light are removed (subtracted). The primary colors of subtractive color mixing include cyan, yellow, and magenta. As you can see from Figure 3.10, if you mix all three primary colors, you are removing all possible wavelengths of light and will be left with black. Recall that black is perceived when all of the wavelengths of light are absorbed.

Color mixing with light is different. Light projected onto a white surface reflects any wavelengths presented. The important point to understand about mixing colored lights is that all of the wavelengths that are reflected individually are added together and reflected when combined. This is why mixing light is referred to as **additive color mixture**. The primary colors in additive color mixing are red, green, and blue. As you can see from Figure 3.11, if you mix all three primary colors of light, you end up with white (not black).

The reason you see white light is because white is a reflection of all the wavelengths *added together*, whereas in subtractive color mixing, black is seen because the mixed paints *absorb* all of the wavelengths.

THE TRICHROMATIC THEORY   The **trichromatic** (tri = three; chroma = color) **theory of color vision** states that there are three different receptors, which we now know as cones, that are each sensitive to varying wavelengths of light. According to this theory, light stimulates certain receptors in a particular way and the pattern of activity among the three receptors is what gives rise to our experience of color. This theory was first proposed by Thomas Young in 1802 and later refined and promoted by Hermann von Helmholtz in 1852, which is why it is sometimes referred to as the *Young-Helmholtz theory of color vision*. The trichromatic theory was derived from observations regarding the color mixing of light discussed in the previous section. Helmholtz conducted color-matching experiments where he showed subjects a light of a particular wavelength (i.e., color) and then gave individuals three lights of various wavelengths. The participants were instructed to adjust and combine the three lights to match the original light presented. He discovered that a minimum of three lights were required to match any color that was presented. After this discovery, he deduced that we must have three different types of receptors, each sensitive to a different range of wavelength.

It wasn't until the 1960s that researchers confirmed the existence of three different cones (Brown & Wald, 1964):

1. Short-wavelength cones, which absorb up to 419-nm (Blue cones)
2. Medium-wavelength cones, which absorb up to 531-nm (Green cones)
3. Long-wavelength cones, which absorb up to 558-nm (Red cones)

According to this theory, the perception, or experience, of color comes from a combination of the cones that are stimulated and the relative strength of that stimulation. For example, the perception of yellow results from a large response from both green and red cones and a small response from the blue cones.

The trichromatic theory provides a good rationale to explain "true" color-blindness. Technically, to be truly color blind, a person would have no functioning cones and therefore not be able to perceive any color. This rare condition is referred to as *monochromatism*, and gives new meaning to 50 Shades of Grey. Most people with color-deficiency (which is the more appropriate term) experience *dichromatism* and see some color, usually a range of colors that can be made from two primary colors (or two sets of functioning cones). Dichromatism is an inherited condition that comes from a deficient gene on the X chromosome. Females have an X chromosome from both their mother and father and *each* X chromosome would have to have the defective gene in order for the female to experience color deficiency. Males however, only

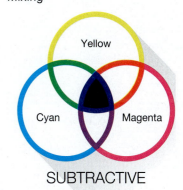

Figure 3.10 Subtractive Color Mixing

subtractive color mixture

when adding additional colors removes (subtracts) wavelengths of light, eventually resulting in black (e.g., mixing paints)

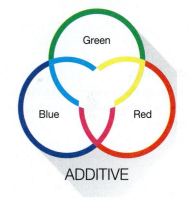

Figure 3.11 Additive Color Mixing

additive color mixture

a process involving the mixing of light, where additional wavelengths are added together and reflected, eventually creating white light

trichromatic theory of color vision

a theory that there are three different types of retinal receptors that are each sensitive to varying wavelengths of light; also called Young-Helmholtz theory of color vision

have one X chromosome, so the mother may be a carrier of the gene, which will cause the son to be color-deficient. This is why this condition has been found to affect 1 out of every 12 males compared to 1 out of every 200 females (Deeb & Motulsky, 2011).

Tests for Color Deficiency

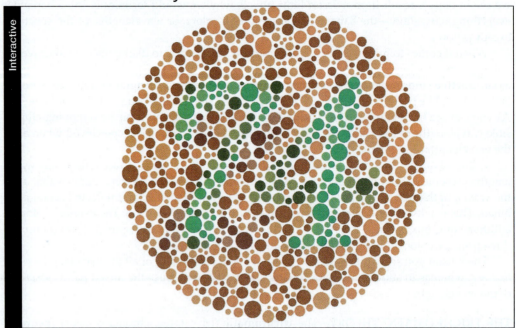

THE OPPONENT PROCESS THEORY The trichromatic theory offers a good explanation of color vision, but Ewald Hering noted in the late 1800s that there were certain color combinations we could never see. For example, what do you think reddish-green looks like? How about blueish-yellow? It seemed that there were "pairs" of colors that worked in "opposition" to each other. Another interesting phenomenon that suggested that there was more than just the trichromatic theory was that of afterimages. An **afterimage** is an image that remains within the visual field once the stimulus has been removed. Try the following activity to experience an afterimage for yourself.

Stare at the white dot in the middle of the flag for 30 seconds. After 30 seconds, shift your gaze to the empty white box.

Experience an Afterimage

What you just experienced is referred to as a **negative afterimage**. It is called "negative" because the colors that are seen after staring at the picture are the *opposite* of what was originally presented. If you stare at green, you will see red once you shift your gaze to a white background. The trichromatic theory could not explain this phenomenon; leading Hering to propose the **opponent-process theory**, which states that there are three special receptors that work in an opposing manner (Hering, 1964; Hurvich & Jameson, 1957).

As depicted in Figure 3.12, the first receptor may have an excitatory response to blue and an inhibitory response to yellow, or vice versa. The second receptor shown might exhibit an excitatory response to green and inhibitory response to red. Finally, the third receptor may have an excitatory response to white light and an inhibitory response to black, or the absence of light (De Valois, 1960). The presence of these "opponent neurons" was confirmed

afterimage

an image that remains in the visual field once the stimulus has been removed

negative afterimage

an afterimage where the colors seen are the opposite of those originally presented

opponent-process theory

theory of color vision stating there are three special visual receptors that work in pairs and in an opposing manner

Figure 3.12 The Opponent-Process Theory of Color Vision

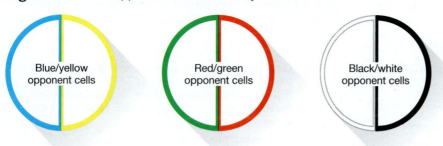

Blue/yellow opponent cells

Red/green opponent cells

Black/white opponent cells

by researchers in the 1950s and 1960s when they were found in the retina and the brain (De Valois et al., 2000).

The presence of opposing neurons adequately explains negative afterimages. Staring at a colorful picture for a minute, with little blinking, can cause certain receptors to fatigue and effectively stop working. Remember that when one color is on, the other is off, and vice versa. Therefore, if you are staring at a yellow wall for 30–60 seconds and then look away to a white wall, you will see which color? If you said "blue," then you're right! By staring at the yellow wall, you have worn out your "yellow on", "blue off" receptor. Now the yellow turns off because it is tired, which then pops the blue on, and is why you would see a blue afterimage. Typically, the receptors in your eye don't tire much because our eyes are constantly making small, jerky movements called **microsaccades**, which allow neurons to "share the load" and have small intervals of time to refocus. Here's one last afterimage to view, which is quite astonishing. This is a negative photo afterimage. Stare at the person's nose for at least 30 seconds. Then, shift your gaze to the white space to the right.

microsaccades

small, jerky movements of the eye, which allow neurons to rest, therefore preventing exhaustion

A Different Type of Afterimage

Interactive

This afterimage is a great example of how the different intensities and brightness of wavelengths can affect the colors we see. It is also a good example of how our brain processes other information such as "Hey, this is a human face, so the hair should look brown" (or another typical hair color).

When faced with two theories that explain a complicated phenomenon in different ways, it is tempting to want know "Which one is right?" For years, researchers argued about this very thing. Most experts would now agree that *both* theories of color vision are correct. That seems difficult to understand given how different the theories are, but it makes more sense if you think about the fact that receptors predicted by both theories have been found in the eye and brain (Hardie & Stavenga, 1989; Neitz & Neitz, 2008; Stoughton & Conway, 2008). It appears that seeing in color involves various stages of processing sensory information. The first stage seems to involve the red, green, and/or blue cones in the retina as described by the trichromatic theory, whereas the neurons further down the line in the brain are more consistent with the opponent process theory.

Quiz for Module 3.4–3.6

1. Which structure of the eye first makes contact with light?

a. Pupil   b. Cornea

c. Iris   d. Retina

2. An 80-year-old man may have trouble with reading on the computer because of which condition?

a. Visual habituation   b. Myopia

c. Presbyopia   d. Visual accommodation

3. When a person drives on a dark road at night, which receptor cells in the retina help detect the low levels of light to navigate the road?

a. Ganglion cells   b. Bipolar cells

c. Cones   d. Rods

4. Maeve spent the day in the Museum of Modern Art enjoying all the paintings and artwork. She was amazed at the fact that her visual system could take in all the motion, color, depth, and form and convert it into an exceptional art appreciation experience in her brain. This is called _____.

a. parallel accommodation   b. visual accommodation

c. sensory processing theory   d. parallel processing

5. Jamal stared at a green screen for a long time and then looked at a white piece of paper. The _____ theory of color vision would predict that Jamal would see the color _____ when he looked at the white paper.

a. opponent process; red

b. trichromatic; red

c. trichromatic; yellow

d. opponent process; yellow

6. Which theory of color vision states that we have three different cone receptors that are sensitive to varying wavelengths of light?

a. Trichromatic theory of color vision

b. Afterimages theory

c. Opponent process theory

d. The color mixing theory

Module 3.7–3.8: The Auditory System

The average person may not be able to use echolocation like dolphins or bats, but the series of events that lead to hearing the sounds of the world around us is nothing short of amazing. With the help of our ears and brains, we gracefully convert sound waves, caused by the vibration of air, into meaningful noises.

Auditory Stimuli and the Ear

LO 3.7   **Label the anatomy of the ear.**

sound wave

a change in air pressure caused by molecules of air or fluid colliding and moving apart

If you traveled into deep space, you wouldn't hear a single sound. Why? A **sound wave** is a change in air pressure caused by molecules of air or fluid colliding and moving apart. In deep space, there are no molecules to collide with each other. Sound cannot exist in a vacuum.

Like light waves, sound waves have wavelength, amplitude, and purity. The **frequency** of the sound waves, which determines the pitch, is measured in cycles per second, or hertz (Hz). The tighter the sine waves are together, the higher the pitch. So, the frequency of a tuba might look like this:

frequency

the rate of a sound wave measured in cycles per second, or hertz (Hz); determines the pitch of a sound

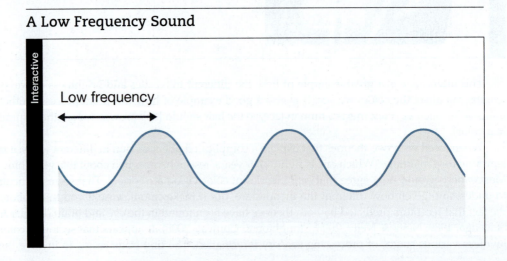

A Low Frequency Sound

Interactive

Low frequency

A flute, which makes a much higher sound would have sound waves that are much closer together and might look like this:

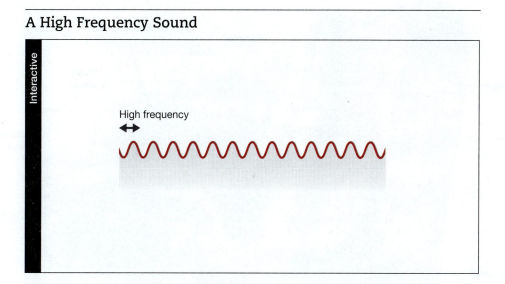

A High Frequency Sound

Interactive

High frequency

The human ear is able to hear sounds that range from 20 to 20,000 Hz. This makes us practically pitch deaf compared to dolphins, who can hear up to an astonishing 200,000 Hz.

The amplitude, or height, of a sound wave is interpreted as its volume—how loud or soft something sounds. Volume is measured in decibels, which is a standardized measure of sound pressure. The absolute threshold for hearing is set at 0 decibels, and prolonged exposure to anything above 85 decibels can produce hearing loss (Daniel, 2007; Rabinowitz, 2000). Musicians often play at a whopping 140 decibels at close range, making it remarkable that they (and their die-hard fans) are able to hear at all.

Have you ever covered your ears in horror while listening to early *American Idol* or *The Voice* auditions? The disillusioned contestants probably need to work on the quality of their sound (in addition to their pitch.) The quality of their sound includes the purity and complexity of their tone and is referred to as **timbre** (TAM-ber). A helpful judge on a talent reality show will be able to provide useful feedback to the contestants about ways to improve their sound.

LOCATING SOUNDS   Have you ever wondered why our ears are on either side of our head, rather than at the front or back? It is more than just an aesthetic reason—the location of our ears enables us to hear *stereophonically*, which means to hear from two different sources. When a dog to our left starts barking, the sound reaches our left ear a bit sooner and slightly more intensely than our right ear. Our heads cast a **sound shadow**, meaning that a sound has to go through or around our head in order to reach the other ear (Van Wanrooij & Van Opstal, 2004). As the sound travels around the head, it weakens, providing an extra clue as to the location of the sound.

THE ANATOMY OF THE EAR   As with vision, the process of hearing involves a series of stages beginning with sensation and ending with the perception of sound. Stimuli from the environment in the form of sound wave vibrations are transduced in the ear from pressure signals to electrical signals, which are then interpreted in the brain to indicate the specifics of the sound (e.g., pitch, loudness, timbre).

There are many small and intricate structures in the ear and it is easiest to think about the anatomy starting from the outside. Imagine sound coming in from the environment and going through a long and windy maze before leaving the ear for the brain. The anatomy of the ear can be broken up into structures of the outer ear, middle ear, and inner ear (see Figure 3.13).

The outer ear acts as a funnel for sound waves, which travel to the **ear drum** (also known as the tympanic membrane), causing it to vibrate. Then, the three small bones of the middle ear, the *hammer, anvil*, and *stirrup* strike each other and pass the vibration on to the *oval window* and on to the **cochlea** in the inner ear. The fluid in the cochlea is moving, which causes ripples in the basilar membrane. The **basilar membrane** is a stiff, structural component of the cochlea, which is lined with thousands of hair cells. These hair cells contain **cilia** on their tips that stimulate receptor cells

timbre

referring to sound; the purity and complexity of tone

sound shadow

the absorption of sound by the head; sound waves hit one ear first, then are dampened by the head, which aids in the location of sound

ear drum

part of the outer ear that vibrates in response to sounds in the environment

cochlea

a fluid-filled structure in the inner ear that receives vibrations from the small bones of the middle ear (hammer, anvil, and stirrup)

basilar membrane

a stiff, structural component of the cochlea, which is lined with thousands of hair cells

cilia

hair cell receptors in the ear that send messages through the auditory nerve to the auditory cortex in the brain

Figure 3.13 Anatomy of the Ear

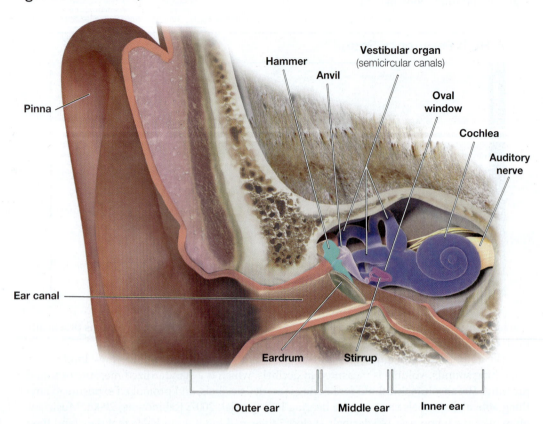

and send messages through the auditory nerve to the auditory cortex in the temporal lobe of the brain. The volume of a sound affects the number of hair cells that are activated and too much noise can permanently damage hair cells, and therefore impair hearing, by destroying or fusing the hair cells together (Kujawa & Liberman, 2015; Pienkowski & Eggermont, 2012). Watch the video *The Auditory Process* and then see if you can put the steps of hearing in the correct order.

The Auditory Process

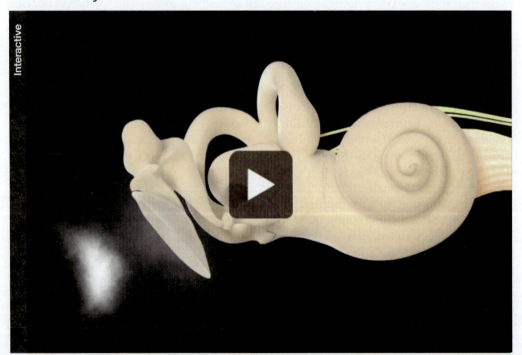

Steps of Auditory Processing

Interactive

Imagine you are walking down the street and hear someone calling your name. Arrange the following processes in order from beginning to end to explain the process of you hearing the sound and recognizing that sound as someone calling your name.

1	The pinna, or outer ear, funnels in sound waves from the environment
2	Sound waves travel to the ear drum causing it to vibrate
3	Cilia stimulate action potentials through the auditory nerve
4	Vibrations are sent to the cochlea in the inner ear
5	Fluid in cochlea causes ripples in basilar membrane
6	Cilia on the top of hair cells in basilar membrane are stimulated
7	The auditory nerve carries sound messages to the auditory cortex of the brain
8	The hammer, anvil, and stirrup strike each other and send vibrations to the oval window

Check Answers

Theories of Hearing

LO 3.8   Describe the different theories of hearing and types of hearing impairment.

It makes sense that vibrations are sensed in the ear and that those vibrations are transduced into electrical impulses. But, exactly how does your brain know how loud something is, or how to distinguish the high-pitched screech of an ambulance siren from the low pitch of a truck driving down the street?

Louder sounds carry and release more energy in the cochlea. Therefore, more hair cells on the basilar membrane move, or are displaced, in response to a louder stimulus. Think of it like picking and blowing the seed heads of a dandelion flower. If you blow softly, maybe only half of the seeds would move and blow away. However, if you blow harder (i.e., use more energy) you will release many more of the seeds. The dried seeds are like the hair cells in your ear and the more of them that are moved in a particular area, the louder the stimulus is perceived (Harris, 2001).

Blowing softly on a dandelion will release only a few seeds. A similar process occurs in the ear, where quieter sounds lead to less movement of the hair cells.

More seeds are released when they are blown off with more energy. Louder sounds release more energy in the cochlea and therefore move more of the hair cells.

place theory

theory of hearing; states that different pitches activate different sets of hair cells along the cochlea's basilar membrane

frequency theory

theory stating the pitch of a sound is perceived by the brain based on the rate (i.e., the frequency) of neural firing; best explains low pitched sounds

volley principle

theory of hearing, suggesting neurons take turns firing thereby combining forces to create a more complicated neural signal

Pitch then, is not determined by the *number* of hair cells moved, but instead by a combination of the *location* and the *rate* at which the hair cells are moved. High pitched sounds are best explained by **place theory**, first proposed by Hermann von Helmholtz, which states that different pitches activate different sets of hair cells (i.e., at different *places*) along the cochlea's basilar membrane (Von Békésy, 1963; Von Békésy & Wever, 1960). The **frequency theory**, which was initially proposed to explain both high pitched and low-pitched sounds, states that lower pitched sounds are perceived by the brain based on the rate (i.e., the *frequency*) at which the neurons fire. Interestingly, at one time it was suggested that the rate of firing of the neurons roughly matched the frequency of the sound (Rutherford, 1886). The problem with this theory is that we can perceive pitches at a higher frequency than neurons can fire. This difficulty led to the incorporation of the **volley principle** into pitch perception. This principle suggests that neurons take turns firing and by combining forces can create more power (i.e., overall neural signal) to the brain for interpretation (Wever, 1949). To see how this works, try this: Your goal is to tap your index finger on a table as many times as you can. You can use both your right and left index fingers, but you can only use one finger at time. Start with one finger and tap it as many times as fast as you can. When you feel your finger fatiguing and slowing down, switch to your other index finger. When that finger gets tired, switch back to the first finger you used. Switch back and forth a few times. Do you see what happens? Taking just a small break, allows the neurons in your finger to rest and "reset" to get ready to move quickly again. This is essentially what the volley principle suggests; that the neurons on the basilar membrane in the cochlea take turns firing back and forth to communicate pitch information. Most researchers now agree that discerning pitch involves the position of neuronal activity and the temporal pattern of firing within and between neurons (Moore, 2012). That is, place theory best explains high frequency stimuli (high pitch) and frequency theory is best suited to understand low frequencies (low pitch). The volley principle appears to come into play for the low and moderate frequencies (Wever, 1949).

HEARING IMPAIRMENT It is estimated that 20 percent of individuals over the age of 12 have some degree of unilateral (one ear) hearing loss and that 12.7 percent of Americans demonstrate some degree of bilateral (both ears) hearing loss (Lin et al., 2011). Workers in mining, manufacturing, and construction industries appear to be at particularly high risk for hearing impairment (Masterson et al., 2013).

There are three types of hearing impairment: sensorineural, conductive, and mixed hearing loss. **Sensorineural hearing loss** results from damage to the cochlea in the inner ear or from damage to the nerve pathways from the inner ear to the brain. This type of hearing loss is usually a result of damage to the outer and inner ear hair cells and is the most common type of permanent hearing loss. What is surprising is just how many conditions (medical and environmental) can lead to this type of hearing impairment. Various illnesses and over 200 medications can cause sensorineural hearing loss (Cone et al., 2015). The aging process is also associated with this type of hearing loss, as is exposure to loud noises. As listening to music via headphones has become more portable and accessible, concern about hearing loss as a result of this practice has arisen. In a recent study of students between the ages of 18 and 30 years old, 8 percent of students who reported listening to music via earphones for at least two hours per day were found to have high frequency sensorineural hearing loss (Naik & Pai, 2014). While 8 percent may not sound like much, keep in mind that these were individuals younger than 30 years old! The World Health Organization recently released a report estimating that 1.1 billion teenagers/young adults were at risk for hearing loss due to unsafe listening practices (WHO, 2015).

Individuals with mild to moderate hearing impairment can likely be helped by the use of a hearing aid. A hearing aid merely amplifies the sounds that exist in the environment and the sound is processed in the same way through the ear and brain as someone without hearing loss. For those who experience severe to profound hearing loss, which is sometime referred to as "nerve deafness", cochlear implants provide an opportunity for hearing and speech that 50 years ago wouldn't have been available (Hearing Loss Association of America, n.d.). A **cochlear implant** is a small, complex, and truly fascinating piece of technology that takes sounds from the external environment and converts them to electrical signals to be interpreted by the brain. Unlike hearing aids, the cochlear implant completely bypasses the ear and directly stimulates the auditory nerve. There is now clear evidence that the earlier a child can receive a cochlear implant (e.g., even by 6 months or 1 year old), the better chance they will have at developing normal speech, language and cognitive abilities (Colletti et al., 2012; Colletti et al., 2011).

sensorineural hearing loss

hearing loss that results from damage to the cochlea in the inner ear or from damage to the nerve pathways from the inner ear to the brain

cochlear implant

a hearing device that takes sounds from the external environment and converts them to electrical signals to be interpreted by the brain

As long as children receive a cochlear implant while they are in the sensitive period for language development (even if it is after infancy), they should make significant progress (Szagun & Stumper, 2012; Tobey et al., 2013). Watch the video *Cochlear Implant* to see how this device can change the world for someone with hearing impairment.

Cochlear Implant

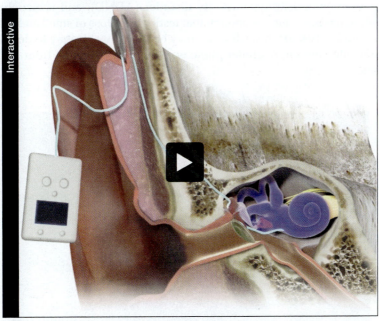

Conductive hearing loss is a type of hearing impairment where the sound is not *conducted* properly through the outer or middle ear. Individuals with this type of hearing loss experience an overall reduction in sound level and/or have difficulty hearing faint sounds. Typically, there are medical reasons (e.g., ear infections, allergies, impacted earwax, swimmer's ear) that explain the problem in the conduction of sound and often can be corrected through the use of medication or surgery. **Mixed hearing loss** involves a combination of both sensorineural and conductive hearing loss, which taken together, can mean damage to the outer, middle, and inner ear. Active middle ear implants have been used with some success to treat individuals with mixed hearing loss (Luers et al., 2013; Verhaert et al., 2013).

conductive hearing loss

a type of hearing impairment where sound is not conducted properly through the outer or middle ear

mixed hearing loss

hearing impairment that involves a combination of both sensorineural and conductive hearing loss

Quiz for Module 3.7–3.8

1. Which characteristic of a soundwave represents its volume?
   a. Frequency
   b. Timbre
   c. Amplitude
   d. Hertz

2. What are the names of the three small bones in the middle ear?
   a. Ear drum, hammer, and stirrup
   b. Hammer, ear drum, and stirrup
   c. Basilar membrane, cilia, cochlea
   d. Hammer, anvil and stirrup; sound vibrations on to the inner ear

3. Place theory suggests that people hear differing high-pitched sounds by the activation of different sets of _____ along the cochlea's _____.
   a. hair cells; auditory nerve
   b. hair cells; basilar membrane

   c. neurons; basilar membrane
   d. neurons; auditory nerve

4. Harper was born with severe hearing loss. She received a cochlear implant just after her first birthday and was able to hear clearly for the first time. The cochlear implant helped Harper to hear by _____.
   a. amplifying sounds from the environment
   b. directly stimulating the hair cells on her basilar membrane
   c. directly stimulating her auditory nerve
   d. mechanically stimulating the bones of her inner ear to pass the sound on for processing

Module 3.9–3.10: The Chemical and Body Senses

Our senses of smell, taste, and touch are intertwined in a way that is providing novel ways of obtaining information about diseases. For example, smell and taste dysfunction have been found to be early biomarkers of many neurodegenerative diseases, such as Parkinson's, Alzheimer's, attention-deficit/hyperactivity disorder (ADHD), and schizophrenia (Field, 2015). This finding has been reliable enough that testing for a loss of smell and taste in people who are considered at-risk for these diseases may become a viable way to determine who is in need of early intervention. A similar photo was part of a blog post from an Alzheimer's support website.

The Relationship Between Smell and Taste

LO 3.9   **Explain how the senses of smell and taste work together.**

You have probably heard people with a cold complaining that everything tastes like cardboard. Our senses of smell and taste are inextricably linked because the back of the mouth cavity is connected to the nasal cavity. Pinch your nostrils, close your eyes and have a friend feed you chunks of apple and raw potato. You will probably find that you are unable to tell the difference. Children seem to intuitively understand this connection between smell and taste because they quickly figure out that "yucky" medicine can be made more palatable by plugging their nose while drinking it.

olfaction

the sense of smell

SMELL   Smell is a chemical sense. **Olfaction** is the technical term for our ability to smell odors. Molecules of a substance are carried through the air to the receptor cells at the top of our nasal cavities, meaning that we effectively inhale part of everything we smell. This is not so bad if you are breathing in the scent of rose petals on a summer's day, but you might want to hold your breath the next time you drive past a sewage treatment plant.

Your sense of smell can serve as an early warning system that helps you detect danger. Think about an experience that you've had where you entered a room and experienced immediate concern and asked, "What's that smell?" Interestingly, there are some smells, particularly unpleasant smells that not only activate our olfactory system, but impact our somatosensory system as well. There are nerve endings in our nose that are also sensitive to touch, temperature, and pain (Brand, 2006). This is why people who have completely lost their sense of smell can still detect many odorous substances. Rather than activating the olfactory receptors, these smells are stimulating touch receptors and can actually cause pain (Fox, 2009).

Our sense of smell is not as acute as our eyesight or hearing, and it's downright pitiful compared to the smelling abilities of dogs, which each possess at least 300 million scent receptors (compared to a paltry 5 million for humans). It has often been stated that humans can distinguish at least 10,000 different odors, but recent research involving psychophysiological testing has calculated that humans can discriminate at least *one trillion* stimuli (Bushdid et al., 2014).

As molecules travel to the top of our nasal cavity, they reach olfactory receptor sites—large protein molecules on the olfactory neurons that bind to specific odorants. When a particular odor is encountered, it fits like a key into the receptor that is sensitive to that individual smell. The chemical stimuli are then transduced into electrical messages that travel along the *olfactory nerve* that leads to the brain for processing. Since we do not have a distinct receptor for each of the trillions of smells we encounter, it is likely that each odor triggers combinations of receptors, and it is those combinations that produce our experience of each specific smell. Watch the short animation *The Process of Smell* to see how odor molecules are eventually interpreted by our brain as a particular smell.

The Process of Smell

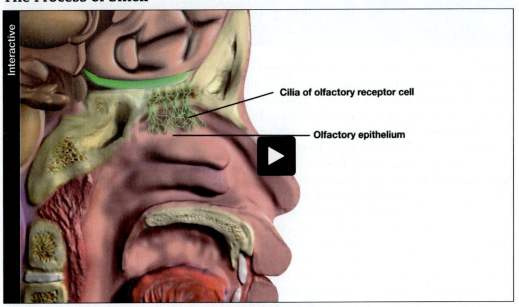

Cilia of olfactory receptor cell

Olfactory epithelium

Olfactory cells are special because they regenerate throughout the life cycle (Yang et al., 2015). This feature, coupled with the discovery that olfactory cells also exist outside the olfactory system (Kang & Koo, 2012), has led to the use of olfactory cells in spinal cord injury patients (see LO 2.5).

Have you ever caught a whiff of a fragrance and been reminded of a particularly emotional time in your past? Maybe the scent of a particular perfume or cologne immediately reminds you of your first love. We recently discovered that both of us have strong, emotional reactions to the very distinctive smell of the soap at our local hospital. Having both spent some scary days and weeks in that hospital while her premature baby was in the neonatal intensive care unit (BW) and while her husband was recovering from a broken back (DH), even years later the smell of that soap makes us feel like we are back in those moments. This reaction makes sense, because the area of the brain that receives information from receptor cells in the nasal cavities is closely linked to the limbic system, which is associated with memories and emotions. Furthermore, smell signals don't have to travel through the thalamus; they have direct links to the brain's emotion and memory centers like the amygdala and the hippocampus. Thus, odors have the ability to quickly evoke memories and feelings (Masaoka et al., 2012; Sullivan et al., 2015). Whether these memories are happy or sad depends on our earliest experiences with the particular smell (Herz, 2001). Watch *Can Smells Alter Mood and Behavior* to see what happens in the brain when smells are introduced and why smells have the quickest ability to change our moods.

Can Smells Alter Mood and Behavior?

TASTE   If our ancestors had enjoyed the taste of milkweed, we might not be around today. Fortunately, our natural inclination to avoid bitter-tasting foods developed as a result of the natural defense mechanism of many poisonous plants to produce a bitter-tasting substance. Even if you place a bitter substance on a newborn baby's tongue, the baby will react with a disgusted expression similar to one an adult might make (Rosenstein & Oster, 1988). Chemical companies use the same technique when they introduce bitter-tasting chemicals into cleaning products to discourage people from ingesting them. Pharmaceutical companies are doing the opposite: They are trying to develop medicines that don't have a bitter taste associated with them in an effort to increase medication compliance in children (Mennella et al., 2013).

taste buds

taste receptor cells located in the fungiform papillae on the tongue

Taste receptor cells, more commonly known as **taste buds** are embedded in the tongue's *papillae*—the little bumps you can see on your tongue. *Microvilli* are tiny hairs at the tips of the taste receptor cells that generate a nerve impulse, interpreted in the brain as a particular taste. When we eat, saliva dissolves the chemical substances in food, which slip between the papillae in order to reach the taste buds. Taste signals are passed to the limbic system and the cerebral cortex. A team of researchers conducted live imaging of the tongue of a mouse while tasting and was able to clearly identify the papillae and microvilli at work. (Choi et al., 2015).

The Process of Tasting

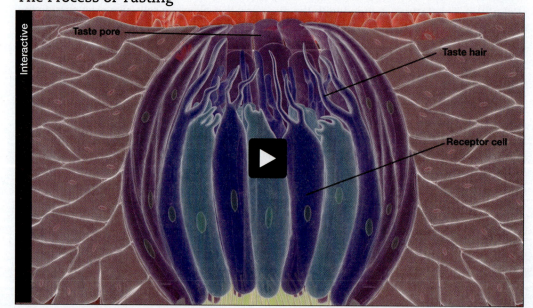

Psychologists recognize five basic tastes: sweet, salty, sour, bitter, and umami (a Japanese word that describes the taste of foods such as soup, chicken, cheese and anything containing monosodium glutamate). In recent years, researchers have confirmed our ability to also *taste* fat (what has come to be known as *oleogustus*), leading some to propose that "fat" should be added to the list of basic tastes (Running et al., 2015; Running & Mattes, 2016). Taste receptor cells are located throughout the tongue, mouth, and throat, with some types more prevalent than others in certain areas, particularly on the tip and the edges of the tongue. You can find a cluster of taste buds on the roof of your mouth where the hard and soft palates meet. If you wet your finger and dip it in salt and then run your finger along the roof of your mouth until you feel the end of the bone under the hard palate, all of a sudden you will experience a flash of saltiness and will know exactly where your taste buds exist (Bartoshuk & Snyder, 2013).

Are you surprised when you meet someone who says they don't like any sweets? While it is possible this is a learned preference, for some, eating high fat, high sugar food is associated with taste sensations so intense that they make the experience entirely unpleasant. Scientists have discovered that some people have an unusually high number of taste buds, affecting not only their food preferences but also their food *experiences* (Duffy et al., 2003). Yale University researcher Linda Bartoshuk named these people with higher densities of taste buds "supertasters." You can determine the likelihood that you are a supertaster by putting a drop of blue food coloring on your tongue and then swishing it around with water. Your taste buds will not absorb the blue coloring as much as the other cells on your tongue, so it will allow you to count the number of taste buds in a small area at the tip of your tongue. The average person has about 20 taste buds, whereas it isn't uncommon for "supertasters" to have 50 or more in a small area (de Lange, 2013).

Many supertasters would dispute the notion that they are blessed with a gift. Since each taste bud is associated with clusters of pain fibers, people with high numbers of taste buds experience intensified taste sensations to the point of pain. The burning sensation from a hot pepper may be unbearable, while the feel of fat may irritate the touch sensors on the taste buds.

Being a supertaster and avoiding certain foods has the potential to bring both positive and negative health outcomes. For example, although supertasters dislike the texture, and possibly taste, of fatty foods (Besnard, 2016; Running & Mattes, 2016), they also find particular fruits and vegetables extremely bitter. A supertaster may therefore be thinner than the average person because he or she avoids eating high fat, high sugar foods, but they are also at a higher risk of developing diseases such as colon cancer that could be prevented by consuming more fruits and vegetables (Basson et al., 2005; Dinehart et al., 2006; Duffy & Bartoshuk, 2000).

Body Senses

LO 3.10 Identify important components of the body senses including touch, pain, and the kinesthetic and vestibular senses.

While not typically the first to come to mind, the body senses include a number of different senses, many of which involve various systems and parts of the body. Our ability to recognize where our foot is when kicking a soccer ball, why some people can't even look at spinning rides at amusement parks without feeling nauseous, and how our body interprets and responds to touch and differentiates that from pain, all involve one or more of the body senses.

TOUCH With approximately 21 square feet of skin on your body, you can imagine that includes a lot of receptor cells for the sense of touch. Most people don't realize that our skin is the heaviest organ of our body, comprising approximately 16 percent of our body weight. The skin is constantly regenerating and shedding dead cells to make way for the new ones. It is hard to believe, but humans lose about 30,000–40,000 skin cells every minute! Yes, that is approximately 50 million skin cells each day.

The power of touch has long been understood as means to communicate affection, reassurance, and even promote developmental growth (Ardiel & Rankin, 2010; Honda et al., 2013). Parents of preterm infants are instructed in "Kangaroo Care," which involves placing the infant in an upright position on the mother's bare chest with their head turned to position their ear over the mother's heart. The research is clear that this method of care significantly reduces preterm infant mortality (Boundy et al., 2016).

Our sense of touch is part of the *somatosensory system*, which is responsible for all the different sensations we may feel. There are several different types of receptors cells in layers of the skin that process pressure, temperature, and pain. The density and sensitivity of the receptors vary across different parts of your body and often respond relatively, rather than in an absolute fashion. For example, jumping into a cold lake feels much colder if you have been out in the hot sun compared to an already chilly day. The temperature of the lake is the same, so it is not that your temperature receptors detect the exact temperature, but rather, they sense the relative difference in temperature between two objects or between the temperature of your skin and the temperature of the water. If you have ever heard people talk about their pain tolerance, then you know that pain can also be relative, and our perception of pain has a large psychological component.

PAIN   We may not appreciate it, but we are really lucky that we have the ability to feel pain. Pain is your body's way of telling you that placing your hand on a hot oven or running into a brick wall is a bad idea. It encourages us not to try those things again, which prolongs our survival. While many of the other senses have only one type of stimulus (e.g., light) from the environment that is transduced into electrical signals, pain is sensed by *nociceptors* (no-si-sep-ter), which detect potentially harmful pressure, chemicals, or temperatures (Dubin & Patapoutian, 2010).

Have you ever thought about why when we hit our funny bone, or slam our shin into something that our first instinct is to grab onto the injured area and rub it? Doesn't it seem strange that our instinct is to touch that painful spot? In 1965, Ronald Melzack and Patrick Wall proposed the gate control theory of pain, which provides a nice explanation for this phenomenon. The **gate control theory of pain** states that there are two different types of nerve fibers that relay information to our spinal cord; one thin fiber that carries the pain signal and another thicker fiber that transmits touch, pressure, and vibration. The sensation that ends up being perceived the most is the one with the biggest input. Therefore, rubbing, squeezing, or pushing around the painful area can stimulate the larger nerve fibers and crowd out (or close the gate) on the nerve fibers that communicate pain. The following video, *Managing Pain*, provides more information about this theory and the role our body and mind can play in pain perception.

gate control theory of pain

theory suggesting information about pain is conveyed through two different nerve fibers (a thin fiber for pain and a thicker fiber relaying touch, pressure, and vibration); pain can be inhibited by activating larger nerve fibers, which closes the smaller pain gates

Managing Pain

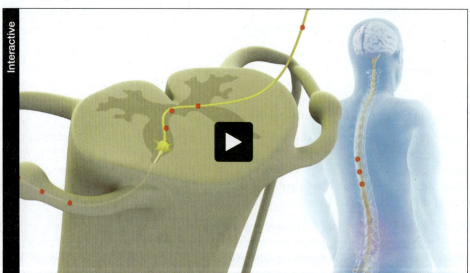

Pain Management   The current understanding of pain includes three interrelated dimensions: (1) the sensory-discriminative, which includes the intensity, location, quality, and duration of pain; (2) the affective-motivational, which includes the negative experience of pain and desire to flee painful circumstances; and (3) the cognitive-evaluative dimension, which involves the individual's interpretation of the pain and the surrounding context, which includes cultural values and expectations (Moayedi & Davis, 2013).

It makes sense that the most effective pain management strategies address each of these different dimensions. Pain can be either acute or chronic and the method for controlling pain is determined in part by the type of pain experienced. Acute pain, particularly involved with painful medical procedures can be effectively managed with the use of virtual reality video games (Choo et al., 2014; Garrett et al., 2014; Hoffman et al., 2011).

Chronic pain management often involves a combination of pharmacological (medicines), psychological, and alternative therapies (Shrestha et al., 2013; Sturgeon, 2014). Opioids (e.g., morphine, fentanyl, hydrocodone, methadone, oxycodone) are commonly prescribed by medical doctors to manage chronic pain (see the *Piecing It Together* module) but often lead to abuse and dependence (Sehgal et al., 2012). Cognitive behavioral therapy is an effective psychological method of managing pain through its focus on the patient's cognitive interpretation and affective (or emotional) experience of the pain (Burns et al., 2015; Ehde et al., 2014). Stress management and mindfulness-based interventions are other psychological treatments that have efficacy for some chronic pain conditions (Hannibal & Bishop, 2014; la Cour & Petersen, 2015). Complementary and alternative medicine (CAM) is considered a diverse group of medical and health care practices and products not generally considered part of conventional, western medicine. CAM can be classified into five different categories including: (1) whole medical systems (e.g., naturopathy, Chinese medicine, homeopathy); (2) mind-body medicine (e.g., meditation, prayer, yoga); (3) biologically based therapies (e.g., herbs, special diets); (4) body manipulative (e.g., massage, acupuncture, chiropractic); and (5) energy healing (e.g., reiki) (Mao et al., 2011; Terry et al., 2012).

Virtual reality video games have become a popular distraction for children undergoing painful procedures or as part of the treatment for psychological disorders.

BODY POSITION AND MOVEMENT   Our kinesthetic sense provides information to our brains about the positions and movements of our muscles and joints. Without it, we would be unable to walk in a straight line, raise a glass to our lips, or bend down to pick up a pencil. Our kinesthetic sense helps us not knock our cup of coffee over when we go to reach for it first thing in the morning. Signals from specialized nerve endings, or **proprioceptors** in our muscles, tendons, and joints provide a constant stream of information from our body parts through our spinal cords and into the cortex of the parietal lobe.

proprioceptors

sensory receptors that provide information about body position and movement

The vestibular sense monitors the body's position in space. It enables a person to determine body orientation (e.g., whether you are right-side up or upside down), gather a sense of direction and speed of movement, and maintain balance. The vestibular sense originates in the inner ear, which is why you sometimes lose your sense of balance when you have an ear infection. Hair cells in the *semicircular canals* send messages to the brain as they move back and forth and provide feedback about body rotation. Gravitation and movement also stimulate tiny crystals in the *vestibular sacs*, which connect the canals to the cochlea. The crystals bend the hair cells when moved and send messages to the cerebellum, enabling it to maintain the body's sense of balance. If you have ever participated in gymnastics, cheerleading, or dance, you've probably been told to "spot your turns." Spotting involves picking a constant spot in your visual field to focus on throughout your movement. This strategy helps maintain balance by providing constant feedback via your visual system. However, this strategy can also result in motion sickness due to the conflicting messages sent to the brain. For those who are susceptible to motion sickness, reading and riding in the car don't mix. This is because your vestibular sense is detecting movement, but the steady gaze at your book is suggesting to your brain that you are stationary. Your brain doesn't like the conflicting information and your stomach then, doesn't like your brain. This is why you may have heard the advice to "look out the window" when riding in the car (so your visual system and vestibular system will obtain corresponding information.)

Pilots must learn a lot about the vestibular sense because flying puts them at high risk for *vestibular illusions*. These illusions result from intense angular accelerations or decelerations or by a sudden change in gravity and are more likely to occur when the visual field is impaired (e.g., when it is dark or cloudy). Vestibular illusions can create serious spatial disorientation (e.g., feeling as though you are flying straight when in fact, you are turned or feeling as though you are upside down when you aren't.) Pilots have flight simulators to acclimate their body and brain to these types of effects and can find information online, in the *Skybrary*, about various aspects of these illusions.

A Review of Sensation

Drag and drop the following descriptions into the appropriate place in the table. Once you complete the table, you will have a good summary of the important components of each of the senses discussed in the modules.

Sense	Sense Organ	Stimulus	Receptor Cells
Vision	Eyes	Wavelengths of light	Rods and cones
Hearing	Ears	Sound waves	Hair cells in cochlea
Taste	Mouth	Food/ chemicals dissolved in saliva	Taste buds
Smell	Nose	Odor molecules in the air	Receptors at the top of the nasal cavity
Pain (from the sense of touch)	Skin, internal organs	Pressure, heat, cold, or tissue damage	Nociceptors
Kinesthetic sense (body position and movement)	Sensors in muscles and joints	Change in body position; movement of body parts	Proprioceptors in muscle and joints
Vestibular sense (balance)	Semicircular canals and vestibular sacs	Gravitational changes in body causing movement of fluids in inner ear	Hair-like receptors in the inner ear

Start Over

Quiz for Module 3.9–3.10

1. What are the five basic tastes that humans recognize?

  a. Sweet, sour, salty, bitter, pungent

  b. Sweet, sour, salty, bitter, umami

  c. Sour, salty, bitter umami, fatty

  d. Sour, sweet, bitter, fatty, brothy

2. Brandi loved the smell of chocolate chip cookies because it reminded her of her grandmother. Brandi learned that smell can evoke vivid memories because it is directly related to which brain structures?

  a. Amygdala; hypothalamus

  b. Amygdala; hippocampus

  c. Thalamus; hypothalamus

  d. Hippocampus; thalamus

3. Specialized nerve cells in our muscles, tendons, and joints called _____, provide a constant stream of information from our body parts through our spinal cords and into the cortex of the parietal lobe.

  a. receptor cells

  b. vestibular sacs

  c. semicircular canals

  d. proprioceptors

4. Our sense of pain is experienced by _____, which can detect harmful pressure, chemicals, or temperatures.

  a. nociceptors

  b. proprioceptors

  c. joints

  d. sensory neurons

Module 3.11–3.15: The Science of Perception

Perception is the way we organize and give meaning to sensory information from the outside world. No two people perceive the world the same way. One person may perceive a beautiful work of art, while another sees only blobs of color that have no meaning. The painting is the same, but the perception of the painting is very different.

Perception occurs when we take the sensations from our environment, and through the process of transduction, interpret them as meaningful data. Rather than seeing patterns of light and darkness, we are able to perceive a frog hopping into a pond, or a car whizzing past us on the freeway. Instead of sound waves and vibrations, we hear a pleasing melody of a song. But how do we create meaning from all of the sensory data that bombards us every day?

Theories of Perception

LO 3.11 Distinguish top-down from bottom-up processing.

Perception most often involves a combination of a gathering of the *raw data* and then an interpretation of what that data means. Understanding human behavior comes from a process of collecting information about the way people think, feel, and behave and then analyzing, or interpreting that information to come to meaningful conclusions. Understanding human behavior starts with the raw data, but hopefully ends with perceptions about the meaning of the data. Our everyday perceptions in the world follow a similar process. Stimuli from the environment is collected through our sense organs and then sent to the brain for interpretation. **Bottom-up processing** refers to the type of processing of information that starts with the raw data, or the stimuli from the environment. In bottom-up processing, our sense receptors gather the data and send it up to the brain for further processing. For an example of bottom-up processing and top-down processing, click through the following activity.

bottom-up processing

method of perception that involves processing information from the raw data, or environmental stimuli, up to the brain

Bottom-Up vs. Top-Down Processing

Interactive

top-down processing

perception that relies heavily on previous knowledge and experience; also known as knowledge-based processing

The way we perceive the world is affected by our beliefs, experiences, and expectations, just as the way you perceived that picture. This aspect of perception is referred to as **top-down processing**. Top-down processing is sometimes called *knowledge-based processing* because it relies heavily on your previous knowledge and experience to influence perceptions. Businesses with successful marketing strategies know this fact and often their goal is to have you associate a simple stimulus with their store. One of your authors realized the power of this when her oldest daughter, who was no more than two years old at the time, saw a picture like this

and said, "Ooooooo, I like Target" (referring to the store).

Most perception (as was the case with the honey jackfruit) involves a combination of both bottom-up and top-down processing. Our senses gather the raw data from the environment (bottom-up) and our brain interprets that information in the context of our life experiences and knowledge (top-down).

Adaptive Pathway 3.3: Theories of Perception

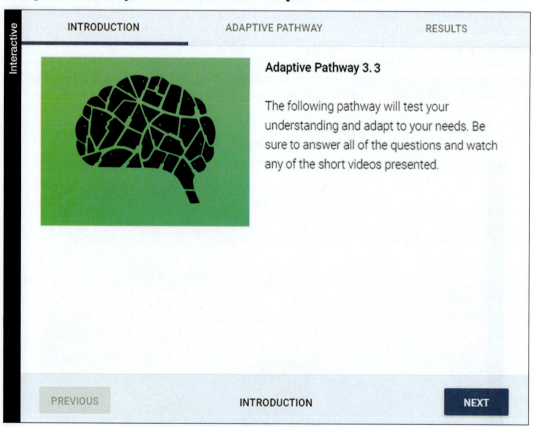

| INTRODUCTION | ADAPTIVE PATHWAY | RESULTS |

Adaptive Pathway 3.3

The following pathway will test your understanding and adapt to your needs. Be sure to answer all of the questions and watch any of the short videos presented.

PREVIOUS   INTRODUCTION   NEXT

Perceptual Constancies and Perceptual Sets

LO 3.12   Recognize how perceptual constancies and perceptual sets help to organize sensations and guide perception.

Our perceptual processes are continually at work to help us make sense of the world. Imagine if every time we perceived something in our environment, it was like seeing it for the first time. That is, imagine if we had to use bottom-up processing to understand everything around us.

Luckily, our evolved brain and life experiences aid us in perception, but as we'll see, this is not a perfect process and at times, results in some interesting errors.

PERCEPTUAL CONSTANCY One perceptual aid involves the tendency to maintain **perceptual constancy**, which is the idea that our perception of a stimulus remains the same even though some its characteristics may have changed. For example, we don't panic and think that our kids are shrinking as they run away from us to play at the park. Thanks to **size constancy** we know that it isn't their size that is changing, but the distance they are from us. Likewise, we don't look at this figure to the right and see the man in the background and think, "That man in the background is the smallest person I've ever seen!" We intuitively know, because of perceptual constancy, that the "small man" is just a man who is further behind the "larger man".

We also have perceptual constancy for color and for shape. With respect to color, we know that a red apple is red regardless of whether or not it is seen in brightly lit sun or at dusk. Interestingly, the wavelengths of light that are reflected from the apple do change in different environments but because of **color constancy**, we still perceive the apple as red.

Shape constancy refers to the fact that despite the retinal images cast by objects from different viewpoints, we still perceive the object to be the same shape. For example, the three viewpoints of the doors in Figure 3.14 are actually three different shapes (outlining the doors helps you to see this). However, if asked what the shape of the door was, because of shape constancy, you would reply that it was a rectangle. Perceptual constancies develop over time and through the experience of interacting with our world (Kavšek & Granrud, 2012; Mulak et al., 2013).

perceptual constancy

the perception of a stimulus remains the same even though some of its characteristics may have changed

size constancy

the perception of an object's size doesn't change, regardless of changes in distance

color constancy

recognizing that the color of an object doesn't change even though the reflected wavelengths of light change in different environments; for example, knowing a red apple is red regardless of whether or not it is seen during the day or at dusk

shape constancy

objects are perceived as the same shape even though the retinal image may change as a result of different viewpoints

perceptual set

the tendency for previous experiences and expectations to influence how situations or objects are perceived

Figure 3.14   Shape Constancy

PERCEPTUAL SETS Our previous experiences and expectations give us a mental predisposition, or **perceptual set**, that influences the way we perceive things. For example, if a child hands you a page scrawled with scattered squiggles in brown crayon and tells you he has drawn a picture of a horse, you will be more likely to perceive the messy brown scribble as a horse. Top-down processing enables us to use preexisting knowledge to create a coherent image in our brains. Therefore, a perceptual set is our tendency to view things in a specific way that is influenced by our motivations, expectations, emotions, attitudes, and culture.

Bruner and Minturn (1955) showed how the context can impact how you read the number/letter in the middle of this picture (see Figure 3.15). Is it the letter "B" or the number "13"? The answer is, "It depends." It depends on whether or not you are reading from top to bottom or left to right. The interesting fact about this demonstration is that it illustrates how our perceptual sets can vary *within* the same stimulus.

Figure 3.15 Perceptual Set

A

12   13   14

C

Figure 3.16 The Devil's Trident

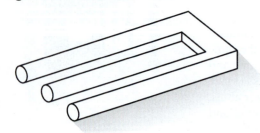

Figure 3.17 Illusory Contour

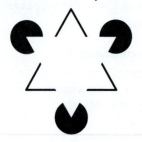

illusory contour

a visual illusion where lines or contours are perceived but do not exist

proximity

tendency to perceive objects close to one another as part of the same group

similarity

principle of interpersonal attraction that the more two people have in common, the more likely they are to experience increased attraction to that person

closure

Gestalt principle of perception involving the tendency to perceive images as complete objects

continuity

Gestalt principle of perception involving the tendency to view intersecting lines as part of a continuous pattern, rather than as a series of separate lines

Have you ever misheard something one of your friends said because you were expecting her to say something else? Perceptual sets are not just restricted to vision. We can play certain rock songs backward and not think anything of them. But if someone tells us that certain disturbing words or phrases can be heard among the backward sounds, we are far more likely to perceive the evil messages (Vokey & Read, 1985), which is why in the past some people considered it a form of subliminal messaging. Gary Greenwald, a Christian minister, maintained that Led Zeppelin's *Stairway to Heaven* when played backward contained the phrase "There's no denying it, here's to my sweet Satan." When told what to listen for, Greenwald's religious supporters agreed that the song did in fact contain the heretical line. In fact, there is apparently a whole lot more in the song than just that one line:

Oh here's to my sweet Satan. The one whose little path would make me sad, whose power is Satan. He'll give those with him 666, there was a little toolshed where he made us suffer, sad Satan.

If you Google "backmasking" and "songs" you'll find various examples of this phenomenon.

Since our perceptual set is determined by our previous experiences, it is easily influenced by culture. For example, individuals from developed countries are likely to perceive diagrams differently than people raised in less developed countries. We can find evidence of this with a diagram commonly known as the Devil's Trident (see Figure 3.16). Europeans and North Americans have a natural desire to interpret it as a three-dimensional object, yet people from different cultures (e.g., Africa) are able to view the diagram as two-dimensional—just a series of lines and circles (Deregowski, 1969).

Our brains have a natural desire to create logic and order. Just as in the Devil's Trident, our brain wants to see it as either two prongs or three prongs and it is confusing, and a little frustrating, when it switches back and forth between the two. Often, we create the perception of contours and borders to construct a logical form, even if it is not really there. An **illusory contour** is a visual illusion in which lines are perceived without actually being present. Researchers have discovered that illusory contour images activate specific regions in the visual cortex. Cells in these areas respond as though the contours were formed by real lines or edges (Mendola et al., 1999; Sheth et al., 1996; Von der Heydt et al., 1984). You can see illusory contour at work when you look at Figure 3.17.

Chances are the "white triangle" jumped off the page to you when you first encountered the picture. There appear to be well-defined edges of the triangle but, in fact, there are no edges at all.

Gestalt Principles

LO 3.13 **Explain the different Gestalt principles of perception.**

The German word *gestalt* means "form" or "whole." In psychological terms, it refers to the way in which we naturally group objects together and perceive whole shapes, rather than a number of individual parts. Gestalt psychology developed in Germany at the beginning of the 20th century and its overarching concept is the Law of Pragnanz (or Law of Simplicity), which says that we organize a stimulus into the simplest possible form. Work your way through the following interactive to learn about and see for yourself the various Gestalt principles used to explain perception.

Gestalt principles of grouping examine how individuals organize stimuli into shapes, patterns, and forms. People tend to organize information according to **proximity**, **similarity**, **closure**, and **continuity**.

Gestalt Principles in Action

Interactive

The Necker Cube

Rubin Vase

Reversible Woman

Figure Ground

Gestalt Principles of Grouping

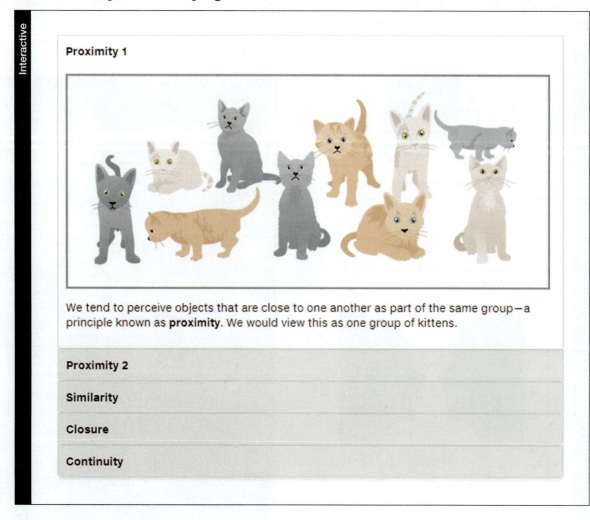

Interactive

Proximity 1

We tend to perceive objects that are close to one another as part of the same group—a principle known as **proximity**. We would view this as one group of kittens.

Proximity 2

Similarity

Closure

Continuity

Depth Perception

depth perception

the ability to judge distances of objects and to see them in three dimensions

This is an example of a child being coaxed across the visual cliff. The results of this research indicate most babies can judge depth by the time they start to crawl.

LO 3.14 **Differentiate monocular cues and binocular cues with respect to depth perception.**

Our retinas process all images in two dimensions. That being the case, then how do we see in 3D? **Depth perception** involves the ability to judge distances of objects and to see them in three-dimensions. You are aware you can see in three-dimensions, but that process does not occur in your eyes. Your brain receives two slightly different two-dimensional images, one from each eye, and puts those together with other cues from the environment to construct our world in three-dimensions.

Thanks to classic research by Eleanor Gibson and Richard Walk, we understand that depth perception is at least partly innate. Gibson and Walk (1960) tested 36 infants ranging in age from 6-14 months old in what is referred to as a "visual cliff." This box is covered with a glass top, but there appears to be a sharp drop-off, or cliff, starting at halfway across. Babies and toddlers were placed on the visual cliff and their mother stood at one side or the other and would coax their child to crawl to them. The purpose of the study was to see if these children would crawl *off the cliff*. Of all of the children tested, only three ventured off the cliff when called by their mother. Most of the children refused to come, went the other direction, or sat where they were and cried. Gibson and Walk concluded that most human infants are able to judge depth by the time they can crawl.

The process of seeing in 3D occurs in the brain, but cues from our eyes and environment signal depth in order to construct our visual field. These cues can be divided into three major groups: oculomotor, monocular, and binocular cues.

OCULOMOTOR CUES   **Oculomotor cues** refer specifically to what is happening *with* and *within* your eyes when you are perceiving depth. Take your right index finger and hold it out at an arm's distance from your face. Now, stare at your finger and slowly move your finger closer to your nose. As you do this, pay attention to the feeling you have in your eyes. As you move your finger toward your face, you should notice that your eyes are looking in toward your nose, which is accompanied by a feeling a tension in your eyes. This inward movement of our eyes that occurs when we look at something close up is referred to as **convergence**. The brain detects the convergence of our eyes and interprets that as "I'm seeing something that is very close." The other feedback your brain gets is directly from your eye. If you recall from an earlier module, the lens of the eye changes shape, a process called *accommodation*, to focus the image on the retina. Part of the shape change of the lens has to do with the distance of the object. So, as you moved your finger further away from your nose, your lens flattens out. The brain is able to use both convergence and accommodation as indicators of depth.

VISUAL CUES: MONOCULAR CUES   There are some cues that indicate depth or distance that can be seen by just one eye. These are called **monocular cues**. Remember that *mono* means one and *ocular* refers to the eye, so you can think "one-eye cues." There are different types of monocular cues. Some cues are related to what is communicated in a two-dimensional picture and others are related to movement.

Pictorial cues involve information about depth communicated through two-dimensional pictures. If you are an artist, you are likely very familiar with these principles for creating the illusion of depth in drawings and paintings. Parallel lines that converge, or come together, at one end of a picture convey distance, which is referred to as **linear perspective**. An object or person seen as smaller *relative* to other objects or people in a picture is assumed to be further away. This pictorial cue of **relative size** capitalizes on the principle of size constancy because you assume the people are *actually* the same size but the smaller size in the picture is an indication of distance. Similarly, the concept of **relative height** suggests that taller objects appear further away. In addition, if one object or person is blocking another, we assume the one being blocked is *behind* the other one. This is referred to as **interposition**. For example, we perceive Figure 3.19 as a picture of one cow standing in front of another cow—not as one very wide cow with two heads and six legs!

The last example of a pictorial cue is **texture gradient**. The closer something appears, the more texture it appears to have. As distance sets in, the texture of the object becomes smaller and smoother. We perceive these textured lily pads as closest to us, while the ones off in the distance seem to have lost their texture.

All of the cues discussed so far work best when we are not moving. Once motion is introduced, other cues for depth perception are introduced. You have likely noticed that when you are looking out a car window, the objects closest to you seem to be whizzing by, where those farther away seem to move more slowly. This phenomenon is known as

Figure 3.19 Two Cows

oculomotor cues

depth perception cues involving the activity within the eyes

convergence

monocular cue of depth perception; the inward movement of the eyes that occurs when looking at something close-up

monocular cues

cues that indicate depth or distance that can be seen with just one eye

pictorial cues

monocular cues that provide information about depth communicated through two-dimensional pictures

linear perspective

a depth perception cue where converging parallel lines suggest distance

relative size

a pictorial cue based on size constancy, suggesting that smaller objects are further away

relative height

a pictorial cue based on the principle of size constancy, suggesting that taller objects are further away

interposition

a depth perception cue; when an object or person blocks another, the one in the back is perceived to be further away

texture gradient

a pictorial cue that assumes that objects with visible texture appear closer than those with little or no texture

motion parallax

a depth perception cue; the sense that objects further away are moving more slowly

binocular cue

a depth perception cue that involves the use of both eyes

retinal disparity

referring to the slightly different images seen by the right and left eye (due to the distance between the two retinas); a primary binocular cue for depth perception

motion parallax and has become a very important strategy to convey depth perception in animation and video games. Motion parallax occurs as a result of the amount an object has to move to be seen by both eyes. If you are riding in the car and notice someone standing on the side of the road, that visual stimulus first hits the retina closest to the person and then your other retina. Because the person is close, the image of them has to move quite a bit from one retina to the other. If this person was standing one block away, they would appear much smaller (because of relative size) and not have to move as much from one eye to the other. The more the image has to move between the eyes (i.e., the closer it is), the faster it has to move to be detected. If you are travelling at a constant speed, you have the same amount of time to view the object whether it is close or far away, but the one that is closer is required to move much further to be seen by both retinas and therefore appears to move faster than the image further away.

VISUAL CUES: BINOCULAR CUES   In addition to all the monocular cues in our environment, there is also an important **binocular cue**; that is, a cue that involves both/two (bi) eyes (ocular). This cue is referred to as **retinal disparity** and is the primary binocular cue for depth. As you know, each of your eyes casts an image onto the retina. The retinal images are slightly different because of the distance between our two eyes. You can see how this works by closing your left eye and holding up the index finger on your right hand about an arm's length in front of you. Now, take your left index finger and hold it about six inches from your nose, and use it to completely cover up the right index finger. As soon as you can't see your right finger anymore, switch eyes by opening your left eye and closing your right eye. What happened to your right index finger? It moved to the left, didn't it? Now, of course you know it didn't actually move because you didn't move it! But, this demonstrates that your right and left eye see things from slightly different angles. Objects that are near have increased retinal disparity. This means, the closer an object is, the larger the difference in the angles between what is seen by the right eye and the left eye. The further away something is, the more similar the image to both eyes, meaning less retinal disparity.

Retinal disparity is an important binocular cue for depth perception. It works well because, even though the eyes see images from slightly different angles, the image itself is focused on the center of the retina of each eye. That way, the brain is able to interpret that both images are from the same object in space. It would be unusual to have two different images focus on the central part of the retina of each eye. But, we can artificially create that situation and when we do, you'll be surprised at the result.

Roll an 8 ½ × 11 sheet of paper lengthwise to make a tube. Close your left eye, and then look through the tube with your right eye, as if looking through a telescope. Focus on something off in the distance. Now, place your left hand up against the side of the tube, at the far end of the tube. Your palm should be facing toward you. Now, open your left eye and, while

A Hole in Your Hand

Interactive

still looking off in the distance, slowly move your left hand up the tube toward your face. Very soon, you should see the hole in your hand!

Can you explain why that happened? The reason is because we forced the center of each retina to register different images by putting a barricade around the right eye (through the use of a rolled-up piece of paper). This meant that the right eye was registering a hole while the left eye was focusing on your hand. Your brain interpreted these images coming from the same place in space (just like if you were holding a pencil out in front of you) and therefore combined the two images into one!

Movies made in 3D take advantage of the principle of retinal disparity by filming a scene with two cameras just a few inches apart (like your eyes). Putting on 3D glasses isolates the images to each eye so that the right eye only sees what was filmed by the "right camera," and the left eye sees what was filmed by the "left camera." Your brain takes these slightly different retinal images and combines them into a 3D experience.

Perceptual Illusions

LO 3.15 **Recognize the different types of perceptual illusions and the factors involved in producing them.**

Throughout this chapter, you have encountered several **perceptual illusions**, where the appearance of a stimulus is different than the actual nature of the evoking stimulus (e.g., seeing a hole in your hand). Illusions can occur with any of the senses; however, optical illusions, those involving the sense of sight, are often the easiest to demonstrate and most dramatic to experience. Illusions and the specific situations in which they are created have been useful to those studying perception because they highlight the processes that underlie normal perception (Eagleman, 2001). Michael Bach has explained that although the term *visual illusions* suggest some kind of problem or malfunction with the visual system, it is actually the unusual context that leads to inappropriate interpretations of the visual scene (see www.michaelbach.de/ot/).

There are three types of visual illusions: (1) **literal** (or sometimes called physical) **visual illusions** are created images that are different from the objects or situations that make them. In physical illusions, the illusion (e.g., a rainbow) has already occurred before light enters the eye; (2) **physiological illusions** result from excessive stimulation to the eyes or brain. The overstimulation of the receptors produces a rebound-type of response. Afterimages are good examples of physiological illusions; and (3) **cognitive illusions** involve higher-order thinking, such as our knowledge and assumptions about the world. Cognitive illusions involve the most interaction between our sensory and perceptual systems. There are many types of cognitive illusions, including those that involve ambiguous or "impossible" pictures, or distortions of geometrical shape or size. Here is an example of the **Müller-Lyer illusion** in a real-life context.

perceptual illusions

an experience where the perception of a stimulus is different than the actual evoking stimulus

literal visual illusions

illusions that create images different from the objects or situations that make them (e.g., a rainbow)

physiological illusions

illusions that result from excessive stimulation to the eyes or brain

cognitive illusions

type of visual illusion that involves higher-order thinking, such as an individual's knowledge and assumptions about the world; examples include ambiguous or impossible pictures

Müller-Lyer illusion

a geometric illusion where the length of lines appears shorter or longer, depending on whether the arrowheads are pointing in or out

The Müller-Lyer Illusion

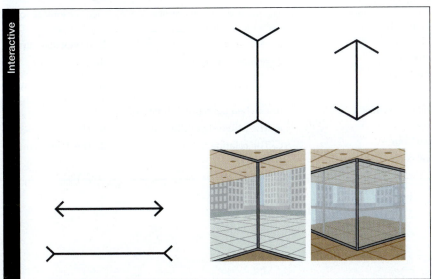

Interactive

The lengths of the windows certainly appear to be different; however, they are the same size. Since 1889, when this illusion was discovered, scientists have been proposing explanations to explain it. Although no longer universally accepted (Howe & Purves, 2005), one of the first theories was proposed by Richard Gregory (1968), which involved the concepts of *depth perception* and *size constancy*. According to *depth theory*, the perspective cues provided by the arrow heads suggest that the window on the left is further away than the window on the right. However, the retinal image of the corner of each window is the same (because the lengths of the lines are the same). This combination of stimulus and monocular cues sets up an impossible situation for our brain—images that are different distances away from us can't appear the same size *unless* one object is actually longer than the other (Gregory, 1997). Therefore, the perceptual process in our brain takes over and says, "that line with the outward-pointing arrowheads is further away and therefore longer than the other line with the inward-pointing arrowheads."

Numerous studies were conducted demonstrating cultural differences in the perception of the Muller-Lyer illusion, with people from non-westernized cultures less likely to see the illusion (Segall et al., 1963). The "carpentered world" explanation suggested it was the regular exposure to the rectangular corners of rooms and buildings in western societies that trained the visual system to respond in this particular way. However, given the fact that both fish (Sovrano et al., 2016) and computer programs (Zeman et al., 2013) were trained to discriminate the length of lines and both demonstrated the visual illusion, the answer to the reason for the Muller-Lyer illusion is likely to be contained with the visual system itself, rather than the outside world (García-Garibay & de Lafuente, 2015).

Quiz for Module 3.11–3.15

1. A person who steps outside first thing in the morning to smell the air, feel the breeze on their face, and see the rays of light as the sun rises would be doing which type of processing?

   a. Bottom-up processing

   b. Top-down processing

   c. Both bottom-up and top-down processing

   d. Neither bottom-up nor top-down processing

2. Processing that relies heavily on previous knowledge and is influenced by our beliefs, expectations, and experiences is called _____.

   a. top-down processing   b. bottom-up processing

   c. experience processing   d. parallel processing

3. As Gina's boyfriend Omar walks toward her, the image on Gina's retina will change the closer he gets. However, Gina's perception of Omar's size does not change. She does not perceive him as growing bigger or taller because of _____.

   a. color constancy   b. shape constancy

   c. size constancy   d. retinal constancy

4. When viewing an ambiguous picture, we will tend to see an image that is consistent with our own culture and experience. This phenomenon is called _____.

   a. perceptual set   b. illusory contour

   c. size constancy   d. perceptual constancy

5. A group of preschoolers are taken on a field trip and given matching hats to wear. The teacher is making use of what Gestalt principle to easily identify the children?

   a. Similarity   b. Proximity

   c. Figure-ground   d. Continuity

6. The ability to see in 3D comes from the brain, which receives two slightly different images from each _____ and puts those together with cues from the _____ to construct the world in three dimensions.

   a. brain hemisphere; occipital lobe

   b. eye; environment

   c. brain hemisphere; environment

   d. eye; occipital lobe

7. The inward movement of our eyes when we look at something close up is called _____.

   a. binocular cues   b. monocular cues

   c. retinal disparity   d. convergence

8. Which perceptual illusion has been shown to vary across cultures and as a result is one of the most well-known and extensively researched perceptual illusions?

   a. The Müller-Lyer illusions   b. The lilac chaser

   c. The rotating mask   d. The devil's trident

Module 3.16: Piecing It Together: Chronic Pain

LO 3.16 **Analyze how the cross-cutting themes of psychology apply to the management of chronic pain.**

As discussed in this chapter, pain can be either acute or chronic. Acute pain often occurs in response to something that is damaging the body. Acute pain is our body's way of saying, "Stop doing that!" However, pain can also become chronic, lasting months or years. *Chronic pain syndrome*, although not currently well defined, is typically diagnosed in a person experiencing pain for either 3 or 6 months. Sometimes, chronic pain is defined as pain that lasts longer than the expected period of healing for a given injury or condition.

The understanding and management of pain is truly an interdisciplinary undertaking. Pain is one of the few conditions that all medical doctors (regardless of specialty) and psychologists will encounter in their practices. Pain has biological, psychological, and sociocultural components and therefore has been conceptualized according to a *biopsychosocial model* (Gatchel et al., 2007; Kamper et al., 2015). Despite a number of documented approaches to managing pain that don't involve the use of drugs (i.e., opioids), the prescription of narcotics such as Oxycodone, Hydrocodone, and Fentanyl is often one of the primary methods of pain management (Dowell et al., 2016), with approximately 60 million prescriptions dispensed per calendar quarter in 2013 (Dart et al., 2015). In 2014, a total of 20,000 people died as a result of an opioid overdose and approximately 2 million people met the diagnostic criteria for a substance-use disorder involving opioids (Olsen, 2016).

According to the Centers for Disease Control and Prevention (CDC), the sales of prescription opioids in the United States quadrupled between 1999 and 2014, which paralleled the four times higher rate of opioid overdose deaths. There appears to be significant variability in prescribing rates between states regarding opioid painkillers, which has led to federal and state regulations aimed at reducing the access to these medicines (Dart et al., 2015). The following map details the geographic differences in opioid prescribing rates. The categories represent the number of retail opioid prescriptions dispensed per 100 persons in 2016.

Explore State by State Opioid Prescribing Rates

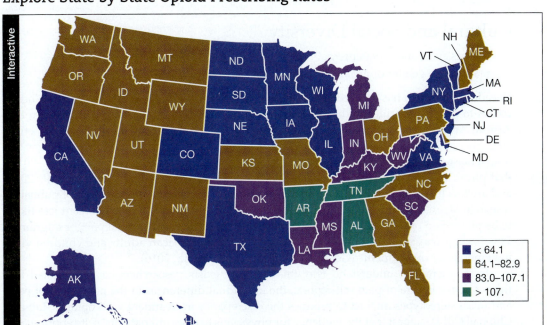

■	< 64.1
■	64.1–82.9
■	83.0–107.1
■	> 107.

In response to the number of opioid-related deaths and addicted individuals, in 2016, the CDC published a set of 12 recommendations regarding the use of opioid treatment for pain (Dowell et al., 2016). Some examples of these recommendations include:

- Nonpharmacologic and nonopioid treatment (i.e., exercise and cognitive behavioral therapy) are the preferred method of treatment for chronic pain.
- Prior to initiating opioid therapy, doctors should establish treatment goals with the patient and regularly monitor progress toward those goals.
- Doctors should prescribe immediate-release opioids instead of extended-release opioids when initiating treatment for acute pain.
- The lowest effective dose should be used first, and only a few pills should be prescribed for the treatment of acute pain. Three days or less should be sufficient, with it being rare that a patient is prescribed opioids for seven days or more.

Variations in Human Functioning

- Is all pain the same?
- Are there different types of chronic pain?

There are several different kinds of chronic pain (Gould, 2007). Click through each of the tabs to learn about the different kinds of chronic pain people can experience.

Types of Chronic Pain

Interactive

Nociceptive: Somatic Pain

Somatic pain is a type of nociceptive pain (detected in the body by specialized sensory receptors called nociceptors). Somatic pain is detected by the sensory nerves in your skin, muscles, and soft tissue.

Examples of Somatic Pain: Tension headaches, Arthritis

Nociceptive: Visceral Pain

Neuropathic Pain

Idiopathic Pain

Cultural and Social Diversity

- Does everyone experience pain in the same way?
- Are there gender or racial inequities in the way opioids are prescribed?

Decades of research has focused on individual differences in the perception of pain. When it comes to racial disparities, a disappointing picture has emerged. Despite the evidence that African Americans have lower pain thresholds and tolerances than Caucasians (Riley et al., 2002; Sheffield et al., 2000; Tait & Chibnall, 2014), there is plenty of data to show that Caucasians hold a biased belief that African Americans feel less pain than others (Trawalter et al., 2012), that physicians underestimate the severity of pain among minorities (Wandner et al., 2012) and are less likely to prescribe opioids for pain relief. After examining 20 years of published research, Meghani et al. (2012) concluded that African Americans were 34 percent less likely to be prescribed opioids for certain conditions such as back or abdominal pain or migraines. This finding was subsequently replicated with African American adults and children visiting emergency departments (Goyal et al., 2015; Singhal et al., 2016).

In an attempt to understand why this disparity exists, researchers have suggested that the subjective nature of pain self-reports, the individual differences in the perception of pain, and racial stereotypes interact to produce the discrepancy in treatment with opioids. Tait and Chibnall (2014) suggest that the tendency for physicians to discount patients' self-reported pain when it is reported to be very high, creates uncertainty about the validity of the patient's report.

Figure 3.20 A Model of Pain Report, Stereotypes, and Opioid Prescriptions

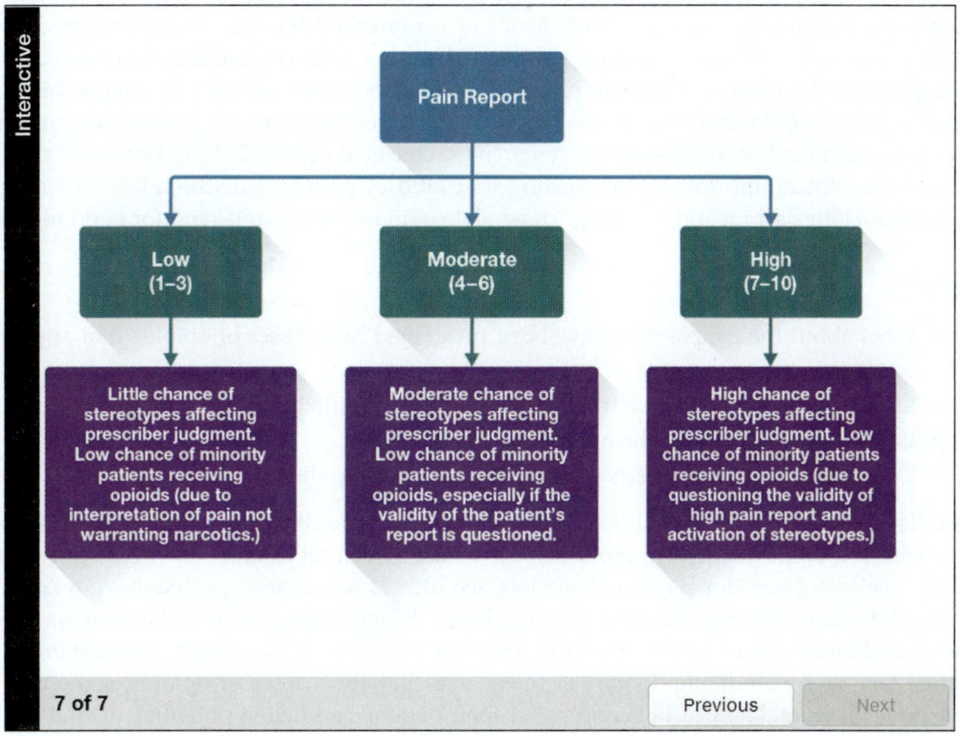

Uncertainty has been shown to activate implicit stereotypes, which benefits those patients who fit the positive stereotype (e.g., Caucasians) and creates disadvantages for those who don't (e.g., African Americans).

Journal Prompt: Your Conclusions

What do you conclude from examining the figure you just completed above? What kinds of changes could be made to modify the outcome for minority patients?

Research Methods

- How is pain researched in laboratory settings?
- Is pain experienced in a lab the same as the pain experienced outside of an artificial environment?

Pain can be experienced in any part of the body and different types of injuries or illnesses produce different types of pain. Laboratory studies are frequently conducted to measure tolerance to pain in an attempt to understand the factors that contribute to differences between people and within the person themselves. Since not all pain is experienced in the same way, some people are more tolerant of certain kinds of pain, which can be influenced by psychological and social factors (Racine et al., 2012b).

Many researchers attempt to mimic acute and chronic pain in the laboratory (Racine et al., 2012a). The following is a list of some of the different types of pain that people can experience:

1. Cold Pain—pain induced by placing a body part (typically hand or arm) into cold water.
2. Heat Pain—pain created through various means of producing heat (e.g., hot water, heat lamp, laser.)
3. Pressure Pain—many studies use a *pressure algometer*, which is a device the monitors the force place on a particular area (tender points or non-tender points) of the body.
4. Muscle Pain—muscular pain that is induced either through exercise or by injecting solutions into the muscles.
5. Electrical Pain—administering electrical stimulation to the skin at various sites on the body.

As discussed earlier, we have different types of pain receptors (i.e., nociceptors) that are sensitive to different types of pain. While people don't typically refer to pain in the way it is mimicked in the laboratory, you have likely heard or experienced the type of pain referred to as: burning, squeezing, twisting, pushing, cramping, buzzing, and/or shocking. Some researchers have questioned whether or not pain produced in the laboratory can truly be used to approximate the pain people experience in real life and have called for more *ecologically valid*, meaning more generalizable to real-life settings, research (Racine et al., 2012a, 2012b). However, you can imagine the ethical implications of creating that kind of pain in a research lab—researchers can't induce long-lasting and, at times, irreversible pain to participants (and for good reason!)

Ethics

- What about the people who have been prescribed high doses of opioids that appear to be effective?
- Is it ethical to discontinue a treatment because the guidelines have changed?
- What about the people who are already addicted?
- Do we, as a society, have any ethical obligation to help them?

There is no question that the United States has a problem with opioids. In 2015, the state of Massachusetts confirmed 1,379 opioid-related deaths, which represented an increase of 41 percent in just two years (for more information, see http://www.mass.gov/eohhs/gov/departments/dph/stop-addiction/current-statistics.html). Federal and state laws have changed and new guidelines (such as those created by the CDC) have been published. While there is no explicit language mandating doctors to lower their patient's doses of opioids, some doctors have done just that, likely out of concern for their patient's addiction potential, overall health, and because of the potential scrutiny of their own prescribing practices. But what about all of the people who are on high doses of opioids (and aren't experiencing the harmful effects of addiction) and as a result are able to function better in life with less pain? A doctor's primary oath is to "do no harm" but there seem to be ethical implications on both sides of this situation.

Journal Prompt: What Do You Think?

Do you think doctors should automatically lower the dose for patients who are prescribed high doses of opioids? Why or why not?

In June 2016, Gloucester, MA Police Chief, Leonard Campanello, opened police station doors to heroin addicts who want help. Addicts are assured they will not be arrested even if drugs are in their possession.

One of the concerns those who work in the field of addictions have about restricting access to prescribed opioids is that it leads people to look to other sources of the drug, such as heroin and other variations bought on the street. Some reports examining the rates of prescription opioids and heroin use have demonstrated that as prescription opioid abuse has decreased in recent years, heroin abuse has been on the rise (Dart et al., 2015). However, others have cautioned against a causal link since it appears that the increase in heroin use preceded many of the state laws regulating opioid prescriptions (Compton et al., 2016).

Regardless of the exact reason, heroin abuse is on the rise and frequently responsible for overdose deaths. Massachusetts, one of the states with a serious opioid abuse problem, is also leading the way in novel approaches to addressing addiction. In 2016, Gloucester Police Chief, Leonard Campenello was honored at the White House as a "Champion of Change" for his program that allows opioid addicts to come into the police station for help. Addicts are promised that they will not be arrested, even if they are possessing drugs, and that they will be connected with a volunteer who is familiar with addiction (often a former drug addict) who will offer moral support and help them find appropriate treatment. Campanello's idea has spread to over 100 other police departments around the country.

Some people question the ethics of allowing someone to avoid arrest. Does this really help solve the problem of addiction, or does it encourage the behavior since people know they won't get arrested if they make their way to the police department? This is a philosophical and ethical dilemma inherent in the *harm reduction* approach movement to the treatment of addiction (see LO 4.10).

Quiz for Module 3.16

1. How long does a person typically have to experience pain to be diagnosed with chronic pain syndrome?

    a. 3–6 weeks   **b.** 4–5 months

    c. 3–6 months   **d.** 4–5 weeks

2. During the period of time from 1999 to 2014, what was the relationship between opioid prescriptions and opioid overdose deaths?

    a. Both prescriptions of opioids and opioid deaths decreased dramatically.

    b. Both prescriptions of opioids and opioid deaths increased dramatically.

    c. As opioid prescriptions increased, the number of opioid overdose deaths actually decreased.

    d. As opioid prescriptions decreased, the number of opioid overdose deaths actually increased.

3. Pain detected by the sensory nerves in your skin, muscles, and soft tissue, which can lead to tension headaches or arthritis, is known as _____.

    a. neuropathic pain   **b.** somatic pain

    c. visceral pain   **d.** idiopathic pain

4. A 34-year-old Black man arrives at the emergency room complaining of severe abdominal pain. What is the likelihood of the man receiving a prescription for opioid pain killers?

    a. He is more likely to be sent to a long-term chronic pain management clinic.

    b. No different than any other race or gender

    c. More likely than if he were not a minority

    d. Less likely than if he were not a minority

5. What is one potential negative side effect of restricting access to prescribed opioids?

    a. People may look to find other sources of the drug such as heroin.

    b. Pharmaceutical companies will stop investing in development of opioids.

    c. People will not be able to afford other non-opioid pain medications.

    d. There will be increased pressure on physicians to prescribe opioids.

Summary: Sensation and Perception

Module 3.1–3.3 The Science of Sensation

Sensation is the process by which our sensory systems detect physical energy from the environment. **Receptor cells** in the sense organs are stimulated by physical energy, which is converted to electrical signals through a process called **transduction**. This sensory information is selected, organized, and interpreted by the brain during the process of **perception**.

    Psychophysics is the study of the relationship between physical characteristics of stimuli and the sensory experiences that accompany them. Some important concepts in psychophysics include the **absolute threshold**, which refers to the smallest amount of energy needed for an individual to detect a stimulus at least 50 percent of the time. Not everyone has the same absolute threshold and **signal detection theory** attempts to explain the factors involved in the varying responses people have to stimuli. The **difference threshold** involves the minimum detectable difference between two stimuli that occurs at least 50 percent of the time. The difference threshold is also referred to as the **just noticeable difference**. **Weber's Law** refers to the fact that the difference threshold varies proportionally to the initial size of the stimulus. It is possible for stimuli to fall below an individual's absolute threshold, yet still be perceived at an unconscious level. This experience of **subliminal perception** can have a limited influence on future behavior, which is known as **subliminal persuasion**. Prolonged exposure to an unchanging stimulus can lead to **sensory adaptation**, where the senses stop registering the existence of the stimulus and therefore the stimulus is no longer perceived.

Module 3.4–3.6 The Visual System

Vision is a sense that tends to decay with age. **Presbyopia** is characterized by blurred vision, which typically occurs after the age of 35. Vision is based on the availability of light, which is described in terms of **wavelengths** in the electromagnetic spectrum. Light enters the eye through the **cornea**, which is the eye's protective cover. It then travels through the **pupil**, a small hole in the eye that is controlled by the **iris**, the colored muscle that dilates or constricts depending on the amount of light. The **lens** lies behind the pupil and accommodates, or changes shape, to focus the image on the **retina**. The retina is the receptor-heavy tissue at the back of the eye that converts the light energy into neural signals to be sent to the brain. There are two types of photoreceptors in the retina: the **rods** are found in the periphery of the retina and respond to varying degrees of light and dark; and the **cones**, which are located more toward the center, or **fovea** of the retina and are responsible for detecting the color and clarity of objects. When light strikes the retina, the neural images are passed through a series of receptor cells to the **optic nerve**, which travels out of the eye to the brain for processing. There are no receptors on the retina where the optic nerve leaves the eye, creating a **blind spot** in the visual field. Half of the visual information from each eye crosses in the brain at the **optic chiasm.** The brain receptors work simultaneously, known as **parallel processing**, to determine various features at the same time. Certain areas of the brain contain specialized receptors for particular tasks. Damage to particular areas of the primary visual cortex can cause blindness in certain parts of the field of vision. Some people have experienced a condition referred to as **blindsight**, where they report no conscious ability to see yet appear to be aware of what was in their visual field.

Color can be characterized by its **hue** (the actual wavelength of light that hits the eye), its **saturation** (richness of the color), and its **brightness** which is affected by the amplitude, or height of the wavelengths of light. When talking about color, it is important to distinguish between the color of objects and the color of light. Objects reflect light and therefore mixing paints is considered a **subtractive color mixture** process because some of the reflected light is being removed once paint colors are mixed. Color mixing with light is referred to as **additive color mixture** because white surfaces reflect all light and adding in other light increases the amount of reflected light.

There are two primary theories of color vision. The **trichromatic theory of color vision** proposes that there are three different types of cones (blue, green, and red) and the perception of color comes from the combination and relative strength of stimulation between the cones. The trichromatic theory of color vision has been useful in explaining color deficiency. The trichromatic theory doesn't sufficiently explain **afterimages**; an image that remains in the visual field after the stimulus has been removed. **Negative afterimages** are afterimages that appear in the colors that are opposite to what was originally presented. Afterimages are typically noticed because of **microsaccades**, the frequent, small, jerky movements made by the eyes. The **opponent-process theory** explained the phenomenon of afterimages by suggesting that humans have three pairs of special receptors (blue/yellow; red/green; black/white) that work in an opposing manner. Color vision occurs as a result of processes explained by both theories with the trichromatic theory occurring primarily in the retina and the opponent-process theory taking place in the brain.

Module 3.7–3.8   The Auditory System

Hearing occurs as a result of **sound waves** in the environment. The **frequency** refers to the pitch of a sound, the **amplitude** refers to volume, and the **timbre** represents the quality and complexity of tone. The **sound shadow** cast by our heads helps to determine location of sounds. Sound waves are funneled through the outer ear to the **ear drum**, causing it to vibrate. The vibrations are sent through the middle ear via the three small bones, the hammer, anvil, and stirrup on to the oval window and **cochlea** of the inner ear. The fluid in the cochlea moves, causing ripples in the **basilar membrane**, a part of the cochlea that is lined with hair cells. The tips of the hair cells contain **cilia**, which stimulate receptor cells and send auditory messages to the brain. **Place theory,** a theory of hearing which states that different pitches activate different sets of hair cells along the cochlea's basilar membrane, seems to best explain hearing high-pitched sounds. With respect to lower-pitched sounds, the **frequency theory** suggests that they are heard based on the rate of firing of the neurons. The **volley principle** takes into account the finite speed that neurons can fire, and suggests that neurons take turns firing to produce the signal that is then interpreted by the brain. Individuals can experience three types of hearing loss including: **sensorineural hearing loss**, which results from damage to the inner ear or nerve pathways to the brain; **conductive hearing loss** is more of a mechanical problem where the sound is not conducted properly from the outer ear to the middle ear; and **mixed hearing loss** involves a combination of both

sensorineural and conductive hearing loss. **Cochlear implants** are most effective for sensorineural hearing loss and appear to be most efficacious if implanted when children are young.

Module 3.9–3.10   The Chemical and Body Senses

Olfaction (smell) and taste are intertwined senses. Odor molecules in the air travel to the top of nasal cavity where receptors convert the stimuli to messages for the olfactory nerve to carry to the brain for processing. Taste receptors, or **taste buds**, are embedded in the bumps on the tongue, referred to as **papillae**.

The **gate control theory of pain** suggests that while small nerve fibers sense pain and open the gate of the pain pathway, large nerve fibers will respond to normal sensations of touch and pressure that can inhibit the pain by closing the gate. Effective pain management often includes addressing the sensory aspect of pain, the affective-motivational component of pain, and the cognitive-evaluative dimension of an individual's pain.

Module 3.11–3.15   The Science of Perception

The perception of sensation is a complex process that involves both raw data from the environment combined with knowledge and experience of the individual. **Bottom-up processing** starts perception from sensing the basic stimuli in the environment and is followed by interpretation by the brain. **Top-down processing** starts from the brain and uses an individual's knowledge, experiences, and expectations, to guide the interpretation of stimuli in the environment. Accuracy in perception is guided by **perceptual constancy**, the idea that our perception of a stimulus remains the same even though some characteristics of the stimuli may have changed. **Size constancy, color constancy,** and **shape constancy** are examples of perceptual constancies. Previous experiences or expectations, which is referred to as **perceptual set**, can influence the way things are perceived and offer some explanation for individual differences in perception of everyday experiences as in the case of ambiguous figures.

Perception has been explained by Gestalt principles, which involves seeing objects as wholes rather than parts. Perception involves being able to distinguish the **figure**, or object of focus, from the **ground**, or its surroundings. **Reversible figures** often have interchangeable figure and ground making perception difficult. Gestalt principles include those of: **proximity** (perceiving objects that are close together as part of a group); **similarity** (perceiving similar objects as part of a pattern or group); **closure** (perceiving images as complete objects even if they are incomplete); and **continuity** (perceiving intersecting lines as a pattern rather than separate lines).

Depth perception involves the ability to judge distances of objects and to see them in three-dimensions. Many indicators including oculomotor cues, monocular cues, and binocular cues are used to inform the perception of depth. **Oculomotor cues** involve cues directly from your eyes including **convergence**, the extent to which your eyes move inward the closer an object appears. **Monocular cues** are sometimes referred to as pictorial cues and are those that are seen by just one eye. **Linear perspective, relative size, relative height, interposition, and texture gradient** are all examples of stationary monocular cues for depth. When moving, **motion parallax**, or the sense that objects further away are moving more slowly, is an important cue for depth perception. **Binocular cues** involve the use of both eyes. **Retinal disparity** involves the slightly different retinal image received by both eyes and provides an important cue for perceiving depth. Perception is a constructive process and **perceptual illusions**, where the stimulus is different than the experience of the event, can result at the sensory or perceptual level. Perceptual illusions can be classified as either **literal** (physical), **physiological**, or **cognitive**. The **Müller-Lyer illusion** is a well-known optical illusion of size that has yet to be fully explained by science.

Chapter 3 Quiz

1. Which of the following is a good example of a physiological illusion?

   a. A rainbow

   b. Müller-Lyer illusion

   c. Rubin Vase

   d. Afterimages

2. Strong bright lights will cause sensory neurons to _____ fire while dim low lights will cause sensory neurons to _____ fire.

   a. slowly; rapidly   **c.** strongly; weakly

   b. rapidly; slowly   **d.** weakly; strongly

3. Which part of the ear carries the message to the brain?

   a. Hammer, anvil, and stirrup

   b. Cochlea

   c. Basilar membrane

   d. Auditory nerve

4. What is the function of the outer ear?

   a. To protect our ears from loud sounds

   b. To vibrate the middle ear bones

   c. To funnel sound waves to the ear drum

   d. To funnel sound waves to the cochlea

5. The interpretation of raw stimuli from our senses into meaningful information is called _____.

   a. sensation

   b. perception

   c. transduction

   d. neuron communication

6. Leander was really hungry before being interviewed about his study habits. Researchers whispered "taco truck" several times during his interview although he didn't hear the words. He was then given the opportunity to eat food from a taco truck or from the cafeteria. Leander would most likely choose the taco truck. He was subjected to what researchers call _____.

   a. subliminal priming   **c.** subliminal persuasion

   b. subliminal perception   **d.** manipulation

7. Weber's law states that detectable differences between stimuli involve the _____ difference between them.

   a. actual

   b. absolute

   c. minimal

   d. percentage

8. According to the visual cliff experiment, when can most humans judge depth?

   a. By the time they can walk

   b. By the time they can crawl

   c. At 36 months of age

   d. At 18 months of age

9. List the three layers of cells in the correct order that transmit neural signals from the retina to the optic nerve.

   a. Nasal retina, rods and cones, bipolar cells

   b. Ganglion cells, rods, nasal retina

   c. Cones, ganglion cells, bipolar cells

   d. Rods and cones, bipolar cells, ganglion cells

10. Helmut is at a crowded park walking his dog. He is looking for a friend and finally sees his friend's face among the crowd. He is using his _____ neurons to detect faces.

    a. feature detector

    b. simple cell

    c. nasal retina

    d. complex facial

11. Mixing objects (such as paint) is referred to as _____ color mixing; whereas, mixing colors of light is called _____ color mixing.

    a. subtractive; additive

    b. trichromatic; opponent process

    c. opponent process; trichromatic

    d. additive; subtractive

12. You are attending a lecture with your friend but can't quite hear what the presenter is saying. Once your friend tells you the title of the lecture is "Psychology in Oscar-Winning Movies," you are able to understand much more of what was being said. This is an example of _____.

    a. bottom-up processing   b. top-down processing
    c. parallel processing   d. perceptual constancy

13. The _____ is the colored muscle of the eye that dilates and constricts according to the amount of light.

    a. lens   b. iris
    c. pupil   d. retina

14. Kendra likes to listen to soft music while studying. Each time her roommate Layla comes in, Layla turns the music up by one. Kendra doesn't always notice the change, but she does notice it more than 50 percent of the time. This is an example of _____.

    a. sensory receptor change
    b. Weber's law
    c. just noticeable difference
    d. absolute threshold

15. The place theory of hearing explains _____; the frequency theory explains _____; and the volley principle explains _____.

    a. high frequencies; low frequencies; low and moderate frequencies
    b. low frequencies; high frequencies; low and moderate frequencies
    c. moderate frequencies; high frequencies; low frequencies
    d. low frequencies; low and moderate frequencies; high frequencies

16. Marcus loves to listen to music, podcasts, and radio talk shows. He usually falls asleep while listening to something on the Internet and has his earphones in almost 5–6 hours a day. He has noticed lately that he seems to be asking his wife to repeat what she said several times before he can hear it. What type of hearing loss may Marcus be experiencing?

    a. Sensorineural hearing loss
    b. Conductive hearing loss
    c. Mixed hearing loss
    d. Nerve deafness

17. Where are the olfactory receptor sites located?

    a. At the bottom of the nasal cavity
    b. At the top of the nasal cavity
    c. Behind the sinus cavities
    d. In the semicircular canals

18. Anita has a severe reaction to chili peppers—they actually cause her pain—and she finds kale and broccoli too bitter to eat, while oranges are too sweet. Anita may have many more taste buds than the average person, which would make her a _____.

    a. testtaster   b. supertester
    c. supertaster   d. tastemaster

19. Preterm infants have been found to thrive when their sense of _____ is stimulated by their mother.

    a. vision   b. sound
    c. taste   d. touch

20. Which sense originates in the inner ear and can cause you to lose your balance when you have an ear infection?

    a. Vestibular sense
    b. Kinesthetic sense
    c. Skin sense
    d. Hearing

21. Which theory of color vision states that we have three special receptor cells to process color that work in an opposing manner?

    a. Trichromatic theory
    b. Opponent process theory
    c. Opposite receptor cell theory
    d. Afterimage theory

22. The _____ is comprised of multilayered tissue at the back of the eye and is responsible for visual transduction.

    a. receptor cells   b. lens
    c. retina   d. cornea

23. Stephan convinced his friend Derek that if he played a Beatles song backward, he would hear it whispering, "Worship Satan." Derek tried it and did hear the words "Worship Satan." Derek's perception of these words was probably influenced by _____.

    a. perceptual constancy
    b. bottom-up processing
    c. perceptual set
    d. perceptual processing

24. What concept explains how a person can perceive lines in a diagram, even though distinct lines are not actually part of the diagram?

    a. Perceptual set
    b. Color constancy
    c. Size constancy
    d. Illusory contour

25. What does the term Gestalt mean for psychological purposes?

a. It refers to how we naturally group objects together and perceive whole shapes instead of individual parts.

b. It refers to how individual parts must be broken down before the whole shape can be understood.

c. It refers to the science of understanding perception and processing.

d. It refers to the constant changing nature of shapes and objects.

26. When a person is shown a series of disconnected curved lines in a circular pattern, the brain will interpret it as a circle. Which Gestalt principle is this example illustrating?

a. Closure   b. Proximity

c. Similarity   d. Figure ground

27. Most perception involves which type of processing?

a. Bottom-up processing

b. Both bottom-up and top-down processing

c. Top-down processing

d. Perceptual set processing

28. Humans receive images on their retinas from two slightly different angles. This binocular cue is referred to as

_____.

a. convergence   b. interposition

c. retinal disparity   d. monocular cues

29. Research has determined that our brain is capable of sensing stimuli without conscious awareness of that stimuli. This is called _____.

a. subliminal perception

b. subliminal persuasion

c. unconscious detection

d. subliminal advertising

30. Why has the Müller-Lyer Illusion intrigued psychological researchers for years?

a. There are reliable cultural differences in perception of the illusion, but no consensus regarding why the differences exist.

b. There are reliable gender differences, with women being more apt to see visual illusions.

c. Babies can see the illusion even before they can talk.

d. The illusion is more prevalent in non-Western countries.

Chapter 4
Consciousness

Chapter Outline and Learning Objectives

Module 4.1–4.2: What is Consciousness?

LO 4.1 Describe the different states of consciousness.

LO 4.2 Identify the different aspects of attention involved in consciousness.

Module 4.3–4.7: Sleep and Dreaming

LO 4.3 Explain how the circadian rhythm is related to sleep.

LO 4.4 Describe the function of sleep and consequences of sleep deprivation.

LO 4.5 Differentiate the various stages of sleep in the sleep cycle.

LO 4.6 Distinguish the various sleep disorders and their treatments.

LO 4.7 Recognize the different theories proposed to explain the function of dreams.

Module 4.8–4.10: Psychoactive Drugs

LO 4.8 Recognize the symptoms associated with a substance use disorder.

LO 4.9 Differentiate depressant and stimulant psychoactive drugs and their effects on the body.

LO 4.10 Describe the effects of narcotic and hallucinogenic psychoactive drugs.

Module 4.11: Piecing It Together: Hypnosis

LO 4.11 Analyze how the cross-cutting themes of psychology apply to hypnosis.

Daydreaming, Sleepwalking, and Murder

Your Different Levels of Consciousness

Interactive

Have you ever had the experience of driving home only to realize once you got there that you had no memory of *actually* driving home?

○ Yes

○ No

Has anybody ever told you that you sleepwalk?

○ Yes

○ No

Scott Falater was an average man. He had a wife and family, was an active member of the local church, and worked as a product engineer at a nearby plant. However, on January 19, 1997, he brutally stabbed his wife to death. A neighbor witnessed the scene and informed police, who arrested Falater on the spot. In a strange twist, however, Scott Falater claimed to have been sleepwalking during the murder. Officials were confused. No one could determine a motive for the act; in fact, Falater's sister and close friends of the family described the marriage as a happy one and the relationship between husband and wife as warm and affectionate. But how could a man carry out such a precise crime—even going so far as to hide the body and eliminate incriminating evidence—in his sleep? The jury didn't see how this was possible either, and Falater was convicted of first-degree murder and sentenced to life in prison without the possibility of parole.

In a similar case, but with a different outcome, Kenneth Parks drove 14 miles to his mother-in-law's house and stabbed her to death while she slept. Parks was asleep and claimed to have been sleepwalking throughout the entire ordeal, waking at some point on the drive home. Covered in blood, he went to a nearby police station looking for help. Experts testified that Parks's brain activity during his sleep was extremely abnormal and not able to be faked. In 1992, he was acquitted for the murder. Parks experienced an abnormal state of consciousness that led to tragic results for his family.

Scott Falater claimed to have murdered his wife while sleepwalking. The jury found him guilty of murder and he is currently still serving life in prison in Arizona.

Module 4.1–4.2: What is Consciousness?

Have you ever tried to define consciousness? It's not an easy task. Rather than a precise definition, you might generate examples that involve an experience of consciousness—that moment when you were just about to fall asleep and said something that made no sense, or a time when your consciousness was divided, and you drove all the way home and then realized you had no memory of it because you were busy thinking about something else. Consciousness can be a mystical and intriguing concept. In fact, its complexity was a career changer for one of your author's, Dr. Hudson's, husband. After graduating from business school, he worked as a senior financial analyst, with no intention of leaving the corporate world—until he saw a daytime talk show where a doctor was working with a patient with chronic pain. At first, the patient had difficulty moving due to intense

One way acupuncture can affect states of consciousness is by producing a relaxation response.

consciousness

awareness of the internal and external environment

meditation

an alerted state of consciousness that may involve focused and regulated breathing, specific body positions, minimization of external distractions, mental imagery, and/or mental clarity

focused attention meditation

type of meditation that involves directing attention toward an object for the entire meditation session

back pain. After a short time, without taking any medicine, the patient was mobile and reported feeling little to no pain. What happened? How was this possible? It turns out the patient had a session of acupuncture to help manage the pain.

Dr. Hudson's husband was so intrigued that he eventually quit his job and went back to school to study Chinese medicine and acupuncture, which has been his career ever since.

States of Consciousness

LO 4.1   Describe the different states of consciousness.

Most psychologists define **consciousness** as the awareness of our internal and external environment; however, this definition may be deceptively straightforward. The study of consciousness is one of the few topics that remains firmly rooted in both psychology and philosophy. René Descartes, the 17th-century French philosopher, is famous for his statement on consciousness: "I think, therefore I am." Descartes was convinced the mind, or what he referred to as the soul, was separate from the body. Although Descartes's hypothesis was subsequently disproved, the debate about consciousness still exists.

The debate has shifted to include neuroscience, offering newer theories in an attempt to unlock the mystery of consciousness. For some, like philosopher David Chalmers, consciousness is more than the sum of the parts of the brain. However, defining exactly *what* that is can be more difficult. He writes, "There is nothing that we know more intimately than conscious experience, but there is nothing that is harder to explain" (Chalmers, 1995). For others, like the modern-day philosopher Patricia Churchland, consciousness is merely a problem to be solved by science in the same way many puzzles of the past were explained (e.g., in the 17th century, it was believed that light wasn't physical and must occur outside of the laws of nature.) Churchland believes that eventually neuroscience will show that consciousness is simply a matter of different brain states (Burkeman, 2015).

We each look at the world from a slightly different perspective; therefore, our observations and experiences tend to be subjective. Since none of us see the world, or ourselves, in the same way, it is likely that consciousness is a unique experience for every person.

Consciousness can be divided into two groups: *waking consciousness*, in which an individual is alert and aware of his or her surroundings, and *altered states of consciousness*, which represent any measure of arousal different from the normal waking state. Altered states of consciousness can range from sleeping to a decreased level of consciousness because of depressant drugs or alcohol or an increased state of consciousness arising from intense exercise, stimulant use, or sensation-seeking behaviors. Watch the following video, *Altered States of Consciousness*, for an explanation of what occurs in the brain during these different levels of consciousness.

An altered state of consciousness doesn't just refer to someone who is *unconscious*. As you saw in the last video, many activities can produce an altered state of consciousness, which will be discussed throughout the remainder of this chapter. One such activity involves the practice of meditation (Srinivasan, 2015; Thomas & Cohen, 2014). **Meditation** may involve focused and regulated breathing, specific body positions, minimization of external distractions, mental imagery, and/or mental clarity. Meditation has been described as an approach to train the mind, similar to the way exercise and fitness is used to train the body (Inner IDEA, 2014). Meditation has been practiced since ancient times and was typically associated with religious traditions or beliefs. Today, meditation is a collective term, analogous to our use of the word "sports" and does not necessarily have a religious component. Dr. Richard Davidson, from the University of Wisconsin-Madison, created the Center for Healthy Minds, which uses science and meditation to discover how the mind can enhance well-being and relieve suffering.

There are numerous different types of meditation, most of which fall into one of two general categories: (1) focused attention meditation and (2) open monitoring meditation. **Focused attention meditation** involves directing attention toward an object for the entire meditation session. The object may be internal (e.g., the breath) or external (e.g., a rock), and the session

Altered States of Consciousness

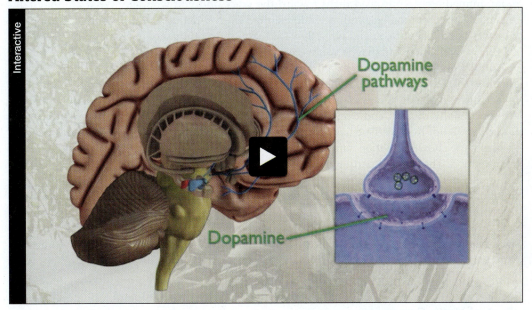

may last for hours. The idea is to focus your attention in a way that blocks out all distractions (which can be extremely difficult, if you have never tried it.) *Samatha*, a type of meditation practiced by Buddhists, is an example of focused meditation. **Open monitoring meditation** doesn't focus on just one object or experience. Instead, you become a nonjudgmental observer of all aspects of experience (e.g., thoughts, emotions, sounds.) You recognize and acknowledge all the experiences within and around you, but do not judge or attempt to change any of them (also, incredibly difficult to do when you first try it.) Mindfulness meditation is probably the most well-known form of open monitoring meditation and is incorporated into several treatments for psychological disorders. You might think the goal of meditation practice is to become drowsy and in a trance-like state, but experienced practitioners often describe an altered state of consciousness that includes a *heightened* sensitivity and awareness of their life and environment (Kabat-Zinn, 2005).

open monitoring meditation
type of meditation that involves nonjudgmental observation of all aspects of experience (e.g., thoughts, emotions, sounds)

Selective Attention, Inattention, and Divided Attention

LO 4.2   **Identify the different aspects of attention involved in consciousness.**

Our ability to be conscious of information, and to move some pieces of information in and out of consciousness as necessary, gives us a significant advantage when it comes to survival. If we were completely unaware of ourselves and our environments, we wouldn't last long in a group of predators (or on a four-lane highway.) At the same time, if we were conscious of everything going on around and inside us, we would likely be completely overwhelmed and unable to function effectively. Fortunately for us, we're able to focus our consciousness by paying attention only to the most important things at a given time.

SELECTIVE ATTENTION   Thanks to complex neural processes in our brain, we don't waste our attention on information not immediately relevant to our situations. This restrictive function allows us to exercise **selective attention**, or a conscious focus on one stimulus or perception at a given time. For example, when you take an exam, selective attention allows you to focus on reading and answering the questions without becoming preoccupied by the feeling of your shirt against your skin or the pressure of the pencil against your finger. Selective attention is also responsible for what has been referred to as the **cocktail party phenomenon**, or our ability to selectively tune *into* particular messages while filtering out others in a crowded, noisy, or chaotic environment (Arons, 1992; Bronkhorst, 2015). You have most likely experienced the cocktail party phenomenon when you were talking with a friend or small group of people in a large gathering. You may have been listening intently to your friend's description of the

selective attention
a conscious focus on one stimulus or perception at a given time

cocktail party phenomenon
ability to selectively tune into particular messages while filtering out others in a crowded, noisy, or chaotic environment

latest movie he just saw and then suddenly hear someone mention your name from across the room. Immediately, your head turns toward the voice and you wonder, "What are they talking about?" In that moment, your attention shifted from listening to your friend to finding out who was talking about you and what they said. You didn't think you were paying attention to another conversation, but maybe you were?

Intuitively, it makes sense that in order to be aware of something, you have to first pay attention to it (Cohen et al., 2012; Mole, 2008). However, this idea has not been widely accepted. In fact, many researchers now claim that although attention and consciousness are related, they are functionally distinct and even operate at different stages of cognitive processing (Eimer & Grubert, 2015; Koch & Tsuchiya, 2012; Norman et al., 2013). In support of this perspective, studies have shown attention can occur without awareness—and awareness can occur without attention. The cocktail party phenomenon is an example of *attention without awareness* and subliminal perception is an example of *awareness without attention*. In the case of subliminal perception, a person has actually perceived something, but it occurred at a level below conscious perception. Therefore, the person may experience awareness of a phenomenon without having paid any conscious attention to the situation. In the activity *A Test of Your Concentration*, you'll see a number of people passing a basketball. Watch the video and count how many times the team wearing black shirts passes the ball.

A Test of Your Concentration

selective inattention/
inattentional blindness

environmental stimuli that are screened out or ignored while attention is selectively focused on something else

As you may have experienced in the video you just watched, **selective inattention**, or *inattentional blindness*, is the flipside of selective attention, which refers to the environmental stimuli screened out or ignored while your attention is selectively focused on something else. This phenomenon can be seen in action much more, now that smartphones have become so intricately woven into daily life. How many times have you seen someone (or a video of someone) walking and texting only to walk into a pole, another person, or even worse, fall into a manhole or fountain? You may have even had an unfortunate experience like this at some point in your life. You *think* you are paying attention to your surroundings, but in reality you are blind to certain aspects of your environment because your attention is focused on something else.

Several classic studies have demonstrated the strength of selective inattention. Beginning in the 1970s, researchers demonstrated people can "miss" the detection of unexpected events when asked to perform an attentional task while watching a video (Neisser & Becklen, 1975).

In a variation of his original research, Neisser (1979) describes a study where he showed a video of six basketball players (three in black shirts and three in white shirts) passing a ball back and forth and asked participants to pay attention to only one team of players and press a bar each time the ball was passed. After about 30 seconds, when the participant is engrossed in the activity, a woman carrying an open umbrella walks right through the middle of the scene (for a total of four seconds). Only 21 percent of the participants reported noticing the woman with the umbrella, even when they were directly asked about it at the end of the study!

Is it possible the woman with the umbrella was just not "noticeable" enough? In another variant of this study, Simons and Chabris (1999) added a condition with a different unexpected stimulus. One condition included a woman with an umbrella walking through the scene, and the other condition involved a person wearing a gorilla suit walking through the scene, turning to the camera, thumping its chest, and walking off (just like the re-creation you watched at the beginning of this section). In this comparison, even fewer people noticed the gorilla (44 percent) than the woman with the umbrella (65 percent).

What accounts for the difference between those who see the unexpected event and those who don't? It has been shown that this phenomenon is a limit of perception, not memory (Ward & Scholl, 2015) and that children are more likely to experience inattentional blindness, especially when asked to engage in more cognitively taxing tasks (Remington et al., 2014). Some psychologists have suggested that being skilled at the task or having a level of expertise (e.g., being a basketball player) can protect against inattentional blindness (Becklen & Cervone, 1983; Memmert, 2006). In a cleverly titled paper, "The invisible gorilla strikes again: Sustained inattentional blindness in expert observers," researchers asked radiologists (doctors who are trained to detect small changes) to search through lung CT scans and identify any lung nodules (i.e., areas of concern). In the final set of scans, the researchers inserted an image of a gorilla into the lung that was 48 times the average size of a nodule (look in the top right corner of the photo on the left if you are having trouble spotting the gorilla).

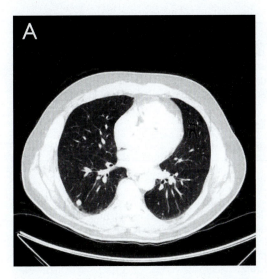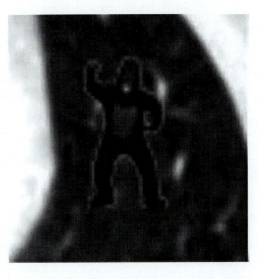

The photo on the left is the actual stimuli used in the Drew et al. (2013) research with radiologists. The photo on the right is a close-up of the gorilla image added to the lung.

The findings were quite remarkable: 83 percent of radiologists tested failed to notice the gorilla embedded in the CT scans even though all participants reported they could see the gorilla after it was pointed out at the end of the study (Drew et al., 2013).

Most people wonder how they can miss something that seems so obvious once it is pointed out to them. **Change blindness** is a form of inattentional blindness where the visual stimuli in the environment change during a moment of interruption but go unnoticed by the

change blindness

a form of selective inattention where large changes in the environment are overlooked resulting from a break in the visual field or lack of attention observer. This inability to detect large changes in the environment between glances suggests we retain very little visual information in short-term memory (Gibbs et al., 2016; Simons & Levin, 1997). As with selective inattention, most people aren't aware of how much they miss in their environment because most of us believe we are good at multitasking and therefore can pay attention to everything around us.

multitasking

attention divided among two or more stimuli or activities

DIVIDED ATTENTION: "I'M REALLY GOOD AT MULTITASKING"   There has never been a time in history where so many people regularly engage in **multitasking**, which is nothing more than attention divided among two or more stimuli or activities. The millennial generation (people born between the 1980s and early 2000s) appears to be defined by their "ability" to multitask because they can squeeze 10 hours and 45 minutes of media content into 7 hours and 30 minutes of actual media usage (Rideout et al., 2010).

While there are situations where multitasking is possible, especially when engaging in well-learned tasks or activities that don't require much cognitive attention (Chinchanachokchai et al., 2015; Medeiros-Ward et al., 2014), in many other situations the consequences of multitasking can be negative and even deadly. Despite that fact that many people believe multitasking is beneficial and they are good at it (Carrier et al., 2015; Grinols & Rajesh, 2014), study after study has shown that multitasking during lecture, class, or while studying interferes with learning and leads to lower grades and GPA in college (Hembrooke & Gay, 2003; Junco, 2012; Junco & Cotten, 2012; Karpinski et al., 2012).

Similar, but even more tragic results have been found when examining the effects of multitasking (i.e., texting/talking on a cell phone) while driving. Drivers distracted by cell phones are 2–4 times more likely to be involved in a crash, and inexperienced drivers appear to be at the highest risk (Klauer et al., 2014; Llerena et al., 2014; Stavrinos et al., 2013). Despite laws in some places requiring the driver to use a hands-free device for talking, there has been no difference between the two methods in terms of their likelihood of contributing to a crash (Fitch et al., 2013). Distracted driving stems from the impaired cognition caused by the redirection of attention from the road to the phone conversation—not by whether or not a person is holding the phone while talking.

Journal Prompt: Multitasking and Driving

Many people think they are good at multitasking and therefore can "handle" texting and driving. What information presented in this chapter so far suggests people are inaccurate in their perceptions of their multitasking abilities?

Quiz for Module 4.1–4.2

1. Most psychologists define consciousness as the awareness of our _____ and _____ environment.
   a. brain; physical
   b. internal; external
   c. mind; social
   d. brain; familial

2. This altered state of consciousness involves training the mind by using focused and regulated breathing, minimization of distractions, and mental imagery.
   a. Hypnosis
   b. Medication
   c. Brain training
   d. Meditation

3. Syed is sitting in a bustling restaurant listening to his friend talk about the test he just took. Syed is interested in the conversation because he is taking the test tomorrow but all of a sudden his interest is drawn across the room because he heard his name spoken. This is called _____.
   a. change blindness
   b. focused attention
   c. cocktail party phenomenon
   d. attention deficit phenomenon

4. Sasha has her laptop open in class and is watching funny cat videos while the professor talks. After class is over, she hears the other students talking about the quiz they are having Friday. Which phenomenon explains why Sasha didn't hear her professor talk about the quiz?
   a. Selective attention
   b. Selective inattention
   c. Multitasking
   d. Selective consciousness

5. Multiple studies have shown that when students multitask during class or studying:
   a. they do not learn effectively, which leads to lower grades.
   b. they complete homework more quickly because they are more productive.
   c. they are rewarded with a higher GPA.
   d. they perceive that they struggle to learn but actually perform better on exams.

Module 4.3–4.7: Sleep and Dreaming

Sleep has long been an intriguing topic to many people. A few years ago, the only "real" way to measure the quality or quantity of sleep was to participate in an expensive and inconvenient sleep study at a local hospital. While this is still the most accurate way to obtain sleep data, especially if you are being evaluated for a sleep problem, many of us who are just curious about our own sleep patterns have turned to sleep tracking devices.

Many people have found the information presented from these devices to be enlightening and have been able to use the data to modify their own sleep patterns. One of your authors did just that a few years ago. Realizing she was not getting a healthy amount of sleep each night, she set a goal to average at least 7 hours of sleep a night. With the help of a sleep tracking device, she was able to modify her own behavior to the point of sleeping, on average, 7 hours and 10 minutes each night! It was a small victory, but one that has numerous health benefits.

There are many forms of sleep tracking devices available that can provide relatively accurate information about sleep quantity and quality.

Our Biological Clock

LO 4.3 **Explain how the circadian rhythm is related to sleep.**

Sleep, or the daily, natural loss of consciousness, is just one of the important bodily functions controlled by our brain. Our bodies operate according to a **circadian rhythm**, which can be thought of as biological clock that regulates various bodily functions on an approximately 24-hour cycle. Circa is Latin for "about a" or "around" and diēs means "day." Not only does our circadian rhythm affect whether we are awake or asleep, it's also responsible for changes in our body temperatures and levels of arousal during periods of sleep and wakefulness. Our body temperature, and therefore our alertness, rises in the morning, peaks during the day, and declines both in early afternoon (ever had a 2 p.m. class?) and before we go to sleep. Research suggests thinking and memory peak consistently with circadian arousal. While this peak occurs at different times for different people (Fabbri et al., 2013), it seems to occur at increasingly earlier times of the day as we age (Knight & Mather, 2013). This explains why many older adults rise at dawn, eat dinner by 5 p.m., and are asleep by 8 or 9 p.m. Moreover, research also indicates young adults experience an improvement in performance throughout the day, but older adults experience a decline in performance throughout the day (May & Hasher, 1998). This data helps explain why many traditionally-aged college students report they feel lively and energetic at night but struggle to make it to 9 a.m. classes.

The following video, *Circadian Rhythms*, provides a brief overview of how the sleep rhythms work and the factors that affect them. As described in the video, circadian rhythms are an inherent part of our biology; however, they are not immune to effects from external factors. For example, light can alter or reset our circadian clocks. How? When light hits the eye, it activates

sleep

the daily, natural loss of consciousness controlled by the brain

circadian rhythm

biological clock that regulates various bodily functions on approximately a 24-hour cycle

Circadian Rhythms

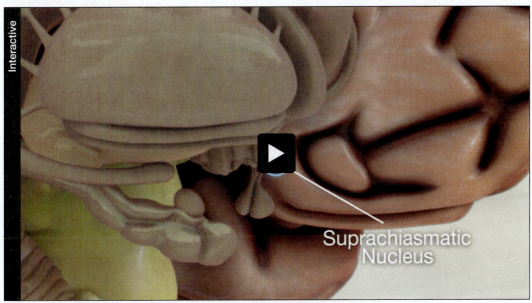

Suprachiasmatic Nucleus

suprachiasmatic nucleus (SCN)

small part of the hypothalamus that controls the circadian clock

light-sensitive proteins in the retina. These in turn signal the **suprachiasmatic nucleus (SCN)**—the small part of the hypothalamus that controls the circadian clock. The suprachiasmatic nucleus sits on top of the optic chiasm, which is how it got its name. Supra is Latin for "above," and you can see the word "chiasm" in the name as well. When put together, you get "above the chiasm." The suprachiasmatic nucleus causes the *pineal gland* to either increase (in the evening) or decrease (in the morning) the production of *melatonin*, a sleep-inducing hormone.

Brain Structures Involved in Sleep

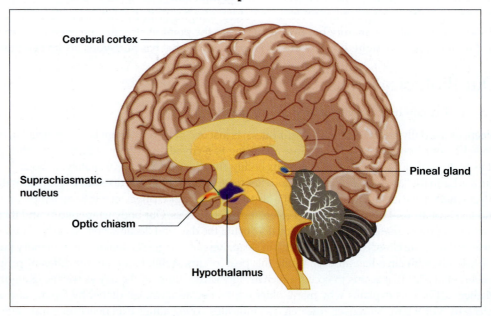

When we stay up until 1 a.m. reading or socializing in a well-lit place, we're exposed to artificial light, which tricks our brain into producing less melatonin at a time when it should be producing more, delaying sleep and pushing back our biological clocks (Jones et al., 2015). As a result, many young people today operate on a 25-hour cycle because they stay up late and don't rise until late morning or early afternoon. This doesn't just happen to humans: Most animals placed under a constant light source will develop a biological clock that lasts more than 24 hours per day (De Coursey, 1960; Oren & Terman, 1998). Therefore, natural light serves an important purpose by resetting our biological clock back to a 24-hour cycle. This is the reason the advice for managing jet lag involves staying up until a reasonable bed time in the new time zone, and then immersing yourself in natural light the next day. These two strategies will help override your circadian rhythm (from the previous time zone) by resetting your biological clock.

Kenneth Wright Jr. and colleagues (2013) conducted an interesting study where they took participants camping in the Rocky Mountains and recorded their sleep times, wake times, and melatonin production. After just 1 week of being surrounded by natural light (no electric lights), the participants' biological clocks reset to where they were going to sleep earlier and waking up earlier. The researchers measured the amount of melatonin in the body and found that the increases and decreases in melatonin shifted to 2 hours earlier and corresponded much more closely to natural light-dark conditions.

Because the SCN plays a key role in regulating sleep, damage to this area of the brain can have devastating effects such as causing random periods of sleep throughout the day and/or the disruption of regulation of body temperature (Cohen & Albers, 1991). One case study describing a 38-year-old woman who had been shot through the right temple reported that while she often slept more than 8 hours during a 24-hour period, her sleep was fragmented throughout the day and night. As a result, she had frequent awakenings throughout the night and numerous naps throughout the day (DelRosso et al., 2014). You might think of damaging the SCN akin to taking batteries out of the circadian clock.

What else can influence our circadian rhythms? As anyone who has pulled an all-nighter likely knows, caffeine is one answer. Under normal circumstances, *adenosine*, another sleep-inducing hormone, increases as the night wears on, inhibiting certain neurons and making us drowsy. However, if we need to hold off adenosine's tranquilizing effects late into the evening, we can block its activity by ingesting a few cups of coffee, a Red Bull, or any other potent source of caffeine. However, the problem with this approach is that you may only have needed the caffeine to help you stay awake for an additional hour or two, yet caffeine typically lasts in the body for 5–6 hours. This situation produces the frustrating experience of feeling exhausted yet not being able to fall asleep. Because of these effects, one contributor to *Forbes* magazine referred to caffeine as "The Silent Killer of Success" (Bradberry, 2012).

Why We Need to Sleep

LO 4.4 **Describe the function of sleep and consequences of sleep deprivation.**

If you've ever tossed and turned in bed all night or nodded off in a lecture hall, you know that sleep often seems like it's beyond our control. In fact, it is often paradoxical—the harder you *try* to fall asleep, the less likely you will fall asleep, or when you really want to stay awake but just can't keep your eyes open. We all know sleep is important and that we feel terrible when we don't get enough of it. But, why is it so important? What is the purpose behind sleeping each night?

THE FUNCTION OF SLEEP While psychologists have a fairly solid understanding of what happens in the brain and body as we sleep, exactly *why* we sleep remains a topic of debate. Several theories, summarized in the following interactive table, provide some reasons behind the purpose of sleep.

The Many Functions of Sleep

Interactive

Read each of the different theories about the function of sleep, then drag and drop the appropriate description to each theory.

Theory	Description
Preservation and Protection	Sleep is an evolutionary adaptation that keeps us out of harm's way when darkness sets in.
Body Restoration	The body tires during the day and needs to sleep to recuperate and function at maximal capacity.
Learning, Memory, and Synaptic Plasticity	Sleep promotes learning and memory partly due to the changes in neurons that result from sleep.
Growth	The pituitary gland releases growth hormone during deep sleep, which plays an important role in the growth process.

Check Your Understanding

Do you get enough sleep each night? Chances are your answer is "no." It's generally believed that a "good night's sleep" should be between 7 and 9 hours each night, but the amount of sleep needed for optimal functioning varies between individuals and throughout the lifespan (Dillon et al., 2014; Hirshkowitz et al., 2015). Newborns spend about two-thirds of their day asleep, while most adults doze for about half that time. Sleep needs decrease as you age, which is why seniors often get up so early in the morning (see Figure 4.1).

You might think more sleep is always better, but you'll notice there is an upper limit on the sleep duration recommendations. Many studies have suggested a U-shaped curve when it comes to the amount of sleep and risk of death. That is, adults who consistently sleep *less than 7 hours* or

Figure 4.1 Sleep Duration Recommendations

The recommended hours of sleep each night decreases with age. Even within each age group, a range of appropriate hours of sleep exists. It is important to find the number of hours of sleep that is right for your age, body, and lifestyle.

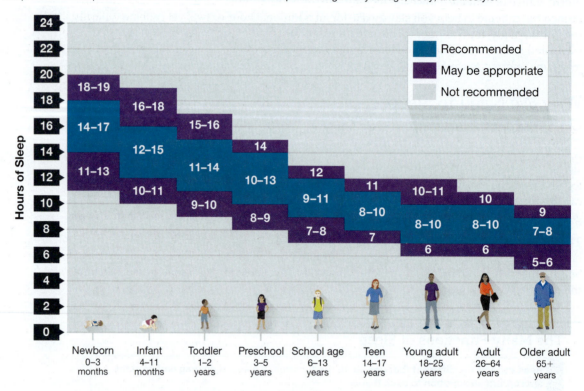

more than 9 hours each night have a significantly greater risk of dying from coronary heart disease (Cappuccio et al., 2011; Xiao et al., 2014). However, in some cases, when researchers controlled for preexisting health conditions, this relationship disappeared—suggesting that people who are already unhealthy tend to either sleep too much or too little (Kurina et al., 2013; Magee et al., 2013).

Genetics appear to play some role in our individual sleep patterns, with the heritability of sleep duration somewhere between 30 and 50 percent (de Castro, 2002; Watson et al., 2012). When researchers studied the sleep patterns of identical and fraternal twins, they found only the sleep patterns of identical twins were similar (Sletten et al., 2013). However, environmental situations also influence our sleep patterns. As mentioned earlier, indoor lighting has had a significant impact on our sleep patterns. In addition, cultural habits, such as engaging with the bright screens of mobile devices before going to bed (Cain & Gradisar, 2010; Chang et al., 2015; Lemola et al., 2015), have been implicated in the explanations for various sleep problems and why people sleep much less nowadays than they did a century ago.

SLEEP DEPRIVATION   A recent report compiling data from more than 300,000 Americans confirmed that we are getting less sleep than we did in the past. In 1985, adults reported sleeping an average of 7.40 hours each night. By 2012, the average amount of sleep each night had decreased to 7.18 hours, with 29.2 percent of adults reporting they consistently sleep less than 6 hours each night (Ford et al., 2015).

Young people, especially adolescents, are highly prone to skimping on sleep. Teenagers need about 8–10 hours of sleep each night, but on average, they clock only about 7 hours (Maslowsky & Ozer, 2014). A recent study examining more than 270,000 adolescents found that self-reported sleep has decreased in the past 20 years. The largest increase in those reporting less than 7 hours of sleep each night was among 15-year-old adolescents (Keyes et al., 2015). There appears to be a clear relationship between age and adequate sleep, with self-reported adequate sleep decreasing throughout adolescence, reaching the lowest level during the last year of high school and the year following high school, and rebounding some by age 19. Cultural differences have also been observed with Asian adolescents observing later bedtimes, obtaining less sleep overall, and reporting greater levels of daytime drowsiness, compared to North American and European adolescents (Gradisar et al., 2011).

Age and Adequate Sleep

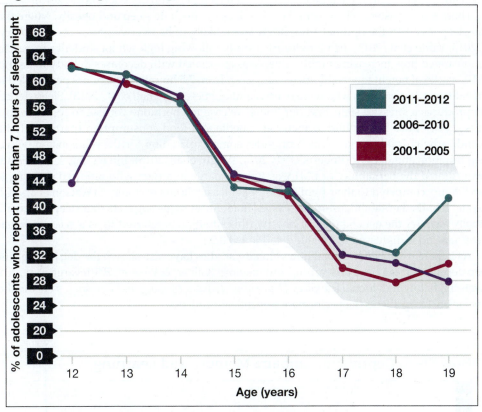

Journal Prompt: Sleep Deprivation

Have you ever gone through a period where you have been sleep deprived (i.e., getting 6 hours or less of sleep each night for at least a week)? If so, how did you feel, and what kinds of effects (if any) did this sleep deprivation have on your life? After you answer this question, read the next section to see if you can relate to any of the effects of sleep deprivation discussed.

Many students are sleep deprived and experience difficulty studying, irritability, fatigue, a lowered rate of productivity, and a tendency to make mistakes. In a study examining predictors of academic performance, getting enough sleep and the quality of sleep were 2 of the 5 primary predictors of end of semester grades (Gomes et al., 2011). These results suggest that if maintaining a high GPA is your goal, it's a good idea to make sleep a priority.

Unfortunately, the effects of sleep deprivation are not limited to merely feeling lethargic or moody; studies and examples show that sleep deprivation can, in fact, have tragic consequences. One year, traffic records showed an 8 percent increase in car accidents during the morning after the initiation of daylight savings time, when people changed their clocks and lost an hour of sleep. This increase disappeared in the fall when clocks were turned back for an extra hour of sleep (Coren, 1996). Sleep deprivation also leads to slowed reaction times and increased errors on visual tasks (Cain et al., 2011; Daviaux et al., 2014), resulting in potentially catastrophic mishaps both for drivers and for those whose jobs rely on these skills such as pilots, airport baggage screeners, surgeons, and X-ray technicians (Drummond et al., 2012).

Sleep deprivation can also have dire consequences for our physical and mental health. Sleep deprivation weakens our immune system, which explains why exhaustion and illness seem to go hand in hand as well as why we sleep more when we feel sick (Besedovsky et al., 2012; Ruiz et al., 2012; Wilder-Smith et al., 2013). Not sleeping enough, or not experiencing good-quality, restful sleep has also been associated with the onset of depression (Lemola et al., 2015; Short et al., 2013). In addition, sleep problems are a symptom of depression itself. Ultimately, sleep deprivation changes our metabolic and endocrine systems in ways that resemble aging, making us more susceptible to hypertension, memory loss, and obesity (Dettoni et al., 2012; Gangwisch, 2014; Havekes et al., 2014; Palagini et al., 2013; van Heugten–van der Kloet et al., 2015).

There is a consistent relationship between lack of adequate sleep and obesity, where those who sleep less than the optimal amount are more likely to be overweight or obese (Sperry et al., 2015; Valrie et al., 2015). In a longitudinal study following high school students, researchers demonstrated how increasing nightly sleep was associated with decreases in body mass index (BMI), a ratio of height to weight. Increasing sleep from 7.5 hours to 10.0 hours per day led to 4 percent fewer 18-year-olds who were overweight or obese (Mitchell et al., 2013). Sleep deprivation produces a stressful state, and our bodies release the hormone cortisol in response to the stress. Cortisol has been found to increase appetite and food consumption (particularly high fat and carbohydrate snacks), which provides some explanation for the relationship between sleep duration and obesity (Roberts et al., 2014; Wright et al., 2015). Interestingly, a twin study demonstrated the heritability of BMI was twice as large in a twin who reported sleeping less than 7 hours compared to their twin who slept at least 9 hours each night (Watson et al., 2012). The fact that the heritability estimate *changed* in identical twins suggests that sleep deprivation actually *increases* the genetic risk for obesity (this situation is referred to as a *gene-environment interaction* and is discussed in greater detail in LO 8.9.)

As if there wasn't enough bad news already, studies have also shown the detrimental effect sleep deprivation can have on learning and memory (Gilbert & Weaver, 2010; Varga et al., 2014). Watch the following video, *How Sleep Deprivation Impairs Memory and Learning*, to learn about how lack of sleep affects the performance of college students.

How Sleep Deprivation Impairs Memory and Learning

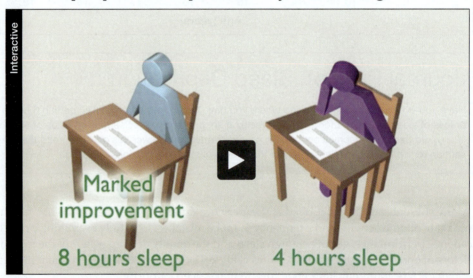

Stages of Sleep

LO 4.5 **Differentiate the various stages of sleep in the sleep cycle.**

Before the 1950s, scientists assumed all sleep was essentially created equal, that is, they believed there were no distinguishing physiological or psychological factors between the sleep you experience in the first 10 minutes after lying down and the sleep that occurs in the middle of the night. In 1952, however, University of Chicago graduate student Eugene Aserinsky discovered a connection while studying his son sleeping. He recognized a relationship between his son's brain activity, his eyes darting back and forth, and his report of dreaming. Aserinsky realized this collection of experiences was indicative of a distinct stage of sleep—**rapid eye movement (REM)**, a recurring stage of sleep during which vivid dreams usually occur.

Aserinsky went on to collaborate with his mentor, Nathaniel Kleitman, and discovered other sleep stages characterized by specific brain wave activity (Aserinsky & Kleitman, 1953).

rapid eye movement (REM)/ stage R

a deep stage of sleep consisting of rapid eye movement (REM) typically associated with dreaming; sometimes referred to as paradoxical sleep

We now know, through the use of EEGs on sleeping participants, that the sleep cycle comprises five distinct stages we cycle through about every 90 minutes. The original publication that defined and distinguished these sleep stages was published in 1968 by Rechtshaffen and Kales and became known as the "R and K" rules. In 2007, and again in 2012, the American Academy of Sleep Medicine published changes to the system that had been in use for almost 40 years. Five stages are still recognized in a sleep cycle, which are contained within three distinct categories: wakefulness (W), non-REM (NREM), and REM (R). A typical pattern of sleep starts from a wakened state, progresses through deeper stages of sleep (i.e., N1, N2, and N3), and eventually ends with a period of REM sleep. N3 represents the deepest stage of sleep, after which sleep will become lighter, ending in a period of REM. After REM, you might briefly wake up (which you may or may not remember) or transition back to a NREM stage and then back to REM. This cycle repeats itself about 4–5 times throughout the night.

STAGES W AND N1   If you used an EEG to measure the brain activity of someone who was on the verge of falling asleep, what would you discover? You'd most likely see evidence of a few different types of brain waves. Brain waves are typically described by how they look in terms of their *amplitude*, the height of the wave, and *frequency*—how close the waves are to one another. High amplitude brain waves look tall and high frequency brain waves are tightly squeezed together. Low amplitude brain waves look short, and low frequency brain waves are separated by more space (see Figure 4.2).

Figure 4.2 Amplitude and Frequency of Brain Waves

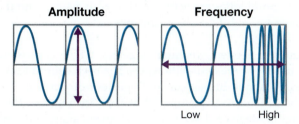

As we prepare for sleep, our brains transition from producing the low-amplitude, high frequency, and irregular **beta waves** that characterize active wakefulness to producing the slower **alpha waves** that characterize a relaxed or drowsy state. As we enter the first stage of sleep referred to as **N1**, alpha wave activity decreases and larger, slower **theta waves** become more active. Stage N1 doesn't last very long and only makes up about 5 percent of the total sleep time. During this time, your eyes move slowly under your eyelids and your muscles relax. Since you are so close to a wakeful state, it is very easy to be woken up while in this stage. If you have ever experienced just getting to sleep only to be woken up by your roommate coming home and slamming the door, you were probably in the N1 stage of sleep.

Several strange, often disconcerting sensations can occur during this period of transition between wakefulness and sleep that typifies stage N1. One of these is the *hypnagogic jerk*—a sudden jerk of the body just as one is drifting off to sleep. Many people wake up when this happens and report feeling as though they were falling. Some people also report feeling as though they were floating weightlessly above the bed during the hypnagogic period. Although there's nothing otherworldly about these strange sensations, their existence may explain some individuals' accounts of alleged alien abductions or other "supernatural" experiences (McNally & Clancy, 2005). *Hypnagogic hallucinations* are another odd experience you may experience in this early stage of sleep. As the name suggests, some people report seeing or hearing things that don't exist, just as they are drifting off to sleep.

STAGES N2 AND N3   As we continue to doze, we become increasingly relaxed, and soon we enter stage **N2**, a period of light sleep. This stage lasts about 10–25 minutes and is accompanied by the cessation of eye and body movements, a slower heart rate, and a decrease in body temperature. Overall, we spend about 50 percent of our total sleep time in stage N2.

beta waves

low-amplitude, high frequency, and irregular brain waves present during active wakefulness

alpha waves

high frequency, low amplitude brain waves characteristic of a relaxed or drowsy state

N1

the first stage of sleep where alpha wave activity decreases and larger, slower theta wave activity increases

theta waves

brain waves associated with the transition to sleep; may be present in N1 and N2 stages of sleep

N2

the second stage of sleep characterized by increased relaxation and a period of light sleep

An EEG records theta waves that continue from stage N1, but stage N2 is also marked by the periodic appearance of K-complexes and sleep spindles. *K-complexes* are large, well-defined, pointed brain waves that last at least half a second (see Figure 4.3).

K-complexes clearly stand out from theta waves because of their amplitude and are typically followed by a *sleep spindle*, or rhythmic burst of activity lasting between ½–1 second (see Figure 4.4).

Figure 4.3 Example of a K-Complex

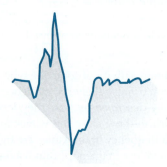

Figure 4.4 Example of a Sleep Spindle

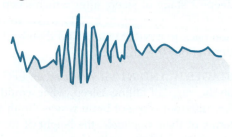

Although the exact physiological roles of K-complexes and sleep spindles are still unclear (De Gennaro & Ferrara, 2003), research involving the use of fMRI has linked K-complexes and sleep spindles to specific areas of the brain (Kaufmann et al., 2006). The thalamus and temporal lobes are active during both events, and it has been suggested that these events help to maintain sleep and promote memory consolidation (Caporro et al., 2012).

As sleep continues to deepen, we enter stage **N3**, which consists of higher amplitude **delta waves**. The pattern of repeated delta waves has been said to look like a series of skyscrapers and makes up about 20 percent to 25 percent of our total sleep time. People in stage N3 are usually difficult to wake up and, if they are awoken, they tend to be groggy and disoriented; yet, this stage of sleep is the most restful stage and tends to be reported as the aspect of sleep that reduces feelings of sleepiness and restores the body. This is also the stage where night terrors, bed-wetting, and sleepwalking occur (see upcoming discussion of parasomnias.)

STAGE R   About an hour after we fall asleep and complete one cycle of the three NREM sleep stages, we enter **stage R**, which refers to rapid eye movement (REM) sleep, which can last anywhere from a few minutes to an hour. We spend about 20–25 percent of an average night in REM sleep, which is also the stage most associated with dreaming. Have you ever heard someone say they don't dream? Even people who report that they never dream will remember the details of a dream if they are awakened during stage R sleep (Muntean et al., 2015; Yu, 2014).

At the beginning of stage R, our brain waves resemble those that appear during stage N1 sleep. In contrast to stage N1, however, stage R sleep is a time of physiological arousal rather than increasing tranquility: Our heart rate increases, our breathing becomes rapid and irregular, and our eyes dart around behind our eyelids in quick bursts of activity approximately every 30 seconds. And yet, amid all this excitement, we are unable to regulate our temperature (which explains why you sometimes wake up freezing cold or burning up), and our muscles remain relaxed. For these reasons, REM sleep is also referred to as paradoxical sleep; even though the brain's motor cortex remains active, neurons in the brainstem and spinal cord are unable to transmit messages to the rest of the body. This causes our muscles to be still to the point of paralysis. It is generally thought that the muscle paralysis associated with stage R occurs to prevent the body from acting out the dreams that occur during this stage and therefore avoiding potential injuries (Brooks & Peever, 2012).

Although some sleep researchers have suspected the rapid eye movements characteristic of REM sleep are related to the visual aspects of dreaming, most scientists believe these eye movements are a result of overflow to the active nervous system (Fraigne et al., 2014;

N3

the third stage of sleep consisting of deep sleep characterized by higher amplitude delta waves

delta waves

higher amplitude, lower frequency brain waves that appear when sleep deepens; characteristic of sleep stage N3.

stage R/rapid eye movement (REM)

a deep stage of sleep consisting of rapid eye movement (REM) typically associated with dreaming; sometimes referred to as paradoxical sleep

Keenan & Hirshkowitz, 2011). As the night wears on, we tend to spend more time in stage R sleep and less time in deep sleep (i.e., stage N3.) Our periods of REM sleep generally increase in both duration and frequency the longer we sleep, which is why you are most likely to remember your dreams from early in the morning rather than the period after you first went to sleep.

The following video, *Stages of Sleep*, will summarize this information. Watch the video, then complete the interactive activity to check your understanding.

Stages of Sleep

Types of Brain Waves During Sleep

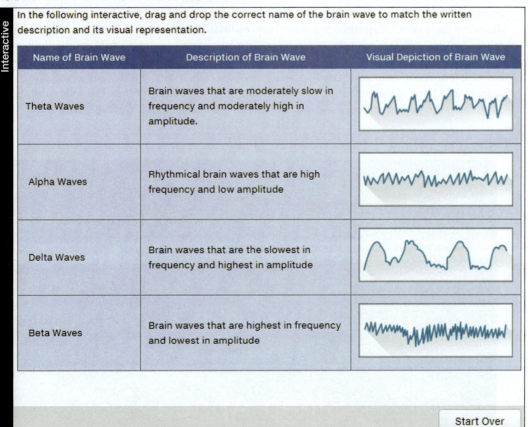

In the following interactive, drag and drop the correct name of the brain wave to match the written description and its visual representation.

Name of Brain Wave	Description of Brain Wave	Visual Depiction of Brain Wave
Theta Waves	Brain waves that are moderately slow in frequency and moderately high in amplitude.	
Alpha Waves	Rhythmical brain waves that are high frequency and low amplitude	
Delta Waves	Brain waves that are the slowest in frequency and highest in amplitude	
Beta Waves	Brain waves that are highest in frequency and lowest in amplitude	

Start Over

Adaptive Pathway 4.1: Brain Waves and Sleep

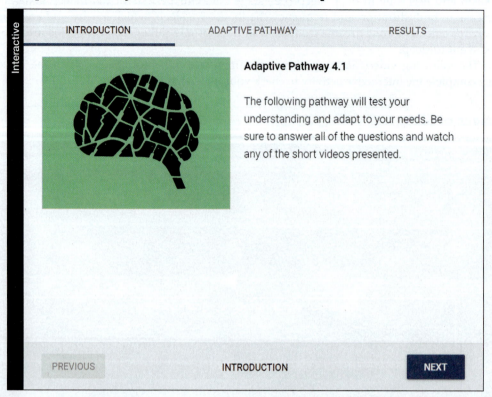

Sleep Disorders

LO 4.6 **Distinguish the various sleep disorders and their treatments.**

Did you know there are more than 70 different sleep disorders? According to the National Institutes of Health (NIH), at least 40 million Americans suffer from long-term, chronic sleep disorders each year. Sleep disorders have been estimated to cost $16 billion each year in direct medical costs, with the indirect costs in terms of missed work and decreased productivity to be much higher (National Institute of Neurological Disorders and Stroke, n.d.). Many people experience intermittent sleep issues that typically resolve on their own, but for some, the symptoms worsen and have significant effects on their happiness and functioning. The following video, *Sleep Disorders*, provides an overview of the various problems people can have with sleep.

Sleep Disorders

INSOMNIA Sleep deprivation is often a by-product of a busy schedule that allows little time for sleep. Sometimes, however, sleep debt is accumulated as a result of **insomnia**, a sleep disorder characterized by dissatisfaction with sleep quality or duration (Morin & Benca, 2012). Several specific problems are related to sleep that can qualify for a diagnosis of insomnia, including:

insomnia

a sleep disorder characterized by dissatisfaction with the duration or quality of sleep

- Difficulty falling asleep at bedtime

- Difficulty maintaining sleep throughout the night

- Waking up too early in the morning and not being able to get back to sleep

- Nonrestorative or poor quality sleep (meaning you don't feel well-rested after a full night's sleep)

People who experience one or more of these symptoms for some time often report low energy, daytime sleepiness, changes in mood, and difficulty concentrating. Research has confirmed with neuropsychological tests that those suffering from insomnia perform worse on measures of cognitive functioning, especially memory (Fortier-Brochu et al., 2012).

If you sometimes have difficulty sleeping, or if anxiety or excitement keeps you awake from time to time, you shouldn't be alarmed—most people face occasional sleep issues and, unless these issues happen frequently, they usually aren't symptomatic of insomnia. In fact, about 25 percent of people report occasional problems with insomnia, with only approximately 10 percent having problems severe enough to warrant a diagnosis of insomnia (Morin & Benca, 2012; Pigeon, 2010).

As tempting as it might be, people who experience insomnia should avoid relying on "quick fixes" such as alcohol and sleeping pills, which can make the problem worse by reducing REM sleep and creating next-day fatigue. Moreover, people who use these substances on a regular basis can quickly build up a tolerance, leading to unpleasant withdrawal and worsening insomnia if and when the "sleep aids" are discontinued (Lugoboni & Quaglio, 2014).

Several environmental and behavioral activities contribute to sleep problems, which are collectively referred to as *sleep hygiene*.

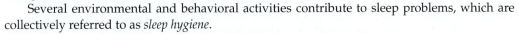

Your Sleep Hygiene

Interactive

Time for a checkup. How is your sleep hygiene? Answer the following questions about your sleep in the past month.

1. Have you taken more than one nap in the past month?

○ Yes
○ No

2. Do you go to bed and wake up at different times throughout the week?

○ Yes
○ No

Previous   Next

Promotion of good sleep hygiene practices can be helpful in preventing further sleep problems but has been generally ineffective as a stand-alone strategy for those suffering from diagnosable insomnia (Edinger & Carney, 2008). Good sleep hygiene principles are more often included as a component of larger cognitive-behavioral treatment programs for insomnia (Morin & Benca, 2012). Cognitive-behavioral treatment of insomnia also typically includes keeping a sleep diary, temporary sleep restriction to ensure the patient is sleepy at bedtime, and changing routines and bedtime behaviors to break bad habits and promote healthy sleep.

Even though improved sleep hygiene isn't a cure for insomnia, poor sleep hygiene has been found to be predictive of future development of insomnia, particularly in college students. Gellis and colleagues (2014) conducted an interesting study where they collected data on college students' sleep hygiene habits. The findings are probably unsurprising—in general, college students engaged in many behaviors consistent with poor sleep hygiene. Of more interest, however, is they found of all poor sleep hygiene behaviors, the only one that predicted *future* insomnia was "improper sleep scheduling." Therefore, the takeaway from this study might be that if you choose to only focus on one thing to help protect yourself from future insomnia, you should attempt to go to bed and get up at the same time each day (yes, even on weekends) and avoid daytime naps.

narcolepsy

a sleep disorder characterized by excessive daytime sleepiness and periodic, uncontrollable sleep attacks

NARCOLEPSY In stark contrast to insomnia is **narcolepsy**, a sleep disorder characterized by excessive daytime sleepiness and periodic, uncontrollable sleep attacks. These unexpected periods of sleep usually last less than 5 minutes, but because they occur at unexpected times—in the middle of a conversation, for example, or while driving—they can seriously impair one's quality of life, not to mention safety (Mets et al., 2012; Ozaki et al., 2012).

Narcolepsy is often accompanied by *cataplexy*, a sudden loss of voluntary muscle tone, where the individual becomes "paralyzed" yet remains conscious (which distinguishes it from a seizure). Although cataplexy can happen spontaneously, strong emotions and laughter have been reported as the most common trigger (Dauvilliers et al., 2007).

Narcolepsy is a brain disorder involving a dysregulation of normal sleep-wake cycles. Contrary to what most people think, people with narcolepsy don't actually spend more time in sleep over a 24-hour period. While they do spend more time in sleep throughout the daytime hours, their sleep tends to be fragmented with frequent awakenings throughout the night.

Less than 1 percent of the population suffers from narcolepsy, and there is hope for those individuals. For those who experience cataplexy with narcolepsy, neuroscientists have found a relative absence of neurons that produce *hypocretin*, an alerting neurotransmitter that promotes wakefulness (van den Pol, 2000). Several genes have been identified as possibly playing a role in the development of narcolepsy. However, the specific pathological process related to the development of hypocretin has only been identified in certain breeds of dogs (i.e., Dobermans, Labradors, and Dachshunds) at this point. Did you know that dogs can have narcolepsy? While there is no specific cure for narcolepsy, it can be treated with stimulant medication (for sleep attacks) and/

Mabel the Narcoleptic Dog

or antidepressant medication (for cataplexy) and lifestyle changes. Behavioral changes include practicing good sleep hygiene and scheduling regular naps at the times of day when the person feels most sleepy. In the following video, you'll meet *Mabel the Narcoleptic Dog*.

SLEEP APNEA **Sleep apnea** is a sleep disorder involving regular interruptions of breathing during sleep. People with sleep apnea intermittently stop breathing during sleep, which in turn causes the level of oxygen in the blood to plummet, resulting in an awakening (the person may not remember waking up, but the brain wakes up and has to start the sleep cycle over again). The severity of sleep apnea is measured by how many times a person wakes up each hour and in severe cases can be more than 30 times an hour! These excessive, nonstop interruptions deprive sufferers of slow-wave sleep, leaving them chronically groggy and irritable during the day. Because they often don't remember waking up repeatedly during the night, many people suffering from sleep apnea don't even realize they have the disorder. Sleep apnea is particularly common among those who are overweight; and, as obesity rates have risen in the United States, so too have the rates of sleep apnea. Currently, about 26 percent of people between the ages of 30 and 70 suffer from sleep apnea (National Health Sleep Awareness Project, 2014).

While lifestyle changes (e.g., losing weight, quitting smoking, changing pillows) are recommended first, for those who do not respond to these interventions, more aggressive treatment for sleep apnea is necessary. Treatment for the most common type of sleep apnea (technically referred to as *obstructive sleep apnea*) involves wearing a mask that uses air pressure to keep the airway open during sleep. This machine is referred to as **continuous positive airway pressure** and is called a CPAP for short. CPAPs come in many variations and can be a very effective treatment option, although some people have a difficult time adjusting to the feel and noise of the machine.

PARASOMNIAS: NIGHTMARE DISORDER, SLEEP TERRORS, AND SLEEPWALKING Nightmares, sleep terrors, and sleepwalking are considered **parasomnias**, which refer to abnormal behavioral, experiential, or physiological events that occur in conjunction with sleep. Parasomnias tend to be divided into those occurring during NREM sleep and those associated with REM sleep.

Nightmares are scary dreams that share many characteristics with other nonscary dreams. Nightmares, like most dreams, occur almost exclusively during REM and therefore are more typical in the second half of the sleep cycle (remember, the amount of time in REM sleep increases over the course of the night). Nightmares typically end as soon as the person wakes up and can typically be described in detail. Upon awakening, the individual is usually not disoriented and quickly returns to being fully alert (American Psychiatric Association, 2013). *Nightmare disorder* can be diagnosed if an individual is experiencing repeated nightmares that cause distress or clinically significant impairment in the individual's life.

Sleep terrors and **sleepwalking**, which is also referred to as *somnambulism*, are manifestations of what the DSM-5 calls *nonrapid eye movement sleep arousal disorders* and most commonly occur in children. As the name suggests, both sleepwalking and sleep terrors occur during NREM sleep, typically at some point during the first 2 hours of falling asleep (which is when we spend the most time in NREM deep sleep). These events occur in response to an abnormal transition from deep sleep (e.g., Stage N3) to either REM sleep or a lighter stage of sleep (Howell, 2012; Meltzer & McLaughlin Crabtree, 2015). In contrast to nightmares, children who experience **sleep terrors** may scream, have increased autonomic nervous system activity, appear very distressed, and not be comforted by a caregiver. Despite the person's eyes being open, they are asleep and therefore appear very groggy and disoriented. There is significant overlap between sleep terrors and sleepwalking, as they share similar origins and often occur together. While it is not dangerous to wake a person during a sleep terror or sleepwalking episode, it will likely extend the length of the event (Meltzer & McLaughlin Crabtree, 2015). Typically, amnesia accompanies the event so the individual will have no memory of the dream, being scared, or walking around. There appears to be a strong family history to both of these parasomnias with the prevalence of sleepwalking reaching 61.5 percent among children whose mother and father experienced sleepwalking as a child (Petit et al., 2015). Nonrapid eye movement sleep arousal disorders appear to be triggered by sleep deprivation, which is often how researchers study these disorders in the lab: They deprive their participants of sleep in the days leading up to the sleep study with the hope of increasing the probability of a sleepwalking or sleep terror episode.

sleep apnea

a sleep disorder involving regular interruptions of breathing during sleep

continuous positive airway pressure (CPAP)

treatment for sleep apnea, which involves wearing a mask that uses air pressure to keep the airway open during sleep

parasomnias

abnormal behavioral, experiential, or physiological events that occur in conjunction with sleep

nightmares

scary dreams, which almost always occur during REM sleep

sleepwalking

a parasomnia that occurs during NREM sleep in response to an abnormal transition from deep sleep (e.g. Stage N3) to REM or a lighter stage of sleep

sleep terrors

a parasomnia characterized by scary dreams and increased autonomic nervous system activity; typically occurs during NREM sleep and therefore can be accompanied by movement

Remember the murder cases of Scott Falater and Kenneth Parks described at the beginning of this chapter? Both claimed to be sleepwalking while committing the murder. Falater was found guilty of murder, and Parks was acquitted of the charges. In a recent review of sleep-related murder cases, only three of the nine murder trials resulted in a conviction of murder (Ingravallo et al., 2014).

Distinguishing the Sleep Disorders

Read the following descriptions of fictional patients and match the correct sleep disorder to their symptoms.

Emily is 8 years old and frequently wakes up crying from scary dreams. The dreams tend to happen in the early morning hours, and she can often remember the content.	Nightmares
Donna reports that she is often sleepy during the day. She reports that she has no trouble falling asleep. However, when she wakes up in the middle of the night, she struggles to get back to sleep and sometimes is awake for 2 hours.	Insomnia
Carlos feels sleepy all the time. Sometimes, he nods off during work meetings. He reports an unusual symptom of experiencing muscle weakness most times when he laughs.	Narcolepsy
Garrett's wife contacted his doctors because she is concerned about his loud snoring. She said that there seems to be times during the night when Garrett stops breathing for a short period. Garrett has no memory of any of this, but does report experiencing daytime sleepiness.	Sleep Apnea
Wenxi has been told by her parents that often within a couple hours of going to bed, she starts screaming and lashing out in her bed. Her parents report that her eyes are open and she looks awake, but Wenxi has no memory of this event in the morning.	Sleep Terrors

Start Over

Dreams

LO 4.7 **Recognize the different theories proposed to explain the function of dreams.**

dreams

the sequences of images, feelings, ideas, and impressions that occur during sleep

Dreams, the sequences of images, feelings, ideas, and impressions that pass through our minds as we sleep, are among the most fascinating aspects of human consciousness. They can produce a wide range of intense emotions, transport us through time, and make the impossible seem possible. Often, they're completely nonsensical. This fact hasn't stopped humans from *attempting* to decipher dreams, however. How often do you wake up from a memorable dream and wonder, "What was that about?" Have you ever felt like a dream you had the previous night was trying to tell you something? Did it seem so cryptic that you decided it must have a deeper meaning and couldn't resist trying to decode it? You've likely heard about or experienced some of the more common dreams.

All the interpretations you just read suggest that dreams mean something. But, is that always the case? Can't you just dream about something just because.....? In their studies of dreams and dreaming, psychologists ask similar questions: What are dreams, and what function does dreaming serve?

The most vivid dreams are experienced during REM sleep and can involve bizarre imagery and vivid, though highly illogical, plots. Nevertheless, when we dream, we uncritically accept these strange elements and, at times, even confuse them with reality. Despite the belief that dreams are always fantastical, research has demonstrated that our dreams tend to be consistent over time and involve (albeit sometimes dramatized) aspects of our life and waking thoughts (Domhoff, 2007; Schredl & Hofmann, 2003). For example, people tend to have nightmares after traumatic events (Valli et al., 2006), and studies have shown that people who play video games

What Might Your Dreams Mean?

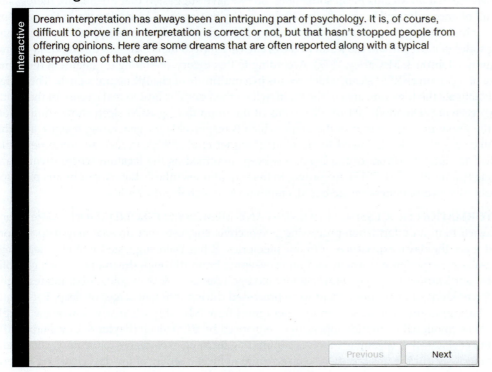

Interactive

Dream interpretation has always been an intriguing part of psychology. It is, of course, difficult to prove if an interpretation is correct or not, but that hasn't stopped people from offering opinions. Here are some dreams that are often reported along with a typical interpretation of that dream.

Previous   Next

for several hours before sleep are highly likely to report emotional dreams involving images related to their games (Gackenbach & Kuruvilla, 2008; Stickgold et al., 2001).

Many people believe our dreams can help us solve the problems of our waking lives or give us clues about our futures. Just as several different theories attempt to explain why we sleep, there are also many competing theories regarding the purpose behind our dreams.

FREUD AND THE INTERPRETATION OF DREAMS Sigmund Freud, who published *The Interpretation of Dreams* in 1900, based much of his theory on the significance of dreams and dream analysis. He argued that dreams allow us to fulfill our wishes and express our unacceptable feelings in a safe environment. He classified the content of dreams into two types: the manifest content and the latent content. **Manifest content** refers to what we explicitly remember about a dream—its storyline, characters, and details. Manifest content may incorporate sensory stimuli from the sleeper's environment. For instance, people who had cold water lightly sprayed on their faces while sleeping were more likely to dream about water (Dement & Wolpert, 1958). Other experiments have found less specific results. For example, when researches presented a pleasant smell (i.e., roses) to sleeping participants, they were much more likely to report having a pleasant dream compared to those who were presented with a noxious smell (i.e., the smell of rotten eggs) (Schredl et al., 2009). You may have even had the experience of when your alarm goes off in the morning, you incorporate that sound into your dream.

Freud described **latent content** as the more interesting and informative aspect of the dream, as it is said to involve the unconscious, repressed wishes and drives of the dreamer. The manifest content is viewed as a protective cover over the "real," but unconscious, desires of the individual. Freud theorized that most adults' wishes expressed through dreams are erotic, even when overt sexual imagery is not present. Dream research has confirmed that dreams with overtly sexual content occur much less than you might expect—somewhere between 5 percent and 9 percent of reported dreams (i.e., the manifest content) contain content of a sexual nature (Domhoff, 2005a).

Freud probably wouldn't be surprised by this statistic because he was less interested in the manifest content of dreams. He believed our inner conflicts and unconscious desires, contained in the latent content, could be identified and analyzed through the process of dream interpretation. There are, however, plenty of critics of Freud's dream theory. Some of these critics point out that dreams can be interpreted to mean nearly anything, depending on the creativity of the interpreter; others argue that dreams don't hide anything below the surface and don't seem to contain subtle clues to our unconscious desires (Fisher & Greenberg, 1985; Grünbaum, 1992).

manifest content

the actual, remembered content of a dream, including the storyline, characters, and specific details

latent content

the underlying meaning of a dream where the unconscious, repressed wishes, and drives of the dreamer are expressed

activation-synthesis hypothesis

theory of dreaming that dreams are the result of the brain's attempt to make sense of random neural activity

AN ATTEMPT TO DERIVE MEANING FROM BRAIN ACTIVATION   In opposition to Freud's insistence that all dreams mean something, others have suggested that dreams are merely the result of uncoordinated brain activity. While we may be unconscious during sleep, the neurons in our brain fire away even while we slumber. The **activation-synthesis hypothesis** of dreaming states that dreams are the result of the brain's attempt to make sense of this random neural activity (Hobson & McCarley, 1977). According to this theory, dreaming originates in the same area of the brain as REM sleep, which results in a multitude of chaotic neural signals. These signals activate the forebrain area of the brain, which then does its best to make sense of the input it is receiving (Domhoff, 2005b). PET scans of the brain during REM sleep show stimulation in the visual processing area of the brain, which is responsible for generating images, and the limbic system, which is linked to emotions (Maquet et al., 1996). In fact, an entire network, called the *default network* of the brain, has been identified as the location where dreams are made (Domhoff & Fox, 2015). According to the activation-synthesis theory, our brains produce dreams by weaving these image-based, emotion-laced signals into stories.

INFORMATION PROCESSING: LEARNING AND MEMORY CONSOLIDATION   More recent research from an information-processing perspective, suggests that dreams may help us sort and place the day's experiences into our memories. It has been suggested that after learning, our waking experience is reactivated in the sleeping brain (through dreaming), which consolidates our learning into long-term memory storage (Wamsley & Stickgold, 2011). Interestingly, different kinds of memories appear to be processed during different stages of sleep. For example, basic episodic memories seem to benefit most from NREM (particularly slow-wave sleep), whereas emotional memories appear to be enhanced by REM sleep (Baylor & Cavallero, 2001; Smith et al., 2004). If dreaming involves committing learning experiences to memory, you might wonder why our dreams are often so bizarre and not just a replay of the day's learning experiences. Sleep and dream researcher Erin Wamsley (2014) says we shouldn't expect our waking experiences to appear in our dreams in their original form because the process of memory consolidation involves compiling many different experiences, with the goal of identifying particular themes. It is a similar process in some ways to studying: When you study, you aren't simply trying to memorize word for word what is written in your text (or at least you shouldn't be). Instead, you are organizing many pieces of information into meaningful chunks and developing a story that makes sense in order to help you remember the overall themes and theories. Dreaming may be our brain's way of studying what we learn in day-to-day life.

Quiz for Module 4.3–4.7

1. Our _____ is a biological clock responsible for the regulation of body temperature and levels of arousal during our sleep and wake cycle.
   - **a.** sleep rhythm
   - **b.** hypothalamus
   - **c.** biological rhythm
   - **d.** circadian rhythm

2. One of the many reasons psychologists believe we need to sleep is that our bodies tire during the day, and sleep helps the body recuperate and function at maximum capacity. This is a description of which theory?
   - **a.** Body restoration
   - **b.** Circadian
   - **c.** Growth
   - **d.** Preservation and protection

3. In which stage of sleep do vivid dreams typically occur?
   - **a.** N3; non-REM
   - **b.** N1; non-REM
   - **c.** REM
   - **d.** N2; non-REM

4. The brain waves with the highest amplitude are referred to as _____ waves.
   - **a.** beta
   - **c.** alpha
   - **b.** delta
   - **d.** theta

5. Beta waves are associated with _____, while theta waves are characteristic of the _____ stage.
   - **a.** drowsiness; N2
   - **b.** alert wakefulness; REM
   - **c.** drowsiness; N1
   - **d.** alert wakefulness; N2

6. Billy is having trouble with insomnia. He has difficulty going to sleep and wakes up numerous times throughout the night. Based on what you know about sleep hygiene, what should you recommend he start doing?
   - **a.** Stop drinking anything with caffeine
   - **b.** Engage in intense exercise 1 hour prior to going bed
   - **c.** Go to bed and get up at the same time each day
   - **d.** Read a book on his phone before going to sleep

7. According to Freud, the latent content of our dreams is _____ and contains the repressed _____ and drives of the dreamer.
   - **a.** conscious; memories
   - **b.** unconscious; wishes
   - **c.** unconscious; memories
   - **d.** conscious; wishes

Module 4.8–4.10: Psychoactive Drugs

Marilyn Monroe, Corey Monteith, Whitney Houston, Phillip Seymour Hoffman, and Prince......
What do all of these people have in common? They are just a few of the many celebrities who
have died from a drug overdose. The costs of drug abuse are high, both in terms of the risk of
death and the economic impact on society. It has been estimated that the annual costs associated
with the abuse of tobacco, alcohol, and illicit drugs is more than $700 billion, which includes costs
related to crime, health care, and lost work productivity (National Institute on Drug Abuse, 2017).

However, the news is not all bad. National surveys over the past 20 years, through the National
Institute on Drug Abuse, have reflected a decrease in cigarette and alcohol use, especially among
high school students. Nonetheless, as progress is made in some areas, newer drugs of abuse are
discovered (e.g., bath salts, 2C-1/smiles, phenazepam), new methods of administration are introduced (e.g., e-cigarettes, vaporizers), and laws regulating the recreational use of certain drugs have
been changed (e.g., legalization of marijuana in Washington, Oregon, Colorado, and Alaska), which
create difficulties for researchers in their ability to "keep up" with monitoring the effects drugs can
have on individuals and society (Cerdá et al., 2012; Grana et al., 2014; Oyemade, 2012).

National Trends in Alcohol, Cigarette, and Illicit Drug Use

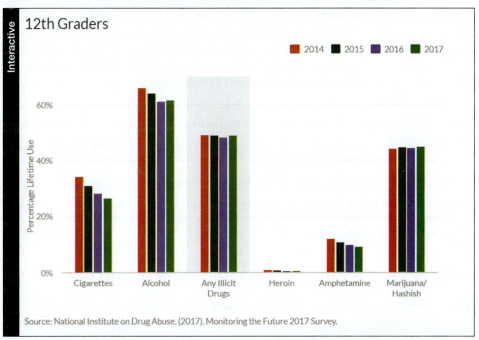

Source: National Institute on Drug Abuse. (2017). Monitoring the Future 2017 Survey.

Substance Use Disorders

LO 4.8 **Recognize the symptoms associated with a substance use disorder.**

A **psychoactive drug** is defined as a chemical substance that alters brain function resulting in
changes in consciousness, perception, and/or mood. Psychoactive drugs have many different
uses and in some cases can be extremely helpful (taking a prescribed oxycodone after having your wisdom teeth removed) and in other cases incredibly harmful (needing to take oxycodone on a daily basis to be able to function). Many drugs have the capability of producing
physiological dependence, which is where the body becomes physically dependent on the drug.
Physiological dependence typically includes aspects of tolerance and withdrawal. **Tolerance** involves
the body becoming used to, or tolerant of, the drug. The result of tolerance is the need to increase the
dosage to experience the same effects as in the past. As tolerance develops, an individual often also
experiences withdrawal symptoms. **Withdrawal symptoms** are physiological symptoms produced
by the body when the drug is absent from the system. For example, in the case of prolonged heroin
use, the withdrawal symptoms of anxiety, sweating, vomiting, and diarrhea are often what drive the
individual to continue to use the drug, in many cases despite their intentions to quit. Drugs change
the brain in ways that produce physiological symptoms, but they also change the brain in ways that
produce psychological dependence. **Psychological dependence** has been described as emotional or

psychoactive drug
a chemical substance that alters
brain function, resulting in changes
in consciousness, perception, and/
or mood

psychological dependence
the emotional or motivational
symptoms associated with repeated
drug use, such as intense cravings,
inability to concentrate on other
nondrug-related activities, and/or feeling restless when not taking the drug

tolerance
a form of physiological dependence
where the body becomes used to a
drug, resulting in an increased need
for the drug to achieve the same
effects

withdrawal symptoms
physiological symptoms produced
by the body when a drug is absent
from the system

physiological dependence
process in which the body becomes
physically dependent, or reliant,
on the drug; typically involves
tolerance and/or withdrawal

motivational symptoms that include intense cravings for the drug, inability to concentrate on other nondrug-related activities, and/or feeling restless when not taking the drug. Wise and Koob (2014) describe the process of physiological dependence as one that develops from the increases in dopamine and the neuroadaptation that occurs *after* the administration of drugs. In contrast, they suggest that the psychological dependence is based on memory traces, or memories of the drug experiences, that occur from the first administration. Therefore, the psychological dependence can be established long before the signs of physiological dependence are evident.

It has been well-established for some time that psychoactive drugs exert a powerful effect on the brain, particularly in the dopamine-rich area of the brain associated with experiencing reward (Wise & Bozarth, 1987). Animals that are given the opportunity to self-administer alcohol and most psychoactive drugs will continue this behavior at the expense of most other life-sustaining behaviors (Deneau et al., 1969). In a classic study led by Bozarth and Wise (1985), 90 percent of rats who were given unrestricted access to cocaine died within 30 days as a result of their inability to focus on anything else other than administering cocaine.

The terms *addiction*, *substance abuse*, and *substance dependence* are often used interchangeably. Even medicines that are prescribed and taken as directed can produce physiological dependence, but that doesn't necessarily mean the patient is addicted. However, many people who are functioning adequately at work and deny having any problems with drugs, are in fact, addicted.

substance use disorder

a psychological disorder characterized by a pattern of drug use leading to distress or significant impairment in functioning

The DSM-5 is currently used by most mental health practitioners to diagnose substance-related problems. It separates drugs into 11 different classes and provides criteria that must be met to be diagnosed with a substance use disorder within any of the classes. This diagnostic manual defines a **substance use disorder** as a "cluster of cognitive, behavioral, and psychological symptoms indicating that the individual continues using the substance despite significant substance-related problems" (APA, 2013, p. 483). General substance-related problems may include:

- Impaired control over the substance use (e.g., cravings, inability to cut down or stop)
- Social impairment, including failure to fulfill responsibilities at work, school, or home
- Using the substance in risky situations (e.g., driving, continued use despite medical or psychological problems)
- Physiological dependence as evidenced by tolerance or withdrawal

A substance use disorder is diagnosed when a pattern of drug use leads to significant impairment or distress in the person's life. There must also be two of the specific diagnostic criteria present within a 12-month period to receive a diagnosis.

The Ways Substance Use Disorders Can Interfere With Life

Read the following situations and match them to the general substance-related problem described below.

Impaired control over the substance use	Despite waking up every day and telling herself she wasn't going to take any more diet pills, Addison can't resist the urge and continues to take more than the recommended dose.
Social impairment, including failure to fulfill responsibilities at work, school, or home	Leon is frequently hungover and unable to make it to work on time. Last week, he was fired from his job because of his lack of reliability.
Using the substance in risky situations	Jill hides a bottle of vodka in her desk at work. She drinks throughout the day and then drives home at 5:00.
Physiological dependence as evidenced by tolerance or withdrawal	Phillip used to only take one pain pill each day for his bad back. Now, he has to take three pills to experience any relief.

Interactive

Start Over

Depressants and Stimulants

LO 4.9 **Differentiate depressant and stimulant psychoactive drugs and their effects on the body.**

Psychoactive drugs can be legal or illegal and come in various forms. Many drugs differ in their effects on the body and on how quickly those effects are experienced. Therefore, drugs tend to be grouped together in categories with substances that share similar pharmacological properties. There is some variation in the way to classify psychoactive drugs, but a common method includes the classes of depressants, stimulants, narcotics, and hallucinogens (see Figure 4.5).

Figure 4.5 Classes of Drugs

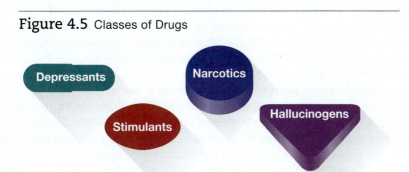

DEPRESSANTS As the name suggests, **depressants** are drugs that depress or slow down the central nervous system and other bodily functions. The most common depressants include alcohol, barbiturates, and benzodiazepines.

Alcohol Alcohol is a liquid derived from the distillation or fermentation of grains, fruits, or vegetables. Alcohol is ingested orally and metabolized by the stomach and liver. One common misconception is that one "drink" constitutes what is considered one serving of alcohol. One drink could be a 1-ounce shot of vodka, an 8-ounce glass of wine, or a pint (20 ounces) of beer. Each of these drinks has a different amount of alcohol, which makes it difficult to assess when you should stop drinking if you are only counting drinks. Technically, one serving of alcohol is .6 fluid ounces of pure alcohol (which is the same as a 12-ounce beer with 5 percent alcohol content). Most cocktails contain more than this amount of alcohol and therefore constitute more than one serving per drink.

depressants

class of drugs that depress or slow down the central nervous system and other bodily functions

How Much Do You Know About Alcohol?

Interactive

Let's try a quick true or false quiz and see how much you know about alcohol and its effects.

1. Heavier people can drink more alcohol before feeling its effects and becoming impaired.

○ True
○ False

2. People who have a low percentage of body fat will become intoxicated faster than those with a higher level of body fat.

○ True
○ False

3. Women become intoxicated more quickly than men.

○ True
○ False

4. People first experience impairment when their blood alcohol level reaches 0.08 percent.

○ True
○ False

Previous   Next

It typically takes about 30 minutes to start feeling the effects of alcohol, although there are several factors that can affect how long it takes for the effects to be noticeable and the intensity with which these effects are felt.

So, how did you do on the quiz? Perhaps you learned something you didn't already know about alcohol. Many aspects of alcohol are counterintuitive, meaning what we think is obvious is actually incorrect (and often the opposite of what we thought). For example, consider the fact that alcohol is classified as a depressant. Most people associate alcohol with feelings of euphoria (happiness) and a loss of inhibitions and self-control. This doesn't seem to fit with the idea of a depressant. But, in reality, alcohol indirectly stimulates the release of GABA (an inhibitory neurotransmitter), which slows down and inhibits (or depresses) the brain (Behar et al., 1999). One of the first areas of the brain to be affected by alcohol (and therefore GABA), is the frontal cortex, the area of the brain responsible for impulse control and good judgment (Aron et al., 2014; Tsujii et al., 2011). Think of it as a double negative equaling a positive. Alcohol inhibits inhibitions, resulting in a more outgoing, carefree, and sometimes inappropriate person.

Gregarious behavior and decreased inhibitions are a few of the effects of alcohol commonly sought after by students on college campuses. Many colleges report problems with students engaging in *binge drinking*, which is defined as consuming four (for women) and five (for men) drinks during a single occasion. Binge drinking is associated with short-term risks such as injuries, sexual assault, other violent acts, and alcohol poisoning. The following video, *The Physical Effects of Alcohol*, describes the effect of alcohol on the brain and some of the longer-term problems that can arise from the overuse of alcohol.

The Physical Effects of Alcohol

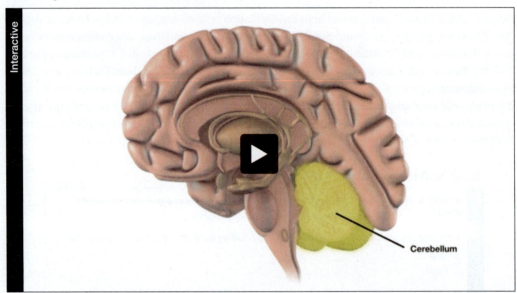

Cerebellum

According to the Centers for Disease Control and Prevention (CDC), excessive drinking over time can lead to chronic health conditions such as high blood pressure, heart disease, liver problems (e.g., cirrhosis), cancer, depression, anxiety, and a variety of occupational, familial, and social problems. In addition to the longer term physical and psychological consequences of drinking, researchers have demonstrated that binge drinking while in college has a negative effect on a student's critical thinking abilities over the course of their college career (Trolian et al., 2016). Furthermore, it appears that the students most at risk for alcohol's negative effects on critical thinking were those students who had the weakest critical thinking abilities when entering college.

Barbiturates Barbiturates, such as Seconal or Luminal (generic name phenobarbital), are also classified as depressants because they decrease the functioning of the central nervous system; because of this, they are sometimes referred to as "downers." Their effects can range from mild sedation to coma and death. Before their addictive potential and lethality were fully realized, barbiturates were frequently prescribed as sleep aids. Barbiturates can be particularly dangerous because of the tendency for those who are abusing them to combine them with other depressants, such as alcohol. Many people have died (either accidentally or by intended suicide) as a result of the additive effect of ingesting multiple drugs from the same class (Weathermon & Crabb, 1999).

Benzodiazepines Compared to barbiturates, benzodiazepines (also known as tranquilizers) are now most often prescribed for those with difficulty sleeping. Benzodiazepines, which are also frequently prescribed for anxiety, are a central nervous system depressant; and, while they can produce dependence, they are much less likely to result in death from overdose than barbiturates. Among the most common benzodiazepines today are Valium, Xanax, Ativan, and Klonopin. Xanax (generic name alprazolam) is a prescription drug commonly abused on college campuses (Brandt et al., 2014; Droppa et al., 2014). Its high potency, rapid onset of action, reinforcing effects, and short half-life make people highly susceptible to physical and psychological dependence (Chen et al., 2014). The withdrawal symptoms can be intense and include insomnia, shaking, nausea/vomiting, increased anxiety, and depression.

STIMULANTS Stimulants have an opposite physiological effect compared to depressants. **Stimulants** excite or increase the functioning of the central nervous system and speed up the body. The most common stimulants include caffeine, nicotine, amphetamines, and cocaine.

stimulants
a drug that excites or increases the functioning of the central nervous system

Caffeine Although not typically thought of as a psychoactive drug, caffeine is the world's most widely used drug (Meredith et al., 2013). Caffeine is a naturally-occurring substance found in many different plants and is consumed in a variety of ways (e.g., coffee, tea, energy drinks, cold/headache medicines, sodas, chocolate, and weight loss aids). More than 85 percent of adults and children consume caffeine on a regular basis (APA, 2013), with the average adult intake between 200 mg and 300 mg/day. For reference, one cup of drip coffee can contain anywhere from 95–200 mg of caffeine. Most people think a shot of espresso contains a large dose of caffeine; however, it has about half the amount of caffeine contained in a cup of coffee. High doses of caffeine, typically 500 mg or more, can cause intoxication, and prolonged usage can result in withdrawal symptoms (Bergin & Kendler, 2012). Caffeine headaches (or really, lack-of-caffeine headaches) and fatigue are among the most common withdrawal symptoms. These withdrawal symptoms were found to be significant enough that *caffeine withdrawal* has been added to the most recent list of disorders in the DSM-5 (APA, 2013).

Nicotine Another legal stimulant drug is nicotine, which is contained in all tobacco products, including cigarettes and smokeless tobacco. Cigarette smoking is the leading cause of preventable disease and death throughout the world. According to the CDC, cigarette smoking causes more than 480,000 deaths in the United States each year (CDC, 2017). Smoking has been found to harm nearly every organ in the human body and yet each day 3,200 adolescents smoke their first cigarette, a behavior that can quickly lead to a powerful addiction.

While they don't necessarily look like cigarettes, e-cigarettes can deliver just as much or more nicotine to the user through vaporized liquid.

Electronic cigarettes (e-cigarettes), which have become more popular in recent years, simulate smoking by vaporizing a liquid solution (known as e-liquid). Rather than delivering nicotine through smoke, the drug is inhaled as a vapor.

It is possible to purchase e-liquids without nicotine; however, the majority of people using e-cigarettes are doing so because they wish to remove the additional harmful effects of smoking tobacco. Successful marketing of e-cigarettes has promoted them as a healthier alternative to smoking cigarettes and as a potential strategy for those wishing to quit smoking all together. While there is evidence that e-cigarettes can be a less harmful alternative to smoking tobacco cigarettes (Farsalinos & Polosa, 2014), other studies point to the fact that e-cigarettes are not toxic free, and the long-term

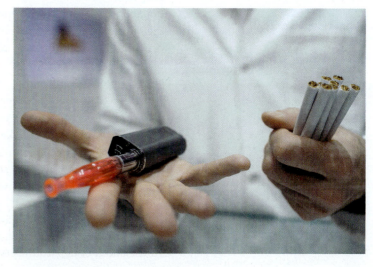

In 2013, more than **a quarter million** middle and high school students **never** smoked regular cigarettes but **had** used e-cigarettes...

3 times as many as 2011!

In 2014, the CDC published a press release to bring attention to the concern that adolescents don't view e-cigarettes as harmful.

negative effects are not yet known (Drummond & Upson, 2014). In an effort to standardize the materials and chemicals used in the devices, the Food and Drug Administration did not announce its plan until 2014 to regulate e-cigarettes in the same way as other tobacco products.

Despite the marketing, there is little scientific evidence that e-cigarettes assist in smoking cessation better than any of the other already-approved methods such as: nicotine gum, nicotine patches, and certain medications (Cobb & Abrams, 2014; Rom et al., 2015). One major concern is that adolescents, the population most vulnerable to start smoking, will believe that e-cigarettes aren't harmful. A 2014 study reported that 8.7 percent of eighth-grade students had used an e-cigarette within the past month, compared to only 1.4 percent who reported smoking a traditional cigarette (Schraufnagel, 2015).

Amphetamines Amphetamines are stimulant drugs synthesized by combining various compounds. There are legal, medicinal uses for amphetamines that include the treatment of narcolepsy, obesity (amphetamines were once commonly used as diet pills because of the side effect of decreased appetite), and attention-deficit hyperactivity disorder (ADHD). *Methylphenidate* (not to be confused with methamphetamine) is a modified amphetamine marketed under the names Ritalin and Concerta and is used in the treatment of ADHD. It may seem odd that doctors prescribe a stimulant to people who are already hyperactive, but one way to think about ADHD is that the individual's brain is in need of stimulation and therefore the person looks to provide that high level of stimulation in the environment. It is a form of self-stimulation, which expresses itself as hyperactivity, distractibility, inattention, and inability to follow instructions. Therefore, stimulant drugs can fulfill the brain's need by stimulating dopamine and norepinephrine neurotransmitters in the prefrontal cortex (Arnsten, 2006). Rather than seeking stimulation from the external world, the person receives that stimulation through medicine, which alleviates the common symptoms associated with ADHD.

Methamphetamine Methamphetamine is a highly addictive and potent central nervous system stimulant that comes in various forms (e.g., powder, liquid, clear chunks) and is known by a variety of names (e.g., meth, crystal meth, ice, crank, speed, glass, etc.). Any fan of the hit television series, *Breaking Bad*, can tell you about the devastating effects methamphetamine has on individuals, families, and society. Methamphetamine causes large amounts of dopamine and serotonin to be released in the brain, which is responsible for the initial intense, euphoric high described by users. After the initial high, the other effects (increased activity, decreased appetite and need for sleep, enhanced sexual arousal) can continue for an additional 6–12 hours. Due to this relatively long half-life (the length of time the drug stays in the body), the withdrawal symptoms are particularly intense and long-lasting, which also contributes to the desperate need to continue to use the drug. It has been shown that methamphetamine destroys dopamine receptors in the brain (Nordahl et al., 2003), leaving the user "chasing a high" like they experienced their first time using the drug. This becomes an impossible feat because the drug has destroyed the very receptors needed in the brain to experience such intense feelings of euphoria.

Cocaine Cocaine is another powerful central nervous system stimulant made from the leaves of the coca plant. It comes in powdered form, which can be snorted, dissolved in water and injected, or smoked. Interestingly, cocaine is the only drug known to be both a central nervous system stimulant and a local anesthetic. As you can see in the following animation, *How Cocaine Effects the Brain*, cocaine exerts its effects on the brain by blocking the reuptake of dopamine, which leaves more dopamine in the synapse to stimulate the postsynaptic neuron.

According to a 2013 national survey on drug use, 0.6 percent of people 12 years or older were currently using cocaine, with the largest group involving 18- to 25-year-olds (Substance Abuse and Mental Health Services Administration, 2014).

How Cocaine Affects the Brain

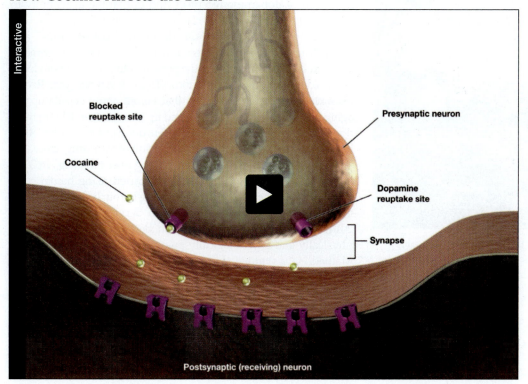

Interactive

Blocked reuptake site

Cocaine

Presynaptic neuron

Dopamine reuptake site

Synapse

Postsynaptic (receiving) neuron

Narcotics and Hallucinogens

LO 4.10 **Describe the effects of narcotic and hallucinogenic psychoactive drugs.**

Some ingredients found in certain drugs are naturally occurring (e.g., opium, mushrooms), which gives some people the impression they can't be dangerous if they are "organic." Both narcotics and hallucinogens can contain chemicals found naturally, and drugs from both classes can have devastating effects when misused.

NARCOTICS **Narcotics** are a type of depressant used medically in the management of pain. They work by stimulating the body's internal pain management system (i.e., endorphins), which aids in the relief of pain (Minozzi et al., 2012). They can also produce feelings of euphoria due to their actions in the reward areas of the brain. Narcotics are also referred to as *opiates* or *opioids* because they are all derived from opium, which comes from the opium poppy.

The most commonly prescribed narcotics for pain include codeine, morphine, hydrocodone (e.g., Vicodin, Lortab), and oxycodone (e.g., OxyContin, Percocet). Because of their effects, these drugs are also commonly abused by either crushing them into a powder and snorting or taking significantly more than the recommended dose. Physical dependence can develop, even among those taking narcotics as prescribed, meaning withdrawal symptoms will be experienced when the drug has been metabolized or excreted from the body.

One of the most dangerous narcotics is **heroin**, which is made from morphine. Heroin activates specific opioid receptors in the brain, which in turn stimulates dopamine in the reward centers of the brain causing the sensation of pleasure (Blum et al., 2012). Users describe these feelings as a "rush," and they are often accompanied by a feeling of warmth, heaviness in the extremities, and possibly nausea/vomiting and/or itching. Research using brain scan technology has been able to confirm that heroin directly reduces stress-related emotions through its effects in the left amygdala, providing some explanation for the continued desire for the substance (Schmidt et al., 2013). After the initial effects, heroin causes drowsiness and slows down heart rate and breathing, which has the potential to lead to permanent

narcotics

a category of drugs used medically in the management of pain

heroin

a narcotic that activates specific opioid receptors that stimulate dopamine in the reward centers of the brain, causing feelings of intense pleasure

Opium, which is used to make many narcotics, is derived from the seeds of an unripe opium poppy.

Many people are under the false impression that if something is "organic" or found in nature, that it can't be dangerous. Psilocybin, or better known as "magic mushroom" can be found in nature, but can also produce powerful hallucinogenic, and sometimes dangerous effects.

brain damage, coma, or death. Over time, heroin use leads to a reduction of dopamine receptors and dopamine availability to the brain (Martinez et al., 2012).

You have likely seen those disturbing "before drugs" and "after drugs" photos often used to deter people from experimenting with drugs. In most cases, the person in the "after" photo looks years older—even if the change took place in less than a year. Recent research has actually confirmed that heroin abuse speeds up the aging process at the cellular level and in terms of overall brain functioning (Cheng et al., 2013). Heroin users don't just look older—they have actually aged at a faster rate as a result of their drug abuse.

While heroin use has been increasing over time (e.g., in 2012, almost double the number of people started using heroin compared to 2006), the number of teens using heroin has been decreasing (Substance Abuse Mental Health Services Administration, 2014) (see LO 3.16). Recovery from heroin addiction can be a physically and psychologically painful process (Fox et al., 2013). Methadone, a synthetic form of heroin, which is taken orally and has a much longer half-life, is prescribed to some patients as an alternative to heroin. Advocates of this *harm-reduction approach* argue that using methadone decreases the risks of crime (e.g., stealing to get money to buy drugs), infection/disease (e.g., hepatitis and HIV from sharing needles), and overdose because it is provided to the patient by a doctor and monitored by medical staff (Alavian et al., 2013; Sees et al., 2000). For many people attempting to recover from heroin addiction, methadone and other related medications have been shown to increase the probability of recovery by keeping patients in treatment (Proctor et al., 2014).

hallucinogens

class of drugs that can produce unusual sensations, distortions in the perception of reality, and intense emotional mood swings

HALLUCINOGENS Sometime referred to as *psychedelic drugs*, **hallucinogens** can be naturally occurring (e.g., magic mushrooms) or manufactured in a laboratory (e.g., LSD). Hallucinogens produce unusual sensations, distortions in the perception of reality and, in some cases, intense emotional mood swings. Although the types of hallucinogens can be quite varied, most appear to influence the neurotransmitter serotonin (Lee & Roth, 2012). Synthetic drugs such as LSD (d-lysergic acid diethylamide) are synthesized from an acid found in a particular fungus that grows on rye and other grains and is one of the most potent mood-altering drugs (National Institute on Drug Abuse, 2016). Psilocybin is found in certain naturally growing mushrooms and can produce unreliable and variable effects due to the variations of the drug and other hallucinogenic compounds found in the mushrooms. Psilocybin is one drug that can't be inactivated through cooking or freezing, which is why they are sometimes used to make "tea" or "brownies." So why are drugs like magic mushrooms referred to as psychedelic? Substances from this class of drugs appear to alter consciousness and interact with the brain to produce widely varied and often intense sensory experiences. In a complicated but informative study, a group of researchers in Italy mapped the connection and relationship among networks of brain cells in a "normal brain" (see Figure 4.6) and a psilocybin-influenced brain (see Figure 4.7) (Petri et al., 2014).

Figure 4.6 Mapped Connections of a Drug-Free Brain

Figure 4.7 Mapped Connections of a Brain on Psilocybin-"Magic" Mushrooms

Even if you don't have much of a background in neuroscience, you can probably see from these figures why people under the influence of hallucinogens might taste colors, feel sounds, and see smells (a condition called *synesthesia*).

Although its effects are much less intense than other hallucinogens, **marijuana** can produce some altered sensations, feelings of well-being, and changes in cognition (e.g., difficulty thinking and impaired memory). Marijuana is made from the dried flowers, leaves, stems, and seeds of the hemp plant, which contains the chemical *tetrahydrocannabinol* (THC). Marijuana is typically smoked, although the practice of *dabbing* has become widespread recently. Dabbing involves the inhalation of concentrated THC that is created through butane extraction. This process can create a crystalized product close to 80 percent THC concentration (Stogner & Miller, 2015). Users of both marijuana and "dabs" have noted higher tolerance and withdrawal symptoms, with dabbing suggesting a higher addictive potential (Loflin & Earleywine, 2014).

Marijuana use is one of the few drugs (either legal or illegal) that continues to be on the rise, particularly among high school students (Substance Abuse and Mental Health Services Administration, 2014). According to Dr. Nora Volkow, the Director for the National Institute on Drug Abuse, 1 in 15 high school seniors use marijuana daily. This increased use is accompanied by what she refers to as "myths of marijuana," including the beliefs that marijuana is safer than other drugs, not addictive, and can be beneficial (National Institute on Drug Abuse, 2013). While messages in our environment are likely driving many of these beliefs, Dr. Volkow highlights the importance of getting the facts from research out to adolescents (see Figure 4.8).

marijuana

a drug containing tetrahydrocannabinol (THC); can produce altered sensations, feelings of well-being, and changes in cognition

Figure 4.8 Marijuana's Effect on the Developing Brain

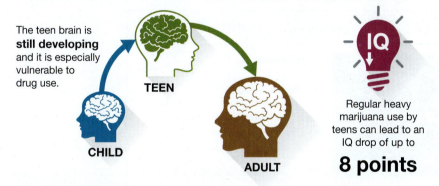

MARIJUANA MAY HURT THE DEVELOPING TEEN BRAIN

The teen brain is **still developing** and it is especially vulnerable to drug use.

TEEN

CHILD

ADULT

Regular heavy marijuana use by teens can lead to an IQ drop of up to

8 points

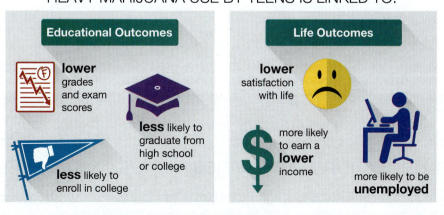

HEAVY MARIJUANA USE BY TEENS IS LINKED TO:

Educational Outcomes

lower grades and exam scores

less likely to graduate from high school or college

less likely to enroll in college

Life Outcomes

lower satisfaction with life

more likely to earn a **lower** income

more likely to be **unemployed**

Classes and Actions of Drugs

Interactive

Now, that we have described the different classes of drugs and how they work, it is time to test your understanding. Study the table below. When you are ready, test yourself by dragging and dropping the correct class of drug to its properties.

Class of Drugs	Primary Action or Effects	Examples of Drugs from This Class
Depressants	• Decrease the functioning of the central nervous system • Produce feelings of relaxation	Alcohol Barbiturates Benzodiazepines
Stimulants	• Increase the functioning of the central nervous system • Produce feelings of energy and excitement	Caffeine Nicotine Amphetamine Methamphetamine Cocaine
Narcotics	• Mimic endorphins • Produce feelings of euphoria and pain relief	Morphine Oxycodone Heroin
Hallucinogens	• Affect serotonin in the brain • Produce a state of altered consciousness and creates perceptual distortions	LSD Psilocybin (mushrooms) Marijuana

Check Your Understanding

Adaptive Pathway 4.2: Drugs and Dependence

Interactive

INTRODUCTION	ADAPTIVE PATHWAY	RESULTS

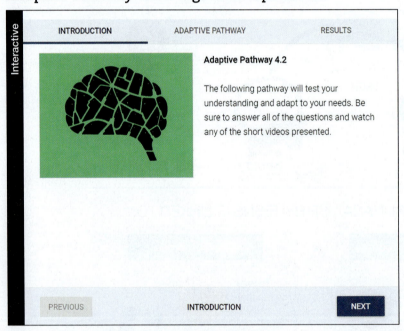

Adaptive Pathway 4.2

The following pathway will test your understanding and adapt to your needs. Be sure to answer all of the questions and watch any of the short videos presented.

PREVIOUS   INTRODUCTION   NEXT

Shared Writing: Harm Reduction Approaches: Helpful or Harmful?

Harm reduction is both a philosophy and a set of practical strategies aimed at reducing the detrimental consequences of drug use. Harm reduction approaches include needle exchange programs (where heroin users can exchange dirty needles for clean ones); specialized housing that keeps drug users off the streets and allows illegal drug use while living in the housing; and free or inexpensive methadone (synthetic heroin) given to heroin users as a substitute for injected heroin from the streets, where the purity is unknown. There are pros and cons to this approach. Do you think harm reduction is a good strategy in addressing drug use and users? Why or why not?

Quiz for Module 4.8–4.10

1. Physiological dependence on a substance typically includes
_____ and _____.

   a. emotional cravings; restlessness

   b. tolerance; emotional cravings

   c. withdrawal; memory loss

   d. tolerance; withdrawal

2. Markita promised her parents she would stop smoking marijuana. Every time she worried about school and bills, she would remember how marijuana relaxed her and made her feel good. She ended up smoking again and again, even though she hated disappointing her parents. This is an example of what type of dependence?

   a. Psychological

   b. Physiological

   c. Tolerance

   d. Psychiatric

3. Rina works hard all week long. On the weekend, she engages in binge drinking with her friends. How many drinks must she have in one night for it to be considered binge drinking?

   a. 10   **b.** 7

   c. 4   **d.** 5

4. Which neurotransmitter receptors does methamphetamine destroy in the brain?

   a. Endorphin

   b. Dopamine

   c. Serotonin

   d. Noreprinephrine

5. Benzodiazepines come from the class of drugs called
_____, which _____ the functioning of the central nervous system.

   a. depressants; decrease

   b. narcotics; decrease

   c. depressants; increase

   d. narcotics; increase

6. Heroin is classified as a _____ and directly _____ stress-related emotions.

   a. hallucinogen; decreases

   b. narcotic; increases

   c. stimulant; increases

   d. narcotic; decreases

Module 4.11: Piecing It Together: Hypnosis

LO 4.11 **Analyze how the cross-cutting themes of psychology apply to hypnosis.**

What comes to mind when you hear the term *hypnosis*? You might think of the stage-show magician who convinces his subjects to act like chickens or the highway billboard that touts hypnosis as a quick fix for obesity or smoking. These popular conceptions of hypnosis—as a form of entertainment or a miracle cure—can obscure the term's true meaning, and merits, within the field of psychology. At its most basic level, hypnosis is an exercise in suggestion. The American Society of Clinical Hypnosis describes **hypnosis** as "a state of consciousness involving focused attention and reduced peripheral awareness characterized by an enhanced capacity for response to suggestion" (Elkins et al., 2015). At a basic level, hypnosis involves an altered state of consciousness; it has sometimes been likened to using a magnifying glass to focus the rays of the sun and make them more powerful. This image represents the idea that when our mind is focused, we can use it in powerful ways.

Despite some misperceptions that hypnosis is a passive state, focused on the directions of the hypnotist, hypnosis is viewed as a resource for the patient or participant. Hypnosis is seen as a solution-oriented strategy, focused on the patient's overall potentials (Häuser et al., 2016).

During hypnosis, one person, the hypnotist, makes suggestions to another person regarding the perceptions, feelings, thoughts, or behaviors that the subject can expect to experience. It is ultimately up to the participant whether or not they will choose to accept the hypnotic suggestions. The mystique around hypnosis has contributed to some misunderstanding of the process by which it works (or doesn't work). Nonetheless, many people are intrigued by this strategy that affects our level of awareness or consciousness. In the following sections, we'll

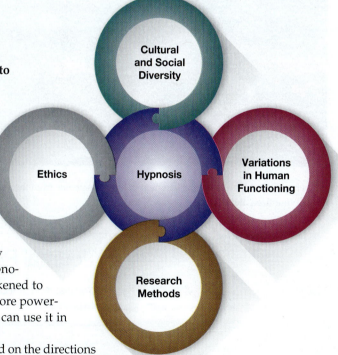

hypnosis

a state consciousness involving focused attention and reduced awareness of surroundings, accompanied by an enhanced state of suggestibility

Hypnosis involves an altered state of consciousness. Despite what many people think, a person can't be hypnotized against their will.

Stage hypnosis is a form of entertainment that invites people from the audience to be hypnotized and become the stars of the show.

explore a few of the questions people may have when it comes to hypnosis.

Variations in Human Functioning

- Can everyone be hypnotized?
- Are there certain characteristics that make some people more likely than others to be successfully hypnotized?

All hypnosis involves suggestion; however, there are various types, reasons for, and applications of hypnotic suggestion. *Medical hypnosis* involves the alleviation of somatic or medical symptoms or the reduction of mental stress during medical procedures. *Hypnotherapy* is more psychological in nature and focuses on improvements in problem solving, changes in behavior, thoughts, or emotions and/or the resolution of emotionally stressful events. *Hypnotic communication* occurs when a patient receives suggestions while awake or while under general anesthesia (but not in a hypnotic trance). This form of hypnosis has been found effective in improving the doctor-patient therapeutic relationship and communication (Häuser et al., 2016). Finally, *stage hypnosis* involves a demonstration of hypnotic events with the sole purpose of entertaining an audience.

Hypnosis has been effectively used in all of the modalities mentioned above for a variety of reasons and conditions (Schaefert et al., 2014; Tefikow et al., 2013). Specifically, medical hypnosis and hypnotherapy have demonstrated efficacy for the treatment of chronic lower back pain (Tan et al., 2015), depression (Alladin, 2012; Alladin & Alibhai, 2007; Shih et al., 2009), anxiety (Golden, 2012), stress (Cardeña et al., 2013), irritable bowel syndrome (Schaefert et al., 2014), controlling vital signs during surgery (Behnaz & Solhpour, 2016); relief from nausea and vomiting (Dupuis et al., 2017), pregnancy and childbirth (Beevi et al., 2016; Werner et al., 2013), and many other conditions.

There appear to be both personal and situational factors that can affect the success of hypnosis. For example, it has been determined that mid-morning is the best time to be hypnotized, and afternoon is the time when people are least susceptible to hypnotic suggestion (Green et al., 2015).

Journal Prompt: The Best Time to Be Hypnotized

You just read that certain times of day are better than others to be hypnotized. Why do you think hypnosis is more effective mid-morning compared to afternoon?

You may have heard people talk about whether or not a person is "susceptible" to hypnosis. In fact, in the late 1950s and early 1960s, groups of researchers from Stanford University and Harvard University independently published hypnotic susceptibility scales (Shor & Orne, 1962; Weitzenhoffer & Hilgard, 1962). These scales are still often used today when people, often researchers, want to classify participants into "highs" (highly susceptible to hypnotic suggestion) or "lows" (much less susceptible to hypnotic suggestion). There are other shorter susceptibility tests available as well. This Arm Movement Suggestibility Test takes just a couple of minutes to administer and can be done anywhere. Would you like to try?

Take a Hypnosis Susceptibility Test with Dr. John Mohl

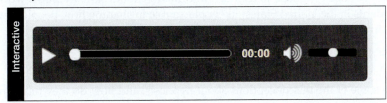

So.....did you feel your arms move? This test is a good one for hypnotists because they can gauge if a person would be a good candidate for hypnosis by how freely their arms move in response to the suggestion.

Researchers have had a difficult time finding reliable psychological differences (e.g., personality traits) between people with varying levels of susceptibility (Cardeña & Terhune, 2014). However, it has been suggested for some time that people who have a tendency to become completely absorbed in activities such as reading a good book, watching a movie, or listening to music possess a trait that will allow them to become absorbed in the hypnosis process. A study attempting to operationalize this "trait" found those who were highly susceptible to hypnosis were also more likely to report dissociative experiences (i.e., detachment from reality) in everyday life. They were also found to experience increased sensitivity and empathy toward others (Facco et al., 2017). Neurological research has also found differences in brain activity between "highs" and "lows" that is thought to represent differences in attentional processes with those who are highly susceptible better able to focus or control attention (Cojan et al., 2015; Santarcangelo, 2014).

Cultural and Social Diversity

- Does hypnosis really work?

- Is hypnosis the same throughout different countries and cultures?

The Variations in Human Functioning section suggested that neurological differences can account for some of the differences between people with respect to their ability to be hypnotized. It is likely, however, that other factors, including where someone lives and the culture within which they are raised, can influence how hypnosis is practiced or perceived.

Hypnosis has a long history, although historically its roots have been found in shamanism. A "shaman" has been described as a healer who heals others by manipulating the power of spirits by using a trance technique. Shamanism is a practice that exists in many cultures around the world, including Asia, Africa, and the Americas.

Hypnosis grew out of shamanism and other spiritual healing rituals (Woodard, 2005). Shamans and hypnotists are similar in that they both serve to attempt to relieve suffering, in part due to the relationship built with their clients and being viewed as a respectable authority. However, unlike hypnotists, shamans are in a much more visible position within the community and are often seen as responsible for the overall health of the community.

There is some recognition, in both shamanism and hypnotism, of the role that expectancies may play in the healing process. That is, if a person believes they can be healed, they will more likely experience success. While some studies have compared cultural views and attitudes about hypnosis and found similarities (Green et al., 2006), others have not found consistent similarities across cultures. Jacquith et al. (1996) conducted research with Malaysian students attending college in Malaysia, compared to

Shamanism is an ancient healing tradition practiced in many indigenous cultures around the world. Modern-day hypnosis is believed to have roots in Shamanism.

Malaysian students attending college in the United States. They found that the typical relationship between hypnotizability, the ability to become absorbed in an activity, and responding to waking suggestions by another person was not found among Malaysian students attending college in Malaysia. However, the relationship was evident among Malaysian students studying in the United States. The researchers concluded that culture-based expectancies (the students in Malaysia had not been exposed to as much information about how hypnosis works compared to those students in the United States) likely play a role in shaping how people respond to, and experience, hypnosis.

Ethics

- What are some of the misconceptions about hypnosis, and how do they relate to ethical concerns that may arise when working with a person who is in a highly suggestible altered state of consciousness?

Every mental health practitioner is expected to adhere to an ethical code. For those who practice hypnosis, additional issues must be considered due to the nature of the practice and potential for misuse and/or harm. There are numerous misconceptions about hypnosis, and it is thought that these misunderstandings lead to fear and negative opinions about hypnosis.

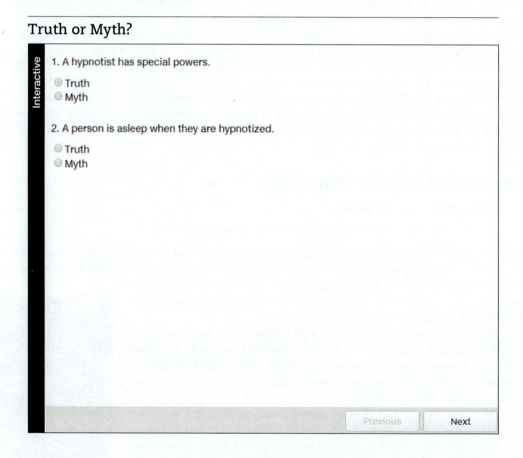

Truth or Myth?

Interactive

1. A hypnotist has special powers.

  ○ Truth
  ○ Myth

2. A person is asleep when they are hypnotized.

  ○ Truth
  ○ Myth

Previous   Next

Even though many of the beliefs people hold about hypnosis are incorrect, there is no question that the hypnotist is in a unique and powerful position with their patient. Therefore, professional organizations such as the Society for Clinical and Experimental Hypnosis have suggested the following standards for the use of hypnosis (Voit & DeLaney, 2005):

- The hypnotist is in good standing with their professional organization.
- The use of hypnosis is restricted to the hypnotist's area of expertise.
- Hypnosis is only used to promote health, not entertainment.
- Any advertising is responsible and accurate.
- Hypnosis is used to contribute to the welfare of the patients or research participants.

Research involving hypnosis can be conducted where the hypnotic state itself is the focus of the research, or where other psychological phenomena is of interest and hypnosis is used as part of the methodology to answer the research question(s). For example, hypnosis has often been investigated as a strategy for managing pain. In these cases, experiments involve the purposeful induction of both pain and hypnosis (both of which tend to raise ethical concerns). All research studies must be approved by an ethical review committee. With respect to research involving hypnosis, the committee will pay special attention to the following ethical principles (Enea & Dafinoiu, 2011):

- Informed consent by the participant

- Protection of the participants from mental or physical harm

- Allowing the participant to withdraw from the research at any time without penalty

- Confidentiality and protection of the participant's personal information

- Debriefing at the end of the study, which is especially important if any deception was used in the research

In the final piece of this puzzle, we will examine aspects of research focused on hypnosis and some of the important methodological considerations when conducting this type of work.

Research Methods

- How has research been conducted with hypnosis, and has anyone figured out what is really happening in the brain during hypnosis?

If we know that highly suggestible people are the ones most likely to benefit from hypnosis, is it possible that it is merely the *placebo effect* that is responsible for any posthypnotic change, rather than the hypnosis itself? A placebo effect is a beneficial effect in response to an inert substance believed to exist as a response to an individual's belief or expectancy of change. Rates of the placebo effect vary widely, but it is common to see ranges from 15 percent to 50 percent of people responding to "placebo treatments" (Enck et al., 2011).

If highly suggestible people undergoing hypnosis are experiencing the placebo effect, then you would expect a correlation (i.e., a relationship) between how susceptible someone is to hypnotic suggestion and how likely they are to respond to a placebo medicine. One group of researchers set out to empirically test this question. Sheiner et al. (2016) assessed participants with a test of hypnotic susceptibility (similar to what you experienced in the Variations of Human Functioning section). They were then given a placebo capsule: One group was told it was an inert substance, and the other group was told the pill contained a heavy dose of an herbal sedative.

Research Methodology

Interactive

In the study described above, the group that was told the pill was an inert substance and should have no effect is called the _____ group.

In the study described above, the group that was told the pill contained a heavy dose of herbal sedative and should make them feel sleepy and relaxed is called the _____ group.

WORD BANK
- experimental
- control

Start Over   Check Answers

The researchers found a small, but significant correlation ($r = .29$) between hypnotic suggestibility and self-reported ratings of drowsiness. That is, the higher a person scored on a measure of hypnotic suggestibility, suggesting a better response to hypnosis, the more likely they were to report feelings of drowsiness when told they were given a strong sedative (even though they weren't given any active substance). Given the results of this study, it might be tempting to conclude that hypnosis and a placebo response are similar experiences, with different names.

However, an important part of science involves the ability to replicate research findings. Shortly after the researchers completed the study described above, they performed another very similar study in an attempt to replicate their results. Despite similar methodology, the researchers were unable to demonstrate the same relationship between suggestibility and subjective relaxation (Lifshitz et al., 2017). In fact, this time they found a correlation between suggestibility and an objective decrease in heart rate of those in the experimental group. The differing results of these studies led the researchers to highlight the complexity of individual differences, the role of expectancies, and how situational variables can interact with these factors to produce a variety of responses to a placebo. These two studies demonstrate the importance of replication in science. Had the second study never been conducted, what would people have concluded about the relationship between hypnotic suggestibility and placebo effects?

As is the case nowadays with many questions regarding psychological phenomena, researchers have turned to brain imaging techniques to understand the underlying mechanisms of hypnosis.

Figure 4.9 Patient Undergoing an fMRI

Hypnosis in the Brain

Interactive

MRI

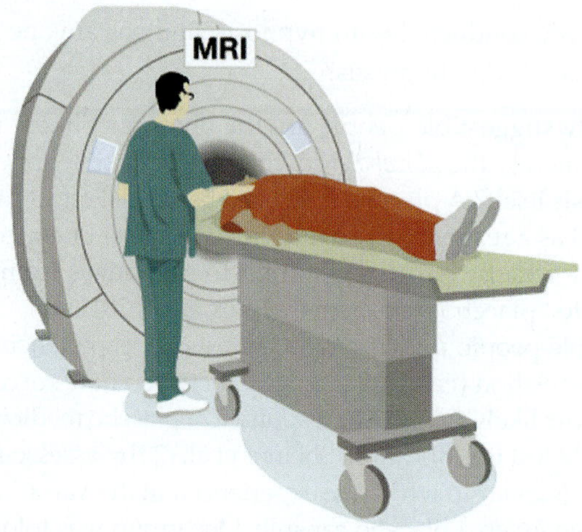

In 2016, a group of researchers attempted to understand the brain activity associated with a hypnotic state (Jiang et al., 2016). They used functional *magnetic resonance imaging (fMRI)* to examine the connectivity between different areas of the brain when an individual is hypnotized.

1 of 6   Previous   Next

Quiz for Module 4.11

1. Hypnosis is a state of _____ involving focused _____ and reduced peripheral awareness characterized by an enhanced capacity for response to suggestion.
   - **a.** awareness; drive
   - **b.** consciousness; attention
   - **c.** awareness; attention
   - **d.** consciousness; drive

2. Hypnosis has been shown to be effective in the treatment of:
   - **a.** depression and anxiety.
   - **b.** schizophrenia and personality disorders.
   - **c.** cancer and lupus.
   - **d.** cancer and depression.

3. Zsolt is planning to try hypnosis to help him stop smoking. Based on your knowledge of the best time of day for most people to be hypnotized, when should he make his appointment?
   - **a.** Early morning
   - **b.** Late afternoon
   - **c.** Mid-morning
   - **d.** Noon

4. What is a common test of hypnosis susceptibility?
   - **a.** Watch the watch test
   - **b.** Finger steeple test
   - **c.** Count back from ten test
   - **d.** Finger tapping test

Summary: Consciousness

Module 4.1–4.2   What Is Consciousness?

Consciousness represents the awareness of our internal and external environment. **Meditation,** one of many activities that can produce an altered state of consciousness, can involve focused or regulated breathing, specific body positions, minimization of external distractions, mental imagery, and/or mental clarity. **Focused attention meditation** involves directing attention toward an internal or external object for the entire meditation session. In contrast, **open monitoring meditation** doesn't focus on just one object or experience, but requires the person to become a nonjudgmental observer of all aspects of experience (e.g., thoughts, emotions, sounds). **Selective attention** allows for the focus on one stimulus or perception at a given time. An example of selective attention is the **cocktail party phenomenon,** or our ability to selectively tune into particular messages while filtering out others in a crowded, noisy, or chaotic environment. **Selective inattention** (or **inattentional blindness**) is the opposite of selective attention, which refers to the environmental stimuli that are screened out or ignored while your attention is selectively focused on something else. **Change blindness,** a form of selective inattention, occurs when large changes in the environment are overlooked due to an interruption in the visual field. **Multitasking** is nothing more than attention divided among two or more stimuli or activities, where attention is switched from one activity to another (rather than attending to more than one activity at the same time.)

Module 4.3–4.7   Sleep and Dreaming

Sleep refers to the daily, natural loss of consciousness and operates roughly on a 24-hour cycle called a **circadian rhythm.** This rhythm is controlled by the **suprachiasmatic nucleus (SCN),** a small part of the hypothalamus that sits on top of the optic chiasm. Sleep consists of several predictable stages called non-REM (NREM) and one additional period referred to as **rapid eye movement (REM),** a recurring stage of sleep during which vivid dreams usually occur. While awake and active, the brain is characterized by low-amplitude, high frequency **beta waves. Alpha waves** are slower and are present in a relaxed/drowsy state. As the first stage of sleep (**N1**) is entered, alpha wave activity decreases and larger, slower **theta waves** appear. **N2** is the next stage and is characterized by light sleep. As sleep continues to deepen, we enter stage **N3,** which consists of higher amplitude **delta waves.** After about an hour of sleep, and once the three NREM sleep stages have been completed, **stage R,** which represents rapid eye movement (REM) sleep, is entered. There are numerous disorders of sleep, including **insomnia** (a sleep disorder characterized by dissatisfaction with sleep quality or duration), **narcolepsy** (a sleep disorder characterized by excessive daytime sleepiness and periodic, uncontrollable sleep attacks), and **sleep apnea** (a sleep disorder involving regular interruptions of breathing during sleep, leading to low oxygen, and wakening). Some types of sleep apnea are best treated with a **continuous positive airway pressure (CPAP)** machine that uses air pressure

to keep the airway open during sleep. **Parasomnias** refer to abnormal behavioral, experiential, or physiological events that occur in conjunction with sleep. Examples of parasomnias include **nightmares** (scary dreams that occur during REM sleep), **sleepwalking** (rising from bed and walking around while the brain is still asleep), and **sleep terrors** (scary dreams, accompanied by autonomic arousal, that occur in NREM sleep and are often accompanied by movement and/or talking or screaming.) **Dreams** are the sequences of images, feelings, ideas, and impressions that pass through the mind during sleep. Sigmund Freud claimed that the content of dreams could be classified into either **manifest content,** the explicit details remembered from the dream, and **latent content,** which he described as the true, underlying meaning of the dream that involved the unconscious wishes and drives of the dreamer. More modern theories of dreams, such as the **activation-synthesis hypothesis,** see dreams as the result of the brain's attempts to make sense of the random neural activity that occurs while sleeping.

Module 4.8–4.10   Psychoactive Drugs

A **psychoactive drug** is defined as a chemical substance that alters brain function resulting in changes in consciousness, perception, and/or mood. Drugs can cause **physiological dependence,** where the body becomes physically dependent on the drug and is typically characterized by **tolerance** (when the body becomes used to the drug and more of the drug is needed to achieve the same effect) and **withdrawal** (physiological symptoms produced by the body when the drug is absent from the system.) **Psychological dependence** can also occur, which involves emotional or motivational symptoms that include intense cravings for the drug, inability to concentrate on other nondrug-related activities, and/or feeling restless when not taking the drug. A **substance use disorder** is diagnosed when an individual experiences a number of negative symptoms as a result of the drug use but continues to use the drug despite these significant substance-related problems. Drugs that share common properties are organized into different classes. **Depressants** are drugs that depress or slow down the central nervous system and other bodily functions, whereas **stimulants** excite or increase the functioning of the central nervous system and speed up the body. **Narcotics** are a type of depressant, often used medically to treat pain, that stimulate the body's internal pain management system. **Heroin** is a particularly dangerous narcotic that activates specific opioid receptors in the brain, which in turn stimulates dopamine in the reward centers of the brain, causing an intense sensation of pleasure. **Hallucinogens,** which can be naturally occurring or synthesized, represent another class of psychoactive drugs. Hallucinogens produce unusual sensations, distortions in the perception of reality, and in some cases intense emotional mood swings. Although its effects tend to be less intense than other hallucinogens, **marijuana,** which is made from the hemp plant, can produce some altered sensations, feelings of well-being, and changes in cognition.

Chapter 4 Quiz

1. Janel goes to sleep at night around 11 p.m. and usually drifts off quickly. She wakes up every morning at 3:45 and tosses and turns for 2 hours until she falls into a restless sleep to wake up at 6:30 feeling tired and groggy. She struggles throughout her day to stay awake and concentrate. Janel most likely suffers from which sleep disorder?

   a. Sleep apnea   **b.** Insomnia

   c. Restless legs syndrome   **d.** Narcolepsy

2. This type of meditation trains a person to become a non-judgmental observer of all their thoughts and emotions.

   a. Focused attention meditation

   b. Open monitoring meditation

   c. Samatha meditation

   d. Hatha meditation

3. _____ perception is an example of awareness without attention.

   a. Focused   **b.** Divided

   c. Subliminal   **d.** Subclinical

4. Which of the following can lead to a decreased level of consciousness?

   a. Alcohol

   b. Nicotine

   c. Running

   d. Focused meditation

5. Justin installed a blue tooth device in his car. He now believes he will be safe from distracted driving because he does not have to use his hands to hold his phone. Justin doesn't understand that distracted driving stems from impaired _____caused by redirection of _____.

   a. attention; perception

   b. perception; attention

   c. attention; cognition

   d. cognition; attention

6. This small part of the hypothalamus controls the circadian clock and is responsive to light.

   a. Pineal gland

   b. Hypothalamus

   c. Suprachiasmatic nucleus

   d. Optic chiasm

7. Quincy notices that he feels much more focused and aware later in the day and struggles to concentrate in his 8 a.m. meeting at work. Based on his circadian rhythm, Quincy is most likely in what age group?

   a. 20–25   **b.** 40–45

   c. 50–55   **d.** 65–70

8. In order to study sleep in natural conditions, researchers took people out to camp in the woods for one week. What did they discover about the influence of natural light on the participant's biological clocks?

   a. No change was noted in their biological clocks.

   b. It shifted the increase and decrease of melatonin in their bodies to 2 hours earlier to correspond with the natural light-dark conditions.

   c. It shifted the increase and decrease of melatonin to 2 hours later each night.

   d. Their biological clocks were reset so they were sleepy at 5 p.m. and wide awake at noon.

9. Cyan told her friend that she believes her dreams are just random neural activity and they have no deeper meaning. Cyan believes in:

   a. Freud's manifest content.

   b. the information-processing theory.

   c. the activation-synthesis hypothesis.

   d. the activation-information mode model.

10. Adolescents need _____ hours of sleep each night but on average only get _____ hours of sleep each night.

   a. 8–10; 7   **b.** 7–9; 8

   c. 10–12; 9   **d.** 9–10; 7

11. Jaebok stayed up studying most of the night for his calculus final. He only slept about 4 hours. According to research, his memory and cognitive functioning will be decreased by approximately what percentage?

   a. 50%   **b.** 30%

   c. 75%   **d.** 10%

12. Petra feels really alive and an overwhelming sense of well-being after her 4-mile morning run. We could say Petra has entered a(n) _____ state of consciousness after exercise.

   a. altered   **b.** waking

   c. meditative   **d.** intentional

13. Andre sometimes will wake himself up because his body jerks as he is drifting off to sleep and he says it feels like he is falling. Researchers refer to this bodily sensation as a _____.

a. drifting hallucination

b. hypnagogic hallucination

c. hypnagogic jerk

d. hypnopompic perception

14. Drugs that alter brain functions resulting in changes in consciousness, perception, and/or mood are called _____ drugs.

a. depressant

b. psychoactive

c. stimulant

d. narcotic

15. This disorder involves excessive daytime sleepiness and periodic, uncontrolled sleep attacks that may leave the sufferer falling asleep at odd and inconvenient times.

a. Insomnia

b. Sleep apnea

c. Narcolepsy

d. Cataplexy

16. Katie who is 10 years old will occasionally find herself asleep at the foot of her parents' bed in the morning, even though she went to sleep in her own bed. She never remembers leaving her room and walking to her parents' room. Katie is experiencing _____, which tends to occur during _____ sleep.

a. sleepwalking; NREM

b. sleep terrors; REM

c. nightwalking; NREM

d. sleepwalking; REM

17. Cal was worried because of how much his newborn son was sleeping. He called the doctor to check how many hours a typical 2-month-old sleeps. The doctor told him newborns are supposed to sleep _____ hours each day.

a. 10–13   b. 14–17

c. 12–15   d. 11–14

18. The information-processing perspective on dreaming suggests dreams allow us to consolidate experiences from the day into _____.

a. brain waves   b. memories

c. unconscious wishes   d. stories

19. People commonly dream of their teeth falling out; if you ascribe to the idea that dreams have hidden meanings, what is a way to interpret this dream?

a. Anxiety about self-image and appearance

b. Worried about going to the dentist

c. Phobia about brushing teeth

d. Anxiety about a test

20. _____ waves emerge in sleep Stage N1 and continue into Stage N2.

a. Delta   b. Alpha

c. Beta   d. Theta

21. A person can be diagnosed with a substance use disorder when the pattern of drug use causes _____ impairment or _____ in the person's life.

a. cognitive; dysfunction   b. significant; distress

c. social; distress   d. school; dysfunction

22. Mia gets so drunk at college parties that she passes out and wakes up in a different location. She is not concerned about her behavior; however, her actions would fit into which diagnostic criteria for substance use disorder?

a. Using the substance in risky situations

b. Social impairment—failing to fulfill responsibilities

c. Impaired control over the substance (cravings)

d. Physiological dependence, including tolerance and withdrawal

23. What is one of the most commonly prescribed benzodiazepines on college campuses?

a. Ativan   b. Valium

c. Xanax   d. Seconal

24. What is the most widely used stimulant drug in the world?

a. Caffeine   b. Nicotine

c. Methamphetamines   d. Ritalin

25. Ritalin, a stimulant drug, is used to treat attention deficit hyperactivity disorder. How does a stimulant help people who already have difficulties with distraction and hyperactivity?

a. By calming down the nervous system so they can focus and be less hyper

b. By helping them sleep better and therefore think more clearly

c. By reducing the amount of neurotransmitters in the brain

d. By providing internal stimulation of neurotransmitters within the brain instead of the person seeking external stimulation

26. Narcotics are a type of _____ that work by stimulating the body's internal pain management system or _____.

    a. depressant; endorphins

    b. stimulant; endorphins

    c. depressant; opiates

    d. stimulants; opiates

27. Sam has been taking opioids she buys from her friend for more than a year. She has spent all her savings on buying these pills and is considering dropping out of school so she can work more to make more money to buy drugs. If she goes too long without taking a pill, she begins to sweat and feel nauseated. Sam is experiencing _____.

    a. a substance use disorder and physiological dependence

    b. a substance use disorder but no physiological dependence

    c. physiological dependence but no substance use disorder

    d. neither physiological dependence nor a substance use disorder

28. Drew is an 18-year-old senior in high school. He has been using marijuana for 2 years on a daily basis and believes it has no long-term side effects. What does the research show as a potential side effect for Drew?

    a. Feeling more calm and rational

    b. Lower IQ score

    c. Higher test scores from reduced anxiety

    d. Decreased conflict with parents in adolescence

29. In a study on inattentional blindness, what percentage of radiologists failed to detect the intentional insertion of the image of a gorilla in CT scans?

    a. 83%   b. 8%

    c. 88%   d. 13%

30. The American Academy of Sleep Medicine changed the sleep cycle system in 2012 and now recognizes which stage of sleep as the deepest stage?

    a. N3   b. N4

    c. N2   d. Stage R (REM)

Chapter 5
Learning

Chapter Outline and Learning Objectives

Module 5.1–5.3: Classical Conditioning

LO 5.1 Identify the components of classical conditioning.

LO 5.2 Recognize how emotional responses can be classically conditioned.

LO 5.3 Explain different factors that affect the acquisition and extinction of classically conditioned responses.

Module 5.4–5.7: Operant Conditioning

LO 5.4 Recognize the similarities and differences between classical conditioning and operant conditioning.

LO 5.5 Distinguish between positive and negative reinforcement.

LO 5.6 Distinguish between positive and negative punishment.

LO 5.7 Identify how the different schedules of reinforcement affect behavior.

Module 5.8–5.9: Modifying Behavior with Operant Conditioning

LO 5.8 Identify how behaviors are modified through the process of shaping.

LO 5.9 Describe applied behavior analysis.

Module 5.10–5.11: Observational Learning

LO 5.10 Identify the role of mirror neurons in learning.

LO 5.11 Recognize the characteristics necessary for observational learning.

Module 5.12–5.13: Learning and Cognition

LO 5.12 Explain the cognitive theory of insight learning.

LO 5.13 Define latent learning.

Module 5.14: Piecing It Together: Violent Video Games

LO 5.14 Analyze how the cross-cutting themes of psychology are related to the topic of violent video games.

What is Learning?

If psychology is the scientific study of behavior and mental processes, then it might be difficult to find a more relevant topic than learning. How do people learn to behave and think? Under what circumstances does learning occur? Can learning be automatic, or does it always require significant effort? Why does it seem relatively effortless to learn your native language, but trying to learn a second language can be an entirely new ballgame? These are just a few examples of the types of questions that psychologists have explored when it comes to the concept of learning.

learning

a relatively permanent change in behavior due to experience

Learning has been defined as a relatively permanent change in behavior due to experience. If you think about that definition for a moment, you'll notice two distinct components of learning: (1) learning leads to a relatively permanent change in behavior, and (2) learning is a result of experience.

Psychologists have discovered that learning actually involves biological changes in the brain. For example, early studies of the biological underpinning of learning indicate that repeated experiences lead to the increased synaptic strength between neurons (Kandel, 2001; Nithianantharajah & Hannan, 2013). The connections between neurons lead to the development of long-lasting neural pathways. These findings suggest that learning is considered generally permanent, even if memory may not be perfect. For example, what was one of your favorite songs when you were in high school? If you can remember one, can you sing the words? Many of us will have a hard time remembering something like that. But, what would happen if you heard that song start playing the next time you were out? Chances are, you could immediately start singing along and remember all of the words! In order to remember something, you must have learned it in the first place.

As this chapter explains, a variety of "experiences" lead to learning. For example, your experiences may lead you to associate two events in your mind (e.g., going to the movie and craving popcorn), or you may learn to avoid a situation because of a negative prior experience (e.g., avoiding walking in a neighborhood where you got mugged), or you might learn something new by the simple experience of observing someone else (e.g., watching a cooking show). All of these "experiences" can lead to learning through a variety of mechanisms, which will be explained throughout this chapter.

Journal Prompt: Examples of Learning in Your Life

Provide a personal example of a time when you learned something by:

a) associating two events in your mind, b) avoiding a situation because of past negative consequences, or c) observing others

Of all the issues discussed in this course, learning and memory are perhaps the most relevant to your role as a student. After all, your primary "job description" is to learn new information through your coursework and remember that information so you can apply it not only for exams but in your future career and relationships. Therefore, as you read and interact with the materials in this chapter, be sure to think about how to apply the concepts to your own study habits. For example, you will discover that learning is often increased when behavior is followed by immediate consequences. When you encounter a question or task in the chapter, it's important to receive immediate feedback (another word for "consequences") on your response (or "behavior"). This feedback is designed to decrease any misconceptions and increase accurate understanding of the topic. To put this learning concept into further action, you could consider writing your own quiz questions after each topic has been covered. Make sure you immediately review the material so that both the question and the answer match the concepts presented in the material. This simple task will likely improve your learning overall, which will lead to many positive consequences—a great exam grade, improved metacognition (see Prologue: Learning to Learn), and skills that can be applied across a variety of settings.

Module 5.1–5.3: Classical Conditioning

If you have different ringtones on your cell phone for different people in your life, you've probably experienced an emotional response as a result. When you hear your mother's ringtone, do you feel suddenly happy, or do you tense up in anticipation of a difficult conversation? How do you feel when you hear the ringtone associated with your significant other—or your boss on a day you're supposed to be off work? These examples are an excellent demonstration of **classical conditioning**, or learning that occurs by associating two events that are repeatedly paired so that you eventually respond to a neutral stimulus in the way you responded to the naturally occurring stimulus.

Cell phone ringtones can become classically conditioned to elicit an emotional response. Just by hearing your mother's ringtone, you might experience a number of different emotions depending on your relationship with your mother and/or whether or not you want to talk to her at that particularly point in time.

Pavlov and His Salivation Research

LO 5.1   Identify the components of classical conditioning.

Like many important findings, the first discovery of classical conditioning was somewhat of an accident. Russian physiologist Ivan Pavlov (1849–1936) was interested in studying the physiology of digestion. He used dogs as his research subjects and collected and measured the saliva produced by dogs during food consumption. As a part of his experiment, the dogs were provided food, which would trigger a reflexive salivation response. This is true of all animals, including humans—if you put food in your mouth, you'll naturally respond by increasing your saliva production. One of the problems Pavlov and his team encountered was that the dogs started to salivate at times before the food was provided. This discovery changed the focus of Pavlov's research for the rest of his career. Pavlov noticed that the dogs would begin to salivate in response to people (e.g., the lab assistant who typically fed the dogs) or sounds that signified the dogs were about to be fed. Similarly, if you've ever fed an animal canned food, you'll notice that the animal soon learns to come running at the sound of the can opener. Pavlov labeled the dogs' salivation in response to a stimulus that suggested food was coming a "psychic secretion" and began to earnestly study the nuances of reflexive learning.

In trying to understand classical conditioning, let's first start with the idea that stimuli elicit a natural or reflexive response. These stimuli are labeled the **unconditioned stimulus (UCS)**. In other words, the responses are unconditioned because they are naturally occurring without prior experience. The naturally-occurring, or reflexive response, to an unconditioned stimulus is labeled the **unconditioned response (UCR)**. Some examples of unconditioned stimuli and unconditioned responses include:

1. UCS = puff of air ⟶ UCR = blinking
2. UCS = smell or taste of food ⟶ UCR = salivation
3. UCS = a loud unexpected noise ⟶ UCR = increased heart rate

Pavlov decided to test whether or not he could condition his dogs to salivate to a previously **neutral stimulus** (a stimulus that doesn't elicit the reflexive/desired response) by pairing the neutral stimulus with an UCS to lead to a **conditioned response (CR)**. The CR occurs when a previously neutral stimulus (NS) leads to the response originally associated with the UCS. At first, Pavlov established that the sound of a metronome was a NS that did not elicit salivation in the dogs. Then, he paired the two stimuli (NS and UCS) by first making a metronome tick (NS) and then presenting the food (UCS). After preceding the food repeatedly, the sound of the metronome began to cause the dogs to salivate—even in the absence of the food. In this case, the bell became a **conditioned stimulus (CS)**. See Figure 5.1 for a step-by-step walkthrough of this experiment. The CS is the previously neutral stimulus that comes to predict the UCS so that it produces the response previously elicited by the US.

classical conditioning

an automatic or reflexive type of learning that occurs by making associations between different events and stimuli

unconditioned stimulus (UCS)

stimuli that elicit a natural or reflexive response without prior experience

unconditioned response (UCR)

the naturally occurring or reflexive response to an unconditioned stimulus

neutral stimulus

a stimulus that doesn't naturally elicit the reflexive/desired response in classical conditioning

conditioned response (CR)

occurs when a previously neutral stimulus leads to the response originally associated with the unconditioned stimulus

Figure 5.1 Pavlov's Study

After the metronome is paired with the food repeatedly, the metronome becomes a conditioned stimulus (CS) that leads to salivation, or the conditioned response (CR), even when the food is not present.

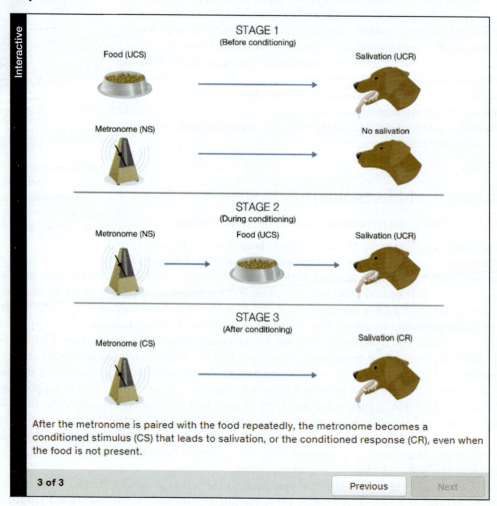

After the metronome is paired with the food repeatedly, the metronome becomes a conditioned stimulus (CS) that leads to salivation, or the conditioned response (CR), even when the food is not present.

conditioned stimulus

during classical conditioning, when a previously neutral stimulus comes to produce the conditioned response because of an association with the unconditioned stimulus

If you consider the examples of unconditioned stimuli and unconditioned responses above, you can imagine pairing a neutral stimulus such as a flashing light with the puff of air that causes blinking. If you flash a light (NS) and then produce a puff of air (US) that causes blinking (UR) repeatedly, eventually the flashing light (CS) itself will lead to blinking (CR).

After Pavlov's studies demonstrated that classical conditioning of physiological responses (e.g., salivation) was possible, later psychologists sought to discover whether or not other types of responses (e.g., emotional responses) could also be classically conditioned.

Little Albert and Classically Conditioned Emotional Responses

LO 5.2 **Recognize how emotional responses can be classically conditioned.**

Psychologist and professor John B. Watson and his graduate student Rosalie Rayner (Watson & Rayner, 1920) set out to examine whether or not classical conditioning could be used to condition an emotional response. They first tested a 9-month-old infant, referred to as "Little

Albert," by presenting him with a series of objects and animals (e.g., rat, rabbit, monkey, burning newspaper) to see if the child demonstrated any natural fear. They discovered that Little Albert did not demonstrate any fear behavior in response to these animals or objects. On the other hand, they discovered that Little Albert appeared startled and began to cry when a metal pipe was struck with a hammer behind his back (imagine that!). When Little Albert was 11 months old, Watson and Rayner began the process of classically conditioning him to fear a white rat. They began by presenting Albert with a white rat. As Albert reached out to touch the rat, a metal pipe was struck behind his head. After only a few pairings of the rat and the loud noise, Albert began to demonstrate a fear response after seeing a rat alone, as shown in the *Little Albert Study* video.

Little Albert Study

What became of Little Albert after the fear conditioning experiment? Watson reported that Little Albert and his mother moved away before the "deconditioning" portion of the study could be conducted. For years, students and psychologists have wondered what became of Little Albert. In 2009, a paper was published that potentially identified Little Albert as Douglas Merritte, a child who died at age 6 (Beck et al., 2009). If Little Albert was truly Douglas Merritte, this would be concerning on many levels because Merritte appears to have been neurologically impaired from birth. The original Little Albert study has been criticized for many years based on the ethics of conditioning a child to experience fear, but if Watson and Reyner actually conducted the research on a neurologically impaired child, the ethical concerns would have been even greater. Thankfully, several scholars have recently cast significant doubt on the identification of Little Albert as Douglas Merritte and provided substantial evidence that Little Albert was more likely Albert Barger, a healthy and neurologically normal child (Digdon et al., 2014; Powell et al., 2014). The Little Albert case was one of psychology's most notorious studies, and today researchers continue to investigate the findings from 95 years ago.

While the original intent of the Little Albert case was to determine if fear could be classically conditioned, the principles of classical conditioning have since been applied to help people *reduce* negative emotions and behaviors such as fear, anxiety, and substance abuse. For example, phobias (a persistent, irrational fear of a specific object or situation) have been successfully treated by teaching people to pair states of deep relaxation with anxiety-provoking situations. These types of treatments will be discussed in more detail in Chapter 16 (LO 16.5).

Little Albert being held by Rosalie Raynor while Watson observes his initial response to a white rat.

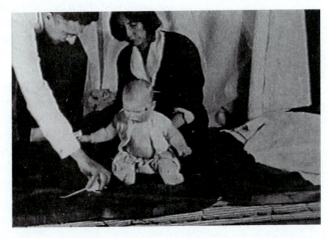

Identifying the Components of the Little Albert Experiment

While the white rat is initially a neutral stimulus, when it is paired with a loud noise (unconditioned stimulus) repeatedly, the white rat becomes a conditioned stimulus that elicits fear from Little Albert.

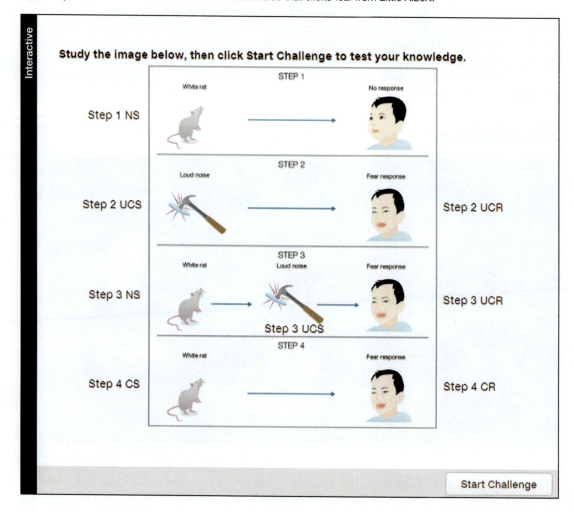

Assuming you've not been the subject of ethically questionable childhood research, you might wonder if the examples provided by Pavlov and Watson's work have much application to your daily life. In fact, you likely experience classically conditioned responses throughout your day. Let's go back to the example of the cell phone ringtone from the beginning of this discussion. In this example, talking to your mother is the unconditioned stimulus (US) because it elicits a natural, unconditioned response (good or bad). Your mother then gets paired with the particular sound of the ringtone you assign to her in your cell phone. Every time your mother calls and you hear the ringtone, you've paired an unconditioned stimulus (your mother) with a neutral stimulus (the ringtone). After enough pairings of your mother (UCS) and the ringtone (NS), you will eventually have an emotional response to the sound of the ringtone alone. The ringtone is now called the conditioned stimulus (CS), and the emotional response is now a conditioned response (CR). Again, a conditioned response occurs when a previously neutral stimulus (e.g., a ringtone) leads to the response originally associated with the UCS (e.g., your mother). Imagine your friend has the same ringtone programmed on his/her phone, and it starts to play while you're having lunch together one day. You will quite likely experience a conditioned response to the sound of the ringtone, even though it has nothing to do with your mother.

Adaptive Pathway 5.1: Classical Conditioning

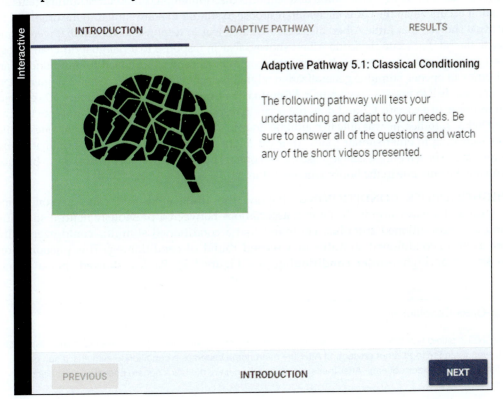

Interactive

INTRODUCTION   ADAPTIVE PATHWAY   RESULTS

Adaptive Pathway 5.1: Classical Conditioning

The following pathway will test your understanding and adapt to your needs. Be sure to answer all of the questions and watch any of the short videos presented.

PREVIOUS   INTRODUCTION   NEXT

Factors That Affect Conditioning

LO 5.3 **Explain different factors that affect the acquisition and extinction of classically conditioned responses.**

You may be wondering if classically conditioned responses last forever. Will the ringtone associated with your mother still cause you to have an emotional reaction when you hear it again in 5 years? And, how would you respond if you heard a ringtone that was similar—would it lead to the same emotional response? To answer these questions, it's important to understand a few important factors that affect conditioning.

ACQUISITION, EXTINCTION, AND SPONTANEOUS RECOVERY   The **acquisition phase** occurs while the neutral stimulus and the CS are repeatedly paired and the association between the neutral stimulus and the CR becomes strengthened. In Pavlov's study, this was the phase when the food and the metronome were repeatedly paired and classical conditioning had occurred the first time the metronome was presented alone and led to salivation. During the acquisition phase, the association between the neutral stimulus and the CR will typically be the strongest when the neutral stimulus is presented immediately prior to the UCS. For example, if the food was provided to the dogs after a 5-minute delay in playing the metronome, the association between food and the bell would be very weak or even nonexistent.

When the CS is no longer paired with the UCS, the response will eventually be subject to **extinction**. Extinction occurs when the CS no longer elicits the CR. If you change your ringtone for your mother, you will eventually stop having an emotional response when you hear the previous ring tone. Similarly, after the metronome is repeatedly presented without food to the dogs, the salivation response will decrease. Interestingly, after a period of time when a CS is not presented, there will be a brief reappearance of the CR—even if there had been an extinction phase previously. For example, if the dog stops salivating to the sound of the metronome because it's repeatedly presented without food (extinction) but hears the metronome a week later, there will likely be a **spontaneous recovery** of the initial CR. This effect is short lived, and extinction will be rapid if the UCS is not presented again with (or before) the CS.

acquisition phase

the period of time during classical conditioning when the neutral stimulus comes to evoke the conditioned response

extinction

the disappearance of a learned behavior when the behavior is no longer reinforced or no longer associated with the unconditioned stimulus

spontaneous recovery

the brief reappearance of a previously extinguished response

stimulus generalization

responding to stimuli similar to but distinct from the original stimulus

stimulus discrimination

responding to the original stimulus only without responding to other stimuli

higher-order conditioning

when a conditioned stimulus eventually acts as an unconditioned stimulus in a second round of conditioning

STIMULUS GENERALIZATION AND DISCRIMINATION   Pavlov and Watson also demonstrated that stimulus generalization and stimulus discrimination can occur. **Stimulus generalization** occurs when the CR is elicited in response to stimuli that are similar to the original CS. Watson showed that Little Albert also demonstrated fear in response to stimuli that were similar to the rat. For example, Little Albert showed fear in response to a rabbit, a fur coat, a dog, and even a Santa Claus beard. If your cat becomes classically conditioned to the sound of an electric can opener, stimulus generalization might occur if the cat begins to expect dinner when you use a drill to make a home repair. **Stimulus discrimination** occurs when the CR is elicited in response to a specific CS and does not occur in response to stimuli that are similar to the CS. In Pavlov's studies, he was able to condition dogs to salivate in response to specific tones while not salivating to other similar tones. Your cat might demonstrate stimulus discrimination by expecting to be fed only when you use the can opener but not when other people do so because you are the only one in the house who feeds the cat.

HIGHER-ORDER CONDITIONING   Pavlov also discovered that classical conditioning doesn't always stop with the first associations between a previously neutral stimulus and an unconditioned stimulus. He found that a conditioned stimulus could eventually act as an unconditioned stimulus in a second round of conditioning. This phenomenon is known as **higher-order conditioning** (see Figure 5.2). Pavlov showed that a sound

Figure 5.2 Higher-Order Conditioning

1) When the metronome (NS) is paired repeatedly with the food (UCS), the metronome becomes a conditioned stimulus (CS) which leads to salivation (CR) even when the food is not present. 2) After the metronome becomes a conditioned stimulus, it can be paired with a neutral stimulus (e.g., a black square). After these are repeatedly paired, the black square becomes a conditioned stimulus (CS) leading to salivation (CR).

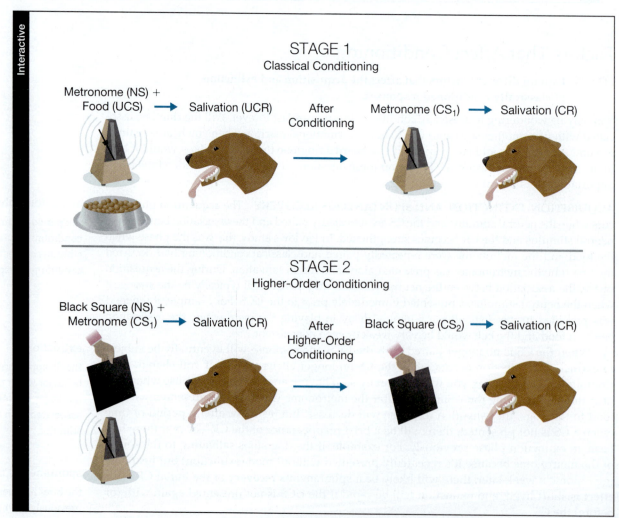

(e.g., metronome) could be paired with food so that dogs eventually salivate in response to the sound alone. He then further demonstrated the process of higher order conditioning by pairing the sound with an image of a black square. Because the sound had already been conditioned to elicit salivation, by pairing the sound *and* the black square, the black square eventually led to salivation on its own. Importantly, the original UCS (food) was never actually presented in the higher order conditioning paradigm!

For an example in your life, consider the fact that music often serves as a conditioned stimulus for people. Certain music becomes associated with certain events or people in your life. For example, many couples identify a song as "their song." This song can lead to a conditioned positive emotional response—or a conditioned negative emotional response if there's a nasty break-up! After the break-up, every time you hear the song, you may feel sad or angry. Imagine watching a commercial later that uses the song as part of the advertisement. You might develop a negative response to the product advertised through the process of higher-order conditioning. Smart marketers understand this phenomenon well, so they are always attempting to pair their products with stimuli that already have a positive association for most people.

CONDITIONED TASTE AVERSIONS Do you think any stimulus can be classically conditioned? Pavlov stated that "any natural phenomenon chosen at will, may be converted into a conditioned stimulus…" (Pavlov, 1928). However, after many years of research, the answer appears to be that some stimuli are much easier to associate with certain responses than other stimuli (Desimone & Duncan, 1995). Take the example of food and illness. While in college during a particularly brutal winter, one of the authors (BW) decided to drink coffee to warm up. She added a ton of sugar and creamer and began drinking a cup between classes each day. One day, hours after returning home from class, she came down with a nasty stomach virus. All she had to eat or drink that day was, of course, coffee. As a result, she developed a **taste aversion** to coffee, or a classically conditioned dislike and avoidance of a certain food following illness. More than 20 years later, she still has not had a single sip of coffee despite the growing popularity of coffee and coffee bars over that timeframe.

taste aversion

classically conditioned dislike and avoidance of a certain food following illness

When teaching introductory psychology, we've heard from many students who provide funny (and disgusting) examples of taste aversions they have developed. This may seem to be a simple application of classical conditioning in our lives until you look a little closer. First of all, the CS (coffee) was only paired with the UCS (stomach virus) on one occasion, and the timing between the CS and UCS was not seconds or minutes apart but rather hours apart. How can such strong conditioning occur after hours of separation between the CS and UCS? Why wasn't something else associated with the UCS that occurred more closely in time? Researchers have discovered that humans and other animals appear to have a certain **biological preparedness** to develop associations between certain types of stimuli and responses. If you are an animal foraging in the woods and then become ill, it makes sense that you would have a biological tendency to associate your illness with food rather than something else in your environment so that you would avoid that food in the future. Garcia's famous studies with rats showed that he could easily condition rats to develop taste aversions when he paired flavored water with an injection that produced illness. The rats avoided the flavored water when it was presented in the future. On the other hand, he was unable to condition rats to associate a certain taste with an electric shock or associate illness with a noise (Garcia & Koelling, 1966). Likewise, Seligman (1971) further pointed out that humans appear to be biologically prepared to develop fear responses to certain stimuli (e.g., snakes, spiders, heights, tightly enclosed spaces) much more readily than others. One theory is that we are biologically prepared to be afraid of objects or situations that were a threat to people throughout evolution. While many more people are injured or killed in car accidents than by snake bites today, it remains much easier to condition people to experience a fear response to snakes than to cars.

biological preparedness

an organism's predisposition to develop associations between certain types of stimuli and responses based on evolutionary survival

Shared Writing: Advertisements and Classical Conditioning

Marketing campaigns often use classical conditioning techniques so that people will have positive associations with a product. Describe an advertisement that uses classical conditioning, and identify the NS, UCS, CS, and CR. Next, discuss how stimulus discrimination and stimulus generalization related to the advertised product could lead to higher or lower sales of the product.

Quiz for Module 5.1–5.3

1. The neutral stimulus, when paired with an unconditioned stimulus, becomes a(n) _____ in classical conditioning.
   a. conditioned response
   b. conditioned stimulus
   c. unconditioned response
   d. unconditioned stimulus

2. Every week, Jade spends her allowance on ½ pound of sour lemon gummy candies, even though they always make her mouth water. One day, as she is walking down the street, Jade sees a girl carrying a little white bag that looks like a candy shop bag! Jade notices that her mouth is puckering and overflowing with saliva. In this example, the unconditioned stimulus is the _____.
   a. puckering and saliva
   b. sour lemon gummy candy
   c. allowance money
   d. little white bag

3. Normally, when food is placed in the mouth of any animal, the salivary glands start releasing saliva to help with chewing and digestion. In terms of Pavlov's analysis of learning, salivation would be referred to as a(an) _____.
   a. voluntary response
   b. conditioned response
   c. digestive reflux
   d. unconditioned response

4. In Watson and Rayner's "Little Albert" study, each time the rat was presented to the boy, it was accompanied by a loud noise which eventually led Albert to cry when presented with the rat. In this experiment, Albert's reaction of fear upon seeing the rat was a(n) _____ response.
   a. counterconditioned
   b. latent
   c. conditioned
   d. unconditioned

5. In the past, thunder has made you flinch because the loud noise scares you. Lightning always comes before the thunder and after time, you begin to flinch as soon as the lightning strikes. In this scenario, lightning can be interpreted as a(n) _____.
   a. conditioned stimulus
   b. conditioned response
   c. unconditioned response
   d. unconditioned stimulus

6. In classical conditioning, _____ occurs when the conditioned stimulus is no longer paired with the unconditioned stimulus.
   a. extinction
   b. spontaneous recovery
   c. stimulus generalization
   d. stimulus distinction

7. Martha trains her cat Whiskers to salivate to the sound of a bell. She rings the bell every 15 minutes and doesn't follow it with food for Whiskers. Whiskers salivates less and less and finally stops salivating at the sound of the ringing bell. A week later, she finds Whiskers salivating to the sound of a ringing bell. Which of the following terms explains this response?
   a. Stimulus discrimination
   b. Spontaneous recovery
   c. Instinctive drift
   d. Counterconditioning

Module 5.4–5.7: Operant Conditioning

The discovery of classical conditioning highlighted that learning can occur when a neutral stimulus is presented *before* a reflexive behavior such as salivation. On the other hand, learning can also occur—depending on what happens *after* a behavior is performed.

The Beginning of Operant Conditioning

LO 5.4   Recognize the similarities and differences between classical conditioning and operant conditioning.

Remember the discussion about the emotional response you can have merely from hearing a particular ringtone? When you experience that emotion, your body is also responding physiologically. Your heart rate increases, you start breathing more rapidly, and you may even start to sweat. Imagine you are at home eating dinner when suddenly you hear the ringtone associated with an ex you haven't spoken to in more than 6 months. In this example, you probably didn't *voluntarily* choose to have your heart start racing when you heard the ringtone (we aren't specifying whether your heart racing is a good or a bad thing—that's for you to decide!). Regardless, through repeated associations of that specific ringtone to that specific person, your body *passively* and *reflexively* began to respond to the ringtone in the same way it would in the presence of that person. Sometimes, people refer to classical conditioning as involving *respondent behavior* because your behavior is a passive and reflexive response to a particular stimulus.

Whereas classical conditioning occurs *before* the reflexive and involuntary response, **operant conditioning** is a type of learning that occurs *after* we *voluntarily* engage in a behavior. This type of conditioning is much more *active* and is based on the *consequences* that occur after a particular behavior is performed. While you may not always be aware that your behavior is shaped through operant conditioning, you almost always have some choice in how you are going to behave. For example, do you remember when you were a child and your mother said "make sure to take a jacket with you because it is going to be cold"? You might have thought "I'll be fine" and ignored her advice and then you froze and were miserable the entire time. You made the choice not to listen to your mother and, as a result, you suffered the consequences.

operant conditioning

learning related to voluntary behavior that occurs through the application of consequences after a particular behavior is performed

So, what likely happened the next time you were about to go out and your mother told you to take a jacket? You probably chose to take a jacket because you had learned (through operant conditioning) to listen to your mother. The interesting thing about operant conditioning is that it easily explains how we can both *increase* and *decrease* the frequency of behaviors. In fact, operant conditioning can be defined as a type of learning in which behavior is strengthened or diminished, depending on its desirable or undesirable consequences (Hahn, 2013).

There are also similarities between classical conditioning and operant conditioning. Both types of learning involve making associations between stimuli and responses. In addition, the concepts of extinction, generalization, and discrimination apply to both classical conditioning and operant conditioning.

In the late 19th century, American psychologist Edward Thorndike (1874–1949) studied learning processes in animals. Having worked under the supervision of two of psychology's forefathers (William James and James McKeen Cattell), at age 24 Thorndike published a paper in which he described the ability of animals to learn through association and as a result of consequences of their behavior. Thorndike built what he called a "puzzle box," a wooden cage that required a simple act (such as pushing a lever) to open it (see Figure 5.3). He would place a hungry cat inside the box and a delicious meal of fish just outside the door of the cage so that the cat could see it. To reach the food, the cat had to figure out how to press the lever to open the door, a process Thorndike timed. After pushing and rubbing up against the walls of the cage, the cat accidentally stood on the lever, opening the door. The cat did not immediately learn the connection between the lever and the road to freedom. However, after numerous trials, the cat was able to open the door very quickly, demonstrating that it had learned an association between the lever and the path to food and freedom (Thorndike, 1898). This line of research led Thorndike to develop the **law of effect**, which simply states if a response produces a *satisfying effect*, the response is likely to occur again.

Thorndike's work provided the foundation for B. F. Skinner (1904–1990), who, along with John B. Watson, paved the way for behaviorism to become a dominant school of thought in psychology by the mid-20th century. Although Watson and Skinner are often grouped together as "behaviorists," they were actually representatives from different behavioral camps. Watson was very clear that the only behavior he believed worthy of study was outward behavior, or behavior that can be seen by others. This camp is referred to as *methodological behaviorism* and is known for its beliefs that thoughts are unimportant in learning. Skinner however, did not believe that thoughts had no value in learning; he merely viewed thoughts as a form of "inner behavior" that were subject to the same contingencies, or rules, of outward behavior. Skinner's view represents the camp of behaviorism referred to as *radical behaviorism*. Skinner believed all behaviors (internal and external) were a result of factors in the individual's environment.

Skinner's theory of operant conditioning focused on the ways in which the environment can *operate* on a person or animal (Skinner used the word *organism* when referring to any living thing) to either increase or decrease behavior. Let's discuss the principles related to *increasing* behavior first.

law of effect

if a response produces a *satisfying effect*, the response is likely to occur again

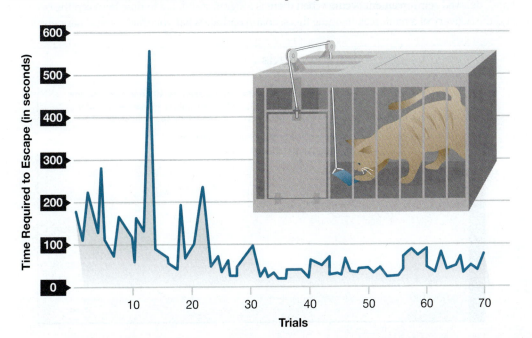

Figure 5.3 Picture of Thorndike's Puzzle Box

The cat becomes quicker at escaping the puzzle box to receive the food over time.

Principles of Reinforcement

LO 5.5 **Distinguish between positive and negative reinforcement.**

Building on Thorndike's law of effect, Skinner (1938) developed some of the principles of behavior control. He developed his own version of a puzzle box, called a "Skinner box," or "operant-conditioning chamber." By pressing a bar in the chamber, a rat could release food pellets or water, while a device recorded the animal's responses. Skinner discovered, as did Thorndike, that animals can learn to perform a behavior quickly when it is followed by a desirable outcome. Skinner referred to this desirable outcome (in this case, the food) as a *reinforcer*. The most important thing you can remember at this point is that whenever you see any form of the word *reinforcement*, it involves the goal of *increasing behaviors*. Think about the idea of adding "reinforcements" to something you are building. The reason you do this is because you want to make the object *stronger*. Reinforcement serves a similar function in the theory of operant conditioning; it refers to any event/thing/outcome that strengthens a preceding response. Skinner demonstrated the ability of animals (and humans) to learn, sometimes very complex behaviors, as a result of reinforcement. For example, Skinner taught pigeons to turn in circles to the left or the right and to play ping pong with each other, and he even consulted with the military about training pigeons to guide missiles in World War II (Skinner, 1953).

Let's think about your own behavior. If you spend a few hours a week working out at the gym, what motivates you to go? Achieving a good level of personal fitness? Reducing your stress level? Avoiding the aches and pains you experience when you stop working out? There are many health-related reasons to jump on a treadmill, but there are also fringe benefits such as spending time with your gym buddies, avoiding an unpleasant household chore, or studying for that next exam. For every repeated action we take, you can guarantee reinforcement played a role in strengthening that behavior. Think of another behavior you engage in on a regular basis. Why do you continue to do this? What are you "getting" out of it? That is, what has been your reinforcement for that behavior?

CHARACTERISTICS OF REINFORCERS   Remember, all reinforcers strengthen behavior, but reinforcers can have different characteristics. A **primary reinforcer** satisfies a basic biological need, such as hunger or thirst. Both Thorndike and Skinner used primary reinforcers (i.e., food) in their work with animals. A **secondary reinforcer** becomes satisfying or pleasurable through its association with primary reinforcers. For example, you can use money (a secondary reinforcer) to purchase food (a primary reinforcer). Other examples of secondary reinforcers are praise or recognition. You learn the value associated with a secondary reinforcer over time as it becomes associated with a primary reinforcer.

Reinforcers can also vary in their effectiveness based on timing. **Immediate reinforcement** typically occurs when the behavior and the delivery of a reinforcer occur very close in time. On the other hand, **delayed reinforcement** occurs when there is a significant delay in time between the behavior and the delivery of a reinforcer. Imagine this scenario and see what you think would happen:

primary reinforcer

naturally reinforcing stimuli because they satisfy a basic biological need such as hunger or thirst

secondary reinforcer

something that becomes satisfying or pleasurable through its association with a primary reinforcer

immediate reinforcement

when the desired behavior and the delivery of a reinforcer occur very close in time

delayed reinforcement

a significant delay in time between the desired response of an organism and the delivery of a reinforcer

Delayed vs. Immediate Rewards

Interactive

1. Children ages 4–6 were brought into a laboratory and presented with one marshmallow. They were told that they could eat it immediately, but if they waited 15 minutes to eat it, they would receive an additional marshmallow. What do you think the children did?

○ They ate the first marshmallow before the 15-minute time limit.
○ They waited 15 minutes and received the second marshmallow.

Previous   Next

This study demonstrates that immediate reinforcers are typically preferable to delayed reinforcers. You might think this only applies to children, but reconsider the previous example of going to the gym. Some of the positive effects (or reinforcement) associated with exercise include maintaining a healthy weight and improved fitness. However, these are often very delayed reinforcers, which helps explain why people sometimes find it difficult to forgo a nap (immediate reinforcer) and head to the gym.

POSITIVE AND NEGATIVE REINFORCERS   Reinforcers can also vary in terms of whether something is *added* or *removed*. **Positive reinforcers** strengthen a response by adding a pleasurable consequence. The consequence can be something tangible (e.g., money, stickers, candy) or intangible (e.g., a feeling of pride after receiving a compliment, feeling empowered after taking your recycling to the local recycling center, or donating blood to the blood bank). If you have ever spent any significant time with young children, you have seen just how powerful positive reinforcement can be. Kids will do just about anything for a sticker!

Having young children, your authors would be remiss if we didn't acknowledge practicing what we preach. For example, Dr. Hudson used to struggle on a daily basis to get her children (ages 6, 5, and 2 at the time) out of the house and into the car in under 20 minutes. One day, she came across some "star stickers" and made a big deal of whichever child was engaging in a behavior that would eventually lead to getting into the car. She exclaimed loudly and dramatically to the first child, "Wow, I like how quickly you are getting your shoes on and heading to the car. You get a gold star!" At that point, her daughter received a gold star sticker and responded as if she had just won the lottery. It didn't take long for the others to come running in an attempt to claim their prize—2nd place received a silver sticker and 3rd place a bronze. What do you think happened the next time they needed to leave the house? Dr. Hudson announced, "It is time to go. Let me find my stickers" and guess what? Yes, they all came running, and we had created a new Olympic sport! Even a year later, long after the stickers were all gone, Dr. Hudson would merely state who received the gold, silver, and bronze sticker and would achieve a similar outcome. At that point, even imaginary stickers worked as reinforcers for increasing the speed at which they could leave the house. As this example demonstrates, positive reinforcement involves strengthening a behavior by adding a pleasurable or desirable consequence.

In contrast, **negative reinforcers** strengthen a response by *removing* an undesirable consequence, or what is sometimes referred to as an aversive stimulus. We rock a baby to sleep to stop it from crying. You pick up your dirty clothes off the floor to stop a significant other or roommate from nagging. Sometimes, students get confused by the word "negative" by thinking it is synonymous with "bad." Remember what we said before about the word "reinforcement"? Any time you see that word, you should think about *increasing* or *strengthening* a behavior. So, negative reinforcement is still referring to strengthening behavior. In this case, the word "negative" refers to the fact that something undesirable is *removed* or taken away. Think of "take away" as in "subtract" and when you see the term negative reinforcement, picture a subtraction sign. Conversely, when you see the term *positive reinforcement*, you should picture an addition sign (i.e., something positive is added) (see Table 5.1).

Praise or stickers are examples of positive reinforcement.

positive reinforcers
something that strengthens or increases a response by adding a pleasurable consequence

negative reinforcers
strengthening or increasing a response by removing an unpleasant consequence

Table 5.1 Two Ways to Increase Behavior

	Reinforcement
Positive **+**	*Adding* something desired or pleasurable after a behavior occurs
	Example: Receiving a bonus check for meeting a sales target at work
	Explanation: Receiving money (a secondary reinforcer) is strengthening the behavior associated with making sales (e.g., working hard)
Negative **−**	*Removing* (subtracting) or avoiding something undesirable or annoying
	Example: A child screaming that they don't like broccoli and the parent takes it off their plate
	Explanation: The child screaming when they don't like something has been negatively reinforced by the parents removing what was undesirable (the broccoli); removing the broccoli will now strengthen or increase the screaming behavior of the child

Negative reinforcement is about the positive experience you have after something annoying or undesirable has been removed. Have you ever driven in a car that has a very loud and irritating buzzer that goes off until you buckle your seatbelt? Why would the car company design a car like this? What are they trying to accomplish? Yes, they are trying to influence your "seatbelt wearing behavior" by using negative reinforcement. Think about how you feel after you click in your seatbelt and the annoying noise stops. Most people would describe a feeling of relief, which is a positive (and reinforcing) feeling. With negative reinforcement, the behavior is still being strengthened as a result of experiencing something positive. The difference is in the way the positive event arises (i.e., in response to the removal of an annoying or aversive stimulus). If you know anyone who suffers from some form of anxiety, then you can now understand how much of their anxious behavior is maintained through negative reinforcement. Most people who experience extreme anxiety about going somewhere, doing something, or interacting socially with someone begin to avoid the situations and experiences that make them most anxious. While this may seem like an intuitive thing to do, it is in fact the worst choice because the avoidance behavior (i.e., removal of the anxious state) leads to an overwhelming sense of relief and therefore negatively reinforces the avoidance behavior (Rosqvist, 2012). So, in this example, the avoidance behavior is strengthened, which means the next time the person is presented with an opportunity to engage in an activity that produces some anxiety, there is an increased likelihood that they will choose to avoid the situation.

Positive vs. Negative Reinforcement

Interactive

You will be provided with 4 scenarios. Identify each as an example of either positive reinforcement or negative reinforcement.

Positive Reinforcement	Negative Reinforcement
You give your dog a treat after he sits.	The buzzer in your car stops after you secure your seat belt.
Your roommate says "thanks" after you clean up the kitchen.	Your headache is relieved after taking aspirin.

Start Over

Punishment

LO 5.6 Distinguish between positive and negative punishment.

Most of us probably remember being punished for bad behavior at some point during childhood. Were you sent to your room to "think about what you had done"? Ever been grounded or lost special privileges? What about receiving a spanking? As you think back on those experiences, ask yourself, "Did that work?" Was the punishment you received effective in terms of decreasing undesirable behavior? So far, we have only discussed principles of increasing behavior. Whereas reinforcement increases or strengthens a behavior, **punishment** *decreases* or *weakens* a behavior (Skinner, 1953).

Sometimes distinguishing between reinforcement and punishment can be tricky. It is helpful to consider the response to the situation rather than the situation itself. For example, think of the following situation: You have an annoying family member who loves to ask you personal questions in front of other family members. Over the years, you have politely said to them that this makes you uncomfortable, but there has been no change in their behavior. Finally, at the summer family reunion, you can't take it anymore and when asked about your current love

punishment

consequences for behavior that decrease the probability of that behavior occurring again

Distinguishing Reinforcement from Punishment

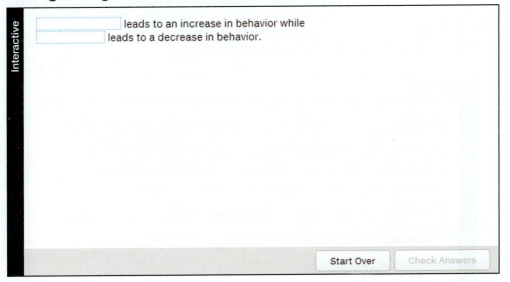

_____ leads to an increase in behavior while
_____ leads to a decrease in behavior.

Start Over   Check Answers

life, you yell "It's none of your business!" and stomp off. Now, was yelling at the person a form of punishment? Well, it depends on the outcome. Did your outburst lead to a decrease in your family member's meddling ways, or was your outburst just the response they were looking for and has now helped them to figure out exactly what to ask in order to get a rise out of you in the future? If the behavior stopped or decreased, then losing your temper was a form of punishment. But, if your outburst led to an increase in that family member's behavior, then it was most definitely a reinforcer.

Just like our discussion about reinforcement, punishment can also take two forms: **positive punishment** (adding something undesirable after a behavior) and **negative punishment** (removing something desirable or enjoyable after a behavior). Click through the following table to learn about positive and negative punishment.

positive punishment
adding something undesirable after a behavior with the intention of decreasing the likelihood of that behavior occurring again in the future

negative punishment
removing something desirable or enjoyable after a behavior with the intention of decreasing the likelihood of that behavior occurring again in the future

Two Ways to Decrease Behavior

Positive Punishment = _____ something _____ after a behavior with the intention of decreasing the likelihood of that behavior occurring again in the future.

Negative Punishment = _____ something _____ after a behavior with the intention of decreasing the likelihood of that behavior occurring again in the future.

WORD BANK
- unpleasant or undesirable
- Removing (subtracting)
- pleasant or enjoyable
- Adding

Start Over   Check Answers

ISSUES RELATED TO THE EFFECTIVENESS OF PUNISHMENT The issue of punishment is one of the topics in the field of psychology that stimulates great debate among people, including psychologists. For example, consider the issue of spanking as a discipline technique in childhood. You've likely been exposed to strong opinions both for and against the practice of spanking. Let's walk through the research regarding spanking.

Was your answer to the question at right based on your own experience as a child? If so, did your guess about the scientific research mirror the method of discipline you experienced as a child? That wouldn't be unusual. Simons and Wurtele (2010) conducted a study with 102 families and found that the parents who experienced frequent spankings as children were more likely to view spanking as acceptable and reported spanking their own children frequently. Furthermore, the children of these parents who experienced frequent spankings tended to also agree that spanking was an acceptable form of discipline.

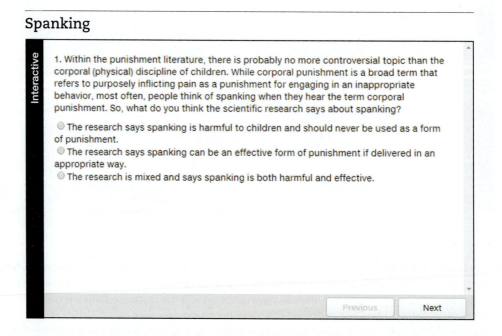

Spanking

1. Within the punishment literature, there is probably no more controversial topic than the corporal (physical) discipline of children. While corporal punishment is a broad term that refers to purposely inflicting pain as a punishment for engaging in an inappropriate behavior, most often, people think of spanking when they hear the term corporal punishment. So, what do you think the scientific research says about spanking?

○ The research says spanking is harmful to children and should never be used as a form of punishment.
○ The research says spanking can be an effective form of punishment if delivered in an appropriate way.
○ The research is mixed and says spanking is both harmful and effective.

Previous   Next

Learning how to think critically about real-world issues by reading scientific literature or even articles you find on the Internet is an important skill. It takes practice to seek out *all* relevant information, even if we don't agree with that information. For example, the *confirmation bias* states that once we establish an opinion on a particular topic, we tend to only look for evidence to support our position.

Research on Spanking

Below you will find a list of statements or conclusions derived from, or used in actual psychological research related to, corporal punishment (e.g., spanking). Drag and drop the following statements into the column that best represents each statement.

Spanking Has No Serious Detrimental Effects and Its Use Should Be At the Discretion of the Parents	Spanking is Ineffective and/or Harmful and Should Not Be Used
The use of corporal punishment is not always associated with poor outcomes; however, there is no added benefit to spanking over other discipline practices (Simons et al., 2013).	Recent findings showed that spanking was associated with 13 negative outcomes and no positive outcomes. Detrimental outcomes were not only associated with spanking that verged on physical abuse. Researchers found that any spanking at all can be harmful to a child (Gershoff & Grogan-Kaylor, 2016).
Prudently used, spanking can effectively accomplish its limited goals with no more harm than alternative disciplinary tactics (Baumrind, 1996).	Many parents who spank their children often spank them more than recommended (Holden et al., 2014). Evidence suggests that corporal punishment can easily escalate into abuse (Hall, 2013).
When not overused, spanking has been found to have beneficial outcomes, including increased compliance, in children from ages 2–6 (Larzelere, 2000; Larzelere & Kuhn, 2005).	Being spanked more than 2 times in the past month, at age 3, by either mother or father, is associated with increased child aggression at age 5 (Lee et al., 2013).
	Currently, 37 countries have made corporal punishment illegal in the home (GITEACPOC, 2014).

Start Over

Now that you've had a chance to review the research on spanking and realize it is a complicated topic, let's consider the issues related to punishment in general. Skinner and other behaviorists discovered that punishment was not as effective in changing behavior as reinforcement (Skinner, 1974). Imagine having a roommate who is very messy and never picks up her belongings. If your goal is to increase your roommate's cleaning behavior, you will probably be more successful by finding a way to reward her when you see her pick up something and put it away than if you simply criticize her when you find something on the floor. Why is this true? It turns out that punishment only provides information that the behavior was not correct or acceptable, but it does not inform the person about what behavior to perform instead. By rewarding appropriate behavior, your roommate would clearly know what behavior leads to a positive response from you. This does not mean that punishment is ineffective. Research has suggested that punishment can be effective if it is:

1. Immediately applied after the behavior

2. Consistently applied every time the behavior occurs

When you consider how punishment is actually used in our society, it becomes clear that these two criteria are rarely applied. The practice of incarcerating people who break the law is meant to serve as a punishment with the hopes of reducing future criminal behavior. However, this is often ineffective, and one reason is the delay in time between the criminal behavior and the incarceration. In fact, sometimes it takes years for the legal process to transpire. Consistency is another important consideration when thinking about the effectiveness of punishment. For example, sometimes when you speed while driving, you receive a speeding ticket (a form of positive punishment). However, this form of punishment is not likely to be very successful at reducing your speeding behavior because it is not consistently applied every time the behavior occurs. Imagine if you had a computer monitor built into your car that alerted the police every time your car went over the speed limit and you were sent a ticket in the mail. This would be a much more effective way of using punishment to reduce speeding behavior!

In this section, you have been reading about and experiencing different ways to change behavior through the principles of operant conditioning. You've seen how to increase behaviors through positive and negative reinforcement and decrease behaviors through positive and negative punishment. In the next section, we'll look at the way in which you present the reinforcement and how it can impact the resulting behavior.

Adaptive Pathway 5.2: Operant Conditioning

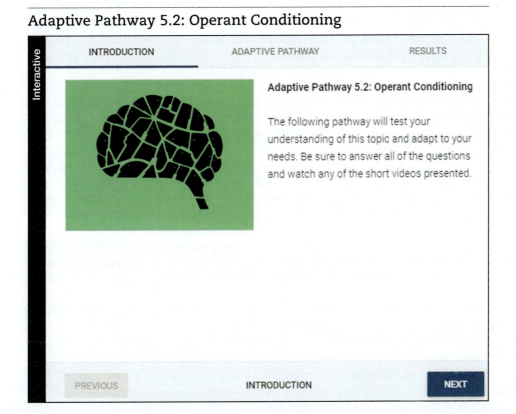

Schedules of Reinforcement

LO 5.7 **Identify how the different schedules of reinforcement affect behavior.**

Not only can we change behavior through the use of reinforcement, but the rate at which the reinforcement is delivered can alter future behavior patterns (Ferster & Skinner, 1957). Skinner referred to this as *schedules of reinforcement* and, through a series of studies, he concluded that animals and humans respond in a very predictable pattern based on the schedule of the delivery of their reinforcement.

continuous reinforcement

when a desired response is reinforced every time it occurs; this schedule results in rapid learning, but if the reinforcement stops, extinction also occurs rapidly

The most straightforward schedule is **continuous reinforcement**, which means the desired response is reinforced every time it occurs. This schedule results in rapid learning; but, if the reinforcement stops, extinction also occurs rapidly. If a rat suddenly stops receiving food pellets every time it presses a bar, it will soon give up and stop pressing it. Many activities we engage in on a daily basis exist as a result of continuous reinforcement. For example, when you push a button for an elevator, you are rewarded by the elevator doors opening eventually. Assuming the elevator is working properly, the behavior of pushing the button will be reinforced every time the behavior is performed. What do you do if you push the button and no elevator comes after a couple of minutes? You will likely very quickly give up and find another elevator or take the stairs. This is the process of extinction discussed earlier. However, if you are like most people, you probably won't give up right away. In fact, you may find yourself pushing that elevator button over and over with great enthusiasm, hoping your perseverance will open the doors. Rats do the same thing when they are initially deprived of reinforcement. That is, when the food is removed, they rapidly push their lever over and over in hopes of obtaining another pellet (Weissman, 1960). This behavior is called an **extinction burst**, and it often occurs in response to the removal of previous reinforcement (Lerman & Iwata, 1995; Lerman & Iwata, 1996).

extinction burst

a burst of responding following the removal of previous reinforcement

Journal Prompt: Extinction Bursts

Can you give an example of an extinction burst, maybe one you have experienced or witnessed?

partial (intermittent) reinforcement

when responses are only occasionally reinforced; this produces slower initial learning, but the learning is more resistant to extinction

Partial (intermittent) reinforcement occurs when responses are only occasionally reinforced. This produces slower initial learning, but the learning is more resistant to extinction. Never knowing when the reinforcement will be presented maintains the behavior for a longer period of time. There are several types of partial reinforcement, and they exist along two dimensions. The first dimension is related to the *rate* at which the reinforcement is provided. The rate can either be *fixed,* meaning the reinforcement is provided according to a set and unchanging schedule, or the rate can be *variable,* meaning the reinforcements are delivered according to a random or unpredictable schedule. The second dimension involves the *reason* for the reinforcement. If the reinforcement depends on the number of responses, then it is said to be a *ratio* schedule (think "r" for ratio and "r" for responses). If the reason for the reinforcement has to do with the amount of time that has passed, then it is considered an *interval* schedule (think about people who do circuit training for exercise—they may engage in a particular exercise for two-minute *intervals* and then move on to the next one). Specific schedules of reinforcement merely involve all four possible combinations of these variables: fixed ratio, variable ratio, fixed interval, variable interval.

fixed-ratio schedules

when a behavior is reinforced after a set number of responses; fixed-rate schedules produce high rates of responding with only a brief pause following reinforcement

Fixed-ratio schedules reinforce behavior after a *set number* of *responses*. For example, you might get one free latte after every 10 purchases at the local coffee shop. Fixed-rate schedules produce high rates of responding with only a brief pause following reinforcement.

variable-ratio schedules

reinforcing behavior after varying and unpredictable numbers of responses; have high response rates and produce behavior that is difficult to extinguish

Variable-ratio schedules reinforce behavior after *varying* and *unpredictable numbers* of responses. A gambler at a slot machine may put in thousands of coins and receive no payout, or insert a single quarter into the slot and win thousands of dollars. Variable-ratio schedules have high response rates and produce behavior that is difficult to extinguish.

fixed-interval schedules

when a behavior is reinforced after a fixed time period; fixed-interval schedules produce rapid responses at the expected time of reward and slower responses outside of those times

With **fixed-interval schedules**, behavior is reinforced after a *fixed time period*. If we know our dinner is almost ready, we will check the oven more frequently, producing rapid responses at the expected time of reward and slower responses outside of those times.

Variable-interval schedules reinforce behavior after *variable* periods of *time*. We may obsessively check our phones for new text messages and be rewarded for our efforts at varying time intervals. This schedule generally produces slow and steady behavioral responses.

variable-interval schedules

reinforcing behavior after variable periods of time; generally produce slow and steady behavioral responses

Schedules of Reinforcement

Interactive

1. You have been asked to sell cookie dough as a way of raising money for your school. After every 5 tubs of cookie dough that you sell, you will earn a $5.00 Visa gift card. [_____]

2. You work at a store that is part of a chain. Your manager is responsible for your store and the 4 other stores in town. Your manager typically shows up to your store at least once each week, but you never know which day. [_____]

3. You are playing a video game where if you die, you have to wait 5 minutes before your character is regenerated. [_____]

4. You are learning about psychology, and you can earn "surprise" bonus points after correct responses on quizzes. Sometimes you can get an extra point after 3 correct responses and sometimes it takes 10 correct responses. [_____]

WORD BANK
- variable interval
- fixed ratio
- fixed interval
- variable ratio

[Start Over] [Check Answers]

Rates of Responding Based on Different Schedules

Fixed and variable ratio reinforcement lead to high response rates. Fixed interval reinforcement leads to higher response rates at the expected time of reinforcement. Variable interval reinforcement leads to very steady response rates.

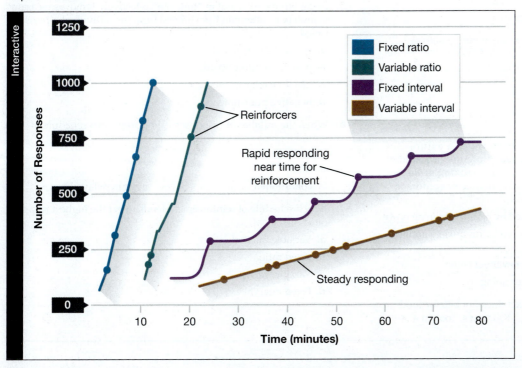

Adaptive Pathway 5.3: Schedules of Reinforcement

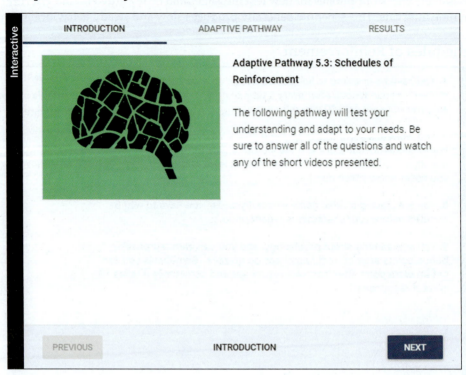

Quiz for Module 5.4–5.7

1. Discrimination, generalization, and extinction occur in_____.
   a. classical conditioning only
   b. operant conditioning only
   c. both operant and classical conditioning
   d. neither operant nor classical conditioning

2. _____ reinforcement occurs when something pleasant follows a behavior.
   a. Positive
   b. Negative
   c. Neutral
   d. Compound

3. Fred is afraid of spiders. He won't even watch a nature show on TV about them. When he sees a picture of a spider, he has a panic attack, but when he avoids looking at the image, his panic goes away. Fred's avoidance of spiders is _____ .
   a. positively reinforced; he is rewarded by his anxiety going down
   b. negatively reinforced; he is rewarded by his anxiety going down
   c. recovered spontaneously; he will never get better
   d. extinguished; he feels anxious after doing so

4. Kyla wants to make sure her dog Axel does not beg for food from the table. Every time Axel begs, Kyla says, "no" in a sharp, scolding voice and she never gives in. Kyla is using _____.
   a. stimulus generalization
   b. negative reinforcement
   c. positive punishment
   d. negative punishment

5. Being grounded or put in "time out" effectively removes pleasant stimuli (e.g., attention from others) from the individual. This is called _____.
   a. positive punishment
   b. positive reinforcement
   c. negative reinforcement
   d. negative punishment

6. When the number of responses is important to a schedule of reinforcement, that schedule is called a _____ schedule.
   a. ratio
   b. interval
   c. conditioned
   d. time-delayed

7. Which schedule of reinforcement tends to get the highest response rate?
   a. Variable interval
   b. Fixed ratio
   c. Variable ratio
   d. Fixed interval

Module 5.8–5.9: Modifying Behavior with Operant Conditioning

The principles of operant conditioning have broad applications to all sorts of behaviors for both people and animals. Have you ever seen a seal balance a ball on its nose at an aquarium? Or have you seen a child throwing a tantrum in public while his/her parent appears to be ignoring the behavior completely? If so, you've witnessed how operant conditioning principles can be applied to modify behaviors.

Operant conditioning is the basis of animal training--whether you are teaching your dog to sit or a seal to balance a ball.

Shaping

LO 5.8   Identify how behaviors are modified through the process of shaping.

The process of **shaping** behavior uses reinforcers to guide an individual's or animal's actions toward a desired behavior (Kazdin, 2012). This new behavior is achieved by using *successive approximations*, or behaviors that are incrementally closer to the overall desired action. Most amazing animal tricks are taught according to this method, as shown in the video *Shaping Techniques*.

shaping

the use of reinforcement of successive approximations of a desired end behavior

Shaping Techniques

One method of shaping complex behavior is referred to as **chaining**. A chain is a combination or series of responses performed in a particular order (Kazdin, 2012). The reward is ultimately tied to the full sequence of behaviors; but, during training, reinforcement of the successive approximations (each behavior in the chain) is used to shape the overall sequence of behaviors. This is exactly how Skinner managed to train a rat to wait to hear the "Star-Spangled Banner" before sitting up on its hind legs, pulling a string to hoist the U.S. flag, and finally saluting the banner in a remarkable display of rodent patriotism.

chaining

a method of shaping complex behavior by rewarding a combination or series of responses performed in a particular order

Applied Behavior Analysis

LO 5.9   Describe applied behavior analysis.

One of the most exciting aspects of psychology is the ability to learn something new and then immediately apply it to your own life. **Applied behavior analysis (ABA)** has been defined as the systematic extension of the principles of operant psychology to problems and issues of social importance to people (Baer et al., 1968). In recent years, researchers and clinicians have favored the use of the name *applied behavior analysis* (rather than behavior modification) because of its less negative connotation (Cooper, 1982; Fielding et al., 2013). You can use techniques from ABA to change some of your own behaviors, or you can use it with others to alter their behavior patterns. True to the principles of operant conditioning, applied behavior analysis can be employed to either increase or decrease behaviors through the use of reinforcement and punishment. These techniques have been and continue to be applied to many aspects of life such as school, work, home, sports, and relationships. It is likely that you have experienced these techniques in your own life—maybe without even knowing it!

applied behavior analysis (ABA) or behavior modification

using the principles of operant psychology to address problems and issues of social importance to people

Antecedent The environment prior to the behavior of interest	→	Behavior	→	Consequence What happens after the behavior of interest occurs

EDUCATIONAL APPLICATIONS Skinner believed it was possible to achieve an ideal education. He stated: "Good instruction demands two things. Students must be told immediately whether what they do is right or wrong and, when right, they must be directed to the step to be taken next." (Skinner, 1961). Think about what you are doing right now. This introductory psychology program is focused on providing you with (1) immediate scores and feedback on your performance related to the questions you answer and (2) directions to the next step along the learning pathway based on your performance. Skinner's thinking was well ahead (about 55 years ahead!) of technology, but hopefully, through this program, you are experiencing the benefits of his contributions to education.

Premack principle

high probability (or preferred) behaviors can be used to reinforce low probability (or nonpreferred) behaviors

As we have seen, enticing rewards tend to be good motivators. The **Premack principle** states that people (and animals) are more likely to engage in a low probability activity if they know it will be followed by a high probability activity they enjoy (Premack, 1959). That is, promising yourself some kind of reward for completing a task you are not excited about can motivate you to begin and finish the task quickly (e.g., "I'll get a snack after I finish reading this chapter."). The Premack principle is a very useful strategy when it comes to completing homework or studying for exams.

Journal Prompt: Premack Principle

Write an example of how you could use the Premack principle in your own life right now.

In order to use the Premack principle, you must know how or be capable of performing the behavior required to obtain the reward.

APPLICATIONS TO THE TREATMENT OF AUTISM In recent years, ABA has often been discussed most often in terms of its treatment potential for *autism-spectrum disorders (ASD)*. ABA interventions are personalized based on individual needs but typically focus on communication, sociability, self-care, play, and academic skills (www.autismspeaks. org). For example, an ABA therapist may help a child with autism learn how to communicate hunger in an appropriate way rather than throwing a tantrum. The therapist would break the skill down into small components and provide reinforcements for performing the small steps. First, they may focus on making the sounds of the words, "I'm hungry." Then, they may work on having the child sign the word for "eat." Finally, if they are at home, they may encourage the child to go to the kitchen when they are hungry. Each of these skills would be taught discretely (one at a time), and then the therapist would work with the child to put them all together.

An ABA therapist uses positive reinforcement after a child performs a desired behavior.

According to recent data, the rates of ASDs are the highest they have ever been with 1 in every 68 children aged 8 years are diagnosed with ASD (Developmental, D.M.N.S.Y, & 2010 Principal Investigators, 2014). These rates have increased from 1 in every 88 children in 2008 and 1 in every 150 children in 2002 (Mandell & Lecavalier, 2014). It isn't clear whether the increased rates are a result of more children developing ASD or simply a consequence of greater public awareness, increased advocacy, wider screening with better assessment techniques, and/or earlier detection (Neggers, 2014). Regardless of the reasons for the increased numbers, early intervention utilizing applied behavior analysis has been an effective treatment for ASD (Eikeseth et al., 2012; Reichow, 2012). With the recent increase in the number of states mandating insurance companies to cover the cost of applied behavior analysis for ASD (Johnson et al., 2014), many colleges and universities are offering training and credentialing of behavior analysts at the undergraduate, masters, and doctoral levels.

BUSINESS APPLICATIONS   Outside of autism and education, applied behavior techniques are evident in most modern successful businesses—a field of study referred to as organizational behavior management (Abernathy, 2013). There may be no better company example of this than Google—a leader in developing a corporate culture that empowers, self-motivates, and rewards employees for creative innovation and contributions to the company. According to Cook (2012),

> Many talented people work for Google, Inc. because of their unique culture, rewards, and perks. At the Googleplex, employees can show up to work anytime they want, bring their dog, wear pajamas, eat gourmet food for free, enjoy a free fitness center and trainer, see the onsite doctor if they are sick, wash their clothes and partake in free espresso at each corner of their "office." This relaxed, fun environment has worked well for Google, Inc. because it provides a psychological benefit to encourage employees to become more committed, more creative, and more productive.

Google has gone further than other companies in terms of personalizing rewards for its employees. So, rather than having a static reward system where everyone earns the same reward if they meet a certain goal or objective, Google has empowered its managers to truly get to know each of their employees and decide what types of rewards would be most meaningful to them. Just think: Wouldn't you work harder and more effectively if you knew you could potentially earn a trip to a destination you have always wanted to visit?

This strategy of keeping employees happy through the use of reinforcement has certainly been rewarding to Google founders Larry Page and Sergey Brin who in 2017 made the Forbes list of billionaires with a net worth of more than $44 billion each! While most of us are probably never going to work for Google, that doesn't mean we can't use some of the principles from ABA to become more productive, learn new skills, or promote positive behavior changes.

TOKEN ECONOMIES   If you have ever been to Chuck E. Cheese, have a frequent flyer account, or have one (or 50) coffee shop punch cards, then you have participated in a token economy. A token is anything (e.g., a sticker, a coin, a point, a cotton ball) that represents a currency that can be cashed in for something rewarding (Doll et al., 2013). Therefore, a **token economy** is an interconnected system of token production, token accumulation, and token exchange for desirable goods or services (Hackenberg, 2009). A token is considered a conditioned reinforcer because it becomes associated with a primary or secondary reinforcer (Kazdin, 1982). Getting a punch on your coffee card isn't inherently rewarding, but over time it becomes rewarding because it is associated with receiving free coffee (which is very exciting for most coffee lovers).

token economy
providing tokens (e.g., stickers, coins, points) for desired behaviors that can be exchanged for something rewarding

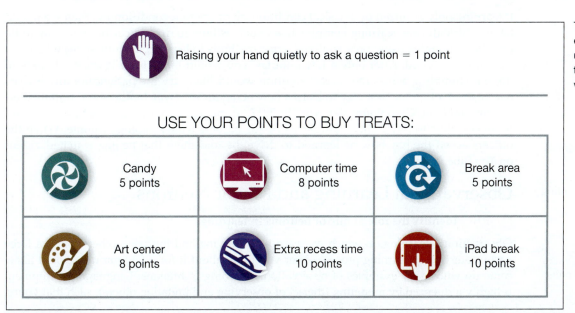

This is an example of a token economy system that could be used in a classroom where the teacher defines what behavior will earn a point.

Raising your hand quietly to ask a question = 1 point

USE YOUR POINTS TO BUY TREATS:

Candy 5 points	Computer time 8 points	Break area 5 points
Art center 8 points	Extra recess time 10 points	iPad break 10 points

Token economies were initially developed as a technique to manage the behavior of patients in psychiatric wards by providing tokens for specific desirable behaviors such as daily self-care, interacting with others in nonaggressive ways, and demonstrating responsibility. These tokens could be exchanged for things like movies and well-located beds (Atthowe & Krasner, 1968). Token economies are still used in some psychiatric facilities today to promote healthy behaviors such as exercise (Kokaridas et al., 2013). The use of token economies has been generalized to other populations (e.g., individuals with developmental disorders) and situations such as classrooms (Hulac & Briesch, 2017; Nelson, 2010). In fact, Dr. Hudson distinctly remembers the token economy from her 7th grade classroom where little pieces of blue paper with one hole punched in the middle could be earned for good behavior and entered into the drawing at the end of the week for a new record. (Yes, they were called "record stickers" and yes—that was a long time ago!)

ABA offers a number of strategies to change your own behavior or the behavior of others. Many colleges offer an entire psychology course in applied behavior analysis, with a project that involves developing your own behavior change plan.

Quiz for Module 5.8–5.9

1. _____ is the process of reinforcement of complex behaviors by rewarding the small steps in the overall sequence of behaviors.

   a. Observational learning   **b.** Operant conditioning

   c. Chaining   **d.** Classical conditioning

2. Gary trains his hamster to roll a marble. First, he reinforces the hamster when it walks toward the marble, then he reinforces when it touches the marble with its nose. Finally, the hamster learns to roll the marble and is reinforced for it. This example illustrates _____.

   a. shaping   **b.** counterconditioning

   c. classical conditioning   **d.** the Premack principle

3. The application of operant-conditioning techniques to teach new responses or to reduce or eliminate maladaptive or problematic behavior is called _____.

   a. applied behavior analysis   **b.** counterconditioning

   c. higher-order conditioning   **d.** stimulus generalization

4. Ms. Wang gives a sticker for each book her 3rd grade students read. At the end of the year, any student with more than 10 stickers gets to attend a pizza party. What behavioral technique is Ms. Wang using?

   a. Classical conditioning technique   **b.** Shaping

   c. Negative reinforcement   **d.** Token economy

5. Promising yourself some kind of reward for completing a task you are not excited about is an example of _____.

   a. a token economy   **b.** the Premack principle

   c. positive punishment

   d. negative punishment

Module 5.10–5.11: Observational Learning

If learning only occurred by classical conditioning or operant conditioning, then we would have a difficult time learning complex tasks such as how to drive a car or even how to tie our shoes. Imagine using only trial-and-error methods to learn to tie your shoes when you were a young child. After only a few minutes, you would likely have learned what *not* to do, but stumbling across the correct solution would likely try the patience of any 5-year-old. Instead, often the best way to learn a new behavior is to watch others and imitate their actions. Take the Ohio youngster who, in 2017, at the age of 8, drove his 4-year-old sister to McDonald's to buy a cheeseburger while his parents were sleeping at home. When the officers asked the boy how he learned to drive, he told them that he just watched videos on YouTube.

observational learning

learning by observing and imitating others

Observational Learning and Mirror Neurons

LO 5.10   **Identify the role of mirror neurons in learning.**

modeling

the act of observing behavior exhibited by someone else in order to imitate the behavior

Observational learning, in which we learn by observing and imitating others, plays a large part in our overall learning process. After you think about it for a few minutes, you'll likely come up with many examples of observational learning in humans. Language development is highly influenced by **modeling** (the act of observing and imitating others), such that young

Primates often learn by observing the behavior of fellow primates.

Children learn many behaviors such as how to repair a bicycle through the process of observational learning.

children learn the vocabulary and even the accent of the language(s) they are exposed to the most. Observational learning can also help protect us. For example, you don't have to be hit by a car (which would be very "punishing" in an operational learning sense) to learn that it is dangerous to walk across the street without looking carefully. Likewise, observational learning does not occur in humans alone. Many nonhuman animals provide excellent examples of observational learning, which is also referred to as "social learning." Learning how to obtain safe foods, how to identify predators, and how to select a mate have all been shown to have a strong social learning component. Consider the experiment by Whiten et al. (1996) in which researchers showed chimpanzees and human children (ages 2–4) different human models accessing an "artificial fruit" by different methods. Similar to the way a banana must be peeled, the artificial fruit had some sort of covering or "shell" that had to be removed in a certain way in order to access the "treat" inside. The human models demonstrated how to "peel" the fruit. The researchers found that the chimpanzees successfully copied some of the methods they witnessed. The human children were even more successful in imitating the adult model's methods, demonstrating that humans are very adept at imitation and social learning. Outside of the laboratory, examples of social learning in many species can be found. Songbirds such as the sparrow learn to sing their songs by listening to and imitating other sparrows in their territory (Beecher, 2008; Beecher et al., 1994). Young cheetahs are often taught how to hunt by being provided with injured prey (Eaton, 1970).

Over the past 25 years, there has been a surge in research on social learning in human and nonhuman animals (Nielsen et al., 2012). One current debate focuses on the difference between *imitation* (copying the actions of others) and *emulation* (reproducing the end results of the actions of others through different means) (Call et al., 2005; Subiaul & Schilder, 2014; Whiten, 2017; Whiten et al., 2009) with significant evidence suggesting that primates are more adept at imitation than other animals. The fact that humans are very adept at imitation may help explain why human cultures have become so rich and diverse—the ability to imitate another person and then further that learned skill and teach the next generation sets humans apart from other nonhuman animals.

Research advances have also demonstrated the importance of specific types of neurons in the brain to explain how social learning works. Like many important scientific findings, these neurons were first discovered by accident. In the early 1990s, a group of Italian scientists implanted electrodes into macaque monkeys' brains to study brain activity involved in various motor movements such as grasping food. One day, as one of the researchers reached for his own food, he noticed that neurons in the monkey's prefrontal cortex had fired just by watching the researcher reach for food. The monkey's brain responded to watching the researcher reach for his food in the same way as if the monkey were reaching for its own food (Di Pellegrino et al., 1992). These neurons, which were named **mirror neurons**, fire not only when a monkey engages in a particular action, but also if a monkey observes another monkey (or human) engaging in the same action (Di Pelligreno et al., 1992, Gallese et al., 1996, Rizzolatti & Sinigaglia, 2016;

mirror neurons

neurons that fire not only when an animal engages in a particular action, but also if the animal observes another animal engaging in the same action

Rizzolatti & Craighero, 2004). Much indirect evidence that primarily comes from fMRI studies strongly suggests that humans also have mirror neurons (Molenberghs et al., 2012). This means that anytime you watch another person make a face after biting into a sour lemon or flinch in pain when receiving a painful injection, your brain also simulates the experience.

These findings have very important implications to a wide variety of issues. Recent research has discovered that mirror neurons not only allow us to imitate, but they also allow us to infer the intention behind an action. Mirror neurons have been linked to the experience of empathy (the ability to understand and share the feelings of another). One adaptive response when people experience pain is to either freeze or escape. One study showed that watching a person have a needle injected into his hand led the observer to experience the same type of disinhibition (or "freezing") response as the person receiving the injection. This response did not occur when the individual observed the person being touched with a nonpainful Q-tip or when they watched a tomato being injected with the same needle (Avenanti et al., 2005). Studies like this have demonstrated that mirror neurons provide us with the ability to actually experience the pain, joy, or sadness of others. While these findings are fascinating, other scientists have cautioned about overinterpreting research findings related to mirror neurons (Hickok, 2014).

Bandura's Experiments

LO 5.11 **Recognize the characteristics necessary for observational learning.**

One of the first studies of observational learning was conducted by psychologist Albert Bandura. He conducted a famous experiment in which he attempted to evaluate the nature of observational learning in children with respect to aggressive behavior (Bandura, 1961). Watch the video *Bobo Doll Study* to see an overview of this experiment.

Bobo Doll Study

Bandura pointed out that some key "ingredients" must be present for observational learning to occur (Bandura, 1986). The first of these is *attention*. In order to learn something by watching others, an individual must be paying attention to the model. For example, if an art professor is demonstrating a particular painting technique, the students must be paying attention to the demonstration to actually learn how to use that technique. *Retention* is the second process of successful observational learning. Retention is the ability to encode and store the information so that it can later be retrieved from memory. Sometimes, when observing a complicated lesson (e.g., watching a gourmet cooking show), the reason you can't replicate the model's behavior (baking a perfect soufflé) is because you weren't able to accurately retain the information in your memory for later recall. The third process important in observational learning is *motor reproduction*. You must be capable of reproducing the action that was observed for observational learning to be successful. Simply watching a talented gymnast demonstrate how to complete a complicated tumbling pass will not be sufficient for most people to learn how to engage in that same behavior because they don't have the motor ability to do so. Finally, Bandura pointed out that *motivation* is the final ingredient for successful observational learning. To replicate the behavior of someone else, the individual needs to be motivated to do so by some sort of incentive. While observing, if the model's behavior is followed by a positive consequence (positive reinforcement), then the observer will be more likely to attempt to imitate the behavior. If the consequences are negative, the observer is less likely to be motivated to imitate the behavior.

Observational Learning

Drag and drop the observational learning process that best represents each example.

Example	Observational Learning Process
Juan stared off into space while the guide demonstrated how to secure the harness to the zipline. When handed his harness, he was embarrassed to admit he didn't know what to do.	Attention
Because she had just learned how to make the letter "P," preschooler Meg was successfully able to reproduce the letter "B" after her teacher provided an example on her paper.	Motor Reproduction
Alec was hesitant at first, but after watching a fellow student be awarded extra credit points for volunteering for a class demonstration, he quickly raised his hand the next time the instructor asked for volunteers.	Motivation
Aleni was able to recreate the first three steps in the process of assembling the display like her supervisor had demonstrated, but she couldn't remember the last two steps.	Retention

Interactive

Start Over

Quiz for Module 5.10–5.11

1. A _____ neuron fires not only when an animal engages in a particular action, but also if an animal observes another animal (or human) engaging in the same action.
   a. motor
   b. chaining
   c. mirror
   d. reflex

2. Research on mirror neurons shows that these neurons fire when an animal _____.
   a. engages in a particular behavior only
   b. watches another animal engage in a particular behavior only
   c. is at rest
   d. either engages in a particular behavior or watches another animal engage in the behavior

3. Michael grows up in a home where his father is generally unloving toward his mother. He observes his father yell and degrade his mother, and he notices that his mother never resists this treatment. Based on the work of Bandura, what might we predict about Michael's own relationships when he is older?
   a. Michael may treat women with discourtesy and disrespect, as he repeats the behavior he saw in his father.
   b. Michael will probably have no relationships with women, as his father has taught him that relationships are not worth having.
   c. Michael will always be very distant from his father, as he has learned that his father does not care about anyone but himself.
   d. Michael will probably treat women very well, as he rebels against the behaviors he saw in his father.

4. For observational learning to occur, each of the following must happen *except* _____.
   a. being reinforced for imitating the model
   b. doing what the model did
   c. remembering what the model did
   d. paying attention to what the model does

Module 5.12–5.13: Learning and Cognition

After studying classical conditioning, operant conditioning, and observational learning, you might assume all learning involves some type of conditioning or observation. However, have you ever had an "aha moment" where the solution to a problem seems to come to you out of the blue? If you're anything like the authors, these moments are rarely timely (e.g., a sudden brainstorm while in the shower or better yet, while trying to go to sleep), but they do suggest the possibility that **cognition**, or mental events, can lead to learning without other forms of conditioning or observation taking place. To provide an example, take a moment and try to find the solution to the following problem:

cognition

mental processes, including thinking, knowing, judging, problem solving, and remembering

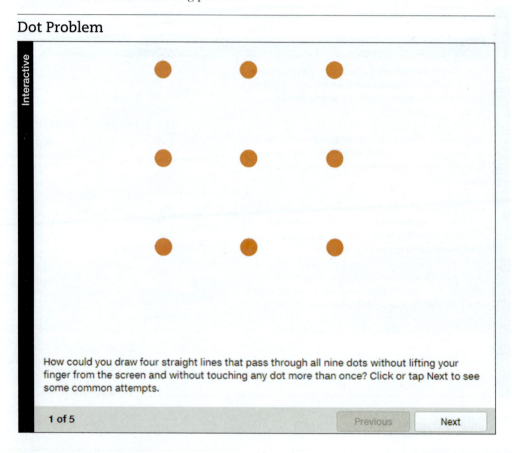

Dot Problem

How could you draw four straight lines that pass through all nine dots without lifting your finger from the screen and without touching any dot more than once? Click or tap Next to see some common attempts.

1 of 5   Previous   Next

Insight Learning

LO 5.12 **Explain the cognitive theory of insight learning.**

In the 1920s, Wolfgang Köhler was conducting research on problem solving in chimpanzees. One chimpanzee, Sultan, became famous for developing excellent problem-solving skills. In one experiment, Köhler placed Sultan in a cage and provided him with a stick that was reachable just outside the cage. Köhler then placed some bananas a short distance away. Sultan quickly became adept at using the stick to retrieve the bananas. One day, Köhler moved the bananas out of the reach of the stick. Sultan had access to two sticks and, after approximately an hour, Sultan appeared to suddenly discover that he could fit the two sticks together and retrieve the bananas. Köhler argued that Sultan's abrupt inspiration on how to use the sticks to retrieve the bananas was not achieved through shaping, or gradual reinforcement of behavior. Rather, Sultan appeared to experience a flash of insight that led the chimpanzee to come up with a solution to the problem. In another of Köhler's experiments, the chimpanzees were left in a room with several boxes and bananas hanging out of reach. The chimpanzees learned to stack the boxes on top of one another to be able to access the fruit. Köhler argued that it is possible for **insight learning** to occur when you suddenly realize how to solve a problem (Köhler, 1927) which does not exclusively occur through trial and error. This theory was very influential in the development of models of learning that focused on the role of cognitions.

insight learning

sudden realization of how to solve a problem that does not occur as a result of trial-and-error

The chimpanzee learns to stack the boxes in order to reach the food through a process Kohler labeled insight learning.

Latent Learning

LO 5.13   Define latent learning.

Around the same time Köhler was working with his chimpanzees, psychologist Edward Tolman was conducting experiments with rats. Tolman was timing how long it took rats to learn to navigate successfully through a maze. In one of his most famous experiments (Tolman & Honzik, 1930), Tolman divided his rats into three different groups and measured how quickly the rats were able to navigate a maze, taking into account the number of mistakes the rats made on each trial through the maze. The first group received a food reward every time they successfully reached the end of the maze. The second group never received any reinforcement (i.e., food) upon reaching the end of the maze. The third group did not receive any reinforcement for the first 10 days, but the experimenter added a food reward to be waiting for the rat at the end of the maze on the 11th day of the study. A simple behavioral prediction would be that the first group of rats would learn to navigate the maze faster than the other two groups because they were being reinforced. That is exactly what happened. The rats in group one quickly learned to navigate the maze, while the rats in the unreinforced groups meandered slowly through the maze, appearing to find the end by accident. However, the interesting finding came after day 11 when the third group of rats received a reinforcer. The next day, those rats showed a drastic increase in their speed at navigating the maze, making their performance equivalent to the rats who had received rewards all along. Tolman proposed that the rats who were not reinforced until later were not simply wandering through the maze without learning anything. Rather, he argued that the rats experienced **latent learning**, or learning that is not immediately expressed and occurs without any obvious reinforcement. See Figure 5.4 for a graph of the study's results.

Years later, Tolman hypothesized that spatial latent learning might be due to the development of a *cognitive map*. That is, prior experience in a setting such as a maze may lead the rat (or other animal) to develop a mental map of the environment that can later be accessed if necessary or if a reward incentivizes the behavior (Tolman, 1948).

Prominent behaviorists of the time, including Clark Hull and Edwin R. Guthrie, responded by developing and testing behavioral theories with a more traditional "stimulus-response" focus (e.g., that learning occurs when associations are made between a stimulus such as a maze, and a response, such as turning left or right) that could potentially explain Tolman's results. Ultimately, a 30-year debate on latent learning ensued with the results characterized as a "stalemate" (Jensen, 2006) between more traditional

latent learning

learning that is not immediately expressed and occurs without any obvious reinforcement

behavioral models and behavioral models such as Tolman's that focus on the intervening role of cognitions between stimuli and responses. Overall, the evidence for cognitive maps has been limited (e.g., Bennett, 1996; Jensen, 2006), but Tolman's work was instrumental in moving behavioral theories forward by evaluating and considering the role of cognition in learning.

Figure 5.4 Results from Tolman's Study

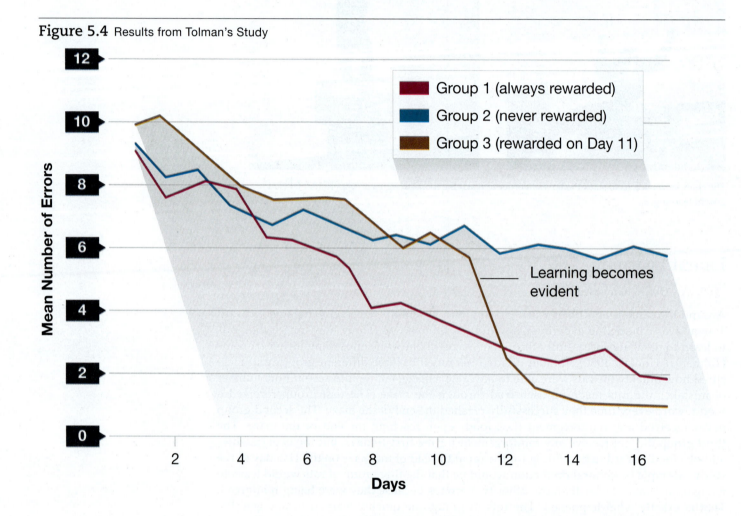

Quiz for Module 5.12–5.13

1. You need to remove a broken light bulb from a lamp. Without a pair of gloves, you are likely to cut yourself on the jagged glass. Suddenly, it occurs to you that you can use a cut potato to remove the light bulb from the socket. You have just demonstrated _____.

   a. generalization   **b.** insight learning

   c. discrimination   **d.** latent learning

2. Scientists like Tolman and Köhler conducted important studies to help determine the role of _____ in learning.

   a. reinforcement   **b.** classical conditioning

   c. cognition   **d.** operant conditioning

3. Rats that have never received any reinforcement for finding the end of a maze are presented with food the next time they complete the maze. According to the theory of latent learning, the next time the rats enter the maze, their performance will be _____.

   a. slower than rats who have always received reinforcement

   b. the same as when they were not reinforced

   c. slower than when they were not reinforced

   d. as fast as rats who have always received reinforcement

4. What is it called when learning has taken place but has not yet been demonstrated?

   a. Latent learning   **b.** Observational learning

   c. Classical conditioning   **d.** Instinctive drift

Module 5.14: Piecing It Together: Violent Video Games

LO 5.14   Analyze how the cross-cutting themes of psychology are related to the topic of violent video games.

The relationship between playing violent video games (VVGs) and aggression includes a tale of academic bickering, methodological intricacies, political maneuvering, and even the U.S. Supreme Court. This issue is important to consider as video game sales have surpassed movie box office sales for several years, and statistics indicate that more than half of Americans play video games on a regular basis (Kamenetz, 2013). While many games are nonviolent, there have been concerns about certain games such as "first person shooter" games that position the player to act violently. There are games that simulate gang activity, encouraging players to target innocent characters and use chain saws to attack, maim, and kill. Some games use guns, swords, grenades, bombs, and other weapons and focus on the dismemberment, decapitation, and death of the opponents. New technology has allowed these games to become so realistic that the next generation of games has been touted as having "a film-like quality to the action in the games, creating a deeper feeling of immersion in the narrative" (Frum, 2013).

Given Bandura's theory of observational learning, psychologists have long been interested in the effects of exposure to violence in the media. Hundreds of research studies have been conducted to try to determine if a relationship exists between playing violent video games and aggressive behavior. If you looked at each individual study, you would likely conclude that the findings are mixed—some studies show that violent video games are related to increased aggression, and some do not. One statistical technique that is helpful in situations like this is called *meta-analysis*. This is a way of taking large amounts of data from a variety of studies and pooling it together to see if an overall conclusion about the findings can be made. In 2010, a group of researchers conducted a meta-analysis that included 130 studies and a total of 130,296 participants (Anderson et al., 2010). They found evidence of a causal link between playing violent video games and aggressive behavior, aggressive cognitions, and aggressive affect (or emotions). They also found that violent video games were related to decreased empathy, desensitization to violence, and a reduction in prosocial behavior. Given these results, you would expect these games to be highly regulated (e.g., not sold to minors) and that the American Psychological Association (APA) would be strongly and publicly opposed to the sale and promotion of violent video games. In fact, the Supreme Court ruled in 2005 on the *Brown v. Entertainment Merchants Association* against California's ban of the sale of certain violent video games to minors without parental supervision. The court argued that video games were protected speech under the First Amendment. The video game industry responded by voluntarily instituting a rating system, and some video distributors will not sell games rated as "mature" to minors. The APA released a public statement in 2005 confirming the link between aggression and playing violent video games and advocated a reduction in all video game violence in games targeting children and adolescents. However, after a different set of meta-analyses was published in 2007 with results questioning the established link between aggression and VVGs (Ferguson, 2007), the APA withdrew its policy. In August 2015, the APA released an updated

More money is spent on video games than movies now, and over 50% of Americans play video games regularly.

policy that called for more investigation despite continuing to confirm that evidence shows consistent links between VVGs and increased aggression.

Why has this issue been so difficult to sort out? The next section on research methods will discuss the various methodological concerns that have contributed to these muddy waters.

Research Methods

- How has this issue been studied in the past, and what are the limitations of these experiments?

- How do researchers measure aggressive behavior?

The following is only a brief list of some of the methodological issues surrounding the debate about VVGs and aggression.

1. **Correlational studies versus experimental designs:**

   As you have learned, it is difficult to determine the nature of the relationship between two variables in a correlational study. It's possible that a third variable could account for the correlation between VVGs and aggression. For example, it's possible that people who watch VVGs and engage in aggression may also be more likely to have certain personality characteristics, and these characteristics might be the *cause* of both the choice to play VVGs and the aggression. Much of the research on VVGs and aggression has been correlational, but in recent years, there have been more experimental designs, and researchers have used more advanced statistical techniques to establish whether or not a causal relationship exists between these two variables.

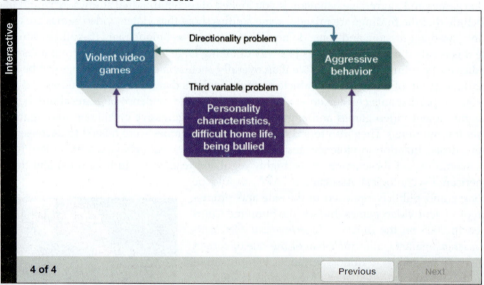

The Third Variable Problem

2. **How we measure aggression is important**

   Obviously, if we are interested in determining if playing VVGs leads people to act more aggressively, we need an accurate and consistent way to measure aggression. However, few studies measure aggressive behavior the same way, and the majority of the research has focused on mild aggressive behavior. As a society, we are much more interested in whether VVGs can lead some people to engage in acts of extreme violence such as the mass school shootings that have occurred with alarming frequency in the past decade.

3. Is there bias in which studies get published?

Some authors have argued that studies associating VVGs with aggressive behavior are more likely to be published than studies that show no such link. These researchers are concerned that "null results" (when the results don't show any relationship between variable A and variable B) are less interesting or don't conform to an underlying social or political agenda and therefore may not be selected for publication in academic journals. However, other authors have suggested that this potential bias could work in the opposite direction. Given the lobbying power of the video industry, it's possible that there could be pressures to avoid publishing studies that suggest VVGs have harmful effects.

Measuring aggression consistently across research studies is difficult, and most studies examine only mild aggressive behavior.

4. Is the relationship between VVGs and aggression meaningful in the real world?

In the 2010 meta-analysis, the authors found an overall effect of VVGs on aggression to be $r = .19$.

Meaningful Correlations

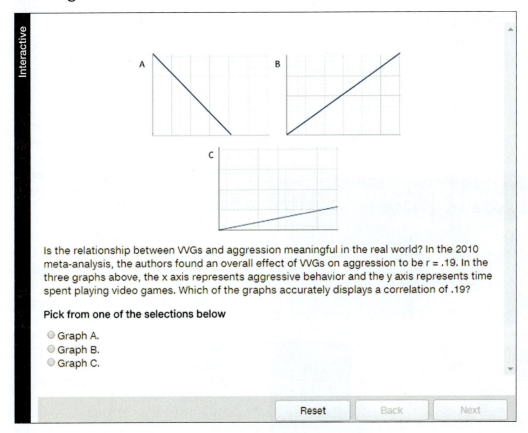

Is the relationship between VVGs and aggression meaningful in the real world? In the 2010 meta-analysis, the authors found an overall effect of VVGs on aggression to be r = .19. In the three graphs above, the x axis represents aggressive behavior and the y axis represents time spent playing video games. Which of the graphs accurately displays a correlation of .19?

Pick from one of the selections below

○ Graph A.
○ Graph B.
○ Graph C.

| Reset | Back | Next |

Ethics

- Given the methodological problems with current research, why can't someone design a good experimental study that avoids these problems and gives us an answer to the question of whether or not exposure to VVGs causes aggressive behavior?

Take a minute to design the best experimental study possible to answer the question, "Does playing VVGs lead people to act more aggressively?" Don't worry about making your study possible to implement. Instead, brainstorm an "ideal" study without regard for the limitations or ethics involved. Use the following steps to help you design the study:

1. Develop your hypothesis.
2. Identify the independent and dependent variables.
3. Consider who will be in the control group and experimental group.
4. Think about the outcome that would support your hypothesis.
5. Next, consider any ethical concerns with your design. Discuss any issues related to random assignment to groups, informed consent, and causing harm to participants.

Journal Prompt: Design Your Own Study

Discuss any issues related to random assignments to groups, informed consent, and causing harm to participants.

Cultural and Social Diversity

- Are VVGs the same across different cultures?
- Are there any cultural differences that would make some people less susceptible to the effect of VVGs?

It is interesting to consider if cultural differences might impact how VVGs affect levels of aggression. There has been interesting research on media violence in Eastern versus Western countries. While the amount of violence in the media is often similar between Eastern and Western countries, there are differences in the portrayal of violence. For example, there is an increased focus on the suffering of the victims, and "heroes" often suffer more violence than "villains" in Eastern countries (Kodaira, 1998). In this cultural context, it is possible that individuals would respond differently to VVG exposure.

Research conducted using participants from the United States and Japan, however, found no differences in how individuals from these countries respond on measures of aggressive behavior and aggressive cognition after exposure to VVGs (Anderson et al., 2008; Anderson et al., 2010). A large-scale study examining VVG exposure and aggressive behavior in individuals from seven different countries (Australia, China, Croatia, Germany, Japan, Romania, and the United States) found no differences in the impact of

Researchers have studied cultural differences in the impact of VVGs but have generally found that the relationship between VVGs and aggressive behavior is the same across cultures.

culture on aggressive behavior. In fact, across all countries, the relationship between violent behavior and VVG exposure was significant, and VVG exposure was the second highest risk factor for aggressive behavior (Anderson et al., 2017).

Variations in Human Functioning

- While examining cultural differences as a whole is important, what specific characteristics might predict how one individual might respond to playing VVGs?

It is intuitive to think some characteristics or personality traits might cause certain individuals to respond more negatively to playing VVGs, and research findings have supported this theory. Studies have shown that individuals with high levels of trait hostility (a tendency to be hostile across a variety of situations) or aggressiveness tend to respond to playing VVGs with increased levels of aggression when compared to other individuals (Gentile et al., 2004). These findings are concerning because individuals with high levels of trait hostility are likely to be the very people who are most drawn to playing VVGs.

One recent 3-year study of more than 3,000 adolescents in Singapore confirmed the relationship between playing VVGs and aggressive behavior. As shown in Figure 5.5, however, prior aggressiveness was not an important predictor of aggressive behavior following VVG exposure, suggesting that the negative impact of playing VVGs is not limited to those with prior aggressive tendencies (Gentile et al., 2014).

Figure 5.5 Levels of Aggression After Exposure to VVGs

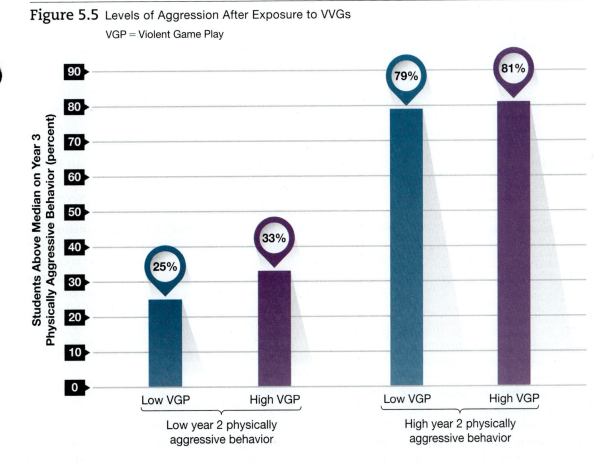

VGP = Violent Game Play

Quiz for Module 5.14

1. Which of the following statements is most accurate about the relationship between exposure to violent video games (VVGs) and aggressive behavior?

   a. While there have been some individual studies with mixed findings, the overall evidence suggests a causal link between playing VVGs and aggressive behavior.

   b. The findings have been so mixed that it is too difficult to conclude if there is a relationship between playing VVGs and aggressive behavior.

   c. The data strongly suggests no causal link between playing VVGs and aggressive behavior.

   d. Not enough research has been conducted to make any conclusions about the relationship between playing VVGs and aggressive behavior.

2. Research examining the association between violent video games and aggression is limited by which of the following?

   a. Finding an accurate and consistent way of measuring aggression has been difficult.

   b. Many studies have reported correlational results rather than experimental results.

   c. There may be a bias in the way studies are selected for publication.

   d. All answers are correct.

3. Imagine a study that examines levels of aggression among people who play violent video games (VVGs) and people who do not. What is the primary limitation of this type of study?

   a. People who play VVGs are unlikely to consent to being research participants.

   b. People were not randomly assigned to either play VVGs or not play VVGs, so differences between groups cannot necessarily be attributed to VVGs.

   c. There is no dependent variable in the study.

   d. There is no independent variable in the study.

4. Which of the following statements is true regarding findings across different cultures about the impact of violent video game (VVG) exposure and aggressive behavior?

   a. People in Western cultures are more likely to exhibit aggressive behavior after exposure to VVGs than people in Eastern cultures.

   b. People in Eastern cultures are more likely to exhibit aggressive behavior after exposure to VVGs than people in Western cultures.

   c. No cultural differences have been found in the impact of VVGs on aggressive behavior.

   d. Cultural differences have only been studied in a few countries with very small sample sizes.

5. Studies have shown that individuals with high levels of ____ tend to respond to playing violent video games (VVGs) with increased levels of aggression when compared to other individuals.

   a. anxiety   b. depression

   c. hostility   d. introversion

Summary: Learning

Module 5.1–5.3:   Classical Conditioning

Learning is a relatively permanent change in behavior due to experience. Most learning can be explained through the process of connections between behavior and the environment. **Classical conditioning**, discovered by Ivan Pavlov, is an automatic or reflexive type of learning. This type of learning occurs through the associations between stimuli (i.e., things). That is, when pairing a stimulus like food (**unconditioned stimulus**) that naturally causes salivation (**unconditioned response**) with a previously neutral stimulus like a metronome, the metronome (**conditioned stimulus**) will eventually come to signal to the person or animal that food is coming and will lead to salivation (**conditioned response**) all on its own. In this chapter, you learned about Pavlov's famous salivating dogs but also about how classical conditioning could be at work in your own life. John B. Watson was famous for his work in the ability to condition emotional responses. His famous study with "Little Albert" demonstrated how emotions can be classically conditioned. Many factors can affect classical conditioning such as how similar stimuli can lead to similar responses (**stimulus generalization**), how **discrimination** allows us to differentiate between stimuli that are not the same, the process of **acquisition** of a classically conditioned behavior, and how such behaviors can be extinguished through **extinction** or temporarily re-occur through **spontaneous recovery. Higher order conditioning** occurs when a conditioned stimulus eventually acts as an unconditioned stimulus in a second round of conditioning. Researchers have discovered that humans and other animals appear to have a certain **biological preparedness** to develop associations between certain types of stimuli and responses. For example, **taste aversions** are a classically conditioned dislike and avoidance of a certain food following illness.

Module 5.4–5.7:   Operant Conditioning

Classical conditioning occurs *before* a response occurs, whereas **operant conditioning** occurs as a result of the consequences that happen *after* a behavior is exhibited. Operant conditioning is based on voluntary behavior, whereas classical conditioning is based on reflexive behaviors. B. F. Skinner, one of the most famous behaviorists, taught us about the powerful role reinforcement and punishment plays in our life. Reinforcement refers to consequences that strengthen the preceding response. Reinforcement is always about *increasing* behavior. A **primary reinforcer** satisfies a basic biological need, such as hunger or thirst. Both Thorndike and Skinner used primary reinforcers (i.e., food) in their work with animals. A **secondary reinforcer** becomes satisfying or pleasurable through its association with primary reinforcers. **Immediate reinforcement** typically occurs when the behavior and the delivery of a reinforcer occur very close in time. On the other hand, **delayed reinforcement** occurs when there is a significant delay in time between the behavior and the delivery of a reinforcer. **Positive reinforcement** involves strengthening behavior through the addition of something desirable, whereas **negative reinforcement** involves strengthening behavior by removing something undesirable or aversive. **Punishment** involves consequences for behavior that ultimately decrease the probability of that behavior occurring again in the future. So, punishment is always about *decreasing* behavior. As with reinforcement, punishment can also be delivered by adding something negative or by taking away something positive. Reinforcement can be delivered according to different schedules or timings and, as a result, produces very predictable patterns of responding. The most straightforward schedule is **continuous reinforcement**, which means the desired response is reinforced every time it occurs. When continuous reinforcement is removed, an **extinction burst** (rapid rate of responding) often occurs. **Partial (intermittent) reinforcement** occurs when responses are only occasionally reinforced. This produces slower initial learning, but the learning is more resistant to extinction. **Fixed-ratio schedules** reinforce behavior after a set number of responses. **Variable-ratio schedules** reinforce behavior after varying and unpredictable numbers of responses. With **fixed-interval schedules**, behavior is reinforced after a fixed time period. **Variable-interval schedules** reinforce behavior after variable periods of time.

Module 5.8–5.9: Modifying Behavior with Operant Conditioning

The principles of operant conditioning have broad applications to all sorts of behaviors for both people and animals. The process of **shaping** behavior uses reinforcers to guide an individual's or animal's actions toward a desired behavior by using *successive approximations*, or behaviors that are incrementally closer to the overall desired action. One method of shaping complex behavior is referred to as **chaining**, which includes a combination or series of responses performed in a particular order. **Behavior modification** refers to the application of primarily operant conditioning principles to modify behaviors and has been referred to more recently as **applied behavior analysis** (the field of study concerned with the application of operant conditioning principles to

learn new behaviors and solve every day problems). Applied behavior analysis techniques have been widely implemented in homes, schools, hospitals, and the workplace. The **Premack principle** states that people (and animals) are more likely to engage in a low probability activity if they know it will be followed by a high probability activity they enjoy. A **token economy** is an interconnected system of token production, token accumulation, and token exchange for desirable goods or services. A token is considered a conditioned reinforcer because it becomes associated with a primary or secondary reinforcer.

Module 5.10–5.11: Observational Learning

In addition to learning by association and as a result of consequences, people also learn by observation. In this module, you learned about Albert Bandura and how his famous "Bobo Doll" study contributed to the understanding of **observational learning,** or learning by observing and imitating others. Research advances have also demonstrated the importance of specific types of neurons in the brain to explain how social learning works. These neurons, named **mirror neurons**, fire not only when an animal engages in a particular action but also if an animal observes another animal (or human) engaging in the same action. Much indirect evidence that primarily comes from fMRI studies strongly suggests that humans also have mirror neurons. **Modeling** is the act of observing and imitating others. The ability to learn by observing and imitating a **model** requires that a person pay *attention* to the model, *remember* the behavior being modeled, have the necessary *motor skills* to engage in the behavior, and have the *motivation* to learn.

Module 5.12–5.13: Learning and Cognition

Theories of learning tend to involve observable behavior; however, researchers have also pointed to the important role **cognition** (or thinking) can have. Based on his work with Sultan the chimpanzee, Wolfgang Köhler argued that it is possible for learning to occur through **insight** when you suddenly realize how to solve a problem, and it does not exclusively occur through trial and error. Around the same time Köhler was working with his chimpanzees, Edward Tolman was conducting experiments with rats. Rats who did not receive any reinforcement for successfully navigating a maze performed slower than rats who were rewarded. However, once rewards were provided, their performance became equivalent to the rats who had received rewards all along. Tolman argued that the rats experienced **latent learning**, or learning that is not immediately expressed and occurs without any obvious reinforcement. Years later, Tolman hypothesized that spatial latent learning might be due to the development of a *cognitive map*. Overall, the evidence for cognitive maps has been limited, but Tolman's work was instrumental in moving behavioral theories forward by evaluating and considering the role of cognition in learning.

Chapter 5 Quiz

1. Bill hates to clean up after dinner. One night, he volunteers to bathe the dog before cleaning up. When he finishes with the dog and returns to the kitchen, his wife has cleaned everything up for him. Which of the following statements is most likely true?

   a. Bill's wife has negatively reinforced him for bathing the dog.

   b. Bill will never bathe the dog again.

   c. Bill's wife has positively reinforced him for bathing the dog.

   d. Bill will start cleaning up the kitchen before he bathes the dog.

2. Which of the following is true of research on insight?

   a. Researchers have found that apes are capable of insight only after being taught this by humans.

   b. Researchers have proven that all creatures, even one-celled organisms such as the amoeba, are capable of insight learning.

   c. Researchers have found support for the existence of both human and animal insight learning.

   d. Researchers have found that only human beings are capable of insight learning.

3. John Watson offered a live, white rat to Little Albert and then made a loud noise behind Albert's head by striking a steel bar with a hammer. Eventually, the white rat alone made Albert cry. The white rat served as the _____ stimulus in this study.

   a. unconditioned   b. counterconditioning

   c. conditioned   d. discriminative

4. Watson's experiment with Little Albert demonstrated that fears might be _____.

   a. based on the principals of observational learning

   b. deeply rooted in the innate unconscious of infants

   c. based on Skinner's analysis of positive reinforcement

   d. based on classical conditioning

5. In Pavlov's studies, he was able to condition dogs to salivate in response to specific tones while not salivating to other similar tones. This is called _____.

   a. stimulus discrimination   b. stimulus generalization

   c. extinction   d. behavior modification

6. After Little Albert acquired a conditioned fear of rats, Watson wanted to see how he would react to a white rabbit, cotton wool, and a Santa Claus mask. He was studying whether or not _____ had occurred.

   a. stimulus generalization   b. extinction

   c. stimulus discrimination   d. behavior modification

7. You decide to condition your dog to salivate to the sound of a metronome. You give the dog a biscuit, and then a second later you sound the metronome. You do this several times, but no conditioning seems to occur. This is probably because _____.

   a. you should have had a longer interval between the metronome and the biscuit

   b. the metronome should have been sounded before the dog ate the biscuit

   c. Pavlov found that the CS and UCS must be only seconds apart to condition salivation

   d. the metronome was not a distinctive sound

8. _____ classical conditioning, operant conditioning requires the organism to voluntarily produce the _____.

   a. Unlike; consequence   b. Like; stimulus

   c. Unlike; response   d. Like; response

9. You spend days wandering aimlessly around a park with many different paths that end at different parts of the park. One day when you arrive at the park, you get a call on your cell phone from your cousin whom you haven't seen for years, and she says she is waiting for you in a particular section of the park. Even though the paths are complicated and twisted, you manage to find the shortest route to your cousin. Tolman would explain your efficient passage through the park as an example of _____.

   a. formation of a cognitive map

   b. insight

   c. unconscious trial-and-error imagery

   d. spontaneous recovery

10. Of the following, _____ would serve as a primary reinforcer for most people.

    a. food   b. praise

    c. money   d. attention

11. Sal's dog loves to go on a walk and starts spinning in circles and wagging his tail in excitement when his lead is clipped onto his collar. Eventually Sal begins to notice that his dog starts to act excited when he puts on his tennis shoes before a walk. His dog's behavior of spinning in circles and wagging his tail when Sal puts on his tennis shoes is a _____.

    a. conditioned response   b. conditioned stimulus

    c. unconditioned response   d. unconditioned stimulus

12. Phil wants to train his parrot to kick a ball into a soccer net. Which of the following should he do?

  a. Use positive punishment until the parrot kicks the ball into the net.

  b. Use negative punishment until the parrot kicks the ball into the net.

  c. Wait until the parrot kicks the ball into the net on its own and then give it a food treat.

  d. Begin by reinforcing when the parrot goes near the ball.

13. Cheryl is trying to teach her son to do the laundry by watching her. According to observational learning theory, what must occur for Cheryl to be effective?

  a. Her son must be motivated to learn how to do the laundry.

  b. Her son must be able to complete other tasks while watching her.

  c. Her son must always model the behavior immediately.

  d. Cheryl must show her son how to do the laundry while she is making dinner.

14. A reinforcer is a consequence that _____ a behavior, while a punisher is a consequence that _____ a behavior.

  a. motivates; stimulates
  b. weakens; strengthens
  c. inhibits; motivates
  d. strengthens; weakens

15. You put a dollar in a soda machine and are rewarded with a bottle of root beer. When you put in another dollar, you get another soda. Assuming that the machine has a limitless supply of root beer, which kind of reinforcement schedule does this machine operate on?

  a. Continuous reinforcement
  b. Ratio reinforcement
  c. Interval reinforcement
  d. Partial reinforcement

16. Reinforcement given for a response emitted after each hour and a half (e.g., 10 a.m., 11:30 a.m., 1 p.m.) is most likely a _____ schedule.

  a. fixed-interval
  b. fixed-ratio
  c. variable-interval
  d. variable-ratio

17. Al must build 25 radios before he receives $20. What schedule of reinforcement is used?

  a. A variable-ratio schedule
  b. A fixed-ratio schedule
  c. A fixed-interval schedule
  d. A continuous schedule

18. _____ is an operant-conditioning procedure in which successive approximations of a desired response are reinforced.

  a. Spontaneous recovery
  b. Stimulus generalization
  c. Shaping
  d. Stimulus discrimination

19. Dr. Sardis provides his students with extra credit points every time they speak in class to encourage class participation. Dr. Sardis is using _____.

  a. negative punishment
  b. positive reinforcement
  c. negative reinforcement
  d. positive punishment

20. The application of operant-conditioning techniques called _____ has been used to help children with autism.

  a. applied behavior analysis
  b. counterconditioning
  c. higher-order conditioning
  d. stimulus generalization

21. In order to get her 3rd grade students to memorize the poem written on the chalkboard, Mrs. Thyberg gives the students stickers for each poem they can recite from memory. After earning five stickers, a student gets to pick a prize out of the goody box. Mrs. Thyberg is using _____ to modify the children's behaviors.

  a. a token economy
  b. shaping
  c. negative reinforcement
  d. classical conditioning

22. What type of neurons fire if a monkey observes another monkey engaging in an action?

  a. Magnetic neurons
  b. Mirror neurons
  c. Sensory neurons
  d. Motor neurons

23. Which type of learning occurs when we observe how other people act?

  a. Operant conditioning
  b. Classical conditioning
  c. Observational learning
  d. Insight learning

24. After watching her father slide through pictures on his smartphone using his index finger, Laura, a 5-year-old, learns to use her finger to slide the screen on his smartphone. Laura acquired this behavior through _____.

  a. operant conditioning
  b. counterconditioning
  c. classical conditioning
  d. observational learning

25. When a stimulus is removed from a person or animal resulting in a decrease in the probability of response, it is known as _____.

  a. negative reinforcement
  b. positive reinforcement
  c. negative punishment
  d. positive punishment

26. Dad is watching a home improvement show about how to install a new sink. He really wants to do it and watches the show intently. He knows his wife will reward him when he is done. However, when he tests the new sink, water spurts everywhere. Taking the new sink apart, he finds that he has left out the crucial washers in the faucet assembly even though this was emphasized in the TV show. What part of Bandura's theory of the necessary components of observational learning is most likely the reason for this disaster?

    a. Memory
    b. Imitation
    c. Motivation
    d. Inadequate motor skills

27. John has been working on a math problem late at night without success, and he falls asleep. Upon awakening, he suddenly realizes how to answer the problem. This scenario best illustrates _____ learning.

    a. cognitive
    b. insight
    c. latent
    d. observational

28. In a conditioning experiment, a sound is paired with a brief puff of air to the eye of a rabbit. After several pairings, the rabbit ultimately blinks its eye when it hears the sound. Which of the following is true?

    a. The puff of air serves as the conditioned stimulus.
    b. The puff of air serves as the unconditioned stimulus.
    c. The blinking of the eye serves as the conditioned stimulus.
    d. The blinking of the eye serves as stimulus.

29. Learning that occurs but is not immediately reflected in a behavior change is called _____.

    a. insight
    b. innate learning
    c. reflexive learning
    d. latent learning

30. Reflexive learning is related to _____, while learning related to voluntary behaviors is known as _____.

    a. observational learning; classical conditioning
    b. operant conditioning; classical conditioning
    c. classical conditioning; observational learning
    d. classical conditioning; operant conditioning

Chapter 6
Memory

Chapter Outline and Learning Objectives

Module 6.1–6.2: Models of Memory

LO 6.1 Recall Atkinson and Shiffrin's three-stage model of memory.

LO 6.2 Describe the core features of contemporary connectionist models of memory.

Module 6.3–6.6: Acquiring and Storing Memories

LO 6.3 Recognize the types and characteristics of sensory memory.

LO 6.4 Distinguish between short-term memory and working memory.

LO 6.5 Apply effective strategies for encoding information into long-term memory.

LO 6.6 Differentiate the various types of memory contained within long-term memory.

Module 6.7–6.9: Retrieving Memories

LO 6.7 Recognize factors that influence the retrieval of information.

LO 6.8 Identify how flashbulb memories differ from other memories.

LO 6.9 Describe situations that can lead to inaccuracies in memory.

Module 6.10–6.11: Forgetting

LO 6.10 Identify reasons for forgetting related to encoding and retrieval failures.

LO 6.11 Distinguish between the different types of amnesia.

Module 6.12–6.13: The Biological Basis of Memory

LO 6.12 Recognize that memories are located in various places in the brain.

LO 6.13 Recall the role of neurons in creating long-term memories.

Module 6.14: Piecing It Together: False Memories

LO 6.14 Analyze how the cross-cutting themes of psychology apply to the issue of false memories.

What is Memory?

What Comes to Mind?

Interactive

Type in the name of one of your favorite athletes.

[Reset]   [Next]

Which athlete came to mind? A football player? Soccer player? Maybe your favorite baseball player? While it would be difficult to predict exactly whose image you would conjure up, we can be quite certain you are *not* imagining Joshua Foer. Joshua Foer is a "memory athlete" who won the USA National Memory Championship in 2006.

What's interesting about Joshua's story is that one year prior to winning the competition, he was merely working as a scientific journalist and writing a story about the people who entered national and international memory contests. In 2005, Joshua had an average memory and believed people in these competitions had a gift that could not be learned. In his 2012 TED talk on his experience, Joshua describes his own journey into learning to train his brain to memorize massive amounts of information (in the contest he won, he set a new record in the "speed cards" event by memorizing a shuffled deck of 52 playing cards in 1 minute and 40 seconds). One of the purposes of the book he wrote and his TED talk was to demonstrate that anyone can develop an exceptional memory through practice and the use of various memory techniques.

Our memory serves many important functions, many of which have been crucial to our survival as a species. Researchers who work in *adaptive memory* have asked important questions such as, "What is memory for?" and "Why do we have the ability to remember experiences that occurred at a certain place and at a certain time in the past?" The ability to create and access memories is an evolutionary advantage. Results from adaptive memory research labs indicate that memory has evolved to address specific problems that can threaten survival, such as remembering the location of food, sources of contamination, and characteristics of predators (Nairne, 2015).

Joshua Foer used psychological principles of memory to become a memory champion. He also showed he could learn the vocabulary of an obscure language from the Republic of Congo in just 22 hours.

While memory is an essential human attribute, it is far from perfect. In terms of accuracy, memory is not the same as simply hitting rewind and replaying an event in your mind like you would when watching a video. Memory doesn't always present us with a clear, factually accurate account of events. Like a video, though, our memories can be edited, tampered with, or lost forever. The rest of this chapter will focus on the building blocks involved in the creation of memories and the factors that can lead to inaccurate or forgotten memories.

In addition to information about how memory works, this chapter will also provide important information and tools to improve your own memory and even your class performance. The reality is that *learning* and *memory* go together. In order to learn, you have to be able to remember; and, if you can understand how memory works and the techniques used to improve memory, then you are likely to be more successful in learning.

Module 6.1–6.2: Models of Memory

What exactly is memory? **Memory** is a collection of information and experiences stored in our brain for retrieval at a later time. Memory is our brain's system for filing away new knowledge and retrieving previously learned information. The concept of memory can be difficult to understand: Sometimes it is used as a noun, as in our definition of memory, and sometimes it is described as a verb, as in memory is the *active process of storing and retrieving information*. Which definition is right? Well … they are both technically correct. Memory has a structure, but it can also be a process.

A general theory used to understand memory involves what has been called the **information processing approach**, which suggests that our memory works in a way similar to having our own administrative assistant. Just as an assistant organizes hundreds of files, puts them away in specific filing cabinets, and finds your stored files for you when you need them, your memory *encodes* information, *stores* it away, and *retrieves* it for later use (see Figure 6.1).

In an effort to simplify and explain the important components of memory, researchers have developed various models of how memory works. Early models of memory were helpful for the initial conceptualization of memory and paved the way for more contemporary memory models that incorporate principles from neuroscience.

memory

a collection of information and experiences stored in the brain for retrieval at a later time

information processing approach

general theory of memory stating memories are encoded, stored, and retrieved later when needed

---

Figure 6.1 An Information-Processing Approach to Memory

The information processing approach to understanding memory involves the encoding of information, storing that information, and then retrieving the information when needed.

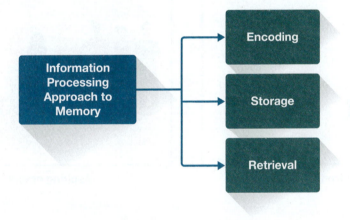

A Historical Perspective: The Three-Stage Model of Memory

LO 6.1   **Recall Atkinson and Shiffrin's three-stage model of memory.**

Richard Atkinson and Richard Shiffrin (1968) proposed a model of memory that can help us start to understand some of the important components of memory. While this model of memory is no longer accepted as an accurate picture of the way our memory truly works, its development was important as it stimulated further research that has led to more contemporary theories of memory (see LO 6.2).

Atkinson and Shiffrin's model addressed two different dimensions of memory. One dimension included the permanent or structural part of memory and the other was the more malleable part of memory. They used the analogy of a computer (yes, even in 1968) to clarify the distinction between the two parts. When you buy a new laptop, certain structural components can't be easily changed: the screen, keyboard, and many of the hardware components inside. This is similar to our basic memory storage facilities. Atkinson and Shiffrin proposed three fixed memory storage units that provide the structural foundation for our memory. However, much of our memory is under our control. Like your new laptop, you may not be able to easily change the hardware, but you can choose how your computer is going to run by choosing which type of programs to install. That is, you have some control over how your computer will function within the structural constraints. Our memory is the same way: We all have a similar basic structure of memory, but the processes or strategies we use to function make for the variation in memory we see between people. The good news about this, just like Joshua Foer discovered, is that working to strengthen the aspects of memory we can control may produce life-changing results.

According to Atkinson and Shiffrin, the *structure* of memory could be divided into three distinct memory stores, or types of memory (i.e., sensory memory, working memory, and long-term memory). The *processes* of memory involved how information moved from one store to another. They proposed that information from the external world is detected by our senses and first enters *sensory memory* for a very brief period of time. We are constantly bombarded with numerous pieces of information from our environment, so a lot of stimuli can enter sensory memory.

As we discuss the structure and process of memory consider the analogy of a casting call for actors needed for a new Netflix series. Stimuli that enters into sensory memory is similar to the set being bombarded by numerous, hopeful actors looking for their big break after the announcement is made for a casting call (see Figure 6.2a).

Figure 6.2a Atkinson and Shiffrin's Three Stage Model of Memory: Sensory Memory

SENSORY MEMORY — Taste, Hearing, Sight, Touch

Stimuli from environment

CASTING CALL

Aspiring actors

At the casting call, the director may encounter hundreds of actors, but only a small percentage of them will actually move on to the next stage of the audition. What has to happen for an actor to progress in the audition process? That actor will have to do something to catch the director's eye and gain the director's attention. This is the same principle with respect to sensory memory. In order for information to be captured in sensory memory and progress to the next memory structure, we must pay attention to it (part of the process). Just as only a small percentage of actors make it to the next round of auditions, only a small percentage of information is moved from sensory memory to short-term memory, the next memory storage facility. The process by which the information is moved involves giving it the appropriate amount of **attention** (see Figure 6.2b)

Short-term memory, as proposed by Atkinson and Shiffrin, is a memory storage facility that has a slightly longer duration, but much lower capacity. Initially, this memory store was viewed as a passive facility, just as the waiting room holding all the actors invited to the call-back audition. However, short-term memory is now more accurately described as *working memory*, a more complex short-term memory store that contains different active systems and types of information. In the casting call scenario, the actors wouldn't be just sitting passively in the waiting room; they would be actively practicing their skills. One person might be focusing on improvisation, another on vocal ability, and others role-playing a scene. They are still in a waiting room, but they are actively engaged in various activities. Again, not all actors are going to make it to the final audition and be offered a part. Similarly, not all information in working memory is going to be committed to *long-term memory*, is the last

attention

the act of directing cognitive resources in a particular direction

Figure 6.2b Atkinson and Shiffrin's Three-Stage Model of Memory: The Role of Attention

SENSORY MEMORY

Taste

Hearing

Sight

Touch

CASTING CALL

Attention

Attention

SHORT-TERM MEMORY

CALL-BACK AUDITION

Figure 6.3 A Netflix Analogy of the Three-Stage Model of Memory

CASTING CALL

Attention

CALL-BACK AUDITION

Rehearsal/Meaningful Performance

CAST IN THE ROLE

structural component, or memory storage facility. The primary process involved in moving memories from working memory to long-term memory involves various active strategies such as repetition, making the information meaningful, and connecting it to some form of prior knowledge.

Journal Prompt: Your Memory Strategies

What are some of the strategies you use to successfully commit information to long-term memory? Are there any strategies you no longer use because you've discovered they are ineffective?

Long-term memory is said to have an unlimited capacity (Brady et al., 2008), but typically only a very small amount of information that crowds our sensory memory is eventually stored in our long-term memory—just as very few actors will actually get cast in the roles at the end of the audition process. For the final actors to be chosen, they must have *rehearsed* and delivered a *meaningful* performance that made a lasting impression on the casting director or director for the movie (see Figure 6.3).

The three-stage model of memory emphasized both the structure and the processes associated with memory. See if you can put the whole model together in the interactive activity below.

Putting the Three-Stage Model of Memory Together

Contemporary Models of Memory

LO 6.2 Describe the core features of contemporary connectionist models of memory.

While Atkinson and Shiffrin's three-stage model is the most well-known memory model, it has been highly criticized for not accurately capturing the way memory truly works (Baddeley & Hitch, 1974; McClelland, 1995). The three-stage model assumes that one stage is completed at a time and that activities within each stage happen one at a time (e.g., a short-term memory task where you must decide if you have seen a number of pictures before). This method of recognition memory is referred to as *serial processing*, but in reality there is evidence that some of these processes can occur at the same time, called *parallel processing* (Ratcliff, 2014; Townsend & Fifić, 2004). For example, you can simultaneously process a number of different characteristics of the pictures you are seeing (e.g., the shape, color, size) and compare more than one picture at a time to those images in your short-term memory. These findings highlight the simplicity of our computer analogy. Even though computers can process information extremely fast, they still follow a sequential, or serial, pattern. Furthermore, unlike humans, computers don't have a host of other factors (e.g., thoughts, emotions, and motivations) that can influence the process of memory.

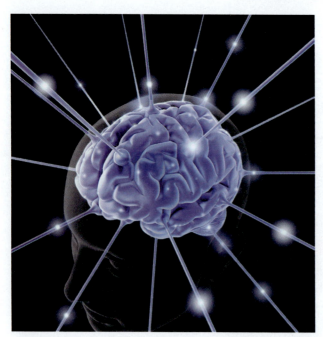

Modern explanations of memory include connectionist models, which view the brain as an interconnected network of neurons.

connectionist models of memory

an approach in cognitive science that describes memory as interconnected networks in the brain

parallel distributed processing model of memory

example of a connectionist memory model that states memories are distributed throughout the brain and represented in the pattern of activation between neurons

More contemporary models of how memory works, which account for the parallel processing that occurs, are referred to as neural network or **connectionist models of memory**. The concept of connectionism is an approach in cognitive science, based on the work of Donald Hebb, which describes cognitive processes as interconnected networks in the brain. The individual units that make up the network are the neurons in the brain. A core assumption of connectionism is when neural units are activated together, the connection between them becomes stronger. The strength of connection between these units is the biological basis of learning and memory. Therefore, memory isn't viewed as a sequentially processing computer, but rather a set of instructions neurons send to each other that create patterns of activity among neurons (McClelland, 2000).

The **parallel distributed processing model of memory** is an example of a connectionist model. In this model, memories are constructed through a pattern of activation among neurons: A neuron is either *excitatory* and passes the information on to the next neuron, or *inhibitory* and does not stimulate the nearby neuron(s). In this model, memory is said to be distributed throughout the brain as a pattern of activation among neurons (McClelland & Rumelhart, 1985). As a concrete example, imagine your brain as a large connect-the-dots game and each time you have an experience, multiple pathways of dots (i.e., neurons) simultaneously connect. The more you have that experience or think about that experience, the stronger those connections become (see Figure 6.4)

Therefore, when someone says the word "airplane," you likely have a number concepts that come to mind all at the same time. Some may be common and recalled by most people

Figure 6.4 Parallel Distributed Processing as a Dot Game

The parallel distributed model of memory describes memory as a pattern of connections between neurons that strengthen over repeated activations. Some memories (i.e., the red lines) are stronger than others (i.e., the blue lines). And, some memories are just beginning to be formed (i.e., the green dotted lines.)

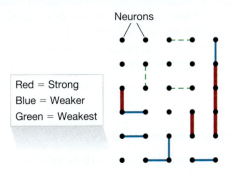

Red = Strong
Blue = Weaker
Green = Weakest

Figure 6.5 Different Patterns of Connections Representing Memory

Each of these figures could represent a person's memories related to the word "airplane." The figure on the left is likely a person who knows a lot about airplanes or who has taken an airplane many times. The figure on the right could represent the memory of a child who has only flown on an airplane once.

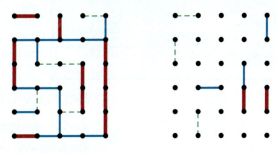

such as method of transportation and flies in the sky. And others may be more specific to you; a particular airline you always fly, or your first time on an airplane and the vacation that was part of that experience. Or, if you happen to have a flying phobia, the word airplane might conjure up news of airplane crashes and the time you had a panic attack on a plane. As you can see, your "connect-the-dots" will have a particular pattern of connections, and this will likely be different from your friend's "connect-the dots" in relation to the word airplane (see Figure 6.5). In this sense, memory is viewed as a constructive process and, as we will see later in this chapter, memory is also a reconstructive process.

According to the parallel distributed processing model, it is not possible to retrieve a specific memory from a specific place in your brain (as the three-stage model would suggest.) The memory is contained within the connections themselves and distributed throughout various connections in the brain (McClelland, 2011). Connectionist models have been help-ful in understanding the neural basis of the creation and storage of memories but tend to be less focused on understanding the process of and factors associated with the acquisition and storage of memories.

Quiz for Module 6.1–6.2

1. The approach suggesting our memory works like an administrative assistant that encodes, stores, and retrieves information is called the _____.

   a. information-processing approach

   b. memory activation approach

   c. three-stage processing approach

   d. connectionist approach

2. According to Atkinson and Shiffrin, the structure of memory can be divided into three distinct types. What are these three aspects of memory?

   a. Iconic memory, short-term memory, and long-term memory

   b. Sensory memory, productive memory, and long-term memory

   c. Sensory memory, working memory, and long-term memory

   d. Sensory memory, working memory, and procedural memory

3. Atkinson and Shiffrin used the example of a _____ to help describe memory in their 1968 theory.

   a. casting call for the theatre   b. bank

   c. computer   d. filing cabinet

4. According to the connectionist model of memory, memory is viewed as a set of interconnected _____ in the brain.

   a. life experiences

   b. computer chips

   c. serial pictures

   d. neural networks

5. When someone says the words "ice cream," most people will have numerous images pop into their head. Those images may be common like a picture of an ice cream cone as well as more specific like their favorite flavor. This is an example of which model of memory?

   a. Parallel distributed processing model

   b. Information-processing approach

   c. Serial position approach

   d. Three-stage approach

Module 6.3–6.6: Acquiring and Storing Memories

We are now going to take a more detailed look into each of the components and processes associated with memory. We're going to answer the questions, "How do we form new memories?" and "How can we be sure to commit information to long-term memory?" As you read through this module, think about how this information applies to your own process of learning and remembering information. Consider trying some of the techniques discussed to see if you can notice a difference in your ability to understand and retain the information in this chapter.

Sensory Memory

LO 6.3 **Recognize the types and characteristics of sensory memory.**

Regardless of the specific content, a memory is the product of a sensory experience—a series of images, sounds, tastes, smells, and feelings. We constantly use our five senses to collect information about the world around us. This information is the raw material from which memories are formed. Information from the environment is transmitted from the senses into the brain's sensory registers, which together make up sensory memory, the first structural stop along the road to developing a long-term memory. These registers are capable of holding large amounts of data, but if we don't pay attention to the information, it disappears in less than a second. In many ways **sensory memory**, or the brief retention of sensory stimulation, is merely an extension of perception. Technically, each of our senses has a sensory register, but it is sight and hearing that have been studied the most.

ICONIC MEMORY Do you remember playing with sparklers when you were a kid? If you waved the sparkler through the air around you, what would happen? Maybe you'd see something like the photo below. Even though it looks like the sparkler is leaving a long trail of light, it really isn't. The trail of light that you see is the brief *persistence* of the image that remains after you perceive the light. This fleeting, visual aspect of sensory memory is referred to as **iconic memory** and explains why we perceive the light and a tail to the light. Iconic memory comes from the Greek word "icon" meaning "image" and typically lasts for a few tenths to one half of a second (Bradley & Pearson, 2012; Rensink, 2014; Sperling, 1960).

sensory memory

according to the 3-stage model of memory, the first memory store that retains sensory stimulation for a short time; an extension of perception

iconic memory

part of sensory memory that involves the ability to briefly and accurately remember visual images

echoic memory

part of sensory memory that involves the ability to briefly and accurately remember sounds

ECHOIC MEMORY Has someone ever asked you a question you didn't immediately understand, so you respond with "What?" But, just as you say "what" you suddenly understand what they asked you and promptly answer their question? Just like visual information, auditory stimuli are also funneled to a sensory register. Our ability to briefly and accurately remember sounds is called **echoic memory**—think of how the word "echo" makes up "echoic" to remind you that this has to do with sound. Like iconic memory, echoic memory comes and goes quickly but not as quickly as visual information. If we are not paying attention to a sound, we are only able to recall it from our echoic memory for about three or four seconds before it disappears. We hear information quicker than we process it, which is why you sometimes think you don't hear what someone asked you. In reality, you needed just a few seconds to pay attention and process what was said by moving the information out of sensory memory, which allows you to respond.

Regardless of the modality (or specific sense), sensory memory appears to have a few key characteristics (Figure 6.6):

- It has a large capacity
- It can only hold information for a very brief period of time
- The acquisition of information into sensory memory is primarily an unconscious process
- The information that is stored in sensory memory is "as is," meaning it is relatively unprocessed

Figure 6.6 Sensory Memory

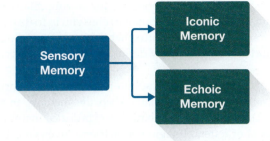

As we move along to the next memory structure, take note of the process involved in moving information out of sensory memory and into short-term memory.

Test Your Iconic Memory

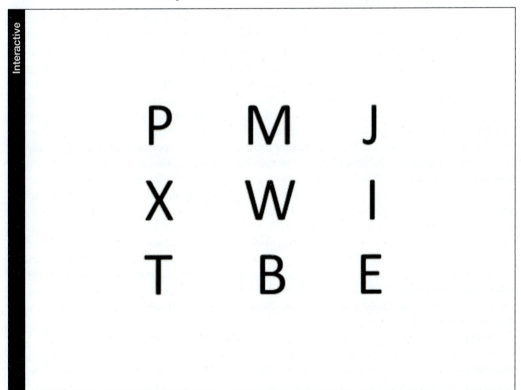

Short-Term Memory and Working Memory

LO 6.4 **Distinguish between short-term memory and working memory.**

What steps are necessary in order for the information captured in sensory memory to move into short-term memory? What is required for you to read this sentence and understand what it is saying? The answer to both questions is "attention": You've likely had the experience where you are reading something but *not* truly paying attention to it only to quickly realize that you have absolutely no idea what you just read! People are generally aware that they must pay attention to whatever they are doing in order to be able to recall it later. What this means is attention is necessary for information to move from sensory memory to short-term memory. At any given moment, we are processing dozens of images, sounds, and other sensory information from our environment, but we're not necessarily paying attention to all

short-term memory

the structural component of memory responsible for storing relatively small amounts of information for a short time

maintenance rehearsal

memory strategy that involves repeating or rehearsing information to maintain it in short-term memory

decay

short-term memory loss due to information disappearing over time

interference

explanation for short-term memory loss whereby new information interferes with the information currently in short-term memory

of these sensory memories. When a sensation grabs our attention, however, we're likely to direct attentional resources to it and transfer it to our short-term memory. **Short-term memory** is the structural component of memory responsible for storing relatively small amounts of information for a short time. The name itself can help clue you in to its properties: *short-term = short amount of time*. If you are paying attention while you are reading this sentence, then it has made it to your short-term memory. By definition then, short-term memory is focused on the present.

Researchers have concluded that the duration of short-term memory is about 15–30 seconds, unless something is done to intentionally keep the memory in the present moment (Atkinson & Shiffrin, 1971). You have likely had this experience many times when trying to remember a list of numbers or letters. Imagine your friend gives you their password so you can order something from their online account. You don't want to write their password down anywhere, so what do you do? You will likely just repeat the password to yourself over and over again until you get to a computer or your phone to type it in. This strategy is referred to as **maintenance rehearsal**, and simply involves repeating or *rehearsing* the information over and over again to *maintain* it in your short-term memory. Maintenance rehearsal can be good for relatively small amounts of information that you need to keep active for a brief period of time. Think about that password…what is the likelihood that you will remember it after you have placed your order? If it took more than 20–30 seconds to order your item, it is unlikely you will remember your friend's password.

Information can be lost from short-term memory for one of two reasons. First, an interval of time longer than approximately 20–30 seconds will lead to the process of **decay**, which refers to the fact that the information disappears over time. If you've ever composted before, you've seen the process of how organic material *decays*, or breaks down, over time. Memories decay much more quickly than yard and food waste, but you can use this analogy to help you understand what it means for memories to decay. The second reason information is lost from short-term memory involves the role of interference. **Interference** refers to new information that grabs your attention and *interferes* with the information currently in your short-term memory. Interference is often what is responsible for the common experience of having something "go in one ear and out the other." Many people have this experience when being introduced to someone new. Imagine you are at a party and your friend introduces you to another person. You say "hi" and introduce yourself and immediately realize that you have already forgotten their name! You may have even thought to yourself, "How could I forget their name? They just told me what it was." The reality is, when you were being introduced to that person, you had a number of other things you were thinking about that monopolized your attention and interfered with your ability to remember their name. In this situation, it can be helpful to remind yourself that you are likely to forget names, which will help focus your attention on the person when the introduction is made. In this situation, the more consciously you can process the information, the more likely you are to focus your attention and remember the person's name at a later point in the evening.

Information can be processed for storage in short-term memory both consciously and unconsciously. As in our example of meeting someone new, conscious processing, also called *effortful processing*, requires paying explicit attention to the information to be remembered. Unconscious processing, also called *automatic processing*, refers to the fact that we often pay attention to certain things without being consciously aware that we are doing so. If someone asks you where you were at 6 p.m., you can say, "I was at dinner," even though it's unlikely that you took a few seconds at 6 p.m. to note and explicitly memorize your location. You are using automatic processing even as you read this paragraph: You can store the last few words you read in your working memory without even thinking about it.

THE CAPACITY OF SHORT-TERM MEMORY Although information remains in short-term memory longer than it can be held in sensory memory, short-term memory does not have a particularly large capacity for storage. If we were to read you a list of numbers and ask you to repeat them back, you would likely be able to remember somewhere between four and nine numbers.

We could be pretty confident in estimating how many numbers you could remember thanks to research that has been conducted since the 1950s. In his famous paper, "The Magical Number Seven, Plus or Minus Two," George Miller (1956) declared that our short-term memory is limited in its capacity to process information and that this capacity is quite uniform across people. Miller found that the majority of people have the ability to hold between 5 and 9 items in short-term memory (i.e., 7 plus or minus 2). In more recent years, this magical number has been reduced to 4 plus or minus 1 (Cowan, 2001, 2010) to account for the retention of more complex information (e.g., remembering a list of directions, rather than just a list of single digit numbers). Regardless of the *actual* number of pieces of information, the point is that without engaging in any specific memory techniques, the capacity of our short-term memory is quite small.

What can be done to increase the amount of information we can hold in short-term memory?

Test Your Short-Term Memory

Interactive

L T O M O B G T L W M I

We know our short-term memory tends to hold anywhere from 3–9 pieces of information at one time. Miller (1956) also described that these pieces of information do not have to be *individual pieces* of information but could be *chunks* of information. **Chunking** is the strategy of combining individual small units of information into larger meaningful units. In keeping with our computer analogy from earlier, a chunk has also been described as maximally compressed code (Mathy & Feldman, 2012). The chunk itself becomes one unit; so rather than remembering L–O–L, you process those letters as a chunk, LOL, and may even say to yourself "laugh out loud." Chunking information is a process that links the external environment to internal cognitive processes (Gobet et al., 2001). In our example, trying to remember a string of random letters becomes much easier if you organize that information into meaningful chunks, which is a form of effortful processing. This internal cognitive process also relies somewhat on information from your long-term memory, as you have to know what LOL means for it to be an *effective* chunk.

CODING INFORMATION INTO SHORT-TERM MEMORY We have been discussing different ways to process information, which can ultimately improve your memory. Understanding how our brains process information can also be helpful in identifying the best strategies for you to improve your memory. The way in which our brains code information depends on the type of information being processed. **Visual coding** involves processing images (e.g., looking at a map or a floor plan), **auditory coding** is the coding of sounds (e.g., remembering phone numbers by the pattern of sounds of the numbers rather than what the numbers look like), and **semantic coding** is processing information based on its meaning (e.g., remembering chunks of letters based on what they mean). Sometimes pieces of information can be coded in multiple ways: If you look at a pie chart that shows the results of a political poll, you can code it both

chunking
strategy of combining individual small chunks of information into larger meaningful units

visual coding
a type of processing that is based on visual images

auditory coding
a type of processing used by the brain based on sounds

semantic coding
a type of processing that is based on meaning

visually (by remembering what it looks like) and semantically (by thinking about what the poll results mean for each candidate) (Baddeley, 2012).

Although we are capable of encoding images, sounds, and meanings, not all types of encoding are equally effective. In general, we find it easier to remember information that means something to us. A 20-letter sentence in a textbook, for example, is much easier for us to remember than a random, meaningless string of 20 letters. Experiments investigating the three types of encoding have demonstrated that semantically encoded information is likely to be retained longer than information processed through visual or auditory encoding (Craik & Tulving, 1975), and audiovisual information that is presented with semantically-related cues is more likely to be remembered than information with neutral semantic cues (Heikkilä et al., 2014). For example, you would be much more likely to remember the word "cow" if it was presented at the same time as the sound "moo" (i.e., semantically-related) then if it was presented with the sound of a phone ringing (i.e., semantically-neutral).

SHORT-TERM MEMORY EVOLVES INTO WORKING MEMORY There is no question that the conceptualization of short-term memory as a memory structure was a useful starting point. Since the days of Miller, Atkinson, and Shiffrin, research has demonstrated that the component of memory that exists between sensory memory and long-term memory is much more than a simple storage unit, as originally suggested. In fact, this structure is actively working to manipulate and move information into long-term memory and then again to retrieve information out of long-term memory when it is needed. Consider what it takes to divide 324 by 6 in your head. You start by dividing 32 by 6, which is 5, with 2 left over. Not only do you have to remember the 5, but you now have to subtract 30 from 32, which leaves you with 2. Continuing to keep the 5 in your memory, you bring down the 4, making the leftover 2 into 24. Now, divide 24 by 6, which thankfully is a whole number, 4. Bring the 4 up beside your 5 and there you have it, 54! Easy, right? Not really. Doing these kinds of mental calculations involves a significant amount of cognitive processing *and* short-term memory. Through this example, you can see that short-term memory is much more than a brief storage facility.

Baddeley and Hitch (1974) proposed a model of *working memory* to account for some of the newer research findings. **Working memory** is defined as a structural component of the memory system that allows for the manipulation of information for cognitively complex tasks (e.g., learning, reasoning, comprehension) and for the limited and temporary storage of that information. Working memory is much more complex than short-term memory. In fact, there are three separate components of working memory that can each function independently, which also means they can all be working at the same time (Cowan, 2008).

The three components of working memory include the phonological loop, the visuospatial sketchpad, and the central executive (See Figure 6.7). The *phonological loop* holds verbal and auditory information for a brief period of time through the process of maintenance rehearsal. This is the most active part of your working memory when you are trying to remember an email address someone recites for long enough to write it down. The *visuospatial sketchpad*, as

working memory

structural component of memory that allows for the manipulation of information for cognitively complex tasks and for the limited and temporary storage of that information

Figure 6.7 The Components of Working Memory

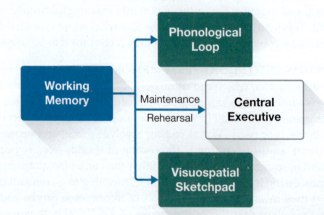

the name suggests, holds both visual and spatial information. Anytime you are visualizing the layout of a location, or recalling something in your "mind's eye," your visuospatial sketchpad is hard at work. Finally, the *central executive* is the triage nurse of working memory, focusing attention where necessary and coordinating the activities between all departments of working memory.

A good example of how this all works together is to think about using GPS on your phone to guide you to a new location in the city. Picture yourself driving with the music playing loudly in the car. You are driving on the highway and notice a slightly robotic voice coming from inside the car. As you realize this is your phone talking to you with directions, the central executive of your working memory quickly focuses your attention on the voice, while simultaneously guiding you to turn down the music. The auditory information of "turn left at the next intersection" is repeating over and over again in your phonological loop. At the same time, the central executive is guiding your vision toward the map on your phone and the road in front of you. As you recognize the upcoming street on the map, your visuospatial sketchpad is pulling up a picture of that area of town and you realize this is close to your friends' old house and one of your favorite cupcake stores. There is a lot for your working memory to cognitively process in this common situation, which is why it is easy to miss your turn if you lose focus and let your attention shift elsewhere. Your authors may or may not have driven 30 miles in the wrong direction on the way to a conference once because they were talking and not paying attention to the directions from the phone.

Distinguishing Short-Term Memory and Working Memory

Interactive

As a quick review, drag and drop the appropriate descriptions to distinguish short-term memory from working memory.

Short-Term Memory	Working Memory
Includes multiple components that work together	Only stores information
Stores and manipulates information	Includes only a single component

Check Answers

Encoding Strategies: How to Make Learning Stick

LO 6.5 Apply effective strategies for encoding information into long-term memory.

Pay attention! This may be the most important learning objective you will read in this course. Becoming aware of, and practicing effective strategies to move information from working memory to long-term memory, is what *learning* is all about. If you can figure out how to do this successfully, you will be much more successful in your college courses and life in general. We realize this is a lofty promise, but these are the evidence-based strategies this introductory psychology program has been built upon and that have been part of our research for years.

This section is going to focus on the *process* that occurs between working memory and long-term memory. In general, this process refers to how we encode information in order to solidify it in our long-term memory. You'll notice the term *encoding* is similar to the term *coding* we used earlier. While some people use these terms interchangeably, we prefer to keep them distinct by referring to *coding* as the *form*, or *way*, that information is presented. Recall that information can be presented in various *forms*. The first way information can be coded is visually.

Retrieval Practice: Coding of Information

Interactive

Can you remember the other way information can be coded? Type in your answer.

1. Visual

2. Auditory

3. [   ]

Start Over | Check Answers

encoding

process used to consolidate information from working memory to long-term memory

Encoding refers to the *process* used to consolidate information from working memory to long-term memory. Keeping with our earlier computer analogy, imagine you come across an amazing picture on the Internet that you want to use as the wallpaper on your screen. You could click on the picture, and it will be visible on your screen at that moment (this is similar to being held in short-term/working memory). However, if you want that picture to *permanently* become your wallpaper, you would have to actively make some changes in the control panel on your computer. This *process* of clicking various buttons to make the picture your wallpaper forever is similar to the active process we have to go through to commit information to our long-term memory.

So far, we have discussed one strategy for holding information in working memory. It is moderately effective, in that it will keep a small amount of information active for as long as you are devoting cognitive energy to it. It is not, however, a very efficient strategy and not one that is particularly effective to get that information into long-term memory. Do you remember the name if it? You have likely engaged in this *maintenance rehearsal* strategy before when studying. It is often referred to as "rote memorization." Think about a time when you tried to just memorize a list of items, definitions, or calculations. What made this so difficult? Usually, we struggle with this approach because rote memorization suggests no need to *truly understand* what you are memorizing. In that sense, does rote memorization really have anything to do with learning? You may have had some teachers say to you in the past, "Don't just memorize this—be sure you understand it." Your initial thought may have even been, "Sure, easy for you to say!" But, taking the time and effort to actually understand a concept sets up a situation where you rarely have to "just memorize." Of course, this does take time and energy, which

effortful processing

using time and energy to processing information deeply to aid understanding and memory; opposite of maintenance rehearsal

is why the most effective encoding strategies involve **effortful processing**. Learning doesn't happen by osmosis—you know that just showing up for class isn't enough. The best encoding strategy that involves effortful processing is referred to as elaborative rehearsal (Raaijmakers & Shiffrin, 2003).

In many ways, elaborative rehearsal is the opposite of maintenance rehearsal. **Elaborative rehearsal** focuses on *meaning* by (1) truly understanding the meaning of the information and (2) *elaborating* on the material by making it meaningful to you. Psychology is a great subject to study to do this because no matter what the topic, you can almost always find some way to connect the information to your own life or experiences. Even with respect to the information in this learning objective; if you think of something from your past that you learned very well, or a particular exam you aced, and you think about what it took for you to achieve mastery, you'll likely realize you engaged in some sort of effortful processing and/or elaborative rehearsal. Connecting *that* memory to *this* content is a form of elaborative rehearsal and will help you understand and consolidate this information into your long-term memory. Another way to demonstrate the power of elaborative rehearsal is by discussing some of the *levels of processing* research findings, which are important concepts to understand if you are interested in improving your memory.

elaborative rehearsal

an effortful processing strategy that focuses on elaborating on the information and making it personally meaningful

LEVELS OF PROCESSING Shortly after the work of Atkinson and Shiffrin was published on their model of memory, researchers from Canada proposed the idea that encoding can take a variety of forms and that those forms vary in terms of depth (Craik & Tulving, 1975). More importantly, they discovered that information that was processed *deeply* was far more likely to make it to long-term memory than information processed in a *shallow* way.

Rote memorization is a form of shallow processing because it focuses only on the physical features (i.e., the words themselves) and does not have any real meaning associated with it; whereas, elaborative rehearsal is a form of deep processing because it involves focusing your attention and manipulating the information in a meaningful way. The more deeply you process information, the more likely it will make it to your long-term memory (Rose et al., 2015; Schott et al., 2013; Ward & Walker, 2008).

Deep processing can take various forms. Here's another strategy you could use if you needed to remember a list of words, or even a set of terms, concepts, or instructions. Imagine you had to remember the following words: plant, twister, keys, rabbit, phone, cards, window, prince. You could try making a story that involves you walking through your house and encountering each of the items on the list. The more vivid and bizarre you can make your story, the more likely you are to remember it (and the items) when it is time for recall. Maybe your story might go something like this (see Figure 6.8):

> I walked in my front door to see a giant **plant** with a banner that read "Surprise!" Walking around the plant I saw that my friends had transformed my living room into a county fair. There were people playing **twister**, a game show host holding sets of **keys** that unlocked prizes and a magician pulling a **rabbit** out of a hat. I reached for my **phone** and started to walk over to take a picture. As I was walking I suddenly slipped on some playing **cards**, falling and putting my hand through a **glass** window. As my friend was driving me to urgent care, I thought it was ironic that *Let's Go Crazy* by **Prince** was playing on the radio.

Figure 6.8 The Method of Loci for the List of Words Presented

If you actually took the time to write that story yourself, what do you think the likelihood is that you would remember all 8 words? It is extremely likely that you would remember all 8 of them! This is the exact technique that Joshua Foer uses to memorize all kinds of things (including his TED talk that he gave on this very topic). Joshua didn't invent this technique. In fact, it is called the *Method of Loci*, and he traced it back 2,500 years ago to Ancient Greece. As a result of his TED talk, Joshua brought the term "elaborative encoding" into popular culture and showed people that anyone can become a memory athlete if they understand and practice elaborative encoding, which is a form of deep processing.

USING ELABORATIVE REHEARSAL TECHNIQUES TO IMPROVE LEARNING   You may not aspire to become a memory athlete. But, chances are you would be interested in learning how to use some of these techniques to become more efficient in your studying and more effective when learning. Here are a few tips that we would encourage you to start practicing right away:

1. *Visualize*   Create pictures in your mind's eye of how something works, relationships between concepts, or crazy stories that include all of the information you need to know. Even as your professor is lecturing, you might try to tie the material to vivid images, which will make it easier to recall later (Burkard et al., 2014; Miller et al., 2012). The adaptive videos you encounter in this program are one way we are trying to bring some visual imagery to difficult concepts in an effort to help you make meaningful connections.

mnemonics

memory strategies that connect information to be learned to something else that then serves as a trigger for retrieval

2. *Use Mnemonics*   **Mnemonics** are memory strategies that connect the information to be learned to something else that can serve as a trigger for you to retrieve the learned material. Successful mnemonics often have a visual component and can include the use of acronyms, where the first letter of each word is used to make a new word (e.g., ROYGBIV), or where the first letter of each word is used to create a new word that becomes a full sentence (e.g., Please Excuse My Dear Aunt Sally). The popular *peg-word system* is a more complex mnemonic where images to remember are connected with specific image pegs. To use this method, you must first memorize the rhyme *"one is a bun, two is a shoe, three is a tree etc...."* Then, you can visually pair the first image you need to remember, with a *bun* and so on. Given what we know about the importance of making information meaningful, the best mnemonics are ones that have some personal meaning to you (Hampstead et al., 2012; McCabe, 2015; McDaniel & Pressley, 2012). You'll notice throughout the text and in the adaptive videos that we try to give you various mnemonics to help you understand and remember important and/or challenging content.

3. *Teach Someone Else*   As you are processing information, always think to yourself, "Could I teach this concept to someone else?" We often say to students, "Imagine that a family member calls and says, *Tell me what you learned in psychology today.*" Could you explain to her all of the components to the model of memory we have discussed so far? Both of us can attest to the fact that we learned the most about psychology when we had to start teaching it to college students. Engaging in a writing task, whether through journal prompts or writing assignments, is a way to get you into the mindset and habit of explaining content in a way that could be understood by others.

4. *Organize Information*   Developing your own organization system for information you need to learn is extremely important. Students often talk about rewriting their notes as a method of studying. Merely rewriting what you already have on your page, is not studying, it's copying information, which requires little attention and effort. Therefore, it is a form of shallowing processing, at best. Making a new set of study notes can be an excellent strategy if it is done in a way that organizes and consolidates information. It is the *act of making the notes* that promotes learning, not the rote rehearsal of the notes after they are made. The more visual imagery you can bring to your notes the better; draw diagrams, make flow charts and hierarchies. Many of the interactive activities you are completing in this program are geared toward helping you to deeply engage with the material and organize it in a different way. Making your own concept maps or illustration is also an

excellent way to study. Research has shown that the process of generating information yourself can have tremendous effects on the learning and retention of information (Bjork & Bjork, 2011; Staniland et al., 2015; Weinstein et al., 2010).

5. *Test Yourself*   Finally, as we discussed in the Learning How to Learn chapter, we cannot stress enough the power of the testing effect. Repeatedly engaging in the testing of to-be-learned material is one of the best ways you can ensure the internalization and retention of that material (Carpenter, 2012; Karpicke & Aue, 2015; Meyer & Logan, 2013; Roediger & Karpicke, 2006). Testing can take various forms including flashcards, multiple choice questions, fill-in-the-blank, essay questions etc. The impact of learning through testing is the primary reason you encounter so many "test" questions in this program. So, the next time you are completing an interactive activity or posttest, remind yourself that you are engaging in an excellent learning opportunity.

6. *Interleaving (Mixing Up Your Practice)*   As we discussed in the Learning How to Learn chapter, interleaving tends to be counterintuitive to most people. Interleaving involves studying several different concepts during the same study session (e.g., some information from one chapter and a section from a previous chapter). For example, if you are learning a new mathematical formula, interleaved practice would involve completing practice questions utilizing that new formula, but also tackling questions requiring you to practice other previously learned formulas. Most students tend to study in a linear fashion; however, most likely, the exam questions are not going to be presented in the same organized fashion. Interleaving *feels* difficult and people perceive that they are not learning during the process, but the research suggests that interleaved practice produces superior results in learning and memory (Carvalho & Goldstone, 2017; Sana et al., 2017). In the following video, *Making It Stick*, Drs. Robert and Elizabeth Bjork discuss the importance of interleaving your practice.

Making it Stick

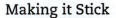

Long-Term Memory

LO 6.6   **Differentiate the various types of memory contained within long-term memory.**

We've just seen the importance of using effective encoding strategies as a way of increasing the chances that certain information will be stored in long-term memory. **Long-term**

long-term memory
according to the 3-stage model of memory, the structure where information is stored for long periods of time

memory, the last component of our model of memory, is the structure where information is stored for long periods of time. It is also the *largest* memory structure. This is, in fact, one of the primary differences between working memory and long-term memory: working memory is limited and long-term memory is unlimited. Long-term memory can store memories from something that happened when you were 5 years old, to the last thing your friend said to you 45 seconds ago. The clarity and ease with which you can retrieve those memories certainly varies with time, but the fact that all kinds of memories exist from your entire life is quite remarkable. An important point to remember is that although the name long-term memory suggests it is a "place" in the brain where specific memories are stored, our memory doesn't actually work that way. Rather than having complete memories saved in a specific place in the brain, our connected brain has many parts that work together to encode, store, and then retrieve individual components, or pieces of information, that ultimately become a consolidated memory.

Memories that stay with us manifest themselves in two forms: explicit memories and implicit memories. **Explicit memories**, which are also sometimes referred to as *declarative memories*, are memories of which we are consciously aware: We remember certain facts or experiences, and we are able to state that we remember these things. There are two kinds of explicit memories. Some explicit memories are **semantic**—that is, they contain factual and conceptual information not directly linked to life events. If you bought a dozen pizzas for a party, how many pizzas did you buy? When you answered "12," you accessed a semantic memory: The word *dozen* means "12." This information is an example of one of the vast number of semantic facts stored in your long-term memory. Trivia contests focus almost exclusively on semantic memory.

explicit memories

conscious memories of facts or experiences

semantic memories

type of explicit memories that contain factual and conceptual information

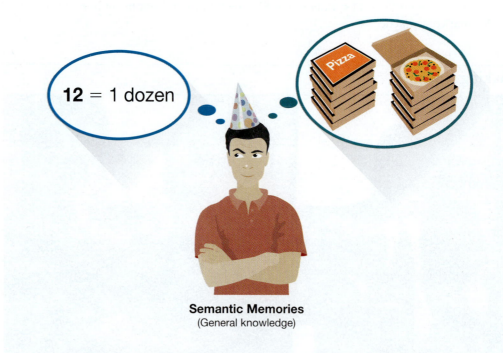

Semantic Memories
(General knowledge)

episodic memories

a type of explicit memory involving entire sequences of events; memories tend to be autobiographical

Often, though, we don't just remember bare-bones facts; we remember entire sequences of events, or episodes, which are referred to as **episodic memories**. When you think about the process of solving a long division problem, you're accessing an episodic memory, or a specific sequence of events. Many episodic memories are autobiographical. If, for instance, you and your friends became horribly lost on the way to pick up your dozen pizzas, arriving at the party so late that it was already over, you would probably have a vivid personal memory of this experience. Another good example of episodic memory is if you were asked to recall a favorite childhood vacation. Could you tell a friend about the vacation and why it was your favorite? This is an episodic memory because it contains information from various *episodes* of your life.

Episodic Memories
(Personal recollections)

There are also memories of which we are not consciously aware, which are called **implicit memories**, or *nondeclarative memories*. When we remember information implicitly, that information is retained in our minds, but we are not necessarily aware that we have remembered it. You might be thinking, "But if we're not conscious of our own implicit memories, how do we know that implicit memories exist at all?" This is a legitimate question and one that scientists have attempted to answer with creative research. Some evidence for the existence of implicit memory comes from the phenomenon of **priming** (Bargh, 2006). In psychological studies, researchers prime subjects by quickly presenting them with a stimulus (typically below their level of conscious awareness) before asking the subjects to complete a task. The stimulus is designed to activate certain unconscious associations in the subjects' minds. In their seminal research on priming and implicit memory, Graf and Schacter (1985) primed subjects with a list of words. Later, they gave the subjects several unfinished words and asked the subjects to complete the words. The results of the study suggested that people who see the word *trees* on a list, for example, are likely to complete the word *tre_____* as *trees*, even if they don't remember seeing *trees* on the original list. People who were not primed with the word *trees* were much less likely to complete the stem *tre_____* as *trees*.

The idea that people process information unconsciously, and even make better complex decisions when *prevented* from consciously deliberating (Dijksterhuis et al., 2006), has been somewhat controversial, but numerous laboratory and real-life studies have supported the role of priming (Bargh, 2011) and its association with implicit memory.

One type of implicit memory, **procedural memory**, consists of the habits and skills that we perform. Riding a bike and playing a musical instrument are both examples of procedural memory. Both of these skills take time and practice to learn, but once they're learned, they are stored in long-term memory, and we don't need to consciously access the memory to perform the procedure.

One thing that's interesting about procedural memories, is often when you try to consciously recall them, you can't. For example, most people have a routine they follow when they take a shower. That is, they engage in the *same* behaviors

implicit memories

memories that exist below the level of conscious awareness

priming

aspect of implicit memory involving presenting a stimulus that activates unconscious associations that then lead to a predictable response

procedural memory

type of memory consisting of habits and skills

Priming

Procedural Memories
(Knowing how to do something)

in the *same* order each time. If you were asked to list out all the steps of your shower routine, could you do it? Chances are right now you are trying to picture yourself taking a shower from the beginning to attempt to trigger your memory. Your showering routine is a procedural memory (pay attention the next time you take a shower), but it is not as easily recalled as your explicit memories. Now, let's put the whole model together to see the various types of long-term memories.

Types of Long Term Memories

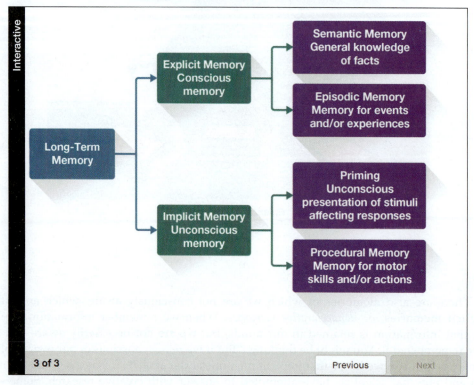

Adaptive Pathway 6.1: Components of Memory

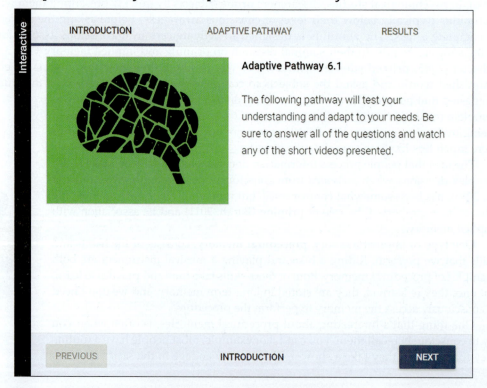

Quiz for Module 6.3–6.6

1. Iconic memory is a type of _____ memory and handles our _____ senses.
   - **a.** sensory; auditory
   - **b.** echoic; auditory
   - **c.** echoic; visual
   - **d.** sensory; visual

2. Echoic memory lasts for _____?
   - **a.** 1–2 minutes
   - **b.** 3–4 seconds
   - **c.** 3–4 minutes
   - **d.** ¼ to ½ second

3. What is the duration of short-term memory?
   - **a.** 1–2 seconds
   - **b.** 7–9 seconds
   - **c.** 15–30 seconds
   - **d.** 45–60 seconds

4. Working memory is said to be used for more complex _____ tasks, while short term memory functions as primarily a _____ facility.
   - **a.** executive; map reading
   - **b.** mathematical; storage
   - **c.** cognitive; storage
   - **d.** storage; cognitive

5. Henna is having difficulty with her psychology class. She visited with her professor and she told her to try to understand and remember the meaning of a concept by connecting that concept to a personal story. What is this strategy called?
   - **a.** Elaborative rehearsal
   - **b.** Rote memorization
   - **c.** Method of Loci
   - **d.** Maintenance rehearsal

6. Shania needed to remember to pick up seven items at the grocery store. She didn't want to write them down so she made up a story in her head imagining herself walking through her house and visualizing each item in a different room in the house. This is called the _____ technique.
   - **a.** method of loci
   - **b.** rote rehearsal
   - **c.** storytelling
   - **d.** interleaving

7. The memory of a student's first semester of college, when they were stressed and anxious, is considered what type of long-term memory?
   - **a.** Procedural
   - **b.** Episodic
   - **c.** Semantic
   - **d.** Implicit

8. Howard has not ridden a bike in 10 years. He first learned to ride a bike when he was 5 years old and enjoyed riding throughout his childhood. He recently bought a new bike and had no problem riding it around the block. The type of memory that allows him to recall this skill is called?
   - **a.** Episodic
   - **b.** Procedural
   - **c.** Semantic
   - **d.** Explicit

Module 6.7–6.9: Retrieving Memories

Quickly, off the top of your head—can you name all of Snow White's seven dwarfs? In attempting this task, you likely felt a rush of "Oh, I know this!" followed by some frustrating moments of trying to remember those last couple of names. This feeling of being consciously aware of the fact that the information you are trying to retrieve from your memory is temporarily inaccessible is referred to as the *tip-of-the-tongue phenomenon* (Schwartz & Metcalfe, 2011). Research has shown that if we could prime you (i.e., present you) with words containing syllables from the dwarfs' names (e.g., donut—Dopey, cheese—Sneezy), you would be much more likely to experience the "aha" moment of suddenly retrieving the name you couldn't remember (James & Burke, 2000). The process of remembering is not always an easy one and, as we will see, not always trustworthy.

Retrieval Cues

LO 6.7 **Recognize factors that influence the retrieval of information.**

So far, we have focused on how to get the information *into* your memory. However, that is only half of the equation. The other important part of memory involves **retrieval**, or getting that information *out of* your long-term memory when you need it. When you retrieve information from memory, it is typically through the process of recall or recognition. **Free recall** involves pulling information directly from long-term memory without the help of any kind of retrieval cues. **Retrieval cues** are bits of information that can trigger the information in long-term memory to become available to you (Tullis & Benjamin, 2015). Asking you to recall from memory all the seven dwarfs is an example of free recall.

retrieval

the ability to access information from long-term memory when needed

free recall

retrieval of information from long-term memory without the help of any kind of retrieval cues

retrieval cues

bits of information that trigger the memory to become available

Free Recall

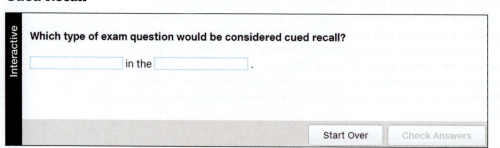

The question you just answered about free recall is itself a free recall question. We didn't provide any cues or hints; you just had to rely on your own retrieval process from long-term memory to come up with the answer. Another kind of recall is called **cued recall** because it involves the use of retrieval cues. As you can imagine, this type of recall is found to be easier than free recall.

cued recall

information from long-term memory becomes available after a retrieval cue is presented

Cued Recall

Which type of exam question would be considered cued recall?

[   ] in the [   ] .

Start Over   Check Answers

Can you see how this question is a cued recall question? You are provided with two of the words from the correct answer and the lines themselves can serve as cues because we have become accustomed to seeing lines of that length used to represent fill-in-the-blank questions. Finally, retrieval can come in the form of **recognition**, which is where the correct answer is provided among a group of possible answers.

By now you have likely caught on that this multiple-choice question is an example of recognition retrieval. As you are probably already aware, this type of question is most preferred by students taking exams (Mizrahi, 2013).

recognition

retrieval of information that occurs after seeing the correct answer provided among a group of possible answers

Recognition

Interactive

1 question

1. Which of the following type of exam question is an example of recognition retrieval?

- ○ Essay
- ○ Fill-in-the-blank
- ○ Multiple choice
- ○ Short-answer

Next

THE SERIAL POSITION EFFECT   Over the past 50–60 years, researchers have conducted studies to better understand how memory retrieval works and the factors that can influence the process of retrieving information from long-term memory. One robust finding has involved what has been called the **serial position effect**, which refers to the fact that when recalling a list of words/ items, most people can remember the words from the beginning *and* the end of the list (Murdock, Jr., 1962). If we were to read a list of 20 words to a group of people and then ask them to recall as many of the words as they could, the results would look something like this (see Figure 6.9).

serial position effect

when recalling a list of words/items most people can remember words from the beginning and the end of the list

Figure 6.9 The Serial Position Effect

IMMEDIATE RECALL

As you can see from the graph, most people tend to remember the words at the beginning and at the end of a list. Specifically, the ability to remember words at the beginning of the list is called the **primacy effect**, and the tendency to easily recall words at the end of the list is referred to as the **recency effect**. What we have come to understand about how our memory works can explain both of these effects. The recency effect is most easily explained by the concept of working memory: The items at the end of the list are most *recently* in your working memory and therefore easier to access. In a classic study, Glanzer and Cunitz (1966) demonstrated that they could eliminate the recency effect by having participants immediately count backward for 30 seconds after studying the words. The act of switching tasks and counting backward (which requires cognitive resources) effectively replaced the last words on the list in working

primacy effect

the tendency to remember words at the beginning of a list

recency effect

tendency to easily recall words at the end of the list

memory. The primacy effect, however, still remained strong. It turns out that the primacy effect is explained by the fact that the words that appear at the beginning of a list have more time to be rehearsed than those at any other place in a list (Rundus, 1971). In this digital age, we rarely have to memorize lists anymore; however, if you ever have to remember a list of items, be sure to construct the list with the most important items at the beginning and at the end of the list.

THE ROLE OF EXTERNAL CONTEXT   When it comes to acquiring and retrieving memories, context is important. Have you ever had an experience where you visited a place you hadn't been since you were a child, only to get there and suddenly be flooded with childhood memories you thought had been long forgotten? What about hearing an old song that immediately brings back very specific memories from the seventh grade? The principle of **encoding specificity** states that information is encoded along with its context and therefore memories are most easily recalled when the retrieval context *matches* the context in which the memory was initially encoded (Moscovitch & Craik, 1976; Tulving & Osler, 1968; Tulving & Thomson, 1973).

Context-dependent memory is related to encoding specificity and refers to how the context during encoding can aid in improving recall. Think of how you might remember your favorite vacation—you don't just remember where you went, but you also remember all kinds of contextual details: who you were with, the feel of the temperature, maybe even the smells around you. Even though you may not necessarily plan on it, the context becomes tied to the memory when they are encoded together. Therefore, the next time you are in a situation where even one of those salient cues is present (e.g., the smell of coconut), all the memories from your favorite beach vacation come flooding back.

Have you ever noticed how smell can be one of the strongest sensory retrieval cues you encounter? Smell is the one sense that does not pass through the thalamus before being processed by the brain. Instead, smell is processed directly by the amygdala, and the amygdala is connected to the hippocampus. Since the hippocampus plays such an important role in learning and memory, it makes sense that smell would be a contextual cue that can quickly and easily be associated with memories. A person under stress (which releases chemicals that activate the hippocampus and amygdala) is even more likely to have better memory when the same smell is present on both encoding and retrieval (Wiemers et al., 2013). So, context-dependent memory doesn't always refer to the encoding that takes place in a particular location.

In a classic experiment that involves location and context-dependent memory, Godden and Baddeley (1975) had a group of students learn a list of words and then attempt to recall those words 24 hours later. The creative part of this study involved the context in which the participants learned the list of words: either on dry land or underwater. The words learned underwater were best recalled when underwater and the words learned on dry land were best recalled on dry land (see Figure 6.10).

encoding specificity

information is encoded along with its context; memory recall is best when the retrieval context matches the encoding context

Figure 6.10 Results of Dry Land vs. Underwater Memory Experiment

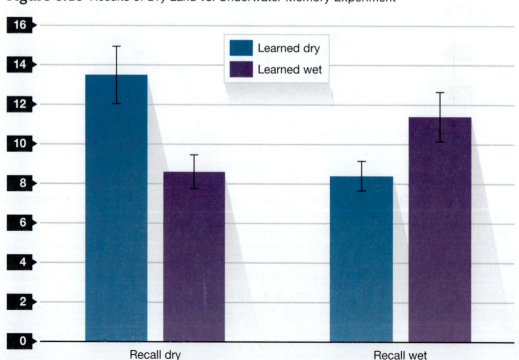

The results of this study support the principle of context-dependent memory and can offer some important tips for studying and learning. If you've ever had a professor tell you that you should study in the same type of environment in which you will be tested, context-dependent memory is the reason behind the advice. This principle is not so rigid as to say that you have to study in the exact room you'll be taking the exam (although that would be ideal), but it does mean that you should study in a quiet, nondistracting environment, which is the same context you would expect when taking an exam. Even though many students argue that they study best with music playing in the background, context-dependent memory would suggest this is not a good strategy, since you aren't likely going to be allowed to listen to music while taking your exam.

Journal Prompt: Encoding Specificity and Online Courses

Many students have taken at least one online course while pursuing their degree. Online courses often require students to take exams in a Proctoring Center, either on or off campus. What implications could context-dependent memory have on exam performance in these situations?

THE ROLE OF INTERNAL CONTEXT Just as the external context can influence the encoding and retrieval of memories, so too can the internal context. An internal context is referring to an internal state, such as the mood or level of awareness an individual experiences. The principle of *state-dependent learning* is similar to encoding specificity, but it is related to a match between an individual's *internal state* at encoding and again at retrieval. That is, if you are studying for an upcoming exam with the newest love of your life, you'd be best off taking that exam while in a good mood. Internal stimulation from alcohol or drugs is another common internal context that can have important implications for memory. Sanday et al. (2013) administered caffeine to rats prior to a learning task and found that the rats demonstrated the best memory for the task when they received the same dose of caffeine prior to retrieval. The same effect with caffeine has also been found in humans (Kelemen & Creeley, 2003).

Factors Affecting Memory Retrieval

Interactive

In this section, we've discussed the different factors that research has shown can impact the retrieval of information. Match each of following principles to their respective definitions.

Context-Dependent Memory	Memory is best when an individual's external environment during retrieval matches the external environment that existed during encoding.
Serial Position Effect	When attempting to recall a list of items, memory is best for those items that come at the beginning and at the end of the list.
State-Dependent Learning	Memory is best when an individual's internal state during retrieval matches their internal state during encoding.
Encoding Specificity	Memories are most easily recalled when the retrieval context (either external or internal) matches the context in which the information was encoded.

Start Over

Emotional Memories

LO 6.8   Identify how flashbulb memories differ from other memories.

Throughout our history, there have been certain events that we claim we will never forget. The memories seem to be burned into our brains. One of your authors can remember growing up hearing her parents vividly recalling the moment they heard about the assassination of President John. F. Kennedy. Other events for us have included the space shuttle Challenger explosion in 1986, the death of Princess Diana in 1997, the horrific day of the terrorist attacks on September 11, 2001, and the heartbreaking day of the Sandy Hook Elementary massacre in 2012 (sadly, many more incidents could be included in this list).

Brown and Kulik (1977) were first to call these types of memories "flashbulb memories." The name came out of their description of how learning about extremely emotional events (positive or negative) causes the moment to stop, as if a picture was being taken. They also claimed that the "picture" of that moment in time was extremely vivid, accurate, and resistant to fading. Many people report positive flashbulb experiences: receiving an acceptance letter to college, getting married, or giving birth (Liu et al., 2012).

Common Flashbulb Memories

Interactive

Challenger Explosion

1 of 5   Previous   Next

flashbulb memories

vivid, long-lasting memories about the circumstances surrounding the discovery of an extremely emotional event

Flashbulb memories are most commonly defined as vivid, long-lasting memories about the circumstances surrounding the discovery of an extremely emotional, public event. While details of the event itself (called the *event memory)* are included in the memory, the flashbulb memory is more centered on the moment you heard the shocking news. In these circumstances, people can often vividly recall what they were doing, what they were wearing, the weather outside, and various other peripheral details not typically encoded with other less salient events.

Since Brown and Kulik's original paper on the subject, many researchers have continued to research the characteristics of flashbulb memories and question various aspects of their original theory. For example, just because the memory is vivid, does it mean it is more accurate? Watch the video *Flashbulb Memories* to learn about how stress impacts the accuracy of a flashbulb memory.

Flashbulb Memories

Interactive

The events of September 11, 2001, provided a unique opportunity to study flashbulb memories; since then, more than 20 scientific studies featuring memories surrounding this day have been published in academic journals. The most recent and thorough examination of flashbulb memories included a 10-year follow-up of some participants who originally participated in the study immediately after the attacks (Hirst et al., 2015). For the most part, the results of this study echoed those conducted earlier (e.g., Phelps & Sharot, 2008; Talarico & Rubin, 2007). Here is a summary of their findings and a synopsis of what we know about flashbulb memories to date:

- There was rapid forgetting of the event and the flashbulb memory within the first year.
- Forgetting tended to level off after the first year with people remembering approximately the same amount of information (event and flashbulb) even 10 years later.
- The confidence people have in "ordinary" memories decreased over time; however, the confidence people have in flashbulb memories remained extraordinarily high. This is an interesting result especially since the data indicated that people tended to forget aspects of their flashbulb memory to the same extent that they forgot details of the actual events and other more "ordinary" memories around the same time. Therefore, despite the lack of consistency (accuracy) of the flashbulb memory over time, people continue to have great confidence in their recollection.
- Only the inaccurate event memories *self-corrected* over time. That is, only the details of the event, not the flashbulb memory, became more accurate over time. It is thought that exposure to media (e.g., news stories, books, movies) and discussions with others help to restore accurate details of the event.

The fact that even memories for extremely emotional events, ones we think we'll never forget, degrade and change over time suggests that our memories are anything but an accurate recording of events and circumstances.

How Accurate Are Our Memories?

LO 6.9 **Describe situations that can lead to inaccuracies in memory.**

Despite what many people might intuitively think, our memory is much more than the playback of recorded scenes in our life. The analogy of a computer doesn't help much to dispel this myth, since the act of retrieving a computer file is much more precise. If you are working on a paper for one of your classes and save a draft of it, you know that the next time you open that file, it will be the same as you left it. Our memory is much more puzzle-like in structure in that whole memories are not stored together, but in fact, pieced back together during the process of retrieval (Kolodner, 1983). And, it is common that during this retrieval process, certain details get lost or changed in some ways (Loftus & Loftus, 1980; Mantonakis et al., 2013a; Patihis et al., 2013). Imagine if the draft of your term paper was broken up into various sections and sentences and when you opened the file from your hard drive, the computer had to quickly reconstruct your entire paper. During this process, certain points you made or references you cited were forgotten and maybe even other similar paragraphs from other papers you have written were inserted instead. In the end, you have something that looks similar to your original draft, but it is not a perfect replica. Our memories work much the same way. **Reconstructive memory** is a term used to suggest that the act of remembering requires the reconstruction of previous events (Roediger & DeSoto, 2015). The reality of memory is that circumstances and events that occur before, during, and after memory creation can affect the accuracy of the memory. Memories are often influenced by either the *source* of the information, our *general knowledge*, and/or the *suggestions* supplied by others.

SOURCE MONITORING ERRORS   Can you recall having the experience of knowing something but you can't remember where you first heard it? Was it from the news? Your friend? Or, did you read about it in a blog online? *Source monitoring* involves the process of determining the origins, or source, of our memories, beliefs, or knowledge (Johnson et al., 1993; Luna & Martín-Luengo, 2013). A **source monitoring error** occurs when we recall a memory but attribute it to the wrong source. Source monitoring errors are quite common and in some cases can occur without any conscious awareness (Lindsay, 2014). *Cryptomnesia* is a special type of source monitoring error and refers to the unconscious plagiarism of another person's work. At one point, during the feud with Marvin Gaye's family, Robin Thicke argued that he had no intention or awareness of the similarity of the 2013 hit "Blurred Lines" to Gaye's "Got to Give It Up." Was he claiming to have suffered from cryptomnesia? The jury apparently didn't think so, and they awarded Gaye's family $7.3 million.

Source monitoring and its errors are viewed as happening when the memory itself is created. All experiences, and subsequent memories are encoded with the primary information about the event, but also include an individual's thoughts and emotions, general knowledge of the world, cultural factors, and other events that occurred around the same time (Mitchell & Johnson, 2009). Familiarity with a concept can easily lead to source monitoring errors. For example, researchers developed a study where they influenced participants' judgments about whether the name they viewed was someone famous or not by exposing them to that name 24 hours earlier (Jacoby et al., 1989). Specifically, Jacoby and his colleagues showed students a list of names (e.g., Sebastian Weisdorf) and told them these were names of people who were not famous. Immediately after the presentation of the names, participants could judge with certainty whether or not they saw various names and that they were names of nonfamous people. However, after only 24 hours the nonfamous names were significantly more likely to be judged as famous. Why? The participants experienced a familiarity with the name, but were unable to distinguish whether or not they knew the name because it was on the initial nonfamous study list of names or because it truly was a famous person whose name they had seen before. Claiming that Sebastian Weisdorf was famous is a source monitoring error.

THE EFFECT OF GENERAL KNOWLEDGE ON MEMORY   In the following activity you will see a list of words. Don't write them down, but do your best to remember as many as you can.

General Knowledge and Memory

Survey: General Knowledge and Memory

Was the word Aardvark in the list?

○ Yes

○ No

Was the word Sleep in the list?

○ Yes

○ No

---

reconstructive memory

the act of remembering requires a reconstruction of previous events

source monitoring error

memory error that involves attributing it to the wrong source

As the interactive activity you just completed shows, our real-world knowledge can affect the reliability of our own memory. All of the words presented fit into an overall category, or *schema*, about sleeping. The idea that we have schemas for many aspects of life fits well with the connectionist models of memory discussed earlier in this chapter. You may have a schema for "vacation" that includes many pieces of information (e.g., beach, drinks with umbrellas, the smell of coconut) represented by the strengthened connections between neurons along specific neural pathways. Since many of those aspects of vacation have been associated with each other over time, thinking about just one piece of information (e.g., beach) often ends up activating the entire schema. Since our memory is reconstructive, it makes sense that we are going to make some errors, especially when we are accustomed to certain things going together.

Here is another example of the type of study a memory researcher might conduct to show how our underlying knowledge can affect our memory.

Sentence Completion Task

The baby was sick all night.

Participants in a similar study to the interactive activity you just completed were presented with a number of sentences to study and then provided with fill in the blank sentences to complete. Approximately one-third of the participants made errors by including words that were never listed, even though they had just read the actual sentences not long before (McDermott & Chan, 2006). These wording changes reflect **pragmatic inference**, which refers to the effects that real-world knowledge and experience can have on people's expectations and ultimately their memories (Brewer, 1977). It is certainly possible that the quarterback ran a touchdown; however, those who have knowledge of the game know that it is much more likely that the quarterback is going to throw the ball. When a situation or context is unclear, pragmatic inference is more likely to occur and there is now evidence that different areas of the brain are activated when a person is engaging in this cognitive strategy (Feng et al., 2017).

pragmatic inference
the effects real-world knowledge and experience can have on the accuracy of memories

THE MISINFORMATION EFFECT   So far, we have been talking about events that happen prior to, or at the time of forming a memory that can lead to inaccuracies when the memory is recalled. However, people are suggestible and information presented after the fact can also influence how information is remembered. Since memory involves the reconstruction of events and details, information encountered after the initial encoding of the memory has the ability to impact the way in which the "facts" are remembered. An event or situation occurring after the initial memory that modifies that memory is referred to as the **misinformation effect**. In a classic study demonstrating this effect, Loftus and Palmer (1974) had participants watch films of car accidents and then answer questions immediately after viewing the films and again one week later. The control

misinformation effect
when an event or situation occurring after the initial memory modifies that memory and affects the accuracy of recall

group received the question, "About how fast were the cars going when they *hit* each other?" and the experimental group answered the question, "About how fast were the cars going when they *smashed* each other?" Figure 6.11 presents the average responses of the participants based on the question they were asked (keep in mind that only one word was changed in the question):

Figure 6.11 Results from Loftus and Palmer's 1974 Classic Study on the Misinformation Effect

LEADING QUESTION:

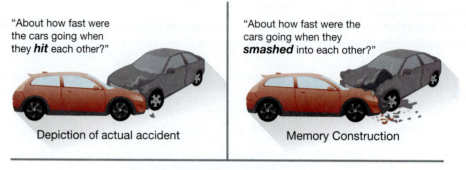

"About how fast were the cars going when they **hit** each other?"

Depiction of actual accident

"About how fast were the cars going when they **smashed** into each other?"

Memory Construction

Average speed data:

Key Word "**HIT**" > Estimated Speed 34.0 mph

Key Word "**SMASHED**" > Estimated Speed 40.8 mph

Percentages saying yes to broken glass in the different conditions:

HIT 14%

SMASHED 32%

Not only did the choice of words affect the judgment of the speed, but in a follow-up experiment participants who viewed an accident followed by the question containing the word "smashed" were significantly more likely to say "yes" to the question "Did you see any broken glass?" when they returned to the lab one week later. That is, the information presented *after* the initial memory was encoded actually changed the memory for the original event.

FALSE MEMORIES   Numerous research findings have provided convincing evidence that our memories are not 100 percent reliable. It is not just that the facts associated with memories can be altered, but a number of research studies have shown how completely new memories can be "implanted" or produced through the power of suggestion (Hyman et al., 1995; Loftus, 1997; Porter et al., 1999; Thomas & Loftus, 2002).

One of your authors had the opportunity as a psychology undergraduate to work as a research assistant on the Porter et al. (1999) study cited above. For this study, she was trained as a memory interviewer and met with participants to interview them about childhood experiences that may or may not have happened to them. Prior to coming in for the first interview, a questionnaire was sent to their parents asking about whether their child had experienced any of the events listed (e.g., a serious medical procedure, getting lost, a serious animal attack). In the first interview, one real and one false event were chosen and the participant was asked to recall as many details as they could about the event. At first, no participants recalled any memories of the false events. Through a series of three interviews each involving techniques utilizing minor social pressure and visual imagery, participants began to "remember" the false events. In fact, by the end of the third interview, 56 percent of the participants had recalled some details of the memory for this false event. Of these participants, 26 percent of them recalled vivid, detailed, and complete memories of a childhood event that *did not* happen. Stephen Porter and his colleague Julia Shaw recently completed another similar study where they created false memories in participants, where some participants recalled a memory of committing a crime. In this case, 70 percent of participants developed false memories of committing a crime in adolescence that led to police contact (Shaw & Porter, 2015). For more information on this study, see LO 6.14.

It is not difficult to see the importance of this research and the potential implications the findings have for our legal system. Results from the studies discussed in this module have been used to inform policies and procedures related to police line-ups, the types of questions allowed in court, and the use of eye-witness testimony (Bornstein et al., 2012; Mickes et al., 2012; Schacter & Loftus, 2013). In the video, *Memory and Eyewitness Testimony*, some of the variables that can affect the memory of eye witnesses are discussed.

Memory and Eyewitness Testimony

As discussed in the video you just watched, eyewitness testimony can be notoriously unreliable. In fact, it was found that eyewitness misidentifications contributed to more than 300 convictions that have since been overturned by DNA evidence (Hsu, 2013). However, more recent research has discovered a *system variable* (as described in the video) that can be changed to increase the usefulness of eyewitness testimony. For example, studies have confirmed that specifically looking at the confidence levels of eye-witnesses at the time of suspect identification (i.e., in a police line-up rather than at trial) can be a highly reliable indicator of accuracy (Wixted et al., 2015). Small changes in our legal system, such as those mentioned in the video and in this section, can have a significant impact on the lives of many people affected by criminal activity.

Shared Writing: Eyewitness Testimony

You have just witnessed a crime. You realize that you may be called in the future to testify as an eye-witness. What are some things that you could do (or not do) in the moment and in the days following the crime to ensure the accuracy of your memory?

Quiz for Module 6.7–6.9

1. Leeann was telling her friend about a movie with her favorite actor. She wanted her friend to guess his name so she gave her friend the first initial to his first and last name. Leeann provided a _____ for her friend.

   a. contextual cue
   b. memory cue
   c. learning cue
   d. retrieval cue

2. _____ states that context is encoded along with information and therefore memories are most easily retrieved when the context of the retrieval matches the context of the encoding.

   a. The recency effect
   b. The serial position effect
   c. Encoding specificity
   d. Cued recall

3. Aashna remembers exactly where she was, what she was wearing, and who she was with when she first heard the news of the terrorist attacks on September 11, 2001. Aashna has a _____.

   a. flashbulb memory
   b. explicit memory
   c. episodic memory
   d. echoic memory

4. Spencer believes he learned about the famous "Stanford Prison Experiment" from his psychology class. His professor tells him they haven't covered that topic yet so he must have heard about it from someone else. Spencer experienced a _____.

   a. pragmatic interference
   b. misinformation error
   c. source monitoring error
   d. false memory

5. Selma witnessed a robbery at a convenience store. She watched various news reports about the robbery prior to being interviewed by police. When she was interviewed, she remembered some inaccurate details. Selma has experienced _____.

   a. the misinformation effect
   b. encoding specificity
   c. retroactive interference
   d. proactive interference

Module 6.10–6.11: Forgetting

Despite our best efforts, not all information we store in long-term memory can be retrieved. When you come to think of it, would you really want to be able to remember every single detail, of every single moment, for your entire life? This is the case for Jill Price, and in the video, *The Woman Who Cannot Forget*, she points out there are pros and cons to having such an impressive memory.

The Woman Who Cannot Forget

Interactive

Unlike Jill Price, most of us have no problem forgetting many things from our past. In fact, forgetting helps us to conserve brain energy and focus on remembering more important details (Wenner, 2007). German psychologist Hermann Ebbinghaus (1850–1909) was one of the first scientists to systematically study memory and specifically, the process of forgetting. He used himself as his only subject and spent his days memorizing lists of nonsense syllables (e.g., WEC, NIN) and then measuring how many of those syllables he could recall immediately and then over the next 30 days. His results, depicted graphically, became known as the *forgetting curve* (see Figure 6.12). This curve suggests that we are quick to forget most things we learn. But, after a few days, our rate of forgetting levels off. That is, if we haven't forgotten something after 6 days, we're likely to remember it after 30 days.

Figure 6.12 Ebbinghaus's Forgetting Curve

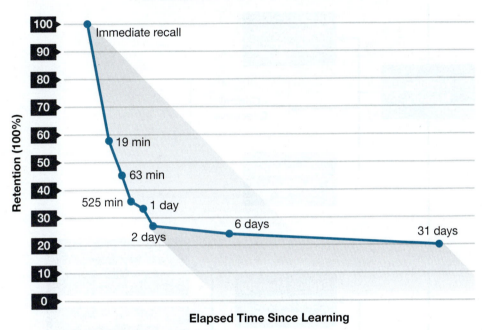

THE EBBINGHAUS FORGETTING CURVE

There are two important points to take away from Ebbinghaus's work. He specifically chose to work with meaningless information in order to get a more accurate picture of our *raw* memory abilities. Although this information is useful, it doesn't always translate well when it comes to studying and learning. Recall from our earlier discussion the importance of making information meaningful and how that elaborative processing will increase the likelihood of it being remembered in the future (Roberts et al., 2014). So, studying does not have to be as hopeless as the forgetting curve might suggest. The other important information that comes from Ebbinghaus's work has to do with *when* we study material. He found the information was much more resistant to forgetting if he *spaced* out, or *distributed*, his practice, rather than studying all at one time. For example, Ebbinghaus's findings suggest that you will retain more information if you study for 20 minutes on three separate days rather than studying for one hour on one day. This discovery from over 100 years ago is still one of the most common pieces of advice given by instructors to college students, "Don't cram. Spaced (or distributed) practice is a more effective way to learn and remember information." However, even when we space out our studying and engage in elaborative processing by creating meaning around the material, we still forget some information. What is actually happening when we forget? It turns out that a number of different theories explains why information either isn't retained or can't be accessed from memory.

Why We Forget

LO 6.10   Identify reasons for forgetting related to encoding and retrieval failures.

As we continue to discuss forgetting, it is helpful to review the model of memory discussed earlier in the chapter. When put together, it might look something like Figure 6.13.

Figure 6.13 A Full Model of Memory

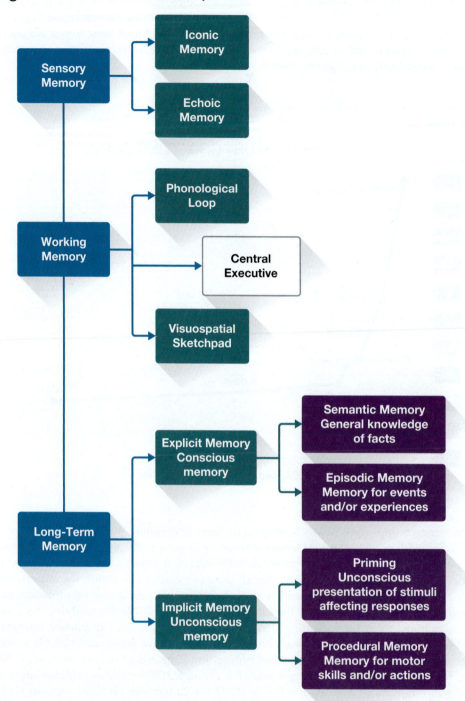

ENCODING FAILURE When the encoding process goes well, information from sensory memory moves to working memory and from there is further encoded into long-term memory. But what happens when something interferes with the encoding process? One cause of forgetting is ineffective or interrupted encoding of information (Brown & Craik, 2000). For instance, imagine that your friend is talking to you about his weekend plans while you're trying to finish up a good book. This situation is causing you to have to divide your attention, which we know doesn't usually lead to good memory (Mickley-Steinmetz et al., 2014; Turk et al., 2013). If you start paying attention to what your friend is saying, then you're not really paying attention to your book, even though you might still be reading the words on the page. After your friend leaves, you'll probably find it difficult to remember what you just read, and have to go back and reread a few pages.

It is also possible, that while you think you're encoding information as you attempt to read, your attention has been interfered with to the point that you haven't actually stored any information in working memory at all. As a result, when you go to retrieve your memories and find them missing, it may be because they were never encoded into working memory, and therefore long-term memory, in the first place. Technically, this isn't an example of forgetting information—it's impossible to forget something you never really learned in the first place. But, it does provide one explanation for why some information is not available to us at a later point.

Encoding must occur for information to move from working memory to long-term memory. There are many experiences in daily life that demonstrate how information can repeatedly enter working memory, but never really get encoded into long-term memory. Think of how many texts or messages of some kind you send every day. Also, think of how much time you spend on a computer for your college classes. Now, can you recite the top row of letters on a standard keyboard from right to left? Chances are you will

find this very difficult because despite the fact that many of us have contact with a keyboard every day, we have never really encoded that information into an explicit long-term memory. You do however, likely have a procedural memory related to typing, which is why when you start to type your fingers just seem to take over and do the rest. In fact, the more you think about it, the harder it becomes to type. In an effort to remember the top row of letters, you may have even tried imagining yourself typing a sentence, which could serve as a retrieval cue for the letters themselves. Still, the order of the letters on the keyboard themselves have probably never been encoded into an explicit, long-term memory. Now, had we asked you to recall the top row of the keyboard from left to right, some of you may have been able to do that (at least half of the row) because you may have learned the word "qwerty", which is the first six letters of a standard keyboard. In fact, standard keyboards are called *qwerty keyboards*. Learning the word "qwerty" means you have encoded information about the first six letters of a keyboard— and if you didn't know the first six letters of a standard keyboard before, you probably do now.

STORAGE DECAY THEORY It makes some intuitive sense that memories fade over time—it fits with the "use it or lose it" phenomenon. Indeed, long-term memories were initially proposed to *decay*, or disappear over time (Brown, 1958). While the decay of information seems to explain what happens during the transition from sensory memory to working memory and even within working memory itself (Baddeley & Scott, 1971; Barrouillet et al., 2012), this theory has been more controversial when it comes to explaining what happens to the memories already in long-term memory. We can remember many things from a very long time ago, some of which we haven't thought of in years, so why don't those memories decay? It has been suggested that the memory doesn't actually go away but gets "lost" among all of the other memories, some of which have interfered with your ability to access the original memory. Imagine the analogy of getting separated from your friends at a busy concert. You find yourself scanning the audience to try to find them, but can't see them because there are so many other people in the way. Your friends aren't gone—they are just obscured by others. While this theory of interference has garnered significant support over the years (e.g., Mensink & Raaijmakers, 1988; Raaijmakers & Jakab, 2012; Underwood & Postman, 1960; Wixted, 2004), there are still researchers committed to the role of decay in long-term memory (Altmann & Gray, 2002; Hardt et al., 2013) and the debate about how forgetting occurs, that began in the 1800s, is far from over (Ricker et al., 2016).

RETRIEVAL FAILURE As illustrated in our previous example of losing your friend in a crowd, forgetting in long-term memory often occurs not because our memories have necessarily disappeared or been overwritten but because we are unable to access them. Retrieval failure can happen for a number of reasons.

Most of us have forgotten more than a handful of email passwords, computer logons, and PINs in our lives. Maybe you just changed your email password and, although you can't remember what your new password is, you have no trouble remembering the old one. This phenomenon is known as **proactive interference**, and it occurs when previously learned information interferes with your ability to recall new information (Jonides & Nee, 2006; Loosli et al., 2014). Conversely, maybe it's been a while since you've changed your password, and now that you've gotten used to the new password, you no longer remember what your old one was. This is an

proactive interference

forgetting occurs when previously learned information interferes with the ability to recall new information

retroactive interference

forgetting occurs when new information interferes with the ability to recall older memories

example of **retroactive interference**, which occurs when new information causes you to forget older memories (Dewar et al., 2007; Eakin & Smith, 2012). Proactive and retroactive interference can be easily confused. One of the tricks we use to distinguish proactive from retroactive interference is by remembering that proactive starts with "p," which can then be associated with the word *previously*. So, *proactive interference is where previously learned information interferes with new information*. If you can remember that "proactive = previously learned"—then retroactive is just the opposite, where new information interferes with old memories (see Figure 6.14).

Figure 6.14 Proactive vs. Retroactive Interference

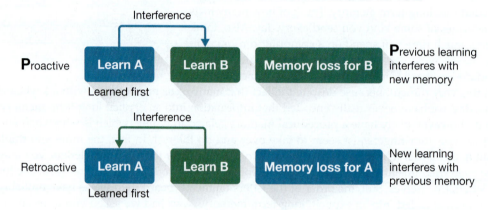

Proactive vs. Retroactive Interference

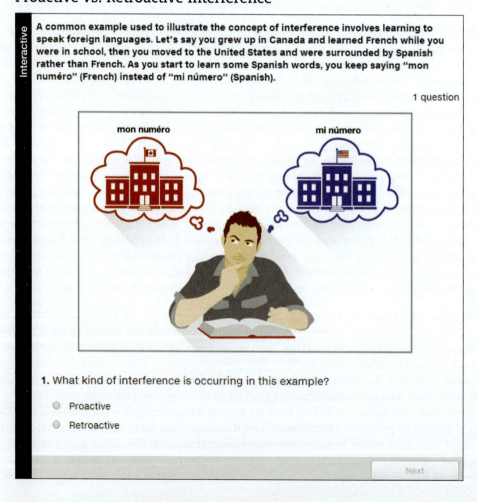

Let's recall our rule from earlier. *Proactive interference is where <u>previously</u> learned information interferes with new information.* Our example is a true story, one of your authors did grow up in Canada and couldn't remember the Spanish words because of her *previous* knowledge of French. So, the previous learning interfered with new information, which makes this an example of proactive interference.

Distinguishing Proactive and Retroactive Interference

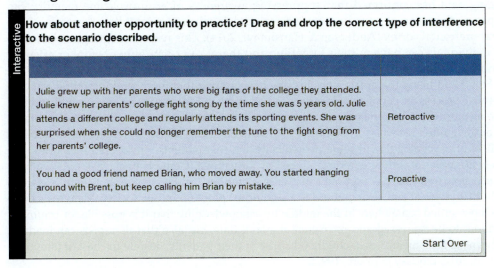

An interesting and very applicable finding from this area of research involves the important effect that sleep has on the consolidation (i.e., strengthening) of memories, both through the neurobiological activities that occur during sleep and the protection from interference (Abel & Bäuml, 2014; Atherton et al., 2014; Stickgold & Walker, 2007). The idea that sleep provides a protective mechanism from retroactive interference was first proposed by Jenkins and Dallenbach (1924), who demonstrated that individuals who learned information prior to going to sleep had superior recall of that information compared to the times where they had to learn and recall the information after the same interval of time, but without having slept. Jenkins and Dallenbach assumed that sleep played a passive role in memory by merely protecting the individual from encountering new information that could potentially interfere with the existing memory. Studies with rats have shown them to also have superior memory in the morning (after having slept) than in the evening hours. When these same rats were sleep-deprived, their morning memory abilities vanished (Binder et al., 2012).

Research into the mechanisms that explain these findings have highlighted the important role of non-REM, deep sleep in promoting memory consolidation and that REM sleep may even play an important role in "rescuing memories" that have already been disrupted by retroactive interference (Deliens et al., 2013; McDevitt et al., 2015; Sheth et al., 2012). These findings suggest that sleep plays a much more active role in the promotion of memory than was once thought.

To summarize, it appears that humans (and rats) replay daily events during sleep, which consolidates and strengthens the memory. Sleep deprivation not only leads to fatigue, but it also robs you of the opportunity to consolidate information from the day into long-term memories. The take home message of this research is that you should ***study and then sleep on it!***

MOTIVATED FORGETTING   Sometimes forgetting is the goal. There are some cases where **motivated forgetting**, or increased forgetting of unwanted experiences through active processes, occurs in response to an unfortunate or traumatic situation (DePrince et al., 2012). You may have had an experience in your life that you wish you could forget. In some cases, people can actively avoid memories to the point where those memories are not easily accessible. Whether or not these memories are truly forgotten is a controversial topic, but there is no question that some people are able to push memories out of conscious awareness (Anderson & Hanslmayr, 2014).

motivated forgetting
the active forgetting of experiences, typically in response to a stressful or traumatic situation

The concept of motivated forgetting has been around for a long time. In fact, Sigmund Freud proposed that *repression* was a prominent defense (self-protective) mechanism. Freud's psychodynamic theory focused on the idea that many sexual and/or aggressive impulses or traumatic memories were repressed, or pushed down deep into the unconscious.

One difficulty with Freud's theory, and psychodynamic theory as a whole, is that it is difficult to test and conduct research on something that is, by definition, not accessible to the conscious mind. In more recent years however, scientists have been working to understand motivated forgetting from a neuroscience perspective. Behavioral and neuro-imaging data has confirmed that suppressing awareness of an unwelcome memory can happen at the stage of encoding or retrieval and involves the inhibitory controls of the lateral prefrontal cortex (Anderson & Hanslmayr, 2014). This research highlights the active role individuals can have in their forgetting and that it can occur either before or after the memory is firmly established.

Freud and many therapists since his day have argued that motivated forgetting can be a protective process for people who experienced physical and/or sexual abuse as a child and that these memories can be remembered, or recovered, at a much later date. Either the spontaneous or the guided recovery of memories of childhood sexual abuse is a controversial topic in the field of psychology, with some people believing that patients' "recovered memories" are merely examples of false memories induced by a therapist (Geraerts et al., 2007). As we have already discussed, there is no doubt that false memories can be created, but there is also no doubt that physical and sexual abuse is a significant problem in our society. Many psychologists have settled somewhere in the middle by acknowledging that it is possible for traumatic memories to be repressed and recovered at a later date, but also that therapists can inadvertently create false memories of childhood abuse in their patients, despite the best of intentions (Brewin, 2012; Lindsay & Briere, 1997).

Improving Study Strategies: You're in Charge

> After everything you have been learning about memory, you decide to start a tutoring service to help your friends improve their academic performance. Your plan is to help them figure out the source of their difficulties and then provide them with helpful tips that could improve their grades. Let's begin.

Reset   Back   Next

Amnesia

LO 6.11   Distinguish between the different types of amnesia.

"According to Hollywood," writes neuropsychologist Sallie Baxendale, "[amnesia] is something of an occupational hazard for professional assassins." Baxendale is referring to *The Bourne Identity* movies and other popular shows that, although they feature characters who struggle from various forms of memory loss, hardly ever present an accurate picture of amnesia (Baxendale, 2004, p. 1481). Outside the borders of the silver screen, there are two distinct types of amnesia: retrograde amnesia and anterograde amnesia. **Retrograde amnesia** is characterized by the loss of past memories. Because of the process of consolidation discussed earlier,

retrograde amnesia

type of amnesia characterized by the loss of past memories

amnesia that is the result of an injury tends to be graded, meaning the amnesia is most intense for the recent past with more remote memories less likely to be affected (Winocur et al., 2013). **Anterograde amnesia**, in contrast, affects future memories. People with anterograde amnesia can remember events from their past, but they struggle to create new long-term memories.

Both types of amnesia are linked to brain damage, which is often caused by an accident, surgery, or illness. The type of amnesia a patient develops depends on the affected area of the brain: A patient with a disease, like dementia, that affects the whole brain (particularly the hippocampus) may show signs of retrograde amnesia, while someone who sustains a frontal lobe injury in a car accident will likely have difficulty encoding memories and may suffer from anterograde amnesia.

The famous patient Henry Molaison, or better known as "H. M." developed anterograde amnesia in 1953 when doctors removed his temporal lobes in an attempt to cure his severe epilepsy. After the surgery, H. M. could no longer create new long-term memories, but his working memory remained functional, as did many of his procedural memories. Watch the following video, *When Memory Fails*, to learn more about H. M. and how his unique circumstances have helped researchers understand the biological connections between memory, memory loss, and the brain.

anterograde amnesia

type of amnesia characterized by the inability to form new memories; people with anterograde amnesia can remember events from their past, but have difficulty creating new long-term memories

When Memory Fails

Interactive

After H.M.'s death in 2008, his brain was sent to University of California, San Diego, to be sliced into thousands of cross-sectional pieces (Annese et al., 2014). The image you see below is an actual slice from H. M's brain. This detailed level of analysis has allowed researchers to make discoveries about H. M.'s brain that have helped contribute to their understanding of how memory works. The research team plans to publish a free online map of H. M.'s brain that will be zoomable to a microscopic level. This is no small task given that they have 2,401 slices of brain to digitize and publish.

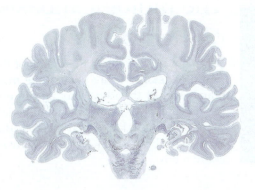

Retrieval Practice: Types of Amnesia

Match each scenario to the appropriate type of amnesia.

Roland was in a severe car accident was he was 47 years old. He recovered quite quickly and had minimal physical injuries. He experienced a concussion and, after the accident, had difficulty remembering any new information. Memories from before the accident appeared to be undisturbed. Roland is suffering from [   ] amnesia .

Judy fell off a ladder, hit her head, and sustained a concussion. She was in the hospital for a short time and didn't have many lasting injuries. She couldn't remember the day of the fall or much information in the few days leading up to the fall, but otherwise her memory appeared to be fine. Judy is experiencing [   ] amnesia

WORD BANK
- anterograde
- retrograde

Start Over   Check Answers

Quiz for Module 6.10–6.11

1. Given what you know about Ebbinghaus's research on forgetting, what advice about studying would you give your friend?

   a. Make flashcards quickly before you forget the information.

   b. Don't cram—engaging in distributed practice over a few days or weeks is more effective.

   c. Cram right before the test because it's the best way to recall the information.

   d. Make the material you're studying into nonsense material so you can remember it.

2. Trent just moved and has to list all addresses on a job application. He has no problem remembering the new address, but when the application requests his old address he cannot remember it. Trent is experiencing which type of interference?

   a. Retroactive interference

   b. Proactive interference

   c. Encoding interference

   d. Storage interference

3. What is it called when some people work to actively forget memories of trauma or abuse?

   a. Deliberate decay

   b. Motivated forgetting

   c. Proactive interference

   d. Extreme memory loss

4. Caroline has dementia and can no longer remember the names of her grandchildren. She is experiencing which type of amnesia?

   a. Neurocognitive dementia   b. Alzheimer's amnesia

   c. Retrograde   d. Anterograde

5. The famous patient known as H.M. developed anterograde amnesia after having his temporal lobes removed. This led to him no longer being able to create _____ memories, but his _____ memory remained functional.

   a. long-term; working   b. procedural; working

   c. working; long-term   d. working; procedural

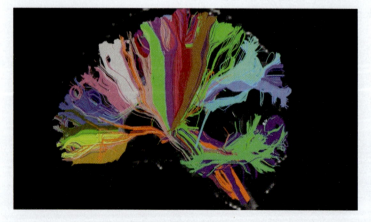

Module 6.12–6.13: The Biological Basis of Memory

For many people, when they think of their memories, they picture them stored away one-by-one in a particular area of the brain—sort of the same way all of your socks are stored in a particular drawer. Thanks to a number of scientists over the past century, we now know that memory does not exist in just one place in the brain. In fact, the socks are scattered throughout the entire room.

Brain Structures Involved in Memory

LO 6.12 **Recognize that memories are located in various places in the brain.**

In the early 1900s, a psychologist named Karl Lashley believed there was a specific area in the brain that held what he referred to as an *engram*, or a physical memory trace. Lashley provides us with a great example of how the process of science is supposed to work. He had a hypothesis—that memories were localized to a specific area of the brain—and he conducted studies to test his hypothesis. Lashley trained rats to run through a maze and then lesioned (destroyed) parts of their brains to see if he could "remove" the memory. Much to his surprise, although the lesions produced some memory problems, the rats still remembered how to run through the maze (Lashley, 1950). He replicated his results and eventually concluded that his hypothesis was not supported and in fact he had evidence to suggest that the opposite was true: that memories were widely distributed throughout the entire cortex.

Since Lashley's days, the pendulum has swung slightly back toward the idea of localization. Currently, most scientists would agree that while there is no specific brain area for all memories, certain types of memories seem to be grouped together in specific areas of the brain. Think of it like having multiple socks drawers; separate drawers for dark colored socks, light colored socks, and athletic socks, etc.

Explicit and implicit long-term memories don't just seem different to us; they're actually processed in different areas of the brain. Short-term memory/working memory has been localized to the hippocampus and frontal lobe (Yoon et al., 2008), specifically the prefrontal cortex (D'Esposito & Postle, 2015), which is thought to play an important role in encoding, updating, and maintaining information in working memory (D'Ardenne et al., 2012). As you can see in Figure 6.15, the hippocampus, which is located in the medial temporal lobe, is largely responsible for processing our explicit memories, and is assisted by some areas of the frontal lobe (Rosenbaum et al., 2014). After semantic and episodic memories are formed in the hippocampus, they are sent to other regions of the brain for storage. The hippocampus and frontal lobes are also pivotal to the recognition and recall of long-term memories: People and animals with hippocampus damage struggle to remember explicit memories (Clark & Maguire, 2015; Dede et al., 2013; Sherry & Vaccarino, 1989). Research with rats has demonstrated that by using a light to "turn off" cells in the hippocampus, a previously intact memory can be essentially erased by interfering with the neurons needed for the retrieval process (Tanaka et al., 2014). However, subsequent studies using a similar methodology have fine-tuned some of these findings and suggest, for the first time, a copy is made of every memory that is created. Through brain imaging, researchers from MIT showed that mice simultaneously created two memories for the same event: one in the hippocampus and one in the cortex (Kitamura et al., 2017). Their research also suggested that if the memory is recalled in the first few days after formation, the hippocampus was involved in its retrieval. But, after the connections between the hippocampus and cortex were given time to develop, memory retrieval was shown by activation of the cortex. It appeared that the short-term memory weakened in the hippocampus, but the long-term memories were consolidated over time in the cortex.

So far, we have been focusing only on explicit memories. As discussed earlier in the chapter, implicit memories are quite different from explicit memories and different areas of the brain are involved in the consolidation and storage of these unconscious and/or skill-based memories. As with explicit memories, the hippocampus plays an important role with implicit memories. However, the cerebellum and the basal ganglia are also intricately involved in the formation and storage of implicit long-term memories (Lu, 2013; Lum & Conti-Ramsden, 2013; Packard & Knowlton, 2002). Because both the cerebellum and the basal ganglia are linked to the development of motor skills, they are necessary for the formation of procedural memories and habits related to movement. The basal ganglia and the cerebellum may be linked to different types of motor skills, but patients with damage to either area have difficulty creating new procedural memories (Doyon et al., 2009; Gabrieli, 1998).

The amygdala is a small brain structure important for processing and experiencing emotion, particularly strong emotions like fear. It follows that emotional memories, including flashbulb memories discussed earlier would involve the amygdala (Davidson et al., 2005; Phelps & Sharot, 2008).

Figure 6.15 Neuroanatomy and Memories

Despite what many people think, memories are not just stored in one area of the brain. There are numerous brain structures that play a role in the consolidation and storage of memories.

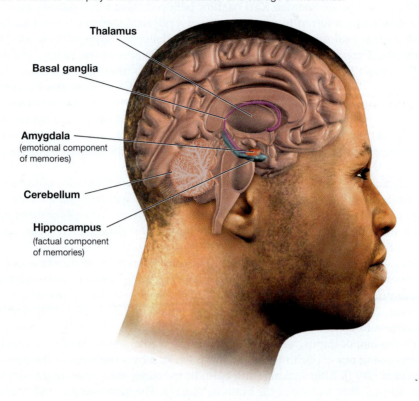

We have determined that our memories are spread throughout various parts of our brain and that connections between neurons are an important part of the memory process. However, that still doesn't explain exactly what is taking place in the brain. What are the biological building blocks of memories and what happens when a memory is formed?

The Role of Neurons in Memory Formation

LO 6.13   Recall the role of neurons in creating long-term memories.

Research into the biology of memory tends to focus on two primary areas: (1) the parts of the brain involved in long-term memory storage and (2) the individual neurons and their synapses (the areas between neurons across which nerve impulses travel from one neuron to the next.) When we learn something new, neurons "talk" to one another through the release of neurotransmitters. Each time we review that information, those specific neural connections are strengthened, and it becomes easier for neurotransmitters to travel across those synapses and impact the next neuron. Think about what happens when there is a big snowfall. At first, the snow might be light and fluffy and fun to walk through. Trying to get from your driveway to your front door could be a challenge because there is no visible path. But time after time of walking up to your front door creates a well-worn path of packed snow. This snow is no longer fluffy but compacted and solid. The walkway of compacted snow develops from the repeated use of the path, similar to the way receptors and neurotransmitters develop efficient connections through the repeated action potentials. Have you heard of the phrase, "neurons that fire together, wire together?" In the case of memories, at a basic biological level, neurons activated at the same time develop a connection and, if repeated, become a memory.

long-term potentiation (LTP)

biological explanation for the development of long-term memories; memories are formed as a result of strengthened neural connections

Back in 1949, psychologist Donald Hebb first theorized that a relationship existed between strong neural connections and the creation and maintenance of memories. When Hebb's theory was confirmed in the 1970s, scientists referred to this strengthening of neural connections as **long-term potentiation (LTP)**. As Hebb suggested, LTP is part of the biological basis for memory: Strong neural connections lead to long-term memories.

Noble prize winner Eric Kandel has devoted his life to understanding the nature of learning and memory at the biological level. When he began his work as a medical student in the 1950s, he initially concluded that higher functions of the brain (such as in human brains) were too sophisticated to study immediately and that he must take a reductionist approach to discover exactly how memories were created. He settled on studying *Aplysia californica*, a giant marine slug.

Why the sea slug? Kandel described that Aplysia californica is made up of only 20,000 central nerve cells (considerably less than the 100 billion neurons in the human brain) and, unlike human neurons, many of the sea slug's nerve cells are large enough to be seen by the naked eye (Kandel, 2001). Kandel and his colleagues were able to show that after the sea slug experienced an electric shock on its tail, which would produce a reflexive withdraw of its gill, it *learned* to withdraw its gill when any innocuous stimulus was applied to its tail. If the sea slug *learned* to protect itself in the future, that meant that it must have developed a *memory* for the initial aversive event (Pinsker et al., 1973). This research was the beginning of decades of research on the biology of memory and allowed Kandel and others to discover what was actually happening at the synaptic level and how that differed depending on whether short-term or long-term memories were being studied (Bliss & Collingridge, 1993; Cai et al., 2012; Herdegen et al., 2014). Watch the video, *Long-Term Potentiation*, for a review of Kandel's pioneering work in long-term memory.

Long-Term Potentiation

Even before any specific memory is created, many of our neurons have some existing "relationship" where the presynaptic neuron releases neurotransmitter into the synapse thereby communicating with the post-synaptic neuron. In the case of short-term memory, where the memory is available to you for only a short period of time (about 15–20 seconds) there is a *functional* strengthening between those two neurons. That is, the process of neurotransmission becomes more efficient and effective (this is the example of forging a path through the snow that we discussed earlier). In the case of long-term memories, however, there is also a *structural* change in the neurons. When information is repeated/learned/memorized, and as a result of LTP, that target neuron experiences a change in the expression of its genes and grows *new synaptic connections*. This means there is an actual anatomical change, typically developing new, additional receptors, in the post-synaptic neuron to account for that memory. This process is an excellent example of the concept of *neuroplasticity*—the fact our brain actually changes as a result of experience. Think of it like this: If you remember anything at all after reading this chapter (and we certainly hope you do), and if you can recall that information a week later, then you know your brain actually changed as a result of your experience of working through the material in this chapter.

Adaptive Pathway 6.2: Neuroanatomy and Memory

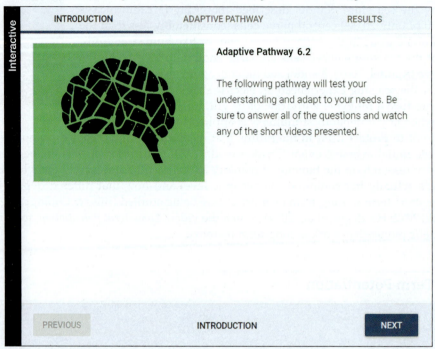

Quiz for Module 6.12 – 6.13

1. Short–term memory or working memory has been localized in the _____ and the _____.
   a. hippocampus; frontal lobe
   b. amygdala; frontal lobe
   c. cerebellum; basal ganglia
   d. hippocampus; cerebellum

2. Which parts of the brain are necessary for procedural memories and habits related to movement?
   a. Hippocampus; cerebellum
   b. Amygdala; thalamus
   c. Cerebellum; basal ganglia
   d. Basal ganglia; thalamus

3. Which brain structure plays an important role in processing emotions, especially strong emotions like fear?
   a. Hippocampus
   b. Amygdala
   c. Thalamus
   d. Hypothalamus

4. The strengthening of neural connections, which is considered the biological basis of memory, is called _____.
   a. synaptic connection potential (SCP)
   b. long-term neuron connection (LTC)
   c. long-term potentiation (LTP)
   d. synaptic neuron potentiation (SNP)

5. When a new concept or behavior is learned, repeated, and practiced, there is a _____ change in the neurons, which often involves the growth on new receptors.
   a. chemical   b. schematic
   c. structural   d. functional

6. Maria has decided to learn to play the piano at the age of 55. She knows this will be good for her brain because as she learns something new her brain actually changes as a result of the experience. What is this proces called?
   a. Neuroplasticity
   b. Long-term memory formation
   c. Synaptic connections potentia
   d. Neurocognitive potential

Module 6.14: Piecing It Together: False Memories

LO 6.14 Analyze how the cross-cutting themes of psychology apply to the issue of false memories.

What Do You Think?

Interactive

1. People who develop false memories of autobiographical events (i.e., a detailed memory for an event that never occurred) are a select group of people who are more likely to have a psychological disorder and a history of trauma.

○ True
○ False

Previous   Next

One of the most controversial topics within the field of memory involves false memories for events, the extent to which this phenomenon occurs, and the impact false memories can have on future behavior. The interest in exploring whether or not people could be induced to remember an event that did not happen rose in the 1990s when there was a notable increase in the number of recovered memories of childhood abuse that were claimed to have been repressed for many years (Loftus, 1993). The debate was less about whether or not is was *possible* to repress memories of childhood abuse, but more about whether or not therapists were in a position to intentionally or unintentionally create false memories of abuse. Data from research studies and legal cases provided various sources of evidence to suggest that false memories existed and that therapists were in a unique position to create such memories (Berk & Parker, 2009; Ost et al., 2013; Pope, 1996).

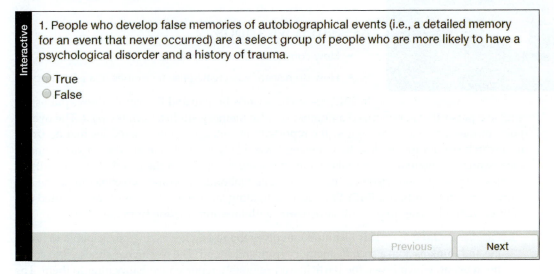

The American Psychological Association highlights the need for more research but acknowledges the possibility of false memories related to abuse by pointing to the following facts (American Psychological Association, 2017):

- Childhood sexual abuse is an unfortunate and often devastating part of our culture.
- Dissociation, the process of making a memory inaccessible, has been seen as a form of coping with traumatic experiences.
- Memory is a reconstructive process and is susceptible to inaccuracies.
- It is possible for people to remember "false events" in great detail and with great confidence.

With an issue such as this that has potential legal and life-long implications, it is necessary to ask important questions and study all aspects of false memories. For example, are there certain people who are more susceptible to developing false memories? Are there techniques interviewers can use to increase the likelihood of creating a false memory? What are the ethical implications involved in creating false memories in people, and is it possible this technique can be used in a positive way? A review of the research will help highlight some of the controversy within the field and answer some of these questions.

Research Methods

- How common are false memories?
- How do researchers create false memories in a laboratory?

In 2017, researchers Chris Brewin and Bernice Andrews published a review paper that summarized a number of false memory studies from the past. The overall point of their paper was to suggest the reported percentages of false memories that occurred in research studies (often close to 40 percent) was likely an overestimate due to variations in the research methodology, how false memories were defined, and the fact that the majority of studies have been conducted in a highly-controlled laboratory setting, which is unlike the real world (Brewin & Andrews, 2017). Studies investigating false memories have typically used one of three methodologies to present participants with false information from their past:

1. *Imagination Inflation*   This technique involves the researcher asking participants to imagine and think back to a specific memory from childhood. The researcher chooses the childhood event, which is one the participant previously reported *not* happening to them. The participant is encouraged to concentrate and imagine details of the event and then answer questions about the memory. This method often results in the participant's increase in their *belief* that the event occurred but tends not to produce vivid details of the memory itself.

2. *False Feedback*   Another methodology involves providing false feedback to participants. Again, participants are asked about childhood experiences and are then presented with feedback (either from a computer or a person posing as a therapist) suggesting that the event happened, but they are just unable to remember it *right now*. Participants may then be asked to imagine the event and/or answer questions about the event (similar to the imagination inflation procedure.)

3. *Memory Implantation*   This methodology, which has also been called the Parental Informant Paradigm (Porter & Baker, 2015), combines the previous two approaches and relies on the explicit corroboration from an authoritative source, typically a parent. In this situation, both the participant and parent complete a childhood experiences questionnaire. The researchers choose an experience that both participant and parent reported did *not* happen (e.g., having a serious medical procedure) and then tell the participant that even though they can't

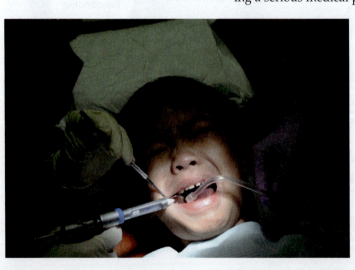

remember it, their parent said it happened. In some cases, participants are even shown an edited photograph depicting the event. Sometimes, but not in all cases, participants are asked to imagine the event occurring prior to being asked to recall the memory.

The highest rates of fully-formed memories tend to come from the Memory Implantation Technique. Brewin and Andrews (2017) demonstrated how widely the rates of false memories vary depending on how the memory for the event was defined. Using the study described earlier in the chapter (Porter et al., 1999), the rate of false memories varied from 56 percent (reported in the published paper) to 26 percent when a more stringent definition of recollective memory was used. This finding does not mean that 26 percent is a more accurate estimate of false memories but that the prevalence of an outcome can vary, even within the same study, with minor wording changes to how questions are asked and variables are defined.

Brewin and Andrews' study has become near as controversial as the subject of false memory itself. Numerous memory researchers subsequently published their own papers and commentaries suggesting the researchers' conclusions about the overestimation of false memories are incorrect. Brewin and Andrews have been accused of hand-picking the studies to be included in their analysis (Otgaar et al., 2017), failing to recognize how their conservative estimate may not generalize to people outside of the laboratory, like psychiatric patients in a clinical setting (McNally, 2017), and downplaying the significance of what a 15 percent rate of false childhood memories could mean. Nash et al. (2017) point out that the lifetime prevalence rate of Posttraumatic Stress Disorder (PTSD) is only 6.8 percent (less than half their estimate of false memories), but that no one would suggest people not be concerned about PTSD and its effect on patient's lives. Finally, in a somewhat unusual and pointed attack, Nash et al. (2017) claim that Brewin and Andrews' paper was not even peer-reviewed prior to publication (an accepted practice in scientific research) and is therefore better viewed as an op-ed piece than a scientific research article.

Critics of the Brewin and Andrews paper point instead to a methodologically rigorous and inclusive study conducted that recoded 423 participant transcripts from various published studies across the world (Scoboria et al., 2017). Using their own coding scheme, these researchers determined that false memories were created, depending on the specific methodology used, in 22 to 46 percent of participants, which appears to be more consistent with the literature over the past few decades. These studies highlight that the controversy over false memories that began in the early 1990s is far from over.

Variations in Human Functioning

- Are some people more prone to experience a false memory?

- If so, what individual characteristics are associated with false memories?

Your Memory for United 93 Crash

Interactive

As you may know, on September 11, 2001, United Airlines Flight 93 crashed in a field near Shanksville, Pennsylvania, killing all 44 people on board. Video footage of the plane crashing, taken by one of the witnesses on the ground, has been well publicized both by the news media and on the Internet.

Previous   Next

While it would be appealing to have a list of characteristics that could identify those individuals most susceptible to developing false memories, the research is far from clear on this issue. However, researchers have identified some individual differences in both participants and research assistants that can account for some of the variability seen in rates of false memories. In one study that examined false memories for both positive and negative events, physiological differences, including increased skin conductance (sweating) and muscle tension, were found between true and false memories (Faulkner & Leaver, 2016). Participants who reported remembering a false *positive* event (e.g., meeting someone famous, being given a surprise party) experienced the most physiological changes, including increased heart rate. Just as physiological measures have been used as an indicator of whether or not someone is lying, perhaps one day these same measures and other neuroimaging techniques (e.g., fMRI) will be able to distinguish real from false memories (Bernstein & Loftus, 2009b)?

Other studies have attempted to identify personality traits or individual characteristics of people who tend to report false memories. Some of the most-often reported characteristics include the extent to which an individual engages in mental imagery (e.g., an active and vivid imagination) and has dissociative experiences (e.g., spacing out while driving) (Hyman & Billings, 1998; Porter et al., 2000). In the study discussed earlier about the United 93 plane crash, factors such as familiarity with the news story, frequency of negative emotions after the event, and higher consumption of alcohol in addition to fantasy and dissociation proneness, were all related to false memory production. These results suggest that factors specific to the content of the study itself can also be important determinants of outcome. In the largest false memory study to date, more than 5,000 participants were asked about their memories of political events, where three of the four events were true and one was fabricated. Half of the participants reported that they remembered the false event happening with 27 percent of those individuals saying they saw it on the news (Frenda et al., 2013). The most interesting aspect of this study, however, was that political preference appeared to guide the development of the false memories (i.e., conservatives were more likely to remember a false, negative story involving Barack Obama, and liberals were more likely to falsely remember a negative George W. Bush event.) The researchers concluded that our prior attitudes can produce a feeling of familiarity when presented with information from the past, which increases the likelihood we believe the memory to be true.

While most studies have focused on the individual characteristics of participants, one study conducted analyses of the personality characteristics of the student interviewers who were part of the research team. Porter et al. (2000) found that susceptibility to memory distortion was related to the personality trait of extraversion in both the participant *and* the research assistant conducting the interview. That is, interviewers who scored in the mid to high range on extraversion were more likely to elicit a false memory, especially if the participant scored low on extraversion (i.e., was an introvert.)

Cultural and Social Diversity

• What implications does this research have for the legal system, particularly for individuals who have been charged with a crime?

Given the decades of controversy and research regarding false memories, you might notice yourself thinking, "So what? What does it really matter if the percentage of false memories is this versus that?" When you think about our legal system and how much we rely on the memory of others (e.g., picking a suspect out of a lineup or testifying in court to what they witnessed), it is acutely obvious that this issue is one of life or death for some people.

There is no question, due to the reconstructive nature of memory, that people and circumstances can influence the quality and truthfulness of a witness's memory (Loney & Cutler, 2016; Schacter & Loftus, 2013), which has led to psychologists playing an important role in the revision of eyewitness identification procedures (Wells & Quinlivan, 2009; Wells et al., 1998).

But what about for the individuals who have been suspected of a crime? It might be hard to believe, but there have been documented cases where a suspect develops a false memory of committing a crime and subsequently confesses (Porter & Baker, 2015). In the laboratory, researchers have demonstrated the ability to create false memories of committing a crime. Shaw and Porter (2015) reported 70 percent of their participants eventually falsely remembered committing a crime. The following simulation will take you through the procedure of their study. As you read through it, ask yourself if you think you would have been in the 70 percent that reported a false memory.

False Memories of Committing a Crime

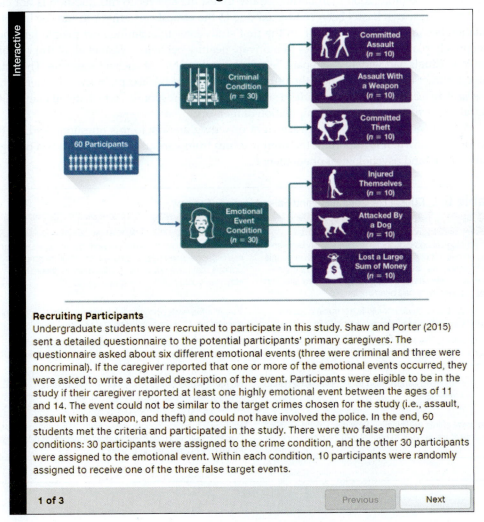

Recruiting Participants

Undergraduate students were recruited to participate in this study. Shaw and Porter (2015) sent a detailed questionnaire to the potential participants' primary caregivers. The questionnaire asked about six different emotional events (three were criminal and three were noncriminal). If the caregiver reported that one or more of the emotional events occurred, they were asked to write a detailed description of the event. Participants were eligible to be in the study if their caregiver reported at least one highly emotional event between the ages of 11 and 14. The event could not be similar to the target crimes chosen for the study (i.e., assault, assault with a weapon, and theft) and could not have involved the police. In the end, 60 students met the criteria and participated in the study. There were two false memory conditions: 30 participants were assigned to the crime condition, and the other 30 participants were assigned to the emotional event. Within each condition, 10 participants were randomly assigned to receive one of the three false target events.

1 of 3   Previous   Next

Ethics

- Even if we know how to create false memories in people, is it ethical to do so?

Journal Prompt: The Ethics of Implanting Memories

Most people, we hope, would agree that implanting false memories of abuse or committing a crime is unethical. However, what if memories could be implanted that would only have positive outcomes? For example, if you could develop false memories about your love of exercise and desire to eat healthy foods, would that still be unethical? Why or why not?

The manipulation of memory through the implantation of false memories or even more invasive memory erasure techniques involving deep brain stimulation may sound like the theme of a science fiction movie, but these are real issues facing researchers and health-care practitioners today (Robillard & Illes, 2016). The possibility of interfering with an individual's memory—and therefore their history and understanding of who they are—is inherently fraught with ethical concerns. While the majority of false memory research has focused on neutral or negative events, some researchers have started exploring if implanting false memories can result in positive behavior change such as eating a healthier diet or drinking less alcohol (Bernstein & Loftus, 2009a; Bernstein et al., 2015; Mantonakis et al., 2013b).

Ethical dilemmas are typically faced with the question, "Will this procedure/experience/ treatment cause more good than harm?" Many times, the answer to this question is not clear because the research hasn't been conducted due to the ethical concerns. You can see how this situation becomes a dilemma itself. In the first study ever to examine how people felt about deceptively planting false memories to motivate healthy behavior, Nash et al. (2016) revealed that individuals had widely discrepant beliefs about the ethics of such a procedure. Their data helped extract the reasons behind the public's beliefs about the acceptability of implementing *false memory therapy*. Table 6.1 provides a summary of these responses, which detail many of the ethical concerns regarding the manipulation of memory.

As you can see, there isn't an easy right or wrong answer to this question. And, as this section has shown, it is important to examine issues from various perspectives when trying to truly understand psychological phenomenon.

Table 6.1 Ethical Reasoning Behind False Memory Therapy

Reasons False Memory Therapy Is Unethical	Reasons False Memory Therapy Is Ethical
Psychological consequences (the effects of discovering something once believed was false; leading people to question their own identity and past); social consequences (how relationships could be affected after finding out a memory had been implanted)	Some people need the extra support; the recognition that many people need help and have tried other treatment options that have not worked; false memory therapy, if effective, could help to change people's lives
Integrity: The ends *do not* justify the means. Even if there is a potential to help, it is wrong to lie to someone	Integrity; the ends *do* justify the means; helping people and possibly saving lives outweighs any potential risks
High potential for abuse; police could elicit false confessions of a crime or therapists could use for their own personal or professional gain	More treatment options; all options should be provided to patients and left up to them to decide which ones they would like to pursue
Lack of consent; people need to provide permission to receive treatment	No harm would be done; memory is a reconstructive process anyway, so this is no different from normal remembering
Removal of free will; planting false memories would rob people of the free will to control their own behavior	No worse than alternatives; other ineffective treatments are currently practiced, so if this worked, it would be better than those other ones that don't work

Quiz for Module 6.14

1. Why was there an increased interest in the 1990s to explore if false memories could be created?

   a. There was a notable increase in the number of recovered memories of childhood abuse.

   b. There was a notable increase in the number of court cases based on false memories.

   c. There was a notable number of clients claiming their therapists intentionally implanted false memories.

   d. There was a notable increase in the reports of childhood sexual abuse.

2. This technique to test the feasibility of false memory implantation asks research participants to vividly recall a childhood event that did not happen to them. What is this technique called?

   a. False feedback

   b. Imagination inflation

   c. Memory Implantation

   d. Fake imaging feedback

3. Research has attempted to identify individual differences or personality characteristics associated with people more likely to experience false memories. The most often reported characteristics are_____ and _____.

   a. dissociative experiences; poor memory skills

   b. vivid imagination; dissociative experiences

   c. vivid imagination; habitual lying

   d. poor memory skills; vivid imagination

4. How has research into the reconstructive nature of memories influenced the legal system?

   a. A psychologist must always be present when an eyewitness is interviewed.

   b. Eyewitnesses are not allowed to be cross-examined more than twice.

   c. Eyewitnesses are not allowed to watch news coverage of the crime.

   d. Eyewitness identification procedures have been revised to decrease the likelihood of false memories.

5. Isaac asked his therapist to implant memories that he loves to exercise and prefers vegetables over potato chips. This issue of whether therapists should use psychological techniques to mislead their clients is inherently a(n) _____ one.

   a. ethical

   b. legal

   c. medical

   d. cultural

Summary: Memory

MODULE 6.1–6.2   Models of Memory

Memory is the collection of information and experiences stored in the brain for retrieval at a later time. The **information processing approach** suggests memory involves the encoding, storage, and retrieval of information. **Attention,** which involves directing cognitive resources in a particular direction, is necessary for the creation of memories. More contemporary memory models that can account for the simultaneous processing that occurs, are referred to as neural network or **connectionist models of memory.** An example of a connectionist model is the **parallel distributed processing model of memory.** In this model, memories are distributed throughout the brain and represented in the pattern of activation between neurons.

MODULE 6.3–6.6   Acquiring and Storing Memories

Memory is the product of a sensory experience including, images, sounds, tastes, smells, and feelings. **Sensory memory, or** the brief retention of sensory stimulation, is an extension of perception. The visual aspect of sensory memory is referred to as **iconic memory,** while our ability to briefly and accurately remember sounds is called **echoic memory.** According to the three-stage model of memory, when attention is given to sensory information, it moves to **short-term memory,** the structural component of memory responsible for storing relatively small amounts of information for a short time. The duration of short-term memory is relatively limited unless something is done to intentionally keep the memory in the present moment. **Maintenance rehearsal** is the practice of repeating or rehearsing the information over and over again to maintain it in short-term memory. Information can be lost from short-term memory because of **decay,** which refers to how information naturally disappears over time or **interference,** which occurs when new information interferes with the information in short-term memory. **Chunking** is another memory strategy that involves the combining of individual small chunks of information into larger meaningful units. The way in which the brain codes information depends on the type of information being processed: **Visual coding** involves processing images (e.g., looking at a map or a floor plan), **auditory coding** is the coding of sounds (e.g., remembering phone numbers by the pattern of sounds of the numbers), and **semantic coding** is processing information based on its meaning (e.g., remembering chunks of letters based on what they mean). **Working memory** is a structural component of the memory system that allows for the manipulation of information for cognitively complex tasks (e.g., learning, reasoning, comprehension) and for the limited and temporary storage of that information. **Encoding** involves the process of consolidation of information from working memory to long-term memory. The most effective encoding strategies involve **effortful processing.** An example of an effortful processing strategy is **elaborative rehearsal,** which focuses on elaborating on the information and making it meaningful. **Mnemonics** are memory strategies where information

to be learned is connected to something else that can serve as a trigger for retrieval. All of these strategies increase the likelihood that information will be stored in **long-term memory,** the structure where information is stored for long periods of time. Memories manifest themselves in two forms: (1) **explicit memories**—memories of which we are consciously aware and (2) **implicit memories**—memories below the level of conscious awareness. Explicit memories include **semantic memories,** which are memories that contain factual and conceptual information not directly linked to life events. **Episodic memories** are the explicit memories that contain entire sequences of life events. Evidence for the existence of implicit memories comes from the phenomenon of **priming,** which involves presenting a stimulus that activates unconscious associations that then lead to a predictable response. One type of implicit memory, **procedural memory,** consists of habits and skills such as riding a bike or driving a car.

MODULE 6.7–6.9   Retrieving Memories

Retrieval refers to the ability to access information from long-term memory when needed. **Free recall** involves pulling information directly from long-term memory without the help of any kind of **retrieval cues,** which are bits of information that can trigger the memory and make it accessible. **Cued recall** involves the use of retrieval cues. **Recognition** is another form of recall where the correct answer is provided among a group of possible answers. The **serial position effect** refers to the phenomenon that when recalling a list of words/items most people can remember the words from the beginning and the end of the list. The ability to remember words at the beginning of the list is called the **primacy effect,** and the tendency to easily recall words at the end of the list is referred to as the **recency effect.** The principle of **encoding specificity** states that information is encoded along with its context and therefore memories are most easily recalled when the retrieval context matches the context in which the memory was initially encoded. **Flashbulb memories** are vivid, long-lasting memories about the circumstances surrounding the discovery of an extremely emotional, often public event. **Reconstructive memory** refers to the fact that remembering requires the reconstruction of previous events and is therefore prone to errors. **Source monitoring errors** occur when a memory is recalled but attributed to the wrong source. The effects real-world knowledge and experience have on memories is referred to as **pragmatic inference.** An event or situation occurring after the initial memory that modifies that memory is referred to as the **misinformation effect.**

MODULE 6.10–6.11   Forgetting

Forgetting can result from **proactive interference,** which occurs when previously learned information interferes with the ability to recall new information, or **retroactive interference,** where new information interferes with the ability to recall older memories. **Motivated forgetting** involves the active forgetting of experiences, typically in response to a traumatic situation. Another way that memory is impaired is through amnesia: (1) **retrograde amnesia** is characterized by the loss of past memories or (2) **anterograde amnesia** involves the inability to create and retain new memories.

MODULE 6.12–6.13 **The Biological Basis of Memory**

The biological basis of memory involves the strength between neural connections. **Long-term potentiation (LTP)** refers to the process whereby strong neural connections, which arise from being repeatedly activated, lead to long-term memories.

Chapter 6 Quiz

1. Shandra is prompted to change her password on her work computer every 4 months. She tries to make new ones that are similar to her old ones. After returning from vacation for a week, she could only remember her old password. This is an example of which type of memory failure?

   a. Retroactive interference   b. Proactive interference

   c. Storage decay   d. Encoding failure

2. In the case of the creation of a short-term memory, there is a _____ strengthening between neurons.

   a. dynamic   b. quick

   c. structural   d. functional

3. The goal of false memory research is to demonstrate that _____.

   a. most people will report remembering something even if they don't, just to satisfy the researchers

   b. people can be forced to remember inaccurate details when they are distressed

   c. is impossible to convince someone to remember something that never happened to them

   d. some people will report remembering an event that didn't happen to them just because the researcher suggested it did happen

4. The parallel distributed processing model of memory has been likened to which game?

   a. Tic-tac-toe   b. Poker

   c. Connect-the-dots   d. Jenga

5. When Jamal thinks about the first time he played hockey, he remembers the smell of the ice, the sound of his stick hitting the puck, and how much he loved the game. In retrieving this memory, Jamal is accessing _____ in his brain.

   a. multiple connections   b. a specific connection

   c. specific files   d. one neural pathway

6. Sensory memory is primarily a(n) _____ process.

   a. unconscious   b. conscious

   c. lengthy   d. manipulative

7. Anika has just asked her son to pick up his toys. Even though he heard her, he responds with "what did you say?" He is experiencing the echoic memory delay, which means we _____ information quicker than we can _____ it.

   a. process; hear   b. hear; process

   c. see; process   d. process; see

8. Which of the following events will most likely become a flashbulb memory?

   a. Your wedding day

   b. Your first day of a new semester at college

   c. Receiving a speeding ticket

   d. Getting a bad grade on an exam

9. The brain processes and codes information in three different ways, which include _____, _____, and _____.

   a. sensory; visual; auditory

   b. encoding; storage; retrieval

   c. sensory; short-term; long-term

   d. visual; auditory; semantic

10. Enrique is practicing new study strategies. His professor told him that he needs to make sure he is effectively encoding information. Which strategy or strategies should Enrique use?

    a. Effortful processing   b. Elaborative rehearsal

    c. Deep processing   d. All answers are correct

11. The technique of studying several different concepts or mixing information from different chapters during the same study session is called?

    a. Interleaving   b. Interweaving

    c. Encoding   d. The testing effect

12. Andre will never forget where he was or what he was wearing when he heard the news about the mass shooting at an outdoor concert in Las Vegas. Which area of the brain would have significant involvement in the creation of Andre's memory for this event?

    a. Amygdala   b. Medulla

    c. Basal ganglia   d. Cerebellum

13. When Johann drives his car to school, he does not have to think about every step in the process of driving, yet he does have memories of the steps to take. This type of memory is called _____.

    a. episodic   **b.** semantic

    c. implicit   **d.** explicit

14. Lars went to the grocery story but accidentally left his list at home. He remembered coffee and chocolate because those were the first things on the list. This phenomenon is called the _____ effect.

    a. procedural   **b.** contextual

    c. recency   **d.** primacy

15. If you study for your exam in a noisy, crowded restaurant that smells like fried foods, the best place for you to take the exam is a noisy, crowded restaurant that smells like fried food. This phenomenon is referred to as _____.

    a. context dependent   **b.** state dependent
        memory   memory

    c. serial position effect   **d.** implicit memory

16. To increase the capacity of short-term memory, you can combine small bits of information into larger meaningful units. What is this strategy called?

    a. Maintenance rehearsal   **b.** Chugging

    c. Chunking   **d.** Coding

17. Research with people who reported flashbulb memories from the September 11 terrorist attacks showed that most forgetting of the event occurred within _____.

    a. 1 month   **b.** 1 year

    c. 6 months   **d.** 3 months

18. Your friend wants to hear all the details from your birthday party last year. Recalling the details of this memory is a _____ process.

    a. reliable   **b.** restorative

    c. reconstructive   **d.** slow

19. According to the connectionist model of memory, memory is viewed as a _____.

    a. file cabinet with a series of files to be accessed sequentially

    b. sequentially processing computer

    c. set of instructions neurons send to each other that create a pattern of activity among neurons

    d. set of blueprints for the location of memories in the brain

20. Trina typically reads her textbook while watching her favorite Netflix series. She later has difficulty remembering what she read and starts to wonder if she has memory problems. What is Trina experiencing?

    a. Encoding failure   **b.** Storage decay

    c. Proactive interference   **d.** Retroactive interference

21. What role does sleep play in memory formation?

    a. It consolidates and strengthens the memory.

    b. It has no impact on memory.

    c. It plays a passive role by allowing our brains to rest.

    d. It protects against the interference of new material.

22. The three-stage model of memory emphasized both the _____ and the _____ associated with memory.

    a. patterns; processes   **b.** structure; processes

    c. neurons; connections   **d.** structure; patterns

23. Julianna was in an accident that left her unable to form new long-term memories. What type of amnesia does Julianna have?

    a. Proactive   **b.** Retroactive

    c. Anterograde   **d.** Retrograde

24. Identify the area(s) of the brain where long-term memories are stored.

    a. There is no single area where all memories are stored.

    b. Hippocampus

    c. Hippocampus and amygdala

    d. Prefrontal cortex and amygdala

25. Semantic and episodic memories are formed in the _____ and then sent to other areas of the brain for _____.

    a. hippocampus; storage   **b.** frontal lobe; storage

    c. hippocampus; retrieval   **d.** frontal lobe; retrieval

26. Lucy has been studying for her psychology exam and thinks she knows all the facts and concepts. Her conscious memory of the facts is what type of memory?

    a. Nondeclarative   **b.** Explicit

    c. Implicit   **d.** Procedural

27. Which two brain structures are involved in the formation and storage of implicit memories?

    a. Cerebellum and amygdala

    b. Cerebellum and basal ganglia

    c. Basal ganglia and amygdala

    d. Frontal lobe and hippocampus

28. When we learn something new, what happens at the neuron level?

    a. Neurons shut down to consolidate the learning process.

    b. Hormones are released throughout our body.

    c. Neurons communicate with each other through the release of neurotransmitters.

    d. Neurons release glucose to help solidify the learning.

29. Fill in the blanks to complete the correct order of the structures and processes associated with Atkinson and Shiffrin's three-stage model of memory: sensory memory, _____, _____, elaborative rehearsal, _____.

    a. attention; working memory; long-term memory

    b. short-term memory; working memory; long-term memory

    c. attention; long-term memory; retrieval

    d. working memory; long-term memory; retrieval

30. Eric Kandel worked with marine slugs to understand how memory works at the synaptic level in humans. The strengthening of the connections between neurons resulting in the development of memories is called _____.

    a. long-term memory formation

    b. long-term potentiation

    c. synaptic plasticity

    d. an action potential

Chapter 7
Cognition and Language

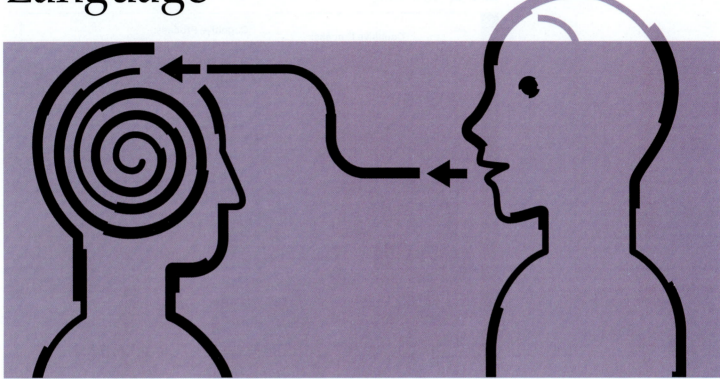

⌄ Chapter Outline and Learning Objectives

Module 7.1–7.2: Concepts

LO 7.1 Distinguish between formal and natural concepts.

LO 7.2 Describe the hierarchical model of concept classification.

Module 7.3–7.4: Problem Solving

LO 7.3 Identify different types of problem-solving strategies.

LO 7.4 Describe different problem-solving difficulties.

Module 7.5–7.7: Decision Making

LO 7.5 Identify different theories about how people make decisions.

LO 7.6 Recognize obstacles that can hinder decision making.

LO 7.7 Describe the role of confirmation bias in decision making.

Module 7.8–7.9: Creativity

LO 7.8 Distinguish between convergent and divergent thinking.

LO 7.9 Explain Sternberg's theory of creative thinking.

Module 7.10–7.14: Language Structure and Development

LO 7.10 Identify the basic structure of language.

LO 7.11 Describe theories of language acquisition.

LO 7.12 Identify milestones in language development.

LO 7.13 Explain the relationship between language and thought.

LO 7.14 Identify the areas of the brain associated with language.

Module 7.15: Piecing It Together: Cognition in Nonhuman Animals

LO 7.15 Analyze how the cross-cutting themes of psychology are related to the topic of cognition in nonhuman animals.

What is Cognitive Psychology?

The mental processes associated with seemingly simple tasks are surprisingly intricate. For example, a job waiting tables at a restaurant involves multiple different forms of mental processing.

Mental Processing

Cognitive Process: ATTENTION
Does anyone need a drink refill?

Cognitive Process: DECISION MAKING
What's the best way to carry all these dishes without dropping one?

Cognitive Process: MEMORY
Who ordered which dish?

Cognitive Process: COMMUNICATION
How should a difficult customer be approached with the news that the kitchen is backed up and the order will be late?

cognition

the mental activities associated with thinking, knowing, remembering, and communicating

Whether we're learning, creating, solving problems, reasoning, making judgments and decisions, or communicating, we rely on cognition to live our daily lives, go to school, do our jobs, and make sense of our world. The study of **cognition**, the mental activities associated with thinking, knowing, remembering, and communicating, has been an active field since the 1950s and 1960s (Miller, 2003). Before this, however, many psychologists were behaviorists who tended to dismiss the study of cognition. Instead, they preferred to study mental processes that were readily observable. In opposition to the behaviorists before them, cognitive psychologists such as Noam Chomsky and Jean Piaget argued that we must go beyond the directly observable and examine cognition in order to truly understand behavior.

Module 7.1–7.2: Concepts

Think about everything you've learned and all of the information you've collected in your life so far. Directions to the city's recycling center; the poem you memorized when you were 8; the blog post about your cat that you're composing in your head; a litany of dates, facts, and events....How can we possibly keep track of everything stored in our brains? The video *Concepts, Prototypes, and Mental Images* provides an overview of this process.

Concepts, Prototypes, and Mental Images

Concept: a set of ideas that represent a class of objects

Formal and Natural Concepts

LO 7.1 **Distinguish between formal and natural concepts.**

One way we organize and remember information is through the use of **concepts**. Concepts are mental groupings of similar objects, events, and people. We are able to comprehend vast amounts of information with concepts by creating a mental representation that categorizes shared features of related objects, events, or other stimuli. For example, the concept *car* contains everything from a shiny BMW to a rusty old Jeep to the Batmobile. Examine the following description of a scene:

> The sun's last sliver of pink was just slipping past the horizon over the sea while the triangle sails flapped half-heartedly in the quiet breeze.

This description provides several examples of different types of concepts. Without the use of concepts in language, our descriptions and writing would become much more laborious and long-winded. For example, the same description without the use of concepts might read as follows:

> The large circle of bright light in the sky, a mix of reddish-whitish color, was just slipping past the horizontal line where the large body of water meets the sky while the three-sided pieces of cloth hanging from ropes on a floating vessel moved back and forth in the quiet currents of moving air.

Formal concepts (also known as logical concepts) have a rigid set of rules or parameters for membership. For example, scientific classifications often include specific rules that clearly denote whether an individual case is included or excluded from the category. An example might include classifying something as a solid, a liquid, or a gas.

The concept of a triangle is a good example of a formal concept. The "rules" for deciding whether an object is a triangle include: a closed object with 3 sides and 3 angles totaling 180 degrees. In fact, all geometric shapes are examples of formal concepts. Formal concepts are sometimes referred to as *artificial concepts* because many of our experiences cannot be easily sorted into such clear-cut and inflexible categories. Most of our concepts develop through our own experiences in the world and are known as **natural concepts**. Because there are no rigid rules for these concepts, the boundaries between categories are often a bit fuzzy. Colors are a good example of a natural concept. How do you know the difference between red and orange? You've probably even debated a color with someone who

concepts

mental groupings of similar objects, events, and people

formal concepts

concepts that have a rigid set of rules or parameters for membership

natural concepts

concepts that develop through our own experiences in the world

says a particular shirt is red, while you believe it's clearly orange. Despite these moments of disagreement, many natural concepts have general agreement from most people regarding classification. There are even some cases where formal concepts exist but are not typically used by the average person. For example, do you think of a tomato as a fruit or a vegetable? Botanists have a formal concept of fruits and vegetables, and tomatoes clearly fall into the category of fruit. However, as you develop your own experiences with fruits and vegetables beginning in childhood, you likely use different guidelines to establish the difference between the two categories. Most people think of fruits as having a sweet taste, while vegetables are more savory. Thus, the natural concept of a tomato might place it into the vegetable category in your own mind.

Find the Concepts

Review the previous passage to see if you can identify examples of both formal concepts and natural concepts. Write (formal) next to formal concepts and (natural) next to natural concepts.

The **sun's** (_____) last sliver of **pink** (_____) was just slipping past the **horizon** (_____) over the **sea** (_____) while the **triangle** (_____) **sails** (_____) flapped half-heartedly in the quiet breeze.

Start Over   Check Answers

Sometimes, we form concepts by definition much like the way formal concepts are determined. We might define an athlete as one who excels in one or more sports. However, we also form concepts by creating a mental image or a typical example that exhibits all of the features associated with a certain category. This mental image or example is called a **prototype**. We more readily identify something as an example of the concept if the object closely resembles the prototype (Rosch, 1978).

prototype

a mental image or a typical example that exhibits all of the features associated with a certain category

Category Examples

Name the best example of each category:

Vehicle:

Fruit:

Reset   Next

You most likely generated an example of a prototype for the concept of a vehicle and a fruit. As Table 7.1 demonstrates, most people generate the same examples using prototypes for these concepts. Prototypes form because a specific example is considered highly representative of the characteristics associated with a concept. For example, think of the concept "bird." The characteristics you associate with this concept may include "flying," "feathers," and "beak," which would make a robin very representative because it has all three defining characteristics. However, a penguin would be less representative because it swims instead of flies and its feathers are less recognizable. Rosch and Mervis (1975) studied the concepts of vehicles and fruit and discovered that people were most likely to generate examples that represented prototypes. However, if your answers do not match the prototypes found in this study (or align with the less typical examples), it doesn't imply you are wrong. In fact, the prototypes that people develop over time are highly influenced by culture (Owens, 2015; Schwanenflugel & Rey, 1986; Wassmann & Dasen, 1994).

Table 7.1 From Prototypes to Unusual Examples

Rosch & Mervis (1975) found that people were most likely to generate the examples at the top of the lists (representing prototypes) and least likely to generate the examples at the bottom of the lists.

Vehicles	Fruit
Car	Orange
Bus	Apple
Train	Peach
Bicycle	Grape
Airplane	Strawberry
Boat	Grapefruit
Wheelchair	Watermelon
Sled	Date
Skates	Tomato
Elevator	Olive

SOURCE: Adapted from Rosch & Mervis, 1975, p. 576.

In addition to definitions and prototypes, we may also form concepts by using an **exemplar** approach, or a "specific remembered instance." In order to categorize new information, new stimuli encountered are compared to past experiences stored in memory (Anderson & Bower, 2014; Ashby & Maddox, 1992; Ashby & Ells, 2001). Therefore, instead of developing an abstract notion of a prototypical bird, exemplar theory states that when you encounter something "bird-like," you will compare the new stimulus to your own memory of all the birds you've encountered in the past. This means that the more often you encounter a certain type of bird (e.g., robin, sparrow), the more "remembered instances" of those birds you'll have and the more easily they will be recalled from memory. If the new "bird-like" object has enough similarities to your memory of other birds, you will likely classify it under the concept of bird.

exemplar
a specific remembered instance used in the formation of new concepts when a new stimulus is encountered

Classification of Concepts

LO 7.2 **Describe the hierarchical model of concept classification.**

Once we form a concept category, we can classify it even more by using **hierarchies of concepts** that progress from broad to narrow. The categories that are the broadest, or include the most concepts, are called **superordinate concepts**. Examples of superordinate categories include animal, food, or furniture. Superordinate concepts are global categories and don't actually provide much specific information about a stimulus because they are so broad and include many other underlying concepts. For example, the superordinate concept of animal applies both to your Aunt Sally and an earthworm, which are unlikely to have many similarities.

hierarchies of concepts
a method of classifying concepts that progresses from broad to narrow

superordinate concepts
the categories that are the broadest or include the most concepts

basic concepts

this level of concept provides significantly more specific information than superordinate concepts

Underlying superordinate concepts are **basic concepts**. This level of concept provides significantly more information than the superordinate concepts. For example, the concept of "dog" is a basic level concept falling under the superordinate concept of "animal." An animal is any living organism that isn't a plant, meaning that there is not much specific information about any individual organism classified as an animal. However, the classification of "dog" provides much more specific information about an individual organism, including that it has four legs, a tail, a fur coat, and is a carnivore.

The most specific type of concepts fall into the subordinate level, which includes the narrowest categories. An example of a subordinate concept would be a golden retriever or a chihuahua. **Subordinate concepts** provide the most specific level of information about included members. Not only do golden retrievers meet all the criteria to be included in the concept of "dog," but they also have several other distinguishing characteristics that further classify them into a specific breed at the subordinate level (e.g., large in size, water-repellant coat, light-to-dark golden in color).

subordinate concepts

the most specific type of concepts that includes the narrowest categories

Figure 7.1 A Concept Hierarchy

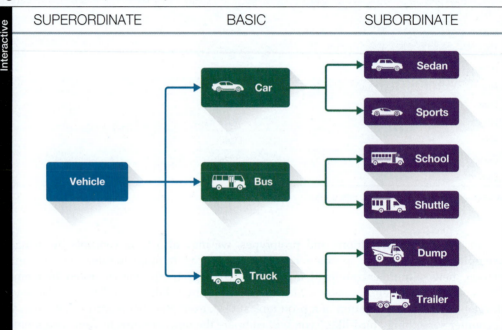

While steak and parsley may have very little else in common, they both fall under the superordinate concept of "food."

Cognitive scientists point out that people are most likely to use basic-level concepts when describing stimuli as opposed to superordinate or subordinate level concepts (Anderson & Matessa, 2014; Murphy & Lassaline, 1997; Rosch et al., 1976). For example, someone who witnesses an accident is most likely to describe seeing a "car" run a red light rather than a "vehicle" or a "sedan." Children also learn basic concepts more readily than other levels of concepts. For example, a 3-year-old child in a park will likely point to an animal and say "doggie" much more commonly than "animal" or "labrador." However, the use of more specific categories (e.g., subordinate concepts) increases when people have more knowledge or expertise (Harel, Kravitz, & Baker, 2013; Johnson & Mervis, 1997; Rogers & McClelland, 2004). For example, a zookeeper doesn't present an animal as a "bear" but rather as a specific type of bear (e.g., "panda bear").

Make A Concept Hierarchy

Interactive

Use the following word bank to place the terms into the correct locations within the hierarchy. The level of concept is listed up top and the examples will be used to correctly complete the hierarchy below. Drag the terms below into the appropriate dotted boxes.

Superordinate	Basic	Subordinate
	Table	Stool
		Hammock
Furniture	Chairs	Coffee Table
		Recliner
	Bed	Kitchen Table
		Bunks

Check Answers

Quiz for Module 7.1–7.2

1. _____ are mental groupings of similar objects, events, and people.

   a. Classifications   b. Thinking

   c. Organizations   d. Concepts

2. What type of concept develops through our experiences and has no rigid rules of classification?

   a. Formal concept   b. Natural concept

   c. Prototype   d. Cognitive concept

3. Which category of concepts is the broadest and contains very little specific information?

   a. Specific concept   b. Subordinate concept

   c. Superordinate concept   d. Basic concept

4. What is an example of a subordinate concept?

   a. Cat   b. Chair

   c. Animal   d. Persian cat

Module 7.3–7.4: Problem Solving

A 2015 survey summarized in Figure 7.2 by the National Association of Colleges and Employers (NACE) found that employers rated problem-solving skills as the fourth most important quality in considering new college graduates for employment (National Association of Colleges and Employers, 2014). Obviously, these skills are very important if you want to be successful,

Figure 7.2 Executives Who Say Employees Are Not Proficient in These Skills

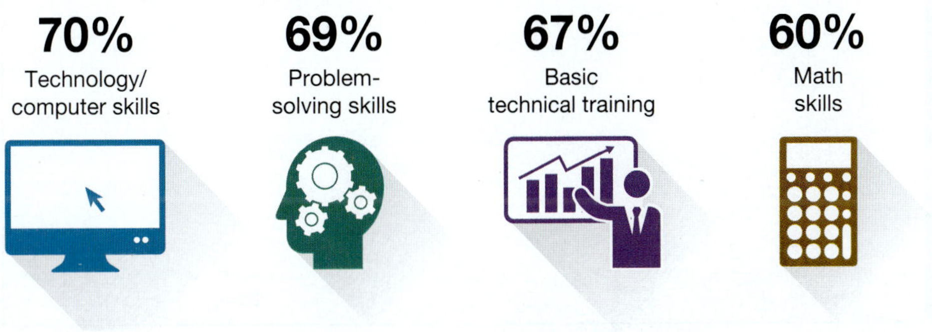

70%
Technology/
computer skills

69%
Problem-
solving skills

67%
Basic
technical training

60%
Math
skills

The GPS systems that tell us how to navigate from one location to the next depend on an algorithm model of problem solving.

problem solving

the act of combining current information with information stored in your memory to find a solution to a task

initial state

state during problem solving in which there is incomplete or unsatisfactory information

goal state

the state one is working toward when engaged in problem solving

set of operations

the steps you need to take in problem solving to reach the goal state from the initial state

but what are they? **Problem solving** is the act of combining current information with information stored in your memory to find a solution to a task.

Problem-Solving Strategies

LO 7.3 **Identify different types of problem-solving strategies.**

Think about the last time you got lost. What did you do to find your way? You might have checked GPS on your phone to get back on track. Maybe you forgot your phone and had to use trial and error, trying different routes until you arrived at your destination. You may have just asked someone for directions. Whatever strategy you chose, you were most likely able to ultimately reach your destination—thanks to finding and implementing a successful problem-solving strategy.

Newell and Simon (1972) defined a *problem space* in terms of the **initial state**, the **goal state**, and the **set of operations**. In the initial state, you have incomplete or unsatisfactory information. You are trying to reach the goal state, or the state in which you have all the information you need. The set of operations consists of the steps you need to take to reach the goal state from the initial state. Typically, the first steps in problem solving include identifying the initial state and the goal state (Davidson & Sternberg, 2003; Russel et al., 2003). Essentially, you need to define the problem and what the outcome will be once a successful solution has been found. In the example above, the initial state is that you are lost, and the goal state would be arriving at your destination. This may seem obvious, but many times in life people fail to adequately identify a problem or the desired outcome. For example, someone might state, "I hate my job," but to actually engage in problem solving, the underlying problem needs to be more specifically identified and understood. Perhaps the real problem is that the person has difficult coworkers or has to commute too far to work each day. The goal state is actually quite different, depending on which of the two concerns is at the root of the person's dissatisfaction at work. One problem might require the person to successfully deal with interpersonal problems at work, while the other problem might require a transfer to a closer location.

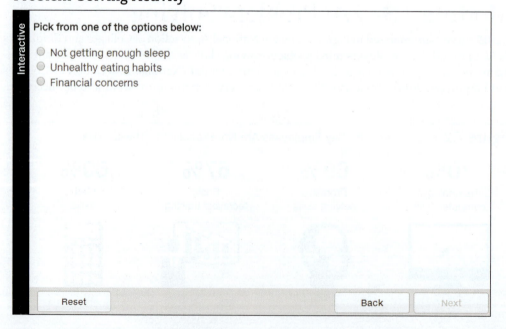

While it is important to be able to identify a problem and know the desired outcome, you are also going to need to determine how to achieve a solution. We use a variety of different methods, or set of operations, for solving different kinds of problems. People sometimes attempt to solve a problem by using **trial and error**, which involves trying a potential solution and discarding that option if it fails while moving on to the next potential solution (Durkin, 1937). If you can't remember which key fits a particular lock, you might choose a key at random on your keyring and then keep trying different keys until you find the one that fits. Trial-and-error methods are useful when there are a limited number of possible solutions and when the consequences of making a mistake are not severe (Durkin, 1937; Salamatov, 1999). For example, you wouldn't want an air traffic controller to use a trial-and-error approach to directing planes on the landing strip by trying one strategy and, if it fails (e.g., planes crash), move on to the next possible strategy.

Because trial-and-error techniques can be haphazard and therefore not very efficient, a more systematic form of trial and error is known as the algorithm method. **Algorithms** are step-by-step procedures we can follow to guarantee the ability to discover a solution to a particular problem. In order to do long division or decipher an encoded message, you might follow the steps of an algorithm. As long as you follow the correct process, you will eventually come up with the correct solution (Lin & Kernighan, 1973). Formulas from geometry are a good example of an algorithm approach to problem solving. You can reliably calculate the area of a circle by squaring the radius of the circle and multiplying times pi. Algorithms are good problem-solving strategies when they are an option because they guarantee the discovery of the correct solution. However, some problems don't come with a handy algorithmic solution (e.g., how to prepare a last-minute meal with the few ingredients in your refrigerator) and some problems that could be solved using an algorithm would take too long to be practical. For example, if you want to solve the anagram for "dormitory," (when you rearrange the letters in one word to form a different word or words), you could use an algorithm approach by writing every possible combination of letters. However, this strategy might take you a while—there are a total of 362,880 different letter combinations from the original 9 letters in the word (to save you the trouble, the anagram solution to "dormitory" is ironically "dirty room")!

Current research on problem solving has suggested that problem-solving strategies are not as universal as suggested by the original Newell and Simon (1972) model of initial state, goal state, and set of operations (Ohlsson, 2012). However, the original model's focus on the use of heuristics, or mental shortcuts, is still an important focus of current models of problem solving. Like rules of thumb, **heuristics** are informal rules that make solving problems or decision making quicker and simpler. We use them all the time; in fact, psychologists Daniel Kahneman and Amos Tversky (1973) argue that human judgment rests more heavily on heuristics than on purely rational analytic processes. While heuristics are much less reliable than algorithms, they are also much more efficient by reducing the number of possible solutions to be tested (Davidson & Sternberg, 2003). One example of a heuristic that is often helpful when solving problems is called a means-end analysis. **Means-end analysis** depends on examining the difference between the initial state and the goal state and then forming subgoals that will get you closer to the goal state. In reality, most problems can't be solved in one simple step and breaking the larger goal into smaller subgoals helps focus your efforts and move you incrementally to the goal (Anderson, 1993). For example, imagine you receive a text alert that your checking account is overdrawn when you were certain you had plenty of money left to cover your expenses for the month. You would likely use a means-end analysis to help you solve the problem. You might break it down into subgoals that include looking up your account information online and (1) adding up all your monthly deposits and (2) subtracting all your payments. If the balance you calculate is the same as the bank notification, you could then review each individual withdrawal to see if any errors had been made. When you find that an online payment for an item was mistakenly deducted twice, you would tackle the next subgoal of contacting the bank and working to get the error corrected.

Working backward is another useful heuristic that can assist in problem solving. Using this strategy, you start at the goal state and then work your way backward to determine a solution (Gick, 1986). Imagine you have a flight departing at 7:00 AM and you are wondering what time to set your alarm. One useful strategy would be to start with

trial and error

type of problem solving that involves trying a potential solution and discarding that option if it fails while moving on to the next potential solution

algorithms

step-by-step problem-solving procedure that guarantees the ability to discover a solution to a particular problem

heuristics

informal rules or mental shortcuts that make solving problems or decision making quicker and simpler

means-end analysis

examining the difference between the initial state and the goal state in problem solving and then forming subgoals that will ultimately lead to the goal state

working backward

when you start at the goal state and then work your way backward to determine a solution to a problem

Working backward is often how we decide when we need to set our alarm in the morning.

the flight time and work your way backward to the necessary wake-up time. If your flight leaves at 7:00 AM, you probably need to be at the airport by 5:30 AM. You then subtract the time you need to drive to the airport (30 minutes) and the time you expect to need to get ready (20 minutes because you are skipping a shower). You then arrive at your wake-up time: 4:40 AM (ouch!).

Sometimes, of course, we don't need to use algorithms or analyses or complicated methods to solve problems. On those rare and wonderful occasions, we experience **insight**: Without warning, the solution we've been looking for suddenly pops into our heads. If you've ever had a flash of inspiration while taking a test or struggling with a seemingly impossible project, you're probably familiar with the joys that insight can bring. It turns out that scientists can spot insight in the brain. Recently, psychologists used fMRI and EEG imaging technology to map the brains of participants who were solving word problems. The researchers noticed that when participants had an insight that helped them solve a problem, there was increased activity in the participants' right temporal lobes (Chu & MacGregor, 2011; Gerlach et al., 2011; Jung-Beeman et al., 2004; Shen et al., 2017). Insight has also been connected to heightened brain activity in the cingulate, lateral, prefrontal, and posterior parietal cortices (Kovács et al., 2014; Schaafsma et al., 2015; Vogeley et al., 2001).

insight

when a solution to a problem presents itself suddenly

Summary of Problem-Solving Strategies

Drag the box below to its appropriate spot on the table.

Problem-Solving Strategy	Description	Example
Trial and error	Trying a potential solution and discarding that option if it fails while moving on to the next potential solution	Trying to remember a password by typing in every past password you've used that you remember until you find the correct one
Algorithm	Step-by-step procedures that we can follow to guarantee the ability to discover a solution to a particular problem	Trying to solve the combination to a lock by entering every possible number combination systematically
Means-end analysis	Examining the difference between the initial state and the goal state and then forming subgoals that will get you closer to the goal state	You decide that you want to work as a doctor who treats children with cancer. You consider your current job and imagine all the steps you'll need to achieve before you can start practicing as a doctor.
Working backward	Starting at the goal state and then working your way backward to determine a solution	You have $50 to spend at the grocery store so each time you put an item in your cart, you subtract the amount from $50
Insight	When the solution you've been looking for suddenly pops into your head	You are trying to fit a large piece of furniture through a door and suddenly realize how to angle the furniture so that it will fit

Start Over

CULTURAL INFLUENCES ON PROBLEM SOLVING Culture is also an important influence on the process of problem solving. For example, people from Eastern cultures tend to engage in more **holistic thinking**, or a focus on the "whole" or interconnectedness of systems and objects. Westerners, on the other hand, engage in more **analytic thinking**, or a focus on breaking down the whole into parts or details (Miyamoto, 2013; Nisbett et al., 2001; Nisbett, 2010). Holistic thinking focuses on context to a greater degree, while analytic thinking involves more formal logic. You can imagine that these different ways of perceiving and thinking about the world lead to different strategies and strengths/weaknesses when it comes to problem solving. For example, medical problems are treated differently based on Eastern holistic approaches (e.g., focusing on total health including mind, body, and spirit) versus Western approaches that are more analytical (e.g., focusing on and treating the specific symptom or problem).

holistic thinking

a focus on the "whole" or interconnectedness of systems and objects

analytic thinking

breaking down a problem into multiple parts to find a solution

Challenges with Problem Solving

LO 7.4 Describe different problem-solving difficulties.

In March 2005, Elaine Bromiley was wheeled back to surgery for a fairly routine procedure to straighten her nose and clear her sinuses. Her husband, Martin Bromiley, drove their 6-year-old son and 5-year-old daughter back home as the surgery was conducted. Martin then received a life-changing call saying that Elaine was not waking up from the anesthesia. He arrived back at the hospital to be informed that she had responded poorly to the anesthesia and had been deprived of oxygen while the physicians struggled to intubate her. Elaine died after being in a coma for a week. After an investigation, Martin discovered that her death was caused by a simple error. As the team of surgeons and anesthesiologists struggled to get the tube down her throat that would provide oxygen, they became so focused on getting her intubated that they forgot that there was another solution to the problem—perform a tracheotomy to provide the much-needed oxygen. After 25 minutes of oxygen deprivation, they were successfully able to intubate Elaine, but it was too late. As a pilot who had been specifically trained to detect and avoid these types of errors, Martin instantly recognized the cognitive trap called fixation (Leslie, 2014). **Fixation** can be described as the inability to see a problem from a fresh perspective because of our tendency to become stuck in our thinking. Because of his personal experience, Martin Bromiley has been leading a movement to reduce the risk of medical errors related to fixation that focuses on the training that pilots have been undergoing for years. While most problems are not as critical as the one faced by surgeons or pilots, they are susceptible to the same types of cognitive errors that we all face in our attempts to solve problems.

One type of fixation is known of as a **mental set**, or a preexisting state of mind we use to solve problems because it's helped us solve similar problems in the past. A mental set is especially helpful for simple, everyday tasks. However, our mental sets can sometimes interfere with problem solving when a different strategy needs to be considered (Koppel & Storm, 2014). Consider the example in the following video.

fixation

the tendency to become entrenched in thinking a certain way, which leads to the inability to see a problem from a fresh perspective

mental set

a preexisting state of mind used to solve problems because it helped solve similar problems in the past

Problem Solving Difficulties: Confirmation Bias, Functional Fixedness, and Mental Sets

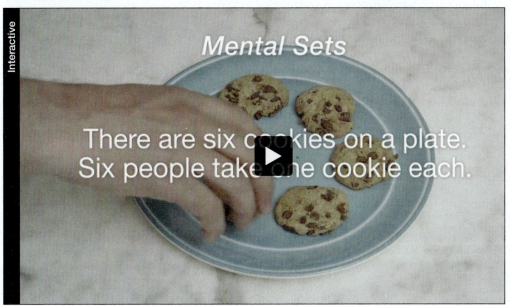

Some research has shown that expertise in a certain domain can actually make us more susceptible to mental sets (Ricks et al., 2007; Wiley & Jarosc, 2012). One of the reasons you want an expert to complete your root canal is that he or she has done the same procedure successfully hundreds of times before. However, if any anomalies exist, an expert may find it more difficult than someone with less experience to engage in problem solving because it can be challenging to "think outside the box."

Functional Fixedness

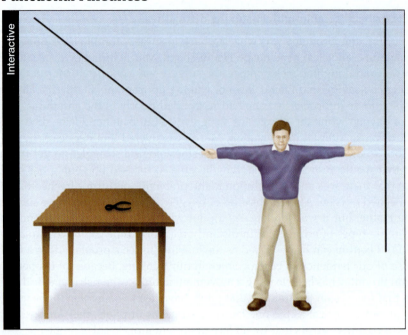

Interactive

Now consider the problem above. How can this person tie the two strings together if he can't reach both at the same time? Any ideas? In fact, he could use the pliers as a pendulum to swing the second string close to him.

How'd you do? If you couldn't find the solution, you probably were a victim of **functional fixedness**, a bias that limits your ability to think about objects in unconventional ways. You might not have considered an unconventional use of the pliers, which were the key to solving the problem. By attaching the pliers to the end of one string, you could swing them like a pendulum to reach the other string and tie a knot (Maier, 1931).

As the "two strings" problem demonstrates, it can help to take a novel perspective or pay attention to unusual or seemingly unimportant elements when you're trying to solve a difficult problem. It also doesn't hurt to keep a positive attitude: Your mood can affect your success with a problem (Fredrickson, 2000; Vacharkulksemsuk & Fredrickson, 2013; Vogelgesang et al., 2014). When you are in a bad mood, your perceptions and thoughts become restricted, and you will probably find it harder to "think outside the box."

functional fixedness

a bias that limits the ability to think about objects in unconventional ways

Quiz for Module 7.3–7.4

1. When you are faced with the problem of needing to figure out how to feed 10 people with the food currently in your refrigerator, what is the initial state of the problem?

   a. No idea for a meal to feed a large group of people quickly

   b. Final solution of making soup

   c. Inventory of all the items in your refrigerator

   d. List of recipes that you know how to prepare

2. Max wants to bake a cake for his girlfriend for her birthday. He has never done this before, but he finds a recipe for a seven-layer chocolate cake and proceeds to follow the instructions step-by-step. The result is a wonderful cake that impresses his girlfriend. What problem-solving strategy did Max use?

   a. Algorithm   **b.** Trial-and-error

   c. Heuristic   **d.** Goal state

3. The inability to see a problem from a different perspective is called _____.

   a. mental set   **b.** fixation

   c. functional fixedness   **d.** confirmation bias

4. An expert may become susceptible to this problem-solving difficulty because they are used to solving problems in the same way each time with success.

   a. Confirmation bias   **b.** Functional fixedness

   c. Expertise fixation   **d.** Mental set

Module 7.5–7.7: Decision Making

There are times when problem solving leads directly to decision making. For example, when there are several potential solutions to a problem, how do people decide which option to pursue? Decisions have to be made constantly throughout your day, and the following images demonstrate just a few of the decisions you have to make just to begin each day.

Daily Decisions

Just how do people make decisions? What parts of the brain are most active in the process of decision making? Are there systematic errors that everyone makes when confronted with decisions related to uncertainty?

How People Make Decisions

LO 7.5 **Identify different theories about how people make decisions.**

Imagine your friend asks you to sign up for the latest trend in fitness classes (e.g., trampoline cardio, aqua cycling, or indoor surfing). Would you consider signing up, or would you be skeptical? You have probably formed an opinion about these methods using your **judgment**. Judgment is a skill that allows us to form opinions, reach conclusions, and evaluate situations objectively and critically. Judgment informs our **decision making**—the process of selecting and rejecting available options.

THEORIES OF DECISION MAKING   Once we've been given a decision to make, how do we arrive at a conclusion? **Rational choice theory** states that we make decisions by determining how likely each outcome of that decision is as well as the positive or negative value of each outcome (Coleman & Fararo, 1992; Dekker, 2017; Jennings & Beaudry-Cyr, 2014; Scott, 2000). If you needed to decide whether to purchase a tablet versus a laptop, what would you do?

According to rational choice theory, you'd determine the pros and cons of buying each device as well as the likelihood of each of these pros and cons. Then, if the value of buying a tablet outweighed the value of buying a laptop, you'd likely make the purchase. While this sounds ideal, criticism has focused on the fact that the assumptions underlying rational choice theory may be inaccurate (Blais, 2000; Hodgson, 2012). For example, to make decisions according to this model, people must (1) have access to all relevant information and (2) be able to adequately and efficiently analyze the information (Coleman & Fararo, 1992; Jennings & Beaudry-Cyr, 2014; Scott, 2000). You can likely think of many times when you did not have all

judgment

a skill that allows people to form opinions, reach conclusions, and evaluate situations objectively and critically

decision making

the process of selecting and rejecting a course of action from several available options

rational choice theory

the theory that decisions are made logically by determining how likely each outcome of that decision is as well as the positive or negative value of each outcome

Rational Decision Making

Interactive

the relevant information that would be helpful in making a decision (e.g., how often do people need to replace their laptop versus tablet?) or the time to be able to adequately research or analyze the information (e.g., school starts tomorrow and you need to bring either a laptop or tablet with you to your first class).

Kahneman and his colleague Tversky proposed an alternate decision-making theory called **prospect theory**, which describes how people make decisions in situations that involve elements of risk. In general, we avoid risk in situations where we stand to gain, but our behavior becomes more risk seeking when we face a loss (Barberis, 2012; Camerer, 2004; Kahneman & Tversky, 1979). Imagine you are a contestant on a game show. The host gives you a check for $1,000. You can either keep the check, thereby guaranteeing $1,000, or you can exchange the check for the envelope in the host's hand. There's a 50 percent chance that the envelope contains $2,500, but there's a 50 percent chance that the envelope contains nothing at all. In this situation, most people choose to avoid risk and stick with the $1,000 they are sure to win. However, try to imagine a slightly more sadistic game show: The host says that if you do nothing, he's going to take $1,000 from you. However, he offers you another envelope. There's a 50 percent chance that the envelope contains a card that will let you keep all your money, and there's a 50 percent chance that it contains a card that will allow the host to take $2,500 from you. Do you take the envelope and risk losing $,2500, or do you refuse the envelope and hand over $1,000? Faced with this decision, most people would rather run the risk of losing $2,500 to have a chance to keep all their money. Prospect theory suggests that we have different attitudes toward risk depending on the situation we're facing.

prospect theory

the tendency to avoid risk in situations where we stand to gain but to become more risk seeking when facing a potential loss

NEURAL CONTRIBUTIONS TO DECISION MAKING   When your friend makes a decision you don't agree with, you may wonder what could possibly have been going through her brain when she made that choice. What *was* going through her brain? One answer might be the neurotransmitter dopamine. Research has found that the presence of dopamine in the brain helps us make decisions that lead to good outcomes and avoid bad outcomes (Dalley & Roiser, 2012; Jenni et al., 2017; St. Onge & Floresco, 2008; Treadway et al., 2012). A large amount of dopamine is present in the basal ganglia, an area of the brain that seems crucial to decision making (Thibaut, 2016). When we're faced with a decision, activity in the basal ganglia picks up, and bursts of dopamine help us choose the most rewarding or favorable potential outcome.

What happens, though, if a choice that makes us feel good isn't necessarily the best choice for us? For instance, if you want to eat more healthily, you probably don't want to decide to eat a delicious frosted cupcake, but the dopamine in your brain will cause you to identify that cupcake as a tasty reward. Luckily, your brain has executive control systems that inhibit the pleasurable response to the cupcake so you can stick to your original plan and snack on something healthier instead. These systems are generally thought to be centered in the brain's frontal regions (with significant additional input from the thalamus) (Gläscher et al., 2012; Wunderlich et al., 2009).

Obstacles in Decision Making

LO 7.6   Recognize obstacles that can hinder decision making.

Most people can quickly recall at least a short list of poor decisions they have made in the past. Have you ever made an impulse purchase you later regretted? Has peer pressure ever played a role in getting you to do or say something you wish you hadn't? The process of decision making is complex, and several obstacles can lead people astray when making decisions.

Our framework for understanding decision making is often based on the assumption that this process involves logical and voluntary cognitive processes like the rational choice theory suggests. However, there are times when decisions must be made quickly and automatically without time to rationally consider the options at hand. For example, if someone pulls out in front of you on the road, you have to make an immediate and automatic decision—do you slam on the brakes, swerve the car to the right or left, or do both simultaneously? Daniel Kahneman, the only psychologist to ever receive a Nobel Prize, published a book, *Thinking, Fast and Slow*, (2011) outlining two different types of thinking that lead to decisions. He described System 1 thinking, which is automatic and effortless. On the other hand, System 2 thinking is slower, more deliberative, and requires more cognitive effort. Figure 7.3 outlines the differences between System 1 and System 2 thinking.

When you are asked to compute a simple sum (e.g., 2 + 2) you are using System 1 to answer; however, when you are asked to compute a more difficult problem (e.g., 17 × 24), you are using System 2 to answer. System 2 works in the background and can monitor System 1 to some extent. However, for the most part, System 1 is the engine behind many of our day-to-day decisions and actions and can often lead us to make predictable errors in judgment. Several of the heuristics discussed in this section have been the focus of Kahneman and his colleagues over decades of research.

FRAMING   The way a decision or problem is presented, or the **framing**, of an issue can greatly influence the decisions we make. To understand more about framing, consider the following questions on the next page:

If you've ever watched a political debate, you have witnessed the powerful impact of framing. Using the same set of statistics, two people can frame the numbers in a way that actually supports each of their differing views. For example, one candidate can tout that his/her policy has been shown to be effective for 90 percent of people and the opposing candidate can also point out that the opponent's policy will fail for one out of ten people with equal validity.

framing
the way a decision or problem is presented

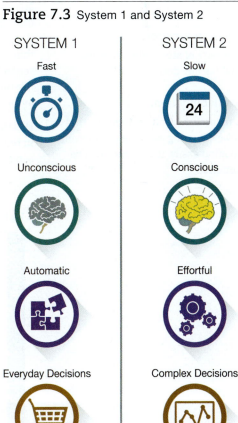

Figure 7.3 System 1 and System 2

SYSTEM 1	SYSTEM 2
Fast	Slow
Unconscious	Conscious
Automatic	Effortful
Everyday Decisions	Complex Decisions
Error Prone	Reliable

The Importance of Framing

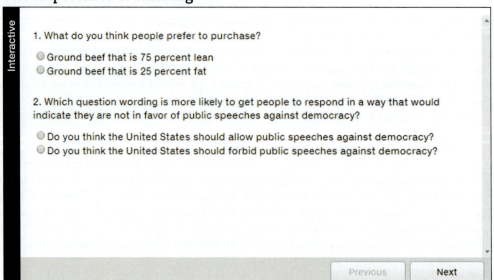

1. What do you think people prefer to purchase?

○ Ground beef that is 75 percent lean
○ Ground beef that is 25 percent fat

2. Which question wording is more likely to get people to respond in a way that would indicate they are not in favor of public speeches against democracy?

○ Do you think the United States should allow public speeches against democracy?
○ Do you think the United States should forbid public speeches against democracy?

Previous   Next

Framing has been a powerful component of social and economic policies, media, and advertising. A recent study examined the impact of framing on people's willingness to spend more money on certain products that are believed to contribute to combatting climate change. People were more willing to incur an increased cost when it was described as a "carbon offset" than when it was described as a "carbon tax" (Hardisty et al., 2010). Sometimes, if we're presented with a decision that can be viewed through too many conflicting frames, or if we have too many alternatives to choose from, we develop **decision aversion**, the state of attempting to avoid making any decision at all.

decision aversion

the state of attempting to avoid making any decision at all

HEURISTICS   As with problem solving, people often use heuristics, or mental shortcuts to aid in making decisions. One common mental shortcut, the **availability heuristic**, tells us that if we can bring examples of an event to mind easily, that event must be common.

availability heuristic

a mental shortcut that tells us that if we can bring examples of an event to mind easily, that event must be common

Estimating Cause of Death

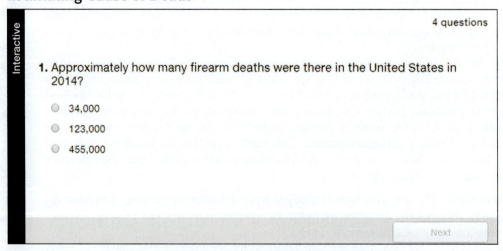

4 questions

1. Approximately how many firearm deaths were there in the United States in 2014?

○ 34,000

○ 123,000

○ 455,000

Next

Consider your estimates to the questions above. Like most people, you may have overestimated the number of deaths due to firearms. This is likely due to the availability heuristic—on the evening news, a firearm death, and especially a homicide, is likely to receive more attention than a death related to heart disease or choking. This means that many examples can quickly be accessed when you are asked about the number of firearm deaths, leading you to overestimate their frequency. Suicides are actually the most common form of firearm death but they receive much less media coverage and are therefore often underestimated in terms of frequency. The following video provides a few more examples of the availability heuristic.

The Availability Heuristic

Availability heuristic
a mental shortcut used to judge the likelihood or frequency of events based on information available in memory

Tversky and Kahneman (1973) were the first to identify the availability heuristic, and they suggested that this is an unconscious process in which people quickly judge how easily they can think of examples as an accurate assessment of reality. Consider the earlier anagram problem for "dormitory" again. Rather than using the laborious algorithm approach, you could look at all the letters and determine which ones would be most likely to be at the beginning of a word using the availability heuristic. For example, how quickly can you think of words that start with the letter "d" versus the letter "o"? You will mostly likely think of many more words that start with "d" which will lead you to assume that this is a more common first letter (and you are correct). Therefore, you would spend more time looking for a solution to the anagram that starts with "d" than "o." The availability heuristic can be very helpful in narrowing down options when solving problems or making decisions. However, as the first example demonstrates, using this heuristic can actually lead you to make mistakes.

Make A Guess

Survey: Make A Guess

Read the following description:

"Tom W. is of high intelligence, although lacking in true creativity. He has a need for order and clarity, and for neat and tidy systems in which every detail finds its appro-priate place. His writing is rather dull and mechanical, occasionally enlivened by somewhat corny puns and by flashes of imagination of the sci-fi type. He has a strong drive for competence. He seems to feel little sympathy for other people and does not enjoy interacting with others. Self-centered, he nonetheless has a deep moral sense."

Tom is currently a graduate student at a university that has 50 percent of graduate students enrolled in humanities and education, 25 percent of students enrolled in social science and social work, 15 percent of students enrolled in business, and 10 percent of students enrolled in engineering. Given what you've read about Tom, which of the following programs do you think he is currently attending?

○ Humanities and education

○ Social science and social work

○ Business

○ Engineering

You just participated in a version of an experiment conducted by Kahneman and Tversky (1973), showing that people tend to ignore important information about the base rate (or how often something normally occurs) in favor of information that fits with our own experiences or beliefs. In this study, the base rate chance of any individual being in an engineering program is only 10 percent, but because the description of Tom may fit with your preexisting notion of engineers, you are likely to ignore the base rate and predict that Tom is in an engineering program much more often than other programs. This phenomenon was termed the *representativeness heuristic* by Kahneman and Tversky.

Representativeness Heuristic

representativeness heuristic

solving problems or making decisions about the probability of an event under uncertainty by comparing it to our existing prototype of the event

The **representativeness heuristic** is used when trying to solve problems or make decisions about the probability of an event by comparing it to our existing prototype of the event. For example, if you hear that you will be meeting an older woman who is a great cook and loves children, you might assume she is a grandmother because the description fits with your own idea, or prototype, of what a grandmother is like. Once again, this mental shortcut helps us in our attempt to solve problems quickly or make rapid decisions but it can also lead us astray.

Are You a Safe Driver?

Survey: Are You a Safe Driver?

We would like to know about what you think about how safely you drive an automobile. All drivers are not equally safe drivers. We want you to compare your own skill to the skills of other people taking this psychology course. By definition, there is a least safe and a most safe driver in this group. We want you to indicate your own estimated position among your peers in this course. Of course, this is a difficult question because you do not know all the people in this course much less how safely they drive. But please make the most accurate estimate you can.

"I estimate that I am as safe a driver as _____ of my classmates." (Higher percentiles represent a judgment that you are a safer driver).

0–10%	11–20%	21–30%	31–40%	41–50%	51–60%	61–70%	71–80%	81–90%	91–100%

OVERCONFIDENCE AND BELIEF BIAS   Did you estimate that you were a safer driver than at least 50 percent of your classmates? If so, you are not alone. An early famous study showed that 93 percent of Americans rated themselves as better drivers than the median, the 50 percent point (Svenson, 1981). Clearly, these estimates cannot be accurate, demonstrating that we are sometimes more confident in our own abilities or decisions than we are accurate. Have you ever been 100 percent sure you were right about something, only to find out you were completely mistaken? One common error in reasoning is **overconfidence**, or our tendency to think we are more knowledgeable or accurate than we really are. The subprime mortgage crisis that reared its head in 2008 was due in part to overconfidence on the part of both lenders and home buyers, many of whom were wrongly convinced they'd be able to make payments on time or make huge amounts of money from home sales. Of course, many people who didn't get caught up in this housing debacle believed after the fact that they'd never have gotten involved in such a risky action, but this response may simply be an example of a form of overconfidence called **hindsight bias**, our tendency to overestimate our previous knowledge of situations.

Our own belief systems can also impact our reasoning and decision making at times. Consider the following statements:

- Premise 1: Women enjoy watching romantic comedies.
- Premise 2: Men are not women.
- Conclusion: Men do not enjoy watching romantic comedies.

Does this conclusion sound logical to you? If it does, you've fallen victim to **belief bias**, the effect that occurs when our beliefs distort our logical thinking. The two premises allow for the possibility that some men might like watching romantic comedies, but your own beliefs about men's preferred movies might have led you to conclude the opposite. Our beliefs have incredible power over our judgments and reasoning skills: Even when we are presented with evidence that refutes our beliefs, we find it difficult to abandon those beliefs. This tendency is known as **belief perseverance**. We are particularly vulnerable to belief perseverance if our beliefs have been stated publicly or if the erroneous belief enhances our self-image in some way (Guenther & Alicke, 2008).

overconfidence
the tendency to think we are more knowledgeable or accurate in our judgments than we really are

hindsight bias
our tendency to overestimate our previous knowledge of situations

belief bias
the effect that occurs when our own beliefs distort or bias our ability to reason logically

belief perseverance
a tendency to hold on to beliefs, even when we are presented with evidence that refutes our beliefs

Adaptive Pathway 7.1: Heuristics

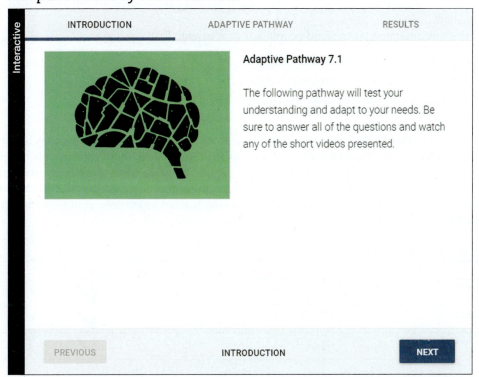

Confirmation Bias

LO 7.7 **Describe the role of confirmation bias in decision making.**

If you are a sports fan, you've probably had the experience of watching "your" team play while sitting near a fan of the opposing team. Invariably, the referee/official/umpire will make a questionable call at some point. Replay after replay, you simply cannot see how anyone else could not agree with your side of the argument (which, of course, is in favor of your team). Meanwhile, your friend feels equally convinced that the call should have gone in favor of the opponent (the team he/she supports). In these situations, who is right? It turns out that we are all susceptible to specific types of cognitive bias related to these situations. When we already believe something is true, we tend to look for evidence that proves our beliefs, and

When a referee makes a call against "your" team, it's very difficult to understand how anyone else would agree with the call. This is due, in part, to the confirmation bias.

confirmation bias

the belief that something is already true and the tendency to therefore look for evidence that proves our beliefs while failing to notice evidence that disproves those beliefs

we tend not to notice evidence that disproves those beliefs. This phenomenon is known as **confirmation bias**—although we may think we're being objective, we're actually trying to confirm our previously held opinions. For example, if you already think the media are biased against your particular political beliefs, you're more likely to notice those news stories that *are* biased against your beliefs, but you may not notice those stories that are unbiased or those that are biased *toward* your beliefs.

The confirmation bias has been coined "the mother of all biases" by prominent psychologist Scott Lilienfeld (2015), and Nickerson (1998) who wrote "If one were to attempt to identify a single problematic aspect of human reasoning that deserves attention above all others, the confirmation bias would have to be among the candidates for consideration" (p. 175). Everyone appears susceptible to the confirmation bias, and the consequences of this cognitive bias are often mild. However, Lilienfeld points out that there can also be very serious effects as "virtually all violent regimes fan the flames of extreme confirmation bias in their citizens, especially their youth, by presenting them with only one point of view and assiduously insulating them from all others" (Lilienfeld et al., 2009 p. 391).

The confirmation bias can lead people astray in essentially three ways:

1. Influencing how we seek information
2. Influencing how we interpret information
3. Influencing how we remember information

BIASED INFORMATION SEEKING Imagine your teacher tells you to play a game. She puts up three numbers on the screen (2, 4, 6) and says she is creating these three numbers using a rule in her head. Your job is to guess the rule. You're going to guess the rule by giving the teacher three numbers, and she will tell you if they do or do not follow the rule. Click on the numbers that each student provided along with the teacher's response about whether they meet the rule or not.

DOES IT FIT THE RULE?

	Numbers Proposed	Does It Meet the Teacher's Rule?
Student 1	2, 4, 6	✔
Student 2	8, 10, 12	✔
Student 3	30, 32, 34	✔

What Is the Rule?

> **Interactive**
>
> 1. Student 4 decides to guess the rule. He says that the rule is "increasing even numbers."
> How confident are you that he is correct?
>
> ○ 0 percent
> ○ 25 percent
> ○ 50 percent
> ○ 75 percent
> ○ 100 percent
>
> | Previous | **Next** |

Actually, the teacher's rule was "three increasing numbers." When confronted with this problem, most people get it wrong. This is due to our tendency to seek out information that confirms our beliefs or hypotheses while neglecting to seek out information that would be disconfirming. For example, it's easy to understand why someone would hypothesize that the rule was "increasing even numbers," given the first three numbers the teacher presented. Most people then seek to confirm their hypothesis by testing out numbers that would fit within the rule. However, people rarely think to seek feedback about numbers that would disconfirm their hypothesis. For example, asking about uneven increasing numbers (3, 5, 7) or decreasing numbers (8, 6, 4) would help rule out a hypothesis.

Like this exercise demonstrates, once people have a theory or hypothesis about something, they tend to seek out information in a biased manner. Rather than looking for information that might disconfirm a theory or belief, people tend to be biased to search for information that would prove them right. This tendency is called a *positive test* because you are seeking out information that would be positive toward your theory or belief. A *negative test*, on the other hand, would be seeking out information or asking questions that would disconfirm your original hypothesis. Remember the game of "20 questions" where one person thinks of some object and the other person gets to ask 20 yes/no questions to try to correctly identify the object? After you've determined that the object is alive, smaller than a bread box, and has four legs, you may develop a theory that the person is thinking of some type of pet. A positive test in this case would be the question "is it a pet?" while a negative test would be the question "is it a wild animal"? Both are equally valid questions, but people are much more likely to use positive tests when seeking out information (Klayman & Ha, 1987; Zuckerman et al., 1995), making them potentially vulnerable to obtaining skewed or biased information.

One example of the tendency to seek out information that confirms our existing beliefs comes from studies examining the habits of people who identify themselves as politically conservative or liberal. According to a 2014 Pew Research Center survey described in Figure 7.4, people who already have liberal or conservative beliefs tend to seek out sources of news and reading material that are the most consistent with their views (Mitchell et al., 2014). In fact, reading information in online formats has actually contributed further to this phenomenon as search engines and social networking sites automatically analyze your search histories and preferences and filter out information in opposition to your views while serving up only information perceived to be consistent with your interests (Pariser, 2011). After the tumultuous 2016 U.S. presidential election, some social psychologists further studied this phenomenon. One recent study showed that both liberals and conservatives turned down a chance to win money if it required them to read about opposing views regarding same-sex marriage (Frimer et al., 2017).

BIASED INTERPRETATION Once we have a theory or belief about something, we tend to interpret any data or evidence we encounter in ways that confirm our original hypothesis. This tendency has been supported in numerous laboratory experiments (Baron, 2000;

Figure 7.4 Liberal versus Conservative

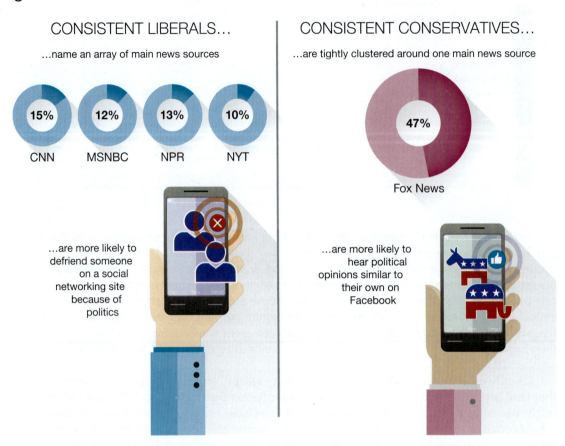

CONSISTENT LIBERALS...

...name an array of main news sources

| 15% | 12% | 13% | 10% |
| CNN | MSNBC | NPR | NYT |

...are more likely to defriend someone on a social networking site because of politics

CONSISTENT CONSERVATIVES...

...are tightly clustered around one main news source

47%

Fox News

...are more likely to hear political opinions similar to their own on Facebook

Journal Prompt: Biased News Exposure

What are the potential consequences (both personal and societal) of exposure to news that only fits with your worldview? How does this relate to the confirmation bias?

Devine et al., 1990; Kida, 2006; Kunda, 1999), but this effect is also found in real-world examples. Consider a recent legal case that appears to have been highly influenced by the confirmation bias.

In 2000, David Camm returned home from playing basketball with his friends to discover his wife and two young children murdered in their garage. The police suspected Camm early on, and he was convicted of the murders in two separate trials. However, both convictions were overturned on appeal, and he was later acquitted in 2013 in his third murder trial. It turned out that his conviction was made almost entirely on the evidence of 8 small blood stains on his shirt. Camm claimed that the stains were incurred when he embraced his daughter's body, but the prosecutor's blood splatter analyst testified that the stains were caused by splatter from the gunshots themselves. It turns out that there was DNA evidence from a convicted felon, Charles Boney, at the scene. When this evidence was finally presented in 2005, the prosecution convicted Boney but continued in their attempt to prosecute Camm as an accomplice because Boney claimed that Camm was the actual shooter. When it was discovered that (1) the blood splatter analyst in the first trial actually knew little to nothing about blood splatter (he had read one book on the subject years before); (2) the DNA from Boney was actually found on two of the victims, contradicting his claim that he never touched the victims; and (3) the prosecutor had pressured a forensic expert to falsely claim that Camm's DNA had also been found, Camm was finally acquitted. It is likely that the police and prosecutor's early suspicion about

Camm's guilt led them to dismiss any evidence to the contrary and misinterpret any ambiguous information as evidence of his guilt.

BIASED MEMORY Even when people are confronted with data that is contrary to their beliefs or expectations, they may not recall that information as well as confirmatory information (Greenwald, 1980; Scherer et al., 2013; Schwartzstein, 2014). For example, one study provided participants with a description of a week in the life of "Jane," which included examples of both introversion and extraversion. A few days after reading the description, the participants were asked to judge if Jane would either be a good real estate agent or a good librarian. The participants who were asked if she would be a good real estate agent remembered Jane as being extraverted, while the participants who were asked if she would be a good librarian remembered Jane as being introverted. Then, when participants were asked about Jane's suitability for the other position, the participants stuck with their initial assessment, saying that she would be unsuited for the real estate position if they had first evaluated her as introverted or saying she would be unsuited for the librarian position if they had first evaluated her as extraverted (Snyder & Cantor, 1979).

Quiz for Module 7.5–7.7

1. Stuart is trying to make a decision on whether to spend money to remodel his kitchen. He makes a list of the pros/cons for each choice and the possible outcomes for each choice. Stuart is engaging in which decision-making theory?
   a. Logical choice theory
   b. Judgment theory
   c. Prospect theory
   d. Rational choice theory

2. Which neurotransmitter helps people make decisions that lead to good outcomes.
   a. Endorphin
   b. Serotonin
   c. Dopamine
   d. GABA

3. Maria is telling Lupe that she is going to meet a friend of hers who is a doctor, loves to play golf, and drives a red sports car. Lupe is surprised when Maria's friend shows up and is a female. Lupe has engaged in what type of heuristic?
   a. Representativeness heuristic
   b. Availability heuristic
   c. Stereotype heuristic
   d. Overconfidence bias

4. Regan frequently hears stories on the news about cars being stolen. In a criminology class, he was asked to guess how frequently vehicles are stolen. According to the availability heuristic, Regan is likely to _____ the frequency.
   a. underestimate
   b. overestimate
   c. bias accurately estimate
   d. be unwilling to estimate

5. Even when we are presented with information that shows our beliefs to be incorrect, we often find it difficult to abandon those beliefs due to _____.
   a. belief nonadherence
   b. confirmation bias
   c. belief perseverance
   d. hindsight bias

6. When we have a strongly held belief, we sometimes seek out information to prove the belief while ignoring information that might disprove the belief. What is this phenomenon called?
   a. Consideration bias   b. Hindsight bias
   c. Belief bias   d. Confirmation bias

7. People tend to seek out news sources that are consistent with their own political views, which is an example of _____.
   a. hindsight bias   b. biased interpretation
   c. biased memory   d. biased information seeking

Module 7.8–7.9: Creativity

Imagine you are a contestant in a new reality television show. You are told that you will be left stranded in an unknown area for an indeterminate period of time with uncertain supplies. You get to have a role in choosing your teammates by designating certain characteristics you think would be helpful in this situation. While characteristics such as physical strength and confidence would certainly be helpful, your best bet might be to choose the most creative thinker to be on your team. After all, it wasn't necessarily the brawn that won the day in books/movies like *The Hunger Games*, but the brain of characters like Beetee and Wiress who were able to creatively adapt to the situation.

Convergent and Divergent Thinking

LO 7.8 **Distinguish between convergent and divergent thinking.**

What exactly do we mean by creativity? Because creativity can be expressed in such diverse ways, defining the concept can be a bit tricky. After all, the inventor of the remote control, Eugene Polley, and J. K. Rowling (author of the *Harry Potter* fiction books) likely have little in common, but both are clearly creative thinkers. Defined broadly, **creativity** is the ability to come up with new ideas that can lead to a particular outcome. There are two components of the definition. First, in order for an idea to be considered creative, it must be novel and not simply the extension of a preexisting idea. Second, the idea must be functional or workable in some way.

You might be wondering if creativity and intelligence are the same thing. Discussed in detail in Chapter 8, intelligence is defined as the ability to learn and adapt from experience, solve problems, and apply knowledge in new situations (Legg & Hutter, 2007). While there is certainly some overlap in the concepts of intelligence and creativity, it also appears that there are some differences. A meta-analysis evaluating the correlation between intelligence and creativity in 21 different studies with 45,880 participants found that the correlation between the two variables was only .17, suggesting that the two variables are not that closely related (Kim, 2005). The relationship between intelligence and creativity appears to be one in which a certain level of intelligence is necessary for someone to think creatively, but being intelligent doesn't necessarily guarantee that someone is creative. The **threshold theory of creativity** states that above average intelligence (typically defined as an IQ of at least 120) is a necessary condition for someone to be able to engage in the thinking processes that lead to creativity (Guilford, 1967). While evidence has sometimes been mixed regarding the threshold theory (e.g., Cho et al., 2010; Fuchs-Beauchamp et al., 1993; Preckel et al., 2006; Welter et al., 2016), data from a recent study supported the threshold theory (Jauk et al., 2013). However, this study did not necessarily support a cutoff IQ of 120, showing that there were also changes in the relationship between creativity and intelligence with an IQ cutoff of 104. So perhaps, only an average to slightly above average IQ is needed for creativity to develop as shown in Figure 7.5.

creativity

the ability to come up with new ideas that can lead to a particular outcome

threshold theory of creativity

states that above average intelligence is a necessary condition for someone to be able to engage in the thinking processes that lead to creativity

Figure 7.5 Threshold Theory of Creativity

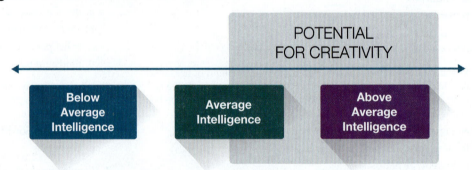

Guilford (1967) was the first to discuss the difference between convergent and divergent thinking and how they relate to creativity. **Convergent thinking** occurs when we are confronted with well-defined, straightforward problems that have a right/wrong answer. Most of the tasks you are required to perform in school require convergent thinking. For example, multiple choice, fill-in-the-blank, and true/false exams are all forms of assessment that rely on convergent thinking strategies. Accuracy and speed are often goals of convergent thinking tasks, and this type of thinking relies on logical step-by-step processes in order to reach the desired outcome.

Divergent thinking, on the other hand, includes thought processes used to generate many different possible solutions to a problem. For example, think about the following question: "How many uses can you think of for a piece of string?" This type of question leads to divergent thinking. As this example demonstrates, divergent thinking is very similar to the process of brainstorming where you try to generate many possible solutions to a problem. Problems that don't have a right/wrong answer are particularly conducive to divergent thinking strategies. Many tests of creativity are actually measures of divergent thinking strategies.

convergent thinking

thinking that occurs when we are confronted with a well-defined, straightforward problem that has a single right/wrong answer

divergent thinking

thought processes used to generate many different possible solutions to a problem

Divergent vs Convergent Thinking

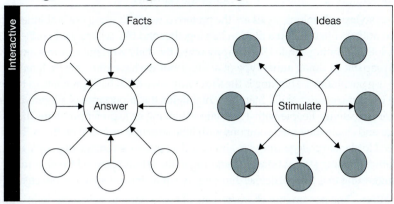

Sternberg's Theory

LO 7.9   **Explain Sternberg's theory of creative thinking.**

Robert Sternberg and his colleagues have proposed the **investment theory of creativity**, which outlines the critical ingredients for creative thinking (Sternberg & Lubart, 1991, 1992, 1995). This theory is based on the economic principal of "buy low and sell high," referring to the fact that creative people are able to take ideas that are new or not highly valued and transform them through the process of creativity to become valuable. According to this theory, six different ingredients must be present for creativity to emerge (Sternberg, 2006).

investment theory of creativity
theory that creative people are able to take ideas that are new or not highly valued and transform them through the process of creativity to become valuable

1. **Intellectual skills:**   As the previous discussion highlighted, some relationship exists between intellectual skills and creativity. Sternberg highlights three different intellectual skills particularly critical for creativity, which include: (a) the ability to see problems in a new light, (b) the ability to think critically about ideas and to know when to pursue an idea and when to give up, and (c) the ability to effectively communicate your ideas to others so that the ideas will be valued. These three abilities interact to discover and promote creative products.

2. **Knowledge:**   To make a meaningful contribution in any field, you must have a certain level of knowledge about the topic in terms of the history and current state of the field. For example, if you have an idea for an app that will help people manage their finances, you need to have an understanding of personal finance, how current technology has attempted to solve the problem, and the obstacles to implementing your idea. However, it's also true that knowledge can sometimes blind us because the more we know about something, the harder it becomes to think about things outside of our entrenched frameworks. The story of the school bus that got stuck trying to go under an overpass illustrates this idea. The bus driver and other experts floated several ideas to remove a portion of the bridge or cut

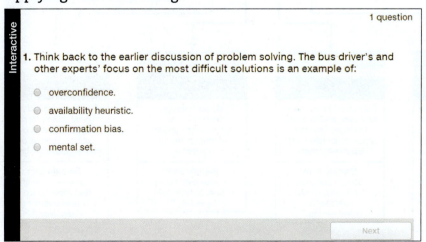

Applying Your Knowledge

1 question

1. Think back to the earlier discussion of problem solving. The bus driver's and other experts' focus on the most difficult solutions is an example of:

○ overconfidence.

○ availability heuristic.

○ confirmation bias.

○ mental set.

Next

off the top of the bus. However, it took an inexperienced child to point out a much better solution—simply let some of the air out of the bus tires.

3. **Thinking styles:**   Thinking styles are the preferred ways for using one's abilities. For example, your text authors often attend a fitness class together and BW is happy when the daily workout features lots of running, while DH is happy when the daily workout features more weights. We are both capable of doing either type of activity, but we have different preferences in how we want to use our abilities. Thinking is the same way—we often have preferences for the ways we want to use our cognitive skills. Sternberg highlights the importance of a *legislative thinking style* in fostering creativity. People with a legislative thinking style prefer problems that require them to design and create their own solutions with little structure imposed on them. Turki (2012) surveyed 800 Jordanian college students and found a higher percentage of people endorsed using a legislative thinking style who were majoring in the arts as opposed to other major specializations, suggesting that this particular thinking style may indeed lead to more creativity.

4. **Personality:**   The personality characteristic of being open to new experiences appears to be the most predictive of creativity among people who already demonstrate adequate levels of intelligence (Chamorro-Premuzic & Reichenbacher, 2008; Jauk et al., 2013). The trait of openness leads to the curiosity and imagination necessary to think "outside the box."

   Sternberg also emphasizes the importance of being willing to take risks and refusing to conform to convention as personality characteristics that are particularly conducive to creativity.

5. **Motivation:**   When it comes to motivation, intrinsic motivation appears to be the key to creativity (Amabile, 2012). People are intrinsically motivated when they engage in a behavior for its own sake rather than the desire to obtain an external goal or reward. In other words, to be the most creative, people have to be truly interested in and passionate about their work.

6. **Environment:**   Finally, for creativity to be fostered, the environment must inspire, support, and reward creative ideas. For example, work environments foster creativity when employees are presented with the right level of challenge (not too much and not too little), overspecialization is not encouraged, fear of failure is low, and creative dissent is encouraged (Montuori, 2011).

One the most compelling components of Sternberg's investment theory of creativity is that it de-emphasizes natural creative talent while focusing instead on the fact that thinking creatively is a choice most people are capable of making. Sternberg discusses creativity as a "habit" that must be developed through effort and conscious decision making. This approach has significant implications for educational settings and in the workplace. To improve your own creativity, Robert Epstein and colleagues have suggested four skills you can cultivate (Epstein et al., 2008) see box on page 306.

"Thinking outside of the box is difficult for some people. Keep trying."

Components of Creativity

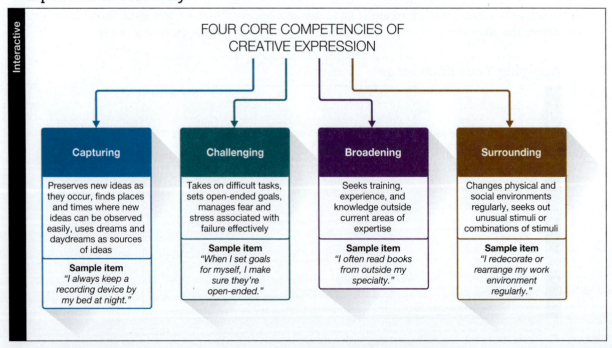

Interactive

FOUR CORE COMPETENCIES OF CREATIVE EXPRESSION

Capturing	Challenging	Broadening	Surrounding
Preserves new ideas as they occur, finds places and times where new ideas can be observed easily, uses dreams and daydreams as sources of ideas	Takes on difficult tasks, sets open-ended goals, manages fear and stress associated with failure effectively	Seeks training, experience, and knowledge outside current areas of expertise	Changes physical and social environments regularly, seeks out unusual stimuli or combinations of stimuli
Sample item *"I always keep a recording device by my bed at night."*	**Sample item** *"When I set goals for myself, I make sure they're open-ended."*	**Sample item** *"I often read books from outside my specialty."*	**Sample item** *"I redecorate or rearrange my work environment regularly."*

When Epstein and his colleagues used these four skills to implement creativity training for 74 city employees, they found these employees had increased their rate of generating new ideas by 55 percent, which was attributed to an increase of $600,000 in new revenue and a savings of $3.5 million due to innovative ways of implementing costs savings. In essence, this study demonstrated that creativity certainly pays.

Quiz for Module 7.8–7.9

1. What type of thinking allows many different solutions to a problem?

   a. Convergent thinking

   b. Divergent thinking

   c. Creativity

   d. Brainstorming

2. An example of convergent thinking would be a(n) _____.

   a. free writing exercise

   b. brainstorming session

   c. multiple-choice test

   d. open ended question

3. According to Sternberg's investment theory, which of the following is NOT an ingredient of creativity?

   a. Social skills

   b. Motivation

   c. Personality

   d. Intellectual skills

4. Which personality characteristic is the most predictive of creativity?

   a. Neuroticism

   b. Extraversion

   c. Introversion

   d. Openness to new experiences

Module 7.10–7.14: Language Structure and Development

Imagine traveling to a foreign country where you don't speak a word of the native language and no one there speaks English. Most English speakers traveling abroad rarely encounter this situation because English has become the most widely taught foreign language across the globe. In fact, an estimated 1 billion people are nonnative English speakers (British Council, 2014). But, if you found yourself in this situation, how would you communicate (assuming you can't use a translation app)? Facial expressions and body language would only get you so far. For example, if you want to know how much an item costs—how are you going to understand how to ask the question or understand the answer if you are able to convey the question? Spending one day in a situation like this will likely provide all the evidence necessary to prove that language is one of our most important cognitive abilities.

Language Structure

LO 7.10   **Identify the basic structure of language.**

Language—the system of symbols that enables us to communicate our ideas, thoughts, and feelings—plays a vital part in how we think. While an estimated 7,000 languages are spoken worldwide (Lewis et al., 2015), most languages have similar basic building blocks.

PHONEMES   **Phonemes** are the smallest units of sound possible in a language. Do you remember learning to read and being asked to try to "sound out the word?" If you saw the word "dog," you would sound the word out using its component phonemes. The "duh" sound of the "d" is one phoneme, the "ah" sound of the "o" is the second phoneme, and the "guh" sound of the "g" is the third phoneme. Phonemes are not always represented by single letters, however. For instance, the sound of letter blends such as "sh" or "th" represent as single phoneme. Conversely, a single letter can also represent more than one phoneme as is the case with different "g" sounds in words like "golf" versus "gesture." Phonemes in English are different from phonemes in other languages, making learning a second language challenging when phonemes significantly differ. For example, a Spanish speaker learning English might have difficulty with the sound of the "i" in the word "sit" because there is no equivalent phoneme in Spanish. Often, the word "sit" will sound more like "seat" when pronounced by a native Spanish speaker. On the other

language

the system of symbols that enables us to communicate our ideas, thoughts, and feelings

phonemes

the smallest units of sound that are possible in a language

hand, ask any English speaker who has taken Spanish classes, and they will tell you the trilled "rr" sound in Spanish is difficult to master because it has a different sound and meaning than a word pronounced with an "r" sound, a difference that doesn't exist in English. If you were to mispronounce the Spanish word "perro" (meaning "dog") without the trilled "rr" sound, you would be using an entirely different word (pero = but).

Spanish/English Phonemes

While hundreds of phonemes have been identified across all languages, no language uses all of them. The English language has somewhere between 40 and 44 distinct phonemes, which is a lot compared to Rotakas (a language spoken in Papua New Guinea) with only 11 phonemes but minimal compared to !Xóõ (a language spoken in Botswana) with 112 phonemes (Gordon, 2005).

Count the Phonemes

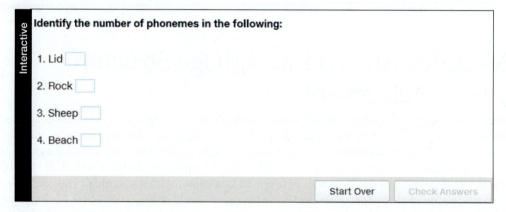

morphemes

the smallest units in a language that have meaning

MORPHEMES **Morphemes** are the smallest units in a language that have meaning. Morphemes are the next building block of language and consist of one or more phonemes. A word that has a prefix and a suffix actually has at least three morphemes. For example, the morpheme "dis" combined with the morphemes "connect" and "ed" makes the word "disconnected." There are actually three meaningful units in the word disconnected because each of the three morphemes conveys meaning (e.g., dis = apart; connect = to join or link together; ed = past tense). There are only two morphemes that consist of only one phoneme.

Morphemes with Only One Phoneme

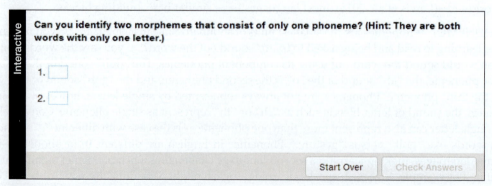

SYNTAX Syntax refers to the rules about how words are to be arranged to form sentences in a given language. Syntax involves word placement. For example, sentences in English must contain both a noun phrase and a verb phrase. Syntax also specifies the order in which words should appear in a sentence. In English, the article comes before the word it modifies (e.g., "A book is…" rather than "Book a is…") and the adjective typically comes before the noun (e.g., "The yellow flower…" rather than "The flower yellow…"). Word order can also be important in determining the accuracy of a sentence. For example, the word order "Sally hit Tim" is much different than "Tim hit Sally" because the two sentences actually identify a different person who did the "hitting."

syntax

the rules about how words are to be arranged to form sentences in a given language

SEMANTICS Semantics refers to the meaning of words and sentences in a given language. It's possible for the syntax of a sentence to be correct but the semantics to be incorrect. For example, famous linguist Noam Chomsky provided the following two example sentences (1957):

1. Colorless green ideas sleep furiously.

2. Furiously sleep ideas green colorless.

Chomsky pointed out that these two sentences provide an example of the difference between syntax and semantics. The first sentence has proper syntax—that is, the placement of the adjective, verb, and noun are appropriate for English. However, the sentence is meaningless (e.g., something can't be colorless and green at the same time) and therefore violates the rules of semantics. The second sentence violates rules of syntax and semantics. It's also possible to think of examples when a sentence has incorrect syntax but is semantically acceptable. Consider the sentence of a toddler trying green peas for the first time: "I no like." This sentence may have poor syntax but the meaning is clear, which makes the semantics acceptable. Punctuation can also change the meaning of sentences. For example, you may have seen a meme highlighting the importance of punctuation like the following:

semantics

the meaning of words and sentences in a given language

THE IMPORTANCE OF GRAMMAR DEMONSTRATED BY SIR PAUL McCARTNEY

HERE'S A SONG I WROTE YESTERDAY

HERE'S A SONG I WROTE - YESTERDAY

Cordell

Grammar actually combines syntax and semantics to provide a system of rules that governs the way people compose and use language. This is why you had to learn all of the parts of a sentence and punctuation when you studied grammar in school, so you could put the pieces together like a puzzle to communicate meaning.

grammar

combines syntax and semantics to provide a system of rules that governs the way people compose and use language

Structures of Language

Interactive

Review the following structures of language. When you are ready, click "Check Your Understanding" below.

Language Structure	Definition
Phonemes	the smallest units of sound possible in a language
Morphemes	the smallest units in a language that have meaning
Syntax	the rules about how words are to be arranged to form sentences in a given language
Semantics	the meaning of words and sentences in a given language
Grammar	combines syntax and semantics to provide a system of rules that governs the way people compose and use language

Check Your Understanding

Adaptive Pathway 7.2: Language Structure

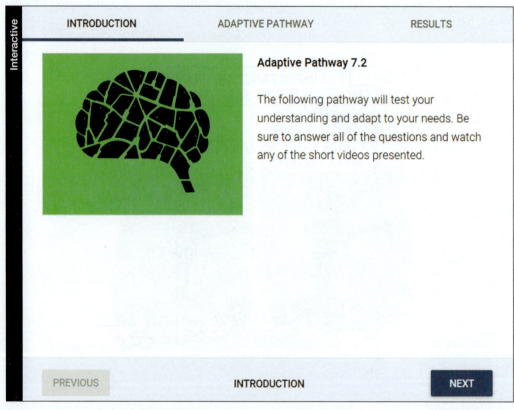

INTRODUCTION   ADAPTIVE PATHWAY   RESULTS

Adaptive Pathway 7.2

The following pathway will test your understanding and adapt to your needs. Be sure to answer all of the questions and watch any of the short videos presented.

PREVIOUS   **INTRODUCTION**   NEXT

Influences on Language Acquisition

LO 7.11 Describe theories of language acquisition.

After learning about the structure of language, you might wonder how we ever learn all these seemingly complex rules about syntax, semantics, and grammar. If a nonnative English speaker asked you to identify what is wrong with the sentence "I likes cookies," you might not be able to identify the exact grammatical violation (e.g., a subject/verb agreement error), but you would certainly know something was wrong with the sentence. How did you learn this? How do psychologists explain how people acquire language?

BEHAVIOR THEORY B. F. Skinner proposed one of the earliest theories of language acquisition. Based on the behavioral model, Skinner believed that children acquire their native language through the process of reinforcement (Skinner, 1957). Nothing is more exciting to a parent than hearing their young child start to use their first words. The first utterance of "dada" will earn the child loud claps and smiles from his father with an instant request to "say it again." The child will find this attention and response rewarding, which increases the likelihood of repeating the word in the future. The behavioral theory argues that language is developed through this process of associating certain sounds with meaning and reinforcement. It seems unlikely however, that this simple theory can explain all of the complexities that underlie the process of language acquisition.

CHOMSKY'S THEORY In response to Skinner's theory, linguist Noam Chomsky argued that the rules and structures of language are so complex that children would never become fluent in a language by the process of imitation and reinforcement alone (Chomsky, 1959). Instead, Chomsky believed that humans are born with an innate capacity for acquiring language. He suggested that children are born with a **language acquisition device** (LAD), or the innate ability to learn the rules of grammar in any language (Chomsky, 1965). Chomsky and other proponents of the *universals of language* argue that humans are born with prewired knowledge of universal grammar rules such as the relationship between nouns and verbs. When children are exposed to language, they simply plug in the vocabulary to their preexisting knowledge of grammar. In support of this theory, before the age of 5, many children are able to produce and understand sentences they have never heard before (Fisher et al., 2010; Kline et al., 2011).

B.F. Skinner proposed that language was learned like other behaviors—through the process of reinforcement.

Noam Chomsky proposed that language capabilities are innate.

language acquisition device (LAD)

the innate ability to learn the rules of grammar in any language

Skinner vs Chomsky

Interactive

Drag the answers below to their appropriate spot on the table to indicate which theorist emphasized environment versus biology more.

Skinner's theory	Environment
Chomsky's theory	Biology

Check Answers

CRITICAL PERIOD HYPOTHESIS When you consider the theories of Skinner and Chomsky, which theory focuses on the role of environment in language acquisition versus the role of biology?

While Skinner's behavioral theory of language development has fallen out of favor, that does not mean environmental factors are not important in influencing how language is acquired. Did you ever wonder what would have happened to Mowgli from the *Jungle Book* if he hadn't happened to be raised by wolves who spoke English? There's no doubt in anyone's mind that a child who has no exposure to language will not be able to understand or produce speech. But, is it ever too late for a child or adult to learn language?

The **critical period hypothesis** (CPH) suggests that there is a limited window of opportunity for children to effectively learn language. According to the CPH, children are most

critical period hypothesis (CPH)

suggests a limited window of opportunity for children to effectively learn language

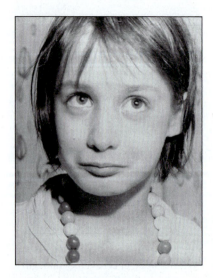

"Genie" was discovered at age 13 with no language capabilities after years of neglect and abuse.

amenable to language acquisition in the first few years of life, and the ability to adequately acquire language after that point becomes increasingly problematic (Lenneberg, 1967). One early case study provided some support for the notion of a critical period in language development. Child welfare authorities in Los Angeles discovered a 13-year-old child, "Genie," who had been severely neglected and abused. She was kept in social isolation tied to a child's potty chair or a crib. She had extremely limited exposure to language and when she was discovered, she did not have any language. After years of intense rehabilitation, Genie was able to make considerable improvements in her vocabulary but she remained unable to use grammar.

Journal Prompt: Critical Period Hypothesis and Genie

Researchers are limited in their ability to use Genie's case as confirmatory evidence for the critical period hypothesis. Can you explain why?

In the case of Genie, it is impossible to know if she had some cognitive deficits prior to her abuse and isolation that might have led to language deficits. The only way to truly test the CPH would be to randomly assign normally developing children to either receive exposure to language or not—a study that thankfully has not, and will not, be conducted. However, other avenues of investigation have provided additional support for the CPH. Researchers have examined language acquisition among deaf children who were not exposed to sign language until later in childhood or adolescence. One study followed the case of E.M. who was born deaf and not exposed to education or any language until he received a hearing aid at age 15. After 4 years of being exposed to Spanish, he continued to demonstrate significant language deficits (Grimshaw et al., 1998).

The CPH has also been applied to the acquisition of second languages. Children who acquire a new language before age 7 can develop near-perfect fluency, and you would find it difficult to distinguish them from native speakers (Long, 1993; Ortega, 2014). Asian immigrants to the United States were given a grammar test, which showed that those who had arrived in the country as young children understood American English grammar as proficiently as native speakers (Johnson & Newport, 1991). However, fluency tends to decrease with age, even when learning sign language (Meier, 1991; Strong & Prinz, 1997).

Adults can learn second languages after this critical period has passed. They use different cognitive strategies than babies and young children. Indeed, the brains of people who learn a second language late in life look different from the brains of people who are bilingual from infancy (Marian et al., 2007), at least in the early stages of learning. While second languages are acquired through the same neural structures, there is more neural activity when people use their native language until the proficiency of the second language is increased (Abutalebi, 2008; Leonard et al., 2010).

Language Development

LO 7.12 Identify milestones in language development.

During those critical first years of language development, most children develop language in a natural progression even if each child develops at his or her own pace. Children typically develop **receptive language skills** (the ability to understand language) much sooner than they develop **expressive language skills** (the ability to communicate with others using language). For example, by age 4, most children can say approximately 2,300 words while they actually understand approximately 8,000 words (Stone et al., 2005). As any parent can attest, young children understand what you mean when you say "stop doing that" much earlier than you realize—a fact that any toddler will exploit to the fullest.

receptive language skills
the ability to understand language

expressive language skills
the ability to communicate with others using language

Table 7.2 Language Development Milestones, from Birth to Age 5

Age	Receptive Language Skills	Expressive Language Skills
Birth to 3 months	• Recognizes caregiver's voice and calms down if crying • When feeding, starts or stops sucking in response to sound • Reacts to loud sounds • Calms down or smiles when spoken to	• Coos and makes pleasure sounds • Has a special way of crying for different needs • Smiles when he or she sees caregiver
4 to 6 months	• Follows sounds with his or her eyes • Responds to changes in tone of voice • Notices toys that make sounds • Pays attention to music	• Babbles in speech-like way and uses many different sounds, including sounds that begin with p, b, and m • Laughs • Babbles when excited or unhappy • Makes gurgling sounds when alone or playing with someone
7 months to 1 year	• Turns and looks in the direction of sound • Listens when spoken to • Understands words for common items such as "cup," "shoe," or "juice" • Responds to requests ("come here")	• Babbles using long and short groups of sounds ("tata, upup, bibibi") • Babbles to get and keep attention • Communicates using gestures such as waving or holding up arms • Imitates different speech sounds • Has one or two words ("hi," "dog," "Dada," or "Mama") by first birthday
1 to 2 years	• Knows a few parts of the body and can point to them when asked • Follows simple commands ("roll the ball") and understands simple questions ("where's your shoe?") • Points to pictures, when named, in books	• Acquires new words on a regular basis • Uses some one- or two-word questions ("where kitty?" or "go bye-bye?") • Puts two words together • Uses many different consonant sounds at the beginning of words
2 to 3 years	• Increases their understanding of object names • When asked, points to a picture of something named (such as "where is the cow?" or "show me the airplane")	• Has a word for almost everything • Uses two- or three-word phrases to talk about or ask for things • Uses k, g, f, t, d, and n sounds • Speaks in a way that is understood by family members and friends • Names objects or asks for them or to direct attention to them
3 to 4 years	• Hears when you call from another room • Hears the television or radio at the same sound level as other family members	• Answers simple "who?" "what?" "where?" and "why?" questions • Talks about activities at daycare, preschool, or friends' homes • Uses sentences with four or more words • Speaks easily without having to repeat syllables or words
4 to 5 years	• Pays attention to a short story and answers simple questions about it • Hears and understands most of what is said at home and in school	• Uses sentences that give many details • Tells stories that stay on topic • Communicates easily with other children and adults • Says most sounds correctly, except for a few (l, s, r, v, z, ch, sh, th) • Uses rhyming words • Names some letters and numbers • Uses adult grammar

Within the first 3 months, infants will start to make basic "cooing" noises and will recognize a caregiver's voice. Around age 4 to 6 months, babies start to make "babbling" noises that sound like speech, and by age 7 months to a year, babies start to babble in multiple syllables and use their first recognizable words. A toddler's vocabulary grows from age 1 to 2, and he/she often begins to put two words together. At this age, toddlers demonstrate what is referred to as **telegraphic speech** because it resembles an old-fashioned telegram. The sentence "I would like some milk" is shortened to "want milk," which is not grammatically correct but conveys the same meaning. Between ages 2 and 3, children begin to use short phrases, and they use full sentences by ages 3 to 4. Table 7.2 provides a summary of receptive and expressive language milestones from birth through age 5 (National Institute on Deafness and Other Communication Disorders, 2010).

We know that children from ages 1 to 3 experience a significant increase in their vocabulary. The average 18-month-old can produce around 50 words. By age 2, a child typically uses 200–300 words and, by age 3, an average child has 500–1,000 words in their expressive vocabulary (Paul & Norbury, 2012). Each unfamiliar word a child encounters is a puzzle to be solved. A child must decipher the meaning of the word and then produce the word in an appropriate novel situation. There are some instances when a child only has to encounter a new word once before it is learned. The ability to acquire and retain new words or concepts with minimal exposure is called **fast mapping** (Carey & Bartlett, 1978). In the original Carey and Bartlett (1978) study, they asked preschoolers to "Bring me the chromium tray, not the blue one, the chromium one." There were two trays the children could choose between—one that was blue and another that was an olive-green color. Children correctly assumed that "chromium" referred to the olive-green tray and retained this information a week later during a comprehension test. Parents across the globe may have been dismayed when observing

telegraphic speech

the two-word stage of language development in early childhood when speech resembles an old-fashioned telegram

Right before baby's first text.

fast mapping

the ability to acquire and retain new words or concepts with minimal exposure

slow mapping

when a new word is acquired through a gradual process that requires repeated exposures

the process of fast mapping after uttering a curse word accidentally in front of a child on only one occasion. However, not all words or concepts are learned after one exposure. The process of **slow mapping** occurs when a child acquires a word through a more gradual process that requires repeated exposures (Deák, 2014; Swingley, 2010).

Language and Thought

LO 7.13 Explain the relationship between language and thought.

If someone said "penny for your thoughts," how would you describe the thoughts going through your mind this instant? You would most likely discover that you were thinking with words. Most of our thoughts are language based, which leads us to wonder about the relationship between thinking and language. Experts tend to agree that thinking and language are interrelated (see Figure 7.6), and this topic has been one of the most interesting and controversial topics in the area of linguistics.

Figure 7.6 Relationship Between Language and Thought

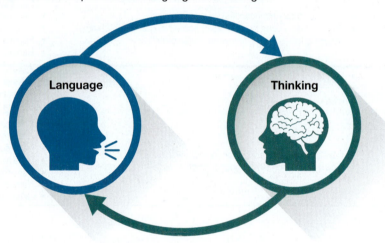

IS LANGUAGE INFLUENCED BY THOUGHT? Is the way you verbally describe your world influenced by the way you think? For example, do people from different cultures perceive the world differently? Many studies suggest that they do (Lee, 2000; Mercier et al., 2015; Nisbett & Norenzayan, 2002; Peng & Nisbett, 1999). A group of Japanese and American students were shown an animated underwater scene in which one larger, "focal" fish swam among smaller fish and other aquatic life. When asked to describe what they saw, the Japanese students were much more likely to begin by describing the background and how the parts of the scene related to one another—the rocky pool, the color of the water, the fish swimming past seaweed. In contrast, American students were far more likely to begin by describing prominent individual aspects of the scene—the largest, fastest, brightest fish. Nisbett and his colleagues found that the Japanese were similarly sensitive to context in the social world and could pick up how situational pressures were affecting people's behavior far quicker than Americans.

In addition, English and other European languages have an egocentric frame of reference. In other words, space is represented with ourselves at the center. You might describe a local grocery store as being 2 miles from your house, whereas someone with an absolute frame of reference might give the specific geographic location. These examples suggest fundamental differences in the way people from different cultures perceive the world which in turn has an influence on the way they use language.

IS THOUGHT INFLUENCED BY LANGUAGE? If the way we communicate about the world can be influenced by our thinking, what about the opposite? Does the language we use actually

Examples of the Linguistic Relativity Hypothesis

Guugu Yimithirr, a language spoken in an area of Australia, uses directional words (e.g., north, south, east, and west) rather than front, back, left, or right. Do people who speak Guugu Yimithirr think about directions differently than English speakers?

| 1 of 2 | Previous | Next |

impact how we think? The **linguistic relativity hypothesis** states that the way people think is strongly affected by their native language (Whorf, 1956). The following activity provides examples of situations that the linguistic relativity hypothesis has been seen as relevant.

For example, the linguistic relativity hypothesis proposes that the number of words a language has to describe colors will influence how an individual perceives the color spectrum. If your language has few words for color, you will perceive fewer differences between stimuli than if your language has more words for color. Kay and Kempton (1984) studied English speakers and Tarahumara speakers (Native Americans from northwestern Mexico) on a task of color discrimination between blue and green. English language differentiates between blue and green, while Tarahumara language does not. However, contrary to the linguistic relativity hypothesis, Tarahumara speakers were able to differentiate between blue and green stimuli. Interestingly, more recent work suggests that language may actually affect color perception—but only in the right visual field. Because images in the right visual field are processing in the language-dominant left hemisphere, it appears that language has more of an impact on perception in the right visual field than the left visual field (Regier & Kay, 2009).

While research has failed to find strong support for the notion that language *determines* our conceptions of reality, there is significant evidence that the language we speak certainly *influences* our perceptions of the world (Boroditsky, 2011). Consider the fact that many languages specify nouns as either masculine or feminine. In French, a table (la table) is feminine, while an airplane (le avion) is masculine. While these distinctions are generally considered purely grammatical (as opposed to meaning that a table is truly more feminine), Phillips and Boroditsky (2003) found that speakers of languages who differentiate between masculine and feminine nouns actually rated people and objects of matching gender (e.g., a table and a woman) as more similar than people and objects that didn't match (e.g., a table and a man).

People who are bilingual also appear to be influenced by the language they use. When speaking one language, individuals will often endorse different personal preferences than the same person does when speaking a different language. For example, (Ogunnaike et al., 2010) found that

linguistic relativity hypothesis
hypothesis that the way people think is strongly affected by their native language

people who were English-Spanish bilinguals actually indicated a higher preference for Spanish names when speaking in Spanish than when the same person was speaking in English. In other words, the cultural values associated with a particular language appear to be activated when someone uses that language as opposed to a different language with different cultural values.

The Brain and Language

LO 7.14   Identify the areas of the brain associated with language.

Receptive and expressive language abilities, including reading, talking, listening, and writing, are complex abilities that depend on many brain structures. In 1861, French physician Pierre Paul Broca encountered a patient who had developed aphasia, or the inability to speak. This patient could only say only one word: "tan." After the patient died, Broca performed an autopsy, which revealed that the individual had damage to his brain in the frontal lobe of the left cerebral hemisphere (Broca, 1861). Based on his work, this area of the brain associated with the production of speech has since been known as "**Broca's area**." When this area of the brain is damaged, people can still understand language but when trying to speak, they are often slow, laborious, and slurred. Listen to the following clip in Revel for an example of speech affected by damage to Broca's area.

Broca's area

the area of the brain in the left frontal lobe associated with the production of speech

A Patient with Broca's Aphasia

Wernicke's area

the area of the brain in the left temporal lobe focused on language comprehension

Several years later, Karl Wernicke discovered a second area in the left cerebral hemisphere that caused different types of language problems when damaged. This area, now referred to as "**Wernicke's area**" is in the temporal lobe, slightly farther back and lower in

Broca's Area and Wernicke's Area

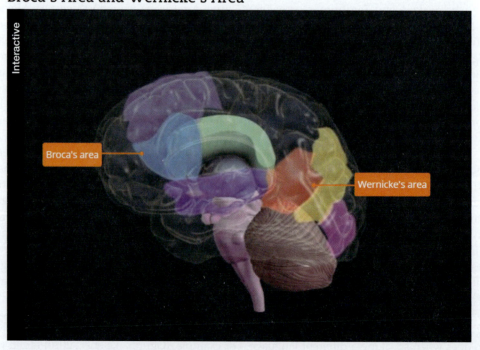

A Patient with Wernicke's Aphasia

the brain than Broca's area. Whereas Broca's area is considered the speech production center, Wernicke's area in the brain is focused on language comprehension. People who have damage to Wernicke's area struggle to understand language and although they may be able to produce understandable words, their speech doesn't make sense and has been referred to as "word salad." Listen to the following clip in Revel for an example of speech affected by damage to Wernicke's area.

Connecting Broca's and Wernicke's areas is a tract of nerves called the **arcuate fasciculus**. When there is damage to the arcuate fasciculus, people develop what is called **conduction aphasia**. Interestingly, these individuals can understand and produce speech, but they are unable to repeat words or sentences spoken by other people. The **angular gyrus** is another area of the brain associated with language that lies between Wernicke's area and the visual cortex of the occipital lobe. The angular gyrus is particularly important in tasks of reading and writing, and damage to this area has been associated with problems such as alexia (inability to read) and dyslexia (difficulty with reading). Figure 7.7 demonstrates the location of Broca's area, Wernicke's area, the arcuate fasciculus, and the angular gyrus in the brain.

Modern technologies, including PET scans, EEG, MRIs, and fMRIs, continue to affirm the role of Broca's area and Wernicke's area, which are both found in the left hemisphere. However, these new technologies have also demonstrated that the right hemisphere plays a critical role. For example, the process of sentence comprehension appears to focus on the left hemisphere for issues of syntax and the right hemisphere for issues of semantics (Friederici, 2011). Overall, scientists now understand that language processing occurs in different regions of the brain, and effective communication between these brain areas is critical for all aspects of language to work well (Duffau et al., 2014; Friederici, 2012; Friederici & Gierhan, 2013).

arcuate fasciculus

tract of nerves connecting Broca's and Wernicke's areas that when damaged leads to conduction aphasia

conduction aphasia

when individuals can understand and produce speech but are unable to repeat words or sentences spoken by other people

angular gyrus

area of the brain associated with language that lies between Wernicke's area and the visual cortex of the occipital lobe that is particularly important in tasks of reading and writing

Figure 7.7 Language Areas in the Brain

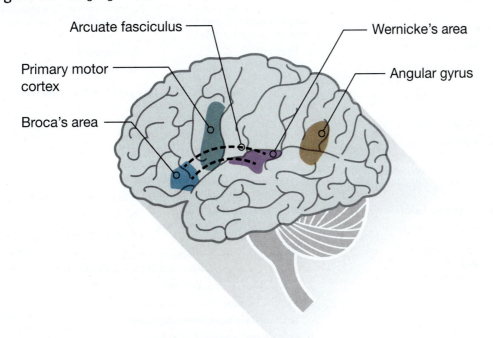

Adaptive Pathway 7.3: Broca's Area and Wernicke's Area

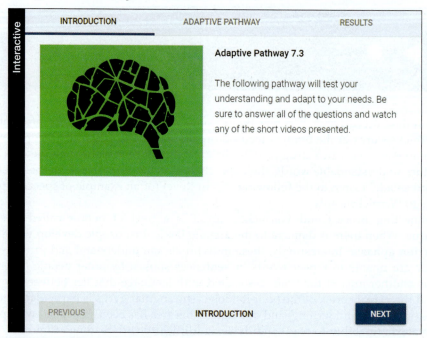

Quiz for Module 7.10–7.14

1. The system of symbols that allows people to communicate thoughts, ideas, and feelings is called _____.
   a. morphemes
   b. phonemes
   c. syntax
   d. language

2. Larissa is 5 years old and learning to read. Her parents have her sound out each letter in the words as she is trying to read. Each letter that she sounds out is considered what part of the building blocks of language?
   a. Semantics
   b. Morphemes
   c. Phonemes
   d. Syntax

3. In the English language, adjectives typically come before nouns in a sentence, which is an example of _____. On the other hand, _____ refers to the meanings of words and sentences in a given language.
   a. phonemes; morphemes
   b. syntax; semantics
   c. semantics; syntax
   d. morphemes; phonemes

4. Noam Chomsky believes that children are born with a(n) _____, or an innate ability to learn the rules of grammar in any language.
   a. acquired knowledge device
   b. language knowledge device
   c. language acquisition device
   d. acquired language device

5. Genie was severely neglected and abused until the age of 13. When she was discovered, she had no language and never fully developed language abilities. This case supports which theory of language development?
   a. Critical period hypothesis
   b. Early language development
   c. Behavioral theory of language
   d. Critical development period

6. A baby that has the ability to understand language but not express themselves has developed which type of language skills?
   a. Receptive language skills
   b. Expressive language skills
   c. Telegraphic speech
   d. Babbling

7. Mia is learning language quickly; she knows about 50 words and can put simple phrases together like: "go bye-bye." What is the most likely age for Mia?
   a. 18 months
   b. 3 months
   c. 4 years
   d. 3 years

8. _____ states the way people think is influenced by their native language.
   a. Language relativity device
   b. Language acquisition device
   c. Linguistic relativity hypothesis
   d. Linguistic acquisition hypothesis

9. What area of the brain is associated with the production of speech?
   a. Arcuate fasciculus
   b. Angular gyrus
   c. Wernicke's area
   d. Broca's area

10. _____ is located in the left temporal lobe and _____ is located in the left frontal lobe.
    a. Broca's area; Wernicke's area
    b. Wernicke's area; Broca's area
    c. Arcuate fasciculus; Wernicke's area
    d. Broca's area; arcuate fasciculus

Module 7.15: Piecing It Together: Cognition in Nonhuman Animals

LO 7.15   **Analyze how the cross-cutting themes of psychology are related to the topic of cognition in nonhuman animals.**

Reflect for a moment on the topics covered in this chapter such as problem solving, categorization, decision making, and language. Now, think about your favorite pet—your dog, cat, hamster, or bird—and consider whether your pet shares these cognitive abilities. Do nonhuman animals (referred to as "animals" from here on) engage in similar types of cognitive processes as humans? What, if any, are the differences in the cognitive abilities of animals and humans? This field of study is known as **comparative psychology**, or the scientific study of nonhuman animal mental processes and behavior. Click through the following gallery to read about researchers in the field of comparative psychology from 1871 until the present (Beran et al., 2014).

These examples are only a few highlights of the thousands of current and past studies in comparative psychology examining cognitive processes in animals across a variety of species. When considering the field of comparative psychology, several important issues/questions need to be considered. We will discuss these questions in the following pages.

Research Methods

- What types of research methods are employed when studying animals?

Perhaps it is important to begin a discussion of research on animals with the question "why?" Why is it necessary or important to conduct research using animal participants? According to the American Psychological Association (APA), psychologists conduct research with nonhuman animals "to learn more about behavior and how knowledge of behavior can be used to advance the welfare of people and animals" (APA, 2012). Most psychologists would agree that much of the foundation of our knowledge about topics such as learning, sensation, medications, and the functioning of the central nervous system has been established through research with animals.

While animal research is considered vital in many areas, only about 7–8 percent of research in psychology involves animals, and approximately 90 percent of animal studies rely on rodents and birds. Animals are usually studied when there are reasons why conducting research with human participants is not feasible or ethical. For example, some studies of the process of aging would require a human sample to be followed over a lifespan that might last 70 to 80 years. Studying aging among animals with much shorter lifespans speeds up the discovery process significantly. However, there are some specific considerations when conducting research with animals.

1. Research with animals is highly regulated and evaluated with regards to ethics. While this topic will be addressed further in the ethics section, it is important to note that psychological research with animals is carefully considered and several safeguards are in place to ensure that animals are treated humanely and ethically. The APA Code of Ethics outlines ethical standards for conducting research with animals. The U.S. federal government also enforces the Animal Welfare Act about the care and use of animals in research. In addition, the broader scientific community maintains accreditation processes to oversee research involving animals.

2. *Anthropomorphism*, or the assignment of uniquely human traits to nonhumans, has been one area of concern in conducting research with nonhuman animals. For example, using emotional terms to describe the experience of an animal (e.g., a "despondent" chimp, or a "joyful" cat) can be considered as an instance of anthropomorphism. Because it

comparative psychology

the scientific study of nonhuman animal mental processes and behavior

Comparative Psychology Then and Now

Interactive

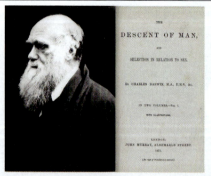

Darwin's (1871) *Descent of Man*

Harry Harlow's 1958 study of maternal deprivation in monkeys (Harlow & Zimmermann, 1958)

Dr. Irene Pepperberg's study of gray parrots demonstrating numerical abilities (e.g., counting) (1994).

J. David Smith at the University at Buffalo presents evidence of animal metacognition in dolphins – that is, they may share humans' ability to reflect upon, monitor, or regulate their states of mind (2009).

Margaret Floy Washburn's (1909) influential *The Animal Mind: A Text-Book of Comparative Psychology*

Sue Savage-Rumbaugh's work with two bonobos, Kanzi and Panbanisha, investigating their linguistic and cognitive abilities using lexigrams and computer-based keyboards (Savage-Rumbaugh et al., 1998).

Jonathan Crystal and colleagues at Indiana University's work demonstrating episodic and source memory in rats (Babb & Crystal, 2006; Crystal et al., 2013).

is difficult to know exactly what an animal is feeling or thinking, scientists can only describe what the animal *looks* like it is feeling. When studying cognitive processes in animals, however, it can be difficult to avoid all cases of anthropomorphism. After all, it is also difficult to know with certainty what humans are feeling at all times, but people rarely argue that prescribing emotions to human behavior would be inappropriate. The key when it comes to research involving animals appears to be making sure that terms are clearly operationally defined. That is, if a researcher describes an animal as demonstrating signs of "happiness," the term should be clearly defined in terms of behavioral observations and an agreement among others that those behaviors are representative of "happiness" (Mitchell & Hamm, 1997).

For example, one research team recently examined how dogs can communicate with subtle differences in the wagging of their tails. They discovered that dogs can wag their tails more on the right or more on the left, which has an impact on the behavior of an observing dog. By having dogs watch silhouettes of different tail-wagging directions, researchers could infer different emotional responses (Siniscalchi et al., 2013).

The researchers found that dogs who observed another dog "wagging to the left" demonstrated a "stress/anxiety" response, while dogs who observed another dog "wagging to the right" demonstrated a "relaxed/neutral" response (see Figure 7.8). This study

Figure 7.8 Effect of Direction of Tail Wag

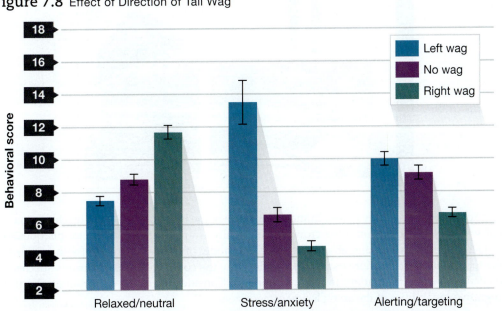

provides an example of scientists' attempts to avoid using anthropomorphic terminology to describe behavior.

Journal Prompt: Describe the Behavior

Think about your knowledge of dog behavior, and hypothesize about what kinds of behaviors indicate "stress/anxiety" and what kind of behaviors indicate "relaxed"? If these behaviors were observed in humans, would we describe them differently?

3. Can data from animal studies be reliably used to predict human outcomes? This topic has been the source of much debate and controversy. Studies of cognition in animals are not always conducted with the goal of translating the data into human models; however, sometimes research with animals is primarily motivated by a desire to learn more about human functioning. In those cases, it is important to know that the data from studies with animals can be meaningfully used to provide insight about humans. In recent years, several studies have demonstrated that findings in animal studies are not always able to be replicated in a human sample (Ferdowsian & Beck, 2011). For example, Hackman and Redelmeier (2006) evaluated 76 animal research studies of various diseases and found that only a third of those studies was successfully translated to human random trials.

Cultural and Social Diversity

- How much diversity is there in cognitive processes across different animal species?

Do you think you can classify animals in terms of their cognitive abilities?

Which Animals are the Most Intelligent?

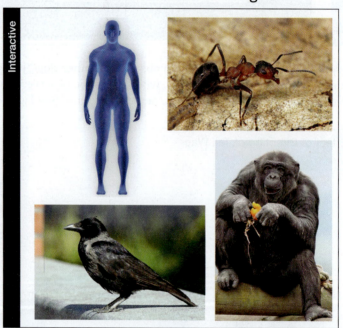

Interactive

You may have quickly placed humans at the top of the hierarchy followed by chimpanzees, but what about the ants and the crows? There really isn't a "right" answer to this question. In fact, rather than thinking about a hierarchical model of animal cognition (with humans at the top), it has become more useful to consider how the cognitive skills of various species are related to the ability to adapt to the environment. Consider the following findings about the cognitive capabilities of the animals you categorized.

- **Ants:** They have the ability to transmit precise information about the location of food (Reznikova, 2007).
- **Crows:** Studies show they are capable of creating tools (e.g., making a hook in a straight wire), which is considered a hallmark of advanced intelligence (Emery & Clayton, 2004).
- **Chimpanzees:** Research has shown that chimpanzees have an amazing ability to remember numerical sequences that surpasses that of many humans (Inoue & Matsuzawa, 2007).

evolutionary cognition

field of study focused on the fact that cognitive abilities develop across different species over time based on what skills/abilities help a species adapt to a particular environment and provide a survival advantage

The concept of **evolutionary cognition** has gained support in recent years. This field of study focuses on the fact that cognitive abilities develop across different species over time based on what skills/abilities help a species adapt to a particular environment and provide a survival advantage (De Waal, 2016). For example, black-capped chickadees can remember the locations of seeds they store in hundreds of different places every day. Consider that memory feat the next time you are searching for your keys or cell phone for what seems like the hundredth time. From the perspective of evolutionary cognition, these birds have developed this skill because being able to remember where the seeds are located means there is a higher chance of survival and therefore the likelihood of passing along those "memory" genes to the next generation. So, rather than thinking about cognition across different species in terms of "greatest to least," it is likely more accurate to consider cognitive abilities across species in terms of evolutionary advantage and adaptations to specific environments.

Variations in Functioning

- What do we know about animals and the capacity for language?

One of the important questions about differences in cognition between humans and animals is related to language abilities. Consider the following definition of language presented earlier in this chapter: the system of symbols that enables us to communicate our ideas, thoughts, and feelings.

Journal Prompt: Do Animals Have Language?

Do you think animals have language abilities? What are the differences between humans and animals when it comes to language?

When considering this issue, it is important to distinguish between the concepts of language and communication. *Communication* can be thought of as the transfer of information from an individual or group to another individual or group. It is very clear that all animals can communicate, whether it's the color, shape, or texture of their skin or the sounds they make. Language, on the other hand, is the use of words and/or symbols used for the purpose of communication. Language has several properties that tend to separate it from the communication of most animals. Some of these properties include:

- Discreteness—language consists of small, discrete units that are repeatable and used in combination to create meaning
- Displacement—language can be used to communicate about things that are not immediately present (either spatially or temporally)
- Productivity—language can be used to create an infinite number of messages

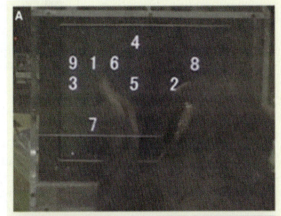

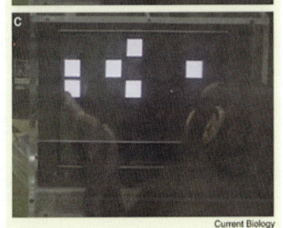

Current Biology

Chimpanzee Ayumu remembers where the numbers were located after they are covered up by white squares.

Examples of Different Language Properties

Interactive

Drag the language property below to its appropriate spot on the table.

Language Property	Example
Discreteness	Phonemes in human language
Displacement	A child talking about what she wants to be when she grows up
Productivity	The game of Scrabble (e.g., using a limited number of letters to generate many words)

Check Answers

Many animals have demonstrated one or more of these properties in their communication abilities. For example, a honeybee returns to the hive and uses an elaborate dance to tell other bees about a source of nectar with details such as the distance, direction, and quantity of nectar. Because the bee is communicating about something not immediately present, the bee is demonstrating displacement (Trask & Stockwell, 2007). However, the general consensus currently is that while many animals exhibit *some* of the properties of human language, there are no animals that exhibit *all* of the properties of human language (Beran et al., 2014). Even among famous primates such as Washoe (the first chimpanzee to learn American Sign Language) and Koko (reported to understand more than 1,000 hand signs), most researchers agree that their communication falls short of all the properties of human language.

Ethics

- What types of ethical concerns must be considered when conducting research with animals?

Like research conducted on human participants, animal experimentation has many ethical considerations. Unlike experiments using humans, studies using animal participation are not able to rely on informed consent to help alleviate some ethical concerns. In addition, many studies are conducted using animals because they are considered too risky for human experimentation (e.g., either there is the potential for too much pain/suffering or the outcome is too dangerous or possibly too unknown). Table 7.3 demonstrates the number and type of animals used in research in the United States in 2015. However, this data does not include mice, rats, and fish because the use of these animals is not covered or tracked by the Animal Welfare Act. Given the United Kingdom reports that 97 percent of all animal studies are conducted on mice, rats, fish, and birds, it is safe to assume that the total number of animals used in research in the United States is likely to be around 25 million when all animals are included. Approximately 62,000 nonhuman primates were used in research in 2015 in the United States.

One of the guiding principles for conducting animal research is the notion of *harm versus benefit*. According to this principle, research involving animals is acceptable if, and only if, suffering is minimized and human benefits are gained that would otherwise not have been possible with different methods.

In addition, research using animals has been guided by the following "three Rs":

1. Reduction = reducing numbers of animals used in experiments
2. Refinement = refining experiments to reduce animal suffering
3. Replacement = replacing animal research with alternatives

Table 7.3 Animals Used in Research in the United States in 2015

Animals used in research in 2015	Total number of animals	% of total	% change from 2014
Guinea Pigs	172,864	22.5%	2.0%
Hamsters	98,420	12.8%	−19.3%
Rabbits	138,348	18.0%	−8.0%
Dogs	61,101	8.0%	2.9%
Non-Human Primates	61,950	8.1%	7.3%
Pigs	46,477	6.1%	2.4%
Sheep	10,678	1.4%	3.5%
Other Farm Animals	27,786	3.6%	1.4%
Cats	19,932	2.6%	−5.5%
All Other Animals	130,066	16.9%	−24.1%
Total Animals Used	**767,622**	**100%**	−8.0%

CC-BY: www.speakingofreseach.com

However, some experts have argued that the three R's may not be enough and that our newly developing understanding of animal cognition can better inform us about the use of animals in research. For example, research has demonstrated that animals can experience pain and distress (Gregory, 2004). Conducting invasive procedures or depriving animals of their natural habitats and/or socialization are all sources of harm to animals (Ferdowsian & Beck, 2011), which should be considered when moving forward to reevaluate the ethical considerations of using animals in research.

Shared Writing: Benefits vs Risks

Some people feel the benefits of using animals to advance science and medicine outweigh the risks to the welfare of animals. Other people feel the welfare of the animals should be the first consideration in determining whether research with animals is acceptable or unacceptable. What do you think, and why?

Quiz for Module 7.15

1. What is the scientific study of nonhuman animal mental processes and behavior?
   a. Comparative psychology
   b. Clinical psychology
   c. Animal psychology
   d. Behavioral psychology

2. Which of the following statements about research with nonhuman animals is true?
   a. Animal research makes up the majority of research in psychology.
   b. Animal research makes up less than 10 percent of all the research in psychology.
   c. Animal research is always considered the first step before conducting research with humans.
   d. There are not many ethical standards regarding the use of animals in research.

3. When conducting research with animals, one concern that scientists share is the assigning of uniquely human traits to animals. This is called _____.
   a. anthropomorphism
   b. anthropology
   c. agnosticism
   d. apolgism

4. Human language has several properties that separate it from animal language that include the properties of _____, displacement, and _____.
   a. directness; productivity
   b. discreteness; grammar
   c. phonemes; morphemes
   d. discreteness; productivity

5. One ethical guideline states "using animals in research is only acceptable if and only if suffering is minimized and human benefits are gained that would not otherwise be possible." This is called

   _____.
   a. replacement versus harm
   b. reduction and refinement benefit
   c. harm versus replacement
   d. harm versus benefit

Summary: Accordian

Module 7.1–7.2: Concepts

Cognition is the study of mental activities associated with thinking, knowing, remembering, and communicating. **Concepts** are mental groupings of similar objects, events, and people that we use to comprehend vast amounts of information. **Formal concepts** (also known as logical concepts) have a rigid set of rules or parameters for membership. Most of our concepts develop through our own experiences in the world and are known as **natural concepts** with fuzzy boundaries between categories. Concepts can be formed by creating a mental image or a typical example that exhibits all of the features associated with a certain category called a **prototype.** We more readily identify something as an example of the concept if the object closely resembles the prototype. We may also form concepts by using an **exemplar** approach whereby new encounteres are compared to past experiences stored in memory. Once we form a concept category, we can classify it even more by using **hierarchies of concepts** that progress from broad to narrow. The categories that are the most broad, or include the most concepts, are called **superordinate concepts** (e.g., animal). Underlying superordinate concepts are the **basic concepts** (e.g., dog), which provide more specific information. The most specific type of concepts fall into the **subordinate** level, which includes the most narrow categories (e.g., golden retriever).

Module 7.3–7.4: Problem Solving

Problem solving is the act of combining current information with information stored in your memory to find a solution to a task. A *problem space* has been defined in terms of the **initial state** (when you have incomplete information), the **goal state** (when you have all the necessary information), and the **set of operations** (the steps you need to take to reach the goal state from the initial state). We use a variety of different methods for solving different sorts of problems, including **trial and error** (trying a potential solution and discarding that option if it fails and moving on to the next potential solution). A more systematic form of trial and error is **algorithms** (step-by-step procedures we can follow to guarantee the ability to discover a solution). Because of the limitations of the algorithmic approach, many problems are solved using some form of mental shortcut, or **heuristic.** One example of a heuristic that is often helpful when solving problems is called a **means-end analysis** (forming subgoals that will move you closer from the initial state to the goal state). **Working backward** is another heuristic that involves working your way backward to determine a solution. There are also times when you don't need complicated methods to solve problems due to **insight** (when the solution suddenly pops into your head). People from Eastern cultures tend to engage in more **holistic thinking,** or a focus on the "whole" or interconnectedness of systems and objects, while Westerners engage in more **analytic thinking,** or a focus on breaking down the whole into parts or details. Difficulties during problem solving can be due to **fixations,** or the inability to see a problem from a fresh perspective because of our tendency to become stuck in our thinking. One type of fixation is known as a **mental set,** or a preexisting state of mind we use to solve problems because it's helped in the past. **Functional fixedness** is a bias that limits your ability to think about objects in unconventional ways.

Module 7.5–7.7: Decision Making

Judgment is a skill that allows us to form opinions, reach conclusions, and evaluate situations objectively and critically. Judgment informs our **decision making**—the process of selecting and rejecting available options. **Rational choice theory** of decision making states that we make decisions by determining the likelihood and the positive or negative value of each potential outcome. **Prospect theory** states that we avoid risk in situations where we stand to gain, but our behavior becomes more risk seeking when we face a loss. Research has found that the presence of dopamine in the brain helps us make decisions that lead to good outcomes and avoid bad outcomes. Your brain also has executive control systems that inhibit pleasurable responses that would have negative consequences. The way a decision or problem is presented, or the **framing,** of an issue can greatly influence the decisions we make. If we have too many alternatives to choose from, we develop **decision aversion** (attempting to avoid making any decision at all). One common mental shortcut used in decision making, the **availability heuristic,** tells us that if we can bring examples of an event to mind easily, that event must be common. The **representativeness heuristic** is used when making decisions about the probability of an event by comparing it to our existing prototype of the event. One common error in reasoning is **overconfidence,** or our tendency to think we are more knowledgeable or accurate than we really are. A form of overconfidence called **hindsight bias** refers to our tendency to overestimate our previous knowledge of situations. **Belief bias** refers to the effect that occurs when our beliefs distort our logical thinking, and **belief perseverance** occurs when we maintain a belief despite being confronted with evidence that refutes the belief. Our tendency to seek out evidence in favor of our existing beliefs is called the **confirmation bias.** Confirmation bias can (1) influence how we seek information, (2) influence how we interpret information, and (3) influence how we remember information.

Module 7.8–7.9: Creativity

Defined broadly, **creativity** is the ability to come up with new ideas that can lead to some outcome. The **threshold theory of creativity** states that above average intelligence is a necessary condition for someone to engage in the thinking processes that lead to creativity. **Convergent thinking** occurs when we are confronted with well-defined, straightforward problems that have a right/wrong answer. **Divergent thinking,** on the other hand, has been used as a measure of creativity and includes thought processes used to generate many different possible solutions to a problem. Sternberg proposed the **investment theory of creativity,** which outlines the critical ingredients for creative thinking, including intellectual skills, knowledge, thinking styles, motivation, and environment.

Module 7.10–7.14: Language Structure and Development

Language—the system of symbols that enables us to communicate our ideas, thoughts, and feelings—plays a vital part in how we think. **Phonemes** are the smallest units of sound that are possible in a language, and **morphemes** are the smallest units in a language that have meaning. **Syntax** refers to the rules about how words are to be arranged to form sentences in a given language, while **semantics** refers to the meaning of words and sentences in a given language. **Grammar** combines syntax and semantics to provide a system of rules that governs the way people compose and use language. Based on the behavioral model, Skinner believed that children acquire their native language through the process of reinforcement. Noam Chomsky suggested that children are born with a **language acquisition device** (LAD), or the innate ability to learn the rules of grammar in any language. The **critical period hypothesis** (CPH) suggests a limited window of opportunity exists for children to effectively learn language. Children typically develop **receptive language** skills (the ability to understand language) much sooner than their **expressive language skills** (the ability to communicate with others using language). A toddler begins to put two words together in what is referred to as **telegraphic speech** because it resembles an old-fashioned telegram. The ability to acquire and retain new words or concepts with minimal exposure is called **fast mapping,** while the process of **slow mapping** occurs when a child

acquires a word through a more gradual process that requires repeated exposures.

The **linguistic relativity hypothesis** states that the way people think is strongly affected by their native language. While research has failed to find strong support for the notion that language *determines* our conceptions of reality, significant evidence suggests that the language we speak certainly *influences* our perceptions of the world.

The area of the brain associated with the production of speech is called **Broca's area,** and when damaged, people can still understand language but struggle to produce language. **Wernicke's area** in the brain is focused on language comprehension, and people who have damage to Wernicke's area struggle to understand language; and, while they string words together, their speech doesn't make sense. Connecting Broca's and Wernicke's areas is a tract of nerves called the **arcuate fasciculus**. When there is damage to the arcuate fasciculus, people develop what is called **conduction aphasia**. Interestingly, these individuals can understand and produce speech, but they are unable to repeat words or sentences spoken by other people. The **angular gyrus** lies between Wernicke's area and the visual cortex of the occipital lobe and is particularly important in reading and writing.

Chapter 7 Quiz

1. Skinner believed that children learn language through _____.

   a. brain development
   b. conditioning
   c. reinforcement
   d. punishments

2. Which strategy involves establishing subgoals to reach the goal state?

   a. Working backward
   b. Trial-and-error
   c. Algorithms
   d. Means-end analysis

3. People more readily use which type of concept when describing an object, event, or person?

   a. Prototype
   b. Subordinate
   c. Basic
   d. Superordinate

4. A sports car is an example of which level of concept?

   a. Basic
   b. Superordinate
   c. Prototype
   d. Subordinate

5. Which of the following is an example of the representativeness heuristic?

   a. When asked if he got along with his brother, Rick could only think of instances when they argued.
   b. An online dating profile described a person as "smart, introverted, and loves to read." When asked to guess the person's job, most people selected "librarian" rather than the correct response "waitress."

   c. After hearing about a jogger getting mugged, Darius decided it was too risky to run outside any longer.
   d. Lucy can only remember the good times during her childhood.

6. A car is a typical example of a vehicle. This is known as a _____.

   a. concept
   b. prototype
   c. formal concept
   d. natural concept

7. Aaron is 2 years old and is trying to communicate his needs to his parents. He says "I bye-bye now go." This sentence may have _____ errors, but it does have clear _____.

   a. syntax; grammar
   b. semantics; syntax
   c. grammar; syntax
   d. syntax; semantics

8. When we need to "think outside the box," what can get in our way?

   a. Positive attitude
   b. Working backward
   c. Mental set
   d. Divergent thinking

9. Jamal believes that all cheerleaders are snobbish and vain. Therefore, when he encountered Tonya who he had seen cheering at the basketball game, and she was obsessing about a stain on her dress and seemed too busy to give him directions, Jamal believed her behavior confirmed his belief about cheerleaders. He did not consider any other explanation for Tonya's behavior. What specific aspect of the confirmation bias was Jamal engaging in?

a. Biased interpretation
b. Biased memory
c. Biased information seeking
d. Biased evaluation

10. People's decisions become more risk-seeking when they face a loss. This decision-making theory is called _____.

a. prospect theory
b. rational choice theory
c. prejudgment theory
d. risk averse theory

11. Sayla is attempting to pick which college she should attend. She is overwhelmed with the choices and the prices. She does not know if she should go to a large, public in-state school or a small, private liberal arts school. She has heard that state schools are cheaper but private schools give more scholarships. Sayla just decides not to make a decision and has stopped answering her parents when they ask her about her choices. She is experiencing _____.

a. decision weariness
b. decision meltdown
c. decision aversion
d. decision avoidance

12. Rashaad does not know how much time he will need to study for each of his classes this semester to make the A's he needs to keep his scholarships. He decides that he will just try different tactics and see what works. He starts by studying 30 minutes a week for each class, but ends up with a D on his first exams. He decides to try to double his study time to an hour a week for each class. Rashaad is using which problem-solving strategy for his semester?

a. Trial-and-error
b. Algorithm
c. Heuristics
d. Means end analysis

13. Damage to the _____ can negatively impact reading and writing, while damage to the _____ can cause conduction aphasia (or the inability to repeat words or sentences).

a. Wernicke's area; Broca's area
b. Broca's area; Wernicke's area
c. arcuate fasciculus; angular gyrus
d. angular gyrus; arcuate fasciculus

14. The three ways that confirmation bias can lead people astray are 1) influencing how people seek information, 2) _____, and 3) influencing how people remember information.

a. influencing how people sell information
b. influencing how people publish information
c. influencing how people use information
d. influencing how people interpret information

15. Which of the following is a criticism of the rational choice theory of decision making?

a. There is too much focus on decision making in unlikely situations.
b. This model emphasizes the role of avoidance of risk too heavily.
c. People must rely on intuition too much according to this model.
d. People must have access to all the relevant information to be able to make decisions according to this model.

16. The two components of creativity include generating novel and unusual ideas and _____.

a. generating ideas that are liked by many people
b. generating ideas that are functional or workable in some way
c. generating ideas that create excitement
d. generating ideas that can be available to mass audiences

17. Japanese students were more likely to describe the _____ of a scene, while American students were more likely to describe the _____ of a scene during a study to test how people perceive the world differently.

a. background; natural elements
b. background; prominent features
c. prominent features; background
d. natural elements; background

18. _____ is based on the fact that creative people are able to take ideas that are new or not highly valued and transform them through the process of creativity to become valuable.

a. Divergent thinking
b. Threshold theory of creativity
c. Investment theory of creativity
d. Convergent thinking

19. Which type of thinking style lends itself to the creative process?

a. Legalistic
b. Authoritative
c. Representative
d. Legislative

20. What are the smallest meaningful units in language called?

    a. Morphemes

    b. Phonemes

    c. Syntax

    d. Grammar

21. If you can only see one use for a hammer (e.g., to pound nails) and you fail to see other uses for the hammer, you are experiencing _____.

    a. mental set

    b. functional fixedness

    c. fixation

    d. confirmation bias

22. What is the system of rules that governs how language is composed and used?

    a. Syntax   b. Grammar

    c. Semantics   d. Phonemes

23. A rigid set of rules for classifying objects, events, or people is considered a _____.

    a. formal concept   b. natural concept

    c. prototype   d. concept

24. Children who learn a second language before what age develop a near perfect fluency?

    a. 10   b. 13

    c. 2   d. 7

25. The ability for a child to acquire new words or concepts with little exposure is called _____.

    a. expressive language

    b. telegraphic speech

    c. fast mapping

    d. fast napping

26. Ramon smiles at his mom when she holds him and makes cooing sounds when talked to. Ramon is probably what age?

    a. 3 months old   b. 1 month old

    c. 1 year old   d. 9 months old

27. Studies show that to engage in creative thinking, a person needs what level of intelligence?

    a. Above average only

    b. Average to above average

    c. Superior

    d. Below average to average

28. Imagine you discovered people who lived on the moon who had no words in their language for describing weather, which led them to perceive and think about temperature changes differently. This would provide evidence in support of the _____.

    a. receptive language theory

    b. critical period hypothesis

    c. linguistic relativity hypothesis

    d. language acquisition device

29. The tendency to judge how common an event is based on how easy it is to think of examples or instances is called _____.

    a. belief perseverance

    b. representativeness heuristic

    c. availability heuristic

    d. hindsight bias

30. Which hemisphere of the brain processes the semantics of language?

    a. Right   b. Left

    c. Both   d. Equally distributed

Chapter 8
Intelligence

Chapter Outline and Learning Objectives

Module 8.1–8.3: Theories of Intelligence

LO 8.1   Recognize why we study intelligence.

LO 8.2   Distinguish between traditional theories of intelligence.

LO 8.3   Describe expanded theories of intelligence, including emotional intelligence and Gardner's multiple intelligences.

Module 8.4–8.5: Measuring Intelligence

LO 8.4   Explain how intelligence was measured historically.

LO 8.5   Explain how intelligence is measured currently.

Module 8.6–8.7: Test Construction

LO 8.6   Explain the process of test standardization.

LO 8.7   Describe the importance of establishing reliability and validity in constructing intelligence tests.

Module 8.8–8.9: Nature and Nurture

LO 8.8   Describe the evidence for genetic influences on intelligence.

LO 8.9   Understand the impact of environmental factors on intelligence.

Module 8.10–8.12: Group and Individual Differences

LO 8.10   Describe the findings regarding racial and ethnic differences in intelligence.

LO 8.11   Understand the concept of stereotype threat.

LO 8.12   Explain individual differences in intelligence, including intellectual disability and giftedness.

Module 8.13: Piecing It Together: Intelligence and Test Bias

LO 8.13   Analyze how the cross-cutting themes of psychology are related to the topic of test bias.

What is Intelligence?

Journal Prompt: How Do You Define Intelligence?

How would you define "intelligence?" What do you think makes someone "intelligent" or not?

Even though we often use the word "intelligent" to describe people, it turns out that this concept is anything but simple. First, the construct of intelligence is notoriously difficult to define. Second, even if a definition can be agreed on, establishing appropriate measures of intelligence is a whole different challenge. Finally, understanding the unique contribution of genetics and the environment on intelligence is yet another complicated matter. This chapter delves into each of these issues to help you better understand this complex topic.

Intelligence: What Do You Think?

Module 8.1–8.3: Theories of Intelligence

Not everyone processes information the same way. Some of us are adept at solving complex math problems, while others are able to memorize mind-boggling amounts of text. Which skill is a better indication of mental prowess? For more than a century, psychologists have argued various theories of intelligence. But is intelligence really that easy to define? While we use adjectives such as "bright," "smart," and "intelligent" frequently in our day-to-day lives, when it comes to actually defining and understanding intelligence, the field of psychology has struggled for many decades. Is intelligence a specific "thing" you either have or don't have? Is it a group of abilities or characteristics? Does culture influence the way we define intelligence? These questions have motivated extensive research on the nature of intelligence and, while we may not know all the answers, most people agree that intelligence is an important characteristic.

Why Do We Study Intelligence?

LO 8.1   Recognize why we study intelligence.

What does it mean to be intelligent? If you've seen the classic version or the 2016 reboot of the TV show *MacGyver*, you've witnessed MacGyver's amazing ability to solve problems by being resourceful. In any given episode, MacGyver might make explosives from a select combination of jungle weeds or repair a crashing helicopter with duct tape. MacGyver obviously exhibits a great amount of practical and scientific intelligence. Does this mean he would also score well on the math section of the SAT? Would he be able to express himself eloquently in his writing? The answer might depend on what theory of intelligence is the most accurate.

A discussion of intelligence must start with a definition of the term. **Intelligence** is defined as the ability to learn and adapt from experience, solve problems, and apply knowledge in new situations (Legg & Hutter, 2007). Underlying this definition is the notion that intelligent people are able to use their cognitive abilities to interact effectively within their environment. When you think about it this way, it makes sense that *demonstrating* intelligence may actually differ from one culture to another or across time. For example, one research group studied children in Kenya. A highly adaptive skill that Kenyan children develop is the ability to correctly identify and utilize natural herbal medicines (Sternberg, 2004). This ability fits with every component of the previously stated definition of intelligence (namely, the ability to learn and adapt from experience, solve problems, and apply knowledge in new situations). Most Western children don't have these same abilities but they might show other capabilities that are more adaptive in their own environments.

The study of intelligence is important in the field of psychology for many reasons. First, intelligence is an individual characteristic that people view as important—both for themselves and others. For example, a past survey of high school students found that intelligence was rated as the second most desirable personal attribute, with 92% of the students surveyed rating intelligence as either "extremely important" or "important" (Brim, Jr., et al., 1969). Additionally, when people are looking for a future mate, both men and women rate intelligence as a top five personality characteristic in potential dating partners (Botwin et al., 1997; Li et al., 2002; Stone et al., 2012).

Additionally, intelligence is used to make decisions in a number of important arenas. For example, estimates of intelligence are often used in education settings (e.g., to identify students in need of special assistance or those who are gifted), when making employment decisions, and in clinical settings (e.g., evaluating people with brain injuries or dementia).

Intelligence (as measured by tests of intellectual abilities) has also been found to be predictive of numerous factors including school performance (Heaven & Ciarrochi, 2012), job success (Boyatzis et al., 2012; Gottfredson, 1997; Ree & Earles, 1992), quality of life (Palmer et al., 2002; Salguero et al., 2012), and even relationship success (Ciarrochi et al., 2002; Frederickson et al., 2012). One unique study conducted in Scotland was able to follow almost an entire birth cohort, or children born in the same year. In 1932, all Scottish children born in 1921 underwent intelligence testing and this population of children was then followed until age 76. As shown in Figure 8.1, researchers found that intelligence at age 11 actually predicted *morbidity* (or rate of illness or disease) and *mortality* (or rate of deaths) over the lifespan of the individuals (Deary et al., 2004; Gottfredson & Deary, 2004). One explanation for these findings is that intelligent people are better equipped to prevent chronic diseases and accidental injuries through superior problem-solving skills and reasoning abilities (Gottfredson & Deary, 2004).

Studies examining the relationship between intelligence and academic achievement in areas of reading, writing, and math have shown strong positive correlations (.80 or above) between these variables (Kaufman et al., 2012). As many intelligence experts have long pointed out, higher levels of intelligence are related to success in school (Duckworth & Seligman, 2005; Gottfredson, 2004; Kuncel et al., 2010; Lubinski, 2004) and to scores on college entrance exams such as the SAT (Frey & Detterman, 2004). While intelligence is not the only factor in determining academic success, evidence clearly points to intelligence playing a significant role.

Given the breadth of findings relating intelligence to a variety of life outcomes, the use of intelligence testing in decision making, and the importance that most individuals place on the notion of intelligence, studying intelligence as a construct is important. Because of the implications of studies of intelligence, it is critical for psychologists to (1) understand what comprises the concept of intelligence and (2) develop accurate and effective measures of intelligence.

intelligence

the ability to learn and adapt from experience, solve problems, and apply knowledge in new situations

Figure 8.1 IQ at Age 11 and Longevity

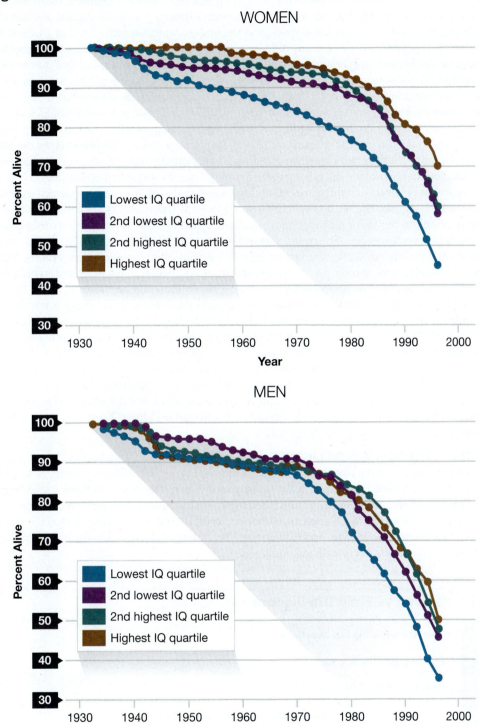

Traditional Theories of Intelligence

LO 8.2   Distinguish between traditional theories of intelligence.

For more than a century, psychologists have proposed and debated about various theories of intelligence. Some theorists have proposed that intelligence is a single characteristic and the "driving force" behind many abilities. Other theorists have argued that intelligence is more complicated and includes a compilation of different cognitive abilities.

general intelligence (or *g*)

represents a broad mental capacity that influences performance on mental tasks

SPEARMAN'S THEORY OF GENERAL INTELLIGENCE   Psychologist Charles Spearman proposed a theory of **general intelligence (or *g*)**, arguing that *g* represents a common factor that underlies certain mental abilities. According to Spearman's theory, *g* includes mental abilities that are distinct from memory, physical abilities, and the senses. An individual's level of *g* would impact the person's performance on many different mental tasks such as abstract reasoning, problem solving, or quickly learning new information (Spearman, 1904). Keep in mind that *g* represents mental *aptitude* (or your overall capability or potential), which is not always the same as actual performance or achievement. For example, your math aptitude can be differentiated from your performance on a math test. You may perform poorly on an exam due to a number of factors (e.g., you were sick or you forgot one key formula), despite having a generally strong math capability. Likewise, *g* should also be distinguished from *acquired knowledge*. Being a trivia buff is not the same as having high levels of general intelligence, although very often *g* and acquired knowledge levels are related because *g* provides an advantage in learning capacity and speed of learning.

specific intelligence (or "s")

represents abilities related to a specific single mental activity

Spearman believed that measures of intelligence should seek to assess *g* as much as possible while limiting what he termed **specific (or "s")** factors. These factors are abilities related to a specific single activity. For example, playing music by ear is likely to be an ability that is high in *s* and relatively lower in *g*. Spearman showed that two factors that are high in *g* would often be positively correlated, while two factors high in *s* would often have low correlations. Many years of research have shown that performance on many mental tasks is related, which provides some support for the notion of an underlying general intelligence factor (Carroll, 2003).

In other attempts to identify what makes up general intelligence, psychologists have found that quick speeds in processing information often contribute to high scores on intelligence tests (Deary, 2001; Robitaille et al., 2013). A person's high capacity for working memory has also been identified as an important factor in general intelligence (Conway et al., 2011; Kyllonen & Christal, 1990; Tourva et al., 2016). Besides these factors, mental self-monitoring also appears to play a role. Researchers find that strong **central executive functioning** (the set of mental processes that governs goals, strategies, and coordination of the mind's activities) is related to higher intelligence (Barbey et al., 2012; Duncan, 2000; Royall & Palmer, 2014), and brain activity has been documented to support these ideas.

central executive functioning

a set of mental processes that involves mental control and self-regulation

CATTELL'S THEORY OF INTELLIGENCE   In contrast, psychologist Raymond Cattell argued that intelligence was not a single entity, but that different types of intelligence were, in fact, distinct from one another. He defined **fluid intelligence (Gf)** as the ability to think logically and solve problems. Abilities requiring fluid intelligence include pattern recognition, abstract reasoning, and problem solving. Cattell also described **crystallized intelligence (Gc)** as the mental ability to use skills, knowledge, and experience. Vocabulary and general knowledge tests have been used as measures of crystallized intelligence.

fluid intelligence

the ability to think and reason abstractly and solve problems

crystallized intelligence

the ability to use learned skills, knowledge, and experience

Crystallized vs Fluid Intelligence

Answer the following two questions:

1. Entomology is the science that studies [_____].

2. What comes next: 2   4   8   16   32 [____]

Identify which type of intelligence (crystallized intelligence or fluid intelligence) is most closely related to each question above:

1. [_____]

2. [_____]

Start Over   Check Answers

Figure 8.2 Fluid Intelligence versus Crystallized Intelligence Over the Lifespan

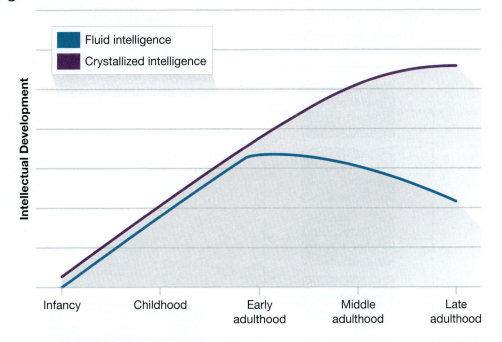

The distinction between crystallized and fluid intelligence has been particularly interesting in research examining the impact of aging on intelligence. As demonstrated in Figure 8.2, Cattell's research found that as people age, they accumulate more crystallized knowledge, but their fluid intelligence levels decrease (Cattell, 1963; Horn, 1982; Schroeders et al., 2015; Thorsen et al., 2014). Many current intelligence tests have adopted a form of Cattell's model in the development of their tests. However, there has been some confusion about how to define Gc, what abilities actually constitute Gc, and how to measure it (Keith & Reynolds, 2010; Schipolowski et al., 2014). Additionally, measuring *purely* crystallized intelligence or *purely* fluid intelligence is not possible, given that any task includes components of both. In the previous example, recognizing the pattern in the numbers is typically considered a task of fluid intelligence, but it also requires some crystallized intelligence, or acquired knowledge (e.g., recognizing numbers).

Cattell's theory has been expanded in recent years to incorporate the work of John Horn and John Carroll into the **Cattell-Horn-Carroll (CHC) model of intelligence**, which includes nine different broad ability areas (with more than 70 narrow abilities within these categories): (1) crystallized intelligence, (2) fluid intelligence, (3) quantitative reasoning, (4) reading and writing ability, (5) short-term memory, (6) long-term storage and retrieval, (7) visual processing, (8) auditory processing, and (9) processing speed (McGrew, 2005; McGrew, 2009; Newton & McGrew, 2010). Shown in Figure 8.3, this model has been called the "most comprehensive and empirically supported psychometric theory of the structure of cognitive and academic abilities to date" (Alfonso et al., 2005, p. 185). It was developed in a series of studies using a statistical procedure known as *factor analysis*. Factor analysis is used to examine if there are different underlying variables in a set of test items. For example, you have presumably been exposed to some standardized testing in school in the past, and those tests usually are broken into subtests (e.g., reading and math). If you took every student's answers to all of the items assessing reading and math and subjected their scores to factor analysis, the results would likely show that the measure included two underlying variables—reading skills and math skills. The CHC model of intelligence has received support from studies using factor analysis (Lichtenberger & Kaufman, 2009; Niileksela et al., 2013; Schneider & McGrew, 2012; Weiss et al., 2013a).

Cattell-Horn-Carroll (CHC) model of intelligence

a hierarchical model of intelligence that includes nine different broad ability areas broken down into more than 70 narrow abilities

Figure 8.3 Cattell-Horn-Carroll Model of Intelligence

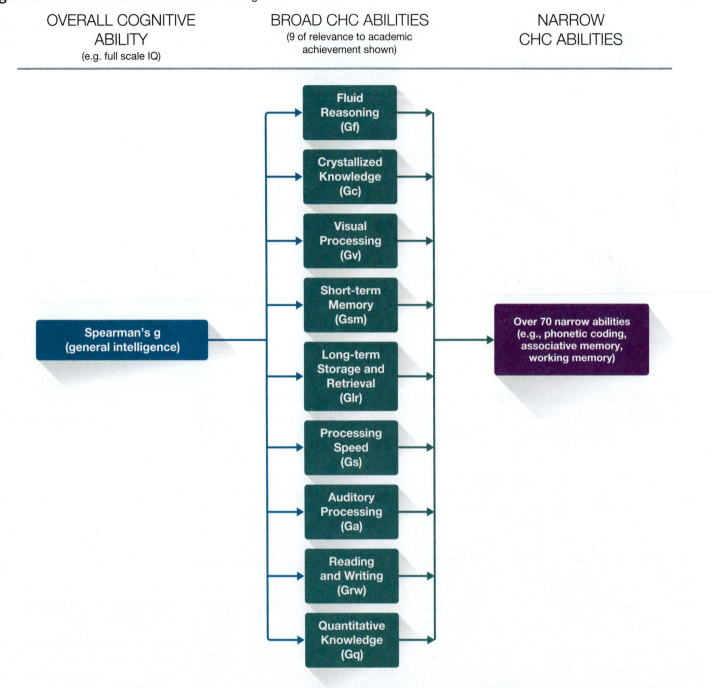

OVERALL COGNITIVE ABILITY
(e.g. full scale IQ)

BROAD CHC ABILITIES
(9 of relevance to academic achievement shown)

NARROW CHC ABILITIES

Spearman's g (general intelligence)

Fluid Reasoning (Gf)

Crystallized Knowledge (Gc)

Visual Processing (Gv)

Short-term Memory (Gsm)

Long-term Storage and Retrieval (Glr)

Processing Speed (Gs)

Auditory Processing (Ga)

Reading and Writing (Grw)

Quantitative Knowledge (Gq)

Over 70 narrow abilities (e.g., phonetic coding, associative memory, working memory)

analytic intelligence

one of Sternberg's three types of intelligence that includes the ability to analyze and evaluate ideas, solve problems, and make decisions

creative intelligence

one of Sternberg's three types of intelligence that includes a person's ability to adapt to new situations, come up with unique ideas, and think of novel solutions to problems

STERNBERG'S TRIARCHIC THEORY OF INTELLIGENCE As the following video points out, Robert Sternberg (1985) proposed a model that includes three aspects of successful intelligence. The aspect most people probably think of when they hear the word *intelligence* is **analytic intelligence**, or academic problem-solving intelligence. This is the type of intelligence generally assessed by intelligence tests that present well-defined problems with only one correct answer. The second aspect, **creative intelligence**, isn't just referring to a skill possessed by those people in the creative arts. If you're a creative thinker—meaning, if you can adapt to new situations; come up with unique, unusual ideas; and think of novel solutions to problems— then you have creative intelligence. **Practical intelligence**, the third aspect in Sternberg's theory, is the ability to find many solutions to complicated or poorly defined problems and use those solutions in practical, everyday situations. For example, when you discover the train you normally take to work isn't going to arrive that morning, you might use practical intelligence to hash out an alternative transportation plan that still gets you to work on time.

Sternberg's Theory of Intelligence

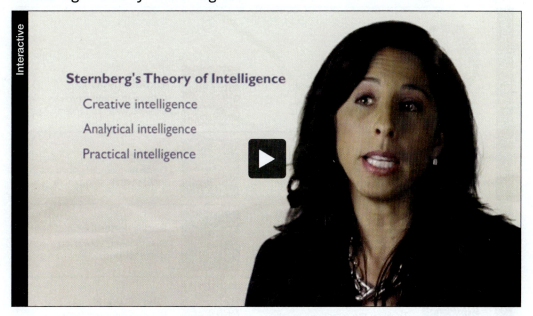

Sternberg's work has been influential in highlighting the importance of the *application* of cognitive skills to one's environment. The study discussed previously examining adaptive cognitive skills among children in Kenya was conducted by Sternberg and his colleagues. To highlight the importance of understanding the role of culture in studying intelligence, Sternberg (2004) stated that "intelligence cannot be fully or even meaningfully understood outside its cultural context" (p. 325). However, one critique of this theory is the fact that the empirical support for the triarchic theory is not as impressive as the support for *g*, or a general intelligence factor and that practical intelligence is likely highly related to *g* (Gottfredson, 2003). Additionally, the relationship between creativity and intelligence in many studies has actually shown to be quite small, suggesting that creativity may not be as integral to intelligence as Sternberg has proposed (Kim, 2005).

practical intelligence
one of Sternberg's three types of intelligence that includes a person's ability to find solutions to problems and use those solutions in practical, everyday situations

Expanded Theories of Intelligence

LO 8.3   **Describe expanded theories of intelligence, including emotional intelligence and Gardner's multiple intelligences.**

The theories of intelligence that have been discussed thus far have all generally viewed intelligence as a single complex construct or a set of constructs that are related. Some theorists have proposed that intelligence actually comprises relatively independent abilities that might not be captured adequately by our current intelligence tests. Two of the more well-known theories based on this model are Gardner's theory of multiple intelligences and the theory of emotional intelligence.

GARDNER'S THEORY OF MULTIPLE INTELLIGENCES   Howard Gardner's (1983, 2004) **theory of multiple intelligences** is fairly well-known today. Gardner argued that traditional measurements of intelligence were too limited and that people have a range of different "intelligences," including the following nine factors: (1) musical-rhythmic, (2) visual-spatial, (3) verbal-linguistic, (4) logical-mathematical, (5) bodily-kinesthetic, (6) interpersonal, (7) intrapersonal, (8) naturalistic, and (9) existential. Depicted in Figure 8.4, each of Gardner's nine intelligences is distinct from the others, which means we may be very talented in some of these areas and completely untalented in others. Someone who's a great dancer may have bodily–kinesthetic intelligence, musical intelligence, and spatial intelligence, but she might have difficulty making friends or interacting with people—meaning that interpersonal intelligence is probably not her strong suit. Unlike the CHC theory, Gardner does not propose that each of the nine intelligences is a subcomponent of overall *g*.

Gardner's theory has been of particular interest to educators who hoped to tailor their lesson plans according to individual students' strengths and weaknesses. For example, a musical learner might find it easier to memorize facts if the teacher encouraged that learner to create

theory of multiple intelligences
theory of intelligence that proposes nine specific modalities of intelligence rather than a single general ability

Figure 8.4 Gardner's Multiple Intelligences

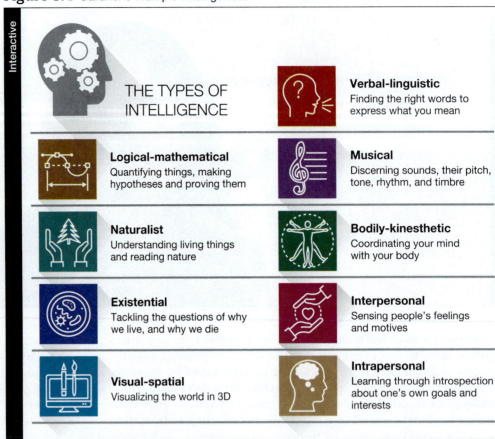

a song or rhyme incorporating the information. While this approach may seem intuitive, and as much as we would like to believe that everyone can be smart in some way, there simply isn't any strong empirical evidence in support of multiple intelligences or its effective application in the classroom (Gottfredson, 1998; Visser et al., 2006a; Visser et al., 2006b, Waterhouse, 2006a; Waterhouse, 2006b). Much like the findings related to learning styles, no evidence suggests that students learn better when instruction is targeted to a student's specific intelligence. Additionally, it turns out that many of the nine intelligences proposed by Gardner correlate with the *g* factor, which actually provides support for Spearman's theory of a single underlying construct of intelligence (Visser et al., 2006a). Finally, another weakness of Gardner's theory is the difficulty involved in actually measuring nine different intelligences.

SOCIAL AND EMOTIONAL INTELLIGENCE   Can you squeeze yourself into any social group with ease? Do you know when to speak and when to remain silent? How well do you tune in to others' emotions and adjust your own behavior accordingly? You might not identify with all these characteristics, but all of us probably know a few individuals with these skills. This ability to negotiate new social environments has been called *social intelligence* (Cantor & Kihlstrom, 1987). If you are socially intelligent, you can easily understand social situations and the part you should play to be a successful group member. Consider a salesperson as an example. If you've ever made an impulsive purchase after an interaction with a salesperson, you realize the unique skill of these people. A successful salesperson has the ability to read the client and be persistent and persuasive but not come across as too pushy.

One important facet of social intelligence is **emotional intelligence**, or a person's ability to perceive, understand, manage, and utilize his or her emotions. Emotional intelligence as a theory of intelligence was first proposed by Peter Salovey and John Mayer in 1989. After the publication of the best-selling book *Emotional Intelligence* by Daniel Goleman in 1995, the theory received significant attention in both scientific and popular circles. According to the original model proposed by Salovey and Mayer (Mayer et al., 2001; Mayer & Caruso, 2004; Mayer & Salovey, 1993; Mayer et al., 2008; Salovey & Mayer, 1989), emotional intelligence includes the following four components:

emotional intelligence

a person's ability to perceive, understand, manage, and utilize his or her emotions

1. Ability to accurately perceive emotions in oneself and others
2. Ability to use emotions to facilitate thought
3. Ability to understand emotions and emotional knowledge
4. Ability to effectively regulate emotions

The concept of emotional intelligence has certainly struck a mainstream chord. For many years, *Forbes* magazine actually published a list each year of the "Top 10 Emotional Intelligence Moments." Psychological research into the nature of emotional intelligence and its ability to predict outcomes has also exploded. Applying the notion of emotional intelligence to successful job performance has been a particularly prolific research area. On the whole, studies have shown that while cognitive intelligence (e.g., g) has continued to be the top predictor of job performance (Schmidt et al., 2008), emotional intelligence can also provide additional predictive information about job performance even after cognitive intelligence is known (O'Boyle et al., 2011; Van Rooy & Viswesvaran, 2004). Interestingly, research has found that people who suffer brain damage that impairs their emotional intelligence tend to have unimpaired levels of cognitive intelligence (Bar-On et al., 2003). This finding provides biologically-based support for the idea that we may have distinct and independent types of intelligence.

Of course, the theory of emotional intelligence is not without its criticisms. One of the concerns with the theory is that there have been several different definitions and conceptualizations of emotional intelligence, which makes it difficult to interpret all of the findings in this area (Conte, 2005; Landy, 2005; McCleskey, 2014; Murphy, 2014). Perhaps more problematic are the criticisms that this is too broad a definition of intelligence (Locke, 2005). Are the abilities described in the theory of emotional intelligence truly aspects of intelligence, or could they better be conceptualized as personality characteristics? The debate about these issues continues and isn't likely to be resolved any time soon.

Theories of Intelligence

Look at the following table summarizing the theories of intelligence. Use the clues within the table to correctly drag and drop the information below into the correct position in the table.

Theory	Description	Strength	Criticism
Spearman's Theory of General Intelligence (g)	Intelligence can best be represented by a single factor underlying many mental tasks.	Measures of different abilities (e.g., verbal and spatial skills) tend to be correlated suggesting an underlying common factor.	A single general intelligence factor cannot adequately capture the diversity of human abilities.
Emotional Intelligence	A type of intelligence related to a person's ability to perceive, understand, manage, and utilize his or her emotions.	Evidence suggesting that this type of intelligence is particularly related to job performance.	May be too broad a definition of intelligence and may actually capture a personality characteristic instead.
Gardner's Multiple Intelligences	Theory that there are nine different types of intelligence.	Highlights the importance of many other skills in addition to verbal and spatial skills.	(1) Limited empirical support, (2) many of the factors correlate with g, (3) difficult to measure some proposed intelligences.
Sternberg's Triarchic Theory	Model of intelligence including three major aspects: analytic, creative, and practical intelligence.	Focuses on the importance of creative and practical abilities in a cultural context.	The practical component of intelligence appears to be heavily influenced by g suggesting an underlying general intelligence. Also, studies show that creativity and intelligence are not strongly related.
Cattell (Gc and Gf) and Cattell-Horn-Carroll (CHC) Model	Model that initially divided g into two subcategories and was later expanded to a total of nine broad abilities.	The distinction between the two factors of intelligence has been useful in research on intelligence over the lifespan and the expanded model has support from factor analyses.	Crystallized intelligence has not been consistently defined or measured.

Interactive

Start Over

Quiz for Module 8.1–8.3

1. _____ is the ability to learn and adapt from experience, problem solve, and apply knowledge to new situations.
   a. Street smarts
   b. Achievement
   c. Academic success
   d. Intelligence

2. Intelligence can predict positive outcomes in different areas of life such as _____.
   a. school performance, marital satisfaction, and quality of life
   b. job success, increased mental health, and quality of life
   c. job success, marital satisfaction, and quality of life
   d. school performance, job success, and quality of life

3. General intelligence (g) is related to a person's _____, or their overall potential or capability, while _____ are abilities related to a specific single activity.
   a. knowledge; nonspecific factors
   b. attitude; specific factors
   c. aptitude; specific factors
   d. skills; nonspecific factors

4. A puzzle is a measure of _____ intelligence, while a trivia quiz is a measure of _____ intelligence.
   a. general; specific
   b. skill-based; knowledge-based
   c. crystallized; fluid
   d. fluid; crystallized

5. According to Gardner, if Mitch is a phenomenal baseball player but fails most of his classes in college, Mitch would be said to have a strength in what type of intelligence?
   a. Naturalist
   b. Spatial
   c. Bodily-kinesthetic
   d. Interpersonal

6. The four components of emotional intelligence include: the ability to perceive emotions in oneself and others, _____, the ability to understand emotions and emotional knowledge, and _____.
   a. the ability to effectively regulate emotions; the ability to suppress emotions
   b. the ability to use emotions to facilitate thought; the ability to suppress emotions
   c. the ability to use emotions to facilitate thoughts; the ability to effectively regulate emotions
   d. the ability to effectively regulate emotions; the ability to use gut instinct

"'IQ'? — I thought this was a *haiku* test!"

Module 8.4–8.5: Measuring Intelligence

One of the most important issues in studying intelligence is to determine how to accurately measure intelligence. The findings relating intelligence to academic performance, physical health, and job performance are based on correlations between these variables and some measure of intelligence. Additionally, measurements of intelligence can have a significant impact on individual lives. Therefore, it's extremely important that the tools we develop to assess intelligence are (1) accurately measuring the construct and (2) used appropriately in decision making. Unfortunately, as the following video points out, the field of intelligence testing has not always succeeded at these two tasks.

Intelligence Testing, Then and Now

Historical Measures of Intelligence

LO 8.4 **Explain how intelligence was measured historically.**

The history of intelligence testing starts in the early 1900s in France. From that point until now, the intelligence tests and the ways the scores have been used have changed significantly.

Historical Measures of Intelligence

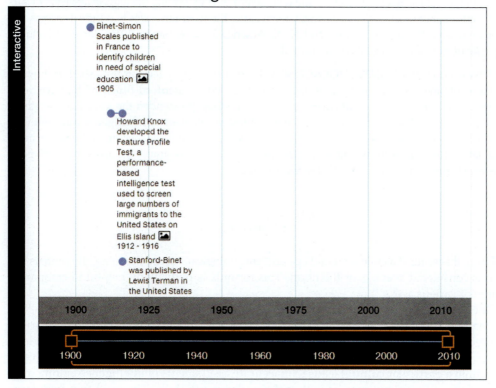

Interactive

Binet-Simon Scales published in France to identify children in need of special education 1905

Howard Knox developed the Feature Profile Test, a performance-based intelligence test used to screen large numbers of immigrants to the United States on Ellis Island 1912 - 1916

Stanford-Binet was published by Lewis Terman in the United States

| 1900 | 1925 | 1950 | 1975 | 2000 | 2010 |

| 1900 | 1920 | 1940 | 1960 | 1980 | 2000 | 2010 |

Table 8.1 Binet-Simon Sample Items

Age level 3

1. Point to various parts of a face
2. Repeat two digits forward

Age level 4

1. Name familiar objects
2. Repeat three digits forward

Age level 5

1. Copy a square
2. Repeat a sentence containing ten syllables

Age level 6

1. State age
2. Repeat a sentence containing sixteen syllables

Age level 7

1. Copy a diamond
2. Repeat five digits forward

Age level 8

1. Recall two items from a passage
2. State the differences between two objects

Age level 9

1. Recall six items from a passage
2. Recite days of the week

Age level 10

1. Given three common words, construct a sentence
2. Recite months of the year in order

Age level 11

1. Define abstract words (for example, *justice*)
2. Determine what is wrong with absurd statements

Age level 12

1. Repeat seven digits forward
2. Provide the meaning of pictures

Age level 13

1. State the differences between pairs of abstract terms

BINET-SIMON SCALES In 1904, French psychologist Alfred Binet and psychiatrist Theodore Simon were asked to develop a test that could help teachers identify students with special needs. At that time, France had passed a law mandating universal education for all children. There was a need to be able to identify children who were thought to have intellectual deficiencies in order to provide them with special education assistance. Binet and Simon developed a battery of assessments from the existing resources of the time and arranged the tests according to age level. For example, the digit span test (measuring the longest list of digits that a person can repeat back in the correct order immediately after presentation) would be administered by starting with the average number of items remembered by children of the same age. If the child answered correctly, he/she would progress to a higher age level. If

Binet-Simon scales

the first widely used intelligence test developed by French psychologist Alfred Binet and psychiatrist Theodore Simon to help teachers identify students with special needs

Stanford-Binet Intelligence Scale

a standardized intelligence test measuring cognitive abilities in children and adults that was originally an English adaptation of the Binet-Simon scales in French

intelligence quotient (IQ)

a number representing a person's overall intellectual ability that used to be based on the relationship between an individual's actual age and his/her mental age but is now based on a standard score with a mean of 100 and a standard deviation of 15

mental age

a measure of an individual's intellectual level based on the age at which it takes an average individual to reach the same level of attainment

culture-bound

valid only within a particular culture

the child was incorrect, he/she would be administered a lower age-level item. This process would continue until the child's "intellectual level" could be determined by finding the highest age level of successful performance (Boake, 2002). This test, known as the **Binet-Simon scales** was a great success and was administered throughout Europe and North America (Binet & Simon, 1916). Table 8.1 includes sample items from the original Binet-Simon scales.

THE STANFORD-BINET INTELLIGENCE SCALE   In 1916, Lewis Terman published an English adaptation of Binet's test through Stanford University, called the **Stanford-Binet Intelligence Scale** (Terman, 1916). This test was particularly significant because it extended the test to assess adults as well as children. The Stanford-Binet was the first test to calculate an **intelligence quotient (IQ)** based on the relationship between an individual's actual age and his/her **mental age** (or intellectual level). Remember from your math class that a "quotient" is simply the answer to a division problem. Therefore, IQ refers to the following formula:

$$IQ = \frac{Mental\ age}{Chronological\ age} \times 100$$

Using this scale, if a child's mental age and chronological age are the same, the score is 100 which is considered average, or the norm. This formula is particularly helpful in comparing children of various ages.

One of the limitations of the early Stanford-Binet was its sole emphasis on verbal skills. This made it difficult to accurately assess intelligence among people who were hearing-impaired or had limited English-speaking abilities. As discussed earlier in the video *Intelligence Testing, Then and Now*, using questions that are heavily **culture-bound** (valid only within a particular culture) leads to inaccurate assessments of intelligence among individuals from different cultures or with different language skills. The need to screen large numbers of immigrants to the United States in the early 1900s led to an emphasis on developing performance-based measures of intelligence. Such measures were developed for use in the assessment program at Ellis Island in New York. An example of a performance-based measure used on Ellis Island is shown in Figure 8.5. This task presented the person with a random array of pieces that were to be quickly put together like a puzzle. Theoretically, measures that require an individual to physically "perform" a task rather than verbally recite an answer would reduce the influence of culture and language on the results.

Figure 8.5 Example of Ellis Island Performance Task

INTELLIGENCE TESTING AND THE U.S. ARMY Intelligence testing became much more widespread during World War I. At that time, the U.S. Army needed a way to screen recruits quickly and effectively to determine (1) if they were cognitively capable of serving at all; (2) what job classification would be best for a particular individual; and (3) the individual's potential, if any, for a leadership role. Psychologists developed two versions of a brief intelligence test that could be quickly administered in large group formats. The Army Alpha test was similar to the verbal tests in the Stanford-Binet and was group-administered to literate, English speakers. The Army Beta test was similar to the performance-based tests used on Ellis Island and was group-administered to illiterate or non-English proficient recruits. From 1917 to 1919, records suggest that the Army Alpha and Beta tests were administered to a staggering 1,726,966 recruits (Yerkes, 1921).

Intelligence was evaluated using the Army Alpha and Army Beta tests during World War I.

Current Measures of Intelligence

LO 8.5 **Explain how intelligence is measured currently.**

Currently, intelligence tests continue to be widely administered. Today's intelligence tests are often still referred to as IQ tests, yet for the most part they use standard scores that allow scores from different IQ tests to be directly compared. The Stanford-Binet is now in its fifth edition (SB5) and can be administered to individuals from ages 2 through 85. Unlike its primarily verbally-focused predecessor, the current version of the Stanford-Binet includes both verbal and nonverbal domains. However, despite the longevity of the Stanford-Binet test, the Wechsler scales have reigned supreme in the world of intelligence testing for several decades (Kaufman & Lichtenberger, 2005).

THE WECHSLER SCALES Heavily influence by his experiences as an Army examiner, Wechsler developed a derivative of the Army Alpha and Army Beta tests to assist him in his work with adults at Bellevue Hospital in New York City. He first published the Wechsler Adult Intelligence Scale (WAIS) in 1939 (Wechsler, 1939). The current version of the Wechsler scale for the assessment of intelligence in adults is the Wechsler Adult Intelligence Scale Fourth Edition (WAIS-IV), which was published in 2008 (Wechsler, 2008). The WAIS-IV can be administered to people from the age of 16 to 90 by a qualified professional. The latest edition of the WAIS-IV included a notable change from previous editions. All prior versions of the Wechsler scale had provided a verbal score and a performance score which both equally contributed to what is called a Full Scale IQ (FSIQ). The WAIS-IV structure changed so that four different index scores now contribute equally to the calculation of the FSIQ. These four index scores include:

1. *Verbal Comprehension Index*
   - measure of verbal concept formation, verbal reasoning, and knowledge acquired from one's environment
2. *Perceptual Reasoning Index*
   - measure of perceptual and fluid reasoning, spatial processing, and visual-motor integration
3. *Working Memory Index*
   - measure of working memory abilities, which involve attention, concentration, mental control, and reasoning
4. *Processing Speed Index*
   - measure of the ability to quickly and correctly scan, sequence, and discriminate simple visual information requiring short-term visual memory, attention, and visual-motor coordination

The WAIS-IV includes 10 core subtests used to calculate each of the four index scores and the FSIQ. The table below provides a description of 4 of the 10 subtests and an example of the subtests. Take a minute to read the information and then drag and drop the subtests into the correct index score.

WAIS-IV Factors

Take a minute to read the information and then drag and drop the subtests into the correct index score.

Subtest Name	Subtest Description (Lichtenberger & Kaufman, 2009)	Example Item	Index Score
Block Design	Working within a specified time limit, the examinee views a model and a picture, or a picture only and uses red-and-white blocks to recreate the design.		Perceptual Reasoning Index
Coding	Using a key, the examinee copies symbols that are paired with numbers within a specified time limit.	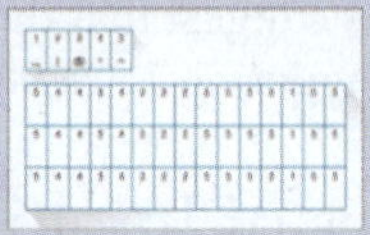	Processing Speed Index
Similarities	Examinee is presented two words that represent common objects or concepts and describes how they are similar.	"In what way are copper and brass alike?"	Verbal Comprehension Index
Arithmetic	Working within a specified time limit, the examinee mentally solves a series of arithmetic problems.	"Greg has 15 pens and 4 friends. If he gives each friend an equal number of pens, how many will he have left?"	Working Memory Index

Check Your Understanding

There are also two Wechsler scales designed to measure intelligence in children. The Wechsler Intelligence Scale for Children Fifth Edition (WISC-V) is administered to children ages 6 to 16, and the Wechsler Preschool and Primary Scale of Intelligence Fourth Edition (WPPSI-IV) is administered to children as young as 2 years and 6 months and as old as 7 years and 7 months. The latest edition of both scales has been published since the release of the WAIS-IV in 2008 and has expanded on the four-factor structure of the WAIS-IV to now include five index scores. The Perceptual Reasoning Index was split into two different score domains, including the Visual Spatial and the Fluid Reasoning Index scores (see Figure 8.6). The new factor structure most closely aligns with the Cattell-Horn-Carroll (CHC) theory of intelligence. From the previous figure depicting the CHC model, you can see that the new WISC-V and WPPSI-IV factor structure in Figure 8.7 includes five of the nine broad abilities proposed in the model (now shown in red in Figure 8.7), and this model has been supported empirically (Benson et al., 2010; Weiss et al., 2013a, 2013b).

Figure 8.6 New Factors in WISC-V and WPPSI-IV

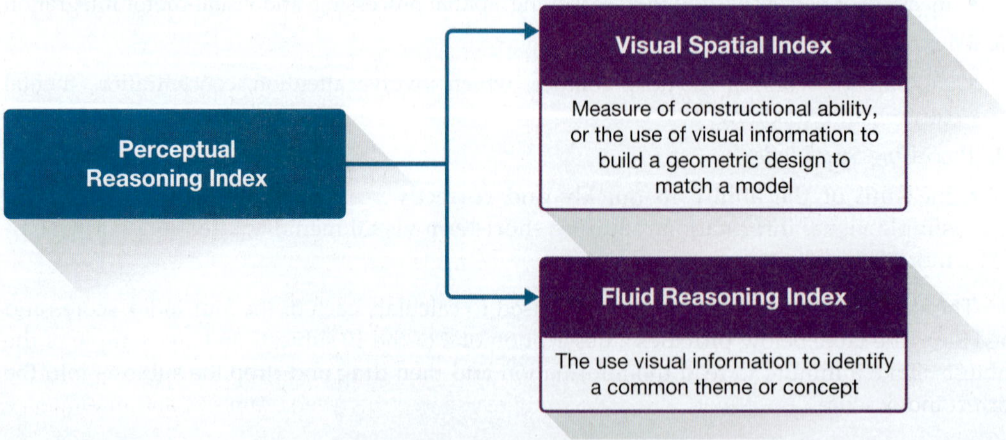

Perceptual Reasoning Index

Visual Spatial Index

Measure of constructional ability, or the use of visual information to build a geometric design to match a model

Fluid Reasoning Index

The use visual information to identify a common theme or concept

Figure 8.7 Using the CHC Model in the New Wechsler Intelligence Tests

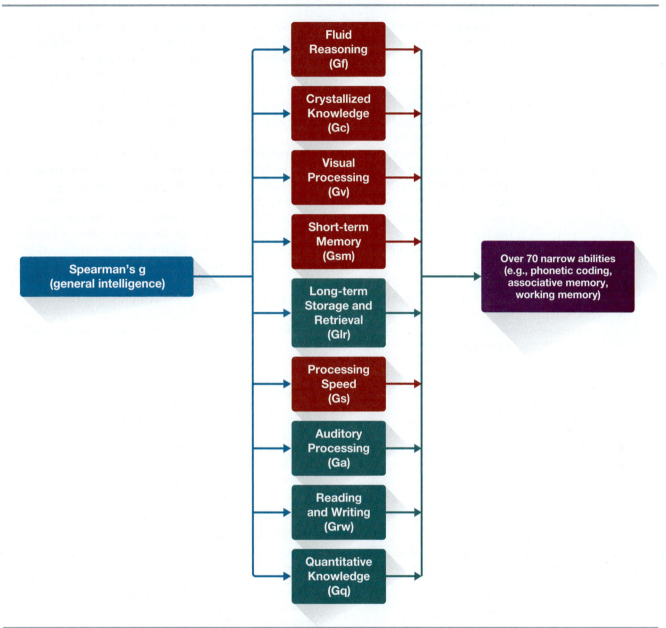

OVERALL COGNITIVE ABILITY
(e.g. full scale IQ)

BROAD CHC ABILITIES
(9 of relevance to academic achievement shown)

NARROW CHC ABILITIES

Spearman's g (general intelligence)

Fluid Reasoning (Gf)

Crystallized Knowledge (Gc)

Visual Processing (Gv)

Short-term Memory (Gsm)

Long-term Storage and Retrieval (Glr)

Processing Speed (Gs)

Auditory Processing (Ga)

Reading and Writing (Grw)

Quantitative Knowledge (Gq)

Over 70 narrow abilities (e.g., phonetic coding, associative memory, working memory)

You may be wondering if an intelligence test can really be accurate for a preschooler. Generally, the older the child is at the first assessment, the higher the correlation with IQ in adulthood. While measures of IQ before age 4 have shown significant correlations with measures in adolescence and early adulthood (ranging from .36 to .59), one study by Schneider et al. (2014) suggested that stability increases with increased age. For example, in this study, the correlation between IQ at age 7 and IQ in adolescence and early adulthood ranged from .88 to .95, which was substantially higher than the correlations with IQ in children ages 4 and younger. A longitudinal study examining the stability of IQ over the lifetime found that the correlations between IQ measured at age 7 and later adulthood (Deary et al., 2000; Deary et al., 2004; Deary et al., 2013; Gow et al., 2011) are generally high and stable until the late 80s.

NEUROLOGICAL MEASURES OF INTELLIGENCE Since larger muscles often indicate greater strength, you might think that a larger brain indicates greater intelligence. In fact, several studies have indicated that there is a slight correlation between brain size and intelligence

(Jerison, 2012; Passingham, 1979; Ritchie et al., 2015). Prefrontal cortex areas show an increased activity during difficult tasks, and prefrontal cortex size is linked to intelligence more closely than the size of any other area in the brain (Schnack et al., 2014; Sternberg, 2012). However, uncontrolled variables such as nutrition and environmental stimulation, could cause both above-average intelligence and large brains, so it's not clear that brain size is directly a function of intelligence.

Instead, the neural component of intelligence might be more closely related to the brain's *plasticity*, or its flexible ability to grow and change. A study by neuroscientist Philip Shaw and his colleagues (2006) on a group of children who were "highly intelligent" according to intelligence tests revealed a link between the thickening and thinning rate of the brain's cortex and intelligence: Very intelligent children tended to have a thinner cortex than their peers during childhood, but the cortex thickened more rapidly during the pre-teen years. These results suggest a relationship, at least in childhood, between the rate at which the brain matures and IQ.

Does intelligence reside in a particular part of the brain? Some believe there is a "global workspace for organizing and coordinating information" in the brain's frontal lobe (Duncan, 2000), but this assertion is the subject of hot debate among intelligence researchers. However, there are a few correlations that may help us pin down the connections between intelligence and the brain. First of all, there are correlations between a person's intelligence test score and his or her **perceptual speed**, or the time it takes a person to perceive and compare stimuli. People with higher scores tend to take in perceptual information more quickly than their lower-scoring counterparts. There also seems to be a relationship between high intelligence test scores and the speed and complexity of activity in the brain. People with high intelligence scores tend to exhibit complex, fast-moving brain wave activity in response to simple stimuli. While this finding is certainly interesting, its significance is uncertain: We still don't know why fast reactions to simple tasks should be a good predictor of intelligence.

perceptual speed

the ability to quickly and accurately compare letters, numbers, objects, pictures, or patterns

Quiz for Module 8.4–8.5

1. Which of the following was the first intelligence test to be developed?
   a. Army Alpha and Army Beta
   b. Stanford-Binet Intelligence Scales
   c. Wechsler Adult Intelligence Scale
   d. Binet-Simon Scales

2. The Stanford-Binet Intelligence Scale was the first test to calculate the _____ based on the relationship between a person's actual age and his/her mental age.
   a. intelligence score
   b. intelligence quotient
   c. mathematical formula
   d. mathematical ability

3. Which intelligence test is the most widely administered today?
   a. Stanford-Simon Scales
   b. Stanford-Binet Scales
   c. Binet-Simon Scales
   d. Weschler Scales (WAIS-IV)

4. The WAIS-IV includes four index scores that contribute equally to the calculation of the _____.
   a. verbal and performance intelligence quotient (VBIQ)
   b. full scale intelligence quotient (FSIQ)
   c. flat out intelligence quotient (FOIQ)
   d. perceptual reasoning intelligence quotient (PRIQ)

5. Ahna complained of problems with spatial skills and visual-motor skills and was administered only part of an intelligence test. She was asked to rearrange blocks to match a picture and solve puzzles. She was most likely being assessed on which of the four index scores of a WAIS-IV?
   a. Processing Speed Index
   b. Working Memory Index
   c. Perceptual Reasoning Index
   d. Verbal Comprehension Index

Module 8.6–8.7: Test Construction

Is a person's measured IQ a true indicator of intelligence? After all, the whole point of intelligence tests is to accurately measure the underlying construct of intelligence. However, simply administering a bunch of tests that look like they should be related to intelligence and calling the results an IQ score doesn't mean it is actually measuring intelligence. You've probably seen those quickie-IQ tests pop up on Facebook or other online formats, but what makes those tests any different from the Wechsler scales?

Standardization

LO 8.6 **Explain the process of test standardization.**

Wechsler was critical of the Stanford-Binet because of the difficulty in using a mental age/chronological age scoring system with adults. After all, what does it really mean to say that you are actually 35 years old with a mental age of 25, or 45? Instead, the Wechsler scale implemented a *standard score* approach that helps transform a raw score into a meaningful piece of information. Simply knowing how many digits a person can remember doesn't actually provide you with meaningful information unless you know how to compare that person's performance with other people of the same age. **Standardization** involves the process of establishing test norms and the guidelines for uniform administration and scoring.

NORMS   The Wechsler scales used the standardization process to establish **test norms**, or a way to compare an individual's score relative to the performance of others. The accuracy of this comparison depends significantly on the way the norms were established in the first place. For example, the most widely used test of personality and psychopathology, the Minnesota Multiphasic Personality Inventory (MMPI), was first published in the 1940s (Hathaway & McKinley, 1943). To establish the norms of the test, the researchers administered the questionnaire to a fairly small group of mostly young, Caucasian, married individuals from Minnesota. The performance of these individuals was used as a comparison group for everyone else who completed the test for more than 50 years when the norms were updated and improved.

standardization

the process of establishing test norms and the guidelines for uniform administration and scoring

test norms

a way to compare an individual's score relative to the performance of others

Journal Writing Prompt: Problems with Normative Samples That Are Not Representative

Explain why it might be problematic to use a very specific group of people when establishing the norms of a test that is then administered to all different types of people.

In essence, if you are trying to establish what is "normal" or "average," you need to make sure you collect data from a representative sample to establish your norms. A *representative sample* is a randomly selected group that matches the population on important characteristics. When developing the norms for an intelligence test, it is critical that the normative sample include a range of people from different (1) regions of the country (if the test is to be used only in the United States), (2) socioeconomic backgrounds, and (3) ethnic/racial backgrounds. Ideally, you want your normative sample to look identical to the population at large. For example, using the racial composition of the U.S. population in the most recent 2010 census as shown in Figure 8.8, an ideal normative sample would comprise 75 percent White, 14 percent African American, 6 percent Asian, etc.

The current Wechsler scales have gone to great lengths to make sure the normative samples are representative of the U.S. population. The WAIS-IV used a standardization sample, including 2,200 people living in the United States. The sample was *stratified* (the process of dividing members of a population into subgroups) by age, gender, education level, ethnicity, and region. Additionally, because intelligence test scores are often used to make clinical decisions, additional normative data was collected on specific clinical populations (e.g., individuals with dementia, individuals with intellectual disability).

ADMINISTERING AND SCORING THE TEST   After you have selected a representative sample to establish your test norms, you must also focus on standardizing the instructions for the administration and scoring of the test. In order to compare one individual's performance to the established group norm, you must be certain that the content of the test, the scoring rules of the test, and the administration of the test were identical for the individual and the group to which he/she will be compared. For example, for tests that have a time limit, it is critical that each examiner use the same time limit for every individual examinee in order for the results to be meaningful. One of your text's authors has taught graduate students to administer intelligence tests in the past. One semester, as she was reviewing one student's administration, she discovered that the examinee had scored extremely low on two subtests. These happened to be measures of processing speed, and both subtests required examinees to complete as many problems as possible in 120 seconds. As your author questioned the trainee, she discovered that

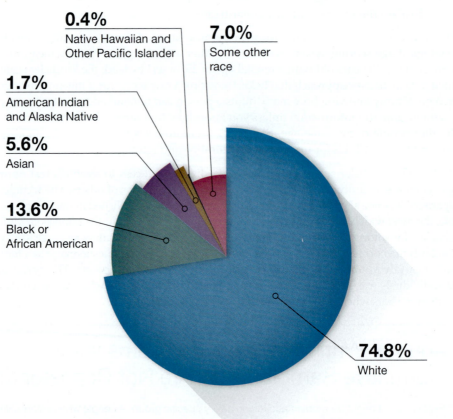

Figure 8.8 U.S. Population

0.4%
Native Hawaiian and
Other Pacific Islander

7.0%
Some other
race

1.7%
American Indian
and Alaska Native

5.6%
Asian

13.6%
Black or
African American

74.8%
White

normal distribution

a bell-shaped frequency distribution showing that most scores cluster in the middle of the graph and the rest taper off symmetrically toward either end

standard deviation

a measure of the typical distance between the scores of a distribution and the mean, which indicates how widely individual scores in a group vary

he had mistakenly interpreted the 120-second time limit to mean 1 minute and 20 seconds. The entire interpretation of the scores was based on a serious administration error. It turns out that this is one of the most common mistakes new trainees make in learning to administer IQ tests.

The role of subjective scoring criteria should also be minimized as much as possible. For example, an essay test would typically have a high degree of subjective scoring, where as a true/false test would not be subjectively scored. Most of the subtests on the Wechsler scales are objectively scored (e.g., items have a clear "correct" answer), and the subtests that require some degree of examiner judgment are the focus of extensive training.

CLASSIFYING SCORES To understand the concept of standard scores, let's start with the notion of a normal distribution. A variable is considered **normally distributed** if a graph of the scores shows that most scores cluster in the middle and the rest taper off symmetrically toward either end. For example, look at the graph in Figure 8.9.

When variables follow a normal distribution, the graph of the results looks like a bell curve shape. The top of the "bell" represents the score of the largest percent of the population. Another piece of useful information you can obtain when looking at the graph is the standard deviation. The **standard deviation** refers to a numerical value used to indicate how widely individuals in a group vary. In a normal distribution, 68 percent of the scores will fall within one standard deviation from the mean (or average) score. Another 28 percent of people will score between one and two standard deviations above or below the mean. Once a score is more than two standard deviations from the mean, it is pretty rare (only 4 percent of scores fall above or below 2 standard deviations from the mean). A good example of a normal distribution would be height. If you measured the height of all American men in the world and then graphed the data, it would look very similar to the bell curve graph in Figure 8.9. The mean height for American men is 5'10" with a standard deviation of three inches. Use the curve below to answer the questions in the following interactive.

HOW WOULD YOU SCORE THIS?

WHERE IS
CHILE?

IN THE
CANNED
VEGETABLE
DEPARTMENT?

SCHOOL
PSYCHOLOGIST

Figure 8.9 Distribution of IQ Scores

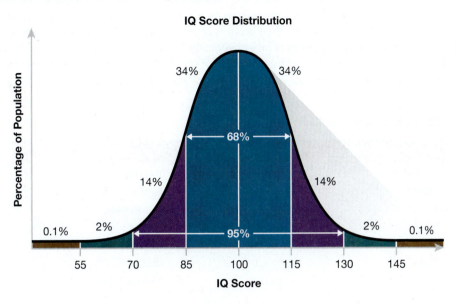

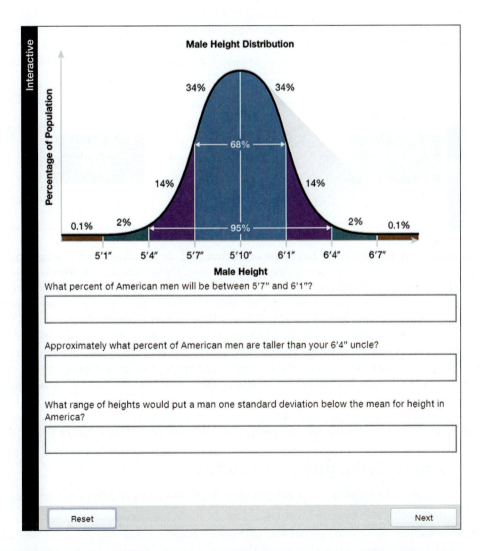

What percent of American men will be between 5'7" and 6'1"?

What percent of American men are taller than your 6'4" uncle?

What range of heights would put a man one standard deviation below the mean for height in America?

Reset   Next

Beginning with the Wechsler scales, measures of intelligence have been converted into standard scores that are normally distributed. This means that the sums of scores across all subtests would be converted into one standard score. For example, each time a Wechsler scale is updated, the average score for a 20-year-old is converted into a mean score of 100 and a standard deviation of 15 points. By converting scores on the Wechsler subtests into a standard distribution, a score of 115 means the same thing for a 10-year-old child as it does for a 60-year-old adult. Furthermore, if you know that someone has an IQ (which no longer has anything to do with quotients) of 115, you also know that their score is one standard deviation above the mean, and they performed better than 84 percent of other people their age (look back to the fill-in activity you just completed to see how we figured this out). Use of standard scores has allowed for better classification of different scores. Table 8.2 demonstrates how IQ scores are currently classified.

Table 8.2 Wechsler Classifications

Standard Score Range	Percentile Rank Range	Wechsler Classification
130 and above	98 to 99.99	Very Superior
120–129	91 to 97	Superior
110–119	75 to 90	High Average
90–109	25 to 73	Average
80–89	9 to 23	Low Average
70–79	2 to 8	Borderline
69 and below	.01 to 2	Extremely Low

What about someone who receives an IQ score of 119? Does this mean the person's true cognitive abilities fall in the High Average range? After all, the score is only one point shy of falling into the range classified as Superior. With any psychological test that attempts to capture an individual characteristic with a numerical value, it's important to keep in mind the notion of the *observed score* versus the *true ability*.

Error in Measurement

Interactive

| Observed Score | = | True Ability | + | Random Error |

Basically, any measurement has some error involved. In the case of an intelligence test, the potential error could be related to the examinee (e.g., the person didn't sleep well or was extremely anxious, which affected his/her performance), the examiner (e.g., the administrator made a scoring error or failed to provide the correct instructions), or even the environment (e.g., the room was noisy or had poor lighting). In the end, the observed IQ score includes some degree of measurement error in addition to the accurate measure of the individual's true ability. Measurement error can either inflate (make higher) or suppress (make lower) true scores. Because we can never completely eliminate all error, intelligence tests provide confidence intervals. A **confidence interval** takes into account the error associated with the measure and provides a range of scores that most likely encompass the "true" score. For example, the person with an IQ of 114 would have a 95 percent confidence interval of 106–120. This means that there is a 95 percent chance that the person's *true* IQ falls within the range of 106–120.

confidence interval

provides a range of scores that most likely encompass the "true" score to take into account the error associated with a measure

Establishing Reliability and Validity

LO 8.7 Describe the importance of establishing reliability and validity in constructing intelligence tests.

Intelligence tests are designed to measure an unobserved construct. After all, you can't "see" intelligence, and it doesn't show up on a blood test. Therefore, it's critical that tests be carefully developed so that there is plenty of evidence supporting the validity and reliability of the scores obtained from the test. **Validity** refers to the accuracy of a measure, meaning that the test is accurately measuring the construct it is designed to measure. On the other hand, **reliability** refers to the consistency of a measure. To better understand these concepts, consider the example of target practice. The goal is to

validity

a test's ability to accurately measure the construct it is designed to measure

reliability

the consistency of a measure

hit the middle of the target like the goal of an intelligence test is to accurately measure the construct of intelligence. If you are reliable (e.g., consistent), you will hit the target in the same place repeatedly. However, it's also possible to hit the wrong spot over and over again, which shows high reliability but low validity (e.g., accuracy). The ideal outcome is to consistently hit the target on the bullseye, which represents both reliability and validity. Notice that it's possible to be reliable (or consistently hit the target in the same place) but have low validity by hitting the target consistently in the wrong spot. One of your text authors' high school basketball coach used to love to quote Vincent Lombardi stating "Practice does not make perfect. Perfect practice makes perfect." In other words, if you keep hitting the target in the wrong spot, you'll end up being very reliable but also very inaccurate.

Reliability and Validity

Drag the label to the correct bullseye.

Interactive

Neither Valid nor Reliable

Question 1 of 3   End Challenge

So, how do you actually determine if a psychological test is valid and reliable? Scientists attempt to evaluate characteristics of tests in several ways. First, a test must demonstrate reliability in order to establish validity. It's not possible for an unreliable test to be valid. There are several types of reliability that can be measured for a specific test. Reliability refers to the stability of a score over time, between different raters, or within the test items themselves. **Test-retest reliability** involves evaluating the consistency of test scores over time. For example, WAIS-IV scores for the same individual tested at two different time points should be highly correlated. In fact, the Wechsler scales have test-retest reliability estimates of more than .90, which is very high (remember that 1.0 is a perfect correlation from L.O. 1.9). **Interrater reliability** measures the degree of consistency between two different observers of the same behavior. For intelligence tests, interrater reliability is established by showing that two different examiners would score the same answers from an examinee in the same way. Today's intelligence tests go to great lengths to standardize the administration and scoring instructions to maximize the interrater reliability of the tests. One of the ways graduate students are graded on intelligence tests is to examine the interrater reliability between the way they score test items compared to an "expert grader," in this case, the instructor. Finally, the **internal consistency** of a test refers to the consistency within the test items themselves. For example, the WAIS-IV subtest of Arithmetic demonstrates high internal consistency, which means that every item on the Arithmetic test appears to be measuring the same underlying construct (e.g., mental manipulation of information, attention, and memory). If one item on the Arithmetic test required examinees to recite the first five digits of *pi*, that item would likely have poor internal consistency because it would be measuring something different than the other items on the subtest. Overall, the Wechsler scales and the current Stanford-Binet (SB-5) have demonstrated very high reliability across all domains.

test-retest reliability
evaluating the consistency of test scores over time

interrater reliability
a measure of the degree of consistency between two different observers of the same behavior

internal consistency
a measure of how well the items on the test measure the same construct

construct validity

the degree to which a test measures the construct it claims to measure

aptitude

a person's capacity to learn

achievement

a person's level of knowledge in a particular area

predictive validity

the degree to which a specific test predicts future behavior

Validity can also be broken down into different subtypes. One of the most important forms of validity as it relates to intelligence tests is the notion of construct validity. **Construct validity** refers to the degree to which a test measures the construct it claims to measure. In the case of intelligence tests, the most important thing to establish is that the test is, in fact, measuring the underlying construct of intelligence. It's easy to confuse a test of intelligence with the construct of intelligence. But, a quick look at the history of intelligence testing can demonstrate the error of this assumption. Francis Galton, an English aristocrat, made one of the earliest attempts to measure intelligence in the late 19th century. He believed that intelligence could be measured by physiological tests such as reaction time (e.g., how quickly you can detect a sound and hit a button) and grip strength. However, one way to evaluate the construct validity of a test is to see if the test scores are related to other established measures that should be theoretically related to the construct. For example, it makes sense that variables such as class rank in school and occupational status should be related to a test designed to measure intelligence. Galton's physiological tests that he believed were measuring intelligence were not actually related to such variables, showing that his intelligence tests actually had very poor construct validity (Eysenck, 1984; Lagoy, 2012; Naroll, 1961). Remember, just because a test is called an "intelligence test" doesn't mean it is actually measuring intelligence until it has demonstrated adequate construct validity. In the case of the current Wechsler scales and Stanford-Binet test, construct validity has been demonstrated by showing a strong relationship between the scores and other related measures of cognitive abilities as well as tests of academic achievement.

Also remember that intelligence tests are designed to measure **aptitude**, a person's potential ability, rather than **achievement**, a person's knowledge and academic progress. However, critics question if aptitude is really measurable. Test questions are inherently bound to tap into the subject's factual knowledge, despite efforts to mostly test common knowledge (Ackerman & Beier, 2005; Cianciolo & Sternberg, 2008). These concerns directly relate to the construct validity of intelligence tests.

A second type of validity that is a particularly important consideration of intelligence tests is known as predictive validity. **Predictive validity** is the degree to which a specific test predicts future behavior. It wouldn't be particularly informative to know someone's level of intelligence if that knowledge didn't give you any meaningful information about the person's abilities, skills, or potential. As outlined at the beginning of the chapter, current tests of intelligence have demonstrated that IQ scores can be useful in predicting a number of life outcomes, including academic success (Heaven & Ciarrochi, 2012; Mandelman et al., 2016), job performance (Boyatzis et al., 2012; Gottfredson, 1997; Ree & Earles, 1992), and even mortality/morbidity over time (Palmer et al., 2002; Salguero et al., 2012).

Different Forms of Reliability and Validity

Interactive

Read each example and use the word bank to select which type of reliability or validity is being described.

1. Rico took an IQ test when he was 11 years old. He took the test later, and his scores were compared. [_____]

2. A scientist developed a new test of intelligence. She administered the new test and the WAIS-IV to a large group of people and then correlated the scores. [_____]

3. Two examiners separately score an individual's answers while administering an intelligence test to evaluate whether they are scoring the test consistently. [_____]

4. A group of fourth graders were administered an intelligence test. When they graduated from high school, a researcher correlated their earlier IQ score with their high school GPA (grade point average). [_____]

5. A researcher wanted to make sure that all the items of a test designed to assess verbal comprehension skills were actually measuring the same thing. [_____]

WORD BANK
- Test-retest reliability
- Interrater reliability
- Construct validity
- Internal consistency
- Predictive validity

Start Over   Check Answers

Adaptive Pathway 8.1: IQ Scores

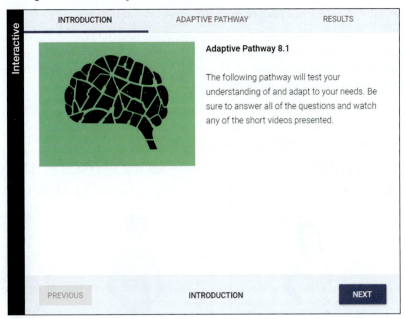

Quiz for Module 8.6–8.7
Quiz for Module 8.6–8.7

1. _____ are used to compare an individual's score to the performance of others.
   a. Abnormal distributions
   b. Standard deviations
   c. Test norms
   d. Standardization practices

2. Which of the following is an example of a variable that is normally distributed?
   a. Income among all Americans
   b. Grades on an easy exam
   c. Grades on a difficult exam
   d. Body weight

3. For a test to be considered _____, it has to actually measure what it is designed to measure; and for a test to be considered _____, it has to be consistent each time.
   a. reliable; valid
   b. valid; reliable
   c. predictable; reliable
   d. predictable; valid

4. Ethan takes a WISC test at age 6 and obtains a FSIQ of 135; he is retested at age 16 and obtains a FSIQ of 138. This means the Weschler scales have high _____.
   a. construct validity
   b. test-retest reliability
   c. interrater reliability
   d. internal consistency

5. An important factor in intelligence tests is the ability to determine future behavior based on the score received on the test. This construct is known as _____.
   a. achievement validity
   b. aptitude validity
   c. predictive validity
   d. future predictability

Module 8.8–8.9: Nature and Nurture

In the newly published book, *Great Myths of Child Development*, authors Stephen Hupp and Jeremy Jewell tackle the question of whether or not showing infants and toddlers videos such as *Baby Einstein* or having them play with "educational" apps on mobile devices actually leads to improved intelligence. The popularity of such products has been immense, with $1.9 billion spent in 2015 on children's games for mobile devices—many of which claim to be "educational" (Barseghian, 2012; Grubb, 2015). Parents appear to believe these "educational" videos, games, and apps lead to enhanced cognitive functioning as one study demonstrated that 85 percent of college students and 69 percent of parents agreed with the statement "Showing cognitively stimulating videos to infants boosts their intelligence" (Hupp et al., 2017). However, there is no evidence suggesting that these types of videos, games, or apps lead to increases in intellectual development or language skills (Hupp & Jewel, 2015). Apparently, this "nurture" strategy to improve intelligence is not effective. Are there any effective environmental influences on intelligence, and to what degree is a child's intelligence predetermined by his or her genetics?

Genetic Influences on Intelligence

LO 8.8   Describe the evidence for genetic influences on intelligence.

To understand the influence of genetics on intelligence, the best data comes from studies examining monozygotic (identical) twins, dizygotic (fraternal) twins, and adopted siblings (see LO 9.2 for further discussion of twin studies). Figure 8.10 demonstrates how twin studies can help tease apart the impact of genetics and environment.

Figure 8.10 Twin Studies Tease Apart Environment and Genetics

DIZYGOTIC TWINS RAISED TOGETHER	MONOZYGOTIC TWINS RAISED APART

Different DNA | Same Environment

If intelligence is the same, it must be due to environment.

Same DNA | Different Environment

If intelligence is the same, it must be due to genetics.

Decades of research have repeatedly confirmed that individual intelligence appears to be an inherited characteristic (McGue et al., 1993; Plomin & Deary, 2015). Heritability estimates of intelligence are around .50 (Chipuer et al., 1990; Devlin et al., 1997; Loehlin et al., 1989; Petrill et al., 2004), indicating that about half of the population variance in intelligence is due to genetic differences between individuals (see LO 14.10 for a full explanation of heritability).

If genetic factors are the most important in determining an individual's IQ, then the correlation between IQ among family members should increase as the familial relationship becomes closer (e.g., a parent–child relationship shares significant genetic overlap, whereas grandparents and grandchildren have fewer genes in common). Table 8.3 below demonstrates

---

Table 8.3 Familial IQ Correlations

Type of Relationship	Correlation Between IQ Scores (Kaufman, 2009)
Same Person Tested Twice	.95
Identical Twins—Reared Together	.86
Identical Twins—Reared Apart	.76
Fraternal Twins—Reared Together	.55
Fraternal Twins—Reared Apart	.35
Biological Siblings—Reared Together	.47
Biological Siblings—Reared Apart	.24
Unrelated Adults—Raised Together As Children	.04

the IQ correlations between different family relationships. Keep in mind that when comparing relationships with the same amount of shared genetics (e.g., identical twins raised together versus raised apart), having a shared environment will lead to a higher IQ correlation than being raised apart.

These findings are so robust that 34 twin studies examining 4,672 pairs of monozygotic twins raised together found that the average correlation between IQ scores was around .86 (Bouchard & McGue, 1981). This correlation is nearly as high as that found through test-retest reliability studies testing the same individual twice (average test-retest correlation of .90–.95) (Jensen, 1998; Kaufman, 2009). On the other hand, the average correlation between IQ scores among dizygotic twins was .60 among a total of 5,546 pairs of twins (Bouchard & McGue, 1981), demonstrating that a closer genetic relationship leads to a stronger IQ correlation.

What about twins raised apart or adopted siblings raised together? Studies of these groups confirm that genetics appears to play a more important role in determining intelligence than environment. There are some effects of environment such that the correlation between twins or siblings raised together is generally higher than between those raised apart (Kaufman, 2009). However, studies examining adult adoptive siblings have found that the IQ correlation is about the same as that between two strangers, while adult biological siblings consistently have an average IQ correlation of around .60 (Bouchard, 1998).

If evidence suggests that genetics plays the largest role in your intelligence level at birth, you might assume that the environment will slowly have a greater and greater impact as you grow and develop into adulthood. After all, having loving parents, the opportunity to travel, excellent nutrition, and attending the best schools should have an impact on intelligence over time, right? While it might seem intuitive to believe that the environment plays an increasing role in intelligence over the lifespan, a recent study has actually shown the opposite to be true. Haworth and colleagues (2010) reported that the genetic influence on intelligence actually increases over the lifespan. They studied 11,000 pairs of twins recruited from four different countries and found a heritability rate of 41 percent at age 9, 55 percent at age 12, and 66 percent at age 17.

It is clear that individual intelligence has a high heritability rate and that the degree of genetic influence increases from childhood to adulthood. But which genes actually influence intelligence? Like most complicated human characteristics, the answer appears to be that intelligence, or *g*, is determined by many different genes, each of which has only a small overall impact (Benyamin et al., 2014; Davies et al., 2011; Deary et al., 2012). A review of genetic studies by Antony Payton (2009) found that more than 50 different genes have been identified in previous research as associated with high cognitive functioning. However, despite the large number of genes that have been identified as related to intelligence, each individual gene has been found minimally responsible (e.g. less than 1 percent) for variations in intelligence (Butcher et al., 2008; Chabris et al., 2012).

Environmental Influences on Intelligence

LO 8.9 **Understand the impact of environmental factors on intelligence.**

Evidence from adoption studies and high heritability estimates suggest that genetic factors are most influential in determining intelligence. But, does the environment play a role at all? Before we jump to the conclusion that the environment has *no* influence, consider the fact that genetic scientists have long pointed to the importance of the interplay between genes and environment in explaining measurable human traits. When discussing the relationship between genes and environment, it's important to think about both gene-environment interactions and gene-environment correlations (Plomin et al., 1977). First, you need to remember that *genotype* is a collective term for the genes in our DNA that are responsible for a specific trait, whereas *phenotype* refers to the observable physical expression of that trait. For example, your DNA carries the gene responsible for eye color (genotype), but the fact that your eyes are blue is an example of the phenotype, or the physical expression, of the gene. Figure 8.11 illustrates the difference between gene-environment interactions and gene-environment correlations.

When it comes to intelligence, both gene-environment interaction and gene-environment correlation are important. Figure 8.11 provides examples of both. The data regarding the

Figure 8.11 Gene-Environment Interactions and Correlations

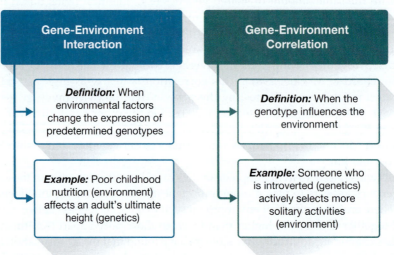

Gene-Environment Interaction	Gene-Environment Correlation
Definition: When environmental factors change the expression of predetermined genotypes	**Definition:** When the genotype influences the environment
Example: Poor childhood nutrition (environment) affects an adult's ultimate height (genetics)	**Example:** Someone who is introverted (genetics) actively selects more solitary activities (environment)

increased influence of genetics over the lifetime has been discussed in terms of gene-environment correlation. To explain their findings, the study authors suggest that "the developmental increase in the heritability of *g* lies with genotype-environment correlation: as children grow up, they increasingly select, modify and even create their own experiences in part on the basis of their genetic propensities" (Haworth et al., 2010, p. 1120). This means that people who are genetically predisposed to higher levels of intelligence are more likely to select environments that tend to nurture their intellectual development. Highly intelligent people may choose more intellectually stimulating activities (e.g., read more or enjoy brain teasers or puzzles), select more rigorous curriculums in school (e.g., AP or honor's classes), and opt for more intellectually challenging careers. These environments in turn reinforce the genetic tendency toward higher intelligence scores over time.

On the other hand, the opposite relationship can also exist. It is possible for the environment to impact the expression of a genetic intellectual tendency. Much of the research in this area has focused on the role of deprivation on intelligence. One research group has conducted longitudinal research on children living in highly impoverished orphanages in Romania (Nelson et al., 2007).

The researchers assessed 136 institutionalized young children (less than 3 years old) who were abandoned at birth. Approximately half of the children were then randomly assigned to be placed in foster care, while the other half remained in the orphanages.

Studies have shown that institutionalization has a negative impact on children's intelligence.

The average age of foster care placement was 21 months. At age 4.5, the children were reassessed using the WPPSI as a measure of intelligence. As shown in Figure 8.12, there was a significant difference in IQ scores between the children who were placed in foster care and those who remained institutionalized with the foster care children scoring higher (around 8 points, or half of a standard deviation). Furthermore, the difference was most pronounced for children who were placed in foster care at the youngest ages, suggesting that impoverished environments in infancy/toddlerhood are the most detrimental on cognitive and intellectual development.

Studies of noninstitutionalized children have also demonstrated that poverty can have significant negative effects on intellectual development. Research has shown that children as young as age 2 who are living in poverty have significantly lower IQ scores than children who are not living in poverty

Figure 8.12 Impact of Institutionalization on IQ

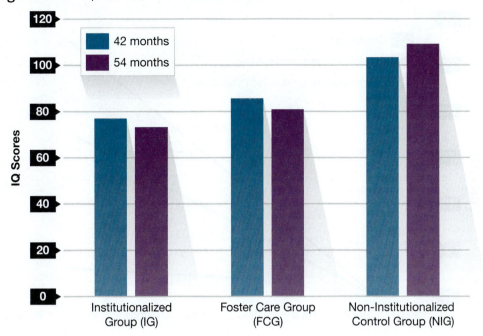

(Barajas et al., 2007; Duncan et al., 1994; Hanson et al., 2013; Klebanov et al., 1998). One recent study followed nearly 15,000 children from ages 2 to 16 who were administered intelligence tests nine different times (von Stumm & Plomin, 2015). They found that children from low socioeconomic status (SES) homes had an average IQ that was 6 points less than that of children from high SES homes. Furthermore, these differences increased significantly and almost tripled by the time the children were 16 years old (i.e., more than a standard deviation difference).

Additional evidence for the environmental impact on intelligence comes from decades of data showing that the average IQ score in most places in the world has been increasing since the 1930s. In 1984, James Flynn published a paper describing this trend in IQ scores over a 66-year period (Flynn, 1984), which has become known as the **Flynn Effect**. Intelligence tests have to be updated on a regular basis to make sure the items are not obsolete, the latest research on intelligence is incorporated, and the norms are current. When each test is updated, the normative sample takes the test, and the average score becomes the "new" IQ of 100. However, one way to examine the validity of the new test is to have an individual take the new test and the older version of the test to see if the scores are related. When the same person takes the new test and the older version, they typically score higher on the older version, suggesting that the average person's IQ has increased over time. Each time a test has been updated, Flynn demonstrated that the new normative sample (which was younger than the last normative sample) scored significantly higher than the previous cohort. Over the course of 46 years, Flynn found that the average IQ score increased by 13.8 points. As shown in Figure 8.13, on the Wechsler scales, people in the United States appear to gain about 3 IQ points per decade (Flynn, 1984, 2012; Trahan et al., 2014).

The Flynn effect has been called "one of the biggest puzzles in intelligence research" (Woodley et al., 2014, p. 27). Numerous explanations for the Flynn effect have included improved nutrition (Daley et al., 2003; Flynn, 1987; Lynn, 2009), increased access to education (Husen & Tuijnman, 1991; Woodley, 2012), improved test-taking strategies (Woodley et al., 2014), and the increased cognitive demand of math curricula over time (Blair et al., 2005). A single explanation for the Flynn effect has not been established. However, because these changes have occurred too quickly to be accounted for by genetic selection (Blair et al., 2005), it is clear to most scientists that the explanation for the phenomenon has some environmental basis.

Flynn effect

the phenomenon in which there is a significant increase in average IQ scores over time

Figure 8.13 Flynn Effect

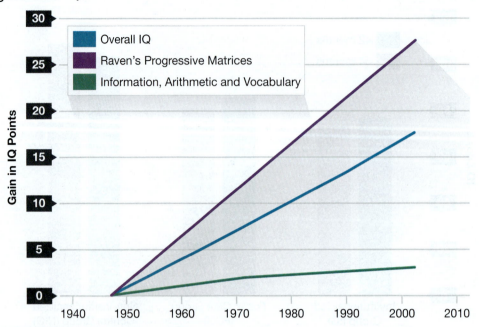

Adaptive Pathway 8.2: Gene-Environment Interactions and Correlations

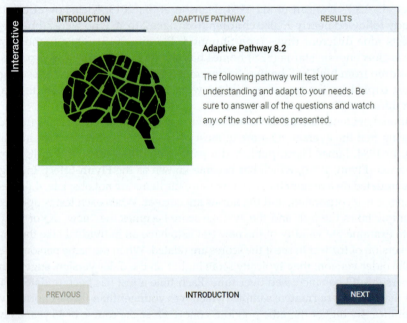

Quiz for Module 8.8–8.9

1. What percentage of intelligence is considered an inherited characteristic?

   a. .33   **b.** .25

   c. .86   **d.** .50

2. Emma and Carter are identical twins who have been raised in the same household from birth. If Emma scores a 125 on an IQ test, what is the most likely score for Carter?

   a. 124   **b.** 150

   c. 90   **d.** 100

3. Which of the following statements about genes and intelligence is true?

   a. While there are many genes involved in determining intelligence, less than five appear particularly influential.

   b. There are two primary genes responsible for determining an individual's level of intelligence.

   c. Intelligence appears to be influenced by many different genes, but any individual gene has only a minimal influence alone.

   d. The evidence for genetic influences on intelligence is weak.

4. Prae was a child who loved to read books and learn about the world. She always wanted to explore new ideas and engage in intellectually stimulating games. Prae scored a 143 on an IQ test at age 8. Prae is an example of a _____ that can help explain how genetics can impact the environment.

   a. gene-environment interaction

   b. gene-environment correlation

   c. deprived environment interaction

   d. intellectual institutional-ization interaction

5. Research on young children who have been institutionalized shows that _____.

   a. intelligence is more likely to be negatively impacted when children are institutionalized at later ages

   b. intelligence is not impacted by environmental conditions

   c. intelligence can be negatively impacted by impoverished environments

   d. the relationship between environment and intelligence is unclear

6. Evidence suggests that IQ scores have been increasing since the 1930s. What is this phenomenon called?

   a. Gene environmental effect

   b. Adaptive learning effect

   c. Environmental interaction effect

   d. Flynn effect

Module 8.10–8.12: Group and Individual Differences

The history of intelligence testing has an ugly side. As soon as the first tests were developed, scientists began to study the possibility of group differences in intelligence based on categorizations such as race, ethnicity, and gender. Many decades of research support the fact that there are indeed group differences on intelligence tests. However, despite not having a clear understanding about the cause of such group differences, many people jumped to the conclusion that such differences were genetic and therefore unalterable (Hernstein & Murray, 1994). Proponents of this view have used the data to argue for racial segregation, gender discrimination, and even eugenics—selective breeding to improve humans' genetic composition (Fischer et al., 1996; Herrnstein & Murray, 2010; Kincheloe et al., 1997). This dark side of the science has been less and less influential over recent decades as increasing evidence suggests that environment may play a more significant role in group difference in IQ scores than previously thought (Nisbett et al., 2012a). Gender differences in IQ scores are discussed in Chapter 11 (see LO 11.4), and the following discussion of group differences focuses on racial and ethnic differences.

Interestingly, while the majority of research has focused on group differences in intelligence, these studies tell us nothing about any particular individual. Decisions based on IQ scores related to education or employment are made at the individual level and knowing someone's group status (e.g., male or female) isn't helpful when making predictions about one specific person. Individual scores fall along the entire bell curve and the implications for a particular individual at either end of the curve have been of interest to researchers.

Racial and the Ethnic Differences

LO 8.10 Describe the findings regarding racial and ethnic differences in intelligence.

When discussing differences in IQ scores, the terms "race" and "ethnicity" should first be distinguished. *Race* has traditionally been referred to as a biological category with genetically distinct populations. *Ethnicity*, on the other hand, refers to a shared cultural heritage. Race is presumably represented in phenotypic physical characteristics (e.g., skin color, facial characteristics), while ethnicity is not a "visible" characteristic.

While the term race is used frequently in many domains, the scientific evidence for racial distinctions is not universally agreed on. Some social scientists have argued that race is primarily a socially constructed concept without real biological markers (Lopez, 1994; Mukhopadhyay & Henze, 2013; Omi & Winant, 2014; Smedley & Smedley, 2005). They point to the fact that multiracial backgrounds have become more and more common, and many times race is a self-identified characteristic (e.g., how do you decide which race box to "check" if you have a White mother and an Asian father?) that may or may not correlate with your genetic markers. For example, a person who has light skin may have genetic markers that trace his/her ancestry to Africa, and a person who has dark skin may have European ancestry. Furthermore, the notion that significant genetic differences exist among races has not been supported as humans have been found to be 99.9 percent identical genetically. When the human genome results were first presented in 2000, Crag Venter (chief private scientist involved with the Human Genome Project) claimed that "race" was not a scientifically valid construct and that there is only one race—the human race (Shampo & Kyle, 2011). Conversely, other researchers have argued that new capabilities in genetics research have allowed scientists to identify ancestry through genetic analyses, suggesting that there are some biological markers for race (Fujimura et al., 2014; Risch et al., 2002; Shim et al., 2014). Additionally, some people have advocated for the importance of continuing to consider racial distinctions in the areas of biomedical research and medical practice (Burchard et al., 2003).

The debate about whether race is biological or socially constructed continues, but one thing is clear: According to current racial classifications, there are significant differences among racial groups on intelligence tests which are depicted in Figure 8.14. When group means are compared, the latest WAIS-IV standardization sample showed that the Asian mean was approximately 3 points higher than the White mean, the White mean was approximately 11–12 points higher than the Hispanic mean, and the Hispanic mean was approximately 3 points higher than the Black mean (Lichtenberger & Kaufman, 2009). The IQ difference between Blacks and Whites has been researched the most and research has consistently shown that this difference in IQ scores has been approximately 15–18 points (or 1 standard deviation) (Roth et al., 2001; Rushton & Jensen, 2005).

Ethnic differences in IQ scores have also been found. One of the best studies examining IQ scores in different nations was conducted in 1981. This study was unique in that the same intelligence measure was used to assess IQ in 21 different European countries (Buj, 1981). As Table 8.4 demonstrates, the difference in average IQ between the Danish and French people was approximately 13 points—almost approaching the average Black-White difference. Another notable series of studies conducted by Richard Lynn and Tatu Vanhanen (Lynn & Vanhanen, 2002; Lynn & Vanhanen, 2006; Lynn & Vanhanen, 2012) attempted to establish the average IQ in more than 200 different nations. They showed marked differences in IQ worldwide with

Figure 8.14 IQ Scores by Race and Ethnicity

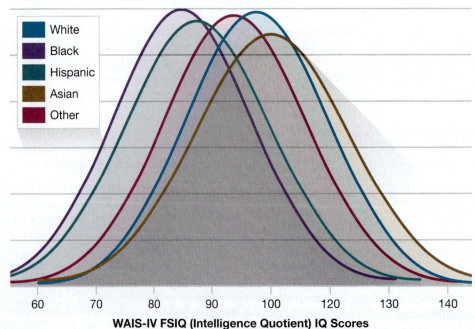

WAIS-IV FSIQ (Intelligence Quotient) IQ Scores

Table 8.4 Mean IQ Values in European Countries

	Country	Town	No. of subjects	Mean IQ	Standard deviation	Standard error of the mean
1.	Holland	Amsterdam	333	109.4	16.1	0.9
2.	Germany	Hamburg	1,572	109.3	22.4	0.6
3.	Poland	Warsaw	835	108.3	29.7	1.0
4.	Sweden	Stockholm	205	105.8	25.8	1.8
5.	Yugoslavia	Zagreb	525	105.7	34.1	1.5
6.	Italy	Rome	1,380	103.8	35.2	0.9
7.	Austria	Vienna	187	103.5	15.3	1.1
8.	Switzerland	Zurich	163	102.8	19.4	1.5
9.	Portugal	Lisbon	242	102.6	18.7	1.2
10.	Great Britain	London	1,405	102.0	19.3	0.5
11.	Norway	Oslo	100	101.8	11.6	1.2
12.	Denmark	Copenhagen	122	100.7	13.3	1.2
13.	Hungary	Budapest	260	100.5	21.4	1.3
14.	Czechoslovakia	Bratislava	363	100.4	25.9	1.4
15,	Spain	Madrid	848	100.3	34.7	1.2
16.	Belgium	Brussels	247	99.7	23.5	1.5
17.	Greece	Athens	220	99.4	25.6	1.7
18.	Ireland	Dublin	75	99.2	17.3	2.0
19,	Finland	Helsinki	120	98.1	26.6	2.4
20.	Bulgaria	Sofia	215	96.3	34.7	2.4
21.	France	Paris	1,320	96.1	27.1	0.7

nations with colder temperatures generally having higher average IQ scores. However, their work has been subject to significant criticism, some of which is due to the fact that many of the average IQs for nations were estimated rather than actually measured (Barnett & Williams, 2004; Wicherts et al., 2010).

While the fact that racial and ethnic IQ differences exist is generally accepted, the cause of such differences is certainly disputed. We know that genetics plays an important role in explaining *individual* differences in intelligence, but what about *group* differences? Remember that the concept of race itself as a biological construct is not widely accepted, and most studies examining racial differences in IQ rely on people to self-identify their own race. Because racial categories are not genetically determined in these studies, it's difficult to know what role, if any, genetics plays in these group differences. On the other hand, a wealth of possible environmental explanations have been considered, including socioeconomic environment (Lawson et al., 2014; Turkheimer et al., 2003), educational differences (Jensen, 2011; Rushton & Jensen, 2005), and differences in health and nutrition (Daniele & Ostuni, 2013; Neisser, 1998). In addition, criticisms of the intelligence tests themselves have arisen, suggesting that the tests are culturally biased (see the Piecing It Together section for a full discussion of test bias). Evidence of the phenomenon known as "stereotype threat" (details to come) has also provided support for the notion that the environment plays a critical role in group IQ differences. In fact, Nisbett et al., (2012b) argue that the evidence for environmental causes of racial IQ differences is strong enough to account fully for them without assigning any responsibility to genetics.

To summarize the findings related to racial and ethnic differences in IQ, there are two primary "take home" points: (1) significant racial and ethnic IQ differences do exist, and (2) while there is no consensus on the cause of these group differences, compelling evidence suggests that environment plays a significant role.

Stereotype Threat

LO 8.11 **Understand the concept of stereotype threat.**

Stereotype Threat and Intelligence Tests

Imagine you are part of a group that is subject to certain stereotypes based on your gender, race, or even the color of your hair. You are told that members of your particular group tend to perform poorly on certain types of tasks, and then you are asked to complete a similar task. How well do you think you would perform?

stereotype threat

when worry about confirming a negative stereotype leads to under-performance on a test by a member of a stereotyped group

The research suggests that your performance would actually be negatively impacted by your knowledge of the stereotype. This phenomenon has been called **stereotype threat**, and it occurs when people are aware that they must work against a stereotype and risk confirming the negative stereotype by their behavior (Steele & Aronson, 1995). The first study to identify this phenomenon was conducted by Claude Steele and Joshua Aronson in 1995. They evaluated a group of Black and White college students' performance on a verbal subtest of the Graduate Record Examination (GRE). Participants randomly assigned to the stereotype threat condition were told the test was diagnostic of intelligence, which theoretically activated the negative stereotype regarding inferior intellectual abilities among Black participants. In the "nondiagnostic" group, students were told they would be completing a laboratory problem-solving test that was nondiagnostic of ability. When the results for the two different groups were analyzed, they found that the White participants were unaffected by the instructions, while the Black students who were told the test was diagnostic of intelligence performed much worse than those who were told the test was nondiagnostic (see Figure 8.15).

Since the Steele and Aronson (1995) publication, hundreds of new studies investigating the role of stereotype threat have been published (Stroessner & Good, 2011). These studies have found additional evidence for the role of stereotype threat in the area of academic/intellectual achievement for Blacks but the phenomenon has also been investigated in terms of female performance on tests of math and/or spatial skills (Cadaret et al., 2017; Inzlicht & Ben-Zeev, 2000; Johns et al., 2005; Shapiro & Williams, 2012) and in terms of performance on tests of memory or physical abilities for older adults (Horton et al., 2010; Lamont et al., 2015). Schmader and Johns (2008) proposed a model of stereotype threat suggesting that performance is impaired when negative stereotypes are activated for members of the stereotyped group because of "(1) a physiological stress response that directly impairs prefrontal processing, (2) a tendency to actively monitor performance, and (3) efforts to suppress negative thoughts and emotions in the service of self-regulation." Basically, each of these mechanisms consumes some of the vital cognitive resources that would otherwise be available to improve performance on the task itself.

Encouraging data from some studies suggests that the effects of stereotype threat can be mitigated in some cases. One way to combat the impact of negative intellectual stereotypes is to actually challenge people's views of intelligence. For example, if you believe intelligence is a

Figure 8.15 Impact of Stereotype Threat on Performance

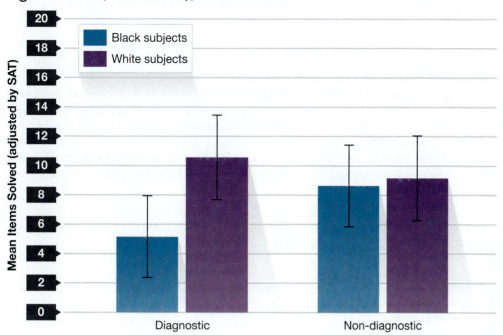

fixed characteristic out of your control, a negative stereotype about the intelligence of your own in-group can certainly appear threatening. However, if you view intelligence as a malleable or changeable characteristic, such stereotypes may not seem as personally threatening. The work of Carol Dweck (e.g., Dweck, 2000) has consistently shown that a *fixed view* of intelligence can have negative repercussions, while a more malleable viewpoint tends to lead to better outcomes (see LO 10.9). Aronson and colleagues (2002) found that Black college students who were encouraged to view intelligence as malleable rather than fixed actually ended up with a higher grade point average than members of control groups.

While stereotype threat is likely not the only reason for Black-White differences in IQ scores, the fact that negative stereotypes can cause significant performance difficulties only serves to highlight the complicated role of environment in group IQ differences. If stereotype threat can be a powerful player in performance, imagine the impact of nutrition, poverty, and education.

Intellectual Disability and Giftedness

LO 8.12 **Explain individual differences in intelligence, including intellectual disability and giftedness.**

As the normal curve suggests, most people (68 percent) have IQ scores between 85 and 115, and another 27 percent fall within 1 and 2 standard deviations either above or below the mean. Scores more than 2 standard deviations above (>130) or below (<70) the mean of 100 are statistically rare and potentially indicative of either intellectual disability or intellectual giftedness.

Intellectual disability (previously referred to as mental retardation), as defined by the American Psychiatric Association (APA, 2013), includes the following traits:

1. Deficits in intellectual functions confirmed by both clinical assessment and individualized, standardized intelligence testing, including:
   - Reasoning
   - Problem solving
   - Planning
   - Abstract thinking
   - Judgment
   - Academic learning
   - Learning from experience

intellectual disability

includes deficits in intellectual functioning with accompanied deficits in adaptive functioning

2. Deficits in adaptive functioning that result in failure to meet developmental and sociocultural standards for personal independence and social responsibility, including:

- Communication
- Social participation
- Independent living

To diagnose intellectual disability, the IQ score is approximately 2 standard deviations below the mean, and most clinicians use a cutoff of scores below 70. However, significant intellectual deficits alone are not enough to receive a diagnosis of intellectual disability. In addition to a significantly below average IQ score, there must be evidence of problems in adaptive functioning across one or more daily life activities. Intellectual disability has been discussed in terms of conceptual, social, and practical domains. Some of the limitations in each of these three areas include:

Domains of Intellectual Disability

Interactive

Conceptual Domain

difficulty with academic skills (e.g., reading, writing, math), difficulty managing money, poor understanding of time

Social Domain

Practical Domain

There are many known causes of intellectual disability, although in about two-thirds of cases, the cause is unknown (Daily et al., 2000; Simpson et al., 2016). Intellectual disability can be caused by any condition that impairs normal brain development during pregnancy, childbirth, or childhood. Some of the most common causes of intellectual disability include:

1. Genetic conditions (e.g., Down syndrome)
2. Problems during pregnancy (e.g., alcohol/drug use, infections)
3. Problems during childbirth (e.g., oxygen deprivation, prematurity)
4. Accidents or injuries (e.g., meningitis, brain injury)

intellectual giftedness

intellectual abilities that are significantly higher than average

On the other end of the IQ spectrum are individuals with extremely high intellectual functioning. While there is no real definition for **intellectual giftedness**, most schools with gifted programs and most research involving gifted individuals rely on IQ scores in the top 2 percent (>130), which you now know is 2 standard deviations above the mean. As part of the No Child Left Behind Act that was passed in 2002 in the United States, gifted students were defined as "Students, children, or youth who give evidence of high achievement capability in areas such as intellectual, creative, artistic, or leadership capacity, or in specific academic fields, and who need services and activities not ordinarily provided by the school in order to fully develop those capabilities" (U.S. Department of Education, 2002).

One of the oldest longitudinal studies still ongoing today started with Lewis Terman's study examining a total of 1,528 gifted children born between 1900 and 1925 and living in California at the time. These children were followed for decades (and the few remaining alive today are presumably still being tracked). One of the goals of Terman's research was to evaluate the negative stereotype of gifted children as being sickly, socially inept, and not well-rounded. The findings generally supported Terman's hypothesis that giftedness would not lead to poor outcomes. The "Termites," a nickname for the study participants, have been tracked for more than 90 years now, through nearly all the milestones of life (Burks & Jensen,

1930; Oden 1968; Sears, 1977; Terman, 1925; Terman & Oden, 1947; Terman & Oden, 1959). Some of the major findings of the study include:

- As children, they:
  - Were generally physically healthy
  - Were generally socially adept and well-adjusted
  - Performed better in school

- As adults:
  - Many were highly educated (two-thirds obtained bachelor's degrees, which was 10 times higher than average at the time, and there were 97 PhDs, 57 MDs, and 92 attorneys) (Leslie, 2000)
  - They had significantly higher incomes
  - They were generally well-adjusted

While Terman's methodology has been criticized (e.g., he was overly involved in the lives of his participants, there was a lack of diversity in his sample, and he relied on teacher referrals to identify his initial test pool) (Block & Dworkin, 1976; Chapman, 1988; McClelland, 1973; Minton, 1988), his study was ground-breaking because it showed that having an extremely high IQ should not be viewed as problematic. That does not mean that certain gifted individuals do not struggle with social or emotional difficulties (Winner, 2000) but, as a group, gifted individuals are quite successful.

Shared Writing Prompt: Educational Needs of Gifted Students

Do you think intellectually gifted students need to receive specialized gifted education? Why or why not?

Quiz for Module 8.10–8.12

1. _____ is traditionally considered a biological category with genetically distinct populations, whereas _____ refers to a shared cultural heritage.
   - **a.** Genome; ethnicity
   - **b.** Ethnicity; race
   - **c.** Race; ethnicity
   - **d.** Ethnicity; genome

2. Which of the following statements regarding ethnic and racial IQ differences is accurate?
   - **a.** Environmental causes of differences have been ruled out.
   - **b.** These differences are due to genetics.
   - **c.** There are no differences in IQ between different racial and ethnic groups.
   - **d.** The cause of these differences is not entirely known.

3. _____ occurs when performance on an intelligence test is negatively impacted by knowledge of a stereotype.
   - **a.** Performance anxiety
   - **b.** Stereotype threat
   - **c.** Mental illness
   - **d.** Stereotype evaluation

4. Which of the following populations has not demonstrated evidence of stereotyped threat?
   - **a.** Females in the area of math or spatial skills
   - **b.** Black individuals in the area of intellectual/academic achievement
   - **c.** Asian men in the area of intellectual/academic achievement
   - **d.** Older adults in the area of memory

5. A person with an IQ score below 70 who also shows deficits in problem solving, social relationships, and daily living skills would be considered to have an _____.
   - **a.** average intelligence
   - **b.** above average intelligence
   - **c.** intellectual gift
   - **d.** intellectual disability

6. One of the major findings of Terman's longitudinal study of intellectually gifted individuals is that generally they _____.
   - **a.** were socially well adjusted
   - **b.** were socially inept and eccentric
   - **c.** were physically weak
   - **d.** had poor adjustment in school

Module: Piecing It Together: Intelligence and Test Bias

LO 8.13   Analyze how the cross-cutting themes of psychology are related to the topic of test bias.

Test Bias in Intelligence Testing

The evidence for gender, racial, and ethnic differences on intelligence tests has led many people to wonder if these tests are biased. Have we developed tests of so-called "intelligence" that actually focus on skills/abilities that are not equally valued by all groups of people, and then used the scores to discriminate against certain people? As you consider this issue and work through the material below, you'll soon recognize that this is a very challenging topic for psychologists. In fact, there are even different meanings of the term "test bias," which impact how current intelligence tests are viewed.

Cultural and Social Diversity

Ethics

Test Bias

Variations in Human Functioning

Research Methods

RESEARCH METHODS

- What does it really mean to say an intelligence test is "biased"?

- How do we determine if bias exists in an intelligence test?

Discussions of bias in intelligence tests have been occurring for decades. In order to really evaluate this issue, a clear definition of what it means for a test to be biased must be established. Remember that one of the key elements of research is making sure the concepts being studied have been clearly *operationally defined*, or defined precisely with specifics about how the construct can be measured. Experts in the area of assessment have discussed two different ways of defining "bias" in terms of intelligence tests. The first type of bias is called *technical bias*. When a test is "technically" biased, it has differential validity for different groups of people (Sattler, 1992). This means the scores represent valid estimates of intellectual functioning in some groups of people, but not others. As discussed earlier in the chapter, different types of validity are particularly important when considering intelligence tests. Both *construct validity* (the degree to which a test measures the construct it claims to measure) and *predictive validity* (the degree to which a specific test predicts future behavior) are important when evaluating whether or not a test is technically biased.

Which Type of Validity?

Interactive

Read each scenario and decide whether or not it describes a problem with <u>construct validity</u> or <u>predictive validity</u>.

Example:
An intelligence test was administered in English to people who were nonnative English speakers. It turns out that the test was actually measuring proficiency in English, as opposed to intelligence in that group of people.
This describes a problem related to...

Example:
A new intelligence test was used to predict how well certain students would do in college. The test was very good at predicting college GPA among female students but was not able to accurately predict college GPA among male students.
This describes a problem related to...

Start Over   Check Answers

In order to make sure a test is not technically biased, it must measure the intended construct similarly in all populations, and it must be equally predictive of some future outcome among all groups. In addition, technical bias can be associated with bias in test item selection, for example, if an item for an intelligence test is selected based on the experiences of one group more than some other group. For example, imagine asking people to identify the image on the right.

Asking someone to identify this image would likely be a poor question for an intelligence test because many younger people may have never seen a rotary phone.

Some people would easily and quickly identify this as a "telephone." However, other people might have no idea what the image represents. What do you think would differentiate the people who answer correctly from the people who answer incorrectly? Most likely, the older you are the more likely you are to accurately name this image. If you are a child or teenager, it's possible you've never even seen a rotary phone. In this case, the ability to recognize a rotary telephone has more to do with age than intelligence. Therefore, if an item like this was included in an intelligence test, it would represent bias in test item selection.

What evidence is there to suggest that intelligence tests either are or are not technically biased? In terms of predictive validity, if an intelligence test accurately predicted school performance or SAT scores for Whites but not Blacks, this would be evidence of technical bias. Current intelligence tests, including the Wechsler scales, have shown that the IQ scores derived from the test are equally predictive across different groups (Neisser et al., 1996; Scheiber & Kaufman, 2015). These findings support the notion that intelligence tests are not biased in terms of having differential predictive validity for different groups.

When considering construct validity, it is important to determine if a test is measuring the same underlying construct across all groups of people. Remember that a Full Scale IQ on the WAIS-IV is derived from four different factors, including the Verbal Comprehension Index, Perceptual Reasoning Index, Working Memory Index, and Processing Speed Index. Each of these factors is hypothesized to measure a distinct facet of intelligence. In order to establish that there is no bias related to the construct validity of an intelligence test, the underlying factors would need to be shown to be equally distinct and important across different groups of people. There has been evidence of equivalent factor structures of some intelligence tests across different groups of people (Georgas et al., 2003; Weiss et al., 2013). However, when new editions of an intelligence test are released, there are often changes to the factor structure. When changes occur, they need to be validated again across different groups of people to establish that the test is free from any technical bias related to construct validity. For example, while studies examining the WAIS-III generally showed the same factor structure for Whites and Blacks (Shuttleworth-Edwards et al., 2004), there has not been adequate research to test the new WAIS-IV factor structure among Blacks (Thaler et al., 2015).

CULTURAL AND SOCIAL DIVERSITY

- Can cultural background impact performance on intelligence tests?
- Is it possible to develop intelligence tests that are "culture free"?

In addition to technical bias, a second type of bias is called *social bias*. Social bias occurs when an individual's performance is affected by his/her experiences and cultural background. Remember the definition of intelligence is the ability to learn and adapt from experience, solve problems, and apply knowledge in new situations. When considering this definition in relation to the concept of social bias, it is easy to understand how someone's cultural background can make a significant difference in how the person solves problems and learns or adapts from experience.

Because the majority of students are members of the dominant culture, it can sometimes be difficult to understand how culture might impact someone's performance on an intelligence test. To help provide some insight about the role of culture in measuring intelligence, take a moment to complete the following intelligence test that was developed for Australians living in the Edward River Community.

Australian Test of Intelligence

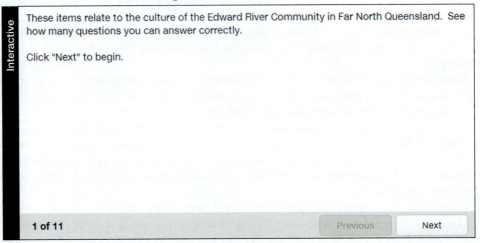

Chances are good that you did not perform very well on this "intelligence" test, highlighting the important role of experiences and cultural background in measuring intelligence. How would you feel if you had just moved to Australia and were told you were significantly less intelligent than the average person because of your score on this test? Because of the acknowledgment that social bias is inherent in many tests of intelligence, and the recognition of the negative impact this bias can have, attempts have been made to develop tests that are less impacted by cultural background.

Journal Prompt: "Culture-Free" Intelligence Test

How would you develop an intelligence test that is "culture free," or not influenced to any degree by experiences or cultural background? What kind of items would you include, and what types of items would you not include?

The notion of "culture-free" tests of intelligence might be ideal, but most experts agree that it is not possible to develop a test that is not impacted by culture at all. One past assumption was that nonverbal tests of intelligence would be much less influenced by culture than tests that rely on verbal stimuli or responses. Theoretically, the ability to identify a pattern in an image would be less likely to be influenced by cultural background than defining a particular vocabulary word. However, nonverbal tests appear to be influenced by culture just as much as verbal tests (Benson, 2003; Reynolds & Ramsay, 2003). It turns out that the types of images people see and their experience with detecting patterns in rows and columns in their culture can impact performance on nonverbal tests just as much as their exposure to language can impact their performance on verbal tests. Therefore, while it is important to reduce cultural influences as much as possible when developing and evaluating intelligence tests, it is impossible to design a test completely devoid of social bias.

Because the notion of "culture-free" intelligence tests is unrealistic, striving for tests considered "culturally fair" is important. Test fairness refers to the social consequences of specific test results (Gregory, 2004) and whether those consequences are fair or unfair for different groups of people. If a test unfairly prevents people in certain groups or from certain backgrounds from being selected by a college for admission or by employers for a job, then that test is unfair and should not be used. Therefore, intelligence tests should be evaluated not only in terms of technical bias, but also with respect to fairness (Ford, 2005).

VARIATIONS IN HUMAN FUNCTIONING

- What other variables may impact someone's performance on an intelligence test?

When considering the topic of test bias, it's also important to think about any variable that can impact an individual's intelligence test scores other than the underlying construct of intelligence.

Variables that Influence Test Performance

Interactive

1. In the box below, list any of the following variables you think could impact a person's performance on an intelligence test:

- Educational background
- Motivation
- Anxiety
- Sleep deprivation
- Drug or alcohol use

1 of 1   Reset   Next

In fact, all of these variables can impact performance on an intelligence test. For example, the amount of education a person has (e.g., years of education) as well as the overall quality of a person's education have both been associated with outcomes on intelligence tests (Thaler, 2015; Whiting, 2009). One study highlighted the fact that motivation plays a significant role in performance on intelligence tests.

Angela Lee Duckworth and her colleagues (2011) conducted a study to determine the impact of motivational factors on IQ scores. They found that people tend to perform better on intelligence tests if they were provided some sort of incentive (e.g., money) to complete the test. On average, having an external incentive when being tested led people to score 9.6 points higher on an IQ test (.64 standard deviations). This effect was even stronger for people who had lower IQ scores to begin with—meaning that people who scored lower than average tended to have greater improvements in their scores as a function of receiving any incentive than people who scored higher than average.

Duckworth et al. (2011) also examined the issue of predictive validity of IQ tests considering the impact of motivation. They examined a group of approximately 500 boys who had taken an intelligence test in 1987. Each of the testing sessions was videotaped, so Duckworth's research team was able to view the tapes and rate each boy's performance in terms of motivation (e.g., did the boys indicate they wanted the testing over or have other behavioral indicators of low/high motivation). They were able to use those motivational ratings along with IQ scores to predict later outcomes, including employment, criminal convictions, and academic achievement. As expected, IQ scores were significant predictors of these outcomes. However, they also found that motivational levels also predicted the life outcomes, and when they removed the impact of motivation from the IQ scores, the predictive power of the IQ score was reduced. These results suggest that motivation may be playing a significant role in making IQ scores highly predictive of life outcomes.

Studies like the Duckworth et al. (2011) experiment serve to highlight the need to continually examine intelligence tests and IQ scores for potential confounding variables. When individual variables such as motivation can significantly impact IQ scores, these scores need to be interpreted carefully, and efforts need to be made to make sure individuals have appropriate levels of motivation when administering intelligence tests.

Potential IQ Score Confounds

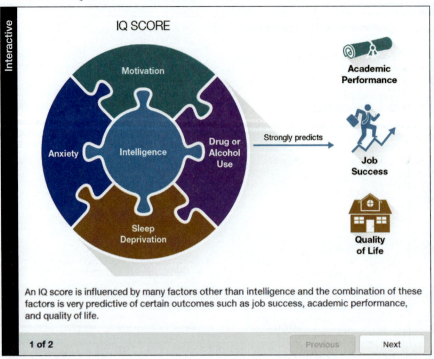

An IQ score is influenced by many factors other than intelligence and the combination of these factors is very predictive of certain outcomes such as job success, academic performance, and quality of life.

1 of 2   Previous   Next

ETHICS

- What kind of ethical or legal difficulties have been associated with intelligence testing?
- How can intelligence tests be used in a way that upholds both ethical and legal standards?

The topic of test bias has been examined from a research perspective, but it has also been evaluated from legal and ethical perspectives. The table on the following page includes a brief summary of some of the most influential legal cases concerning intelligence tests.

While these legal cases highlight how the issue of test bias has been viewed through the courts, it is also important to remember that concerns related to test bias can also be seen as an ethical issue. From an ethical standpoint, the following recommendations are

Legal Cases Related to Test Bias

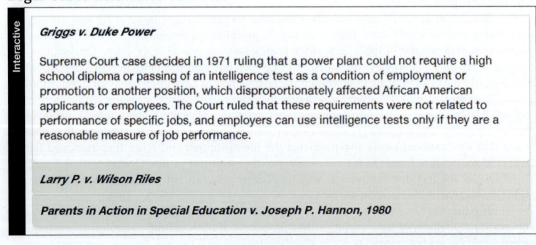

Griggs v. Duke Power

Supreme Court case decided in 1971 ruling that a power plant could not require a high school diploma or passing of an intelligence test as a condition of employment or promotion to another position, which disproportionately affected African American applicants or employees. The Court ruled that these requirements were not related to performance of specific jobs, and employers can use intelligence tests only if they are a reasonable measure of job performance.

Larry P. v. Wilson Riles

Parents in Action in Special Education v. Joseph P. Hannon, 1980

important to utilize intelligence test data in a way that minimizes the impact of any potential test bias:

- Translate tests into the language of the examinee.
- Examine all items to see if groups perform differently and then eliminate such items.
- Consider examinee's background when making interpretations of test scores.
- Never base decisions on one test or one score; try to include a culture-fair or culture-reduced test as part of the assessment whenever possible.

These recommendations incorporate information discussed in each of the pieces of this puzzle on test bias. There is no quick and easy answer to the question about whether or not intelligence tests are biased, but there are a number of important dimensions to consider with respect to the administration, scoring, and interpretation of these tests.

Quiz for Module 8.13

1. Two groups of people take an IQ test. The test shows strong predictive validity for one group but not the other group. This test has demonstrated _____.

   a. social bias   **b.** construct validity

   c. technical bias   **d.** exclusivity bias

2. Tamika did poorly on the intelligence test her school counselor gave her because she did not understand the context of the questions. Tamika was raised in a restrictive culture where she was not allowed to access current books, media, or culturally relevant material. Tamika may have experienced _____ bias in the IQ testing process.

   a. content   **b.** social

   c. gender   **d.** ethnic

3. If the idea of a "cultural-free" intelligence test is unrealistic, what do psychologists strive for in the development of IQ tests?

   a. Culturally unbiased tests   **b.** Culturally relevant tests

   c. Culturally fair tests   **d.** Culturally irrelevant tests

4. Angela Duckworth's research demonstrated that _____ plays a significant role in performance on intelligence tests.

   a. academic success   **b.** sleep deprivation

   c. test anxiety   **d.** motivation

5. What is one recommendation to minimize the impact of any potential test bias?

   a. Never consider the examinee's background or culture.

   b. Never base decisions on one test or one score.

   c. The test should be written and given only in the majority culture's language.

   d. All items on the test should be given in the manner they were originally designed.

Summary

Module 8.1–8.3: Theories of Intelligence

Intelligence is defined as the ability to learn and adapt from experience, solve problems, and apply knowledge in new situations. The study of intelligence has been important in the field of psychology for many reasons such as (1) intelligence is an individual characteristic that people view as important; (2) intelligence is used to make decisions in a number of important arenas; and (3) scores on intelligence tests have also been found to be predictive of numerous factors, including school performance, job success, quality of life, relationship success, morbidity (or rate of illness), and mortality (or rate of deaths).

Charles Spearman proposed a theory of **general intelligence** (or *g*), arguing that *g* represents a common factor that underlies certain mental abilities. Spearman believed that measures of intelligence should seek to assess *g* as much as possible while limiting what he termed **specific** (or "**s**") factors related to a specific single activity. Support for Spearman's theory comes from studies showing that quick processing speeds, working memory, and strong **central executive functioning** (the set of mental processes that governs goals, strategies, and coordination of the mind's activities) are related to higher intelligence. Raymond Cattell argued that intelligence was not a single entity, but that different types of intelligence were distinct from one another. He defined **fluid intelligence** (also referred to as Gf) as the ability to think logically and solve problems and **crystallized intelligence** (also referred to as Gc) as the mental ability to use skills, knowledge, and experience. Cattell's model was expanded to the **Cattell-Horn-Carroll (CHC) model of intelligence** that includes nine different broad ability areas (with more than 70 narrow abilities within these categories): crystallized intelligence (Gc), fluid intelligence (Gf), quantitative reasoning (Gq), reading and writing ability (Grw), short-term memory (Gsm), long-term storage and retrieval (Glr), visual processing (Gv), auditory processing (Ga), and processing speed (Gs). Robert Sternberg proposed a model that includes three aspects of successful intelligence: **analytic intelligence** (academic problem-solving intelligence), **creative intelligence** (adapt to new situations, come up with unique, unusual ideas, and think of novel solutions to problems), and **practical intelligence** (the ability to find solutions to problems and use those solutions in practical, everyday situations). Howard **Gardner's theory of multiple intelligences** proposes nine intelligences that are distinct from one another and include categories such as musical intelligence, interpersonal intelligence, and existential intelligence. One facet of social intelligence is **emotional intelligence,** or a person's ability to perceive, understand, manage, and utilize his or her emotions. Emotional intelligence theory states that it includes four components: (1) the ability to accurately perceive emotions in oneself and others, (2) the ability to use emotions to facilitate thought, (3) the ability to understand emotions and emotional knowledge, and (4) the ability to effectively regulate emotions.

Module 8.4–8.5: Measuring Intelligence

The first widely used intelligence test was the **Binet-Simon scales,** developed by French psychologist Alfred Binet and psychiatrist Theodore Simon to help teachers identify students with special needs. The **Stanford-Binet Intelligence Scale** was an English adaptation of the Binet-Simon scales, which calculated an **intelligence quotient (IQ)** based on the relationship between an individual's actual age and his/her **mental age** (or intellectual level). The early Stanford-Binet emphasized verbal skills, which made the test heavily **culture-bound** (valid only within a particular culture) and led to inaccurate assessments of intelligence among individuals from different cultures or with different language skills. During World War I, psychologists developed two versions of a brief intelligence test that could be administered in large group formats: (1) the Army Alpha test (verbal tests administered to literate, English speakers), and (2) the Army Beta test (performance-based tests administered to illiterate or non-English proficient recruits). Heavily influence by his experiences as an Army examiner, David Wechsler developed a derivative of the Army Alpha and Army Beta tests and first published the Wechsler Adult Intelligence Scale (WAIS) in 1939.

The Wechsler Adult Intelligence Scale Fourth Edition (WAIS-IV) is the latest version of the Wechsler scales and was published in 2008. The WAIS-IV can be administered to people ages 16 to 90 by a qualified professional. The WAIS-IV provides a Full Scale IQ (FSIQ), along with four different index scores: (1) Verbal Comprehension Index (VCI), a measure of verbal concept formation; (2) Perceptual Reasoning Index (PRI), a measure of perceptual and fluid reasoning; (3) Working Memory Index (WMI), a measure of working memory abilities; and (4) Processing Speed Index (PSI), a measure of the ability to quickly and correctly scan, sequence, and discriminate simple visual information). Two Wechsler scales are designed to measure intelligence in children. The Wechsler Intelligence Scale for Children Fifth Edition (WISC-V) is administered to children ages 6 to 16, and the Wechsler Preschool and Primary Scale of Intelligence Fourth Edition (WPPSI-IV) is administered to children as young as 2 years and 6 months and as old as 7 years and 7 months.

The latest editions of both scales have expanded the four-factor structure of the WAIS-IV to now include five index scores and most closely aligns with the Cattell-Horn-Carroll (CHC) theory of intelligence. Studies examining the stability of IQ scores from childhood into adulthood have shown these scores to be quite stable over time, and the stability increases with age.

Module 8.6–8.7: Test Construction

The Wechsler scale implemented a *standard score* approach. This approach utilizes the procedure of **standardization,** a process that helps transform a score into a meaningful piece of information. The new Wechsler scale used the standardization process to be able to establish **test norms,** or a way to compare an individual's score relative to the performance of others. A variable is considered **normally distributed** if a graph of the scores shows that most scores cluster in the middle and the rest taper off symmetrically toward either end. The **standard deviation** refers to a numerical value used to indicate how widely individuals in a group vary. Beginning with the Wechsler scales, measures of intelligence have been converted into standard scores normally distributed with a mean score of 100 and a standard deviation of 15. It's important to keep in mind the notion of the *observed score* versus the *true ability*. The observed IQ score includes some degree of measurement error in addition to the accurate measure of the individual's true ability. Because we can never completely eliminate all error, intelligence tests provide **confidence intervals,** which takes into account the error associated with the measure and provides a range of scores that most likely encompass the "true" score.

Once a test has been developed with a strong theoretical foundation, the process of **standardization** begins (the process of establishing test norms and the guidelines for uniform administration and scoring). It's important to select a representative sample to establish the test norms and standardize the instructions for the administration and scoring of the test. The **validity** (the accuracy of a test) and **reliability** (consistency of a test) are both important when establishing that a test is actually a good measure of intelligence. There are several types of reliability, including **test-retest reliability** (evaluating the consistency of test scores over time), **interrater reliability** (the degree of consistency between two different observers of the same behavior), and **internal consistency** (the consistency within the test items themselves). Intelligence tests are designed to measure **aptitude,** a person's potential ability, rather than **achievement,** a person's knowledge and academic progress, which relates to the validity of intelligence tests. Validity also contains different subtypes, including **construct validity** (the degree to which a test measures the construct it claims to measure) and **predictive validity** (the degree to which a specific test predicts future behavior). The current Wechsler scales have demonstrated both strong reliability and validity.

Module 8.8–8.9: Nature and Nurture

Research has repeatedly confirmed that individual intelligence appears to be an inherited characteristic with heritability estimates of intelligence around 50 percent. Correlations between IQ scores of monozygotic (identical) twins are significantly higher than correlations between scores of dizygotic (fraternal) twins. Adoption studies examining adult adoptive siblings have found that the IQ correlation is about the same as that between two strangers, while adult biological siblings consistently have an average IQ correlation of around .60. The degree of genetic influence also increases from childhood to adulthood. Additionally, intelligence is determined by many different genes, which each have only a small overall impact. *Gene-environment interactions* occur when environmental factors change the expression of predetermined genotypes. On the other hand, *gene-environment correlations* occur when the genotype influences the environment. The **Flynn Effect** also provides evidence for the environmental impact on intelligence, showing that the average IQ score in most places in the world has been increasing since the 1930s.

Module 8.10–8.12: Group and Individual Differences

Gender, racial, and ethnic differences on IQ scores have been found. *Race* has traditionally been referred to as a biological category with genetically distinct populations. *Ethnicity*, on the other hand, refers to a shared cultural heritage. While the fact that racial and ethnic IQ differences exist is generally accepted, the cause of such differences is disputed. The concept of race itself as a biological construct is not widely accepted, and it's difficult to know what role, if any, genetics plays in these group differences. On the other hand, a wealth of possible environmental explanations has been considered, including socioeconomic environment, educational differences, and differences in health and nutrition. In essence, research shows that (1) significant racial and ethnic IQ differences do exist, and (2) while there is no consensus on the cause of these group differences, compelling evidence suggests that environment plays a significant role.

The phenomenon known as **stereotype threat** occurs when people are aware that they must work against a stereotype and risk confirming the negative stereotype by their behavior. Steele and Aronson (1995) published the first paper showing that Black students performed worse when they were told that a test was diagnostic of intelligence than when they were told the test was not diagnostic of intelligence, while the instructions did not affect the performance of White students. This effect has been replicated many times, and researchers have proposed explanations that focus on the use of vital cognitive resources (e.g., anxiety, performance monitoring) that otherwise would be available to improve performance on the task itself. One way to combat the impact of negative intellectual stereotypes is to actually challenge people's views of intelligence as either fixed or malleable.

Scores more than 2 standard deviations below (IQ <70) or above (IQ >130) the mean of 100 are statistically rare and potentially indicative of either intellectual disability or intellectual giftedness. **Intellectual disability** includes deficits in intellectual functioning with accompanied deficits in adaptive functioning. Intellectual disability has been discussed in terms of conceptual (e.g., difficulty with academic skills, money/time management), social (e.g., interpersonal difficulties, problems with social judgment), and practical (e.g., difficulties with tasks of daily living) domains. Intellectual disability can be caused by any condition that impairs normal brain development during pregnancy, childbirth, or childhood. **Intellectual giftedness** is most associated with IQ scores in the top 2 percent (IQ >130). Based in part on Lewis Terman's longitudinal study of gifted children, research has generally supported the notion that most gifted children are quite successful and well-adjusted.

Chapter 8 Quiz

1. Maya has been working as a media relations specialist for 6 months. Her boss is demanding and difficult to get along with. Maya has learned to read her boss's mood and to understand that her reactions to those moods are temporary. Maya knows that if she can get along with her boss and not take the moodiness personally, she will be promoted. She helps others in the company process the demands and makes friends with the people on the team. Maya is considered to be high in what type of intelligence?

   a. Fluid intelligence

   b. Emotional intelligence

   c. Intrapersonal intelligence

   d. Interpersonal intelligence

2. One reason to study intelligence in school or educational settings is to _____.

   a. establish classroom groups based on intelligence

   b. provide assistance to intellectually disabled or intellectually gifted students

   c. make decisions on which students receive further education

   d. give more financial aid to the schools for the students

3. In Sternberg's theory of intelligence, what is meant by "creative intelligence"?

   a. Being artistic and having the skills of an artist

   b. Academic problem-solving skills

   c. Adaptability to new situations, problem solving with unique solutions, and generating unusual ideas

   d. Adaptability to academic and difficult work, problem solving every day issues, and generating practical ideas to problems

4. Which model of intelligence includes 9 broad abilities and over 70 narrow abilities?

   a. Sternberg's triarchic model of intelligence

   b. Cattell's crystallized versus fluid model of intelligence

   c. Spearman's *g* model of intelligence

   d. Cattell-Horn-Carroll model of intelligence

5. One of the limitations of the early Stanford-Binet test was the sole emphasis on _____ skills.

   a. verbal

   b. written

   c. performance

   d. spatial

6. What does the evidence suggest about Gardner's theory of multiple intelligences in regard to learning in the classroom?

   a. Musical and bodily movement should be used to improve students' learning capabilities.

   b. Evidence suggests that students learn better if their specific intelligence is targeted for learning.

   c. There is no evidence that students learn better if their specific intelligence is targeted for learning.

   d. Social and emotional means should be used to improve students' learning capabilities.

7. Imagine discovering a previously unknown group of people who value skills related to surviving in the wild. Tests of these skills should be included in an intelligence test for this group of people because _____.

   a. intelligence tests should include evaluations of people in their natural environments

   b. the notion of intelligence would not apply to their culture

   c. existing intelligence tests do not measure adaptive capabilities

   d. it would provide a measure of their ability to interact effectively in their environment

8. A criticism of the theory of emotional intelligence is that _____.

   a. it has not been researched enough

   b. it is not correlated with other traditional measures of intelligence

   c. it is too broad of a concept and may be more a personality characteristic

   d. no one truly understands the definition

9. During World War I, the U.S. Army screened recruits using the _____ to determine if the recruits were cognitively capable of serving in the military and what job classification would be appropriate.

   a. Wechsler Adult Intelligence Scale

   b. Army Alpha and Army Beta tests

   c. Stanford-Binet Intelligence Scale

   d. Binet-Simon scale of intelligence

10. Sternberg's theory of intelligence is important because it highlights the significance of _____.

    a. knowledge as the most important factor in intelligence

    b. creativity being essential to overall intelligence

    c. the application of cognitive skills to one's environment

    d. factor analysis in supporting the ideas of intelligence

11. The Wechsler Preschool and Primary Scale of Intelligence Fourth Edition (WPPSI-IV) is administered to individuals in what age range?

    a. 4 to 15

    b. 6 to 16

    c. 3 years 6 months to 7 years 7 months

    d. 2 years 6 months to 7 years 7 months

12. If an individual is asked "in what way are blue and red alike?" they are likely taking a subtest of the WAIS-IV designed to measure _____.

    a. processing speed

    b. verbal comprehension

    c. perceptual reasoning

    d. working memory

13. Riley was clearly athletically gifted from birth. She always chose physical activities over academic activities, played every sport in school, and majored in physical education in college. This is an example of a _____.

    a. environmental selection effect

    b. genetic predisposition

    c. gene-environment correlation

    d. gene-environment interaction

14. You are told that you obtained a score of 35 on a psychological test, and the examiner tells you that "there's a 95 percent chance that your true score falls somewhere between 30 and 40." This statement is an example of a(n) _____.

    a. error resolution

    b. reliability estimate

    c. normal distribution

    d. confidence interval

15. Loki took an intelligence test and obtained an IQ score of 130. When comparing his score to the others on the normal curve, he realized that his score was _____.

    a. 2 standard deviations above the mean and higher than 98 percent of others

    b. 1 standard deviation above the mean and higher than 86 percent of others

    c. 1 standard deviation below the mean and lower than 44 percent of others

    d. average and higher than 50 percent of others

16. Rory is a graduate student in psychology administering her first intelligence test. She knows that her scores and her professor's scores for the same student need to match. This is an example of _____.

   a. internal consistency   **b.** test-retest reliability

   c. interrater reliability   **d.** construct validity

17. Logan is a 2-year-old who demonstrated normal abilities at birth but since that time, he has been left in his crib for days. No one answers his cries, reads to him, or rocks him. He does not get fed on a regular basis and is underweight for his age. As a result of this neglect, he does not speak, is just now pulling up to walk, and his IQ is measured at 65. This is an example of

_____.

   a. a gene-environment correlation

   b. a gene-environment interaction

   c. a developmental delay

   d. Down's syndrome

18. Intelligence tests are designed to measure _____ rather than _____.

   a. physiological reactions; mental reactions

   b. achievement; aptitude

   c. aptitude; achievement

   d. mental reactions; physiological reactions

19. The correlation between IQ will be highest among which two people?

   a. Siblings of different ages

   b. Mother and daughter

   c. Fraternal brothers

   d. Identical twin sisters

20. Research shows that _____ plays a more important role in intelligence than _____.

   a. genetics; environment

   b. environment; genetics

   c. nutrition; socioeconomic status

   d. socioeconomic status; nutrition

21. One recent research study showed that the genetic influence on intelligence _____ over the lifespan.

   a. have little effect

   b. decrease

   c. have no effect

   d. increase

22. If you hit a bullseye consistently in the upper right corner repeatedly, you are showing high _____ but low _____.

   a. validity; reliability

   b. reliability; validity

   c. internal consistency; validity

   d. validity; internal consistency

23. What area of the brain is most closely linked to intelligence?

   a. Limbic system

   b. Corpus callosum

   c. Prefrontal cortex

   d. Cerebral cortex

24. Which of the following are possible explanations for the Flynn effect?

   a. Improved test taking strategies

   b. Increased access to education

   c. Improved nutrition

   d. All answers are correct

25. In the past, evidence of ethnic and racial differences in intelligence was inaccurately assumed to be due to _____, which led some people to argue for racial segregation, gender discrimination, and even eugenics.

   a. genetics

   b. environment

   c. culture

   d. family background

26. To qualify for an intellectually gifted program, a student usually has an IQ score _____ standard deviations above the mean, which translates to an IQ score of _____ or above.

   a. 1;115   **b.** 2; 130

   c. 3; 145   **d.** 4; 160

27. In a research study examining stereotype threat, a group of Black students were told that the test they were taking was indicative of intelligence. The students who took the test did _____ on the test compared to the White students who were told the same thing.

   a. better

   b. worse

   c. the same

   d. slightly better

28. Viewing intelligence as _____ rather than _____ is one way to combat the effects of stereotyped threat.

a. fixed; malleable

b. genetic; culturally bound

c. malleable; fixed

d. culturally bound; genetic

29. If a 25-year-old individual with an IQ of 67 cannot remember to take a bath and spends all their money on candy and games, there is a deficit in the _____ domain of intellectual disability.

a. genetic

b. conceptual

c. practical

d. social

30. What are possible environmental explanations for the differences in IQ scores between racial and ethnic groups?

a. Socioeconomic environment

b. Educational differences

c. Nutritional and health differences

d. All answers are correct

Chapter 9
Human Development

Chapter Outline and Learning Objectives

Module 9.1–9.2: Studying Human Development

LO 9.1 List the various types of research designs used in the study of human development.

LO 9.2 Summarize the debates over nature and nurture, continuity and discontinuity, and stability versus change in human development.

Module 9.3–9.6: Development in Infancy and Childhood

LO 9.3 Recognize the stages of prenatal development.

LO 9.4 Describe the physical changes that occur during infancy and childhood.

LO 9.5 Compare and contrast theories of cognitive development.

LO 9.6 Describe the social and emotional development that occurs during infancy and childhood.

Module 9.7–9.11: Development in Adolescence

LO 9.7 Describe the physical changes of puberty.

LO 9.8 Explain the impact maturation of the frontal lobes has on adolescent reasoning.

LO 9.9 Identify Kohlberg's theory of moral reasoning.

LO 9.10 Describe the impact adolescents' newly formed identities have on their relationships with others.

LO 9.11 Describe the features of the life stage of emerging adulthood.

Module 9.12–9.14: Development in Adulthood

LO 9.12 Describe some of the physical and neurological changes that occur in adulthood.

LO 9.13 Explain how some types of memory and intelligence change during adulthood.

LO 9.14 Describe the social and emotional development associated with adulthood.

Module 9.15: Piecing It Together: Development and Body Image

LO 9.15 Analyze how the cross-cutting themes of psychology relate to the topic of body image and development.

What Is Developmental Psychology?

Somewhere in the attic or on an old hard drive you may find photos, videos, and baby books that preserve important moments throughout your life so far: that first tentative step, your first lost baby tooth, a traumatic first day of school, that regrettable fourth-grade haircut. Just as parents sometimes track their children's progress, **developmental psychologists** study the physical, cognitive, and social changes that we experience throughout our lifespans.

Many people think of developmental psychology as focused solely on human development in childhood and adolescence. While we do tend to see the most rapid changes from infancy through adolescence, the field of developmental psychology extends to studying changes throughout the lifespan. After all, people are just as different (physically, cognitively, and socially) in their 20s as in their 60s, and these changes over time are studied by developmental psychologists.

developmental psychologists

psychologists who study the physical, cognitive, and social changes that humans experience throughout the lifespans

Choose Your Ideal Age

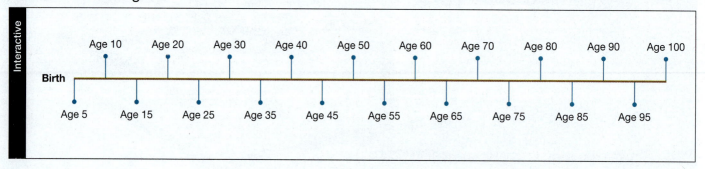

What is the ideal age? Do you think childhood with its lack of responsibilities is the perfect age? Would you prefer early adulthood with its peak physical performance or perhaps later adulthood with the accompanying maturity? A recent survey conducted by *Time* magazine showed that, on average, people would prefer to "stop the clock" at age 50. However, if you look at the age of the respondents, you'll notice an interesting trend. People actually tended to choose an age that is very close to their current age. For example, survey respondents between ages 18 and 36 chose 38 as the ideal age while people between the ages of 49 and 67 chose 55 as the ideal age (Waxman, 2013). Interestingly, people appear to think their own age is very close to ideal. We tend to think this in our 20s, and we continue to think this in our 50s! As you read about the physical, cognitive, and social development throughout the lifespan, consider the unique advantages and challenges present at every stage.

Module 9.1–9.2: Studying Human Development

Does birth order affect personality? Do short-term memory capabilities stay the same across the lifespan or decline with age? Does bullying affect the self-esteem of children in the long run? How important is nutrition in infancy and early childhood for brain development? These are only a few examples of the types of research questions examined by developmental psychologists. Because developmental psychologists conduct research documenting developmental changes over the lifespan, selecting the appropriate research design is particularly important. In addition, developmental research also tends to focus on specific themes such as questions of nature-nurture, which will be discussed in the current module.

Developmental Research

LO 9.1 List the various types of research designs used in the study of human development.

Researchers use **normative investigations** to determine the landmarks of development, or characteristics present at certain ages or stages of development. By identifying norms, or standard development patterns, researchers can differentiate between **chronological age**—the amount of time someone has spent alive—and **developmental age**—the point at which someone falls within a developmental continuum. Have you ever heard a preteen described as "12 going on 25"? This would describe a child whose developmental age (whether it be physical, cognitive, or social) is ahead of his or her chronological age. Tests of reading fluency often use the notion of a difference between actual grade level and the demonstrated reading grade level. For example, a child who is in the sixth grade but is reading at a fourth grade level is demonstrating a discrepancy between his chronological age/grade level and his developmental age/ability.

Developmental psychologists tend to rely on three types of studies to frame their research questions. **Cross-sectional studies** observe different individuals of different ages at one point in time to track differences related to age. While these studies are relatively quick, inexpensive, and easy to conduct, they cannot control for differences among **cohorts**—groups of people raised during the same time period. For example, cross-sectional studies have been used to examine how aging affects intelligence. A researcher might examine a group of 20-year-olds and compare them to a group of 70-year-olds. However, any differences in intelligence between the two groups may not be entirely due to the process of aging. There are many differences in the experiences of 20-year-olds and 70-year-olds based on the historical and social time period in which they were born and raised, including their access to education, nutrition, and technology. For example, high school graduation rates were lower in the 1950s compared to today, so far fewer 70-year-olds were likely to have completed a high school education compared to the 20-year-olds.

Another commonly used research design in developmental studies is a **longitudinal study**, in which the same individuals are observed over a period of time to track changes related to age. To assess changes in intelligence over time using a longitudinal design, researchers would examine the same group of individuals repeatedly over time (e.g., at age 20, 30, 40, 50, etc.). While they often provide very valuable insights and can control for cohort effects, longitudinal studies require a great deal of time, money, and effort. For example, imagine waiting to publish your research findings for 30 or more years. In addition, longitudinal studies sometimes have problems related to selective

normative investigations

research studies performed with healthy ("normative") participants to establish normal behavior or average performance in a population

chronological age

the amount of time someone has been alive

developmental age

a measure of a child's development using age norms

Cross-Sectional Research Study

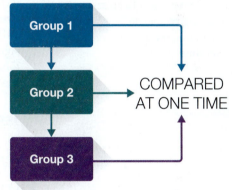

cross-sectional studies

studies that observe different individuals of different ages at one point in time to track differences related to age

cohorts

a group of people who share a common temporal life experience

longitudinal study

a type of study in which the same individuals are observed over a period of time to track changes over time

Longitudinal Research Study

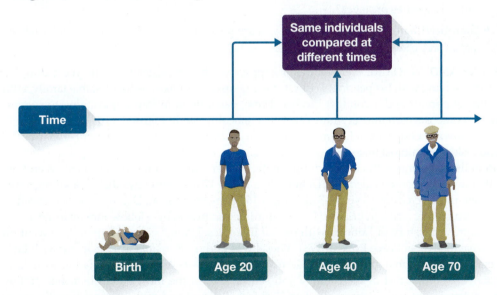

Table 9.1 Research Designs Used to Study Development

	Type of Design	Description of Design	Design Advantages	Design Disadvantages
Interactive	Cross-Sectional	Different individuals of different ages are observed at one point in time to track differences related to age.	• Quick • Inexpensive • Easy to conduct	• Can't control for cohort effects
	Longitudinal	The same individuals are observed over a period of time to track changes related to age.	• Controls for cohort effects • Can track an individual over time	• Takes a long time • Expensive • Requires significant effort • Problems related to selective drop-out
	Cross-Sequential	Examines several different cohorts over time	• Can provide immediate cohort comparisons and longitudinal comparisons	• Requires significant effort • Expensive

drop-out. For example, if people in the lowest intelligence range tend to drop out of the study as the years go on at a greater rate than people in the highest intelligence range, your results would be skewed in the end.

The third type of research design is called a **cross-sequential study**. This type of study includes a combination of both cross-sectional and longitudinal designs by examining several different cohorts over time. Using a cross-sequential design to study changes in intelligence over time, a researcher might study different age groups (e.g., ages 20, 40, 60, 80) in the year 2015 and again in the year 2025. This study would still take 10 years to complete and requires significant resources, but you would have both immediate cross-sectional data to examine and longitudinal information without having to wait for your group of 20-year-olds to turn 80. See Table 9.1 for a comparison of the three research designs.

cross-sequential study

a type of study which includes a combination of both cross-sectional and longitudinal designs by examining several different cohorts over time

Issues in Development

LO 9.2 Summarize the debates over nature and nurture, continuity and discontinuity, and stability versus change in human development.

Developmental psychologists often frame their questions around three major issues:

- **Nature/nurture:** How do both your genetics and your life experiences influence your development?
- **Continuity/Discontinuity:** Is development a continual, gradual process, or do we develop in a series of stages?
- **Stability/Change:** What aspects of you are present throughout your life, and what aspects have changed across your development??

NATURE AND NURTURE Jeffrey was a happy, bubbly youngster who enjoyed riding his bike and playing with his pet dog, Frisky. Growing up in the 1960s, he had a stable family, with two loving parents and a younger brother. There was little in Jeffrey's upbringing to suggest that he should develop into anything other than a healthy, well-adjusted adult.

On July 22, 1991, Jeffrey Dahmer was arrested at his Milwaukee apartment. What police found inside was almost unspeakable. Gruesome photos of dismembered body parts, a severed head in the refrigerator, three more heads in the freezer—the list of atrocities went on and on. Further investigation revealed that Dahmer had killed 17 men and boys during a killing spree that went undetected for 13 years. Following a 160-page confession, Dahmer was sentenced to 15 consecutive life terms in prison. He was murdered in prison by a fellow inmate in 1994.

Contrast the story of Dahmer with that of Elie Wiesel, a holocaust survivor who went on to receive the Nobel Peace Prize in 1984. Wiesel was born in Romania in 1928 to a Jewish family that was placed in a ghetto by the German Nazis in 1944. Wiesel and his father were later separated from the rest of their family and sent to two of the most notorious concentration camps: Auschwitz and Buchenwald. For 11 months, Wiesel endured the most horrific of circumstances, culminating in his father's death in the crematoriums. Many years after the war, Wiesel went on to become a prolific author and is most famous for his autobiographical book,

"So, how do you want to play this? Nature, nurture, or a bit of both?"

Night, which has sold millions of copies. He became a citizen of the United States in 1955, and he was awarded the Nobel Peace Prize for his activism against violence, repression, and racism.

The stories of Jeffrey Dahmer and Elie Wiesel underscore one of the biggest and most enduring issues faced by psychologists. Do our human traits develop through experience, or does a genetic blueprint determine who we will become? Are we primarily defined by **nature**—inherited characteristics that influence personality, physical growth, intellectual growth, and social interactions, or by **nurture**—environmental factors such as parental styles, physical surroundings, and economic issues? Although Dahmer was not subjected to the abuse or neglect that many serial killers experience during childhood, there were several incidents in his past that could have factored into his decline into sadism. However, like the case of Elie Wiesel, many people deal with far more traumatic life experiences without engaging in violence. Was there something inherent in Dahmer's biological makeup that made his sadistic killing spree inevitable? Was there something inherent in Elie Wiesel's genetics that made him capable of overcoming such a traumatic experience?

To ideally study the contribution of genetics versus environment, comparisons can be made between two groups: (1) children who are genetically identical but who were raised in different environments and (2) children raised in identical environments but who have differing levels of genetic similarity. Therefore, researchers often look to studies of twins and children who have been adopted. **Monozygotic**, or identical, twins develop when one egg is fertilized by one sperm. After fertilization, the egg splits in half, and two fetuses develop with identical genetic makeup. **Dizygotic**, or fraternal, twins develop when two eggs are released and are both fertilized by two different sperm. While fraternal twins share a uterus and have a similar upbringing to identical twins (because simply being a twin can lead to different treatment), they are no more genetically similar than any other siblings. Instead of having to share your toys with your little brother or big sister, you literally have to share a womb with a fraternal twin. In terms of studying the impact of environment and genetics, studies of fraternal versus identical twins offer a chance to control for environment while genetics is varied. For certain conditions, such as schizophrenia or bipolar disorder, researchers often examine the twin **concordance rate**, or the probability that one twin will develop the condition if the other twin has been diagnosed. For example, if you study a large group of twins in which one of the twins has schizophrenia, the concordance rate would be the probability that the other twin also has (or will develop) schizophrenia.

nature

inherited characteristics that influence personality, physical growth, intellectual growth, and social interactions

nurture

environmental influences such as parental styles, physical surroundings, and economic issues

monozygotic twins

identical twins that develop when one egg is fertilized by one sperm and then the egg splits into half and two fetuses develop with identical genetic makeup

dizygotic twins

fraternal twins that develop when two eggs are released and are both fertilized by two different sperm

concordance rate

the probability that one twin develops a condition if the other twin has it

Concordance Rate

> Interactive
>
> 1 question
>
> 1. For conditions with a large genetic component, which would be higher: the concordance rate between identical twins or fraternal twins?
>
> ○ identical
>
> ○ fraternal
>
> Next

Adoption studies also provide insight into the nature-nurture debate. Whereas twin studies control for environment, adoption studies can control for genetics. If you have identical twins who are raised apart, you can compare them to identical twins raised together to try to tease apart characteristics that are due to environment versus genetics. Since 1979, the Minnesota Study of Twins Raised Apart has evaluated more than 100 twin-pairs who were raised separately, and that data has contributed significantly to our knowledge about the contribution of heritability and environment on different traits (Bouchard et al., 1990). More recently, researcher Nancy Segal has been studying Chinese twins who were adopted and raised separately by parents in the United States (Segal, 2017) and twins born in Korea who were raised separately in the United States and France (Segal & Cortez, 2014). In addition, a new category of "virtual twins" have been studied, which includes same-age unrelated adopted siblings (Segal, et al., 2015).

Environment vs. Genetics

Interactive

1 question

1. For traits with a high environmental component, would you expect identical twins raised apart to be highly similar or different on that trait when compared to identical twins raised together?

○ different

○ similar

Next

heritability estimates

an estimation of how much variability in a trait is due to genetics

As scientific and technological advancements have been made, researchers have been able to more accurately pinpoint the degree to which genetics (or nature) contributes to different human traits or characteristics. **Heritability estimates** provide us with an estimation of how much variability in a trait is due to genetics. Researchers have been able to identify traits that are considered high heritability (e.g., eye color), moderate heritability (e.g., body weight), and low heritability (e.g., specific language). See if you can identify the heritability of various traits in Table 9.2.

The nature-nurture issue raises interesting questions for contemporary psychologists. Are people with mental illnesses predisposed to suffer particular conditions, or do stressful life events or other environmental factors trigger mental disorders? How do children learn language—through repetition and education, or via a preprogrammed mechanism that stimulates the development of grammar? The answers to one question in particular may have

Table 9.2 Teasing Apart Nature and Nurture

High Heritability (Nature)	High Environmental Component (Nurture)	Low Heritability and Low Environmental Influence
The trait is more similar among twins raised apart than adoptive siblings.	The trait is more similar among adoptive siblings than twins raised apart.	The trait is no more similar among twins raised apart or adoptive siblings.

fascinating social implications: Can people change? Is there hope of rehabilitation for men like Jeffery Dahmer, or is a serial killer always a serial killer? Could all Holocaust survivors have gone on to develop the mental fortitude and productivity displayed by author Elie Wiesel, or did something in Wiesel's biological makeup awaken in him a sense of determination rather than one of hopelessness? As the debate continues, researchers attempt to find answers to these important questions.

CONTINUITY AND DISCONTINUITY   In addition to the issue of nature-nurture, developmental researchers have long considered whether human development occurs in a continuous or discontinuous pattern. Proponents of the **continuous model** argue that development occurs as a gradual but consistent process over time. A good analogy for the continuous theory of development is the notion of a path winding up a mountain. Each step up the path takes you higher in elevation and as long as you continue to walk steadily along the path, you will eventually reach the peak. If you've ever interacted with an infant or young child, you may have noticed that they seem to grow and change in subtle ways that you may fail to even notice on a day-to-day basis. Each visit to the pediatrician may surprise you at how much the child has grown in height and weight over a short period of time, although you were unable to detect small changes that were occurring every day. Proponents of continuous theories of development argue that physical, cognitive, and social development occur in a steady and smooth fashion.

In contrast, proponents of the **discontinuous model** maintain that development occurs in distinct steps or stages. In the mountain analogy, the discontinuous model would be best represented by a stair-step path. As you climb the mountain, you take larger steps up the staircase which represents a more abrupt elevation increase than the smooth path. You may reach a plateau where you stay for some time before beginning your upward climb again. While many of the changes in an infant or toddler seem gradual, several developmental milestones, such as starting to walk, appear abruptly—one day the child was not able to engage in the behavior and the next day the child could. Jean Piaget, Erik Erikson, and Lawrence Kohlberg all proposed *stage theories* of development based on the discontinuous model that will be discussed within this chapter.

STABILITY VERSUS CHANGE   Another issue for developmental psychologists is the question of **stability versus change**. To what degree do you remain unchanging from infancy to adulthood? What aspects of your personality are relatively stable and unchanging over years of growth and maturation? On the other hand, what traits or characteristics are more malleable and change

continuous model
model of development suggesting that human development occurs as a gradual but consistent process over time

discontinuous model
a model of developmental suggesting that development occurs in distinct steps or stages

stability versus change
the degree to which traits remain stable and unchanging versus malleable over years of growth and maturation

A winding path is similar to a continuous model of development.

A stair step path with flat portions is similar to a discontinuous model of development.

over the course of your development? Regardless of your current age, you can likely look back into your past and identify some aspects of your personality that you know have always been true of you. Likewise, you may look back at certain times in your life and find it hard to reconcile the person you were then with the person you are now. Researchers in the area of development often focus on trying to identify which of our traits, characteristics, or abilities appear to remain stable throughout the lifespan and which appear to change more readily over time.

Journal Prompt: Stability versus Change

Write about at least one aspect of your personality that has been stable throughout your life and one aspect that has changed significantly throughout your life.

Quiz for Module 9.1–9.2

1. What type of research study examines individuals of different ages at one point in time to track the differences related to age?

   a. Longitudinal   b. Cohort study

   c. Cross-sectional study   d. Cross-sequential study

2. Darius is a 6-year-old boy who can throw and catch a ball like a 10-year-old. Researchers would say that his developmental age is more advanced than his _____.

   a. normative age

   b. chronological age

   c. cross-sectional age

   d. cohort age

3. The question of whether a person's development is more influenced by genetics or by life experience is considered _____.

   a. nature vs. stability   b. nature vs. nurture

   c. stability vs. change   d. continuity vs. discontinuity

4. Ellie is a healthy 12-month-old baby. She has been crawling for several months but her mother recently looked up to see Ellie walking over toward her in a wobbly fashion. When her mother described the day to Ellie's pediatrician, she stated, "it was like she took a giant step over night in her development." This is an example of which type of developmental model?

   a. Nurture model   b. Stability model

   c. Continuous model   d. Discontinuous model

Module 9.3–9.6: Development in Infancy and Childhood

Development from infancy through adolescence is a truly incredible process. Physically, infants are born unable to control their own arm and leg movements and in a relatively short period of time, babies learn to sit, crawl, walk, and run. In fact, some of the most amazing physical feats of athleticism are performed by children before the age of 13 in sports such as gymnastics.

In infancy, our cognitive skills are very limited as we are born with minimal communication skills and awareness of how the world works. By the age of 3, most children have already amassed a significant vocabulary and by the time many children are 12 years old, they can think abstractly and even solve algebra problems (Bjorklund & Causey, 2017). Social development is no less impressive during these years. Early in childhood, the social bonds that form between parents and children are very critical and complex. By late childhood, children have developed significant social relationships with their peers that sometimes even last a lifetime. The following sections provide a summary of physical, cognitive, and social development of this amazing period of development.

Many gymnasts compete at the elite level before they are even teenagers.

Prenatal Development

LO 9.3   **Recognize the stages of prenatal development.**

It's hard to think of anything more miraculous than the process of human reproduction. Two tiny human cells combine to form a single cell that eventually becomes a unique human being. To understand the process of prenatal development, we must start from an understanding of the unique role of each parent.

CONCEPTION AND STAGES OF PRENATAL DEVELOPMENT At birth, women have all the immature eggs, or **ova**, they will ever have. Of these ova, only one in 5,000 are ever released from the **ovaries**, the female reproductive organ where ova are produced and released. Eggs are 85,000 times the size of one **sperm** (male sex cells). While sperm are much smaller in size than eggs, many more sperm are produced than eggs. Starting at puberty, males produce sperm cells 24 hours a day, and an average of 200 million sperm are released during a single act of intercourse. Only a few sperm make it to the egg. As soon as one sperm penetrates the egg's protective coating, the egg blocks the other sperm out and uses fingerlike projections to pull the lucky guy in. In less than half a day, a sperm and egg have fused into a single fertilized cell, or **zygote**.

After fertilization, the zygote enters the **germinal stage** of development. This stage lasts two weeks and includes a period of rapid cell division and culminates with the implantation into the female's uterus. After implantation, the **embryonic stage** begins and lasts from around two weeks to eight weeks of gestation. The **fetal stage** occurs from around eight weeks until birth. Click through Table 9.3 to learn more details and see images related to each stage of development.

TERATOGENS During the embryonic period, the developing baby is most susceptible to damage from harmful agents that include certain medications, street drugs, alcohol, toxins, and viruses. However, all stages of prenatal development can be negatively affected by **teratogens**, or agents that can have a negative impact on the development of an embryo or fetus. Teratogens can include a wide range of substances. Because the developing embryo is attached to the uterus and shares a blood supply with the mother, anything in the mother's blood stream can potentially affect the developing baby.

Alcohol use during pregnancy has received a significant amount of attention and research due to **fetal alcohol spectrum disorders (FASD)**. FASD causes physical and cognitive abnormalities in children resulting from a pregnant mother's alcohol intake. Researchers do not know how much alcohol or at what point in the pregnancy alcohol use can cause FASD; however, there is also no known "safe" amount of alcohol for a pregnant woman (Centers for Disease Control and Prevention, 2015a; Ikonomidou et al., 2000;

ova
immature eggs contained in the ovaries

ovaries
the female reproductive organ where ova are produced and released

sperm
male sex cells

zygote
a single fertilized cell

germinal stage
stage of development that the zygote enters after fertilization that lasts two weeks and culminates with the implantation into the female's uterus

embryonic stage
stage of prenatal development that occurs after implantation into the female uterus around two weeks after conception and continues until eight weeks of gestation

fetal stage
stage of prenatal development that occurs from around eight weeks of gestation until birth

teratogens
agents that can negatively impact the development of an embryo or fetus

fetal alcohol spectrum disorders (FASD)
physical and cognitive abnormalities in children resulting from a pregnant mother's alcohol intake

Table 9.3 Stages of Prenatal Development

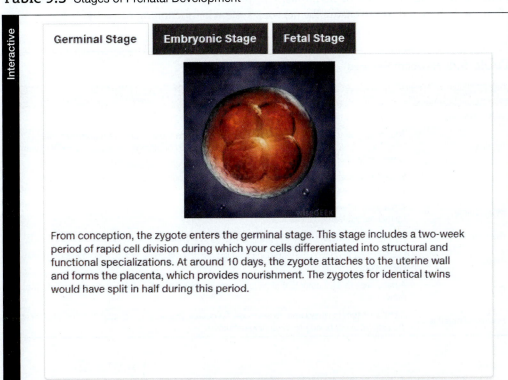

Germinal Stage | **Embryonic Stage** | **Fetal Stage**

From conception, the zygote enters the germinal stage. This stage includes a two-week period of rapid cell division during which your cells differentiated into structural and functional specializations. At around 10 days, the zygote attaches to the uterine wall and forms the placenta, which provides nourishment. The zygotes for identical twins would have split in half during this period.

Nykjaer et al., 2014). Alcohol negatively affects the fetus because it passes freely through the placental barrier. The fetus' liver is not yet capable of detoxification and is therefore exposed to alcohol in the amniotic fluid for much longer than an adult would be (Behnke & Smith, 2013; Ornoy & Ergaz, 2010). FASD can cause growth deficiencies and noticeable facial abnormalities and is the leading cause of intellectual disability (Ornoy & Ergaz, 2010; Streissguth et al., 1991; Suttie et al., 2013).

Nicotine is another potential teratogen. Smoking not only increases the chance of miscarriage during pregnancy, it is also associated with higher rates of premature births and birth defects (Hackshaw et al., 2011; Pineles et al., 2014; Sullivan et al, 2015; Tuan, 2016). Additionally, babies whose mothers smoked during pregnancy also have a higher risk of **sudden infant death syndrome (SIDS)**, the unexplained death of a seemingly healthy infant (Galland & Elder, 2014; McDonnell-Naughton et al., 2012).

The use of street drugs and certain medications during pregnancy can also be harmful for a developing embryo. In addition, viruses such as influenza can also be teratogens. Recent findings have highlighted the risk of the Zika virus for pregnant women. This virus can cause microcephaly (a birth defect that causes a baby's head to be smaller than normal) and other severe fetal brain defects (Centers for Disease Control and Prevention, 2016b; Marrs et al., 2016; Miner et al., 2016).

sudden infant death syndrome (SIDS)

the unexplained death of a seemingly healthy infant

Physical Development in Infancy and Childhood

LO 9.4 Describe the physical changes that occur during infancy and childhood.

The physical development that occurs from infancy through childhood is truly incredible. Consider the fact that infants find it very challenging to coordinate the activities of sucking, swallowing, and breathing (which is why feeding a newborn can take so long). By the age of two, most children are running circles around their parents and feeding themselves easily, demonstrating that infancy and childhood are periods of intense physical development.

NEWBORN REFLEXES   Even before a newborn infant has time to adjust to being outside of the amniotic sac, hardwired reflexes help prepare the infant to interact with the world. At birth, an infant begins breathing air, regulating its temperature, and crying when hungry. Table 9.4 shows some of the **reflexes**, or involuntary responses, that newborn babies exhibit. Doctors often check these reflexes to ensure the nervous system is functioning correctly.

reflexes

involuntary responses

Table 9.4 Newborn Reflexes

Reflex	Baby's Physical Reaction
Withdraw/Pain	A baby will pull his or her limb away from a source of pain.
Rooting	Touching a baby's check causes him to turn toward the touch, open his mouth, and search (or "root") for the nipple. Finding the nipple causes initiation of other reflexes (e.g., sucking, swallowing without choking).
Babinski	Stroking the sole of the baby's foot will cause his big toe to extend up while the other toes stretch down and fan out.
Moro/Startle	A baby will extend his arms when startled by a loud noise or sensation of falling, even though he has not yet learned these fears.
Grasping	A baby will hold tightly onto a finger or anything else placed in his hand.
Stepping	Holding a baby up with his feet touching a flat surface will cause him to move his legs in a walking motion.
Crying	A baby cries to alert parents that he is hungry. Since parents find this sound unpleasant, the baby is fed.
Restricted breathing	A baby will turn his head from side to side if a cloth is placed over his face. He may also hit at the cloth to avoid having his breathing restricted.

Now watch the following videos to see if you can correctly identify each of the reflexes.

Identify the Reflexes

BRAIN DEVELOPMENT The rate of brain development from conception through childhood is equally impressive to the degree of physical development that occurs during this time period. Only 16 days after conception, the foundation for the spinal cord and the brain has already developed. By 5 weeks after conception, neurons begin to form at a rapid pace. During the most rapid phase of neuron development in the second trimester, a fetus creates 250,000 neurons per minute (Budday et al., 2015). By birth, the cortex of the brain basically contains all of the neurons it will ever have (Egorov &, Draguhn, 2013; Rakic, 2006). In addition to the rapid rate of neuron development, the fetus is also developing synapses to connect neurons. So many synaptic connections are developed in utero and during the first two to three years of life that by birth, an individual neuron may be connected to as many as 2,500 other neurons; and, by the age of 2 to 3, there are approximately 15,000 synapses per neuron (see Figure 9.1) (Blakemore & Firth, 2005; Huang et al., 2015; Philips & Shonkoff, 2000). This is twice the number of synapses that will be present in adulthood, and excess synapses (those connections that are not used) are gradually reduced during childhood in a process called **synaptic pruning**.

synaptic pruning
a process in which excess synapses are gradually reduced during childhood

Figure 9.1 Synaptic Density

Synaptic connections increase throughout the first 2 years, with the greatest density occurring at the end of toddlerhood.

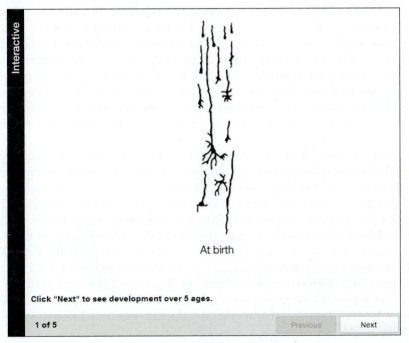

At birth

Click "Next" to see development over 5 ages.

1 of 5   Previous   Next

motor development

the emergent ability to execute physical actions

cephalocaudal rule

the tendency for motor skills and physical growth to emerge in sequence from top to bottom

proximodistal rule

the tendency for motor skills to emerge in sequence from inside to outside

MOTOR DEVELOPMENT As your muscles and nervous system developed, so too did your physical coordination. **Motor development**—the emergent ability to execute physical actions—tends to occur in a universal sequence. Like most other babies, you likely rolled over before you could sit up and crawled before you could walk. This sequence also tends to be true for visually impaired children, suggesting that these behaviors do not merely reflect imitation (Elias & Berk, 2002).

Two general rules govern the development of motor skills. The **cephalocaudal rule** is the tendency for motor skills and physical growth to emerge in sequence from top to bottom. Recall the rooting reflex, which causes the baby to move his or her head, open his or her mouth, and search for a nipple; as a baby, your head had very capable motor skills long before your legs would allow you to walk. The **proximodistal** rule is the tendency for motor skills to emerge in sequence from inside to outside. As a child, the center of your body possessed motor skills before the periphery. Do you remember learning to write? You probably started out by holding the pencil far from the tip because you initially used your shoulder to make the pencil move. The source of movement then worked its way down to your elbow, and finally to your fingers and thumb (Payne & Isaacs, 1987).

While the sequence of motor skill development is generally universal, the timing can vary based on an individual's genetics or experiences. However, experience can do little to rush motor skills before adequate muscular and neural maturity have been reached. Most babies are ready to walk at around one year, when the cerebellum has developed enough to enable physical coordination and balance. A parent could try to beg or cajole a 6-month-old infant into walking earlier than his or her peers, but it will have little positive impact. Other physical skills, such as bowel and bladder control, are also resistant to being hurried along.

Cognitive Development in Infancy and Childhood

LO 9.5 Compare and contrast theories of cognitive development.

How do we develop the ability to think? When do we begin to remember our early experiences? How do we learn to communicate? Psychologists study **cognition**, the mental activities associated with sensation and perception, thinking, knowing, remembering, and communicating to find answers. Theories of cognitive development vary in terms of how much emphasis is placed on the role of the environment versus how much the role of biology is emphasized. In addition, some theories suggest that infants start out with relatively few cognitive capabilities, while other theories proposed that newborns are born with more cognitive abilities (Newcombe, 2013).

cognition

the mental activities associated with sensation and perception, thinking, knowing, remembering, and communicating, to find answers

schemas

concepts or frameworks around which we organize and interpret information

assimilation

the process through which we incorporate new experiences in terms of existing schemas

accommodation

the process through which we adjust and refine our schemas to incorporate new information

PIAGET'S THEORY OF COGNITIVE DEVELOPMENT Jean Piaget's early 20th-century observations of children's innate interest in learning led him to believe that children didn't simply know less than adults, but that they instead understood the world around them differently. His revolutionary ideas presented children's minds not as miniature adult minds but rather as minds that develop by an intrinsic motivation to explore and understand. Piaget's theory described two processes by which we adjust our **schemas**—concepts or frameworks around which we organize and interpret information. For example, if you hear someone refer to a "zoo," you probably automatically think of a number of concepts associated with a zoo such as giraffes, lions, tigers, and zookeepers. That is, you have a schema for "zoo." Schemas are useful because they save time in having to recall a variety of information associated with a topic. Using **assimilation**, we incorporate new experiences in terms of existing schemas. When people encounter a new animal at the zoo (e.g., an alpaca), they will typically assimilate this new information into their existing zoo schema so that their schema for a zoo now includes alpacas. Under this process, a child might visit an aquarium for the first time and call it a "zoo" because both a zoo and an aquarium have animals that you go to see. However, once the child learns the differences between zoos and aquariums, he or she will use **accommodation** to adjust and refine the zoo schema to incorporate new information about the differences between zoos and aquariums. See Figure 9.2 for another example of assimilation versus accommodation. The main idea of Piaget's theory is that mental development derives from children's interactions with the world around them.

Figure 9.2 Assimilation versus Accommodation

In the top image, the child assimilates his schema for "mammals" with new information about a zebra. In the bottom image, the child accommodates his schema for horse when he discovers that a zebra is not a horse.

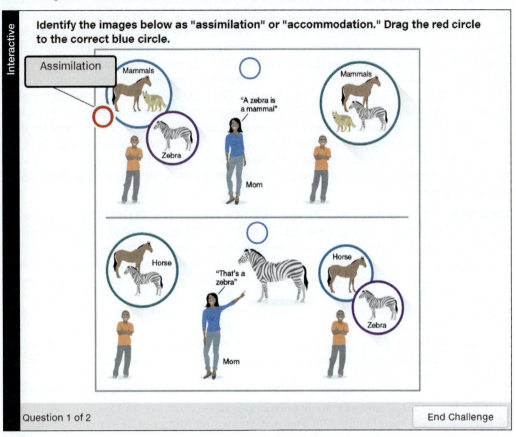

Piaget proposed that cognitive development occurred in a series of four stages from infancy to adulthood. These stages focus more on sequencing than the age at which milestones are reached. The following page includes a brief description of each of Piaget's stages and an example of one cognitive task associated with the stage.

Piaget's Stages of Development

Piaget's work has been very influential in advancing research about the cognitive development of children based on his notion that children think differently than adults and are active participants in seeking out information from the environment (Hopkins, 2011). However, research studies did not necessarily support the qualitative differences between the stages as cognitive development appears to be more fluid and continuous than Piaget's stage theory suggests. In addition, significant evidence suggests that Piaget may have underestimated children's cognitive abilities (Martin & Rodriquez, 2012). While Piaget thought babies couldn't think before age 2, researchers have found that babies do possess some logic: They look longer at unexpected scenes, such as a car passing through a solid object (Baillargeon, 1995, 1996, 2004; Denison et al, 2013; Wellman & Gelman, 1992) or numerically impossible outcomes (e.g., where a doll was added behind a screen to another doll, but when the screen was removed only one doll was present) (Slater et al., 2011; Wynn, 1992, 2000). These findings suggest that theories like Piaget's that focus on actively constructing knowledge from the environment (called constructivism) and theories that focus on the innate cognitive capabilities (called nativism) can both offer important contributions to our knowledge about cognitive development.

VYGOTSKY'S SOCIOCULTURAL THEORY OF COGNITIVE DEVELOPMENT Leading the case for social influence on cognitive development was Russian psychologist Lev Vygotsky, who believed that development occurs on a social level before it occurs at the individual level. Unlike Piaget, who took the view of the child as a scientist with the goal of developing logic skills, Vygotsky believed the child was more like an apprentice with the goal of developing the ability to function effectively in adult society. According to Vygotsky, children want to participate in activities central to their culture. As a result, the cognitive development of children is influenced by their specific cultural experiences—their homes, schools, and meeting places. While a child in an industrialized country may learn math in a formal school environment, a child in a nonindustrialized country may learn arithmetic through interactions with others in the community.

One key aspect of Vygotsky's theory is the **zone of proximal development**—the difference between what a child can do alone versus what a child can do together with a more competent person (see Figure 9.3). The process of providing appropriate assistance to a learner, which is removed gradually as the learner becomes more independent, is called **scaffolding**. For example, imagine a child who can independently recognize letters and understand basic phonics (i.e., what he can do alone). When teaching the child to read, a teacher or assistant can help the child use context cues and other word recognition

zone of proximal development

a key component of Vygotsky's theory of cognitive development that highlights the difference between what a child can do alone versus what a child can do together with a more competent person

scaffolding

the process of providing appropriate assistance to a learner which is removed gradually as the learner becomes more independent

---

Figure 9.3 Zone of Proximal Development

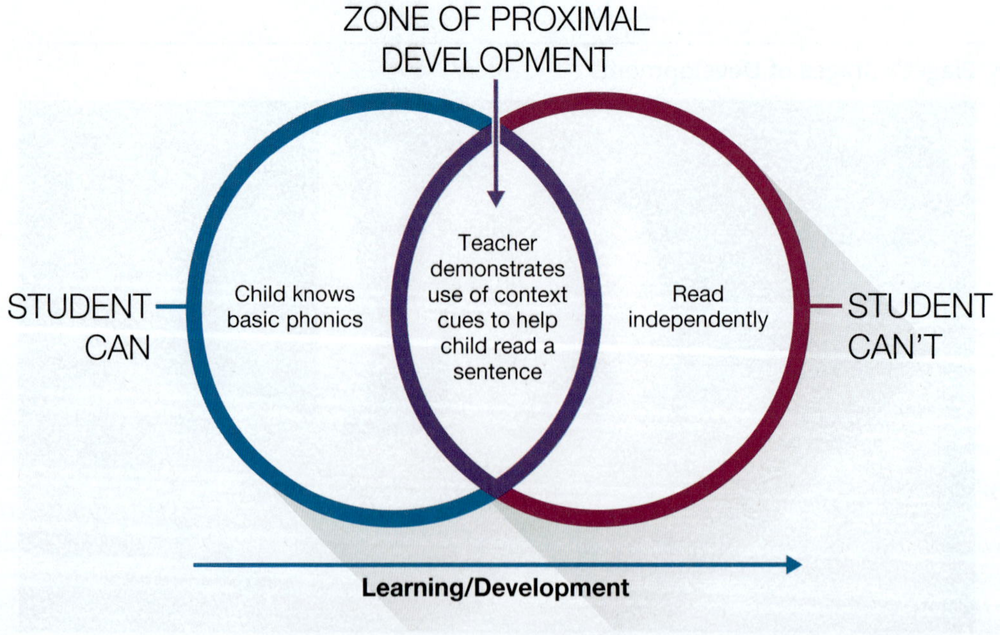

strategies to help decipher a sentence (i.e., what the child can do together with a more competent person). As the child becomes more adept at using these strategies, the teacher provides less and less assistance.

Vygotsky's work has been influential in education models focusing on *reciprocal teaching*, a model of teaching that uses scaffolding as a reciprocal dialogue between teacher and student (Palincsar, 2012). Vygotsky's theories have not been as heavily scrutinized as Piaget's theories, but the primary criticism focuses on the fact that the role of the individual is ignored by Vygotsky's theories while the role of sociocultural influences may be overemphasized (Liu & Matthews, 2005).

INFORMATION PROCESSING THEORY OF COGNITIVE DEVELOPMENT   Like Vygotsky's model, information processing theories also focus on the role of the environment in cognitive development. However, rather than focusing on the role of culture, information processing theories emphasize how information from the environment is actively processed through the systems of attention, memory, and perception (Klahr, 1992; Proctor & Vu, 2006). A computer analogy has been often used to explain the information processing model by describing the human mind as a "computer processor" that encodes, stores, and transforms information to produce some output. As children mature, they are able to process information more efficiently, selectively attend to information, and have increased capacity for working memory. According to this model, maturation causes changes to the "hardware" (e.g., the nervous system) and "software" (mental processes) that leads to cognitive development. Rather than developing in distinct stages like Piaget's theory proposed, the information processing model emphasizes a more continuous pattern of development.

An example of the information processing model can be found in research examining the development of arithmetic skills. To be successful in your college algebra class, you need to have successfully developed many mathematical skills from recognizing differences in quantities (e.g., 5 is greater than 3) to learning basic computational skills (e.g., 10 + 8 = 18) and eventually grasping advanced abstract reasoning (e.g., solving an equation for x). Information processing models have been applied to studies of children's developing arithmetic skills to better understand how improvements in working memory, problem solving, and processing speed translate into better arithmetic skills (Bjorklund, 2017; Menon, 2010; Siegler & Braithwaite, 2017). Researchers have also recently been investigating the neural underpinnings of arithmetic skill development (e.g., Cho et al., 2011, Price et al., 2013), demonstrating how work in neuroscience can complement the work being done to evaluate and refine theories of cognitive development.

Adaptive Pathway 9.1: Theories of Cognitive Development

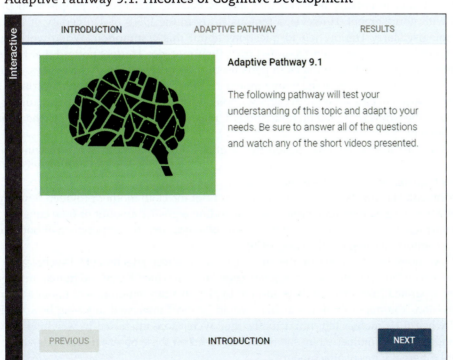

Interactive

INTRODUCTION   ADAPTIVE PATHWAY   RESULTS

Adaptive Pathway 9.1

The following pathway will test your understanding of this topic and adapt to your needs. Be sure to answer all of the questions and watch any of the short videos presented.

PREVIOUS   INTRODUCTION   NEXT

Social and Emotional Development in Infancy and Childhood

LO 9.6 **Describe the social and emotional development that occurs during infancy and childhood.**

The emotional and social domains are additional critical aspects of human development. As a toddler, one of your authors used to scream and cry when mad or scared to the point of holding her breath until she passed out—at home, in the middle of a street, or even at the doctor's office. While this behavior may be mildly alarming or even somewhat amusing from a toddler, this same behavior would be very shocking from an adult, indicating that significant social and emotional changes occur throughout the process of development. Throughout the stages of infancy and childhood, social and emotional development allow children to learn how to express and manage emotions and develop meaningful relationships with others.

attachment

the emotional bond newborns share with their caregivers

stranger anxiety

a fear of strangers that is a survival strategy that enables babies to perceive unfamiliar faces as potentially threatening

INFANT ATTACHMENT The emotional bond that newborns share with their caregivers is called **attachment**, a term developed by psychologist John Bowlby in the 1950s. Bowlby believed that emotional ties between a child and caregiver developed out of instinct (Bowlby, 1969). Babies will smile and coo when they are near their caregivers and whimper when the caregivers go away. They recognize familiar faces and voices and show preferences for them. At about 8 months old, this preference becomes even stronger and develops into a fear of strangers, called **stranger anxiety**. If you have ever attempted to greet an infant sitting next to you in a restaurant and been met with loud, disapproving screams, you should not take it personally. Stranger anxiety is a survival strategy that enables babies to perceive unfamiliar faces as potentially threatening.

Why Do Babies Bond?

Interactive

Survey: Why Do Babies Bond?

Why do you think infants/children bond with their caregivers?

○ Because their caregivers are a source of nourishment or food

○ Because their caregivers are a source of physical contact or comfort

Harry Harlow discovered that monkeys separated from their mothers at birth preferred the cloth artificial mother over the wire artificial mother that provided nourishment.

Psychologists initially believed that infants become attached to people who provide them with nourishment. However, a famous study in the 1950s by University of Wisconsin psychologist Harry Harlow led to questions about this assumption. While working with infant monkeys who had been separated from their mothers, Harlow noticed that the infants became strongly attached to the cloth pads used to cover the floors of their cages. When the cloths were taken away from the young monkeys, they threw violent temper tantrums. Infant monkeys raised in bare wire-mesh cages without a cloth pad survived with difficulty, if at all. Although the cloths provided no nourishment, they seemed to be important to the monkeys' development.

To test his theory, Harlow created two artificial mothers. One was a bare wire cylinder, while the other was a wooden cylinder covered in sponge rubber and soft terry cloth. Both types of surrogate mothers were placed in the monkeys' cages, but only one type provided nourishment. Harlow discovered that whether or not the cloth mother provided nourishment, the infant monkeys invariably preferred it, spending a greater amount of time clinging to the cloth surrogate than the wire surrogate. His results indicated the importance of body contact from a comforting caregiver (Harlow, 1958).

How does the behavior of the main caregiver affect attachment? Psychologist Mary Ainsworth (1979) developed a "strange situation" test, in which 1-year-old human infants were briefly separated from their mothers and left to play in a new environment under a stranger's supervision. You might think researchers would be most interested in seeing how the babies acted when their mother left, but actually, they were more interested in watching how they responded to their mother when she returned. Based on these observations, Ainsworth noted several different types of attachment:

- **Secure attachment:** The majority of infants that Ainsworth studied were labeled as secure. These children were quite happy to play in their new environment while their mothers were present, became upset when she left, but were soon comforted by parental contact upon their mother's return.

- **Anxious-ambivalent/resistant attachment:** Ambivalent/resistant infants were ill-at-ease to begin with and became extremely distressed when their mothers left the room. They were difficult to soothe, even when their mothers returned. Infants often displayed a mixed reaction to their mothers' return, simultaneously demanding to be picked up and pushing or kicking their mothers away.

- **Anxious-avoidant attachment:** Avoidant children did not appear particularly distressed when their mothers left the room. Upon their mothers' return, infants actively ignored their mothers and instead focused on a toy or other object in the room.

Subsequent researchers added a further category to Ainsworth's findings (Main & Hesse, 1990):

- **Disorganized-disoriented attachment:** Infants who were labeled disorganized did not have a consistent response to their mothers' return. They seemed unable to decide how they should react, suggesting a lack of a coherent coping pattern.

Ainsworth's results correlated with the behavior of the infants' mothers. Mothers who were loving, warm, and sensitive to their child's needs tended to have secure babies, while mothers who were unresponsive or insensitive tended to have anxious, insecure children. However, critics of Ainsworth's test have pointed out that placing young children in an unfamiliar situation may not capture the interaction between mother and child in less stressful circumstances. Some researchers also believe that this test is not a valid measurement of attachment in all cultures (Keller, 2013). For example, Japanese infants are rarely separated from their mothers (Miyake et al., 1985), and other cultures (e.g., the Brazilian Piraha Indians and the Beng people of Cote d'Ivoire in West Africa) do not ascribe to the notion of "stranger as dangerous," making the concept of stranger anxiety less relevant (Everett, 2009). The **temperament** of the infant, or aspects of personality considered innate and not learned, may also affect the mother's reaction, suggesting that attachment does not depend exclusively on the behavior of the mother. For example, a child with a highly reactive, or generally anxious, temperament is naturally hard to soothe, no matter how attentive the mother. Alexander Thomas and Stella Chess (1977) studied infants over time and identified three different temperament types: 1) **easy temperament** (infants with regular eating/sleeping patterns who adapt easily to change and can tolerate frustration, 2) **difficult temperament** (infants with irregular eating/sleeping patterns who are slow to adapt to change and respond negatively to frustration), and 3) **slow-to-warm temperament** (infants with generally regular eating/sleeping patterns who can adapt to change with repeated exposure and have mildly negative responses to frustration).

PARENTING STYLES In addition to studies of attachment, parenting styles have also been the focus of investigation. Developmental psychologists strive to identify which parenting strategies led to the best outcomes for children. Diana Baumrind's work (Baumrind, 1966, 1967) led her to identify three different parenting styles. Later, an additional category was added by Maccoby and Martin (1983). Parenting styles were classified along two dimensions, including parental demandingness and parental responsiveness. A parent considered high in demandingness is one who exerts control, provides supervision, expects maturity, and confronts disobedience. A parent considered high in responsiveness is involved in the child's life and expresses warmth and acceptance. Each of the four parenting styles described below varies according to these dimensions.

1. *Authoritarian*: These parents exert high levels of control over their children, expect unquestioning obedience, and are very punitive. When a child asks "why" he or she must do something, an authoritarian parent would invariably answer "because I told you to." Children and adolescents from authoritarian families tend to perform moderately well in school and to be less involved in problem behaviors than children and adolescents from permissive families. However, boys raised in authoritarian homes have higher levels of hostility and resistance while girls are more dependent and submissive (Baumrind, 1991; Pascual-Sagastizabal et al., 2014).

secure attachment

children who are upset when their mother leaves but are soon comforted by parental contact upon their mother's return

anxious-ambivalent/resistant attachment

infants who are insecure and overly emotional in their relationship with their caregiver so that they are extremely distressed when their mothers leave the room and difficult to soothe, even when their mothers return

anxious-avoidant attachment

infants who do not seek contact with a caregiver when distressed so that they do not appear to be particularly distressed when their mothers leave the room and actively ignore their mothers upon their return

disorganized-disoriented attachment

infants who do not have a consistent response to their mother's absence or return, appearing to be confused or hesitant and display contradictory behaviors

temperament

aspects of personality considered innate and not learned

easy temperament

infants with regular eating/sleeping patterns who adapt easily to change and can tolerate frustration

difficult temperament

infants with irregular eating/sleeping patterns who are slow to adapt to change and respond negatively to frustration

slow-to-warm temperament

infants with generally regular eating/sleeping patterns who can adapt to change with repeated exposure and have mildly negative responses to frustration

authoritarian

a style of parenting in which parents exert high levels of control over their children, expect unquestioning obedience, and are very punitive

permissive

a style of parenting in which parents are warm and very involved in the lives of their children but they place very few limits on behavior

neglectful/uninvolved

a style of parenting in which parents make few demands on their children and they are also unresponsive to their children's needs or behavior

authoritative

a style of parenting in which parents are warm and affectionate but also sensitive and responsive to their children's behavior and needs

2. *Permissive*: These parents are warm and very involved in the lives of their children. However, they place very few limits on behavior and generally allow their children to do what they want. For example, imagine the young child who does not have any set bedtime or the adolescent who never has a curfew. Children of permissive parents have demonstrated poorer self-control (Piotrowski et al., 2013), higher rates of drug/alcohol use (Lamborn et al., 1991), and lower achievement orientation (Baumrind, 1991).

3. *Neglectful/Uninvolved*: These parents are not affectionate or warm in their interactions with their children. While they make few demands on their children, they are also unresponsive to their children's needs or behavior. Consider a child who is never made to complete homework assignments and a parent who never attends school activities or parent-teacher conferences. It's not hard to imagine that this parenting style can be very harmful on the development of a child. Children with neglectful/uninvolved parents tend to have higher levels of stress/anxiety, increased behavior problems, poorer academic performance, and poorer social skills (Brown & Whiteside, 2008; Hildyard & Wolfe, 2002; Kim & Cicchetti, 2010; Kotch et al., 2008; Pinquart et al., 2017; Shipman et al., 2005).

4. *Authoritative*: These parents are warm and affectionate, but they are also sensitive and responsive to their children's behavior and needs. They have high standards and enforce limits on behavior but also respect their children as independent individuals. An authoritative parent may respond to a child who complains of still being hungry after a meal by providing several nutritious snack options but refusing to allow the child to eat anything he or she wants. Children with authoritative parents are independent, self-reliant, academically successful, and generally more competent than children of other types of parenting styles (Pinquart, 2017; Steinberg, 2001).

Use Table 9.5 to try to identify the various parenting styles.

Table 9.5 Parenting Styles

Interactive

Try to identify the various parenting styles for yourself. Drag the style to its appropriate spot on the table.

	Low Responsiveness	High Responsiveness
Low Demandingness	Neglectful/ Uninvolved	Permissive
High Demandingness	Authoritarian	Authoritative

Check Answers

It is important to note that parenting is also highly influenced by culture. The cultural context in which a child is raised plays an important role in shaping parents' expectations for their children and providing social norms for how parents care for their children (Bornstein, 2013). For example, in Western cultures, parenting styles that encourage autonomy and independence are highly valued whereas Asian, African, and Latin American cultures favor parenting styles that encourage interdependence (Fu & Markus, 2014; Johnson et al., 2013; Richman & Mandara, 2013; Tseng, 2004).

ERIKSON'S MODEL OF SOCIAL DEVELOPMENT Erik Erikson (1902–1994) proposed a model that encompassed the process of social development from infancy through late adulthood. He focused on developmental milestones that occur throughout the lifespan, emphasizing that social development is a continual process and doesn't end at a specific age or stage. Erikson's model focuses on an individual's social needs at each stage. He suggested that the outcome of each stage depended on how well the individuals' needs were met, and he presented the possible outcomes of each stage on a continuum from poor to good. Erikson's model includes a total of eight psychosocial stages, four of which occur during childhood (see Table 9.6). Each of the eight stages is summarized in the table below, but the first four stages are specific to childhood. In essence, Erikson focuses on the primary challenges of childhood such as feeding, toilet training, exploration/play, and school, and his theory outlines the social needs at each stage of development. If the challenge is successfully met, the child will develop the positive characteristic (e.g., autonomy) associated with that stage; however, if the challenge is not successfully met, the child may experience the negative characteristic (e.g., shame/doubt) associated with that stage.

Table 9.6 Erikson's Stages

Stage	Approximate Age	Important Event	Description
Basic Trust vs. Basic Mistrust	Birth to 12–18 months	Feeding	To develop a sense of basic trust, the infant's basic needs must be met by responsive caretakers.
Autonomy vs. Shame/Doubt	18 months to 3 years	Toilet Training	Toddlers are able to assert their independence/autonomy without excessive restraint or punishment.
Initiative vs. Guilt	Ages 3–6	Exploration/Play	Children need freedom and encouragement to play and explore. If discouraged or dismissed, children will develop a sense of guilt.
Industry vs. Inferiority	Ages 6–12	School	Children need encouragement to master new skills and develop self-confidence in their abilities.
Identity vs. Role Confusion	Teen years into the 20s	Peer Relationships	Adolescents develop a sense of self, or become confused about who they are.
Intimacy vs. Isolation	Early Adulthood (20s to early 40s)	Love Relationships	Develop intimate and loving relationships to avoid feelings of loneliness and isolation.
Generativity vs. Stagnation	Middle Adulthood (40s to 60s)	Work and Parenthood	Adults broaden their focus to family, society, and future generations, or they feel a lack of purpose.
Ego Integrity vs. Despair	Late Adulthood	Reflecting on Life	Elderly people develop a sense of satisfaction about their lives, or feel a sense of failure.

Quiz for Module 9.3 – 9.6

1. During which stage of pregnancy is the developing baby most susceptible to damage from harmful agents like drugs or alcohol?

   a. Conception

   b. Germinal period

   c. Fetal period

   d. Embryonic period

2. Brittany is 12 weeks pregnant and has been drinking a few beers followed by a glass or two of wine a night. She hasn't told her doctor, but she knows from looking online that alcohol is considered a(n) _____ that can have an extremely negative impact on the development of her baby.

   a. teratogen

   b. stimulant

   c. addiction-potential

   d. zygote

3. During the second trimester, a fetus creates _____ neurons a minute.

   a. 1,500

   b. 250,000

   c. 2,500

   d. 15,000

4. Tyrone is a 12-month-old who, like most other children, was able to hold his head up, roll over, and sit up before he could walk. This sequence of motor skill development follows the _____.

   a. synaptic pruning

   b. motor development rule

   c. cephalocaudal rule

   d. proximodistal rule

5. DeShawn learned to call his father "Daddy" and then began calling other men "Daddy," including the police officer, mail carrier, and nurse. This is an example of Piaget's process of _____.

   a. accommodation

   b. schemas

   c. preoperational

   d. assimilation

6. A 5-year-old may struggle to complete a puzzle by himself, but when his mother helps him he is able to accomplish the task. This is an example of what Vygotsky called _____.

   a. conservation

   b. assimilation

   c. the zone of proximal development

   d. adaptive learning

7. Harry Harlow's famous study in the 1950s about infant attachment could be summarized in these few words:

   a. Nourishment or food from the caregiver is the primary way that attachment is formed.

   b. Physical contact from a caregiver is more important than nourishment or food when attachments are being formed.

   c. There is no difference between physical contact or nourishment from the caregiver in regard to attachment.

   d. Attachment is solely based on the child's temperament.

8. Keesha grew up in a home where there were guidelines and rules. She was expected to complete chores, do her best in school, and be respectful. Her parents also gave her praise when she did well, hugged her before she left for school, and told her they loved her. She was able to talk to them about her ideas and offer her own opinions, even if they differed from her parents. This is an example of what type of parenting?

   a. Authoritarian
   b. Permissive
   c. Authoritative
   d. Neglectful/Uninvolved

Module 9.7–9.11: Development in Adolescence

adolescence

the period of transition from childhood to adulthood that usually occurs around age 10–12 and continues until age 18–21

The onset of **adolescence**—the period of transition from childhood to adulthood—usually occurs around age 10–12 and continues until age 18–21. While the changes from infancy through childhood are profound, adolescence is also marked by significant physical, social, and cognitive development. Think about yourself at age 10 compared to yourself at age 18. Most likely, your entire appearance, thought processes, and social skills underwent a significant transformation.

Physical Development in Adolescence

LO 9.7 **Describe the physical changes of puberty.**

puberty

period of physical development when the physical changes that lead to sexual maturation occur

Adolescence begins with a process known as **puberty**, when adolescents' bodies go through the physical changes that lead to sexual maturation. Puberty is initiated by brain signals to the gonads (ovaries in girls and **testes** in boys) which lead to an increase in hormone concentrations and resulting changes in the body. These changes include growth spurts in height, changes in body shapes, and development of **primary sex characteristics**—reproductive organs and external genitalia—and **secondary sex characteristics**—nonreproductive traits, such as breasts and hips in girls, facial hair and deeper voices in boys, and pubic and underarm hair for both boys and girls.

testes

male gonads

primary sex characteristics

reproductive organs and external genitalia

secondary sex characteristics

nonreproductive traits that develop during puberty such as breasts and hips in girls, facial hair and deeper voices in boys, and pubic and underarm hair for both boys and girls

Figure 9.4 Trends in Age of Menarche

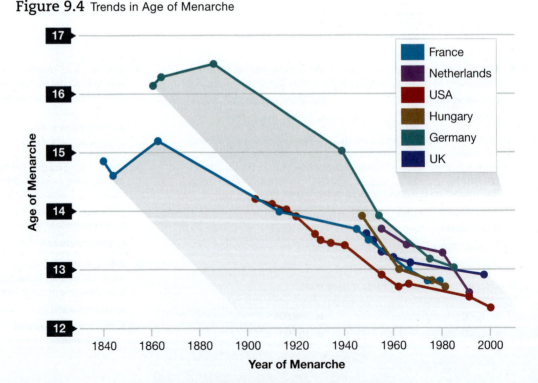

In North America, the average age for the onset of puberty is 10 for girls and 12 for boys. This represents a significant change in North America over the past 125 years when the average age of the onset of puberty occurred approximately 4 years later. A similar trend is evident with **menarche** (the onset of menstruation in girls), which tends to occur between ages 12–13 in North America today and between ages 16–17 in the 19th century (see Figure 9.4). Factors such as changes in nutrition (Jansen et al., 2016) and decreased incidence of disease are believed to contribute to the relatively early onset of puberty in North America.

While girls develop physically earlier than boys, the onset of sexual interest occurs at the same time for both boys and girls. This suggests that **adrenal androgen**, the hormone that increases in production during puberty, plays an important role in the development of sexual interest.

Sexuality can be a confusing issue for adolescents. Although teens have the ability to reproduce, they are not socially accepted as adults. While bombarded with sexually sugges- tive advertisements, websites, and television shows, teens are expected to abstain from sexual activity, and those who are sexually active are often associated with delinquency. The United States has the highest teen pregnancy rate in the Western world, including Canada and the United Kingdom. Most of these pregnancies occur outside of marriage, and nearly one-third end in abortion (U.S. Department of Health and Human Services, 2014). The future of a young unmarried mother is generally bleaker than it is for women who delay pregnancy until later in life. Teen moms are less likely to graduate from high school, less likely to improve their eco- nomic status, and less likely to sustain long-term marriages (Hoffman & Maynard, 2008; Wolfe & Rivers, 2008).

While these statistics may seem alarming, the teen pregnancy rate in the United States is actually the lowest it has been in the past 30 years (see Figure 9.5) (U.S. Department of Health and Human Services, 2014). Research suggests this decrease is due primarily to a decrease in sexual activity and an increase in the use of contraceptives from 1988–2002 (Martinez et al., 2011; Santelli et al., 2007). Since 2002, further declines in teen pregnancy rates have been attributed to an increase in the types of contraceptive methods utilized by teenagers (Martinez et al., 2011).

menarche

the onset of menstruation in girls

adrenal androgen

the hormone that increases during puberty and plays an important role in the development of sexual interest

Figure 9.5 Birth Rates per 1,000 Females Ages 15–19, by Race/Ethnicity, 1990–2012

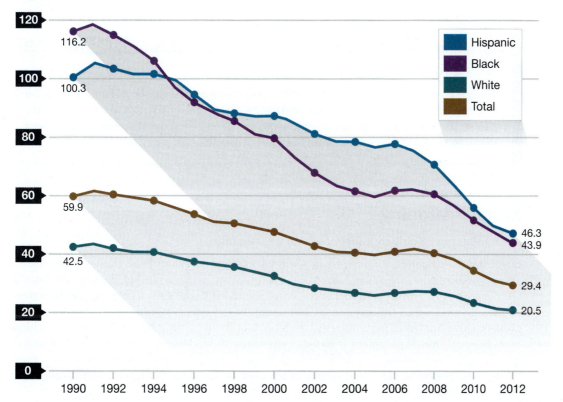

The Teen Brain: It's Just Not Grown-Up Yet

reason

the ability to organize information and beliefs into a series of steps leading to a conclusion

Better sex education in schools and parents' increased willingness to discuss sex openly with their children and teenagers have also been implicated in the declining teen pregnancy rates in the United States.

Cognitive Development in Adolescence

LO 9.8 **Explain the impact maturation of the frontal lobes has on adolescent reasoning.**

Until puberty, brain cells are increasing their connections; however, during adolescence, the brain adopts a "use it or lose it" policy and selectively prunes neurons and connections that aren't being used (Crews et al., 2007; Durston et al., 2001). Adolescents are also dealing with different rates of development in their brains. The maturation of the limbic system, which controls emotions, occurs more quickly than the maturation of the frontal lobe. As you will recall, the frontal lobe is a region of the brain responsible for functions such as problem solving, judgment, and impulse control to name only a few (see LO 3.8). Teens may feel like adults and have adult-like emotional reactions, but they lack the ability to make sensible, well-thought-out decisions (Baird & Fugelsang, 2004; Duell et al., 2016) because their frontal lobes aren't fully developed until their early 20s. Couple this with surging hormones and you have a perfect storm, resulting in the impulsive and risky behaviors for which adolescents are infamous. It would probably take only a few seconds for you to think of several decisions from your own adolescence that were less than prudent. As the frontal lobes become more fully developed in the later teenage years and early 20s, most young adults will experience a marked improvement in judgment, impulse control, and the ability to plan for the future (Bennett & Baird, 2006; Casey, 2015; Qu et al., 2015).

As the frontal lobes develop, they enable us to **reason**—to organize information and beliefs into a series of steps leading to a conclusion. As they become increasingly capable of abstract logic, they can reason hypothetically, reach conclusions, and identify flaws in others' opinions. Looking back, do you remember a point at which you suddenly had not only strong opinions but also the reasoning skills to back them up? You may have felt a new kind of social awareness and moral judgment during adolescence. These developing personal convictions can often be the cause of conflict with parents and other authority figures as adolescents develop their own thoughts and beliefs about the world.

Shared Writing Prompt: Juveniles and Criminal Behavior

Teenage immaturity can lead to significant consequences if adolescents go so far as to break the law. In 2005, a Supreme Court ruling against capital punishment for juveniles legally recognized a biological deficiency in their judgment. Given what you now know about cognitive development during adolescence, how should society deal with juvenile criminal behavior?

Moral Reasoning

LO 9.9 **Identify Kohlberg's theory of moral reasoning.**

If you found 20 dollars on the street, would you keep it? What if the money were inside an unmarked wallet with no identification? Now imagine you saw the money fall from a stranger's jacket. Would you pocket the cash or hand it back? As adolescents develop new abilities to reason and think abstractly, their ability to engage in moral reasoning also progresses. Developmental psychologist Lawrence Kohlberg (1981, 1984) built on Piaget's idea that children's moral judgment is based on their cognitive development. He assessed moral reasoning by presenting people with hypothetical scenarios and asking them how they thought the person in the scenario should act. Here is one of Kohlberg's scenarios called the "Heinz Dilemma":

In Europe, a woman was near death from a special kind of cancer. There was one drug that the doctors thought might save her. It was a form of radium that a druggist in the same town had recently discovered. The drug was expensive to make, but the druggist was charging ten times what the drug cost him to make. He paid 200 dollars for the radium and charged 2,000 dollars for a small dose of the drug. The sick woman's husband, Heinz, went to everyone he knew to borrow the money, but he could only get together about 1,000 dollars, which is half of what it cost. He told the druggist that his wife was dying and asked him to sell it cheaper or let him pay later. But the druggist said: "No, I discovered the drug and I'm going to make money from it." So Heinz got desperate and broke into the man's store to steal the drug for his wife (Kohlberg, 1969, p. 379).

Should Heinz have stolen the drug? Kohlberg was not interested in people's beliefs, but rather in how they reached their conclusions. He believed that moral reasoning developed through a series of six stages, progressing from simplistic and concrete to abstract and principled. To reach each stage, people had to progress through the stage before it. Kohlberg believed that not everyone reached the highest level of moral development, with most faltering at the fourth stage, and many not progressing beyond the second or third stage. While the stages of moral development were not linked to specific ages, Kohlberg proposed that adolescence and young adulthood were the most likely times in which a person may advance to higher levels (see Table 9.7).

Table 9.7 Kohlberg's Theory of Moral Reasoning

Levels of Moral Reasoning	Stages of Moral Reasoning	Description	Example
Preconventional Morality	1. Punishment/ Obedience	Right and wrong depend on which one leads to punishment.	If Heinz saves his wife, he will be a hero.
	2. Self-Interest	Right and wrong depend on what leads to a reward.	
Conventional Morality	3. Good Boy/Good Girl	Being good is whatever pleases others with a focus on obtaining approval.	If Heinz steals the drug, everyone will think he is a criminal.
	4. Law and Order	Obey laws without question by respecting authority and doing your duty to society.	
Postconventional Morality	5. Social Contract	Right and wrong defined by personal values so that morally right and legally right are not always the same. Mutual benefit and reciprocity are key.	Everyone has the right to life. Therefore, Heinz is justified in stealing the drug.
	6. Universal Ethical Principles	Living based on deeply held moral principles that transcend laws, mutual benefit, and reciprocity.	

Preconventional morality.   Individuals at this stage (most often preadolescent children) tend to view morality in terms of punishment and reward. Behavior that is rewarded is right, while behavior that is punished is wrong.

Conventional morality.   By this stage (often early adolescence), morality is defined by convention—caring for others and conforming to social laws is right simply because they are the rules within society.

Postconventional morality.   The highest levels of moral reasoning are based on abstract principles such as justice, liberty, and equality. People who reach this level may not necessarily agree with societal norms but follow their own personal set of ethics.

If you are able to reason that handing a 20-dollar bill back to a stranger is the right thing to do, does that necessarily make you a good person? One criticism of Kohlberg's theory is the fact that there are differences between moral reasoning and moral action. It is often easy to theorize the correct moral choice, but it's not quite as simple in a real-world situation. In 1994, top government officials from the Hutu majority in Rwanda ordered soldiers to massacre 500,000–1,000,000 Tutsi minorities in what is now called the Rwandan genocide. Most

preconventional morality

Kohlberg's lowest level of moral reasoning in which behavior that is rewarded is viewed as right, while behavior that is punished is viewed as wrong

conventional morality

Kohlberg's second level of moral development in which morality is defined by convention—caring for others and conforming to social laws is right simply because they are the rules within society

postconventional morality

Kohlberg's highest level of moral reasoning in which moral reasoning is based on abstract principles such as justice, liberty, and equality

---

Identify the Level of Moral Reasoning

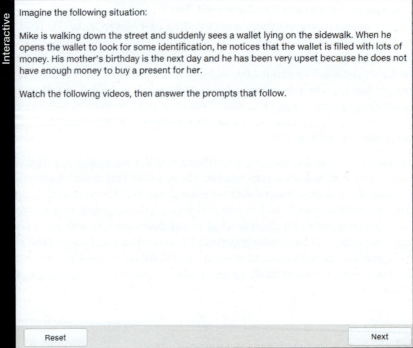

Imagine the following situation:

Mike is walking down the street and suddenly sees a wallet lying on the sidewalk. When he opens the wallet to look for some identification, he notices that the wallet is filled with lots of money. His mother's birthday is the next day and he has been very upset because he does not have enough money to buy a present for her.

Watch the following videos, then answer the prompts that follow.

Reset   Next

---

of those soldiers likely considered themselves good people with strong morals before following the orders to commit genocide. On a smaller scale, we all know that we should conserve natural resources, buy fair-trade products, and reduce our energy consumption, but how many of us actually live this way consistently?

How do adolescents' thoughts and experiences contribute to their moral development? Psychologist Daniel Hart and his colleague studied 15 New Jersey youths from a low-income, inner-city neighborhood of Camden, who had been identified as morally exemplary by various community organizations. The teens had resisted involvement in criminal activities and spent much of their time volunteering in soup kitchens, shelters, counseling groups, and community gardens.

According to Kohlberg's theory, the teens should have been motivated by abstract thoughts of right and wrong, but Hart discovered that the volunteers were motivated simply by wanting to do what was right. Part of their self-image was tied up with a desire to set a good example to others. Hart also noted that the teens' self-ideals were much closer to those of their parents than a matched comparison sample of peers who did not participate in volunteer work (Hart & Fegley, 1995). This study suggests that social factors such as parental influence can contribute to moral development.

As members of industrialized countries, are we responsible for ensuring the basic rights of workers around the world? According to Jonathan Haidt's **social intuitionist** account of morality, you instantly thought of a "yes" or "no" response to that question and then justified it with reasons. Haidt theorized that we have an instant gut reaction to moral situations, which precedes moral reasoning (Haidt, 2001; Haidt, 2013). He believed that our moral reasoning convinces us of what we feel intuitively.

Take one of Haidt's less wholesome examples: A brother and a sister are on vacation in France. They drink some wine, one thing leads to another, and they decide they want to have sex. They use two different kinds of contraception and enjoy it but decide they won't do it again. Haidt presented this scenario to people and asked for their reactions. Invariably, people said it was morally wrong and when pushed for a reason, most pointed to the possibility of birth defects. Upon being reminded that the brother and sister used two forms of contraception, the interviewees were stumped but still adamant that the scenario was immoral. Haidt referred to this phenomenon as "moral dumbfounding," supporting his theory that we have an initial gut reaction to moral situations. Why might this be? Acceptable reactions to socially prohibited concepts such as incest are drilled into us from a very young age. We hear negative comments of friends and family members and read terms such as *deviant* and *twisted* in the media. Over time,

social intuitionist

Haidt's theory that we have an instant gut reaction to moral situations, which precedes moral reasoning

our responses of disgust become automatic, so that when given Haidt's scenario, we produce an instant gut reaction. Similarly, children of parents who consistently reiterate the values of honesty and integrity are more likely to hand back a 20-dollar bill they saw falling out of a stranger's pocket than children who have been given mixed moral messages from their parents.

Adaptive Pathway 9.2: Moral Development

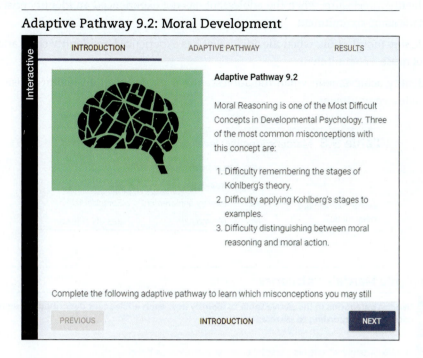

Interactive

| INTRODUCTION | ADAPTIVE PATHWAY | RESULTS |

Adaptive Pathway 9.2

Moral Reasoning is one of the Most Difficult Concepts in Developmental Psychology. Three of the most common misconceptions with this concept are:

1. Difficulty remembering the stages of Kohlberg's theory.
2. Difficulty applying Kohlberg's stages to examples.
3. Difficulty distinguishing between moral reasoning and moral action.

Complete the following adaptive pathway to learn which misconceptions you may still

PREVIOUS   INTRODUCTION   NEXT

Social and Emotional Development in Adolescence

LO 9.10 **Describe the impact adolescents' newly formed identities have on their relationships with others.**

We've all been through it—one day everything makes sense and the next we are moody, confused, and asking the notorious question "who am I?" Adolescence is the period in life in which our **identity**, or our sense of self, becomes a critical part of our development and our relationships with others.

identity

our sense of self

IDENTITY DEVELOPMENT   Do all teenagers go through an identity crisis? As previously discussed, theorist Erik Erikson (1963) believed that every stage of life has a crisis in need of a resolution (refer back to Table 9.3). According to Erikson, the plight of the adolescent is to experience identity versus role confusion—establishing a sense of self by deciding on individual beliefs and value systems. Which political party should I support? What do I think about religion? Which career path should I choose? Adolescence is a time of transition and confusion.

To form an identity, most adolescents will find themselves trying out different roles—the diligent student at school, the clown among friends, the moody teenager at home. Eventually, as the adolescent develops a stronger sense of self, these roles fuse into one cohesive identity. However, Erikson noticed that some adolescents form their identities much earlier than others by taking on parents' values and expectations. Other adolescents adopt a negative identity that deliberately opposes their parents' views, while still others align themselves with a particular peer group, proving there is an element of truth to teen movies and television shows like *Mean Girls, Glee, Easy A,* or *Perks of Being a Wallflower* that group together stereotypical goths, jocks, and geeks. Erikson believed that only when we have a clear and comfortable self are we ready to develop intimacy—close relationships with others.

Erikson's work on adolescent identity development was expanded by Canadian psychologist James Marcia. Marcia theorized that adolescent identity development focuses on the two processes of conflict (a time of upheaval when values and choices are reevaluated) and commitment (an investment in a particular identity)(Kroger et al., 2010; Marcia, 1966,

1980, 1993; Marcia et al., 1993). Marcia uses the following four categories to denote whether an adolescent has experienced a crisis or made an identity commitment (see Table 9.8).

- Identity diffusion: when the adolescent has not experienced an identity crisis and has not yet made a commitment
- Identity foreclosure: when the adolescent has not experienced an identity crisis but has made some commitment
- Identity moratorium: when the adolescent has experienced an identity crisis and has not yet made a commitment
- Identity achievement: when the adolescent has experienced an identity crisis and has made a commitment

Table 9.8 Marcia's Identity Development

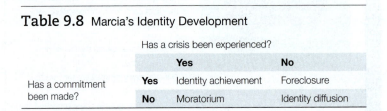

		Has a crisis been experienced?	
		Yes	**No**
Has a commitment been made?	**Yes**	Identity achievement	Foreclosure
	No	Moratorium	Identity diffusion

Applying Marcia's Categories

Use the categories in the above table to identify how each adolescent described would be categorized according to Marcia:

1. Alex strongly adopts his parents' political and religious beliefs without exploration or question. ☐

2. Renae drifted through high school and ended up in college with no idea about a major or future goals. ☐

3. Despite being raised in a religious family, Tanya took her first world religion class and is now questioning everything she previously believed. ☐

4. After discussing political views with his parents and friends, Thomas discovered that he did not always agree with their opinions. In his first election, he read about each candidate and party platform and conducted follow-up research before casting his vote.
☐

Interactive

Start Over   Check Answers

RELATIONSHIPS WITH FAMILY AND FRIENDS Adolescence can be a difficult time, but are teenagers really as rebellious and scornful as pop culture suggests? Actually, studies frequently demonstrate that most teens admire their parents and support or adopt their religious and political beliefs (Eaves et al., 2008; Jennings et al., 2009). Conflicts usually arise over deceptively minor topics such as hair styles and clothing, but these parent–child spats often boil down to a much more basic issue—control. Adolescents want to be treated as adults, while parents worry that allowing their teens too much freedom exposes them to potential dangers such as alcohol and drugs. Intense conflict usually occurs during the early teen years. The battle for independence is usually resolved in the late teens, when many adolescents and their parents manage to establish some sort of balance between childhood dependence and self-sufficiency.

Adolescents also increasingly turn to their peers for emotional support, enabling greater independence from their parents and a stronger sense of self. If your heart was broken in high school, it's likely that the first person you called to help you through that traumatic experience was a friend rather than a parent. Australian researcher Dexter Dunphy (1963) identified two kinds of peer groups: cliques and crowds. **Cliques** are small, same-sex groups of three to nine members who share intimate secrets and see themselves as best friends. However, even if you pinky-swore to be best friends forever with Tori and Lisa in seventh grade, you may have found that by tenth grade, your soul mates had become mere passing acquaintances. Cliques tend to break down by mid-adolescence, giving way to more loosely associated groups. **Crowds** are larger, mixed-sex groups who tend to get together socially on weekends, often for parties. Cliques of boys and girls interact, and the gender barriers that were so firmly established in childhood break down, increasing the number of opposite-sex peers in an adolescent's social network.

If you've ever been dumped by a former best friend or shunned online or in the cafeteria, you're well aware that social ostracism, especially among teens, can be vicious and painful. Being a social outcast as an adolescent is often seen as a fate worse than death, resulting in groups of teen clones all anxious to fit in by talking, dressing, and acting like their peers. For many parents, the possibility of negative peer pressure luring their child into a world of alcohol, drugs, and casual sex is a constant source of worry. Research suggests that these fears are well-founded—teenagers of the same friendship group usually indulge in similar risky behaviors, and teens who start smoking usually do so because one of their friends offered them cigarettes or made it look cool (Rose et al., 1999; Simons-Morton & Farhat, 2010). While the selection effect—choosing friends who have similar interests and behaviors—partly explains peer similarities, friends usually become increasingly similar to each other in terms of frequent smoking, drinking, or other risky behavior. Additionally, although peer pressure is usually seen in a negative light, it can have positive effects. For example, teens in China often meet to do homework together and encourage each other to do well academically. Parents and teachers in China often view peer pressure as a positive influence.

Emerging Adulthood

LO 9.11 **Describe the features of the life stage of emerging adulthood.**

A generation or two ago, people were expected to reach sexual maturity, find a job, get married, and have children—all within a couple of years. But increasing opportunities for higher education, combined with numerous career choices, has meant that in industrialized cultures, adolescents are taking more time to finish college, leave the ever-comfortable nest, and establish their independence. In the United States, the average age for a first marriage has increased by more than 6 years since 1960 (to age 29 for men and age 27 for women) (Barkhorn, 2013; Copen et al., 2012).

In the Western world, it's not unusual for people in their 20s to ask their parents for a little help paying the rent, buying a car, or moving into a new apartment. As adolescents reach adulthood, emotional ties with parents loosen. But during their early 20s, many people still depend greatly on their parents for financial and emotional support. This phase of life, which Jeffrey Arnett has dubbed **emerging adulthood** (Arnett, 2000; Arnett, 2001; Arnett, 2007), typically occurs between ages 18 and 25 and differs in many ways from both adolescence and early adulthood. Most adolescents live with their parents, are unmarried, and attend school. By the age of 30, most people live independently from their parents, are married, and are no longer attending school. The time between these periods is unique in that there are no demographic "norms," and this stage is marked by exploration and unrestricted by defined roles. One 23-year-old may live at home with her parents working part-time jobs while another 23-year-old may have finished college and be married. In addition, people between the ages of 18 and 25 in industrialized societies don't identify themselves as either adolescents or adults. As shown in Figure 9.6, when asked if they viewed themselves as adults, most people in their late teens and early twenties indicated a degree of ambiguity (e.g., in some ways yes, and in some ways no).

This period of exploration, uncertainty, and identity formation is usually resolved by the later 20s, when people tend to achieve total independence from parental support and develop the ability to empathize with others as fellow adults.

The stage of emerging adulthood is typically discussed in terms of Western industrialized societies. This period of prolonged exploration and development is possible primarily due to economic development and prolonged lifespans. In fact, one of the top predictors of the average age at first marriage is a country's income level with more prosperous countries having a much later age of first marriage than less affluent countries (Mayyasi, 2013).

cliques

small, same-sex groups of three to nine members who share intimate secrets and see themselves as best friends

crowds

larger, mixed-sex groups who tend to get together socially on weekends

emerging adulthood

a period of time between adolescence and adulthood in primarily Western cultures during which emotional ties with parents loosen, but dependence on parents for financial and emotional support remains

Figure 9.6 Answering the Question: Do You Think You Have Reached Adulthood?

People in their late teens and early 20s respond to the question, "Do you think you have reached adulthood?" with a degree of ambiguity but respond "yes" more frequently around their mid-20s.

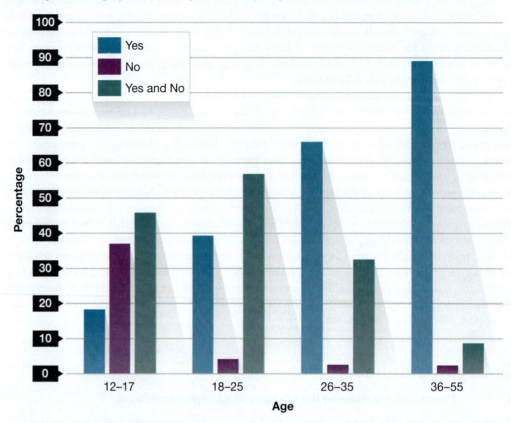

Journal Prompt: Influences on Emerging Adulthood

Explain why economic development and prolonged lifespans would contribute to whether or not a society supports a stage of emerging adulthood.

Quiz for Module 9.7–9.11

1. What are the physical changes in an adolescent's body that lead to sexual maturation called?
   a. Menopause
   b. Adrenal androgens
   c. Hormonal shifts
   d. Puberty

2. Which hormone increases in production during puberty and plays an important role in the development of sexual interest?
   a. Testosterone
   b. Adrenal androgen
   c. Estrogen
   d. Adrenaline

3. Which part of the brain is not fully developed in adolescence?
   a. Frontal lobes
   b. Limbic system
   c. Occipital lobes
   d. Temporal lobes

4. Luke is an 18-year-old who argues with his parents about politics. He feels very strongly that the United States should have a comprehensive socialized medicine program. This demonstrates his ability to _____, or organize information and his beliefs into coherent arguments.
   a. think concretely
   b. reason
   c. judge
   d. have conceptual thoughts

5. Nunzio, an 8-year-old boy, stole a candy bar from the grocery store. His parents never found out about it, and Nunzio didn't feel it was wrong because he was never punished for it. This level of reasoning would fit into which of Kohlberg's stages?
   a. Postconventional morality
   b. Conventional morality
   c. Social justice
   d. Preconventional morality

6. According to Kohlberg, someone who makes a moral decision by focusing on the opinions of others and conforming to social laws is likely at which level of moral reasoning?

a. Conventional   b. Postconventional

c. Punishment/obedience   d. Preconventional

7. According to Erikson's theory, which crisis is to be resolved in adolescence?

a. Identity foreclosure

b. Intimacy vs. isolation

c. Identity diffusion

d. Identity vs. role confusion

8. Keneesha, Tory, and Bev have been best friends since the seventh grade. They do everything together and share all their secrets. They gossip about boys, and when one of them has a problem they call each other rather than their moms. This is considered which type of peer group?

a. Crowd   b. Clique

c. Besties   d. Cohorts

9. The developmental period of emerging adulthood typically occurs between the ages of _____.

a. 15 and 18   b. 30 and 40

c. 18 and 25   d. 25 and 30

Module 9.12–9.14: Development in Adulthood

At what age do people buy their first house? How old are first-time parents? When should we aim to retire? Whereas childhood and adolescence are punctuated by formal rites of passage that occur at roughly the same time, development in adulthood is less predictable. In today's society, not everyone enters the workplace at 18 and retires at 65. Some people become parents in their 20s, and some people decide to forgo parenthood completely. Likewise, physical and cognitive changes occur at varying times and rates compared to childhood and adolescence. Because the term adulthood encompasses such a large span of time, researchers typically divide this stage into *early adulthood* (approximately ages 25–40), *middle adulthood* (approximately ages 40–65) and *late adulthood* (beginning approximately at age 65).

Physical Development in Adulthood

LO 9.12 **Describe some of the physical and neurological changes that occur in adulthood.**

One of the advantages of successfully navigating through adolescence and emerging adulthood is the peak physical abilities of early adulthood. As with the onset of puberty, women tend to peak earlier than men. For people in their mid-20s, muscles are strong, reaction times are quick, and most people barely notice the early signs of physical decline, such as decreased vision/hearing and speed/agility.

As people move into middle adulthood, physical vigor becomes less to do with age and more to do with our health and exercise habits. No longer can we stay out until the early hours, eat pizza for breakfast three times a week, and still feel fit enough to run a marathon. Smokers, heavy drinkers, and sunbathers are more likely to look and feel older than those who avoid unhealthy behaviors, pay attention to nutrition, exercise, and reduce stress (Helfrich et al., 2008; Morita, 2007; O'Shea et al., 2010). However, there is generally little we can do to fully combat the inevitable declines in fertility, hearing, vision, metabolism, and physical strength.

In late adulthood, declines in physical abilities become more noticeable. Declines in vision, muscle strength, reaction time, stamina, hearing, distance perception, and sense of smell are part of the aging process (Merrill, 2015; Rabbitt, 2014). The aging body is also vulnerable to many things it could have easily handled in youth, such as hot weather and falling (Bloch et al., 2010; Kenney et al, 2014). Although older adults are less likely to suffer common short-term ailments because of all the antibodies they have accumulated over a lifetime, their inability to fight off other diseases makes them susceptible to life-threatening ailments like cancer and pneumonia (World Health Organization, 2014).

REPRODUCTIVE CHANGES Peak female fertility rates are typically associated with late adolescence and emerging adulthood. At the same time, the trend for women to delay having children until their late 20s or early 30s has continued, as shown in Figure 9.7. In 2012, the birth rate for women in their 20s declined, but the birth rate for women in their 30s and early 40s increased (Martin et al., 2013). This pattern has persisted over the last couple of years (Centers for Disease Control and Prevention, 2015b). In the United States, the average age of a woman

Figure 9.7 Birth Rates by Age of Mother

The birth rate among women in their 30s and 40s has increased significantly over the past decades.

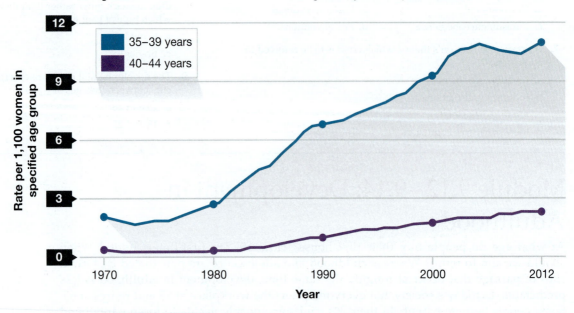

giving birth to her first child was 26.3 in 2013 and up to age 30 in one study in 2016, and women in many European countries have been delaying child birth even later (Centers for Disease Control and Prevention, 2015; OECD, 2016).

The reasons why women have been delaying motherhood vary but include increasing educational attainment for women, the potential conflict between careers and motherhood, and economic uncertainty (Mills et al., 2011). In fact, it is more common than ever for women and couples to remain childless. In 2014, the U.S. Census data showed that 15.3 percent of women ages 40–44 had never given birth compared to only 10.2 percent in 1976 (U.S. Census Bureau, 2014). More people are choosing not to become parents, but some are unable to conceive due to fertility problems. Despite the sociocultural reasons for delaying child-rearing, the biology of fertility remains unchanged. For women between the ages of 35–39, a single act of intercourse is half as likely to result in pregnancy as it would be for a 19- to 26-year-old (Dunson et al., 2002). Many women find themselves in a position of delaying pregnancy until a point at which their fertility may have long passed its peak. Mindful of the changing trends in parenthood, popular Silicon Valley corporations such as Apple and Facebook—in order to recruit top employees—have recently included healthcare benefits that allow women to freeze their eggs (Sydell, 2014).

Regardless of when or whether women choose to become mothers, within a few years of age 50, most women begin **menopause**—the end of the menstrual cycle and ability to bear children. Menopause is accompanied by a reduction in estrogen, which can have uncomfortable effects, such as hot flashes. As with aging in general, a woman's psychological response to menopause will depend on her attitude and the cultural messages she has received. For example, the Japanese term for menopause, *konenki*, actually means "time of renewal," which provides a positive context for this new phase of development. One study of postmenopausal women found that most of them recalled feeling "only relief" when their periods ceased, and only 2 percent felt "only regret" (Goode, 1999). Some women may lose a sense of their femininity and experience a decreased interest in sex, while others may celebrate that they no longer have to bother with birth control methods and a monthly hassle.

Aging men experience more gradual sexual changes than women. What some call **andropause** (Carruthers, 2001; Samaras et al., 2012) includes decline in sperm count, testosterone level, and speed of erection and ejaculation. If testosterone levels decline too rapidly, men may experience depression, irritability, insomnia, impotence, or weakness—effects that can be treated with testosterone replacement therapy. For men, psychological reactions to a

menopause

the end of the menstrual cycle and ability to bear children in women

andropause

gradual sexual changes that occur in aging males; includes decline in sperm count, testosterone level, and speed of erection and ejaculation perceived decrease in virility may be tempered by the relatively long-term and subtle onset of these changes.

For both women and men, a decline in fertility does not necessarily mean a decline in sexuality. When the American Association of Retired Persons (AARP) surveyed adults over 45, they found that the majority of people who have a current or recent sexual partner reported that they have sex at least once a month, and 57 percent reported being satisfied with their current sex life (Fisher, 2010). While frequency of sexual behavior does appear to decline for some people as they age, individuals with a positive attitude about sex and who have physically satisfying relationships tend to engage in more frequent sexual behavior (DeLamater & Moorman, 2007).

CHANGES IN THE BRAIN   The process of healthy aging involves the gradual loss of brain cells. This process begins in early adulthood and causes a 5 percent reduction in brain weight by age 80, which includes a decline in gray and white brain matter (Resnick et al., 2003). The region of greatest cell loss tends to occur in the frontal lobes, which handle memory storage and other higher-mental functions (Giorgio et al., 2010). This decline is slower in women and active adults. Exercise, which causes increased oxygen and nutrient flow, not only enhances muscle strength, bone strength, and energy and prevents obesity and heart disease, it also stimulates the development of brain cells and neural connections (Bherer et al., 2013; Cotman et al., 2007; Davis et al., 2011; Van Praag, 2009).

Atypical aging can also be associated with more severe brain decline. **Dementia** (also known as a neurocognitive disorder) is associated with a progressive loss of cognitive functioning in areas such as memory, reasoning, planning, decision making, and social functioning. Dementia can be caused by many different conditions, but Alzheimer's disease is the most common form of dementia and accounts for 60–80 percent of cases (Alzheimer's Association, 2013; Hyman et al., 2012). **Alzheimer's disease** is a condition characterized by progressive and irreversible declines in memory, thinking, and language. The exact cause of Alzheimer's disease is not known, but the impact of this disease on the brain is significant (Alzheimer's Association, 2013). Alzheimer's disease leads to significant shrinkage of the cortex with particularly severe reductions in the size of the hippocampus (associated with memory functioning) (Hyman et al., 2012; Schneider et al., 2009). In addition, an overall reduction in neurons and connections between neurons is found in the brains of people with Alzheimer's disease. This degradation of neurons is associated with the presence of **amyloid plaques** (the accumulation of protein fragments between nerve cells) and **neurofibrillary tangles** (twisted strands of protein within neurons) (Hyman et al., 2012).

Cognitive Development in Adulthood

LO 9.13   **Explain how some types of memory and intelligence change during adulthood.**

In addition to physical declines, cognitive declines are also associated with aging. Neural processing slows, and older adults take more time than younger adults to react, solve perceptual puzzles, and remember names (Cabeza et al., 2016; Cargin et al., 2008; Fjell et al., 2014; James et al., 2008; Richardson & Vecchi, 2002; Tun & Lachman, 2008).

CHANGES IN MEMORY   As with physical vigor, some types of learning and memory peak in early adulthood. While younger adults have higher recall than older adults (for example, being asked to remember a list of words in a memory test), they don't have higher recognition (for example, being shown a list of words and asked to point out which words were in the memory test), as shown in Figure 9.8 (Craik & Rose, 2012; Danckert & Craik, 2013). Additionally, older people tend to make more errors than younger people when trying to recall meaningless information such as nonsense syllables and unimportant events (Gordon & Clark, 1974) or names (Burke & MacKay, 1994; Surprenant, 2007; Wright & Holliday, 2007).

Alzheimer's and the Brain

Brain of Alzheimer's patient (at left) compared to normal brain (at right) showing shrinkage of the cortex and enlargement of the ventricles (fluid-filled spaces within the brain).

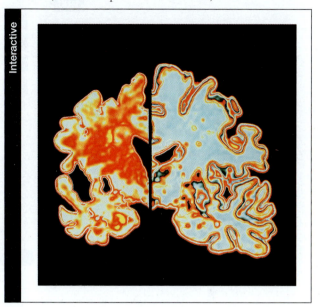

Interactive

dementia

a progressive loss of cognitive functioning in areas such as memory, reasoning, planning, decision making, and social functioning

Alzheimer's disease

the most common form of dementia characterized by progressive and irreversible declines in memory, thinking, and language

amyloid plaques

the accumulation of protein fragments between nerve cells which is often found in people with Alzheimer's disease

neurofibrillary tangles

twisted strands of protein within neurons often seen in individuals with Alzheimer's disease

Figure 9.8 Recognition versus Recall as We Age

Younger adults clearly perform better than older adults on tasks of recall (on the left), but these differences are less pronounced on tests of recognition (on the right).

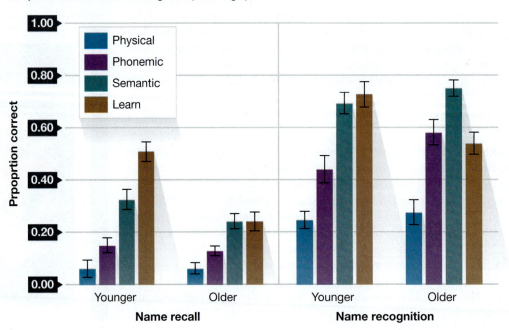

prospective memory

remembering to perform a specific action such as calling someone back or bringing lunch to the office

Although meaningful information is more easily remembered, older adults take longer than younger adults to produce their memories. **Prospective memory**—remembering to perform a specific action such as calling someone back or bringing lunch to the office—remains strong if time management and reminder cues are used (Macan et al., 2010; Mahy et al., 2014). Time-based and habitual tasks (e.g., taking medications at a certain time each day), however, are challenging. The good news for older adults is that their ability to learn and remember skills declines less than their verbal recall ability.

We might lose some cognitive abilities as we age, but at least one good thing comes from aging—we begin to tune out bad memories. Mather and Carstensen (2005) conducted a series of experiments in which they showed young adults (ages 18–29), middle adults (ages 41–53), and late adults (ages 65–80) pictures displaying positive, negative, and neutral scenes. Each group was then asked to recall and describe as many pictures from memory as possible. The results showed that older people recalled fewer scenes overall, indicating a decline in memory with age. However, whereas the younger group remembered both positive and negative scenes, the older group recalled more positive images than negative images, suggesting that as we age, we are able to pay selective attention to the positive.

Neurological studies may have an answer as to why more mature brains selectively remember positive events. An older adult's amygdala, a center of emotion in the brain, is likely to show less activity in reaction to negative events than a younger adult's amygdala does; however, both elderly and younger brains show the same responsiveness to positive occurrences (Mather et al., 2004). In other words, it appears that as we get older, we learn not to let negative emotions drag us down.

AGING AND INTELLIGENCE Understanding intelligence in later adulthood has been challenging and controversial. David Wechsler, perhaps best known for his intelligence scales, believed that deterioration of mental ability is an inherent part of aging. Kaufman et al. (1989) conducted a cross-sectional study comparing individuals from ages 20–74 split into seven different age ranges and found significant declines in intellectual functioning related to age. But, as discussed earlier in this chapter, these two groups differ in age and cohorts, so it is difficult to determine if the cognitive differences are a result of aging or the time period in which each group was raised.

Journal Prompt: Aging and Intelligence

Can you recall some of the confounding factors that could also explain the difference found in a cross-sectional study of aging and intelligence?

In contrast to cross-sectional studies, results from longitudinal studies have somewhat lessened concerns about declining intelligence across the lifespan, with findings that some aspects of intelligence remain stable into later adulthood (Gow et al., 2011; Salthouse, 2009; Sternberg et al., 2013). However, longitudinal studies also have their challenges. By the end of a study that spans decades, only a portion of the original participants will still be available for inclusion in the study. The important question becomes whether or not the participants who are no longer available differ in some substantial way from those who stay in the study. For example, what if the participants who live long enough and are healthy enough to stay in the study had higher scores to begin with than the participants who dropped out along the way? It is possible that individuals who survived to the end of the studies were those with intelligence least likely to deteriorate.

Social and Emotional Development in Adulthood

LO 9.14   **Describe the social and emotional development associated with adulthood.**

Work life and family life play critical roles in how people navigate through the social and emotional challenges of adulthood. Establishing and maintaining meaningful intimate relationships through marriage, friendships, parenthood, and extended family is critical for most people to experience happiness and fulfillment in life. In addition, Confucius once said that "if you find a job you enjoy, you never have to work a day in your life." Since most people spend about a third of their adult lives working, it makes sense to choose a job that doesn't fill you with a growing sense of dread every Sunday evening at the thought of returning to work the next day.

LOVE AND MARRIAGE   What defines an adult? Erikson's lifespan theory proposes that the ability to establish intimate, caring relationships and find fulfillment are primary tasks of early and middle adulthood.

People are often said to be "insanely in love," a phrase that implies that romance and sanity aren't altogether compatible. While being in love won't actually drive you crazy, it does cause specific brain activity. The neural and hormonal mechanisms of mating bonds between two adults are similar to the bonds between an infant and a caregiver. Partners feel most secure and confident when they are together, and they may even show physiological evidence of distress when they are separated. In fact, the mortality rate increases significantly for people who have lost a spouse through death, an effect referred to as the "widowhood effect" (Elwert & Christakis, 2008).

Studies have shown that people's descriptions of their adult romantic attachments are closely related to their recollections of early relationships with their parents. For example, those who were rated as having more positive, loving relationships with their mothers as children became more trusting adults—a finding that supports Erikson's theory of social development. As a result, they were more likely to seek comfort from their romantic partners and enjoy an open and honest relationship with them (Black & Schutte, 2006).

So, how can we become part of a happily married couple? Is living together prior to marriage (called cohabitation) to iron out any potential problems an effective strategy to prevent divorce? Until recently, the research seemed to suggest the opposite as several studies showed that couples who live together before marriage are more likely to divorce than noncohabiting couples (Myers, 2000). However, the most recent findings show that it's not actually the act of living together that is associated with higher rates of divorce, but it's the age at which people move in together that serves as a risk factor for divorce (Kuperberg, 2014). There has been a strong relationship between age of marriage and likelihood of divorce such that the younger people marry, the higher the risk of divorce. However, researchers had previously failed to take into account the age of first cohabitation. It now appears that the age at which people first decide to cohabitate has likely been the driving force behind the increased divorce rates associated with

Figure 9.9 Does Age of Marriage or Cohabitation Matter?

The percent of dissolved marriages after 10 years differs depending on the age of first cohabitation. People who married at age 23–24 had similar rates of dissolution as people who first began to cohabitate at age 23–24.

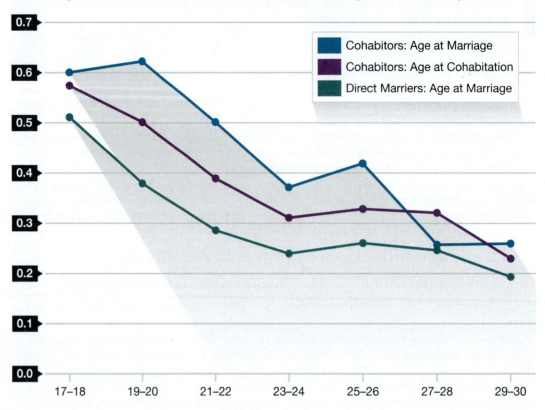

cohabitation (see Figure 9.9). When you control for the age of first cohabitation, differences in divorce rates between people who cohabitated versus those who were "direct marriers" (marrying without first cohabitating) become much smaller and in some cases disappear altogether. This is encouraging news, given the ever-increasing numbers of couples who are cohabitating. A recent CDC report found that 48 percent of women between 2006 and 2010 reported cohabitating prior to marriage—a significant increase from 34 percent in 1995 (Copen et al., 2012).

Despite the alarming divorce statistics, the institution of marriage is showing no signs of collapse. Gay couples have recently won the right to marry in the United States. In Western cultures, approximately three in four adults who divorce will remarry (Bramlett & Mosher, 2002; Sweeney, 2010), although their second marriage has a slightly higher chance of also ending in divorce (Bumpass & Raley, 2007). Marriage is a good general predictor of happiness, health, sexual satisfaction, and income level. Surveys of Americans since 1972 show that 40 percent of married adults report being "very happy," compared to only 23 percent of unmarried adults. Married lesbian couples also report being happier than single lesbian women (Wayment & Peplau, 1995; Wienke & Hill, 2008). Furthermore, if you live in a neighborhood with a high marriage rate, you are likely to benefit from a low crime rate, few delinquent teenagers, and low numbers of children with emotional disorders (Myers, 2000).

EMPLOYMENT At its best, work has the same psychological benefits for adults as play does for children. It brings people into social contact with peers outside of their family, presents problems to be solved, and offers us a chance to improve our physical and intellectual skills. Erikson also believed that employment offered an opportunity for adults to contribute to society in meaningful ways that would outlast their own lifetimes.

Most people report that they enjoy work if it is complex rather than simple, varied rather than routine, and not closely supervised by another (Gray, 2013). Despite what we might assume, job satisfaction is only minimally related to pay (Judge et al., 2010). Jobs with high occupational self-direction enable a worker to make many choices and decisions throughout the day. Surprisingly, despite the high demands that these jobs pose, most people find them less stressful than jobs in which workers make few decisions and are under close supervision (Van den Broeck et al., 2008).

As of 2013, 57.2 percent of women were employed outside of the household compared to 38 percent in 1963 (Lyles, 2013; U.S. Department of Labor, n.d.a; U.S. Department of Labor, 2016). When you look at women with children under the age of 18, the percent of women who are employed increases to 69.9 percent. The combination of raising children, completing housework, and holding down a paid job has become a fine balancing act. Although men are more involved in housework and childcare than they were 30 years ago, women continue to report doing more housework (e.g., cleaning, laundry) and physically caring for children than men (U.S. Department of Labor, 2016). According to the Bureau of Labor Statistics, on a typical day, 49 percent of women reported doing housework compared to 19 percent of men. Additionally, women reported spending an hour a day physically taking care of children while men reported spending 26 minutes on the same tasks. Despite the additional workload, most women report that having a paid job increases their self-esteem (Elliott, 1996) and protects them from depression (Etaugh, 2008). Additionally, most women say they would continue to work, even if they didn't need the money (Schwartz, 1994).

SOCIAL DEVELOPMENT AS WE AGE Baby boomers, those multitudes of Americans born between the end of World War II and the early 1960s, are throwing 65th birthday celebrations across the country even as you read this. Thanks to improved medical care, life expectancies in general are increasing (as of 2016, the average life expectancy in the United States was 78.8) (Centers for Disease Control and Prevention, 2016a). As a result of these factors, among others, the United States has a rapidly aging population. In 2013, 14.1 percent of Americans were over the age of 65 (U.S. Census Bureau, 2014). There are now more Americans over the age of 65 than at any other time in history. Women outlive men by 4 years throughout the world and 5 to 6 years in the United States, Canada, and Australia. **Gerontology**, is a budding interdisciplinary field that studies the process of aging and the aging population.

Ageism, or prejudice against the elderly, often leads to negative stereotyping that can cause isolation and poor self-image among members of the older community. To combat negative stereotypes, one recent study found that implicit positive messages about aging can actually improve physical functioning (Levy et al., 2014). Researchers tested individuals who were 61–99 years old and randomly assigned them to be exposed to either (1) implicit (or subconscious) positive stereotypes about aging, (2) explicit positive stereotypes about aging, (3) a combination of explicit and implicit stereotypes about aging, or (4) neutral implicit and explicit messages (control group). The participants completed the study sessions once a week for 4 weeks. They found that exposure to the implicit positive stereotypes not only led to improvements in the participants' perceptions of aging, but the participants also experienced improved physical functioning that lasted for 3 weeks and was greater than that achieved by a 6-month exercise intervention. These results suggest that perceptions and beliefs can play an important role in physical decline (or not!) as people age.

> Age is an issue of mind over matter. If you don't mind, it doesn't matter.
>
> —Mark Twain (1835–1910), novelist

Erik Erikson suggests that older adulthood is an important time for people to reflect on their lives and develop a sense of meaning and satisfaction about their experiences and accomplishments. If this does not occur, Erikson suggests that people may experience feelings of bitterness and despair.

Luckily, research suggests that most older adults navigate the challenges of aging quite well. Ratings of life satisfaction actually increase after middle age (Mroczek, 2001; Sütterlin et al., 2012). In a surprising "paradox of aging," elderly people report greater enjoyment of life than middle-aged people, who in turn report greater enjoyment of life than young adults.

Depending on how we perceive the aging process, physical changes can bring about varying psychological responses. Western cultures tend to view aging negatively—a perception that can lead to the stereotype of the midlife crisis. However, research suggests that only 10 percent of adults reported experiencing a midlife crisis (Brim et al., 2004; Brim, 1992). Despite the reality that midlife crises are actually not all that common, an overall obsession with age is evident in Western culture—just watch some late night infomercials or walk down the cosmetics aisles

gerontology
an interdisciplinary field that studies the process of aging and the aging population

ageism
prejudice against people based upon their age

disengagement theory of aging

theory that elderly people gradually and willingly withdraw themselves from the world around them in preparation for death

activity theory of aging

suggests that elderly people are happiest when they stay active and involved in the community

socioemotional selectivity theory of aging

theory that suggests that as people grow older and realize that the time they have left is limited, they focus on enjoying the present rather than looking to the future

at the grocery store. However, some findings suggest that aging is viewed less negatively in some Eastern cultures (Löckenhoff et al., 2009). Recent studies have also shown that differences between Eastern and Western perceptions of aging may be more related to socioeconomics and the rate of aging within the population rather than due to differences in cultural values (Löckenhoff et al., 2014).

Researchers have examined how people tend to address the process of aging. For example, after retirement, what motivates people when they no longer have to get up for work in the morning? How do parents feel when their children suddenly stop needing parental support? According to the **disengagement theory of aging** (Cumming et al., 1961; Johnson & Mutchler, 2014), elderly people gradually and willingly withdraw themselves from the world around them. In preparation for death, members of the older generation sever all social ties and become increasingly preoccupied with their own memories, thoughts, and feelings. Cumming and Henry theorized that this withdrawal enables a transfer of power from the older generation to the younger generation, making it possible for society to continue functioning after its individual members die.

In contrast, the **activity theory of aging** (Havighurst, 1957; Johnson & Mutchler, 2014) suggests that elderly people are happiest when they stay active and involved in the community. Contrary to the view that the elderly willingly disengage themselves from the outside world, the activity theory proposes that disengagement takes place only when people are forced to retire or are no longer invited to social engagements.

Recent research has shifted from the question of whether elderly people prefer to be active to questions about the types of activities they choose and their reasons for choosing those activities. Laura Carstensen (1991; 2006) proposed the **socioemotional selectivity theory of aging**, suggesting that as people grow older and realize that the time they have left is limited, they focus on enjoying the present rather than looking to the future. Elderly people pay more attention to people with whom they have close emotional ties, and spend less time with casual acquaintances. Couples in long-term marriages become closer; marital satisfaction increases; and ties with children, grandchildren, and long-term friends are strengthened. Those who continue working into old age report a higher level of enjoyment than they did when they were younger because they are more interested in maintaining social relationships with colleagues than with career progression.

Older adults who maintain an active lifestyle tend to be the most satisfied.

Quiz for Module 9.12–9.14

1. The trend for women to delay childbirth until their late 20s or early 30s has _____ while the peak years for female fertility are _____.

   a. increased; early to mid-thirties

   b. decreased; late adolescence and emerging adulthood

   c. continued; late adolescence and early adulthood

   d. continued; early to mid-thirties

2. The Japanese term for menopause, "konenki," means _____.

   a. "time of renewal"   **b.** "aging"

   c. "sadness"   **d.** "fatigue"

3. Tyrone is 18 years old and challenges his 55-year-old father to a memory test. Tyrone would be most likely to win a memory test based on _____.

   a. recall of information   **b.** recognition of information

   c. memory of past events   **d.** short-term memory

4. Older adults recall more _____ events, while younger adults recall both _____ events.

   a. social; social and work

   b. negative; positive and negative

   c. positive; positive and negative

   d. work; social and work

5. In general, marriage is a good predictor of _____, health, _____, and income level.

   a. instability; mental illness

   b. contentment; conflict resolution

   c. happiness; longer life

   d. happiness; sexual satisfaction

6. For most people to enjoy their work, it needs to be complex, varied, and _____.

   a. not closely supervised   **b.** pay a high salary

   c. supervised   **d.** closely supervised

Module 9.15: Piecing It Together: Development and Body Image

LO 9.15 **Analyze how the cross-cutting themes of psychology relate to the topic of body image and development.**

Body image, defined as your mental image of your own body, is an interesting topic related to human development. Body image develops over time and includes elements of physical development, cognitive development, and social development. Obviously, your body image depends to some degree on your actual *physical* appearance. Are you tall, short, dark-skinned, or freckled with fair skin? Body weight and shape are also important characteristics that influence body image. *Cognitively*, one important aspect of body image pertains to the thoughts and feelings a person has about his or her appearance. *Social* factors are also extremely important with research pointing to the influence of media, peers, and family in the development of body image. The following contains a brief summary of how body image develops across the lifespan.

Childhood: As Piaget pointed out, children do not have an accurate understanding of themselves as unique entities until around age 2 when they are able to understand the concept of "me." From that point on, children are beginning to develop a sense of their body image. Body size concerns can be seen in children as young as 5–6 years old (Smolak, 2011; Tremblay et al., 2011). The cultural emphasis on thinness and anti-fat biases are present in young children (Spiel et al., 2012), and children who are overweight by age 7 already report feeling dissatisfaction with their bodies (Taylor et al., 2012). By age 4, children already subscribe to the "thin ideal" suggesting that images from the media, toys (e.g., Barbie dolls), and messages from family and peers have already solidified the notion that thinness is attractive (Brown & Slaughter, 2011).

Adolescence: With the physical changes that accompany adolescence, it's not surprising that body image often becomes very important at this stage (Wertheim & Paxton, 2011). For girls in particular, puberty results in increased fat deposits in areas such as the breasts and hips. Because of the prevalence of the thin ideal, these changes in body size and shape often lead girls to express dissatisfaction with their bodies. Girls appear to have increasing levels of body dissatisfaction as they get older (Calzo et al., 2012). Both boys and girls who are overweight report higher levels of body dissatisfaction than their normal weight peers, but as adolescence progresses, even healthy weight girls reported increasing body concerns. Adolescent body image is highly influenced by the media (e.g., television, magazines, and social media), and peer groups become even more influential during the teenage years.

Adulthood: Body image remains an important developmental topic throughout early, middle, and late adulthood. While the physical changes related to aging would lead you to assume that body image becomes more negative as people age, research findings suggest that body image may actually become more positive throughout middle and late adulthood (Gagne et al., 2012). While weight and shape remain important to many people in adulthood, body image begins to focus more on the appearance of youth.

From this brief overview of the topic, you are likely left with many questions, which we will discuss in the following pages.

Research Methods

- How do researchers study body image?
- How is body image measured?

Body image has been widely studied in different age groups, across genders, and in different ethnic/racial groups. One of the challenges for researchers is determining how to accurately measure body image. Researchers have identified two primary aspects of body image, including attitudinal components (e.g., your thoughts and feelings about your body and appearance) and perceptual components (e.g., how accurately you perceive your body size and shape). Each component of body image has been studied extensively in an effort to develop a reliable and valid form of measurement.

- **Measuring Body Image Attitudes**

All attitudes have three components: the *cognitive component* (the thoughts and beliefs people hold), the *affective component* (your emotions or feelings), and the *behavioral component* (how you act). Each of these three components has been measured as they relate to body image. Cognitions related to body image include both positive and negative thoughts about one's appearance, body shape, or weight. Most assessment tools developed to measure the cognitive component of body image use self-report questionnaires asking individuals to rate the frequency with which they experience certain positive or negative body image related thoughts. Measuring the affective, or mood, component of body image can be a bit trickier. While some people describe "feeling fat" at a given moment, "fatness" is not technically an emotion. However, feelings such as disgust and shame have been associated with negative body image (Franzoni et al., 2013). Behavioral measurements of body image have been classified into two categories: those measuring avoidance behaviors (e.g., avoiding wearing certain clothes such as a swimsuit due to negative body image) and those measuring body checking behaviors (e.g., repeatedly weighing yourself or checking your appearance in a mirror).

Assessing Different Components of Body Image

Read the following questions and see if you can correctly identify them as measuring the cognitive, affective, or behavioral component of body image. Drag the box below to its appropriate spot on the table.

On a scale of 1–7 (1 = never and 7 = always), please rate the frequency that you check your body shape/size by trying on specific clothing.	Behavioral
On a scale of 1–7 (1 = never and 7 = always), please rate the frequency that you experience the following thought: "I am fat."	Cognitive
When thinking about your body shape/size, rate how often you feel... Depressed Content Shameful Happy	Affective

Start Over

- **Measuring Body Image Perceptions**

If you were asked to accurately estimate your body shape and size on a computer screen or even by sketching your own outline on a large piece of paper, how accurate do you think you would be? Research suggests that certain people tend to overestimate their body size while other people tend to underestimate their body size. But, how do we accurately measure whether your estimation is accurate or not? Perceptual measures of body image are designed to answer this question. Typically, these measures include a series of figures that vary according to dimensions such as thinness or muscularity. People are asked a variety of questions about the images such as (1) which image best represents your actual body size/shape, and/or (2) which image best represents your ideal body shape? Take a moment to complete the assessment below, which is a replication of a measure used in a recent study (Grossbard et al., 2011).

Ideal versus Actual Body Size

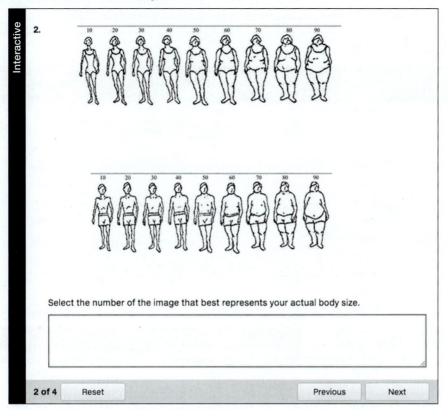

Select the number of the image that best represents your actual body size.

2 of 4   Reset   Previous   Next

Variations in Human Functioning

- What gender differences have been discovered in terms of body image?
- When do gender differences begin to emerge?

Did your assessment results show a discrepancy between your current and ideal body size? The results from an actual research study show that women and men respond somewhat differently. Women clearly chose an ideal body size that is thinner than their actual body size. Men chose an actual and an ideal image that were basically the same with the stimuli assessing preferred levels of thinness. However, men did report a desire for a more muscular ideal body size compared to their own actual level of muscularity with the stimuli assessing preferred levels of muscularity. When it comes to understanding what body type the opposite sex finds most attractive, both men and women appeared to get it somewhat wrong. Women consistently report believing that men prefer a thinner female body size than men actually report themselves. On the other hand, men also seem to believe that women prefer a more muscular body size for men than the women actually reported.

The findings of this study provide a good example of gender differences in body image. Over decades of research, body image dissatisfaction has been higher among women. Boys and girls tend to have similar levels of body concerns in childhood, although boys are more concerned with muscularity while girls are concerned with thinness. These gender differences suggest that children have internalized gendered messages of attractiveness in their social world (e.g., watching cartoons that have positive muscular male characters and positive thin female characters) (Klein & Shiffman, 2006). By adolescence, girls consistently report higher levels of dissatisfaction than boys, and this trend continues throughout adulthood (Calzo et al., 2012).

Ethics

- Many people use cosmetic surgery to address perceived defects in their physical appearance. At what age, if any, is cosmetic surgery a good option?

Negative body image may lead some individuals to consider cosmetic surgery. Concerns have been raised in recent years about adolescents seeking cosmetic surgery. Table 9.9 shows the statistics on individuals ages 13–19 who received cosmetic surgery in 2012. As the data suggests, this age group comprises a very small percentage of overall procedures. However, there were more than 230,000 procedures performed on adolescents in 2012.

Table 9.9 Cosmetic Surgery Procedures Across Different Ages

COSMETIC SURGICAL PROCEDURES	AGE 13–19 2012 TOTAL	AGE 13–19 % OF TOTAL PROCEDURES	AGE 13–19 % CHANGE 2012 vs 2011
Breast augmentation (augmentation mammaplasty)^	8,204	3%	−8%
Breast implant removals (augmentation patients only)^	76	0%	−1%
Breast lift (mastopexy)	1,591	2%	−3%
Breast reduction in men (gynecomastia)	15,142	73%	5%
Chin augmentation (mentoplasty)	1,592	9%	−12%
Dermabrasion	3,176	4%	−1%
Ear surgery (otoplasty)	7,406	29%	−1%
Eyelid surgery (blepharoplasty)	1,926	1%	2%
Lip augmentation (other than injectable materials)	243	1%	−2%
Liposuction	3,191	2%	−2%
Nose reshaping (rhinoplasty)	33,673	14%	−1%
TOTAL COSMETIC SURGICAL PROCEDURES	**76,220**	**5%**	**−1%**

COSMETIC MINIMALLY–INVASIVE PROCEDURES	AGE 13–19 2012 TOTAL	AGE 13–19 % OF TOTAL PROCEDURES	AGE 13–19 % CHANGE 2012 vs 2011
Botulinum toxin type A (Botox®, Dysport®)***	17,447	0%	8%
Chemical peel	6,024	1%	4%
Laser hair removal	72,778	7%	5%
Laser skin resurfacing	25,241	5%	7%
Laser treatment of leg veins	20,954	9%	−4%
Microdemabrasion	9,576	1%	7%
Sclerotherapy	1,961	1%	2%
Soft tissue fillers	6,155	0%	0%
Calcium hydroxylapatite (e.g., Radiesse®)	926	0%	−2%
Collagen	228	0%	−6%
Fat	560	1%	−6%
Hyaluronic acid (e.g., Juvederm Ultra®, Juvederm Ultra Plus®, Perlane®,Prevelle Silk®, Restylane®)	2,535	0%	7%
Polylactic acid (Sculptra®)	1,906	1%	−5%
TOTAL COSMETIC MINIMALLY–INVA SIVE PROCEDURES	**160,136**	**1%**	**4%**
TOTAL COSMETIC PROCEDURES	**236,356**	**2%**	**2%**

Journal Prompt: Cosmetic Surgery

Thinking about adolescent cognitive and social development, what are some concerns about cosmetic surgery to improve body image among this age group? You might want to address such ethical topics as informed consent or developmental concerns related to decision making.

Cultural and Social Diversity

- Are there differences between ethnic/racial groups in terms of body image in the United States?
- Are there cultural differences in body image around the globe?

A large body of research examining different subgroups within the United States has demonstrated that factors such as ethnicity and sexual orientation can have an impact on an individual's body image. Gay men have consistently reported higher levels of body dissatisfaction than heterosexual men, but the differences between lesbian and heterosexual women are negligible

(Morrison et al., 2004; Morrison & McCutcheon, 2011). People have theorized that the gay male subculture strongly emphasizes appearance and body shape thus placing more pressure on gay men to achieve an ideal image (Peplau et al., 2009). On the other hand, the thin ideal for women is so pervasive that sexual orientation does not appear to play an important role in the development of body image among women.

Research has also found that African American women in the United States report having a larger ideal body size and are more satisfied with their bodies than their white female counterparts (Grabe & Hyde, 2006; Kronenfeld et al., 2010). On the other hand, Asian American women tend to report higher levels of body dissatisfaction and increased risk of eating disorders than other ethnicities (Cummins & Lehman, 2007).

Degree of **acculturation**, or the extent to which a member of one cultural group adopts the beliefs and behaviors of another group, has also been shown to be an important factor in predicting the degree of body dissatisfaction among Hispanic/Latina girls and women (Cachelin et al., 2006).

Across the globe, there are significant differences in idealized images of attractiveness and body image. In 2010, the International Body Project surveyed more than 7,000 individuals across the globe about their own body image and body ideals. This study demonstrated that exposure to Western media predicted body dissatisfaction in women such that women who were exposed to more Western media reported higher levels of body dissatisfaction. In addition, socioeconomic status (SES) was also related to preference for thinness in that higher SES locations preferred a thinner ideal than lower SES locations (Swami et al., 2010).

acculturation

the extent to which a member of one cultural group adopts the beliefs and behaviors of another group

Quiz for Module 9.15

1. Your mental image of your own body is called your
_____.
 a. body focus
 b. body image
 c. body assessment
 d. shape impression

2. Rea was asked to view a series of silhouettes ranging from very thin to very overweight and identify her current body size and ideal body size. She was completing a(n) _____ measure of body image.
 a. perceptual
 b. attitudinal
 c. cognitive
 d. affective

3. In measurements of perceptual body image, women tend to rate their ideal image as _____ than their current image and think men prefer a _____ female image than men actually report.
 a. thinner; larger
 b. larger; larger
 c. thinner; thinner
 d. larger; thinner

4. Men tend to report a desire for a more _____ body shape than their own perceived level.
 a. defined
 b. larger
 c. thinner
 d. muscular

5. Black women in the United States reportedly have a _____ ideal body shape and report being more _____ with their bodies than their White female counterparts.
 a. larger; satisfied
 b. thinner; satisfied
 c. larger; critical
 d. thinner; critical

Summary: Learning

Module 9.1–9.2 Studying Human Development

Developmental psychologists study the physical, cognitive, and social changes that we experience throughout our lifespans. To study human development, researchers distinguish between **chronological age** (the amount of time someone has been living) and **developmental age** (the point at which someone falls using developmental stages) in conducting **normative investigations** to determine developmental landmarks. Researchers use **cross-sectional studies** examining different individuals at different ages, **longitudinal studies** examining the same individuals over time, and **cross-sequential studies** which combine both cross-sectional and longitudinal designs by examining several different cohorts over time. The question of whether we are primarily

defined by our inherited characteristics (i.e., "**nature**") or environmental factors (i.e., "**nurture**") has been the focus of much debate and research. To help determine the influence of genetics versus environment, the study of **monozygotic**, or identical, twins compared to **dizygotic**, or fraternal twins in terms of **concordance rates** (the probability that one twin develops the condition if the other twin has it) has been helpful. Ultimately, most psychologists agree that we become the people we are through a unique combination of hereditary and environmental factors. Developmental researchers have also debated the issue of whether or not development occurs in a **continuous** (steady but gradual process over time) or **discontinuous** (through distinct steps or **stages**) pattern as well as the question of stability versus change.

Module 9.3–9.6   Development In Infancy And Childhood

Human development begins when the **ova**, or female egg, is released by the **ovaries** and fertilized by a male sex cell called a **sperm**. The single fertilized cell is called a **zygote**. For two weeks following fertilization, the **germinal stage** of prenatal development leads to rapid cell division, implantation in the uterus, and the development of the fetus. The **embryonic stage** occurs from two to eight weeks following fertilization and is associated with organ development and the first heartbeats. The **fetal stage** occurs from eight weeks after fertilization until birth. **Teratogens** are agents that can negatively affect the development of an embryo or fetus. **Fetal alcohol spectrum disorders (FASD)** can be the result of alcohol use during pregnancy. Nicotine is another potential teratogen associated with **Sudden Infant Death Syndrome (SIDS)**, the unexplained death of a seemingly healthy infant.

Infants are born with certain **reflexes**, or involuntary responses, including the withdraw/pain, rooting, Babinski, Moro/startle, grasping, stepping, crying, and restricted breathing reflexes. By five weeks after conception, neurons begin to form at a rapid pace. By birth, the cortex of the brain basically contains all of the neurons it will ever have. The fetus is also developing synapses to connect neurons, and by birth an infant will have twice the number of synapses that will be present in adulthood. Excess synapses are gradually reduced during childhood in a process called **synaptic pruning**. **Motor development**, the emergent ability to execute physical actions, is governed by (1) the **cephalocaudal rule,** or the tendency for motor skills to emerge in sequence from top to bottom, and (2) the **proximodistal** rule, or the tendency for motor skills to emerge in sequence from inside to outside.

Jean Piaget's theory of cognitive development described two processes by which we adjust our **schemas**—concepts or frameworks around which we organize and interpret information. Using **assimilation**, we interpret new experiences in terms of existing schemas, and we use **accommodation** to adjust and refine schemas to incorporate the new information. Piaget proposed that development occurs in a series of four stages. Lev Vygotsky focused on social influences on cognitive development and proposed that children learn best in the **zone of proximal development** (the difference between what a child can do alone versus with assistance) and can be best assisted through the process of **scaffolding**, or providing appropriate assistance to a learner, which is removed gradually. The information processing theory of cognitive development emphasizes how information from the environment is actively processed through the systems of attention, memory, and perception. A computer analogy has been often used to explain the information processing model by describing the human mind as a "computer processor" that encodes, stores, and transforms information to produce some output. The emotional bond that newborns share with their caregivers is called **attachment;** at around 8 months of age, this preference for familiar caregivers leads to **stranger anxiety**, or fear of strangers. The results of Harlow's famous study of infant monkeys removed from their mothers demonstrated the importance of physical contact between infants and caregivers. Mary Ainsworth's strange situation test demonstrated that children tend to show one of four patterns of attachment: (1) **secure** (upset when mother leaves but easily comforted on her return), (2) **anxious-ambivalent/resistant** (difficult to soothe even when mother returns), (3) **anxious-avoidant** (unconcerned when mother

leaves and ignores her return), and (4) **disorganized-disoriented** (inconsistent response to mother's return). Other researchers have pointed to the role of the infant's **temperament** (innate aspects of personality) that might affect the mother's reaction. Three different temperament types have been identified: (1) **easy temperament** (infants with regular eating/sleeping patterns who adapt easily to change and can tolerate frustration, (2) **difficult temperament** (infants with irregular eating/sleeping patterns who are slow to adapt to change and respond negatively to frustration), and (3) **slow-to-warm temperament** (infants with generally regular eating/sleeping patterns who can adapt to change with repeated exposure and have mildly negative responses to frustration).

Parenting styles have also been classified into four categories, including **authoritarian** (high demandingness and low responsiveness), **permissive** (low demandingness and high responsiveness), **neglectful/uninvolved** (low demandingness and low responsiveness), and **authoritative** (high demandingness and high responsiveness). Erik Erikson proposed a stage model of social development that focuses on the major social challenges that must be successfully navigated at each age. Erikson's four childhood stages include basic trust versus mistrust (birth to 12–18 months with a focus on feeding), autonomy versus shame/doubt (18 months to 3 years with a focus on toilet training), initiative versus guilt (ages 3–6 with a focus on play), and industry versus inferiority (ages 6–12 with a focus on school).

Module 9.7–9.11   Development in Adolescence

Physically, **adolescence** (the period of transition from childhood to adulthood) is marked by **puberty,** or the process of sexual maturation. Brain signals to the gonads (**ovaries** in girls and **testes** in boys) lead to the development of **primary sex characteristics**—reproductive organs and external genitalia—and **secondary sex characteristics**—nonreproductive traits such as breasts in girls and facial hair in boys. **Menarche** (the onset of menstruation in girls) typically occurs between ages 12 and 13 and has been occurring at earlier ages over the past centuries. **Adrenal androgen,** the hormone that increases in production during puberty, plays an important role in the development of sexual interest for both boys and girls.

As the frontal lobes develop, they enable us to **reason**—to organize information and beliefs into a series of steps leading to a conclusion. This ability to reason leads to increased ability to engage in moral reasoning. Lawrence Kohlberg developed a model that classified moral reasoning into **preconventional morality** (focus on punishment and reward), **conventional morality** (conformity to social laws), and **postconventional morality** (based on abstract principles). In contrast, Jonathan Haidt's **social intuitionist** account of morality suggests that we have an instant gut reaction to moral situations, which precedes moral reasoning.

Social development in adolescence is marked by a search for **identity,** or our sense of self, and Erikson's model proposes that adolescents go through the stage of identity versus role confusion during which the focus is on peer relationships. Adolescence is also marked by two kinds of peer groups: **cliques** (close-knit same-sex groups of three to nine members) and **crowds** (larger, mixed-sex groups).

Emerging adulthood typically occurs between ages 18 and 25 and differs in many ways from both adolescence and early adulthood. This period of exploration, uncertainty, and identity formation is usually resolved by the later 20s, when people tend to achieve total independence from parental support and develop the ability to empathize with others as fellow adults. The stage of emerging adulthood is typically discussed in terms of Western industrialized societies.

Module 9.12–9.14 Development in Adulthood

Physical aging in women is marked by **menopause**, or the end of the menstrual cycle and ability to bear children. For men, **andropause** leads to a decline in sperm count, testosterone level, and speed of erection and ejaculation. Aging is associated with a decline in vision, muscle strength, reaction time, stamina, hearing, distance perception, and sense of smell. Overall, Western cultures appear more concerned with the aging process, while Eastern cultures embrace aging for the wisdom and stability that often accompany it.

Dementia (also known as a neurocognitive disorder) is associated with a progressive loss of cognitive functioning in areas such as memory, reasoning, planning, decision making, and social functioning. **Alzheimer's disease** (a condition characterized by progressive and irreversible declines in memory, thinking, and language) is the most common form of dementia. An overall reduction in neurons and connections between neurons is found in the brains of people with Alzheimer's disease. This degradation of neurons is associated with the presence of **amyloid plaques** (the accumulation of protein fragments between nerve cells) and **neurofibrillary tangles** (twisted strands of protein within neurons).

There are also cognitive declines associated with aging such as some types of learning and remembering. **Prospective memory**—remembering to perform a specific action, can be preserved with good reminder cues. Using cross-sectional designs to measure intelligence in different age **cohorts** (groups of people raised during the same time period) have likely overestimated declines in intelligence with age. Longitudinal studies also have their shortcomings, but these types of studies have shown much less intellectual decline associated with aging.

Erikson's theory suggests that between ages 20 to 40, people enter the stage of intimacy versus isolation during which the focus is on love relationships. From age 40 to 60, Erikson's theory proposes that people enter the stage of generativity versus stagnation during which the focus is on work and parenthood.

Gerontology is a budding interdisciplinary field that studies the process of aging and the aging population. **Ageism,** or prejudice against the elderly, often leads to negative stereotyping. Erikson suggests that older adulthood is an important time for people to reflect on their lives, proposing the stage of ego integrity versus despair occurs during late adulthood. According to the **disengagement theory of aging,** elderly people gradually and willingly withdraw themselves from the world around them. In contrast, the **activity theory of aging** suggests that elderly people are happiest when they stay active and involved in the community. Recent research has shifted from the question of whether elderly people prefer to be active to questions about the types of activities they choose and their reasons for choosing those activities. The **socioemotional selectivity theory of aging** suggests that as people grow older and realize that the time they have left is limited, they focus on enjoying the present rather than looking to the future.

Chapter 9 Quiz

1. Sa'dia is an 18-month-old girl whose parents use flash cards to teach her the alphabet and simple words, they use videos and music to teach her other languages, and they use infant swimming and movement classes to improve her coordination. Despite all these classes, Sa'dia walked at 12 months and spoke her first word at 13 months. What would developmental psychologists tell Sa'dia's parents?

  a. Keep up the good work, and it will eventually pay off with advanced developmental abilities.

  b. Overstimulation can result in a decrease in motor skills.

  c. There is little one can do to rush motor skill development. Babies have to have adequate muscular and neural maturity to reach developmental milestones.

  d. Increase the rate of classes and rewards so that your child can reach her full developmental peak.

2. While longitudinal studies produce valuable data, there are some limitations to these research designs. What are two of the problems?

  a. Dropout rate of participants; large amount of time and effort required

  b. Cohort effects; dropout rate of participants

  c. Dropout rate of participants; researchers are not interested in these types of studies

  d. Large amount of time and effort required; cohort effects

3. Once a sperm and egg have fused into a single fertilized cell, it is called a(n) _____.

  a. zygote   **b.** ovary

  c. blastocyst   **d.** embryo

4. As a child, Liam was an outgoing boy who made friends easily. Today, he is the top salesman in his company and he is still outgoing and engaging. Liam's case would be interesting to developmental psychologists studying the consistency of traits and characteristics over time to answer the question of _____.

  a. developmental age versus chronological age

  b. continuity versus discontinuity

  c. nature versus nurture

  d. stability versus change

5. Marcy was 3 years old when she went to the zoo for the first time. She saw her first leopard and called it a "kitty." Her mother responded, "that is a leopard, which looks like a kitty but is much bigger and has spots." The next time Marcy saw a leopard, she said "leopard!" This is an example of Piaget's notion of _____.

a. assimilation   b. schemas

c. accommodation   d. concepts

6. Dr. Tomas is interested in studying how a person's biological makeup vs. environment affects criminal behavior. Who would be the ideal candidates for this study?

a. Teenagers who have been in juvenile lockup

b. Prison inmates with criminal parents

c. Monozygotic twins raised in different homes and dizygotic twins raised together

d. Monozygotic twins raised together and dizygotic twins raised apart

7. After baby Lorenzo was born, the nurses checked him for these five reflexes to make sure he was functioning normally.

a. Stepping, Babinski, grasping, Moro, and rooting

b. Sucking, rooting, hearing, seeing, and grasping

c. Grasping, sucking, stepping, breathing, and rooting

d. Hearing, seeing, sucking, stepping, and rooting

8. Dr. Samuelson wants to study the impact of social media on the friendships of 20-, 40-, 60-, and 80-year-olds. He plans to follow each age group for 10 years and study their use of social media and their relationships. What type of study is Dr. Samuelson conducting?

a. Cross-sectional study

b. Longitudinal study

c. Cross-sequential study

d. Normative study

9. At which month of pregnancy does the fetus have fully developed organs and a chance of survival if born prematurely?

a. 7 months   b. 5 months

c. 4 months   d. 6 months

10. Which of the following stages of cognitive development occur first according to Piaget's theory?

a. Sensorimotor stage

b. Formal operational stage

c. Preoperational stage

d. Concrete operational stage

11. During the civil rights movement in the 1960s, people broke state laws so that Black people could sit where they wanted to on the bus or drink from the same water fountain or use the same bathroom as white people. Kohlberg would say these people were operating at which stage of morality?

a. Conventional morality

b. Preconventional morality

c. Postconventional morality

d. Ethical social justice

12. Baby George is 4 months old. He typically has a hard time falling asleep and then only sleeps 2 hours at a time. George doesn't like it if the routine changes and usually responds with crying and frustration. He only wants to be held and fed by his mother and cries when passed off to another person. George would be considered what type of temperament?

a. Easy   c. Anxious

b. Slow-to-warm   d. Difficult

13. Chen is a 3-year-old who likes to dress himself and insists on helping with the dishes, even though he makes a mess cleaning them up. He likes to feed the family dog, even though he spills the food all over the place. He insists that he can do things by himself. Which of Erikson's psychosocial stages would Chen be in?

a. Trust vs. mistrust

b. Industry vs. inferiority

c. Autonomy vs. shame/doubt

d. Initiative vs. guilt

14. Ross has decided that he is a Republican just like his parents and embraces their religious values as well. He has never questioned his parents' beliefs or ideas. He has also decided to attend the university they chose for him and the course of study they believe he needs to pursue. According to Marcia's categories, Ross is in which stage?

a. Foreclosure

b. Identity achievement

c. Identity diffusion

d. Moratorium

15. Julie is 15 years old and has her first long-term serious boyfriend. He is pressuring her to have sex, but she is concerned about getting pregnant. She just read a brochure that stated that teen moms are less likely to _____.

a. graduate from high school

b. drop out of high school

c. be good parents

d. divorce their partner

16. Henry is 16 years old and has had his driver's license for 2 months. He and his friend are drinking beer while driving around town one night. They decide to drive down country roads with the lights off as fast as they can. This is an example of lack of maturation in which part of the brain?

a. Frontal lobe   b. Amygdala

c. Parietal lobe   d. Temporal lobe

17. Which of the following abilities is most affected by functioning of the frontal lobes of the brain?

a. Expression of anger

b. The ability to identify right from wrong

c. Problem-solving

d. Visual perception

18. Latetia, age 5, has learned to do simple addition problems through using small objects in her environment like toys. Her teacher has assisted her in this process and now is challenging Latetia to use subtraction in her work. As Latetia gains confidence in each stage, the teacher allows her to do the problems on her own. Latetia's teacher is using the process of scaffolding based on which theory of cognitive development?

    a. Vgotsky's theory of cognitive development
    b. Piaget's theory of cognitive development
    c. Information-processing theory of development
    d. Social emotional theory of development

19. One criticism of Kohlberg's theory of moral development is that there is no distinction between _____.

    a. thoughts and feelings
    b. conventional and postconventional reasoning
    c. preconventional and postconventional reasoning
    d. moral reasoning and moral action

20. You forget to pay for the big bag of dog food on the bottom of your cart at Wal-Mart, and your neighbor in the next checkout lane notices. If you go back to pay for the dog food because you want to be seen as a good person to your neighbor, this is an example of which stage of Kohlberg's morality?

    a. Conventional morality
    b. Postconventional morality
    c. Right versus wrong
    d. Preconventional morality

21. Shania has been looking for her breasts to develop since she was in fifth grade. She thinks she is the only girl in seventh grade who does not have a bra. She has noticed some underarm hair growing and is hopeful that she will start developing breasts soon. Shania is worried about the development of _____.

    a. ovaries
    b. hormones
    c. primary sex characteristics
    d. secondary sex characteristics

22. Prejudice against the elderly is called _____.

    a. stereotyping   b. racism
    c. sexism   d. ageism

23. Seyon is a 24-year-old college graduate with a job that does not pay enough for him to pay rent. He lives with his parents and works at the local Starbucks while he looks for a job. His parents pay his cell phone bill and his car insurance. He is considering going back to school to get a graduate degree. He is in the stage of life called _____.

    a. early adulthood   b. late adolescence
    c. emerging adulthood   d. boomerang children

24. At what age do most people in Western societies achieve total independence and identify themselves as adults?

    a. Mid-20s   b. Early 20s
    c. Early 30s   d. Late 20s

25. Neural processing slows in older adulthood, which means older adults take more time to react and remember _____.

    a. past events
    b. names
    c. vocabulary words
    d. how to perform certain tasks

26. Sofia, a 65-year-old woman, can't seem to remember if she has eaten breakfast each day. She also doesn't remember that her granddaughter called to tell her she was going to stop by to visit. She seems to be forgetting more things and doesn't want her family to know. Sofia may be showing signs of _____.

    a. dementia   b. brain tumor
    c. menopause   d. Parkinson's disease

27. It is rare to see a baseball player or football player stay in the professional game past age 40. What contributes to this phenomenon?

    a. Increase in illnesses
    b. Drug use and steroid overdose
    c. Decline in vision, strength, reaction time, and stamina as we age
    d. Younger players push them out of the game

28. _____ research designs show a decline in intelligence with age, while _____ research designs show more stability in intelligence over time.

    a. Longitudinal; cross-sectional
    b. Cross-sectional; longitudinal
    c. Case study; population study
    d. Population study; case study

29. The conflicts that parents and adolescents engage in while the adolescent is in the process of forming their own identity are usually about _____.

    a. friends   c. attending church
    b. control   d. curfew

30. The _____ theory of aging suggests that elderly people are happiest when they stay active and involved in the community.

    a. Erikson
    b. disengagement
    c. socioemotional selectivity
    d. activity

Chapter 10
Motivation and Emotion

Chapter Outline and Learning Objectives

Module 10.1–10.3: Physiological Theories of Motivation

LO 10.1 Explain the instinct theory of motivation.

LO 10.2 Describe the drive-reduction theory of motivation and the limitations of this theory.

LO 10.3 Explain how the Yerkes-Dodson law applies to the optimal arousal theory of motivation.

Module 10.4–10.5: Hunger

LO 10.4 Identify the physiological, social, and cultural influences on hunger.

LO 10.5 Identify some of the factors that impact obesity.

Module 10.6–10.9: Beyond Biology: Other Theories of Motivation

LO 10.6 Identify Maslow's hierarchy of needs from the most basic needs to the needs highest on the pyramid.

LO 10.7 Distinguish between intrinsic motivators and extrinsic motivators.

LO 10.8 Explain the roles of autonomy, relatedness, and competence in self-determination theory.

LO 10.9 Summarize Dweck's self-theory of motivation.

Module 10.10–10.12: Components of Emotion

LO 10.10 Identify the biological factors associated with emotions.

LO 10.11 Identify some of the ways we detect and express emotions.

LO 10.12 Explain how our thoughts can influence our emotions.

Module 10.13–10.14: Theories of Emotion

LO 10.13 Differentiate between the James-Lange and Cannon-Bard theories of emotion.

LO 10.14 Distinguish between the two-factor theory, the cognitive mediational theory, and the facial feedback hypothesis of emotion.

Module 10.15: Piecing It Together: Obesity Treatment

LO 10.15 Analyze how the cross-cutting themes of psychology are related to the topic of motivation and emotion through the issue of obesity treatment.

What is Motivation and How Does It Relate to Emotion?

Motivation is the need or desire that energizes and directs behavior. It is made up of internal factors—*dispositional forces*—and external factors—*situational forces*—that drive us to do specific things in a particular situation. When we experience a subjective reaction to an object, event, person, or memory, we are experiencing **emotion**. The relationship between emotion and motivation is multifaceted such that emotions can certainly motivate behavior, but people are sometimes motivated to act in order to achieve a certain emotional outcome. For example, people often engage in leisure activities out of a pursuit of positive emotional states such as happiness.

Journal Prompt: Motivated by Emotion

Describe a time when you were motivated to act because of a strong emotion.

Consider the stories of amazing heroism that emerged from the 2012 school shooting at Sandy Hook in Newtown, Connecticut. On that December day, 20 children and 6 adult staff members were shot and killed. One teacher, 27-year-old Victoria Soto, sacrificed her own life while trying to hide her small students. She told the gunman Adam Lanza that the children were in the gym; when the children began to run from the closet where she had hidden them, she threw her own body in front of the gunman, resulting in her death (Conner et al., 2012). Many factors probably motivated this act of bravery, but the extreme emotions triggered by the situation likely played a significant role in inspiring Soto and others to act.

Module 10.1 – 10.3: Physiological Theories of Motivation

Many of the early theories of motivation focused almost exclusively on how physiological needs served to motivate behavior. For example, if you think about day-to-day behaviors in your life, you will notice that many of them appear driven by some sort of physiological need. You wake up and likely head straight to the restroom—a biological need that is very motivating indeed! You will eat several times a day, and make sure you leave time for sleep. These are all examples of behaviors motivated primarily by physiological needs, and psychologists have developed several theories about how and why our physiological states serve to motivate our behavior.

Instinct Theory

LO 10.1   **Explain the instinct theory of motivation.**

Charles Darwin's theory of natural selection focused on the notion that characteristics that enhance an individual's ability to survive and reproduce will be passed down to the next generation. He described these characteristics that evolved through the process of natural selection as instincts (Darwin & Beer, 1951). As Darwin's theory of evolution became popular, so did the labeling of human instincts. William James (1890) believed that **instincts**—unlearned complex behaviors with a fixed pattern throughout a species—are purposeful in humans and other animals. Early theories of motivation focused on instincts as being the primary motivator of human behavior. Instincts are discussed in terms of the evolutionary perspective—those behaviors that help a species to survive will become instinctual through the process of natural selection. One of the earliest proponents of the instinctual theory of human motivation, William McDougall (1926) first proposed a list of 18 core human instincts, which included such things as the instincts for repulsion, curiosity, and flight when afraid. However, within 20 years of McDougall's first list of 18 instincts, the inventory of instincts had expanded to more than 10,000. This theory grew out of favor for several reasons. Primarily, it became difficult to prove

motivation

a need or desire that energizes and directs behavior

emotion

a subjective reaction to an object, event, person, or memory that includes physiological arousal, expressive behavior, and cognitive experiences

instincts

unlearned complex behaviors with a fixed pattern throughout a species

that many human behaviors were motivated purely by biological instincts. To qualify as an "instinct," a behavior must be (1) unlearned (occurs naturally without any prior experience) and (2) follow a fixed pattern across all members of a species.

Instinct or Not?

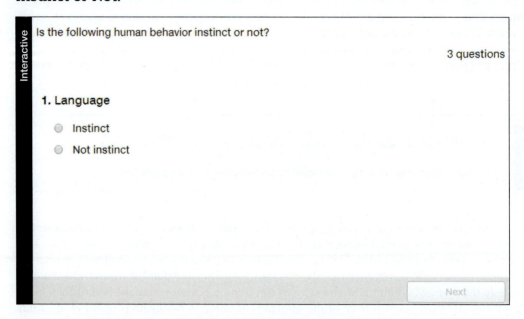

It's not difficult to think of several examples of instincts among nonhuman animals. Migratory patterns in birds, hibernation in bears, and even the way a dog shakes its fur when it becomes wet are all examples of instinctual behavior. We also know there are human instincts such as the infant rooting reflex (turning the head in response to facial touch in an effort to nurse). However, most psychologists now believe human behavior is motivated by a combination of biological and psychological states and that humans don't often engage in purely instinctual behavior.

Drive-Reduction Theory

LO 10.2 **Describe the drive-reduction theory of motivation and the limitations of this theory.**

drive-reduction theory

Clark Hull's theory that we act when a physiological need creates an aroused state that drives us to reduce the need. Based on the premise that humans are motivated to maintain a state of homeostasis

homeostasis

a state of balance or equilibrium

primary drives

drives based on innate biological needs such as hunger and thirst

secondary drives

drives learned though conditioning such as money

According to Clark Hull's **drive-reduction theory**, we act when a physiological need creates an aroused state that drives us to reduce the need. This theory is based on the premise that humans are motivated to maintain a state of **homeostasis**—a state of balance or equilibrium. Our use of indoor heating in the winter months and air conditioning in the summer months is a good example of homeostasis. When we are too cold, we turn the thermostat up; and, when we are too hot, we turn the thermostat down. You can imagine Hull's drive-reduction theory as our biological drive to keep the thermostat at a perfect 72 degrees. When we act to restore homeostasis, the resulting reduction in physiological tension reinforces the behavior (Hull, 1943, 1952). **Primary drives**, such as hunger and thirst, lead us to eat or drink and therefore preserve homeostasis. However, humans are motivated to do much more than simply eat, drink, or keep the temperature at 72 degrees. While primary drives are innate (e.g., thirst, hunger, sex), **secondary drives** are learned through conditioning (e.g., money). Money becomes associated with the things it can buy such as food to reduce primary drives.

Hull's theory was extremely ambitious in that he attempted to develop a theory to understand all human behavior. He even developed elaborate mathematical formulas to explain human behavior and his theories were also notable because they lent themselves to laboratory testing. For thirty years, this theory influenced the entire field of psychology. However, two significant limitations to the theory ultimately led to its loss of influence in the field. First, it is difficult to understand how secondary reinforcers serve to immediately reduce drives. Although money can be a very strong reinforcer, receiving a paycheck does nothing to reduce physiological needs in the moment. Second, Hull's theory is unable to explain why humans are sometimes motivated to behave in ways that actually increase arousal and disrupt homeostasis.

Journal Prompt: Thrill-Seeking and Drive Reduction Theory

Name some thrill-seeking behaviors, and explain why these behaviors would not fit well with Hull's drive-reduction theory.

For example, why do you choose to watch a horror movie or ride a death-defying roller coaster? Have you ever eaten dessert despite already being quite full? It turns out that "balance and equilibrium," the very definition of homoeostasis, can actually be undesirable to people in certain situations. Therefore, thrill-seeking behaviors are difficult to explain in terms of Hull's drive-reduction theory.

Optimal Arousal Theory

LO 10.3 **Explain how the Yerkes-Dodson law applies to the optimal arousal theory of motivation.**

Rather than being driven to achieve homeostasis, the **optimal arousal theory** of motivation states that people are driven to achieve an ideal level of arousal. Every individual is unique in determining his or her optimal level of arousal. This theory may explain why some people are drawn to risky or thrill-seeking behaviors such as sky diving or mountain climbing to achieve their ideal level of arousal while others are quite satisfied with the arousal provided by watching a movie or going on a hike. Given that our individual needs for arousal appear to be different, what do we know about the ideal level of arousal to perform our best on various tasks? Distance runners, like most athletes, capitalize on the fact that a little anxiety or arousal can actually improve their performance. Most people training for a marathon never run the full 26.2 miles before race day. In fact, many training programs only have people train up to a 20-mile run. On the actual race day, having a mild to moderate case of nerves can actually help you run longer and even a little faster than you did on your more monotonous training runs. The **Yerkes-Dodson law** states that performance generally peaks with a moderate level of arousal (Yerkes & Dodson, 1908). Performance levels increase as arousal increases, but only up to a certain point. After that, performance levels decrease as arousal increases. This means that a moderate level of arousal on race day will be beneficial but very high levels of arousal can be detrimental. Sports psychologists often work with athletes who have high levels of performance anxiety to achieve the perfect balance of arousal and performance.

optimal arousal theory
the theory that people are motivated to achieve an ideal level of arousal

Yerkes-Dodson law
law that states performance generally peaks with a moderate level of arousal

Graph the Yerkes-Dodson Curve

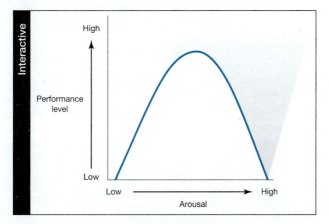

While this inverted U graph provides a simple explanation of the relationship between arousal and performance, research suggests that it's a bit more complicated. The optimum level of arousal actually depends on the type of task. Easier tasks (e.g., sorting colors of crayons) have higher optimal levels of arousal, and more difficult tasks (e.g., multitasking by sorting colors of crayons while also counting backward by sevens) have lower optimal levels of arousal. Tasks requiring persistence also generally require more arousal than intellectual ones. Therefore, optimal arousal to compete in a sport would be higher than to play chess.

Graph the Yerkes-Dodson Curve Considering Task Difficulty

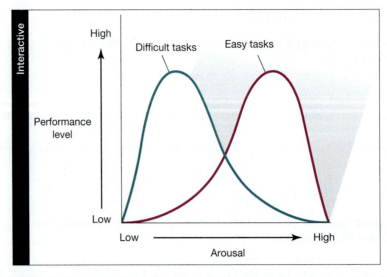

Researchers have only recently been able to test the Yerkes-Dodson law by measuring blood levels of corticosterone (or stress hormones) in rats (Salehi et al., 2010). One study introduced "stress" to a group of rats by either lowering or raising the temperature of the water while training the rats to navigate through a water maze (Diamond et al., 2007; Salehi et al., 2010). The "highest" temperature led to the lowest levels of corticosterones, while the "lowest" temperature led to the highest level of corticosterones. They indeed found evidence for the "inverted U" relationship between stress levels and performance on learning and remembering the path through the water maze.

Review the Theories

Review the following theories, their descriptions, and their pros and cons. When you are ready, click "Check Your Understanding" below.

Theory	Description	Pros	Cons
Optimal Arousal Theory	Theory stating that people are driven to achieve an ideal state of arousal.	Helps explain why some people are motivated to engage in risky or thrill-seeking behaviors.	The theory does not encompass all human behavior.
Drive Reduction Theory	Theory stating that people act in response to a state of physiological arousal to achieve homeostasis.	Provided a testable theory of all human behavior.	(1) Doesn't account properly for the role of secondary reinforcers. (2) Thrill-seeking behavior that serves to increase arousal is not explained by this theory.
Instinct Theory	Biological theory of motivation focusing on the role of unlearned, fixed patterns of behavior that serve to aid in natural selection.	Uses an evolutionary perspective on the study of human motivation.	It became difficult to identify human behaviors that were (1) unlearned, and (2) fixed patterns across all humans.

Check Your Understanding

Quiz for Module 10.1–10.3

1. _____ are unlearned complex behaviors with a fixed pattern throughout a species.
   - **a.** Drives
   - **b.** Motivations
   - **c.** Instincts
   - **d.** Fears

2. When Mattea yawns in class, her professor told her not to feel guilty because this is an unlearned reflexive behavior. What theory of motivation was her professor trying to demonstrate?
   - **a.** Drive reduction theory
   - **b.** Instinct theory
   - **c.** Optimal arousal theory
   - **d.** Maslow's theory

3. When you are working outside in the 90-degree heat and are so thirsty that you take a drink from the garden hose, you are responding to a _____ drive, according to the drive-reduction theory.
   - **a.** secondary
   - **b.** primary
   - **c.** homeostasis
   - **d.** instinctual

4. One limitation of the drive reduction theory is the inability to explain people's motivation to _____.
   - **a.** drink when they are thirsty
   - **b.** maintain a balance in their lives
   - **c.** restore homeostasis
   - **d.** increase arousal and disrupt homeostasis

5. Yanni feels at his best when he has a challenging rock face to climb. He loves the feeling of exhilaration he gets when he attempts a difficult climb, but he has a hard time staying motivated when he has to read an article assigned by his biology professor. What theory would best explain Yanni's preference for risky adventures?
   - **a.** Maslow's hierarchy of needs theory
   - **b.** Drive reduction theory
   - **c.** Instinct theory
   - **d.** Optimal arousal theory

6. Eleza has been training for her 10k race for months. The morning of her race, she feels ready but has a few butterflies in her stomach. She knows she has a moderate level of nerves (arousal), which leads to the best performance, according to the _____.
   - **a.** moderate level arousal principle
   - **b.** Yerkes-Dodson Law
   - **c.** drive reduction theory
   - **d.** kick butt runner's law

Module 10.4–10.5: Hunger

Regardless of whether or not you previously felt hungry, simply seeing or smelling a favorite food like pizza can trigger sensations of hunger.

You might wonder why the topic of hunger is discussed in relation to motivation. In fact, hunger and eating behavior are great examples of how motivation has many different facets. Consider the question "why do people eat?" The simple answer is that people eat because they feel hungry. In other words, sensations of hunger *motivate* people to consume food. However, if you've ever reached for dessert after already overeating at a family holiday meal, you probably realize that hunger is not the only reason why people eat. Did you see the above photo of a pizza and feel a little twinge of hunger? Understanding the basic physiological mechanisms and social and cultural influences underlying hunger provides an example of the complexities of one of our most powerful motivated behaviors. As obesity has become an increasing public heath challenge, understanding the physiological, social, and psychological aspects of our motivation to eat has become extremely important.

Factors Influencing Hunger

LO 10.4   Identify some of the physiological, social, and cultural influences on hunger.

The experience of hunger can be triggered by both internal and external cues. For example, if you've been busy working or studying for hours, you might notice that your stomach starts to growl and your attention wonders to your next meal. These are internal cues that it's time to re-fuel. We can also experience hunger in response to external cues such as walking past a bakery and smelling freshly baked bread. These hunger signals work together in a complex interplay between physiology, social cues, and cultural influences.

THE PHYSIOLOGY OF HUNGER   If you've ever skipped breakfast before an early morning class, you've probably experienced the embarrassment of your stomach growling loud enough to alert everyone in the room of your hunger. A. L. Washburn swallowed a balloon to monitor stomach contractions and discovered that feelings of hunger did indeed correspond to stomach contractions (Cannon & Washburn, 1912). But removing the stomach in rats and humans did not eliminate hunger, leading to the need for new theories about its source.

glucose

level of blood sugar that helps determine hunger and satiety

insulin

a hormone released by the pancreas that tells the body to convert glucose to fat

lateral hypothalamus

area of the hypothalamus that controls the experience of hunger

orexin

a hormone secreted by the lateral hypothalamus that produces feelings of hunger

ventromedial hypothalamus

part of the hypothalamus that controls the experience satiety center

Hormones   Levels of blood **glucose**—blood sugar—help determine hunger and satiety (feeling full). When glucose levels drop, we feel hungry. If glucose levels rise, the hormone **insulin** is released, telling the body to convert glucose to fat. As the body monitors these chemical levels, it sends messages to the brain about whether to eat or not.

The Brain and the Dual Center Model   Early research had shown that the hypothalamus plays a role in regulating hunger according to a *dual center model*, the idea that there are two distinct "centers" in the brain; one for hunger and one for satiety. The hunger center involves the **lateral hypothalamus** where the hormone **orexin** is secreted and subsequently initiates feelings of hunger. When the lateral hypothalamus was electrically stimulated, rats that already felt full started eating. When the area was damaged or removed, even starving rats had no desire to eat (Sakurai et al., 1998). The satiety center includes the **ventromedial hypothalamus**, which suppresses hunger and sends out signals that stop an animal from eating. If the ventromedial hypothalamus is destroyed, an animal will overeat and eventually become obese. On the other hand, if the ventromedial hypothalamus is stimulated it will cause an animal to stop eating.

More recent findings have demonstrated that the process of regulating hunger and satiety in the brain is more complicated than a simple "on" switch in the lateral hypothalamus and an "off" switch in the ventromedial hypothalamus (Simpson et al., 2008). There are complex neural circuits involved in the experience of hunger (Huang, 2015; Sternson et al., 2013; Sternson & Atasoy, 2014) and specific neurotransmitters such as Neuropeptide Y (NPY) play a role in communicating the need for food to various brain regions (Bakos et al., 2016; Stanley & Leibowitz, 1985). Studies have shown that other areas of the hypothalamus are also important. For example, recent research has focused on the role of the paraventricular nucleus and the arcuate nucleus of the hypothalamus (Hussain et al., 2015; Krashes et al., 2014; Sechler et al., 2014) is also involved in hunger regulation. When the paraventricular nucleus of a rat is damaged, the rat will eat a very large quantity of food at each meal.

Lateral and Ventromedial Hypothalamus

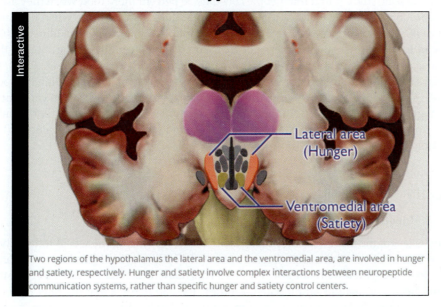

Two regions of the hypothalamus the lateral area and the ventromedial area, are involved in hunger and satiety, respectively. Hunger and satiety involve complex interactions between neuropeptide communication systems, rather than specific hunger and satiety control centers.

PSYCHOLOGICAL AND SOCIOCULTURAL INFLUENCES ON HUNGER Not all hunger originates in internal body states. Many people seem to have room for dessert even when they already feel full after a meal. In this case, the **gustatory sense**—taste—also impacts hunger. Satiety also involves sensory stimuli in the environment. The dessert looks appetizing, so we feel like eating it. Animals that eat a certain food until they feel satisfied will eat again if introduced to a novel food or taste. The sweet taste of dessert presents a new taste compared to the savory one of the meal, and therefore helps to override the messages from our brain telling us that we shouldn't eat anymore. We also appear to have an innate preference for sweet, high-fat foods because consumption of these foods would have provided an evolutionary advantage (Breslin, 2013; Drewnowski, 1997; Ulijaszek, 2002).

gustatory sense

sense of taste

Factors that Influence Eating Behavior

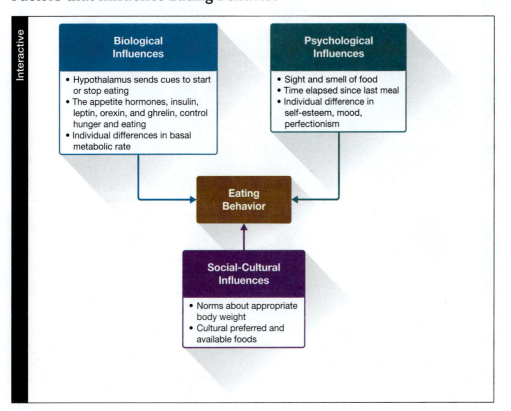

How much we eat and what types of foods we consume can also depend on the context. For example, one study found that people consume 30 percent more food when they are offered larger portion sizes (Rolls et al., 2002). Children and adults also eat more when they are in the presence of others as opposed to eating alone (Herman, 2015; Lumeng & Hillman, 2007;) and they tend to model the eating patterns of their companions (e.g., by eating more if the companion eats more and eating less if the companion eats less) (Vartanian et al., 2015). Culture also plays an important role in our selection of foods and the availability of different foods. For example, some people from Western cultures might experience disgust when confronted with the Shanghai dish chou doufu (tofu that has been fermented and has a strong odor), while many people from China experience a similar disgust reaction to the notion of eating cheese (basically made from curdled milk).

Obesity

LO 10.5   Identify some of the factors that impact obesity.

Obesity is one of the most difficult public health challenges facing the world today. The health care costs associated with obesity are estimated at $147 billion–$210 billion a year in the United States alone. Despite the number of resources contributed to combatting obesity in the form of public health campaigns and research funding, the bad news is that the rates of obesity are continuing to rise. In fact, the number of individuals classified as overweight or obese has increased approximately 40 percent between 1980 and 2013 (Ng et al., 2014).

Simply stated, obesity is caused by an imbalance between energy consumed and energy spent. However, when trying to understand the cause of obesity, the answer is far from simple. A complex interplay of biological and sociocultural factors each contribute to the current obesity epidemic.

Adult Obesity Rates in the U.S.

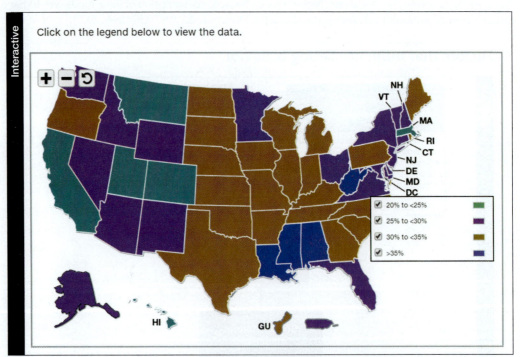

DEFINING OBESITY   Obesity is defined as an excessive accumulation of body fat and is often assessed using Body Mass Index (BMI). BMI is simply a mathematical formula that uses a ratio of height and weight to estimate a person's health status related to percentage of body at. Take a moment to calculate your own BMI and determine your BMI classification in Table 10.1.

BMI calculator

$$\text{weight (lb)} / [\text{height (in)}]^2 \times 703$$

Table 10.1 Adult Body Mass Index (BMI)

Body Mass Index (BMI) is a ratio of a person's height to weight. BMI is an indicator of level of body fat.

- If your BMI is less than 18.5, it falls within the underweight range.
- If your BMI is 18.5 to <25, it falls within the normal.
- If your BMI is 25.0 to <30, it falls within the overweight range.
- If your BMI is 30.0 or higher, it falls within the obese range.

Obesity is frequently subdivided into categories:

- Class 1: BMI of 30 to <35
- Class 2: BMI 35 to <40
- Class 3: BMI of 40 higher. Class 3 obesity is sometimes categorized as "extreme" or "severe" obesity.

BMI is not perfect when it comes to estimating weight status. It is particularly inaccurate for people whose weight may be higher than normal due to high muscle mass. For example, extreme athletes may find themselves falling into the "overweight" or "obese" categories despite having very low body fat percentages. For those individuals, more accurate methods of assessing body composition are preferable such as bioelectrical impedance (Böhm & Heitmann, 2013; Talma et al., 2013), underwater weighing (Fields et al., 2002), and dual energy x-ray absorptiometry (DXA) (Toombs et al., 2012). However, for the average individual, BMI is an efficient and accurate way to estimate weight status.

BIOLOGICAL FACTORS Simply stated, obesity is caused by an imbalance between energy consumed and energy spent. That is, consuming more calories than you burn on a regular basis. While this may seem to be a simple equation, many complex systems are involved in the regulation of eating and weight. Significant research has been conducted to try to determine the biological factors that contribute to obesity with evidence suggesting that genetics and the metabolic system both play important roles.

Twin and adoption studies along with family studies have consistently demonstrated that the heritability of obesity and BMI in general is very high (Silventoinen et al., 2010). Trying to determine exactly what role genetics plays in obesity is complicated. Monogenic obesity, or obesity caused by dysfunction of one specific gene, is very rare (e.g., estimated to affect only 1-2 percent of obese adults) (Hinney et al., 2006; Hinney et al., 2010). The most recent evidence suggests that at least 97 sites on the human genome have been linked to obesity (Albuquerque et al., 2015; Early Growth Genetics Consortium, 2012; Locke et al., 2015).

In addition to genetic contributions, the metabolic system also plays a role in obesity. **Basal metabolic rate (BMR)** is an estimate of how many calories the body burns when at rest. Basically, if you lay on the couch all day watching Netflix, your BMR is the number of calories you would burn during that day. BMR for an individual depends on a number of variables including body weight, gender, and age. **Set point theory** suggests that our body is biologically programmed to defend a certain body weight and BMR is one tool that can be used to make us burn more calories when we overeat or burn fewer calories when we don't eat enough in order to maintain the same weight (Farias, 2011; Harris, 1990). Our metabolic system relies on a variety of hormones to function properly. In the normal process of hunger regulation, the hormone *leptin* is released from the fat cells as a satiety cue to notify the brain that enough energy has been stored in the fat cells. Mice with mutated genes who are unable to produce leptin become obese, suggesting that leptin may also play a role in human obesity (Friedman & Halaas, 1998; Farooqi & O'Rahilly, 2014; Tartaglia et al., 1995). However, in obese humans, leptin levels are often high, suggesting that the brain isn't receiving the message that would signal satiety (Bouret et al., 2015; Clement et al., 1998).

basal metabolic rate (BMR)

an estimate of how many calories the body burns when at rest

set point theory

a theory that suggests that our body is biologically programmed to defend a certain body weight

A comparison of a mouse unable to produce leptin thus resulting in obesity (left) and a normal mouse (right)

SOCIOCULTURAL FACTORS The rates of obesity have increased so sharply over the past few decades that genetics and other biological explanations cannot be solely responsible for the phenomenon. The role of culture and the environment have been the primary targets in pinpointing the cause of the rising obesity epidemic. In fact, obesity rates have increased dramatically wherever Westernized diets have been introduced and assimilated. Rates of obesity in China were historically low, but over the past 30 years, China has experienced skyrocketing rates of obesity. In one rural Chinese province, the rates of overweight and obese children increased 60-fold from .5–8 percent to 20.6–30.7 percent from 1985–2014 (Zhang et al., 2016). During this same time period, it comes as no surprise that Western-style fast food restaurants (e.g., McDonald's, Kentucky Fried Chicken, Pizza Hut) have become increasingly popular in China.

There are two main environmental contributors to the obesity epidemic: (1) diets based on processed foods high in fat and carbohydrates and low on nutrients and (2) lack of physical activity. A recent study showed that approximately 60 percent of the calories consumed by people in the U.S. come from highly processed ready-to-eat foods (Poti et al., 2015). In addition to eating more highly processed foods, people are also eating more overall. From 1971–2000, the average American man consumed 168 calories more per day and the average American woman consumed 335 more calories per day (CDC, 2004). One of the challenges facing society is the fact that buying the ingredients to prepare a nutritious meal with fresh fruits and vegetables is much more expensive than consuming ready-to-eat processed foods. This economic problem is demonstrated by the fact that obesity rates are highest among people living in poverty (Levine, 2011). This problem has led some researchers and public health policy experts to advocate for increasing taxes on junk food while subsidizing fresh, nutritious foods (Franck et al., 2013).

To further exacerbate the problem of increased consumption of food, there has also been a trend toward reduced physical activity (see Figure 10.1). In 2015, a total of 81.6 million Americans above the age of 6 reported being physically inactive. As technology and economic growth has led to improvements in many areas of life, these improvements have also led to reduced physical activity at work, home, and via transportation. The importance of physical activity has been repeatedly demonstrated and one recent large-scale study demonstrated that being sedentary puts someone at more risk of death than being obese (Ekelund et al., 2015).

Figure 10.1 Inactivity Rate from 2010–2015

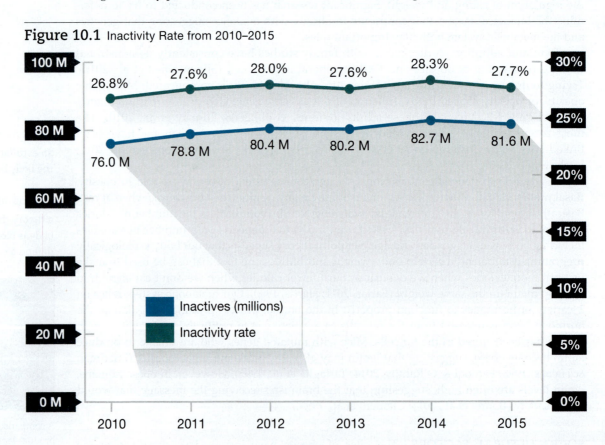

Quiz for Module 10.4–10.5

1. Which hormone in the body helps regulate hunger cues?

   a. Glucose   **b.** Cortisol

   c. Insulin   **d.** Adrenaline

2. The satiety center of the brain is located in the _____, which suppresses hunger and sends out signals that stop an animal from eating.

   a. thalamus

   b. amygdala

   c. lateral hypothalamus

   d. ventromedial hypothalamus

3. Myra just finished a big meal when her friends called and asked her to go out for ice cream. She went but didn't plan to eat anything. As soon as her friends got their ice cream cones, Myra felt hungry for ice cream. What influenced her hunger cues?

   a. Sociocultural reasons

   b. Psychological reasons

   c. Biological reasons

   d. Reduced willpower

4. What is the mathematical formula used to calculate obesity levels?

   a. BMI (body mass index)

   b. BMR (basal metabolic rate)

   c. Set point theory

   d. The water test

5. Lin Su went away to college and started eating more chips, pop tarts, and cereal. She also does not get much exercise anymore because she is studying and watching Netflix in her downtime. This is very different than her life at home where her family's diet consisted of plant-based meals and they walked and rode their bikes everywhere. As a result, she has gained 20 pounds in 6 months. These two main environmental contributors of obesity are:

   a. missing family, stress of school

   b. lack of physical activity; stress of school

   c. stress of school; diets based on processed foods

   d. diets based on processed foods; lack of physical activity

Module 10.6–10.9: Beyond Biology: Other Theories of Motivation

Humans are motivated by more than just physiological needs--they are also motivated by social and psychological needs.

So far, the theories of motivation that you learned about have focused heavily on how we are motivated by physiological states. However, most current theories of motivation also emphasize the role of psychological needs. For example, most people feel a need for love or companionship that motivates them to seek out dating partners or friendships. This type of behavior appears to be motivated by both psychological and physiological needs and the following theories attempt to incorporate both aspects of motivation.

Maslow's Hierarchy of Needs

LO 10.6 Identify Maslow's hierarchy of needs from the most basic needs to the needs highest on the pyramid.

Have you ever experienced a time in your life when you were very concerned about something (e.g., studying for final exams) one day, only to have some unexpected and life-changing event occur the next day (e.g., a house fire that destroys all your belongings)? Suddenly, those final exams seem really unimportant compared to your need to find clothes and food and a place to sleep at night. These times in our life clearly highlight that different needs take priority at different points in time.

hierarchy of needs

a model proposed by Maslow focusing on the fact that some needs must be fulfilled before we will be motivated to achieve other higher goals

In 1943, Abraham Maslow proposed that our behavior is motivated in order to fulfill a need, and the "need" that is most salient in the moment depends on what needs have previously been satisfied. Thus, he proposed the **hierarchy of needs**, a model focusing on the fact that some needs must be fulfilled before we will be motivated to achieve other higher goals. Maslow (1943) stated that "It is quite true that man lives by bread alone—when there is no bread. But what happens to man's desires when there is plenty of bread and when his belly is chronically filled?" (p. 375). According to Maslow, we can focus on higher needs only if our most basic needs have been satisfied. For example, you're unlikely to pay much attention to your need for love if you are desperate for a glass of water. Maslow's hierarchy makes sense from an evolutionary perspective: our most basic needs are those most immediately linked to survival. Maslow divided the needs into two categories: deficiency needs and growth needs. *Deficiency needs* are those that are based on a lack of something, while *growth needs* are higher up on the hierarchy and focus on the desire to grow as an individual or reach one's potential. While Maslow's original theory proposed five levels of the hierarchy, his later writings include additional levels. While there continues to be debate about whether to consider only the original five levels or to include a sixth or seventh level, recent scholars have argued that the entirety of Maslow's work appears to support the six level heirarchy above (Koltko-Rivera, 2006).

Maslow's Hierarchy of Needs

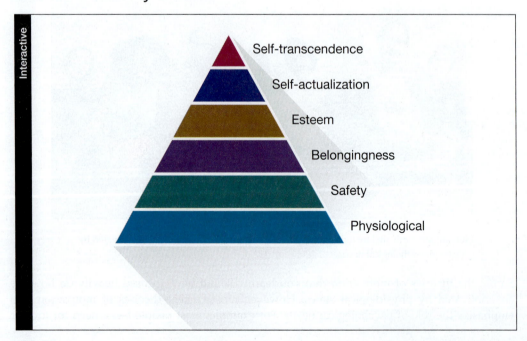

The deficiency needs include the physiological, **safety**, **belongingness**, and **esteem** needs. The highest two levels on the hierarchy include *self-actualization* and **self-transcendence**. Self-actualization is the experience of becoming your "real self" and realizing your full potential (see LO 14.3). Maslow (1970) stated that only about 2 percent of people actually become "self-actualized" and reach their true potential. He studied a group of 18 people who he considered to be self-actualized which included people like Abraham Lincoln, Albert Einstein, and Henry David Thoreau to develop a list of characteristics of self-actualized people (Maslow, 1970). These characteristics included things such as being able to perceive reality accurately, acceptance of the self and others "as is," and being problem-centered rather than self-centered.

Self-transcendence was added to the hierarchy based on Maslow's later work. While self-actualization is the process of reaching one's own personal potential, self-transcendence actually goes beyond the focus of the self. People who are already self-actualized appear to continue to move upward in the hierarchy to focus on what Maslow (1969) described as "peak experiences," or "moments of highest happiness and fulfillment" (p. 62). These experiences can be aesthetic (e.g., related to art and beauty), emotional, or mystical/spiritual. At the level of self-transcendence, people seek to engage in activities that have a higher purpose and serve the greater good.

Critiques of Maslow's theory have focused on the fact that people are often motivated to achieve higher levels on the hierarchy despite not having fulfilled something lower on the hierarchy. For example, people living in impoverished countries still report a desire for belongingness which would not be predicted by Maslow's particular order of the hierarchy (Hagerty, 1999; Soper et al., 1995; Yawson et al, 2009). Furthermore, there is ample evidence of people in concentration camps during WWII who engaged in "higher" level behaviors despite being continually threatened and malnourished. Viktor Frankl is perhaps the best example of how devastating circumstances can sometimes lead people to live at a motivational level that is much higher than expected given their circumstances. Frankl's best-selling book, *Man's Search for Meaning*, was originally published in Vienna in 1946 after he spent three years in concentration camps. His book has been considered one of the most influential books in the United States and had sold more than 10 million copies by the time he died in 1997.

self-transcendence

level six in Maslow's hierarchy of needs that focuses on the need to go beyond the self and experience oneness with the greater whole or higher truth

Adaptive Pathway 10.1: Maslow's Hierarchy of Needs

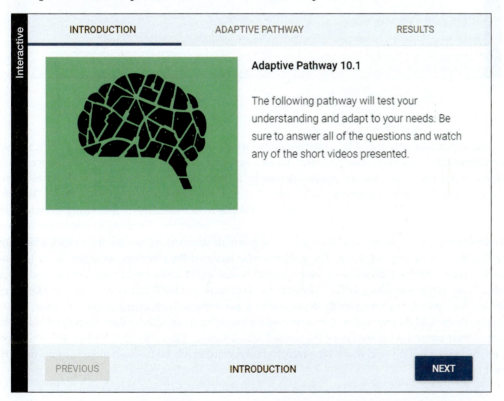

Interactive

| INTRODUCTION | ADAPTIVE PATHWAY | RESULTS |

Adaptive Pathway 10.1

The following pathway will test your understanding and adapt to your needs. Be sure to answer all of the questions and watch any of the short videos presented.

PREVIOUS   INTRODUCTION   NEXT

Intrinsic and Extrinsic Motivation

LO 10.7 **Distinguish between intrinsic motivators and extrinsic motivators.**

extrinsic motivation

when people are motivated to engage in a particular behavior to gain a reward or to avoid a negative outcome

intrinsic motivation

engaging in a behavior for the sake of enjoyment

Have you ever stopped to think about why you attend class or show up to work? You would likely think about the external motivators for these behaviors such as getting a good grade or receiving a paycheck. **Extrinsic motivation** occurs when people are motivated to engage in a particular behavior to gain some sort of reward or to avoid some negative outcome. Examples of extrinsic motivation include things such as agreeing to work a holiday for extra pay, competing in a sporting event to win an award, or doing a favor for someone to avoid his/her disapproval. People can also be motivated by internal factors. You typically do not need to offer children an external incentive to get them to play pretend games. In fact, we are often internally motivated by our own interests, desires, or values. **Intrinsic motivation** is defined as engaging in a behavior for its own sake rather than the desire to obtain an external goal or reward. Examples of intrinsically motivated behaviors are reading an article because you are curious, playing a sport because you find it exciting, or working on a project because you find it challenging.

Intrinsic or Extrinsic Motivation?

> **Read the following scenarios and type the letter "E" if it describes extrinsic motivation or "I" if it describes intrinsic motivation.**
>
> Playing a board game with friends because you enjoy the friendly competition. ☐
>
> Asking a question in class so that the teacher will praise you. ☐
>
> Washing the dishes so that your roommate will be happy. ☐
>
> Reading a book that you find interesting. ☐
>
> Start Over   Check Answers

Research suggests that there are situations when using extrinsic motivators is effective at increasing a particular behavior and other times when intrinsic motivation may be more successful. However, for behaviors that are already driven by intrinsic motivation, adding an external incentive can actually serve to decrease motivation. For example, two classic studies in the 1970s demonstrated that providing an external incentive to people who were already inherently interested in a task or activity actually reduced interest in the activity over time. Deci (1971) instructed college students to work on puzzles and then gave one group of students money for their work while not paying the other group anything. The students who received the payment were less likely to continue working on the puzzles once the payments had stopped compared to students who did not receive any payments (Deci, 1971). Furthermore, Lepper et al. (1973) found that the expectation of reward for a previously intrinsically motivated task led to the reduction in interest over time. When children were told they would receive a reward for engaging in an activity they already found interesting, their interest decreased once the reward was removed. However, the children who received a reward unexpectedly and those who received no reward at all did not lose interest in the activity over time.

While these results might seem surprising at first, they can be explained by the **overjustification effect**, or people's tendency to pay more attention to external rewards rather than their own internal motivation, leading them to assume they were only engaging in the behavior because they were receiving some sort of incentive. These findings suggest that giving rewards for behaviors that are intrinsically motivated may serve to actually reduce the motivation for the behavior in the end. This means that offering people money to do something they had been volunteering to do might make them want to do it less in the end. For example, offering children rewards for reading books they enjoy might actually lead to them have less interest in reading in the long run. Have you ever been paid for getting good grades? How would you answer a parent if they asked you "Should I pay my kids for getting good grades?"

So, are external incentives or rewards always a bad thing? Actually, there are times when using extrinsic motivation might be a good idea such as when you want to encourage a behavior or activity that is not already inherently appealing. For example, using an incentive to motivate a young child to swallow a nasty-tasting antibiotic might be a useful strategy, which is an example of positive reinforcement. Verbal rewards have actually been shown to improve intrinsic motivation under certain circumstances:

1. When the praise communicates that success is related to effort and under the person's control rather than purely about ability (e.g., "you are such a hard-worker" rather than "you are so smart")

2. When the praise provides messages of competence about the individual rather than simply a positive social comparison (e.g., "you are great at time management" rather than "you manage your time better than your coworker")

3. Praise that communicates attainable and realistic standards rather than low or unrealistically high standards (e.g., "I am impressed that you are able to consistently meet deadlines" rather than "I know I can count on you to never miss a single deadline.") In addition, rewards that are unexpected have also been shown to preserve intrinsic motivation (Deci et al., 1999; Henderlong & Lepper, 2002; Zentall & Morris, 2010, 2012).

Self-Determination Theory

LO 10.8 **Explain the roles of autonomy, relatedness, and competence in self-determination theory.**

The study of intrinsic and extrinsic motivation has expanded in recent years to focus on the specific intrinsic needs that are most likely to result in self-determination when fulfilled. Edward L. Deci and Richard Ryan proposed a model of intrinsic motivation called **self-determination theory (SDT)**. According to this theory, it is part of human nature to be "curious, vital, and self-motivated" (Ryan & Deci, 2000, p. 68), and there are environmental conditions that can act to either enhance or stifle our natural tendencies. They proposed a model including three basic, universal psychological needs that must be satisfied in order to facilitate a natural tendency toward human growth. These three needs are autonomy, relatedness, and competence.

Autonomy refers to "volition," or the ability/freedom to make your own choices (Carabelea et al., 2005; Ryan et al., 1995). Have you ever felt disinclined to do something simply because someone else told you to do it? This likely offended your sense of autonomy, or your desire to make your own decisions and to "choose your own destiny." **Relatedness** refers to the need to feel connected to other people in meaningful ways (Blatt, 2008). Why do you join organizations, take face-to-face classes, or spend time with friends and family? You are most likely behaving in response to your basic need for relatedness. Finally, **competence** is defined as the need to feel effective when interacting in the environment (Deci & Ryan, 2000; Fernandez et al., 2012; Van den Broeck et al., 2010). When people praise your skills or abilities, it is especially gratifying because of our need to feel competent in our activities.

overjustification effect

when an external incentive is added to behaviors that are already driven by intrinsic motivation, thereby decreasing internal motivation

self-determination theory (SDT)

theory that all humans have three universal psychological needs including autonomy, relatedness, and competence that must be satisfied in order to facilitate a natural tendency toward human growth

autonomy

the need to be causal agents of one's own life without being controlled by others

relatedness

the need to feel connected to other people in meaningful ways

competence

the need to feel effective when interacting in the environment

Self-Determination Theory

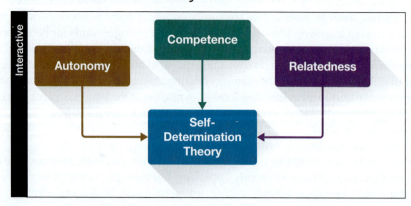

Self-determination theory proposes that under the right circumstances, these three basic psychological needs will be satisfied. When these needs are fulfilled, there are a number of positive outcomes (Vansteenkist & Ryan, 2013), including increased self-esteem (Deci et al., 2001), reduced levels of the stress hormone cortisol (Quested et al., 2011), and greater feelings of gratitude (Weinstein et al., 2010) across a variety of domains including at work (Van den Broeck et al., 2010), at school (Vlachopoulos et al., 2011), and in sports (Lonsdale & Hodge, 2011). On the other hand, if people are frustrated in their ability to satisfy their needs for autonomy, competence, and relatedness, studies have shown a variety of negative outcomes such as increased psychological distress (Soenens et al., 2008; Soenens et al., 2008), dissatisfaction at work (Ferner et al., 2013; Vander Elst et al., 2012), and diminished motivation and well-being (Ryan & Deci, 2000).

One explanation for the negative impact of providing external incentives on intrinsic motivation is the notion that it undermines autonomy. Studies have shown that restricting and controlling environments that stifle autonomy can decrease intrinsic motivation (e.g., Amabile et al., 1976; Gagne & Deci, 2005) while environments that allow people to make free choices tend to increase intrinsic motivation (Amabile, 1993; Cho & Perry, 2012; Deci et al., 1989; Zuckerman et al., 1978). This theory helps explain why people find it so difficult to maintain their motivation to exercise or engage in physical activity. Many times, people have external reasons for exercising such as to lose weight or change their body shape/size, and people often report that they exercise out of necessity rather than internal desire (Teixeira et al., 2010). In addition, people who are not physically active can question their own competence and experience the feeling that "I am not good at it." In fact, research has suggested that people who experience autonomous motivation to exercise, and have goals related to affiliation and skill development are more likely to engage in exercise behavior (Teixeira et al., 2012).

There has been significant evidence across different populations and settings in support of self-determination theory. One question that has been debated within the field is the cross-cultural generalizability of self-determination. Is this model most appropriate for individuals in Western cultures? Or, is this theory more universal in describing motivation in both Eastern and Western cultures? This question remains important as some studies have demonstrated support of the model cross-culturally (e.g., Church et al., 2013; Deci et al., 2001; Nie et al., 2015; Ryan & Deci, 2016) while other work has questioned the validity of the theory among Eastern cultures (e.g., Iyengar & Lepper, 1999).

Dweck's Self-Theory of Motivation

LO 10.9 **Summarize Dweck's self-theory of motivation.**

Do you think that believing in your own abilities will help you become a successful student? Carol Dweck's self-theory of motivation proposes that such a belief in your own abilities may actually backfire when you are confronted with a challenging class or an academic failure. Dweck (2000) suggests that successful people have "*mastery-oriented*" qualities that include a love of learning, seeking challenges, valuing effort, and persistence in the face of obstacles. Her research has focused on the identification of beliefs that people hold about themselves that serve to either enhance or diminish mastery-orientation. This theory stems from the notion that people hold different beliefs about the nature of intelligence. People who have a **fixed mindset** of

fixed mindset

the belief that our abilities are inborn and unchangeable

intelligence view intellectual ability as "an entity that dwells within us that we cannot change." On the other hand, people who prescribe to the **growth mindset** of intelligence believe that intellectual ability is a malleable construct that can be changed with effort. The Khan Academy's slogan of "You Can Learn Anything" is a testament to its growth mindset related to intelligence.

Take a moment and try to imagine the consequences of holding either belief. The following provides you with several different academic scenarios. Try to hypothesize how you would react differently to each scenario based on whether you hold a fixed mindset or growth mindset view of intelligence.

growth mindset
the belief that one's abilties can be developed through effort and dedication

Fixed vs. Growth Mindset

Read the following scenarios and type the letter "F" if it describes a fixed mindset or "G" if it describes a growth mindset.

You fail a test and think "I am not smart enough and I probably shouldn't be in this class/major/university."

When deciding between an easy class and a hard class you conclude: "The only way I will increase my intelligence is to challenge myself and put a lot of effort into my classwork—so the easy class would be a waste of time."

After failing a test, you think to yourself: "I definitely need to put more effort into this in order to be successful next time."

When faced with a task that requires significant effort you think: "If I have to put a lot of effort into something, it means I didn't have enough ability to succeed easily."

Start Over   Check Answers

Diener and Dweck (1978, 1980) studied a group of fifth and sixth graders by giving them a set of problems that included eight that were solvable and four that were too difficult to solve. They examined how the students approached and persisted on the difficult problems and considered the students' thoughts and feelings while working on the problems. They found that about half of the students demonstrated a "mastery response" while the other half demonstrated a "helpless response." The students who demonstrated helplessness were quick to make negative comments about their own abilities/intelligence and they even lost faith in their ability to complete the easy tasks that they had just successfully completed. These children also experienced a biased perception of their own performance. Despite having answered two-thirds of the problems correctly, the students who responded with helplessness believed they had answered more problems incorrectly than correctly. On the other hand, students who showed a mastery response did not give up easily, remained confident about their success, and thrived on the challenging aspect of the difficult problems. It is important to note that these students did not differ in terms of their *actual* ability to complete the tasks (their performance on the easy tasks was equivalent) but their internal interpretation of the reason for their success or failure had a significant impact on their mood, persistence, and future success.

In fact, research supports the notion that people's beliefs about intelligence can significantly impact their success (Bandura, 1993; Hossein et al., 2011). Dweck's self-theory suggests that even the most gifted students might struggle if they have too much "easy" success early on. If someone has always found academic tasks to be easy and require little effort, that person runs the risk of feeling incapable of persisting when challenged or demoralized in the face of failure due to a fixed mindset approach to intelligence. Additionally, providing praise to children about being "smart" or possessing other positive "entities" such as being "good at math" or having an "advanced vocabulary" might actually lead them to adopt a fixed mindset of intelligence. When those children are confronted with challenges or failures, they will tend to interpret the fact that they are struggling as threatening. Instead, praising a child for effort or persistence will likely lead them to be more likely to confront difficulties as a challenge and an opportunity for growth.

Shared Writing Prompt: What's Your Mindset?

It's likely that you have a fixed mindset about some of your abilities and a growth mindset about others. Describe one example of each type of mindset in your life, and explain how this mindset has affected the way you have responded to a challenge or failure.

Quiz for Module 10.6–10.9

1. Fredrick has so many student loans, he can't afford rent on an apartment. Most of the time, he lives in his car and even though he has a job, he can't seem to make enough to save for the deposit and rent payments. He rarely gets a full night's sleep and as a result he has difficulty concentrating at work. He is jumpy and scared at night and worried all the time. Fredrick is struggling to fulfill which two of Maslow's needs?

   a. Physiological; self-actualization
   b. Safety, belongingness
   c. Physiological; safety
   d. Esteem; safety

2. Maslow's hierarchy was based on two categories of needs that included _____ and _____.

   a. biological needs; esteem needs
   b. growth needs; biological needs
   c. deficiency needs; esteem needs
   d. deficiency needs; growth needs

3. Macy decides to eat all the vegetables on her plate so she can get a cookie after dinner. What type of motivation is Macy responding to?

   a. Extrinsic
   b. Intrinsic
   c. Reinforcers
   d. Natural consequences

4. Harry loves to read and will do it on his own without his mother telling him to read. This is an example of what type of motivation?

   a. Extrinsic
   b. Intrinsic
   c. Internal
   d. Basic

5. Shakir has always been good at math. She usually earns the top score on her math tests. When she took a standardized math test and only received an 85 percent, she felt horrible for a week and refused to leave her room. Shakir's need for _____ was shaken.

   a. autonomy
   b. relatedness
   c. competence
   d. self-esteem

6. A college student's desire to join organizations and hang out with friends is explained through which self-determination need?

   a. Social
   b. Relatedness
   c. Competence
   d. Autonomy

7. Dweck's 4 mastery-oriented qualities include a love of learning, _____, valuing effort, and _____.

   a. seeking challenges; persistence in the face of obstacles
   b. being good at learning; believing in your self
   c. high intelligence; high self-esteem
   d. believing in yourself; persistence

8. Omar failed his first psychology test and thought "I'm just not smart enough for college." This is an example of what type of mindset according to Dweck's self-theory of motivation?

   a. Fixed
   b. Growth
   c. Set
   d. Changing

Module 10.10–10.12: Components of Emotion

valence

a positive or negative value along a continuum assigned to an emotion

All emotions have a **valence**, a positive or negative value along a continuum, and an arousal level. An unpleasant feeling, anger has a negative valence. As a strong emotion, its high arousal makes you act quickly in a threatening situation. Because people don't enjoy feeling bored, boredom would have a negative valence but a low arousal, as a low-energy emotion. By contrast, elation has a positive valence and a high arousal; an elated person feels happy and excited. Sadness has a negative valence and low arousal, sadness feels unpleasant but does not feel particularly stimulating.

Arousal and Valence

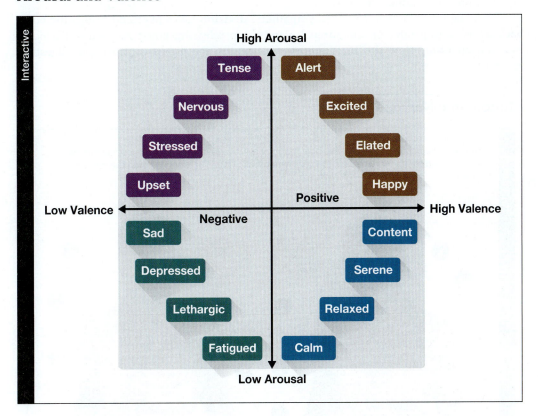

Emotion also includes three distinct but related parts: *physiological arousal, expressive behavior*, and *cognitive experience*. If your heart pounds in fear as you walk to the edge of a diving board or you feel choked up watching a sad movie, you are experiencing physiological arousal. If you turn around and run back down the diving board ladder or cry during the film, you are exhibiting expressive behaviors. Your cognitive experience on the diving board might include telling yourself "I'm such a chicken" or while watching the sad movie you might think "I know exactly how that character feels."

Physiology and Emotions

LO 10.10 **Identify the biological factors associated with emotions.**

Although emotions may seem entirely psychological in nature, the experience of a particular emotion is actually associated with a series of biological events.

EMOTIONS AND THE NERVOUS SYSTEM: FIGHT OR FLIGHT If you've ever had a near-miss car accident, you've experienced the sudden physiological response we call the "fight-or-flight" response. Your heart starts pounding in your chest, your breathing becomes rapid and shallow, you shake uncontrollably, and you may even start to sweat. When this fight-or-flight response occurs, the *autonomic nervous system (ANS)* prepares our bodies for action and controls unconscious processes such as perspiration and respiration (see LO 2.5). The two divisions of the autonomic nervous system help us prepare for and recover from emotionally charged actions.

To prepare for action, the *sympathetic division* of the ANS initiates the fight-or-flight response. This system does its work primarily through spinal neurons and connections to peripheral sympathetic ganglia. When the sympathetic nervous system is stimulated, it induces a cascade of adrenaline from the adrenal medulla. The binding of adrenaline to adrenergic receptors throughout the body results in the fight-or-flight response. The firing of sympathetic neurons, along with the release of adrenaline, causes dilated pupils, decreased salivation, increased perspiration and respiration, accelerated heart rate, and inhibited digestion. From an evolutionary perspective, these changes allow the body to be optimally prepared to either fight off another predator or flee as fast as possible. Of course, in the event of a near-miss car accident, the fight-or-flight response may not be particularly helpful. But, if you find yourself in a burning

parasympathetic division

division of the autonomic nervous system that brings the body back to its resting rate following the fight-or-flight response

building or hear someone trying to break into your house, this state of arousal would likely be very helpful in preparing you to act.

Once the crisis is over, the **parasympathetic division** takes over and brings the body back to its resting rate. As the adrenal glands stop releasing stress hormones, the heart rate and breathing slow down, perspiration decreases, the pupils contract, and digestion resumes.

Autonomic Nervous System

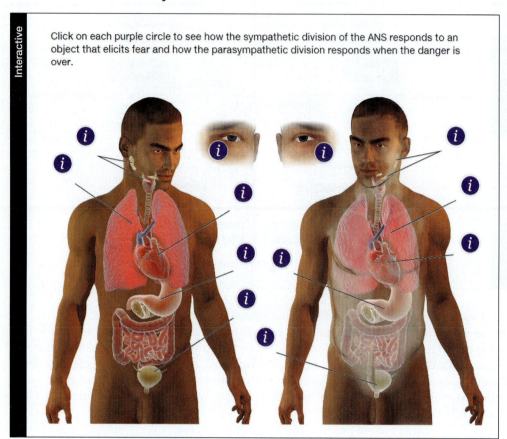

Click on each purple circle to see how the sympathetic division of the ANS responds to an object that elicits fear and how the parasympathetic division responds when the danger is over.

exposure effect

when the familiarity of a stimulus primes us to react with a certain emotion

rapid subcortical pathway

the "low road" where messages are sent directly from the thalamus to the amygdala without going to the cortex, enabling quick behavioral responses without first making a cognitive interpretation

slower cortical pathway

the "high road" where messages are sent from the thalamus to the visual cortex and then back to the amygdala, allowing your perceptions (or interpretations) to affect your emotions

EMOTIONS AND THE BRAIN Robert Zajonc argued that some emotional reactions can bypass our conscious minds (1980, 1984). A flashed image of a smiling or angry face influenced people's emotions, although they had no conscious awareness of having seen the face (Duckworth et al., 2002; Murphy et al., 1995). Prior experience of a stimulus causes an **exposure effect**; the familiarity of the stimulus primes us to react a certain way (Zajonc, 1968).

Some messages can go directly to the amygdala, a structure in the brain essential for unconscious emotional responses such as the fight-or-flight response, leaving our cortex to process the information afterward (see LO 2.8). More messages go to the cortex from the amygdala than the other way around. The amygdala receives projections from sensory organs via the thalamus, the brain's message-directing center, by way of the **rapid subcortical pathway**, which has also been referred to as the "low road" by neuroscientist Joseph LeDoux (Le Doux, 1994). The amygdala can analyze sensory data even before it reaches the cortex. If you hear a loud noise, the thalamus may direct that message directly to the amygdala so that you feel startled and jump. You might turn around and see that the loud noise came from the wind slamming a door shut, and you would relax. In that case, the **slower cortical pathway** or the "high road" would have sent messages from the thalamus to the visual cortex and then back to the amygdala, allowing your perceptions (or interpretations) to affect your emotions (see Figure 10.2).

Figure 10.2 High Road vs Low Road

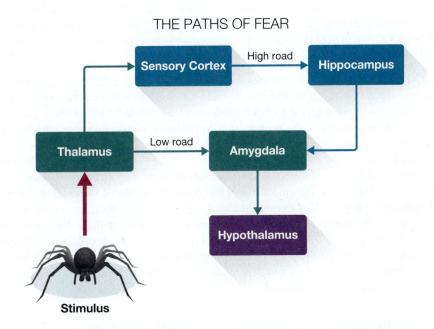

THE PATHS OF FEAR

A famous study examined the amygdala in monkeys to determine the impact of removing this part of the brain on the experience of emotions. When researchers removed monkeys' amygdalae and parts of their temporal lobes, the monkeys had an extraordinary response. They developed what is called *psychic blindness*—they saw and approached objects that ordinarily would frighten them (e.g., a rubber snake) but seemed to feel no fear or anger and became indifferent to the object's emotional significance (Kluver & Bucy, 1937).

At the anterior of the frontal lobes, the prefrontal cortex is essential for the cognitive experience of emotion. As a treatment for severe mental disorders, from 1949 to 1952, about 50,000 people in the United States, including John F. Kennedy's sister Rosemary, received **prefrontal lobotomies** (NPR, 2005). Disabling the prefrontal area of the brain left people feeling less intense emotions but also unable to plan or manage their lives. Because the prefrontal cortex receives input from the amygdala and the somatosensory cortex in the parietal lobes, emotion may be essential to the prefrontal cortex's ability to carry out the life functions it controls, such as planning, setting goals, and reasoning.

Just as your heart might pound as a result of nervousness over an exam or an attractive person, arousal levels for many emotions are similar. Many emotions have physiological similarities. Being ecstatic about winning the lottery produces the same heart rate increase as the fear you might feel while running away from a wild animal. So how can you tell if you're feeling ecstatic or afraid?

You might want to think of emotions as recipes: Each emotion is made up of different physiological ingredients that set it apart. Anger changes finger temperature more than joy or sadness. Anger, fear, or sadness, will increase your heart rate far more than happiness, surprise, or disgust. Fear moves different muscles in the face than joy, and the amygdala becomes much more active in someone looking at a fearful rather than an angry face.

Positive and negative emotions also engage different sides of the brain. Negativity, such as resentment or guilt, activates the right side of the prefrontal cortex more than the left. Depressed people often show less activity in the left side of the frontal cortex, which is associated with positive emotions. Electrical stimulation of the nucleus accumbens in depressed people releases dopamine and triggers smiling and laughing.

prefrontal lobotomies
psychosurgery in which the connection between the frontal lobes and the parts of the brain that control emotions is severed

Behavior and Emotion

LO 10.11   Identify some of the ways we detect and express emotions.

What is the "behavior" of emotions? Aren't emotions an internal experience? Think for a moment about the emotion of sadness. How would another person be able to detect that you are feeling sad? Likely you would give some nonverbal cues about your internal experience. For example, you might hang your head, droop your shoulders, draw down the corners of your mouth, or even cry. These nonverbal cues are often called "body language" and it's impressive how much we're able to communicate to each other about our emotional states without words: With just a "look," two people who know each other well can communicate when they want to leave a party or if they are annoyed by a comment.

FACIAL EXPRESSIONS   Facial expressions are strong communicators of emotional states. In *The Expression of the Emotions in Man and Animals*, Charles Darwin's **universality hypothesis** proposed that facial expressions are understood across all cultures (1872/1965). Past research conducted by Ekman supports the universality hypothesis, suggesting that certain facial expressions may be universally associated with specific emotions across cultures (Ekman & Friesen, 1971; Ekman & Friesen, 1975; Ekman et al., 1987; Ekman, 1994). Blind children who have never seen facial expressions will express emotions with the same expressions as sighted people, a fact that argues for the innate biological basis of emotional expression (Matsumoto, 2009). Ekman and Friesen (1971) examined facial expressions of emotions across a variety of cultures including preliterate areas of New Guinea to determine if there are universal facial expressions or if these are simply learned through exposure to other people and cultures. Their results confirmed their hypotheses, demonstrating that people could universally identify six facial expressions. Click on the link and see if you can identify the original six universal expressions that Ekman and Friesen proposed.

universality hypothesis

Darwin's hypothesis that facial expressions are understood across all cultures

Simulate: Recognizing Facial Expressions of Emotions

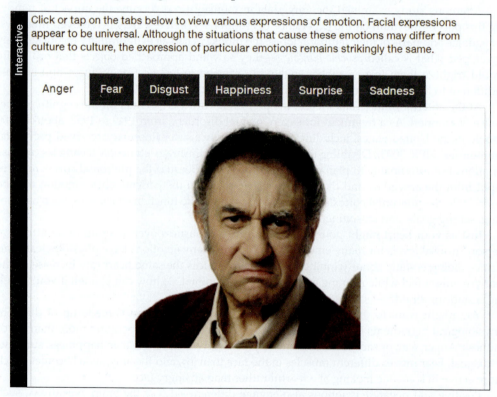

Interactive

Click or tap on the tabs below to view various expressions of emotion. Facial expressions appear to be universal. Although the situations that cause these emotions may differ from culture to culture, the expression of particular emotions remains strikingly the same.

| Anger | Fear | Disgust | Happiness | Surprise | Sadness |

Ekman later expanded the list of basic emotions to include amusement, contempt, contentment, embarrassment, excitement, guilt, pride in achievement, relief, satisfaction, sensory pleasure, and shame. After 40 years of research on emotions, Ekman's most recent (1999) theories focus heavily on the evolutionary perspective. He argued that the human species developed specific ways of responding to life tasks over time. For example, dealing with rivals, facing danger, and parental devotion are not modern situations. Rather, humans have experienced these events throughout time and the associated emotional responses have been passed down through the ages.

While the notion of universal facial expressions of emotions has been widely accepted and disseminated, a recent study actually challenged Ekman's findings. Gendron et al., (2014) used a different paradigm to evaluate the universality hypothesis. Most prior research had people from different cultures match images of facial expressions to words describing emotion (e.g., "angry"). Gendron and her colleagues argued that this provided a conceptual context for participants to interpret the facial expressions. When her research team had people from Namibia sort images of different facial expressions into piles by emotion type, they found that the piles did not conform to the universally hypothesized categories. This recent finding highlights the fact that sometimes a simple change in methodology can lead to new discussions and research about theories that previously seemed to be widely embraced.

Interestingly, not all expressions draw our attention equally. We seem to have radar for threats and will more easily pick out angry faces from a set of different facial expressions (Fox et al., 2000; Hansen & Hansen, 1988; LoBue et al., 2013). Experience also influences which emotions we see more easily. When shown a picture of a face that combined fear, sadness, and anger, physically abused children more frequently classified the expression as angry (Pollak et al., 2000).

Gender also informs how we read and express emotions. When it comes to expression of specific emotions, women have demonstrated the ability to express happiness better than men, and men have expressed anger better than women (Becker et al., 2007; Coats & Feldman, 1996). Studies have also shown that there are likely sex differences in the perception of facial expressions. In general, women can detect and interpret nonverbal cues better than men (Hall, 1984, 1987; McClure, 2000). There are also gender differences in the perception of specific emotional cues. For example, Williams and Mattingley (2006) demonstrated that men were able to detect angry male faces more quickly than women, but women were quicker to detect happy, sad, surprised, or disgusted faces. Click on the following interactive for a simulation of the types of stimuli used in studies examining people's abilities to detect and express different emotions.

Gender and Emotion Detection

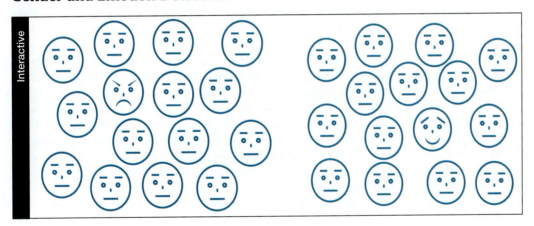

These results suggest that there are sex differences in the perception of emotional cues. While men and women appear to have different abilities when it comes to detecting emotions, are there gender differences in the ways that men and women actually experience emotions? The answer to this question depends. Some research suggests that women report experiencing more empathy (understanding and sharing the feelings of others) than men. However, actual physiological measures or secret observations of nonverbal cues do not support such sex differences (Eisenberg & Lennon, 1983; Michalsak et al., 2013). This means that the subjective experience of emotion (e.g., how much you *think* you feel a certain emotion) may not be the same as objective measures of emotions (e.g., heart rate, facial expressions).

CULTURE AND EMOTIONAL EXPRESSION   Although facial expressions may be universal, physical gestures and degree of emotional expression vary among cultures. For instance, Norwegians who saw President George Bush's 2005 inauguration interpreted his University of Texas "Hook 'em Horns" salute as the sign of the devil. The "A-OK" hand gesture or showing someone a "thumbs-up" in the United States indicates agreement or a positive communication. However, these same hand gestures in many other countries are the equivalent of showing someone the middle finger in the United States.

There are also cultural differences in what type of emotional expressions are viewed as acceptable or unacceptable. Cultural display rules are defined as culturally prescribed rules that influence the degree and type of emotional expressions (Matsumoto & Hwand, 2012). For example, one study demonstrated that Japanese display rules were different from North American display rules such that powerful emotions were seen as less acceptable and positive emotions in general were expressed less often (Sadfar et al., 2009).

DECEPTIVE EXPRESSION   Interestingly, expressions of genuine emotions actually differ from false ones (Bartlett et al., 2014; Calvo et al., 2013; Porter & Ten Brinke, 2008). If you are pleased to see someone but act overjoyed, you're showing *intensification*, exaggerating your emotions. In public, someone feeling intense grief might find it necessary to use *deintensification* to mute some of their emotions in order to be sociable. Showing one emotion while feeling another is called **masking**. Poker players routinely maintain the "poker face," neutralizing whatever they feel, so their opponents have no clues about their hands.

False expressions involve different muscle groups than real ones, and studying their *morphology*, or shape, can tell us if the expressions are real. Sincere emotions have more symmetry than insincere ones, so both sides of the face show the same expression equally. Real expressions last about half a second; false ones can have a longer or shorter duration. Temporal patterning also differs in false and real emotions; sincere expressions come and go smoothly, but insincere ones start and end abruptly (Frank et al., 1993).

What about detecting truth from lies? **Polygraph tests** are machines designed to measure physiological characteristics including heart rate/blood pressure, skin conductivity, and respiration. Based on these measurements, the polygraph is designed to assist in making inferences about the truthfulness of a person's statement. The theory underlying polygraph machines is that when someone lies, his or her body shows signs of arousal, which the polygraph test measures. However, since many emotions evoke physiological arousal, a person feeling nervous or afraid may appear to be lying. Conversely, spies famously tricked polygraphs because they knew how to control their physiological reactions or confuse results by showing arousal for baseline questions. Because of the concerns about the unreliability of polygraph tests, they are not currently admissible in a court of law (APA, 2004).

masking

when you express one emotion outwardly while experiencing a different emotion internally

polygraph tests

machines designed to measure physiological characteristics including heart rate/blood pressure, skin conductivity, and respiration in order to make inferences about the truthfulness of a person's statement

Cognition and Emotion

LO 10.12   Explain how our thoughts can influence our emotions.

Cognition, or thought, can influence what we feel or believe we feel. Interestingly, our thoughts are so powerful in influencing our emotional experiences that we can feel extremely fearful in a situation that is not actually threatening, or we can feel calm in a situation that is actual very dangerous. As a college senior, one of the authors (BW) was flying on an airplane with the university basketball team. As the plane was landing, there were some loud bumps and a cracking noise before the plane came to a stop. The passengers had to deplane on the runway where they were surrounded by police and fire trucks, and the runway was in rubble. It became clear that the pilots had landed at the wrong airport with a runway that was far too short for the large jet. Not a single person on the plane had been afraid during the landing due to their lack of awareness of the situation, but it turned out to be very lucky that there was not a major crash. On the other hand, many people experience extreme anxiety while flying because of their fearful thoughts about a possible plane crash, despite the fact that most of the time, the situation poses less real threat than driving a car every day. The difference between these situations lies not only in the presence of a real or imagined threat, but also in the way that people interpret the events. In essence, thinking fearful thoughts can lead to, or intensify, the emotional experience of fear.

Arousal from one event can spill also over into the emotions we experience about other events. For example, if someone insults you just after you've completed a long run, you might react more angrily than usual because your body is physiologically aroused from physical exercise. Misattribution sometimes leads people to attribute their arousal to the wrong stimulus. In a classic study, Dutton and Aron (1974) had an attractive female confederate (a member of the research team) approach male participants to complete a questionnaire. The participants were interviewed while either walking across a very tall suspension bridge or once they had reached the end of the bridge and had rested. The female confederate told all of the participants that she would be available for any follow-up questions and provided the men with her name and phone number. As shown in Figure 10.3, they found that the men who were interviewed while walking across the suspension bridge were more likely to call the female and ask her out on a date following the study than the participants who were interviewed after they had reached the end of the bridge. The authors hypothesized that the physiological arousal (e.g., increased heart rate, rapid breathing) of walking on the tall bridge led men to misattribute their feelings to attraction to the female interviewer. In essence, the men found themselves physiologically aroused, and they assumed their arousal must be caused by attraction to the female confederate. This research certainly has implications for dating. If you really want someone to like you, don't take them out to a quiet romantic dinner. Instead, take them somewhere that will get their adrenaline flowing such as riding roller coasters, watching a horror film, or even skydiving. You might be able to capitalize on a misattribution so that the person assumes their arousal is associated with attraction to you!

Figure 10.3 Dutton & Aron (1974) Bridge Study

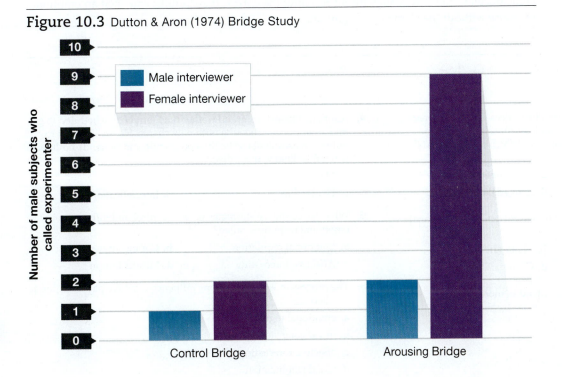

mood-congruent processing

the tendency to selectively perceive stimuli congruent with one's emotional state

Sometimes our emotions can influence what we choose to perceive through **mood-congruent processing**. Depressed patients noticed stimuli related to sadness more than to other emotions (Elliott et al., 2002; Erickson et al., 2005). Have you ever noticed that when you're in a bad mood, it seems like nothing goes right? In part, this could be a result of mood-congruent processing. When you are already feeling irritable, you pay much more attention to the person who cuts you off in traffic. When your mood is content, you are much less likely to pay attention to the rude driver. Research suggests that in general, people will selectively perceive stimuli congruent with their emotional state (Cacioppo et al, 2000; Joormann & Arditte, 2013).

Journal Prompt: The Impact of Emotions

Write about a time when your own emotions (positive or negative) changed how you perceived a situation.

---

emotion regulation

the use of cognitive strategies to control and influence our own emotional responses

When we engage in **emotion regulation**, we use cognitive strategies to control and influence our own emotional responses. For example, if you see your boyfriend or girlfriend animatedly talking to another person, you could stop yourself from feeling jealous or worried by reappraising the situation and deciding that talking does not necessarily indicate romantic involvement. Teaching emotion regulation strategies is a core component of treatment for borderline personality disorder. In fact, the emotion dysregulation characteristic of individuals with borderline personality disorder has been linked to an exaggerated amygdala response to emotional stimuli (Hazlett et al., 2012; Koenigsberg et al., 2014). It has recently been found that after patients learn improved emotion regulation strategies, they experience a reduction in amygdala overactivity when confronted with emotional stimuli (Goodman et al., 2014). Thoughts can also help us make better decisions. You might have perused college Web sites to decide where to apply and imagined yourself as a student at each school. If so, you engaged in **affective forecasting**, imagining how you would feel about something that might happen in the future.

affective forecasting

predictions about one's future emotional state

Sometimes emotions do not reach our cognitive pathways or even have a cognitive element at all. People tend to prefer an image they have seen before, even if they didn't know they saw it (Elliott & Dolan, 1998). Since the message about the stimulus goes directly from the thalamic nuclei to the amygdala without reaching the cortex, the stimulus can elicit an emotional response without the element of cognition.

Quiz for Module 10.10–10.12

1. Adaline is watching a horror movie. She notices that in response to the scary scenes, her heart races and her muscles tense. She knows this is the fight-or-flight response. Which part of the ANS activates these reactions?

   a. Parasympathetic division   **b.** Sympathetic division

   c. Adrenal medulla   **d.** Amygdala

2. Which part of the brain is essential in our unconscious emotional responses?

   a. Amygdala   **b.** Thalamus

   c. Visual cortex   **d.** Cortex

3. Which emotions do people seem to attend to more easily?

   a. Disgust and shame

   b. Sadness and fear

   c. Joy and happiness

   d. Anger and fear

4. Samra just heard his grandmother died, but he is scheduled to go into an important meeting with new clients. He really needs to impress these clients so he puts on a smile and pretends nothing is wrong. What is this called?

   a. Masking   **b.** Deception

   c. Leadership   **d.** Intensification

5. What are cognitive strategies used to control and influence our emotional responses called?

   a. Emotional regulation   **b.** Coping strategies

   c. Affective forecasting   **d.** Misattribution

6. The process in which emotions influence what we pay attention to is called _____.

   a. emotional regulation

   b. mood congruent processing

   c. affective forecasting

   d. mood stabilization

Module 10.13–10.14: Theories of Emotion

The same physiological emotional response (e.g., crying) can be triggered by very different experiences.

Emotions have a physiological, behavioral, and cognitive component, but exactly how do these three factors interact to produce our experience of emotions? Do we cry because we are sad, or are we sad because we are crying? Because there is so much overlap in the physiological aspects of different emotions, how do we differentiate between fear, anger, or even love? After all, each of these three emotions can leave us with our hearts pounding and feeling short of breath. Do we think about a situation and then communicate the resulting emotion through our facial expressions? Several theories of emotions help provide answers to these questions.

Historical Theories: James-Lange and Cannon-Bard

LO 10.13   Differentiate between the James-Lange and Cannon-Bard theories of emotion.

Many psychologists have attempted to answer the question of whether the physiological experience, the expression, or the awareness of an emotion comes first and produces the other parts.

JAMES-LANGE THEORY   At the end of the 19th century, American psychologist William James and Danish physiologist Carl Lange both simultaneously, but independently, arrived at the same theory of emotion. They believed the physiological experience of emotion precedes our cognitive understanding of it. Instead of fear causing your heart to race or sadness causing tears to flow, the **James-Lange theory** proposes that the physiological experience of heart pounding or tears flowing causes you to feel afraid or sad (James, 1890/1950; Lange, 1887).

One avenue for testing the James-Lange theory has been through spinal cord injury patients. Essentially, James-Lange's theory suggests that people who suffer a spinal cord injury impacting the sympathetic nervous system will have less intense emotional experiences. However, in studies examining the emotional experience of individuals with spinal cord injuries, no differences were found between people with or without spinal cord injuries in terms of arousal, valence, or intensity of the emotion (Cobos et al., 2002). Despite the lack of strong empirical support, current researchers in the field of emotion have credited the James-Lange theory with highlighting the importance of physiological sensations in the experience of emotion (Dalgliesh, 2004).

CANNON-BARD THEORY   Walter Cannon and Philip Bard, on the other hand, believed that physiological reactions were not a prerequisite for emotional experiences. According to

James-Lange theory of emotion
theory that emotions are the result of physiological arousal

William James and Carl Lange (pictured here) argued that physiological experience precedes emotion. In other words, you experience the emotion of sadness because you are crying.

Cannon-Bard theory

proposes that the cognitive and physiological components of emotions happen simultaneously

Walter Cannon (pictured here) along with Philip Bard, argued that emotional perception and physiological arousal occur simultaneously. In other words, you experience sadness and begin to cry at the same time.

two-factor theory

theory developed by Schachter and Singer that the cognitive evaluation following physiological arousal leads to the experience of emotion

the **Cannon-Bard theory**, the mental and physiological components of emotions happen simultaneously (Cannon, 1927). Cannon and Bard argued that the James-Lange theory was inaccurate because (1) emotion can still exist even when access to physiological sensations is denied, and (2) the physiology of different emotions is too subtle to account for the richness of emotional experiences reported by people. To test this first assumption, Cannon removed the sympathetic nervous system from cats and showed that cats continued to demonstrate emotional responses such as anger in response to a barking dog (Cannon, 1927).

The Cannon-Bard theory also has some support from basic neuroscience regarding the way that sensory information is transmitted. When some form of external stimulation occurs (e.g., seeing an oncoming car), sensory information is transmitted to the thalamus. The thalamus then relays that information to both the autonomic nervous system and the cerebral cortex. The stimulation of the autonomic nervous system leads to increased physiological arousal (e.g., increased heart rate, tensing of muscles) while simultaneously, the stimulation of the cerebral cortex leads to the perception of emotion (e.g., fear).

Modern Theories

LO 10.14   Distinguish between the two-factor theory, the cognitive mediational theory, and the facial feedback hypothesis of emotion.

In addition to the James-Lange and Cannon-Bard theories of emotion, more recent theories have focused on the role of cognition in our experience of emotion.

SCHACHTER AND SINGER'S TWO-FACTOR THEORY   In the 1960s, Stanley Schachter and Jerome Singer (1962) developed the **two-factor theory of emotion**, which states that the cognitive evaluation following physiological arousal creates the emotion we experience. Labels become important since physiological experiences can be very similar. For example, if you encounter a man holding a gun, you are likely to experience a racing heart and rapid breathing. The two-factor theory of emotion states that you will interpret these sensations in light of the original stimulus (e.g., the man holding a gun) and label the experience as "fear." However, if you had encountered a man yelling racial slurs and then noticed the same sensations (e.g., heart racing and rapid breathing), you might be more likely to label the experience "anger." Having to decide what emotion a physiological response indicates could lead to misattribution. If you are taking an exam while sitting next to someone, you might think you feel attracted to that person, when in fact you are simply terrified of failing the exam.

Support for this theory was found in the early work of Schachter and Singer (1962). Some participants in this famous study were told they were receiving a vitamin injection when they actually received an injection of epinephrine. Epinephrine causes increased heart rate, trembling, and dry mouth—which are often associated with strong emotional reactions. Participants were assigned to one of four groups, including those who (1) received an epinephrine injection and were uninformed about the effects of the injection, (2) received an epinephrine injection and were informed about the effects of the injection (e.g., they were told to expect increased heart rate, trembling, etc.), (3) received an epinephrine injection and were misinformed about the side effects (e.g., they were told to expect numb feet and headaches), or (4) received a placebo injection that would have no effect and were uninformed about any possible effects. After participants received the injections they were then randomly assigned to sit in a waiting room with either an "angry" confederate of the study (who complained loudly and tore up his questionnaire) or a "euphoric" confederate of the study (who was exuberant and entertaining). When the participants were later asked to report on their own emotional experiences, the results were very interesting. The researchers found that the participants who had either no explanation for their symptoms of arousal or those who were misinformed about their symptoms tended to report being either angry or happy, depending on which confederate they had been with in the waiting room. If a participant was exposed to the angry confederate while feeling symptoms of physiological arousal, the participant tended to "catch the emotion" and report being angry. Likewise, if a participant was exposed to the happy confederate while feeling symptoms of physiological arousal, the participant tended to report being happy. These results supported the two-factor theory of emotions in that the participants used the original stimulus to help them interpret and label their physiological arousal. However, critics of this theory have pointed out that the two-factory theory over-emphasizes ANS arousal while ignoring emotional experiences (e.g., "low road" experiences such as hearing a loud noise) that appear to bypass the cortex and lead to unconscious emotional responses such as the fight-or-flight response.

Table 10.2   Schachter & Singer (1962)

Situational Cues	Participants' Expectation	
	Informed (expected symptoms of arousal)	Misinformed (did not expect symptoms of arousal)
Confederate is angry	Participants' emotions are generally unaffected	Participants tend to exhibit **anger**
Confederate is happy	Participants' emotions are generally unaffected	Participants tend to exhibit **happiness**

COGNITIVE MEDIATIONAL THEORY   Richard Lazarus (1991) argued that we have to think about the stimulus prior to experiencing either a physiological response or an emotional response. According to the **cognitive-mediational theory**, your cognitive interpretation of an event or stimulus "mediates" (or comes before) the physiological arousal or emotional experience. For example, if you see a snarling dog, you must first interpret the situation as threatening before you experience physiological arousal or the emotion of fear. If the snarling dog is actually a Chihuahua behind a fence, your physiological arousal would be minimal and you would not experience fear. If the snarling dog is a Doberman pulling a broken chain, your arousal would be much higher and you would likely feel afraid. The cognitive-mediational theory focuses on the individual's interpretation of the stimulus as a mediating factor that determines the level and intensity of the physiological arousal and the emotional experience.

Lazarus (1995) himself pointed out that there are several limitations to this theory. Once again, the cognitive-mediational theory does not provide an explanation for unconscious emotional responses believed to be caused through direct stimulation of the amygdala. Additionally, Lazarus points out there is not enough evidence yet to determine if the cognitive-mediational theory can be applied universally across all cultures.

cognitive-mediational theory
the theory of emotion proposed by Lazarus that the cognitive interpretation of an event or stimulus mediates, or comes before the physiological arousal or emotional experience

FACIAL FEEDBACK HYPOTHESIS   Darwin (1872) wrote in *The Expression of the Emotions in Man and Animals* that "free expression by outward signs of an emotion intensifies it." The **facial feedback hypothesis** says that a person who makes a certain facial expression will feel the corresponding emotion, as long as the person is not feeling some other competing emotion. When people were asked to frown while watching sad films, they felt even sadder than they did while watching the films without frowning (Larsen et al., 1992; Soussigna, 2002). In another example, people who held pencils in their teeth, effectively forcing them to smile, while looking at cartoons, reported that the cartoons were more amusing and enjoyable (Strack et al., 1988; Neal & Chartrand, 2011). Ekman and Friesen (1983) extensively studied the facial muscles involved in emotional expressions and found that the muscles make 46 unique movements, or *action units*. For instance, the zygomatic major on the cheek and orbicularis oculi around the eye move when we smile. These findings suggest that expressing emotions seems to intensify, not diminish, how we feel them. However, a recent attempt to replicate some findings related to the facial feedback hypothesis were unsuccessful, suggesting that further study is necessary in order to fully understand the relationship between facial expressions and emotional experiences (Wagenmakers et al., 2016). Figure 10.4 demonstrates how each of the theories of emotion would explain how someone might respond to hearing the sound of broken glass.

facial feedback hypothesis
theory that facial expressions can influence emotional experiences

Figure 10.4 Theories of Emotion

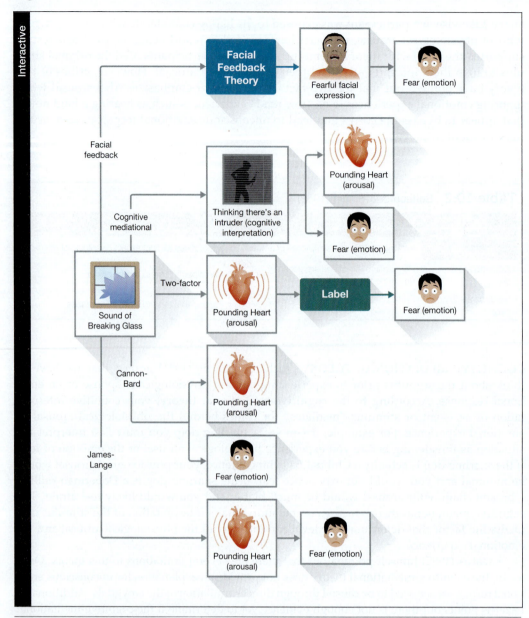

Adaptive Pathway 10.2: Theories of Emotion

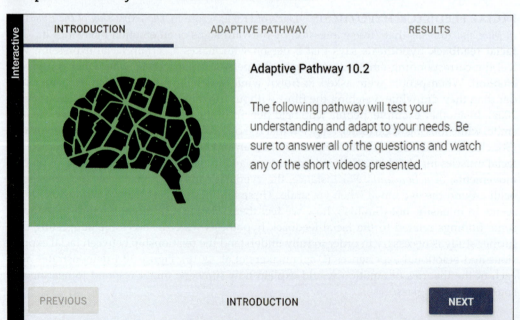

Quiz for Module 10.13–10.14

1. Tim's heart pounds really fast when he watches a horror movie, but he doesn't recognize he is afraid until he notices the pounding heart first. This is an example of which theory of emotion?

   a. Cognitive mediational theory

   b. Cannon-Bard theory

   c. James-Lange theory

   d. The two-factor theory

2. This theory suggests that our hearts pound and we experience fear simultaneously.

   a. The two-factor theory

   b. Cognitive mediational theory

   c. James Lange theory

   d. Cannon-Bard theory

3. Cognitive labels become important in evaluating our emotional experience because physiological arousal can be very similar in differing situations. This statement summarizes which theory of emotion?

   a. Two-factor theory

   b. James-Lange theory

   c. Facial feedback hypothesis

   d. Cognitive mediational theory

Piecing It Together: Obesity Treatment

LO 10.15 **Analyze how the cross-cutting themes of psychology are related to the topic of motivation and emotion through the issue of obesity treatment.**

As the chapter highlighted, obesity has become one of the most difficult public health challenges facing the world today with obesity-related costs in the hundreds of billions of dollars in the United States alone. To combat this epidemic, researchers and physicians are developing and evaluating a variety of treatments over the past decades with mixed success. As you are likely aware, there are many different obesity treatments. The following provides a brief summary of the different treatment options available:

1. **Behavioral Modification/Lifestyle Changes:** The goal of these types of programs is to change unhealthy eating habits and increase physical activity to promote weight loss. Programs focusing on lifestyle modifications can take place in a clinical setting with licensed healthcare providers, or they can be commercially based using a self-help or support group model.

To help people make healthy eating choices, the United States Department of Agriculture uses this MyPlate image.

2. **Medication:** Several different over-the-counter and prescription medications are used to promote weight loss. Many of the medications promote appetite suppression, while other medications prevent the absorption of dietary fat.

Currently, there are nine FDA-approved prescription medications for weight loss.

3. **Weight-Loss Surgery:** Weight-loss surgery (called bariatric surgery) involves different procedures used to reduce the size of the stomach and therefore reduce the amount of food that can be consumed.

Weight loss surgery has been increasing in frequency over the past decade.

When considering these different obesity treatments, several important issues should be considered. We will discuss these in the following pages.

Research Methods

- What about "fad" diets and other questionable treatments for obesity?

- How can you determine if a specific treatment is empirically supported?

Because obesity has become such a widespread problem, there is a big market for products and diet plans to help people lose weight. The chances are good that you can name at least three popular "diet" plans that you or someone you know has tried. It's hard to browse the Internet, listen to the radio, or watch television without being exposed to some type of advertisement for a weight loss product. However, it can be difficult to determine which weight loss methods are scientifically supported and which are not. The term "fad diet" describes weight loss plans that promise quick and drastic results through methods that are not healthy and don't promote long-term weight loss. To evaluate the claims made in an advertisement for a particular product or diet plan, recall the steps of critical thinking from LO 1.5:

1. Consider any underlying motives for making a particular claim. Is the person or company impartial or unbiased with respect to the claim being made? Or, is there a reason that your belief in the claim would be advantageous to the person or company?

- Does the person or company promoting the weight loss plan stand to make a profit if people use the product?

- Was the research being used to demonstrate the effectiveness of the product conducted by the company or individual who is promoting the product? Has there been any independent research that supports the claims?

2. Evaluate the quality of the evidence used to support the claim. A thorough examination of the author's use of the scientific process is required to determine whether the claim is reliable. Consider if the research was conducted using the steps of the scientific method or if support for the claim is not based on sound scientific principles.

   - Was a control group part of the study?

   - Have follow-up studies been conducted to determine the long-term effectiveness of the product?

   - Was the study subject to a peer review so that other scientists could review and critique the methodology or results?

3. Consider any alternative explanations for the results. Look just as hard for disconfirming information as confirmatory information. Is there a different explanation that might explain the results just as well (or even better) than the reason provided?

   - For example, if someone shows you research findings demonstrating that taking a certain pill was associated with weight loss, try to think of alternative explanations for the results. For example, were people eating the same and exercising the same amount before and after taking the pill? Perhaps dietary and activity changes—rather than the pill itself—led to weight loss.

   - If people lost large amounts of weight rapidly using the product or plan, be skeptical about the cause of the weight loss. Dehydration, for example, can cause people to rapidly lose weight—and then just as rapidly regain the weight.

4. Avoid using emotions or personal experiences when evaluating the claim.

   - This means you should ignore evidence based on testimonials alone. Just because a product or plan worked for one person does not mean it will work for most people. Look for data from well-controlled group research studies to evaluate the weight loss product.

Cultural and Social Diversity

   - What is the link between poverty and obesity?

   - Are there social policies that could help address this problem?

Figure 10.5 Obesity Rates by State in 2015

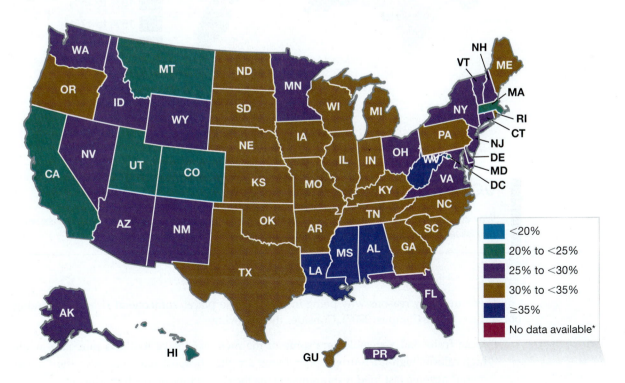

When you consider the rates of obesity in different states (See Figure 10.5), you begin to notice some concerning trends. For example, in 2015, Louisiana had the highest rates of obesity (36.2 percent) followed closely by Alabama (35.6 percent), West Virginia (35.6 percent), and Mississippi (35.6 percent). These were the only four states with obesity rates above 35 percent (Centers for Disease Control and Prevention, 2016; The State of Obesity, 2016). However, states with the highest obesity rates appear to have something else in common—high poverty rates (See Figure 10.6). In fact, the four states with the highest obesity rates in 2015 were ranked 45th (West Virginia), 46th (Alabama), 49th (Louisiana), and 51st (Mississippi) when it comes to poverty, meaning that these states had four of the six highest poverty rates in the country (Poverty USA: A CCHD Initiative, 2014). Studies have further established the link between poverty and obesity (Demment et al., 2014; Lee et al., 2014).

Figure 10.6 Poverty Rates by State

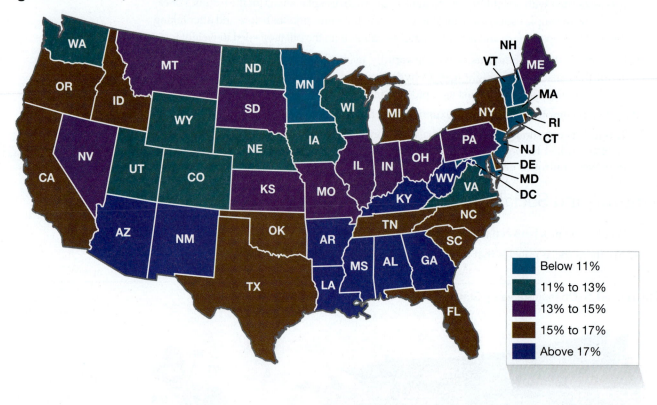

![teal]	Below 11%
![green]	11% to 13%
![purple]	13% to 15%
![brown]	15% to 17%
![blue]	Above 17%

Journal Prompt: Poverty and Obesity

Why do you think the risk for obesity is greater among the poor? Consider both nutritional issues and issues related to physical activity.

There are many reasons why being in poverty also places someone at risk for becoming obese (Brownell & Campos, 2007). Consider the following:

- Fresh fruits and vegetables are some of the most expensive foods to purchase, while high-calorie/high-fat nutrient-poor foods are the cheapest (e.g., consider the "dollar menu" at some fast food restaurants versus the cost of buying fresh produce).

- There are fewer and fewer supermarkets in inner cities but increasing numbers of fast-food chains and small food markets, which limit access to healthy foods and instead provide easier access to cheap, high-fat foods.

- Poor individuals have less leisure time for physical activity, are less likely to be able to afford gym memberships, and access to free parks, trails, or playgrounds is limited. Impoverished schools have worse facilities and fewer opportunities for organized sports.

- Due to safety concerns, children in impoverished neighborhoods are often unable to walk or bike to school and spend much of their time indoors.

Because of the link between poverty and obesity, some experts have focused on the need to address the problem through public policy changes. The goal of these policies is to find a way to make healthy foods more affordable and encourage active lifestyles through public programs, tax policies, and health initiatives. Kelly D. Brownell, a psychology professor at Yale University and director of the Rudd Center for Food Policy and Obesity, has been a leading voice in the debate about how to best use public policy to reduce the link between poverty and obesity (Yach et al., 2006). Some of the initiatives of the Rudd Center for Food Policy and Obesity have included the following:

- Regulating food advertising targeting children

- Menu labeling in chain restaurants

- Taxes on sugar-sweetened beverages

- Improving meals at schools

The Rudd Center for Food Policy and Obesity implemented a recent community campaign focused on reducing consumption of sugary drinks in Howard County, Maryland (Schwartz et al., 2017). A 3-year effort that included changing public policies, community outreach, and media strategies led to a significant reduction in sales of sugary drinks in supermarkets.

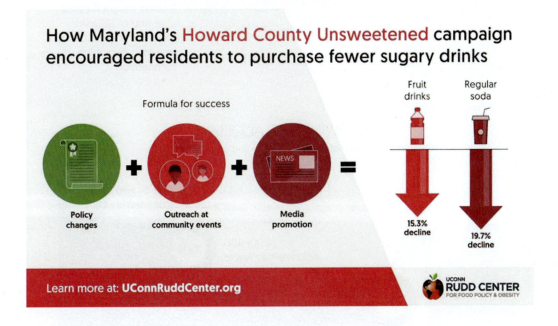

Variations in Human Functioning

- Are obesity treatments effective over the long run?

The Biggest Loser, a 30-week weight loss reality television competition show has been watched by millions of viewers since the first season in 2004. The show has had significant success over the years as millions of people tune in each week to watch the contestants engage in a weekly routine of grueling exercise and diet regimens. The contestants undergo amazing physical transformations. The winners have lost anywhere from 37–60 percent of their original body weight over the course of the competition. However, in 2016, a team of researchers completed a 6-year follow-up of 14 of the 16 competitors from Season 8 of *The Biggest Loser*. After 6 years, most of the contestants had regained a significant amount of weight, and 5 of the 14 contestants were within 1 percent of their pre-show weight (See Figure 10.7). Concerningly, the contestants also showed a significant drop in their metabolism when they lost weight during the competition (meaning they could eat significantly fewer calories to avoid gaining weight). However, their metabolic rates remained low 6 years later, even though many of them had gained much of the weight back. Those contestants who had

Figure 10.7 Biggest Losers Fight a Slower Metabolism

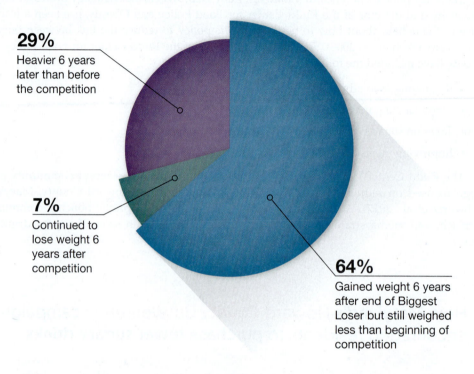

29%
Heavier 6 years later than before the competition

7%
Continued to lose weight 6 years after competition

64%
Gained weight 6 years after end of Biggest Loser but still weighed less than beginning of competition

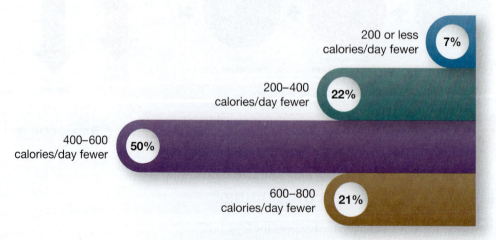

A SLOWING METABOLISM
Calories burned at rest 6 years after the end of the competition

200 or less calories/day fewer — 7%

200–400 calories/day fewer — 22%

400–600 calories/day fewer — 50%

600–800 calories/day fewer — 21%

maintained the greatest weight loss over 6 years also had the greatest metabolic slowing, making it even harder for those individuals to keep the weight off.

In light of these disheartening results, it is important to consider whether obesity treatments focusing on lifestyle change in the "real world" work over the long term. If people can lose weight by altering their diet and increasing their physical activity in the short run, but they eventually gain the weight back and their metabolism is permanently lowered, are programs focusing on lifestyle change actually beneficial? What about medications or surgery? Below is a summary of the current findings regarding the long-term effectiveness of different obesity treatments. As the table demonstrates, the research suggests that it is possible to lose weight and maintain the weight loss, but that drastic results like those depicted on shows like *The Biggest Loser* and those promised by certain fad diets are most certainly unrealistic in the long run.

Treatment Type	Summary of Research Findings
Weight Loss Medications	• After 1 year, 35–73% of patients achieved at least a 5% weight loss using an obesity medication, which was prescribed with lifestyle interventions. [Yanaovski & Yanovski, 2014]
	• At week 52, participants who were prescribed a weight loss medication in combination with lifestyle modification were more than twice as likely as those in the placebo group to have lost greater than or equal to 5% of their weight. [Aronne et al., 2014]
	• In a 12-week trial which tested the efficacy of a medication for weight loss, a dose-response relationship was found (i.e., higher doses = more weight lost). However, as the dose increased, so did side effects of the medication. [Kim et al., 2015]
Weight Loss Surgery	• A review of bariatric surgery outcomes after at least 2 years showed that patients had lost between 51 and 78% of excess weight [Puzziferri et al., 2014]
	• A mean of 47% of excess weight lost 10 years or longer following bariatric surgery (laparoscopic adjustable gastric banding) [O'Brien et al., 2013]
	• A review comparing bariatric surgery and nonsurgical weight loss outcomes found that patients lost significantly more weight, had reduced medication usage, and increased quality of life. [Gloy et al., 2013]
Lifestyle Modification	• After 8 years of an "intensive lifestyle intervention" program by Look AHEAD (Action for Health in Diabetes), 50% of the patients had sustained at least a 5% reduction in weight. [Look AHEAD Research Group (2014)]
	• In a long-term study of self-reported weight loss and behavior change, mean weight loss was 31.3 kg at baseline, 23.8 kg at 5 years, and 23.1 at 10 years. [Thomas et al., 2014]
	• In a year-long weight loss program, all three groups lost modest amounts of weight, but only two of the three groups were able to maintain their weight loss a year after baseline. [Lutes et al., 2017]

Ethics

- When should a drastic treatment such as bariatric surgery be considered?

- At what age is it appropriate?

It appears that bariatric surgery can be an effective strategy for treating obesity for some people. However, at what age should this treatment approach be considered? After all, childhood obesity now affects one in every five school-aged children in the United States (Ogden et al., 2016). Should surgery be an option for a severely obese adolescent? Some of the concerns unique to adolescence that must be considered when reflecting on this issue include the following:

- Can adolescents fully understand and evaluate the risks and benefits of undergoing bariatric surgery?

- Are adolescents capable of managing the postoperative lifestyle changes the surgery demands?
- Does surgery pose any unique medical risks to an adolescent's developing body?
- Have there been long-term studies in adolescents to demonstrate the safety and effectiveness of bariatric surgery?

In 2011, a survey demonstrated that two-thirds of parents felt that bariatric surgery should not be considered in adolescents under the age of 18 (C.S. Mott Children's Hospital National Poll on Children's Health, 2011). A large majority of parents believed that adolescents should attend a pre-surgery program for at least a year (See Figure 10.8). Interestingly, parents with their own personal experience with bariatric surgery were more likely to be open to considering surgery for an adolescent under age 18.

Figure 10.8 How Long Should Adolescents Attend Pre-Surgery Programs?

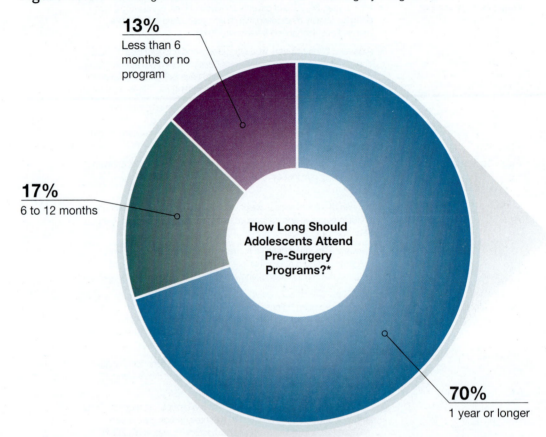

13%
Less than 6 months or no program

17%
6 to 12 months

How Long Should Adolescents Attend Pre-Surgery Programs?*

70%
1 year or longer

*Non-white parents and those with personal experience considering bariatric surgery were more likely to endorse a shorter time in a weight loss program prior to surgery.

However, adolescents with severe obesity are also at risk for other significant health conditions including type 2 diabetes, high blood pressure, nonalcoholic fatty liver disease, and sleep apnea (Childerhose & Tarini, 2015; Zwintzer et al., 2013). One recent study examined the long-term impact of bariatric surgery in adolescents. Prior to surgery, the adolescents had a mean BMI of 58.5 and after an average of 8 years post-surgery, their mean BMI was 41.7. Even though the individuals were generally still obese, they had sustained significant weight loss and they had also had significantly reduced their blood pressure and had lower rates of type 2 diabetes (Inge et al., 2017). These results do show some promise for the effectiveness of bariatric surgery as a treatment option among adolescents who are severely obese and who have other significant related health risks.

Quiz for Module 10.15

1. When a person switches to eating fruits, vegetables, and lean proteins from a diet high in processed foods while also beginning an exercise program, they are using which method to lose weight?

   a. Medications

   b. Weight loss surgery

   c. Behavioral modification/lifestyle changes

   d. A combination of all of these

2. A company selling diet pills claims that people taking the pill lost an average of 5 pounds in 2 days. It would be important to evaluate this claim by

   a. evaluating the quality of the evidence used to support the claim.

   b. considering the underlying motive of the person or company making the claim.

   c. considering any alternative explanations for the results.

   d. All of the answers are correct.

3. States with the highest rates of obesity are also the states with the highest rates of _____.

   a. income

   b. processed food companies

   c. poverty

   d. taxes on fruits and vegetables

4. What are two reasons why poverty has been linked with obesity?

   a. Fewer supermarkets in low-income neighborhoods; lack of interest in eating a healthy diet

   b. Lower cost of highly processed food; lack of motivation to work out

   c. Lack of motivation to work out; less education about healthy nutrition

   d. Higher cost of fresh fruits and vegetables; less time for physical activity

5. What does the research suggest about the long-term effectiveness of obesity treatment?

   a. It is possible to lose weight and maintain the weight loss, but drastic results are unrealistic.

   b. It is possible to lose weight, but maintaining the weight loss is not possible.

   c. Drastic weight loss and maintenance of the weight loss is certainly possible.

   d. Most people are unable to lose enough weight to make a difference in their health status.

Summary: Motivation and Emotion

Module 10.1–10.3: Physiological Theories of Motivation

Motivation is the need or desire that energizes and directs behavior. It is made up of internal factors—*dispositional forces*—and external factors—*situational forces*—that drive us to do specific things in a particular situation. People like William James and William McDougal believed that **instincts** (unlearned complex behaviors with a fixed pattern throughout a species) motivate human behavior. This theory grew out of favor because it became difficult to prove that many human behaviors were motivated purely by biological instincts. According to Clark Hull's **drive-reduction theory,** we act when a physiological need creates an aroused state that drives us to reduce the need. This theory is based on the premise that humans are motivated to maintain a state of **homeostasis**—a state of balance or equilibrium. **Primary drives,** such as hunger and thirst, lead us to eat or drink and therefore preserve homeostasis. While primary drives are innate (e.g., thirst, hunger, sex), **secondary drives** are learned through conditioning (e.g., money). Rather than being driven to achieve homeostasis, the **optimal arousal theory** of motivation states that people are driven to achieve an ideal level of arousal, and the **Yerkes-Dodson law** states that performance generally peaks with a moderate level of arousal.

Module 10.4–10.5: Hunger

Sensations of hunger *motivate* people to consume food. In terms of physiology, levels of blood **glucose**—blood sugar—help determine hunger and satiety (feeling satisfied). When glucose levels drop, we feel hungry. If glucose levels rise, the hormone **insulin** is released, telling the body to convert glucose to fat. The lateral hypothalamus secretes the hormone **orexin,** which also brings on feelings of hunger. The ventromedial hypothalamus suppresses hunger and sends out signals that stop an animal from eating. Not all hunger originates in internal body states. For example, the **gustatory sense**—taste—can mediate hunger. Complex neural circuits are involved in the experience of hunger, and specific neurotransmitters such as Neuropeptide Y (NPY) play a role in communicating the need for food to various brain regions. Studies have shown that other areas of the hypothalamus such as the paraventricular nucleus and the arcuate nucleus are also important. How much we eat and what types of foods we consume can also depend on the context. For example, people eat more when they are in in the presence of others as opposed to eating alone, and they tend to model the eating patterns of their companions.

A complex interplay of biological and sociocultural factors each contribute to the current obesity epidemic. Obesity is defined as an excessive accumulation of body fat and is often assessed using Body Mass Index (BMI). Twin and adoption studies along with family studies have consistently demonstrated that the heritability of obesity and BMI in general is very high.

In addition to genetic contributions, the metabolic system also plays a role in obesity. **Basal metabolic rate (BMR)** is an estimate of how many calories the body burns when at rest, and **set point theory** suggests that our body is biologically programmed to defend a certain body weight. BMR is one tool that can be used to make us burn more calories when we overeat or burn fewer calories when we don't eat enough in order to maintain the same weight. In the normal process of hunger regulation, the hormone *leptin* is released from the fat cells as a satiety cue to notify the brain that enough energy has been stored in the fat cells. However, in obese humans, leptin levels are often high suggesting that the brain isn't receiving the message that would signal satiety. The role of culture and the environment have been the primary targets in pinpointing the cause of the rising obesity epidemic. There are two main environmental contributors to the obesity epidemic: diets based on processed foods high in fat and carbohydrates and low on nutrients and lack of physical activity.

Module 10.6–10.9: Beyond Biology: Other Theories of Motivation

Abraham Maslow proposed that our behavior is motivated in order to fulfill a need, and the "need" that is most salient in the moment depends on what needs have previously been satisfied. He developed a theory based on a hierarchy of needs and divided the needs into two categories: *deficiency needs* (based on a lack of something) and *growth needs* (focusing on the desire to grow as an individual). Maslow's six-level hierarchy in ascending order includes **physiological** (physical requirements needed for human survival), **safety** (the need to feel safe and secure), **belongingness** (the need for affection, love, friendship, and intimacy), **esteem** (the need for self-esteem, achievement, independence, and prestige), **self-actualization** (realizing your potential as a person by seeking personal growth), and **self-transcendence** (the need to go beyond the self and experience oneness with the greater whole or higher truth by seeking peak experiences).

Extrinsic motivation occurs when people are motivated to engage in a particular behavior to gain some sort of reward or to avoid some negative outcome, and **intrinsic motivation** is defined as engaging in a behavior for its own sake. For behaviors already driven by intrinsic motivation, adding an external incentive can actually serve to decrease motivation through the **overjustification effect,** or people's tendency to pay more attention to the external rewards rather than their own internal motivation.

According to **self-determination theory (SDT),** three basic, universal psychological needs must be satisfied to facilitate a natural tendency toward human growth. These three needs include **autonomy (**"volition," or the need to be causal agents of one's own life), **relatedness (**the need to feel connected to other people in meaningful ways), and **competence** (the need to feel effective when interacting in the environment).

Carol Dweck's self-theory of motivation proposes that successful people have "*mastery-oriented*" qualities that include a love of learning, seeking challenges, valuing effort, and persistence in the face of obstacles. Dweck differentiates between people who prescribe to the **fixed mindset** of intelligence (viewing intellectual ability as an entity that dwells within us) and people who prescribe to the **growth mindset** of intelligence (believing that intellectual ability is a malleable construct that

can be changed with effort). Research supports the notion that people who ascribe to the incremental theory of intelligence are often more successful.

Module 10.10–10.12: Components of Emotion

When we experience a subjective reaction to an object, event, person, or memory, we are experiencing **emotion.** All emotions have a **valence,** a positive or negative value along a continuum, and also vary in degree of arousal. Emotion includes three distinct but related parts: *physiological arousal, expressive behavior,* and *cognitive experience.* The *autonomic nervous system (ANS)* prepares our bodies for action and controls unconscious processes such as perspiration and respiration. The **sympathetic division** of the ANS initiates the fight-or-flight response and the **parasympathetic division** brings the body back to its resting rate. The amygdala is a small structure in the brain that can analyze sensory data before it reaches the cortex by receiving projections from sensory organs via the thalamus, the brain's message-directing center, by way of the **rapid subcortical pathway,** or the "low road." The slower **cortical pathway,** or the "high road," allows your perceptions (or interpretations) to affect your emotions. When researchers removed monkeys' amygdalae and parts of their temporal lobes, the monkeys developed what is called *psychic blindness*—they did not experience fear or anger when confronted with previously frightening objects. At the anterior of the frontal lobes, the prefrontal cortex is essential for the cognitive experience of emotion. **Prefrontal lobotomies** involved disabling the prefrontal area of the brain and caused less intense emotional reactions as well as problems with other life functions such as planning and reasoning.

Charles Darwin's **universality hypothesis** supposes that facial expressions are understood across all cultures. Ekman's research supported the notion of six universal facial expressions including: happiness, sadness, surprise, fear, disgust, and anger. People appear to detect anger more easily. Gender and culture play a role in both detection and expression of facial expressions and body language. True expressions of emotion actually differ from false ones. *Intensification* (exaggerating your emotions), *deintensification* (muting emotions), or **masking** (showing one emotion while feeling another) are all examples of deceptive emotional expression. False expressions involve different muscle groups than real ones, and studying their *morphology,* or shape, can sometimes tell us if the expressions are real. **Polygraph** tests are machines designed to measure physiological characteristics, including heart rate/blood pressure, skin conductivity, and respiration to assist in making inferences about the truthfulness of a person's statement. Because of the concerns about the unreliability of polygraph tests, they are not currently admissible in a court of law.

Cognition, or thought, can influence what we feel or believe we feel. Arousal from one event can spill also over into the emotions we experience about other events and misattribution sometimes leads people to attribute their arousal to the wrong stimulus. Sometimes our emotions can influence what we choose to perceive through **mood-congruent processing** (the tendency to selectively perceive stimuli congruent with their emotional state). When we engage in **emotion regulation,** we use cognitive strategies to control and influence our own emotional responses. **Affective forecasting,** or imagining how you would feel about something that might happen in the future, is a way that people use thoughts to improve decision-making.

Module 10.13–10.14:   Theories of Emotion

The **James-Lange theory** of emotion proposes that the physiological experience of heart pounding or tears flowing causes you to feel afraid or sad. According to the **Cannon-Bard theory,** the mental and physiological components of emotions happen simultaneously. Conversely, the **Schachter and Singer two-factor theory** says that the cognitive evaluation following physiological arousal creates the emotion we experience. While cognition may be part of emotion, Robert Zajonc believed that some emotional reactions can bypass our conscious minds and prior experience of a stimulus can cause an **exposure effect** (when the familiarity of the stimulus primes us to react a certain way). According to Richard Lazarus' **cognitive-mediational theory,** the cognitive interpretation of an event or stimulus "mediates" (or comes before) the physiological arousal or emotional experience. The **facial feedback hypothesis** says that a person who makes a certain facial expression will feel the corresponding emotion, as long as the person is not feeling some other competing emotion.

Chapter 10 Quiz

1. Juan has been in a wheelchair since an accident damaged his spinal cord. Despite this injury, he laughs and cries and experiences a full range of emotions. Juan's experience _____ the James-Lange theory of emotion.

   a. does not support

   b. supports

   c. validates

   d. neither supports nor fails to support

2. Loki loves to organize and clean his house. He does it because it makes him feel peaceful and happy. His parents decide to pay him $5 every time he cleans and organizes some part of the house. After being paid a few times, he feels less interested in cleaning or organization. What explains this behavior?

   a. Extrinsic overuse

   b. Intrinsic motivation

   c. Overjustification effect

   d. Interest overload

3. When people feel they have a choice in their life, are connected in positive ways to friends and family, and feel a sense of effectiveness in their life, they have a reduced level of which stress hormone?

   a. Peptids

   b. Cortisol

   c. Adrenaline

   d. Insulin

4. Ian loves to bungee jump off bridges. He loves the heart pounding excitement that comes before, during, and after the jump. Ian's behavior is NOT a good example of _____ theory.

   a. balance

   b. secondary drive

   c. optimum arousal

   d. drive reduction

5. Depressed people show less activity in the _____ side of the _____ cortex.

   a. left; frontal

   b. right; temporal

   c. left; occipital

   d. right; parietal

6. Huang has a difficult final to take and has to decide between staying up to study 2 more hours or getting sleep. He has already studied 4 hours for the final and is really tired and extremely anxious. Which would be the better choice for Huang according to the Yerkes-Dodson law?

   a. Getting more sleep to calm his nerves

   b. Staying up all night studying and drinking energy drinks

   c. Studying 2 more hours and not going to sleep, but eating a good breakfast

   d. Taking a sleeping pill and going to bed because he really doesn't care anymore if he sleeps through his final

7. _____ is the need or desire that energizes and directs behavior.

   a. Motivation   b. Emotion

   c. Instinct   d. Homeostasis

8. Myra teaches at a public middle school where she does not get to determine her curriculum or how many students will be in her classroom. As a result of her lack of choice, she feels frustrated and depressed most days at work. Which psychological need is not being met, according to the self-determination theory?

   a. Autonomy

   b. Relatedness

   c. Competence

   d. Esteem

9. Frankie has lost 10 pounds through exercise and diet, but now she has stalled in her weight loss. It seems that doing the same things she has for the last 2 months to lose weight is not working anymore. How could this be explained?

   a. Decrease in leptin

   b. Hypothalamus

   c. Basal metabolic rate

   d. Set point theory

10. _____ is an estimate of how many calories the body burns when at rest.

   a. Basal Metabolic Rate (BMR)

   b. Body Mass Index (BMI)

   c. Set point theory

   d. Obesity

11. According to Maslow, self-actualization is _____ while self-transcendence is _____.

   a. realizing your full potential; seeking to serve the greater good

   b. seeking to serve the greater good; realizing your full potential

   c. the need for self-esteem; the need for belonging

   d. the need for belonging; the need for self-esteem

12. Which of the following is the correct order of Maslow's hierarchy of needs?

   a. safety; physiological; esteem; belongingness; self-actualization; self-transcendence

   b. physiological; safety; belongingness; esteem; self-actualization; self-transcendence

   c. physiological; safety; esteem; belongingness; self-actualization; self-transcendence

   d. safety; physiological; belongingness; esteem; self-actualization; self-transcendence

13. What do most psychologists now believe about the instinct theory for human behavior?

   a. Human behavior is instinctual based on the evolutionary perspective of survival.

   b. Human behavior is motivated by a combination of biological and psychological states.

   c. Human behavior has 18 core instincts that help with survival and adaptation.

   d. Human behavior is motivated only by physiological needs.

14. Sayla wants to communicate to her daughter Lola that she is proud of her grades and behavior in school. She wants Lola to continue working hard in the future even if she fails at something. What type of feedback would be best for Sayla to improve her daughter's intrinsic motivation?

   a. "Lola, I am glad you are such a perfect student."

   b. "Lola, I know you will always get A's."

   c. "Lola, I think you are such a smart girl."

   d. "Lola, I am so proud of how hard you work in school."

15. What are the three needs according to the self-determination theory?

   a. Autonomy, relatedness, competence

   b. Achievement, connectedness, independence

   c. Relatedness, self-esteem, achievement

   d. Autonomy, achievement, relatedness

16. Damien just finished a very satisfying meal of meat and savory potatoes at his friend's house. He is full and doesn't intend to eat dessert. His friend breaks out a seven-layer chocolate cake and Damien feels hungry for the cake. This could be explained by

   a. insulin and leptin being released at the smell of the cake.

   b. the fact that he is trying to lose weight, so he is craving sweets.

   c. the gustatory sense: dessert presents a new appetizing taste.

   d. The fact that he wants to gain weight, so knows dessert is a good way to pack on the pounds.

17. When we eat before we get too hungry to prevent overeating, Hull would say we are maintaining a state of balance called _____.

   a. secondary drive

   b. primary drive

   c. homeostasis

   d. equilibrium

18. Lebron has always believed he is good at basketball, but he thinks the effort he puts into his practice is what will help him win more games and get a college scholarship. He is the last one to leave the court at practice, and the first one to get there every morning. According to Carol Dweck, Lebron has a _____.

a. belief system

b. fixed mindset

c. growth mindset

d. challenging mindset

19. Judy decided to do an experiment to test what her grandmother always told her: "Turn that frown upside down, and you will feel better." Judy went around frowning all day long and even though she started the day in a good mood, she ended up feeling sad for most of the day. Which theory explains this sad tale?

a. Facial feedback hypothesis

b. Two-factor theory

c. James-Lange theory

d. Canon-Bard theory

20. Mateeka loves to play soccer and her team has finally made it to the championship game; however, her coach has been screaming at them for days and Mateeka has had a stomach ache and has not been able to sleep. She is extremely nervous going into the game and doesn't feel well. She performs poorly as do her teammates and they lose the game. How does the Yerkes-Dodson law explain this?

a. High levels of arousal can be detrimental to performance in difficult situations.

b. Moderate levels of arousal are beneficial to performance.

c. Low levels of arousal are required for difficult situations.

d. High levels of arousal are needed for most tasks to gain the best performance.

21. The "high road" in emotional responses is _____ than the "low road" and allows _____ to affect your emotions.

a. slower; interpretations

b. faster; interpretations

c. slower; instincts

d. faster; instincts

22. Certain facial expressions universally associated with specific emotions across all cultures is known as the _____ hypothesis.

a. facial feedback

b. universality

c. emotional expression

d. cultural literacy

23. What gender differences have been found regarding how we perceive and express emotions?

a. Women pay attention to the more important cues than men.

b. Men express happiness better than women.

c. Women can generally detect and interpret nonverbal cues better than men.

d. Women are able to detect angry faces more quickly than men.

24. Rashad is in the middle of an intense workout at the gym. He is running sprints in between sets of weights. His heart is pumping and he feels good. An attractive woman walks by and smiles at him. He thinks he might want to get her number because he feels attracted to her. According to the Dutton and Aron study, this might be

a. normal gym behavior.

b. physiological attraction.

c. mood congruent processing.

d. misattribution.

25. Bianca is going to meet her future in-laws for the first time over Thanksgiving. She imagines a positive experience with laughing and joking while playing games and watching movies together. She is engaging in _____.

a. affective forecasting

b. mood congruent processing

c. daydreaming

d. emotional regulation

26. You are on a hike in the woods and a bear runs across your path. Your heart races and you feel fear at the same time. This explanation for your emotional reaction would be best explained by which theory?

a. James-Lange theory

b. Cannon-Bard theory

c. Two-factor theory

d. Cognitive mediational theory

27. Susan has grown up in the United States and eaten a Western style diet. She is shopping at the farmer's market and is starting to get hungry. She smells the strong odor of kimchi and becomes nauseous and no longer feels hungry. Her feelings of hunger were influenced by

a. biological predisposition.

b. psychological and cultural background.

c. hormones released when smelling food.

d. the hypothalamus.

28. Lars walks into a dark room, flips on the light, and 30 people yell "Surprise!" His heart is racing and his breathing is rapid. He feels happy and excited because he recognizes that his friends remembered his birthday. He has interpreted the event as positive. Which theory of emotion explains his reaction?

    a. Cognitive mediational theory

    b. Facial feedback hypothesis

    c. Two-factor theory

    d. Cannon-Bard theory

29. Sheila walks into a room and everyone laughs. She thinks, "I bet someone just told a funny joke; I wonder what it was." Due to her thoughts about the event, Sheila is curious and not upset. Which theory does this best represent?

    a. Canon-Bard theory

    b. Two-factor theory

    c. Facial feedback hypothesis

    d. Cognitive-mediational theory

30. Students who do not give up easily on tests and persist in the face of challenges demonstrate what Dweck calls a _____.

    a. fixed response   c. helpless response

    b. growth response   d. mastery response

Chapter 11
Human Sexuality and Gender

⌄ Chapter Outline and Learning Objectives

Module 11.1–11.3: Gender Development

LO 11.1 Describe biological bases of gender development.

LO 11.2 Recognize how social and cultural influences affect gender development.

LO 11.3 Explain transgender experiences.

Module 11.4–11.5: Gender Similarities and Differences

LO 11.4 Explain gender differences in cognitive abilities, including intelligence and memory.

LO 11.5 Describe gender differences related to social behaviors.

Module 11.6–11.7: Sexual Orientation

LO 11.6 Recognize the definition and prevalence of various sexual orientations.

LO 11.7 Understand the research findings about the causes of sexual orientation.

Module 11.8–11.9: Human Sexual Behavior

LO 11.8 Describe the phases of the sexual response cycle.

LO 11.9 Recognize the cognitive and sociocultural influences on human sexual behavior.

Module 11.10–11.12: Sexual Disorders and Sexually Transmitted Infections

LO 11.10 Define and describe sexual dysfunctions.

LO 11.11 Define and describe paraphilic disorders.

LO 11.12 Recognize the definition and ways to prevent various sexually transmitted infections.

Module 11.13: Piecing It Together: Sexualization of Girls

LO 11.13 Analyze how the cross-cutting themes of psychology are related to the topic of the sexualization of girls.

Understanding Sexuality and Gender

In the summer of 2015, the Supreme Court of the United States ruled that states must allow same-sex marriage. In 2016, President Obama issued a directive informing all public school districts in the country to allow transgender students to use the bathrooms that match their gender identity. Less than a year later, the new Trump administration rescinded this order. In the fall of 2017, explosive allegations of sexual harassment and assault against Harvey Weinstein, a prominent American film producer, brought discussions of sexual harassment to the forefront. These are just a few recent examples of how the topics of gender and human sexuality are complicated and rapidly evolving. Figure 11.1 clearly demonstrates how views about sexual morality have shifted dramatically over the past 50 years.

Changing Beliefs About Sexuality

A recent study examined changes in American's attitudes about sexual behavior from 1972 to 2012. See if you can accurately predict how people responded to the questions in 1972 and in 2012.

What percent of people said that premarital sex is "not wrong at all" in...
1972?

2012?

Reset | Next

Figure 11.1 Public Attitudes about Sexual Morality

The figure shows how public attitudes about these issues have changed over this time.

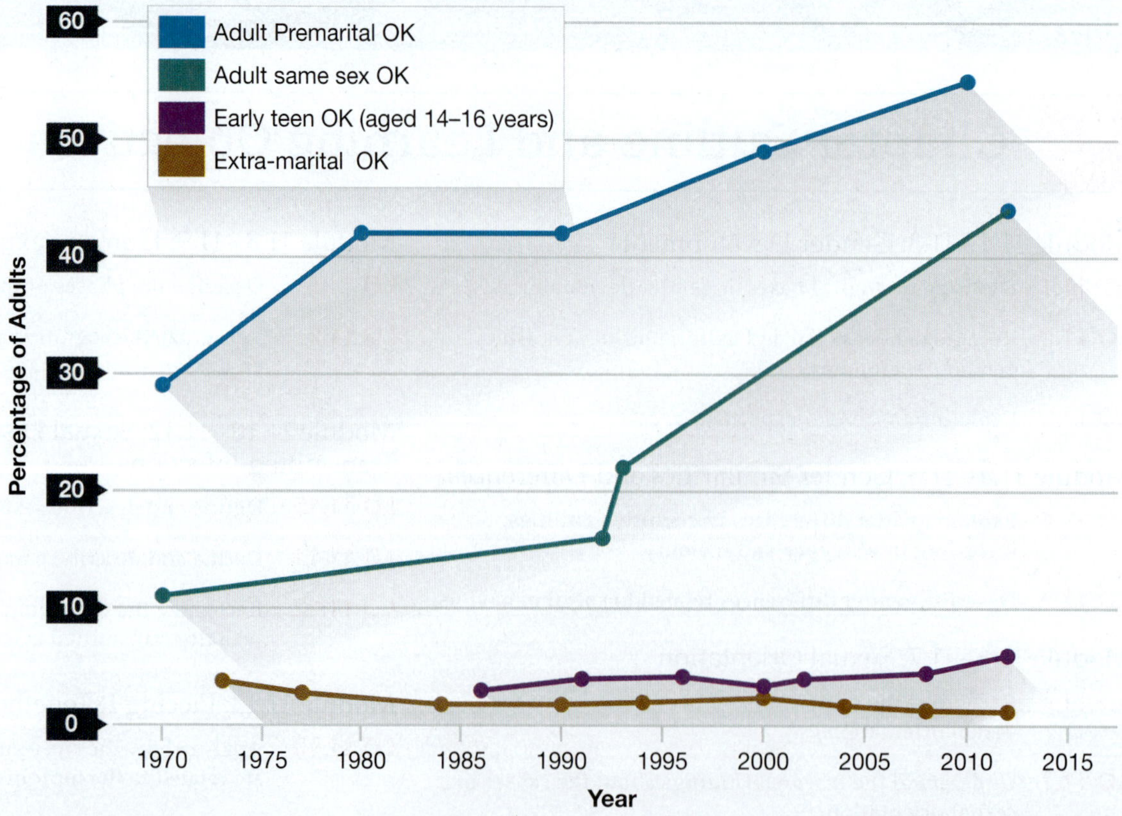

Legend:
- Adult Premarital OK
- Adult same sex OK
- Early teen OK (aged 14–16 years)
- Extra-marital OK

Y-axis: Percentage of Adults
X-axis: Year (1970, 1975, 1980, 1985, 1990, 1995, 2000, 2005, 2010, 2015)

Even though opinions have changed dramatically in the past 50 years, that does not mean there is agreement or consensus today. Topics related to gender and sexuality continue to motivate significant debate, strong emotions, and political upheaval. Before wading into these highly charged topics, it's important to consider each issue from the standpoint of psychological science. Examining the research about gender identity, sexual orientation, and human sexuality can provide a more neutral groundwork for considering topics that can often lead to strong reactions. The specific language used to describe topics related to gender and sexuality is one of the issues that must be carefully considered. Like public opinion, language has evolved over time so that terminology once widely accepted may change in meaning or become associated with negative or disparaging views. With this in mind, the terminology was carefully selected throughout this chapter. However, given the rapidly fluctuating nature of these topics, it is possible that new terminology can become more accepted within a very short timeframe.

Module 11.1–11.3: Gender Development

While being circumcised in 1966, 7-month-old David Reimer (born as "Brian" Reimer) lost his penis due to severe burns. His distraught parents consulted with John Money, a well-known psychologist of the time who believed that gender was primarily a social construct that could be successfully altered early in life. At Dr. Money's advice, David Reimer's parents decided to have their 22-month-old child undergo surgery to become female. After surgery to remove his testes, David became Brenda and was raised as a little girl. This case provided a unique opportunity to better understand the contributions of biology and socialization on gender development. Unfortunately, this particular case ended in tragedy. David failed to identify with a female gender despite taking female hormones and dressing as a girl since infancy. At age 14, after learning the truth from his parents, David decided to assume a male identity and underwent multiple surgical procedures to revert to his biological sexual identity. At age 38, after a failed marriage, David Reimer committed suicide by shooting himself in the head (Colapinto, 1997, 2000; Walker, 2004).

David Reimer, who underwent gender transitions as a male newborn (Brian) to a female young child (Brenda) and ultimately a male adolescent (David).

In contrast, consider the case of Christine Jorgensen. She was born a biological male named George Jorgensen in 1926 in the Bronx, New York City. George was drafted into the U.S. Army in 1945, and after many years of experiencing a state of *gender dysphoria* (feeling a mismatch between biological sex and gender identity), became one of the earliest individuals to undergo gender affirmation surgery and be prescribed female hormones. In the *New York Daily News*, the headline in 1952 read "Ex-GI Becomes Blonde Bombshell," and Christine Jorgensen went on to become a spokesperson for the rights of transgender individuals (Summers, 2004; Zack, 2009).

Christine Jorgensen was born as a biological male named George before she transitioned to female.

To many people, the words *sex* and *gender* mean pretty much the same thing. When we're asked to identify our sex or gender on a standardized test, many of us fill in the bubble marked *male* or *female* without much thought. However, as the cases of David Reimer and Christine Jorgensen demonstrate, sex and gender are not always synonymous. While David Reimer's case provides evidence for the biological nature of gender, cases such as Christine Jorgensen also highlight that gender is not always as simple as a dichotomy based on biological sex. In fact, the process of gender development is complex and involves both biological and social processes.

The Nature of Gender

LO 11.1 Describe biological bases of gender development.

Our **sex** is our biological classification as male or female based on the sex chromosomes contained in our DNA, our reproductive organs, and our anatomical features. Most females have two **X chromosomes**, one from each parent. Most males have an X chromosome from the mother and a **Y chromosome** from the father. You may be surprised to learn there are actually six different biological sexes, which include the following:

- X: occurring in roughly 1 in 2,000 to 1 in 5,000 females (called Turner syndrome)
- XX: most common form of female
- XXY: occurring in roughly 1 in 500 to 1 in 1000 males (called Klinefelter syndrome)
- XY: most common form of male
- XYY: occurring in roughly 1 out of 1,000 males (called Jacob's syndrome)
- XXXY: occurring in 1 out of 18,000 to 1 in 50,000 males

Gender, on the other hand, is the set of behaviors and characteristics that define the degree to which someone is masculine or feminine. In other words, while sex is a biological phenomenon, gender is psychological. Identifying with a particular gender is a process that involves the influences of both biology and our interactions with society.

sex

our biological classification as male or female based on the sex chromosomes contained in our DNA, our reproductive organs, and our anatomical features

X chromosomes

A sex chromosome, two of which are normally present in female cells (designated XX) and only one in male cells (designated XY)

Y chromosome

a sex chromosome that is normally present only in male cells, which are designated XY

gender

the set of behaviors and characteristics that define the degree to which someone is masculine or feminine

Gender on a Continuum

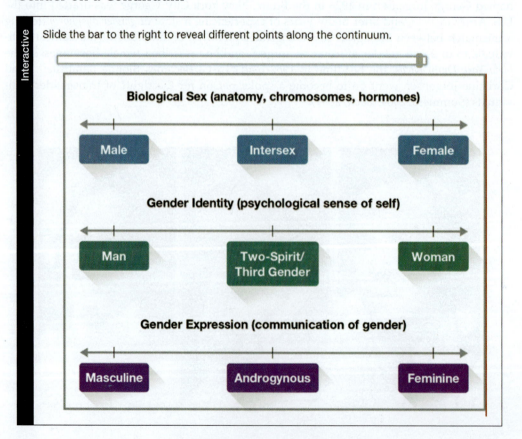

Interactive

Slide the bar to the right to reveal different points along the continuum.

Biological Sex (anatomy, chromosomes, hormones)

Male — Intersex — Female

Gender Identity (psychological sense of self)

Man — Two-Spirit/Third Gender — Woman

Gender Expression (communication of gender)

Masculine — Androgynous — Feminine

In the vast majority of cases, gender is aligned with biological sex: Someone born with two X chromosomes will come to identify herself as female, and someone born with one X chromosome and one Y chromosome will come to identify himself as male. However, this is not always the case. Some people with two X chromosomes feel more like men than women, and some people who are genetically male identify as female. Gender is not always a black and white experience between male and female, either. Gender is conceptualized on a continuum, and it's possible for people to feel varying degrees of gender intensity. Some people experience gender fluidity and do not have a fixed gender identity but instead identify as masculine at some times and feminine at other times. There is also a difference between gender identity and gender expression (or the communication of gender in behavior, clothing, etc.).

PRIMARY VERSUS SECONDARY SEX CHARACTERISTICS   The process of identifying with a gender begins long before our awareness of it. As soon as our **primary sex characteristics**—the sexual organs present at birth and directly involved in human reproduction—are visible to doctors, nurses, and parents, they begin to treat us a certain way. This moment used to occur at birth, but ultrasound technology has led many parents to choose to find out the sex of their child during pregnancy. In fact, it has become the norm for parents to find out the sex before birth while waiting until the moment of delivery has become more rare (Carroll, 2007; Italie, 2013). Regardless of when the sex is identified, from that moment on, the process of gender development is underway. The minute we are swaddled in a pink or blue hat and onesie embroidered with dainty butterflies or big, tough fire trucks, we have not only a sex but a gender, too.

primary sex characteristics
sex-specific reproductive organs

Primary and Secondary Sex Characteristics

Interactive

Review the primary and secondary sex characteristics. When you are ready, click "Check Your Understanding."

	Primary Sex Characteristics	Secondary Sex Characteristics
Males	• penis and scrotum • testes (maturation during puberty)	• enlargement of the genitalia • lowering of the voice pitch • redistribution of the muscle tissue and fat • pubic, facial, body, and armpit hair
Females	• vagina and other internal genitalia • vulva and other external genitalia • ovaries (maturation during puberty)	• enlargement of the genitalia • development of the breasts • pubic and armpit hair

Check Your Understanding

Primary sex characteristics, including gonads, internal sex organs, and external genitalia, emphasize the primary ways in which males and females are different—their roles in reproduction. However, you might be surprised at just how similar male and female primary sex characteristics are for much of prenatal development. The first sex organs to develop are the gonads, which are identical in male and female fetuses for the first four weeks of prenatal development. After the first four weeks, if a Y chromosome is present, it activates the enzyme that turns gonads into testes for males. If the Y chromosome is absent, however, the fetus is female, and it begins to develop ovaries.

Until the third month of pregnancy, the fetus, regardless of its sex chromosomes, has both the **Müllerian system**—the precursor of female sex organs—and the **Wolffian system**—the precursor of male sex organs. During the third month, a male's testes will secrete **androgens**, or

Müllerian system
a female reproductive system

Wolffian system
a male reproductive system

androgens
male sex hormones

male sex hormones, to initiate the Wolffian system to develop. The testes will also produce an anti-Müllerian hormone to stop development of the female sex organs. In the absence of these androgens, the Müllerian system will develop and the Wolffian system will wither away; in other words, the fetus will develop female sex organs.

The development of **external genitalia**—the penis and scrotum in males and the labia, clitoris, and external vagina in females—also depends on the presence or absence of androgens. In rare cases in which the fetus's receptors for androgens fail to function, **complete androgen insensitivity syndrome (CAIH)** causes a genetic male to develop external female genitalia. Varying degrees of androgen insensitivity can cause males' testes to develop internally or cause boys to develop breasts during puberty.

When we reach reproductive age, our bodies change to prepare for reproduction and alert others that we're physically ready to reproduce. These changes involve the development of **secondary sex characteristics**—sexual organs and traits that develop at puberty but are not directly involved in reproduction. Both sexes begin to grow pubic hair and experience an overall growth spurt. Females begin this development about two years before males, which explains why most of the girls towered over most of the boys in your seventh-grade class. Females grow breasts and their hips widen to prepare for childbirth, while males grow facial hair and chest hair. Both males and females develop lower, more adult voices, but this change is particularly noticeable in boys, who sometimes seem to change from sopranos to basses with astonishing speed.

HORMONAL INFLUENCES As you've probably already figured out, hormones play a significant role in the development of our sex characteristics. The androgen **testosterone** is the principal male hormone. The male's Y chromosome includes a single gene that triggers the testes to produce testosterone. In females, the ovaries produce testosterone, but to a much lesser extent. Many studies have examined the impact of atypical concentrations of testosterone in genetic males and females on the development of **gender identity**—our self-identification as male or female, a blend of both, or neither (e.g., Hines, 2006; Imperato-McGinley et al., 1979; Lamminmäki et al., 2012; Yang et al., 2010).

Evidence from several cases suggest that while excess androgens in female embryos may create more "masculine" girls, these male hormones don't cause girls to identify themselves as boys. If a female embryo exposed to excess androgens is born with male-looking genitals, doctors may surgically change the genitals by making them appear female. Although these girls tend to be typical tomboys, act more physically aggressive than most girls, and play in ways more typical of boys than girls, their gender identification as girls is not altered by the excess male hormones (Berenbaum & Snyder, 1995; Hönekopp & Watson, 2011; Jordan-Young, 2012; Money & Matthews, 1982; Money & Norman, 1987). Research into other species from rats to monkeys shows that female embryos exposed to male hormones go on to develop a masculine appearance and act more aggressively than typical females of their species (Brody, 1981; Ramirez et. al., 2010).

Some genetic males with typical male hormones are born with penile deformity, causing some well-meaning parents to raise their sons as daughters as in the case of David Reimer. However, genetic males who are raised as females often come to reject their female gender identity. In the past, the medical community often recommended genital surgery for genetic males born with deformed or very small penises to remove the testes and replace with female genitalia. One study of 14 such cases found that six of these individuals later identified as men and five identified as women, while the remaining three had unclear gender identities (Reiner & Gearhart, 2004).

The Intersex Society of North America advocates for the rights of **intersex** individuals, or those born with ambiguous genitalia. New terminology was introduced in 2006 and some in the medical community have begun using the term "disorders of sex development" (DSD) rather than intersex conditions (Hughes, 2008), although concerns have been expressed about pathologizing individuals with these conditions by using the term "disorder." One outcome of the research and advocacy for intersex individuals has been a more cautious approach to genital surgeries in infancy and childhood. As the medical community has come to understand more about the complexities of gender, doctors

---

external genitalia

the penis and scrotum in males and the labia, clitoris, and external vagina in females

complete androgen insensitivity syndrome (CAIH)

a condition that causes a genetic male fetus to develop external female genitalia because the receptors for androgens fail to function

secondary sex characteristics

the sexual organs and traits that develop at puberty and are not directly involved in reproduction

testosterone

the principal male sex hormone

gender identity

our self-identification as male or female, a blend of both, or neither

intersex

when someone is born with ambiguous genitalia

have become more willing to leave intersex individuals' genitalia intact and are far less eager to surgically alter infants' anatomical features. Even when an individual chooses to have surgery performed as an adult, the process isn't undertaken hastily. Gender has such a powerful impact on our lives that people who choose to have this type of surgery must undergo extensive counseling to ensure they are fully informed about—and comfortable with—their decision. In addition, support for intersex individuals has begun to focus less on gender assignment and genital appearance and more on addressing stigma and overall well-being.

EVOLUTIONARY EXPLANATIONS   Evolutionary theory also contributes to our understanding of gender. The evolutionary approach to psychology explores how human behavior has evolved because of its beneficial effects on survival. Certain human behaviors or psychological traits are more likely to be passed on from one generation to another because those characteristics were beneficial for survival or reproduction (Confer et al., 2010). When thinking about gender from an evolutionary lens, consider gender differences in terms of which characteristics make reproduction and the survival of offspring more likely. According to Charles Darwin, **sexual selection** is the preference by one sex for certain characteristics in individuals of the other sex (Darwin, 1871). Across most animal species, the male is in competition with other males for access to the female. The males are "competitors" and the females are "choosers" in this system, and characteristics that lead to a female choosing a male will be passed on genetically. Traits that allow males to (1) succeed in competition with other males and (2) be chosen by females are the traits most likely to be passed on to future generations. A great example in the animal kingdom is the male elk. Male elks with large antlers are better able to compete with other males, and large number of points on the antlers signify health and longevity to females, making them more likely to be selected as mates (Brennan, 2012; Frances 2013).

The large antlers of a male elk provide a competitive advantage and signify health to potential mates.

How does this apply in humans? According to sexual selection, differences between the sexes have evolved so that men and women can attract members of the opposite sex and ensure reproductive success. This can help explain why men are typically bigger and stronger than women because these traits would have given them a competitive advantage in the past. One recent study examined male beards as a possible trait that women use when selecting potential sexual partners. A man's ability to grow a full beard is an indicator of sexual maturity, good health, and masculinity. However, when women were asked to rate the attractiveness of various beard lengths, they appeared to prefer "heavy stubble" as opposed to "full beards" (Dixson & Brooks, 2013). The authors hypothesize that women may prefer the heavy stubble to the full beard because of the costs associated with mating with a man who is perceived as too masculine and therefore potentially aggressive and dominant.

sexual selection

a type of natural selection in which the preference by one sex for certain characteristics of the other sex or a competitive advantage of certain traits leads the sexes to evolve in different forms

Women rated the attractiveness of these images in the Dixson & Brooks (2013) study.

CLEAN-SHAVEN   **LIGHT STUBBLE**   **HEAVY STUBBLE**   **FULL BEARD**

The Nurture of Gender

LO 11.2 Recognize how social and cultural influences affect gender development.

It's hard to deny that we all have ideas about gender that go beyond just what nature determines. For example, when we see a baby, we look for external clues about its gender so we know how we're supposed to act around it. One famous study measured how adults interacted with a 3-month-old baby when they were told the infant was either a boy, girl, or they were given no gender information (Seavey et al., 1975). The researchers discovered that the perceived gender of the infant influenced which toys the adults presented to the baby and how the adult interacted with the baby. Interestingly, adults who were not provided with any gender information were asked to predict the child's gender, and many of them reported using stereotypical characteristics to do so. For example, adults who guessed that the baby was a girl cited reasons such as "softness" and "fragility" while adults who guessed that the baby was a boy cited reasons such as the strength of the baby's grip or the lack of hair. Knowing that we begin to treat children differently from the moment their sex is revealed demonstrates that social factors are indeed important in the development of gender. Gender ambiguity—whether a girl baby mistaken for a boy or vice versa—generally causes discomfort in a society in which gender is such a significant part of a person's identity.

SOCIAL CONSTRUCTIONS OF GENDER   Although it is clear that biology plays a part in our sense of gender identity, many of the behaviors and ideas associated with each gender are socially constructed. Women may be viewed as emotional, nurturing, and passive, while men may be viewed as rational, dominant, and aggressive (e.g., Lindsey, 2015; Rosenkrantz et al., 1968). These associations come primarily from people who are highly **gender typed**—boys and men who show traditionally masculine traits and behaviors (called **instrumental traits**) and girls and women who show traditionally feminine traits and behaviors (called **expressive traits**).

Although gender was traditionally viewed as an either/or dichotomy, psychologist and gender studies researcher Sandra Bem developed a sex role inventory (known as the BSRI) to measure the degree to which people ascribe to both masculine feminine traits. Those who rate themselves equally high on both masculine and feminine traits are called **androgynous**. Bem and others believe that androgynous people are highly functioning and effective because, rather than limiting themselves according to gender typing, they are comfortable displaying whatever behaviors and traits are most appropriate in a given situation (Bem, 1975, 1981, 1993; Gartzia & van Engen, 2012; Mitchell & Allen, 2011; Rath & Mishra, 2013). An individual who scores high on the characteristic of androgyny would endorse high levels of both feminine/expressive traits (e.g., affectionate, gentle) and masculine/instrumental traits (e.g., independent, dominant).

The majority of people who experience a form of gender dissonance in adolescence or adulthood, including David Reimer and Christine Jorgensen, report having had such feelings since childhood. David's mother recalls him clawing at a dress the first time she dressed him in one, and his brother recalls David preferring the rough-and-tumble play of boys to dolls and tea parties (Colapinto, 1997). This early gender expression also suggests roots in both society and biology. Additionally, several examples of a third gender exist throughout the world. In 2005, India included a designation on passports for the *Hijra*, a distinct gender that is neither man nor woman. *Hijra* are typically born male or intersex, and they adopt a feminine dress but reject both the terms *man* and *woman*. The *kathoeys* of Thailand and the *winkte* of indigenous North American cultures are other examples of third genders living in the world today. When not all males are men and not all females are women, it becomes easier to see how sex and gender don't always go hand in hand.

As the Seavey et al. (1975) study demonstrated, babies are treated differently as soon as their sex is known. A father may talk to his son about cars while he's still in the womb, and a mother may read stories about princesses to her *in utero* daughter. As infants, boys and girls are dressed and treated differently. Girls tend to be talked to more often and treated more gently than boys, who are played with more roughly (Brody & Brody, 2009; Chaplin, 2015; Maccoby, 1998). Children are often given gendered toys to

gender typed

boys and men who show traditionally masculine traits and behaviors and girls and women who show traditionally feminine traits and behaviors

instrumental traits

traditionally masculine traits and behaviors

expressive traits

traditionally feminine traits and behaviors

androgynous

people who have both masculine and feminine traits

Hijra individuals in India.

play with and may even be discouraged from playing with toys typical of the other gender. Lego introduced a new line of building blocks called Lego Friends marketed to girls with pastel colors that focused on activities like baking, hair salons, and pool parties. This led to a backlash about gendered toys in general with a push to develop and market gender-neutral toys (Martin, 2012). In fact, the retail chain Target stopped labeling toy aisles with "boy" and "girl" designations in 2015 (Hains, 2015).

Gendered Toys

Ride-on toys for very young children are often targeted to specific genders.

Some researchers have found that male babies as young as one year show a preference for balls, guns, and trucks, while girls show a preference for dolls, stuffed animals, and cookware (Caldera et al., 1989; Goble et al., 2012; Wong & Hines, 2015). Studies with nonhuman primates have revealed similar preferences (Alexander & Hines, 2002). While these findings may suggest some biological influence, we are still left to wonder what use a female monkey of any age would have for cookware.

Perhaps more detrimental are the different assumptions that adults have about the interests and abilities of school-age boys and girls. These assumptions can lead to unequal treatment. For example, adults tend to offer more help and comfort to girls, while they expect boys to solve problems on their own (Biddulph, 2013; Eagly, 2013; Maccoby, 1998). Boys often receive more encouragement and instruction in math and science than girls (Gunderson et al., 2012; Sadker, 2000), who tend to pursue careers in these fields less often than their male counterparts (Cheryan, 2012). Proponents of single-gender education claim that without classroom competition between genders, both boys and girls receive equal opportunities and encouragement (Hughes, 2007).

SOCIAL THEORIES OF GENDER   Psychologists consider not only what aspects of gender are learned, but also how that learning occurs. The **social learning theory** assumes that children learn gendered behavior by observing and imitating adults and responding to rewards and punishments (Bussey & Bandura, 1999). For example, a little boy observes his father turn his ball cap backward and then goes to his closet, grabs his own ball cap, and puts it on backward. Chances are, this behavior will result in the child being complimented (i.e., rewarded) on how he looks like "a little man" or how he's "Daddy's little boy." His mother

social learning theory

a theory of gender development stating that children learn gendered behavior by observing and imitating adults and responding to rewards and punishments

may even ask him to pose for a picture with dad. These subtle comments serve to reinforce the child's behavior of imitating his father. On the other hand, if the same little boy gets into his mother's closet and puts on her high heels, the response might be less positive. Even parents who would never scold or criticize this behavior might laugh at the little boy which could be interpreted as negative feedback. The social learning theory suggests that over time, repetition of these observations, imitations, and reinforcements lead children to adopt a specific gender role.

Social Learning Theory

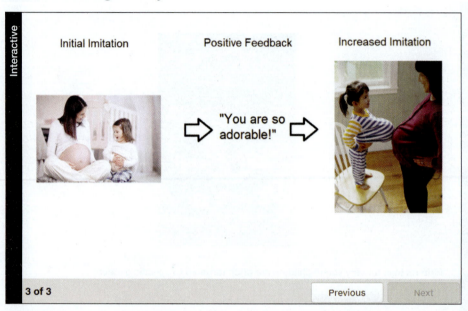

gender schema theory

a theory of gender development stating that children develop schemas for what is "male" and what is "female" through the process of social and cognitive learning

The **gender schema theory**, however, combines the social learning theory with the element of cognition. A *schema* is a cognitive framework that helps us organize and interpret information. According to gender schema theory, the process of gender differentiation begins at a very young age as children develop schemas for what is "male" and what is "female." Before the age of one, children learn to differentiate between male and female faces and voices (Martin et al., 2002). For example, a child's schema for "male" might include a deep voice and facial hair while the schema for "female" might include a higher-pitched voice and smooth facial skin. As children develop schemas for their own gender they also begin to adjust their behavior to align with it. As they begin to learn language, children are forced to organize words based on gender, whether through male and female pronouns or through masculine and feminine classifications. Studies show that by age three, children prefer to play with members of their own sex; they generally reach the peak of gender rigidity at age five or six (Aboud & Spears Brown, 2013; Bem, 1993; Hartley et al., 2013).

gender roles

expectations about the way women and men behave based on their gender

social role theory of gender

theory proposed by Alice Eagly stating that inherent physical differences between men and women lead to the formation of gender roles in the division of labor in the home and at work

GENDER ROLES AND STEREOTYPES Children may be treated differently according to the **gender roles**—expectations about the way women and men behave—they are expected to fill. Alice Eagly proposed the **social role theory of gender**, which focuses on how the inherent physical differences between men and women lead to the formation of gender roles in the division of labor in the home and at work (Eagly, 1987). This has led to various occupations being traditionally associated with one gender. For example, a survey in 2015 showed that 99 percent of speech-language pathologists are female and 99 percent of electrical power-line installers are male (United States Department of Labor, 2015).

The underrepresentation of women in STEM (science, technology, engineering, and mathematics) majors and careers has been a concern for many years. Despite the fact that women comprise an increasing percentage of the college-educated workforce (from 46 percent in 2000 to 49 percent in 2009), women only make up 24 percent of the STEM workforce (Beede et al., 2011). As educators and scientists work to narrow this gender gap, messages about gender roles in childhood and adolescence have been implicated as playing a role in the STEM gender gap. A combination of stereotyped messages from parents, educators, and the media about the typical roles and educational interests of men and women likely has an

Gender Schema Theory

A girl may have developed a schema that trucks are for boys and dolls are for girls. The chart demonstrates how gender schema theory might lead a girl to decide to play with the doll rather than the truck.

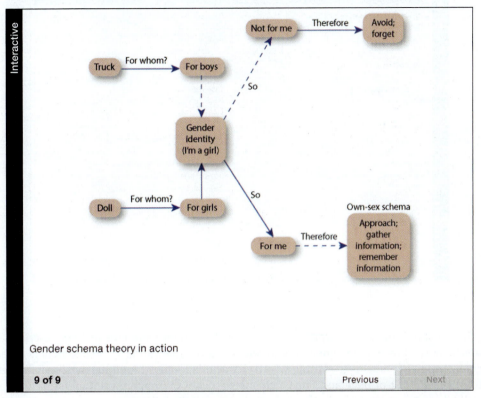

Gender schema theory in action

impact on college major and career choices. The infamous talking Barbie doll sold in 1992 that was programmed to say "math class is tough" served as a clear example of how messages of gender roles can be pervasive ("COMPANY NEWS: Mattel Says It Erred; Teen Talk Barbie Turns Silent on Math", 1992). The outcome of these messages can be self-perpetuating in that fewer girls interested in STEM subjects lead to fewer female role models in STEM careers. The exposure to encouraging role models is an important component in both social learning and gender schema theories.

Gender roles can and do change. Women's roles around the globe have changed vastly in just the last century. In the early 1900s, the only place where women had the right to vote was New Zealand. In 2015, Saudi Arabia became the last country to grant women the right to vote. In just 50 years, the number of U.S. law students who were women rose from 1 in 30 in 1960 to 1 in 2 in the early 21st century (American Bar Association, 2012). In less than a decade, the percentage of women who agreed that married women should be full-time homemakers dropped from about 45 percent in 1967 to 15 percent in 1972 (Glater, 2001). Currently, 51 percent of women report that they would prefer to work outside the home rather than stay at home and take care of the house and family (Saad, 2012). There have also been significant shifts in the roles of men in recent decades. Only 49 percent of men agreed that working mothers could have as good a relationship with their children as stay-at-home mothers in 1977; however, by 2008, 67 percent of men agreed with this statement (Galinsky et al., 2009). As women and mothers have moved into the workforce, the role of fathers has also shifted. In 1977, fathers spent 2.4 hours per workday with their children while today's fathers spend an average of 4.3 hours per workday with their children (Galinskey et al., 2009).

You've likely been exposed to **gender stereotypes**, or widely held concepts about a person or group of people based only on gender. There are numerous such stereotypes about both genders. One particularly interesting study conducted in 1968 asked a group of college students to imagine the characteristics of an average adult male or an average adult female (Rosenkrantz et al., 1968). Click on the table below to see which traits they used to describe males versus females.

gender stereotypes

widely held concepts about a person or group of people that are based only on gender

Gender Stereotypes

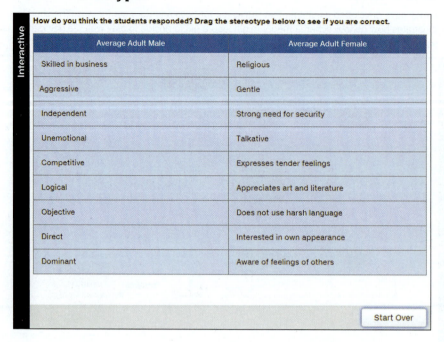

It probably came as no surprise to you to see that college students in 1968 described the characteristics of men and women very differently. More interestingly, the researchers asked a different group of students to identify which characteristics they found the most socially desirable. When the list of male and female characteristics was compared to the list of generally socially desirable characteristics, the authors discovered the following.

Gender and Socially Desirable Characteristics

The authors found that the socially desirable characteristics were much more likely to be associated with the descriptors of an average adult male than the average adult female.

2 of 2   Previous   Next

As the table demonstrates, the authors found that the socially desirable characteristics were much more likely to be associated with the descriptors of an average adult male than the average adult female.

Another research team replicated this study 30 years later to see if gender stereotypes have persisted despite significant changes in gender roles during that same time period (Nesbitt & Penn, 2000). While the more recent study still showed that male and female gender stereotypes were strongly present, the data related to social desirability had shifted significantly. In the 2000 study, characteristics more likely ascribed to women were rated as more socially desirable than characteristics ascribed to men. These results demonstrate not only how persistent stereotypes can be, but also how changing gender roles over time can lead to changes in whether a stereotype is viewed as positive or negative. Gender stereotypes have both positive and negative characteristics. For example, in many cultures, women are commonly stereotyped as nurturing and empathetic, but they are also stereotyped as overly emotional and irrational. Stereotypes portray men as powerful and rational, but also as aggressive and inattentive.

These gender stereotypes often lead to **sexism**—prejudice and unfair treatment (i.e., discrimination) based on gender stereotypes. Schoolteachers who call on boys more often than girls in math and science classes may not even realize that their bias is a result of sexism. Sexism can be more blatant, too. Ben Barres, a transgender Stanford neurobiology professor who attended MIT as Barbara Barres, knows all about sexism. According to Barres, his colleagues' treatment of him has changed noticeably since he changed his gender, and this change in treatment has led Barres to believe that sexism in the scientific community is likely responsible for the relatively small number of women who hold tenured academic positions in the sciences. Barres describes one fellow scientist who mentioned to him that Barres's work was much better than that of his "sister," Barbara. Barres's academic ability hadn't changed at all, but his change in gender altered people's perceptions of his work (Dean, 2006).

Another type of sexism is more insidious. **Benevolent sexism** is the acceptance of positive stereotypes or favorable biased behavior that propagates unfairness and inequalities based on gender (Becker & Swim, 2012; Glick & Fiske, 2001). Certain aspects of chivalry could be considered examples of benevolent sexism. When men open doors for women and insist on footing the bill for every romantic evening out, both the men who act "chivalrously" and the women who expect them to do so are perpetuating the sexist idea that women are helpless, weak, and unable to provide for themselves. Of course, holding the door for someone isn't inherently sexist, but in order to eliminate the effects of benevolent sexism, both men and women should be willing to hold open doors for people of any gender.

sexism

prejudice and discrimination based on gender

benevolent sexism

the acceptance of positive stereotypes that propagates unfairness and inequalities based on gender

Adaptive Pathway 11.1: Gender Theories

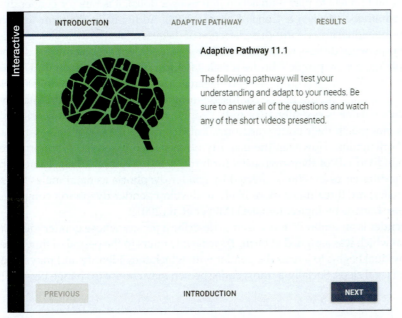

INTRODUCTION ADAPTIVE PATHWAY RESULTS

Interactive

Adaptive Pathway 11.1

The following pathway will test your understanding and adapt to your needs. Be sure to answer all of the questions and watch any of the short videos presented.

PREVIOUS INTRODUCTION NEXT

Transgender Experiences

LO 11.3 **Explain transgender experiences.**

Gender identity has been discussed frequently in the media over the past few years. Caitlyn Jenner, a former Olympic gold medalist, publicly changed her name in April 2015 and has become one of the most well-known transgender women in the world. Watch the video *Travis: Transgender Experiences* for another example.

Travis: Transgender Experiences

gender dysphoria

persistent feelings of identification with the opposite gender and discomfort with the sex assigned at birth

GENDER DYSPHORIA Unlike androgyny, which involves a combination of masculinity and femininity, **gender dysphoria** (previously known as gender identity disorder) causes a person to feel that he or she was born with a physical body that is not consistent with his or her gender identity which causes distress. Gender dysphoria is a diagnostic category found in the fifth and most recent version of the Diagnostic and Statistical Manual of Mental Disorders (DSM-5; American Psychiatric Association, 2013). While it is not uncommon for some children to express a degree of gender dysphoria in childhood (e.g., the little girl who says she doesn't want to be a girl, refuses to wear dresses, and prefers to play with action figures over dolls), it is rare for gender dysphoria to persist into adulthood (Wallien & Cohen-Kettenis, 2008). Additionally, the term "dysphoria" implies that the individual experiences dissatisfaction or distress related to their biological sex. People who do not experience distress related to their cross-gender identification are not diagnosed with gender dysphoria, nor are people who are satisfied following a gender transition.. Ultimately, a diagnosis of gender dysphoria is quite rare and is seen in less than 1 percent of adults (Zucker, 2010).

Gender dysphoria should not be confused with the concept of sexual orientation (the gender to which someone is sexually attracted). People with gender dysphoria believe that their gender does not match their body's anatomy, but this mismatch is not necessarily associated with sexual orientation. However, the majority of people with gender dysphoria are sexually attracted to individuals of their own *natal* (or birth) sex (Lawrence, 2010). There appear to be some gender differences in who is affected by gender dysphoria as natal males (those born as biological males) are three times more likely to develop gender dysphoria compared to natal females (those born as biological females) (Meyer et al., 2001).

transgender

umbrella term used to describe a person whose gender identity is different from that which was assigned at birth

Transgender is an umbrella term used to describe a person whose gender identity is different from that which was assigned at birth. *Transitioning* refers to the period of time when a transgender individual begins to live as the gender with which they identify and may include social, medical, and legal steps. Socially, a transgender person may choose to change his/her first name and manner of dress or grooming. Medical options for transitioning may include taking hormones or undergoing surgical procedures. A variety of surgical procedures can be considered, including breast augmentation/removal and/or alterations of the genitals. Legal steps in transitioning can include changing legal documents such as a birth certificate, driver's license, and social security card. The ability to change gender on a driver's license currently varies by state with the most restrictive states requiring proof of surgery, a court order, or an amended birth certificate. Whenever a transgender person has to use documents that identify him/her incorrectly in terms of gender, the experience can lead to awkwardness, embarrassment, and even harassment or discrimination.

The process of transitioning can be both economically and socially costly. Like any medical procedure, choosing a surgical route has some inherent risk, and the cost of these procedures is also quite high. So, why would someone choose to transition? For many people, the experience of gender dysphoria is so distressing that they are willing to endure the costs and associated difficulties in an attempt to live a life consistent with who they believe themselves to be. Research has confirmed the high degree of distress experienced by these individuals by documenting a higher than normal risk of suicide (Glicksman, 2013; James et al., 2016) and high rate of additional psychiatric conditions such as substance abuse (Hepp et al., 2005). Following gender transitioning, studies have shown that individuals report improved quality of life and a reduction in gender dysphoria (Johansson et al., 2010; Wierckx et al., 2011), suggesting that the treatment may provide significant benefit to some individuals. Watch *Travis: Transgender Experiences: Part 2* to learn more about Travis's life after his transition.

MPL Video Series Travis: Transgender Experiences Part 2

Interactive

Journal Prompt: Travis Video Review

After watching the videos describing Travis' experiences, describe the transition process that Travis underwent to transition from female to male.

Quiz for Module 11.1–11.3

1. _____ is our biological classification while _____ is our psychological classification along the continuum of maleness and femaleness.

   a. Gender; sex

   b. Sex; gender

   c. X chromosome; Y chromosome

   d. Y chromosome; X chromosome

2. _____ are the sexual organs present at birth which are directly involved in human reproduction.

   a. Primary sex characteristics

   b. Secondary sex characteristics

   c. Mullerian system

   d. Wolffian system

3. Ben is a nurse who is known as gentle and nurturing with his patients. On his days off, he plays soccer with his children. Ben's wife Nikki is a president of a bank and is known for making tough decisions and being an independent thinker. Her hobbies are cooking and sewing. Both Ben and Nikki exhibit what Sandra Bem calls _____ traits.

   a. androgynous

   b. gender-typed

   c. masculine

   d. neutral

4. When Suki was asked what role she wanted in the school play about the Wild West, she said she would be the cook for the cowboys because girls aren't rowdy. Which theory of gender development best explains Suki's behavior?

   a. Androgynous behavior

   b. Gender development

   c. Gender schema theory

   d. Social learning theory

5. Which theory of gender development focuses on the role of observational learning and reinforcement?

   a. Social learning theory

   b. Role theory

   c. Gender schema theory

   d. Gender identity development theory

6. _____ refers to the period of time when a transgender individual begins to live as the gender with which they identify.

   a. Transgender

   b. Gender identity disorder

   c. Homosexuality

   d. Transitioning

7. _____ refers to a mismatch between gender and biological sex resulting in distress, while _____ refers to the gender to which someone is sexually attracted.

   a. Sexual identity; sexual orientation

   b. Sexual orientation; gender dysphoria

   c. Gender dysphoria; sexual orientation

   d. Sexual orientation; sexual identity

Module 11.4–11.5: Gender Similarities and Differences

Before the 2008 Beijing Olympics, organizers created a "gender determination lab" where female athletes could be given genetic tests to determine whether or not they were truly female. The decision to create this lab was most likely made in the spirit of fair play, based on the idea that men are generally physically stronger than women and would have an innate biological advantage if they posed as women and competed against female athletes. The mere fact that sporting events, including the Olympic Games, are almost always divided into men's competitions and women's competitions reinforces this generalization. But are men and women really so different? And what are the ethical implications of testing athletes' sex? How do transgender athletes, intersex athletes, and others who blur boundaries of sex and gender fit into the picture? Even at the "gender determination lab," the question of differences and similarities between genders persists.

While much effort has been made to emphasize the equality of men and women, some studies have found ways in which they are consistently different. However, if we were to focus on the studies that find no differences between the genders on various physical, cognitive, or emotional characteristics, the summary of such studies could fill the entire book. One recent group of researchers evaluated hundreds of studies examining gender differences (Zell et al., 2015), and Figure 11.2 represents the average differences on all traits between males and females. Keep in mind that the tallest point of the curve represents the average, or mean, score on a trait for a particular gender. Can you predict the average degree of difference between the

Figure 11.2 Average Difference Between Genders

This graph represents a difference between two groups that is similar in size to the average gender differences found on psychological variables.

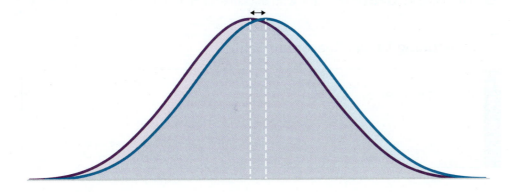

genders by placing the "peaks" of the curves either close together (to represent very small gender differences) or far apart (to represent very large gender differences)?

Zell and colleagues essentially found support for an overall "gender similarities" hypothesis, the fact that men and women are similar in most but not all psychological variables. Even when gender differences have been found, they tend to be quite small. The correct graph provides an example of what the average difference on a given trait looks like for men and women. Notice how much overlap exists between the distribution of male and female "scores." This graph provides an important lesson in how to interpret statistical data. While the average scores between two groups may be significantly different, that does not mean that those differences are large or even meaningful. Additionally, these gender differences represent a slight difference between the average scores of males and females. If you were to consider an individual male or female, you can see by looking at the graph that it's quite possible for an individual male to outperform an individual female.

When differences are found between the genders, these differences are likely not rooted in biology alone. After all, 45 of our 46 chromosomes are unisex. The way that parents, siblings, peers, and society as a whole treat people differently according to gender certainly has an influence on the ways in which they are different. Often, our expectations about the ways we think people will act become a self-fulfilling prophecy. We should also remember that variation among individuals is much greater than generalized variation between genders.

Gender Differences in Cognitive Abilities

LO 11.4   **Explain gender differences in cognitive abilities, including intelligence and memory.**

While scientific evidence of gender dissimilarities is less prevalent than you might expect (Hyde, 2014), there are certainly some clear-cut difference between the genders. Women have a longer average life expectancy and men tend to have a higher basal metabolic rate. But what about gender differences in intelligence or memory? Studies of male and female differences in cognitive abilities are much more complicated than evaluations of other physical differences.

INTELLIGENCE   *Intelligence*, defined as the capacity to reason, solve problems, and acquire new knowledge, has been studied for many years. While a variety of theories have been developed to understand the concept of intelligence, most experts tend to agree that both verbal reasoning skills and spatial reasoning skills are important subcomponents of intelligence. *Verbal reasoning skills* include the ability to analyze information and solve problems using language-based reasoning. Verbal reasoning skills typically require the ability to understand a question, draw from past experiences, develop a response, and express thoughts verbally. For example, if you took the SAT for college entrance, you likely encountered a test of verbal analogies. This exam requires the test-taker to recognize the underlying relationship between two words and choose a second set of words with the same relationship.

Demonstrating Verbal Reasoning Skills

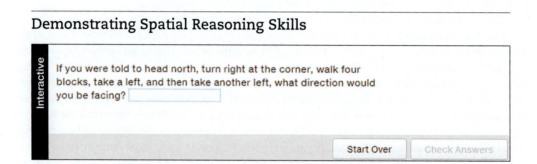

On the other hand, *spatial reasoning skills* include the ability to understand, remember, and even manipulate in your "mind's eye" the spatial relationships between objects. For example, see if you can answer the following problem.

Demonstrating Spatial Reasoning Skills

Of all the components that comprise measurements of intelligence, verbal reasoning skills and spatial reasoning skills have been some of the most highly researched in terms of differences between the genders. Studies in both areas showed a reliable difference between males and females such that females performed better on certain measures of verbal skills (e.g., particularly in *verbal fluency*, or the ability to generate words in a category quickly) while males performed better in terms of spatial skills (Dabbs et al., 1998; Hyde, 2014; Hyde & Linn, 1988; Maloney et al., 2012; Voyer et al., 1995). However, it's important to recognize that these differences were still quite small, particularly with regard to the female advantage in certain verbal skills.

Research has also focused on potential gender differences in mathematic abilities. The majority of studies until the 1990s showed that males had a small but significant advantage over females in terms of math skill (Hyde et al., 1990). This difference was more pronounced for the math skill of complex problem solving in high school students. These findings prompted significant concern given the gender disparity in STEM fields and the focus on mathematical complex problem solving within these fields. Some recent data has shown that the gender gap in mathematic ability overall and complex problem-solving skills specifically has all but disappeared (Hyde et al., 2008; Hyde, 2014; Lindberg et al., 2010), while other studies continue to show gender differences favoring males in mathematics (Reilly, et al., 2015). It appears that progress has been made toward obtaining gender equity in math achievement, but more work remains to be done.

Researchers have attempted to understand why these differences seem to exist. They have found that, consistent with these generalizations, the part of the parietal lobe associated with spatial perception is thicker in adult men than it is in adult women, who have a thicker part of the frontal lobes associated with verbal fluency than their male counterparts (Bramen et al., 2012; Gur et al., 1999; Pangelinan et al., 2011). It would make sense to conclude that these brain differences are the cause of men's and women's different strengths. Evolutionary theories may help explain why these brain differences and resultant spatial skills differences exist (Jones et al., 2003). However, scientists still know very little about how our brains work, and it's just as likely that repeated practice with spatial puzzles thickens that area of the brain in men, who may have more exposure to these puzzles than women due to gender-targeted toys (e.g., video games) and education. The same principle could hold true for the findings related to verbal fluency, since female babies are generally spoken to more and are encouraged to interact verbally with others (Van Hulle et al., 2004).

Which Research Study?

Interactive

If you were to conduct a research study to attempt to definitively answer this question about brain size and specific intellectual abilities, would a cross-sectional or longitudinal research study be best suited to provide you with an accurate answer?

Start Over | Check Answers

MEMORY   In addition to intelligence, memory is another cognitive ability that has been studied in terms of gender. Similar to intelligence, the term memory encompasses a variety of processes and abilities. Figure 11.3 demonstrates some of the divisions of the memory system. For the most part, researchers have not found gender differences in memory functioning. However, there have been some consistent differences found within certain aspects of memory.

Specifically, gender differences in explicit memory have been found. Explicit memory is defined as the information you can consciously recall. That is, your explicit memory is *what you know that you know*. Several studies have shown that females tend to have better **episodic memory** (memory of specific events or experiences) (Herlitz et al., 1997), and this difference is greatest for events that are emotional in nature (Burton et al., 2004; Williams et al., 2009). For example, one study with adults revealed that women recalled more childhood events of an emotional nature than men (Davis, 1999). In addition, studies have shown a general female advantage in memory for object location (Voyer et al., 2007).

episodic memory

memory of specific events or experiences

Figure 11.3 Memory and Gender Differences

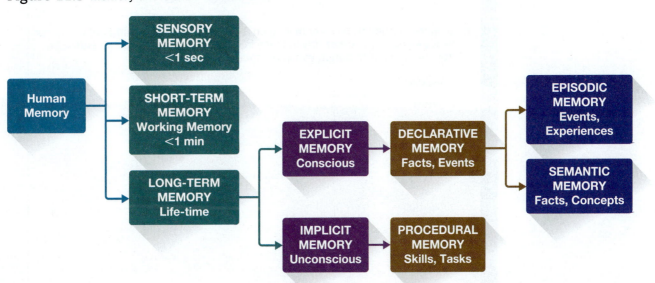

However, despite the findings of some specific gender differences, it's important to note that overall memory functioning appears to be quite similar across genders. A study examining gender differences among children and adolescents on 14 different tests of memory components only found two consistent differences such that girls showed a slight advantage on verbal tasks and boys showed a slight advantage on spatial tasks (Lowe et al., 2003). However, there were no gender differences found on the other 12 domains of memory suggesting that memory, like intelligence, is actually very similar across genders.

Gender Differences in Social Behavior

LO 11.5 Describe gender differences related to social behaviors.

In addition to differences in cognitive abilities, gender differences in social behaviors have also been widely examined. It's important to evaluate the nature of gender stereotypes such as "men are more aggressive" and "women are more emotional" because such stereotypes are often used as the basis for social policies related to access to education or sharing of power and decision making.

AGGRESSION Aggression is defined as any purposeful behavior intended to cause physical or psychological harm to others. When it comes to studying aggression and gender, it is important to distinguish between different types of aggressive behavior. **Physical aggression** includes any behavior that threatens physical harm or actually causes physical harm to another person. For example, hitting someone or threatening to hit someone are both acts of physical aggression. **Verbal aggression**, on the other hand, includes verbal communication that is intended to cause psychological harm rather than physical harm. While both physical and verbal aggression can be forms of **direct aggression**, people can also engage in indirect aggressive behavior. **Indirect aggression** (also referred to as *relational aggression*) includes acts that do not directly involve the target of the aggression such as spreading rumors, avoiding, and attempting to persuade others not to like the targeted individual. While early studies of gender differences in aggressive behavior unequivocally claimed that men are more aggressive than women by nature, more recent researchers have pointed out the importance of defining the type of aggression when studying gender differences. (Björkqvist et al., 1992).

aggression

any purposeful behavior intended to cause physical or psychological harm to others

physical aggression

includes any behavior that threatens or causes physical harm to another person

verbal aggression

includes verbal communication that is intended to cause psychological harm rather than physical harm

direct aggression

aggressive acts that directly target an individual

indirect aggression

includes acts that do not directly involve the target of the aggression but are used to harm a person's relationships or social standing

Different Forms of Aggression

Interactive

Identify the type of aggressive behavior by first indicating whether the example involves physical or verbal aggression and then indicating whether the example is direct or indirect.

4 questions

1. Pat is rear-ended by a driver talking on a cell phone. After getting out of the car, Pat walks up to the other driver, leans in close with a balled up fist, and yells, "You idiot! I want to punch you in the face!"

○ Physical

○ Verbal

Next

Gender stereotypes would lead most people to believe that men are more likely to engage in physical and direct aggression while women would be more likely to engage in verbal and indirect aggression. Like many stereotypes, some evidence supports these assumptions but other findings are contradictory to the stereotypes.

Surveys, experiments, and observed cultural behaviors lend support to the idea that physical aggression is more prevalent in men than in women (Archer, 2004; Card et al., 2008; Eagly & Steffen, 1986). One study found that men are more likely than women to administer what they believe are more painful shocks to another person (Bettencourt & Kernahan, 1997). Men also commit more violent crimes; the male-to-female arrest ratio is eight to one in the United States (United States Department of Justice, 2015) and seven to one in Canada (Statistics Canada, 2003; 2008; 2015). These differences even appear to extend to opinions regarding the use of aggression. A recent paper outlining gender differences on public opinions of the use of military force in the United States from 1980–2013 showed that women were less likely to support the use of military force in each instance of military operations from El Salvador in the 1980s and early 90s to the most recent conflicts in Iraq, Afghanistan, Libya, and Syria (Eichenberg, 2016). Some theorists have hypothesized that socialization of gender roles has played an important role in socializing men to be more physically aggressive than women through media exposure, marketing of aggressive toys to boys (e.g., toy guns and other weapons), and reinforcement of aggressive behavior in boys but not girls (Berkowitz, 1993; Fortuna, 2014). However, as gender roles have changed over the past decades, there has not been a corresponding increase in female physical aggression nor a decrease in male physical aggression. The more likely explanation for male physical aggression is an evolutionary one. Males who were physically dominant and aggressive were able to gain status and protect their families and belongings which led to these traits being inherited by future generations of men (Bus & Duntley, 2006; Gat, 2010).

In terms of indirect or verbal aggression, individual studies have found some evidence that women are more likely to engage in such behavior, but meta-analyses in which data from many studies is aggregated have shown that the gender differences between adults in terms of indirect aggression are very small (Archer, 2004), and no gender differences have been found for indirect aggression among children and adolescents (Card et al., 2008).

SOCIAL POWER AND SOCIAL CONNECTEDNESS   Think about the most powerful individuals in your state, country, or the world. Of the individuals who quickly came to your mind, what percent were male versus female? It's likely that at least the majority of the people you thought about were male. In fact, in 2016, the U.S. Treasury Department reported that it will be replacing Andrew Jackson on the $20 bill with Harriet Tubman who will become the first women shown on U.S. currency. The simple fact that every form of U.S. currency in the past has had the image of a man underscores that gender has been a powerful determinant in the arena of social power.

Men tend to be more socially dominant in most cultures (see Figure 11.4). Not only are men often the leaders in groups, such as juries and companies (Colarelli et al., 2006), but they also held 77 percent of seats in the world's governing parliaments in 2015 (Inter-Parliamentary Union, 2015). Studies comparing male and female leaders have found that men tend to be more directive, autocratic, and opinionated and more likely to talk assertively, interrupt, initiate touching, stare, and are less likely to smile, while women tend to be more democratic, more welcoming of subordinates' participation in decision making, and more likely to express support (Aries, 1987; Cheng & Lin, 2012; Eagly & Johnson, 1990; Hall, 1987; Kark et al., 2012; Major et al., 1990; van Engen & Willemsen, 2004; Wood, 1987).

On the other hand, studies have found that women tend to have higher levels of social connectedness. The term **social connectedness** refers to the quality and number of meaningful relationships an individual may have among friends, family, and the community. Psychologist and feminist Carol Gilligan (Brown & Gilligan, 1993; Gilligan, 1982; Gilligan et al., 1990) and her colleagues described the desire for social connectedness as largely female and the desire for a separate identity as largely male. While it is unclear if these gender differences exist across all cultures, one recent study confirmed that adolescent girls demonstrated higher levels of social connectedness than adolescent boys in South Africa (Schulze & Naidu, 2014). Many studies show how this pattern begins in childhood and persists throughout adulthood. Gender segregation in childhood play is extremely common. It is reinforced not only by adults but also by other children who ridicule any peers who don't seem to buy into the dominant "girls versus boys" mind-set. The kinds of play seen in these separate groups are also distinct. Boys tend to play in large groups that focus on activity over discussion, while girls tend to play in smaller groups or pairs with little competitiveness and more focus on social relationships (Rubin et al., 2007; Rudman & Glick, 2012).

social connectedness

the quality and number of meaningful relationships an individual may have among friends, family, and the community

Figure 11.4 Leadership Roles and Gender

The global map demonstrates that most countries have either never had a female leader or have had one for less than 5 years. As the infographics demonstrates, women are also unequally represented in other areas of U.S. government and businesses, with women of color being particularly poorly represented in leadership positions.

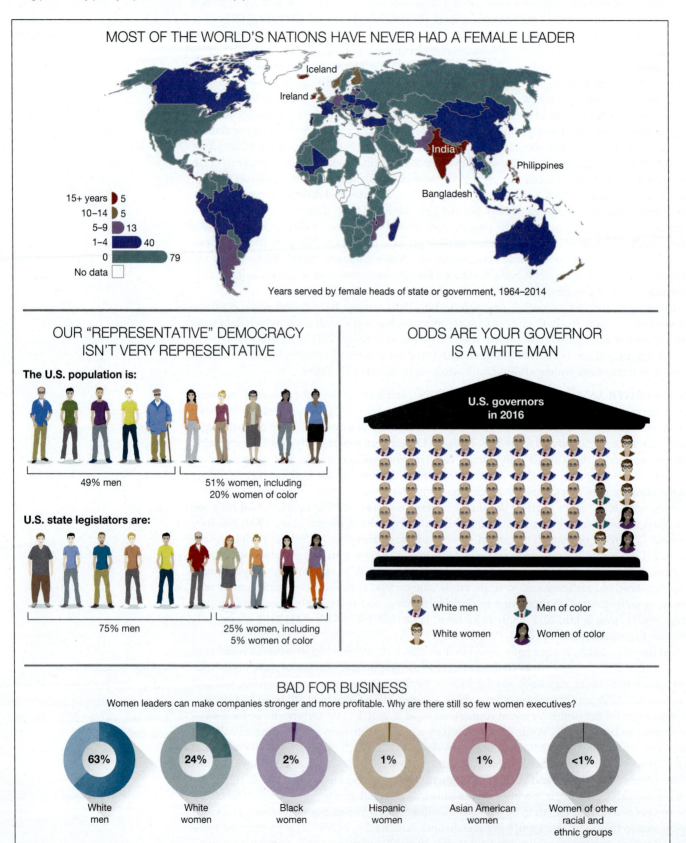

MOST OF THE WORLD'S NATIONS HAVE NEVER HAD A FEMALE LEADER

Iceland
Ireland
India
Bangladesh
Philippines

15+ years 5
10–14 5
5–9 13
1–4 40
0 79
No data

Years served by female heads of state or government, 1964–2014

OUR "REPRESENTATIVE" DEMOCRACY ISN'T VERY REPRESENTATIVE

The U.S. population is:

49% men
51% women, including 20% women of color

U.S. state legislators are:

75% men
25% women, including 5% women of color

ODDS ARE YOUR GOVERNOR IS A WHITE MAN

U.S. governors in 2016

White men   Men of color
White women   Women of color

BAD FOR BUSINESS

Women leaders can make companies stronger and more profitable. Why are there still so few women executives?

63%	24%	2%	1%	1%	<1%
White men	White women	Black women	Hispanic women	Asian American women	Women of other racial and ethnic groups

As the play of childhood gives way to the conversations of adulthood, men and women continue to exhibit differences. Women tend to be more interdependent, using conversation to explore social relationships (Tannen, 1990) and to cope with stress (Tamres et al., 2002; Taylor, 2002). Interestingly, both women and men report having more intimate, enjoyable, and nurturing friendships with women (Hall, 1984; Kahneman et al., 1999; Sapadin, 1988).

Quiz for Module 11.4–11.5

1. Erin has excelled on the debate team in high school. She is skilled at understanding complex concepts, developing arguments to support her ideas, and expressing those arguments verbally. This set of skills is known as _____.
   a. intelligence
   b. processing speed
   c. spatial reasoning skills
   d. verbal reasoning skills

2. Overall, research suggests that gender differences in the areas of intelligence and memory are _____.
   a. minimal
   b. moderate
   c. significant
   d. nonexistent

3. According to several studies, females perform slightly better at which type of memory tasks?
   a. Episodic
   b. Procedural
   c. Semantic
   d. Sensory

4. Tomas is a 5th grader who is caught at recess throwing rocks at the girls and kicking some of the boys. This type of behavior is known as _____.
   a. distinct aggression
   b. physical aggression
   c. verbal aggression
   d. indirect aggression

5. Men are more likely than women to engage in _____ aggression, while some studies have shown that women are slightly more likely than men to engage in _____ aggression.
   a. verbal; direct
   b. verbal; physical
   c. indirect; direct
   d. direct; indirect

Module 11.6–11.7: Sexual Orientation

Imagine you were born left-handed surrounded by a majority of right-handed people. Approximately 90 percent of people are right-handed. Being part of the 10 percent of left-handed people is not a big deal unless you imagine a world in which being left-handed is stigmatized and considered to be a sign of moral weakness. Imagine left-handed people are discriminated against when it comes to employment or job advancement, and left-handed people are not allowed to marry. At a young age, if you are suspected of being a "lefty," then your parents might hide your "disability" from others and try to retrain you to only use your right hand to write or throw a ball. If those efforts were unsuccessful, you might receive public ridicule in school for writing with your left-hand and you would never excel in sports because you would not be allowed to shoot a basketball with your left hand, or bat left-handed in baseball. You would often be told that you are "choosing" to use the wrong hand and could easily change your behavior if you had the willpower to do so.

This example may sound absurd, but left-handedness actually was considered pathological or "evil" at times in our history. One famous 19th century criminologist stated that being left-handed "may contribute to form one of the worst characters among the human species" (Kushner, 2011). Have you ever stopped to consider that the synonym for the word "right" is "correct?" If you receive a "left-handed compliment" it actually means that you've been the recipient of an unflattering comment. In fact, many Asian cultures continue to encourage or force left-handed children to use their right hands, particularly for writing and eating. School children in the United States used to be forced to write right-handed and if caught using the left-hand, children would often receive a slap on the wrist or hand (Binns, 2006).

The issue of sexual orientation has several interesting parallels to the consideration of being left-handed in a right-handed world. **Sexual orientation** refers to the pattern of a person's sexual attractions. Three of the most common categories of sexual orientation include attraction to members of one's own sex (*gay men or lesbians*), members of the other sex (*heterosexual*), or both sexes (*bisexual*). However, these are not the only categories of expression of sexual orientation. Also, keep in mind that *sexual orientation* (the gender(s) to which one is sexually attracted) is different from *gender identity* (personal experience of one's gender). As the following sections will detail, current research suggests that sexual orientation is not something we choose but

sexual orientation

refers to the pattern of a person's sexual attractions

rather reflects the way we are born much like being left-handed or right-handed. However, there has been a long history of discrimination and stigmatization of individuals who are not heterosexual. In addition, there have been many attempts to try to "change" an individual's sexual orientation under the assumption that it is a choice.

Sexual Orientation: Definitions and Prevalence

LO 11.6 **Recognize the definition and prevalence of various sexual orientations.**

A 2012 Gallup poll asked people to self-identify as either heterosexual, gay, lesbian, bisexual, or transgender. They found an overall LGBT (lesbian/gay/bisexual/transgender) prevalence rate of 3.8 percent (Newport, 2015). Although there are inherent limitations of asking people to self-identify in terms of sexual orientation or gender identity (e.g., possible underreporting due to concerns about discrimination), this finding was very consistent with other studies showing that 2–4 percent of men and 1–2 percent of women identify their sexual orientation as gay or lesbian (Chandra et al., 2013; Fredriksen-Goldsen et al., 2013). Also, the 3.4 percent prevalence rate in the Gallup poll is inflated because the Gallup poll includes people who identify as gay, lesbian, or bisexual in addition to people who identify as transgender which is associated with gender identity rather than sexual orientation. Individuals from racial/ethnic minorities appear to self-identify as LGBT more often than White Americans. For example, the 2012 Gallup poll showed that 4.6 percent of African-Americans, 4.0 percent of Hispanics, 4.3 percent of Asians, and 3.2 percent of white Americans identified as LGBT. Bisexual orientation appears to be even less common than gay or lesbian orientation, with a recent large-scale study showing that only 0.7 percent of Americans self-identify as bisexual (Miller et al., 2013).

These statistics may provide a false sense of sexual orientation as being a dichotomous or an either/or issue. In fact, most experts now believe that sexual orientation falls more along a continuum ranging from exclusive heterosexuality to exclusive gay or lesbian orientation. Ground-breaking studies by Kinsey in the 1940s helped advance our understanding of sexual orientation which had previously been viewed as a one-dimensional construct.

Sexual Orientation on a Continuum

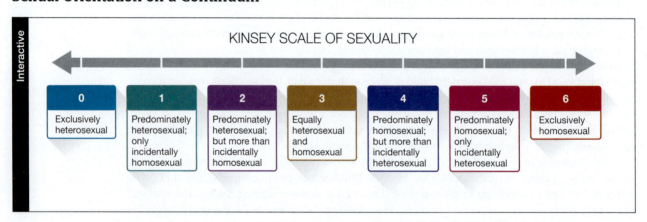

The previous dichotomous model of sexual orientation made the following assumptions: (1) people describe their sexual orientation as clearly either heterosexual or gay/lesbian, (2) the way people behave sexually defines their sexual orientation, and (3) sexual orientation is an enduring and unchanging disposition (Garnets & Kimmel, 2013). However, research over the past few decades has failed to support these three assumptions. Currently, according to the American Psychological Association, "someone does not have to be exclusively homosexual or heterosexual, but can feel varying degrees of both" (American Psychological Association, 2009). It is therefore helpful to distinguish between terms such as sexual orientation, *sexual orientation identity* (group membership or self-labeling), and sexual attraction/behavior when attempting to understand the complexities of sexual orientation. For example, a higher percentage of people report engaging in sexual activity with members of the same sex than the percentage of people who describe their sexual orientation as gay or lesbian. A 2016 National Health Statistics Report found that 17.4 percent of women and 6.2 percent of men had engaged in same-sex sexual activity in their lifetimes whereas in that same survey 3.9 percent of men and 6.8 percent of women classified themselves as gay, lesbian, or bisexual (Copen et al., 2016). Therefore, it is possible for individuals to engage in same-sex sexual behavior without identifying themselves as gay or lesbian.

Development of sexual orientation has generally been shown to occur in childhood and adolescence (Bailey & Zucker, 1995; Saewyc, 2011; Tolman & McClelland, 2011). However, this process has shown to be somewhat more fluid among females than males. Diamond (2007) studied a group of nonheterosexual young women over a period of 10 years from ages 16 to 23. When these women were asked to identify their sexual orientation, two-thirds of them changed their identity label at least once over the course of the study. Additionally, one-fourth of the women changed their identified sexual orientation more than once. Findings such as these led to the concept of **erotic plasticity** for women, meaning that their sexuality tends to be less strongly felt and can be more fluid than men's (Baumeister, 2000; Diamond, 2008; Farr et al., 2014).

erotic plasticity

the degree to which sexual attraction tends to be fluid

Because humans are part of the larger animal kingdom, it can be helpful to examine sexual behavior among other animal groups in order to better understand issues related to sexual orientation. In fact, humans are not the only animals to engage in homosexual or bisexual behavior. While exclusively homosexual behavior is quite rare among non-human animals, many animal species engage in a variety of same-sex sexual behaviors. Driscoll (2008) quotes sociologist Eric Anderson, "Unlike most humans...individual animals generally cannot be classified as gay or straight: an animal that engages in a same-sex flirtation or partnership does not necessarily shun heterosexual encounters. Rather, many species seem to have ingrained homosexual tendencies that are a regular part of their society. That is, there are probably no strictly gay critters, just bisexual ones. Animals don't do sexual identity. They just do sex." The exception to this appears to be domesticated sheep as approximately 8 percent of domesticated rams are exclusively homosexual (Cloud, 2007; Roselli et al., 2004). Birds, primates, reptiles, and even insects have been found to engage in same-sex sexual behavior (Hogenboom, 2015). Making connections between homosexuality in humans and same-sex sexual behavior in non-human animals is complicated (e.g., humans are some of the only species to engage in sex when procreation is not intended and even use contraceptives to prevent reproduction) but the fact that there are widespread examples of homosexual behavior throughout the animal kingdom provides some evidence that this is likely a natural part of animal life.

Prejudice and discrimination related to sexual orientation have been very common throughout history. Currently, countries around the world view homosexuality in drastically different ways, from full acceptance of same-sex marriage to criminalization of homosexuality that is legally punishable by death.

During the 2014 Winter Olympic Games in Sochi, Russia, controversy broke out regarding Russia's laws restricting gay-rights activities. Leading up to the Olympics, laws were enacted in Russia banning homosexual propaganda, restricting gay couples' ability to adopt Russian-born children, and allowing for the detainment of people (including tourists) for up to 14 days on suspicions of being "pro-gay." Russia's treatment of homosexuality prompted an international backlash, leading to numerous protests and boycotts.

Protests and gay-rights campaigns related to the Sochi Olympics were abundant, and the United States actually sent an official delegation to the Olympics comprised entirely of openly gay athletes. This type of official support of the LGBTQ community in the United States demonstrates a significant shift in public opinion and public policy over the past decades. Until 1973, homosexuality was listed as a mental illness by the American Psychiatric Association. This classification endured until 1993 at the World Health Organization, 1995 in China, and 2001 in Japan. The early work of Evelyn Hooker was pivotal in reversing the view of homosexuality as a mental illness. Hooker (1957) studied a sample of gay and heterosexual men and discovered expert judges were not able to accurately classify the men according to sexual orientation based on psychological data alone. This study demonstrated that psychologically healthy gay men are commonly found, and therefore, defining homosexuality as inherently pathological was inaccurate. Further replications of Hooker's work ultimately led to the removal of homosexuality as a classified mental illness (Gonsiorek, 1991).

International Laws Regarding Homosexuality

Click on the legend in the upper right corner to view the data.

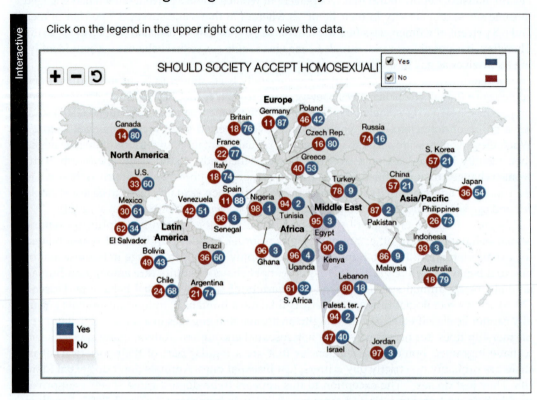

Opinions about same-sex marriage changed significantly in a relatively short period of time from 2001 to 2014. In 2001, only 35 percent of Americans supported same-sex marriage (with 57 percent opposed) but by 2016, this trend had reversed with a majority of Americans now supporting same-sex marriage (with 37 percent opposed). Figure 11.5

Figure 11.5 Changing Views of Same-Sex Marriage

While more people in the United States were opposed to same sex marriage in 1996, that trend has reversed over the last 20 years so that more people are now in support of same sex marriage than in opposition.

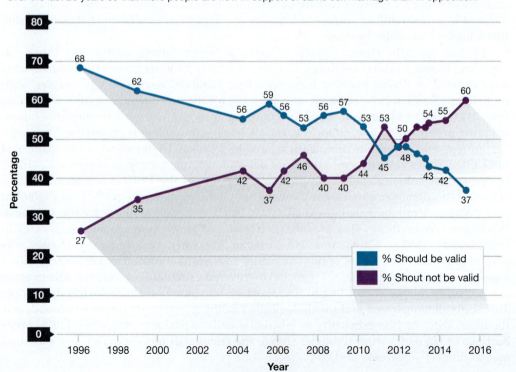

demonstrates how rapidly views have changed about same-sex marriage from 1996–2016. In 2015, a ground-breaking Supreme Court decision legalized same-sex marriage in the United States.

Despite these changes, discrimination against the LGBTQ community continues. For example, hate crimes committed against LGBTQ individuals constitute 21 percent of all hate crimes reported nationally, making homosexuality the second-highest category of hate crimes reported to the FBI in 2014 (Federal Bureau of Investigation, 2014).

Research on the Cause of Sexual Orientation

LO 11.7 **Understand the research findings about the causes of sexual orientation.**

What causes someone to be straight, gay, lesbian, or bisexual? Despite many years of research, the answer to this question unfortunately remains unclear. Many studies have attempted to identify what factors may contribute to the development of sexual orientation and while there is some evidence that certain factors may contribute, no single factor has been identified that causes a person to have a particular sexual orientation. Early psychological theories concluded that sexual orientation was the result of one's upbringing through problematic family dynamics or faulty psychological development. For example, traumatic experiences in early childhood such as childhood sexual abuse were theorized to cause homosexuality. Freud's work was particularly influential with his proposal that homosexuality was maladaptive and caused by unresolved pre-Oedipal conflicts (Freud, 1920; Freud & Strachey, 1921). However, more recent and reliable research has failed to find evidence for early childhood experiences playing a causal role in the development of sexual orientation (Diamond, 1998; Savin-Williams et al., 2012; Calzo et al., 2011). According to the APA in 2011, "[N]o specific psychosocial or family dynamic cause for homosexuality has been identified, including histories of childhood sexual abuse. Sexual abuse does not appear to be more prevalent in children who grow up to identify as gay, lesbian, or bisexual, than in children who identify as heterosexual" (American Psychiatric Association, 2011). Watch the video *Sexuality and Gender* to explore this topic further.

Another widely researched question has been whether or not being raised by a same-sex parent has an impact on the sexual orientation of the children in the household. Research has often demonstrated that children raised by gay or lesbian parents are no more likely to become gay or lesbian compared to children raised by heterosexual parents (Bailey, et al., 1995; Gartrell

Sexuality and Gender: Thinking Like a Psychologist

Interactive

et al., 2005; Biblarz & Savci, 2010) as the majority of children raised by gay or lesbian parents described their own sexual orientation as heterosexual. However, some recent studies have shown that daughters of lesbian mothers are somewhat more likely to report being open to same-sex relationships (Golombok & Tasker, 1996), engaged in more same-sex sexual behavior, and are slightly more likely to describe themselves as bisexual than daughters raised by a comparison group of heterosexual parents (Gartrell & Bos, 2010; Gartrell et al., 2011). These findings may be due to the fact that daughters of openly lesbian women may find it more acceptable to explore same-sex sexual behavior. Also, genetics may play a role such that daughters of lesbians may have an increased likelihood of same-sex attraction.

Current research tends to focus on potential biological factors that may affect sexual orientation. While no single biological marker has been identified that is known to cause a particular sexual orientation, there have been some findings related to genetics, prenatal hormones, and brain structures that are providing some insights into the biological underpinnings of sexual orientation.

THE ROLE OF GENETICS Studies involving twins and family members consistently suggest that genes play at least some role in determining a person's sexual orientation. Gay men and lesbians tend to have a larger proportion of homosexual siblings than heterosexuals (Bailey & Bell, 1993; Bailey et al., 2000; Kendler et al., 2000). Other studies have found that 33 out of 40 gay brothers had the same genes in common in one area of the X chromosome, even though other genes on that chromosome were different (Hamer et al., 1993; Hu et al., 1995; Turner, 1995; Sanders et al., 2015). Since males get their X chromosomes from their mothers, these studies are consistent with those that have found gay men to have more homosexual relatives on their mother's side of the family than on their father's side (Camperio-Ciani et al., 2004).

There is an even more compelling finding for the influence of genetics on sexual orientation. In male identical twins (whose DNA is identical), if one of the twins is gay, the other has a 50 percent chance of also being gay, while the fraternal twin or non-twin sibling of a gay man has only a 15 percent chance of also being gay (Bailey et al., 2000; Dawood et al., 2000; Alanko, 2010). But those percentages mean that one identical twin can be gay and the other can be heterosexual, so we know for certain that there must be more to sexual orientation than genes.

Many researchers think that birth order can play a role in the determination of sexual orientation. According to the **fraternal birth-order effect**, each additional older brother that a male has increases the odds that the male will be gay by 33 percent. The fraternal birth-order effect may be explained by a defensive maternal immune response to foreign substances produced by male fetuses that increases with each consecutive birth (Blanchard, 1997, 2001; Blanchard et al., 1998; Ellis & Blanchard, 2001; VanderLaan & Vasey, 2011; Bogaert & Skorska, 2011).

BRAIN STRUCTURES AND PRENATAL HORMONES Research into the biological origins of sexual orientation has also looked at structures in the brain. While brain structures can be altered by experience, observed differences in postmortem studies reveal certain correlations between some brain structures and sexual orientation. For example, a section of the anterior commissure, which connects the two hemispheres of the brain, is larger in gay men (Allen & Gorski, 1992; Zaidi, 2010), and a set of nodules in the hypothalamus called a hypothalamic cluster is reliably larger in heterosexual men than in gay men (LeVay, 1991; Myers, 2014). Recall that the hypothalamus is the structure of the brain most often discussed in relation to sexual motivation and activity.

Another study has linked the hypothalamus to sexual orientation. In heterosexual women and gay men, the scent of the testosterone derivative AND found in male sweat, activated a hypothalamic response commonly related to sexual behavior. In contrast, heterosexual men showed a similar sexually-linked hypothalamic response to EST, an estrogen derivative present in female urine (Savic et al., 2005). Overall, postmortem studies have found more similarities between gay male brains and female brains than between gay male brains and heterosexual male brains. While few conclusions can be drawn based on these findings, they may eventually lead to a better understanding of the origins of sexual orientation.

There is also evidence to suggest that prenatal androgen exposure may affect sexual orientation. Female infants born with a genetic condition, congenital adrenal hyperplasia (CAH),

fraternal birth-order effect

a finding related to sexual orientation showing that each additional older brother that a male has increases the odds that the male will be gay by 33 percent

are exposed to elevated androgens in utero. Girls with CAH have demonstrated preferences for male-typical toys and activities and have a 30 percent chance of being lesbian or bisexual (Hines et al., 2004; Frisen et al., 2009; Meyer-Bahlburg et al., 2008). Males infants born with *complete androgen insensitivity syndrome* (CAIS) have receptors that fail to respond to the androgens produced by their normally-functioning testes. Almost all males with this condition later describe their sexual orientation as gay (Hines et al., 2015; Hines et al., 2003). These examples illustrate that exposure to prenatal hormones may play a role in the development of sexual orientation later in life.

Adaptive Pathway 11.2: Sexual Orientation

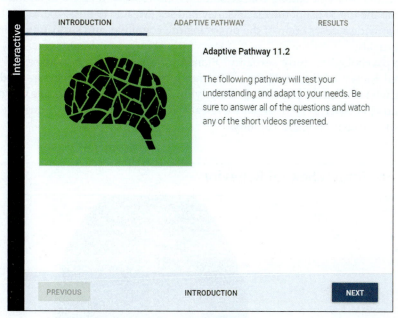

Quiz for Module 11.6–11.7

1. In surveys, what percent of Americans identify themselves as LGBT (lesbian/gay/bisexual/transgender)?
   a. 30 percent
   b. 25 percent
   c. 15 percent
   d. Less than 10 percent

2. The concept of _____ argues that women's sexuality may be less strongly felt and more fluid than men's sexuality.
   a. erotic plasticity
   b. sexual orientation identity
   c. sexual crisis plasticity
   d. erotic orientation identity

3. Which of the following statements regarding sexual orientation is accurate?
   a. The way people behave sexually defines their sexual orientation.
   b. People describe their sexual orientation as clearly either heterosexual or homosexual.
   c. Sexual orientation exists on a continuum.
   d. Sexual orientation and gender identity are the same.

4. The cause of sexual orientation is _____.
   a. environmental factors
   b. unknown
   c. genetic factors
   d. childhood sexual abuse

5. Elliott is 25 and has identified his sexual orientation as gay since he was 15 years old. He has three older brothers and no older sisters. One theory that might help explain his sexual orientation is known as the _____ effect.
   a. sibling sexuality
   b. fraternal birth order
   c. DNA sharing
   d. maternal birth

6. What structure of the brain has been linked to sexual orientation?
   a. Limbic system
   b. Thalamus
   c. Amygdala
   d. Hypothalamus

Module 11.8 – 11.9: Human Sexual Behavior

Sexuality is a core part of being human, and sexual behavior is motivated by an interesting combination of biological drives, psychological factors, and sociocultural influences. Without sex, humans would become extinct, so like other animals, biological sex drives are an important part of sexuality. However, the motivation for sexual behavior is more complex than simple biological urges. After all, people engage in sexual behavior much more frequently than "required" for procreation, and people engage in a variety of sexual behaviors that are not necessarily related to the function of reproduction. Not surprisingly, a study examining motivation for sexual behavior among college students showed that a desire to reproduce didn't even make it to the top 50 list of the reasons they had sex (Meston & Buss, 2007). The following module will provide a description of the physiological, cognitive, and sociocultural influences on human sexuality.

How do psychologists study sexuality? Pioneers in the study of human sexual behavior include Alfred Kinsey who studied the prevalence of various sexual behaviors, and Masters and Johnson, who studied the physiology underlying sexual behavior. Watch the video *Research on Human Sexual Behavior* to learn about these early researchers and their contribution to our current knowledge about human sexuality.

Research on Human Sexual Behavior

Interactive

Physiology of Sex

LO 11.8 **Describe the phases of the sexual response cycle.**

The physiological response to sexual stimulation was widely researched in the 1960s by researchers William H. Masters and Virginia E. Johnson. This research was conducted by having volunteers come into a laboratory and engage in self-stimulation or sexual intercourse while being monitored (Masters and Johnson, 1966). Obviously, this was not considered a "random" or "representative" sample when making generalizations to the general public. But, because Masters and Johnson focused much of their work trying to discover what happens in the body during sexual stimulation, their discoveries about the physiology of sex were groundbreaking.

One of the significant contributions from Masters and Johnson's work was the identification of the human sexual response cycle. There are four phases in the sexual response cycle: (1) **excitement** (arousal phase), (2) **plateau** (period of sexual excitement prior to

excitement phase

the first phase of the sexual response cycle when arousal occurs

plateau phase

the second phase of the sexual response cycle which includes the period of sexual excitement prior to orgasm

Sexual Response Cycle

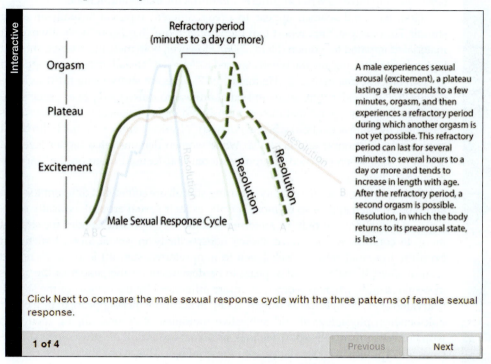

A male experiences sexual arousal (excitement), a plateau lasting a few seconds to a few minutes, orgasm, and then experiences a refractory period during which another orgasm is not yet possible. This refractory period can last for several minutes to several hours to a day or more and tends to increase in length with age. After the refractory period, a second orgasm is possible. Resolution, in which the body returns to its prearousal state, is last.

Click Next to compare the male sexual response cycle with the three patterns of female sexual response.

1 of 4   Previous   Next

orgasm), (3) **orgasm** (climax of the sexual response cycle), and (4) **resolution** (return to normal functioning). Most mammals' sexual drives synchronize with their hormonal levels and chemical signals. The female cyclic production of estrogen and progesterone is the menstrual cycle in humans and the estrous cycle in other animals. For female mammals, estrogen peaks at ovulation, when the female becomes sexually receptive. Testosterone levels in male mammals remain more constant but still influence sexual behavior.

The human female's sex drive synchronizes less with her hormonal levels than in most other mammals. The female sex drive increases somewhat during ovulation but has more to do with testosterone levels than estrogen levels (Harvey, 1987; Meston & Frohlich, 2000; Meuwissen & Over, 1992; Reichman, 1998). Testosterone therapy, such as the testosterone patch, increases sex drive in women who feel a reduced desire for sex due to removal of the ovaries or adrenal glands. In males, testosterone also controls sex drive.

Cognitive and Sociocultural Influences on Sexual Behavior

LO 11.9 **Recognize the cognitive and sociocultural influences on human sexual behavior.**

In addition to physiological factors, cognitive and sociocultural factors are also important in understanding human sexuality. You've likely heard the saying that the brain is the largest sex organ in the body. This cliché certainly has some validity as the brain is responsible for sexual desire, release of sexual hormones, and sexual responsiveness. Additionally, sociocultural influences on sexual behavior include social norms, media, and religion.

COGNITION   One of the most important brain functions when it comes to sexual behavior is the initiation of sexual desire. What makes people think about or desire sex? It turns out that the answer to this question may depend in part on your gender.

To understand how cognition can play a role in sexual behavior, consider that sexual arousal can be caused by both internal (e.g., thoughts, memories) and external stimuli (e.g., erotic images or videos). Furthermore, exposure to external stimuli can trigger internal sexual thoughts and fantasies which lead to sexual arousal or desire for sex. Sexual arousal can be measured in two ways: physiological arousal and subjective (or self-reported) arousal. Both

orgasm phase

the third stage of the sexual response cycle when climax occurs

resolution phase

the fourth phase of the sexual response cycle during which there is a return to normal functioning

the type of stimuli found to be sexually arousing and the form of arousal have been found to have somewhat different patterns for males and females.

First, men and women appear to prefer different types of sexually-arousing stimuli. For example, men report that they prefer more "hard-core" sexually explicit materials compared to women (Hald, 2006). However, both men and women showed higher levels of sexual arousal when exposed to "explicit" sexual materials as opposed to "romantic" sexual materials (Heimann, 1977). A recent study using fMRI technology evaluated gender differences in sexual arousal to different types of erotic stimuli. The researchers found that men demonstrated higher levels of sexual arousal (as measured by brain activation) when exposed to "physical" erotic material (with direct exposure to intercourse and genitalia) while women demonstrated higher levels of sexual arousal when exposed to erotic material that focused more on the storyline (Chung et al., 2013).

Secondly, responses to sexually-arousing stimuli are somewhat different for men and women. Men appear to be more specific in their sexual arousal, typically experiencing sexual arousal only to preferred stimuli (e.g., opposite gender for straight men). In contrast, women have shown nonspecificity in sexual arousal such that exposure to sexual activity itself (even to nonpreferred stimuli) leads to increased arousal. Overall, male arousal appears to be dependent on the gender of the actors in sexual stimuli, whereas women are more influenced by the context of the stimuli (Carvalho et al., 2013; Rupp & Wallen, 2008). In addition, there appears to be a closer link between physiological and subjective measures of arousal among men than women. When men self-report feelings of sexual arousal, their physiological measures are typically in concordance with these ratings. This is not always the case for women as physiological measures do not always show arousal even when women subjectively report feeling aroused (Chivers, 2010). Further evidence of this lack of concordance among women was demonstrated by Hamann and colleagues (2004) by showing that men had higher levels of activation in the amygdala than women, even when psychological ratings of arousal were similar between men and women.

A woman from the Muria tribe in India where sexual permissiveness is the cultural norm.

social norms

the spoken and unspoken rules about what behavior is considered appropriate in a given society

SOCIOCULTURAL INFLUENCES   Sexual activity is an inherently social behavior and is therefore subjected to social norms. **Social norms** are the spoken and unspoken rules about what behavior is considered appropriate in a given society. Social norms regarding sexuality are influenced by a number of cultural factors, including politics, media, and religion. Political influences on defining the cultural norms for sexual behavior have included legislation that legalizes or criminalizes certain sexual behaviors. The politics of same-sex marriage has been one of the more recent examples of this influence. The media also provides frequent messages about what is "normal" or "appropriate" when it comes to sexual behavior. Additionally, many world religions have moral or ethical codes regarding sexuality which may influence an individual's sexual behavior.

Different cultures have different norms when it comes to sexual behavior. For example, societies differ in level of sexual permissiveness, views on contraception, and gender roles related to sexuality. The Muria people of India live in a very sexually permissive society. Children are exposed to nudity and sexual activity at a young age, and premarital sex is encouraged (Martel et al., 2004). Contrast this society with the more sexually restrictive culture of the United States where values regarding abstinence before marriage, monogamy, and limiting children's exposure to sexuality are common. Cultural norms also change over time. For example, in the early 1900s it was considered highly inappropriate for women to even show their ankles in their dresses. Contrast that with today's bikini bathing suits, and you can certainly see how social norms change over time.

Shared Writing Prompt: Evolution and Sexuality

Using evolutionary theory, explain why men might be more sexually aroused when exposed to explicit erotic material, while women might be more aroused when there is a focus on an underlying romantic storyline.

Quiz for Module 11.8–11.9

1. Which two researchers were responsible for groundbreaking findings regarding the physiology of sexual behavior?

    a. Kinsey and Johnson   **b.** Masters and Kinsey

    c. Masters and Johnson   **d.** Johnson and Johnson

2. Joaquin is a 21-year-old college student who enjoys an active sex life. He participated in a survey on the reasons he engages in sexual behavior. One of the reasons that he did NOT likely list was _____.

    a. procreation   **b.** availability of partners

    c. physical enjoyment   **d.** relationship closeness

3. Sexual thoughts that lead to physiological arousal can be caused by both _____ stimuli such as thoughts and memories and _____ stimuli such as erotic images or videos.

    a. external; internal   **b.** internal; external

    c. physical; cognitive   **d.** cognitive; physical

4. Ben and Leslie have been married for 5 years. Their sexual relationship is still active and exciting, but, similar to findings related to gender differences in sexual arousal, they have learned that Ben is stimulated more by _____ and Leslie is stimulated more by _____.

    a. nonphysical images; physical images

    b. romantic images; erotic images

    c. "physically" erotic images; erotic materials with a storyline

    d. erotic materials with a storyline; physically erotic images

5. Sexual behavior can be influenced by _____, or the spoken and unspoken rules about what is considered appropriate.

    a. social behavior   **b.** religious morals

    c. cultural influences   **d.** social norms

Module 11.10–11.12: Sexual Disorders and Sexually Transmitted Infections

According to the World Health Organization (WHO), "[S]exual health is a state of physical, emotional, mental and social well-being in relation to sexuality; it is not merely the absence of disease, dysfunction or infirmity. Sexual health requires a positive and respectful approach to sexuality and sexual relationships, as well as the possibility of having pleasurable and safe sexual experiences, free of coercion, discrimination and violence. For sexual health to be attained and maintained, the sexual rights of all persons must be respected, protected and fulfilled." (World Health Organization, 2006, p.5). The following information focuses on disorders related to sexual functioning and sexually transmitted infections that impair sexual health for millions of people worldwide.

Sexual Dysfunctions

LO 11.10   **Define and describe sexual dysfunctions.**

Movies, television shows, romance novels, and even so-called "reality" TV portray sex as romantic, glamorous, and perfect, and media-based sexual encounters always end in orgasms for all. Exactly like reality, right? "Real" sex is sometimes hard to even reconcile with the embellished media version. People don't bang their heads accidentally or have any awkward moments on television, and certainly "performance failures" are rarely portrayed. In reality, most people experience problems with sexual functioning on occasion. Whether it's a simple lack of desire or difficulty achieving an orgasm, most people encounter these types of difficulties at some point or another. **Sexual dysfunctions**, on the other hand, refer to ongoing problems with sexual functioning that cause distress and impairment for individuals and relationships. According to the DSM-5, sexual dysfunctions are classified as diagnosable conditions when sexual functioning is impaired at least 75 percent of the time and when the problem has lasted at least 6 months (American Psychiatric Association, 2013; IsHak & Tobia, 2013).

Sexual dysfunctions are classified by gender and there are three female conditions and four male conditions. Overall, sexual dysfunctions are among the most prevalent of all disorders. Studies vary, but have generally shown very high prevalence rates with as many as 43 percent of women and 31 percent of men reporting sexual dysfunctions (Burri & Spector, 2011; Christensen, et al., 2011; Laumann et al., 1999; Simons & Carey, 2001). Although these conditions may not be discussed as openly, sexual dysfunctions appear to affect the lives of many more people than other psychological disorders such as depression or schizophrenia. Because these conditions are so widespread, medications such as Viagra (used to treat erectile disorder) have been extremely popular. The pharmaceutical company Pfizer reported

sexual dysfunctions

ongoing problems with sexual functioning that cause distress and impairment for individuals and relationships

sexual interest/arousal disorder

when females experience either a complete lack of or significant reduction in sexual interest/arousal

male hypoactive sexual desire disorder

when males experience either a complete lack of or significant reduction in sexual interest/arousal

female orgasmic disorder

a significant delay, reduction of intensity, or cessation of ability to achieve orgasm in females

erectile disorder

a recurrent inability to achieve or maintain an adequate erection during partnered sexual activities

premature ejaculation

ejaculation with minimal sexual stimulation before or shortly after penetration and before the person wishes it

delayed ejaculation

requiring a prolonged period of sexual stimulation before being able to ejaculate

earnings of $1.69 billion in 2014 from sales of Viagra alone. We may not be discussing sexual dysfunctions very often, but if "money talks," people are certainly interested in finding ways to treat their sexual problems.

Sexual dysfunctions can be associated with any of the first three phases of the sexual response cycle (excitement, plateau, or orgasm). No one has experienced difficulty with having an orgasm end in the resolution stage (or they have not complained about it!). During the excitement stage, females can struggle with **sexual interest/arousal disorder** and men can struggle with **male hypoactive sexual desire disorder**. In these situations, people experience either a complete lack of or significant reduction in sexual interest/arousal (e.g., absence of sexual fantasies/thoughts, reduction or absence of sexual activity). The prevalence of sexual interest/arousal disorder among women is more common than male hypoactive sexual desire disorder (American Psychiatric Association, 2013). Studies have repeatedly shown that men have a stronger sexual desire than women. Men tend to think about sex more often, have more sexual fantasies, desire sexual intercourse more frequently, and initiate sexual activity more often (Baumeister et al., 2001; Schmitt et al., 2012; Baumeister, 2013). However, recent sex researchers have noted that an individual's level of desire (or lack thereof) is not necessarily the most important factor in determining the level of distress or impairment. Much more important is the *desire discrepancy* between sexual partners (Mark & Murray, 2012). If one person desires sexual activity much more frequently than his/her partner, the couple is likely to experience the lower desire as a problem. However, if both partners experience low levels of desire, neither is likely to consider it a problem.

Disorders of the orgasm phase include **female orgasmic disorder** in women and three categories of male disorders: **erectile disorder**, **premature ejaculation**, and **delayed ejaculation**.

Identifying Sexual Disorders

Drag the sexual disorder below to the appropriate spot on the table.

Delayed ejaculation	Being unable to ejaculate during sexual activity after 25 - 30 minutes of continuous sexual stimulation
Erectile disorder	A recurrent inability to achieve or maintain an adequate erection during partnered sexual activities
Premature ejaculation	A feeling of being unable to control orgasm, and climaxing in less than 1 minute after vaginal penetration
Female orgasmic disorder	A significant delay, reduction of intensity, or cessation of ability to achieve orgasm

Start Over

Difficulties with achieving orgasm are particularly common among women. Studies have shown that 20–30 percent of women report an inability to orgasm during vaginal intercourse alone (Harris et al., 2008), and another 4 percent of women report never having achieved an orgasm by any means (Dunn et al., 2002; Garde & Lunde, 1980; Hagstad & Janson, 1984). Studies show that men report being more likely to achieve orgasm when sex includes vaginal intercourse while women are more likely to achieve orgasm when they engage in a variety of sex activities (Herbenick et al., 2010). Interestingly, data shows that around 85 percent of men reported that their female partner had an orgasm during their most recent sexual activity, while only 64 percent of women reported actually having had an orgasm during their most recent sexual activity (Herbenick et al., 2010), suggesting that men are not always able to perceive their partner's orgasm or that the "fake orgasm" is not simply myth.

Attention to the problem of erectile disorder has grown over the past 20–25 years. The prevalence of erectile disorder among men increases with age (Prins et al., 2002), and one study found that at age 40, about 40 percent of men suffered from erectile disorder and by age 70, about 70 percent of men struggled with the condition (Feldman et al., 1994). A gender equality movement called "Even the Score," points out that the FDA has approved 26 drugs for male sexual dysfunctions, while not a single drug has been approved to treat sexual dysfunction in women (Even the Score, 2015). While this fact may have a number of explanations, it's clear that further research and development in this area should be an important future priority.

The last sexual dysfunction, **genitopelvic pain/penetration disorder**, occurs when females experience an involuntary contraction of the pelvic floor muscles around the vagina when any attempt is made to penetrate the vagina. These muscle contractions cause penetration of anything—tampons, gynecological exam instruments, or a penis—to be impossible. Unsurprisingly, women with this condition often have other sexual dysfunctions such as sexual interest/arousal disorder because painful sensations during attempts at sexual intercourse are unlikely to foster high levels of desire. The prevalence of this condition is unknown. However, it is estimated that 15 percent of women in North America report recurrent pain during intercourse (American Psychiatric Association, 2013).

Sexual dysfunctions can be caused by a range of issues influenced by psychological, physiological, sociocultural, and interpersonal/relationship factors. The following demonstrate the wide array of potential influences on the development of sexual dysfunctions.

genitopelvic pain/penetration disorder

when females experience an involuntary contraction of the pelvic floor muscles around the vagina resulting in an inability to penetrate

Causes of Sexual Dysfunctions

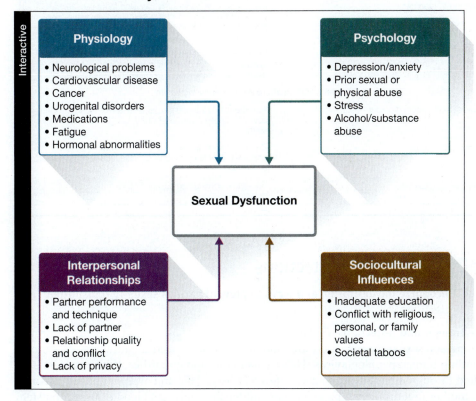

A range of treatment options exist to help people improve their sexual functioning. Medications such as Viagra, Cialis, and Levitra have been successfully used to treat erectile disorder (Giuliano et al., 2010). Currently, there are no FDA-approved medications to improve sexual functioning in women, but sometimes the answer is to actually reduce the dosage of another medication or change medications (e.g., antidepressants can cause sexual dysfunctions). In addition to medical treatment options, sexual dysfunctions can be treated through psychoeducation, behavioral therapy, or sex therapy.

Paraphilic Disorders

LO 11.11 **Define and describe paraphilic disorders.**

While the sexual dysfunctions are associated with problems with normal sexual functioning, the **paraphilic disorders** are a class of disorders related to atypical sexual behavior that (1) cause distress to the person and/or (2) make the person a serious threat to the mental health or physical well-being of others (American Psychiatric Association, 2013). It's important to note that "normal" sexual behavior is not easy to define and depends on a variety of factors, including sociocultural variables. Thus, sexual behaviors considered "unusual" or "atypical" are not to be considered pathological as long as they occur between consenting individuals. Table 11.2 provides a list of the eight paraphilic disorders and a brief description of each.

paraphilic disorders

a class of disorders related to atypical sexual behavior that causes distress to the person, and/or makes the person a serious threat to the mental health or physical well-being of others

Table 11.2 Paraphilic Disorders

Paraphilic Disorder	Description
Disorders involving a nonconsenting victim	
Exhibitionistic disorder	Recurrent and intense sexual arousal from the exposure of one's genitals to an unsuspecting/nonconsenting person
Sexual sadism disorder	Recurrent and intense sexual arousal from the physical or psychological suffering of another nonconsenting person
Frotteuristic disorder	Recurrent and intense sexual arousal from touching or rubbing against a nonconsenting person
Pedophilic disorder	Recurrent, intense sexually arousing fantasies, sexual urges, or behaviors involving sexual activity with a prepubescent child or children (generally age 13 years or younger)
Voyeuristic disorder	Recurrent and intense sexual arousal from observing an unsuspecting/nonconsenting person who is naked, in the process of disrobing, or engaging in sexual activity
Disorders NOT involving a nonconsenting victim	
Sexual masochism disorder	Recurrent and intense sexual arousal from the act of being humiliated, beaten, bound, or otherwise made to suffer
Fetishistic disorder	Recurrent and intense sexual arousal from the use of nonliving objects or a highly specific focus on nongenital body parts
Transvestic disorder	Recurrent and intense sexual arousal from cross-dressing

Sexually Transmitted Infections

LO 11.12 **Recognize the definition and ways to prevent various sexually transmitted infections.**

sexually transmitted infections (STIs)

infections that are spread primarily through person-to-person sexual contact

Sexually transmitted infections (STIs) are infections that are spread primarily through person-to-person sexual contact. There are more than 30 different STIs with the most common STIs including human papillomavirus (HPV), chlamydia, and gonorrhea. While most STIs are transmitted through direct sexual contact, a few STIs (e.g., HIV and syphilis) can be transmitted from mother to fetus during pregnancy or childbirth or through blood or tissue transfers. Table 11.3 includes the symptoms and long-term effects of the most common STIs.

According to the latest CDC data, people ages 15–24 account for half of all newly diagnosed STIs, and adolescent females are particularly at risk with 1 in 4 sexually active adolescent females having an STI (Centers for Disease Control and Prevention, 2015a). The severity of STIs depends on the type of infection with some conditions being treatable with antibiotics, but other conditions can be incurable and have significant medical consequences. Many times, STIs are left untreated because the person doesn't know that he or she is infected. Although chlamydia can be easily treated, if the condition is left untreated for too long it can lead to pelvic inflammatory disease (PID) in women which is the leading cause of infertility. The CDC

Table 11.3 Symptoms and Effects of STIs

	Symptoms and Long-Term Effects				
STI	**Symptom**				**Long term effects/ complications**
	Discharge	**Painful Skin lesions**	**Painless skin lesions**	**May have no clear symptoms**	**Without treatment, STI can lead to:**
Chlamydia	X			X	Pelvic inflammatory Disease (PID), which can lead to infertility, scarring, chronic pain
Gonorrhea	X			X	PID
Syphilis			X		Paralsis, personality changes, blindness, damage to joints, etc.
Trichomoniasis	X			X	Mild to severe inflammation
HSV		X			Recurring symptoms possible
HPV			X	X	Some types of HPV produce genital warts; nay lead to cervical or other cancers

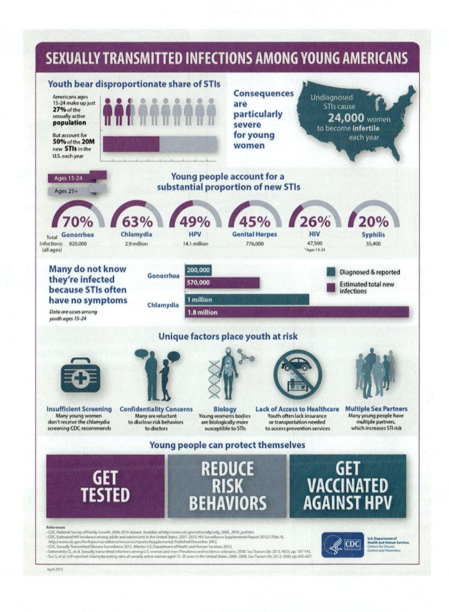

estimates that 24,000 young women become infertile every year due to untreated STIs. There are several barriers for young people to receive proper STI screening and treatment including cost, scheduling conflicts between clinic hours and work/school, stigma associated with seeking screening, and concerns about the confidentiality of testing results (Tilson et al., 2004).

Anyone who is sexually active has some degree of risk associated with developing an STI. Having unprotected vaginal or anal intercourse with an infected partner puts an individual at significant risk of contracting an STI. Oral sex appears to be associated with lower rates of STI transmission, but infections can still be contracted without the use of a condom or other protective device that prevents skin-to-skin contact (CDC, 2016). Having multiple sexual partners also increases the risk of being exposed to an STI (CDC, 2015b). In addition, having a history of an STI places an individual at greater risk for developing another STI (CDC, 2015a). Alcohol and recreational drug use often impact judgement and people are more likely to engage in risky sexual behavior while under the influence of these substances (CDC, 2015b).

Diagnosing and treating STIs as early as possible is clearly an important step in reducing the spread of these infections and minimizing the effects of the conditions. However, prevention of new cases of STIs is even more preferable. Figure 11.6 describes the most effective ways to prevent transmission of STIs.

Figure 11.6 Preventing STIs

PREVENTION STRATEGIES

Practice Abstinence

The surest way to avoid STIs is to not have sex.

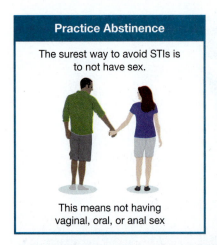

This means not having vaginal, oral, or anal sex

Have Fewer Partners

Agree to only have sex with one person who agrees to only have sex with you.

Make sure you both get tested to know for sure that neither of you has an STI. This is one of the most reliable ways to avoid STIs.

Talk With Your Partner

Talk with your sex partner(s) about STIs and staying safe before having sex.

It might be uncomfortable to start the conversation, but protecting your health is your responsibility.

Use Condoms

Using a condom correctly every time you have sex can help you avoid STIs.

Condoms lessen the risk of infection for all STIs. You still can get certain STIs, like herpes or HPV, from contact with your partner's skin even when using a condom.

Most people claimed they used a condom the first time they ever had sex, but when asked about the last 4 weeks, less than one quarter said they used a condom every time.

Get Vaccinated

The most common STI can be prevented by a vaccine.

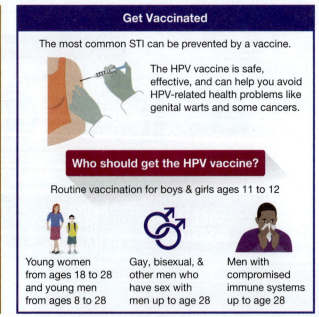

The HPV vaccine is safe, effective, and can help you avoid HPV-related health problems like genital warts and some cancers.

Who should get the HPV vaccine?

Routine vaccination for boys & girls ages 11 to 12

Young women from ages 18 to 28 and young men from ages 8 to 28

Gay, bisexual, & other men who have sex with men up to age 28

Men with compromised immune systems up to age 28

Quiz for Module 11.10–11.12

1. A problem in sexual functioning that causes distress and impairment for individuals and relationships is referred to as a(n) _____.
   a. sexual functioning issue
   b. physiological disorder
   c. sexual dysfunction
   d. erectile disorder

2. Zara and Rohan have been dating for 13 months. At first, their sexual relationship was very healthy. However, for the last 6 months, Zara has shown little interest in sex and usually declines any sexual advances that Rohan makes. Zara may be experiencing what type of sexual dysfunction?
   a. Sexual interest/arousal disorder
   b. Sexual paraphilia
   c. Female orgasmic disorder
   d. Hyperactive sexual desire disorder

3. Sexual behaviors that cause distress to a person or that cause physical or mental distress to another person are referred to as _____.
   a. atypical sexual disorders
   b. paraphillic disorders
   c. pathological sexual disorders
   d. sexual dysfunctions

4. Jared is a 17-year-old male who gets sexually excited and aroused when he exposes his genitals to strangers on the subway. Jared may be experiencing what type of paraphillic disorder?
   a. Voyeuristic disorder
   b. Frotteuristic disorder
   c. Exhibitionistic disorder
   d. Fetishistic disorder

5. What age group accounts for nearly half of all newly acquired STIs (sexually transmitted infections)?
   a. over 50   b. 35–50
   c. 25–34   d. 15–24

6. Catrina had chlamydia when she was 18 years old and she never sought treatment. She is now 30 years old and struggling to become pregnant. What disease related to infertility can be caused by untreated chlamydia?
   a. Pelvic inflammatory disease
   b. Gonorrhea
   c. Human papillomavirus (HPV)
   d. Pelvis pain disorder

Module 11.13: Piecing It Together: Sexualization of Girls

LO 11.13 **Analyze how the cross-cutting themes of psychology are related to the topic of the sexualization of girls.**

The sexualization of girls has been identified by the APA as a growing problem with significant negative consequences for girls. According to the APA Task Force in 2008, sexualization occurs when "a person's value comes only from his/her sexual appeal or behavior to the exclusion of other characteristics, and when a person is sexually objectified, for example, made into a thing for another's sexual use" (Zurbriggen et al., 2007). Girls are increasingly sexualized in television, video games, movies, advertisements, and music videos. For example, dolls targeting girls can be found wearing revealing clothing, heavy makeup, and thigh-high boots. Halloween costumes for girls have become increasingly "sexy," and thong underwear is marketed to pre-adolescent girls. Read on as we consider this topic from a variety of perspectives.

Sexualization of Girl Child beauty pageants have been criticized for sexualizing young girls

Variations in Human Functioning

- First, what kind of impact does sexualization have on girls and young women in terms of mental/physical health?

- Second, is there an impact on society as a whole when girls are repeatedly sexualized in the media?

Let's look at the research about girls and young women first. First, it's important to clearly understand what the term "sexualization" encompasses. According to the APA Task Force report (Zurbriggen et al., 2007), there are four components of sexualization:

Components of Sexualization

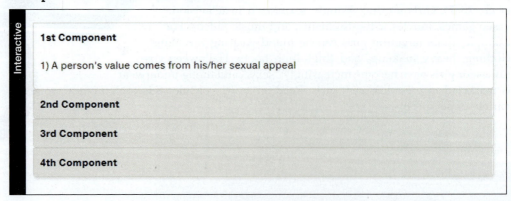

If even one of these components exists in a particular situation, then sexualization has occurred. The third component, **sexual objectification**, occurs when a person is seen as a sexual object for others' use.

One of the consequences of sexual objectification is the fact that girls often begin to self-objectify themselves as a result (Smolak & Murnen, 2011). **Self-objectification** occurs when a girl focuses more on how her body is perceived by others than her own internal perception of her body (Fredrickson & Roberts, 1997). A recent study showed that exposure to magazines and social media were associated with self-objectification in girls ages 12–16 (Slater & Tiggeman, 2015). In a younger sample of girls (mean age of 11–12), researchers found that magazine, Internet exposure, and appearance conversations with friends predicted self-objectification (Tiggeman & Slater, 2015). Another recent study showed that playing a video game as a sexualized avatar led to more self-objectification than playing the game with a nonsexualized avatar (Fox et al., 2013). The evidence appears to show a strong link between exposure to sexualized images in the media and engagement in self-objectification.

Bottle openers in the shape of a female body provide an example of sexual objectification in which a female's body is viewed as a de-personalized object.

What are the consequences associated with self-objectification? Here are some of the most recent findings related to the consequences of self-objectification in young girls:

- Increased body shame, dieting, and eating disturbances (Jongenelis et al., 2014; Slater & Tiggemann, 2016; Tiggeman & Slater, 2015)

- Increased depressive symptoms (Jones 2015)

- Disrupted cognitive performance (e.g., reduced working memory, impaired visual encoding) (Aubrey & Gerding, 2015; Pacilli et al., 2016)

- Poorer sexual self-efficacy (i.e., a girl's belief that she can act upon her own sexual needs in a relationship) and increased rates of unprotected sex (Impett et al., 2006)

sexual objectification

being viewed primarily as an object of sexual desire

Self-objectification

occurs when a person focuses more on how his/her body is perceived by others than his/her own internal perception of his/her body

Research Methods

- What are the societal impacts of the sexualization of girls?

- Does viewing young girls in sexually provocative ways lead to people (who are not pedophiles) to change the way they view children?

The research findings clearly demonstrate that the impact on girls of sexualization and the resulting increased self-objectification is negative. The secondary question is whether or not there are any other widespread societal consequences for the pervasiveness of images that sexualize young girls. To address this question, one study utilized a creative research approach. The researchers examined the impact of viewing "barely legal" pornography. This type of pornography features female models who are actually over age 18, but who look like minors and are posed in a suggestive or promiscuous manner (Paul & Linz, 2008).

The researchers used a lexical decision-making task that looks at the speed with which a person can recognize a word or concept. For example, a person would be asked to click "yes" if the letters they saw represented an actual word or "no" if the letters were not a word. In one type of lexical decision-making task, there are pairs of words, and the participant must decide if both the words are actual words or not. For example:

1.	girl	yiup	Yes	No
2.	sleep	pillow	Yes	No
3.	cord	sample	Yes	No

You would click "no" for item 1 and "yes" for items 2–3. Your speed in making these decisions is the important data. In the original study of this type of task, Meyer and Schvaneveldt (1971) found that people respond more quickly to words that are related to one another (e.g., "sleep" and "pillow") than to words that are entirely unrelated (e.g., "cord" and "sample"). This is because reading words can activate related information stored in memory so that when words are related, we can recognize them more quickly.

Consider this task in terms of exposure to "barely legal" pornography. If such exposure results in an association between youth and sexuality, this association should be measurable using a lexical decision-making task. The authors randomly assigned college participants to view 100 images that were either (1) barley legal pornographic content with models appearing to be under age 18, (2) pornographic content of women appearing to be aged 21–28, (3) pornographic content of women appearing to be aged 31–45, or (4) pornographic content of women appearing to be over the age of 50. A single participant only saw images from the same group. For example, participants assigned to the "barely legal" group only saw pornographic images of women who appeared to be below age 18. After viewing dozens of these images, participants completed the lexical decision-making task. Rather than just seeing words, participants first saw images of models, animals, and objects. The images of models included fully clothed nonsexually explicit women who appeared to be different ages, including 10- to 16-year-olds, 21- to 28-year-olds, 31- to 45-year-olds, and women over age 50. After seeing these images, participants were asked to identify if letters presented represented words or not. There were a total of three neutral words (e.g., window), four nonsense words (e.g., kurstoe), and four words with sexual connotations (i.e., sexy, erotic, arousing, beauty).

For example, a participant might see the following pairs of an image and a word:

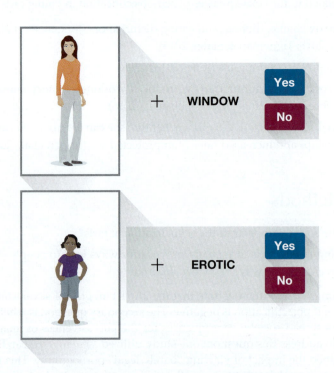

If people have an association between youth and sexuality, they will be quicker to respond "yes" to the second image/word pair than the first image/word pair. The key question in this study was whether or not people exposed to the barely legal pornography would be quicker to recognize the four words with sexual connotations as words right after seeing an image of a child model than people who had not previously been exposed to the barely legal pornography images. In fact, the authors found that both men and women who were exposed to barely legal pornography were faster to recognize sexual words after they saw images of child models. These findings suggest that viewing sexualized images of young girls leads people to associate youth with sexuality.

Identify the Components of the Experiment

Interactive	Identify the components of this experiment.	
	Control Group (group of participants who were either given no treatment or who are given treatment that should have no effect)	The participants who were exposed to the adult pornography rather than the barely legal pornography
	Experimental Group (group of participants who were exposed to the variable being tested)	The participants who were exposed to the barely legal pornography
	Independent Variable (variable that a rsesearcher maniuplates or changes in an experiment)	What type of pornography participants were exposed to (e.g., barely legal, age 21-28, age 31-45, over age 50)
	Dependent Variable (the measurable response to the independent variable)	How quickly participants recognized sexually explicit words

Start Over

Ethics

- Are there ways to reduce the sexualization of girls?
- Can steps be taken to mitigate the negative effects of the sexualization of girls?

In 2010, in response to the 2008 APA report on the sexualization of girls, two U.S. Congresswomen introduced a bill, the Health Media for Youth Act, which sought to increase funding to promote media literacy, provide research funding examining the role of girls and women in the media, and develop youth empowerment programs. However, this bill was not passed.

Media ethics are very difficult to legislate and the movement to address the sexualization of girls has focused more on education and advocacy. One organization in particular was formed to help combat the effects of the sexualization of girls in the media. This organization, known as SPARK (Sexualization Protest: Action, Resistance, Knowledge), focuses on encouraging girls to become change agents by advocating for healthier media images of women.

Cultural and Social Diversity

- Examples of sexualization can be found for both genders, so why is this topic focused on girls?
- What does the data tell us about gender differences in the sexualization of boys and girls or men and women?

One study examined the covers of *Rolling Stone* magazine from 1967 to 2009 and rated the images in terms of sexualization (see Figure 11.7). They found that the majority of images (83–89 percent) of men during that time period were not sexualized, whereas a majority of images of women were sexualized. In fact, images of women during those times became increasingly hypersexualized so that during the 2000s, 61 percent of images of women on *Rolling Stone* covers were hypersexualized (Hatton & Trautner, 2011).

Figure 11.7 Sexualized *Rolling Stone* Images

This figure demonstrates that images of men have been generally non-sexualized and this trend has not changed over time. However, images of women on *Rolling Stone* covers have become increasingly hypersexualized since 1980.

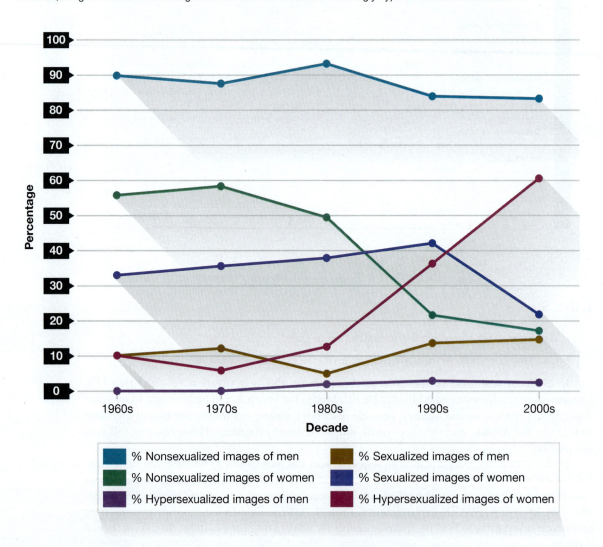

When examining gender differences in sexualization of children and adolescents, there is also evidence that girls are sexualized much more frequently than boys. One study examining "family" films rated G and PG from 2006 to 2011 found that girls and women in these films were sexualized much more frequently than boys or men (Smith et al., 2012). Female teen characters in these films were shown in sexy clothing or partially nude approximately a third of the time (see Table 11.4)

Table 11.4 Hypersexuality Measures by Female Character's Age in Family Films

	Teen 13-20 yrs	Young Adult 21-39 yrs	Middle Age 40-64 yrs
Sexy Clothing	31.6%	37.5%	21.9%
Some Nudity	31.6%	34.5%	21.6%
Thin	49.6%	41.3%	16.5%
Beautiful	23.3%	19%	8.3%

NOTE: Only characters with bodies approximating the human from are included in these analyses. The percentages reflect the proportion of all females within an ages category shown with sexy clothes, exposed skin, think, or beautiful.

The Star and Ferguson (2012) study showed that 6-9 year old girls chose the sexualized images (on the left at the top and on the right on the bottom) as representative of "popular" girls and their own ideal.

Downs and Smith (2010) examined female characters in top-selling video games and found that female characters in video games were depicted in sexually-revealing clothing with unrealistic bodies more often than male characters. Another study evaluating clothes marketed toward girls approximately ages 6–14 found that almost a third of clothing had sexualized characteristics (Goodin et al., 2011). These trends appear to have worsened in recent decades. An analysis of *Seventeen* and *Girls' Life* magazines from 1971 to 2011 showed an increase in sexualized images of girls during the past several decades (Graff et al., 2013). The results of one study are particularly alarming, showing that 6- to 9-year-old girls chose a sexualized paper doll over the nonsexualized paper doll as demonstrating popularity and their own ideal self (Star & Ferguson, 2012).

Overall, the evidence suggests that girls and women are more likely to be sexualized than boys or men, and the consequences are generally negative for everyone. With an advertising culture focused heavily on the notion that "sex sells," the challenge of reducing the sexualization of girls is significant.

Quiz for Module 11.13

1. _____ occurs when a person's value comes only from his/her sexual appeal or behavior to the exclusion of other characteristics, and when a person is sexually objectified, for example, made into a thing for another's sexual use.
   a. Self-objectification
   b. Other objectification
   c. Sexualization
   d. Hyper-feminization

2. Rianna, a 13-year-old girl, always worries about how her body appears to other people. Instead of sitting comfortably in a chair, she positions her body in a way that she thinks would look attractive to others. When she looks in the mirror, she always thinks about how other people would evaluate her appearance. Rianna is demonstrating characteristics of _____.
   a. hyper-sexualization
   b. self-objectification
   c. low self-esteem
   d. decreased sexual interest

3. Studies have found that when people viewed sexualized pictures of young girls, it led them to equate _____ with _____.
   a. middle age; sexuality
   b. sexual behavior; deviance
   c. youth; deviant behavior
   d. youth; sexuality

4. What organization encourages girls to speak up to promote healthier media images of young women?
   a. NOW
   b. Girls and Women Unite
   c. SPARKLE
   d. SPARK

5. When comparing gender differences in sexualization, research has demonstrated that _____ are most often the targets of sexualization.
   a. girls and women
   b. boys and men
   c. older women
   d. young boys

Summary

Module 11.1–11.3: Gender Development

Our sex is our biological classification as either male or female based on the sex chromosomes contained in our DNA. Gender, on the other hand, is the set of behaviors and characteristics that define individuals as boys and men or girls and women in society. Our primary sex characteristics (the sexual organs present at birth and directly involved in human reproduction) develop in utero. Until the third month, every fetus has both the **Müllerian system**—the precursor of female sex organs—and the **Wolffian system**—the precursor of male sex organs. During the third month, a male's testes will secrete **androgens,** or male sex hormones, to initiate the Wolffian system to develop. In the absence of these androgens, the Müllerian system will develop and the fetus will develop female sex organs. The development of **external genitalia** (the penis and scrotum in males and the labia, clitoris, and external vagina in females) also depends on the presence or absence of androgens. In rare cases in which the fetus's receptors for androgens fail to function, **complete androgen insensitivity syndrome** causes a genetic male to develop external female genitalia.

When we reach reproductive age, our bodies develop **secondary sex characteristics**, or sexual organs and traits that develop at puberty and are not directly involved in reproduction. Hormones play a significant role in the development of our sex characteristics, and the androgen **testosterone** is the principal male hormone. Atypical concentrations of testosterone in genetic males and females can affect the development of **gender identity**—our sense of being a boy or girl, man or woman. Advocacy and research about intersex individuals—those born with nonstandard male or female genitals, has led to a more cautious approach to genital surgeries in infancy and childhood. When thinking about gender from an evolutionary lens, **sexual selection** is the preference by one sex for certain characteristics in individuals of the other sex, and traits that allow males to (1) succeed in competition with other males and (2) be chosen by females are the traits most likely to be passed on to future generations.

Any of the behaviors and ideas associated with each gender are socially constructed. People who are highly **gender typed** include boys and men who show traditionally masculine traits and behaviors (called **instrumental traits**) and girls and women who show traditionally feminine traits and behaviors (called **expressive traits**). **Androgynous** people rate themselves equally high on both masculine and feminine traits. The **social learning theory** of gender assumes that children learn gendered behavior by observing and imitating adults and responding to rewards and punishments. According to gender schema theory, gender differentiation begins when children develop schemas for what is "male" and what is "female." Children may be treated differently according to the **gender roles**—expectations about the way women and men behave—that they are expected to fill. The **social role theory** of gender focuses on the fact that inherent physical differences between men and women lead to the formation of gender roles in the division of labor in the home and at work. **Gender stereotypes,** or widely held concepts about a person or group of people based only on gender, often lead to **sexism**—prejudice and unfair treatment (i.e., discrimination) against men or women. **Benevolent sexism** is the acceptance of positive stereotypes or favorable biased behavior that propagates unfairness and inequalities based on gender.

Gender dysphoria causes a person to feel that he or she was born with the body of the wrong sex and should not be confused with the concept of **sexual orientation** (the gender to which someone is sexually attracted). **Transgender** is an umbrella term used to describe people whose gender identities cross over or move between the traditional gender continuum.

Module 11.4–11.5: Gender Similarities and Differences

While the preponderance of the evidence suggests strong similarities between the genders, there are some consistent findings of gender differences. Verbal reasoning skills and spatial reasoning skills have been some of the most highly researched in terms of differences between the genders. Studies in both areas showed that females performed better on certain measures of verbal skills (e.g., particularly in *verbal fluency*, or the ability to generate words in a category quickly), while males performed better in terms of spatial skills. Past research has also demonstrated that males have had a small but significant advantage over females in terms of math skill, but these differences appear to be getting smaller or disappearing altogether. Overall memory functioning appears to be quite similar across genders although several studies have shown that females tend to have better **episodic memory** (memory of specific events or experiences). **Aggression** (any purposeful behavior intended to cause physical or psychological harm to others) can be divided into **physical aggression** (any behavior that threatens or causes physical harm to another person) and **verbal aggression** (verbal communication intended to cause psychological harm rather than physical harm). Additionally, people can also engage in **indirect aggression** (also referred to as *relational aggression*), which includes acts that do not directly involve the target of the aggression (e.g., spreading rumors). Physical aggression is more prevalent in men than in women, but women appear to engage in slightly more indirect or verbal aggression than men. Men tend to be more socially dominant in most cultures, while women tend to have higher levels of **social connectedness** (the quality and number of meaningful relationships an individual may have among friends, family, and the community).

Module 11.6–11.7: Sexual Orientation

Sexual orientation refers to an enduring sexual attraction toward members of the same sex, the opposite sex, or both sexes. Data in American shows a rate of around 2–4 percent of men and 1–2 percent of women identify their sexual orientation as homosexual. Approximately 0.7 percent of Americans self-identify as bisexual. In the past, sexual orientation was viewed as a dichotomous, or one-dimensional issue; research has, however, failed to support this view, and most experts now view sexual orientation on a continuum. Development of sexual orientation generally occurs in childhood and adolescence but this process has shown to be somewhat more fluid among females than males (called **erotic plasticity**). Prejudice and discrimination related to sexual orientation have been very common both historically and currently.

No single factor has been identified that causes a person to have a particular sexual orientation. Research has failed to find evidence for early childhood experiences playing a causal role in the development of sexual orientation. Studies involving twins and family members consistently suggest that genes play at least some role in determining a person's sexual orientation. According to the **fraternal birth-order effect**, each additional older brother that a male has increases the odds that the male is homosexual by 33 percent. Observed differences in postmortem studies also reveal certain correlations between some brain structures and sexual orientation.

Module 11.8–11.9:   Human Sexual Behavior

Sexual behavior is motivated by a combination of biological drives, psychological factors, and sociocultural influences. The four-stage sexual response cycle includes **excitement** (erection in males and vasocongestion in females), **plateau** (additional engorgement in both the male and female genitalia in preparation for orgasm, **orgasm** (muscle contractions leading to ejaculation in males and rhythmic pelvic contractions in females), and **resolution** (body returns to pre-aroused state). Men and women appear to prefer different types of sexually arousing stimuli, and responses to sexually arousing stimuli are somewhat different for men and women. Sexual activity is subjected to **social norms** (the spoken and unspoken rules about what behavior is considered appropriate in a given society), which are influenced by a number of cultural factors, including politics, media, and religion. Societies differ in level of sexual permissiveness, views on contraception, and gender roles related to sexuality.

Module 11.10–11.12:   Sexual Disorders and Sexually Transmitted Infections

Sexual dysfunctions refer to ongoing problems with sexual functioning that cause distress and impairment for individuals and relationships. Sexual dysfunctions are classified by gender; there are three female conditions and four male conditions. The three female conditions include **sexual interest/arousal disorder (**either a complete lack of or significant reduction in sexual interest/arousal), **female orgasmic disorder** (a significant delay, reduction of intensity, or cessation of ability to achieve orgasm), and **genitopelvic pain/penetration disorder** (involuntary contractions of the pelvic floor muscles around the vagina upon penetration). The four male conditions are **male hypoactive sexual desire disorder** (lack of or significant reduction in sexual interest/arousal), **erectile disorder** (a recurrent inability to achieve or maintain an adequate erection during partnered sexual activities), **premature ejaculation** (a feeling of being unable to control orgasm, and climaxing in less than one minute after vaginal penetration), and **delayed ejaculation** (being unable to ejaculate during sexual activity after 25 minutes to 30 minutes of continuous sexual stimulation). **Paraphilic disorders** are a class of disorders related to atypical sexual behavior that cause distress to the person and/or make the person a serious threat to the mental health or physical well-being of others.

Sexually transmitted infections (STIs) are infections that are spread primarily through person-to-person sexual contact. People ages 15–24 account for half of all newly diagnosed STI's. The severity of STIs depends on the type of infection with some conditions being treatable with antibiotics, but other conditions can be incurable and have significant medical consequences. Diagnosing and treating STIs as early as possible is an important step; however, prevention of new cases of STIs is even more preferable.

Chapter 11 Quiz

1. Males have shown a slight advantage in _____ skills, while females have shown a slight advantage in _____ skills.

   a. spatial; verbal   **b.** intellectual; relational

   c. memory; language   **d.** verbal; memory

2. Tobias is a 44-year-old gay man who has researched his family history extensively. Consistent with research findings regarding the genetics of sexual orientation, he discovered that he has numerous male relatives on his _____ side of the family that are also gay.

   a. grandmother's   **b.** grandfather's

   c. fathers'   **d.** mother's

3. In 5th grade, Marcia started noticing that her breasts were developing and that her shorts were getting tighter because her hips were bigger. What are these noticeable changes in the body called?

   a. Adolescence

   b. Primary sex characteristics

   c. Secondary sex characteristics

   d. Müllerian system

4. Darcy identifies as a gay man and Selah identifies as a transgender woman. Darcy is referring to _____ while Selah is referring to _____.

   a. sexual orientation; gender identity

   b. gender identity; sexual orientation

   c. sexual preference; gender identity

   d. sexual behavior; sexual orientation

5. Fraternal 3-year-old twins, Ben and Bella, dressed up in their mother's high heel shoes. Their mom exclaimed "Bella, you look so beautiful!" but said to Ben "those look so silly on you." Ben immediately went and put on his father's loafers instead. Which theory of gender development best explains this scenario?

   a. Social learning theory
   b. Gender schema theory
   c. Stereotype theory
   d. Gender identity theory

6. Which of the following behaviors puts someone at the highest risk of contracting a sexually transmitted infection (STI)?

   a. Unprotected vaginal or anal intercourse
   b. Oral sex
   c. Vaginal or anal intercourse using a condom
   d. Kissing

7. Which hormone influences the sexual drive in both females and males?

   a. Testosterone
   b. Estrogen
   c. Androgen
   d. Adrenaline

8. Natal males (those born as biological males) are _____ likely to develop gender dysphoria compared to natal females (those born as biological females).

   a. equally
   b. less
   c. more
   d. not

9. Marcus and Suri are on a road trip driving across the United States. Marcus states that he should navigate because men have better spatial skills than women. Suri replies that

   a. there are no reliable studies that prove conclusively the differences between male and female brains.
   b. those differences are just because men are told they are better at spatial skills and no real differences exist.
   c. women have superior intelligence in both verbal and spatial skills.
   d. while the differences between male and female verbal and spatial skills have been widely researched, the differences are quite small.

10. Sean is 55 years old and has been married for 20 years. He is still interested in sexual intercourse with his wife, but he suffers from the inability to achieve or maintain an erection at times during sex. What is this disorder called?

    a. Erectile disorder
    b. Premature ejaculation
    c. Hypoactive sexual arousal disorder
    d. Delayed ejaculation

11. Mick and Daphne are adults who enjoy dressing up in each other's clothing and tying each other up during sex. They both consent to this behavior, and it increases their sexual desire. This behavior is considered _____.

    a. pathological
    b. normal because they are consenting adults enjoying their relationship
    c. paraphillic disorder
    d. transvestic disorder

12. Celeste takes unflattering pictures of her classmates and posts them on Instagram, encouraging others to write mean and hateful captions about the pictures. This behavior would be labeled _____ aggression.

    a. physical
    b. indirect
    c. verbal
    d. direct

13. _____ refers to the quality and number of meaningful relationships an individual may have among friends, family, and the community.

    a. Social independence
    b. Social dominance
    c. Social connectedness
    d. Social individualism

14. During a sporting event, two opposing fans get into an argument, and one of them threatens to punch the other in the face. This is an example of both _____ and _____ aggression.

    a. direct; indirect
    b. physical; indirect
    c. indirect; verbal
    d. physical; direct

15. Which of the following statements suggests that sexual orientation exists on a continuum?

    a. Someone does not have to be exclusively homosexual or heterosexual but can feel varying degrees of both.
    b. People clearly identify as either heterosexual, homosexual, or bisexual.
    c. Sexual orientation is an either/or issue.
    d. People experience sexual orientation as a dichotomy between heterosexuality and homosexuality.

16. Huan and Abrielle know they are having a baby girl in 2 months. They have discussed that they want to avoid the stereotypes for gender in regard to colors and toys for their child, but they are not sure they can avoid the way others interact with their child. Research shows that girls are _____ and boys are _____.

    a. left to cry it out; rocked more often
    b. quieter and sleep more; rowdier and sleep less
    c. given toy trucks; given princess dolls
    d. talked to more often and treated more gently; played with more roughly

17. Individuals from racial/ethnic minorities appear to self-identify as LGBT _____ than White Americans.

    a. slightly less often

    b. slightly more often

    c. at rates 2–3 times less often

    d. at rates 2–3 times more often

18. Henry was raised by lesbian mothers. Lola gave birth to him through artificial insemination and the use of donor sperm. He is 15 years old now. What does research suggest about the chances of Henry being gay?

    a. There is a decreased chance of Henry being gay due to being raised by lesbian parents.

    b. There is an increased chance of Henry being gay due to the influence of having two female parents.

    c. Henry is no more likely to be gay than a child raised in the home of heterosexual parents.

    d. There is an increased chance of Henry being heterosexual due to the influence of lesbian parents.

19. Bob was genetically born a male but due to the failure of androgen receptors when he was a fetus, he developed female genitalia. This condition is referred to as _____.

    a. external genitalia syndrome

    b. complete androgen insensitivity syndrome

    c. hermaphroditism

    d. Wolffian syndrome

20. Which sexually transmitted infection can lead to cervical cancer or other cancers?

    a. HIV

    b. Gonorrehea

    c. Syphillis

    d. Human papillomavirus (HPV)

21. What percentage of adults have a diagnosis of gender dysphoria?

    a. 10 percent

    b. Less than 1 percent

    c. 5 percent

    d. More than 15 percent

22. What is the correct order of the phases of the sexual response cycle?

    a. Plateau, excitement, orgasm, resolution

    b. Excitement, plateau, orgasm, resolution

    c. Excitement, plateau, resolution, orgasm

    d. Plateau, excitement, orgasm, resolution

23. Which of the following is an example of a sociocultural influence on sexual behavior?

    a. Religion

    b. Media

    c. Social norms

    d. All of the choices

24. Maria grew up in a culture and home with strict morals about a woman's sexuality. Women were not supposed to have sexual feelings or engage in sexual activity until married. As a result, when Maria married, she thought negatively about sex and was very scared of her own sexual responses. This is an example of _____.

    a. sexual stigma leading to sexual dysfunction

    b. inappropriate reaction to a normal stage in life

    c. appropriate response to new behavior

    d. cultural influences impacting sexual behavior

25. Sexual dysfunctions have a high prevalence rate with as many as _____ of women and _____ of men reporting problems at some point in their lives.

    a. 43 percent; 31 percent

    b. 75 percent; 15 percent

    c. 90 percent; 50 percent

    d. 10 percent; 5 percent

26. Professor Fisher states that men are better than women at math, which is why you see more men in the science and math departments. Rosales, who is a student, replies that

    a. recent research shows a decrease in the gender gap on mathematical performance measures.

    b. men are better naturally at math, but women can work harder and become good at math.

    c. men's brains are just wired to perform mathematical calculations.

    d. research has shown that men are gifted at math and women are gifted at verbal reasoning.

27. Which sex organs are the first to develop?

    a. Gonads

    b. Ovaries

    c. Testicles

    d. Androgens

28. Gerald is a 38 year old man who only becomes sexually aroused by prepubescent children. He states that the children are willing and that they like it. He is considered to have which paraphillic disorder?

    a. Voyeuristic disorder

    b. Sexual sadism disorder

    c. Pedophillic disorder

    d. Exhibitionistic disorder

29. What would be an accurate response to two people arguing about whether sexual orientation is due to genetics or brain structures?

    a. "Actually, the cause of sexual orientation is currently unknown."

b. "The research clearly supports a genetic cause responsible for sexual orientation."

c. "The research clearly supports the fact that brain structures are the underlying cause of sexual orientation."

d. "Neither of you are correct. Sexual orientation is caused by prenatal hormones."

30. Tony is a 5-year-old boy who loves to play with dolls and play house. When he enters kindergarten, he notices that most of the girls do those activities while the boys play ball and tag. He goes home and tells his dad that he is going to start playing ball and tag at recess because that is what boys do. Which theory of gender development best explains Tony's decision to change activities?

a. Gender schema theory

b. Social learning theory

c. Gender conformity

d. Gender learning theory

Chapter 12
Stress and Health

Chapter Outline and Learning Objectives

Module 12.1–12.3: Stress, Stressors, and the Biopsychosocial Model

LO 12.1 Differentiate the concept of stress from stressors.

LO 12.2 Identify the biopsychosocial factors involved in understanding stress and health.

LO 12.3 Describe the role culture plays in the explanation and experience of stress.

Module 12.4–12.5: Responses to Stress

LO 12.4 Recognize the characteristics associated with the physiological responses to stress.

LO 12.5 Identify some of the psychological responses to stress.

Module 12.6–12.7: The Role of Stress in Health and Disease

LO 12.6 Explain the impact of stress on the immune system.

LO 12.7 Describe the role of stress in life-threatening diseases.

Module 12.8–12.10: Managing Stress

LO 12.8 Define various physiological approaches to managing stress.

LO 12.9 Identify different psychological approaches to managing stress.

LO 12.10 Recognize the influence of sociocultural factors involved in stress and health.

Module 12.11: Piecing It Together: Stress, Health, and Smartphones

LO 12.11 Analyze how the cross-cutting themes of psychology apply to smartphone use and its effects on stress and health.

What Does Psychology Have to Do with Health?

Journal Prompt: The Effects of Stress on Your Health

Describe a time when you experienced a lot of stress. What effects did the stress have on your physical and mental health?

If you could easily answer the question above, then you are probably already aware there is a strong connection between our minds and our bodies. Many psychologists study the mind–body connection by examining the ways in which psychological states lead to physical reactions. While stress is a psychological state rather than a physiological ailment, it can significantly increase a person's risk of developing any of the leading causes of serious illness and death such as, heart disease, cancer, chronic lower respiratory diseases, and stroke (National Center for Health, 2014). Unfortunately, as we experience higher levels of stress in our lives, we may be more likely to turn to unhealthy behaviors such as smoking, alcohol abuse, or excessive eating as stress relievers. The physiological changes caused by stress coupled with unhealthy behaviors can negatively impact our overall physical health. Therefore, our behaviors and our mental states can work together to drag us into a vicious and unhealthy cycle. However, it isn't all bad news. Positive states of mind and healthy lifestyle behaviors can also interact in a way to promote long-term happiness and health.

How can we keep ourselves mentally and physically healthy in stressful situations? The answer might lie in the field of **behavioral medicine**, an interdisciplinary approach to medical treatment that integrates medical, psychological, and sociocultural knowledge to increase life expectancy and enhance quality of life. The psychological aspect of behavioral medicine, known as **health psychology**, is focused on the development of strategies people and their doctors can use to eliminate or reduce the risk of illness and disease. For example, health psychologists might develop and implement stress management classes, weight-loss programs, medication adherence plans or community support groups in an effort to encourage individuals to take a holistic, or comprehensive, approach to health. As the name of the field suggests, health psychology places emphasis on the idea that physical health and mental health are closely related: The mind–body connection is real and powerful, and our psychological states can play a major role in our overall health (see Figure 12.1).

behavioral medicine

an interdisciplinary approach to medical treatment that integrates medical, psychological, and sociocultural knowledge to increase life expectancy and enhance quality of life

health psychology

the psychological aspect of behavioral medicine that focuses on the development of strategies to eliminate or reduce the risk of illness and disease

Figure 12.1 The Mind Body Connection

Module 12.1–12.3: Stress, Stressors, and the Biopsychosocial Model

Stress is one of those words that seems to be in everyone's vocabulary. In fact, stress is one of the few English words that remains the same in various other languages (e.g., le stress, il stress, der stress). Despite its linguistic similarities, the word "stress" can represent different things to different people. Something that causes significant stress in your friend may not add any stress to your life. Researchers are paying more attention to stress so they can determine how stress impacts our health. Ultimately, pinpointing the relationship between stress and health can inform us about effective ways to reduce stress levels and improve overall health.

Defining Stress and Stressors

LO 12.1 **Differentiate the concept of stress from stressors.**

You've got an exam coming up, you're trying to repair a strained relationship with an old friend, and you're not sure how you're going to pay off your credit card this month. Even if you've never faced any of these particular circumstances, chances are good you know what stress feels like when you are in a difficult situation. **Stress** was originally defined as "the non-specific response of the body to any demand made upon it" (Selye, 1973, p. 692). Over the years, that definition has evolved into something more descriptive, such as the perceived discrepancy between the physical or psychological demands of a situation and the individual's biological, psychological, or social resources to cope with the demands (Folkman et al., 1986; Lovallo, 2005). As you examine this definition, you'll realize there is a lot of grey area: The situation can be physical or psychological, and the events that happen do not have to be objectively seen as threatening or challenging. Stress is about a response—an individual's response to a situation they feel unprepared for or unable to navigate. A number of people could be presented with the same situation, but not every person will experience that situation as stressful.

In response to these various definitions, a working group of stress researchers has proposed we restrict the definition of stress to include only situations that involve unpredictability and a lack of control (Koolhaas et al., 2011). Think about the stress you have experienced in your own life: Did it tend to involve situations that felt unpredictable or out of control?

The experiences we encounter in life that cause stress are referred to as **stressors**. Stressors tend to involve events we perceive as threatening or challenging. Stressors can produce varying levels of stress and the amount of stress experienced as a result of a stressor can vary between individuals. Which do you think causes more stress: surviving a plane crash or suffering through the traffic jams of your daily commute? Being displaced from your home when a hurricane causes your entire city to flood, or having your basement flood every time it rains? You may be surprised to discover that in some cases, the *cumulative* impact of what we perceive to be minor stressors may be just as significant as the impact of one large-scale event.

Stress is most often described as a response, but it can also be conceptualized as a process—one that involves the interaction between an individual and their environment. Viewing stress as a process can serve as a helpful reminder that we don't live inside a vacuum and that the bidirectional relationship between the experience of stress and the individual's environment leads to the subjectivity inherent in the definition of stress (see Figure 12.2).

stress

the perceived discrepancy between the physical or psychological demands of a situation and the individual's biological, psychological, or social resources to cope with the demands

stressors

the experiences we encounter in life that cause stress; events we perceive as threatening or challenging

Figure 12.2 The Bidirectional Aspect of Stress

If athletes don't learn to cope with physical and mental stress, their performance may suffer.

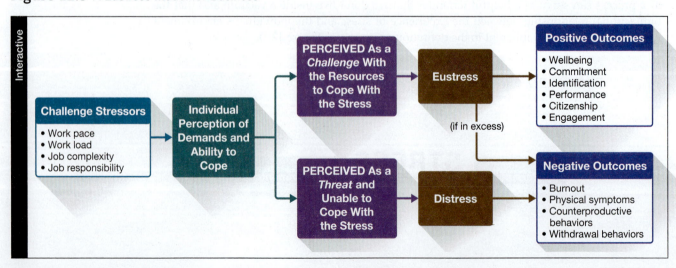

Athletes can also be energized by the stress of a competition, especially when being cheered on by spectators and fans.

distress

the negative effects experienced when confronted with stress

eustress

positive effects that can result from stress; often in relation to positive, yet stressful, situations

DISTRESS VS. EUSTRESS No matter where we encountered stress or how that stress manifested itself in our bodies, we tend to think of stress in negative terms. For most of us, stress is something to be avoided or overcome. In fact, the word **distress** refers to the negative effects often experienced when confronted with stress.

However, while stress can potentially increase your risk for serious illnesses and other health-related problems, it can also help save your life. When stress is short-lived or perceived as a challenge you feel capable of overcoming, it can have positive effects: It can help activate your immune system so you can fight off an illness or heal a wound, it can motivate you to find solutions to problems, and it can teach you to become emotionally resilient. For example, experiencing stress before a big game isn't necessarily a bad thing—that stress might actually help you run faster, throw farther, or jump higher. This positive result from stress is known as **eustress** (Selye, 1975).

An individual's perception of the stressor largely contributes to whether *distress* or *eustress* is experienced. If a stressor is short-term, energizing, and perceived as something to be conquered, it will likely be experienced as eustress. Eustress helps explain why some experiences in life that are generally found to be exciting (e.g., moving away for college, getting married, having a baby) are still considered stressful.

The concept of eustress has become an important one in business and organizational psychology. Human resource departments have recognized the productivity of their employees is best when an appropriate amount of eustress is experienced in the job (Venkatesh & Ram, 2015). So yes, your boss does mean to stress you out! But, it is tricky to find the right amount or combination of stressors, especially since whether a person experiences distress or eustress depends on their own perception of the situation and their abilities to cope with the stress. Hargrove et al. (2015) proposed a theory referred to as the Human Resource Development (HRD) Eustress Model to help companies see how they can turn distress into eustress and increase their productivity and employee satisfaction (see Figure 12.3). Click through a variation of this model below to see the different components.

TYPES OF STRESSORS Stressors come in various forms. Unpredictable, large-scale events are characterized as **catastrophes** (Peters et al., 2012). The terrorist attacks of September 11, 2001, and the numerous natural disasters of 2017, including the hurricanes in Texas, Florida, the Caribbean, and Puerto Rico; the earthquakes in Mexico; and the wildfires in the Western United States are all examples of catastrophes. People who have experienced catastrophes of this magnitude are often at risk for developing PTSD, a psychological disorder caused by persistent re-experiencing of traumatic events. Symptoms of PTSD include sleep and concentration problems, anxiety, nightmares, and flashbacks.

Figure 12.3 A Eustress Model for Business

Interactive				
Challenge Stressors • Work pace • Work load • Job complexity • Job responsibility	**Individual Perception of Demands and Ability to Cope**	**PERCEIVED As a *Challenge* With the Resources to Cope With the Stress**	**Eustress**	**Positive Outcomes** • Wellbeing • Commitment • Identification • Performance • Citizenship • Engagement
		PERCEIVED As a *Threat* and Unable to Cope With the Stress	**Distress**	**Negative Outcomes** • Burnout • Physical symptoms • Counterproductive behaviors • Withdrawal behaviors

(if in excess)

Catastrophic events like these can have extensive, far-reaching implications for stress and health, not just for those directly affected by the catastrophe but also for some people who were merely exposed to images of the tragedy. There is no question that media exposure to disasters and violence can lead to vicarious trauma and other negative health outcomes for those watching the footage (Hopwood & Schutte, 2017). For example, after the 9/11 terrorist attacks, researchers found that many Americans' blood pressure had increased substantially as a result of the attacks and had remained at these increased levels for at least two months (Gerin et al., 2005). Longer term health effects were found as well with documented increases in gastroesophageal reflux (GERD), respiratory illness, and post-traumatic stress disorder (PTSD) (Bowler et al., 2012; Li et al., 2011). Our always-connected digital world, with the option for anyone to publish video to the Internet or stream live on social media (even their own suicide on Facebook Live), just increases the probability of more people being indirectly negatively affected by these images (Jukes, 2016; Meek, 2016).

Fires, such as the California forest fires of 2017, are unpredictable catastrophes that produce significant stress for those affected.

Not all stressors have to be catastrophic to be harmful. More common life events, such as moving out of a childhood home, getting married or divorced, losing a loved one, or changing career paths, can cause large amounts of stress in our lives. Many of these **significant life changes** tend to occur during young adulthood: In your late teens, twenties, and thirties, you may face the challenges and stressors that accompany leaving home for the first time, beginning a career, entering a long-term relationship, starting a family, and coping with the deaths of older relatives. In fact, young adults tend to experience so much change that the term "quarter-life crisis" has been used to describe the stressful, overwhelming feelings that plague may people in their twenties (Johnson, 2015; Stapleton, 2012). Researchers who have studied this type of stress over time have found that reported stress is higher in women and decreases as people get older (Cohen & Janicki-Deverts, 2012).

catastrophes

unpredictable, large-scale, stressful events, such as natural disasters or terrorist attacks

significant life changes

stressful common life events, such as moving out of a childhood home, getting married or divorced, losing a loved one, or changing career paths

Explore Stress Levels by Age and Over Time

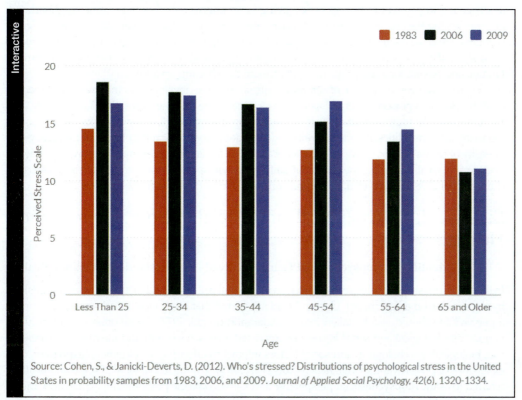

Source: Cohen, S., & Janicki-Deverts, D. (2012). Who's stressed? Distributions of psychological stress in the United States in probability samples from 1983, 2006, and 2009. *Journal of Applied Social Psychology, 42*(6), 1320-1334.

Because of the subjective nature of stress, it can be difficult to find a meaningful way to measure stress. The *Life Experiences Survey* is a 57-item self-report measure designed to quantify the stress brought about by both positive and negative life changes (Sarason et al., 1978). The survey allows

Stressful Life Events

Interactive

Drag the life events below to their appropriate spot in the table.

Rank	Life Event	Value
1	Death of a spouse	100
7	Marriage	50
14	New family member	39
27	Begin or end of school	26
41	Vacation	13

Check Answers

respondents to specify the desirability of the event (was it positive or negative) as well as its impact on their life. The *Social Readjustment Rating Scale* is another widely used measure of life events (Holmes & Rahe, 1967). The following includes a few sample items and their designated values, which provide an estimate of the relative impact each of the stressors have on daily life:

daily hassles

frequent and common stressors experienced in daily life, such as traffic jams, busy schedules, and unexpected delays

The most frequent and common stressors are **daily hassles**, which include such nuisances as sitting in traffic jams, waiting in long lines, having an overly busy schedule, receiving too much e-mail spam, finding the office coffee pot always empty, tripping over your roommate's shoes every time you walk in the door, and so on (Helms & Demo, 2005). While these hassles may seem relatively minor, their effects can add up to create a significant amount of stress (Kotozaki et al., 2014). This type of stress can be even more harmful when exacerbated by socioeconomic or safety-related factors such as struggling to pay rent or buy groceries, living in an impoverished or high-crime neighborhood, or experiencing the effects of racism and other types of prejudice (Jacob et al., 2014). In lower socio-economic areas, where the hassles of everyday life can be plentiful and dangerous, residents tend to show signs of high blood pressure, or hypertension—a physical symptom of a stressful environment. Finding and paying for appropriate medical care can then become an additional stressor.

There have been a number of self-report questionnaires developed to measure the impact of daily hassles on a person's overall level of stress. One of the first measures, the Hassles Scale, lists 117 annoyances in various areas of life (e.g., misplacing/losing things, concerns about owing money, too many responsibilities, having to wait) and produces scores that reflect both the frequency and intensity of the hassles experienced (Kanner et al., 1981). Variations of this measure have been developed to specifically examine the impact of daily hassles in special populations, such as adolescents (Kanner et al., 1987; Wright et al., 2010) and college students (Sarafino & Ewing, 1999).

Biological, Psychological, and Social Factors in Stress and Health

LO 12.2 Identify the biopsychosocial factors involved in understanding stress and health.

In the 1970s, physicians started realizing that an individual's illness couldn't always be fully explained by the standard medical model. George Engel suggested that other factors that were important in a person's life should also be taken into consideration (Engel, 1977). These other factors included various psychological and social issues that impacted a person's health and the disease process. In fact, biological, psychological, and social factors interact to affect the development, expression, and experience of physical and mental health (Suls et al., 2013). This inclusive view of stress and health is referred to as the **biopsychosocial perspective** and has become the predominant explanatory model within the field of health psychology (Sarafino & Smith, 2014; Suls & Rothman, 2004). The video *The Biopsychosocial Perspective in Stress and Health* will provide an overview of this model.

biopsychosocial perspective

a perspective in understanding stress and health that includes biological, psychological, and social factors

Biological factors range from the specific genes inherited by our parents to various structural or physical defects, such as a malfunctioning internal organ or area of the brain. Biological factors

The Biopsychosocial Perspective in Stress and Health

may be visible from birth or, in the case of *gene-environment interactions*, may not become evident unless triggered by certain environmental factors. For example, an individual may inherit a predisposition for high blood pressure but not exhibit the symptoms of high blood pressure until they experience a particularly stressful period in their life. How your body physiologically responds to stress is an important biological factor that we will examine in more detail in an upcoming module.

Psychological factors include many of the *intra*personal (within one person) and *inter*personal (between two or more people) cognitive, emotional, and behavioral aspects of stress. Stress and various psychological factors have a reciprocal relationship—meaning psychological factors can influence the level of stress in one's life and the level of stress experienced can influence various psychological issues. For example, let's consider the situation of starting a new job. Imagine you applied for many jobs and were thrilled when you received a job offer from your first-choice company. This situation is an example of a positive life event, but it is still often experienced as stressful. The *cognitive* psychological factor will involve the beliefs you hold and the thoughts you have about starting this new job. If you believe you were "just lucky" to have landed the job and that you're "never going to be able to live up to the expectations," you are likely going to experience a lot of stress and anxiety heading into your first day. How do you imagine this level of stress will affect your abilities and behaviors on your first day? When we are under significant stress, we tend not to perform at our best, so you may say something or do something to confirm your thoughts of how you weren't qualified for the job—which then leads to more stress. How do you think this scenario's outcome would be different if your thoughts going into the job were, "This is my dream job! I can't wait to impress them with all of my skills and knowledge."

The experience of stress leads to a particular *emotional* experience. In the case of positive life stress, these emotions could be joy or excitement. However, it is much more common to experience negative emotions from stress such as fear, anxiety, sadness, or anger. Fear is an emotion that typically arises when we are confronted with something tangible we experience as threatening whereas anxiety often refers to more a vague sense of uneasiness coupled with a sense that something bad is going to happen in the future. Sadness is another emotion often experienced in response to a stressful event, typically one that involves some kind of loss. Finally, anger is an interesting emotion that often emerges from the frustration experienced at the inability to achieve a goal (e.g., stuck in traffic). Anger has been described as an emotion associated with an entire network of negative emotions and resulting behaviors (Wyer & Srull, 2014). This theory provides some explanation for the observation that many people who report being angry also experience a number of other negative emotions, either consciously or unconsciously, at the same time (e.g., jealousy, rejection, embarrassment).

Stress also has a reciprocal relationship with *behaviors*. That is, there are many behaviors that can lead to stress and the experience of stress tends to motivate certain behaviors. Behaviors resulting from stress typically include strategies to eliminate the stressor (and therefore the stress) or behaviors that promote coping mechanisms for dealing with the stress. Coping mechanisms can be either healthy or unhealthy, and unhealthy coping typically produces more stress in the long run (Evans & Kim, 2013).

So far, we have discussed the biological and psychological aspects of stress. Since we don't live in a social vacuum, we must also examine an individual's social environment when attempting to understand their experience of stress. Social factors include characteristics in the person's surrounding environment (e.g., family structure, social support, socioeconomic status, pollution, natural disasters) that impact stress and health. When you put all of this together—the biological factors, psychological factors, and social factors—it becomes easier to see why the notion of stress is difficult to define and, at times, challenging to understand.

Read the following scenario and then categorize each of the factors into their appropriate category according to the *biopsychosocial model*.

> Lara, a single mother of two children, decided to go back to college to finish her degree with the goal of being admitted into the nursing program. She was 38 years old when she resumed her studies. She worked full time to support her children, which limited her to registering for only online courses. She stayed up very late studying since she was busy with her children in the evenings. She was averaging 4–5 hours of sleep each night. A few big cups of coffee in the morning helped to keep her going. By midterm, she noticed her temper was short and she was worrying if she had made a mistake going back to school. She thought to herself, "I'm not young like these other students. My brain doesn't work as well as it used to. I'm probably going to end up failing and have to quit again." For the most part, her grades were fine, although she did fail one of her midterm exams. On the day of that exam, Lara began to experience chest pains. At first, she thought it was just indigestion because she had been eating a lot of fast food. However, after a few days of intermittent pain she began to worry. Her father died of a heart attack at the age of 55, and her grandmother lived many years with a pacemaker for her heart. She knew she should go see a doctor, but her health insurance was minimal and she didn't have the money to pay for expensive tests. She thought about asking friends for advice but realized she really didn't have any close friendships anymore since she had been so busy with work, kids, and school. Lara started to feel overwhelmed and a little depressed about her future.

Categorizing Biological, Psychological, and Social Factors

How can you explain Lara's stress? Drag and drop the following important pieces of information into the correct category.

Biological	Psychological	Social
Not getting enough sleep	Worry about her physical symptoms	Single mother raising two children
Family history of heart disease (possible genetic factor)	Anxiety about her ability to succeed	Economic stress: needs to work full-time in addition to school
Her age of 38	Irritability	Lack of social support (no friends)
Not eating healthy foods; possibly too much caffeine	Belief that her age is a barrier to success in college	Unable to afford needed healthcare

Start Over

Cultural Factors in Stress and Health

LO 12.3 **Describe the role culture plays in the explanation and experience of stress.**

So far, we have discussed the biological, psychological, and social factors that can influence a person's stress level and overall health. Another important factor that impacts all other aspects of stress and health is *culture*. Cultural factors are often discussed in combination with other social factors (i.e., the sociocultural perspective), but it can be helpful to think of culture as an overarching theme that permeates and influences the biopsychosocial model (see Figure 12.4).

Figure 12.4 The Role of Culture in the Biopsychosocial Model

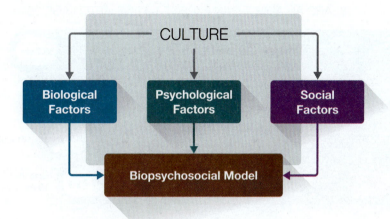

When the term "culture" is presented, most people tend to think about a person's race or ethnicity and while these are two important aspects of culture, they aren't the only important factors. The notion of culture also includes a person's sex/gender, religion, family values/ traditions, and the physical landscape of where they live (Gurung, 2013). Culture can play an important role in determining both an individual's exposure and response to stress.

Economic stress is a sociocultural factor that plays an important role in health and disease because of its relationship with many other stressors and high-risk behaviors. Socioeconomic status (SES) is often used as a measure of an individual's or family's relative economic and social position in society. SES is most commonly calculated using a combination of income and educational attainment. Figure 12.5 highlights the clear link that exists between SES and overall health (Dubay & Lebrun, 2012; National Center for Health, 2012).

Figure 12.5 Self Report of Fair or Poor Health, by Income

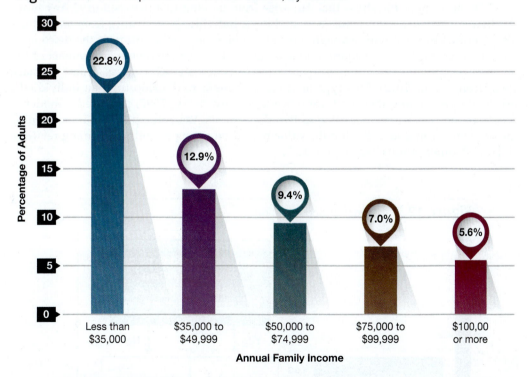

Individuals with lower SES are more likely to have infectious and chronic diseases and more likely to engage in unhealthy behaviors such as cigarette smoking and sedentary behavior (Mathur et al., 2013; Miller et al., 2011; Tandon et al., 2012). As a result, the life expectancy of individuals from lower SES groups can be significantly less than their wealthier counterparts (see Figure 12.6).

It is clear there are several important factors that differ between people who are considered low SES compared to those who have a higher SES. Poorer health may arise due

Figure 12.6 Life Expectancy by Income (1988-1998)

YEARS AN ADULT CAN EXPECT TO LIVE AFTER AGE 25

55.7 yrs	More than 400%
53.8 yrs	201–400%
51.4 yrs	101–200%
49.2 yrs	Less than 100%

Family Income
(percent of federal poverty level)

to increased participation in high-risk behaviors (e.g., drugs, unprotected sex), living in unhealthy environments, and/or less access to healthcare. Regardless of the specific reasons, individuals of low SES are three times more likely to die at a younger age compared to their higher SES counterparts (Signorello et al., 2014). In fact, the gap in life expectancy between low SES and high SES has only increased over time (Singh & Siahpush, 2006). Interestingly, the same pattern of results has been found with respect to people living in rural versus urban areas, with those living in metropolitan, urban areas demonstrating the highest life expectancy (Singh & Siahpush, 2014).

What about the stress of moving from a rural to urban area or from an urban to rural area? Or, how about the stress that can arise from moving to a new country? Any move to a new environment can create stress and those individuals who move from one culture into another are faced with managing the stress of a move in addition to the discomfort that often accompanies the adaptation to a new culture. The psychological impact of living in, or adapting to a new culture is referred to as **acculturative stress** (Smart & Smart, 1995; Torres et al., 2012). This type of stress is thought to develop from an individual's process of negotiating their cultural place in society. Berry (1997) proposed a model of acculturation that varies according to two dimensions: the value placed on maintaining the original cultural identity and the value placed on fitting in and maintaining relationships with other groups. (see Figure 12.7)

acculturative stress

the stress and psychological toll resulting from living in a new culture

Figure 12.7 A Model of Acculturation

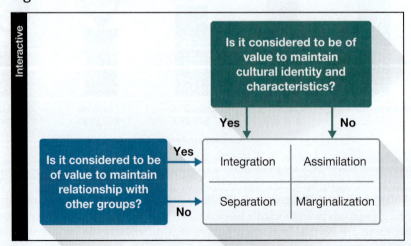

Mental health may vary as a result of these four possible outcomes, with acculturative stress driving both positive (exposure to new cultural experiences, life-long learning) and negative (conflict, anxiety, depression) effects (López-Rocha, 2014; Yoon et al., 2013). With approximately 40 million immigrants living in the United States today, understanding the process of acculturation and the consequences of acculturative stress is important for mental health professionals. Research has shown a variety of pre-immigration and post-immigration factors that contribute to acculturative stress. Living conditions prior to immigration and separation of families during the immigration process increase the risk of negative outcomes for children. Once in the United States, the discrepancy between the expectations of a new life and the reality of starting over in a new country can predict mental health symptoms (Rogers-Sirin et al., 2014). In addition, experiencing negative attitudes and discrimination from non-immigrants unsurprisingly significantly increases acculturative stress, which can lead to harmful effects on well-being (Schmitt et al., 2014).

Since September 11, 2001, Muslim Arab Americans have experienced increased prejudicial attitudes and discrimination (Abu-Ras & Abu-Bader, 2008; Padela & Heisler, 2010). Research with Muslim Arab adolescent immigrants found higher religiosity was associated with a stronger connection to their home country and consequently, less acculturation. However, the longer the adolescent had lived in the United States, the less acculturative stress was experienced (Goforth et al., 2014).

Shared Writing: Socioeconomic Status and Health

Discuss some of the reasons low SES is related to increased levels of stress and poor health. For example, you might note that individuals with lower SES are likely to have a lower-paying job (or no job), which can increase stress in the home. Think about the biological, psychological, and social factors that may be involved.

Quiz for Module 12.1–12.3

1. A contemporary definition of stress includes _____.
   a. a subjective discrepancy between the body's physiological responses and the demands of the situation
   b. an objective discrepancy between a situation and a person's ability to cope with the situation
   c. a subjective discrepancy between a situation and a person's ability to cope with the situation
   d. an objective discrepancy between the body's physiological responses and the demands of the situation

2. An event that is perceived as threatening or challenging is known as a _____.
   a. stress
   b. stressor
   c. distress
   d. eustress

3. If a stressor is short term, energizing, and seen as something to be conquered, it will likely be experienced as _____.
   a. daily hassle
   b. distress
   c. catastrophe
   d. eustress

4. Dr. Banini is a health psychologist. When she conducts assessments of new patients, she is sure to ask about their medical history, family history of illness, any psychological symptoms, and current stressors in their life (e.g., family, work, home environment). Dr. Banini is practicing from a _____ perspective.
   a. bio-stress-environmental
   b. diathesis-stress
   c. gene-environment interaction
   d. biopsychosocial

5. A person may inherit the predisposition for heart disease but not experience the symptoms of heart disease until he loses his job and gets a divorce in the same year. The genetic predisposition is considered a _____ factor in the biopsychosocial model.
   a. biological
   b. inherited
   c. social
   d. psychological

6. The psychological aspect of stress may include feelings of anger. Anger is considered part of the _____ experience of stress.
   a. cognitive
   b. behavioral
   c. emotional
   d. social

7. An individual's _____ should be viewed as an overarching factor that affects other biopsychosocial factors.
   a. religion
   b. culture
   c. ethnicity
   d. socioeconomic status

8. People with lower socioeconomic status (SES) are _____ more likely to die at a younger age than their higher SES counterparts.
   a. no
   b. two times
   c. three times
   d. four times

9. Houmam moved from Syria to England 8 months ago. He is struggling to communicate in English and fit in with his new friends in school. What kind of stress is Houmam experiencing?
   a. Sociocultural
   b. Immigrant
   c. Displacement
   d. Acculturative

Module 12.4 – 12.5: Responses to Stress

Have you ever taken a class with someone who remained calm and unfazed before every exam, regardless of how well-prepared he/she was? Meanwhile, you might have been feeling very anxious and worried about your performance despite putting in hours of study time. We each perceive stressors differently, and each of us has our own strategies for coping with stress. However, we all have very similar immediate physiological responses to stress. Over the years, psychologists have developed several models of our physiological and psychological stress response systems.

The Body's Physical Response to Stress

LO 12.4 **Recognize the characteristics associated with the physiological responses to stress.**

In 1915, American physiologist Walter Cannon observed that extreme cold, lack of oxygen, and emotion-arousing incidents can trigger an increase in the release of the stress hormones epinephrine and norepinephrine from the adrenal glands (Cannon, 1915). This observation demonstrated to Cannon that the stress response is a part of the mind–body system: Although stress is a mental state, it also produces physical symptoms. Cannon described the body's response to emotional arousal the **fight-or-flight response**, a term that describes our evolutionary options when faced with a stressor—fighting back or fleeing to safety. When confronted with a truly stressful or dangerous situation, this response is exactly what we would want from our bodies. Directed by the sympathetic nervous system, a number of characteristic physiological changes make up the fight-or-flight response: heart rate increases to pump more blood to important, large muscles, respiration (breathing) increases to get more oxygen throughout the body, sweating may occur in an effort to cool the body. Some bodily functions slow down or stop altogether, such as digestion, since they are not important when the body is under attack (this is one reason some people get stomach cramps when under stress). The fight-or-flight response is meant to keep us safe. However, there are times when the body's fight-or-flight response occurs in the absence of any stress or danger. Imagine you are just sitting watching television when all of the sudden your body experiences a number of fight-or-flight responses (your heart starts racing, you start sweating, and breathing faster). How do you think you would feel? What would you be thinking? People who have had this experience, which is often referred to as a *panic attack*, describe it as terrifying and very uncomfortable. Just like any other system in our body, our physiological response to stress can malfunction, which if left untreated, can lead to other physical and/or mental health problems. Watch the video *Stress and Your Health* for a review of the body's sympathetic nervous system response to stress.

fight-or-flight response

a physiological response to stress trigged by the release of hormones from the adrenal glands; prepares the body to fight back or flee to safety

Stress and Your Health

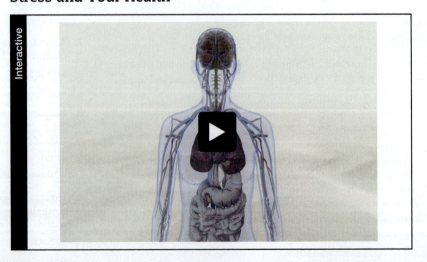

Cannon's description of the fight-or-flight response has become one of the most famous models used to explain animals' responses to stress, but chemically speaking, it doesn't tell the entire story.

Following up on Cannon's research, endocrinologist Hans Selye identified another stress response system that causes the outer part of the adrenal glands to secrete other stress hormones, such as cortisol. Cortisol increases the concentration of glucose (sugar) in the blood to make fuel available to the muscles (in order to fight or flee). The method by which cortisol is released into the bloodstream is slower than the fight-or-flight response, which releases epinephrine and norepinephrine.

The neuroendocrine system responsible for the reacting to stress is called the **hypothalamic-pituitary-adrenal axis**, or just the **HPA axis** (Smith & Vale, 2006). While the name may be long, it is merely referring to the "chain of command" when it comes to stress hormone secretion. The hypothalamus is the president, who directs the pituitary gland to secrete a hormone that tells the adrenal gland to release cortisol. Cortisol and other similar hormones work to defend the body against various forms of stress. The HPA axis doesn't know the difference between the stress you experience because of an upcoming exam and the stress your body experiences when confronted with a pathogen in the environment; the body's response is the same. Just as with the fight or flight response, cortisol and other stress hormones are very helpful when confronted with a stressor, but they are not meant to be a regular part of daily life. In fact, too much cortisol has been linked to a variety of negative outcomes such as increased appetite/weight gain and memory impairment (Manenschijn et al., 2013; Street et al., 2011; Tatomir et al., 2014).

In the 1930s, Selye combined his work with Cannon's to develop a model referred to as the **general adaptation syndrome (GAS)**, which describes how the body adaptively responds to stress over prolonged periods of time. According to the GAS, the body responds in three stages: alarm, resistance, and exhaustion (see Figure 12.8). The *alarm stage* is similar to the fight-or-flight response where the body's initial reaction to a threat causes the heart rate to increase and blood to be diverted to the skeletal muscles. Cortisol is also eventually released but more slowly than the neurotransmitters epinephrine and norepinephrine. During the *resistance stage*, temperature, blood pressure, and respiration remain at high levels; hormones are replenished; and the body stays primed to fight the challenge. During this time, the individual may not show any outward signs of stress, but his/her body is using up many of its resources and therefore may not be able to resist new stressors if they are encountered. If the stress is prolonged, or an individual experiences repeated periods of stress, the *exhaustion stage* occurs when the body exhausts all of its coping resources and depletes its reserves. A chronically stressed person becomes *exhausted* both physically and mentally. This exhaustion causes damage to the internal organs and makes the body more vulnerable to illness and even death. Researchers have confirmed that chronic stress accelerates aging and can lead to physical deterioration (Epel & Lithgow, 2014).

hypothalamic-pituitary-adrenal (HPA) axis

the neuroendocrine system responsible for the reacting to stress; produces cortisol

general adaptation syndrome (GAS)

theory proposed by Hans Selye that describes how the body adaptively responds to stress over prolonged periods of time

Figure 12.8 The General Adaptation Syndrome

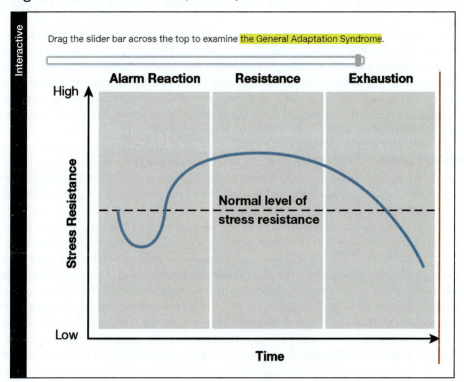

Adaptive Pathway 12.1: The Physiological Stress Response

| Interactive | INTRODUCTION | ADAPTIVE PATHWAY | RESULTS |

Adaptive Pathway 12.1

TThe following pathway will test your understanding and adapt to your needs. Be sure to answer all of the questions and watch any of the short videos presented.

PREVIOUS   INTRODUCTION   NEXT

Psychological Responses to Stress

LO 12.5 **Identify some of the psychological responses to stress.**

So far, we have discussed the physiological changes that occur in our bodies as we respond to stress. Stress can also have effects on an individual's psychological functioning given the connection between the body and the mind. That is, acute and chronic stress can have powerful effects on our emotions, thoughts, and behaviors, and even contribute to the development of psychological disorders. However, unlike the more predictable physiological responses, psychological responses can be broad and varied. You may have found sometimes you respond to stress one way and then other times stress seems to have a different psychological effect on you.

Many people who are under stress experience worry or anxiety, which at times, can be a very appropriate response. Stressful situations are often accompanied by uncertainty about the future, which can be a significant trigger for anxiety and worry (Bomyea et al., 2015; Romero-Sanchiz et al., 2015). In some cases, the anxiety may be the direct result of a stressor (e.g., in the case of a traumatic experience) or the anxiety may be a reaction to the experience of the stress. Worry and anxiety, if left unmanaged have the potential to progress into diagnosable anxiety disorders (Dickson et al., 2012). In fact, research has suggested that chronic stress may alter the brain in a way that makes an individual more susceptible to developing a psychological disorder (Brady & Sinha, 2005; Lupien et al., 2009). Not everyone experiences anxiety as a result of stress. Some people lash out at others with irritability and anger, whereas other others turn their emotions inward, experiencing sadness, which could potentially evolve into depression (Starr et al., 2016).

Our thoughts play an important role in the perception and interpretation of stress and in how we choose to respond to the stress. People have different beliefs about their own ability to cope with stress. Someone who thinks, "I'll never be able to handle it when something really stressful happens" is going to be at a disadvantage compared to the person who thinks, "I know I'm a strong person and I will be able to cope with whatever stress comes my way." While people may tend to hold a particular set of beliefs about their ability to cope, stressful circumstances can challenge, and even change, those beliefs. The concept of *learned helplessness* is an example of the reciprocal relationship between stress, thoughts, and behaviors. Someone who has developed learned helplessness is typically in a stressful situation in which they see no escape and believe to some extent that they are at fault for being in that situation. Imagine a situation where a child was being bullied at school. At first, perhaps the child believed he could handle the situation and tried to stand up for himself, but as a result, the bullying escalated and became worse. In this situation, the child may start to believe that no matter what they do it won't be effective, and that they must be doing something to cause others not to like them. You can imagine that this type of thinking only creates more stress, leaving the student vulnerable to further bullying, with fewer resources to cope. The way we think about stress, and specifically, our beliefs in our own abilities to cope with stress, can have important implications for the effects stress has on our bodies and minds and can even influence the decisions we make while under stress.

How does stress typically affect your behavior? Are you one to seek out social support from friends and family, or do you tend to become more reclusive and withdraw from people? Research has shown that, in general, men and women respond differently to stress. Men are more likely to withdraw socially, whereas women typically seek social support from others (Sonnenberg et al., 2013; Taylor, 2011). Shelley Taylor and colleagues suggested rather than the traditional "fight-or-flight" response, when faced with stress, women are likely to "**tend-and-befriend**" (Taylor, 2006; Taylor et al., 2000), which involves affiliation-related behaviors (e.g., nurturing, seeking care) that appear to be motivated, in part by the hormone oxytocin (Cardoso et al., 2013).

tend-and-befriend

response where women faced with stress seek affiliation-related behaviors (e.g., nurturing, seeking care) that appear to be motivated, in part, by the hormone, oxytocin; alternative to the traditional "fight-or-flight" response

Journal Prompt: Stress and Behavior

What are some behaviors either you or others have engaged in as a result of experiencing stress? Did the behavior(s) help to reduce the stress or add to the stress?

Emotional eating and "comfort food" receives a lot of attention in the media (see Figure 12.9), in part because obesity has become a major public health concern, but also by the way these high fat, high sugar foods are marketed. In fact, certain types of foods have become synonymous with happiness and relief from stress.

Figure 12.9 Stress and Eating

STRESSED spelled backwards is DESSERTS

Emotional eating can occur in response to both negative and positive events and has been shown to exist in children as young as 5 years old (Michels et al., 2012). Numerous studies have documented the relationship between stress and both the urge to eat and the actual consumption of food higher in fat and sugar (Groesz et al., 2012; Rutters et al., 2009). Compared to many other lifestyle variables, emotional eating was the most prominent factor in predicting weight gain in a longitudinal study of 1,562 employees in the Netherlands (Koenders & van Strien, 2011). Brain imaging studies have highlighted similarities in the brain's response to appealing food and illegal drugs (primarily in dopamine-rich reward pathways), which has led researchers to view emotional eating and obesity in the same way they see substance use and addiction (Menzies et al., 2012; Volkow et al., 2011; Volkow et al., 2013a; Volkow et al., 2013b).

No one who is under significant stress thinks that developing an addiction is a good idea. However, the reality is that stress can lead people to engage in various addictive behaviors to try to immediately relieve their stress. Smoking cigarettes, drinking alcohol, and abusing other substances have been used by people to help cope with stress (Garland et al., 2011; Hiscock et al., 2012). It has even been found that stress hormones are present in people during the transition from voluntary (social) to involuntary (addicted) drug use suggesting stress may play a direct role in addiction (Schwabe et al., 2011). It is important to recognize the reason someone first engages in a behavior (e.g., drinking as a way to relieve stress) is not necessarily the same reason the behavior continues (e.g., drinking to prevent withdrawal symptoms). The relationship between stress and unhealthy behavior choices is reciprocal. This means people who engage in unhealthy behaviors as a result of experiencing stress are more likely to become sick or injured, which of course leads to sustained levels of stress (Schneiderman et al., 2005).

Quiz for Module 12.4–12.5

1. Which part of the nervous system directs the fight-or-flight response in times of stress?

   a. Somatic   b. Parasympathetic

   c. Central   d. Sympathetic

2. The neuroendocrine system responsible for releasing cortisol and other stress hormones to defend against stress is called _____.

   a. hypothalamic-pituitary-adrenal axis

   b. amygdala-adrenal axis

   c. parasympathetic nervous system axis

   d. general adaption axis

3. The three stages of the general adaptation syndrome are:

   a. alarm, cortisol, and exhaustion.

   b. alarm, resistance, and exhaustion.

   c. resistance, alarm, and exhaustion.

   d. resistance, exhaustion, and illness.

4. In response to stress, the sympathetic nervous system releases _____, whereas the hypothalamic-pituitary-adrenal system releases _____.

   a. cortisol; epinephrine   b. endorphins; cortisol

   c. epinephrine; cortisol   d. endorphins; insulin

5. All of the following are considered psychological responses to stress EXCEPT

   a. substance abuse.   b. emotional eating.

   c. learned helplessness.   d. bullying.

6. Nathan has a father who yells and tells him he is stupid. His father beats him when he doesn't do his chores quickly enough. Nathan believes he is stupid and that he will never be able to escape his situation at home. What is Nathan experiencing?

   a. Learned helplessness

   b. Anxiety and worry

   c. Ineffective coping

   d. Learned depressed behavior

Module 12.6–12.7: The Role of Stress in Health and Disease

Most people recognize that being sick is stressful, but we don't often think about how stress can influence the likelihood that we get sick or the severity of the illness or disease we experience. As a student, you are likely aware of the relationship between final exams and illness or what some have even referred to as the "post-exam death flu" (Crossley & Kat, 2012).

Stress and Exams

Interactive

Survey: Stress and Exams

Have you ever had an experience where you became ill within a few days of completing final exams?

○ Yes

○ No

Journal Prompt: Post-Exam Illness

What are some of the reasons you think students often get sick after final exams?

While there are a variety of reasons why a person may get sick after final exams, it is clear the heightened stress during this relatively short period of time can have significant effects on overall health due to its impact on the immune system.

Stress and the Immune System

LO 12.6   **Explain the impact of stress on the immune system.**

There is an interdisciplinary field of study called **psychoneuroimmunology** that emphasizes the interaction of psychological, neurological/endocrine, and immunological processes in stress and illness (Ader & Cohen, 1993; Straub, 2014). Watch the following brief animation, *Stress and the Immune System*, for a preview of the information to be presented in this section.

psychoneuroimmunology

an interdisciplinary field of study that emphasizes the interaction of psychological, neurological/endocrine, and immunological processes in stress and illness

Stress and the Immune System

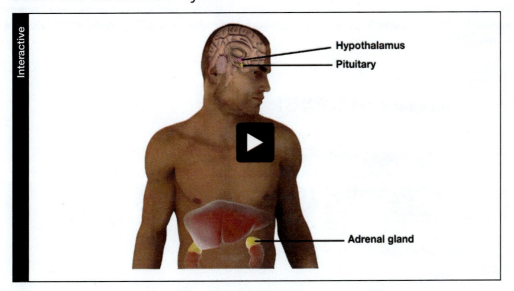

While many people now recognize the mind–body relationship, this understanding is relatively new. In fact, it was only about 30 years ago that psychologist Robert Ader stumbled on the undeniable connection between stress and illness when he was attempting to classically condition rats to avoid drinking sweetened water. In a typical classical conditioning experiment, Ader injected the rats with a drug that made them nauseous every time they took a drink of the sweetened water.

The Effects of Classical Conditioning

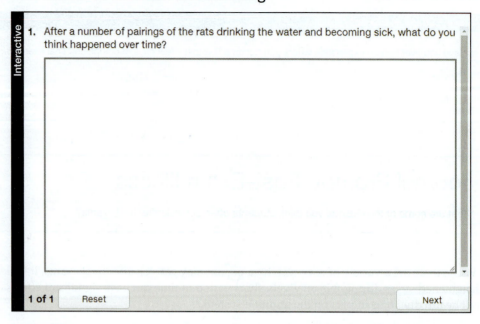

Interactive

1. After a number of pairings of the rats drinking the water and becoming sick, what do you think happened over time?

1 of 1	Reset		Next

Your immune system is like your own built-in bodyguard—it protects you against damage from the diseases and injuries that try to attack it every day. Although the immune system is strong, it isn't invincible. Factors such as your age, your genetic background, your nutritional intake, and the amount of stress in your life can all influence your immune system's effectiveness (Marques et al., 2014; Vitlic et al., 2014). It seems we may even have an intuitive sense of how well our immune system is functioning. In a recent study where people were asked to rate their overall health, those who rated their health as "excellent" were significantly *less* likely to develop a cold when subsequently exposed to a cold virus (Cohen et al., 2015). Can people really sense when they are more likely to get sick? Or, are they using other information in their life, such as their overall stress level, to make this prediction? Based on what you already know about the effects of stress on your overall health, it probably comes as no surprise that when you're under stress, your immune system becomes less able to protect and heal your body quickly and effectively (Dhabhar, 2014; Effros, 2011).

I have a lot of **STRESS**!

lymphocytes

white blood cells that attempt to attack foreign invaders (i.e., antigens) in the body; B cells, T cells and NK cells are all types of lymphocytes

Our immune system contains three types of white blood cells, or **lymphocytes** that play a role in health and disease. When triggered, lymphocytes release proteins called *cytokines* that help to start the process of attacking the unwelcomed cells. *Natural killer (NK)* cells originate in various places in the body (e.g., bone marrow, lymph nodes, spleen) and patrol the body for diseased cells and attack them with lethal chemicals when they are discovered. *B lymphocytes (B cells)* form in the bone marrow and *T lymphocytes (T cells)* form in your thymus and other lymphatic tissue. NK cells, B cells, and T cells all attack foreign invaders, such as bacteria, viruses, and cancer cells (and sometimes even those substances that may not actually be enemies of the body, such as transplanted organs). However, the way these lymphocytes attack foreign invaders, or **antigens**, differs based on the type of white blood cell. B cells attack *indirectly* by producing **antibodies**, which chemically suppress the damaging effects of antigens (this is what happens when you are "immunized," or vaccinated, against certain diseases as a child). When a B cell is stimulated by an antigen, it divides into two different cells: plasma cells, which make thousands of antibodies per second, and longer-lasting memory cells that produce antibodies *and* remember the antigen. That way, if the antigen is ever encountered again, the body responds even faster and stronger than it did the first time. T cells work differently in that they *directly* attack and kill antigens without the help of antibodies. Think of a T cell like a venomous snake: A snake captures its prey, holds it down, and delivers venom through its bite. When a T cell identifies a foreign invader, it locks on to it and directly injects a lethal toxin to kill it. NK cells, like T cells, directly attack antigens. However, NK cells are especially helpful because they can detect some foreign invader cells that get missed by the B cells and T cells (Topham & Hewitt, 2009). This "special power" is why they are called *natural killer cells*—because they don't need to be activated like the other white blood cells.

When these lymphocytes do their jobs properly, they keep you healthy and heal your injuries. However, when your immune system isn't functioning properly, it can respond by either overreacting or underreacting. When it underreacts, it may, for example, fail to fight off those bacteria that enter your body after you touch a dirty doorknob and then rub your eyes, or it may allow cancer cells to multiply. When it overreacts, your immune system may begin attacking your body's own tissues and could cause problems like arthritis, allergies, or lupus, which are referred to as auto-immune diseases (Costenbader et al., 2012). Auto-immune diseases are much more common in women and appear to be related to genetic and hormonal factors (Oertelt-Prigione, 2012; Quintero et al., 2012).

How is stress related to the immune system's functions? We know that during periods of stress, the brain causes increased secretion of stress hormones (e.g., cortisol), which then suppress the disease-fighting activities of the B cells, T cells, and NK cells. So, while cortisol helps the body during times of stress by stimulating glucose release it also puts the body at risk for illness because it decreases the effectiveness of the immune system. Stress also stimulates the sympathetic nervous system, which then diverts much of its energy away from the immune system to the muscles and brain. In a study involving dental students (a group typically under a significant amount of stress), the immune-suppressed response was shown to slow the pace of healing after surgery (Gouin & Kiecolt-Glaser, 2011; Walburn et al., 2009), increase illness, decrease appetite, and increase digestive problems (Elani et al., 2014). In most groups of people, stress has also been found to increase the likelihood of developing a cold after exposure to a cold virus (Cohen et al., 2012).

antigens

a toxin or other foreign substance that induces an immune response in the body, especially the production of antibodies

antibodies

large, Y-shaped proteins used by the immune system to chemically suppress the damaging effects of antigens

Adaptive Pathway 12.2: Psychoneuroimmunology

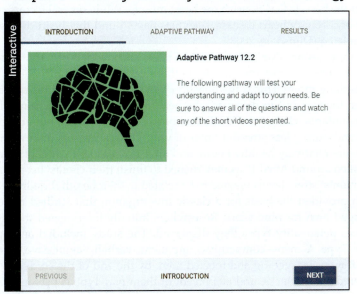

Interactive

INTRODUCTION   ADAPTIVE PATHWAY   RESULTS

Adaptive Pathway 12.2

The following pathway will test your understanding and adapt to your needs. Be sure to answer all of the questions and watch any of the short videos presented.

PREVIOUS   INTRODUCTION   NEXT

Stress and Disease

LO 12.7 **Describe the role of stress in life-threatening diseases.**

Stress doesn't just increase the likelihood of catching a cold. Stress has also been found to play a role in the development and maintenance of life-threatening diseases. For example, heart disease, cancer, and HIV/AIDS are diseases that account for the majority of deaths each year and have all been found to be related to stress (see Figure 12.10).

Figure 12.10 Stress and Disease

coronary heart disease

a condition characterized by the clogging of the vessels that nourish the heart muscle; a leading cause of death in North America

Type A

personality type described as more competitive, impatient, verbally aggressive, ambitious, and outgoing; more likely to experience a heart attack

Type B

personality type described as easy-going and relaxed

STRESS AND THE HEART   High stress levels may help to explain why North America's leading cause of death since the 1950s has been **coronary heart disease**, a condition characterized by the clogging of the vessels that nourish the heart muscle. While several factors contribute to the development of coronary heart disease, scientists have found that heart disease and stress are often closely related (Dimsdale, 2008).

Every April 15, taxes are due in the United States, and every April 15, tax accountants' blood cholesterol climbs to dangerous levels. Is this relationship just a fluke, or could it be indicative of something more? This is the question Meyer Friedman and his colleagues asked in the 1950s when they set out to discover whether stress was related to heart disease. They measured tax accountants' cholesterol levels and blood clotting speeds both during peak tax time (mid-April) and during less stressful times of year. The researchers discovered that while the accountants were relatively healthy before and after tax season, their cholesterol and clotting measures spiked around April 15 as they rushed to finish their clients' tax returns. In other words, the accountants' stress levels seemed to be related to their health (Friedman et al., 1958).

This research provided the basis for a classic investigation that studied more than 3,000 healthy middle-aged men for nine years. Researchers initially interviewed the men to determine which of two personality types they displayed. The study included an approximately equal number of **Type A** men—competitive, impatient, verbally aggressive, easily angered men—and **Type B** men—easygoing and relaxed men. By the end of the study, 257 men in the sample had suffered heart attacks, and 69 percent of them had Type A personalities. Possibly more impressive was the fact that the men who were the most laid-back and relaxed (the most

"Type B-ish" of the Type B men) had all remained heart-attack-free (Rosenman et al., 1975). This study also pointed to other factors already known to contribute to heart disease (e.g., parental history of coronary heart disease, diabetes, and smoking) but this was one of the first times a psychological characteristic, or personality-style, was shown to play a significant and direct role in the development of heart disease.

What made the Type A personality so dangerous? While Type A people and Type B people have similar levels of arousal in relaxed situations, those who have Type A characteristics are more physiologically reactive when they are harassed, challenged, or threatened. For example, their hormonal secretions, pulse rate, and blood pressure increase drastically (Dembroski et al., 1979; Friedman et al., 1975). The hormones cause plaque to accumulate more rapidly on artery walls which leads to hardening of the arteries, raising blood pressure, and increasing the risk of strokes and heart attacks. The active sympathetic nervous system redistributes blood flow to the muscles and away from internal organs such as the liver, which plays a key role in removing cholesterol and fat from the blood. As a result, the excess cholesterol and fat that the blood is carrying are deposited in the heart.

Negative emotions such as depression, anger, and especially hostility (Matthews et al., 2004), may also contribute to Type A toxicity. Adults who react angrily to minor problems or inconveniences are at a higher risk for cardiovascular disease than their calmer counterparts (Allan, 2014; Schneider et al., 2012).

While there has been some suggestion that the relationship between Type A personalities/hostility and coronary heart disease has been overblown (Myrtek, 2001), this relationship is still generally supported and used to drive the development and implementation of interventions for at-risk patients (Blumenthal et al., 2005; Chida & Steptoe, 2009).

In recent years, the attention has shifted to yet another personality type, **Type D** personalities. The "D" stands for "distressed" and describes people who experience increased negative emotions yet tend to avoid self-expression in social interactions (Pedersen & Denollet, 2006; Shanmugasegaram et al., 2014). For example, someone with a Type D personality may feel very depressed and anxious about having received a medical diagnosis. They may dwell on their illness and have catastrophic, negative thoughts about the possible outcomes (see Figure 12.11).

Type D

"distressed" personality type; people who experience increased negative emotions and avoid self-expression in social interactions; negative prognostic factor for those who have experienced a heart attack

Figure 12.11 Identifying Personality Types

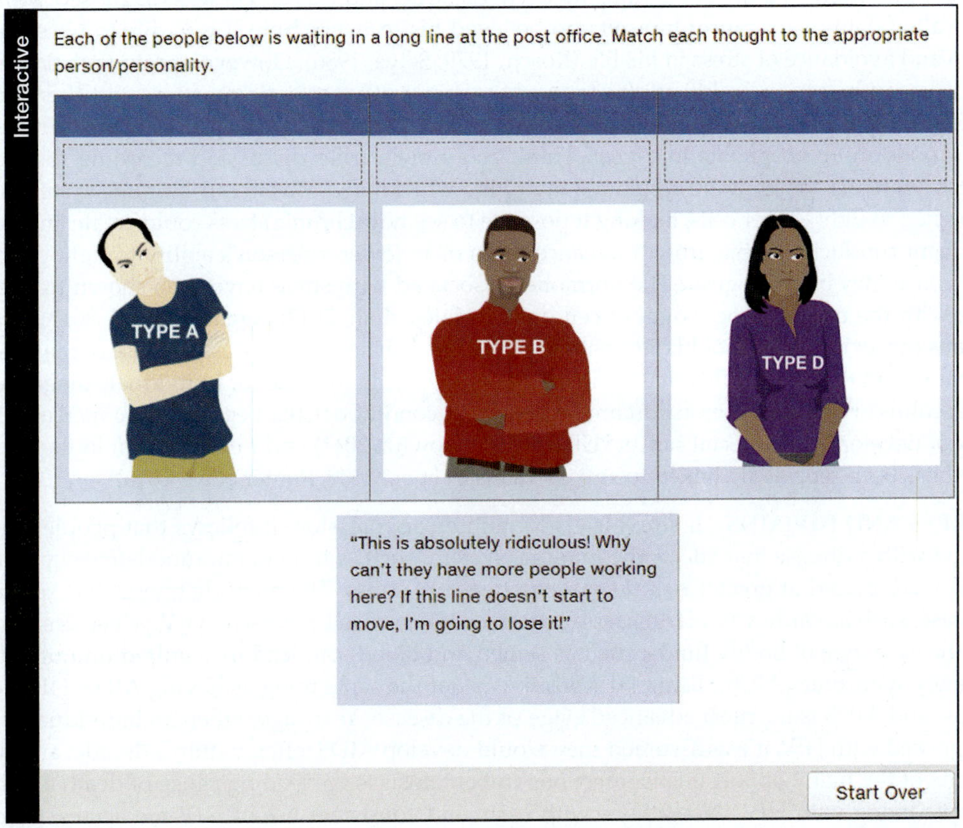

Each of the people below is waiting in a long line at the post office. Match each thought to the appropriate person/personality.

TYPE A

TYPE B

TYPE D

"This is absolutely ridiculous! Why can't they have more people working here? If this line doesn't start to move, I'm going to lose it!"

Start Over

However, when they are in social situations, they are hesitant to share these feelings with others and therefore remain quiet. Their unwillingness to share their distress (and seek social support) could stem from a fear of what others will think of them or from a need to appear unaffected (Compare et al., 2013). This distressed personality style has been found to be related to cardiovascular risk, particularly through unhealthy lifestyle choices (Svansdottir et al., 2012) and impact the prognosis of those who have already been diagnosed with cardiovascular disease. While the influence of the Type D personality on the prognosis of cardiac patients appears to be weaker than originally suspected, it appears that patients can be up to two times more likely to suffer further physical and/or mental health issues after being diagnosed with cardiovascular disease (Grande et al., 2012; Pedersen & Denollet, 2006; Versteeg et al., 2012).

STRESS AND CANCER Just as Type D personalities can impact cardiovascular disease prognosis, stress and negative emotions have also been shown to interfere with the *progression* of cancer. Experiments with animals have demonstrated accelerated tumor growth when the animal is placed in stressful situations (Hassan et al., 2013; Lamkin et al., 2015; Zhao et al., 2015). A recent study in humans provided evidence that women with nonmetastatic breast cancer who underwent cognitive-behavioral stress management after surgery had a significantly reduced risk of death 8–15 years later (Stagl et al., 2015). Therefore, learning to manage stress after a diagnosis of cancer can be an important part of the overall treatment plan. Other psychological treatments, such as mindfulness-based therapy, have also been found effective in reducing the severity of depression and anxiety among cancer patients (Archer et al., 2014; Shennan et al., 2011). The results are difficult to isolate but some evidence suggests psychological interventions can affect physiological changes (or adaptation) and therefore improve survival rates of those diagnosed with cancer (Antoni, 2013).

While it is clear stress can negatively impact the prognosis of an individual already diagnosed with cancer, the more complicated question involves whether or not stress itself can *cause* cancer. This has been a question researchers have debated and investigated for some time. The idea that stress could cause cancer is a sensitive one because no one wants to suggest people choose to get cancer or are at fault because they do develop cancer. Addressing the question is important, however, because the answer to whether the relationship between stress and cancer is correlational or causal has significant implications for treatment and prevention. Hans Selye, who proposed the general adaptation syndrome discussed earlier in this chapter, believed strongly in a direct relationship between stress and cancer. He was diagnosed with a typically fatal type of cancer himself and believed his recovery from it was due to his strong faith and avoidance of stress in his life (Rosch, 1979; Selye, 1986). However, proving that stress directly causes cancer is difficult because of the many ways of defining stress and the many different types of cancer (Todd et al., 2013). Health experts appear to agree that stress makes your body more hospitable to cancer. Think about our earlier discussion regarding the way stress depresses the immune system. Many of the white blood cells in our immune system are designed to fight cancer cells, making it possible to see how chronic stress could create an environment conducive to the growth of cancer cells or to lower a person's ability to fight cancer cells once they begin to grow. The hormones associated with stress have been shown to interfere with the natural progression of cell death (Matés et al., 2012; Nagaraja et al., 2013). This means cancer cells that should die a natural death are resisting this process because of the stress hormones in the body. Inflammation in the body, such as in the case for individuals diagnosed with colitis or Crohn's disease (inflammatory bowel conditions), has been found to increase the risk of developing colorectal cancer (Ullman & Itzkowitz, 2011) and inflammation in the body itself has been repeatedly linked to stress (Khansari et al., 2009; Reuter et al., 2010).

STRESS AND HIV/AIDS If stress leads to immunosuppression, it follows that people diagnosed with a disease that affects the immune system, such as human immunodeficiency virus (HIV), are placed at greater risk by the experience of stress. The mere diagnosis of a serious disease, such as cardiovascular disease, cancer, or HIV, is itself a stressor. HIV, which is spread by the exchange of bodily fluids, such as semen and blood, can lead to acquired immune deficiency syndrome (AIDS). Being HIV positive is not the same thing as having AIDS. HIV is a virus, and AIDS is the most advanced stage of the disease. Years ago, when an individual was diagnosed with HIV, it was assumed they would develop AIDS, often within a decade, and die of one of the many opportunistic infections (tuberculosis is the leading cause of death among people living with HIV.) Nowadays, with early and consistent use of HIV medicines, called antiretroviral therapy (ART), people can control the HIV virus and prevent it from progressing to AIDS (for more information, see www.aids.gov).

Without regular testing for the disease, many people remain unaware they are infected and can therefore unknowingly transmit the disease to others. According to UNAIDS, in 2014 almost 37 million people worldwide were living with HIV. Despite the enormous number of people living with HIV, the number of newly diagnosed cases has decreased 35 percent since 2000 and has led to the UNAIDS organization to set a goal of ending the AIDS epidemic by 2030.

Researchers have found that stress and negative emotions correlate with the progression of HIV to AIDS and can speed the decline of those who already have AIDS (Fumaz et al., 2009; Leserman et al., 2000). Stress reduction interventions appear to have a positive effect on individuals with HIV/AIDS, and programs targeted at decreasing stress report higher quality of life and adaptability to handling stigma associated with disease (Antoni et al., 2002; Riley & Kalichman, 2015).

Quiz for Module 12.6–12.7

1. The interdisciplinary field that emphasizes the interaction of psychological, neurological, and immunological factors in stress and illness is called _____.
   a. psychological neuroscience
   b. biopsychologicla
   c. psychobioimmunology
   d. psychoneuroimmunology

2. The three lymphocytes that play a role in health and disease are _____.
   a. antigens, antibodies, and white blood cells
   b. natural killer cells (NK), B lymphocytes (B cells), and T lymphocytes (T cells)
   c. natural killer cells (NK), antibodies, and antigens
   d. white blood cells, B lymphocytes (B cells), and T lymphocytes (T cells)

3. T cells work directly to kill _____ without the help of _____.
   a. B cells; natural killer cells
   b. antibodies; antigens
   c. antigens; antibodies
   d. C cells; B cells

4. What is the leading cause of death in North America?
   a. Diabetes
   b. Cancer
   c. Coronary heart disease
   d. HIV/AIDS

5. Johann is competitive, easily angered, impatient, and verbally aggressive toward those around him. Johann is considered to have which personality type?
   a. Type A
   b. Type B
   c. Type C
   d. Type D

6. Which personality type predicts subsequent physical and/or mental health issues after the diagnosis of cardiovascular disease?
   a. Type A
   b. Type B
   c. Type C
   d. Type D

Module 12.8–12.10: Managing Stress

In today's fast-paced, connected society, sometimes it's just not possible to alleviate stress. We still have to face daily commutes, juggle work and family life, compete for scholarships and jobs, and tackle overflowing inboxes. However, a variety of stress-management techniques, including physical and psychological strategies, can make our bodies more resistant to the negative effects of stress.

Physiological Approaches to Stress Management

LO 12.8 **Define various physiological approaches to managing stress.**

Since stress has measurable physiological effects on the body and can impact illness and disease, a number of stress management approaches focusing directly on changing the body's physiology have been developed. The goals of these strategies include either reducing the harmful effects of stress or better inoculating the body against the experience of stress in daily life. Biofeedback, relaxation, and exercise are all stress management interventions that have been shown to help reduce and manage stress (Ponce et al., 2008; van der Waerden et al., 2013; van der Zwan et al., 2015).

biofeedback

a form of stress-management therapy that requires participants to monitor and adjust their own physiological states

BIOFEEDBACK **Biofeedback** is a mind-over-matter form of stress-management therapy that requires participants to monitor and adjust their own physiological states. Biofeedback specialists use special electronic equipment to measure people's bodily states such as blood pressure, heart rate, or muscle tension. The equipment then provides feedback designed to help people control their involuntary body functions and reduce stress. For example, a person may not be aware he has particularly tense muscles, but when he sees a flashing light informing him he is experiencing muscle tension, he can make a conscious effort to relax.

Biofeedback has a long history of helping people manage headaches and chronic pain (Flor et al., 1986; Montgomery & Ehrisman, 1976). In the past, patients would have to go to a hospital or research center to be connected to expensive equipment in order to obtain physiological feedback. Currently, there are numerous apps available, some of which require the user to wear a portable heart rate monitor that allow people to engage in biofeedback through their phone or tablet (Wiederhold et al., 2014). As a result of improvements in technology and accessibility, biofeedback is now used to help with a variety of issues among different groups of people, such as those preparing for the military, nursing students, and postpartum patients (Bouchard et al., 2012; Kudo et al., 2014; Lewis et al., 2015; Ratanasiripong et al., 2012).

neurofeedback

a stress management technique that focuses on specifically training individuals to control their own brain activity; similar to biofeedback

Neurofeedback is similar to biofeedback but focuses on specifically training individuals to control their own brain activity. Neurofeedback uses brain imaging technologies, such as EEG and fMRI, to teach individuals how to modify their brain activity in specific regions in real-time (Kober et al., 2013; Zotev et al., 2014). For example, individuals with depression have been taught how to self-regulate their amygdala response, which has resulted in reduced symptoms of depression and anxiety (Linden, 2014; Young et al., 2014). In addition, several studies have been conducted that provide preliminary evidence of the effectiveness of neurofeedback as a method of treatment for children diagnosed with attention-deficit hyperactivity disorder (Arns et al., 2013; Gevensleben et al., 2013; González-Castro et al., 2016); however, researchers are calling for additional well-designed studies to confirm these results (Holtmann et al., 2014).

RELAXATION AND MEDITATION With little to no equipment required, relaxation strategies used to manage physiological responses continue to be a popular therapeutic approach to stress reduction. **Relaxation therapy** involves various techniques that help relax the body and the mind. *Progressive muscle relaxation* focuses on the body's physical source of stress and requires alternate tensing and relaxing of muscle groups in the body in order to relieve tension (McCallie et al., 2006). Relaxed muscles and stress are somewhat incompatible, so learning how to recognize and release the tension in your muscles can be an important strategy to relieving stress. Listen and participate in the following brief demonstration of progressive muscle relaxation. Before you start, take notice of how much tension you feel in your muscles and compare that to how you feel once you finish the exercise.

relaxation therapy

a group of techniques aimed at helping relax the body and the mind

Progressive Muscle Relaxation Demonstration

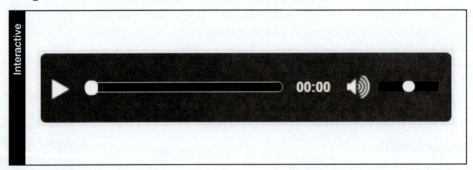

Guided imagery is a mental relaxation strategy that involves focusing attention on a peaceful scene or image in your mind. Guided imagery is typically coupled with deep breathing (from the diaphragm rather than the chest) and works best when focusing on the sensory details of the scene. For example, an individual may be directed to think of themselves laying on a beautiful beach, surrounded by the sound of the waves, the warmth of the sun, and the coolness of the breeze on their skin. Visualization, which is a key component of guided imagery, can be a powerful technique to reduce stress and is particularly appealing to some people because it can be practiced anywhere, at any time, and bring relief within a few minutes.

The aim of any relaxation therapy is to achieve the relaxation response—a condition of reduced muscle tension, cortical activity, heart rate, breathing rate, and blood pressure (Esch et al., 2003). Brain scans of people achieving the relaxation response through meditation reveal many areas of the brain, including the frontal lobe are more active than normal, suggesting the relaxation response is associated with increased attention and autonomic responses (Lazar et al., 2000). Here you can experience a brief example of guided imagery. As with the progressive muscle relaxation exercise, before you start, take notice of how busy or active your mind is and then compare that to how you feel after the exercise.

Guided Imagery Demonstration

Meditation is a practice or discipline that involves training the mind to become present, aware, and open to experiences. Compared to progressive muscle relaxation or guided imagery, meditation typically requires more practice and utilizes many different relaxation strategies. *Mindfulness*, which is often part of meditation, refers to the focusing of attention on the conscious awareness of one's experience, with an attitude of curiosity, openness, and acceptance (Bishop et al., 2004). **Mindfulness-based stress reduction (MBSR)**, initially developed by Jon Kabat-Zinn, combines mindfulness and meditation practices and has been used to help people undergoing medical treatment for chronic health problems (Bohlmeijer et al., 2010; Kabat-Zinn, 1982), those struggling with binge eating (Kristeller et al., 2013), and anxiety and depression (Marchand, 2012). Overall, structured mindfulness-based programs have been found to be helpful for a wide range of physical and psychological problems (Eberth & Sedlmeier, 2012).

EXERCISE Regular **aerobic exercise**—sustained exercise that increases heart and lung fitness, such as walking/jogging, swimming, biking, or Zumba—is not only good for cardiovascular health but also has been shown to reduce stress and symptoms of depression (Josefsson et al., 2014; von Haaren et al., 2015). Some studies have highlighted the calming effect exercise can have on those struggling with anxiety disorders (Fetzner & Asmundson, 2015; Jazaieri et al., 2012), although other researchers have suggested that there is not enough evidence yet to consider aerobic exercise a supported "treatment" for anxiety disorders (Bartley et al., 2013). However, exercise has long been known to have a positive effect on health: It strengthens the heart, keeps blood vessels open, increases blood flow, and lowers blood pressure. If you are like most people, you may feel overwhelmed by the current recommendations of a minimum of 30 minutes/day, 5 days/week (or 150 minutes) of moderate exercise. Many people claim they don't have the time to fit in that much physical activity and, as a result, remain sedentary. However, an all-or-nothing approach to exercise isn't the best approach to take. Recent research examining just how much exercise is needed to provide health benefits has shown that even 5–10 minutes of running (or 15 minutes of brisk walking) each day can reduce your chance of death by 30 percent and increase your life expectancy by three years (Wen et al., 2014; Wen et al., 2011).

In addition to the physical health benefits, researchers have frequently examined the relationship between exercise and stress. Human and animal studies have confirmed that not only does exercise reduce levels of cortisol, but it can stimulate new cell growth and dampen the inflammation and cell damage that occurs as a result of chronic stress (Gleeson et al., 2011; Kannangara et al., 2011; Wisniewski et al., 2015). The American Psychological

meditation

stress management strategy that involves training the mind to become present, aware, and open to experiences

mindfulness-based stress reduction (MBSR)

a structured stress-reduction program based on the principles of meditation and mindfulness

aerobic exercise

sustained exercise that increases heart and lung fitness

Association reports 62 percent of people walk or exercise as a method to effectively manage stress (see Figure 12.12). Interestingly, 43 percent of those people who reportedly exercise to manage stress stated they skipped exercise or physical activity in the past month when they were feeling stressed (American Psychological Association, 2013). While people seem to know what is best for them, they don't always make decisions in their best interest.

Figure 12.12 Stress Management

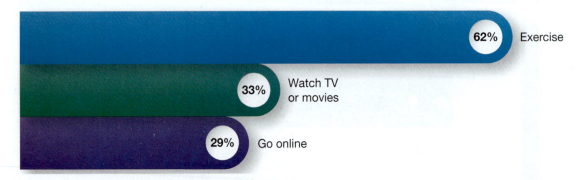

REPORTED EFFECTIVENESS OF STRESS MANAGEMENT TECHNIQUES

- **62%** Exercise
- **33%** Watch TV or movies
- **29%** Go online

Why does exercise help us to feel better more than watching TV or surfing the web? Exercise has been suggested to improve our emotional state by releasing mood-enhancing hormones such as norepinephrine, serotonin, and endorphins, which is how the expression "runner's high" originated. Exercise also helps us feel good by increasing our warmth and body arousal, helping us relax our muscles and sleep more soundly, improving body image, and giving us a sense of accomplishment. We can further enhance the benefits of exercise by taking advantage of diverse, interesting outdoor activities, and exercising with members of our social support groups (Quaresma et al., 2014).

Psychological Approaches to Stress Management

LO 12.9 Identify different psychological approaches to managing stress.

The best approach to stress management is going to involve a combination of physical and psychological strategies. Many psychological strategies tend to be cognitive in nature in that they focus on how a person thinks, interprets, and copes with stress.

PERCEIVED CONTROL In humans and nonhuman animals alike, threats and stressors over which we have no control produce stronger stress responses than controllable threats. When we believe that we have no control over a situation, our stress hormone levels and blood pressure increase and our immune responses decrease. These physiological responses help to explain how perceiving a loss of control over stressors in one's life can lead to increased vulnerability and poor health. When elderly residents in nursing homes have little perceived control over their activities, they tend to experience quicker declines in health and die faster than those who are given more control over their daily activities (Rodin, 2014). Having perceived control seems to be similarly important for people in their work environments: One study found that people who had the freedom to adjust their office furnishings and lighting, and who could control interruptions and distractions, experienced less stress than those who did not have control over their work environment (Wyon, 2000). If we believe we have the power to control our lives and affect change, we are less likely to experience stress. In short, greater perceived control leads to lower stress levels and improved health.

perceived control

the extent to which an individual believes they are in control of a situation

While the reality is that much of what happens in our lives is not under our conscious control, it is the individual's **perceived control**, or the extent to which they believe they have control of the situation, that counts when it comes to stress reduction (Koolhaas et al., 2011). You may face situations that are truly beyond your control, but if you believe you can make a difference to some small aspect of those situations, you may reduce your stress levels and improve your overall health. For example, imagine two people who both find out they are being transferred for work and will have to move within the month. While this experience will no doubt be stressful for both people, the amount of stress experienced can vary based on the level of perceived control. The person who starts focusing on finding a new place to live and thinking about how they will decorate their new office will likely feel less stress compared to the person who stays focused on being mad at their boss and resenting the fact they have to move.

EXPLANATORY STYLE   Do you have a fundamentally positive outlook on life? If so, you may find it relatively easy to cope with stress. One way we can try to reduce and combat stress in our lives is to adjust our **explanatory style**, or the way in which we explain events to ourselves, to be more optimistic. Optimism refers to a confidence someone has about the positive or successful outcomes for their future. Pessimism involves the opposite view of life. Pessimists expect things not to go their way and believe bad outcomes will occur (Scheier & Carver, 1985). Psychologists have found optimists have more perceived control, cope better with stressful events, have better overall health, and have a better prognosis after acute coronary syndrome than pessimists (Huffman et al., 2016; Rasmussen et al., 2009). Furthermore, it appears that an optimistic view of aging actually translates into increased life expectancy. Using a sample of 660 middle-aged adults, researchers concluded that those individuals with optimistic self-perceptions of aging lived, on average, 7.5 years longer than people with less optimistic views (Levy et al., 2002).

COPING WITH STRESS   Altering your view about the amount of control you have in a situation and adjusting your explanatory style may help reduce the amount of stress you experience. However, nobody is going to be able to eliminate all stress in their lives. How we choose to cope with stress can have important implications for our experience of stress and the impact it has on our health.

Take a moment to think about it: How do you cope with stress? Your answer is probably different from your friend's answer or your mother's answer. In fact, there are many different **coping strategies**, or psychological methods to understand and manage stress, each with various advantages and disadvantages. Coping strategies help us to reduce or minimize the effect of stressors. While people vary in their preferred method of dealing with stress, common strategies include cognitive and emotional approaches.

We often react negatively to stressors before we are able to think about them rationally. For example, you might feel incredibly overwhelmed when you look at your schedule for the next week and realize you have three exams in one day, none of which you have begun to study for yet. However, stressors are often much more manageable than we originally assume they are. Just giving them some thought can help to minimize their harmful effects.

How we think about the stressor can have important consequences for the way a stressor is experienced in our lives. A **cognitive appraisal** involves a thoughtful interpretation and evaluation of the stressor. Making a cognitive appraisal is usually a two-step process. First, we make a **primary appraisal**, or an initial evaluation of the seriousness of the stressor and the extent of the demands it will put on us. At this stage, it is helpful to assess the amount of control you have over the situation: Is this stressor something you can change or not? When our kids were in preschool, we noticed the teachers were working to develop these skills in the children. For example, if a 3-year-old came running up to the teacher crying, one of the first questions the teacher would ask was, "Now, is this a *big problem* or a *small problem*?" This question was their attempt to have the children conduct a primary appraisal of the stressful situation. Part of the primary appraisal involves your *perception* of the stressor. Do you view this stressor as a threat or a challenge? Imagine the moment when you discover you have three exams in one day. You may perceive this stressor either as a threat: "This is terrible; there is no way I can study for all three exams. I'm going to fail" or, as a challenge, "I've never had three exams in one day before. This will be an opportunity for me to perform under pressure." In this example, the stressor is either viewed as an obstacle that will be impossible to overcome or as a challenge that will require effort to overcome. Numerous studies have linked people who favor threat appraisals with the experience of increased stress (including increases in cortisol), depressed mood, and burnout (Gaab et al., 2005; Gomes et al., 2013; Kroemeke, 2016; Slattery et al., 2013).

In addition to a primary appraisal, people also make a **secondary appraisal**, or a reassessment that focuses on the actions you need to take and the resources that will help you overcome the stressor. A secondary appraisal focuses more on what can be done in the situation and can help you reevaluate the stressor in a more informed and reasonable way (Peacock & Wong, 1990). You may realize you have a three-day weekend before your exams, which will give you extra time to study,

explanatory style

an approach people use to explain why or how events occurred; style can be optimistic or pessimistic

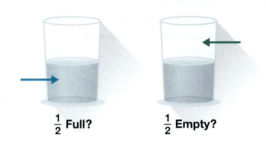

WHICH ONE ARE YOU?

$\frac{1}{2}$ **Full?** $\frac{1}{2}$ **Empty?**

coping strategies

psychological methods used to reduce or minimize stress

cognitive appraisal

cognitive interpretation and evaluation of a stressor

primary appraisal

initial evaluation of the seriousness of the stressor and the demands it will require; part of a cognitive appraisal of stress

secondary appraisal

reassessment of a stressful situation that focuses on the resources and actions needed to help overcome the stressor

or you might decide to seek out study partners to make your exam preparation more effective and fun. By thinking rationally about a stressor and objectively evaluating the resources available to you, you may be able to alleviate your initial emotional reaction and replace it with a plan of action.

When a stressor is already a reality, attempts to alleviate it may be either problem-focused or emotion-focused. People who engage in **problem-focused coping** attempt to alleviate stress directly, either by eliminating the source of a stressor or by changing the way they behave in stressful situations. We tend to opt for this strategy when we feel a sense of control over a situation. If we feel capable of changing our circumstances or our behaviors in response to a problem, we are more likely to be able to tackle the problem itself. For example, if you are dealing with a particularly challenging project at work, you might talk with your supervisor to see if you can delegate some of your workload (changing the circumstances), or you might decide to work extra hours to get the job done (changing your behavior).

If we feel incapable of changing stressful circumstances, we often use **emotion-focused coping**, which involves directing the emotional response to the situation. These strategies may involve attempting to alleviate stress by soothing our stress-related emotions. For example, if your relationship with your neighbor has become particularly stressful and you don't believe you can do anything to change the situation, you might try to make yourself feel better by spending more time with your good friends instead. Or, you might try to redefine the situation, which some people think of as a "positive spin." Rather than thinking about how miserable your neighbor is, you might think how this as a good opportunity to practice dealing with difficult people while not letting it rob you of the joy in your life.

Although emotion-focused coping isn't always the most effective way to deal with a stressor that can be changed, the approach has certain benefits for situations where change is under less control (Wethington et al., 2015). For example, when cancer patients laugh, listen to jokes, or watch old comedies on television, they're using emotion-focused coping to alleviate stress. Cancer patients have little control over their disease, but they can make themselves feel better

problem-focused coping

an attempt to alleviate stress directly, by eliminating the source of a stressor or by changing behaviors that occur during the stressful situations

emotion-focused coping

influencing one's own emotional response to a stressful situation as a method of coping

Stress Management Techniques

Interactive

Read through the following statements someone may make when asked how they are dealing with the stress in their life. Choose the stress management technique being described.

Description	Strategy
"I am managing my stress by focusing on what I can change in the situation and taking steps to solve the problem."	Problem-focused coping
"I am managing my stress by setting aside 20 minutes each night to listen to a script that tells me to imagine various relaxing situations."	Guided imagery
"I am managing my stress by using a heart rate monitor that beeps at me every time my heart rate starts to increase. I use the beep as a cue to take some deep breaths and try to relax."	Biofeedback
"I am managing my stress by just dealing with the emotions that come with the stress. I try to stay busy with activities and challenge myself to think about any positive aspect that could come out of the stressful situation."	Emotion-focused coping
"I am managing my stress by taking time each day to tense different muscle groups and then release the tension so I can encourage my body start to physically relax."	Progressive muscle relaxation
"I am managing my stress by spending time practicing focusing my attention on my conscious awareness while having an attitude of curiosity, openness, and acceptance."	Mindfulness meditation

Check Answers

by tending to their emotional well-being. Learning how to employ both problem-focused coping and emotion-focused coping in the appropriate situations can go a long way for helping to manage stress and, as a result, promote health.

Sociocultural Factors in Stress and Health

LO 12.10 Recognize the influence of sociocultural factors involved in stress and health.

Stress does not develop in a vacuum, and we aren't expected to manage it solely on our own either. People who are most effective at managing their stress draw on many different strategies; some require an individual approach and other methods involve various groups of people. Like other aspects of human behavior, the experience and management of stress must be placed within the individual's cultural context. As we've already seen, not everyone handles stress the same way, and cultural factors can play an important role in understanding the expression and management of stress.

SOCIAL SUPPORT   **Social support**, which can be described as the comfort, caring, and help available to an individual from a network of supportive friends and family members, plays an important role in reducing stress and promoting happiness and health. In fact, people with good social support systems are less likely to die from illnesses or injuries than those without a strong social network (Aizer et al., 2013). While this correlation may be due in part to the stress relief that friends can provide, people with social support also tend to take better care of themselves in other ways. People with supportive friends and marriage partners tend to eat better, exercise more, sleep better, and smoke less—all of which are conducive to coping with stress more effectively (Aschbrenner et al., 2013; Tamers et al., 2011).

social support

the comfort, caring, and help available to an individual experiencing stress, from a network of supportive friends and family members

Although some marital relationships can be fraught with difficulties, they are also positive predictors of health. In successful relationships, a spouse often describes his or her partner as "my best friend." It appears that having someone to confide in plays an important role in our overall well-being. Specifically, researchers have reported that regardless of age, sex, ethnicity, and income, married people tend to live longer, healthier lives than unmarried people do (Huang & Chen, 2014; Su et al., 2014). Siegler et al. (2013) examined middle-aged couples and found that being single or losing a partner and not replacing them were found to significantly increase mortality risk. Certain personality characteristics and risky health behaviors were also found to contribute to mortality but did not eradicate the impact of marital status. It is likely that the social support and ongoing care brought about by a marriage are the "active ingredients" in the marriage and life expectancy recipe. As the legal definition of marriage has broadened and as many people cohabitate and may never get married, there are opportunities for researchers examine whether or not the relationship between marriage and life expectancy generalizes to other committed relationships as well. Frisch and Brønnum-Hansen (2009) conducted a large study of men and women in same-sex relationships in Denmark and determined their life expectancy was better than those who were single, but still not as high as heterosexual couples. The increased mortality risk for same-sex couples was most evident in the early years of marriage (e.g., 1-6 years) and appeared to be related to pre-existing illnesses/diseases.

Interestingly, it is not always *actual* social support that has been found to improve health and well-being, but it is *perceived* social support that appears to have a stronger impact (Lakey & Orehek, 2011). With the prominent role of social networking in today's world, many questions have been raised regarding this relatively new avenue for seeking and receiving social support. A number of studies have contributed to what we know about social networking and social support:

- In addition to individual networks, Facebook is commonly used to connect groups of people who have similar situations/illnesses. The purpose of these groups ranges from fundraising, raising awareness, product/service promotion, and patient/caregiver support (Bender et al., 2011).

- The number of Facebook friends is related to perceived social support. That is, the more friends people have on Facebook, the more they feel supported by others, which in turn leads to reduced levels of stress and illness (Nabi et al., 2013; Oh et al., 2014).

- However, some research has questioned whether or not the relationship between the number of Facebook friends and perceived social support is linear. There is some evidence a curvilinear relationship may exist where the perception of social support is the highest among those who have a moderate number of friends. Once a person has "too many" friends (which is a relative term), they may experience a lack of connection to people similar to those people who don't have many Facebook friends (Kim & Lee, 2011).

- Despite being a useful tool for social support, some people report feeling drained from providing social support to others via social networking. This experience is referred to as *social overload* and is affected by a number of factors such as number of "friends," time spent on social networking sites, subjective social support norms, and whether or not the person seeking support is also an off-line friend (Maier et al., 2015).

Social networking appears to be a part of any culture that includes the Internet and allows for such relationships to exist. However, the extent to which social networking is an integral part of daily life may depend on the cultural context. For example, Chinese students have been found to spend less time, have fewer friends, and view social networking as less important than American students (Jackson & Wang, 2013). Similarly, while Korean and American students were found to have similar motives for social networking, Korean students exhibited a preference for obtaining social support from existing relationships (Kim et al., 2011).

Whether or not a culture is considered individualistic or collectivistic can influence the type of social support sought. Individualistic cultures (more typical of Western cultures) place an emphasis on personal responsibility and individual decision-making. These values might suggest people from individualistic cultures are *less* likely to seek social support compared to those who are part of a more collectivistic culture (more typical of Eastern cultures), which are more oriented toward family, community, and the larger social group. However, research has repeatedly demonstrated that Asians (typically from more collectivistic cultures) are less likely to seek out social support compared to European Americans (Kim et al., 2008).

There are a number of possible reasons to explain differences in seeking social support. And while cultural factors are always important to keep in mind, the fact remains that social support is an important predictor of overall health.

Journal Prompt: Culture and Social Support

Various research studies have shown that individuals from collectivist cultures tend not to utilize social support as a method of coping with stress. What are some possible explanations for the differences between collectivist and individualistic cultures in terms of their likelihood of seeking social support?

RELIGION, SPIRITUALITY, AND FAITH Another common avenue for coping with stress and illness is associated with faith and religion/spirituality. With an estimated 84 percent of the world's population reporting a religious affiliation, faith has the potential to exhibit its effects in a large number of people (Karam et al., 2015). What "effect" does faith (and/or religion/spirituality) have on people? Interestingly, the answer to this question hinges on how it is asked and how the data is examined; that is, whether you are looking at individuals within a country, or large groups of people between countries (Deaton & Stone, 2013). Numerous studies that have examined individuals within different states/countries have demonstrated something that has become known as the *faith factor*. The faith factor is simple: People who are religiously active (which has often been measured by attendance at religious services) live longer compared to those who are not religiously active (Hidajat et al., 2013; Myers, 2000). In fact, when a number of studies were examined together, it was found that being religiously active increased a person's survival, on average, by 37 percent (Koenig, 2012).

Harold Koenig (2012) produced an extensive review and summary of the effects of religion and spirituality on mental and physical health. He reviewed more than 3,300 research studies that investigated the religion/spirituality and health relationship. As you can imagine, if you were reviewing thousands of articles, the results were sometimes mixed (i.e., some studies show a positive relationship between religion/spirituality and X, and some results are in the opposite direction), but in his review, Koenig provided the percentage of studies reviewed that supported the specific result being discussed. Table 12.1 lists all of the psychological and physical advantages that emerged where more than 50 percent of the studies reviewed supported the relationship between religion/spirituality and health outcomes.

Table 12.1 The Relationshiop Between Religion, Spirituality/Faith, and Health Outcomes

Psychological Advantages	Physical Advantages
Coping with adversity	Less cigarette smoking
Positive emotions (hope, optimism, sense of control)	Physical activity and exercise
Happiness/well-being	Healthier diet*
Meaning and purpose to life	Safer sexual behavior
Increased self-esteem	Lower risk for coronary heart disease
Less depression (and suicide)	Lower risk of high blood pressure
Less anxiety	Improved immune system functioning (including the endocrine system)
Less substance abuse	Lower risk of developing cancer, or a better prognosis once diagnosed
More social support	Perception of better health

*Despite the association between religion/spirituality and a healthy diet, the data indicates a positive association between religion/spirituality and weight. Increased weight is the only health behavior associated with religion/spirituality that places people at higher risk for illness.

Based on these and other findings, there is no question that a person's faith and religion/spirituality can have a positive impact on their lives. But what is the exact mechanism responsible for this relationship? While it is impossible to know all the factors involved, many of them have already been discussed in this chapter and are detailed in Figure 12.13.

Figure 12.13 Factors Explaining the Relationship Between Religious Involvement and Health

Quiz for Module 12.8–12.10

1. Neurofeedback has been used to teach individuals with depression and anxiety how to self-regulate their _____ response.
   a. blood pressure
   b. amygdala
   c. hypothalamus
   d. frontal lobe

2. Nikki has a high-pressure sales job. She experiences physiological and psychological stress on a daily basis. Nikki is learning how to systematically tense and relax her muscles to relieve the tension in her body. What is this technique called?
   a. Neurofeedback
   b. Biofeedback
   c. Progressive muscle relaxation
   d. Mindfulness muscle relaxation

3. Hank, who just turned 50, believes he will enjoy his middle and older years and has a positive outlook on the aging process. What implications can this have for the rest of his life?
   a. Hank will live longer than his less optimistic friends.
   b. Hank will have more friends than those who are less optimistic.
   c. Hank will be more likely to participate in mindfulness meditation than his less optimistic friends.
   d. Hank will have a decreased life expectancy compared to his less optimistic friends.

4. Stuart's car breaks down his first week of college. He has just started a new job and needs his car to get to work. He calls around to mechanics to get an estimate of the cost of repairs and compares that to the money he has saved up in the bank. He decides to call his parents and ask if he can borrow half the money needed for the repair. Which strategy is Stuart using to cope with this stress?
   a. Problem-focused coping
   b. Optimistic coping
   c. Emotion-focused coping
   d. Explanatory style coping

5. How does social networking vary between individualistic and collectivistic cultures?
   a. People from individualistic and collectivistic cultures have the same views regarding social networking.
   b. People from individualistic cultures spend more time and have more friends with social networking than those from collectivistic cultures.
   c. People from collectivistic cultures spend more time and have more friends with social networking than those from individualistic cultures.
   d. People from individualistic cultures are less likely to use social networking as a form of social support.

6. A person who is considered religiously active is likely to experience _____ compared to people who are not religiously active.
   a. psychological advantages
   b. physical advantages
   c. psychological and physical advantages
   d. neither psychological nor physical advantages

Module 12.11: Piecing It Together: Stress, Health, and Smartphones

You and Your Phone

Interactive

Survey: You and Your Phone

Imagine you left your house and were going to be gone for 30 minutes. You realize, 10 minutes into your drive, that you forgot your phone at home. Would you turn around and go back to get it?

○ Yes

○ No

○ I don't own a phone

LO 12.11 **Analyze how the cross-cutting themes of psychology apply to smartphone use and its effects on stress and health.**

In 2007, the world changed forever. This statement sounds dramatic, and you wouldn't think it is referring to the invention of handheld technology, but it is. The iPhone was introduced to the market in June 2007, and the roughly 4-ounce gadget has become the most transformative piece of technology in the modern world. According to the 2015 Pew report,

68 percent of Americans owned a smartphone with that number jumping to 86 percent if only considering people between 18 and 29 years old; and, you can imagine that number has only increased in more recent years. Contrary to what you might think, people over the age of 65 were among the fastest-growing group of smartphone users, increasing from 18 percent in 2013 to 42 percent in 2015 (Anderson & Perrin, 2017).

There is no question smartphones have positively impacted our lives in many ways. The convenience of this all-in-one device has enabled us to do more with less. Many children growing up in the digital era will have never seen a paper map, film camera, or even a flashlight.

Smartphones and their applications (i.e., apps) are used extensively by those wishing to improve their physical and/or mental health. Healthcare providers and insurance companies are also relying on health and fitness apps to monitor patients' progress between doctor visits (Higgins, 2016). One example of how smartphones can help improve health involves the Remote Food Photography Method (RFPM), which requires participants to take digital pictures of their food and anything leftover at the end of their meal. These pictures are analyzed in real-time and then provide food intake information and nutritional feedback to the user (Martin et al., 2012). This method of measuring food intake has been found to be reliable and valid in both adults and children and can help people lose weight and improve their overall health (Martin et al., 2014). Smartphones have also been paired with various biosensors (e.g., blood pressure monitor, glucose meter, heart monitor) to provide physiological feedback to the user and their healthcare provider from their natural environment (Bloss et al., 2016) with the hope of improving physical health and decreasing health care costs. In addition to physical health, numerous mental health apps have been developed to provide mental health support and intervention on the user's time and in their own environment (Bakker et al., 2016). A

meta-analysis that examined the results of nine independent, randomized-controlled trials of smartphone-delivered psychological interventions to reduce anxiety found this form of treatment to be both effective and efficient (Firth et al., 2017).

Despite the convenience and positive outcomes associated with smartphones, there are numerous downsides and some troubling trends involving the effects of smartphone use on overall health and wellness. Distracted driving has become a national public safety concern, smartphone addiction has become a regular part of many conversations, and the paradoxical effect of people being more connected yet disconnected in our fast-paced world are just a few of the growing concerns about the negative impact smartphones can also have on our lives.

Variations in Human Functioning

- How can smartphones negatively impact people's health?
- Are people really addicted to their smartphones?

As you were reading the introduction to this section, you may have found yourself thinking "Well, that may be true for some people, but not me. My smartphone doesn't cause me any problems." It is true that many psychological issues should be considered on a continuum and that some statements can't be generalized to the entire population. For this reason, it is important to look at some of the scientific evidence about how smartphones can affect stress levels and health to potentially identify some of the factors that distinguish people who are more severely affected.

Despite various wearable technologies and apps devoted to improving sleep, smartphones appear to be playing a large role in disrupting sleep for many people. Cell phone companies have found that young adults send, on average, 110 text messages per day, some of which occur in the middle of the night. Numerous studies of adolescents have been conducted examining the impact of smartphones on sleep. Owning a smartphone is associated with less sleep overall and an increase in sleep problems among adolescents (Schweizer et al., 2017). One explanation involves the interruption of sleep caused by notifications and compulsions to check their smartphone at night. In one study, 47 percent of college students reported waking up at night to answer text messages (Adams & Kisler, 2013). Not only is cell phone use prior to bed and during the night associated with poor quality sleep, it has also been found to predict symptoms of depression and anxiety (Adams & Kisler, 2013; Lemola et al., 2015).

With so many people owning a smartphone now, you can imagine how many people are walking around each day with a sleep deficit due, in part, to their smartphone. Being sleep deprived affects your ability to think clearly and concentrate. But did you also know the mere presence of your smartphone interferes with your attention and cognitive abilities? Ward et al. (2017) conducted two studies and found people had fewer cognitive resources available to engage in a task that required thought and attention when their smartphone was nearby—even if the smartphone was screen down or completely powered off! Furthermore, the people whose performance was most impaired were those who scored highest in smartphone dependence.

Smartphone dependence, or addiction, is a condition similar to other addictions characterized by excessive use and anxiety when separated from the item/drug. There is even a name for smartphone addiction; *nomophobia* (which comes from *no-mobile-phone phobia* or the fear of being without your smartphone.) In one study of more than 200 people, 13.3 percent were classified as addicted to smartphones (Pearson & Hussain, 2016). Smartphone addiction has been found in students, even among those in middle school, and has been found to be correlated with poor academic performance (Hawi & Samaha, 2016; Samaha & Hawi, 2016).

Are there predictable differences between those who develop a smartphone addiction and those who don't? There appears to be a relationship between smartphone addiction and negative affect, which has been described as depression, anxiety, or the personality trait of neuroticism (Pearson & Hussain, 2016; Yen et al., 2009). Other characteristics, including low self-esteem and low self-control, have also been found to be associated with smartphone addiction (Kim & Shin, 2016).

Journal Prompt: Critically Thinking About Research

Imagine you just read the preceding paragraph to your friend. Your friend responds with, "Wow, so being depressed or anxious and having low self-esteem or self-control causes people to become addicted to smartphones." Is this an accurate statement? Why or why not?

Research Methods

- How does scientific research answer questions about the effects of smartphones on stress and health?
- Why is it important to read the entire study rather than just the summary or bottom line?

The last Journal Prompt encouraged you to think about correlation and causation. That is, do correlational studies provide the opportunity to make casual claims? The answer is "no." Saying smartphone addiction and depression are related is not the same as saying depression *causes* smartphone addiction. It is equally possible that smartphone addiction *causes* people to become depressed. Whether you're reading news headlines or tweets, it is important to read through the research study yourself and determine whether or not causal claims can be made.

Another reason it is important to read original research is because different studies that appear to be measuring similar constructs can reach very different conclusions. For example, Cheever et al. (2014) conducted an experiment where students were randomly placed into two groups. The students in one of the groups were unexpectedly asked to hand over their smartphone to the researcher upon entering the room and the students in the other group were asked to silence their smartphone and keep it out of sight (but still with them.) The researchers measured anxiety levels over time and found people who were separated from their phones experienced anxiety, and this anxiety depended on how attached they were to their phone. High users experienced increasing anxiety over time regardless of the condition they were in, whereas moderate users experienced the most intense anxiety if they were in the condition where they were physically separated from their phone. People who were not dependent on their phones and reported low use didn't experience anxiety in either condition. Let's review a couple of important concepts from research methods that are relevant to this study.

In another study (Ward et al., 2017), researchers were interested in whether or not the mere presence of a person's smartphone would interfere with their ability to sustain attention and perform a cognitive task (e.g., a word find or pattern completion task.) Participants were aware prior to the study that they might be separated from their phones. This research involved a

---

Retrieval Practice: Research Methods

Interactive

Answer the questions below about separation from smartphones and levels of anxiety based on the experiment you just read.

Students who were asked to silence their smartphones and put them away (but still had them with them) were in the [   ] group.

Students who had their smartphones removed from their possession were in the [   ] group.

In this study, the amount of anxiety participants experienced over time was the [   ] variable.

Whether or not the participant kept their phone or had it removed from their possession was the [   ] variable.

WORD BANK

- experimental
- dependent
- independent
- control

Start Over   Check Answers

3 x 2 design. That is, there were two independent variables, one with three conditions and the other with two conditions. Prior to beginning the experiment, participants were asked to either (1) completely silence their smartphones or (2) completely power off their smartphones. Then, participants were randomly assigned to a "smartphone salience" group, meaning they were asked to place their devices screen down on their desk (high salience), in their bag/pocket (medium salience), or in a separate room (low salience). Remember, half of the participants in each "salience group" had their cell phones on silent and the other half had them turned off. The results of this study showed that the *mere presence* of the participant's smartphone, either on their desk or in their bag, reduced their ability to think and complete a cognitive task. As in the previous study we described, the effects were the biggest for those participants who were most dependent on their phones. Furthermore, there was no difference between the groups who had their phones on silent versus those who had them turned off. The researchers concluded that even some of the strategies we have adopted (placing our phones screen down, turning to silent, or turning off) to attempt to improve focus and cognitive performance, are ineffective. The only strategy that was effective was completely removing the smartphone from the room!

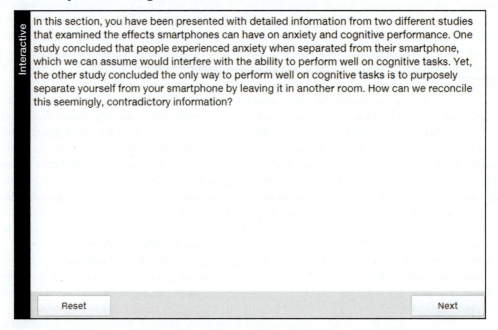

Critically Evaluating Research Conclusions

In this section, you have been presented with detailed information from two different studies that examined the effects smartphones can have on anxiety and cognitive performance. One study concluded that people experienced anxiety when separated from their smartphone, which we can assume would interfere with the ability to perform well on cognitive tasks. Yet, the other study concluded the only way to perform well on cognitive tasks is to purposely separate yourself from your smartphone by leaving it in another room. How can we reconcile this seemingly, contradictory information?

Reset   Next

Cultural and Social Diversity

- Does smartphone ownership vary based on demographics?
- Are men or women more at risk for smartphone addiction?

According to a 2015 Pew Research Center report, more than half of most demographic groups own a smartphone, and there are no significant differences among racial and ethnic groups (Anderson, 2015). The groups of people most likely to have a smartphone were individuals between the ages of 18 and 49 and those from higher income households (see Figure 12.14).

It seems like it should be an easy question to answer: Who is more likely to have a smartphone addiction, men or women? However, the research at this point has not provided us a consistent answer to this question and it may be a more complicated one to address than expected (Al-Barashdi et al., 2015).

Research that has attempted to identify risk factors for smartphone addiction often highlights female gender as one of those risks (Choi et al., 2015; Van Deursen et al., 2015). However, a number of studies examining smartphone use fail to find any significant differences between the number of men and women addicted to their device (Hawi & Samaha, 2016; Liu et al., 2016; Pearson & Hussain, 2016).

It may be the risk factor is less about gender and more about the way in which the smartphone is used. Enez Darcin et al. (2016) found people who used their smartphone primarily to

Figure 12.14 Demographics and Smartphone Ownership

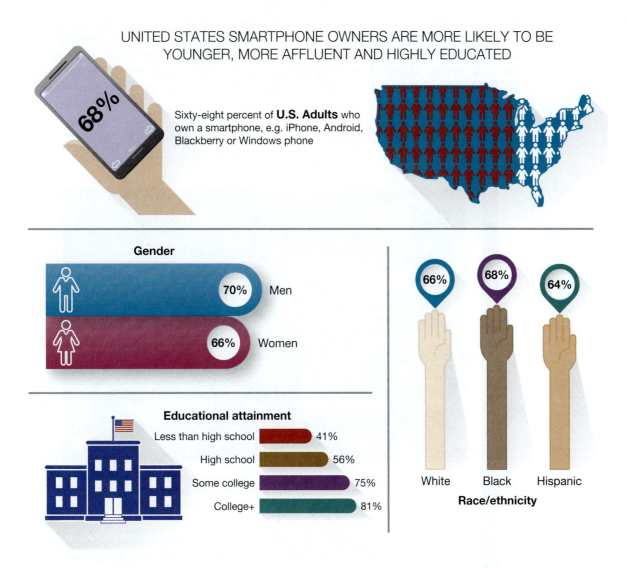

UNITED STATES SMARTPHONE OWNERS ARE MORE LIKELY TO BE YOUNGER, MORE AFFLUENT AND HIGHLY EDUCATED

68%

Sixty-eight percent of **U.S. Adults** who own a smartphone, e.g. iPhone, Android, Blackberry or Windows phone

Gender

70% Men

66% Women

66% White

68% Black

64% Hispanic

Race/ethnicity

Educational attainment

Less than high school 41%

High school 56%

Some college 75%

College+ 81%

access social networking sites were at much higher risk for dependence compared to those who used their smartphone primarily for the Internet or making phone calls. Checking social media has been found to be related to what has become known as FoMO (fear of missing out.) And, we know that one of the risk factors of smartphone addiction is the extent to which the smartphone is used during the day, especially for social purposes (Van Deursen et al., 2015). Therefore, rather than gender per se, FoMO may be the more important risk factor driving the need for individuals to frequently check social media on their smartphone, thereby putting them in a position to become more-easily addicted to their smartphone (Elhai et al., 2017; Elhai et al., 2016).

Ethics

- What are some of the ethical issues related to using smartphones to collect and store personal health data?

The vast majority of people who own a smartphone have a large amount of personal data stored on their device. Most of us have become accustomed to allowing various app permissions and clicking "consent" without reading a single word related to the nature of that consent. In an analysis of over 1 million apps in Google's Android operating system, it was determined that the average smartphone user encounters 235 different kinds of permissions, with the average app requesting five permissions (Olmstead & Atkinson, 2015).

Whether due to "permission fatigue" or the belief that the collection of personal health data will one day lead to improved treatments of medical conditions, most people are generally willing to share personal data via their smartphone if they believe it is going to be used for public health research (Chen et al., 2016). However, constant access to real-time data brings with it a number of ethical concerns yet to be resolved (Jiya, 2016; Nunan & Di Domenico, 2013). Click through each of the following tabs to reveal the primary ethical issues identified by this research.

Smartphones and Ethics

Data Use Concerns

It often isn't clear exactly where personal data is going and for what purposes it will be used. Furthermore, data can be collected at a later date by a third party by merely receiving permission from the app company, not the individual user. For example, researchers at Harvard and Massachusetts General Hospital were able to obtain data from over one million women attempting to get pregnant, who were using a popular fertility app (Lange et al., 2016). All one million of these women likely consented to have their data used at some point in the future. However, providing consent for possible future use opens up the possibility for this data to be used inappropriately. For example, since consent was provided when downloading the app, do you think a fertility app company should be able to sell an individual's personal data to other companies so they can provide direct, targeted marketing to those using the app?

Identity Theft

Privacy Infringement

Quiz for Module 12.11

1. Smartphones have been found to help deliver effective treatments for _____.

   a. obesity

   b. anxiety

   c. high blood pressure

   d. All of the answers are correct

2. Danika spends 20–30 minutes each night before bed scrolling through social media and reading the news on her smartphone. What implications would be predicted based on Danika's behavior?

   a. Poor quality sleep, nightmares, and symptoms of depression

   b. Poor quality sleep, symptoms of depression, and symptoms of anxiety

   c. Nightmares, compulsive behaviors, symptoms of depression

   d. Symptoms of depression, anxiety, and substance use

3. Ceresei, Daenerys, and Jorah agreed to participate in a study of concentration and attention. Ceresei had her phone turned on but in her purse, Daenerys left her phone in her office to charge, and Jorah turned his phone off and placed it face down on the table. Who is likely to perform the best on the concentration and attention task?

   a. Jorah

   b. Daenerys

   c. Ceresei and Jorah will have roughly equal performance

   d. Daenerys and Jorah will have roughly equal performance

4. What is one of the risks for developing a smartphone addiction?

   a. Being male

   b. Using a smartphone for work obligations

   c. Using a smartphone before going to sleep at night

   d. Frequently checking social media throughout the day

5. Using smartphones to store personal and health data presents some ethical concerns. What are some of the ethical concerns discussed in the chapter?

   a. Identity theft, privacy infringement, and inappropriate use of data

   b. Privacy infringement, possible addiction, and curated information based on user behavior

   c. Inappropriate use of data, identity theft, and curated information based on user behavior

   d. Possible addiction, identity theft, and government monitoring programs

Summary

Module 12.1–12.3 Stress, Stressors, and the Biopsychosocial Model

Behavioral medicine is an interdisciplinary approach to medical treatment that integrates medical, psychological, and sociocultural knowledge to increase life expectancy and enhance quality of life. The psychological aspect of behavioral medicine is known as **health psychology,** which is focused on the development of general strategies and tactics people can use to eliminate or reduce stress and the risk of illness and disease. **Stress** is defined as the perceived discrepancy between the physical or psychological demands of a situation and the individual's biological, psychological, or social resources to cope with the demands. **Stressors** are events perceived as threatening or challenging that lead to the experience of stress. **Distress** describes the negative experience caused by stress, but there are times where stress can be experienced in response to positive events and even have positive effects, which is referred to as **eustress.** Stressors can take various forms including **catastrophes, significant life events,** and **daily hassles.** Understanding the reasons for a person's experience of stress requires an examination of the biological, psychological, and social factors in their lives. This view of stress and health is referred to as the **biopsychosocial perspective.** An individual's culture plays an overarching role and informs the biopsychosocial perspective. Cultural factors include, but are not limited to, ethnicity and race, socioeconomic status, and the stress that arises from moving from one culture to another, which is referred to as **acculturative stress.**

Module 12.4–12.5 Responses to Stress

The body has both physical and psychological responses to stress. Physiologically, when faced with a stressor, the sympathetic nervous system releases epinephrine and norepinephrine to initiate a **fight-or-flight response**, which involves preparing the body to fight off or flee from the stressor. In addition, the hormone **cortisol** is released after stress triggers the **hypothalamic-pituitary-adrenal (HPA) axis.** Hans Selye proposed the **general adaptation syndrome (GAS),** which describes how the body adaptively responds to stress over prolonged periods of time. According to the GAS, the body responds in three stages: alarm, resistance, and exhaustion. Stress also produces psychological responses including worry, anxiety, sadness, and/or anger, which left unattended to can progress to a psychological disorder. Stress also influences people's behavior. The **tend-and-befriend** theory suggests that women are more likely to seek social support during periods of stress, whereas men are more likely to withdraw socially. Stress can also lead people to engage in unhealthy coping behaviors, such as emotional eating, or alcohol and drug abuse.

Module 12.6–12.7 The Role of Stress in Health and Disease

Psychoneuroimmunology is an interdisciplinary field that emphasizes the interaction of psychological, neurological and endocrine, and immunological processes in stress and illness. Those who work in this field recognize the powerful impact stress can have on health and disease. Stress decreases the strength and functioning of the immune system: the body's natural defense against viruses, bacteria, cancer, and other **antigens** (i.e., foreign invaders). The immune system contains three types of **lymphocytes,** or white blood cells that attempt to attack antigens and promote health. B lymphocytes, also called B cells, produce **antibodies,** which suppress the damaging effects of antigens. Other lymphocytes attack antigens directly with lethal chemicals. Since chronic stress can suppress the immune system response, people who have stress-filled lives are at risk for developing serious medical conditions such as **coronary heart disease,** which involves a clogging of the vessels that nourish the heart muscle. Personality characteristics have been found to influence the likelihood of developing the disease and the prognosis after diagnosis. People with **Type A** personalities are described as competitive, impatient, verbally aggressive, easily angered, whereas those who are described as **Type B** are easygoing and relaxed. Type A individuals, especially those exhibiting high levels of hostility, are at much higher risk of developing heart disease. The **Type D**, or distressed personality, refers to a person who experiences increased negative emotions, yet tends to avoid self-expressions and social interactions. For those who have already been diagnosed with heart disease, the Type D personality has been found to have a worse prognosis in terms of physical and psychological health.

Module 12.8–12.10   Managing Stress

Many different techniques can be used to manage stress. Physiological approaches can directly change the body's physical responses, resulting in less stress and improved health. **Biofeedback** uses specialized equipment and technology to teach individuals to control bodily states, such as blood pressure, heart rate, or muscle tension. **Neurofeedback** uses a similar approach but focuses specifically on training people to control their own brain activity. **Relaxation therapy** involves a group of relaxation techniques aimed at producing a relaxation response to ease the effects of stress. **Meditation** is a mental practice or discipline that involves training the mind to become present, aware, and open to experiences. **Mindfulness-based stress reduction** is a structured program based on the principles of meditation and mindfulness. In addition to the known health benefits, **aerobic exercise** has also been found to reduce levels of stress and improve mood. Psychological approaches to stress management include: **perceived control,** the extent to which people believe they have control over a situation, and **explanatory style,** which refers to the optimistic or pessimistic way people describe life events. Effective **coping strategies,** or psychological methods to understand and manage stress, can help to minimize the effects of stressors. A **cognitive appraisal** involves a thoughtful interpretation and evaluation of the stressor. Making a cognitive appraisal involves two-steps: (1) a **primary appraisal,** or an initial evaluation of the seriousness of the stressor and (2) a **secondary appraisal,** which focuses on the actions needed, and resources required, to overcome the stressor. Coping can be either **problem-focused,** which attempts to alleviate the stress directly through environmental or behavioral change, or **emotion-focused,** which emphasizes the emotional response to the stressor. A social strategy for managing stress involves **social support,** which can be in-person or online, and includes the comfort, care, and help from friends and family. Cultural factors can play a role in the reasons individuals seek social support and how they seek support from others. Finally, faith and religion/spirituality have been found to help people cope with many aspects of stress and illness.

Chapter 12 Quiz

1. How is Facebook related to social support?

   a. The number of friends a person has on Facebook is positively related to actual social support.

   b. Facebook creates social overload and leaves people feeling disconnected and unsupported.

   c. There is no relationship between the number of friends a person has on Facebook and their experience of social support.

   d. The number of Facebook friends is positively related to perceived social support.

2. Under stress, the hypothalamic-pituitary-adrenal axis releases _____, whereas the sympathetic nervous system releases _____ and _____.

   a. epinephrine; cortisol; norepinephrine

   b. cortisol; epinephrine; norepinephrine

   c. insulin; cortisol; epinephrine

   d. cortisol; epinephrine; insulin

3. What is the function of the natural killer (NK) cells?

   a. They attack foreign invaders indirectly by creating antibodies.

   b. They patrol the body looking for diseased cells and attack them with lethal chemicals.

   c. They release antigens to help increase the number of white blood cells.

   d. They attack antigens indirectly by releasing deadly chemicals into the invading cells.

4. Leesa is excited and nervous to go on her first overseas vacation. She has been thinking about how much the trip will cost and wonders if she is independent enough to manage on her own. Leesa is experiencing which aspect of psychological stress?

   a. Biological   b. Behavioral

   c. Social   d. Cognitive

5. When people feel stressed, they often start eating unhealthy food and stop exercising. These _____ aspects of stress can lead to more stress in the future.

   a. behavioral   b. cognitive

   c. social   d. emotional

6. Mitch was raised in foster care and has no real family to rely on when life becomes overwhelming. He also has difficulty making friends because he does not trust that people won't leave him. Mitch does not have good _____, which can increase the impact of stressors.

   a. coping skills   b. social support

   c. emotional skills   d. genetics

7. Socioeconomic status or SES is most often calculated using a combination of _____ and _____.

   a. income; life expectancy

   b. income; educational attainment

   c. life expectancy; educational attainment

   d. educational attainment; cultural background

8. The group of people who will most likely have the highest life expectancy are those who are _____ and _____.

   a. high SES; live in a rural area

   b. low SES; live in an urban area

   c. high SES; live in an urban area

   d. low SES; live in an urban area

9. Muslim Arabs who are _____ are more likely to experience acculturative stress when trying to adjust to the United States.

   a. less outgoing

   b. more outgoing

   c. less religious

   d. more religious

10. A cognitive appraisal of a stressful situation involves two steps. What are they?

    a. A secondary appraisal and reassessment of the situation

    b. A primary appraisal and optimistic explanatory style

    c. A primary appraisal and a secondary appraisal

    d. Problem-focused coping and emotion-focused coping

11. Increased cortisol production has been linked to what negative outcomes?

    a. Weight gain and memory impairment

    b. Increased sleep and memory consolidation

    c. Decreased weight and memory impairment

    d. Weight gain and memory consolidation

12. A hurricane and an hour daily commute are both considered _____.

    a. stress   b. stressors

    c. eustress   d. distress

13. Women's emotional response to stress typically involves nurturing behaviors that have been called _____.

    a. wine and dine   b. fight or flight

    c. tend and befriend   d. care and cry

14. Marissa's boyfriend broke up with her, and she failed her chemistry test the same day. Marissa feels depressed and worried. Which foods is she most likely to eat in response to her stress?

    a. Fried chicken and French fries

    b. Vegetables and hummus

    c. Miso soup and sushi

    d. Brownies and ice cream

15. Researchers believe that emotional eating and obesity use similar brain pathways as substance use and addiction. Which neurotransmitter is associated with these pathways?

    a. Dopamine

    b. Serotonin

    c. Epinephrine

    d. GABA

16. What factors can influence the functioning of your immune system?

    a. Age, genetics, and nutrition

    b. Caffeine use, exercise, and genetics

    c. Age, alcohol intake, and exercise

    d. Genetics, obesity, and quality of sleep

17. Stress that has a negative impact on people is referred to as _____, whereas the stress that has positive results is called _____.

    a. hassles; eustress

    b. eustress; distress

    c. distress; eustress

    d. catastrophe; hassles

18. During periods of stress, the brain releases cortisol and other stress-related hormones. What impact do these stress hormones have on the immune system?

    a. They kill the T cells, B cells, and NK cells so they can no longer fight infection.

    b. They increase the activity of the white blood cells, which overstimulates the system leading to illness.

    c. They suppress the disease-fighting activity of the T cells, B cells, and NK cells leaving the person more susceptible to illness.

    d. They stimulate antibodies before the B cells can produce them.

19. Which psychological treatment has been shown to reduce anxiety and depression among cancer patients?

    a. Biofeedback

    b. Behavioral therapy

    c. Interpersonal therapy

    d. Mindfulness-based therapy

20. How is stress related to cancer?

    a. Stress can make a person's body more hospitable to cancer.

    b. Stress can cause cancer.

    c. There is no relationship between stress and cancer.

    d. Stress is only a casual factor in people who have a history of cancer.

21. What is the relationship between stress, cortisol, the immune system's functioning, and the risk of illness?

    a. Stress leads to increased cortisol and decreased functioning of the immune system, which increases the risk of illness or infection.

    b. Stress leads to decreased cortisol and decreased functioning of the immune system, which increases the risk of illness or infection.

    c. Stress leads to increased cortisol and increased functioning of the immune system, which decreases the risk of illness or infection.

    d. Stress leads to decreased cortisol and increased functioning of the immune system, which decreases the risk of illness or infection.

22. Biofeedback is designed to help people control their _____ bodily functions as a way to _____ stress.

    a. internal; increase

    b. involuntary; reduce

    c. voluntary; reduce

    d. external; eliminate

23. Quincy is imagining himself lying on a beach. He tries to feel the cool ocean breezes against his skin, hear the quiet lap of the ocean, and see the swaying of the palm trees. He is using which technique to reduce stress?

    a. Meditation

    b. Progressive muscle relaxation

    c. Guided imagery

    d. Neurofeedback

24. Aerobic exercise has been found to _____.

    a. improve cardiovascular health

    b. reduce stress and symptoms of depression

    c. slow down the cellular damage from stress and stimulate new cell growth

    d. All of the answers are correct

25. Reza's parents are going through a divorce. Reza would like to live with his mother, but where he lives will be decided by a judge. Reza feels stressed, in part, because he lacks _____.

    a. coping strategies

    b. perceived control

    c. problem-solving skills

    d. the opportunity to participate in biofeedback

26. What are some of the physiological changes that make up the fight-or-flight response?

    a. Increased heart rate, increased respiration, sweating, decreased digestive function

    b. Increased digestive function, decreased heart rate, increased respiration, sweating

    c. Decreased heart rate, increased respiration, sweating, increased digestive function

    d. Increased heart rate, increased blood pressure, decreased respiration, decreased digestive function

27. Helga was diagnosed with breast cancer and is anxious and worried about the outcome. Her friends have rallied around her, spending time watching funny movies or taking her to comedy clubs. Helga's friends are engaging in which type of coping?

    a. Problem-focused coping

    b. Emotion-focused coping

    c. Distracted coping

    d. Social support

28. Compared to a collectivistic culture, a person from an individualistic culture is likely going to have _____ friends and be _____ likely to seek out social support.

    a. fewer; more

    b. more; less

    c. more; more

    d. fewer; less

29. Some stress researchers have proposed we restrict the definition of stress to situations that involve _____.

    a. unpredictability and lack of control

    b. aggression and violence

    c. natural disasters and catastrophes

    d. daily hassles and frustrations

30. What are some of the positive physical health outcomes associated with being religiously active?

    a. More social support, less depression and anxiety, a sense of purpose in life

    b. Healthier diet, more physical activity, improved immune system functioning

    c. Higher self-esteem, lower risk of developing cancer, and less cigarette smoking

    d. More positive emotions, lower risk for heart disease, and more social support

Chapter 13
Social Psychology

Chapter Outline and Learning Objectives

Module 13.1–13.3: Social Cognition

LO 13.1 Describe how we form impressions of others.

LO 13.2 Identify heuristics used to make decisions about others.

LO 13.3 Distinguish three different attributional biases.

Module 13.4–13.6: Attitude Formation and Attitude Change

LO 13.4 Recognize the three components of attitudes.

LO 13.5 Describe the relationship between attitudes and behaviors.

LO 13.6 Identify factors that influence persuasion.

Module 13.7–13.10: Social Influence

LO 13.7 Differentiate among three approaches to gaining compliance.

LO 13.8 Describe conditions that contribute to obedience.

LO 13.9 Recognize factors that contribute to, and influence, conformity.

LO 13.10 Explain how groups have the power to influence individual behavior.

Module 13.11–13.14: Social Relationships

LO 13.11 Describe explanations for prejudice and ways to reduce prejudice.

LO 13.12 Recognize factors that can lead to aggressive behavior, including intimate partner violence.

LO 13.13 Describe factors that influence attraction, love, and successful relationships.

LO 13.14 Explain factors that can affect helping behavior.

Module 13.15: Piecing it Together: Cyberbullying

LO 13.15 Analyze how the cross-cutting themes of psychology and specific social psychological principles relate to cyberbullying.

What is Social Psychology?

What Do You Think?

Interactive

Do you think people choose to help others truly without caring about themselves or their own self-interests?

○ Yes

○ No

| PREVIOUS | PAGE 1 OF 1 | SUBMIT |

On May 22, 2011, an EF5 tornado (the most severe kind of tornado) ripped through Joplin, Missouri, killing 158 people and injuring more than a thousand. With the cost of the damage estimated at $2.8 billion, it became the costliest tornado in U.S. history. Living approximately an hour from Joplin, we have vivid memories of this horrifying day; however, our memories also involve the incredible response of caring people around the world who wanted to help. On the second anniversary of the tornado, the city reported that 176,869 volunteers had provided 1,146,083 hours of time to the rebuilding and recovery of Joplin.

What motivates people to help others? Is there such a thing as true altruism? Alternatively, while many people were helping, some people chose to take advantage of the wounded city and the people who lived there. As the storm moved out, the looters moved in, looking to take anything that had been left behind. The state's attorney general warned residents to be on the lookout for price gouging on gas, building materials, and fraudulent charities.

Approximately 175,000 volunteers rushed to help Joplin residents after the deadly tornado in 2011.

The aftermath of the 2011 Joplin tornado.

What is it that explains how a natural disaster can bring out both the best and worst in people? Social psychologists are interested in answering these and many other questions related to social interactions and influences and how they impact our thoughts, feelings, and behaviors.

How many times have you thought to yourself, "Why would a person do that?" Or, "What were they thinking?" Have you noticed how differently *you* think and behave in different social situations? Human beings may be individuals, but we are all individuals within a group, and we are all inherently social animals (Adolphs, 1999). This chapter discusses how we are all influenced by our social situations and contexts.

Module 13.1–13.3: Social Cognition

Each of these concepts or characteristics is a topic of interest to social psychologists and can be influenced by the presence or absence of other people.

Social psychologists study how an individual's thoughts, emotions, and behaviors influence and are influenced by the social context. In a classic definition, Gordon W. Allport (1897–1967) defined **social psychology** as "the scientific attempt to explain how the thoughts, feelings, and behaviors of individuals are influenced by the actual, imagined, or implied presence of other human beings" (Jones, 1998, p. 3).

Think back to a situation where you were with a group of people and someone asked your opinion on the death penalty, abortion, war, or other controversial subject. Did you immediately answer? Or, did you take a look around at your audience and consider what some people might think of you after they heard your response? Maybe you suddenly recalled a similar situation in your past that didn't turn out well for you. Did this memory affect your decision in this moment? **Social cognition** is an area in social psychology that focuses on the role of cognitive processes in our social interactions (Aronson et al., 2013). That is, how do people think about the social world and make sense of themselves and those around them? Research in social cognition focuses on the underlying internal processes, such as perception, attention, and memory, that make social behavior possible (Moskowitz, 2005). As we expand our knowledge about the biology of the brain, *social cognitive neuroscience* has become increasingly important in understanding these processes (Fiske & Taylor, 2013). With the ability to utilize neuroimaging techniques such as functional magnetic resonance imaging (fMRI), positron emission tomography (PET), and other technology to see what the brain looks like and how it behaves under certain conditions, scientists are now able to start connecting the dots between social cognitive processes and their neurological counterparts (Lieberman, 2010). For example, biological structures and processes in the brain help us navigate our social environment, whether we're recognizing a friend's face in a crowd, feeling empathy for others, or deciding what we think or how we feel about a particular topic, situation, or person.

social psychology

a field of psychology involving the scientific attempt to explain how the thoughts, feelings, and behaviors of individuals are influenced by the actual, imagined, or implied presence of other human beings

social cognition

an area within social psychology that focuses on the role of cognitive processes in terms of how people think about others

First Impressions

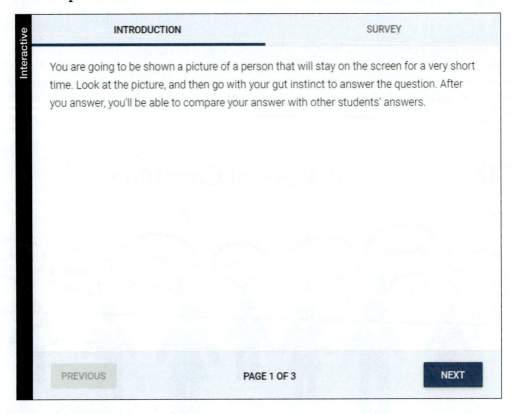

PREVIOUS   PAGE 1 OF 3   NEXT

First Impressions

LO 13.1 **Describe how we form impressions of others.**

Think about when you walk into a new class for the first time. How do you decide where to sit? Do you choose your seat solely based on the location where you typically sit? Chances are, while location may matter, you are also likely scanning the room, examining the people already seated, forming very quick impressions of them, and then deciding where to sit. **Person perception** refers to the different mental processes used to perceive the personality characteristics of others (Oltmanns & Turkheimer, 2009). Person perception involves not only the study of how and why these impressions are formed, but also the impact these decisions have on our behavior.

person perception

refers to the different mental processes used to perceive the personality characteristics of others

The ability to examine another person's face is key in making first impressions, and you don't need very long to make a decision. In fact, most people need about 100 milliseconds, that's 1/10 of a second to make a judgment, about another person (that's how long the picture you saw was presented on the screen). Researchers Willis and Todorov (2006) conducted a series of studies to show that people formed judgments of competence of strangers within a tenth of a second. The research participants were confident in their judgments, and giving them more time did not change their impressions. Subsequent research has shown that our impressions of others can be influenced by information presented subliminally, that is, below our level of conscious awareness. When participants were first subliminally presented with a picture of an untrustworthy face, and then shown a picture of a "neutral" face, they were much more likely to judge the neutral face as untrustworthy compared to participants who were not primed with the untrustworthy subliminal face (Todorov et al., 2009).

Just as face-to-face impressions are formed, impressions of people met online are also produced with very limited information (D'Angelo & Van Der Heide, 2013; Stopfer et al., 2014). For example, it has been found that people tend to make rapid judgments about other people's personality based solely on their Facebook profile pictures. Turner and Hunt (2014) asked a small group of men and women to quickly rate (i.e., in 10 seconds) 52 different Facebook profile pictures of women they had never met. The participants in the study were surprisingly consistent in their impressions of others based only on their profile picture.

However, these impressions shared little relationship to the actual profile picture owner's ratings of their own personality. This result suggests that while certain characteristics about a person in a picture may produce predictable judgments by others, these impressions may not match how the person perceives their own personality.

However, people are not always consistent in their impressions of others. It has been demonstrated that individuals can form different impressions of the same person when pictures are shown at different times and in different social contexts. For example, participants' impressions about the same person changed, depending on whether the picture was presented as an online dating profile or as part of a political campaign (Todorov & Porter, 2014). As you can see, even though there is a neurological basis to forming impressions, the social context plays an important role in directing judgments.

While much of our first impressions depend on visual cues, researchers have found that bodily sensations and biological states can also influence person perception, a field of study referred to as **embodied cognition** (Eerland et al., 2011). For example, when people experienced sensations of "hardness" by squeezing a hard ball, they were much more likely to categorize sex-ambiguous faces as male, whereas those who were primed with sensations of "softness" were more likely to categorize the faces as female (Slepian et al., 2011).

embodied cognition
a field of study that examines how bodily sensations influence person perception

A number of factors are involved in making such quick (less than 1 second) judgments about other people (either in person or online), such as the social norms present in a particular culture (Kitayama & Park, 2010), facial features (Willis & Todorov, 2006) and other physical characteristics (Bar & Neta, 2006), preexisting social categories (Ratner & Amodi, 2013), and aspects of the situation (Andersen & Przybylinski, 2014). So, with all of this information, how are we able to make such rapid assessments of others?

Heuristics: Mental Shortcuts

LO 13.2 **Identify heuristics used to make decisions about others.**

Think back to the picture you just judged. You probably felt quite sure of your judgment of trustworthiness, despite seeing the face for less than a second. How did you do this? Over the course of your life, you have developed a number of strategies to help you make quick decisions. These "rules of thumb" are also referred to as *heuristics*—mental shortcuts aimed at reducing the complexity of our world. Katsikopoulos (2011) describes heuristics as models for making decisions that:

1. Rely heavily on core human abilities;

2. Do not necessarily use all available information, and process the information they use by simple computations; and

3. Are easy to understand, apply, and explain.

Understanding how heuristics work is important in social psychology because many of the decisions we make result from them, which can impact other people. For a review of all heuristics, see LO 7.6.

AVAILABILITY HEURISTIC Researchers in social cognition have identified a number of heuristics that increase the speed in which we make decisions. One example includes the **availability heuristic**, which involves using information that is easily recalled, or *available* to us, when making a decision or judgment. Therefore, just because something can be easily remembered doesn't necessarily mean it is an accurate reflection of reality. As an example, many parents believe their children are unsafe if left alone to play outside. If you were to ask them "why," they would likely cite the number of childhood abductions broadcast on the news and via social media. The *availability* of this information creates a belief that it is more common than it is in reality. In fact, the FBI's data on missing persons suggests that rates of missing children are much lower now than they were 10, 20, and 30 years ago.

availability heuristic
a mental shortcut that relies on information that is easily recalled or readily available

SOCIAL CATEGORIZATION Imagine someone asked you to sort an entire container of buttons. How would you do it? Would you sort by color? Size? Style? Regardless of what process you chose, you would quickly make judgments about each button as to whether or not it possessed the particular characteristics. While humans are certainly more complex than buttons, the process we go through to sort and make quick decisions about them is similar. **Social categorization** involves

social categorization
grouping people or things according to certain characteristics such as age, race, and gender

grouping people or things according to certain characteristics. We often use social categories such as age, race, and gender to make inferences about the people we meet (Bodenhausen et al., 2012). While much of this work has focused on facial features (Freeman & Ambady, 2011), more recent studies have shown that context, including culture, can impact social categorization. For example, in a study examining the influence of culture on social categorization, both American and Chinese students used context (the background landscape picture, which they referred to as "American-typed," "neutral," or "Chinese-typed") to categorize individuals by ethnicity. However, Chinese students began to process the context earlier than American students (Freeman et al., 2013). This finding is consistent with the differences found in Western cultures, which are more independent than Eastern cultures, which are described as more interdependent.

Social categorization involves grouping people according to certain, often visual, characteristics. The approach is similar to one that would be taken to sort a container of various buttons.

implicit personality theory

a heuristic in person perception that involves assuming a person with a particular personality characteristic will think and behave in other ways that are typically associated with that central personality characteristic

IMPLICIT PERSONALITY THEORIES How many times have you heard shocking news about something someone else did and thought to yourself, "No way! They don't seem like that kind of person!" This reaction may be in reference to someone you know quite well or someone you don't know at all (e.g., a movie star or musician). What is the basis for your judgment of this person? Many times, our reaction is based on an **implicit personality theory**, or a set of assumptions people make about the relationship between certain personality traits and the influence they have on an individual's behavior (Schneider, 1973). For example, you might assume that a person who communicates using big words is smart, or that someone who speaks slowly is unintelligent. In 1968, Rosenberg and his colleagues were interested in categorizing which traits tended to stick together and how that group of traits influenced the perception of others. As shown in Figure 13.1, they found that most traits could be categorized along two important

Figure 13.1 Rosenberg's Categorization of Dimensional Traits

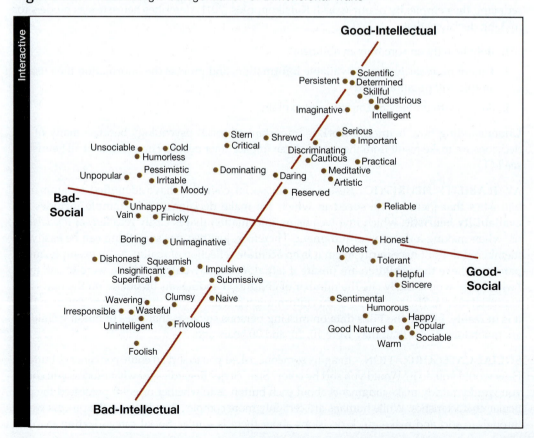

dimensions: *social* good-bad and *intellectual* good-bad, which have repeatedly been replicated in the scientific literature, although they tend now to be referred to as the dimensions of *warmth* and *competence* (Cuddy et al., 2011; Fiske et al., 2007; Kervyn et al., 2010).

Journal Prompt: Using Heuristics

What are some of the advantages and disadvantages of using heuristics?

Attribution Theory

LO 13.3 Distinguish three different attributional biases.

The popularity of reality TV probably wouldn't surprise psychologist Fritz Heider. He believed we are all "naive scientists," naturally interested in analyzing other people's behavior and personalities. In 1958, Heider outlined his **attribution theory**, which states that we understand the behavior of others by attributing their behavior either to their internal dispositions or their external situations. Think of someone on reality TV who really gets under your skin. Let's imagine you watch them behaving in a demeaning way toward other people. Whether you think they are acting that way because they are inherently a bad person or because they think being offensive will help the show's ratings, you are making an **attribution**, which is an explanation about the cause of their behavior.

DISPOSITIONAL AND SITUATIONAL ATTRIBUTIONS When you attribute a person's behavior to his or her personality or personal characteristics, you are making an *internal* or **dispositional attribution**. Alternatively, when you attribute behavior to external factors such as the person's situation or environment, you're making an *external* or **situational attribution**. Of course, the attributions we make about other people can have significant consequences for our own behavior. If your friend stands you up at the movie theater, you might attribute his or her behavior to thoughtlessness or cruelty and send them a snarky text message, not realizing that your friend has actually been delayed because of a parent's illness. The reality is that we are not unbiased when it comes to explaining behavior; however, we tend to be biased in quite predictable ways!

attribution theory

theory that we understand a behavior by attributing it either to an internal disposition or an external situation

attribution

an explanation about the cause of our own or others' behavior

dispositional attribution

attributing our own, or another person's behavior to personality or personal characteristics

situational attribution

attributing our own, or another person's behavior to external factors such as the situation or environment

Name the Attribution

Interactive

Fill in each blank with either "situational" or "dispositional."

1. Your friend, Jacob, tells you that he was just fired from his job. When you ask him what happened, he says that his boss is a terrible person and "was just out to get" him. You know your friend has a tendency to be lazy and think that may have had something to do with it.

In this scenario, Jacob is making a _____ attribution, and you are making a _____ attribution.

2. Despite studying really hard, you did not perform well on a recent exam. You felt that the exam was too hard and focused on picky details.

In this scenario, you are making a _____ attribution.

3. You complain to your friend about the exam, and they suggest that maybe the course is too difficult for you and that you should consider finding a different course to take.

In this scenario, your friend is making a _____ attribution.

Start Over   Check Answers

ATTRIBUTION BIASES We have many reasons for our attributions to be biased. Because we are bombarded with so much information from our environment, we have to take some mental shortcuts to avoid cognitive fatigue. Also, most people are very motivated to interpret the world in a way that leaves them feeling good about themselves (Neff, 2011). Three different biases guide how we tend to explain the behavior of ourselves and others, including the *fundamental attribution error* (Ross, 1977), the *actor-observer bias* (Jones & Nisbett, 1971) and the *self-serving bias* (Heider, 1958).

fundamental attribution error

the tendency to attribute others' behavior to dispositional (internal) rather than situational (external) factors

Both personal characteristics and external factors play an important role in determining our actions. Yet, according to the **fundamental attribution error**, most people tend to attribute others' behavior to dispositional (internal) rather than situational (external) factors. Amazingly, studies have shown that even when people know a situation has actually caused a certain behavior, they still make a dispositional attribution. For example, participants who were told that an experiment collaborator had been instructed to behave coldly or warmly toward them still persisted in believing that the behavior reflected the collaborator's real personality (Napolitan & Goethals, 1979).

actor-observer bias

an attributional bias in which a person attributes their own actions to situational causes, whereas as an observer they make a dispositional attribution for the same event

The **actor-observer bias** explains how our attribution can change depending on whether we are the actor (situational) or the observer (dispositional) in a situation. The actor refers to the person at the center of the situation or behavior (which could be you or someone else), and the observer is you or any other person watching or even hearing about the situation. The actor-observer bias states that "there is a pervasive tendency for actors to attribute their actions to situational requirements, whereas observers tend to attribute some actions to personal dispositions" (Jones & Nisbett, 1971, p. 80). Therefore, the actor-observer bias always includes two attributions of the same event: one from the actor and one from the observer. The bias predicts that those two attributions are going to be opposites. Imagine you met a new coworker who was diagnosed with high blood pressure. The coworker (the actor) knows that he comes from a long line of family members who have high blood pressure, so he tends to make a situational explanation for his diagnosis. You, as the observer, are much more likely to make a dispositional attribution such as assuming that your coworker doesn't lead a healthy lifestyle and therefore has high blood pressure. The actor-observer bias tends to be most prevalent in individuals from Western cultures. Individualistic cultures, such as those in the United States and Canada, place much more value on themselves and view themselves as primarily responsible for their successes and failures (Oyserman et al., 2002). Many studies over the years have demonstrated that non-Western

Figure 13.2 Attribution Biases

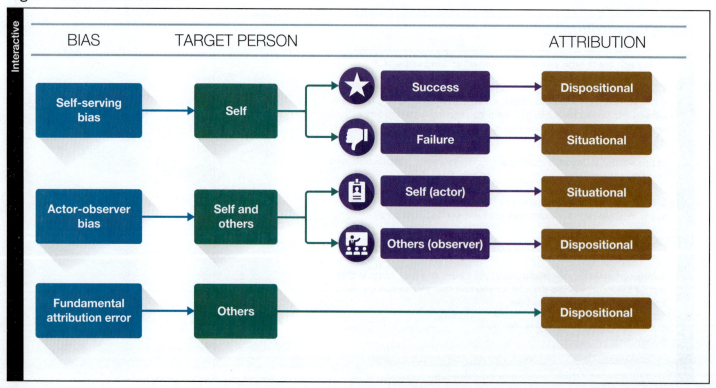

individuals, particularly those of Asian descent, are more collectivistic, and have a much more situation-centered theory of behavior (Morris et al., 1995) and therefore are less susceptible to the actor-observer bias (Choi & Nisbett, 1998).

The self-serving bias, as the name suggests, refers only to situations that involve ourselves and is at work most when a situation threatens our own self-esteem (Campbell & Sedikides, 1999). The **self-serving bias** involves taking personal credit for our own successes, but blaming our failures on external events beyond our control. Imagine you have always been told you are very smart, and a graduate student in clinical psychology asks if they can practice administering an intelligence test on you. You graciously agree and then receive the report that your overall IQ falls within the average range. The self-serving bias would predict that you will experience this information as threatening, by challenging your belief about yourself as a "smart" person, and that you will tend to make a situational attribution for this event (e.g., "the examiner didn't administer the test correctly" or "the room was too noisy.") If, however, the IQ was reported to be in the gifted range, the attribution would likely be a dispositional one (e.g., "I inherited good genes from my parents" or "I work very hard in school.")

To help you distinguish between the three different attributional biases, click to reveal each part of the interactive Figure 13.2, and note how each bias has a different "target person."

self-serving bias

an attributional bias that involves people taking personal credit for their own successes but blaming their failures on external events beyond their control

Adaptive Pathway 13.1: Attribution Biases

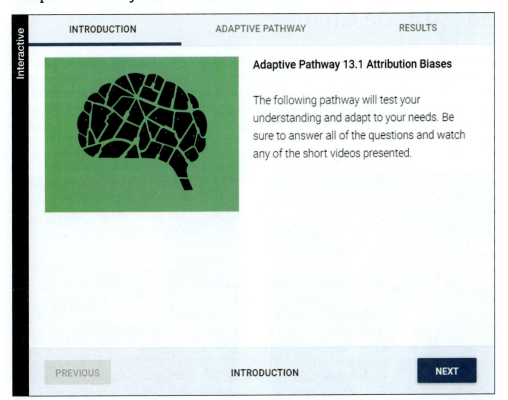

Quiz for Module 13.1 – 13.3

1. Social _____ refers to the role of our thoughts and interpretations in social interactions.

   a. attribution
   b. dissonance
   c. psychology
   d. cognition

2. How long does it typically take a person to formulate a judgment about the trustworthiness of a stranger?

   a. 10 minutes
   b. Less than 1 second
   c. 10 seconds
   d. 1 minute

3. Nate thinks Republicans and Democrats almost never work together in Congress. The reason he believes this is that he finds it much easier to think of examples of politicians from the two parties not working together than to think of examples of them working together. It is likely that the _____ has caused Nate to underestimate how frequently Democrats and Republicans work together.

   a. confirmation bias
   b. social categorization
   c. availability heuristic
   d. framing effect

4. Which of the following statements concerning social categorization is correct?

   a. Social categorization is a relatively new phenomenon.

   b. People who do it tend to be young and naïve.

   c. It is deliberate and conscious.

   d. It occurs without conscious awareness.

5. While stuck in a traffic jam, Yani notices a frustrated driver frequently honking his horn. Yani thinks to himself, "That driver is a real jerk!" This is an example of a _____ attribution.

   a. dispositional

   b. self-serving

   c. prejudiced

   d. situational

6. _____ refers to the tendency to overestimate dispositional influences (and underestimate situational influences) when explaining another person's behavior.

   a. The fundamental attribution error

   b. Diffusion of responsibility

   c. Deindividuation

   d. Cognitive dissonance

7. The self-serving bias involves making _____ attributions for your success and _____ attributions for your failures.

   a. dispositional; dispositional

   b. dispositional; situational

   c. situational; dispositional

   d. situational; situational

Module 13.4–13.6: Attitude Formation and Attitude Change

If you voted in the 2016 presidential election, you probably had some pretty strong opinions or attitudes about the candidates before voting. How did you arrive at your decision? Our attitudes can be complex, and developing attitudes about people, issues, likes, and dislikes is not always a straightforward process. A politician's goal is to speak and act in ways that will change your attitude and, ultimately, your voting behavior. As you'll discover in this module, there are many influences—even genetics—that affect attitude formation and attitude change.

A politician's primary objective is to influence your attitudes and gain your vote.

Attitude Formation

LO 13.4 **Recognize the three components of attitudes.**

An **attitude** is an evaluative belief or opinion about people, objects, or ideas (Ajzen & Fishbein, 2000; Webber, 2013). We have **explicit attitudes**—beliefs or opinions that we hold consciously and can report to others—and **implicit attitudes**—beliefs and opinions that are involuntary or uncontrollable and can automatically influence our actions (Gawronski & Bodenhausen, 2011; Hahn et al., 2014). All attitudes have three components: (1) the *affective*

---

attitude

an evaluative belief or opinion about people, objects, or ideas

explicit attitudes

beliefs or opinions that are held consciously and can be reported to others

implicit attitudes

beliefs and opinions that are unconscious (involuntary or uncontrollable) and can automatically influence behaviors

component, which includes your emotions or feelings toward the attitude object; (2) the *be-havioral component*, which includes how people act, or behave, toward the attitude object; and (3) the *cognitive component*, which includes the thoughts and beliefs people hold about a particular object. Therefore, our thoughts, feelings, and behaviors work together to shape, and display, our attitudes. The easiest way to remember the three components of an attitude involves thinking in terms of the ABCs:

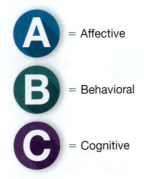

A = Affective

B = Behavioral

C = Cognitive

The ABCs of Attitudes

Drag and drop the following statements into the *Affective*, *Behavioral*, or *Cognitive* categories of attitudes.

Affective	Behavioral	Cognitive
Jayme feels happiest when spending time with animals.	Jayme recently rescued a dog.	Jayme thinks everyone should have a pet.
Jayme loves animals.	Jayme talks about animals all the time.	Jayme believes animals are more loyal and comforting than humans.

Start Over

Evidence suggests that attitudes have a genetic basis (Eaves et al., 1999). In fact, a genome-wide analysis has even identified chromosomal regions of genetic markers (on Chromosomes 2, 4, 6, and 9) to be associated with political preference (Hatemi et al., 2011). However, attitude development also involves the social environment, including the influence of other people. Different types of information or experiences affect the different components of attitudes. For example, relevant facts about an object tend to influence the cognitive component of our attitude. If you are buying a new laptop, your attitude toward a specific brand might be influenced by all of the relevant specs of the computer. But, you could also end up choosing to buy a laptop that was less sophisticated because it was available in a great color. Your feelings about how the laptop looks are the affective component of your attitude, which is more influenced by your values, sensory reactions, or even classical conditioning (Kim & Lennon, 2008).

Here's an interesting example of how corporations attempt to capitalize on the affective components of your attitudes. Many hotels in Las Vegas are determined to sway your attitudes and feelings about their hotel the moment you walk in the door by bombarding you with the smell of fresh flowers. The idea is not just to cover up the smell of cigarettes and alcohol but to create a lasting conditioned response of happiness and enjoyment in response to the scent. For this reason, many hotels market and sell their unique scent in the form of candles and air fresheners so you can continue to be reminded of the hotel—even when you are at home. Since these electronically generated scent systems can cost up to $35,000 each month, we can probably conclude that they have been quite effective in leading to positive attitudes about the hotel.

The Relationship Between Attitudes and Behaviors

LO 13.5 Describe the relationship between attitudes and behaviors.

As clinical psychologists who practice cognitive behavioral therapy, we are well aware of the fact that our attitudes, or our beliefs about something, can affect how we behave and that the way we behave can influence what we believe and think.

Bidirectional Relationship Between Attitudes and Behaviors

Thoughts ⟷ Behaviors

THE INFLUENCE OF ATTITUDES AND BEHAVIORS The entire field of marketing and advertising is based on the assumption that influencing your attitudes toward a product will result in increased buying behavior. Even the way in which you purchase goods is influenced by your attitudes. For example, people are more likely to make online purchases if they believe their financial information will be safe and if they have the skills to complete the purchase (George, 2004). Numerous campaigns have been run to influence people's attitudes about the environment in an effort to change behaviors. As a result, there has been a clear attitudinal and behavioral shift, particularly among the younger generations, with respect to increased recycling, driving hybrid cars, and buying local and organic food (Adams & Solois, 2010; Royne et al., 2011; Schwab et al., 2014). Of course, not everyone who experiences a change of attitude immediately changes their behavior. You may know someone who says they value recycling but because recycling doesn't get picked up at their home, they throw everything in the trash.

The *Theory of Planned Behavior* (Ajzen, 1991) has been often used in the context of predicting health behaviors from people's attitudes (Conner et al., 2013). This theory suggests that behaviors are determined by *behavioral intentions* and that intentions are determined by: (1) the person's attitude about the topic; (2) the subjective norms, meaning the person's perceptions of how other's will react to the behavior; and (3) perceived behavioral control, which refers to how much confidence the person has that they could change their behavior (see Figure 13.3).

Think back to a time in your life when you changed a behavior *after* your attitude had already changed. For example, many people eventually quit smoking because their attitude about the dangers of smoking change to where they truly believe smoking could shorten

Figure 13.3 Theory of Planned Behavior

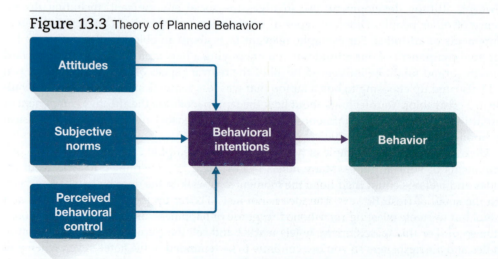

their life. There are numerous examples of behaviors people change as a result of a shift in their attitudes: eating habits, exercise, clothing style, taste in music, environmentally friendly behaviors, to name a few.

Journal Prompt: How Did You Change?

What behavior have you changed in your life? Describe the process you went through of first changing your attitude and then changing your behavior.

Attitudes do not always influence behaviors. We also infer people's attitudes by observing their behavior. When you see someone dressed from head to toe in clothing from a particular sports team, you can make a pretty good guess that they are a fan of that team. Even becoming aware of our *own* behaviors can inform our attitudes. Daryl Bem (1967, 1972) describes this in his **self-perception theory**, which states that people infer (or perceive) their attitudes about various topics by observing their own behaviors. Sometimes, we aren't even consciously aware of our attitude toward something but are able to infer it by examining our own behavior. For example, imagine someone asked you which hair color you found most attractive in a partner, but you'd never really given this a lot of thought. Your response might be something like, "I don't know. I don't really have a preference." But, what if your friend then pointed out that every person you have ever dated had blonde hair? You might then take that behavioral evidence and conclude, "I guess I like blondes." While this way of thinking about attitude formation isn't always intuitive, the reality is that the relationship between attitudes and behaviors is bidirectional: Attitudes can affect behaviors, and behaviors can affect attitudes.

"What fits your busy schedule better, exercising one hour a day or being dead 24 hours a day?"

Most people intuitively understand how your attitudes can affect your behavior. People don't often think as much about how their behaviors can come to shape their attitudes. Exercise is a good example of this. While most people would agree that exercise has numerous health benefits, in 2015 only 21 percent of Americans get the recommended amount of aerobic and muscle-strengthening activity (Ward et al., 2016). So, knowing you should exercise and *actually* exercising are different things.

We often tell people that the way to increase your motivation for exercise is to force yourself to exercise! That is, perform the behavior, and the attitude will follow. How many times have you heard someone say, "I used to hate running/going to the gym/biking, but now I enjoy it"? This principle of behavior change leading to changes in attitudes has been enormously helpful for many people suffering from depression. In fact, this is one of the first things we talk about with patients who are experiencing depression. We discuss the fact that "action precedes motivation" and explain that because of the depression they are often not going to *want* to do many things, and they won't feel *motivated* to go out with friends. But, because we know engaging in behavior influences how we think, participating anyway can help them change the way they think about that situation in the future and ultimately change the way they feel.

COGNITIVE DISSONANCE   If you've ever experienced an uncomfortable feeling because of a disconnect between two contradictory thoughts or between your internal attitudes and your external behavior, then you've experienced **cognitive dissonance**. Let's say you agreed to see a movie with friends, even though you had no interest in watching the movie they chose. Social psychologist Leon Festinger (1959) coined the term cognitive dissonance, and he and others have shown that our desire to counteract cognitive dissonance can play a major role in how we think about and behave in the world. If you are a musician, you likely already understand the concepts of consonance and dissonance. Even if you don't have a background

self-perception theory

people infer (or develop) their attitudes about various topics by observing their own behaviors

cognitive dissonance

a state of psychological tension that develops when a person is faced with two conflicting attitudes or a conflicting attitude and behavior

in music, you will be able to grasp the concept quickly. Click the play button and then answer the following question:

Click on this Sound

If you are like most people, the first chord was probably not your favorite. Most people who hear a similar sound report a feeling of tension, or even irritation. In music, the tension produced from a dissonant chord is resolved by playing a consonant chord (like the second chord you heard). There is a need to resolve the dissonant sound and subsequent feeling. The same is true with people. When our thoughts and behaviors are inconsistent, we are left feeling tense, or uncomfortable, even irritated.

In 1959, in what has become a classic study in social psychology, Festinger and his colleagues asked participants to undertake incredibly boring tasks such as putting spools into a tray and turning square pegs a quarter-turn at a time. The experimenter then asked each participant to tell the next participant that the tasks were enjoyable, intriguing, and exciting. Finally, the researchers asked the participants to rate their own overall enjoyment of the task. Half of the participants were promised $20 in exchange for telling this lie; the other participants were offered $1. Festinger and his fellow researchers discovered that the participants who received $1 rated the tasks they'd performed as significantly more interesting than the participants who received $20. Festinger used his theory of cognitive dissonance to explain these results: If you say something you don't believe, but you don't have sufficient justification (such as a $20 bill) for saying it, you're likely to change your beliefs in order to reduce the effect of cognitive dissonance (Festinger & Carlsmith, 1959).

We have already established that cognitive dissonance occurs when our attitudes or our attitudes and behaviors don't align. We also know that we don't like the uncomfortable feeling of tension that cognitive dissonance produces, so the question is: How do we change it? In order to reduce cognitive dissonance, you have one of three options:

1. Change your behavior so that it is now in line with your cognitions/attitude,

2. Change your cognition/attitude to make it consistent with your behavior,

3. Add another cognition/attitude that helps justify your behavior and therefore does not leave you feeling bad about engaging in the behavior.

Watch the video *Cognitive Dissonance* for a review of this topic and some helpful examples.

Cognitive Dissonance

Adaptive Pathway 13.2: Cognitive Dissonance

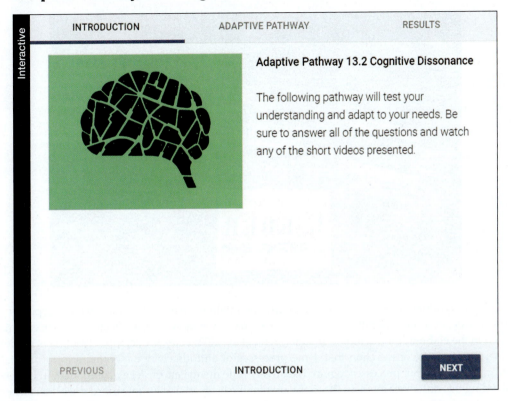

Persuasion

LO 13.6 Identify factors that influence persuasion.

Some attitudes we hold are stronger than others, but nearly all attitudes are susceptible to change. **Persuasion**, a deliberate effort to change an attitude, belief, or feeling, permeates many areas of our lives (Chaiken, 1980). **Persuasive communication** involves actively attempting to change an attitude or belief by delivering a message that advocates a specific side of an issue through a particular medium, such as a speech or an advertisement (Petty & Wegener, 2014). Whether we realize it or not, we are bombarded with persuasive messages on a daily basis through the advertising and marketing of products. Living in a digital world has only increased the methods and opportunities for advertisers. It appears that children who are growing up in a digital world are devoting even more time to media content; they are just accessing it differently than their parents did (Powers & Comstock, 2012).

There is no time where we are more inundated with persuasive messages than during the year preceding a presidential election. Persuasive techniques have become more plentiful and sophisticated in conjunction with the rise in popularity of social media platforms, such as Facebook, that have the ability to curate information. Researchers have found voters who are exposed to online environments containing media bubbles—which are defined as one-sided information environments that prevent a person from considering an issue from both sides (e.g., liberal and conservative)—are more likely to experience intense dislike for members of the opposing party (Lau et al., 2017). It is probably not surprising that this effect, which is referred to as *affect polarization*, is more pronounced when negative political ads are viewed. It has also been found that the persuasive messages encountered in one political campaign can have sustained effects and carryover to subsequent campaigns years later (Gotlieb et al., 2017).

Determining the factors that form an effective persuasive message has been a key area of research for some time. The work of Hovland and his colleagues (1953) was influential in determining the different aspects of persuasion by studying "who says what to whom." That is, who is the source delivering the message? What is the content of the message? And, to what audience is that message delivered?

persuasion

a deliberate effort to change an attitude, belief, or feeling about a particular issue or topic

persuasive communication

actively attempting to change an attitude or belief by delivering a message that advocates a specific side of an issue through a particular medium such as a speech or an advertisement

Components of an Effective Persuasive Message

While working through the above activity, you might have been thinking, "well, it depends." This is true, and the conditions under which persuasion is more or less effective have been outlined in the **elaboration likelihood model** (Flynn et al., 2011; Petty & Cacioppo, 1986). This model emerged from the observation that some processes of attitude change required a lot of mental effort, whereas other processes required relatively little mental effort. A key component in understanding this difference involves the motivation of the listener; that is, how much does the listener care to pay attention to, and *elaborate on* the central idea of the issue or position (Petty et al., 2003)? Attorneys commonly use persuasive techniques to get jury members on their side. The jury might be swayed through the **central route** to persuasion, which involves paying careful attention to strong, well-presented arguments that are personally relevant and that appeal to reason. Or they might be convinced through the **peripheral route** to persuasion, which involves evaluating an argument based on tangential cues rather than on the argument's merits. For example, a juror might be persuaded by a defense attorney's argument based on the attorney's good looks or charming personality rather than on the facts of the case. Emotional appeals can be just as persuasive as appeals to reason, but the former follow the peripheral route, while the latter follow the central route. According to the elaboration-likelihood model, we tend to be persuaded through the central route when our motivation and ability to understand and consider the persuasive message is high. When our motivation is low, however, or when we need to reach a quick decision and we don't have time to think critically, we're more likely to be persuaded through the peripheral route. Watch the video *The Elaboration Likelihood Model* for a review of this concept and an additional example.

elaboration likelihood model

a theory of persuasion that suggests the most effective persuasive technique depends on the motivation of the listener

central route

persuasive technique that focuses on strong, well-presented arguments that are personally relevant and that appeal to reason

peripheral route

persuasive technique that involves evaluating an argument based on tangential cues rather than on the argument's merits

The Elaboration Likelihood Model

Quiz for Module 13.4–13.6

1. Which of the following is *not* one of the three major components of attitudes?

   a. Behaviors

   b. Feelings

   c. Goals

   d. Thoughts

2. Which of the following is the best example of the behavioral component of an attitude?

   a. Bea feels good about herself when she recycles.

   b. Bill struggles to understand the arguments presented by both sides in a debate over a new manufacturing plant.

   c. Bob is upset when he hears a corporation plans to build a polluting plant near his home.

   d. Betty writes a letter to her senator asking for support of a law making corporations responsible for the pollution they cause.

3. Representative Jansen, a U.S. congresswoman, believes in the reproductive rights and welfare of women but voted to ban late-term abortions. Jansen feels very uneasy about the conflict between her beliefs and her behavior. She is most likely experiencing _____.

   a. the fundamental attribution error

   b. cognitive dissonance

   c. cognitive resolution

   d. the just-world hypothesis

4. Which of the following was a finding in the classic study by Festinger and Carlsmith (1959)?

   a. Those who got $1 to perform a boring task said the task was more interesting than did those who got $20.

   b. Those who got $20 to perform a boring task said the task was more interesting than did those who got $1.

   c. Paid groups said the task was less boring than nonpaid groups.

   d. Women performed the tasks for less money than men.

5. Which one of the following activities will *not* reduce cognitive dissonance?

   a. Developing new thoughts to justify the behavior.

   b. Continuing the behavior in spite of the conflicting thoughts.

   c. Changing the thought to justify the behavior.

   d. Changing the behavior to match the attitude.

6. Which communicator would likely be the most persuasive?

   a. A moderately attractive person who is an expert.

   b. An attractive person who is an expert.

   c. An attractive person who has moderate expertise.

   d. A moderately attractive person who has moderate expertise.

7. A local car insurance company advertises their products with television commercials. During those spots, there are flashy lights, attractive dancers wearing skin-tight outfits, and local celebrities talking about how they are customers of the company. The advertisement does not, however, mention any of the features or costs associated with the product. This company is attempting to earn customers through which path of processing?

   a. Tertiary route

   b. Secondary route

   c. Peripheral route

   d. Central route

Module 13.7–13.10: Social Influence

Though we may not always realize it, we often look to others for cues about how to dress, act, and even think. The social influence of others can have powerful effects—whether it is by getting someone to comply with a request, ensuring obedience, or conforming to the majority in a group setting. Let's examine different ways that the real or imagined presence of others can influence thoughts and behaviors.

Compliance

LO 13.7 **Differentiate among three approaches to gaining compliance.**

If you wanted your friend to turn down his obnoxiously loud music or to take care of your cat for you when you go on vacation, you would need to figure out how to get your friend to comply with your wishes. **Compliance** is a change in a person's behavior that occurs in response to a direct request. Hopefully, you can see how this is different than persuasion. Persuasion is about trying to change someone's *attitude* about something and is often attempted in an

The presence of others can provide important cues about how to think or behave in certain situations.

compliance

a change in a person's behavior that occurs in response to a direct request

indirect fashion. Compliance is seen as more active and involves the intentional request of another person, who is hoping to change your overt *behavior*.

Persuasion and Compliance

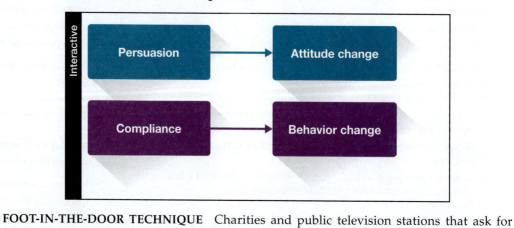

FOOT-IN-THE-DOOR TECHNIQUE   Charities and public television stations that ask for small initial contributions and then follow up with larger and larger requests rely on the **foot-in-the-door technique**, a procedure that involves asking people to comply with a small request and then making a much larger request, to raise funds. Once we've given $10 to our favorite local radio station because we strongly believe in community-supported radio, it can feel inconsistent not to give the station the $50 they ask for in their next email, so we adjust our actions to match our attitudes. Can you see how cognitive dissonance is at work here? One of the most famous foot-in-the-door studies was conducted by Freedman and Fraser in 1966, where researchers called women at home and asked them if they would answer a few questions about the household products they used (small request). Three days later, they called back again and asked if they could send a team of 5–6 men over to their house to go through their cabinets and storage places for 2 hours as part of a larger study on household products. The results of the study showed that the women who answered the questions on the phone were more than twice as likely to allow the men into their homes compared to those women who were just asked if men could come and inventory their homes (Freedman & Fraser, 1966).

foot-in-the-door technique

a compliance technique that involves asking people to comply with a small request first and then, after they agree, making a larger request

The foot-in-the-door technique is used in all kinds of sales tactics and political campaigns and has even been shown to be effective when implemented via email. For example, Guéguen (2002) asked two groups of college students to complete and mail back a 40-item survey about food habits. The experimental group was contacted 30 minutes prior to receiving the larger request and was asked for advice regarding how to send an RTF file in Microsoft Word. As a result of this small request (from a complete stranger), 76 percent of the students in this experimental group completed and *mailed back* the food questionnaire, compared to 44 percent in the control condition (which is still quite an impressive return rate).

door-in-the-face technique

compliance technique that involves making a large request first and then, when that request is refused, making a smaller request that seems reasonable in comparison

DOOR-IN-THE-FACE TECHNIQUE   The **door-in-the-face technique** is the opposite of the foot-in-the-door technique and involves making a large request first; then, when that request is refused, making a smaller request that seems reasonable by comparison. For years, one of your authors told her trainer at the gym that he is the master of the door-in-the-face technique. The conversation usually goes like this:

PAVEL: "Ok, time to kick it up a notch. This time, I want you to do 50 reps."

DR. HUDSON: "What???? Fifty reps! Are you kidding?"

PAVEL: "No. Do I look like I'm kidding?"

DR. HUDSON: "No, but I'm not sure I can do that with this much weight."

PAVEL: "OK fine.....how about 25 reps?"

DR. HUDSON: "Yes, that is much better!" (knowing she has been manipulated because she typically only does 15 reps!)

The door-in-the-face technique has been used in as many contexts as the foot-in-the-door technique. One difference, however, is that the door-in-the-face technique is only effective if the later (less costly) proposition is delivered immediately after the first, larger request (Cann et al., 1975; Guéguen et al., 2011).

LOWBALL TECHNIQUE   Car salespeople, for instance, often use the **lowball technique**, which encourages compliance by offering an attractive deal, only to change the terms of the deal later (Cialdini et al., 1978; Guéguen et al., 2002). Once you have agreed to buy the car, you then find out about all of the "additional" costs that weren't included in the initial offered price. Hidden costs in the lowball technique don't always refer to money. Let's say, for example, your psychology professor describes some interesting research he is conducting and asks if you'd be willing to help out as a research assistant one day the following week. You are flattered by the request and agree to help. Then, your professor tells you that their research involves sleep and that you'll have to stay up all night to monitor the participant's sleep patterns. Do you back out? The lowball technique typically leads people to follow through with the commitment, even though the terms of the request/offer have changed. However, according to this theory, the likelihood that you would have agreed to this request had your professor told you about the overnight work upfront would have been significantly lower.

lowball technique
a compliance technique that involves offering an attractive deal and then changing the terms of the deal later (thus increasing the overall cost of the deal)

Which Compliance Technique Is at Work?

Interactive

Read the following scenarios and drag and drop the appropriate technique to each example.

You go out to buy the newest smartphone. As you are checking out, the cashier tells you that the company requires you purchase the accident/theft insurance for an additional $100. You didn't realize this but still buy the phone.	Lowball
An adolescent asks her parents if she can go to the mall with her friend. She calls from the mall and asks if she can also spend the night. The parents agree.	Foot-in-the-door
A volunteer from a politician's campaign knocks on your door and asks if you would place a large sign supporting the candidate in your front yard. You tell them "no." Then they ask if you would place a small removable sticker on the window by your front door. You agree to do this.	Door-in-the-face

Start Over

obedience
complying with direct requests that come from a person perceived to be in a position of authority

Obedience

LO 13.8   Describe conditions that contribute to obedience.

Obedience involves complying with direct commands that come from a person in the position of authority (Milgram, 1965). The public (via the Internet) beheadings of innocent people by militant, terrorist groups; the genocides in Cambodia, Bosnia, Rwanda, and Darfur; and the Holocaust in Nazi Germany are testaments to the capability of human beings to perform extraordinarily inhumane acts. To understand how and why people obey immoral and unethical commands, Stanley Milgram (1963, 1974) conducted experiments that became some of the most famous (and infamous) studies in psychology.

Obedience to authority is an important value in the military.

In the 1960s, Stanley Milgram, a professor at Yale University, conducted a series of experiments designed to test people's obedience to an authority figure. A research subject was told to act as a "teacher," presenting a series of questions to another person in the room: the "learner." Whenever the learner gave a wrong answer, the teacher was instructed to administer an electric shock. The experimenter demanded that the teacher increase the intensity of the shock by 15 volts for every successive wrong answer, culminating in a 450-volt shock that was clearly marked on the machine as "XXX." As the voltage increased, the learner responded with loud screams of pain and begged to be let out of the room. If the subject questioned the experiment or tried to quit, the experimenter ordered him or her to continue.

What Would You Do?

Milgram designed a study where he told participants they had to deliver increasingly intense electric shocks to other people. The shocks went as high as 450 volts (this voltage would be extremely painful; some death penalty electrocutions started as low as 1,000 volts). Do you think you would be someone who would go all the way to delivering a 450-volt shock just because someone told you to?

○   Yes

○   No

| PREVIOUS | PAGE 1 OF 1 | SUBMIT |

What the participants didn't know was that Milgram's experiment was rigged: The learner was a *confederate* (someone who worked for the experimenter and pretended to be a participant), and no shocks were actually delivered. The true purpose of the experiment was to see how high a voltage subjects were willing to deliver. Milgram found that *65 percent* were willing (even though inflicting the shocks often caused them extreme discomfort) to render shock levels of 450 volts—a potentially lethal dose. Race, class, and gender had no effect on the rate of compliance; given the right set of circumstances, people were willing to inflict pain on others purely because they were told to do so by a person perceived to be an authority figure.

Milgram's experiments provided a fascinating insight into the darkest depths of the human mind and shed light on the behaviors of ordinary Germans during the Holocaust. However, the methods that he and other notable psychologists used before stringent American Psychological Association (APA) guidelines were imposed caused visible stress to participants, creating an ethical conundrum: How can psychologists study natural human impulses without the use of deception? Or, if deception is used in a psychological study, how can psychologists ensure that it does not cause undue mental stress to participants? Under the current APA Ethical Principles of Psychologists and Code of Conduct (APA, 2010), researchers must avoid the use of deception when research might reasonably be expected to cause physical harm or emotional distress.

What allowed average people to behave like sadistic torturers? Milgram determined that certain conditions encouraged participants to follow commands. For example, we generally follow the norm of obeying legitimate authority figures such as the university psychologists who directed the experiment. The experimenter seemed self-assured and accepted responsibility for the outcome of the experiment, making participants feel less responsible for their actions. The experimenter also asked the participants to increase the shocks incrementally; once participants had agreed to give the "learner" a shock of 60 volts, it became more difficult for them to refuse to administer a 70-volt shock.

Milgram's shock machine clearly showed the increasing voltages with the last switch labeled XXX.

Do You Remember?

Interactive

1 question

1. Which method of compliance was Milgram relying on when he asked the experimenter to slowly increase the intensity of the shock over time?

○ Foot in the door

○ Door in the face

○ Credibility technique

○ Lowball technique

Next

Furthermore, participants were placed in a separate room from the learner, increasing their psychological distance from the repercussions of their actions, and participants had no alternative models of behavior to follow—in other words, all they had seen anyone do was comply with the experimenter's requests, so they didn't have a model for refusing to comply. Finally, demand characteristics, or cues in the experimental setting that influenced participants' beliefs about their expected behavior, most likely played a role in participants' decisions to obey authority (see Figure 13.4).

In 2009, psychologist Jerry Burger managed to replicate Milgram's experiment within the APA ethical guidelines by stopping the procedure at 150 volts, carefully screening participants for any potential negative psychological reactions, reiterating that participants could withdraw from the study at any time, and immediately debriefing subjects at the end of the experiment. Burger's results were only slightly lower than those recorded by Milgram nearly half a century earlier and participants suffered no ill effects, suggesting that ethical research methods can achieve effective results without potentially damaging consequences (Burger, 2009).

Figure 13.4 Factors that Increase Obedience

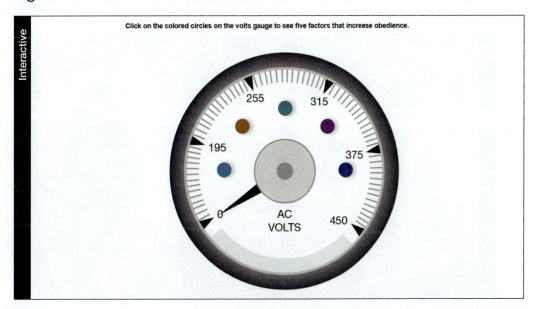

Conformity, or being one of the group, is particularly important during adolescence.

conformity

adjusting one's behavior or thinking to align or conform to a group standard

normative social influence

an explanation for conformity that results from people's desire for others' approval and longing to be part of a group

informational social influence

an explanation for conformity that results from the perceived knowledge of others brought to the group situation

suggestibility

a person's level of susceptibility to the opinions and influence of others

Conformity

LO 13.9 **Recognize factors that contribute to, and influence, conformity.**

Adjusting our behavior or thinking to align or conform to a group standard is referred to as **conformity**. We can feel the pressure to conform in a wide variety of situations, but certain conditions seem to facilitate conformity.

SOCIAL INFLUENCES ON CONFORMITY Whenever people conform by buying the latest style of clothing, joining a club, or ostracizing an outsider, social influence is at work. **Normative social influence**, or influence that draws on our desire for others' approval and our longing to be part of a group, can cause us to conform to the norms or social expectations about attitudes and behaviors that a group values. This is the experience we typically identify as "peer pressure." **Informational social influence**, or influence exerted by information that others give us, can shed new light on the objective nature of an event or situation (Baddeley & Parkinson, 2012; Deutsch & Gerard, 1955). In some cases, the behavior may be the same but come about as a result of either normative or informational social influence. If you are eating at an Ethiopian restaurant for the first time, you may not realize it is customary to eat the food with your hands. While you may not be thrilled with the idea, if you are on a first date, you will likely just eat with your hands out of a desire to be liked and make a good impression (normative social influence). Maybe you aren't on a date but are interested in the cultural experience. Therefore, you will look to others for information about how to "properly" eat with your hands (informational social influence). Normative social influence appeals to the approval motive and our desire to be liked, while informational social influence appeals to the accuracy motive and our desire to obtain correct information.

CLASSIC STUDIES IN CONFORMITY Renowned social psychologist Solomon Asch (1955, 1956) showed how **suggestibility**, or susceptibility to the opinions of others, can cause people to conform. When Asch asked participants in his experiment to match the length of a stimulus line with the length of one of three other lines presented, they had no problem performing this matching task correctly. However, when they were asked to perform the same task in a group with experiment confederates who kept offering the wrong answer, participants changed their answers to conform to those of the group 36 percent of the time. This means that about one out of every three times asked, participants knowingly supplied an incorrect answer as a result of pressures to conform. Think about the implications these results have for society. Watch the video *Conformity* to learn more about the details of Asch's studies.

Conformity: Asch Study

Both normative and informational social influence may have played a role in Asch's results: Normative social influence may have caused participants to change their answers to match the group's answers because they wanted to gain the approval of the group, and informational social influence may have made the participants think that their original perceptions were factually incorrect. After all, if ten other people say two lines are the same and you are the only one who thinks the lines are different, it seems very likely that you've missed something seen by everyone else.

Group Influence

LO 13.10 **Explain how groups have the power to influence individual behavior.**

Groups of people can influence individual behavior in powerful ways. Explicit or implicit pressures from groups can lead people to behave in uncharacteristic ways or not engage in a behavior when it would have been helpful to do so. Let's first examine how the presence of a group can affect individual performance and contribution to the group itself.

Athletes capitalize on the principle of social facilitation when attempting to win the big game.

PERFORMANCE IN GROUPS The mere presence of others can affect how well we perform a task. **Social facilitation** refers to the fact that when we're being observed by others, we tend to perform better as long as the tasks are easy or at least ones that we know well (Bond & Titus, 1983; Guerin, 1986; Zajonc, 1965). Social facilitation is evident in many aspects of sports. For example, athletes consistently have faster times (cycling, running, swimming) when racing in the presence of others versus competing alone. Social facilitation has even been used to explain why individuals eat more when eating among a group of people and that up to a point, food consumption increases as the size of the group increases (Herman, 2015).

Conversely, when people believe their individual efforts don't matter or that they are not personally responsible because they are only one member of a group, they tend to put less effort into a task, a phenomenon called **social loafing** (Harkins & Szymanski, 1989; Jackson & Williams, 1988; Kerr & Bruun, 1983; Latané, 1981; Ying et al., 2014). Social loafing may explain why some students don't like to work on group projects because they have noticed that certain students put forth very little effort and are happy to allow the other members to do the bulk of the work. Researchers have identified ways to reduce social loafing, including (1) making the task more challenging and constructed to where each group member has something unique to contribute, (2) increasing group cohesiveness, and (3) requiring identifiable personal contributions (Simms & Nichols, 2014). Student group projects can become a more enjoyable activity by having each group member submit a set of notes to the instructor for individual grading, prior to the group presenting in front of the rest of the class (Voyles et al., 2015).

DECISION MAKING IN GROUPS Groups not only have the power to affect how a particular individual behaves, but they also have the ability to shift the entire belief system of the group itself. In what has been called the **risky shift**, group decisions are often riskier than they would be if made by individuals alone (Pruitt & Teger, 1969). It is thought that this phenomenon emerges as the members of the group discuss similar opinions, which then leads to more extreme positions as a whole. This phenomenon, known as **group polarization**, strengthens resolve but can also create more extreme opinions, a situation often observed on Twitter when contentious issues such as "abortion" and "right to die" are discussed (Yardi & Boyd, 2010).

Group interactions can also lead to **groupthink** when group members' opinions become so uniform that any dissent becomes impossible (Post & Panis, 2011; Tsintsadze-Maass & Maass, 2014). Such uniformity of opinion may have been responsible for the Bay of Pigs operation in Cuba in 1961, when the members of the Kennedy administration felt so sure of themselves and their decisions that they authorized a botched attempt to overthrow the government of Fidel Castro (Janis, 1972). More recent examples of groupthink include the type of thinking that surrounds some of the newer fads in exercise. You may notice that all of a sudden, people are talking about the great new way to stay in shape. People tend to quickly flock to the newest magic bullet and become absorbed into the group exercise

social facilitation

the tendency to perform easy or well-learned tasks better when observed by others

social loafing

the tendency for people to put less effort into a task when they are part of a group because they believe their individual efforts don't matter or that they will not be held personally responsible for the outcome

risky shift

decisions made in groups become riskier than they would be if made by individuals alone

group polarization

the tendency for like-minded groups to become more extreme in their opinions and positions as a result of being part of the group

groupthink

occurs when group members' opinions become so uniform that any dissent becomes impossible

CrossFit encompasses an element of groupthink that many athletes see as a strength of the CrossFit community.

Riots, like those that occurred in Ferguson, Missouri, are often fueled by deindividuation.

Mardi Gras in New Orleans, Louisiana is a time of celebration and an example of the social identity model of deindividuating effects. Individuals may trade their individual identity for the strong social identity of the group.

deindividuation

a loss of individual identity and personal responsibility that can occur when an individual is part of a group experience

social identity model of deindividuating effects

an explanation for behavior that takes into account the shared social identity of a group and the situational group norms

culture. In fact, in 2014 Jimi Letchford credited the popularity of CrossFit to its "groupthink element." He was quoted as saying, "you suffer through the workout, but you know that you are suffering together" (Lieber, 2014). Given the heated debate that has occurred regarding whether or not CrossFit leads to excessive injuries, one could argue in this example that exercise groupthink could have both positive and negative consequences.

Preventing groupthink from occurring is easier than trying to reverse it once it has taken root. Recommendations for reducing the likelihood of groupthink include having an impartial leader, valuing the importance of exploring all possible alternatives, assigning someone to play "devil's advocate," and bringing outside experts into the group for their opinions and feedback (Janis, 1972; Tsikerdekis, 2013).

DEINDIVIDUATION AND SOCIAL ROLES   Groups can influence performance and decision making. Groups can also increase feelings of anonymity by becoming just one of many people in a group. One thing social psychology has taught us over the years is that a group situation that masks personal identity and reduces a sense of personal responsibility is a potentially dangerous combination. Being part of a group can make us feel less restrained, more physiologically aroused, and willing to act in an anti-normative fashion (Zimbardo, 1969). This process, referred to as **deindividuation**, allows us to relinquish personal responsibility and give ourselves over to the group experience. Rioting after a big sporting event or even disinhibited behavior behind a mask at a Halloween party are examples of behavior that results from deindividuation. Nowadays, the effects of deindividuation are often visible in the comments people write on social media—remarks they would be much less likely to make were the person standing in front of them.

Some researchers have questioned whether or not it is only deindividuation that produces disinhibited behavior or if it is a combination of a loss of individual identity (i.e., deindividuation) that then leads to a strong social identity that reinforces situational group norms (Hite et al., 2014; Postmes & Spears, 1998). This model is referred to as the **social identity model of deindividuating effects** (SIDE; Postmes & Spears, 1998) and takes into account the shared social identity of the group. This helps explain the fact that not all deindividuation leads to antisocial behavior. Perhaps you are at a concert or sporting event and find yourself screaming and clapping with excitement like everyone else. Had the group been smaller, you may not have been screaming so loudly, but the deindividuation produced by being "lost in the crowd" coupled with the social identity of the group (i.e., excited fans) inspired you to behave in a way that was consistent with the social norms of that situation.

Group social identities can also be artificially created when people are asked to act in accordance with a particular social role. Milgram's obedience study discussed earlier probably shares the number one spot for the "most infamous study in psychology" with a current social psychology icon, Philip Zimbardo. In 1971, Zimbardo recruited about 70 young men, mostly Stanford University college students, to participate in a study of the psychological effects of prison life. After completing diagnostic tests to ensure that each participant was psychologically healthy, 24 volunteers were offered $15 a day to participate in the two-week experiment (equal to about $89/day in the present). The participants were arbitrarily divided into two groups with the toss of a coin. Half were told to play the role of prison guards, and half were assigned the role of prisoner. The "prisoners" were booked at a real jail, blindfolded, and taken to a campus building that had been turned into a realistic prison environment with the help of a former convict. Upon arriving at the prison, each prisoner was stripped naked, searched, deloused with a spray, and forced to wear a uniform. Conversely, the prison guards were given a military-type uniform, a pair of mirrored sunglasses, and a wooden baton.

On the second day of the experiment, the prisoners staged a revolt that was quashed by the guards. Some of the guards became more aggressive, forcing the prisoners to perform humiliating tasks such as cleaning toilet bowls with their bare hands. Five prisoners had to be released early because they were so emotionally distressed that they became physically ill. Although the experiment was originally planned to last two weeks, the study was abruptly canceled on the fifth day (Zimbardo, 1971) due to the escalating abuse, harassment, and distress of the prisoners.

While there is no question that Zimbardo's Stanford Prison Study (SPE) is one of the most well-known studies in the field of psychology, its methodology and results have been heavily criticized (Banuazizi & Movahedi, 1975; Bartels, 2015). Even though "psychologically-healthy" individuals were recruited for the SPE, normal variations in personality traits are likely to have interacted with the situation to produce some of the results. In a study investigating the type of people who would be eager to participate in this type of study, Carnahan and McFarland (2007) recruited volunteers in a way similar to Zimbardo and found those who volunteered tended to score higher than average on measures of aggressiveness, authoritarianism, and social dominance. Other criticisms of the SPE have included the fact that Zimbardo himself was part of the simulation (playing the role of Prison Superintendent), providing directions to the guards, which likely influenced the guards to behave in a way consistent with what they thought the experimenter wanted (this is referred to as *demand characteristics*). Perhaps most importantly, given the current emphasis and focus the field of psychology has on replication, similarly developed prison simulation studies have failed to replicate any of the extreme findings found in the original SPE (Lovibond & Adams, 1979; Reicher & Haslam, 2006). As a result, the SPE continues to be an important example, not just for how it relates to social psychology but also for the demonstration of important concepts related to research methods and ethics.

The "guard" from the Stanford Prison Study, selected from a group of college students, was equally likely to have been assigned to the role of "prisoner." The Stanford Prison Study is one of the most well-known studies in psychology, although its methodology has been heavily criticized.

Shared Writing: Ethical Considerations in Research

Much of what we have learned about compliance and obedience has come from psychological studies that would now be considered unethical. Should psychologists be allowed to conduct research that has questionable ethics if they believe the research will lead to discovering new information about human behavior? Why or why not?

Quiz for Module 13.7–13.10

1. Behavior initiated or changed in response to a request, as opposed to a command or direct order, is an example of
   _____.

   a. compliance
   b. conformity
   c. persuasion
   d. obedience

2. Many people hang up on telemarketers, but others will listen politely to their pitches even if they are not interested in the product. Telemarketers know that anyone who agrees to listen to a pitch is more likely to buy the product, thanks to the _____ phenomenon.

   a. foot-in-the-door
   b. door-in-the-face
   c. polarization
   d. risky shift

3. Which method of compliance was at work during Milgram's obedience study?

   a. The door-in-the-face technique
   b. The foot-in-the-door technique
   c. The low-ball technique
   d. The obedience request

4. Which of the following increased the likelihood that participants would disobey in Milgram's obedience study?

   a. Having only one teacher
   b. Having two experimenters issuing the same commands
   c. Having the experimenter in the room with the teacher
   d. Having the experimenter be an ordinary man

5. In what way is compliance different from conformity?

   a. Compliance is a response to a direct request, whereas conformity is a response to indirect social pressure.

   b. Conformity involves direct group pressure for change, whereas compliance involves orders or commands.

   c. Compliance involves eliciting reaction on the part of group members, whereas conformity involves subliminal persuasion.

   d. Conformity and compliance are very similar; the distinction depends on whether one is a male or female.

6. Asch's studies showed that overall conformity to group pressure occurred about _____ of the time.

   a. one-fifth   **b.** one-half

   c. three-fourths   **d.** one-third

7. Cyberbullying is a common form of aggression among adolescents. The concept of _____ would explain the high prevalence of cyberbullying in terms of the presence of anonymity within a group situation.

   a. deindividuation   **b.** diffusion of responsibility

   c. groupthink   **d.** scapegoating

Module 13.11–13.14: Social Relationships

Our life consists of a variety of relationships: parent/child, siblings, friendships, bosses, classmates, romantic partners, ex-romantic partners, and so on. Relationships can be healthy and enrich our lives in meaningful ways, or they can be unhealthy and lead to distress—and even danger. In this module, we'll consider aspects of relationships that can lead to positive and/or negative outcomes. We are also going to examine helping behavior and discover conditions under which people are most likely to help another person. But first, let's discuss prejudice and how it develops.

With issues of prejudice and discrimination continuing to dominate our society, social psychologists attempt to understand how prejudice develops and how it can be changed.

Prejudice

LO 13.11   Describe explanations for prejudice and ways to reduce prejudice.

In recent years, we have started asking our own introductory psychology students at the beginning of the semester what they are most interested in learning about and/or what explanation for human behavior they hope to find by taking this class. While the answers are varied, the overwhelmingly popular responses involve prejudice, discrimination, and aggression. Students (and people in general) want to understand why people hate others in many cases just because they are different in some way.

prejudice

a negative, learned attitude toward individuals or groups of people

discrimination

negative behavior toward members of a group solely as a result of their membership in that group

PREJUDICE, DISCRIMINATION, AND STEREOTYPES Prejudice and discrimination are issues that you, your parents, and your grandparents have likely had to confront in some way while growing up. **Prejudice** comes from the root words *pre* and *judge* and involves a negative, learned attitude toward individuals or groups. Prejudice can be blatant (e.g., belief in the genetic inferiority of a particular race) or subtle (e.g., the defense of traditional values as a way to explain negative feelings toward a particular group seen as behaving in unacceptable ways) and is often used to justify discrimination (Pettigrew & Meertens, 1995).

     Discrimination involves negative *behavior* toward members of a group solely as a result of their membership in that group (Aronson et al., 2013). In the landmark Supreme Court case *Brown v. Board of Education*, attorneys referred to studies by social psychologists Kenneth and Mamie Clark as evidence for the tremendously damaging effects of discrimination. During the "doll test," Black children showed an overt preference for White dolls; and when asked to color pictures of children, they chose white or yellow crayons (Clark & Clark, 1947). By showing how the "separate but equal" education system fostered a sense of inferiority in children, the "doll test" helped end segregation in the United States. Watch *The Black Doll White Doll Experiment* video to see classic footage of this study.

The Black Doll White Doll Experiment

Although the detrimental effects of prejudice have been well documented, prejudice against individuals—because of race, ethnicity, gender, age, sexual orientation, weight, or other factors— still persists. Prejudice is an attitude and, if you recall from earlier in this chapter, attitudes have three components. Do you remember what they are? Does this help trigger your memory?

The ABCs of Attitudes

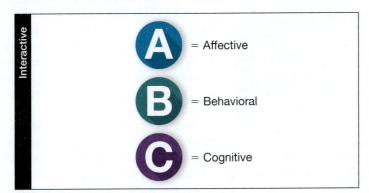

In the case of prejudice, the behavioral component is represented by *discrimination*. The emotional intensity (usually negative) that people experience when they are confronted about, and defend, their prejudice is indicative of the affective component. The cognitive component involves the stereotypes people hold that ultimately lead to prejudice and fuel discrimination. **Stereotypes**, or general beliefs about a group of people, are a type of a heuristic or mental shortcut we introduced at the beginning of this chapter. As discussed, heuristics (which include stereotypes) can be useful schemas for interpreting the world around us. Therefore, stereotypes can help us make rapid determinations about an individual, saving us cognitive time and energy. For example, if you see a man wearing a wedding ring and holding a baby, you might quickly come to the conclusion that the man is committed, mature, and caring—all positive stereotypes associated with happily married fathers. While stereotypes might provide us with some useful basic information, sometimes they can lead us to draw false conclusions and ultimately contribute to the development of prejudice and acts of discrimination.

Sometimes, the mere existence of negative stereotypes can be harmful to individuals within that group. That is, those individuals subject to stereotyping may not be able to perform as well on tasks as they normally would because of a phenomenon known

stereotype

a type of heuristic or mental shortcut involving general attitudes and beliefs about a group of people

stereotype threat

an experience where a person has the knowledge that they must work against an existing stereotype; often includes an awareness of the risk of confirming the negative stereotype as a result of the outcome of the situation

Listing nutritional information on menus has been found to have powerful effects on food choices.

as **stereotype threat**, or the knowledge that they must work against a stereotype and awareness of the risk of confirming the negative stereotype by their behavior (Steele & Aronson, 1995). For example, women who are aware of the stereotype that women are "not supposed to be good at math and science" may feel particularly pressured to perform well on a math test and disprove the stereotype, but the extra pressure they put on themselves may actually hurt their performance, leading them to inadvertently *support* the stereotype. Black students will often experience apprehension when they find themselves in evaluative educational situations due to the stereotype threat that occurs from the existing negative stereotype regarding inferior intellectual abilities.

With nearly 70 percent of Americans either overweight or obese, obesity has become a primary public health concern and a target for stereotypes. Research has confirmed the weight-based stereotypes that others hold regarding obese individuals such as "they are lazy," "they just have poor eating habits," "they lack willpower" (Brochu & Estes, 2011). Weight-based stereotype threat may actually contribute to the problem of obesity by creating an uncomfortable environment that results in obese individuals making poor choices about food and exercise. Paula Brochu and John Dovidio (2014) conducted two interesting studies examining the effects of stereotype threat and menu labelling (listing the calories in each food or beverage item at a restaurant) in overweight men and women. In the first study, they provided participants with a menu that did *not* list the calories and found that those who were overweight *and* who experienced weight-based stereotype threat ordered foods with significantly more calories than those who did not experience stereotype threat (confirming what we already know about how stereotype threat impacts behavior of those stereotyped). However, in their second study, they provided menus with the calories labelled and found that the stereotype threat was eliminated. That is, when overweight individuals are in a stereotype threat situation, presenting them with a menu that includes calorie information can serve as an external cue for self-control and lead to healthier choices. Studies such as this demonstrate the potential of social psychology to contribute to the management of real-world, public health issues.

Recall that attitudes can be either explicit (known and easy to report) or implicit (outside of your conscious awareness and control). Attitudes merely involve an evaluation of something and can be positive or negative. Stereotypes develop from attitudes but specifically involve beliefs about the similarity of people within a particular group. When people hold an **explicit stereotype**, they consciously adhere to a set of beliefs about a group of people. But many beliefs actually operate as **implicit stereotypes**, an unconscious set of mental representations about others that guide attitudes and behaviors. Because of the way our implicit memories function, priming the mind with one concept facilitates the access of associated concepts (the same way we primed you with the ABC figure in the hope it would help facilitate your memory about the components of attitudes). Studies have demonstrated that while most people consciously believe they are not racially prejudiced, many White students more quickly associate positive adjectives with White faces and negative adjectives with Black faces, suggesting that these students hold implicit negative stereotypes about Black Individuals. Black students tend to show the inverse preference (Fazio et al., 1995; Newheiser & Olsen, 2012; Nosek et al., 2002). The Implicit Association Test (IAT), developed by Mahzarin Banaji and Tony Greenwald, is used to access people's implicit attitudes and stereotypes by measuring the time required to pair certain concepts (such as "White" and "good"). The IAT has been used in a variety of contexts and has revealed people's implicit beliefs about race, gender, weight, disabilities, and sexual orientation (Agerstron & Rooth, 2011; Banaji & Greenwald, 1995; Dasgupta & Rivera, 2008; Greenwald et al., 1998, 2002; Hein et al., 2011).

explicit stereotype

a consciously held set of beliefs about a group of people

implicit stereotypes

unconscious beliefs or opinions about a group of people that influence the individual's attitudes and behaviors

FOUNDATIONS OF PREJUDICE   As social animals, humans tend to form groups and derive some portion of their identity from these groups. They treat their own group as the

ingroup and favor their group positions and members; those outside their group might be considered part of an **outgroup** (Tajfel, 1982; Wilder, 1981). When taken to extremes, ingroup and outgroup opposition can erupt into violence, as happens during a time of war or even at sporting events when conflict erupts between supporters of rival teams.

Intense emotions such as frustration, anger, and hostility can motivate people to find someone to blame as a way of managing these emotions. **Scapegoat theory** suggests that prejudice is fueled by people (typically who are part of an ingroup) directing their negative emotions and attitudes toward another group (typically an outgroup). You can see the early signs of this human behavior on the playgrounds of elementary schools, particularly when children are reprimanded for something. Children, just as adults, are quick to turn their attention to "whose fault was it?" Scapegoats are more likely to be identified under times of great stress (e.g., war, economic difficulties, acts of terrorism) since stress typically leads to strong emotions. The terrorist attacks in the United States in 2001, the subsequent years of war, and rise of Islamic terrorist groups throughout the world have been fertile ground for scapegoating. Currently, anti-Muslim sentiment is high (Alibeli & Yaghi, 2012). In fact, some citizens have been questioning whether or not Muslims should be allowed to enter, or stay in the United States, despite the fact that similar situations in history were ineffective and harmful to the vast majority of members of the scapegoated group (Myers, 2016).

In addition to emotion, competition serves as a natural springboard for prejudice and discrimination. The **realistic conflict theory** states that the degree of hostility and prejudice between groups is proportional to the scarcity of resources. That is, conflict (and resulting prejudice and discrimination) will be magnified by real competition for jobs, money, food, status, political power, etc. (Echebarria-Echabe & Guede, 2003; Esses et al., 1998; Sherif, 1966; Zarate et al., 2004).

A number of cognitive processes help people justify both their position at the "top of the food chain" and their poor treatment of those who are "below them." For instance, the **just-world phenomenon** leads us to believe the world is a fair place in which good people are rewarded and bad people are punished. If we convince ourselves that this is really the case, then we conclude that we are doing well because we are good people, while those who are suffering are simply getting what they deserve.

REDUCING PREJUDICE AND DISCRIMINATION Although we might intuitively believe that contact between hostile groups should reduce prejudice, the simple contact between two groups does not usually reverse prejudice unless the groups cooperate with each other to achieve a common goal (Allport, 1954; Dovidio et al., 2003; Pettigrew & Tropp, 2006). This principle of cooperation also works to soothe relationships in the classroom: In "jigsaw" classrooms, each student must manage one part of a project in order for the group to complete the entire assignment (Aronson & Gonzalez, 1988). Researchers Thomas Pettigrew and Linda Tropp (2008) evaluated more than 500 psychological studies devoted to reducing prejudice through intergroup contact. They concluded that three important factors are most responsible for reducing prejudice through intergroup contact:

1. Reducing individuals' anxiety about the intergroup contact.
2. Increasing individuals' empathy and perspective-taking abilities.
3. Enhancing individuals' knowledge about the outgroup.

Aggression

LO 13.12 Recognize factors that can lead to aggressive behavior, including intimate partner violence.

Whether it occurs between warring nations, feuding first graders, dueling drivers on a congested interstate, or as a result of prejudice and discrimination, any purposeful behavior intended to cause physical or psychological harm to others qualifies as **aggression**.

ingroup

the tendency for people to favor their own group positions and members. An explanation for how prejudice can develop

outgroup

the tendency for people to dislike people who are viewed as outside of their own group; an explanation for how prejudice can develop

Many groups who have been the target of prejudice have also been blamed, or scapegoated, for various negative experiences and situations.

scapegoat theory

a concept suggesting that prejudice results from the need to find someone to blame for negative circumstances; scapegoats are typically individuals associated with an outgroup

realistic conflict theory

theory explaining prejudice stating that the degree of hostility and prejudice between groups is proportional to the scarcity of resources in the environment

just-world phenomenon

the belief that the world is a fair place in which good people are rewarded and bad people are punished

aggression

any purposeful behavior intended to cause physical or psychological harm to others

Animals are most likely to display aggression when defending themselves, their territory, or their offspring.

WHAT CAUSES AGGRESSIVE BEHAVIOR? Given the pervasiveness of aggression in animals, it's no surprise that biology influences aggression. From an evolutionary perspective, we can explain aggression as a quality that has developed from a struggle for survival and resources.

Physical aggression among men has historically enabled them to defend their group and perpetuate their genes (Buss, 1989). While direct, physical aggression is consistently more common among males of all ages and in all cultures, females have a tendency to express their aggression indirectly beginning in later childhood and adolescence (Archer, 2004). Indirect aggression includes acts that do not directly involve the target of the aggression such as spreading rumors, avoiding, and attempting to persuade others not to like the target.

Aggression is influenced by both genetic and nongenetic factors. Genetic predisposition to aggression appears to stem mostly from the system of the neurotransmitter serotonin (DeWall & Way, 2014). In the brain, an overactive amygdala combined with inadequate regulation of the prefrontal cortex increases the likelihood of aggressive behavior (Lewis et al., 1986; Pavlov et al., 2012) (see Figure 13.5).

These genetic tendencies are often passed down from generation to generation (Craig & Halton, 2009; Rhee & Waldman, 2002). If a child has a violent temper, his or her siblings are likely to be aggressive, too (Miles & Carey, 1997; Rowe et al., 1999).

Hormones, particularly testosterone and cortisol, also play an important role in the expression of aggressive behavior. It was proposed some time ago that cortisol levels interacted with testosterone to determine aggressive behavior. James Dabbs and his colleagues (1991) discovered that the most violent offenders had high levels of testosterone and low levels of cortisol. This interaction between these two hormones has since been replicated and referred to as the *dual-hormone hypothesis* (Montoya et al., 2012). Recall that cortisol is thought of as the "stress hormone." Therefore, high levels of cortisol tend to biologically evoke a fear/withdrawal response, which is then in opposition to the aggressive behaviors triggered by testosterone. It is as if cortisol cancels out some of the aggressive tendencies brought about by testosterone.

While cortisol may hasten violence, alcohol and violence are commonly linked in the media. The physiological effects of alcohol can increase aggressive behavior; however, most

Figure 13.5 Aggression and the Brain

The amygdala, a small structure in the limbic system, has been found to play an important role in aggressive behavior.

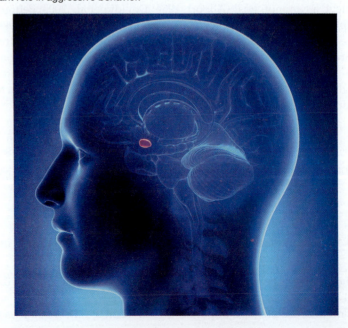

research studies are correlational in nature, therefore making it impossible to determine causality. Correlational studies have shown that neighborhoods with more bars also have more violent crime compared to neighborhoods with fewer alcohol establishments (Toomey et al., 2012). People prone to aggression are more likely to drink and become violent. Studies have demonstrated that four out of every ten violent crimes and three out of four cases of spousal abuse are committed by people who have recently been drinking alcohol (Greenfeld, 1998; Wells et al., 2011; White et al., 1993). This relationship between alcohol and aggression makes sense because alcohol is known to reduce inhibitions by compromising frontal lobe function (Hanson et al., 2011).

While some factors that influence aggression are biological, others are linked to our environments and external situations. Like many other violent criminals, Ariel Castro, who in 2013 pleaded guilty to more than 900 criminal charges (including rape and murder), claimed he had been severely physically and sexually abused as a child. The defense team for Dzhokhar Tsarnaev, one of the Boston Marathon Bomber brothers, attempted to sway the jury away from the death penalty by describing Tsarnaev's childhood as one filled with neglect from his parents. When humans and other animals experience aversive events such as pain and/or abuse, they have a tendency to repeat these patterns in their own life (Berkowitz, 1983; 1989). Hot weather also seems to contribute to hot tempers, and a number of studies point to the influence of uncomfortable heat in aggressive acts (Anderson & Anderson, 1984; Butke & Sheridan, 2010). A study that took place in Dallas, Texas, found that aggravated assault, homicide, and rape increased to a certain point as the temperatures increased (see Figure 13.6). Once temperatures reach 90 degrees, the correlation turned from positive to negative, suggesting that extreme heat may make everyone stay inside, including the criminals (Gamble & Hess, 2012).

If you have ever experienced road rage while stuck in traffic, you will likely agree with the **frustration-aggression hypothesis**, which states that frustration occurs when people feel blocked in obtaining their goals (Dollard et al., 1939). The demonstration of this hypothesis is most easily seen in young children. Before having kids, one of your authors swore she would never use the phrase "Use your words....." Well, after years of watching

frustration-aggression hypothesis

theory suggesting that aggression can occur when people feel frustrated as a result of being blocked from obtaining their goals

Figure 13.6 The Relationship Between Temperature and Aggravated Assault

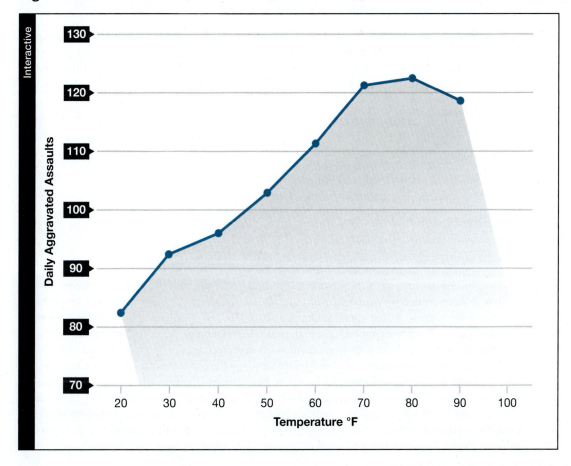

her children and her friends' children become frustrated because they couldn't do or communicate something and then lash out and hit, kick, or scratch their sibling or friend, she realized the wisdom in that phrase. As we get older, we become better at managing our frustration, but certain things such as being stuck in a traffic jam, waiting in line at the post office, or trying to help your parents work their phone or computer can push us over the frustration edge and lead us to act in aggressive ways.

Cultural constraints about acceptable levels of aggression may control how much aggression we feel free to show. In one experiment, American children displayed more verbal aggression than Japanese children in hypothetical situations of conflict (Zahn-Waxler et al., 1996). Even within the United States, acceptable levels of aggression vary regionally. Studies comparing responses to insults in the North and South revealed that the "culture of honor" prevalent in the South meant that "even small disputes become contests for reputation and social status" (Cohen et al., 1996, p. 947; Nisbett & Cohen, 1996; Vandello et al., 2008).

INTIMATE PARTNER VIOLENCE   Violence between romantic partners is a global public health concern, with numerous long-term effects for the victims and their children (Abramsky et al., 2011). Intimate partner violence (IPV) has been defined as "a pattern of purposeful coercive behaviors that may include inflicted physical injury, psychological abuse, sexual assault, progressive social isolation, stalking, deprivation, intimidation and threats" that occurs within an intimate or dating relationship between adolescents or adults (Bair-Merritt, 2010, p. 145). A global study by the World Health Organization (WHO, 2013) produced the following sobering statistics:

- Almost one third (30 percent) of all women who have been in a relationship have experienced physical and/or sexual violence by their intimate partner.

- Across the globe, as many as 38 percent of all murders involving women are committed by intimate partners.

- Women who have experienced IPV report higher rates of health problems such as:

  ○ Delivering low-birth-weight babies

  ○ Almost double the risk of depression

  ○ In some regions, 1.5 times more likely to acquire HIV

The high prevalence of IPV and overall costs to society have led researchers to attempt to identify risk factors for both partners in an effort to develop effective prevention programs. Abramsky et al., (2011) identified the following risk factors for IPV and found that the greatest risk existed when both partners had the following risk factors:

- Alcohol abuse

- Cohabitation

- Young age

- Attitudes supportive of physical violence

- Having outside sexual partners

- Experiencing childhood abuse

- Growing up with domestic violence

- Experiencing or perpetrating other forms of violence in adulthood

Despite the fact that IPV is most often discussed in terms of men being violent toward women, IPV committed by women toward men and among same-sex couples is equally problematic (Hines & Douglas, 2010a; Hines & Douglas, 2010b; Stiles-Shields & Carroll, 2015). One study indicated that 28.5 percent of men have experienced IPV at some point in their lifetime (Black et al., 2011). What do you think your immediate reaction would be if your female friend told you she was being physically abused by her boyfriend? Now how about if your friend was a male and he told you that he was being physically abused by his girlfriend? Do you think your initial reaction would be the same? Many people would admit that their reaction would be different. How would it be different? And why? YouTube contains numerous examples of social experiments related to gender and partner violence. As you might have predicted, the public's reaction tends to be very different, depending on whether a male or female is the target of the abuse: Bystanders are much more likely to intervene if a man is acting aggressively toward a woman compared to a woman behaving aggressively toward a man.

Various interventions have been developed with the goal of reducing IPV. The target group and nature of the interventions are varied and have included women in abusive relationships, adolescent/college girls (De Koker et al., 2014), refugee women (Tol et al., 2017), and fathers with a history of violence (Labarre et al., 2016). An analysis of 42 dating/intimate partner violence interventions found the majority to be effective in the short term but had difficulty maintaining their effectiveness over time (Jennings et al., 2017). Recommendations for improving the effectiveness of IPV interventions include increasing the length of the intervention, focusing on more than one type of IPV, addressing relationship skills, and, for adolescents, providing the intervention in multiple settings (e.g., community and school) and including key adults such as parents, teachers, and community members (De Koker et al., 2014).

Interpersonal Attraction and Love

LO 13.13 **Describe factors that influence attraction, love, and successful relationships.**

With 91 percent of single people in the United States having tried online dating (see Figure 13.7), there is no question that technology has changed the way people connect with one another (Smith & Duggan, 2013; Statistic Brain Research Institute, 2017). In addition to online dating, websites for finding platonic friends, smartphone apps for connecting people with common interests, and online support groups all exist as technology-based communities to connect people. In many ways, the Singles Dance and other face-to-face gatherings have been replaced by screens and video chats that now have the ability to bring people together on a global level. Technology is driving sociocultural changes in the way we develop and maintain

Figure 13.7 Online Dating Statistics

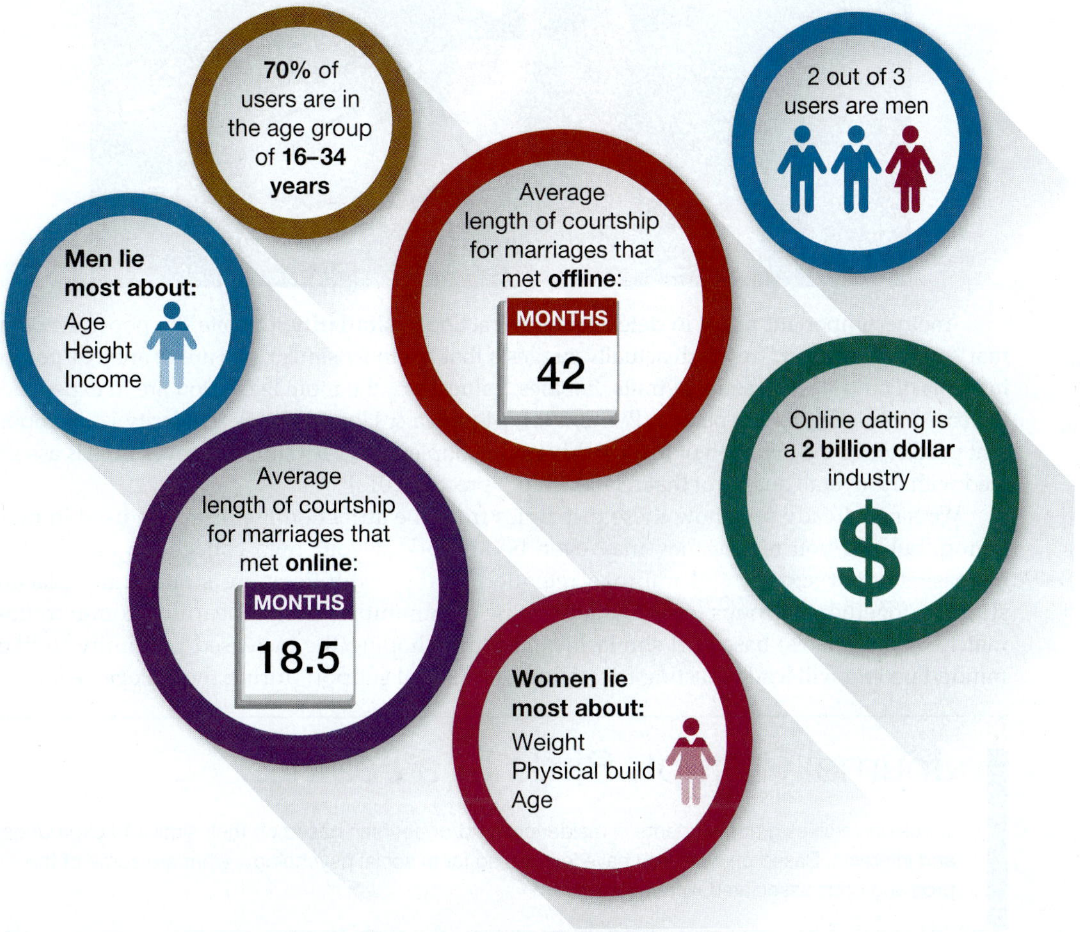

relationships with others. One thing that hasn't changed, however, is the desire of most people to find a compatible partner to share in the ups and downs of life.

FACTORS THAT INFLUENCE ATTRACTION It has long been known within social psychology that **proximity** (i.e., physical distance from someone) plays an important role in the likelihood you will be attracted to that person (Batool & Najma, 2010; Newcomb, 1956; Reagans, 2011). The reason proximity, or what is also called *propinquity*, is thought to be such an important factor in attraction involves the mere exposure effect. The **mere exposure effect** is quite accurately described by its name; that is, it is the mere exposure to other people that leads to feelings of attraction (Moreland & Beach, 1992; Zajonc, 1968). The more exposure you have to someone, the more familiarity you experience, the more likely you are to feel an attraction toward that person (Reis, 2011). This effect has been found repeatedly with various types of people, objects, and situations and is even used in marketing with respect to "product placement," which we discussed earlier in the chapter. People who are exposed to images of products develop an affinity for them without even realizing it (Ruggieri & Boca, 2013).

But what about physical attractiveness? This is a concept we certainly hear a lot about when people are looking for a partner. Watch the video *Secrets of Beauty* to learn about how scientists have determined what makes a person attractive.

proximity

the physical distance between people

mere exposure effect

theory explaining interpersonal attraction that states the repeated exposure to other people leads to feelings of attraction

Secrets of Beauty

similarity

principle of interpersonal attraction that the more two people have in common, the more likely they are to experience increased attraction to that person

Another important factor in determining attraction is **similarity**. Despite the popular notion that "opposites attract," research actually suggests that the more similar you are to another person in terms of attitudes, personality traits, hobbies, values, etc., the more likely you are to experience increased attraction to that person (Byrne, 1961; Montoya & Horton, 2013). Similarity is an important predictor of the initiation of relationships, and couples' *perceived* similarity over time is associated with the overall quality of that relationship (Sprecher, 2013).

We have already seen how these principles from the attraction literature are used in marketing, but did you realize they may even be at work at your own college? In an effort to increase student success and improve retention, many institutions are strategically placing students together in groups (e.g., living-learning communities, circular learning communities, matched roommates) based on similarities and then hoping the increased proximity to like-minded people will lead to lasting friendships and social support during the college years.

Journal Prompt: Birds of a Feather

Some universities group students in residences and/or courses based on their similar backgrounds and interests. Based on what you have learned so far in social psychology, what are some of the pros and cons associated with this plan?

THEORIES OF LOVE   Most people who have been in love will recognize at least two different aspects of love: passionate love and companionate love. **Passionate love** is defined as an intense longing for another person that has physiological, cognitive, emotional, and behavioral components (Hatfield & Sprecher, 1986; Ortigue et al., 2010; Sprecher & Regan, 1998). **Companionate love** consists of the feelings of affection and intimacy we have for another person. Passion and sexual excitement are not part of this kind of love and therefore can be applied to both romantic relationships and close friendships (Berscheid, 2010).

Robert Sternberg has spent his entire career researching love. He proposed the **triangular theory of love**, which states that love has three components: passion, intimacy, and commitment. Passion represents the physical aspect of love, which includes the emotional and sexual arousal in response to another person. Intimacy refers to the emotional connection or feeling of closeness between two people, and commitment involves the short- or long-term decisions about where the relationship is going in the future. When all three components are present, the couple is said to have achieved **consummate love** (see Figure 13.8).

Sternberg recently wrote an article outlining five stages he has progressed through during his career in his attempt to understand love and how love can be successful (Sternberg, 2013). In addition to the triangular theory, he added the importance of understanding "love as a story" as a way to explain the types of love people experience (i.e., where they are on the triangle). He suggests that we all develop our own individual beliefs and expectations of what love can be (our story), which we then seek to fulfill in a relationship (Sternberg, 1995). Most recently, Sternberg added the importance of *compatibility styles*, or the match between your preferred ways and your partner's preferred ways of using your abilities and knowledge and what he refers to as WICS. WICS stands for *wisdom, intelligence, and creativity synthesized*; together with love, it can lead to a successful and satisfying relationship (Sternberg, 2013).

MAKING RELATIONSHIPS WORK   Most people in committed relationships share the goal of longevity and happiness within the relationship. For example, few people start new relationships thinking about it ending or get married thinking they are going to get divorced. Yet, approximately 40 percent of all marriages will ultimately end in divorce (Bramlett & Mosher, 2001; Hurley, 2005). This statistic is noticeably lower than the oft-repeated message that "50 percent of marriages end in divorce" in the media. Some researchers have found that divorce rates among those born after 1980 are stable or even declining, suggesting the possibility that divorce rates could decrease over the next few decades (Kennedy & Ruggles, 2014).

John Gottman has studied hundreds of couples over his 40-year career specializing in relationships. Here are a few key pieces of advice for sustaining healthy relationships that have come out of his work (Gottman & Silver, 1999):

- Low levels of conflict don't equal a good relationship. It is more important to know how to resolve the inevitable conflicts that arise in a relationship.

- The balance of positivity and negativity in the relationship. Gottman's research has shown that a successful relationship will have 5 times more positive interaction/feeling than negativity. Remember that ratio, 5:1, and if you feel that your relationship is going downhill, try inserting more positivity into it to bring it in line with this ratio.

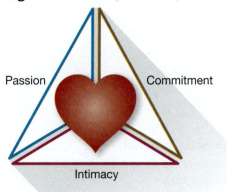

Figure 13.8 Triangular Theory of Love

Passion · Commitment · Intimacy

passionate love

a type of love that involves intense longing and desire for another person that has physiological, cognitive, emotional, and behavioral components

companionate love

one type of love; feelings of affection and intimacy for another person

triangular theory of love

a theory developed by Robert Sternberg describing interpersonal relationships using three components of love: intimacy, passion, and commitment

consummate love

a type of love that includes aspects of all other components of love (i.e., passion, intimacy, commitment)

"I love you"

"Thank you for listening to me"

"You look nice today"

5:1

"You work so hard"

"Why can you never put your dishes in the dishwasher?"

"Everybody wants to be your friend"

An interesting economic study of wedding spending and marriage duration involving more than 3,000 married and divorced couples provided some interesting correlational data (Francis & Mialon, 2014). Remember: Correlation merely refers to a *relationship* between variables and doesn't imply causation. Keeping that in mind, here are a few of the results from the study "A Diamond Is Forever and Other Fairy Tales":

- The amount of money spent on a wedding was positively correlated with divorce. Couples who spent more than $20,000 on their wedding were 3.5 times more likely to end up divorced compared to couples who spent less than half of that.

- The bigger the wedding, the lower the divorce rate. This seems counterintuitive given the last point, but this research found that couples who eloped were 12.5 times more likely to end up divorced than couples who got married with more than 200 guests in attendance. An inexpensive wedding with lots of guests was most highly correlated with marriages that were sustained.

- Take a honeymoon! In this sample, if the couples took a honeymoon, they were 41 percent less likely to get divorced.

Altruism and Helping Behavior

LO 13.14 Explain factors that can affect helping behavior.

In 2014, Malala Yousafzai, at age 17, became the youngest person ever to receive the Nobel Peace Prize for her human rights advocacy for childhood education. Despite receiving multiple death threats, which culminated in an assassination attempt by the Taliban in 2012, Malala continues to advocate for rights for girls and education for all children. What makes some people put the interests of others first, even if risking their own well-being in the process? **Prosocial behavior**, or behavior carried out with the goal of helping others, becomes **altruism** when it is carried out without concern for one's own safety or self-interest (Barasch et al., 2014; Batson, 1990; Penner et al., 2005).

If we examine altruism from a *biopsychosocial* perspective, then we realize that a number of factors are involved in explaining altruistic behavior. Neuroscience has identified areas of the brain, specifically those associated with reward and empathy that are reliably activated when individuals engage in altruistic behavior (Lozada et al., 2011; Masten et al., 2011; Waytz et al., 2012). In fact, when people are taught to be more compassionate (via guided audio instructions 30 minutes/day for two weeks), they tend to behave more altruistically and experience changes in those same areas of the brain (Weng et al., 2013).

Some people would argue that *true altruism* doesn't exist. That is, people help others because they also get something out of it (Feigin, 2014). Maybe it's the warm, fuzzy feeling you experience when you participate in a "random act of kindness"? Or, perhaps underlying your act is the hope that someone will do the same for you in return. The theory of **reciprocal altruism** suggests that people may carry out altruistic acts with the expectation of being the recipient of altruism at some point in the future or because they have been helped by altruism sometime in the past (Trivers, 1971). Maybe you like the way other people think about you when they find out about your selfless behavior? In fact, altruism has even been found to enhance our attractiveness. In one study, college women who perceived certain men to be altruistic evaluated those men as more physically and sexually attractive (Jensen-Campbell et al., 1995). Helping others does seem to help us at certain times, specifically if we are confronted with an acutely stressful experience. Researchers found that people who were intentionally put in socially stressful situations were more likely to engage in an altruistic act as a means of buffering their own stress reaction (von Dawans et al., 2012). So, doing something nice for others can help us manage our own stress!

prosocial behavior

behavior carried out with the goal of helping others

altruism

behavior carried out with the goal of helping others without concern for one's own safety or self-interest

reciprocal altruism

explanation of altruism that suggests people may only carry out altruistic acts because of the expectation of being the recipient of altruism at some point in the future or because they have been helped by altruism in the past

Despite her young age, Malala Yousafzai has modeled altruistic behavior in her advocacy for childhood education.

HELPING BEHAVIOR AND THE BYSTANDER EFFECT Clearly, many people in the world are willing to go to great lengths to help others. But, there are also situations where, despite an obvious and necessary need for help, people don't do anything. One of the most famous events cited in social psychology is the rape and murder of Kitty Genovese in 1964. Apparently, 38 neighbors stood by while she was raped, stabbed, and left to die. Even though much of this story has been refuted (Manning et al., 2007), there is no question that this tragedy led Latané and Darley (1970) to discover one of the most robust effects in social psychology—the bystander effect. The **bystander effect** refers to a situation where someone requires help and predicts that the greater the number of bystanders present, the less likely any individual bystander is to help the person in need. Darley and Latané (1968) performed studies that suggested that most people intervene to help another person having an epileptic seizure when they believe they are the only person who can hear—and help—the seizing individual. If they believe other people can also hear the person in need, they are less likely to help. The explanation for this behavior involves what psychologists call **diffusion of responsibility**. The more people who witness the same event, the more likely each person is to *diffuse the responsibility*, or assume that somebody else is going to take action.

In 2011, a group of researchers conducted a meta-analysis, where they statistically examined all of the bystander studies from the 1960s until 2010. They confirmed that bystanders in critical situations reduce helping responses (Fischer et al., 2011). They also discussed some less well-known, and even counterintuitive, characteristics of bystander situations. For example, bystanders are *more* likely to jump in and help in dangerous situations (compared to nondangerous situations) when there are other people around. This "positive bystander effect" has been found in other research (e.g., Fischer & Greitemeyer, 2013), where it was suggested that bystanders act so fast because potentially dangerous situations are recognized and processed more quickly. Furthermore, the physical support of others helps to decrease the bystander's perceived negative consequences of intervening. But, what about less serious situations? What determines whether or not others will help?

STEPS TO HELPING IN AN EMERGENCY Latané and Darley (1970) described how people go through five decision-making steps before they decide to help someone in an emergency. The following video is a good illustration of how subtle differences in personality or the environment can affect whether or not a person is willing to intervene and help a complete stranger. After watching the video *The Bystander Effect*, test your knowledge of the steps by completing the interactive activity below.

The Bystander Effect

Have you ever had an experience where you are watching something happen and have a feeling you should intervene but don't because there are a number of other people around? Were you assuming someone else would do something?

bystander effect

occurs in situations requiring help where the greater the number of bystanders present, the less likely any individual bystander is to help the person in need

diffusion of responsibility

theory suggesting the more people there are witnessing the same event, the more likely each person is to *diffuse the responsibility*, or assume that somebody else is going to take action

The Stages of Helping

Place the stages of helping in the correct order, and note the reason helping may be blocked at each decision point.

Stage Number	Stage of Helping	Reasons Helping May Be Blocked
1	Notice the event	Observer is distracted and in a hurry.
2	Interpret the event as an emergency	Observer looks to others for clues; no one appears worried.
3	Assume responsibility	Observer diffuses responsibility.
4	Know appropriate form of assistance	Observer lacks skills or knowledge to help.
5	Implement decision to help	The personal cost of helping may be too high.

Start Over

Quiz for Module 13.11 — 13.14

1. Prejudice is a(n) _____ , whereas discrimination is a(n) _____ .
   a. behavior; attitude
   b. hatred; dislike
   c. attitude; behavior
   d. dislike; hatred

2. Increased contact between two warring groups has a tendency to _____ .
   a. solidify preexisting stereotypes and prejudice
   b. prevent prejudicial beliefs from worsening
   c. showcase similarities between the groups and reduce prejudice
   d. reinforce the belief that the out-group is homogenous

3. Which of the following explains why a person may become aggressive?
   a. Genetic predisposition
   b. Alcohol
   c. Excessive heat
   d. All three factors can lead to aggressive behavior.

4. Which of the following is considered a risk factor for intimate partner violence?
   a. Experiencing abuse as a child
   b. Low self-esteem

   c. Listening to music with violent lyrics
   d. Marrying at a young age

5. All of the following are Sternberg's components of love *except* _____ .
   a. commitment
   b. intimacy
   c. loyalty
   d. passion

6. Graycen was walking alone through the mall and suddenly experienced an epileptic seizure. She would be most likely helped if _____ .
   a. the place was crowded with more than 25 people
   b. one person was in the area
   c. a dozen people were in the area
   d. four to five people were in the area

7. A car crash woke John from his afternoon nap. When he looked out his apartment window, he saw several people milling around two smashed cars. He decided not to dial 911 because he assumed someone had already called. John's reaction is an example of _____ .
   a. the bystander effect
   b. pluralistic compliance
   c. obedience to authority
   d. conformity to social norms

Module 13.15: Piecing It Together: Cyberbullying

LO 13.15 Analyze how the cross-cutting themes of psychology and specific social psychological principles relate to cyberbullying.

Bullying has been an important area of concern for teachers, parents, and psychologists for a long time. Over the past decade, as we have come into the digital age, *cyberbullying* has emerged as a serious issue that has resulted in tragic outcomes. Ryan Halligan, Megan Meier, Tyler Clementi, and Amanda Todd are just a few of the names you may recognize of teenagers who committed suicide, presumably as a result of cyberbullying. As of 2011, 95 percent of all adolescents aged 12–17 were online, with 80 percent using social media (Madden et al., 2013). It is likely that those numbers are even closer to 100 percent today.

Cyberbullying has been defined as any behavior performed through electronic or digital media by individuals or groups that repeatedly communicate hostile or aggressive messages intended to inflict harm or discomfort on others (Tokunaga, 2010). Two of the most notable technological advances influencing cyberbullying are the Internet and the cell phone (Kowalski et al., 2012).

Cyberbullying shares a number of characteristics with *traditional* bullying; however, a reporter for MSNBC articulated an important difference when he stated: "Kids can be cruel. And kids with technology can be cruel on a world-wide scale" (Sullivan, 2006). The availability, anonymity, and ease with which people can bully others through the use of technology are what make cyberbullying particularly dangerous.

Here are just a few statistics:

- According to the Cyberbullying Research Center, research from 2004–2014 indicates that on average, 25.2 percent of middle and high school students have experienced cyberbullying at some point in their life.

- An average of 16.6 percent of these students acknowledged that they have cyberbullied someone at some point in their lifetime.

- The 2014 Annual Cyberbullying Report released by *Ditch the Label* in the UK indicates that 70 percent of young people have been victims of cyberbullying, and 37 percent experience it on a very frequent basis.

- According to the Pew Foundation (2013), 95 percent of teen social media users report that they have witnessed cruel behavior on social media and seen others do nothing about it.

- Cyberbullying can occur via email, text, and/or social networking. The social networking sites most frequently mentioned as problematic include Facebook, Ask.FM, and Twitter.

- CyberBullyHotline.com states that 20 percent of the kids who are cyberbullied think about suicide, and 1 in 10 of those kids attempt suicide. Cyberbullying appears to be more strongly related to thoughts about suicide compared to traditional bullying (Gini & Espelage, 2014).

As you read these statistics, you are likely left with many questions. The following sections will examine the issue of cyberbullying from a variety of perspectives and give you an opportunity to consider how psychology may be able to help those affected by cyberbullying.

Cultural and Social Diversity

- Are certain groups of people more likely to be victims of cyberbullying?
- What about other cultures—does cyberbullying happen as much in other countries as it does in the United States?

Unfortunately, kids who are perceived as different from their peers are often the subject of bullying. There is significant overlap between cyberbullying and school bullying (Schneider et al., 2011), and two groups of individuals who tend to experience higher rates of bullying include lesbian, gay, bisexual, or transgender (LGBT) youth and children/adolescents with disabilities.

Journal Prompt: Theories of Bullying

When you think back to the discussion of stereotypes and prejudice, which theory could explain the onset and maintenance of bullying? (Realistic Conflict Theory; Ingroup/Outgroup Bias; Frustration Aggression Hypothesis). Explain how the theory you chose can be applied to bullying.

How might a person's culture affect the extent of cyberbullying? Cyberbullying has been documented in many countries (e.g., Japan, China, Taiwan, Singapore, Norway, Spain, Canada, Australia), but the question may be more about the prevalence of cyberbullying and if there are any aspects within a particular culture that may affect how much or how little bullying takes place. For example, consider Japan and the United States. One might assume that Japan would have higher rates of cyberbullying because they are more technologically advanced than the United States but, in fact, Japan was found to have lower rates of cyberbullying (Barlett et al., 2014).

Retrieval Practice: Cultural Differences

Fill in the blanks below with the most appropriate answer and then check to see if you are correct.

In considering why Japan might have lower rates of cyberbullying compared to the United States, think back to our discussion about attitudes and the *attributions* people make for events. Attributions are either situational or dispositional. Now, recall that western cultures tend to be more [_____], whereas Eastern cultures are more [_____].

WORD BANK
- collectivistic
- individualistic

| Start Over | Check Answers |

Individuals in collectivistic cultures (like Japan) tend to see themselves as part of the overall group and are much more likely to think about themselves within the larger social context (e.g., "If I do something mean or bad to someone else, how will this reflect on my family and community?") As a result, people from collectivistic cultures are also more likely to assume situational factors as the cause for certain events (Masuda & Nisbett, 2001). Therefore, after a perceived attack, American individuals would be more likely to make a dispositional attribution, whereas Japanese individuals would tend to favor a situational explanation. A situational explanation (e.g., that person might just be having a bad day) coupled with their awareness of how their actions can affect their broader social circle, may explain why students in Japan are less likely to exhibit aggression via cyberbullying.

Variations In Human Functioning

- Why is cyberbullying such a problem among adolescents?
- What are the risk factors for being cyberbullied?
- Are there any risk factors for *becoming* a cyberbully?

Cyberbullying can happen at any age; however, the research has shown that adolescents, particularly children aged 12–14, are most susceptible to victimization (Takunaga, 2010). Some reports and websites suggest that girls are more likely than boys to be both the perpetrators and victims of cyberbullying.

You might be wondering if the research has identified other risk factors (for perpetrators or victims). Click on the table to reveal risk factors and see whether they are characteristic of the victim, the perpetrator, or both.

In many cases, individuals are both perpetrators and victims of cyberbullying and it has been shown that *all* of the risk factors listed apply to them (Sourander et al., 2010).

Risk Factors of Cyberbullying

	Victim	Perpetrator
Interactive	Living in a family with anything other than two biological parents	Having less parental involvement or problems at home
	Extent to which the victim perceives difficulty with peers	Hyperactivity
	Emotional (depression/ anxiety) and peer problems	Conduct/ behavioral problems
	Headaches	Low prosocial (helpful) behavior
	Recurrent abdominal pain	Frequent smoking and drunkenness
	Sleeping difficulties	Headaches
	Not feeling safe at school	Not feeling safe at school

Click the Next button to see risk factors for victims and perpetrators of cyberbullying.

15 of 15   Previous   Next

Journal Prompt: Deindividuation and Cyberbullying

Now that you are familiar with the statistics, cultural differences, and risk factors related to cyberbullying, let's use what you have learned in this chapter to attempt to explain why cyberbullying has become such a problem. How does the concept of *deindividuation* relate to cyberbullying?

Research has shown that anonymity is one of the strongest predictors of the frequency of cyberbullying behavior (Barlett, 2013). *The bystander effect* can also be a factor in cyberbullying. A statistic presented earlier is a good example of the bystander effect.

- According to the Pew Foundation, 95 percent of teen social media users report that they have witnessed cruel behavior on social media and have seen others do nothing about it.

Retrieval Practice: Why People Don't Help

Interactive

Fill in the blank below with the most appropriate answer and then check to see if you are correct.

The bystander effect is when people, who are part of a group, witness something that requires intervention, but do nothing about it. What is another term used to describe this phenomenon?

[   ]

Start Over   Check Answers

Now that you are aware of some of the reasons behind cyberbullying, does it give you any ideas of how you could possibly intervene? Schoolwide antibullying interventions appear to be the most effective (Pearce et al., 2011), and one strategy within interventions involves education about the bystander effect and offering strategies to mobilize bystanders to step in and help victims (Desmet et al., 2012). Students from Cupertino High School may have found an inventive way to do just this. Four students worked together to develop *iStander,* an app that student bystanders can use to alert administrators, parents, and other friends when bullying occurs. Would you be more willing to report bullying if you could do it quickly and quietly, without the bully aware of your reporting? This question is one that will likely be answered through research. Once a school puts an intervention in place or a traumatized individual seeks treatment, how do we actually know if those interventions have been successful? The following "Research Methods" section will explore some of the research issues related to studying cyberbullying.

Research Methods

- What should you do if you know someone is being cyberbullied?
- How can we know if prevention/intervention programs are effective?

One of the important methodological issues to take into consideration when conducting research on cyberbullying is:

- How cyberbullying is operationally defined:
  - You can find wide ranges of statistics regarding the prevalence of cyberbullying. Part of the reason for this discrepancy has to do with the way the researchers have defined and then asked about cyberbullying experiences.

Assessing Cyberbullying: The Importance of Choosing Your Words Carefully

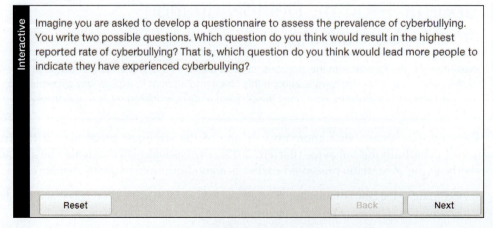

Imagine you are asked to develop a questionnaire to assess the prevalence of cyberbullying. You write two possible questions. Which question do you think would result in the highest reported rate of cyberbullying? That is, which question do you think would lead more people to indicate they have experienced cyberbullying?

Reset   Back   Next

Ethics

- What are some of the potential challenges with conducting research on cyberbullying?
- What are some of the ethical and privacy issues relevant to cyberbullying?

As with any research, ethical conduct needs to be at the forefront of the research design process. Sometimes, balancing ethics and a research study that will provide unbiased information can be challenging. One important ethical issue to consider when researching cyberbullying is informed consent.

- If you were interested in assessing the prevalence of cyberbullying in a particular school and all of the students knew (and agreed) that their cell phone and computer activity would be monitored, how do you think this would affect their behavior?
- *Reactivity* is a term used to describe how people tend to change their behavior when they know they are being watched/monitored/assessed. What impact could reactivity have on the prevalence rates of cyberbullying?
- Do you think it would be ethical to monitor students' social media accounts without their knowledge?
  - One school district in California hired a consulting firm to monitor 14,000 students' social media accounts. They tracked public postings looking for language about truancy, drug use, suicide, and bullying. While it is technically legal for the school to take this action, some students and parents have suggested that this policy interferes with freedom of speech.

Journal Prompt: Privacy Concerns and Cyberbullying

After reading about cyberbullying, do you think it is a good idea for schools to monitor students' social media accounts? Explain your answer.

Quiz for Module 13.15

1. What percentage of teen social media users report observing cyberbullying online?
   a. 25 percent
   b. 50 percent
   c. 75 percent
   d. 95 percent

2. _____ cultures tend to have the _____ rates of cyberbullying.
   a. Individualistic; lowest
   b. Collectivistic; lowest
   c. Collectivistic; highest
   d. Egalitarian; highest

3. Which of the following is a risk factor for being both a perpetrator and a victim of cyberbullying?
   a. Not feeling safe at school
   b. Hyperactivity
   c. Abdominal pain
   d. Sleeping difficulties

4. A researcher plans to test the effectiveness of a new cyberbullying reporting app. She randomly selects one eighth-grade class to receive training on how to install and use the app. The students are assured the reporting is anonymous. The other eighth-grade class is not told about the app. The researcher then measures the rates of cyberbullying in both classes over the next 3 months. This study utilizes which type of research design?
   a. Cross-sectional
   b. Correlation
   c. Experiment
   d. Case study

5. Ethical research involves obtaining informed consent. However, sometimes people change their behavior if they know their behavior is being monitored. What is this phenomenon called?
   a. Self-monitoring
   b. Relative behavior
   c. Selectivity
   d. Reactivity

Summary: Social Psychology

Module 13.1–13.3: Social Cognition

Social psychology is the scientific study of how thoughts, feelings, and behaviors of individuals are influenced by the presence of other people. Social psychologists are interested in **social cognition** or how people think about others. They want to understand how impressions of others are formed, an area of social cognition referred to as **person perception**. People use heuristics, or mental shortcuts, to reduce the amount of information in the environment and make efficient decisions and judgments. Some examples of heuristics include the **availability heuristic**, which involves using information easily recalled to make decisions or judgments. **Social categorization** refers to grouping people or things based on their physical characteristics in order to make quick decisions about them, and **implicit personality theory** relies on the beliefs we hold about the relationship between certain personality traits and prototypical behaviors.

Attributions involve explanations of other people's behaviors and can be **dispositional** (the behavior is attributed to an individual's personal characteristics) or **situational** (the behavior is attributed to features of the external situation). Because we are often making quick attributions with limited information, our explanations of behavior may be biased. **The fundamental attribution error** refers to our tendency to attribute other people's behavior to dispositional (internal) rather than situational (external causes). **The actor-observer bias** involves two people and refers to our tendency to attribute our *own* behavior to situational causes while we attribute the other person's behavior to their personal disposition. When it comes to our own behavior, **the self-serving bias** states that we take personal credit for our successes and tend to blame our failures on external events out of our control.

Module 13.4–13.6: Attitude Formation and Attitude Change

An **attitude** is an evaluative belief or opinion about someone or something and can be either **explicit** (conscious) or **implicit** (unconscious). Attitudes can affect behaviors as a result of **cognitive dissonance**, which is when there is mismatch between two conflicting attitudes or between an attitude and a behavior. In an effort to reduce the uncomfortable feelings produced by cognitive dissonance, individuals will attempt to alter their beliefs, change their behavior, or develop new beliefs consistent with their behavior. Behaviors can also influence attitudes. **Self-perception theory** describes how people sometimes look to their own behaviors to inform them about their attitudes.

Persuasion involves a deliberate effort to change someone's attitude. **Persuasive communication** involves the attempt to change attitudes through a particular medium such as a speech, commercial, or social media. The **elaboration likelihood model** takes into account the motivation of the listener. Listeners who are highly motivated or interested in a topic are most likely persuaded through the **central route**, which involves a strong, well-presented message that appeals to reason. The **peripheral route** to persuasion involves tangential cues, such as credibility and attractiveness of the speaker, and is the most likely route for individuals with low motivation or interest in the topic.

Module 13.7–13.10: Social Influence

Persuasion involves attempting to change a person's attitude about something, whereas **compliance** involves a change in a person's behavior that comes as a result of a direct request. Many techniques exist to gain compliance from others such as the **foot-in-the-door technique**, a procedure that involves asking people to comply with a small request, which is then followed by a much larger request; the **door-in-the-face technique**, which starts with a large and unreasonable request and, when denied, is followed by a smaller request; and the **lowball technique**, which starts with a very attractive deal and then changes the terms of that deal after a person has already agreed to it. **Obedience** involves complying with direct requests that come from a person in the position of authority. **Conformity** involves the adjustment of thinking or behavior to fit a group standard. **Normative social influence** leads to conformity from a need to be part of a group whereas **informational social influence** involves conforming to others because of the perceived knowledge they bring to a situation.

The presence of a group can have powerful effects on attitudes and behaviors. **Social facilitation** refers to the fact that when we're being observed by others, we tend to perform better as long as the tasks are easy or ones that we know well. **Social loafing** refers to the experience where people who are part of a group tend to exert less effort overall because they don't see themselves as personally responsible. When it comes to making decisions as a group, groups can experience a **risky shift**, where the group's decision is riskier than it would have been if individuals made the decision on their own. **Group polarization** occurs as groups with similar opinions move to more extreme views over time. Among groups with uniform opinions and views, **groupthink** may occur, which describes the experience where groups are so rigid in their opinions that the social pressures make any dissent from the group impossible. Groups can also encourage extreme behavior through the process of **deindividuation**, or the perceived loss of identity as a result of being part of a group. The **social identity model of deindividuating effects** takes into account the shared social identity of the group suggesting that disinhibited behavior only occurs when there is a combination of a loss of individual identity, leading to a strong social identity reinforced by the group norms.

Module 13.11–13.14:   Social Relationships

Many relationships are hindered by **prejudice**, a negative attitude toward particular individuals or groups, potentially leading to **discrimination**, or acting in a negative way toward members of a group solely as a result of their group membership. **Stereotypes** are general beliefs about people based on their group membership. People can hold either **explicit stereotypes**, which involve the conscious awareness of a set of beliefs about a group of people, or **implicit stereotypes**, which involve unconscious mental representations about others that guide attitudes and behaviors. In some cases, **stereotype threat**, or the knowledge that one belongs to a particular stereotyped group, creates an environment conducive to failure. Explanations for prejudice include the "us versus them" or **ingroup** versus **outgroup** theory as well as the **scapegoat theory**, which suggests that prejudice is fueled by people (typically who are part of an ingroup) directing their negative emotions and attitudes toward another group (typically an outgroup). The **realistic conflict theory** proposes that prejudice is proportional to the availability of resources. The **just-world phenomenon** is a cognitive process that rationalizes prejudice where people believe that good people are rewarded and bad people are punished. **Aggression** is defined as any purposeful behavior intended to cause physical or psychological harm to another person. The **frustration-aggression hypothesis** specifically highlights that people have a tendency to exhibit aggression when they feel they are blocked from achieving their goals.

Social psychology also examines a variety of social relationships and the conditions that give rise to healthy and unhealthy relationships. **Proximity** and **similarity** to a partner are two characteristics that lead to interpersonal attraction. **The mere exposure effect** suggests that the more exposure we have to someone, the more likely we are going to feel attracted to them. Love has a number of different components such as **passionate love**, which involves an intense longing for another person and **companionate love**, which includes the feelings of affection and intimacy toward another person. The **triangular theory of love** adds the dimension of commitment to intimacy and passion. **Prosocial behavior**, behavior carried out with the goal of helping others, becomes **altruism** when it is carried out without concern for one's own safety or self-interest. **Reciprocal altruism** suggests that people may carry out altruistic acts with the expectation of being the recipient of altruism in the future or because they have been helped by altruism in the past. The **bystander effect** occurs in situations where, despite a number of people watching someone who needs help, no one takes the initiative to help. The more people present, the more **diffusion of responsibility**, or thinking that someone else will take care of it, leading to less help for the person in need.

Chapter 13 Quiz

1. Realistic conflict theory suggests that prejudice arises from _____ .

   a. learned behavior

   b. self-fulfilling prophecies

   c. social categorization

   d. competition over scarce resources

2. Conformity may result from normative social influence, which involves _____ and/or informational social influence, which refers to _____ .

   a. the desire to be part of a group and gain approval; presenting information that can change an opinion

   b. presenting information about the most common response; the overall number of people sharing the same opinion

   c. the overall number of people sharing the same opinion; presenting information about the most common response

   d. presenting information that can change an opinion; the desire to be part of a group and gain approval

3. Tristan became aware that a fellow student had become a victim of bullying. Tristan did all he could to help his classmate, even though he didn't know him well and didn't expect any reward in return. Tristan's behavior is an example of _____ .

   a. altruism

   b. observational learning

   c. role playing

   d. diffusion of responsibility

4. Mental shortcuts used to reduce complex information from the world around us are called _____ .

   a. biases

   b. implicit associations

   c. embodied cognitions

   d. heuristics

5. The fundamental attribution error involves overestimating _____ influences when explaining another person's behavior.

   a. dispositional

   b. situational

   c. external

   d. unconscious

6. Garrett has a tendency to take credit for his good actions, but he attributes his mistakes to factors beyond his control. This is an example of the _____ .

   a. self-serving bias

   b. just-world hypothesis

   c. actor-observer bias

   d. fundamental attribution error

7. You are playing baseball and miss catching a ball that should have been easy to catch. Others watching you are likely to think you aren't good at playing baseball, whereas you are likely to point out that the sun was in your eyes. This is an example of which type of attribution?

   a. The just-world hypothesis

   b. The actor-observer bias

   c. The self-serving bias

   d. The fundamental attribution error

8. A dealer persuades a customer to buy a new car by reducing the price to well below that of his competitors. Once the customer has agreed to buy the car, the terms of the sale are shifted by lowering the value of the trade-in and requiring the purchase of expensive extra equipment. Now the car costs well above the current market rate. This is an example of the _____ technique.

   a. lowball

   b. foot-in-the-door

   c. that's not all

   d. door-in-the-face

9. Roberta is trying to decide whether to vote for a political candidate. Based on what she has read about him, she has concluded that he is not qualified for the position, but she agrees with his political positions. Also, she trusts him and likes his decisive personality. Her trust of the candidate represents the _____ component of her attitude toward him.

   a. cognitive

   b. behavioral

   c. situational

   d. affective

10. In Festinger and Carlsmith's (1959) classic study on cognitive dissonance, participants who were paid $20 for doing a boring task, in contrast to those who were paid $1 for doing the same task, _____ .

    a. liked the task less

    b. liked the task more

    c. liked the task equally as much

    d. were more likely to tell their friends to do the task

11. Which of the following would result in cognitive dissonance?

    a. Violent video games can promote violence; I let my 7-year-old play video games.

    b. Dresses are feminine; Kim Kardashian wears dresses.

    c. Wearing glasses is dignified; a respected political leader wears glasses.

    d. Orange juice is healthy; I drink orange juice.

12. For months, you have been thinking that you need to lose weight to be healthier, yet you are still eating fast food every day. Which of the following approaches will reduce the cognitive dissonance you are experiencing?

    a. Stop eating fast food

    b. Deciding that rather than losing weight, you need to work on being happy with your body the way it is

    c. Telling yourself that this is a particularly stressful time and you'll cut back on fast food next month

    d. All three approaches would reduce cognitive dissonance.

13. Political and other messages should be simple so that the audience can focus on and understand the content without distractions. This example is assuming which type of processing suggested by the elaboration likelihood model?

    a. Under route

    b. Peripheral route

    c. Classic route

    d. Central route

14. Which message is likely to be the most persuasive?

    a. A message that presents only one side of the argument and where it is *not* obvious that it is meant to persuade

    b. A message that presents only one side of the argument and where it is obvious that it is meant to persuade

    c. A message that presents both sides of the argument and where it is obvious that it is meant to persuade

    d. A message that presents both sides of the argument and where it is *not* obvious that it is meant to persuade

15. A person asks you to volunteer to counsel delinquent youth at a detention center for two years. When you refuse, she asks if you could supervise them during a trip to the zoo. She is using the _____ technique.

    a. door-in-the-face

    b. foot-in-the-door

    c. bait-and-switch

    d. lowball

16. Rhianna works in a retail clothing store. Her boss pointed out that she rarely offers help to the overweight customers. When asked about this, Rhianna denied having any negative attitudes toward people who are overweight. Rhianna is verbally expressing a(n) _____ attitude, but her behavior suggests that her _____ attitude may be different.

    a. self-serving; real
    b. implicit; explicit
    c. explicit; implicit
    d. explicit; private

17. What is the difference between obedience and conformity?

    a. Obedience is an indirect request, whereas conformity is a direct request.
    b. In obedience, there is a difference in status between the one who obeys and the one who makes the request.
    c. Conformity requires strict adherence to the rules, whereas obedience does not.
    d. In conformity, there is a perceived difference in status between the one who conforms and the group.

18. People are more likely to be obedient to authority if _____.

    a. no one else is around to see them
    b. they see other people behaving in disobedient ways
    c. the authority figure is perceived as an expert
    d. they are unsure of how to behave

19. Vince has always believed children deserve the best prenatal care available. During a class discussion, he hears the first of several speakers express very negative attitudes toward spending tax money on prenatal care for the poor. When it is his turn to speak, he voices an opinion more in keeping with the previous speakers. Vince's behavior is an example of _____ .

    a. obedience
    b. persuasion
    c. compliance
    d. conformity

20. Which of the following terms is associated with social cognition?

    a. Actions based on emotions
    b. Thinking about others
    c. Obedience to authority
    d. Objective thinking

21. A teacher decides against assigning group projects in which all group members get the same grade. What social-psychological phenomenon might the teacher be concerned about?

    a. Social loafing
    b. Conformity
    c. Social influence
    d. Social facilitation

22. When members of a group discuss similar opinions about a topic, their views on the topic tend to become even more extreme. This phenomenon is referred to as _____ .

    a. groupthink
    b. group polarization
    c. the risky shift
    d. the all-or-nothing law

23. Prejudice is to discrimination as _____ .

    a. behavior is to attitude   b. neutral is to negative
    c. attitude is to behavior   d. stereotype is to feeling

24. Person perception involves the study of _____ .

    a. how impressions of other people are formed
    b. the factors that influence perceptions of a group of people
    c. the behaviors con artists use to manipulate people
    d. why people act differently in different situations

25. Research has shown that males tend to exhibit more _____ aggression, whereas females tend to display more _____ aggression.

    a. direct; indirect   b. verbal; physical
    c. emotional; verbal   d. indirect; direct

26. Intimate partner violence refers to aggressive behavior between which groups of people?

    a. Women and their female intimate partners
    b. Men and their male intimate partners
    c. Men and their female intimate partners
    d. All three groups

27. The mere exposure effect is the tendency of people to _____ .

    a. overestimate their abilities to have predicted an event once the outcome is known
    b. feel more positive toward a person, item, product, or other stimulus that they have seen often
    c. believe that a statement is true simply because it has been repeated a number of times
    d. be unable to distinguish between actual experiences and what they have been told

28. John Gottman has studied relationships for more than 40 years. Which of the following has he identified as an important predictor of a successful marriage?

a. Making sure that every negative interaction is followed by a positive interaction

b. Rarely having conflicts about money

c. Having five times more positive interactions than negative ones

d. The amount of money you spend on your wedding

29. All of the following are decision points in helping behavior *except* _____ .

a. knowing what to do in the situation

b. interpreting the event as an emergency

c. noticing the event

d. diffusion of responsibility

30. Which of the following descriptions best defines implicit personality theory?

a. Personal insights

b. Objective ideas about maladaptive behavior

c. The set of assumptions people have about people, their actions, and their personality traits

d. Unconscious motives for aggressive behavior

Chapter 14
Personality

 ## Chapter Outline and Learning Objectives

Module 14.1–14.2: The Psychodynamic Perspective

LO 14.1 Describe the psychoanalytic theory of personality.

LO 14.2 Identify the neo-Freudians and their contributions to psychodynamic personality theory.

Module 14.3–14.4: The Humanistic Perspective

LO 14.3 Explain the humanistic theory of personality developed by Maslow.

LO 14.4 Summarize the core concepts of the humanistic theory of personality developed by Rogers.

Module 14.5–14.6: The Social Cognitive Perspective

LO 14.5 Recognize the distinguishing features of Rotter's social cognitive theory of personality.

LO 14.6 Describe Bandura's theory of personality, including the concepts of reciprocal determinism and self-efficacy.

Module 14.7–14.10: The Trait Perspective and the Biology of Personality

LO 14.7 Distinguish the trait theories of Cattell and Eysenck.

LO 14.8 Identify the traits described in the five-factor model of personality.

LO 14.9 Recognize how biology and neuroscience have contributed to our understanding of personality.

LO 14.10 Explain how behavioral genetics and the concept of heritability have contributed to personality research.

Module 14.11: Evaluating Different Perspectives on Personality

LO 14.11 Evaluate the strengths and weaknesses of the psychological perspectives on personality.

Module 14.12–14.13: The Assessment of Personality

LO 14.12 Relate the different objective methods of assessing personality to the relevant theories of personality.

LO 14.13 Recognize the most common projective personality tests.

Module 14.14: Piecing It Together: Antisocial Personality Disorder

LO 14.14 Analyze how the cross-cutting themes of psychology and theories of personality relate to antisocial personality disorder.

What is Personality?

Your Personality

Interactive

Have you ever taken a personality quiz online that immediately gave you feedback about your "personality type"?

○ Yes

○ No

If yes, did you generally agree with the website's assessment of your personality?

○ Yes

○ No

In today's world, the term "personality" is used in various situations and contexts. The Internet is filled with self-assessments to determine your personality "type" or even your personality "color." Fashion magazines, websites, and blogs instruct us on how to "express our personalities" through clothing and music, while online dating services promise to analyze the many dimensions of our personalities to successfully find our best romantic match. But, what exactly is personality?

In psychology, personality refers to an enduring and consistent style of thinking, feeling, and behaving in the world. Spending time with friends and family members, you've probably noticed that individual people's behavior tends to remain relatively stable over time. You might have a friend who volunteers to take charge of every situation from working on a major class project to ordering pizza. You might know someone else who is painfully shy and takes a long time to "warm up" to the people around him or her. We are innately interested in, and attuned to, the ways in which people are different from ourselves and from one another. In addition, we tend to focus on the characteristics that make us different rather than those characteristics that we all share. This focus helps us to decide who we should choose as partners and friends, and it provides us with cues for interacting with specific individuals. We often make informal assessments of other people's personalities, but psychologists tend to use more formalized methods of studying personality.

In general, psychologists who study personality rely on five different sources of data, to varying degrees and in varying combinations:

- information you provide about your own thoughts, feelings, behaviors, or qualities;

- information about you provided by friends or family;

- information about specific things you have done;

- information about things that have happened to you; and

- information based on the activity in your body, such as heart rate, blood pressure, and brain activity.

In addition, psychologists interpret the data they collect through the use of two contrasting approaches. The *idiographic approach* is person-centered, focusing on how the unique parts of our personalities form a consistent whole. Studies using this approach are primarily concerned with describing and analyzing individuals' personalities. In contrast, the *nomothetic approach* focuses on finding consistent patterns of relationships among individuals' traits. For example, studying the question of whether or not all introverts enjoy being alone would require a nomothetic approach, while examining how one individual's characteristics of introversion and preference for solitude interact would be an idiographic approach. Studies that use the nomothetic approach often involve many participants and are most concerned with determining general principles and theories of behavior. Both approaches have played, and continue to play, important roles in personality research.

Whether you are taking a broad or narrow approach to studying personality, you might think that there is one "right" way to explain personality. In fact, there are a number of "right" ways to explain personality, depending on the theoretical perspective taken. As discussed in Chapter 1 (LO 1.2), there are a number of different perspectives, or schools of thought, within the field of psychology. The theory characteristic of each school of thought becomes the lens through which personality is observed and explained. So, as you read through each perspective's view of personality, try to remember the core concepts associated with each school of thought, and then predict what the proponents of that particular perspective would say about personality development.

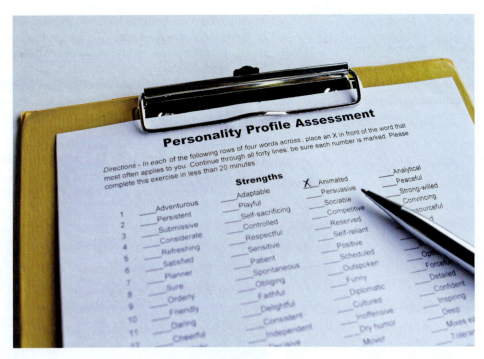

Many personality assessments or quizzes can be found on the Internet but are rarely a scientifically valid measure of personality.

Module 14.1–14.2: The Psychodynamic Perspective

As with many other topics in psychology, the understanding of personality depends on the theoretical perspective from which it is examined. The psychodynamic perspective emphasizes the role of the unconscious, which is thought to contain dynamic forces that shape personality. Psychodynamic theory has deep roots; it is the oldest of all personality theories. The seeds of modern psychodynamic theory were planted in the 1800s by the famous (or some may say, infamous) psychologist, Sigmund Freud.

Freud and the Development of Psychoanalysis

LO 14.1 **Describe the psychoanalytic theory of personality.**

Sigmund Freud pioneered the clinical approach to understanding personality. The image that many of us associate with psychological counseling—a bearded doctor asking his patient (who is usually lying on a leather couch) to "tell me about your mother"—originates here. A controversial figure who shocked Victorian Europe with his theories of sexual repression and aggression, Freud was initially ridiculed for his ideas (Gay, 1998). Today, his theories about the unconscious frequently undergo similar bashings from psychology students, and most professionals view his ideas with great skepticism. However, the influence Freud has had on the modern world is undeniable—ask any member of the public to explain a basic Freudian concept (like someone who is "anal retentive") and they will most likely be able to do so. Despite the professional skepticism toward his theory as a whole, many Freudian concepts still form the basis for modern psychodynamic personality theories.

SIGMUND FREUD: THE FATHER OF PSYCHOANALYSIS Spending most of his life in Vienna, Austria, Sigmund Freud (1856–1939) studied to become a physician with an interest in neurology. He began to see a number of female patients with inexplicable neurologic-like symptoms (e.g., paralysis, visual disorders, and persistent cough). He was first exposed to these patients, who were diagnosed with "hysteria" (derived from the condition of the "wandering womb"), by his mentor and friend, Josef Breuer. Breuer and Freud worked together to develop **psychoanalysis**, a theory of personality development and a psychological treatment that relied heavily on their own case studies and self-analysis (Freud, 1978).

Freud believed that our problems in adulthood are caused by our memories, especially the disturbing ones from childhood. These memories, according to Freud, are impossible for us to access consciously—they're buried deep in the unconscious mind. Freud thought that in order

psychoanalysis

theory and treatment of personality, originally developed by Sigmund Freud, that relies heavily on therapist interpretation of a client's unconscious desires

psychic determinism

belief, typical in the psychanalytic/
psychodynamic perspective, that
unconscious processes underlie all
conscious thoughts and actions

to understand his patients' actions, problems, and personalities, he had to access the contents of their unconscious minds. This concept—that unconscious processes underlie all conscious thoughts and actions—is known as **psychic determinism** (Brenner, 2007) and became the backbone of Freud's theory (Zimring, 2000).

Freud's structure of the mind is often compared to an iceberg that is partly visible above the water, which represents consciousness. However, the much larger portion of the iceberg that is underwater represents the depths of the unconscious mind (see Figure 14.1).

Figure 14.1 Freud's Basic Structure of the Mind

Freud believed the unconscious part of the mind held the secrets to an individual's personality. The unconscious was thought to be much deeper and bigger than the conscious mind, much like an iceberg in the sea.

Freud's psychoanalytic theory was the first personality theory that focused on the interaction of mental forces. His theory was based on two beliefs: (1) we don't usually know what our true motives are (because they are unconscious) and (2) we have defense mechanisms that keep our unpleasant thoughts and motivations in our unconscious mind and therefore out of conscious awareness. How do these "mental forces" interact, why are we unaware of our motives, and what exactly are these defense mechanisms? Freud's psychoanalytic theory provides some interesting answers. As you read on, try to relate these concepts to your own life, even if in a peripheral way. Ask yourself, "How have I seen this concept show up in my own life?" Engaging in this strategy will help you elaborate on the material and make it easier for you to understand and recall later.

FREUD'S DESCRIPTION OF PERSONALITY   Freud conceptualized the mind as three interacting systems: the id, the ego, and the superego. The **id**, which is present at birth, tries to satisfy our basic drives and survival instincts. It operates on the hedonistic **pleasure principle**—seek immediate gratification and pay no attention to societal expectations or constraints (Solms, 2006). You might associate the id with the behavior of an infant, who cries when it needs something and doesn't stop until that need is fulfilled. Maybe you are in close quarters with others, such as an airplane, where a screaming baby won't seem "cute" after about 5 minutes. The baby doesn't care. Babies are all id, and when they want or need something, they will scream until it is provided to them. Freud described the id as "pleasure-striving," fueled by sexual energy and motivation, which he referred to as "libido" (Freud, 1920, p. 116).

As you can probably imagine, life wouldn't turn out well for us if we remained "all id." Take a moment to imagine a day where your id was in complete control—meaning that you

id

Freudian component of personality
that is present at birth and tries
to satisfy basic drives and survival
instincts

pleasure principle

process by which the id seeks
immediate gratification and pays no
attention to societal expectations or
constraints

engage in any behavior that is pleasurable regardless of the consequences. Would you go to work or school that day? Would you eat nutritious meals? Would you restrain yourself if someone is rude to you or cuts you off in traffic? Would you "just say no" to drugs? What if you interacted with an attractive person and you experienced a feeling of sexual desire? Obviously, this day would probably end poorly and you would most likely be spending the night behind bars. Luckily, as the theory states, the infant starts to grow and the ego develops from the id. The **ego** is the rational part of the mind. Its role is to identify the basic drive that the id wants to fulfill and come up with a realistic plan for satisfying that drive. In contrast to the id, the ego operates on the **reality principle**, meaning that it attempts to achieve the id's goals through actions that will be pleasurable rather than painful (Freud, 1992). The ego contains our partly conscious perceptions, thoughts, judgments, and memories. Freud distinguished the id from the ego by stating, "The ego stands for reason and good sense while the id stands for the untamed passions" (Freud, 1961, p. 95).

If the id represents some of your more devilish impulses, then the superego would be the opposite, the proverbial angel on your shoulder. The **superego** forces the ego to consider societal constraints and acceptable forms of behavior. Nowadays, we talk about this as our conscience. Let's say that you're dying to have a shiny new car. If your superego didn't exist, you might steal the car from the lot, paying no attention to laws, social conventions, or a moral sense of right or wrong. Now, if your ego was present, you might still steal the car, but it would help you find a way to do it without getting caught. In addition, your ego would figure out a way to prevent you from feeling any anxiety as a result of your id-driven behavior. Fortunately for you, your superego would probably step in, remind you that stealing is illegal and wrong, and then direct your ego to help you obtain the car in a realistic way: Get a job, earn enough money for a down payment, secure a loan, purchase the car, and continue to make monthly payments. The superego is the last aspect of our personality to develop and Freud suggested that it appears around the ages of 5 or 6. By this age, children have had an opportunity to learn and internalize some of the messages of right and wrong from their parents and society. This doesn't mean that people always behave in a way consistent with the superego (none of us do), but it does mean that people start to feel guilt for some of their poor choices. Watch the video *Freud's Theory of Personality* for a review of these basic concepts.

ego

psychodynamic component of personality that represents the rational part of the mind. Operates according to the reality principle

reality principle

process by which the ego attempts to achieve the id's goals through actions that will be pleasurable rather than painful

superego

psychoanalytic component of personality that considers societal constraints and acceptable forms of behavior

Freud's Theory of Personality

The psychodynamic theory states the id, ego, and superego are competing forces that are constantly trying to achieve balance, or homeostasis. To make these concepts a little more realistic, think of a family with three siblings: the oldest brother, a middle sister, and

the youngest brother. Imagine the little brother sees a stack of freshly-baked cookies sitting unattended on the kitchen counter. His thought is to immediately run over and devour as many cookies as he can. His middle sister notices what is about to happen and urges him to instead tell Mom that he has just cleaned up his toys and then ask if he could please have a cookie. He agrees this is a good idea, but still grabs one cookie and eats it as quickly as possible. The oldest brother walks in just as little brother is finishing the last bite. Older brother proceeds to lecture the little brother about "stealing" and threatens to tell Mom. Middle sister starts to feel anxious for her little brother and rationalizes that Mom probably would have said "yes" to the cookie had she been there. Can you see the id, ego, and superego at work in this example?

Psychodynamic Aspects of Personality

Interactive

Identify each sibling in the scenario described above:

The middle sister [_____]

The older brother [_____]

The youngest brother [_____]

WORD BANK

- Id
- Ego
- Superego

Start Over   Check Answers

defense mechanisms

originate from the ego; mental processes of self-deception that help alleviate worry and anxiety often produced by the id

Figure 14.2 The Role of the Defense Mechanisms

EGO

Protection

Displacement

Repression

Denial

THE ROLE OF DEFENSE MECHANISMS   The ego has a difficult job because the id is not an easy force to control. As a result, there are times when the ego fears losing control of the sexual and aggressive impulses of the id. When this happens, the ego experiences anxiety. According to Freud, we cope with this anxiety through the unconscious use of **defense mechanisms**. These mechanisms, which are mental processes of self-deception, help us alleviate our worry and anxiety (Cramer, 2000). Think of defense mechanisms as the "tools" of the ego that assist the ego in coping with the demands of the id and the resulting anxiety (see Figure 14.2).

According to Freud, the way in which people use defense mechanisms also provides insight about their personality. Freud's daughter and fellow psychoanalyst, Anna Freud, played a major role in developing and studying many of the following defense mechanisms (Freud, 1992).

As with many theories in psychology, there are some parts of psychoanalytic theory that are more scientifically supported and useful than others. Defense mechanisms are an example of this. Many practicing psychologists (even ones who endorse a different theoretical orientation) believe in the validity and utility of the concept of defense mechanisms—the idea that we all have ways of rationalizing our thoughts and behaviors in a way that won't lead us to feel excessive anxiety. As you read through the following types of defense mechanisms in Table 14.1, try to connect this information to a time in your life where you have seen this defense mechanism at work (either by you, someone you know, or a character on TV or in a movie). Following the table, you'll be asked to provide some of your own examples.

Table 14.1 Defense Mechanisms

	Definition	Example
Denial	Refusing to recognize or believe the reality of a situation	A person with obsessive compulsive disorder who says there is nothing wrong with washing her hands 30 times a day (in hot water, with bleach)
Repression	A process that blocks anxiety-provoking thoughts from the conscious mind	A woman was mugged while walking home one night; years later, she has no memory of this event
Regression	A retreat to an earlier stage of development, such as childhood or infancy, due to psychological stress	Curling up in the fetal position after a bad day
Displacement	Redirecting an unconscious and unacceptable wish or drive toward a more acceptable alternative	You argue with your father and have the urge to hit him; you displace this unacceptable aggression by hitting a punching bag instead
Sublimation	A form of displacement where unacceptable urges are redirected into more appropriate activities	An artist who creates paintings that include violent and sexual content
Reaction Formation	Changes an unacceptable desire by adopting the opposite stance	An unfaithful spouse travels the country speaking about the sanctity of marriage
Projection	Attributing an unconsciously experienced impulse or feeling to someone else	A person feels depressed, but instead focuses on their friend who seems depressed
Rationalization	The use of conscious reasoning to explain away anxiety-inducing thoughts and feelings	You lie to a friend, but tell yourself that you did it for their own good

Journal Prompt: Examples of Defense Mechanisms

Provide an example for two of the following defense mechanisms: denial, displacement, sublimation, and projection. These can be real examples from your own life or examples you create.

PERSONALITY DEVELOPMENT: THE PSYCHOSEXUAL STAGES You might have heard of movies or books with sexual overtones or imagery referred to as "Freudian." This description is based on Freud's conception of the human personality as developing through a series of psychosexual stages. Freud believed that sex and aggression were important drives in the formation of our personalities; in fact, he thought that most of the things we do are thinly veiled demonstrations of sexual and aggressive concepts. As a result, the psychoanalytic theory that he developed holds that personality differences are caused by the different ways in which people disguise and channel these drives (Millon, 2012).

Freud outlined five **psychosexual stages**, or developmental stages during which the id's desire for pleasure focuses on many of the body's erogenous zones (see Table 14.2). The idea behind a stage theory is that one stage leads to the next stage. That is, you must successfully negotiate any conflict or discord that arises in one stage before you can move onto the next stage. According to Freud, anxiety or conflict of any sort could cause a person to become stuck at a particular stage, leading to **fixation**, or an unhealthy focus on one particular area, during adulthood. For instance, Freud might trace a child's prolonged thumb-sucking to an oral fixation caused by being abruptly weaned as an infant. Or, someone who is rigidly organized or compulsively neat might be, in Freud's view, fixed at the anal stage as a result of overly strict toilet training (aka "anal retentive"). For Freud, personality was closely linked to childhood experiences.

psychosexual stages

component of psychoanalytic theory focusing on developmental stages during which the id's desire for pleasure focuses on many of the body's erogenous zones

fixation

unhealthy focus on one particular psychosexual stage that continues into adulthood. May be the result of an inability to resolve psychosexual conflicts associated with a particular stage

Table 14.2 The Psychosexual Stages of Development

Freud's Psychosexual Stages of Development					
Age	Psychosexual Stage	Erogenous Zone	Focus	Potential Conflict	Personality Consequences of Fixation
Birth–1½ years	**Oral**	Mouth	Sucking, Chewing, Exploring environment with mouth	Weaning	Abusing alcohol/drugs, nail biting, binge eating
1½–3 years	**Anal**	Anus	Controlling bodily functions; Toilet training	Parents too harsh or too lenient	*Anal Retentive* = rule bound and inflexible *Anal Expulsive* = messy and destructive
3–6 years	**Phallic**	Genitals	Beginning of sexual feelings (initially directed at opposite sex parent) Oedipus Complex Electra Complex	Castration Anxiety (boys) Penis Envy (girls) Autoeroticism	Promiscuity, strive to dominate men (women), vain and overambitious (men) Compulsive masturbation
6 years–Puberty	**Latency**	None	Developing same-sex friendships; Growing physically and intellectually	Seen as a period of sexual calm; period of appropriate maturity	
Puberty–Death	**Genital**	Genitals	Rebirth of sexuality; focus redirected to appropriate targets (others)	Unconscious sexual and aggressive urges	Inability to be successful in work and love

Adaptive Pathway 14.1: Psychodynamic Theory

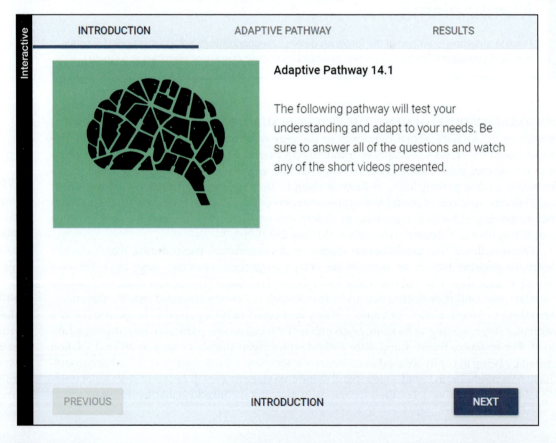

INTRODUCTION	ADAPTIVE PATHWAY	RESULTS

Adaptive Pathway 14.1

The following pathway will test your understanding and adapt to your needs. Be sure to answer all of the questions and watch any of the short videos presented.

PREVIOUS   INTRODUCTION   NEXT

Neo-Freudian Psychodynamic Theorists

LO 14.2   **Identify the neo-Freudians and their contributions to psychodynamic personality theory.**

Freud had a number of followers and disciples who helped spread his ideas into future generations. At the same time, however, few of these disciples agreed with Freud on all points. Many prominent neo-Freudians (meaning "new Freudians"), including Carl Jung, Alfred Adler and Karen Horney, modified or amended Freud's original theories to reflect their own beliefs and concepts regarding personality.

JUNG   Like Freud, Carl Jung (pronounced Yoong, 1875–1961), believed that human personality is strongly influenced by the unconscious. However, Jung placed less emphasis on sexual feelings and pioneered the concept of the **collective unconscious**, a shared pool of memories and images common to all humans (Jung, 1959). For example, the image of a mother as a caretaker and nurturer exemplifies a common idea persistent across time and cultures. Jung called these prototypical images **archetypes** and suggested that they can be seen repeatedly in various forms of art, literature, dreams and religions (Jung, 1959; Stevens, 1982). Jung saw archetypes as an important determinant in personality formation because they guided most people to respond to the environment in predictable ways (Jacobi, 1999).

This picture, dated 1909, shows Freud (front left) with many of his colleagues, who were referred to as neo-Freudians, including Carl Jung (front right).

ADLER   Alfred Adler (1870–1937) agreed with Freud that childhood was an important time for personality development. However, Adler's focus was on each person as an individual and centered on *social* conflicts, not sexual ones. His theory of **individual psychology** described a universal motivation to achieve superiority; however, he emphasized that each person's unique struggle with feelings of inferiority was the key to understanding their personality. Adler believed people often strive for perfection and superiority throughout adulthood in an effort to compensate for feelings of both physical and mental inferiority rooted in childhood. Adler suggested that some of the inferiority experienced as a child resulted from the influence of siblings on the individual's social environment. Adler was one of the first, and probably the most famous psychologist, to discuss the importance of birth order and the effect it had on the development of personality (Eckstein et al., 2010). While not mainstream, Adler's influence in psychology continues today. Currently, there are graduate schools that specialize in Adlerian training in the disciplines of counseling, art therapy, marriage and family therapy, and school counseling.

HORNEY   Psychologist Karen Horney (pronounced Horn-eye, 1885–1952) was deeply influenced by Freud's teachings, but as you might imagine, she did not easily accept Freud's concept of *penis envy*. Instead of rejecting the idea altogether, she proposed the complementary concept of **womb envy** (Aldridge et al., 2014; Bayne, 2011). Horney described womb envy as the jealousy men feel toward a woman's role in nurturing and sustaining life (through pregnancy, birthing and lactation). Horney placed particular emphasis on the importance of social factors, particularly anxiety and the way an individual's parents respond to it, as a strong determinant of our personalities. She incorporated a strong focus on culture and how culture influences gender differences in personality and behavior. As one of the earliest feminists, Horney recognized how cultural norms determined what was seen as acceptable male or female behavior.

Horney is well-known for her theory regarding the development of neurotic personality. Resulting from interactions with others, especially neurotic parental figures, Horney proposed three ways people respond in the world. She suggested people "move toward people", "move against people", or "move away from people." These descriptions and the personality characteristics associated with them, can be seen as foreshadowing the theories to come regarding personality traits. Researchers have attempted to map these three personality styles onto modern-day personality disorders with some success (Coolidge et al., 2001). For example, individuals who "move against people" are seen as aggressive, hostile, and vengeful, which is correlated with the symptoms of antisocial personality disorder (see LO 14.14 for an overview of antisocial personality disorder.)

collective unconscious

Jungian concept reflecting a shared pool of memories and images common to all humans

archetypes

prototypical images from the collective unconscious that can be seen repeatedly in various forms of art, literature, dreams, and religions

individual psychology

theory of personality (Adler) that suggests there is a universal motivation to achieve superiority, while emphasizing that each person's unique struggle with feelings of inferiority is the key to understanding their personality

womb envy

neo-Freudian concept proposed by Horney stating that men experience jealousy due to the woman's role in nurturing and sustaining life (through pregnancy, birthing, and lactation)

Quiz for Module 14.1–14.2

1. Freud divided the personality into three separate systems, which develop at different ages throughout early childhood. Choose the correct order of the systems from earliest to latest development.

a. Superego, ego, id
b. Ego, id, superego
c. Id, ego, superego
d. Id, superego, ego

2. Ten-year-old Diego really likes his classmate Sierra. This feeling makes him uncomfortable because he is unsure if she likes him back. Instead of telling Sierra that he likes her, Diego makes fun of her in front of the other girls. Diego is engaging in which defense mechanism?

a. Rationalization
b. Reaction formation
c. Sublimation
d. Displacement

3. Which of the following represents the correct order of Freud's psychosexual stages of personality development?

a. Oral, genital, anal, latency, phallic
b. Oral, phallic, anal, genital, latency
c. Oral, anal, phallic, latency, genital
d. Oral, anal, genital, latency, phallic

4. Luke Skywalker from the movie *Star Wars* is a young, idealistic person on a mission to save his people. This idea is common to many cultures and stories, and Jung referred to this as:

a. the subconscious.
b. the collective unconscious.
c. an artifact.
d. an archetype.

5. Adler discussed the role of _____ on the development of personality.

a. birth order
b. the collective unconscious
c. superiority
d. conflict

Module 14.3–14.4: The Humanistic Perspective

Despite its popularity at the time, not everyone was a fan of Freud's deterministic and (some would argue) negative theory of personality. Many different theories of personality were developed in the middle of the 20th century as a reaction to the dominance of psychodynamic theories. In many ways, it was Freud who stimulated much of the future work that evolved into the rich and diverse theories of personality in psychology today. One such theory that can be viewed as a direct reaction to the psychodynamic perspective, and to a lesser extent, the mechanistic nature of the behavioral perspective, is the humanistic theory of personality. Humanistic theories of personality share a number of core values including the following ideas:

- **Human Beings Are More Than the Sum of Their Parts:** This holistic view of humans stresses that individuals cannot be reduced to mere components.

- **Focus on the Present:** Now is seen as the most important moment in time. The past is not seen as irrelevant, but isn't something that can be changed. Similarly, the future is unknown, but in some ways can be shaped by focusing on the present.

- **Consciousness Is the Most Important Level of Awareness:** Individuals are aware that they are aware. Furthermore, consciousness includes an awareness of oneself in the context of people around them (Greening, 2006).

- **Every Person Has Value:** Each individual possesses inherent worth. Humanists would go as far as to say that all human beings are inherently good (Morgan & Lilienfeld, 2000). Humanists make a distinction between people making bad *choices* and being a bad *person*.

- **Goal of Life Is Personal Growth:** The primary goal for each individual should be to increase self-understanding through self-exploration. A core belief of humanists is that a person can only be truly happy once they know themselves and have pushed themselves to reach their fullest potential.

Two of the most prominent contributors to the development of humanistic theory were Abraham Maslow and Carl Rogers. The video *Humanistic Theories* will provide a brief overview of the important components of this theory.

Humanistic Theories

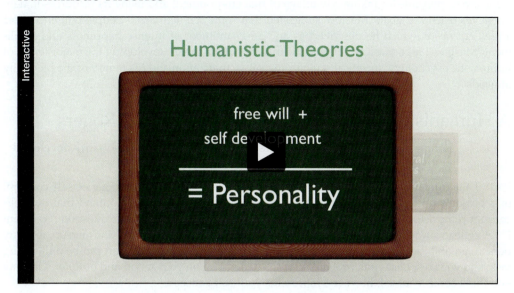

A Humanistic Explanation of Personality: Abraham Maslow

LO 14.3 Explain the humanistic theory of personality developed by Maslow.

Humanistic theories of personality emphasize people's conscious understanding of themselves and their abilities to attain self-fulfillment. With their emphasis on human capacity for generosity, self-improvement, high achievement, and happiness, humanistic theories tend to appeal to the optimists in all of us. Abraham Maslow (1908–1970) disagreed with Freud's assertion that the core of who we are is buried deep in our unconscious. He believed that we are often aware of our drives, motives, and needs and that this awareness leads to a better understanding and acceptance of who we are. While psychoanalysis is based on the concept of determinism, Maslow and other humanistic theorists focus much more on free will and the importance of taking responsibility for behavior (Hansen, 2000).

By focusing on the capacity for psychologically healthy people to grow and achieve happiness, Maslow represented a marked shift from the psychodynamic emphasis on uncovering the roots of individual's psychological troubles. "Tell me about your mother" became "Tell me about yourself—your hopes, dreams, and vision of the future." From Maslow's perspective, our personalities are self-directed and self-determined.

Maslow's most significant contribution to psychology involves his theory of the *hierarchy of needs* (see LO 10.6), which states that our motivation and behavior is driven in an orderly fashion. The theory states that our most basic needs (e.g., food, water, shelter) must be met first before some of the higher, or growth needs (e.g., belongingness, esteem) can be pursued. While there has always been some question about the scientific robustness of Maslow's theory and whether or not people really do have to proceed through the hierarchy in order (Alderfer, 1969; Wahba & Bridwell, 1976), the idea that people generally strive to grow and develop their personality over time is more universally accepted.

Maslow described this personality growth in terms of **self-actualization**, or the experience of becoming your real self and realizing your fullest potential. While Maslow suggested the majority of people never reach self-actualization, the goal of striving toward this level should be part of each person's life. Examples of self-actualized people include, Beethoven, Mother Teresa, and Nelson Mandela. Each of these people provided different contributions to our world, by reaching their own personal, fullest potential. Since everyone is individual and unique, everyone reaches self-actualization differently. However, whatever route you take toward self-actualization, it must be a route you've chosen for yourself. That's not to say that external circumstances play no role in self-actualization. In fact, many humanists would argue

humanistic theories
theories of personality emphasizing the need for conscious understanding and the ability to attain self-fulfillment/self-actualization

self-actualization
an individual's experience of becoming their real self (rather than striving for their ideal self) and realizing their fullest potential as a human being

that we need a nurturing environment in order to achieve full self-actualization. However, we alone are responsible for taking advantage of that environment and using its resources to help ourselves reach our goals. Maslow suggested that some self-actualized people will encounter a *peak experience,* which he described as an "a-ha" moment of intense happiness and fulfillment (Maslow, 1961). Maslow devoted the majority of his career developing the major tenets of humanistic psychology, specifically regarding self-actualization and his theory of the hierarchy of needs.

A Humanistic Explanation of Personality: Carl Rogers

LO 14.4 **Summarize the core concepts of the humanistic theory of personality developed by Rogers.**

self-concept

a person's understanding of who he or she is; this is reflected in the way an individual thinks of themselves

Part of the humanistic approach to personality centers around the principle of **self-concept**, or a person's understanding of who he or she is. Humanistic theories contend that our self-concept comprises a key part of our reality. Take a moment to consider the question, "Who am I?" A college student, a son or daughter, a sister or brother, a friend? A kind person, a funny person, an ambitious person, a laid-back person? Answering this question can be a daunting task, and your responses will probably change depending on your mood and outlook. The way you think about yourself, however, represents your self-concept.

Psychologist Carl Rogers (1902–1987) expanded on the idea of self-concept and created his own theory of personality development. Rogers believed that all people want to be their "actual" selves. In order to achieve this goal, we need to live according to our own wishes rather than those of other people. At the same time, however, other people can help us become our "actual" selves by accepting us, acting genuinely, and showing empathy. When people value us despite our problems and weaknesses, they show us **unconditional positive regard**, an ingredient that Rogers considered crucial to self-development. It is important to recognize that unconditional positive regard for a *person* is not the same as unconditional positive regard for that person's *behavior.* Rogers would not say that he accepted a prisoner's prior criminal behavior, but he would say that he valued that person as a human being. Rogers stated that as a child the primary source of providing unconditional positive regard comes from our parents. If a child does not receive unconditional positive regard, they will develop **conditions of worth**. Conditions of worth are the internalized messages that suggest "I am only a good person if I do _____." Or, "My parents will only love me if I get straight A's in school." Rogers argued that it was impossible for someone to reach self-actualization if they were experiencing conditions of worth (Morgan, 2011; Patterson & Joseph, 2007).

unconditional positive regard

ability to accept and value another person despite their problems or weaknesses

conditions of worth

internalizing message suggesting conditions that one must meet before they are accepted by another person. Develops when someone does not experience unconditional positive regard

For Rogers, our self-concept and access to unconditional positive regard is inextricably linked to our personalities and our interactions with the world at large. A positive self-concept, according to Rogers, manifests itself in positive interactions with the world, productive relationships, and personal satisfaction and happiness. Those people who lack unconditional positive regard and have a negative self-concept tend to struggle with feelings of anxiety or doubt.

Rogers was primarily a psychotherapist, and his principal goal was to help clients achieve a positive self-concept. He suggested that it is the discrepancy between a person's *ideal self* and their perception of their *actual self* that leads to psychological issues (e.g., anxiety, depression, substance abuse etc.) This is an explanation of psychopathology that is still relevant and useful for many practicing therapists today.

Journal Prompt: Your Ideal and Actual Self

Provide an example of a discrepancy between your ideal self (who you ideally want to be) and your actual self (who you actually are). What changes could you make in your life to bring your actual self more in line with your ideal self?

Ideal versus Actual Self

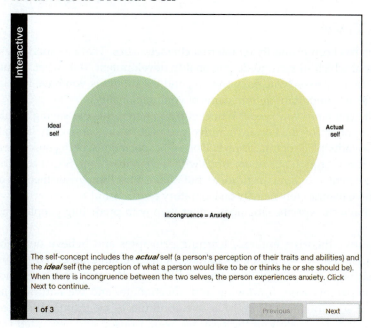

Ideal
self

Actual
self

Incongruence = Anxiety

The self-concept includes the *actual* self (a person's perception of their traits and abilities) and the *ideal* self (the perception of what a person would like to be or thinks he or she should be). When there is incongruence between the two selves, the person experiences anxiety. Click Next to continue.

1 of 3   Previous   Next

Having a positive self-concept is certainly something that can change over time as an individual matures or as situations vary. Women appear to struggle with self-concept more than men during the period of adolescence to adulthood as evidenced by an increased discrepancy between their actual and ideal selves (Block & Robins, 1993). These are important results especially since it has also been found that low self-esteem during adolescence predicts depression two decades later (Steiger et al., 2014).

Quiz for Module 14.3–14.4

1. Anita is struggling to put herself through school, while working a full-time job. Her friends don't understand why she is always so tired and doesn't want to go out with them. Maslow would say Anita is focusing on her _____ needs, whereas her friends are focusing on their _____ needs.

    a. shelter; social

    b. basic; growth

    c. basic; social

    d. physical; self-actualizing

2. Humanistic theory is based on the concept of _____ and _____ for behavior.

    a. free will; taking responsibility

    b. determinism; blaming others

    c. determinism; taking responsibility

    d. free will; the unconscious motivation

3. Tim studied hard for his spelling test but was sad to discover he failed it. When he went home and told his mother about failing the test, she said, "Tim, I love you regardless of the grades you make on spelling tests. I will always be proud that you are my son." Tim's mom was demonstrating what concept in Roger's theory?

    a. Self-concept

    b. Conditions of worth

    c. Unconditional positive regard

    d. Empathy

4. Rogers suggested that a discrepancy between a person's ideal self and actual self could lead to what psychological issues?

    a. Bipolar disorder, substance abuse, or anxiety

    b. Criminal behavior, substance abuse, or schizophrenia

    c. Fixation of the personality, anxiety, or depression

    d. Anxiety, depression, or substance abuse

Module 14.5–14.6: The Social Cognitive Perspective

So far, our focus has been primarily on internal characteristics. That is, experiences that occur inside the person, which in turn guide personality development. But, what about the world that is external to the person? The environment, and the thoughts you have in relation to the environment, are also important determinants of your personality.

"You are the company you keep." Whoever first uttered this old saying would probably have been a proponent of the social cognitive perspective on personality. **Social cognitive theories** of personality place emphasis on beliefs and expectations, both conscious and unconscious, that we form through our interactions with the environment. Social cognitive theories overlap to some extent with humanistic ideas, but unlike most humanistic theories of personality, social cognitive theories rely heavily on laboratory research and are concerned with predicting people's behavior in specific situations rather than with predicting people's more general life choices.

Social cognitive theorists embrace learning principles and believe our behaviors can be traced to our attempts to model, or imitate, what we have observed others doing or to practice what we have learned through conditioning. We are fun-loving and affectionate because our parents were fun-loving and affectionate, and we naturally model their behavior (i.e., observational learning). Or, we continue to be responsible because every time we have acted responsibly in the past, we were praised and rewarded (i.e., operant conditioning).

Psychologists who support social cognitive theories generally believe that our unique perceptions and thinking—about ourselves and our situations—play a major role in determining our behavior. In their view, personality is less determined by underlying traits or childhood traumas than it is by the current situation, our acquired knowledge from past situations, and the way we think about both. For social cognitive psychologists, personality tends to be highly dynamic and reflective of a combination of social cues and norms from the environment as well as individual beliefs, thoughts, and expectancies.

Rotter and Personal Control

LO 14.5 **Recognize the distinguishing features of Rotter's social cognitive theory of personality.**

If you've ever felt like you have no control over a situation, you know that feeling this way can be depressing and difficult. One idea that is central to many social cognitive theories of personality is that of **personal control**, or our sense of having control over our environment rather than feeling as though the environment is controlling us. Julian Rotter, one of the principal founders of the social cognitive perspective on personality, devoted much of his research to exploring the relationship between individuals' sense of personal control and their behaviors, personalities, and states of mind.

Do you act differently when you play a game of pool compared to a game of bingo? In one laboratory study, Rotter (1954) found that people behave differently in different tasks and games, depending on whether they believe that the game requires skill or luck. When we think a game requires skill, we work hard to improve our performance. When we think a game requires only luck, however, we believe that we can't control the game's outcome, so we don't work as hard and as a result, tend not to improve. Based on these findings, Rotter argued that our behavior depends on our perception of the amount of control that we have over a certain situation. He called this disposition the **locus of control**. According to Rotter, people with an **internal locus of control** believe that they control the situation, their own rewards and, therefore, their own fate. People who have an **external locus of control** believe that the situation, rewards, and fate are controlled by outside forces.

---

social-cognitive theories

theories of personality that place emphasis on beliefs and expectations, both conscious and unconscious, that individuals form through their interactions with the environment

personal control

sense of having control over one's environment

locus of control

perception or belief about the amount of control one has over situations

internal locus of control

belief that an individual controls the situation, their own rewards and, therefore, their own fate

external locus of control

belief that the situation, rewards, and fate are controlled by outside forces

Locus of Control

Interactive

Classify each of the following scenarios as having either an external or internal locus of control by filling in the blank.

Jenna's soccer team won their tournament. When her parents congratulated her, she claimed the only reason they won was because the other team didn't know how to play. [____] locus of control

Revi received 98 percent on his term paper. He knew he had worked very hard on it and was pleased with his grade. [____] locus of control

Jackie has been with her company for 10 years; she knows she deserves a promotion but believes the only reason she received one was because her boss is a friend of her husband. [____] locus of control

Salena enjoys playing slot machines and knows whether or not she wins or loses depends on luck. [____] locus of control

Salena's friend, Jack, has studied strategy for Blackjack and believes his winnings come from pure skill. [____] locus of control

Christine tried out for the school musical but didn't receive a lead role. She was disappointed but knew some of the other students were better singers. [____] locus of control

[Start Over] [Check Answers]

Rotter (1966) developed a locus-of-control questionnaire that can be used to identify which locus of control is most characteristic of an individual. Since Rotter's initial experiments, many studies have demonstrated links between scores on this questionnaire and actual behavior. People who demonstrate an internal locus of control are more likely to excel in school, take preventive healthcare measures, and effectively deal with stress (Cascio et al., 2014; Gale et al., 2008; Kirkpatrick et al., 2008). In addition, people who demonstrate an internal locus of control tend to be less anxious and more content with life than people who demonstrate an external locus of control (Arslan et al., 2009; Spokas & Heimberg, 2009; Verme, 2009).

Recent research has explored the idea that we each have many different loci of control, corresponding to a certain area of our lives. In other words, you may feel that your performance in school is entirely in your own hands, but your performance on the soccer team is more or less determined by fate. According to this theory, our **outcome expectancies**, or our assumptions about the consequences of our behavior, greatly influence the degree to which we may exhibit an internal or external locus of control (April et al., 2012; Rotter et al., 1962). For example, imagine you received a low grade on an assignment and felt that the professor unfairly graded your work. Do you go and talk with your professor and make your case as to why you think you deserve a better grade? The answer to this question depends, in part, on your *expectancy of the outcome*. That is, do you think that having this discussion will lead to a positive outcome? Or, maybe your professor has already made it clear that they don't want to "argue about grades" so your expectancy is that the outcome would not be in your best interest. In this example, your outcome expectancy is likely related to whether or not you have an internal or external locus of control regarding your grade in this class.

outcome expectancies assumptions about the consequences of behavior that influence the degree to which an individual may exhibit an internal or external locus of control

Bandura, Reciprocal Determinism, and Self-Efficacy

LO 14.6 Describe Bandura's theory of personality, including the concepts of reciprocal determinism and self-efficacy.

Albert Bandura (b. 1925) was another pioneer of the social cognitive perspective and one whose life-long work was recognized in 2016, when he was awarded the National Medal of Science by President Obama. Bandura's work in observational learning became a part of

reciprocal determinism

social-cognitive concept that highlights the bidirectional relationship between the environment, behavior, and personality

his social cognitive theory. His work continued into the realm of personality where he examined the interaction between an individual and his or her environment (Bandura, 1989). Bandura's social cognitive theory emphasizes the cognitive and affective processes that are involved in acquiring and maintaining patterns of behavior and, as a result, personality (Cervone et al., 2001). At the center of this theory is the idea of **reciprocal determinism**, which provides a basis for understanding how environmental factors coexist with and influence personality, just as personality factors coexist with and influence the environment (see Figure 14.3).

Our personalities are a potent mix of our unique thought patterns, our feelings, our environments, and our behaviors, all of which are engaged in a constant series of cyclical causes and effects. For example, you might love being in the limelight and feel great when you're the center of attention. As a result, you sign up for a drama class and start hanging out with a group of gregarious friends. This new environment reinforces your thoughts and feelings, and soon enough, your behaviors reflect increased extraversion: you audition for *The Voice*; you perform at a local open mic night; you start conversations with strangers while standing in line. Your thoughts and personality helped you choose an environment, which in turn further shaped your thoughts, behaviors, and personality.

Much of Bandura's research also focused on self-efficacy. **Self-efficacy** describes an individual's expectations about their own abilities to perform certain tasks (Bandura,

self-efficacy

an individual's expectations and beliefs about their own abilities to perform certain tasks

---

Figure 14.3 Reciprocal Determinism

Reciprocal determinism is at the heart of the social cognitive theory. Reciprocal determinism describes the bidirectional relationship between personality, behavior, and the environment.

1977). Similar to Rotter, discussed earlier, Bandura also focused on outcome expectancies. However, Bandura focused on distinguishing *outcome expectations* from *efficacy expectations*. Remember, an outcome expectancy is your estimate that a particular behavior *will* lead to a particular outcome. Whereas, an **efficacy expectancy** is the belief you have in yourself that you can perform the behavior required to produce the outcome (Bandura, 1977). Efficacy expectancies have to do with you, which is why Bandura referred to the concept as *self-efficacy*. For example, you might know that achieving a certain number of sales at work will result in you receiving a bonus check at the end of the year (outcome expectancy), but you might not believe in your own ability to produce the number of sales required (efficacy expectancy). Therefore, we might say that you have low self-efficacy in your sales abilities.

Self-efficacy consistently predicts high performance in areas such as academics, physical exertion, and pain tolerance (Bandura & Locke, 2003; Bandura et al., 1987; Cairney et al., 2008; Hsieh et al., 2007; Williams & Williams, 2010). In fact, like the concept of reciprocal determinism, Bandura believed that self-efficacy and outcomes were bidirectional. That is, high self-efficacy not only predicts high performance but it can also cause it (Bandura, 1977). From Bandura's standpoint, the "I think I can" attitude results in actual achievement (Bandura & Locke, 2003). In fact, self-efficacy has been found to be an important ingredient for those attempting to quit smoking and recover from alcohol/drug abuse. Higher self-efficacy has predicted both short-term and long-term successful outcomes related to recovery (Kadden & Litt, 2011; Litt et al., 2013; Ockene et al., 2000; Perkins et al., 2012).

efficacy expectancy

belief an individual has in themselves that they can perform the behavior required to produce a particular outcome

Many inspirational quotes embody the concept of self-efficacy.

Quiz for Module 14.6–14.7

1. Julian took the college entrance exam and didn't obtain the score he wanted. He believed he could achieve a higher score if he studied more and paid for a tutor. Julian is demonstrating which locus of control?

   a. Personal
   b. External
   c. Internal
   d. Decisive

2. People with an internal locus of control tend to be less _____.

   a. anxious
   b. successful
   c. happy
   d. negative

3. Mareeka has always been shy and anxious around people. She recently started a new job as the project manager for an art exhibit. On her first day, she spent most of the time in her office and didn't interact with her team members. She thought about her behavior after work and how some people didn't seem very

welcoming. She recognized that her behavior may have influenced her environment and that the environment influenced her behavior. Bandura described this as _____.

   a. environmental effectiveness
   b. reciprocal determinism
   c. locus of control
   d. outcome expectations

4. Stuart has had a long-term addiction to alcohol. He has finally acknowledged that he needs treatment. If he enters rehab with the attitude that he can overcome his addiction, he is more likely to succeed because of his _____.

   a. high self-esteem
   b. low self-esteem
   c. high self-efficacy
   d. low self-efficacy

Module 14.7–14.10: The Trait Perspective and the Biology of Personality

Quickly think of a few words that describe your personality. Which words did you choose? Chances are good that the words you selected, whether they were *honest* and *kind* or *aggressive* and *ambitious,* are linked to certain personality traits. A **trait** is a relatively stable disposition to behave in a certain way. Traits are part of the person rather than part of the environment, although the environment, by prompting people to behave in certain ways, may play a key role in how traits are revealed.

trait

relatively stable disposition to behave in a particular way

Most people are quick to think of adjectives that describe their own, or other people's, personality. In this module, you will discover how stable some personality traits are over time.

An important distinction exists between traits and *states*. While both traits and states can be examined through someone's observable behavior, traits are long-lasting, while states are transient, or change from moment to moment. Traits and states are definitely related in that a trait can determine the likelihood that someone enters into a particular state. For example, a person who possesses the trait of insecurity is more likely to enter a state of anxiety in a new and uncertain situation compared to someone who is very secure.

Rather than being seen as independent categories (e.g., you are either extraverted *or* introverted), traits are conceptualized as continuous characteristics, meaning that people can differ in the degree to which they express a trait. An extremely sociable person may, for instance, have hundreds of friends, whereas a moderately sociable person may have a dozen friends.

Trait Theories

LO 14.7 Distinguish the trait theories of Cattell and Eysenck.

Since there are numerous traits and words to describe them, it can be challenging for psychologists to describe people's personalities briefly and consistently. For this reason, several researchers have developed **trait theories**, or sets of meaningful and distinct personality dimensions that can be used to describe how people differ from one another. In the 1930s, psychologist Gordon Allport became a pioneer in trait theory when he and his colleague H. S. Odbert attempted to identify all of the possible words in the dictionary that could be used to describe a person's personality. It was a noble goal, but the results were a little overwhelming: They came up with a list of nearly 18,000 trait descriptors (Allport & Odbert, 1936).

CATTELL'S 16 PERSONALITY FACTORS Psychologist Raymond Cattell had a goal of investigating the universal aspects of personality through scientific research (Cattell & Mead, 2008). Starting with Allport's extensive list of traits, Cattell reasoned that not all traits describe personality in the same way. Cattell referred to the traits that are most easily visible in others (e.g., warm, gregarious, outspoken) as **surface traits**—they are the traits we see on the surface of someone's personality. He also argued, however, that those surface traits have to stem from a core common source or cause, which he referred to as **source traits** (Cattell, 1945). Someone who is seen as warm, gregarious, and outspoken likely has a source trait of extraversion. Extraversion itself is difficult to see because it is the source of the surface traits, which are more easily seen and identified (see Figure 14.4).

trait theories

theories of personality that suggest there are sets of meaningful and distinct personality dimensions that can be used to describe how people differ from one another

surface traits

personality traits that are easily visible to others (e.g., warm, gregarious, outspoken) and originate from source traits

source traits

underlying factor or origin of surface traits

Figure 14.4 Source and Surface Traits of Personality

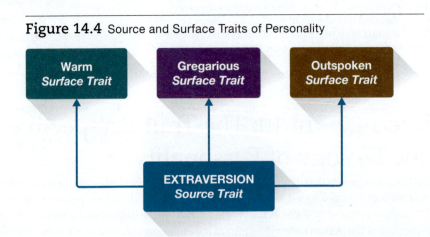

Cattell developed the earliest well-known trait theory by first condensing Allport's extensive list of traits into about 170 distinct adjectives. Next, he had large samples of people rate themselves on each of these adjectives. Cattell then used a statistical technique called **factor analysis** to identify patterns of correlations in these responses. He used these patterns to determine factors, themes around which certain responses tended to cluster. For example, Cattell found that individuals who rated themselves high on perfectionism were also likely to describe themselves as organized and self-disciplined, but unlikely to be described as impulsive or lax. Based on this research, Cattell identified 16 distinct personality dimensions, measured in the *16 PF Questionnaire* ("PF" stands for "Personality Factors"; see Figure 14.5).

factor analysis

statistical technique designed to identify patterns of correlations based on responses to numerous questions

Figure 14.5 Cattell's 16 Personality Dimensions

This figure lists all 16 of Cattell's personality factors on a continuum. Your personality could be described based on where you would fall on the continuum of each trait.

Impersonal, cool	**Warmth**	Warm, outgoing
Concrete thinker, slower to learn	**Reasoning**	Abstract-thinking, fast learner
Emotionally reactive, easily upset	**Emotional Stability**	Emotionally stable, adaptive
Cooperative, submissive, avoids conflict	**Dominance**	Forceful, assertive, aggressive
Serious, restrained	**Liveliness**	Animated, spontaneous
Nonconforming, disregards rules	**Rule-Consciousness**	Conscientious, conforming
Shy, timid, hesitant	**Social Boldness**	Venturesome, uninhibited
Objective, no-nonsense, tough	**Sensitivity**	Sensitive, sentimental, intuitive
Trusting, unsuspecting, accepting	**Vigilance**	Vigilant, suspicious, skeptical
Grounded, practical, solution-oriented	**Abstractedness**	Abstract, imaginative, absent-minded
Open, naïve, forthright, genuine	**Privateness**	Private, discreet, non-disclosing
Self-assured, secure, confident	**Apprehension**	Self-doubting, worried, insecure
Traditional, conservative	**Openness to Change**	Flexible, liberal, open to change
Group-oriented, follower, dependent	**Self-Reliance**	Self-sufficient, resourceful, solitary
Flexible, tolerates disorder, impulsive	**Perfectionism**	Organized, compulsive, self-disciplined
Relaxed, patient, tranquil	**Tension**	Tense, high energy, impatient, driven

Research has demonstrated that our perceptions of our own personality can be quite accurate; however, we tend to have a number of "blind spots," particularly for traits that are very desirable or very undesirable. In these cases, other people can provide a more accurate and balanced picture of our personality (Vazire & Carlson, 2011).

EYSENCK'S CENTRAL DIMENSIONS For some, even 16 dimensions of personality seemed like too much. In the 1950s and early 1960s, psychologists Hans and Sybil Eysenck theorized that personality could be described in terms of two central dimensions: neuroticism (emotional stability versus instability) and extraversion (introversion versus extraversion). Emotional stability referred to the ability to cope with life's stressors in healthy ways and avoid extremes in mood or behavior; extraversion referred to the tendency to be social, high-spirited, and affectionate. The Eysenck Personality Inventory (EPI) was developed to measure these two primary dimensions of personality (Eysenck & Eysenck, 1964), and the dimensions themselves are often represented graphically utilizing a two-axes design (see Figure 14.6).

Figure 14.6 Eysenck's Dimensions of Personality

Eysench believed that personality traits could be described according to two primary dimensions: neuroticism and extraversion.

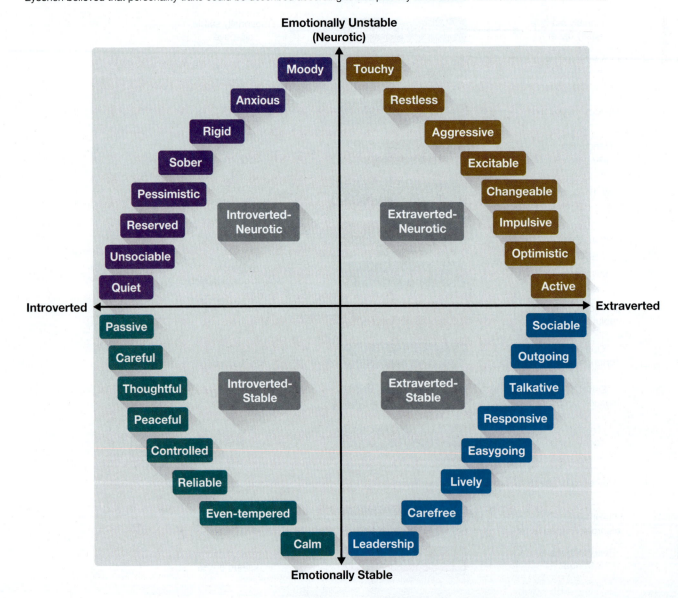

Later, the Eysencks added the somewhat controversial dimension of *psychoticism,* which is a measure of nonconforming, atypical attitudes indicating a lack of socialization or sympathy. Psychoticism has been shown to be related to sensation-seeking behaviors and conceptualized as a component present in many psychopaths and individuals with psychosis (Egorova et al., 2014; Eysenck & Zuckerman, 1978; Eysenck et al., 1985; Heath & Martin, 1990). However, it became controversial because some researchers questioned whether the Eysenck's research on this subscale really measured what it was supposed to measure (Block, 1977). After some revision of the scale, the EPI became the Eysenck Personality Questionnaire (EPQ) which includes this third factor. Both the EPI and the EPQ continue to be used on psychological research today (Barrett et al., 1998; Chapman et al., 2013).

The Five-Factor Model

LO 14.8 **Identify the traits described in the five-factor model of personality.**

Robert McCrae and Paul Costa also believed that Cattell's 16-factor theory was overly complex and redundant. Together, they reanalyzed Cattell's data and identified five, underlying factors of personality (Costa & McCrae, 1992). According to this **Five-Factor Model** (which is also referred to as the "Big Five"), we can describe personality by assessing a person's score on each of the following five dimensions:

You'll notice that if you take the first letter from each of the five factors, it spells the word "OCEAN," which can help you remember the traits associated with the five-factor model of personality. The "Big Five" have become a useful and widely accepted construct for describing personality within the field of psychology (McCrae et al., 2005; Rammstedt et al., 2010). An enormous amount of research, involving different people, cultures, and even other species (e.g., dogs, geese, fish) has been stimulated by this theory of personality. Here is a brief description and example of some of the research findings associated with each trait:

five-factor model

trait theory of personality suggesting five underlying factors (traits) of personality: openness to experience, conscientiousness, extraversion, agreeableness, and neuroticism

penness to experience

onscientiousness

xtraversion

greeableness

euroticism (emotional stability)

- *Openness to Experience* is the most difficult trait to clearly define. It is less about "being open to new experiences" and more a combination of intellect and artistic tendencies. In fact, some researchers refer to this trait as *Openness/Intellect* and use adjectives such as imaginative, curious, and innovative to describe those who are high in this personality dimension. DeYoung et al. (2014) suggest the best description encompassing all aspects of this trait is "cognitive exploration." Individuals who are high in openness to experience tend to be more creative (George & Zhou, 2001; McCrae, 1987), less prejudiced (Flynn, 2005), and more resilient to stress (Williams et al., 2009).

- *Conscientiousness* has been found to be one of the most stable traits over time (Hampson & Goldberg, 2006) and describes those who are seen as organized, thoughtful, and responsible. People who are high in conscientiousness are generally reliable, self-controlled, and motivated to learn (Komarraju et al., 2009; Major et al., 2006).

- *Extraversion*, a trait that involves the desire to be sociable and around people, is another trait that has been found to be very stable over time (Major et al., 2006). Extraverts tend to be fun-loving and gain their energy from being around other people. Introverts, on the other hand, often find large groups of people draining and regain their energy by being alone (See Figure 14.7). Some of the risks associated with extraversion (other than just irritating introverts) include starting to smoke as a teen, reckless driving, and a lower probability of saving money (Harakeh et al., 2006; Hirsh, 2015; Lajunen, 2001).

- *Agreeableness* involves the extent to which someone is helpful, trusting, and generally amiable. This trait is the most predictive of how individuals will view and behave within interpersonal relationships (Jensen-Campbell & Graziano, 2001). Interestingly, it has also been linked with political ideology. In a study that examined two aspects of agreeableness (compassion and politeness), researchers found that compassion was associated with liberalism and politeness was related to conservatism (Hirsh et al., 2010).

- *Neuroticism* is a trait generally thought of as "emotional instability," which was described in Eysenck's work. Individuals who measure high on neuroticism generally experience intense levels of negative affect (e.g., depression, anxiety, worry) (Griffith et al., 2010). Neuroticism is the trait from the Big Five most closely connected with the development of psychological disorders, such as eating disorders (Cervera et al., 2003) and depressive and anxiety disorders (Watson et al., 1988). High levels of neuroticism have even been described as a public health concern because of its broad and detrimental effects (Lahey, 2009).

Together, these five traits can capture and predict many aspects of an individual's personality and behavior. In fact, the Five-Factor Model has been proposed as the basis for an alternative model for assessment and description of personality disorders in the Diagnostic and Statistical Manual of Mental Disorders (Helle et al., 2017).

Figure 14.7 The Introvert's Perspective

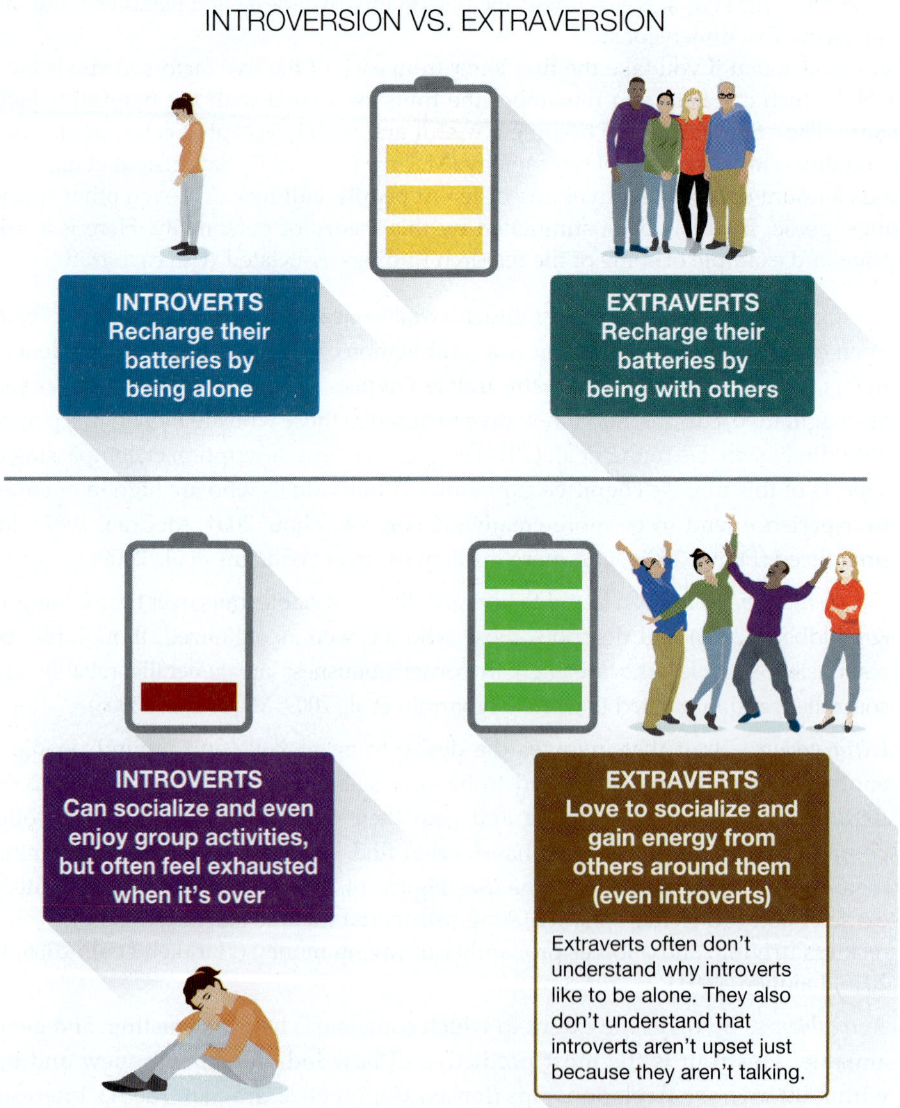

INTROVERSION VS. EXTRAVERSION

INTROVERTS
Recharge their batteries by being alone

EXTRAVERTS
Recharge their batteries by being with others

INTROVERTS
Can socialize and even enjoy group activities, but often feel exhausted when it's over

EXTRAVERTS
Love to socialize and gain energy from others around them (even introverts)

Extraverts often don't understand why introverts like to be alone. They also don't understand that introverts aren't upset just because they aren't talking.

The Five-Factor Model of Personality

	General Description	Those HIGH in this trait tend to be:
Open to Experience	Combination of intellect and general appreciation for new experiences, art, emotion, adventure, and imagination	Divergent/creative thinker Curious (Olson & Weber, 2004)
Conscientiousness	Organized, dependable, self-disciplined; prefer planned experiences	Achievement oriented Motivated to learn Dependable (George & Zhou, 2001)
Extraversion	Gains energy from others and outside experiences, sociable, talkative, positive emotions	Active Sociable Dominant
Agreeableness	Cooperative, compassionate, trusting, interested in social harmony	Sympathetic (Burke & Witt, 2002) Altruistic (Judge et al., 1999) Good-natured
Neuroticism (Emotional Instability)	Easily experience negative emotions (e.g., anger, anxiety, depression)	Emotionally unstable (Elliot & Thrash, 2002) Worry prone Insecure

Decades of research has been devoted to finding additional traits to add to the Five-Factor model. Most of the candidates proposed have been unable to be as reliably produced as the Big Five. However, one factor referred to as "Honesty-Humility" has emerged with strong reliability and validity (Ashton et al., 2014). This factor is part of the *HEXACO model of personality*, which contains six factors: Honesty-Humility (H), Emotionality (E), Extraversion (X), Agreeableness (A), Conscientiousness (C), and Openness to Experience (O). There is some obvious overlap between the five-factor and six-factor models, but their development process was different and there are some subtle differences in what can be measured. For example, individuals who score low on the Honesty-Humility factor tend to exhibit antisocial behavior, narcissism, and manipulative tactics (sometimes referred to as Machiavellianism). This cluster of characteristics is known as the "dark triad" and has been the subject of numerous research studies (Furnham et al., 2013). (See Figure 14.8.)

THE PERSON-SITUATION CONTROVERSY In the early days of the development of trait theories, it was tempting to boil down personality to just a few key traits and it was appealing to think of those traits as the primary determinants of behavior. The 1930s–1960s was a period in psychology's history that encompassed a wealth of new ideas about human behavior, many of which developed as a reaction to the deterministic, yet unobservable, psychoanalytic view of personality development. Given this context, it is easy to see how excited some psychologists must have been to think that personality could be conceptualized by specific, observable, and consistently-expressed traits. In fact, early trait theorists, including Gordon Allport, suggested that these personality dispositions exerted a powerful influence that would lead to consistency, and therefore predictability, in behavior across the majority of situations.

As the social-cognitive perspective began to emerge in the mid-20th century, some researchers began to question if that was really all there was to personality. Walter Mischel, a colleague of Albert Bandura's, ignited an emotional controversy within the field when he suggested that the situation itself may have important influences on behavior and that people may not always behave the same way, even across similar situations (Mischel, 1973). While this doesn't seem like a controversial statement, at that time many interpreted Mischel's critique as to say that personality doesn't exist in the form of stable traits and that the only important aspect was the situation. A debate ensued and became known as the **person-situation controversy** (Kenrick & Funder, 1988). Proponents of the situation side of the argument claimed that although people's traits tended to endure over time, their specific behavior may vary in situations, so traits alone may not always help us predict behavior.

Figure 14.8 The Dark Triad

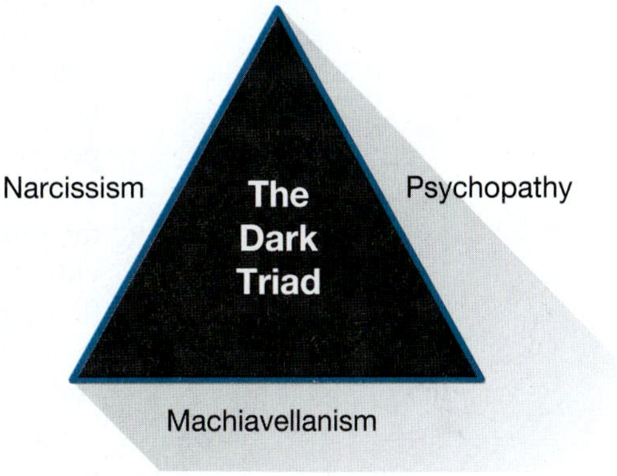

person-situation controversy controversy within the social-cognitive perspective surrounding the extent to which the situation influences an individual's behavior. Developed as a reaction to trait theories of personality suggesting only stable personality traits predicted behavior

cognitive affective processing system (CAPS)

theory stating an individual's response to a given situation depends on the psychological features present in that situation

Mischel and his colleagues developed a model that takes into account both the consistency of a person's behavior over time as well as the variability in behavior across situations (Mischel & Shoda, 1995). The **Cognitive Affective Processing System (CAPS)** states that an individual's response to a given situation depends on the psychological features present in that situation (Shoda et al., 2013). These psychological features include the thoughts, beliefs, and feelings a person experiences in that particular situation and the interaction between them and the individual's personality tendencies. For example, you may have a friend who is high on the trait of introversion; they don't like big crowds, they prefer being alone, and have made a career of computer programming. In most social situations, they prefer to stay in the background. However, that same friend, when attending the Amazon Web Services conference, seems to transform into a different person. They attend every event (including the social ones); they are animated, talkative, and contribute to various discussions. They are, in fact, showing signs of extraversion. This example doesn't mean that your friend's general personality disposition has changed; but in certain situations, in this case, one that involves their career, innovation, and many other people with similar personalities, they may behave in different and unpredictable ways.

CULTURAL INFLUENCES ON PERSONALITY TRAITS If you grew up in Tokyo, Japan, would you have different personality traits than if you grew up in rural Kansas? It is certainly possible. People around the world are exposed to a wide, rich variety of cultural values, philosophies, economic conditions, and expectations for how to behave. One major way in which cultures differ is the degree to which they are formed around collectivistic or individualistic ideals. *Collectivistic cultures* emphasize people's interdependence, whereas *individualistic cultures* place emphasis on each person's individual rights and freedoms and deemphasize the social roles that we play in relation to others (Triandis, 2001; Triandis & Suh, 2002) (see LO 13.3).

The culture in which we're raised affects not only our personality but also our views of the *concept* of personality. If you were raised in a collectivistic culture, the individualist's fascination with personality tests and "finding your true self" might seem bewildering to you since people in collectivistic cultures tend to believe that individual differences stem not from our deep-seated personality traits but from situational or environmental variations. Furthermore, the predominant types of personality traits tend to vary between cultures. For example, individuals who identify with Chinese culture believe in the importance of traits such as harmony (inner peace of mind and harmonious interactions with others), *mianzi* or face (concern with maintaining reputation and/or showing respect for others according to their status in society), and *renqing* (emphasis on the mutual exchange of favors in relationships).

Despite some of these cultural differences in conceptualization or value placed on certain personality dimensions, the traits associated with the Five-Factor Model have been examined and replicated in over 50 countries (Allik & McCrae, 2004; Costa et al., 2001; McCrae & Terracciano, 2005). The results of these studies have led researchers to conclude that personality does have a universal component. The ability to measure personality traits (e.g., conscientiousness) and interpret the results in a meaningful way (e.g., its relationship to economic prosperity) in China, Norway, Ethiopia, and the United States is a relatively rare phenomenon in psychological, cross-cultural research (Schmitt et al., 2007).

The Biology of Personality

LO 14.9 **Recognize how biology and neuroscience have contributed to our understanding of personality.**

With the frequent use of brain-imaging techniques to connect the psychological to the biological, research has been able to confirm that personality and biology are closely tied together. Whether we are talking about a specific area of the brain, the level of arousal in the brain, or the relationship between genetics and personality, biology and neuroscience have contributed to the field of personality research in very meaningful ways.

THE ROLE OF THE RETICULAR ACTIVATION SYSTEM Eysenck believed differences in introversion and extraversion stemmed from individual differences in alertness. He hypothesized that the *reticular activation system,* which contains the reticular formation, a part of the brain that controls arousal, was more sensitive in shy people compared to outgoing people (Eysenck, 1967).

Arousal and the Reticular Formation

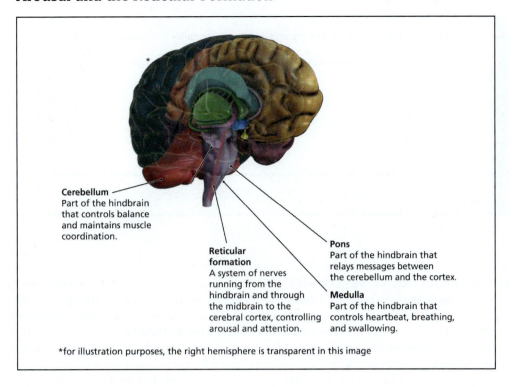

Cerebellum
Part of the hindbrain that controls balance and maintains muscle coordination.

Reticular formation
A system of nerves running from the hindbrain and through the midbrain to the cerebral cortex, controlling arousal and attention.

Pons
Part of the hindbrain that relays messages between the cerebellum and the cortex.

Medulla
Part of the hindbrain that controls heartbeat, breathing, and swallowing.

*for illustration purposes, the right hemisphere is transparent in this image

Eysenck hypothesized that introverts have a more sensitive arousal system, meaning they need less stimulation to feel aroused. This theory also explains why introverted people report becoming easily over-stimulated in noisy, busy, or chaotic environments and why introverts favor more quiet and solitary experiences. The extravert, on the other hand, needs a lot of stimulation to activate the reticular formation, which is why they express preferences for more exciting or sensation-seeking activities. Eysenck and Eysenck (1967) creatively demonstrated their theory by using lemon juice. Just four drops of concentrated lemon juice on the tongues of introverts and extraverts produced significantly different amounts of saliva in response to the stimulation (the lemon juice). This relatively easy experiment to conduct has been a favorite in undergraduate psychology classes and a quick Internet search will reveal numerous DIY lemon juice personality tests. Variations of this test are still regularly studied and written about in books (e.g., Little, 2014) and blogs.

The Lemon Juice Test

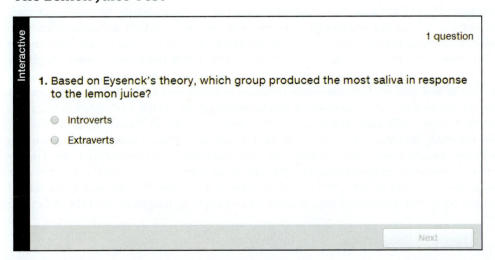

Interactive

1 question

1. Based on Eysenck's theory, which group produced the most saliva in response to the lemon juice?

○ Introverts

○ Extraverts

Next

Personality and the Brain

Interactive

1. According to Eysenck, why would introverts produce more saliva in response to lemon juice?

1 of 1   Reset   Next

---

behavioral activation system (BAS)

brain system that activates approach behavior in response to the anticipation of a reward

behavioral inhibition system (BIS)

brain system that inhibits approach behavior in response to the anticipation of punishment

THE REINFORCEMENT SENSITIVITY THEORY   Jeffrey Gray, another personality researcher and a student of Hans Eysenck's, proposed that two basic brain systems were reflected in Eysenck's two primary personality dimensions (extraversion and neuroticism). According to Gray (1970), the **behavioral activation system (BAS)** activates approach behavior in response to the anticipation of a reward. For example, if a student expects to achieve a high grade by studying hard, activity in the BAS will cause the student to review thoroughly in order to move toward the goal. Gray believed that the BAS is also responsible for the experience of positive feelings such as hope, elation, and happiness. In contrast, the **behavioral inhibition system (BIS)** inhibits approach behavior in response to the anticipation of punishment. Gray believed that the BIS is also responsible for the experience of negative feelings, such as fear, anxiety, frustration, and sadness. Carver and White (1994) developed the BIS/BAS Scales as a way to measure an individual's BAS/BIS sensitivity. This scale has been used in numerous studies and been found to be associated with brain activity, emotional reactions, cognitive control and approach/avoidance motivation (Amodio et al., 2008; Gable & Harmon-Jones, 2013; Gable et al., 2000). The reinforcement sensitivity theory has gone through various revisions over the years with the most recent version identifying three distinct systems: the BAS; the BIS; and the fight, flight, freeze system (FFFS). The FFFS was part of the BIS in the past, but neurobiological research suggests these systems are distinct. The FFFS reacts to all aversive stimuli and is viewed as a general punishment sensitivity system, whereas the BIS is activated in goal conflict situations (e.g., wanting to initiate a conversation with an attractive fellow student, but feeling nervous to do so) and tends to result in the experience of worry and sometimes, avoidance (Corr & Cooper, 2016).

personality neuroscience

field of personality development that utilizes brain imaging techniques to examine the brain's structure and function and how they relate to personality

PERSONALITY NEUROSCIENCE   The emerging field of **personality neuroscience** uses brain imaging techniques to attempt to examine people with shared personality traits to (1) identify particular brain structures that are involved and (2) clarify the relationship between those structures (called *functional connectivity*) and patterns of brain chemistry (referred to as *neurotransmission*). The majority of this work has focused on the traits of extraversion and neuroticism and while progress is being made, the field is complex and results are often difficult to replicate and sometimes controversial (Adelstein et al., 2011; DeYoung & Gray, 2009; DeYoung et al., 2010; Ryman et al., 2011; Taki et al., 2012). For example, the study by DeYoung et al. (2010) has become well-known because of its claims to have found specific areas of the brain tied to each of the Big Five personality traits. For example, extraversion was associated with the size of the medial orbitofrontal cortex (an area involved in processing reward) and conscientiousness was related to the size of the lateral prefrontal cortex (an important area that involves planning, judgment, and the voluntary control of behavior.) Despite this study's popularity, some neuroscience researchers have questioned the methodological and statistical approaches used to interpret this complex data (Anderson, 2012).

Behavioral Genetics

LO 14.10 Explain how behavioral genetics and the concept of heritability have contributed to personality research.

Since the 1970s, substantial time, effort, and money have been devoted to attempting to understand how much of our personality is inherited and how much is derived from our environment. Family members, twins, and adopted individuals provide a unique opportunity to study the role of genetic and environmental influences to personality. *Heritability* is the percentage of phenotype (observable traits) that is associated with variation in genotype (genetics) (Turkheimer et al., 2014) (see LO 2.12). Therefore, with respect to personality, we might ask, "How much variation in the observed characteristics of extraversion (phenotype) can be explained by genetics (genotype)?" Twins have been a very useful group to study, and in behavioral genetics, differences in expressed traits among identical twins can be broken down into three components (see Figure 14.9).

Figure 14.9 Heritability of Twins

Even identical twins can have different expressed traits as a result of the combination of genes, shared familial environment, and each twin's unique variance from their environment.

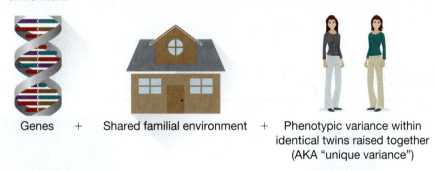

Genes   +   Shared familial environment   +   Phenotypic variance within identical twins raised together (AKA "unique variance")

Turkheimer et al. (2014) provide an excellent summary of the current state of behavioral genetics with respect to personality, which can be summarized into four broad points:

1. **Personality has a genetic component.** At this point, there is no question that differences in personality result to some degree from heredity. Identical twins (who share 100 percent of genes) are more likely than fraternal twins (who share 50 percent of genes, which is the same as non-twin siblings) to have similar personality traits and adopted children have personalities that are more similar to their biological parents than their adopted parents (Bouchard Jr. & Loehlin, 2001; Krueger & Johnson, 2008; Tellegen et al., 1988).

2. **Multiple genes are only part of the explanation.** It has been notoriously difficult to find specific genes and heritability estimates for specific personality traits that can be replicated in different samples. The traits of extraversion and neuroticism have been the most widely researched and have been found to be heritable at approximately 0.4 (Bouchard, 2004; 2014). This means that approximately 40 percent of the population variation in extraversion and neuroticism is due to genetic influences. This is not the same as saying 40 percent of personality is genetic. Rather, a heritability estimate

is a ratio of the amount of genetic variation compared to the total variation within a *specific* population. That is why research with different populations often ends up with different heritability estimates (Visscher et al., 2008). For example, imagine we are interested in studying the heritability of one of the Big Five traits, conscientiousness, and we have been granted access to an entire high school of students. We are able to analyze DNA from the students and their parents, along with self-report measures of personality. In examining our data, we realize that students have very different levels of conscientiousness—some students are very high in this trait and others are very low. That is, there is variation in our population with respect to the trait of conscientiousness. We can think of this total variation in terms of a percentage. That is, all of the variation in this specific population equals 100 percent. Now, the question becomes, "How much of that total variation can be attributed to genetics?" If our DNA analysis revealed that 30 percent of the total variation in conscientiousness was due to genetic influences, then we would say that in this *specific population,* the heritability estimate of conscientiousness is 0.3. This result would mean that among this group of students, 70 percent of the variation in conscientiousness was due to non-genetic influences (e.g., environmental factors).

3. **Shared environment is less important than once thought.** Many people assume that much of identical twins' similarity comes from their shared familial environment (they look the same, are the same age, go to the same school, and therefore are treated similarly by others). The reality is that shared environment contributes very little to variations of twin personalities (Bouchard, 2004; Turkheimer et al., 2014). Creative research conducted by Nancy Segal with *unrelated look-alike pairs* has confirmed the lack of influence of similar environments (the assumption is that people who look alike experience similar treatment by others) by demonstrating that people who look alike, but are not genetically related, have very different personalities and self-esteem (Segal, 2013; Segal et al., 2013). Watch the video *Virtual Twins* to learn more.

Virtual Twins

Interactive

4. **Behavioral genetic research should focus less on genes and more on unique environments.** Finally, the only biological contributor left to explain twin personalities involves the unique environment, which Turkheimer et al. (2014) prefer to call the "phenotypic variance within identical twin pairs raised together" (p. 517). This variation explains the fact that even identical twins that are raised in the same home have some personality differences. That is, even though identical twins share the same genotype,

their phenotype is somewhat different. One twin might be more extraverted than the other twin, despite sharing the same genetics and the same environment. It is in this area where Turkheimer and his colleagues argue we should be now focusing the majority of behavioral genetics research.

Adaptive Pathway 14.2: The Science of Personality

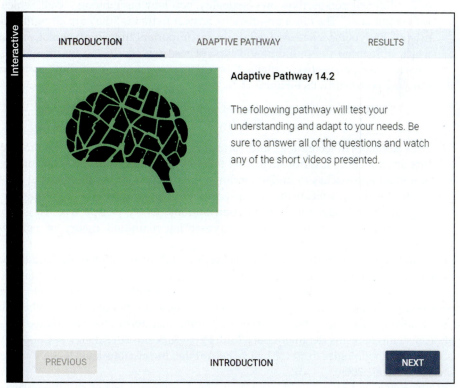

Quiz for Module 14.7–14.10

1. Alisa describes her best friend as funny, outgoing, and the life of the party. She describes herself as quiet, reserved, and thoughtful. Which theory of personality best describes how Alisha distinguishes herself from her best friend?

   a. Self-control theory
   b. Humanistic theory
   c. Social cognitive theory
   d. Trait theory

2. The openness trait in the five–factor model is most closely aligned with which description?

   a. Cognitive exploration
   b. Conscientiousness
   c. Helpful and trusting
   d. Emotionally stable

3. People who are reliable, self-controlled, and motivated to learn score high in which trait?

   a. Extraversion
   b. Reliability
   c. Conscientiousness
   d. Openness

4. According to Eysenck's research, which part of an introvert's brain is particularly sensitive to stimulation?

   a. Medial orbitofrontal cortex
   b. Prefrontal cortex
   c. Behavioral activation system
   d. Reticular activation system

5. The field of _____ uses brain-imaging techniques to identify the brain structures involved in specific personality traits.

   a. personality neuroscience
   b. behavioral genetics
   c. biological psychology
   d. personality psychology

6. The percentage of observable traits associated with genetics is the study of _____ in personality development

   a. environment
   b. gene expressione
   c. behavioral adaptation
   d. heritability

7. Even identical twins raised in the same environment have phenotypic differences. What is said to account for these differences in how they look?

   a. The genome
   b. Multiple genes
   c. Shared environment
   d. Unique environment

Figure 14.10 Perspectives on Personality

PERSPECTIVES ON PERSONALITY

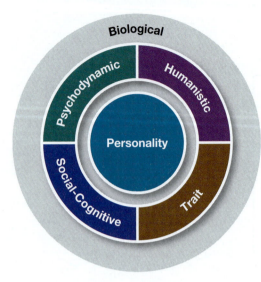

Module 14.11: Evaluating Different Perspectives on Personality

Given the broad definition of personality, you may not be surprised that there are so many different explanations of personality formation. The explanation provided depends heavily on the theoretical perspective it rests upon. After reading about all of the different perspectives on personality, you may be thinking, "Well, which one is the right one?" The often unsatisfying answer to that is "they are all right to some extent." Each perspective evolved during an important time in psychology's history, which influenced the thinking and type of research conducted by researchers. As a result, each perspective contains theories offering unique contributions to understanding personality. (See Figure 14.10.)

LO 14.11 **Evaluate the strengths and weaknesses of the psychological perspectives on personality.**

With advances in technology and various machines available to assess brain structure and function, it is not surprising that neuroscience is currently one of the predominant approaches to understanding human behavior. As the focus of the field shifts that doesn't mean that the psychological perspectives were wrong or that they don't still offer meaningful contributions. Every perspective has strengths and weaknesses when it comes to presenting a unified theory of personality development.

One strength of the psychodynamic perspective is Freud's promotion of the idea that early life experiences shape our personalities. Many psychologists recognize and appreciate much of Freud's foundational concepts and how they played a role in influencing the development of other perspectives within psychology (Westen, 1998). While a number of criticisms claim that it is impossible to empirically test "the unconscious," numerous studies have examined the existence of defense mechanisms (Kramer et al., 2013; Perry & Bond, 2012; Perry & Cooper, 1989) and discovered methodologies to assess beliefs held at the unconscious level (Greenwald et al., 1998; Greenwald et al., 2009).

Most psychologists today would agree that Freud overemphasized childhood sexuality and aggression, at the expense of other more comprehensive explanations of personality. And, while the developmental nature of Freud's stage theory is appealing, it hasn't been supported by observations or studies of children (Kline, 2014). Furthermore, while Freud's theory offers an explanation for personality traits after they have developed, it offers no insight or methods to predict these qualities, making its usefulness more or less limited to after-the-fact analysis (Hall & Lindzey, 1978).

Given these limitations, one might wonder how popular the Freudian approach to personality is today. Despite the eccentric nature of Freud's original ideas and the number of weaknesses associated with this perspective, the psychodynamic (not psychoanalytic) approach is still a popular theoretical orientation for practicing psychologists. In 2012, the American Psychological Association published the results of a survey of its members in which 32 percent of psychologists identified either psychoanalytic (5 percent) or psychodynamic/relational (27 percent) as their primary theoretical orientation (Norcross & Rogan, 2013).

An appealing feature of the humanistic perspective is that it is viewed as holistic; it takes the whole person into account when explaining personality. This approach doesn't reduce people to a set of traits, instincts, or biochemicals, but views them as complex human beings. In addition, the humanistic approach is attractive in nature to many people because the theory is intuitive, relatable, and generally optimistic. The humanistic perspective can be seen in various aspects of life. Humanistic ideas have influenced diverse areas such as counseling, education, parenting, and even contemporary pop psychology. Self-help books and upbeat magazines have probably urged you to read about "finding yourself," "getting in touch with the real you," or "living the life you were meant to live." This type of language has become a ubiquitous part of the self-help literature, talk show chatter, and general conversation.

Despite its presence in a variety of modern-day contexts, a number of criticisms of the humanistic perspective exist. Some psychologists view the humanistic theory as overly optimistic, thereby minimizing the darker side of humanity. Others express concerns that the primary emphasis on the self may lead to selfishness or an overall lack of appreciation for how an individual's behaviors interact with others in the environment. Many of the core concepts associated with humanistic theory are inherently vague and subjective. As a result, people have difficulty envisioning what "self-actualization," "unconditional positive regard," and "self-concept" actually look like. A consequence of this vagueness is difficulty translating these important theoretical concepts into measurable variables that can be empirically tested. For example, Maslow wrote about 15 characteristics of self-actualized people, yet there has been little scientific research conducted to support his description (Heylighen, 1992; Soper et al., 1995; Wahba & Bridwell, 1976).

Despite these limitations, the humanistic perspective and view of personality has made significant contributions to the field of psychology, particularly in the realm of psychotherapy. According to a recent survey of practicing psychologists, 10 percent of clinicians identified their primary theoretical orientation as humanistic/experiential (Norcross & Rogan, 2013).

Unlike the humanistic approach, many aspects of the social cognitive perspective have been scientifically tested and have demonstrated support of the theory. This perspective's emphasis on the relationship between the environment and our thoughts and behaviors is the cornerstone of cognitive-behavioral therapy and has led to many effective treatments for psychological therapies. Twenty percent of psychologists surveyed in 2012 reported cognitive or behavioral as their primary theoretical orientation (Norcross & Rogan, 2013). Some psychologists argue that the social cognitive approach to personality places too much importance on external situations and does not fully appreciate the importance of the roles that biology and genetics play in establishing our inner traits. This criticism is another manifestation of the person-situation controversy discussed earlier.

Proponents of the trait perspective tend to emphasize the enduring dispositions of the individual while still acknowledging that the situation can exert powerful effects. Much of the trait perspective is straightforward, easily communicated and understood by those outside of psychology. One downside to this appeal is that people can easily become "resident experts," which can (and has) led to various trait-based personality tests that have little scientific evidence.

A strength of the trait perspective is that it is dimensional (opposed to categorical) in nature, which allows for a number of features of personality to be described rather than a person being pigeon-holed into one particular category. Looking at personality through the lens of the trait perspective provides us with a number of dimensions to understand the behavior of our friends, our families, and even ourselves. The most recent version of the Diagnostic and Statistical Manual of Mental Disorders (DSM-5) attempted to move to a dimensional diagnostic system to diagnose personality disorders. The significant change from a categorical to dimensional system proved to be too much for this revision, but the proposal still exists in an appendix and will likely be the subject of lively debates when preparing the next revision of the manual.

In the past, some people may have argued the trait perspective effectively described *how* people were different, but it failed to offer much insight into *why* people became that way. The historical work of Eysenck and Gray within the biological perspective helped pave the way for modern neuroscience investigations that are attempting to answer the question of "why." The role of genetics, heritability, brain anatomy, and functional connectivity of networks within the brain have offered many insights and testable hypotheses to understanding personality development.

Shared Writing: Evaluating Personality Theories

Of the different personality perspectives discussed in this chapter (i.e., psychodynamic, humanistic, social-cognitive, trait, and biological), which one do you think does the best job of explaining the development of personality? Explain why you chose this particular theory.

Quiz for Module 14.11

1. Teresa was studying all the different perspectives explaining personality and wondered which perspective was right. Her psychology professor most likely would answer her question with which statement:

   a. "Freud's theories have been completely abandoned because of lack of research."

   b. "They are all right to some extent."

   c. "The humanist theories offer the best explanation for people with and without psychological disorders."

   d. "The only true way to evaluate personality is through neuroscience."

2. Dr. Felix believes people are complex and have the ability to change if they are given unconditional positive regard and respect. He treats his clients with empathy and helps them find the life they were meant to live. Dr. Felix practices from which psychological perspective?

   a. Humanistic   b. Behavioral

   c. Psychoanalytic   d. Cognitive

3. Which psychological perspective has been credited with stimulating thought about personality development and influencing the development of other perspectives?

   a. Cognitive

   b. Behavioral

   c. Humanistic

   d. Psychoanalytic

4. Many personality researchers would like to see the Diagnostic and Statistical Manual of Mental Disorders (DSM) move to a dimensional approach in the diagnosis of personality disorders. Which perspective would most easily align with this approach?

   a. Psychoanalytic

   b. Behavioral

   c. Humanistic

   d. Trait

Module 14.12–14.13: The Assessment of Personality

So far, we have discussed many different theories of personality development and the strengths and weaknesses associated with them. For as many theories of personality that exist in the field of psychology, there are probably 10 times as many personality assessments. As you might imagine, personality assessments also vary according to the perspective that is being used to understand personality. While we will discuss the different types of personality assessments, we can also use this opportunity to review the different perspectives, or schools of thought, and their corresponding theories of personality. If you can connect the perspective with a type of assessment in a meaningful way (because you understand the theory behind it) then you will be much more likely to understand and retain this information. We will discuss four major types of personality assessment and how these can be grouped into two major categories: objective tests and projective tests.

Objective Personality Tests

LO 14.12   **Relate the different objective methods of assessing personality to the relevant theories of personality.**

It doesn't take long on the Internet to come across the latest "personality quiz." While these exercises might be entertaining, they are often not based in science and therefore are unlikely to provide us with meaningful information. Any assessment instrument that is going to be used in research or clinical practice is required to demonstrate both reliability and validity.

     Reliability refers to *consistency*. A reliable assessment will provide you with basically the same results every time you take it. As a result, if you know you are an introvert, then a reliable assessment of this trait will come up with that result each and every time. **Validity** involves

reliability

consistency of an assessment measure

validity

accuracy of an assessment measure

accuracy. That is, does the personality assessment actually assess what it is supposed to, in this case, personality? If you are taking a personality test that is supposed to tell you whether you are an introvert or an extravert, then you want to be really sure that the test is *actually* measuring that aspect of personality. It is possible for a test to be reliable but not valid. Imagine that our personality test was actually measuring social anxiety rather than introversion/extraversion. It reliably measured social anxiety, as demonstrated by the fact that you received the same score on the test every time you took it, but it wouldn't have any validity because it wasn't accurately measuring what it was supposed measure, which was introversion/extraversion (see Figure 14.11).

Figure 14.11 Demonstrating Reliability and Validity

Measures of personality need to demonstrate both reliabilility (consistency) and validity (accuracy) if they are going to be used to assess personality characteristics.

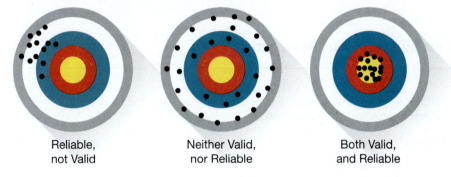

Reliable,
not Valid

Neither Valid,
nor Reliable

Both Valid,
and Reliable

Reliability and validity can be difficult concepts to grasp at first. In the video *Measuring Personality,* these important requirements for a valid assessment are discussed.

Measuring Personality

Interactive

INTERVIEWS Clinical interviews are the most widely used personality test. Any psychologist, regardless of their theoretical perspective, could conduct an interview to assess aspects of an individual's personality. However, the nature of that interview will likely vary based on

structured interviews

standardized interviews that have a specific list of questions, which are administered exactly as written

unstructured interviews

unstandardized interviews that allow the clinician to ask a variety of self-determined questions

behavioral observations

method of assessment that involves observing behaviors (often in a natural environment) to make judgments about an individual's personality

the perspective. Interviews can either be structured or unstructured: **Structured interviews** are standardized, meaning they have a specific list of questions meant to be asked word for word. The answers to those questions can often be scored and subsequently interpreted. Structured interviews are most often used in research settings where it is important to ensure that every participant is treated exactly the same and has the same assessment experience. Most psychologists tend to conduct **unstructured interviews**, which are unstandardized and allow the clinician to ask whatever questions they see as important at the time.

BEHAVIORAL OBSERVATIONS The next category of personality assessment involves **behavioral observations**. As the name suggests, this type of assessment involves "observing behaviors" in order to make judgments about someone's personality. Someone who would conduct behavioral observations would be interested in the "here and now" and the interaction between the person's environment and their behavior.

Reviewing Personality Perspectives

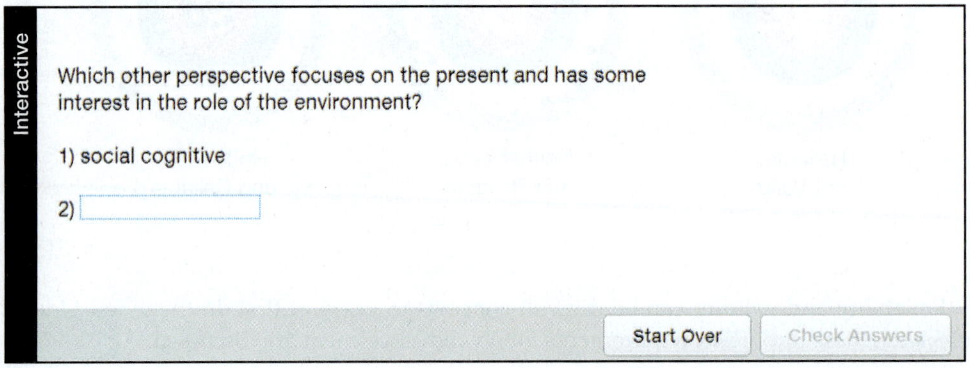

Interactive

Which other perspective focuses on the present and has some interest in the role of the environment?

1) social cognitive

2) [   ]

Start Over   Check Answers

Observing someone's behavior may just be one part of an overall assessment of personality, but it can be an important one because it allows you to see the individual's personality in action. The downside however, is that sometimes people change their behavior when they know they are being watched. This is called "reactivity." Psychologists have developed strategies to attempt to reduce the amount of reactivity present in the assessment. For example, many children who receive evaluations for attention deficit hyperactivity disorder (ADHD) have a classroom observation as part of their overall evaluation. In this case, the child doesn't know they are the one being observed and, in some cases, the teacher doesn't know which child is being observed, either. Both of these strategies are used to minimize reactivity on the part of the student and the teacher.

self-report inventories

objective personality assessments that require the person to read and answer a number of questions; responses to those questions are interpreted by comparing them to standardized norms from a large group of people

SELF-REPORT INVENTORIES The largest category of objective personality tests includes what psychologists call **self-report inventories**. Self-report inventories are also referred to as questionnaires and require the person who is being assessed, or a personal representative (e.g., parent, caregiver, teacher) to read and answer a number of questions. Self-report inventories ask specific questions and then those answers scored are often compared to standardized norms from a large group of people. Self-report inventories still involve interpretation, but the interpretation is guided by the standardized norms and not by the psychologist's personal opinion. Self-report inventories are useful because they can ask a number of specific questions about various dimensions (or aspects) of personality. The trait perspective is particularly well-suited for the assessment of personality via self-report inventories.

Remember Cattell and his 16 factors of personality? He developed the *Sixteen Personality Factor Questionnaire,* which is more commonly called the *16PF*. This self-report inventory contains 185 forced choice questions and in the end creates a profile of the individual's personality according to Cattell's 16 factors.

The Five-Factor Model of personality has a series of self-report inventories used to assess the five traits that characterize this model: **O**penness to Experience, **C**onscientiousness, **E**xtraversion, **A**greeableness, and **N**euroticism. Now in its 4th revision, the *NEO-PI-3* includes 240 items and can be administered to individuals as young as 12 years old (McCrae et al., 2005). There is also a shorter 60-item version called the *NEO Five Factor Inventory-3,* or *NEO-FFI-3* (McCrae & Costa Jr, 2007).

While you may not have heard of the 16 PF or the NEO-PI, you have may have heard of the *Myers-Briggs Type Indicator* or *MBTI.* Have you ever heard people referring to themselves by a 4 letter code? For example, "I'm a ENTJ, what are you?" Developed by a mother (Katherine Cook Briggs) and daughter (Isabel Briggs Myers) team, the MBTI is said to measure personality "types" rather than individual traits. The type is determined by assessing which combination of categories best represents an individual's personality. There are four broad categories:

- Extraversion (E) versus Introversion (I)
- Sensing (S) versus Intuition (N)
- Thinking (T) versus Feeling (F)
- Perceiving (P) versus Judging (J)

In the end, there are 16 different possible personality types. The MBTI has broad appeal (likely because of its simplicity and relatability) and has been used in various educational, occupational, and counseling settings (Armstrong et al., 2012; Harrington & Loffredo, 2010; Kennedy & Kennedy, 2004; Moutafi et al., 2007; Sefcik et al., 2009). However, there is very little scientific evidence to support the validity of these 16 personality types or show that they have any meaningful predictive ability (Hunsley et al., 2003; Michael, 2003; Pittenger, 2005). This example serves as a good reminder that just because something is well-known or often-used in popular culture doesn't necessarily mean it is scientifically supported.

Another well-known *and* scientifically supported measure of personality is called the Minnesota Multiphasic Personality Inventory or MMPI for short. Originally published in 1943, the MMPI is now in its third revision and is referred to as the *MMPI-2 Restructured Form,* or *MMPI-2-RF,* which officially published in 2008 (Ben-Porath & Tellegen, 2008). Of all of the personality assessments mentioned so far, the MMPI-2-RF is the one used most for identifying psychopathology; that is, for determining an individual's type and severity of mental illness. The MMPI-2-RF has 338 true/false items and produces 51 personality scales that are fairly easy to interpret. A unique advantage of the MMPI-2-RF is that it also has built-in validity scales, which are questions or patterns of responding that are analyzed to assess for overreporting, underreporting, and other inconsistent responding that can invalidate the assessment. Thankfully, nowadays computer programs do all of the scoring and even provide an interpretive report. Part of the report will include a personality profile that summarizes much of the information collected in the questionnaire. To the right, is an example of a completed MMPI-2-RF profile.

The MMPI is the most widely used assessment of personality (Archer et al., 2006; Camara et al., 2000) likely because it has everything we would want in a measure of personality: It is reliable, valid (and has the scientific evidence to support that), easy to administer and score, provides meaningful information about an individual's personality, and has built-in validity scales, which allow clinicians to determine if the test-taker is reporting in an honest and forthcoming manner.

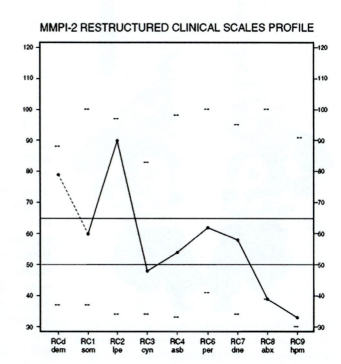

MMPI-2 RESTRUCTURED CLINICAL SCALES PROFILE

Projective Personality Tests

LO 14.13 **Recognize the most common projective personality tests.**

In addition to objective measures of personality, there is another major category of assessments called **projective tests**. In these assessments, the individual is presented with some sort of ambiguous stimuli (e.g., picture, drawing, fill in the blank sentence) and is asked to talk or write about the stimuli. The theory behind projective tests is that the individual will *unconsciously* "project" their personality onto the ambiguous stimuli and then their answers can be *interpreted* by a therapist. Did you see the key words in that description that can give you a clue as to which theoretical perspective is most likely to use projective tests?

projective tests

type of personality assessment that claims to access an individual's unconscious thoughts/wishes. The test typically involves ambiguous stimuli (e.g., picture, drawing, fill in the blank sentence) and the client is asked to talk or write about the stimuli, which is then interpreted by the therapist

Choose the Correct Perspective

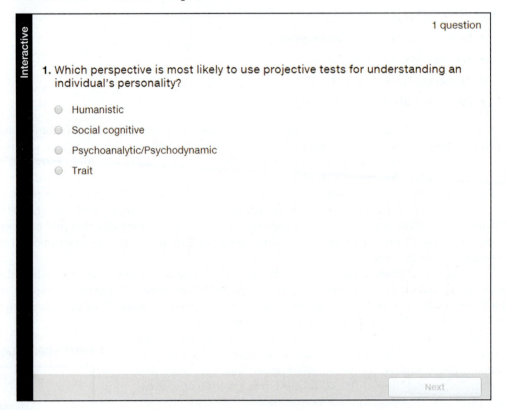

Interactive

1 question

1. Which perspective is most likely to use projective tests for understanding an individual's personality?

○ Humanistic

○ Social cognitive

○ Psychoanalytic/Psychodynamic

○ Trait

Next

Rorschach test

projective personality assessment that presents a series of 10 inkblots to clients, who are instructed to say whatever comes to mind upon viewing them. The responses are interpreted by a therapist and thought to be a window into the client's unconscious

The Rorschach test consists of a series of 10 inkblot cards. Hermann Rorschach had not intended the cards to be used as a projective measure of personality. Rather, they were meant to identify individuals with Schizophrenia or other severe mental disorders.

The most famous projective test is called the **Rorschach test**, which presents a series of 10 inkblots to participants who are instructed to say whatever comes to mind upon viewing them. The test assumes that the interpretations of the inkblots are related to the individual's unconscious thoughts.

For example, if you saw threatening storm clouds in the blurry inkblots, a psychologist might infer that you have feelings of fear or anxiety about something; if you saw a dog, you might be longing for a best friend or trusty companion. While this may seem like an unreliable and subjective way to assess the unconscious mind, psychologists who use this method tend to use a scoring system to measure participants' responses. For example, frequency tables indicate how often a particular response is given by the general population. The scientific evidence is mixed at best regarding the validity of this projective test (Mihura et al., 2013), yet it is still frequently used by primarily psychodynamic clinicians. In the video *The Rorschach Test*, you'll see an example of the administration and interpretation of the Rorschach.

The Rorschach Test

Another famous projective test is called the **Thematic Apperception Test, or TAT** for short. The TAT was developed by Henry Murray and presents people with a series of random, unfamiliar images and asks them to tell a story about what is happening in each picture.

Thematic apperception test (TAT)

projective personality assessment that presents clients with a series of ambiguous images/scenes and asks them to tell a story about what is happening in each picture

This is an example of a Thematic Apperception Test card. All of the cards include an ambiguous scene and the subject is asked to tell a dramatic story about what is happening in the picture.

People who use projective tests claim these stories are a way to access the person's unconscious and discover their inner hopes, fears, and desires.

To help you remember that the psycshodynamic perspective favors projective tests for personality, you can remember that P = P; psychodynamic = projective. Once you recall the

Projective   Psychodynamic

word projective, you can imagine someone "projecting" their inner thoughts and feelings on to ambiguous stimulus as a way of determining their personality.

All of these projective tests are still in use today; however, a number of psychologists continue to question the reliability and validity of these methods of assessment, with mounting scientific evidence that these tests do not do all they claim they do (Erickson et al., 2007; Lilienfeld et al., 2000; May, 2001).

Let's Review

Perspectives	Assumptions of the Perspectives	Key Words to Remember	Type of Personality Assessments
Social-Cognitive	Our personality is shaped through the interaction of our traits and their reciprocal relationship with our environment.	Bandura Reciprocal determinism Self-efficacy	Interviews -unstructured -structured Behavioral observations Self-report inventories
Humanistic	Focus on the psychologically healthy person's need to grow and strive for self-actualization. Distress comes from a discrepancy between the actual and ideal self.	Maslow Rogers Self-actualization Unconditional positive regard Conditions of worth	Interviews -unstructured Self-report inventories
Psychoanalytic/ Psychodynamic	Personality develops from the interaction between unconscious forces (id, ego, super-ego) and their urges and desires (often sexual and aggressive). Childhood experiences play a crucial role in personality.	Freud Unconscious Sexual Aggression Defense mechanisms	Interviews -unstructured Projective tests -Rorschach test -Thematic apperception test
Trait	Our personality is characterized by genetically-influenced, enduring characteristics called traits. Traits are relatively stable over time and can predict behavior.	Cattell Eysenck Gray 5-factor theory of personality	Interviews -unstructured -structured Behavioral observations Self-report inventories -16PF -NEO-PI -Myers-Briggs Type Indicator -MMPI-2-RF

(Interactive)

Quiz for Module 14.12–14.13

1. This type of assessment is the largest category of objective personality inventories and requires a person to answer various questions.

    a. Behavioral observations

    b. Self-report inventories

    c. Structured interview

    d. Personality inventories

2. Lourdes took an online personality test that categorized her as an introvert. When she took the same test a day later, it categorized her as an extravert. Lourdes knew the test wasn't meaningful because it lacked _____.

    a. an interpretation

    b. significance

    c. reliability

    d. validity

3. Which personality assessment involves showing clients abstract pictures and asking them to talk about whatever they see in the picture?

    a. 16PF

    b. MMPI-2-RF

    c. The perception test

    d. Rorschach test

4. Which theoretical perspective is most likely to use projective tests?

    a. Psychodynamic

    b. Trait

    c. Biological

    d. Humanistic

Module 14.14: Piecing It Together: Antisocial Personality Disorder

LO 14.14 Analyze how the cross-cutting themes of psychology and theories of personality relate to antisocial personality disorder.

This chapter has explored the different theories used to understand the development of personality. In most cases, it is assumed the personality that develops is pleasant to be around and functional for the individual. However, this is not always the case. Theories of personality can be used to explain all types of personalities, including the more difficult and even dangerous ones.

A personality disorder is defined as a persistent way of thinking and feeling about oneself and others that significantly interferes with the ability to function in life (American Psychiatric Association, 2013). Personality disorders are long-standing problems that typically develop in adolescence and can be difficult to treat. According to the Diagnostic and Statistical Manual of Mental Disorders, Fifth Edition (DSM-5), Antisocial Personality Disorder (ASPD) is defined as a pervasive pattern of disregard for and violation of the rights of others, occurring since the age of 15. To receive a diagnosis of ASPD, the individual must be 18 years or older, show evidence of *conduct disorder* (children who exhibit persistent and frequent aggressive and disruptive behavior in the home and school) before the age of 15 and exhibit three or more of the following symptoms:

- Failure to conform to social norms with respect to lawful behaviors
- Deception, as indicated by lying, using aliases, or conning others for personal profit or pleasure
- Impulsivity
- Irritability and aggressiveness
- Reckless disregard for the safety of themselves or others
- Consistent irresponsibility (e.g., can't hold down a job or meet financial obligations)
- Lack of remorse toward others (e.g., being indifferent to or rationalizing have hurt, mistreated, or stolen from others)

ASPD and the criminal behavior associated with it has long-captivated the public. There is no doubt that television series such as *Dexter* and *Breaking Bad* have contributed to our current fascination with these individuals. Outside of Hollywood however, ASPD poses a serious societal concern associated with extreme economic costs and suffering by individuals affected by the actions of someone with this diagnosis (Petras et al., 2008). In fact, ASPD has been found to be the second costliest personality disorder (behind Borderline Personality Disorder) with respect to health care utilization (Maclean et al., 2014).

Estimates of the prevalence of ASPD in the general population range from 0.6–4.1 percent (Glenn et al., 2013; Samuels, 2011), with rates increasing drastically to 47 percent for men and 21 percent for women in a prison setting (Fazel & Danesh, 2002). Compared to other personality disorders, a relatively small number of individuals can be responsible for the enormous costs to society. It has been found that 5–6 percent of offenders commit approximately 50 percent of crimes and that these offenders typically continue their behavior throughout the course of their life (National Collaborating Center for Mental Health, 2010). As we consider ASPD in a broader context, a number of questions arise.

Figure 14.12 Personality Theories and ASPD

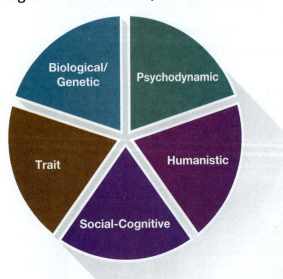

Variations in Human Functioning

- How do the different personality theories explain the development of ASPD?
- What role does genetics play in the development of ASPD?
- Do people with ASPD also have other psychological problems?

Antisocial personality disorder is a complex condition, so it is probably not surprising that there is no easy answer as to why someone would develop this personality disorder. As we have discussed in this chapter, the explanation given for someone's personality depends heavily on the perspective through which personality development is viewed. That is, a psychodynamic explanation of ASPD will likely look quite different than a social-cognitive explanation. Our tendency, when we see varying explanations, is to assume that one is right and the other is wrong. Rather than seeing different perspectives in competition with one another, it can be helpful to see them as working together to provide a thorough explanation for complex human behavior. Think of each perspective as contributing a piece to the overall "pie of understanding," as shown in Figure 14.12.

Explanations for Antisocial Personality Disorder (ASPD)

Jim is 32 years old, unemployed, and has just been convicted of voluntary manslaughter. He has received a number of psychological/psychiatric evaluations. Identify each perspective by dragging and dropping the correct personality perspective on the potential explanation for Jim's development of ASPD.

Explanation	Perspective
Jim grew up in a conflictual family environment. He learned quickly that he could get what he wanted by lying and manipulating others. Due to his parents' neglect, he was rarely caught and never punished for manipulative or aggressive behavior. Jim developed the belief that "you have to do what it takes to get what you want in life." He generally had positive outcome expectancies since he usually found a way to manipulate a situation for his self-interest.	Social-Cognitive
A CT scan and functional MRI revealed that Jim had reduced grey matter and functioning in the frontal lobe of his brain. This is the part of the brain that is particularly important when it comes to making thoughtful choices and learning from punishing consequences.	Biological
Jim's personality is organized in a way that makes it easy for him to behave in ways that aren't consistent with societal norms. He is extremely impulsive, high on extraversion, low on conscientiousness, and low on agreeableness.	Trait
Jim did not feel unconditional love growing up, which led him to experience the conditions of worth imposed by his parents. He had to go to extreme lengths to gain their attention or approval. The choices he continues to make are preventing him from reaching his fullest potential in life (i.e., self-actualization).	Humanistic
Jim did not have his basic needs met as a baby and therefore grew up with a general distrust of his environment. His primary emotions of envy, rage, and excitement are a function of his fixation in a pre-Oedipal stage. His superego was never given an opportunity to fully develop and therefore he experiences a lack of conscience. The id and ego drive his personality leading to impulsive, self-serving choices accompanied by an inability to take any responsibility for his behavior.	Psychodynamic

Check Answers

Since ASPD has its roots in either childhood or adolescence, many researchers have assumed that genetics must play an important role. Recall the earlier discussion of behavioral genetics where variance in observable characteristics (i.e., phenotype) can be partitioned into three sources:

Genetics and ASPD

Ferguson (2010) examined all of the relevant behavioral genetic studies and concluded that the variance in antisocial behaviors could be broken down in the following way: 56%, 31%, and 11%. Drag and drop the percentages to the pictures below to show how the variance in the development of antisocial behaviors is explained.

56%

Genes   +   Shared familial environment   +   Phenotypic variance within identical twins raised together (AKA "unique variance')

Question 1 of 3   End Challenge

Were you surprised by how little the role of shared family environment played in the development of ASPD? While genetics do play an important role, there is a significant amount of individual variation as well. This clinical picture is also complicated by the high rate of comorbidity among those diagnosed with ASPD. In fact, most individuals with ASPD also have other comorbid (co-occurring) psychological disorders (Glenn et al., 2013). The following are the top three comorbid conditions:

1. Substance abuse

2. Anxiety disorders

3. Depressive disorders

Extensive comorbidity is one of the many challenges researchers face when attempting to design and conduct research with individuals diagnosed with ASPD.

Research Methods

- Given the nature of the disorder, what are some of the issues researchers need to consider when drawing conclusions from research with this population?

There are a number of interesting challenges to consider when conducting research on ASPD. Let's continue our discussion of biological factors related to the development of ASPD. Numerous studies have examined the brains of those with ASPD and concluded that their brains look and function differently than people without ASPD (Glenn et al., 2013). Neuroimaging studies have revealed that men with ASPD have a significant reduction in grey matter in the prefrontal cortex compared to control groups (Raine et al., 2000) and that this reduction is suggestive of a serious developmental abnormality (Pemment, 2013). The prefrontal cortex plays an important role in experiencing stress and developing fear in appropriate situations, regulating arousal, and making thoughtful choices. Lack of fear, low level of arousal leading to sensation-seeking behaviors, and impulsive behaviors are characteristic symptoms of those diagnosed with ASPD.

Given that we know there is some (and in some cases substantial) overlap between those with ASPD and other conditions, such as substance abuse, which of the following would be important to consider when developing hypotheses and conducting research? (Choose as many as you think are important.)

- Whether or not the participant has been in jail at some point in their lives.

- Trying to determine if the changes are really a function of ASPD or if they could be a result of the accompanying substance abuse (or other comorbid disorder).

- Whether or not the participant with ASPD is telling the truth during an interview.

If you selected each one of these issues, you're right! These are just a few of the important questions researchers have asked and had to consider. Why would it matter if a participant has been in jail? In addition to a reduction in grey matter in the prefrontal cortex, individuals with ASPD have also been found to have a variety of deficits in *executive functions* such as maintaining attention, shifting between tasks, working memory, problem solving, and inhibition (De Brito et al., 2013; Morgan & Lilienfeld, 2000). These problems are also very consistent with the symptoms of ASPD, but there is one problem. The vast majority of this research has been conducted with participants who are currently incarcerated or who have been in jail for a significant length of time at some point in their lives. Living in any impoverished and sedentary environment has been shown to negatively influence executive functioning (Meijers et al., 2015), and most would agree that a prison setting would qualify as an impoverished and sedentary environment. Therefore, isn't it possible that rather than the deficits in executive functioning causing ASPD, that it is instead the consequence of having ASPD (i.e., going to jail and living with a lack of stimulation) leading to impairments in executive functioning? Many of the studies conducted with individuals with ASPD are correlational in nature and this example is a good reminder that *correlation does not imply causation.*

Journal Prompt: The Role of Substance Abuse

As discovered earlier, substance abuse is the number one co-occurring psychological condition in those with ASPD. How could substance abuse be a confounding variable in the neuroscience research being conducted with individuals with ASPD?

Schiffer and colleagues (2011) conducted a study in an attempt to understand the role that substance abuse may play in the structural differences in the brain that have characterized many individuals with ASPD. The only experimental way to disentangle substance abuse from violent behavior is to examine and compare all possible groups. Therefore, MRIs were performed on four distinct groups of men:

What do you think they found? These researchers found the same results as others (e.g., Raine et al., 2000) in that some of the men had less gray matter in the prefrontal cortex; but, it was the men with the substance use disorders, *not* the violent behavior that displayed these differences in the brain. The violent offenders did have some significant brain abnormalities but these were found in the mesolimbic reward system, including the nucleus accumbens and amygdala (Schiffer et al., 2011). These results suggest that while the biological perspective has much to offer in terms of explaining the origins of ASPD, there are still many unknowns, highlighting the importance of considering various theories of personality when attempting to explain personality development.

Cultural and Social Diversity

- Why are more men than women diagnosed with ASPD?
- Does ASPD look the same in women as it does in men?

One of the most well-established demographic differences in ASPD is the significant difference between the number men and women who receive the diagnosis. Men are two to five times more likely to receive a diagnosis of ASPD and obtain significantly higher scores on measures of ASPD, regardless of whether the symptoms are being measured categorically or dimensionally (Cale & Lilienfeld, 2002; Compton et al., 2005; Dolan & Völlm, 2009). In addition to the differences in prevalence, there is also variation in the expression of the disorder with women having lower rates of violent antisocial behaviors, aggressiveness, and irritability (Alegria et al., 2013). Despite having a lower prevalence rate overall, women with ASPD appear to have experienced significantly more *childhood* adverse events in their life such as:

- Physical neglect
- Verbal abuse
- Physical abuse
- Emotional neglect
- Sexual abuse
- Parental history of mood disorder
- Parental history of antisocial personality disorder

Women are also more likely than men to have experienced *adult* adverse events, including:

- Sexual assault/rape
- Intimate partner violence
- Married to, or lived with, an alcoholic partner

While it is likely that "true" gender difference in the prevalence of ASPD exist, there may be some other possible reasons to explain this gender difference. There may be a diagnostic bias, where clinicians are more likely to view men as aggressive and likely to engage in antisocial behavior and therefore diagnose the disorder more often in men. Furthermore, because the disorder is expressed differently in men and women (women are more likely to engage in nonviolent antisocial behaviors), it is possible that some of the women are overlooked because their antisocial behaviors are less "sensational."

Ethics

- What are some of the ethical concerns to consider when working with a potentially dangerous and often imprisoned population?

There are a number of ethical considerations to keep in mind with respect to ASPD. Consider the following scenario, and see if you can match the potential ethical concern to the various parts of the story. After you correctly select the ethical concern, you will receive more information about the ethics relevant to that situation.

Remember Jim? Jim is 32 years old, unemployed, and has just been convicted of voluntary manslaughter. He recently discovered that his wife of 4 years was having an affair with one of his coworkers. Jim went to a bar where people from his work hung out and, after a heated physical fight, Jim shot his wife's lover in the head. The coworker died at the scene, and Jim was arrested immediately. Despite having a life filled with manipulation, conning others, and theft, Jim had never been arrested as an adult. In fact, he prided himself on his ability to outsmart the cops. His childhood and adolescence were a different story as he was sentenced to juvenile detention on a number of occasions. It was there where Jim learned the "tricks of the trade" that allowed him to get what he wanted in life without getting caught. However, the discovery of his wife's affair was too much for him to handle, and he let his impulsive urges take over.

Jim was interviewed by a forensic psychologist and diagnosed with Antisocial Personality Disorder and Major Depressive Disorder. He was sentenced to 10 years in prison with the possibility of parole after 5 years served. The following interactive will take you through the rest of Jim's story. Can you spot the ethical dilemmas as they arise? What would you do if you were Dr. Shilo?

Ethical Considerations in ASPD

Read through the following fictional account of a person diagnosed with antisocial personality disorder and recently found guilty of a crime. Each stage will present an ethical dilemma. See if you can figure out what the ethical dilemma is before clicking "Next" to advance to the next

1 of 8   Previous   Next

Quiz for Module 14.14

1. Roger is 20 years old and has a history of stealing from his parents, breaking into the grocery store to steal alcohol, and just recently severely assaulted another person. Roger does not feel regret for any of his actions and in fact justifies his behavior by saying people deserve what they get. Which diagnosis seems most appropriate for Roger?

    a. Psychopathic deviant disorder
    b. Borderline personality disorder
    c. Antisocial personality disorder
    d. Conduct disorder

2. Where would you be most likely to find a large number of people diagnosed with antisocial personality disorder?

    a. High school
    b. Prison
    c. Juvenile detention
    d. A political debate

3. Jason has been diagnosed with antisocial personality disorder (ASPD). Which comorbid disorder would Jason be most likely to have?

    a. Substance use disorder
    b. Anxiety disorder
    c. Depressive disorder
    d. Schizophrenia-spectrum disorder

4. Neuroimaging studies examining men diagnosed with antisocial personality disorder have found a pattern of results that includes a reduction of grey matter in which part of the brain?

    a. Cingulate cortex
    b. Temporal lobe
    c. Amygdala
    d. Prefrontal cortex

5. Women diagnosed with ASPD have experienced significantly more adverse events in childhood and adulthood that include

    _____.

    a. sexual assault/abuse, physical abuse, and emotional neglect
    b. being a victim of a natural disaster, loss of a parent, and severe injury
    c. severe injury, sexual assault/abuse, and loss of a parent
    d. sexual assault/abuse, being a victim of a natural disaster, and loss of a parent

Summary

Module 14.1–14.2 The Psychodynamic Perspective

Personality refers to a stable style of thinking, feeling, and behaving in the world. There are various perspectives, or schools of thought, in the field of psychology, and each perspective has its own theories regarding the development of our personalities.

The psychodynamic perspective emerged from the work of Sigmund Freud and his theory of **psychoanalysis.** This theory emphasized the role of the unconscious and its power to direct all thoughts and actions, referred to as **psychic determinism.** Freud saw the mind as three dynamic systems that were often in conflict. The **id** strives to satisfy instinctual needs and operates according to the **pleasure principle.** The **ego** represents the rational part of the mind and utilizes **defense mechanisms** as a way to manage the anxiety caused by the id. The ego operates according to the **reality principle.** The **superego** is the last part of the mind to develop, and serves as the "conscience" by internalizing norms from parents and society and developing a sense of right and wrong. Freud proposed that each person proceeds through a series of five **psychosexual stages** by successfully resolving an internal conflict associated with each stage. If the conflict is unable to be resolved, the individual may become **fixated** in a particular stage, causing problems later in life.

Post-Freud psychodynamic theorists, or neo-Freudians, used many of Freud's basic ideas in the development of their own theories of personality. Jung emphasized the notion of a **collective unconscious,** a shared pool or memories and images common to all humans. He claimed there were a number of prototypical images consistent across people, which he referred to as **archetypes.** Adler's **individual psychology** highlighted every person's desire to achieve superiority. He claimed the key to understanding an individual's personality, was to understand each person's unique struggle with feelings of inferiority. Horney proposed the concept of **womb envy** as the complement to Freud's theory of penis envy, which described the jealousy men feel toward women for their role in nurturing and sustaining life. Her theory emphasized social factors, particularly anxiety, and how these factors influence personality development.

Module 14.3–14.4 The Humanistic Perspective

In part as a reaction to psychodynamic theories, humanistic theories of personality emerged in the mid 1900s. **Humanistic theories** emphasized our conscious awareness and need to achieve self-improvement, happiness, and fulfillment. Maslow stressed the importance of **self-actualization,** the process of becoming your *real self* and achieving your fullest potential. Rogers' theory of personality focused on the individual's understanding of who they were as a person, or their **self-concept.** His theory proposed that all people strive to have minimal discrepancy between their actual self and ideal self. Receiving **unconditional positive regard** from others can help to achieve these results, while not receiving unconditional positive regard can lead to **conditions of worth.**

Module 14.5–14.6 The Social Cognitive Perspective

Social cognitive theories of personality emphasize the interaction between the individual and their environment. Rotter introduced the concept of **personal control**, referring to the sense of control an individual believes he or she has over the environment. This concept was expanded into the theory of **locus of control,** which described the relationship between an individual's behavior and their perception of control over the situation. Those who possess an **internal locus of control** believe they have control over their environment, whereas people who have an **external locus of control** believe that their fate is controlled by outside forces. Locus of control is greatly influenced by **outcome expectancies,** which are our assumptions about the consequences of our behavior. Bandura extended the social cognitive theory by proposing the concept of **reciprocal determinism**, which states that there is a bidirectional relationship between the environment and an individual's personality. He saw the concept of **efficacy expectancies** (i.e., self-efficacy), or an individual's beliefs and expectations about their own abilities to perform a task, as central to their personality and capabilities in life.

Module 14.7–14.10 The Trait Perspective and the Biology of Personality

Theorists prefer to describe personality in terms of **traits**, or enduring characteristics that predispose a person to behave in a particular way. Allport, one of the earliest trait theorists proposed a list of 18,000 traits to describe personality. Cattell referred to traits as either **surface** (those that can be easily seen) or **source** (the underlying factor of the surface traits). He used **factor analysis,** a statistical method of identifying patterns of responses, to reduce Allport's traits down to a total of 16 personality dimensions, which became the basis for his assessment measure of personality. Currently, the most popular trait theory of personality is the five-factor model, also known as the *Big Five.* The Five-Factor Model states that personality can best be described according to five dimensions including: openness to experience, conscientiousness, extraversion, agreeableness, and neuroticism (emotional stability). The **person-situation controversy** unfolded when Mischel began to emphasize the role situations can play in affecting behavior, suggesting the stable personality traits may not have been as predictive as once thought. His **Cognitive Affective Processing System (CAPS)** model states that an individual's response depends on the psychological features present in the situation.

Eysenck proposed that personality could be described according to three primary dimensions and that arousal from the reticular activating system played a central role in personality determination. Similarly, Gray suggested that there were two primary brain systems, the **behavioral activation system (BAS)** and the **behavioral inhibition system (BIS)** that account for the particular personality traits present in an individual. The field of **personality neuroscience** uses brain imaging technology to attempt to understand personality. Behavioral genetics is a field of study that examines the relationship between personality and heredity. **Heritability** refers to the percentage of trait variation that is due to genetics. Most traits that have been researched in this way (e.g., extraversion and neuroticism) have been found to be heritable at approximately 0.4.

Module 14.11 Evaluating Different Perspectives on Personality

There are numerous psychological perspectives that offer varied descriptions and explanations of personality development. All perspectives have strengths and weaknesses and it is important to understand the issues underlying the positive and negative aspects to each of the theories.

Module 14.12–14.13 The Assessment of Personality

Assessment of personality can come in many forms. Regardless of the method, all assessments of personality must possess both **reliability** (consistency) and **validity** (accuracy). Personality assessments can take the form of **structured or unstructured interviews**, projective tests, behavioral observations, or self-report inventories. **Projective tests**, such as the **Rorschach Test** and **Thematic Apperception Test (TAT)**, involve ambiguous stimuli and require the individual to respond to the prompt. This response is said to provide a window into the unconscious, which offers insight into an individual's personality. **Behavioral observations** are present-focused and involve data collection of an individual's behavior in a particular environment. **Self-report inventories** are questionnaire measures of personality. The MMPI-2-RF is often used clinically and has the most empirical support behind its development and interpretation.

Chapter 14 Quiz

1. Rayanne wants to drop out of college to be a roadie for her favorite band. She knows if she did this, it would disappoint her parents who worked hard for her to have the opportunity to attend college. Despite her desires, she attends college, but every weekend she goes to concerts. Freud would say Rayanne is using which part of her personality to fulfill her desire?

   a. Ego

   b. Id

   c. Superego

   d. Subconscious

2. Which of the following represents the correct order of Freud's psychosexual stages of personality development?

   a. Oral, anal, genital, latency, phallic

   b. Oral, anal, phallic, latency, genital

   c. Oral, phallic, anal, genital, latency

   d. Oral, genital, anal, latency, phallic

3. The purpose of defense mechanisms is to help the ego manage _____.

   a. aggressive impulses

   b. sexual impulses

   c. worry and anxiety

   d. unconscious thoughts surfacing

4. Bandura's concept of reciprocal determinism suggests it is the interaction of personality, _____, and _____ that shape who we become.

   a. self-efficacy; environment

   b. environment; behavior

   c. traits; genetics

   d. unconscious; self-worth

5. A good personality assessment must accurately measure what it claims to be measuring. This concept is referred to as _____.

   a. structured

   b. reliability

   c. validity

   d. standardization

6. Compared to the psychodynamic theory of personality, the humanistic theory is more:

   a. focused on the present.

   b. focused on the past.

   c. deterministic.

   d. mechanistic.

7. According to Eysenck, extraverts have a reticular activating system that is _____, and introverts have an _____ reticular activating system.

   a. underactive; overactive

   b. overactive; underactive

   c. activated; inhibited

   d. inhibited; activated

8. Which trait was later added to the Eysenck Personality Inventory, leading to some controversy among psychologists?

   a. Psychoticism

   b. Neuroticism

   c. Extraversion

   d. Introversion

9. Alfonso was raised with high standards about honesty and integrity, which included regular church attendance. He moved away from his parents' home a few years ago and now doesn't attend church. He feels bad about this and wishes he would start going to church again. He also knows his parents would be disappointed in him. According to Rogers, Alfonso is experiencing a discrepancy between his _____ and his perception of his _____.

    a. unconditional positive regard; parents' conditional positive regard

    b. self-concept; actual self

    c. ideal self; parents

    d. ideal self; actual self

10. Dr. Frankel shows his client pictures and asks the client to tell a story about what he sees in the pictures. The client's stories usually involve unresolved anger between parents and children. Dr. Frankel is using the _____ to assess the client's _____.

    a. 16-PF; unconscious mind

    b. NEO-PI; personality conflicts

    c. Rorschach test; emotional mind

    d. Thematic apperception test; unconscious mind

11. Marisha, a 45–year-old mother of three believes she has no control over her children's behavior. They never listen to anything she says and are disrespectful to her. Her beliefs about her ability to control her children lead her to give up quickly when it comes to discipline. Marisha would be considered to have a(n)_____.

    a. external locus of control

    b. internal locus of control

    c. external outcome expectancy

    d. poor self-concept

12. Carl Jung believed in a shared pool of memories and images common to all humans. He referred to this concept as _____.

    a. the subconscious

    b. defense mechanisms

    c. archetypes

    d. the collective unconscious

13. Juan believes when he kicks the soccer ball, it will go where he wants it to go because he believes he is a good soccer player and has practiced kicking the ball daily for many hours. Juan has what Bandura would call high _____ in sports performance.

    a. outcome expectancy   b. reciprocal determinism

    c. self-efficacy   d. self-esteem

14. According to Cattell, surface traits are traits that _____.

    a. most people exhibit in social situations

    b. exist only for a brief time in tense situations

    c. are not easily seen, but form the core of the personality

    d. are most visible in others

15. Adalia is 18 and leaving for college. She thinks of herself as a good student because she worked hard in school. She also has many friends but was never part of the popular crowd because she didn't play sports or join many clubs. She is not sure where she will fit in at college or what her interests will be. Adalia is working on figuring out who she is, an idea Rogers called _____.

    a. self-esteem   b. self-actualization

    c. self-concept   d. self-reflection

16. What are the traits associated with the "Big Five" model of personality?

    a. Openness to experience, conscientiousness, extraversion, agreeableness, and neuroticism

    b. Openness to experience, conscientiousness, excitability, agreeableness, and neuroticism

    c. Openness to experience, extraversion, introversion, anxiousness, and negativity

    d. Openness to experience, consciousness, extraversion, anxiousness, and negativity

17. "Behavior depends on an interaction between the condition an individual is in and their personality traits." This statement summarizes the _____.

    a. trait theory of personality

    b. person-situation controversy

    c. five-factor model

    d. cultural–relativism controversy

18. People from Western cultures are often described as independent and outspoken. These cultures would be described as _____.

    a. open   b. collectivistic

    c. individualistic   d. closed

19. According to Gray, what brain system is responsible for positive feelings such as hope and elation?

    a. Fight, flight, freeze system

    b. Reticular formation system

    c. Behavioral inhibition system (BIS)

    d. Behavioral activation system (BAS)

20. Tony is a therapist who identifies with Maslow's theories of growth and achievement. Most of the time, he starts his assessment of a new client with a question like this:

   a. "Tell me about your relationship with your mother."
   b. "Tell me about yourself and your hopes for the future?"
   c. "Tell me about your childhood."
   d. "Tell me about the behavior you would like to change and the thoughts you have about that behavior."

21. In the fields of personality neuroscience and behavioral genetics, what are the two most widely researched personality traits?

   a. Extraversion and neuroticism
   b. Conscientiousness and agreeableness
   c. Extraversion and agreeableness
   d. Conscientiousness and neuroticism

22. Landon and Logan are identical twins who have been raised in the same family and attended the same schools. As a result, their environments have been very similar. Landon is goal-oriented and driven while Logan is laid back and easy going. How would researchers explain this personality difference?

   a. Since genetics should explain all personality differences, there must have been a genetic mutation.
   b. Shared environment is less important than once thought.
   c. Only 40 percent of personality is inherited.
   d. There is no way to explain their differences.

23. The term genotype refers to which variation in personality development?

   a. Familial
   b. Environmental
   c. Genetic
   d. Expressed traits

24. June read that the heritability of hair color is 73 percent. When her friend asked her what that meant, she said _____.

   a. there is a 73 percent chance that you will have the same hair color as your mother.
   b. there is a 73 percent chance that you will have the same hair color as your father.
   c. hair color is 73 percent inherited.
   d. 73 percent of the variability in hair color between people is due to genetics

25. What is one strength of the psychodynamic perspective?

   a. The emphasis on how to shape a child's personality
   b. The psychosexual stages
   c. The emphasis on childhood sexuality
   d. The focus on how early life experiences shape personality

26. The HEXACO model of personality is similar to the five-factor model, but adds a dimension of _____.

   a. humor
   b. honesty-humility
   c. humanism
   d. humility-happiness

27. Dr. Mira is meeting with a client for the first time. She asks the client a series of questions exactly as they are written on her page. Dr. Mira is conducting what type of assessment?

   a. Structured interview
   b. Unstructured interview
   c. Behavioral observation
   d. Self-report inventory

28. Horney's concept of _____ describes men as jealous of women's role as nurturers and life givers.

   a. superiority   b. inferiority
   c. penis envy   d. womb envy

29. Assessments that involve the presentation of ambiguous stimuli, which are then interpreted by therapists, are called _____ tests.

   a. projective   b. objective
   c. self-report   d. personality

30. LaShawn is a 200-meter runner and is working on qualifying for the Olympics. He believes he has the talent to achieve his dreams through hard work and training. When he is in a big qualifying race, he visualizes winning the race. Rotter would say that LaShawn has an internal locus of control for running due to his _____.

   a. outcome expectancies
   b. behavior and training
   c. personal expectancies
   d. control expectations

Chapter 15
Psychological Disorders

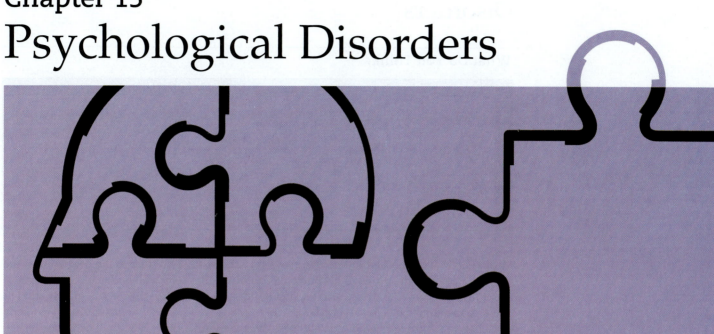

 ## Chapter Outline and Learning Objectives

How Common are Psycholological Disorders?

What Do You Think?

> **Interactive**
>
> **Survey: What Do You Think**
>
> What percentage of people in the United States have been diagnosed with a psychological disorder in the past year?
>
> ○ 5–10%
>
> ○ 11–15%
>
> ○ 16–20%
>
> ○ 21–25%

Most people were shocked to hear the news on August 11, 2014, that Robin Williams, at the age of 63, committed suicide in his home in California. The comedian and actor spoke openly about his struggles with drugs, alcohol, and depression over the years, yet his suicide still left many people thinking *"I had no idea it was so bad."* Many well-known public figures have openly discussed their struggles with mental illness over the years: Elton John, the late Carrie Fisher, Brooke Shields, Gwyneth Paltrow, Lady Gaga, Zoe Sugg, Demi Lovato, Angelina Jolie... The list could go on and yet, despite a shift toward more open disclosure and discussion of personal struggles, there is still an overall lack of knowledge, understanding, and acceptance of people suffering from psychological disorders.

Module 15.1 – 15.3: Understanding Psychological Disorders

Most people agree that a mother who throws herself in front of a train while holding her young child is not behaving normally. But how do we distinguish between someone who is temporarily unable to get out of bed after going through a traumatic divorce and someone who is suffering from severe depression? How do we know which person is likely to recover after a period of grieving, and which person needs immediate counseling? What is the difference between a child with mood and behavioral instabilities who is "just being a kid" and a child who has bipolar disorder?

Definition and Prevalence of Psychological Disorders

LO 15.1   **Recognize the definition and prevalence of psychological disorders.**

Scientists in the field of medicine study *pathology*, which refers to an understanding of the disease process (pathology comes from the Greek word *pathos*, meaning suffering). In attempting to understand the disease process, scientists must uncover knowledge about the causes and effects of diseases. This information is then used to develop treatments and prevention plans for various medical conditions. The field of *abnormal psychology*, or what is technically referred to as **psychopathology**, involves the scientific study of mental/psychological disorders (psycho coming from the Greek origin *psyche*, meaning soul).

What exactly is a psychological disorder? Many terms have been used, somewhat interchangeably, to refer to abnormal disturbances in behavior and mental processes. A precise definition of a psychological disorder is challenging because of the inherent subjectivity of the word "abnormal"—a behavior that one person might see as a symptom of mental illness, another person may view as creative eccentricity.

psychopathology

scientific study of mental/psychological disorders

The American Psychiatric Association's (APA) *Diagnostic and Statistical Manual of Mental Disorders, Fifth Edition (DSM-5)*, which favors the term *mental disorder* rather than psychological disorder (although most psychologists would see the terms as equivalent), is the current gold-standard in the United States for the diagnosis of psychopathology (APA, 2013, p. 310). The DSM-5 defines a **mental disorder** as a clinically significant disturbance in a person's thoughts, emotions, or behavior that reflects dysfunction in mental functioning. The definition continues by emphasizing that a mental disorder is often accompanied by significant distress or disability in social, occupational, or other important activities. Interestingly, the DSM-5 also includes aspects of the definition devoted to what is *not* to be considered a mental disorder, including:

- An acceptable or culturally approved response to a common stressor or loss (e.g., death of a loved one)

- Socially deviant behavior and conflicts between an individual and society (e.g., unusual political, religious, or sexual behaviors), unless these behaviors result in dysfunction for the individual

For the purposes of our discussion, we will use both the terms "mental illness" and "psychological disorder" to refer to individuals struggling with psychological symptoms. Just as physical illnesses can produce particular physical symptoms (e.g., fever, pain), people suffering from psychological disorders also exhibit *symptoms*—characteristic thoughts, feelings, or behaviors that indicate a potential psychological disorder. Many people have symptoms of a psychological disorder, but would not meet the full criteria to receive a diagnosis. In thinking about the difference between having *symptoms* of a psychological disorder and actually *having* a psychological disorder, it can be helpful to remember that psychological disorders affect an individual in various ways. As you'll see in the video *The 4 D's of Psychological Disorders*, a diagnosis tends to involve the 4 D's: distress, dysfunction, deviance, and sometimes danger. After watching the video, see if you can recall examples from each category.

Sometimes a person may suffer from two or more psychological disorders, a condition known as **comorbidity**. For example, many people simultaneously experience both depressive and anxiety disorders (Almeida et al., 2012; Cummings et al., 2014). Often, substance abuse problems such as alcoholism are associated with other psychological disorders. You've likely heard someone talking about "self-medicating" with drugs or alcohol

mental disorder
clinically significant disturbance in a person's thoughts, emotions, or behavior that reflects dysfunction in mental functioning

comorbidity
condition where a person is diagnosed with two or more psychology disorders

The 4 D's of Psychological Disorders

Interactive

Understanding the 4 D's of Psychological Disorders

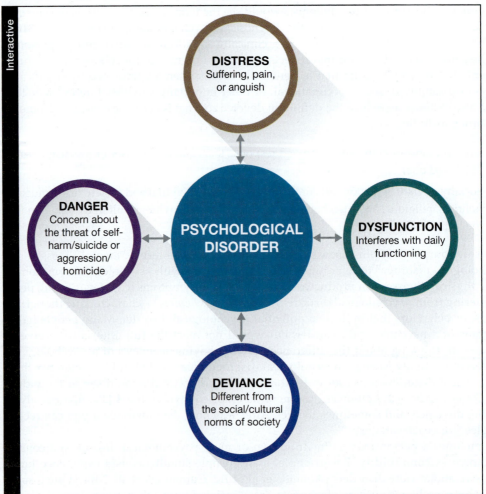

because of an underlying problem with depression or anxiety, which may help explain the high rate of comorbidity between substance use disorders and other psychological disorders (Brady & Sinha, 2014; Havassy et al., 2004; Robinson et al., 2011). The comorbid existence of a substance use disorder with another psychological disorder is referred to as *dual diagnosis*.

PREVALENCE OF PSYCHOLOGICAL DISORDERS As you can imagine, attempting to find the exact number of people suffering from a psychological disorder is an impossible task. However, numerous studies examining large groups of people have been conducted over the years in an attempt to obtain an estimate of the prevalence, or proportion of people who have been diagnosed with a psychological disorder, and the extent to which those rates vary between countries and cultures. In 2000, the World Health Organization published a report comparing lifetime prevalence rates of psychological disorder across countries (World Health Organization, 2000).

Two take-home points can be gleaned from this data: (1) there is substantial variation across countries with respect to the reporting of psychological disorders, and (2) the United States is at the top of the list with close to 50 percent of the sample reporting a diagnosis of a psychological disorder at some point in their lives.

The National Institute of Mental Health has conducted more recent surveys on the prevalence of psychological disorders within the United States. Their report focused on a 12-month period prevalence rate and found that in 2012, 18.6 percent of U.S. adults met the criteria for any psychological disorder *except* developmental and substance use disorders (Substance Abuse and Mental Health Services Administration, 2013). If you add the nearly 8 percent of U.S. adults who have been diagnosed with a substance use disorder in the past year, we have

Psychological Disorders Across Countries

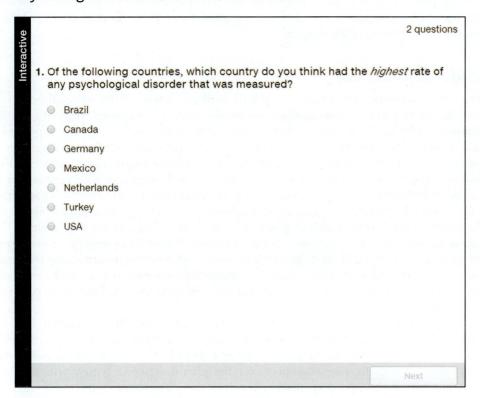

Prevalence of Psychological Disorders Across Countries

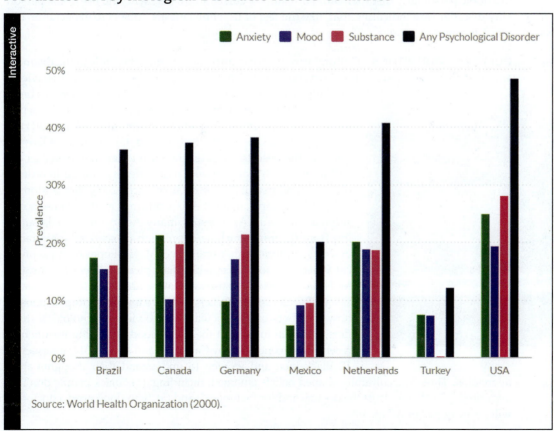

more than 26 percent of Americans who have been diagnosed with a psychological condition in the past year. Just think—on average, one out of every four people in your class has been diagnosed with a psychological disorder *in the past year*. How does this compare to your answer at the beginning of the chapter?

Gender Differences

Overall, more women than men are diagnosed with psychological disorders, although the gender difference varies somewhat when specific disorders are examined. While it's possible that women truly do have a higher rate of psychological disorders, it is also important to consider various cultural and social issues that have the potential to influence diagnoses. In Western society, it's more culturally acceptable for women to discuss their emotional problems than it is for men, so women may be more likely to seek treatment. For example, women are more often diagnosed with depression and anxiety than men (World Health Organization, 2015). Conversely, men have higher rates of substance abuse and antisocial personality disorder than women (World Health Organization, 2015). When men behave abnormally, they are more likely to drink too much and display aggressive behavior, externalizing their stress, whereas women are more likely to become depressed and hopeless, internalizing their emotional pain (Rosenfield & Mouzon, 2013). This distinction suggests that gender-based socialization often plays a significant role in the expression of symptoms and diagnosis of psychiatric disorders.

Diagnoses may also be influenced by clinicians' expectations of each gender. Maureen Ford and Thomas Widiger (1989) conducted a study in which they sent fictitious case studies to clinical psychologists for diagnosis. One case described a patient with antisocial personality disorder (usually diagnosed in males); the other described a patient with histrionic personality disorder (usually diagnosed in females). The subject of each case study was identified as male in some cases and female in others. Ford and Widiger discovered that when the antisocial personality disorder case was identified as male, most clinicians diagnosed it correctly. However, when the subject was identified as female, most clinicians identified it as histrionic personality disorder. Similar results occurred in reverse with the histrionic personality disorder case indicating that, like the rest of us, clinicians are subject to expectation bias when it comes to gender.

cultural relativism

understanding that any individual's behavior or psychological symptom must be evaluated in the context of their own culture

CULTURAL VARIATIONS   Cultural variations can also play an important role in the diagnosis and ultimately, prevalence rates of psychological disorders. What passes for normal behavior in one culture may look remarkably abnormal in another. In a broad sense, **cultural relativism** suggests that any individual's behavior must be evaluated in reference to their culture (Park, 2011).

Applied to psychological disorders, cultural relativism refers to the need to consider the individual characteristics of a culture in which a person with a disorder was raised in order to diagnose and treat it (Lopez & Guarnaccia, 2000; Sam & Moreira, 2012). For example, in most Asian cultures, mental illness is considered shameful. As a result, many Asian individuals suffering from disorders such as depression or schizophrenia report bodily symptoms rather than psychological ones because physical illness is more acceptable than mental illness (Fedoroff & McFarlane, 1998; Kalibatseva & Leong, 2011).

Culturally shaped beliefs can have important implications for how members of a particular culture view psychological disorders, which in turn affect their likelihood of seeking treatment. A recent study conducted by Campbell and Long (2014) interviewed 17 Black men and women to understand their thoughts about depression. Three key culturally shaped beliefs emerged, including: (1) "black people don't get depressed"; (2) "I don't trust the doctors and/or treatment"; and (3) "you don't need a doctor—it will go away, just pray" (p. 48).

Facial tattoos have a long tradition in various cultures and can have different meanings, depending on the cultural context.

Some disorders are known as **culture-bound syndromes**, which means they are limited to specific cultural groups. For example, koro is a psychological disorder primarily found in South Asian and East Asian countries in which the sufferer believes that his or her external genitals (or breasts in females) are retracting into the body, which will ultimately cause death (Chiang, 2015). Tajin Kyofusho (TKS) is a social anxiety disorder found primarily in Japan that causes people to fear they will do something inappropriate in public and cause embarrassment to others (Zhou et al., 2014).

Explanations of Psychological Disorders

LO 15.2 **Describe contemporary explanations of psychological disorders.**

People unlucky enough to be considered "mad" in the Middle Ages were caged, beaten, burned, exorcised, or castrated in desperate attempts to cure them of their aberrant behaviors. Fortunately, the medical model emerged in the 1800s and changed the outcome for those who were suffering from psychological disorders. The **medical model** viewed psychological abnormalities in the same way as physical abnormalities. They were seen as diseases that, like biological diseases, have symptoms, causes, and cures. This *rethinking* of mental illness was important historically because it paved the way for different schools of thought to emerge. Throughout history, many different theoretical approaches have been proposed to understand and explain psychological disorders.

A CONTEMPORARY FRAMEWORK FOR UNDERSTANDING THE CAUSES OF PSYCHOLOGICAL DISORDERS As practicing clinical psychologists, we can tell you that one of the most common questions we are asked by patients (or their parents) is "Why?" People want to understand why they developed a particular psychological disorder. The answer is, of course, complicated and depends somewhat on which psychological disorder is being discussed. In general, however, a useful framework for understanding any psychological disorder involves the 3 P's: predisposing causes, precipitating causes, and, perpetuating causes.

Predisposing causes are existing underlying factors that make an individual particularly susceptible to a certain disorder. Genetics, birth defects, environmentally damaging effects on the brain, toxins such as alcohol, and viruses or bacteria can all be predisposing causes. Predisposing causes are often biological in nature, but they don't have to be. Being born into a home with a high level of marital discord is a predisposing factor for developing psychological difficulties later in life (Brock & Kochanska, 2015).

Let's say you are predisposed to alcohol use with a family history of alcoholism. You have been deliberately staying away from alcohol, but when your new job becomes overwhelming, you suddenly find it harder to resist the urge to drink. **Precipitating causes** are the events in our day-to-day lives that initiate the onset of a particular disorder. You can think of precipitating causes as those environmental situations that were "the straw that broke the camel's back."

Imagine that your alcohol consumption distracts you from pressures at work. You also gain attention of friends and family members, who notice that you appear so much more relaxed and are more fun to be around. **Perpetuating causes** are the consequences of a disorder that help keep it going once it has started. These maintaining factors can involve anything from positive feelings brought about by the behavior, the avoidance of painful memories or relationships, or physical changes in the body that create a more conducive environment for the symptoms.

A useful analogy for the development of psychological disorders involves lighting a match. Imagine you came across a match, recognized what it was, and understood how that little piece of wood could turn into fire. The match contains within it all of the *ingredients* needed to make fire (predisposing causes). However, it will not ignite unless it is provided with the right type of environmental stimuli, which in this case is a surface that will produce frictional heat when contacted (precipitating causes). Once the match is lit, there are certain factors necessary for the fire to be maintained such as a lack of wind or a long enough stick that will continue to burn (perpetuating causes).

culture-bound syndromes

disorders that only exist in specific cultural groups

medical model

perspective that suggests that physical and psychological disorders develop, and should be treated, in the same way

predisposing cause

factor in explaining the development of psychological disorders that focuses on the existing, underlying factors that increase the susceptibility of developing a particular disorder

precipitating cause

factor in explaining the development of psychological disorders that focuses on the events and experiences in daily life that may initiate the onset of a particular disorder

perpetuating causes

factor in explaining the development of psychological disorders that focuses on the consequences of a disorder that helps maintain psychological symptoms

Discovering the Causes for a Psychological Disorder

	Predisposing Causes	Precipitating Causes	Perpetuating Causes
Interactive	Lucy's aunt struggled with anorexia for most of her life.	Lucy's first boyfriend broke up with her and immediately started dating someone she saw as "thinner" than her.	Once she started losing weight, Lucy found that she felt strong and powerful in a way she hadn't felt before.
	Lucy had been involved in ballet since she was 4 years old.	Lucy's ballet teacher told her she would need to lose some weight if she were to ever become a principal dancer.	Lucy noticed that she was receiving more attention from her dance teacher once she lost weight.

CONTEMPORARY VIEWS OF PSYCHOPATHOLOGY   If you recall, there are numerous different perspectives within the field of psychology (see LO 1.2). Likewise, a wide range of contemporary views of psychological disorders also exist. The biological approach grew out of the medical model and looks for physical problems as a root cause of the psychological disorder. Structural abnormalities in the brain, neurotransmitter dysfunction, and genetic factors are all factors at the forefront of the biological approach (Buchsbaum & Haier, 1983; Fowles, 2002).

A clinician using the psychoanalytic or psychodynamic approach investigates unconscious conflicts and other possible underlying psychological factors. Trauma and unresolved unconscious issues are seen as the primary reason behind current psychological problems (Blatt & Levy, 1998). According to this perspective, most of these factors can usually be traced back to childhood (Perry et al., 1987). For example, a woman who was abandoned by her father when she was a young child may be depressed and clingy with romantic partners because she has an unconscious fear of being left alone again.

The behavioral approach focuses on people's current behavior and the learned responses that sustain the behavior (Bandura, 1969). For example, a man develops a fear of flying after a turbulent and traumatic flight experience. Behavioral therapists aim to modify people's dysfunctional behaviors by analyzing and ultimately reorganizing the behavioral contingencies (pattern of reinforcements) that cause the dysfunctional behaviors (Miltenberger, 2012).

The cognitive approach focuses on how thoughts and beliefs contribute to the development and maintenance of psychological disorders (Beck, 1995). Typically, the cognitive approach identifies people's maladaptive (or unhelpful) beliefs and the negative thinking patterns that follow (Beck, 1964). For example, people with depression tend to experience more negative thoughts than those without depression, and this negative thinking is seen as a perpetuating factor in maintaining the depressive state (Levitan et al., 1998; McEvoy et al., 2013). Cognitive and behavioral perspectives are often combined into a cognitive-behavioral approach to understanding psychological disorders (Rush et al., 1975). Cognitive-behavioral theory (CBT) recognizes the reciprocal connection between an individual's thoughts, feelings, and behaviors and how this triad can influence various psychological disorders (Hollon & Beck, 1994).

Sociocultural approaches recognize the importance of taking into account each person's specific social system, which includes social relationships, social and cultural customs, and social and cultural norms. Sociocultural approaches often gather detailed information about the family structure and cultural values and norms prior to making any psychological diagnosis (Fish, 1996).

Today, most mental health professionals take a multidisciplinary approach to understanding psychological disorders, utilizing many of the aforementioned approaches. Collectively, this orientation is referred to as a **biopsychosocial approach**, which acknowledges that psychological disorders are complex conditions with a multitude of factors that must be considered when it comes to understanding the reasons people develop and continue to exhibit various symptoms and disorders (Frankel et al., 2003; Gilbert, 1995, 2013). See Figure 15.1 for a model of this approach.

biopsychosocial approach

theoretical orientation that considers biological, psychological, and sociocultural factors when explaining causes for psychological disorders

Figure 15.1 The Biopsychosocial Model

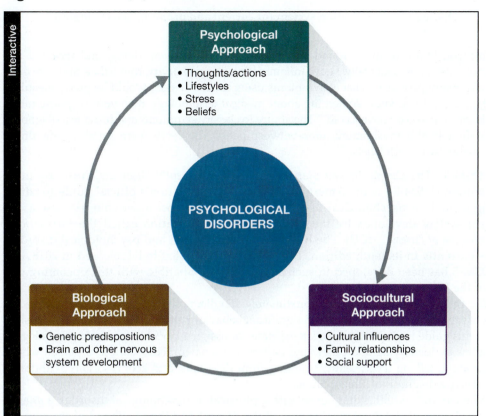

Adaptive Pathway 15.1: Approaches to Understanding Psychological Disorders

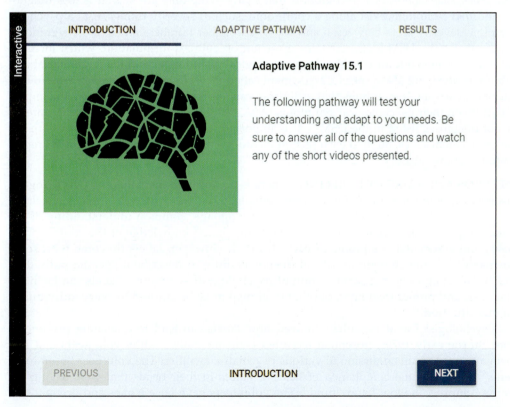

The Classification of Psychological Disorders

LO 15.3 **Discuss the classification system for current and proposed psychological disorders.**

Imagine you bumped into a friend, asked them how they were doing, and received this response: "Well, not great really. I have inflammation of my pharynx, rhinorrhea, and sore muscles." For many people, this list of symptoms using medical jargon would be pretty meaningless. However, if you knew something about medical terminology, then your response might have been, "Oh, so you have a cold." The ability to classify symptoms and provide a diagnostic label definitely aids in communication between people; however, there are also some drawbacks to the use of such labels.

DSM-5

Diagnostic and Statistical Manual for Mental Disorders (5th edition) is the American Psychiatric Association's official guide for diagnosing mental, or psychological disorders

THE DSM-5 The *Diagnostic and Statistical Manual for Mental Disorders*, currently in its fifth edition (**DSM-5**), is the American Psychiatric Association's official guide for diagnosing mental, or psychological disorders (APA, 2013). Most other countries use a categorical system developed by the World Health Organization called the *International Classification of Diseases (ICD)*. The ICD includes all medical and psychological disorders and is currently in its tenth edition. The ICD-11 is scheduled to be released in 2018, and the DSM-5 has been developed in such a way to be compatible with this upcoming version of the ICD.

The DSM-5 provides a list of approximately 250 diagnosable disorders, each defined in terms of specific diagnostic criteria and significant behavior patterns. Mental health professionals use this guide to give a *psychological diagnosis,* or assign a label to a person's psychological symptoms by identifying and classifying patterns of behavior. For example, a person who is hallucinating, talking incoherently, suffering from delusions, and acting socially withdrawn may receive a diagnosis of schizophrenia.

When an individual is diagnosed with a physical or psychological disorder, a *prognosis* (a prediction about the typical course of the disease and the likelihood of recovery) is often made. Just as some people respond to chemotherapy while others succumb to cancer, treatment of psychological disorders and subsequent recovery depends on a number of factors, including the individual patient characteristics and the severity of the disease.

The DSM-5 is the first edition of the manual to attempt to include both *categorical information* (a label reflecting membership to a particular diagnostic group, e.g., schizophrenia) and *dimensional information* (recognition that many symptoms are shared across diagnoses and that symptoms exist along a continuum, such as severity ratings, e.g., a psychosis symptom severity score between 0 and 40, where higher numbers reflect more significant impairment). The DSM-5 also contains a section on cultural formulation, which includes not only a framework for considering psychological disorders within the larger social and cultural context, but also a specific assessment called the *Cultural Formulation Interview*. This interview contains 16 questions that a clinician can ask an individual regarding the impact of culture on their psychological symptoms (APA, 2013). Table 15.1 lists the specific categories of diagnoses listed in the DSM-5. It is important to note that these categories are not diagnoses themselves, but that each section includes a number of different diagnoses representative of the category.

THE PROS AND CONS OF LABELING There is no question that labelling psychological disorders aids in communication between people. Classifying mental illnesses is helpful for clinicians to provide a common shorthand language; common understanding of the causes of particular psychological disorders' and shared knowledge of the course, prognosis, and associated symptoms of each disorder. However, labels do come with some downsides. Giving something a label does very little to describe a specific individual and their struggles with a constellation of psychological symptoms. Labels can facilitate diagnosis and proper treatment, but that treatment must be tailored to every individual's unique situation.

Psychologist David Rosenhan showed how labels can lead to damaging preconceptions. In the early 1970s, Rosenhan recruited eight mentally healthy volunteers and had them attempt to gain admission to various psychiatric facilities. The volunteer "pseudopatients" (fake patients) complained of hearing voices in their heads that were saying the words "empty," "hollow," and "thud." The volunteers gave false names and occupations,

Table 15.1 Categories of Psychological Disorders in the DSM-5

Categories of Psychological Disorders in the DSM-5
Neurodevelopmental Disorders
Schizophrenia Spectrum and Other Psychotic Disorders
Bipolar and Related Disorders
Depressive Disorders
Anxiety Disorders
Obsessive-Compulsive and Related Disorders
Trauma- and Stressor-Related Disorders
Dissociative Disorders
Somatic Symptom and Related Disorders
Feeding and Eating Disorders
Elimination Disorders
Sleep-Wake Disorders
Sexual Dysfunctions
Gender Dysphoria
Disruptive, Impulse-Control, and Conduct Disorders
Substance-Related and Addictive Disorders
Neurocognitive Disorders
Personality Disorders
Paraphilic Disorders
Other Mental Disorders
Medication-Induced Movement Disorders
Other Conditions That May Be a Focus of Clinical Attention

but they answered all other questions truthfully, describing real relationships with friends, colleagues, and family members. All eight were admitted into the psychiatric facilities, and seven were diagnosed with schizophrenia. The clinicians working in the institutions later interpreted normal behavior, such as the volunteers' taking notes or pacing the corridors out of boredom, as symptoms of mental illness (Rosenhan, 1973). On average, it took 19 days (range = 7–52 days) for the pseudopatients to be discharged from the psychiatric hospitals, most with a diagnosis of schizophrenia in remission. This classic study reminds us of the potential that labels have to dehumanize a person, that is, seeing someone as a diagnostic entity rather than a human being.

In addition to the potential dehumanizing effect of labels, a psychological diagnosis can be stigmatizing to those individuals with the diagnosis. Public stigma involves negative attitudes and beliefs about people with mental illness that lead to behaviors involving fear, rejection, and discrimination. Despite evidence to the contrary, people still tend to believe that children and adults with psychological disorders are more dangerous (to themselves and others) and that these beliefs are related to increased social distance, or the desire to stay away from people with mental illness (Parcesepe & Cabassa, 2013). Most research has suggested that the best way to decrease stigmatization is through education about mental illness and increased contact with those who have psychological disorders (Corrigan et al., 2012).

Cultural values, as discussed earlier, not only influence manifestations of particular disorders, but also their labels. It might seem difficult to believe now, but homosexuality was classified as a mental disorder by the American Psychiatric Association until 1973. In the 1940s, smoking was considered a harmless social pastime and less than 40 years later, nicotine dependence was added to the APA's list of psychological disorders. Similarly, there is currently some discussion about adding *caffeine use disorder* and *Internet gaming disorder* to the next edition of the DSM.

Shared Writing: Considering New Psychological Diagnoses

Internet Gaming Disorder is a proposed new psychological disorder. Some of the proposed symptoms of Internet Gaming Disorder include: 1) preoccupation with Internet games, 2) withdrawal symptoms of irritability, anxiety, or sadness when gaming is taken away, 3) tolerance—the need to spend more time playing, 4) unsuccessful attempts to control the amount of game playing, 5) loss of interest in other hobbies and entertainment, 6) excessive participation in Internet gaming despite social or occupational problems. With these criteria in mind, do you think this should become a psychological disorder? Why or why not?

Quiz for Module 15.1–15.3

1. What is psychopathology?
   a. The study of symptoms and how they interfere with an individual's work and social activities
   b. The study of brain abnormalities and how they impact daily functioning
   c. The scientific study of mental/psychological disorders
   d. The scientific study of biological processes and how they interact with environmental stressors to create maladaptive behavior

2. The four D's of a psychological disorder include distress, deviance, _____, and sometimes danger.
   a. dysfunction
   b. disturbance
   c. depression
   d. debilitation

3. Which approach focuses on a person's maladaptive beliefs and negative thoughts to explain psychological disorders?
   a. Cognitive
   b. Psychodynamic
   c. Behavioral
   d. Biological

4. The type of multidisciplinary approach to understanding psychological symptoms is referred to as _____.
   a. sociocultural
   b. biological
   c. cognitive
   d. biopsychosocial

5. Rami has been experiencing a number of concerning symptoms, so he makes an appointment to see a psychologist. After an assessment, the psychologist assigns a label to Rami's psychological symptoms by identifying and classifying them. Rami has received a _____.
   a. prognosis
   b. psychological diagnosis
   c. biopsychosocial opinion
   d. medical diagnosis

Module 15.4–15.5: Anxiety and Anxiety-Related Disorders

Whether we're facing a tough exam or a skydiving expedition, we all feel anxious from time to time. But what if we persistently feel anxious, even though we cannot identify the source of our worries? Or, what if we know what is causing us to feel anxious but feel powerless to control the anxiety? This type of prolonged, uncontrollable, and sometimes vague feeling of anxiety may be a symptom of an **anxiety disorder**. As a group, anxiety disorders are among the most commonly occurring psychological disorders (Kessler et al., 2010).

Understanding Anxiety Symptoms

anxiety disorder

group of psychological disorders characterized by prolonged, uncontrollable, and sometimes vague feelings of worry or anxiety

LO 15.4 **Recognize the symptoms that characterize the different anxiety and anxiety-related disorders.**

People tend to use the words "fear" and "anxiety" interchangeably. Technically, *fear* is an emotional response, accompanied by physiological reactions (i.e., the fight or flight response), that occurs in response to a specific threat; *anxiety* is also an emotion, which may or may not have associated physiological symptoms, that occurs in response to a less clearly defined threat. For example, if you are driving down the highway and an animal suddenly runs in front of your car, you will experience a fear reaction. Your heart will start pounding, your blood pressure will increase, and you may scream something you wouldn't want your mother to hear. You are experiencing fear as a result of a direct and specific threat. Now, the next time you get in the car and are driving along that same stretch of highway, you may notice that you are experiencing some anxiety. In this case, there is no direct threat (i.e., there is no animal on the road), but you do feel a vague sense of uncertainty about what *might* happen. Your heart isn't pounding like before, but you do notice that your palms are a little sweaty and you are gripping the steering wheel tighter than you normally would. Fear can lead to anxiety, and anxiety can lead to fear. These two emotions are very closely related for people who suffer from a specific phobia.

SPECIFIC PHOBIAS Does a photo of a spider cause beads of sweat to appear on your forehead while your heart pounds furiously? If so, you may have *arachnophobia*, which is one of the most common phobias reported by college students (Seim & Spates, 2009). Whenever we ask our students to volunteer to share their phobias, we almost always hear about people's *coulrophobia*, or their fear of clowns.

A **specific phobia** involves a persistent, irrational fear of a specific object or situation. While some species of spiders may be venomous, unless you live in the Amazon rainforest, you are unlikely to encounter one, making your debilitating fear of every eight-legged arachnid unreasonable (even though it doesn't feel that way when you see one). The 12-month prevalence rate of specific phobias in a community population is 7–9 percent (APA, 2013). Specific phobias are more commonly diagnosed in women than men (Fredrikson et al., 1996), although the exact rates vary depending on the phobic stimulus. To be classified as a specific phobia, the fear must be significant enough to disrupt everyday life in some way and have lasted for at least six months. Someone with a *fear* of thunderstorms would not spend a week inside after seeing an ominous weather report, but someone with a *phobia* of thunderstorms might. Take a look at the following groups of phobias classified by the DSM-5.

Coulrophobia, or the extreme fear of clowns, is a common specific phobia.

specific phobia

persistent, irrational fear of a specific object or situation

Categories of Phobias

Animal phobia are the most common type of specific phobias. While snakes, spiders, and dogs are among the most common animal phobia, a person can develop a specific phobia to any animal.

1 of 7   Previous   Next

Some specific phobias make more intuitive sense than others. Psychologist Martin Seligman (1971) suggests that people are genetically predisposed to be wary of objects and situations that posed realistic threats to humans throughout evolutionary history (e.g., venomous snakes and insects, heights). This is certainly not the case for all phobias, however, as any object or situation has the potential to become a phobia (Davey, 2007; Rachman & Seligman, 1976).

SOCIAL ANXIETY DISORDER Social anxiety disorder, which used to be referred to as *social phobia*, has often been viewed as a type of specific phobia. However, **social anxiety disorder** is a distinct diagnosis and refers to individuals who have marked and persistent fears of being

social anxiety disorder

psychological disorder involving marked and persistent fears of being scrutinized by others or embarrassed/humiliated in a public setting

scrutinized by others or embarrassed/humiliated in a public setting. Commonly feared social situations include speaking in public; using public restrooms; writing or eating in front of others; or meeting and engaging in "small talk" with new people. People who suffer from social anxiety disorder find it extremely difficult to engage in daily social interactions such as going to school/work, grocery shopping, or attending group functions. The anxiety they experience typically involves either a fear of doing something to embarrass themselves (e.g., spill their food or drink, say something stupid) or that others will see their nervousness and anxiety (e.g., see them sweating or hear their voice shaking) and evaluate them negatively as a result. Like specific phobias, social anxiety is typically met with a significant amount of avoidance of situations that produce anxiety and must last for at least six months to be diagnosed. The 12-month prevalence rate is 7 percent and equally affects males and females in the general population (McLean et al., 2011). However, in clinical samples (a group of people who are seeking treatment), slightly more men than women are found to have a diagnosis of social anxiety disorder (APA, 2013).

panic attack

sudden episode of intense fear accompanied with physiological symptoms, such as tightening of the chest and shortness of breath, which often occurs unexpectedly

PANIC ATTACKS AND PANIC DISORDER Many people who have a **panic attack** mistakenly believe they are having a heart attack. They suddenly experience a tightening in their chest, shortness of breath, heart palpitations, sweating, and an intense feeling of terror and panic. This attack can happen as a result of being scared, or it can come completely out of the blue. Often, the symptoms reach a peak within about 10 minutes and then begin to decrease (although if you've ever had a panic attack or known someone who did, you know that it seems to last forever!). It is quite common for someone to experience a panic attack (the DSM-5 reports the 12-month prevalence rate as 11.2 percent), but a panic attack by itself is not a psychological disorder. Panic attacks can actually occur on their own or in conjunction with many other psychological disorders. For this reason, the DSM-5 refers to a panic attack as a "specifier" (APA, 2013). Specifiers are meant to be used as additional descriptions that help provide more information about the experience of the patient.

panic disorder

psychological disorder where an individual experiences recurrent panic attacks, some of which are unexpected, followed by feelings of worry or dread about the potential of future panic attacks

In the case of **panic disorder**, an individual experiences recurrent panic attacks, some of which are unexpected (e.g., come "out of the blue" without a noticeable trigger). Feelings of worry and dread often last for days or even weeks after the original attack and lead the individual to begin to change their behavior in an effort to prevent the occurrence of future panic attacks. Most typically, the person begins avoiding situations where they previously experienced a panic attack or situations where they think they *might* have a panic attack. This type of avoidance may start very specifically (e.g., that one restaurant down the street where the first panic attack occurred) but can quickly escalate to include many other situations (e.g., all restaurants). Panic disorder affects approximately 2–3 percent of the general population in a 12-month period (APA, 2013). In the following video, *Panic Attacks and Panic Disorder*, the physiological component of panic attacks are explained and a discussion of how panic attacks can progress to panic disorder is presented.

Panic Attacks and Panic Disorder

For many people, panic disorder can lead to **agoraphobia**, an intense fear of being in a situation from which they cannot escape. The fear of having a panic attack in public often causes sufferers to avoid being in crowds, traveling on trains or buses, or visiting unfamiliar places. In the DSM-5, agoraphobia is a stand-alone diagnosis. That is, it is possible to have excessive fears about entering certain situations that are not accompanied by a history of panic attacks. In our clinical experience, this situation is much less common and the DSM-5 states that at least 30–50 percent of people have a history of panic attacks or panic disorder (APA, 2013). Symptoms of agoraphobia must be present and interfering with an individual's life for at least six months, whereas symptoms of panic disorder only need to be present for at least one month to receive a diagnosis.

GENERALIZED ANXIETY DISORDER   People who worry uncontrollably and are inexplicably tense and uneasy may have **generalized anxiety disorder (GAD)**. While the name of the disorder might give you a false sense that GAD refers to a kind of "free-floating anxiety" and is in some way a type of catch-all category for anxiety symptoms that don't fit elsewhere, that isn't the case at all. GAD is primarily about worry. Individuals with GAD worry excessively about a number of issues.

agoraphobia

intense fear of being in a situation from which escape is difficult or impossible

generalized anxiety disorder (GAD)

psychological disorder involving uncontrollable worry and other cognitive and physiological symptoms

Your Worries

Interactive

What things do you worry about? Respond to each of the statements below.

1. I worry about work/school.

○ Agree
○ Disagree

2. I worry about my health.

○ Agree
○ Disagree

3. I worry about my safety.

○ Agree
○ Disagree

4. I worry about politics.

○ Agree
○ Disagree

Previous   Next

Most worries tend to fall into the categories listed in the poll above (Hirsch et al., 2013; Lee et al., 2014). You may be surprised to see that you're not alone in some of your worries. In fact, most people with GAD worry about similar topics. One distinguishing feature of those individuals with GAD is that they tend to worry about things that might be considered *minor matters*. Minor matters include things like: "What if it rains today and I forget my umbrella?" (but the weather says it is supposed to be sunny); "What if I show up late to meet my friends for dinner?" (but they said to come by anytime). This excessive and exhausting worry must be present for at least 6 months and be accompanied by at least three of the following additional symptoms: restlessness, muscle tension, fatigue, irritability, difficulty sleeping, and difficulty concentrating.

According to DSM-5, approximately 3 percent of people will develop GAD within a 12-month period, with the disorder being more commonly diagnosed in women (APA, 2013). GAD is often comorbid with depression (Klenk et al., 2011), although GAD typically precedes the onset of major depressive disorder (Goodwin & Gorman, 2002).

obsessive-compulsive disorder (OCD)

psychological disorder involving repeated and uncontrollable thoughts, images, or urges (obsessions) that are often followed by repetitive and ritualistic behaviors (compulsions) in an effort to reduce the anxiety brought about by the obsessions

OBSESSIVE-COMPULSIVE DISORDER While **obsessive-compulsive disorder (OCD)** is not technically in the anxiety disorders section of the DSM-5 (it is contained in the obsessive-compulsive and related disorders section), it is associated with extreme anxiety and avoidance. The anxiety or avoidance involves objects or situations thought to have the power to trigger uncontrollable thoughts, which in turn trigger anxiety. Most of us have probably had a sudden fear that we left our car unlocked or forgot to turn off an appliance. In these cases, a quick check is usually enough to put our minds at ease. For many people with OCD, though, a quick check wouldn't be sufficient. *Obsessions* are disturbing and intrusive thoughts, images, or urges that repeatedly interrupt a person's consciousness and cause anxiety, even if the person knows these thoughts are irrational. *Compulsions* are repetitive, ritualistic behaviors usually performed in response to the obsessions. The compulsions are the behaviors that you see, but you should know that they are almost always triggered by the obsessions. The two components typically go hand in hand, although it is possible to have OCD and only have obsessions or compulsions (Woody et al., 2011). Someone with OCD may experience intrusive thoughts about being contaminated and need to repeatedly wash her hands, or experience persistent doubts and have to check to make sure a task has been completed, or have intrusive images of a loved one dying and have to step in and out of a doorway a certain number of times to "make sure the thought doesn't come true."

In order to receive a diagnosis, the obsessions/compulsions must take up a significant amount of time during the day and cause substantial distress and/or impairment. The 12-month prevalence rate of OCD is 1.2 percent, with a slightly higher prevalence in males during childhood and a slightly higher rate of OCD in females in adulthood (Ruscio et al., 2010).

posttraumatic stress disorder (PTSD)

psychological disorder that develops in response to a traumatic event; symptoms must be present for more than one month and include the development of fear, anxiety, and other re-experiencing symptoms in response to the traumatic experience

POSTTRAUMATIC STRESS DISORDER Sadly, many people are exposed to a traumatic situation at some point in their life. Sometimes, the traumatic stress caused by experiencing or witnessing actual or threatened death, serious injury, or sexual violation can lead to **posttraumatic stress disorder**. Posttraumatic stress disorder (PTSD) involves the development of fear, anxiety, and other symptoms in response to the memory of the traumatic experience. It is the only anxiety disorder that actually *requires* the experience of a traumatic event for the diagnosis. Victims of abuse, accident and disaster survivors, people who live in war zones, and combat veterans are all likely to develop PTSD (Davidson et al., 2014; Javidi & Yadollahie, 2012). A report by the RAND Corporation estimates that one in five American soldiers suffer from major depression or PTSD following service in Iraq or Afghanistan (Rand Corporation, 2008).

The DSM-5 has five broad categories of symptoms that comprise the diagnosis of PTSD. The criteria are slightly different for children ages 6 and under. For those over age 6, the diagnosis requires some symptoms from each of the following categories. Click on each of the symptoms to view examples of how they would be experienced by a person with PTSD.

Symptoms of Posttraumatic Stress Disorder

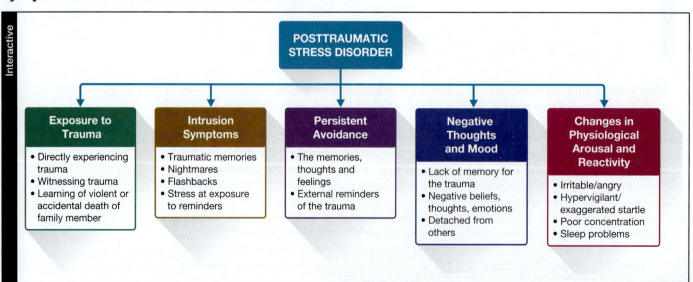

The symptoms of PTSD reach the diagnostic threshold once they have been present and interfering with a person's life for more than one month. Most symptoms begin within three months of the trauma, but it is possible for there to be a significant delay (e.g., six months) in the onset of symptoms. However, as you will see in the following video, *Posttraumatic Stress Disorder*, it is also typical to experience significant distress and impairment immediately after a trauma.

Posttraumatic Stress Disorder

The diagnosis of **acute stress disorder** is similar to PTSD (although there is less rigidity of how many symptoms must come from each category), and it applies to symptoms that occur between three days and one month after the trauma (APA, 2013). It is estimated that approximately 9 percent of the population suffers from PTSD at some point in their lives. The 12-month prevalence rate in U.S. adults is 3.5 percent (APA, 2013). Women are twice as likely as men to develop PTSD (Davidson et al., 2014), a likelihood that increases if the traumatic event took place before the woman was 15 years old (Breslau et al., 1999; Breslau et al., 1997).

acute stress disorder

development of fear, anxiety, and other re-experiencing symptoms in response to a traumatic experience; symptoms last between three days and one month after the trauma

EXPLAINING ANXIETY DISORDERS

LO 15.5   Explain the causes of anxiety disorders.

We inherit Mom's green eyes and Dad's brown hair. Is it also possible to inherit tendencies toward particular psychological disorders? Evidence exists that specific biological factors, such as genetics, contribute to anxiety disorders. Researchers acknowledge that anxiety can be inherited, and specific genetic sites have been identified that may predispose people toward anxiety disorders (Domschke & Reif, 2012; Rapee, 2012). As with intelligence (see LO 8.9), researchers have proposed that gene-environment interactions (e.g., when environmental factors influence the expression of a gene), particularly with early life stress, contribute to the development of anxiety disorders (Nugent et al., 2011). Twin studies have also demonstrated gene-environment correlations, where an individual's genetic predisposition leads them toward specific environmental circumstances. A recent study surveyed 406 pairs of monozygotic and dizygotic twins and found that PTSD symptoms were moderately heritable. The researchers concluded that it is possible that the genetic personality differences influence environmental choices, which have the potential to increase an individual's level of exposure to traumatic situations (Stein et al., 2002).

Research in neuroscience has demonstrated some predictable areas of the brain involved in the experience of anxiety. Recent research has been focusing on functional networks, or collections of brain regions that operate together, and found some consistent similarities across the various anxiety disorders (Sylvester et al., 2012). For example, the amygdala and insula are

Phobias can develop from observing the fearful behavior of other people.

both involved in the experience of fear and anxiety and appear to play a significant role in most anxiety disorders (Bruce et al., 2013; Klumpp et al., 2012; Likhtik et al., 2014). However, functional MRIs have revealed some differences between specific disorders that may explain the diversity of symptoms experienced. For example, abnormalities have been found in the emotional networks of those with PTSD (networks including the medial temporal lobe and limbic system), whereas the somatosensory networks (those related to bodily sensations) have been found to play a central role in panic disorder (Peterson et al., 2014).

As discussed in LO 14.1, Freud described a dynamic relationship between the id, ego, and superego (Freud, 1920). Freud believed all children experience anxiety while growing up and learn to use their ego defense mechanisms as a way to control that anxiety. The psychodynamic approach views some anxiety disorders as the result of powerful, repressed id urges attempting to surface, often in the presence of weak or inadequate defense mechanisms (Leichsenring & Salzer, 2014). In addition, scientific studies have shown the small, but significant impact caregivers can have on their child's subsequent anxiety through overprotectiveness or insecure attachments (Hudson, 2014).

Rather than viewing anxiety disorders as the result of unconscious fears and problematic parental relationships, behaviorists believe that anxious behavior is learned. Remember Little Albert who was taught to fear white rats? The child's fear became a conditioned response after the white rat was repeatedly paired with a scary noise. Classical conditioning provides a good explanation for how some individuals develop phobias in response to seemingly harmless objects (e.g., cotton balls). Any stimulus (i.e., object or situation) repeatedly associated with something that produces fear has the potential to become the object of a phobia.

The behavioral approach also points to the role of reinforcement (particularly negative reinforcement) in maintaining anxiety disorders (Fisak Jr & Grills-Taquechel, 2007). Why does someone with OCD continue to engage in the compulsion of washing their hands in scalding hot water with bleach despite the resulting painful cracked skin? Intuitively, there doesn't seem to be anything *rewarding* about that behavior. It is true, that compulsive handwashing does not provide *positive reinforcement* to most people suffering with OCD. However, compulsive behavior is extremely rewarding as a result of *negative reinforcement*. If you recall, negative reinforcement works to strengthen an existing behavior through the removal of an aversive stimulus (see LO 5.5). In the case of OCD, repetitive, intrusive, and scary thoughts are experienced as aversive; engaging in the compulsion becomes a way to *remove* or *neutralize* those thoughts. Therefore, the compulsive behavior is experienced as very rewarding through the sense of relief it brings by "getting rid" of the obsessions (Rachman, 1997, 2002).

For some people, watching scary scenes in movies, television, or other forms of media can lead to the development of a phobia.

We also tend to learn by observing others. Just as children learned to behave aggressively with the Bobo dolls in Bandura's famous study (Bandura et al., 1961), we can develop anxiety or fears by watching other people behave in anxious and fearful ways. One of your authors can personally attest to this explanation for the development of phobias. As a young child, she loved playing in the woods. She would often spend the afternoon with her neighbors looking to capture snakes. Needless to say, there was little fear of snakes at this point. Then, around 10 years old, she watched the movie *Raiders of the Lost Ark*. She can still remember watching in horror as Indiana Jones dangled above a pit filled with terrifying snakes. After that movie, and ever since, she has had a serious fear of snakes (it thankfully wouldn't be considered a phobia since it doesn't interfere with her life). While learning anxious behaviors can occur outside of conscious awareness and/or thought, often, the environment and the individual's thoughts about the environment are intertwined.

Cognitive psychologists view anxiety disorders as the result of distorted, negative thoughts. People with anxiety disorders tend to overestimate the dangers they are facing and underestimate their ability to cope with them, leading to complete avoidance of the perceived threat. For example, in the case of the development of panic disorder, the cognitive view would explain the condition as stemming from a *misinterpretation* of bodily symptoms (Clark et al., 1997; Rachman et al., 1987; Woud et al., 2014). Instead of your heart just beating more rapidly, it becomes "Oh no! What if I'm having a heart attack?" That anxiety-provoking thought tends to create more anxiety (and more physical symptoms, which causes a vicious cycle of symptoms/misinterpretations).

In the case of GAD, cognitive psychologists have found that people tend to overestimate the probability of danger and hold the belief that worrying will prevent bad situations from occurring (Borkovec et al., 1999; Rowa & Antony, 2008). Furthermore, individuals with GAD demonstrate *intolerance of uncertainty*, where the need to know about future events provokes worry and anxiety (Hanrahan et al., 2013; van der Heiden et al., 2012). While initially described in the context of GAD, intolerance of uncertainty has emerged as an important construct throughout most anxiety disorders and even depression (Carleton et al., 2012; Gentes & Ruscio, 2011; McEvoy & Mahoney, 2012).

Ultimately, anxiety disorders are multidimensional and therefore have a number of different explanations that can help contribute to our understanding of the development, maintenance, and treatment of these conditions. Explaining anxiety disorders offers an opportunity to truly see the *biopsychosocial approach* in action.

Quiz for Module 15.4–15.5

1. You listened to your psychology instructor talk about the symptoms of generalized anxiety disorder (GAD), and you wondered if you qualified for that diagnosis. You recognize that you tend to worry about things, such as passing your classes and what to wear to the party. As you think more about it, you realize you don't experience the three additional symptoms required for the diagnosis. Those three additional symptoms could include

   _____.

   a. social problems, muscle tension, and lack of sleep

   b. difficulty concentrating, irritability, and appetite problems

   c. lack of sleep, lack of motivation, and muscle tension

   d. muscle tension, fatigue, and lack of sleep

2. Which disorder requires an exposure to a terrifying or life-threatening event to qualify for the diagnosis?

   a. Posttraumatic Stress Disorder (PTSD)

   b. Generalized Anxiety Disorder (GAD)

   c. Obsessive Compulsive Disorder (OCD)

   d. Social Anxiety Disorder (SAD)

3. Giada has an irrational fear of dogs. A behavioral psychologist would believe her anxious behavior was _____.

   a. unconscious

   b. socially constructed

   c. learned

   d. genetic

4. Cognitive psychologists view the development and/or maintenance of anxiety as a result of _____.

   a. distorted, negative thoughts

   b. unconscious fear

   c. overactive amygdala

   d. reinforced fear

Module 15.6–15.7: Depressive and Bipolar Disorders

Although we are capable of experiencing emotions ranging from deep despair to intense elation, most of the time we are somewhere in between these two extremes. If you've heard of the expression "polar opposites," then you know this is referencing things being at opposite ends of the spectrum. Emotions are also sometimes referred to in this way. Disturbances in mood can encompass just one pole or can alternate between both poles. In fact, depression has often been referred to as *unipolar depression*, meaning that the emotional experiences are clustered around one (uni) pole, namely, sadness. Another type of disorder involving mood includes a range of extreme emotional experiences that alternate between both (bi) poles and is currently referred to as *bipolar disorder*. Bipolar disorders are separated from depressive disorders in the DSM-5 and placed strategically between the sections on schizophrenia and depressive disorders in an effort to recognize their commonalities with both categories of disorders (APA, 2013; Lichtenstein et al., 2009).

The Symptoms of Depressive and Bipolar Disorders

LO 15.6 **Recognize the symptoms that characterize the different disorders involving mood.**

Clinical depression is different from the slumps we all get into from time to time when nothing seems to be going right. Usually, people can snap out of a bad mood in a relatively short period of time, but when it lasts much longer and interferes with daily functioning, it may be classified as a depressive disorder.

major depressive disorder (MDD)

psychological disorder involving either depressed mood or loss of interest in most activities, accompanied by four other symptoms that last for more than two weeks

DEPRESSIVE DISORDERS There are several types of clinical depression. **Major depressive disorder (MDD)** is characterized by signs of severe depression (defined as either depressed mood most of the day or loss of interest in most activities), accompanied by four other symptoms that last for more than two weeks. These symptoms may include:

- Significant weight loss or weight gain (as a result of changes in appetite)
- Sleep disturbances (insomnia or hypersomnia)
- Noticeable psychomotor agitation (increased movement) or psychomotor retardation (decreased/slowed movement)
- Fatigue, loss of energy
- Feelings of guilt and/or worthlessness
- Poor concentration or inability to make decisions
- Recurrent thoughts of suicide, plan for suicide, or suicide attempt

MDD has a 12-month prevalence rate of 7 percent. It is more commonly experienced (or more commonly diagnosed) in women and occurs at a much higher rate in the 18- to 29-year-old age range (APA, 2013).

persistent depressive disorder

chronically depressed condition that lasts for at least two years for adults and one year for children

Persistent depressive disorder is a chronically depressed condition that lasts for at least two years for adults and one year for children. To meet the criteria for this diagnosis, the individual must experience depressed mood on more days than not accompanied by at least two or more of the other symptoms of depression. The symptoms must cause significant impairment, and the individual cannot have experienced a period of 2 months or more without the symptoms. Overall, persistent depressive disorder is a chronic disorder of mood that can range in severity from depressed mood with two additional depressive symptoms to a full major depressive disorder that has lasted for more than two years.

premenstrual dysphoric disorder (PMDD)

psychological disorder involving significant mood symptoms (e.g., mood swings, irritability, sadness, anxiety) during the week leading up to the onset of menstruation in women

The DSM-5 includes the much-debated diagnosis of **premenstrual dysphoric disorder (PMDD)**, which involves significant mood symptoms (e.g., mood swings, irritability, sadness, anxiety) during the week leading up to the onset of menstruation in women. While many women report some changes in mood, appetite, and sleep during the premenstrual phase of their cycle, PMDD is a diagnosis meant for those women whose symptoms are so intense that they significantly interfere with their life. The DSM-5 states that in order to qualify for a diagnosis of PMDD, women must have experienced these symptoms during *most* menstrual cycles in the preceding year (APA, 2013).

mania

periods of euphoria (feelings of excessive happiness) often accompanied by elevated self-esteem, increased talkativeness, enhanced energy, and a decreased need for sleep

bipolar I disorder

psychological disorder where individuals experience at least one manic episode; most individuals have recurring mood episodes, alternating between periods of mania and major depression

BIPOLAR DISORDERS What do novelists Virginia Woolf, Ernest Hemingway, and Edgar Allan Poe all have in common? They all wrote their masterpieces while suffering from bipolar disorder. People with bipolar disorder experience episodes of **mania**—periods of euphoria (feelings of excessive happiness) characterized by elevated self-esteem, increased talkativeness, enhanced energy, and a decreased need for sleep. While it is true that people in a manic state may initially be more productive and creative, that quickly gives way to behavior marked by poor judgment that can lead to reckless financial decisions, spending sprees, drug use, and unsafe sex. In order to be considered a manic episode, the symptoms must last for at least one week. Individuals who experience at least one manic episode qualify for a diagnosis of **bipolar I disorder**. While not necessary for the diagnosis of bipolar I disorder, the vast majority of people have recurring mood episodes, many of which include a period of major depression. In fact, about 60 percent of manic episodes are followed by a major depressive episode (APA, 2013). The 12-month prevalence rate of bipolar I disorder is 0.6 percent and is roughly equal among men and women. Does the prevalence rate of less than 1 percent surprise you, given how much you have likely heard or read about bipolar disorder? It's important to understand that the *true* prevalence of a disorder (the number of people who truly have a condition despite diagnosis or not) does not necessarily reflect the number of people who are diagnosed with a disorder. The overdiagnosis of bipolar disorder in children (discussed in depth in the *Piecing It Together* module LO 15.14) is an example of how prevalence and diagnosis are not always the same.

A milder form of mania, called **hypomania**, causes less severe mood elevations and does not interfere with normal daily functioning to the same extent as mania. Only four days of symptoms are needed to qualify as a hypomanic episode. In the case of **bipolar II disorder**, a cycle of at least one hypomanic episode and one major depressive episode is required to qualify for this diagnosis. The 12-month prevalence rate of bipolar II disorder in the United States is 0.8 percent (APA, 2013). Because the diagnosis of bipolar II disorder includes hypomania, a less severe form of mania, people intuitively think that bipolar II disorder is *less severe* than bipolar I disorder. In fact, the opposite is true. As illustrated in the following video, *Living with Bipolar Disorder*, individuals with bipolar II disorder are often more chronically ill, spend more time in depressive episodes (which leads to more disability), and tend to be more impulsive, which increases the risk for suicide when in a depressed state (APA, 2013; Baek et al., 2011; MacQueen & Young, 2001).

hypomania

milder form of mania that causes less severe mood elevations and does not interfere with normal daily functioning

bipolar II disorder

psychological disorder where individuals experience at least one hypomanic episode and one major depressive episode

Living with Bipolar Disorder

Interactive

Symptoms of Bipolar Disorder

Depressive Symptoms	Manic Symptoms
Suicidal thoughts	Fast and pressured speech
Poor concentration	Very happy, excited, or euphoric
Poor self-esteem	Impulsive, risky behaviors
Feelings of worthlessness or guilt	Increased self-esteem
Insomnia or hypersomnia	Doesn't feel the need to sleep
Sad mood	Racing thoughts and distracted
Lack of interest in normal activities	Excessive energy
Fatigue or loss of energy	Increased activity/psychomotor agitation

suicide

intentional, self-inflicted behavior resulting in death

SUICIDE **Suicide** refers to an intentional, self-inflicted behavior, which results in the death of an individual. The difference between suicide and some other self-injurious behavior is with suicide the person has the desire and intention to die as a result of their actions.

What Do You Think?

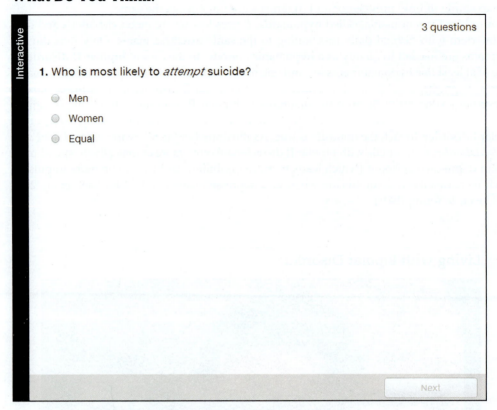

See Figure 15.2 below to examine suicide rates according to age.

Figure 15.2 Suicide Rates by Age from 2000–2013

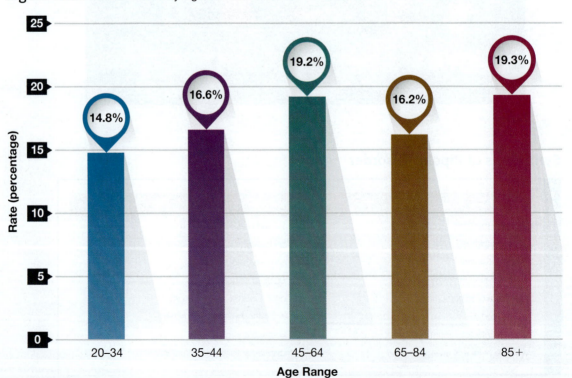

According to the Centers for Disease Control and Prevention (2014), researchers have identified various risk and protective factors related to suicide. In some cases, certain characteristics can be either a risk factor *or* a protective factor depending on the situation. Consider a person's religious beliefs. Do you think religious beliefs would serve as a risk factor or protective factor for suicide? It turns out that religious beliefs can be either a risk or a protective factor depending on the type of beliefs that are held. Those individuals who morally object to suicide based on religious values are less likely to engage in suicidal behavior (Dervic et al., 2004). However, individuals who hold strong beliefs about defending their religious freedom may be more likely to commit suicide. We see this in the case of "suicide bombers" acting out on the Islamic concept of "jihad," meaning to struggle (Gupta & Mundra, 2005; Moghadam, 2009).

Table 15.2 lists a number of protective and risk factors for suicide that have been identified by the Centers for Disease Control (CDC).

Table 15.2 Protective and Risk Factors for Suicide

Protective Factors	Risk Factors
Access to mental health treatment	History of suicide attempts
Family support	Feeling alone/not connected to people
Community support (connectedness)	History of psychological disorders (e.g., depressions, substance use)
Developed problem solving skills	Impulsive or aggressive tendencies
Ability to engage in conflict resolution	History of child maltreatment
Support from ongoing medical and mental health practitioners	Inability to access mental health treatment

Michael Anestis and colleagues have argued that focusing on broad risk factors such as depression is the wrong approach to decreasing suicide. They have conducted interesting research on the role of emotion dysregulation (people who are overwhelmed by, have difficulty tolerating, and try to escape negative emotions) and whether or not an individual will actually commit suicide. Using what they call an ideation-to-action framework (Klonsky & May, 2014), which is a theory for explaining how people move from contemplating suicide (ideation) to attempting suicide (action), Anestis and colleagues suggest that it is not actually the extent of emotion dysregulation that predicts suicide, but the combination of repetitively engaging in painful suicidal behavior (either suicide attempts or self-injury) and the access to a lethal means of death (Law et al., 2015). When examining state laws involving handgun restrictions (required permits, registration, or licensing), they found states that had any handgun laws also had significantly fewer suicides and lower rates of suicide by firearms (Anestis et al., 2015).

Explaining Depressive and Bipolar Disorders

LO 15.7 **Explain the causes of depressive and bipolar disorders.**

Depression has some relationship with the neurotransmitters in our brains—it's often attributed to low levels of the neurotransmitters norepinephrine, dopamine, and serotonin (Dutta et al., 2014; Haenisch & Bönisch, 2011; Saveanu & Nemeroff, 2012; Tye et al., 2013). However, understanding exactly how brain chemistry affects depression is much more complicated. For example, an antidepressant medication will elevate a patient's norepinephrine and serotonin levels in only a few days, but it won't produce any noticeable behavioral changes for approximately two to six weeks. Furthermore, the majority of depressed patients (approximately 75 percent) don't appear to have unusually low levels of either neurotransmitter, suggesting that there's more depression than chemical imbalance (Kemp et al., 2014; Valenstein, 1988).

Neuroimaging studies have shown that localized areas in the brain are affected by depression. People with depression exhibit reduced activity in the ventromedial prefrontal cortex, amygdala, caudate, and hippocampus, while the left temporal lobe and right dorsolateral prefrontal cortex demonstrate increased activation (Ritchey et al., 2011; Saveanu & Nemeroff, 2012). Consistent with these results, studies also indicate that each side of the brain may have a different role to play in the processing of emotions. The right hemisphere is able to identify and process both positive and negative emotions; however, the left hemisphere is only able to identify positive emotions and seems to rely on information from the right hemisphere for the complex processing of negative emotions (Abbott et al., 2013; Shobe, 2014).

Many studies have also shown that some people are genetically predisposed to mood disturbances (Craddock & Sklar, 2013; Nurnberger et al., 2011). Some research has demonstrated that the risks of major depression and bipolar disorder increase if you have a depressed parent or sibling (Sullivan et al., 2000). Other lines of research have focused on twins and have shown that if one identical twin has major depression or bipolar disorder, the chances that the other twin will also develop one of the disorders are between 40 percent to 80 percent (Kieseppä et al., 2004; Müller-Oerlinghausen et al., 2002). The heritability for bipolar disorders is higher than it is for depressive disorders and, in general, the explanations for bipolar disorders tend to be primarily biological (i.e., genetics, brain chemistry, brain structure/function). Biological factors are seen as important with depressive disorders, too; however, psychological factors are also believed to play a prominent role explaining depression.

Psychodynamic explanations of depression have included individual, relational, and developmental explanations. Some theories discuss depression in terms of "narcissistic vulnerability," where the individual behaves as though they have intact self-esteem, but internally they experience a chronic sense of emptiness and depression (Midgley et al., 2013, p. 70). Other psychodynamic theories view depression, particularly in adolescence, as a developmental/identity crisis or the internalization of a real or perceived loss of an important person (Park & Park, 2012). Interpersonal relationships are believed to play an important role in the development and maintenance of depression and are the focus of treatment for both short-term psychodynamic psychotherapy (STPP) and long-term psychodynamic psychotherapy (LTPP) (Lindfors et al., 2012; Zimmermann et al., 2015).

With its roots in philosophy and existentialism, the humanistic approach focuses on each individual's unique and subjective experience (Hansen, 2000). Given this focus, there may be a variety of reasons why a person becomes depressed. One example involves the *self-discrepancy theory*, which suggests that depression results from the discrepancy between a person's ideal self and their actual self (Higgins, 1987). The larger the discrepancy between the two, the more likely the person is to experience depression.

Behavioral explanations of depression tend to focus on the balance of rewards and punishments in a person's life. Research has confirmed that many depressive episodes are preceded by stressful events (Haastrup et al., 2012; Ormel et al., 2001). However, there are numerous people who have struggled with depression who report many positive aspects to their life and don't appear to be able to identify a particular cause of their depression. Many psychologists view depression from a cognitive-behavioral perspective, focusing on the *interaction* between the external environment and the individual's internal thoughts and beliefs that explains the maintenance of depressed mood (Dow, 1993).

The cognitive approach to understanding depression focuses on a person's negative thought and beliefs. Psychologist Aaron Beck noticed that depressed clients tended to engage in *negative thinking* and distort their perceptions of experiences (Beck, 1991, 2005; Beck et al., 1987). They made "mountains out of molehills" by viewing simple, everyday problems as major setbacks. Patients also anticipated that future events would turn out badly and had a habit of overgeneralizing, by interpreting one single negative event as a never-ending pattern of defeat. If you have a habit of using the phrase "Nothing ever goes right" whenever you lose your keys or break a glass, you may be engaging in overgeneralization. Beck found that people who were depressed tended to engage in what he referred to as the **cognitive triad**, which includes negative thinking about themselves, the world, and the future (Beck, 2002; Beckham et al., 1986). A specific type of negative thinking, referred to as *rumination*, has been found to both predict and maintain depressive symptoms (Lyubomirsky et al., 2015; Nolen-Hoeksema, 1991). Rumination is described as repeatedly thinking about the causes and consequences of a negative situation without engaging in any productive coping or problem-solving strategies. Children and adolescents who have a tendency to ruminate are at a much higher risk of developing depression, and it was recently found that exposure to stressful life events was associated with increased engagement in rumination (Michl et al., 2013).

Martin Seligman theorized that depression can be explained by the idea of **learned helplessness**—the tendency to remain in a punishing situation because of a history of repeated failures to escape in the past. Seligman, and his fellow graduate student Stephen Maier, did not

cognitive triad

explanation for mood disorders that includes negative thinking about themselves, the world, and the future

learned helplessness

tendency to remain in a punishing situation because of a history of repeated failures to escape in the past

set out to develop this theory, but instead were studying how classical conditioning impacted future operant conditioning. They classically conditioned dogs to fear the sound of a tone by pairing it with an electric shock. At first, the dogs were strapped into harnesses to keep them in place for the study, which meant they were unable to escape the shock (see Figure 15.3).

Figure 15.3 Example of a Shuttlebox

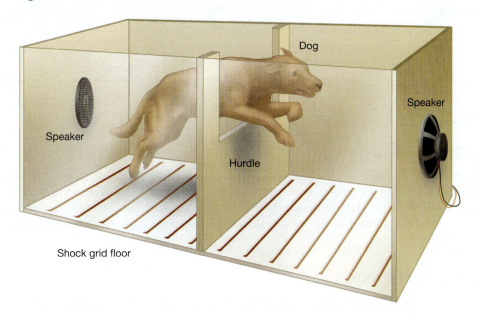

After the fear was conditioned, Seligman and Maier took the harnesses off the dogs and wanted to see how they would react now that they were "free." The *shuttlebox* had a low fence dividing the chamber in half, but still allowed the dogs to jump easily to the other side. Seligman and Maier administered electric shock in one half of the chamber and waited to see how the dog reacted. The dogs who had previously been classically conditioned (and therefore already experienced the shock when they were in the harness) didn't try to escape at all. In fact, they just lay down on the electrified floor and whimpered. The explanation for this behavior was that the dogs had already learned that the shocks were *inescapable*. Dogs that had never been exposed to the inescapable shock before quickly learned to jump the fence to the other half of the shuttlebox where they could find some relief.

Learned helplessness can occur in humans as well and arises from a recurring punishing situation where the person believes there is no escape possible and somehow they are partly to blame for the situation (Overmier, 2014). These negative and hopeless thoughts lead to what may appear as complacency or an inability to make any positive changes. Learned helplessness and the sense of powerlessness experienced may help explain why people living in abusive households eventually stop trying to leave their abusers, even when given the opportunity (Peterson & Seligman, 1983).

Quiz for Module 15.6–15.7

1. What is it called when a person experiences a period of euphoria (excessive happiness), elevated self-esteem, increased talkative-ness, enhanced energy, and a decreased need for sleep?

   a. Manic-depression

   b. Mania

   c. Anti-depression

   d. Depression

2. Major depressive disorder is characterized by either depressed mood or _____ in activities and accompanied by _____ other symptoms that last for more than 2 weeks.

   a. excessive participation; 6

   b. increased interest; 4

   c. loss of interest; 4

   d. lack of interest; 2

3. With respect to suicide, _____ are more likely to attempt suicide, while _____ are more likely to die as a result of their suicide attempt.

 a. White males; Black males

 b. adults; adolescents

 c. women; men

 d. men; women

4. Low levels of which neurotransmitters are linked with depression?

 a. Dopamine, endorphins, and glutamate

 b. Serotonin, endorphins, and glutamate

 c. Norepinephrine, glutamate, and dopamine

 d. Norepinephrine, dopamine, and serotonin

5. Mental health professionals who view depression from a cognitive-behavioral perspective explain it as an interaction between the individual's _____ environment and their _____ thoughts and beliefs.

 a. external; internal

 b. internal; external

 c. family; irrational

 d. internal; internal

Module 15.8–15.9: Eating, Somatic Symptom, and Dissociative Disorders

The disorders discussed so far have tended to focus on mood (i.e., anxiety and depression); however, there are many other psychological disorders in the DSM-5, a number of which focus on the body. While the symptoms manifest in different ways, eating disorders, somatic symptom disorders, and some dissociative disorders all highlight the important connection between the body and the mind.

Eating Disorders

LO 15.8 **Distinguish anorexia nervosa, bulimia nervosa, and binge-eating disorder.**

If you have grown up with any exposure to media, then you have experienced the subtle and not-so-subtle messages about what you should look like, what clothes you should wear, and the "perfect" size for your body. Whether you are male or female, sociocultural factors play an important role in the development of eating disorders. However, individual psychological and familial factors also have a part to play. Each of the eating disorders has a unique set of symptoms, but all of them can have a devastating impact on the life of the sufferer and their families.

anorexia nervosa

eating disorder where an individual purposely loses weight to a point below which is considered healthy

ANOREXIA NERVOSA Anorexia nervosa is an eating disorder where an individual purposely loses weight to a point below which is considered healthy. The DSM-5 uses the World Health Organization's (WHO) classification of the normal weight range as a benchmark for judging the disorder's severity. For adults, the WHO considers a body mass index (BMI) of 18.5–24.9 to be within the normal range. BMI is a ratio of height to weight (wt in kg/ht in meters). Do you know your BMI? If not, you can calculate it here: http://www.nhlbi.nih.gov/health/educational/lose_wt/BMI/bmicalc.htm.

<18.5 kg	18.5–24.9 kg	25–29.9 kg	30–34.9 kg	35+

Underweight	**Normal**	**Overweight**	**Obese**	**Extremely Obese**

Using an online BMI calculator is a quick and easy way to determine your own body mass index.

A diagnosis of anorexia nervosa hinges on being significantly underweight (i.e., a BMI of less than 18.5 for adults or less than what is minimally expected for children and adolescents). However, there are also a number of other required symptoms, including an intense fear of gaining weight or becoming fat and a perceptual disturbance in body image (which refers to the way the individual sees their body weight and/or shape). For example, people with anorexia almost always think and see themselves as bigger than they actually are in reality (Bruch, 1962; Cash & Brown, 1987; Garner et al., 1976; Hagman et al., 2015).

Researchers have also demonstrated that individuals with anorexia nervosa have perceptual abnormalities about their body size even at an unconscious level. Keizer et al. (2013) had participants walk through door-like openings of various sizes while performing a task that required their conscious attention. They found that participants with anorexia nervosa unconsciously started rotating their bodies in openings that were 40 percent bigger than their own bodies compared to healthy subjects who started to turn their shoulders in openings that were only 25 percent larger than their bodies. The researchers suggest that these results demonstrate that individuals with anorexia nervosa exhibit both conscious and unconscious perceptual body disturbances. In some ways, the results of this study provide some evidence that these individuals truly believe they are overweight and adjust their behavior according to that belief.

Bingeing (feeling out of control and eating large amounts of food) and purging (behavior aimed at preventing the absorption of calories) through self-induced vomiting or the misuse of laxative, diuretics, or enemas, can accompany anorexia nervosa. Most people think of bulimia when they hear that someone is engaging in bingeing and purging; however, if these symptoms are occurring in a person who is significantly underweight, then the most appropriate diagnosis is anorexia nervosa. In the following video, *Anorexia Nervosa*, Natasha explains what it was like for her to struggle with anorexia nervosa.

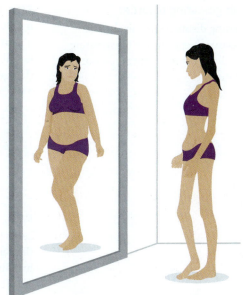

Anorexia nervosa involves a number of different symptoms, including a distorted perception of body image.

Anorexia Nervosa

Interactive

BULIMIA NERVOSA **Bulimia nervosa** is characterized by recurrent episodes of binge eating and purging behaviors meant to compensate for the amount of food eaten. A binge is typically defined as eating an objectively large amount of food in a relatively short period of time (i.e., 2 hours or less). Purging behaviors can consist of those mentioned in conjunction with anorexia nervosa (i.e., self-induced vomiting, laxative, diuretic, or enema abuse) and other methods of compensating for calories including fasting or excessive exercise. As with anorexia nervosa, body image dissatisfaction, fear of gaining weight, and self-esteem tied to shape and weight are the cornerstones of this disorder. However, unlike anorexia nervosa, individuals with bulimia nervosa tend to be normal weight to overweight (Flament et al., 2015; Jordan et al., 2014; Masheb & White, 2012). Both anorexia nervosa and bulimia nervosa are much more common (i.e., ratio of 10:1) in females than males (APA, 2013).

bulimia nervosa

eating disorder characterized by recurrent episodes of binge eating and purging behaviors

binge-eating disorder

eating disorder that involves recurrent episodes of binge eating without subsequent compensatory behaviors

BINGE-EATING DISORDER **Binge-eating disorder** became an official diagnosis in DSM-5, and involves recurrent episodes of binge eating *without* any subsequent compensatory behaviors. As a result, the majority of people with binge-eating disorder are overweight or obese, although it is still possible to be in the normal weight range and receive a diagnosis of binge-eating disorder (Dingemans & van Furth, 2012). To be diagnosed, the binge eating must occur an average of once a week for at least three months and be accompanied by other binge-related symptoms, including:

- Eating faster than normal
- Eating until very full
- Eating large amounts of food, even when not hungry
- Eating alone because of embarrassment
- Experiencing negative feelings after a binge including, disgust, guilt, depression

While the exact numbers vary, the 12-month prevalence of binge-eating disorder (0.8–1.6 percent) tends to be slightly higher than bulimia nervosa (1.0–1.5 percent), which is in turn higher than anorexia nervosa (0.4 percent) (APA, 2013; Kessler et al., 2013). Prevalence rates of all eating disorders are the highest overall among adolescent women (Stice et al., 2013).

It was once assumed that individuals with binge-eating disorder were different from those with the other eating disorders because they didn't hold the same overvalued beliefs about shape and weight. However, research is starting to reveal that a large portion of individuals with binge-eating disorder also experience the undue influence of body shape and weight on their self-evaluation (Grilo et al., 2013), which is associated with more severe eating disorder symptoms and lower psychological functioning. Furthermore, those with overvaluation of shape and weight were less likely to improve with treatment compared to those without these beliefs.

Symptoms of Eating Disorders

	Anorexia Nervosa	Bulimia Nervosa	Binge-Eating Disorder
Interactive	Significantly underweight	Normal weight or overweight	Normal weight or overweight
	May binge eat	Binge eating required	Binge eating required
	May engage in compensatory behaviors	Compensatory behaviors required	Must *not* engage in compensatory behaviors
	Overvaluation of body shape and weight	Overvaluation of body shape and weight	May have overvaluation of body shape and weight

CAUSES OF EATING DISORDERS Do you remember reading earlier about the 3 P's when considering explanations for psychological disorders?

1. Predisposing Causes
2. Precipitating Causes
3. Perpetuating Causes

We even used anorexia nervosa to illustrate because it is such a good example of the importance of taking into consideration the many factors involved in explaining why a person develops a psychological disorder. Table 15.3 outlines some of the factors the research has shown to be important in understanding the development and maintenance of eating disorders.

Table 15.3 Causes of Eating Disorders

Predisposing Causes	Precipitating Causes	Perpetuating Causes
• Genetic factors account for approximately 40–60% of eating disorder development (Trace et al., 2013)	• Participation in athletics, particularly those emphasizing body shape and weight (Bratland-Sanda & Sundgot-Borgen, 2013; Smolak et al., 2000)	• Positive reinforcement from others (Fairburn & Harrison, 2003)
• Perfectionism as a personality trait (Halmi et al., 2000)	• Stressful family and life experiences (Berge et al., 2012)	• Escape from negative emotions (Loeb et al., 2012)
• Diagnosed with an anxiety disorder (particularly OCD) in childhood (Kaye et al., 2004)	• Body dissatisfaction (Machado et al., 2014; Polivy & Herman, 2002)	• Feelings of power and control (Serpell et al., 1999)
• Sociocultural norms and media messages that glorify thinness (Benowitz-Fredericks et al., 2012; Hausenblas et al., 2013)	• Dietary restraint (Fairburn et al., 2014; Jacobi et al., 2004)	• Interpersonal difficulties leading to a lack of social support (Arcelus et al., 2013)

Somatic Symptom and Related Disorders and Dissociative Disorders

LO 15.9 **Recognize the symptoms associated with somatic symptom disorders and dissociative disorders.**

Some psychological disorders are expressed in unusual ways or with symptoms that do not appear to be directly tied to the psychological issue. For example, some psychological disorders are expressed through physical symptoms or affect consciousness, memory, or even self-identity.

SOMATIC SYMPTOM AND RELATED DISORDERS There are some psychological disorders where the prominent symptoms are *somatic* (bodily or physical) in nature and the symptoms cause significant distress or impairment in functioning. **Somatic symptom disorder** involves the combination of the presence of a physical symptom(s) plus abnormal thoughts, feelings, or behaviors in response to the symptom(s). It is typical for these patients to have multiple somatic symptoms, the most common of which involves pain. An example of this disorder would be a woman who has numerous physical complaints, many of which have been medically diagnosed, that are accompanied by a significant proportion of her day worrying about, researching, and consulting various health practitioners regarding her ailments. A diagnosis of somatic symptom disorder does not imply that the physical symptoms aren't "real," but that the patient's response to the symptoms is in excess of what would be expected given the medical presentation. In many ways, the patient's identity is formed around the physical symptoms/diagnoses. Somatic symptom disorder is a new disorder to the DSM-5 and while there was some concern that this disorder would turn medical patients into psychiatric patients (Frances, 2013b), other practitioners and researchers view this new diagnosis as a vast improvement over previously similar diagnoses (Dimsdale et al., 2013; Voigt et al., 2012).

Conversion disorder, which is now also called **functional neurological symptom disorder**, is a related disorder rarely seen in North America and Western Europe (although it was fairly common 100 years ago). Characterized by the sudden, temporary loss of a sensory or motor function, a person may experience blindness, paralysis, deafness, or numbness of particular body parts. In contrast to somatic symptom disorder, none of the conversion symptoms have physical causes that can be medically explained. The explanation of conversion disorder almost always includes exposure to a traumatic event (Roelofs et al., 2005; Sar et al., 2004). For example, there was a high rate of psychological blindness among Cambodian women after the Khmer Rouge reign of terror in the 1970s (Rozée & Van Boemel, 1990).

There are cases where an individual experiences a great deal of dysfunction and impairment, not because of existing physical symptoms, but because of the *fear* of having or acquiring a serious illness or disease. **Illness anxiety disorder**, formerly known as hypochondriasis, involves significant health anxiety and anxiety-related checking and avoidance behaviors.

Exact prevalence rates are difficult to establish in the first few years of a newly named disorder. The DSM-5 suggests that the prevalence for somatic symptom disorder may be 5–7 percent, with a larger range for illness anxiety disorder (1.3–10 percent) in the general population (APA, 2013). There is no question that the prevalence rate for conversion disorder is significantly lower and is likely less than 1 percent of the general population, although it can be as high as 5 percent in neurology patients.

Understanding somatic symptom and related disorders requires a biopsychosocial approach. The DSM-5 describes these disorders as "expressions of personal suffering inserted in a cultural and social context" (APA, 2013, p. 310). Genetic predispositions, early traumatic experiences, learned behaviors including reinforcement for illness behavior, in addition to cultural/social norms that view physical suffering as more acceptable than psychological suffering have all been important factors in understanding somatic symptom and related disorders.

DISSOCIATIVE DISORDERS If you have ever driven the familiar route home and then realized you can't remember anything about how you actually got there, you are already familiar with dissociation. Our conscious minds are able to focus on the term paper due next week, while another part of our brain somehow navigates us through traffic lights and stop signs. **Dissociative disorders** are conditions in which the normal cognitive processes are fragmented, causing a sudden loss of memory or change in personality. These take several forms, and can vary in length from a matter of minutes to many years.

somatic symptom disorder

psychological disorder involving the combination of the presence of a physical symptom(s) plus abnormal thoughts, feelings, or behaviors in response to the symptom(s)

conversion disorder (functional neurological symptom disorder)

psychological disorder characterized by the sudden, temporary loss of a sensory or motor function; symptoms can include blindness, paralysis, deafness, or numbness of particular body parts

illness anxiety disorder

psychological disorder formerly known as hypochondriasis, which involves significant health anxiety and anxiety-related checking and avoidance behaviors

dissociative disorders

group of psychological disorders where the normal cognitive processes are fragmented, causing a sudden loss of memory or change in personality

dissociative amnesia

psychological disorder that causes sudden, selective memory loss, which is usually precipitated by a traumatic event

Dissociative amnesia is a disorder that causes sudden, selective memory loss. It is usually preempted by a traumatic event, such as sexual trauma or childhood abuse (Van Der Hart & Nijenhuis, 2001) and tends to involve primarily autobiographical, retrospective memories. Dissociative amnesia differs from permanent amnesia, in which memory loss is typically caused by a blow to the head rather than a psychological trauma. While dissociative amnesia occurs without any sign of structural damage to the brain, case studies using PET scans have identified an area of the brain (i.e., the right posterior middle temporal gyrus) that is significantly less active in those with dissociative amnesia compared to healthy individuals (Thomas-Antérion et al., 2014). It is thought that this underactivity of the brain may prevent access to certain retrospective memories.

Imagine waking up in a strange place with no idea who you were or how you got there. While it sounds like the plot to a bad Hollywood movie, *dissociative fugue* is a subtype of dissociative amnesia, characterized by a sudden loss of memory accompanied by an abrupt departure from home. A person suffering from dissociative amnesia with dissociative fugue may forget all personal history and take on a whole new identity. Dissociative amnesia *without* fugue is the more common diagnosis (approximately 1–2 percent), with instances of dissociative amnesia with dissociative fugue occurring very rarely (approximately 0–0.2 percent) (Spiegel et al., 2011). In the following video, *Dissociative Amnesia*, Sharon discusses her difficult childhood and symptoms of dissociative amnesia.

Dissociative Amnesia

dissociative identity disorder (DID)

psychological disorder where a person experiences two or more, sometimes vastly different, personalities

Chances are you have heard of multiple personality disorder, which is technically called **dissociative identity disorder (DID)**, where a person seems to experience two or more personalities in one body. DID has been one of the most sensationalized psychological disorders, represented in movies, television shows (e.g., *The United States of Tara*), and courtrooms, with several criminals over the years attempting to obtain an insanity verdict by faking DID (which is referred to as malingering).

In DID, each personality has its own voice, mannerisms, and interests and may or may not be aware of the others. DID is typically accompanied by extensive memory impairment and amnesia for certain events. Patients have explained the amnesia as periods of time where another personality was "out" and prevented the primary personality from knowing what was going on. This explanation provides some understanding for how an individual can, for example, wake up one morning with a hangover, surrounded by empty beer cans, have no memory of a party, and claim that they don't drink alcohol. Yes, this idea is difficult to comprehend. It can be helpful to think of DID not as a collection of *different people* sharing the same body, but instead, as one person who experiences himself or herself as having separate parts of the mind that function with some autonomy.

There is probably no other psychological disorder with as much debate among professionals as to the existence of the condition. There are those who believe that DID is either made up, induced by therapists, or a social cognitive construction (which suggests that sociocultural factors influence certain people to unconsciously enact different "roles" that become a part of their identity) (Boysen & VanBergen, 2013; Lilienfeld et al., 1999, p. 508; Paris, 2012). An entirely different camp of professionals continually argue that DID is in fact "real" and it emerges as an attempt to cope with severe physical and/or sexual abuse experienced in childhood (Lewis et al., 1997; Sar, 2011).

In 1999, Lilienfeld and his colleagues suggested that the social-cognitive model would be shown to be false if certain empirical evidence was presented. This type of evidence included (1) identification of DID across different cultures, (2) demonstrating that all cases of DID include a severe traumatic history, and (3) documentation that people could not fake DID in laboratory studies. Since that time, evidence has emerged suggesting the following:

- DID has been found in various cultural environments (Dorahy et al., 2014; Rhoades & Şar, 2005).

- "Every study that has systematically examined [causes] has found that antecedent severe, chronic childhood trauma is present in the histories of almost all individuals with DID" (Dorahy et al., 2014, p. 408).

- Significant functional brain imaging differences exist between DID patients and those instructed to fake DID symptoms. For those with DID, differences have been documented within the same person but in different personality states. Furthermore, differences have been found between people who have been diagnosed with DID and healthy control participants who were instructed to do their best to simulate DID symptoms and personality states (Dorahy et al., 2014; Savoy et al., 2012; Schlumpf et al., 2013).

Quiz for Module 15.8–15.9

1. What is considered the normal range of body mass index (BMI) for adults?
   a. 10.5–18.5
   b. 25.0–30.0
   c. 18.5–24.9
   d. 30.0–40.0

2. The new eating disorder in the *DSM-5* that involves recurrent episodes of binge eating without any subsequent compensatory behaviors is called _____.
   a. bulimia nervosa
   b. binge-eating disorder
   c. anorexia nervosa
   d. persistent eating disorder

3. This disorder involves the presence of physical symptoms combined with abnormal thoughts, feelings, or behaviors in response to those symptoms.
   a. Conversion disorder
   b. Illness anxiety disorder
   c. Somatic symptom disorder
   d. Pain disorder

4. Joanne has been diagnosed with a psychological disorder characterized by the existence of two or more personalities, marked with periods of memory impairment, and amnesia for certain events. Joanne has the symptoms of which disorder?
   a. Dissociative amnesia
   b. Dissociative fugue
   c. Dissociative identity disorder (DID)
   d. Schizophrenia

5. Which disorder has produced controversy within the field of psychology to where some psychologists don't believe it is a real disorder?
   a. Schizophrenia
   b. Dissociative identity disorder
   c. Dissociative amnesia
   d. Functional neurological symptom disorder

Module 15.10 – 15.11: Schizophrenia

The 2001 movie, *A Beautiful Mind*, is a classic portrayal of schizophrenia. In this movie, Russell Crowe played Nobel-prize winning mathematician John Nash. The movie was not only a blockbuster hit, but provided a window into Nash's real-life struggle with schizophrenia. He was a brilliant man, who suffered to varying degrees throughout his life, who not only contributed to the field of mathematics but also to the world's understanding of schizophrenia.

The Symptoms of Schizophrenia

LO 15.10 Distinguish the various symptoms of schizophrenia.

schizophrenia

severe psychological disorder involving psychosis, which is characterized by delusions, hallucinations, disorganized thinking, abnormal movements, and lack of motivation and emotional expression

Literally meaning "split mind," **schizophrenia** is often confused with dissociative identity disorder, which was sometimes referred to as "split personality." However, schizophrenia actually involves a person's split from reality (referred to as *psychosis*), characterized by delusions, hallucinations, disorganized thinking, abnormal movements, and lack of motivation and emotional expression. In the DSM-5, schizophrenia is just one diagnosis included in the group of disorders that exist along the schizophrenia spectrum.

To be diagnosed with schizophrenia, a person must display two or more of the primary symptoms for at least a month, with continuous signs of disturbance and interference with functioning for at least six months (APA, 2013). There are a total of five primary groups of symptoms and individuals must experience one of the first three in order to receive a diagnosis. To learn more about the categories of symptoms of schizophrenia, refer to Figure 15.4.

Figure 15.4 Diagnostic Criteria for Schizophrenia

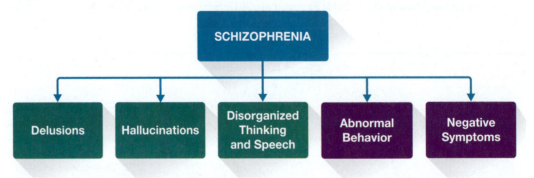

positive symptoms

symptoms of schizophrenia that reflect a pathological excess or additions to normal functions, such as delusions, hallucinations, and disorganized thinking and speech

negative symptoms

symptoms of schizophrenia that represent a pathological deficit, or the absence of emotions or behaviors that are typically present in a psychologically healthy individual

delusions

positive symptom of schizophrenia involving fixed and rigid, false beliefs

All of the symptoms of schizophrenia can be categorized into meaningful clusters. **Positive symptoms** reflect a pathological excess or distortion of normal functions, such as delusions, hallucinations, and disorganized thinking and speech. While these symptoms tend to be the most dramatic, they are also the ones that tend to disappear as the disorder goes into remission. Positive symptoms respond best to antipsychotic medication (Buchanan et al., 2014) and therefore an individual with predominantly positive symptoms will likely have a better prognosis. **Negative symptoms** represent a pathological deficit, or the absence of emotions or behaviors that are typically present in a psychologically healthy individual. The negative symptoms of schizophrenia can look like depression and while they are not always as overt or dramatic as positive symptoms, they tend to be more long-lasting and their presence predicts poor quality of life in the future (Ho et al., 2014; McGurk et al., 2000).

Some of the positive symptoms of schizophrenia include, **delusions**, which are rigid and fixed false beliefs. No amount of contrary evidence is going to convince someone with a delusion that their belief is not real. This is the difference between someone who is stubborn and someone who is delusional. A patient may believe that they are being spied on, that someone is controlling their thoughts and actions, or that a spouse is being unfaithful to them. Some delusions are considered bizarre which involve beliefs that are clearly not plausible (e.g., "An alien from Mars has landed and now lives inside my head").

Hallucinations are false sensory perceptions that a person believes to be real. Auditory hallucinations, or hearing voices, are the most common type of hallucination; many people with schizophrenia report that they hear insulting comments or receive orders from voices inside their heads. Research using fMRI scans shows that auditory hallucinations in people diagnosed with schizophrenia are accompanied by activity in the brain regions normally associated with thought processing, speech generation, and memory (Diederen et al., 2010; Jardri et al., 2011). While auditory hallucinations are most common, people may also see (visual hallucinations), feel (tactile hallucinations), smell (olfactory hallucinations), or taste (gustatory hallucinations) things that aren't really there.

Disorganized thinking and speech is another category of symptoms of schizophrenia. That is, these individuals may think or speak in ways that are jumbled, illogical, or incoherent. They may jump from topic to topic, make up new words, or even speak in rhymes.

Individuals with schizophrenia often also struggle with abnormal motor (movement) behavior, which is technically referred to as **catatonia**. The movements can range from excessive movement and agitation to complete paralysis, which is referred to as a **catatonic stupor**.

The negative symptoms of schizophrenia involve the absence or loss of some kind of functioning, which is why they are referred to as negative symptoms. In this case, "negative" does not mean "bad" but it refers to "the absence" or deficit in an important area of functioning. The best way to remember the negative symptoms is to think of the 5 A's. A prefix of the letter "a" typically signifies "without" or "lack of":

Alogia → Without speech. Individuals with schizophrenia may not speak much, or may take a long time to respond when asked a question. Their answers may be very brief.

Avolition → Without volition, or motivation. They may feel no desire to engage in any activities. This symptom can be similar to that seen in depression.

Anhedonia → Without fun. Nothing is fun anymore. Even if they do force themselves to go out and do something, they don't experience any feelings of happiness or joy.

Affect (blunted or flat) → Without emotional expression. Affect is the behavioral expression of emotion. Their range of emotion tends to be very small (blunted), or they just exhibit no emotion whatsoever (flat).

Asociality → Without interest in social situations. Similar to, and a result of, the other symptoms, individuals with schizophrenia tend to struggle in social situations.

While you watch the video, *Schizophrenia*, see if you can identify some of the positive and negative symptoms of schizophrenia.

hallucinations

positive symptoms of schizophrenia that involves false sensory perceptions

disorganized thinking and speech

group of symptoms of schizophrenia where individuals may think or speak in ways that are jumbled, illogical, or incoherent

catatonia

symptom of schizophrenia involving abnormal motor (movement) behavior

catatonic stupor

extreme form of catatonia that involves paralysis

Schizophrenia

PREVALENCE AND COURSE OF SCHIZOPHRENIA   Approximately 0.3–0.7 percent of people in the world develop schizophrenia (APA, 2013; Bhugra, 2005). The incidence of schizophrenia is slightly lower in women, with gender appearing to affect the expression and prognosis of the disease. Males tend to experience their first psychotic episode in their early to mid-twenties, whereas the onset for females occurs in the late-twenties. Furthermore, men have been found to have worse premorbid functioning (meaning their level of functioning prior to the onset of the illness), lower educational achievement, more negative symptoms, and increased cognitive impairment, all of which lead to a worse prognosis (APA, 2013). Schizophrenia is associated with a high risk of suicide with approximately 20–40 percent of patients with schizophrenia attempting suicide and 5–10 percent of those attempts resulting in death (Erlangsen et al., 2012; Hor & Taylor, 2010).

Adaptive Pathway 15.2: Understanding Schizophrenia

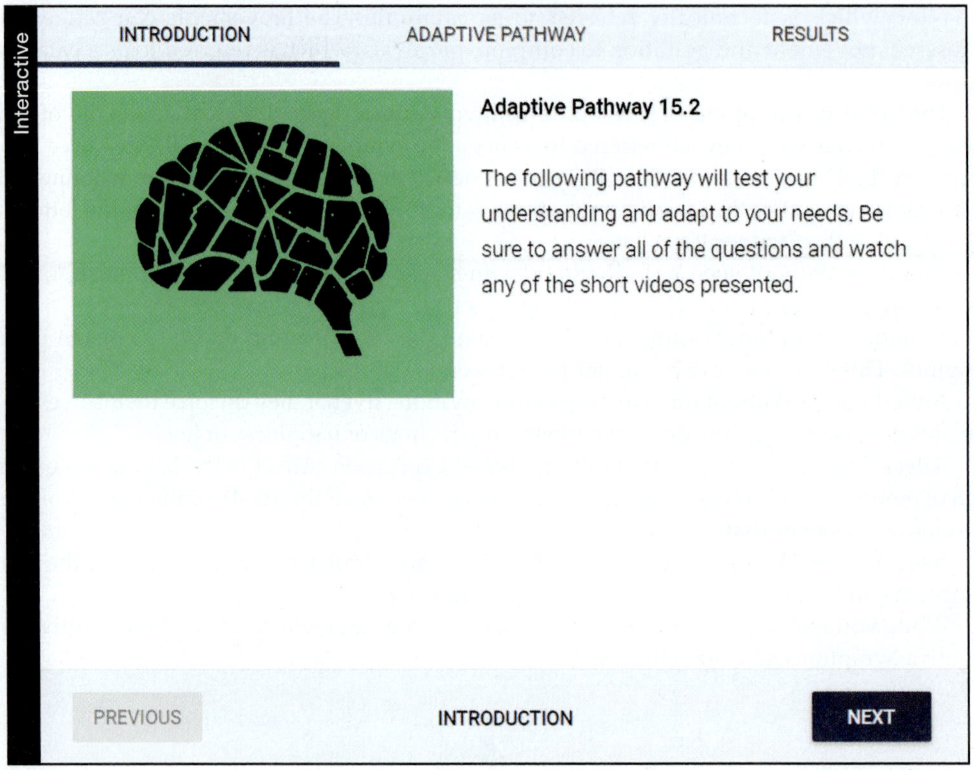

Interactive

| INTRODUCTION | ADAPTIVE PATHWAY | RESULTS |

Adaptive Pathway 15.2

The following pathway will test your understanding and adapt to your needs. Be sure to answer all of the questions and watch any of the short videos presented.

PREVIOUS   INTRODUCTION   NEXT

Explaining Schizophrenia

LO 15.11   **Explain the causes of schizophrenia.**

Schizophrenia is a complex disease and its explanation is equally complex. While a biopsychosocial approach to understanding the causes of schizophrenia is most appropriate, it is fair to say that the majority of research has focused on the biological factors, such as genetics, neurochemistry, and brain structure, to understand what causes this disease.

GENETIC FACTORS   Numerous studies indicate that schizophrenia has a strong genetic component (Gejman et al., 2010). Irving Gottesman compiled data showing that the risk of developing schizophrenia increases with the degree of biological closeness to someone suffering from the disorder. While the general population has approximately a 1 percent risk of developing schizophrenia, the chance of being diagnosed with the disorder increases to 9 percent if a sibling is afflicted (Gottesman, 2001). More recent research has supported a shared genetic link between schizophrenia, bipolar disorder, and autism-spectrum disorder and estimates the heritability of schizophrenia at 64 percent (Lichtenstein et al., 2009; Sullivan et al., 2012).

Twin and adoption studies have provided further evidence for the role of genetics in the development of schizophrenia (see Figure 15.5) (Petersen & Sørensen, 2011). If an identical twin is diagnosed with schizophrenia, the likelihood of the other twin developing the disorder is 48 percent. The fact that fraternal twins show a higher rate of concordance than nontwin siblings (17 percent compared to 9 percent) indicates that the prenatal environment plays a role in developing schizophrenia (Gottesman, 2001).

Figure 15.5 Genetic Influences in Schizophrenia

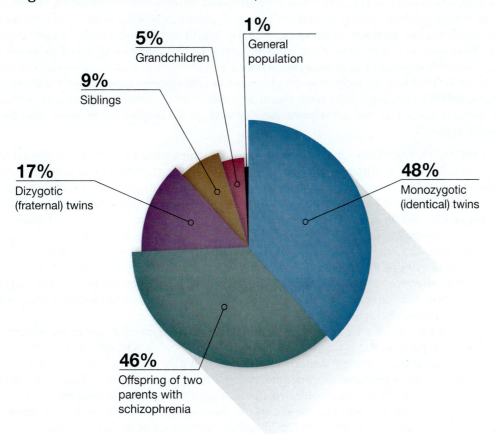

Much of the research today on the causes of schizophrenia focuses on the relationship between genetic and environmental factors to explain its development. After all, if the disease was entirely genetic, then why wouldn't the concordance rate between identical twins be 100 percent? Similar to our discussions in other chapters (see LO 8.9 and LO 12.2), we might ask the question, "Are there environmental factors that activate an underlying genetic predisposition to develop schizophrenia?" This question is asking, "Is there a *gene-environment interaction*?" However, an equally important question to ask is, "Does a genetic predisposition toward schizophrenia lend itself toward particular environments that may influence whether or not the disorder develops?" This question is asking, "Is there a *gene-environment correlation*?" The short answer to both questions is "Yes!"

A specific gene-environment interaction model that has been used to explain schizophrenia is the **diathesis-stress model**, which suggests that some people are genetically predisposed to schizophrenia but will only develop the disorder if they are exposed to environmental or emotional stress during critical developmental periods (Daskalakis & Binder, 2015; Jones & Fernyhough, 2007). As mentioned earlier, one of those critical developmental periods includes the prenatal environment. It has been found that mothers (human and rat) who contract an influenza virus, particularly H1N1, during the second trimester of pregnancy are twice as likely to give birth to offspring who develop the disorder (Brown et al., 2000; Landreau et al., 2012). While it appears that the virus impacts gene expression and dopaminergic neurons

diathesis-stress model

model for explaining schizophrenia that suggests that the disorder develops from a genetic predisposition that interacts with emotional or environmental stress in the developing offspring (Fatemi et al., 2012), it is not clear whether this risk factor is due to the virus itself, the mother's immune response, medications taken to combat the virus, or another, unknown factor. Regardless, this research has informed public policy resulting in the recommendation from the Centers for Disease Control that all pregnant women receive a flu shot. Supporting evidence for this viral theory of schizophrenia also comes from the fact that significantly more (i.e., 5–8 percent) people with schizophrenia are born in the winter or spring months (meaning the second trimester of pregnancy was during the height of flu season) (Suvisaari et al., 2001; Torrey et al., 1997).

Gene-environment correlations also contribute to the explanation of schizophrenia. For example, researchers at Harvard University followed adolescents identified as high-risk for developing schizophrenia (based on having a parent or sibling with schizophrenia) and found that in addition to genetics, prenatal health issues and family environment (e.g., less cohesion and more conflict) were important factors that distinguished those who were high-risk compared to adolescents without any inflated risk of the disease (Walder et al., 2014). That is, even before the development of schizophrenia, individuals with high genetic liability (i.e., high risk) were found to have more stressful environments, which we know is related to the subsequent development of schizophrenia in those who are already at risk.

BIOCHEMICAL FACTORS In addition to genetic factors, neurotransmitter dysfunction can also help explain schizophrenia. Dopamine, serotonin, glutamate, and acetylcholine systems have all been implicated in the development and maintenance of schizophrenia (Kirkpatrick, 2013). When researchers examined the brains of patients diagnosed with schizophrenia after death, they discovered up to six times the normal number of dopamine receptors (Seeman et al., 1993). The researchers believed that this elevated level of dopamine may intensify brain signals in people with schizophrenia, causing positive symptoms such as hallucinations and delusions. Drugs that block dopamine transmission have been shown to be effective at reducing many of the symptoms of schizophrenia, whereas drugs that increase dopamine action, such as cocaine or amphetamines, can exacerbate symptoms (Seeman & Seeman, 2014; Seeman, 2013).

We have known for a long time that dopamine plays an important role in the development of schizophrenia, but it was never clear if individuals with schizophrenia merely had more presynaptic dopaminergic neurons (i.e., a structural difference) or if their existing presynaptic neurons just produced more dopamine (i.e., a functional difference). Two studies that both reanalyzed data from other published studies (i.e., a meta-analysis) were finally able to answer this question. Upon examining the role of dopamine in the striatum, the researchers concluded that there were no structural abnormalities in the number or density of dopaminergic neurons (Fusar-Poli & Meyer-Lindenberg, 2013a). However, they found that patients with schizophrenia had 14 percent more dopamine in this particular area of their brain (Fusar-Poli & Meyer-Lindenberg, 2013b). Taken together, these findings indicate that the positive symptoms of schizophrenia relate to the amount or regulation of dopamine rather than the number of dopaminergic neurons.

Despite this important information, the explanation of schizophrenia is more complicated than just stating, "Schizophrenia results from too much dopamine in the brain." As you have seen, schizophrenia has a wide variety of symptoms and, while an excess of dopamine may explain some of the positive symptoms of schizophrenia, deficits in dopamine in other areas of the brain may explain some of the cognitive impairments (e.g., working memory) that are characteristic of the disorder (Carlsson & Carlsson, 2006; Lewis & Gonzalez-Burgos, 2006).

Recent research also suggests that defects in the receptor molecules for the neurotransmitter glutamate may also cause symptoms of schizophrenia (Keshavan et al., 2011). This discovery accounts for some general cognitive defects as well as the explanation for the effects of street drugs such as PCP (commonly known as "angel dust"), which interfere with glutamate transmission and temporarily induce schizophrenia-like symptoms in people who don't otherwise have a psychological disorder. It has also been hypothesized that the glutamatergic system may have some responsibility for the progressive loss of brain tissue seen in individuals with schizophrenia (Marsman et al., 2013).

ABNORMAL BRAIN STRUCTURE AND FUNCTION Brain scans reveal that people with schizophrenia tend to have abnormal brain structures. Enlarged brain ventricles (the pillow-like sacs filled with cerebral spinal fluid that cushion the brain from the inside) in some patients indicate a deficit in the volume of surrounding brain tissue (Gaser et al., 2014; Sayo et al., 2012), particularly in the medial temporal lobe (Wright et al., 2000).

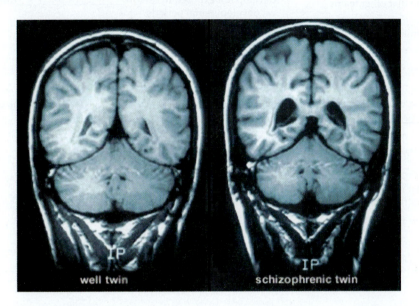

These brain images illustrate the enlarged ventricles (dark spots in the middle of the brain on the right) that often accompany the diagnosis of schizophrenia.

There is also evidence of abnormality in the frontal lobes, anterior cingulate gyrus, thalamus, and left amygdala (Bora & Pantelis, 2015; Pettegrew et al., 1993). Advances in imaging technology have enabled researchers to map a complete set of the brain's network connectivity. In general, findings have supported a widespread, global connectivity deficit among those diagnosed with schizophrenia. In addition, more specific functional connectivity deficits that vary across different situations have also been found, which may explain the individual variation in symptom presentation (Fornito et al., 2012).

These structural and functional changes have been found to occur at various stages of neurodevelopment, including prenatal and perinatal periods, and before, during, and after the onset of schizophrenia (Pantelis et al., 2005).

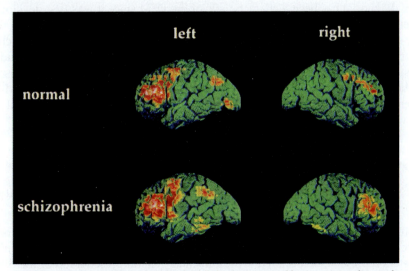

Functional neuroimaging techniques highlight the increased brain activity observed in an individual with schizophrenia.

Quiz for Module 15.10–15.11

1. A person who is experiencing a delusion may:
   a. Believe their baseball team is the best even though the team loses most games, but eventually they concede that other teams have better records and season outcomes.
   b. Hear voices telling them they are lazy and dumb.
   c. See fairies dancing in their backyard.
   d. Believe they are from the planet Mars and have special powers.

2. In schizophrenia, pathological excesses or distortions of normal functioning that include delusions, hallucinations, and disorganized thinking and speech are called _____ symptoms.
   a. positive
   b. negative
   c. additional
   d. residual

3. Nada has been diagnosed with schizophrenia that includes excessive motor symptoms where she often paces frantically. This movement symptom is called _____.
   a. alogia
   b. anhedonia
   c. motoria
   d. catatonia

4. The diathesis-stress model suggests people are _____ predisposed to schizophrenia but will only develop it if exposed to certain _____ during critical developmental periods.
   a. environmentally; genetics
   b. genetically; stressors
   c. chemically; environments
   d. genetically; toxins

5. Which neurotransmitter has been linked to the positive symptoms of schizophrenia?
   a. Glutamate
   b. Endorphins
   c. Dopamine
   d. Serotonin

Module 15.12–15.13: Personality Disorders

Personality disorders are rigid, maladaptive patterns of behavior that make it difficult for individuals to have healthy social relationships. The primary difference between personality disorders and all of the other disorders discussed so far is that personality disorders (by definition) are *long-standing* patterns of thoughts, feelings, and behaviors that interfere with functioning. The symptoms almost always begin in adolescence or early adulthood, even if they aren't diagnosed until years later. Individuals with personality disorders often see the problems in their life as "everyone else's fault." They are not necessarily choosing to blame other people, but they may genuinely lack insight into the problems their behavior is causing.

The categorical approach to personality disorders (i.e., symptom a + symptom b + symptoms c = diagnosis) has been a characteristic of the DSM since it was first developed. During the development of the DSM-5, there was considerable discussion about changing the way personality disorders were conceptualized by moving to a more dimensional approach (i.e., viewing disorders as a series of personality traits that vary along a continuum of mild to severe). This system would have represented a major change in the way personality disorders have always been classified, and it was decided just prior to the publication of the DSM-5 that there wasn't enough research to support the change and the comfort level of the mental health community was too low to go forward with the new system.

personality disorders

long-standing, rigid, and maladaptive patterns of behavior that make it difficult for individuals to sustain healthy social relationships

An Overview of the Personality Disorders

LO 15.12 **Recognize the characteristics associated with the different personality disorders.**

There are 10 recognized types of personality disorders, divided into three clusters: (1) odd or eccentric behaviors; (2) dramatic or impulsive behaviors; and (3) anxious, fearful behaviors. The clusters represent some shared symptoms and general presentation of the disorders that comprise each group. Table 15.4 lists a brief description of all the personality disorders within each cluster

Table 15.4 Personality Disorders

Cluster A	Cluster B	Cluster C
Paranoid Personality Disorder • Extreme suspicion and distrust of others. Jealous and critical of others. Difficult to maintain relationships.	Antisocial Personality Disorder • Criminal and deviant behavior accompanied by a lack of conscience. Observable by the age of 15. Includes people referred to as psychopaths or sociopaths.	Avoidant Personality Disorder • High levels of social anxiety and feelings of inadequacy. These individuals want social interaction, but their extreme shyness and fear of rejection makes it difficult to maintain relationships.
Schizoid Personality Disorder • Loners. Show no interest in relationships with others. Appear cold and unemotional.	Borderline Personality Disorder • Dramatic and erratic emotions and behaviors that often include self-harming behaviors. Unstable self-image, mood, and relationships.	Dependent Personality Disorder • Insecure, clingy, and difficult making decisions on their own. Frequently seeking reassurance from others. Generally, have a difficult time with separation.
Schizotypal Personality Disorder • Peculiar and eccentric mannerisms and expression of personality. Often hold strange beliefs and experience social anxiety. Relationships are difficult to maintain. Sometime considered a mild form of schizophrenia.	Histrionic Personality Disorder • Excessively dramatic and emotional. Manipulative. A need to be the center of attention. Despite an excessive display of emotions, these individuals tend to be emotionally shallow and thrive on the approval and praise of others.	Obsessive-Compulsive Personality Disorder • Concerned with orderliness and perfectionism. Preoccupied with rules, schedules, and order. Difficulty maintaining relationships due to unrealistic expectations and controlling behavior.
	Narcissistic Personality Disorder • Inflated sense of self-worth and importance. A need for the deep admiration from others. Appear conceited and preoccupied with fantasies of their own success.	

Understanding Borderline Personality Disorder

LO 15.13 **Explain the symptoms and causes of borderline personality disorder.**

Two of the ten personality disorders have received the most attention and research into their causes and treatment. The first, *antisocial personality disorder*, was discussed in the *Piecing It Together* module in the Personality chapter (see LO 14.14). **Borderline personality disorder** is the second personality disorder that has been the focus of significant study and is characterized by poor self-image; unstable moods; intense, stormy personal relationships; and impulsive behaviors. The name itself is misleading because some people think it implies that these symptoms are on the "borderline" of a diagnosable disorder. The syndrome was originally described in the early 1900s, and it was noted that some patients exhibited psychotic symptoms in addition to periods of anxiety and depression. In 1938, Adolf Stern, a psychoanalyst, adopted the name *borderline* because he saw the constellation of symptoms to lie on the *border* between neurosis and psychosis (Lilienfeld & Arkowitz, 2012). As you will see, borderline personality disorder bears little resemblance to schizophrenia and other names that have been proposed, such as "emotion-regulation disorder" and "emotionally unstable disorder," are more accurate descriptions of the condition.

SYMPTOMS OF BORDERLINE PERSONALITY DISORDER You can think of borderline personality disorder as involving the 3 I's: *instability* in relationships; *identity* disturbance (poor self-image); and *impulsive* behaviors. Periods of depression and/or anger, excessive spending, drug abuse, or suicidal/self-harming behavior are also characteristics of the disorder (Gunderson, 2011; Leichsenring et al., 2011; Paris, 2002). Fear of abandonment, or what is also referred to as *rejection sensitivity*, is often at the core of this disorder and, as a result, the individual typically engages in desperate behavior to prevent abandonment. In a study comparing individuals with borderline personality disorder to patients receiving outpatient therapy for other psychological disorders, those with borderline personality disorder reported significantly more rejection sensitivity compared to any other diagnostic group (Staebler et al., 2011). Lacking a sense of identity, the person may cling to others, often using suicidal behavior as a form of manipulation. Over time, a self-fulfilling prophecy often emerges where the person with borderline personality disorder engages in so many extreme and intense behaviors that they end up pushing away the very person they are so scared to lose. Frequently lacking insight about the effect their behaviors have on others, the patient sees the partner/friend who is leaving as confirmation that they (the patient) are a bad person and that no one cares for

borderline personality disorder

personality disorder that involves dramatic and erratic emotions and behaviors that often include self-harming behavior

them. These intense feelings of abandonment and loneliness can then trigger other impulsive behaviors such as cutting.

Cutting, or other forms of nonsuicidal self-injury, is common among individuals with borderline personality disorder (Carpenter & Trull, 2013). While it is difficult to understand why someone would want to purposely hurt themselves, some patients have described this behavior as a welcomed alternative to the constant emotional pain they experience (Reitz et al., 2012). From a behavioral perspective, cutting behavior is maintained primarily through negative reinforcement. Cutting, and the experience of physical pain, allows the patient to briefly escape from intense emotional pain. This situation relieves an aversive or negative state, which is therefore experienced as reinforcing. As a result, the cutting behavior is more likely to be adopted again the next time overwhelming emotions are felt. Watch the video *Symptoms of Borderline Personality Disorder* to learn more about one woman's experience with nonsuicidal self-injury.

Symptoms of Borderline Personality Disorder

EXPLAINING BORDERLINE PERSONALITY DISORDER   The prevalence of borderline personality disorder ranges from 1.6–5.9 percent, depending on how it is measured (APA, 2013). The more intense the level of care, the higher the prevalence rate, with about 20 percent of psychiatric inpatients diagnosed with borderline personality disorder. Explanations regarding how borderline personality develops have once again focused on biological factors, environmental factors, and the relationship between biological and environmental influences.

There is a strong genetic component to borderline personality disorder with heritability estimates ranging from 51–75 percent (Leichsenring et al., 2011; Reichborn-Kjennerud et al., 2013). This means that the majority of the variance in the expression of borderline personality among people is due to genetics. Even though the DSM-5 describes the onset of borderline personality disorder in adolescence or early adulthood, researchers have found evidence of borderline personality related characteristics in children who are 12 years old. Following more than 1,000 pairs of twins, Daniel Belsky and colleagues (2012) were able to identify factors at age 5 that predicted borderline characteristics at age 12. In particular, exposure to a harsh family environment through age 10 was a strong predictor of subsequent symptoms. This relationship was the strongest among children who had a family history of psychiatric illness (which also suggests that the child may have inherited a tendency toward developing psychiatric symptoms).

The findings from this study suggest, as with schizophrenia, that a diathesis-stress model is one way to explain the development of borderline personality disorder. Children who inherit a predisposition for borderline personality disorder *and* experience environmental risk factors are more likely to develop the disorder than children without both the genetic and environmental influences.

Marsha Linehan, a leading researcher in the field of borderline personality disorder proposed a type of gene-environment interaction theory called the *biosocial theory*. According to this model, borderline personality disorder develops as a result of the interaction between biological vulnerabilities and environmental risk factors. Poor impulse control is thought to be inherited and develop early in life, followed by extreme emotional sensitivity to the environment. These emotional predispositions interact with an *invalidating family environment* where the child's feelings are not validated, or even punished, resulting in an inability to assess, monitor, and appropriately express their own feelings (Crowell et al., 2009; Kuo & Linehan, 2009).

Childhood sexual, physical, or emotional abuse (an extreme form of invalidation) have long been thought to be an important causative factor in the development of borderline personality disorder in that many patients diagnosed with the disorder report a history of childhood abuse (Kuo et al., 2015). A recent study involving identical and fraternal twins provided evidence to suggest that abuse does not, in fact, have a *causal* effect on the later development of borderline personality disorder. Abuse and certain specific personality characteristics (e.g., impulsivity, negative emotionality) are correlated with borderline personality symptoms, but their relationship appears to be better explained by common genetic influences rather than the environment per se (Bornovalova et al., 2013). This is not to say that environment is not important, but that gene-environment correlations may be a more appropriate way to explain the development of borderline personality disorder (Carpenter et al., 2013).

Quiz for Module 15.12–15.13

1. Angelo has been in and out of prison three times for battery and assault. He recently broke into an elderly woman's home where he robbed and severely beat her. He showed no feelings of remorse or regret about his actions. Which personality disorder would be the most appropriate for Angelo?

   a. Narcissistic   **b.** Avoidant

   c. Obsessive compulsive   **d.** Antisocial

2. The DSM-5 includes _____ clusters of personality disorders.

   a. 3   **b.** 5

   c. 9   **d.** 11

3. Borderline personality disorder is characterized by poor self-image, _____ moods, stormy and intense personal relationships, and impulsive behaviors.

   a. angry   **b.** depressed

   c. manic   **d.** unstable

4. What are the 3 I's in borderline personality disorder symptoms?

   a. Identity problems, intense feelings, and image issues

   b. Instability in relationships, identity disturbance, and impulsive behaviors

   c. Issues management, intensity of feelings, and identity problems

   d. Impulsive actions, issues of stability, and identity fraud

---

Module 15.14: Piecing It Together: Pediatric Bipolar Disorder

LO 15.14   **Analyze how the cross-cutting themes of psychology apply to the misdiagnosis of pediatric bipolar disorder.**

Some psychological disorders may first be evident in childhood. The diagnostic criteria used to assess psychological disorders in children are less standardized and more contextualized than criteria used for adults, and diagnosis can be difficult because symptoms may differ between children and adults. According to the U.S. Surgeon General, one in five children in the United States suffers from a psychological disorder at any given time.

One of the most recent, hotly debated childhood psychological disorders is *pediatric bipolar disorder*. Recall that bipolar disorder in adults is characterized by shifting between periods of depression and often shorter periods of mania. Adults with bipolar disorder typically suffer from numerous impairments in life as a result of their symptoms, and successful treatment is almost always achieved through the use of potent psychotropic medications.

Throughout the 1980s and 1990s, the most discussed childhood psychological disorder was attention-deficit hyperactivity disorder (ADHD). However, that focus has now shifted to pediatric bipolar disorder. Studies have demonstrated phenomenal increases in the number of children (as young as 3 years old) who are diagnosed with bipolar disorder. Research tracking the number

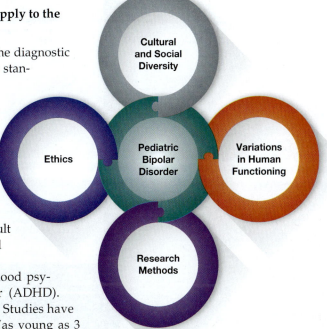

of diagnoses of bipolar disorder in kids determined there was a 4,000 percent increase in diagnoses between 1994 and 2003 (Moreno et al., 2007).

How could that be? Is there a national epidemic of pediatric bipolar disorder? Perhaps inadequate understanding of how bipolar disorder presented in children and lack of appropriate assessment instruments lead to the previous "under-diagnosis." Other prominent figures in the medical community have charged that pediatric bipolar disorder was invented by a few prominent researchers who developed a theory that energized drug companies and gave hope to parents (Frances, 2013a).

In 2010, the National Institute of Mental Health made a commitment to bring the field together to resolve issues and make recommendations, and the recent DSM-5 and ICD-11 work groups also agreed to tackle the issue (Insel, 2010). Despite the agreement to work together to bring clarity to this childhood diagnosis, there is little agreement among professionals in the mental health field to date. Let's explore some of the important psychological perspectives that may help in understanding the complexities of this controversial diagnosis.

Variations in Human Functioning

- How is bipolar disorder expressed in children?

- How are the symptoms of pediatric bipolar disorder distinguished from other childhood psychological disorders?

Bipolar disorder in children is viewed as developmentally different than it is in adults. While the hallmark symptom of bipolar disorder in adults in episodic mania, which is typically expressed in the form of euphoric (i.e., happy/excited) mood, the mood component for children and adolescents is characterized by chronic and severe irritability (Biederman et al., 2004). Evidence mounted to suggest that children with severe irritability did not resemble adults with bipolar disorder nor have the same kind of psychosocial outcomes as adults. Therefore, an attempt to address these differences, while subsequently preventing the continued increase in the diagnosis of pediatric bipolar disorder, involved the creation of a *new* childhood psychological disorder emphasizing emotion dysregulation. As you can see in the timeline below, the process of understanding and labelling chronic, childhood irritability has been ongoing for decades with little evidence that a consensus is in the near future (Parens & Johnston, 2010).

The Changing Diagnostic Label for Chronic Childhood Irritability

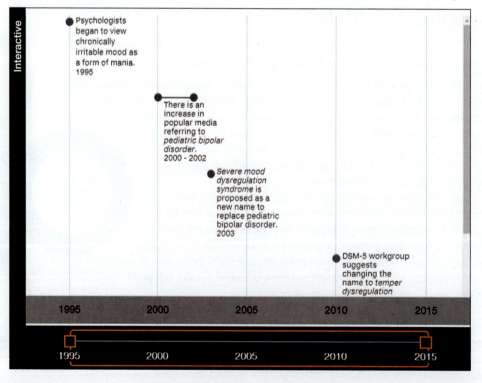

Despite the diagnostic label assigned to the syndrome, the core symptom involves chronic irritability; however, irritability is also a symptom seen in other childhood psychological disorders (Lochman et al., 2015) such as:

- Attention-deficit hyperactivity disorder (inattention and/or hyperactivity symptoms may look like irritability and possibly include temper tantrums)

- Oppositional defiant disorder (diagnosis includes angry/irritable mood and defiant behavior)

- Conduct disorder (diagnosis focuses on violating rules and aggressive behavior)

Piecing It Together: Fill in the Blank

Interactive

Which of the three disorders listed above do you think would be most similar to pediatric bipolar disorder?

Start Over   Check Answers

There are, in fact, many similarities between oppositional defiant disorder (ODD) and disruptive mood dysregulation disorder (DMDD) (Axelson et al., 2011). It appears there may be two different trajectories for kids who develop ODD: one that takes the more traditionally known path toward conduct disorder and a newer proposed path toward internalizing disorders such as depression and anxiety. In fact, recent research has shown that almost all children diagnosed with DMDD also meet the diagnostic criteria for ODD, but not all children diagnosed with ODD have all of the symptoms consistent with DMDD (Cavanagh et al., 2014; Mayes et al., 2016). If this is the case, then why propose a new diagnosis? One argument in favor of the new name indicates that the new disorder would be placed in the "mood" section of the DSM-5 rather than the "disruptive behavior," highlighting that irritability is a mood disturbance (Leibenluft, 2011). Do you think this is a valid reason to create a *new* disorder? Next, let's consider some of the ethical implications associated with the diagnosing and treatment of chronic irritability.

Ethics

- Are the same medications used to treat bipolar disorder in adults safe for children?

- What role, if any, has the pharmaceutical industry played in the increased diagnosis of pediatric bipolar disorder?

One of the concerns that parallels the significant increase in the number of children diagnosed with pediatric bipolar disorder is the corresponding increase in the number of children who are prescribed potent psychotropic medicines such as lithium and antipsychotics (Grimmer et al., 2014; Kreider et al., 2014). In the past decade, it was found that the use of antipsychotics in children and adolescents has increased significantly and to the point where they are prescribed at the same rate in children as they are in an adult population (Olfson et al., 2012). While there is evidence that these medications are effective in treating bipolar disorder in adults, there is a lack of scientific research examining the safety of the use of antipsychotics in children. The studies that exist have focused primarily on adolescents leading the Food and Drug Administration (FDA) to approve the use of some antipsychotics for the acute treatment of children with bipolar disorder between ages 10 and 17 (Olfson et al., 2012). However, there are numerous accounts of "off-label" use (which means using a drug in a way other than what is specifically recommended) of antipsychotics in preschool-aged children.

Journal Prompt: The Use of Antipsychotic Medications in Children

What are some of the pros and cons of prescribing medicines to children that have been shown to be effective only in adults?

Antipsychotics are potent medications that have been shown to have a number of potentially serious side effects in both adults and children (Cohen et al., 2012). In some cases, the side effects (e.g., the onset of type 2 diabetes associated with weight gain from antipsychotic medicines) become additional problems to treat and in some cases can be more serious than the initial symptoms for which the drug was prescribed (Frances & Batstra, 2013; Young et al., 2015).

Some skeptical scientists have pointed to the role of the pharmaceutical industry in promoting the expansion of the diagnosis of pediatric bipolar disorder (see Figure 15.6). After chronic irritability and temper outbursts were viewed as the childhood form of "mania," diagnoses of pediatric bipolar disorder increased 40-fold, which equated to an $18.2 billion increase in spending on antipsychotic medications (Frances & Batstra, 2013; Moncrieff, 2014). One of the reasons cited for the creation of disruptive mood dysregulation disorder (DMDD) is the attempt to decrease the overdiagnosis (and subsequent treatment with antipsychotic medications) of pediatric bipolar disorder. With the number of medications currently under development and investigation for pediatric bipolar disorder, there is a high likelihood that pharmaceutical companies will follow suit with a line of similar medicines to treat DMDD.

Figure 15.6 Profitability of Pharmaceutical Companies

Pharmaceutical companies are motivated to be the first to develop a medication for a new disorder, which can increase their profitability.

TOP 10 PHARMACEUTICAL COMPANIES
Revenue from Pharmaceutical Segment 2016 (USD Million)

Pfizer	Merck	Johnson & Johnson	Roche	Sanofi
#1	#2	#3	#4	#5
$52,824	$35,151	$33,464	$39,494	$35,850

Novartis	Abbvie	AstraZeneca	Gilead	Amgen
#6	#7	#8	#9	#10
$32,562	$25,638	$23,002	$29,953	$22,991

Revenues generated by pharmaceutical products was only one of the seven criteria used to derive an overall company ranking.

Social and Cultural Diversity

- Is the prevalence rate of pediatric bipolar disorder also increasing in other parts of the world?
- Are there any racial differences in the diagnostic rates of pediatric bipolar disorder?

One question we might ask when considering if a particular psychological disorder is being over-diagnosed is, "How do the prevalence rates of pediatric bipolar disorder in the United States compare to other similarly developed countries around the world?" After examining the research, it appears that the prevalence of pediatric bipolar disorder is rising faster in the United States compared to other countries. Consider this:

- In 2010, the United States was the only country to diagnose bipolar disorder in preschool-aged children (Parens & Johnston, 2010).
- In addition to higher rates of diagnosis of bipolar disorder, individuals from the United States have been found to have significantly earlier age of onset compared to various European countries (Bellivier et al., 2011).
- Discharge rates for pediatric bipolar disorder were 12.5 times higher in the United States compared to England (James et al., 2014).

Other trends have been noticed, which continue to raise questions about the diagnostic clarity of pediatric bipolar disorder. While it is certainly possible that real demographic differences exist in the development of this disorder, there has been a disproportionate increase over the past decade in the number of Black males receiving a diagnosis of pediatric bipolar disorder (Blader & Carlson, 2007) and in the number of Medicaid-enrolled children receiving antipsychotic medications (Kreider et al., 2014).

Research Methods

- How will we ever know what, if any, diagnosis is the best for symptomatic children?
- Which research design would be the most appropriate to provide data that can answer questions about pediatric bipolar disorder?

One of the primary criticisms of disruptive mood dysregulation disorder (DMDD) is that no scientific research was conducted on the disorder prior to it appearing in the most recent version of the Diagnostic and Statistical Manual (DSM-5). The DSM work group conducted its own field trials, which measured the diagnostic reliability by examining the agreement between trained clinicians. DMDD fell into the "questionable" range of reliability (Ryan, 2013).

Research Designs in Pediatric Disorders

Summary of Research Study	Research Design
A group of children with disruptive mood dysregulation disorder were compared to a healthy child comparison group to determine if their brains reacted differently to frustrating situations. Children with DMDD had less activation in parts of their brains during frustrating tasks compared to the healthy comparison group. Researchers suggested that the lower levels of activation in key areas of the brain may explain the inability of children with DMDD to regulate their emotions (Deveney et al., 2013).	An Experiment
In a study investigating the treatment effects of the drug, Aripiprazole (Abilify), three groups of children diagnosed with bipolar disorder were randomly assigned to one of three treatment groups. One group received a placebo, one group received a low dose of the drug, and the third group received a higher dose of the drug. Neither the experimenters nor the participants knew which group they were in. Only 32% of the participants completed the 30-week study. Both doses of the drug were found to produce a better response to symptoms compared to a placebo (Findling et al., 2013).	A Double-Blind Experiment
Children of parents diagnosed with bipolar disorder were followed over a period of 7 years in an attempt to identify risk factors for the subsequent development of bipolar disorder. Early, low-level mood symptoms (e.g., hypomania and depressive symptoms) and disruptive behavior disorders were identified as diagnostic risk factors for the future development of mania/hypomania (Axelson et al., 2015).	Longitudinal Research
A study was conducted that examined the relationship between abuse history and pediatric/adolescent bipolar disorder. It was found that both physical abuse and sexual abuse were associated with poorer general functioning, disrupted family environments, and manic symptoms (Schudlich et al., 2015).	Correlational Study

Interactive

Since that time, a number of studies have been published examining children diagnosed with bipolar disorder/chronic irritability/disruptive mood dysregulation disorder. Various research designs have been shown to be reliable and scientifically valid. Can you match these actual studies with their research design?

Quiz for Module 15.14

1. The majority of children diagnosed with disruptive mood dysregulation disorder (DMDD) also meet the diagnostic criteria for which disorder?

   a. Major depressive disorder

   b. Attention deficit hyperactivity disorder

   c. Oppositional defiant disorder

   d. Anxiety disorder

2. Between 1994 and 2003, which psychological diagnosis increased by 4,000 percent?

   a. Conduct disorder

   b. Pediatric bipolar disorder

   c. Attention deficit hyperactivity disorder

   d. Depressive disorders

3. What is the hallmark symptom of bipolar disorder in children?

   a. Chronic and severe irritability

   b. Depressed mood

   c. Extreme emotional outbursts

   d. Mania

4. Based on the information in this module, which statement is the most reasonable with respect to the question of the overdiagnosis of bipolar disorder in children?

   a. Pediatric bipolar disorder has lower prevalence rates in the United States compared to other countries, suggesting other countries may be overdiagnosing the disorder.

   b. Pediatric bipolar disorder has similar prevalence rates in the United States and Europe, suggesting no problem with overdiagnosis.

   c. Pediatric bipolar disorder has higher prevalence rates in the United States, likely due to more American children genuinely developing the disorder.

   d. Pediatric bipolar disorder has higher prevalence rates in the United States, suggesting a problem with overdiagnosis.

5. What is one of the ethical concerns regarding the pharmacological treatment of bipolar disorder in children?

   a. The drugs cost too much money, and families cannot afford to purchase them.

   b. Doctors are prescribing the same medications used in adults with bipolar disorder, and these medicines haven't been adequately tested in children.

   c. These medications have too many side effects for children, including the risk of stunting their growth.

   d. Children cannot be expected to be responsible for taking their medication in a reliable manner.

Summary: Psychological Disorders

Module 15.1–15.3: **Understanding Psychological Disorders**

Psychopathology, or abnormal psychology, is the scientific study of psychological disorders. The American Psychiatric Association favors the term mental disorder, which similarly refers to a clinically significant disturbance in a person's thoughts, emotions, or behavior that reflects dysfunction in mental functioning. Psychological disorders can be characterized by the 4 D's: distress, dysfunction, deviance, and danger. When a person is diagnosed with more than one disorder, it is referred to as **comorbidity. Cultural relativism** suggests that an individual's behavior must be evaluated in reference to their culture. Some disorders only exist in certain cultural groups and are known as **"culture-bound syndromes"**.

The medical model grew out of the period in history where psychiatric patients were treated inhumanely. This **medical model** viewed psychological disorders in the same way as physical diseases in that they were both characterized by symptoms, causes, and cures. The medical model paved the way for more contemporary frameworks for understanding the causes of psychological disorders. In attempting to understand the causes of a psychological disorder, it is helpful to remember the 3 P's:

predisposing causes, those underlying factors that make a person susceptible to developing a disorder; **precipitating causes**, which are the often stressful factors that lead to the emergence of the symptoms; and the **perpetuating causes**, or the internal or external consequences of the disorder that serve to maintain the symptoms. Nowadays, it is common practice to combine many perspectives and take a **biopsychosocial approach** to understanding psychological disorders. The *Diagnostic and Statistical Manual for Mental Disorders*, currently in its fifth edition (**DSM-5**), is the American Psychiatric Association's official guide for diagnosing mental, or psychological, disorders. The DSM-5 provides a list of approximately 250 diagnosable disorders, each defined in terms of specific diagnostic criteria and significant behavior patterns.

Module 15.4–15.5: **Anxiety and Anxiety-Related Disorders**

Anxiety disorders are characterized by unusually high levels of fear, an emotional and physiological response that occurs in response to a specific threat, and anxiety, which is a similar emotion but often in response to a less clearly defined threat. **Specific phobias** involve a persistent, irrational fear of a certain object or situation. **Social anxiety disorder** refers to individuals who have marked and persistent fears of being embarrassed or humiliated in a public setting. As a result, they typically avoid most social situations. A **panic attack** is a sudden onset of numerous physiological symptoms that can mimic a heart attack or other medical catastrophe. A person must experience repeated and unexpected panic attacks followed by concern about future possible panic attacks before being diagnosed with **panic disorder.** Panic disorder can be accompanied by **agoraphobia,** which involves a fear of being in a situation from which escape may be difficult. **Generalized anxiety disorder** is characterized by chronic worry about a number of different events and activities. **Obsessive compulsive disorder** involves intrusive thoughts, images, or urges which trigger anxiety. Often, repetitive and ritualistic behaviors are performed as a way of reducing anxiety. Some people who are exposed to a traumatic event may develop either **acute stress disorder** (if the symptoms emerge between three days and one month) or **posttraumatic stress disorder** (if the symptoms have lasted longer than one month) where they are haunted by the memory of the trauma.

Module 15.6–15.7: Depressive and Bipolar Disorders

Disorders involving mood include depressive disorders and bipolar disorders. A period of two weeks or more with depressed mood or lack of interest in activities accompanied by additional mood-related symptoms is referred to as **major depressive disorder.** A chronic form of depression that lasts for more than two years is diagnosed as **persistent depressive disorder. Premenstrual dysphoric disorder** is a new diagnosis aimed at women who experience significant mood symptoms in the week leading up to menstruation, which interferes with their ability to function normally. Bipolar disorders consist of periods of elevated mood often followed by periods of depression. **Bipolar I disorder** involves at least a one-week period of **mania,** or euphoric mood, accompanied by other behaviors marked by poor judgment that significantly interfere with functioning. **Bipolar II disorder** is diagnosed based on alternating periods of **hypomania,** which is a milder form of mania that only needs to last for four days and does not interfere with functioning, and depression. One concern for those diagnosed with depression or bipolar disorders is the potential for **suicide,** which refers to an intentional, self-inflicted behavior leading to the death of the individual. The cognitive approach suggests that people who are depressed tend to engage in what is referred to as the **cognitive triad,** which includes negative thinking about themselves, the world, and the future. **Learned helplessness,** or the tendency to remain in a punishing situation because of a history of repeated failures to escape in the past, has also been proposed as an explanation for depression.

Module 15.8–15.9: Eating, Somatic Symptom, and Dissociative Disorders

Anorexia nervosa is an eating disorder characterized by an unhealthy low weight, fear of gaining weight, and percep-

tual disturbances in body image. Individuals with **bulimia nervosa** have similar fears about weight gain and high levels of body dissatisfaction but tend to be normal weight or overweight and regularly engage in binge eating and purging behaviors. If the binge eating is not followed by any compensatory behavior, a diagnosis of **binge-eating disorder** may be appropriate.

Somatic symptom disorder involves the combination of the presence of physical symptoms plus abnormal thoughts, feelings, or behaviors in response to the symptoms. Unlike somatic symptom disorder where the physical symptoms have a medical explanation, **conversion disorder** (also known as **functional neurological symptom disorder**) is characterized by the sudden, temporary loss of a sensory or motor functioning with no organic explanation for the symptoms. If the anxiety is focused on the possibility of acquiring a series illness or disease, then **illness anxiety disorder** may be the appropriate diagnosis.

Dissociative disorders are conditions in which the normal cognitive processes are fragmented, causing a sudden loss of memory or change in personality. **Dissociative amnesia** is a disorder that causes sudden, selective memory loss and is usually triggered by a traumatic event. **Dissociative identity disorder** is a condition where an individual experiences two or more personalities within their own body. Almost always prompted by severe childhood abuse, the personalities can have their own voice, mannerisms, and hobbies.

Module 15.10–15.11: Schizophrenia

Schizophrenia, which is often confused with dissociative identity disorder, involves a number of psychotic symptoms that represent a disconnection with reality. **Delusions** (fixed, rigid beliefs), **hallucinations** (false sensory perceptions), **disorganized thinking and speech** (thinking or speaking in ways that are jumbled, illogical, or incoherent), abnormal movements or paralysis (**catatonia or catatonic stupor**), and negative symptoms all characterize the diagnosis of schizophrenia. **Positive symptoms** reflect a pathological excess or distortion of normal functions, such as delusions, hallucinations, and disorganized behavior, whereas **negative symptoms** represent a pathological deficit or the absence of emotions or behaviors that are typically present in someone without schizophrenia. Most explanations of the causes of schizophrenia have focused on biological explanations, including the **diathesis-stress model,** which suggests that some people are genetically predisposed to schizophrenia but will only develop the disorder if they are exposed to environmental or emotional stress during critical developmental periods.

Module 15.12–15.13: Personality Disorders

Personality disorders are long-lasting patterns of inner experience and behavior that are inflexible and pervasive in all areas of life. There are 10 personality disorders in all, and they are categorized within three clusters. **Borderline personality disorder** has been widely researched and involves instability in relationships, poor self-image, and impulsive behaviors (which often take the form of self-injurious behavior like cutting).

Chapter 15 Quiz

1. Greg and Jose have both been diagnosed with schizophrenia. Greg's primary symptoms include lack of motivation and long periods of time where he doesn't speak. Jose's primary symptoms include hearing a voice that makes negative comments about him and a strong belief that the government is responsible for implanting the voice into his head. Greg's symptoms can be categorized as _____, and Jose's symptoms are considered _____.

   a. negative; positive
   b. positive; positive
   c. positive; negative
   d. negative; negative

2. Lilly is 18 years old and terrified of speaking in front of people. She assumes people will laugh at her, notice her crooked tooth, and think she is ugly. She has felt like this since she was 15 years old, but the symptoms have worsened in the past year since she started college. What is a potential diagnosis for Lilly?

   a. Panic disorder
   b. Generalized anxiety disorder
   c. Agoraphobia
   d. Social anxiety disorder

3. Matias is having many negative thoughts about his performance at work. He thinks he is a loser and his boss is out to get him. He believes that only bad things happen to him. He has been feeling extremely depressed lately. Which approach would explain Matias's symptoms by focusing on his negative thought patterns?

   a. Behavioral   b. Psychodynamic
   c. Cognitive   d. Sociocultural

4. Certain underlying factors can make a person susceptible to a mental disorder. These can include genetics, birth defects, and certain toxins such as alcohol or viruses. These factors are called _____ causes.

   a. precipitating   b. predisposing
   c. perpetuating   d. predetermining

5. A person who is significantly underweight, has an intense fear of gaining weight, and a distorted body image could be considered to have _____.

   a. a normal body image for our society
   b. anorexia nervosa
   c. bulimia nervosa
   d. binge-eating disorder

6. The *Diagnostic and Statistical Manual for Mental Disorders-5th Edition (DSM-5)* is the first edition to include _____.

   a. detailed case studies of each diagnosis
   b. an online platform for mental health professionals to check their accuracy
   c. a biological analysis of each disorder
   d. both categorical and dimensional information

7. Bethany unconsciously avoids talking about her childhood whenever possible. Her friend points out that she always changes the subject when her past is discussed. Surprised, Bethany denied this was true. However, her friend quickly replied "denial is a common way of handling unconscious anxiety—I wonder if there's something in your childhood that was traumatic enough for you to have completely repressed the memory?" Bethany's friend's view is typical of the _____ approach to psychological symptoms.

   a. cognitive   b. behavioral
   c. biopsychosocial   d. psychodynamic

8. A behavioral approach to explain a person's fear of flying would focus on _____ patterns of behavior and experiences.

   a. unconscious   b. cognitive
   c. learned   d. biological

9. To be classified as a specific phobia, a fear must be significant enough to disrupt everyday life and have lasted for at least _____ months.

   a. 3   b. 12
   c. 6   d. 4

10. Which two disorders are diagnosed more frequently in women?

    a. Substance abuse and antisocial personality disorder
    b. Depression and anxiety disorders
    c. Bipolar disorder and schizophrenia
    d. Dissociative identity disorder and substance abuse

11. What are some of the environmental factors that play a part in the development of borderline personality disorder?

    a. Poverty and drug/alcohol abuse
    b. Foster care and poverty
    c. Childhood physical, sexual, and/or emotional abuse
    d. Divorced parents and drug/alcohol abuse

12. Which two brain regions are involved in the experience of fear and anxiety and appear to play a significant role in most anxiety disorders?

    a. Prefrontal cortex and hypothalamus

    b. Amygdala and temporal lobes

    c. Insula and hypothalamus

    d. Amygdala and insula

13. The psychodynamic approach to understanding anxiety disorders suggests anxiety is the result of _____.

    a. powerful, repressed id urges attempting to surface

    b. the superego attempting to control thoughts

    c. the guilt produced by the ego

    d. strong defense mechanisms, which produce an overabundance of thoughts

14. Brain scans reveal people with schizophrenia have structural abnormalities in their brain. Which of the following is one of those abnormal features?

    a. Enlarged occipital lobe

    b. Disconnected hypothalamus

    c. Disconnected corpus callosum

    d. Enlarged ventricles

15. Mary has missed the last 3 weeks of classes because she can't get out of bed. She also turns down invitations to go out with friends, hasn't showered in 3 days, and feels like her life is worthless. Mary is likely experiencing _____.

    a. major depressive disorder (MDD)

    b. bipolar disorder

    c. seasonal affective disorder

    d. normal fluctuations in mood

16. What percentage of manic episodes are followed by a major depressive episode?

    a. 20 percent   b. 60 percent
    c. 80 percent   d. 40 percent

17. Natalia is in an abusive relationship with her boyfriend. He has hit her several times. She has tried to leave numerous times, but he always finds her and convinces her that she would never make it without him. Natalia's pattern of behavior is similar to what Seligman studied and called _____.

    a. cognitive triad

    b. maladaptive functioning

    c. learned helplessness

    d. domestic violence

18. What are the three components of Beck's cognitive triad?

    a. Hopelessness, depression, and feelings of worthlessness

    b. Id, ego, and superego

    c. Maladaptive assumptions, overgeneralizations, and defeating thoughts

    d. Negative thinking about the self, the world, and the future

19. Anna consumed two cheeseburgers, two orders of fries, a 32-ounce Diet Coke, and a chocolate milkshake. She consumed all of this in less than 2 hours. She then went to the bathroom to throw up and has been at the gym on the treadmill for an hour and a half. Her behaviors of throwing up and excessive exercise are considered what?

    a. Purging

    b. Bingeing

    c. Restriction

    d. Normal

20. What was the purpose of the classic 1970s study conducted by David Rosenhan, in which he had mentally healthy volunteers fake psychological symptoms, such as hearing voices, to get themselves admitted to a psychiatric facility?

    a. To illustrate the lack of adequate care in psychiatric facilities in the 1970s

    b. To demonstrate that diagnostic assessments are ineffective

    c. To demonstrate that labels such as schizophrenia can be stigmatizing and dehumanizing by emphasizing a person's diagnosis rather than their identity

    d. To illustrate the difficulties that patients have in communicating with doctors and other mental health professionals

21. Henry is always checking his temperature because he worries he may be coming down with something. He has the WebMD app on his phone so he can monitor his symptoms. He worries most of the day about getting sick, despite the fact that he has been very healthy over the course of his life. Henry may be experiencing which disorder?

    a. Specific phobia   b. Illness anxiety disorder

    c. Somatic symptom   d. Conversion disorder
       disorder

22. Hannah was attacked in a parking lot. She woke up in the hospital and cannot remember her name or anything about the attack. The MRI scan shows no brain damage. Hannah is most likely experiencing _____.

    a. head trauma

    b. dissociative identity disorder

    c. dissociative fugue

    d. dissociative amnesia

23. Dissociative identity disorder involves
_____, whereas schizophrenia primarily
involves _____.

   a. psychotic symptoms; two or more personality states

   b. memory loss; multiple personalities

   c. two or more personality states; psychotic symptoms

   d. multiple personalities; memory loss

24. Amir is hearing voices telling him to deliver packages to
the neighbors because he has a special mission to save the
planet. He also believes he is from the planet Krypton and
has x-ray vision. This has been ongoing for six months, and
he lost his job because of the symptoms. Amir is in which
phase of schizophrenia?

   a. Active   **b.** Prodromal

   c. Residual   **d.** Acute

25. Isabella fears she will have a panic attack in the grocery
store and not be able to escape. She thinks every time her
heart beats fast she is having a heart attack. Dr. Meyer
believes Isabella negatively interprets her bodily symptoms and overestimates the danger in public situations.
Dr. Meyer subscribes to which psychological approach to
understanding Isabella's anxiety symptoms?

   a. Biopsychosocial   **b.** Cognitive

   c. Behavioral   **d.** Biological

26. Vladimir has a job as the nighttime janitor of a small factory. There is no one around most of the time, but when he
does encounter someone, he is rude and cold toward them.
His boss has asked him to dinner, but Vladimir turns him
down. He hasn't spoken to his family for years and prefers
it that way. Which personality disorder would these behavior patterns fit most closely?

   a. Schizoid   **b.** Schizotypal

   c. Paranoid   **d.** Antisocial

27. Dependent personality disorder is part of which cluster of
personality disorders?

   a. Cluster C: Anxious or fearful

   b. Cluster A: Odd or eccentric

   c. Cluster B: Dramatic or impulsive

   d. Cluster C: Irrational or illogical

28. Diane, who has had difficulty making friends, finally has
a best friend. She wants to do everything with her friend
Kate. She constantly texts her and calls her late at night
and makes all her plans around Kate. When Kate finally
tells Diane she feels overwhelmed and needs a break from
the friendship, Diane cuts her wrists and writes Kate a letter in blood. This behavior pattern most closely resembles
which personality disorder?

   a. Dependent   **b.** Borderline

   c. Narcissistic   **d.** Histrionic

29. Stefan is a bank executive who has intrusive thoughts
throughout the day about germs and contamination. He constantly worries he will become sick and die from the germs.
He has to interrupt important business meetings to wash his
hands and refuses to shake hands with anyone. The thoughts
have been a persistent problem for him for 10 years. Stefan's
thoughts would be considered _____.

   a. obsessions   **b.** compulsions

   c. anxiety   **d.** traumatic

30. Meg is a 13-year-old girl who wears a super hero cape to
school each day. Even though other students laugh at her,
Meg continues to wear the cape. Meg's behavior fits with
which of the 4 D's of abnormal behavior?

   a. Distress

   b. Deviance

   c. Danger

   d. Dysfunction

Chapter 16
Therapy

Chapter Outline and Learning Objectives

What is Therapy?

Recent statistics suggest that 48 percent of people in the United States will meet criteria for a psychological disorder at some point in their lifetime (Andrade et al., 2014). Therefore, you are very likely to be confronted someday with a friend or family member who is in need of help for a psychological disorder. Or perhaps the person in need of treatment will be you. When the inevitable occurs, how will you know what to do?

Finding Treatment

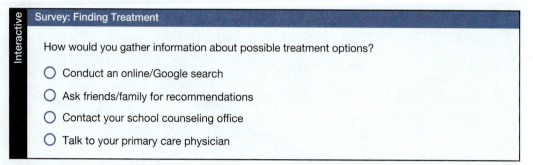

> **Survey: Finding Treatment**
>
> How would you gather information about possible treatment options?
>
> ○ Conduct an online/Google search
>
> ○ Ask friends/family for recommendations
>
> ○ Contact your school counseling office
>
> ○ Talk to your primary care physician

There are many different types of therapy, including psychological therapies (e.g., "talk" therapy), biological therapies (e.g., medications), and sociocultural therapies (e.g., family therapy). How will you know what type of therapy is the most effective for a particular condition? In the same way that you wouldn't seek out an ophthalmologist (eye specialist) for a back problem, you also need to be informed about different treatment options when it comes to psychological disorders.

Module 16.1–16.2: Mental Health Treatment: Then and Now

These days, seeking psychological help from a therapist is very common and less stigmatizing than it used to be. It's not unusual to hear people cite advice or directives from psychological professionals in casual conversations with friends. As you've likely noticed, therapists and therapy sessions also dot the cinematic and television landscape, from reality TV therapist Dr. Drew to VH1's *Couples Therapy* with Dr. Jenn. Whether serious or tinged with humor, as in many contemporary movies and sitcoms, cultural references to psychological treatments have helped demystify and destigmatize such measures for many people. This represents a significant change, and significant progress, within the realm of mental health.

History of Treatment of Mental Illness

LO 16.1 **Describe how mental illness was treated historically.**

From the Middle Ages through the 17th century, most people considered psychological disorders a supernatural phenomenon in the form of demonic possession or witchcraft. Much like today, the treatment of a psychological disorder typically was based on the theory of what was causing the disorder. Therefore, if your symptoms were thought to be caused by a demonic possession, then treatment typically focused on exorcising the demon. Demonic exorcisms, prayers, and charms were common "prescriptions" for psychological symptoms. As a result, treatment was generally ineffective—or even worse. Many "treatment" methods, such as torture, hanging, and burning at the stake, were particularly cruel and inhumane.

Bethlem Royal Hospital, located in London, was one of the first mental hospitals.

During the 18th century in Europe, people with mental illness were sent to live in newly established asylums. When you hear the words "insane asylum," there's a good chance your association is pretty negative. However, an asylum is generally defined as an institution that offers medical assistance to people with mental disorders, which seems innocuous. Unfortunately, the establishment of asylums where mentally ill individuals were often abandoned by overwhelmed family members led to significant abuse and mistreatment.

Bethlem Royal Hospital in England was one of the earliest established (and still currently operating) asylums. Nicknamed "Bedlam," the asylum actually became a tourist attraction where people could pay money to come and observe the patients who were often in chains and living in filthy conditions. People described the "cryings, screechings, roarings, brawlings, shaking of chaines, swearings, frettings, chaffings" in Bedlam (Andrews et al., 2013). In fact, the word bedlam today has become synonymous with words such as "chaos" and "madhouse" because of the horrible conditions and inhumane treatment of the residents of Bethlem.

In 1792, Philippe Pinel, director of a large mental hospital in Paris, initiated the reform movement in the treatment of the mentally ill. He advocated for treating those in mental institutions like patients rather than prisoners. Under his direction, rather than being locked in their rooms or even chained to their beds, patients were allowed to move around freely and exercise outdoors. In 1843, social reformer Dorothea Dix launched the movement for moral treatment of the mentally ill with the publishing of her findings of deplorable conditions in jails and almshouses for the mentally ill in Massachusetts. And in 1919, Clifford Beers helped to steer treatment of the mentally ill toward rehabilitation by co-founding the National Committee for Mental Hygiene.

In the middle of the 20th century, a growing trend of disenchantment with large institutions to house the mentally ill took hold. As a result, the *deinstitutionalization* of psychological disorders began (transferring care from institutions to communities), thanks in part to advances in psychopharmacology. For the first time, some people with severe mental illness were able to live and function independently with the help of carefully monitored medications and treatments.

Nevertheless, the deinstitutionalization movement has hardly been an unqualified success. Lacking adequate transitional support, many patients stop taking necessary medication and end up unemployed, homeless, and unable to care for themselves (Dear & Wolch, 2014). The following graph showing the drastic decline in the numbers of people living in mental institutions beginning in the 1960's looks impressive until you notice that the number of people who are incarcerated in prisons or jails appears to have increased at an equally fast rate. In a 2005 study, the Bureau of Justice reported that more than half of the individuals who were incarcerated in prisons or jails had diagnosable mental health conditions (see Figure 16.1) (James & Glaze, 2006).

Assertive community treatments constitute a new approach toward managing the mental health system. This approach became more popular following a report in 1998 highlighting the gap between the recommendations for treatment of severely mentally ill individuals and the actual treatment provided. Assertive community treatment programs aim to help the severely mentally ill wherever they are in the community. Each mentally ill person is assigned a multidisciplinary team, including a case manager, psychiatrist, nurses, and social workers to help

Where Do You Find the Mentally Ill?

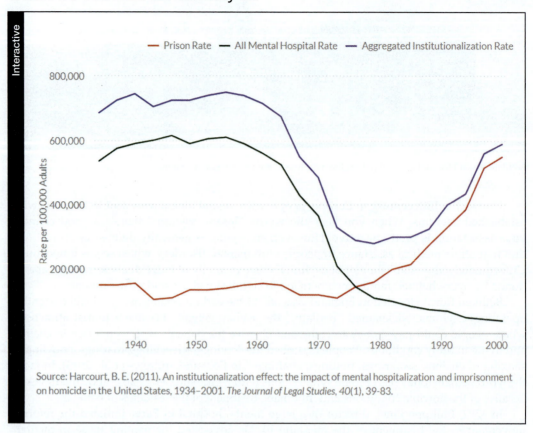

Source: Harcourt, B. E. (2011). An institutionalization effect: the impact of mental hospitalization and imprisonment on homicide in the United States, 1934–2001. *The Journal of Legal Studies, 40*(1), 39-83.

Figure 16.1 Percentage of Inmates with Mental Health Problems

PERCENTAGE OF INMATES WITH MENTAL-HEALTH PROBLEMS AS OF 2004

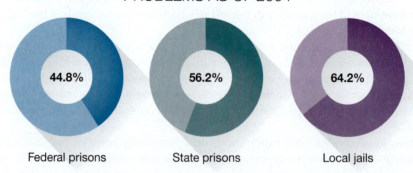

facilitate independent living (Mancini et al., 2015). These programs have been effective in reducing psychiatric hospitalizations, improving housing stability, and improving patients' quality of life (Bond et al., 2001). As you can imagine, these programs are extremely expensive to maintain. However, chronic hospitalization is even more expensive, and because the programs keep mentally ill patients out of hospitals, they may actually save money in the long run.

Current Models of Mental Health Treatment

LO 16.2 Describe current models of mental health treatment.

Clearly, the history of mental health treatment has not been particularly humane or effective. But, what is treatment like today for the millions of people who need it? Like most complex social problems, some progress has been made in terms of accessibility and quality of mental health care, but many challenges remain.

MENTAL HEALTH PROFESSIONALS AND TREATMENT SETTINGS   If you were to conduct an online search for a "therapist" in your city, you might be surprised at just how many different types of professionals would be included in your search results. There are many different educational pathways to becoming a mental health professional, and each type of training tends to provide specialization in different areas. You might think you know enough about different types of mental health professionals to navigate your way successfully with the aid of Google. To test your knowledge, take a look at the different types of professionals listed below and see if you can match them with their appropriate training backg round and treatment specialization:

Mental Health Professionals

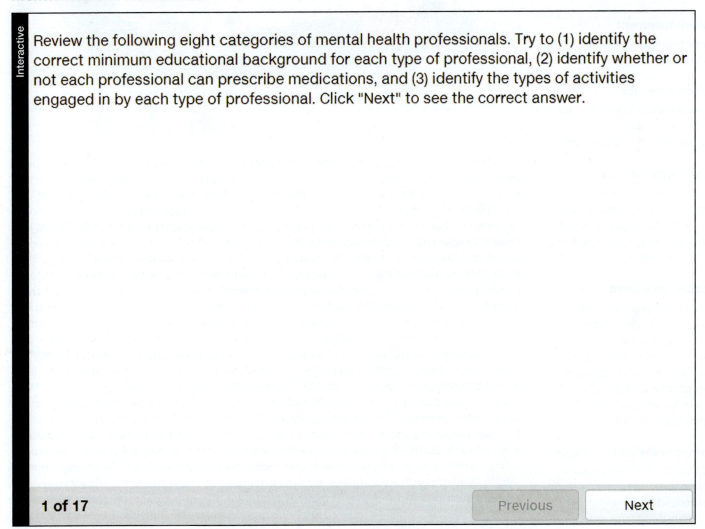

Review the following eight categories of mental health professionals. Try to (1) identify the correct minimum educational background for each type of professional, (2) identify whether or not each professional can prescribe medications, and (3) identify the types of activities engaged in by each type of professional. Click "Next" to see the correct answer.

1 of 17   Previous   Next

If you struggled with identifying the correct information in the table, you are not alone. Each state has different licensure laws for each type of professional, so it is difficult to know exactly what is required in terms of education and training or what types of activities are approved.

Practitioners provide mental health services in a variety of settings as well. Stop for a moment and try to think about the image that comes to your mind when you hear the word "therapy."

Journal Prompt: What Does the Word Therapy Make You Think?

Describe the image that comes to mind when you think of the word "therapy":

Chances are, you think of an image similar to this one:

inpatient treatment

services performed while an individual is hospitalized

residential treatment

treatment provided through a live-in facility where patients receive intense and structured treatment

partial hospitalization

treatment which occurs when an individual still resides in his/her own home but spends up to seven days a week in treatment at a mental health center or hospital

outpatient treatment

mental health treatment which occurs in a variety of outpatient settings (e.g., hospital-based clinics, counseling centers, private practice offices) and are most appropriate for people who are medically stable and able to function independently between appointments

intensive outpatient treatment

treatment which allows people to maintain their work and/or school obligations while still receiving more intensive treatment multiple days a week

preventive care

taking measures to prevent people from developing mental health problems in the first place by addressing the conditions thought to cause or contribute to them

However, this image depicts only one specific form of therapy conducted in one type of treatment setting. In fact, therapy is conducted in a wide range of settings across different levels of care. The level of care for treatment depends on the severity of the condition and the individual's ability to function with less restrictive care. **Inpatient treatment**, or services performed while an individual is hospitalized, is the most restrictive form of treatment and should be reserved for situations when the safety and well-being of the individual would be at risk at a lower level of care. For example, withdrawal from certain substances (e.g., alcohol) can be medically dangerous, requiring a period of detoxification under closely monitored conditions in a hospital setting. **Residential treatment** includes intense and structured treatment but occurs in a home-like setting. For example, several residential treatment programs are devoted to the treatment of eating disorders where individuals go to live for a period of time to receive intensive treatment outside of a hospital setting. **Partial hospitalization** occurs when an individual still resides in his/her own home but spends up to seven days a week in treatment at a mental health center or hospital. Individuals with severe obsessive-compulsive disorder may require a period of partial hospitalization treatment to break the cycle of obsessions and compulsions. The most common level of care for mental health treatment occurs on an **outpatient** basis. People who are medically stable and able to function independently between outpatient appointments are the most appropriate for outpatient care. Outpatient mental health treatment occurs in a variety of settings, including hospital-based clinics, counseling centers, private practice offices, and community/religious offices. Most often, outpatient treatment occurs once a week for approximately one hour but some situations require more frequent visits. **Intensive outpatient treatment** allows people to maintain their work and/or school obligations while still receiving more intensive treatment multiple days a week.

RECENT ADVANCES AND CHALLENGES IN TREATMENT In the past few decades, much of the focus in the field of psychiatric treatment has shifted toward **preventive care**—taking measures to prevent people from developing mental health problems in the first place by addressing the conditions thought to cause or contribute to them. For example, poverty, racism, and abusive households can have an enduring and significant effect on people's abilities to effectively cope with the stresses of life (Albee, 1986; Newman & Newman, 2014; Seabrook & Avison, 2012; Seawell et al., 2012). Advocates for preventive care believe that reducing the occurrence of these traumas in people's lives through social justice programs, community assistance, and educational opportunities will also decrease the number of people afflicted with psychological problems. Obviously, there are no easy solutions for complex social problems such as poverty; however, the investment of time, money, and resources into alleviating some of these issues is a worthy cause both from a social and mental health perspective.

In an odd twist of events, as a part of the October 2008 financial bailout, the U.S. government passed a **mental-health parity law** that forces insurance companies who provide mental health benefits to make the coverage equivalent to coverage for other medical problems (United States Department of Labor, 2010). Prior to the passage of this law, it was common for health insurance companies to either decline coverage for mental health treatment or limit coverage through increased deductibles or co-pays.

Despite passage of the mental health parity law, the availability of care and treatment in the current mental health system remains a challenge for many people because of a shortage of qualified mental health professionals coupled with a difficult-to-navigate system that often neglects the underinsured or uninsured. In 2012, a total of 16.4 percent of Americans had Medicaid (government-provided health insurance for people with very low incomes) (DeNavas-Walt et al., 2013), which has become the largest payer for mental health treatment when compared to other private or corporate health insurance companies (Medicaid: Centers for Medicare and Medicaid Services).

As part of the Affordable Care Act passed in 2010, one avenue for increasing the number of insured Americans has been to expand Medicaid in many states. A higher percent of insured people should translate into an increase in the number of individuals who can obtain mental health care. However, Medicaid reimbursement rates for mental health professionals (the amount Medicaid pays a professional for treating a covered individual) have been so poor that many professionals won't accept Medicaid patients. In fact, one recent study of physicians' willingness to accept new Medicaid patients found that 56 percent of psychiatrists reported that they were unwilling to see new Medicaid patients—the highest rate of any medical subspecialty (e.g., pediatricians, ophthalmologists) (Decker, 2013). Some private insurance reimbursement rates for mental health services have not increased in 10 or 20 years despite increased administrative costs associated with running a practice, leading many mental health care professionals to be unwilling to accept certain insurance coverage. Therefore, increasing the number of insured individuals might not lead to better mental health care as long as professionals continue to be inadequately reimbursed.

Additionally, many state budgets in recent years have instituted significant budget cuts to services designed to assist children and adults living with serious mental illness (Honberg et al., 2011). As the following map demonstrates, a majority of states (26 total) cut funding for

mental-health parity law
law passed in October 2008 that forces insurance companies who provide mental health benefits to make the coverage equivalent to coverage for other medical problems

Changes in Mental Health Spending

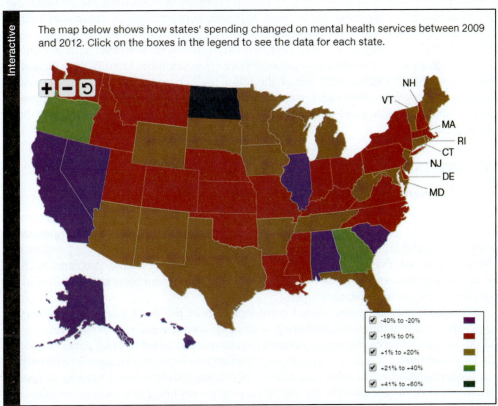

The map below shows how states' spending changed on mental health services between 2009 and 2012. Click on the boxes in the legend to see the data for each state.

mental health from 2009-2012. These cuts have led to reductions in community services and hospital-based programs for serious mental illness and forced more people to seek treatment in emergency rooms or homeless shelters.

As a result of these challenges, many people with psychological problems seek care and don't receive it to an adequate degree or, even worse, simply give up and continue suffering. These individuals' psychological states often continue to deteriorate, with potentially tragic results. While we've come a long way since the Middle Ages, it's clear there is still considerable room for improvement in the mental health system.

Quiz for Module 16.1–16.2

1. During the Middle Ages, what was considered the cause of mental illness?

   a. Imbalance of the four bodily humors

   b. Biochemical imbalances

   c. Disruptive family relationships

   d. Demonic possession

2. In 1792, Philippe Pinel argued that mentally ill patients should be _____.

   a. able to move around freely and exercise outdoors

   b. chained to their beds and punished

   c. given heavy doses of medications

   d. medicated and returned to their home environments

3. What is one reason for inpatient treatment for individuals with mental illness?

   a. To ensure that the medical bills will be paid for by insurance

   b. To ensure that the doctor has access to the patient when necessary

   c. To ensure the safety and well-being of the person receiving treatment

   d. To ensure that the patient will follow through with the treatment

4. In recent years, the focus in mental health care has shifted toward _____.

   a. inpatient care

   b. intensive outpatient treatment

   c. mental health parity law

   d. preventive care

Module 16.3–16.6: Psychological Therapies

psychotherapy

when a trained therapist interacts with someone suffering from a psychological problem with the goal of providing support or relief from the problem

Psychotherapy refers to an interaction between a therapist and someone suffering from a psychological problem, the goal of which is to provide support or relief from the problem. Not all psychotherapies are the same. In fact, each approach to psychotherapy represents a different perspective on how the mind works and how to best address problems. Although some people view psychotherapy as an alternative to medical treatment, it is often used in conjunction with medication or other medical options. While some therapists identify their theoretical orientation as strictly aligned with one of the following perspectives (e.g., as a "behavioral therapist" or a "cognitive therapist"), many therapists identify with a more eclectic approach to psychotherapy. **Eclectic psychotherapy** draws ideas and techniques from a variety of therapeutic approaches.

eclectic psychotherapy

a form of psychotherapy which draws ideas and techniques from a variety of therapeutic approaches

Psychodynamic Approach

LO 16.3 **Summarize the psychodynamic approach to therapy.**

According to psychodynamic theory, unconscious conflicts underlie mental disorders, and these conflicts make their way to the surface through our speech and behavior. **Psychodynamic therapy** views the symptoms of a disorder as side effects of a deeper, underlying problem that needs to be resolved. Psychodynamic therapists tend to trace their clients' problems to childhood or past experiences and focus strongly on understanding symptoms in the context of the client's important personal relationships.

psychodynamic therapy

a form of psychotherapy which views the symptoms of a disorder as side effects of a deeper, underlying problem that needs to be resolved

Although its popularity has waned considerably over the years due to its tendency to be expensive and time intensive (requiring several sessions a week for several years), some psychodynamic therapists still employ classic **psychoanalysis** when treating patients (Goode, 2003). Psychoanalysis is a type of psychotherapy that utilizes Freudian concepts with an emphasis on the influence of the unconscious. Classic psychoanalysis involves a number of specific techniques and strategies, all with the aim of helping clients bring unconscious conflicts into

psychoanalysis

a type of psychotherapy that utilizes Freudian concepts with an emphasis on the influence of the unconscious

conscious awareness, thus gaining "insight." Many of these techniques stem from the theory that the unconscious will be the most accessible at times when the ego is less "on guard." In addition, psychoanalysis focuses on the role of repressed conflicts from early in life, which are least likely to be consciously remembered. For example, according to this perspective, if you directly ask an individual to identify his/her conflicts with a parent during childhood, the person is unlikely to be able to provide accurate or insightful information because (1) the ego's defense mechanisms will be working to protect the person from anxiety or discomfort, and (2) important memories have been repressed and, as a result, aren't consciously accessible. Therefore, the goal of psychoanalysis involves the use of therapeutic techniques designed to provide clues to the unconscious conflicts leading to the manifestation of psychological symptoms.

Free association is a psychoanalytic technique in which the psychoanalyst encourages the client to relax his or her mind and begin reporting every image or idea that enters their conscious awareness. It is important that the client refrains from judging or self-editing the content of their thoughts. Free association is often conducted with the person lying down with closed eyes and out of the sight of the analyst—perhaps very similar to the classic image of therapy we discussed earlier. Theoretically, these seemingly random ramblings will have certain patterns or themes that begin to emerge. The analyst's job is to discern if these outwardly random associations point to particular underlying conflicts or anxieties in the client's unconscious mind.

Freud believed that dreams are the purest forms of free association, and **dream analysis** is another notable psychoanalytic technique. Freud believed that repressed conflicts or memories often surface symbolically in dreams, and interpreting the symbolism within a person's dream is often a key component of psychoanalysis. When analyzing clients' dreams, therapists wade through the **manifest content**—the way the dream is experienced and remembered by the dreamer—in order to uncover the **latent content**, or the unconscious meaning of the dream.

free association

a psychodynamic therapy technique in which the therapist encourages the patient to relax his or her mind and begin reporting every image or idea that enters their conscious awareness

dream analysis

a psychodynamic therapy technique which focuses on discovering repressed conflicts or memories that often surface symbolically in dreams

manifest content

the way a dream is experienced and remembered by the dreamer

latent content

the unconscious or symbolic meaning of a dream

Latent vs. Manifest Content of Dreams

Interactive

For the following examples, type the correct label ("manifest" or "latent") for the descriptions of the dream content.

Dream Example #1: *You dream that you have forgotten to get dressed and are naked in class.*

Being naked in class = [   ] content

You are potentially hiding something and feeling vulnerable that others can see right through you = [   ] content

Dream Example #2: *You dream that you are falling from a tall building.*

There's something in your life (e.g., finances, career, relationships) that is headed in the wrong direction = [   ] content

Falling from a building = [   ] content

[Start Over] [Check Answers]

Throughout sessions in psychoanalysis, analysts remain on the lookout for instances of resistance and transference in their clients. **Resistance** refers to a client's attempts to avoid engaging in the therapeutic process. For example, a client might "forget" to attend sessions or refuse to talk about certain topics. Or perhaps, the resistance might be more subtle, such as changing the topic slightly whenever a certain subject is brought up. During **transference**, a client's unconscious feelings about a significant person in his or her life are instead directed

resistance

a psychodynamic term that refers to a patient's attempts to avoid engaging in the therapeutic process

transference

a psychodynamic term referring to a patient's unconscious feelings about a significant person in his or her life that are instead directed toward the therapist

toward the therapist. From a psychoanalytic perspective, a client who begins to resent her therapist might in fact be transferring her unconscious, unresolved resentment of her mother or other important person in her life.

Several psychologists subscribe to Freud's fundamental ideas but have tweaked or amended his techniques to develop what are known as neo-Freudian therapies. Harry Sullivan, for example, believed that interpersonal relationships have a significant impact on psychological problems (Sullivan, 1938, 1954, 2013). His philosophy contributed to the rise of **interpersonal psychotherapy**, which focuses on helping clients improve their relationships, particularly their current relationships, as a means to resolving their psychological problems. Like traditional psychoanalysis, interpersonal psychotherapy is based on the concept that patients need to uncover the roots of their problems, but it tends to be briefer, less intense, and more practical and immediate than psychoanalysis. This type of therapy seems to be particularly helpful for people suffering from depression (Cuijpers et al., 2011; Klerman & Weissman, 1994; Weissman, 1999) and some studies have shown that interpersonal therapy can also be effective for the treatment of eating disorders (McIntosh et al., 2014; Murphy et al., 2012).

Most current psychodynamic therapy approaches, while still rooted in classic psychoanalysis, have developed a more short-term approach to treatment. As outlined in Shedler (2012), modern psychodynamic therapy includes the following seven features:

1. Focus on expression of emotion

2. Exploration of attempts to avoid distressing thoughts and feelings

3. Identification of recurring themes and patterns

4. Discussion of past experience

5. Focus on interpersonal relations

6. Focus on the therapy relationship

7. Exploration of wishes and fantasies

---

interpersonal psychotherapy

a type of psychotherapy which focuses on helping patients improve their relationships as a means to resolving their psychological problems

---

Adaptive Pathway 16.1: Psychodynamic Therapy

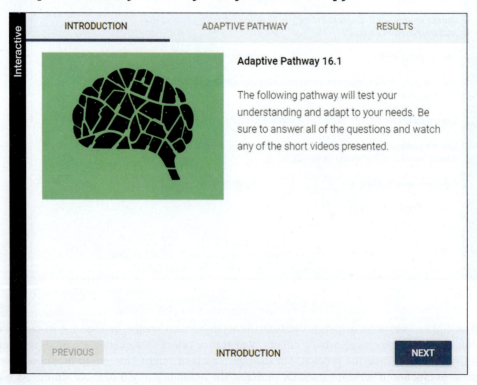

Interactive

| INTRODUCTION | ADAPTIVE PATHWAY | RESULTS |

Adaptive Pathway 16.1

The following pathway will test your understanding and adapt to your needs. Be sure to answer all of the questions and watch any of the short videos presented.

PREVIOUS — INTRODUCTION — NEXT

Humanistic Approach

LO 16.4 **Explain the humanistic approach to therapy.**

If you believe all people have the potential to grow, improve, and become their best selves, you might look at life from a humanistic perspective. The **humanistic approach** to psychology emphasizes humans' promise and our capacities for health, happiness, and generosity toward others. It makes sense then, that humanistic therapies address psychological problems through a lens of positivity and optimism. Psychological problems are not necessarily problems at all, a humanistic therapist might say, but opportunities for us to pause, reflect on our lives, and make changes that enhance our potential. Humanistic therapies tend to focus not on treating illness but on achieving wellness, even greatness, and they're particularly concerned with recognizing and igniting individuals' inner potential for positive growth.

Humanistic therapies center on the notion that when it comes to happiness, the power lies with the people; that is, the choices we make regarding our own behavior can effectively promote our survival and well-being. Humanistic therapists aim to help their clients develop the self-awareness and self-confidence necessary to achieve happiness. They don't "fix" clients, but rather, show clients how to "fix" themselves. You might think of them as the unrelentingly upbeat cheerleaders of the psyche.

Humanistic psychologist Carl Rogers believed that to feel motivated to move forward in life, we have to feel empowered, accepted, and approved of by others, regardless of our flaws. This principle underlies a popular humanistic therapy developed by Carl Rogers (1961, 1966, 1980) called **person-centered**, or **client-centered therapy**. In this model, the therapeutic process focuses squarely on the client's abilities and insights rather than the therapist's thoughts and skills. Person-centered therapists assume the roles of motivators, collaborators, and facilitators of their clients' mental health. They believe their clients are worthy and capable, even when the clients themselves might not agree. The therapists' expressions of genuine acceptance are intended to help clients begin to feel more empowered and self-confident, paving the way for clients to advance on their quest for personal fulfillment (Hill & Nakayama, 2000).

You might have heard a character on TV complain, "You're not really *hearing* me!" or you might have said something similar yourself once or twice. The idea of being "heard," or fully understood and listened to, comes from a key component of Rogers's person-centered therapy called **active listening**. When a therapist actively listens to a client, he or she tries to understand what the client is saying from the client's point of view, without judgment. Active listening involves echoing, restating, and seeking clarification of clients' statements. At the same time, therapists are careful to allow the client to maintain control of the discussion and direct its topics. An active listening session might sound something like this:

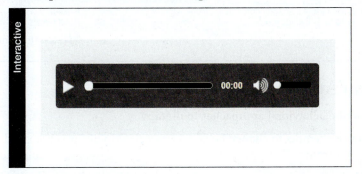

Example of Active Listening

Interactive

According to Rogers, "hearing" clients in this fashion can be a powerful, uplifting force in the lives of those seeking help.

Client-centered therapy focuses on the belief that people are striving to realize their full potential, or *self-actualization*. Because Rogers believed that clients already possess the resources to achieve their potential, the role of the therapist is not to direct the client toward specific thoughts, attitudes, or behaviors. Rather, this form of treatment has been described as nondirective because Rogers believed that telling a person what to do or how to think would provide the false message that the person is unable to address the issue successfully on his/her own, which is the opposite of the empowerment needed for successful change. Instead, the

humanistic approach

approach to therapy that addresses psychological problems through a lens of positivity and optimism

client-centered therapy/person-centered therapy

a form of humanistic psychotherapy in which the therapeutic process focuses on the patient's abilities and insights while the therapist takes a nondirective and supportive role

active listening

a key component of person-centered therapy in which a therapist echoes, restates, and seeks clarification of patients' statements to convey an interest in understanding what the patient is saying

genuineness

a key component of person-centered therapy in which the therapist must be genuine and willing to express their true feelings

unconditional positive regard

a key component of person-centered therapy in which therapists must accept and support the patient regardless of what the person says or does

accurate empathy

a key component of person-centered therapy in which a therapist is able to accurately infer the thoughts and feelings of the patient

therapist's role is to provide an environment for the client that maximizes the person's potential for growth. According to Rogers, such an environment includes the following conditions:

1. **Genuineness.** Unlike psychodynamic therapists who are supposed to maintain a "blank screen" onto which client's project their own thoughts and feelings, a client-centered therapist must be genuine and willing to express their true feelings (Klein et al., 2001; Rogers, 1966).

2. **Unconditional Positive Regard.** Therapists must show complete acceptance and support of the client "as is." While some clients engage in behavior that a therapist may find difficult to accept or support, the therapist isn't required to agree with the client's decisions or choices, but they must approve of the client as a person (Bozarth, 2007; Rogers, 1966). The ability to successfully demonstrate **unconditional positive regard** has been seen as a particularly crucial aspect of successful treatment.

3. **Accurate Empathy.** Rogers defines empathy as "an accurate, empathic understanding of the client's world as seen from the inside. To sense the client's private world as if it were your own, but without losing the 'as if' quality—this is empathy" (Rogers, 1961). A therapist must be able to understand what the client is feeling and accurately understand the client's experiences and viewpoint (Rogers, 1966; Truax & Wittmer, 2012).

Example of Client-Centered Therapy

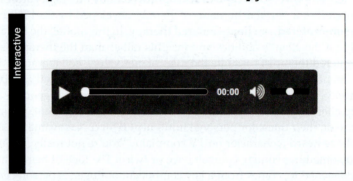

Core Humanistic Therapeutic Conditions

Examples of Genuineness	Examples of Unconditional Positive Regard	Examples of Accurate Empathy
I've definitely had times like that in my life.	I don't think you're stupid at all, actually.	It sounds like you're not really feeling like yourself lately.
And, as much as I wish I could give you that magic bullet, it's actually not possible for me to fix this for you.		So, you wouldn't mind feeling this way if you knew there was a good reason. Is that right?
		You sound really frustrated.

Behavioral Approach

LO 16.5   Describe behavioral approaches to therapy.

behavior therapy

a type of psychotherapy which attempts to change behaviors associated with psychological distress using the principles of learning

Behavior therapy attempts to change behaviors associated with psychological distress using the principles of learning. This type of therapy has three foundational assumptions:

- The maladaptive behaviors associated with psychological problems should be the focus of treatment and do not represent underlying conflicts or repressed impulses.

- Like all behaviors, the behaviors associated with psychological problems are learned, and they are maintained through the process of reinforcement.

- Because these behaviors are learned through conditioning or *modeling*, they can be "unlearned" through similar methods.

As a result of these assumptions, many of the treatment plans behavioral therapists prescribe involve training the mind and body to react differently to various stimuli and situations. Different behavior therapy techniques use either a classical conditioning approach or an operant conditioning approach to modify psychological symptoms.

THERAPIES APPLYING CLASSICAL CONDITIONING PRINCIPLES **Exposure therapy**, a specific type of behavioral therapy, takes the mantra "face your fear" to a clinical level: Over several sessions, people who have a fear or phobia are repeatedly exposed (or *habituated*) to what they fear until they become so accustomed to it that they no longer experience the same level of fear (Wolpe, 1958; Wolpe & Plaud, 1997). You've probably conducted your own exposure therapy by repeatedly forcing yourself to do something you initially found scary or anxiety-provoking. For example, do you remember the first time you jumped off a diving board at the swimming pool? You were likely very scared climbing onto the board the first time but after you jumped repeatedly and "learned" that the experience was actually fun, your anxiety disappeared.

Systematic desensitization is a variation of exposure therapy in which people, within a therapeutic environment, learn to pair states of deep relaxation with anxiety-provoking situations. For example, a therapist might begin a systematic desensitization treatment for a client who is terrified of spiders. The first step in the treatment is to teach the client how to achieve a deeply relaxed, almost drowsy state. Then, the therapist helps the client develop a **fear hierarchy**, or a list of increasingly anxiety-inducing situations associated with spiders. Imagine a fear hierarchy as a series of steps. At the bottom of the steps is the least anxiety-provoking situation, and at the top is the most anxiety-provoking situation. Place the following scenarios in order on the hierarchy from least to most anxiety-provoking.

Making a Fear Hierarchy

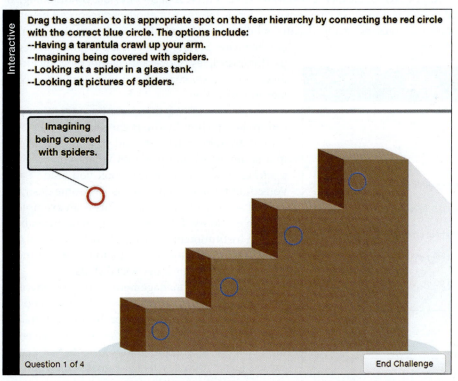

Interactive

Drag the scenario to its appropriate spot on the fear hierarchy by connecting the red circle with the correct blue circle. The options include:
--Having a tarantula crawl up your arm.
--Imagining being covered with spiders.
--Looking at a spider in a glass tank.
--Looking at pictures of spiders.

Imagining being covered with spiders.

Question 1 of 4 | End Challenge

There's actually no "right" or "wrong" answer when creating the fear hierarchy because every individual is different. You'll also notice that the hierarchy contains examples of *in vivo exposure*, or real-life exposure (e.g., looking at a spider in a glass tank), as well as *imaginal exposure*, or visualizing an event (e.g., imagining being covered with spiders). After the fear hierarchy is established, the therapist will direct the person to participate in the exposure exercise, starting at the bottom of the hierarchy while simultaneously engaging in relaxation exercises. Typically, the client will practice with the therapist who is there to provide encouragement and corrective feedback, and then continue to practice on their own for "homework" between sessions. After repeated exposure to the point where the person is no longer anxious at that particular stimulus, the person will move up one step on the hierarchy.

Sometimes in vivo exposure is impractical. Consider someone with a fear of flying—it would be extremely expensive to buy plane tickets only to sit near the boarding gate and then leave. In these types of cases, **virtual reality exposure** provides a helpful alternative. Using computer simulations, clients can learn to be increasingly desensitized to anxiety-inducing

exposure therapy
a type of behavioral therapy in which people are repeatedly exposed to what they fear until they become so accustomed to it that they no longer experience the same level of fear or anxiety

systematic desensitization
a type of exposure therapy in which people learn to pair states of deep relaxation while being exposed to anxiety-provoking situations using a fear hierarchy

fear hierarchy
a list of increasingly anxiety-inducing situations associated with the patient's specific fear that is used in exposure therapy

virtual reality exposure
exposure therapy conducted using computer simulations that help patients learn to be increasingly desensitized to anxiety-inducing situations

flooding

form of exposure therapy that habituates patients by immediately exposing them to their most feared situation (i.e., the top step of their fear hierarchy)

aversive conditioning

a type of conditioning in which the goal is to replace a positive response to a harmful stimulus, such as alcohol, with a negative response

contingency management

a behavior change strategy that typically involves a written agreement between the therapist and patient that specifies the goals for behavioral change, the details regarding the reinforcements that can be earned, and any negative consequences for failing to meet the goal

situations, from speaking in public to taking an airplane ride. Systematic desensitization, whether through in vivo, imaginal, or virtual reality exposure, has been shown to be an effective tool in the treatment of phobias (Augustyn et al., 2013; Davis et al., 2013; Hazel, 2005; McNeil & Zvolensky, 2000; Price et al., 2011; Wang & Chen, 2000).

You might think of **flooding** as the "tough love" approach to exposure therapy. While systematic desensitization eases clients gently into facing their phobias, flooding takes the opposite approach: It habituates clients by immediately exposing them to their most feared situation (i.e., the top step of their hierarchy). Someone with an intense fear of heights, for instance, might experience flooding in the form of spending several hours on the balcony of the top floor of a skyscraper. While flooding is actually quite effective at reducing anxiety in the end, not many people are willing to undergo such an intense and fearful treatment (Khalatbari et al., 2012; Levis & Hare, 2013).

Classical conditioning has also helped psychologists develop treatments based on **aversive conditioning**. The goal of aversive conditioning is to replace a positive response to a harmful stimulus, such as alcohol, with a negative response. For example, a therapist might pair a drink or a cigarette with a nausea-inducing chemical. In this case, when the client drinks or smokes, he or she becomes violently ill and begins to associate drinking or smoking with feelings of sickness. Although aversive conditioning has been shown to treat alcoholism effectively in the short run, its long-term usefulness seems fairly limited (Eysenck, 2013; Wiens & Menustik, 1983) in part due to the need to rely on the motivation of the client to participate in something that produces a punishing response.

THERAPIES APPLYING OPERANT CONDITIONING PRINCIPLES Operant conditioning, or learning that occurs as a result of consequences, forms the basis of another category of behavior therapies. These therapies rest on the idea that reinforcement (or a lack thereof) strongly influences our behavior. Several behavioral treatment strategies use the principles of operant conditioning, including token economies, contingency management, modeling, and extinction.

A *token economy* is an operant conditioning procedure in which individuals earn tokens when they exhibit desirable behaviors. Did you ever participate in a summer reading program where you received a sticker or stamp for every book you read? Later, you could trade in your "tokens" for some desirable reward such as candy or toys. This is an example of a token economy. Token economies have often been used in institutionalized settings such as psychiatric facilities or correctional settings to manage difficult behaviors and/or improve social skills.

Contingency management typically involves a written agreement between the therapist and client that specifies the goals for behavioral change (e.g., "reduce checking behavior by 50 percent"), the details regarding the reinforcements that can be earned (e.g., "each day that the goal is met, 30 minutes of leisure time will be earned"), and any negative consequences for failing to meet the goal (e.g., "if the goal is not met for the day, 30 minutes of extra chores will be completed"). Both teachers and parents often use contingency management with children in the form of *behavioral contracts* that clearly specify rules and consequences (see example at left).

Based on the findings related to observational learning, people don't have to be reinforced directly for behavior change to occur. In some cases, simply watching another person receive positive reinforcement (or punishment) can change the observer's behavior. A therapist may model certain behaviors or instruct the client to observe other people. For example, while treating an individual with a phobia of dogs, one of the authors (BW) "borrowed" a dog

BEHAVIOR CONTRACT

Date:_____

Choose 3 of the following or create your own.

☐ I will go to bed when asked

☐ I will not interrupt

☐ I will not give in to peer pressure

☐ I will get ready for school on time

☐ I will limit my use of technology to ____ hours per day

☐ I will pick up after myself

☐ I will complete my homework on time

☐ I will listen and be attentive when spoken to

☐ I will spend time with my family

☐ I will use good manners

☐ I will treat others with respect

☐ I will eat healthy foods

☐ I will do my chores

☐ I will_____

_____

☐ I will_____

_____

Reward for meeting these expectations: _____

_____

_____

Consequence for not meeting these expectations: _____

_____

_____

Child Signature: _____

Date: _____

Parent Signature: _____

Date: _____

to bring into the session and modeled petting the dog and even brushing the dog's teeth (as a way of exposing the dog's teeth) while the client observed.

In order to eliminate an unwanted behavior, extinction strategies can be utilized to remove all reinforcement for the behavior. Time-outs are a great example of using extinction to eliminate problem behaviors. Each time a child engages in a problem behavior, such as hitting or throwing a toy, the child is removed from all reinforcement (e.g., toys, attention from people) for a period of time.

Cognitive Approach

LO 16.6 Describe cognitive approaches to therapy.

"I think, therefore I am." Even if you aren't an expert in philosophy, you're probably familiar with this statement from René Descartes, 17th-century scholar and thinker. Although Descartes wasn't a psychologist, his belief about the interaction between thought, action, and existence is a convenient starting place for a discussion of cognitive therapy for psychological disorders.

BECK'S COGNITIVE THERAPY Developed by Aaron Beck, **cognitive therapy** first gained notice in the 1960s and is based on the theory that people's psychological problems can be traced to their own illogical or dysfunctional beliefs and thoughts. For example, the cognitive model suggests that people are depressed because they have depressive, self-defeating, negative thoughts, and people are anxious because they have apprehensive, fearful, panic-laced beliefs. Because these maladaptive thoughts and beliefs can make reality seem worse than it is, cognitive therapies attempt to replace them with more realistic cognitive patterns.

So, how can our thoughts affect our feelings or our behaviors? Take a moment and rate your own mood on a 1–10 scale where 1 is extremely down/sad and 10 is extremely happy/satisfied.

cognitive therapy

a form of psychotherapy developed by Aaron Beck based on the theory that people's psychological problems can be traced to their own illogical or dysfunctional beliefs and thoughts

Mood Rating

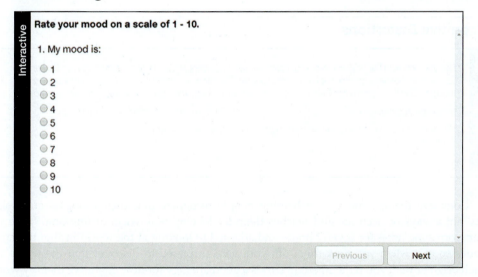

Now, as long as your rating isn't already a 1 or 10, chances are good that you could move your rating in either direction simply by changing what you're thinking about. For example, you could recall the best day of your life and focus on your memories of that day—how you felt, who was with you, and everything that happened. Conversely, you could also think about the most negative experience of your life whether it was losing someone you love through a death or a break-up, a serious injury, or a crushing defeat. Without anything in your current world changing, you could alter your mood with the power of your thoughts. Your thoughts can also impact your behavior. For example, when you think about sad events, you might withdraw to be alone, re-read old emails/texts, or begin to cry.

Because cognition can have such a strong impact on our behavior and mood, it is important to realize that our thoughts, assumptions, and beliefs are not always accurate. In fact, our thinking is often biased. Beck began to notice that his depressed patients appeared to have a number of negative thoughts and assumptions about the world. He called these types of cognitions **automatic thoughts**, and he proposed that depression arises from (1) negative automatic thoughts about the world, the self, and the future, and (2) illogical or distorted thinking patterns (Beck, 1967).

automatic thoughts

thoughts that automatically come to mind and can be negative and/or biased which can lead to depressed mood according to the cognitive model of therapy

Beck's Cognitive Model of Depression

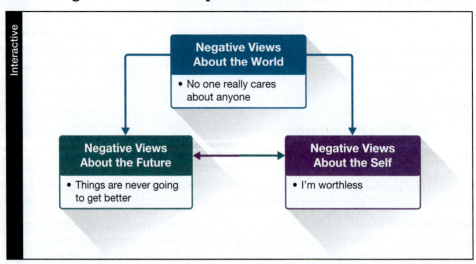

Beck first identified patterns of illogical or distorted thinking patterns, and his student David Burns popularized the term cognitive distortions. Burns identified many different cognitive distortions in his best selling book *The Feeling Good Handbook* (Burns, 1999). Examples of cognitive distortions include **all-or-nothing thinking** (seeing things as black or white, all or none), **overgeneralization** (drawing broad negative conclusions on the basis of a single event), and **mental filter** (focusing only on the negative aspects of a situation and ignoring or "filtering" out any positive aspects).

Cognitive Distortions

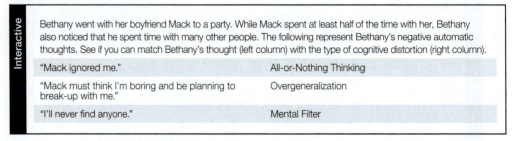

Cognitive therapy focuses on helping people recognize that their thoughts and beliefs may not always be accurate and teaches them to develop new ways of thinking. Have you ever worn sunglasses for several hours and adapted to looking at the world in slightly darker shades so that when you took them off, you were surprised to discover that the world was much brighter than you remembered? This is a good analogy for how cognitive therapy works. Getting people to realize they are interpreting the world inaccurately and providing them with tools to develop more accurate ways of perceiving themselves and the world can help reduce negative feelings such as depression or anxiety.

Cognitive restructuring is an important part of most cognitive therapies. With this technique, therapists teach clients to (1) identify their automatic thoughts, (2) evaluate or test the accuracy of their thoughts, and (3) replace their negative automatic thoughts with more realistic thoughts (Beck et al., 1979). In essence, cognitive therapists encourage people to become more scientific in evaluating their own interpretations by testing their assumptions and evaluating the evidence for and against certain beliefs.

For instance, a client suffering from depression who fails a math exam might be consumed by negative automatic thoughts like, "I failed the test, which means I'm going to fail the class. The only good grades I get are in easy classes that don't matter, and I'll probably never get my degree or a decent job. I'm so stupid." A cognitive therapist applying Beck's technique would encourage the client to understand the illogical reasoning behind this negative interpretation of an isolated situation. The following is an example of a thought record form that is commonly

all-or-nothing thinking

a type of cognitive distortion in which a person sees things in absolute, black or white, terms that leave little room for middle ground

overgeneralization

a type of cognitive distortion that occurs when a person draws broad negative conclusions on the basis of a single event

mental filter

a type of cognitive distortion that occurs when someone focuses only on the negative aspects of a situation and ignores or "filters" out any positive aspects

cognitive restructuring

an important part of most cognitive therapies in which therapists teach patients to identify their negative automatic thoughts, evaluate or test the accuracy of their thoughts, and replace them with more realistic thoughts

used in cognitive therapy. See if you can identify the type of distorted thinking and come up with a more realistic appraisal of the situation.

Cognitive Restructuring

Automatic Thought	Type of Cognitive Distortion	Evidence	More Realistic Alternative Thought
"I failed the exam so I'm going to fail the class."	Overgeneralization	The exam was worth 10% of my final grade in the class.	"Just because I failed one exam doesn't mean I'll necessarily fail the class. If I get some help and study more next time, I'll still be able to pass the class."
"The only good grades I get are in easy classes that don't matter."	Mental Filter	Every grade counts equally toward my final GPA.	If I dismiss my successes, I'll feel bad all the time. In the end, every class counts toward my final GPA, even if it was easy.
"I'll probably never get my degree or a decent job."	All-or-Nothing Thinking	This course is only one of the required courses for my degree.	Just because I'm struggling with this course does not mean I will struggle in all classes or won't get my degree.

(Interactive)

As you can see, cognitive therapy is not simply teaching people to think positively (e.g., putting on rose-colored glasses), but the treatment is actually designed to help people recognize and challenge their distorted thinking in order to view the world more accurately. Ultimately, cognitive therapists aim to move from a teaching to a consulting role in their clients' lives. Therapists hope that with the techniques learned during the therapeutic process, clients can achieve self-directed control of their problems and rely on the therapist for guidance rather than treatment.

COMBINING COGNITIVE AND BEHAVIORAL STRATEGIES In reality, many therapists combine both cognitive and behavioral strategies in treating psychological disorders. The **cognitive–behavior therapy (CBT)** model focuses on the interrelated nature of our thoughts, feelings, and behaviors (see Figure 16.2).

cognitive–behavior therapy (CBT)

a type of psychotherapy which focuses on the interrelated nature of our thoughts, feelings, and behaviors

Figure 16.2 CBT Model

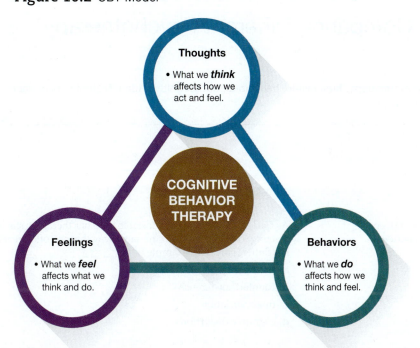

This approach is significantly different from both the psychodynamic and humanistic approaches: The client's primary goal isn't to gain insights into the unconscious mind or to realize personal potential. Rather, CBT asks clients to identify the thought and behavior patterns that create their problems and then make immediate changes to break these patterns. Interestingly, the use of CBT to treat phobias has been shown to have similar brain effects to SSRI treatments: Both reduce amygdala and hippocampus reactivity or activation (Furmark et al., 2002). This finding indicates that there is a biophysiological aspect to CBT and that changing the way you think and act can literally change your brain circuitry. The video *Effective Treatment of Panic Disorder Using CBT* provides a brief discussion by a leading expert of how CBT can be used to treat panic disorder.

Effective Treatment of Panic Disorder Using CBT

Shared Writing Prompt: Comparing Different Psychotherapy Approaches

Compare and contrast the following forms of psychotherapy: humanistic, behavioral, and cognitive. Identify the focus of each approach as well as areas of agreement and difference.

Quiz for Module 16.3–16.6

1. This type of therapy views symptoms as side effects of deeper underlying problems rooted in childhood or past experiences.

   a. Behavioral therapy

   b. Cognitive therapy

   c. Psychodynamic therapy

   d. Humanistic therapy

2. As Carly became more comfortable with her therapist, she began reacting to the therapist in the same way that she often reacted to her father. This is an example of _____.

   a. transference

   b. countertransference

   c. free association

   d. cognitive distortions

3. A key component of Roger's person-centered therapy is a technique that involves echoing, restating, and seeking clarification of a client's statement. This technique is called _____.

    a. unconditional positive regard

    b. genuineness

    c. active listening

    d. accurate empathy

4. Spencer is telling his therapist how he bullied another student at school by posting pictures of the student in the locker room on Instagram. Spencer keeps looking at the therapist to see if she is mad or disgusted with him. Spencer is likely in need of _____ from his therapist.

    a. genuineness

    b. active listening

    c. accurate empathy

    d. unconditional positive regard

5. One of the foundational assumptions of behavioral therapy is _____.

    a. behaviors associated with mental illness are learned and maintained through reinforcement

    b. thoughts produce behaviors that are maladaptive and lead to mental illness

    c. negative childhood experiences are repressed, which leads to psychological illness

    d. maladaptive behaviors are a result of a lack of unconditional positive regard

6. Rosa is afraid of flying but won a free trip to Hawaii. Her therapist instructs Rosa to create a list of things that make her anxious about flying from the least fearful to the most fearful. Rosa and her therapist next work through the list using relaxation techniques to help relieve her anxious responses. What technique is the therapist using?

    a. Systematic desensitization

    b. Flooding

    c. Aversive conditioning

    d. Contingency contract

7. What explanation does the cognitive model give for depression?

    a. People have negative self-defeating childhoods, which leads to depression.

    b. People have behaviors that are negative and self-defeating, which leads to depression.

    c. People engage in negative, self-defeating thoughts, which causes their mood to become depressed.

    d. People have negative experiences in childhood, which later lead to depressed mood.

8. Beck's cognitive triad consists of negative automatic thoughts about the _____, the self, and _____.

    a. future; illogical thoughts

    b. world; the past

    c. world; the future

    d. future; the past

Module 16.7–16.8: Biomedical Therapies

biomedical therapies

physiological treatments designed to reduce psychological symptoms

For some, **biomedical therapies** (physiological treatments designed to reduce psychological symptoms) are an important part of an effective treatment plan. Biomedical treatments have existed for thousands of years, dating back to evidence from the Neolithic times of trephination. Trephination was one of the earliest known psychosurgeries and involves drilling a hole in the skull of an individual suffering from a psychological disorder.

In most cases, trephination was performed to release the evil spirits assumed to cause the psychological abnormality. However, it wasn't until the 1950s that biomedical therapies increased dramatically in effectiveness and popularity with the discovery of several classes of medications designed to treat psychological symptoms.

psychopharmacology

the study of how drugs affect the mind and behavior

This image provides an archaeological example of the practice of trephination.

Drug Therapy

LO 16.7 **Explain the role of drug therapy in treating psychological disorders.**

Over the past 50 years or so, **psychopharmacology**, the study of how drugs affect the mind and behavior, has led to the development of a wide array of drugs used to treat psychological disorders. These medications alleviate symptoms of mental disorders by acting on the bodily processes that may cause those symptoms.

antipsychotic drugs

medications used to treat disorders in which psychotic symptoms, such as hallucinations, paranoia, and delusions, predominate

typical antipsychotics

antipsychotic drugs discovered in the 1950s that work by blocking receptors in the brain's dopamine pathways which are not particularly effective in treating the negative symptoms of schizophrenia and are associated with negative side effects

ANTIPSYCHOTIC DRUGS   Antipsychotic drugs are a class of medications used to treat disorders in which psychotic symptoms, such as hallucinations, paranoia, and delusions, predominate. There are two types of antipsychotic drugs, including the typical and atypical medications. The **typical antipsychotics** were the first to be discovered in the 1950s and the **atypical antipsychotics** were developed later in the 1990s.

Many typical antipsychotics have been around since the 1950s, and they continue to be as effective as newer medications at reducing or eliminating symptoms of disorders like schizophrenia such as delusions and hallucinations. Examples of typical antipsychotics include chlorpromazine (e.g., "Thorazine") and haloperidol (e.g., "Haldol"). These medications work by blocking receptors in the brain's dopamine pathways (Lehman et al., 1998; Lenzenweger et al., 1989; Seeman, 2002). The relative effectiveness of these drugs indicates that excessive dopamine activity plays some role in the symptoms of schizophrenia (Kapur & Seeman, 2014; Pickar et al., 1984; Taubes, 1994; Titmarsh, 2013).

Agonist or Antagonist?

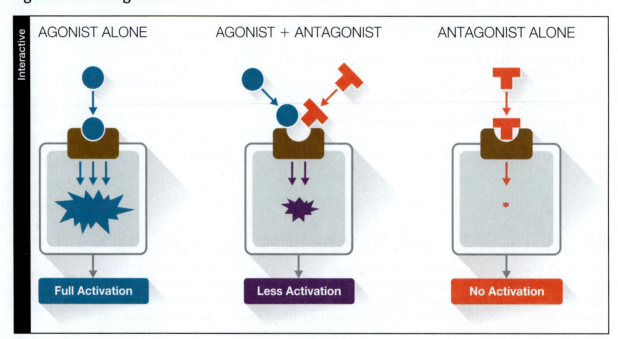

atypical antipsychotics

medications that reduce symptoms of psychosis that are newer and have fewer negative side effects compared to the typical antipsychotics

A notable limitation of typical antipsychotics, however, is that they are relatively ineffective in treating the negative symptoms of schizophrenia (e.g., flat affect, social withdrawal). In addition, side effects of typical antipsychotics can include sluggishness, tremors, weight gain, and even *tardive dyskinesia*, a serious and often irreversible motor disturbance in which the tongue, face, and other muscles involuntarily jerk or contract (Kaplan & Saddock, 1989; Meltzer, 2013; Rummel-Kluge et al., 2012). With such potentially severe side effects, people with psychotic illnesses often find it difficult to continue taking antipsychotics for extended periods of time.

For those struggling with predominantly negative symptoms of schizophrenia, atypical antipsychotics can provide relief for some. These newer medications can alleviate negative symptoms by altering the activity of other neurotransmitters, such as serotonin, in addition to dopamine. They are also less likely to produce the major side effects caused by typical antipsychotics because they target specific dopamine receptors in the brain. Examples of atypical antipsychotics include clozapine (Clozaril), risperidone (Risperdal), and olanzapine (Zyprexa). Although atypical antipsychotics generally produce fewer side effects than typical antipsychotics, both types of drugs can cause symptoms such as dizziness, weight gain, constipation, sexual impotence in men, and nausea.

Typical vs Atypical Antipsychotics

	Examples	Benefits	Limitations
Typical Antipsychotic Medications	chlorpromazine (Thorazine) haloperidol (Haldol)	• Reduces positive symptoms of psychosis	• Not as effective in treating negative symptoms of psychosis • Can lead to serious side effects such as tardive dyskinesia
Atypical Antipsychotic Medications	clozapine (Clozaril) risperidone (Risperdal) olanzapine (Zyprexa)	• Reduces both positive and negative symptoms of psychosis • Fewer serious side effects compared to typical antipsychotics	• Associated with less severe side effects including dizziness, weight gain, constipation, sexual impotence in men, and nausea

ANTIDEPRESSANT DRUGS In 2012, the World Health Organization estimated that 350 million people around the world suffered from depression (Marcus et al., 2012). **Antidepressants** work to regulate mood and alleviate symptoms of depression. Given the prevalence of depression around the world, it's no wonder that the use of antidepressant medications has dramatically increased (Kessler et al., 2005; Pratt et al., 2011). In fact, antidepressant use has increased 400 percent from 1988 to 2008 (National Center for Health Statistics (US), 2010). Between 2005 and 2008, the Centers for Disease Control and Prevention (CDC) reported that antidepressant medications were the third most common prescription drug in the United States with 11 percent of Americans over the age of 12 reporting that they are taking at least one antidepressant medication (National Center for Health Statistics (US), 2010; Pratt et al., 2011).

antidepressants

medications that work to alleviate symptoms of depression

Who Is Taking Antidepressants?

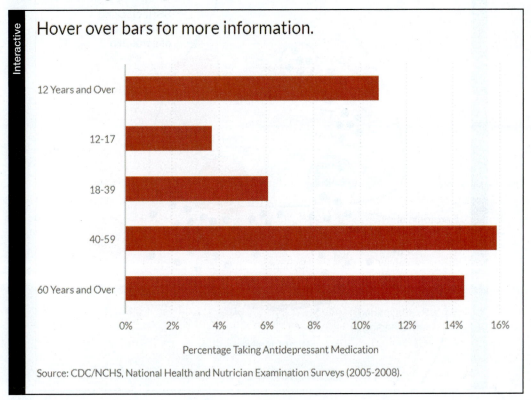

monoamine oxidase (MAO) inhibitors

the earliest antidepressants, which work by inhibiting MAO (an enzyme that metabolizes norepinephrine), also have negative side effects and are often used as a last resort

Most antidepressant medications work by affecting serotonin and norepinephrine, both neurotransmitters associated with arousal and mood. The earliest antidepressants, known as **MAO inhibitors** because they block the enzyme monoamine oxidase, were originally intended to treat tuberculosis but were discovered to be effective at reducing depression. MAO inhibitors metabolize neurotransmitters such as norepinephrine, which allows for increased amounts of norepinephrine in the brain. Because they can have severe side effects, including lethal food and drug combinations, MAO inhibitors are usually used as a last resort for people who don't respond to other drug therapies. Some examples of MAO inhibitors include phenelzine (Nardil) and isocarboxazid (Marplan).

The most popular type of antidepressant from the 1960s–1980s are called the **tricyclics**. Examples include imipramine (Tofranil) and amitriptyline (Elavil). Typically, serotonin and norepinephrine are reabsorbed by the neurons in the brain in a process called reuptake. By blocking the reuptake of these neurotransmitters, which leaves more neurotransmitter available for use, tricyclics can elevate patients' moods.

However, like MAO inhibitors, tricyclics have a number of unpleasant side effects, including dry mouth, fatigue, and blurred vision and are more likely to cause death in the case of an overdose than other types of antidepressants (Anderson, 2000; Anderson et al., 2012; Furukawa et al., 2002; Mulrow, 1999). Given that depression is a risk factor associated with suicide, an antidepressant medication with a lethal overdose potential can be problematic for some individuals. In cases where there is concern about the patient's safety, the doctor may choose to prescribe the tricyclic medication in one-week doses, thereby removing the lethal means to suicide.

Selective serotonin reuptake inhibitors (SSRIs) are a newer alternative to tricyclics. These antidepressants, which began appearing in the mid-1980s, selectively block the reuptake of serotonin in the brain and have fewer side effects than tricyclics. The image below illustrates how SSRI medications work.

tricyclics

antidepressant medications that work by blocking the reuptake of serotonin and norepinephrine that have been associated with worse side effects than newer medications such as SSRIs

selective serotonin reuptake inhibitors (SSRIs)

antidepressant medications that selectively block the reuptake of serotonin in the brain and have fewer side effects than tricyclics

How SSRIs Work

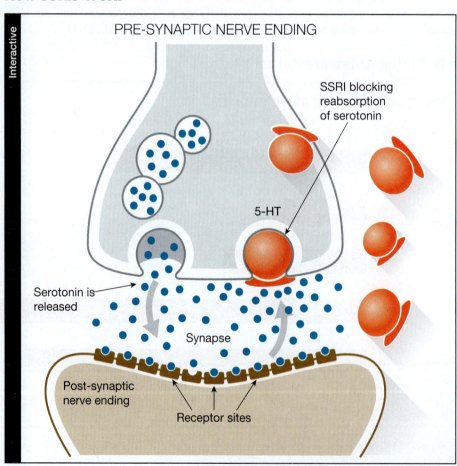

Fluoxetine (Prozac), paroxetine (Paxil), and sertraline (Zoloft) are all SSRIs. Tricyclics and SSRIs tend to have similar effectiveness in treating depression, but because SSRIs have fewer unpleasant side effects, they are more popular (Dharmshaktu et al., 2012; Gold et al., 2015). Testimonial evidence indicates that these drugs can be powerfully effective; ABC News political analyst George Stephanopoulos, actress Brooke Shields, and comedian Rosie O'Donnell have all publicly credited SSRIs with helping them reclaim their lives after episodes of depression. "The gray has gone away. I am living in bright Technicolor," O'Donnell wrote of her experience with the medication (News24, 2001).

The newest types of antidepressants, **atypical antidepressants**, affect neurotransmitters (including serotonin, norepinephrine, and dopamine) in specific combinations. Bupropion (Wellbutrin) and duloxetine hydrochloride (Cymbalta) are examples of these drugs. Interestingly, Wellbutrin, which works as an antidepressant by inhibiting the reuptake of norepinephrine and dopamine, has also been shown to be moderately effective in helping people quit smoking (Cahill et al., 2012; Foulds et al., 2004). Similar to other antidepressants, side effects can occur and may include symptoms such as dry mouth, dizziness, sleep changes, and appetite changes.

atypical antidepressants these include newer medication that affect neurotransmitters (including serotonin, norepinephrine, and dopamine) in specific combinations to reduce symptoms of depression

So, just how effective are antidepressants? This question turns out to be complicated and controversial. Many studies conducted over the past few decades have consistently shown that depressed people feel better after taking antidepressants (Cipriani et al., 2007; Nathan & Gorman, 2015; Sachs et al., 2007). But some researchers argue that taking an antidepressant is the equivalent of taking a sugar pill—the active ingredient being the patient's belief that he or she is taking a medication that will help. The first major review of the literature to come to this conclusion was published by Irving Kirsch and his colleagues (2008). This study was unique because the authors were able to use data from all published and unpublished trials examining the effectiveness of antidepressants submitted to the U.S. Food and Drug Administration. They found no difference between antidepressants and placebos, particularly for individuals with mild to moderate levels of depression. Another study established that there is a bias toward publishing only studies that show antidepressants are effective, while studies demonstrating ineffectiveness are rarely published (Turner et al., 2008). The findings by Kirsch et al. (2008) were upheld by another study in 2011 which also concluded that antidepressants were no more effective than placebos for people with mild depression (Barbui et al., 2011). However, there are also conflicting findings from other large-scale studies showing that antidepressants are effective (Gibbons et al., 2012; Gueorguieva et al., 2011; Linde et al., 2015). Using the same approach of examining data from published and unpublished trials, Gibbons et al. (2012) found that both Prozac and Effexor led to improvements in depression that were greater than those receiving placebos among people with all levels of depression. Among adults receiving Prozac, the improvement rate was approximately 35 percent better than those receiving placebos. In addition, studies have shown that patients receiving antidepressants who were then unknowingly switched to a placebo have higher rates of relapse (Geddes et al., 2003).

Given the inconsistency of the findings about the effectiveness of antidepressants coupled with the extremely high rates of antidepressant usage, it's important for people to carefully consider the use of medications, especially in cases of mild to moderate depression. In addition, some studies showed a correlation between antidepressant use and increased suicide rates among children and young adolescents (Dubicka et al., 2006; Gibbons et al., 2015; Hammad et al., 2006). The Food and Drug Administration issued a public warning about the risk of increased suicidal thoughts or behavior related to the use of SSRI medications by children and young adults (Food and Drug Administration 2004, 2007). However, a later FDA review showed that only 4 percent of children taking SSRI medications experienced suicidal thoughts or behavior (Bridge et al., 2007). The concerns about the effectiveness of antidepressant medications coupled with the potential for negative side effects only strengthen the case for careful consideration prior to prescribing and continuing physician supervision (Gibbons & Mann, 2014; Moreland et al., 2013; Olfson et al., 2006).

Types of Antidepressants

Interactive

	Examples	How the Medication Works	Limitations
MAO Inhibitors	• phenelzine (Nardil) • isocarboxazid (Marplan)	• allow for increased amounts of norepinephrine in the brain by inhibiting the enzymes that break down norepinephrine	• severe side effects, including lethal food and drug combinations
Tricyclics	• imipramine (Tofranil) • amitriptyline (Elavil)	• block the reuptake of serotonin and norepinephrine	• side effects, including dry mouth, fatigue, blurred vision, and increased risk of death in the case of an overdose
SSRIs	• fluoxetine (Prozac) • paroxetine (Paxil) • sertraline (Zoloft)	• block the reuptake of serotonin	• correlation between SSRI use and increased suicide rates among children and young adolescents, according to some studies
Atypical Antidepressants	• Bupropion (Wellbutrin) • duloxetine hydrochloride (Cymbalta)	• affect neurotransmitters (including serotonin, norepinephrine, and dopamine) in specific combinations	• side effects such as dry mouth, dizziness, sleep changes, and appetite changes

anti-anxiety medications

medications that can provide relief for some people suffering from anxiety disorders, often by targeting the physiological symptoms associated with anxiety

ANTI-ANXIETY DRUGS **Anti-anxiety medications** can provide relief for some people suffering from anxiety disorders. These drugs tend to reduce physiological symptoms, such as tension and nervousness, associated with many anxiety disorders by slowing down the central nervous system's activity. The first anti-anxiety drugs were barbiturates, commonly known as *tranquilizers*, and were highly addictive. *Benzodiazepines*, a safer class of drugs, largely replaced barbiturates during the 1960s. These medications, including Valium and Xanax, are most effective in treating generalized anxiety disorder and panic disorder (Bostwick et al., 2012; Hoge et al., 2012; Huh et al., 2011). This class of medications works by enhancing the effect of GABA, an inhibitory neurotransmitter that has a calming or sedative effect in the nervous system. Thus, benzodiazepines work to increase the effectiveness of GABA, which causes an increased inhibitory or calming effect. Side effects of these medications can include drowsiness and a decline in motor coordination and are intensified with the consumption of alcohol. Although benzodiazepines are less addictive than barbiturates, they have several unpleasant withdrawal symptoms. Furthermore, many practitioners believe that anti-anxiety drugs relieve the symptoms of the disorder without addressing the underlying causes, and these practitioners often recommend treatment plans that consist of both medication and therapy. Other anxiety disorders, including OCD and PTSD, are more likely to be treated with antidepressants, specifically SSRIs.

mood-stabilizing medications

medications such as lithium that are prescribed when people experience the drastic mood changes typical of bipolar disorder

MOOD-STABILIZING DRUGS When people experience the drastic mood changes typical of bipolar disorder, doctors often prescribe **mood-stabilizing medications**—namely, lithium—a simple salt element shown to benefit about seven in ten bipolar patients when used on a long-term basis (Solomon et al., 1995). Exactly how and why the drug works is not entirely understood, but it is generally believed to be a complicated process involving multiple mechanisms of action (Jope, 1999; Malhi, 2013). Recent findings have shown that people with bipolar disorder who are taking lithium compared to those who are not have increased brain volumes in the hippocampus and amygdala, which are areas associated with mood regulation (Hallahan et al., 2011; Mahli et al., 2013). These findings point to lithium's possible neuroprotective effect, or the medication's impact on preserving neuronal structures and functions (Diniz et al., 2013). Additionally, lithium has been hypothesized to affect multiple neurotransmitter systems with particular evidence pointing to its impact on glutamate (Dixon & Hokin, 1998). The important thing, however, is that it *does* work for so many affected by the disorder. However, like other medications, lithium has potential negative side effects. It can cause kidney and thyroid dysfunction, so patients must undergo regular tests to monitor drug toxicity levels in the bloodstream.

A commonly used anticonvulsant medication (often used to treat seizures), valproate (Depakote), has also shown promise as a mood stabilizer. This medication has been particularly effective in treating mania (Bowden et al., 2010; Rosa et al., 2011; Smith et al., 2010), although it is less effective in treating depressive episodes (Bowden et al., 2010; Kessing et al., 2011). Because valproate is generally safer than lithium, it has become a popular choice for use with patients with bipolar disorder.

Adaptive Pathway 16.2: Drug Therapy

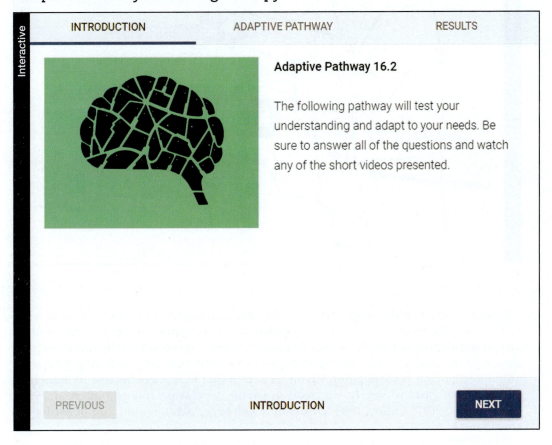

Interactive

| INTRODUCTION | ADAPTIVE PATHWAY | RESULTS |

Adaptive Pathway 16.2

The following pathway will test your understanding and adapt to your needs. Be sure to answer all of the questions and watch any of the short videos presented.

PREVIOUS — INTRODUCTION — NEXT

ECT and Psychosurgery

LO 16.8 **Recognize different medical procedures used to treat mental illness.**

In addition to medications, several other types of medical treatments are used to treat psychological disorders. While these are rarely considered as a first option for treatment due to the potential serious side effects or medical complications, these treatments have provided a beneficial alternative to some who have not had success with any other method.

electroconvulsive therapy (ECT)

electric currents are passed through the brain, intentionally triggering a brief seizure in an attempt to reduce psychiatric symptoms such as severe depression

ECT If you have ever read Ken Kesey's *One Flew Over the Cuckoo's Nest*, or seen the film adaptation, you likely have a very negative impression of **electroconvulsive therapy (ECT)**. Early uses of ECT—which involves sending electric shocks through patients' brains—were largely ineffective and even worse, barbaric. The stigma associated with early uses of ECT and the portrayal of ECT treatment in *One Flew Over the Cuckoo's Nest* have been long-lasting, despite the fact that ECT in the film was used inappropriately—to coerce a patient with a personality disorder without the use of restraints or anesthesia. No wonder the stigma has been so difficult to overcome (Payne & Prudic, 2009).

However, ECT today is administered much differently than it was in the past, as shown in the video *Electroconvulsive Therapy*. Doctors use muscle relaxants and other drugs to block nerve and muscle activity so the patient feels little pain and is not in danger of physical harm resulting from strong convulsions. Next, electrodes are placed on either one or both sides of the patient's head, and electric currents are passed through the brain, intentionally triggering a brief seizure.

Electroconvulsive Therapy

With modern technology and careful medical supervision, ECT is now used to successfully treat severe depression that did not respond to either psychotherapy or antidepressant medications. Imagine having a loved one with severe depression who has not found anything to help relieve their suffering and may have even attempted suicide at some point. If you were told that ECT was effective in more than 80 percent of cases of severe treatment-resistant depression (Bergsholm et al., 1989; Berlim et al., 2015; Coffey, 1993; Ottosson & Odeberg, 2012), would you be willing to consider it?

Over the past 15 years, studies have repeatedly demonstrated that ECT is one of the most effective treatments for severe and resistant depression (Eranti et al., 2007; Khalid et al., 2008; UK ECT Review Group, 2003). As shown in Figure 16.3, one hospital examined 200 patients who received ECT over a 20-year period and found a "good psychiatric outcome" in 90 percent of cases, with 73 percent of the patients reporting ECT as a good treatment (Santos et al., 2013). Similar to lithium, the exact mechanism that makes ECT an effective treatment remains unknown.

Memory loss is typically the most troubling side effect of ECT. Most patients lose their memory for the period of time just prior to the treatment and through the treatment session.

Figure 16.3 Effectiveness of ECT

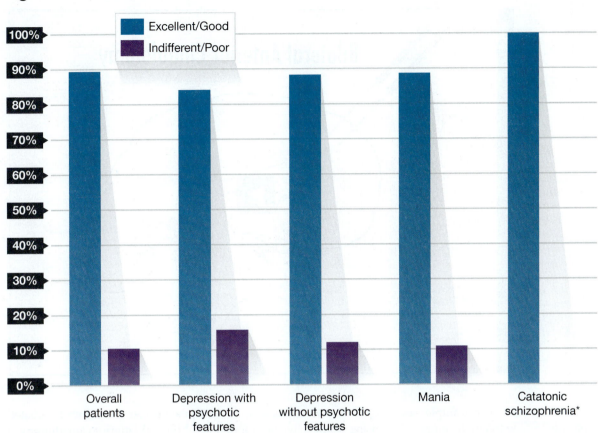

*Statistically superior response rate compared to patients with other diagnoses
(chi-square and Fisher's exact test, $p = 0.02$).

However, there is no long-lasting brain damage and the recent follow-up study showed that only 3 out of 200 patients complained of long-term memory problems.

While ECT continues to be controversial, it is increasingly gaining a reputation as a promising, effective treatment option for those who have been unable to find relief from their depression elsewhere (Consensus Conference, 1985; Eranti et al., 2007; Glass, 2001; Khalid et al., 2008; Parker et al., 1992; UK ECT Review Group, 2003).

OTHER TREATMENTS INVOLVING BRAIN STIMULATION In addition, a newer treatment called **deep brain stimulation** can be used for rare cases of otherwise untreatable OCD. Surgeons implant a thin wire electrode in the patient's brain; when activated, this electrode can stimulate (not destroy) neurons lying near it. Scientists believe this treatment effectively combats OCD by disrupting the ongoing neural loop that may underlie obsessions and compulsions (Chabardes et al., 2013; Garnaat & Greenberg, 2014; Greenberg et al., 2006).

PSYCHOSURGERY Like ECT, *psychosurgery*—in which parts of the brain are surgically altered to treat mental disorders— is another treatment option that often conjures up images of barbaric medical procedures from the past. Fortunately, modern medicine has ended the age of ill-advised **lobotomies** (a procedure that disconnects the frontal lobe from the rest of the brain and results in a near vegetative state) and transformed psychosurgery into a humane treatment option. These refined versions of psychosurgery are highly localized and targeted to specific areas of the brain. Because psychosurgery is irreversible and carries all of the risks of surgery however, it is used only in rare or extreme cases. Watch the video *What Is Psychosurgery?* for more information.

deep brain stimulation

a form of medical therapy in which surgeons implant a thin wire electrode in the patient's brain that when activated can stimulate neurons lying near it

lobotomies

a procedure that disconnects the frontal lobe from the rest of the brain

What Is Psychosurgery?

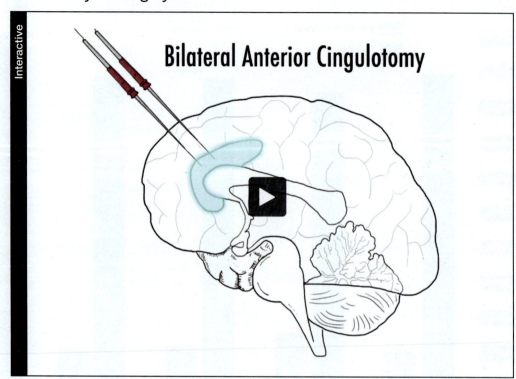

Bilateral Anterior Cingulotomy

bilateral anterior capsulotomy

a surgery that serves to disconnect the circuitry in the orbitofrontal cortex which has been implicated as playing a role in OCD

For example, severe OCD that is untreatable by other means can sometimes be treated with psychosurgery. Promising results have been found in a **bilateral anterior capsulotomy**, a surgery that disconnects the circuitry in the orbitofrontal cortex, which has been implicated as playing a role in OCD (Zou et al., 2013). For patients with severe OCD who have not found any other effective treatment, this surgery has demonstrated its efficacy in the majority of patients who seek out the procedure (D'Astous et al., 2013; Oliver et al., 2002; Rück et al, 2008; Zhan et al., 2014). However, treatment complications and long-term adverse effects from the surgery are not uncommon, and the surgery should only be considered after other less invasive treatments have failed.

Quiz for Module 16.7–16.8

1. Antipsychotic drugs help treat symptoms such as _____, while mood stabilizers help treat symptoms such as _____.
   a. hallucinations; anxiety
   b. depressed mood; hallucinations
   c. hallucinations; mania
   d. mania; hallucinations

2. Which neurotransmitters do most antidepressants affect?
   a. Serotonin and norepinephrine
   b. Serotonin and dopamine
   c. Norepinephrine and dopamine
   d. Glutamate and GABA

3. Olivia will have months of severe depression in which she struggles to complete daily tasks and has overwhelming feelings of sadness. She also experiences periods of euphoria for a week in which she doesn't sleep, has racing thoughts, and thinks she will be the next major movie star even though she never has acted in a movie. The doctor she consulted wants her to try the mood-stabilizing drug _____.
   a. Xanax   b. Lithium
   c. Prozac   d. Wellbutrin

4. What is the effectiveness rate of ECT in severe treatment-resistant depression?
   a. 65 percent   b. 50 percent
   c. 15 percent   d. 80 percent

5. Which disorder responds to bilateral anterior capsulotomy with promising results?
   a. Posttraumatic stress disorder (PTSD)
   b. Generalized anxiety disorder
   c. Obsessive compulsive disorder (OCD)
   d. Depression

Module 16.9–16.10: Sociocultural Influences on Treatment

Nobody lives in a vacuum. Therefore, effective treatments for psychological disorders must take into account the social environment of the client. As illustrated in Figure 16.4, the power of social support (or the lack thereof), the influence of cultural background, and the role of societal stigma related to mental illness are all ways in which sociocultural variables can have an impact on the treatment of psychological conditions.

Figure 16.4 Social Influences

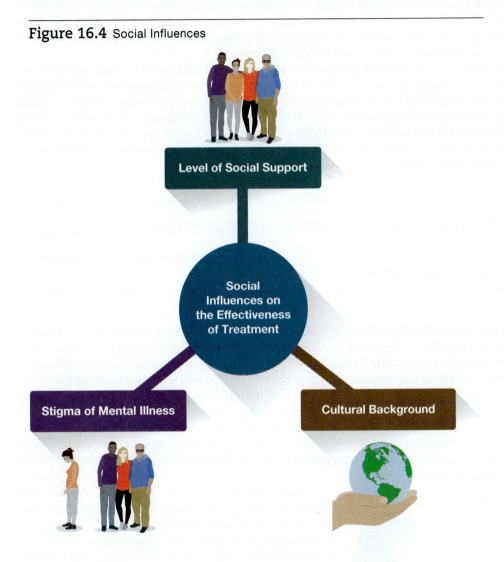

Group Therapy

LO 16.9 **Describe different forms of group therapy.**

There are many reasons why someone might choose to attend therapy in a group setting versus seeing a therapist individually. Have you ever tried to make an important change in your life by partnering with someone else who is also working toward the same goal? What about committing to a new exercise program with a partner or group of people? Having a social support network can be beneficial in many ways by providing social support, encouragement, diverse perspectives, and accountability. **Group therapy** is a form of psychotherapy in which one or more therapists treat a small number of people in a group setting. Group therapy can be a more acceptable alternative for some people since it tends to be less threatening

group therapy

a form of therapy in which one or more therapists treat a small number of people in a group setting

and less expensive than one-on-one sessions with a therapist. Additionally, group therapy gives clients the opportunity to observe others, practice their interpersonal skills, and change their thinking and behaviors based on other people's influence and input. People often find that hearing about others' experiences dealing with similar problems can be enormously comforting and helpful.

Any type of psychotherapy can be conducted in a group format, meaning that group therapy can have a psychodynamic focus, humanistic emphasis, or cognitive-behavioral structure. In addition, group therapy can be conducted in a variety of settings from inpatient hospital-based settings to outpatient clinics or community centers. Certain issues are particularly well-suited for treatment in a group format. For example, group cognitive-behavioral treatment of social anxiety disorder has been demonstrated to be effective (Wersebe et al., 2013; Whitfield, 2010) in part due to the built-in opportunities for exposure to social situations and the ability to test assumptions and beliefs about social interactions.

Irvin Yalom, an emeritus professor of psychiatry at Stanford University, has been one of the most influential figures in the field of group therapy. He proposed that 11 mechanisms are responsible for the positive outcomes related to group therapy. A few examples of these mechanisms include factors such as (1) installation of hope, which creates feelings of optimism; (2) universality, which helps group members realize they are not alone in their experiences; and (3) socializing techniques, which promote social skills and interpersonal behaviors (Yalom, 1995).

Journal Prompt: Group Versus Individual Therapy

What do you think are the pros and cons of receiving group therapy versus individual therapy for someone with social anxiety?

family therapy

a form of group therapy that focuses on the unique interactions of the family unit

FAMILY THERAPY AND COUPLES THERAPY **Family therapy** is one specific form of group therapy that focuses on the unique interactions of the family unit. If someone asked you to describe your family dynamics, your description would probably be influenced by factors such as the size of your family (Are you one of two children, or one of five?), the cultural background of your family (Are your grandparents Italian, or do you have Cajun roots?), and your family values (Does your family emphasize the importance of family meal times, or family vacations?). Because no individual family member exists in a vacuum, psychological issues affecting even one family member can affect the entire family unit. When families experience significant conflict or stress, family therapy might be one good option for help.

Family therapy treats the family as a unique social system and can be an effective tool in helping families cope with and resolve conflict. This type of therapy is based on the assumption that (1) symptoms or problems in an individual may indicate a problem in the family, and the whole family must therefore be treated in order to truly fix the underlying problem; and (2) when one member of a family experiences change, the whole family is affected.

Certain problems have been treated successfully within a family therapy context. Family-based treatments for substance abuse have demonstrated effectiveness for both adolescents and adults and, in many cases, family therapy outcomes are better than those of individual therapy (Rowe, 2012; Stanton & Shadish, 1997). Family-based treatments have also been particularly effective in the treatment of adolescents with anorexia nervosa (Eisler et al., 2007; Lock & Le Grange, 2012).

Couples therapy can help people in relationships to develop new ways to solve problems.

For people involved in relationships who are experiencing distress, **couples therapy** is one treatment option. Although couples therapy has sometimes been referred to as marriage counseling, increasing numbers of unmarried couples are seeking out therapy. One of the limitations of couples therapy is that many couples wait until it is too late to try to mend a damaged relationship, seeing couple therapy as a last resort. A large-scale review of couples therapy over several decades (Benson et al., 2012) identified the following five components of successful couples therapy: (1) changing how relationship problems are viewed, (2) decreasing dysfunctional behaviors in the relationship, (3) reducing emotional avoidance, (4) improving communication, and (5) emphasizing strengths.

SUPPORT GROUPS In contrast to other forms of group therapy, **support groups** do not necessarily have a professionally trained therapist as a group leader. *Professionally operated support groups* are facilitated by professionals while *self-help support groups* typically are peer-led and organized by members on a voluntary basis. Online support groups have also become increasingly popular. The website on-line.supportgroups.com lists hundreds of different support groups with membership in excess of 40,000 in the most popular groups. Probably the most well-known self-help support group, Alcoholics Anonymous (AA) uses a 12-step model to help individuals abstain from alcohol use. AA meetings are generally free and open to anyone, and they focus on supporting attendees through sharing stories, celebrating sobriety, and discussing the 12 steps.

Should you recommend AA to a friend? One study, which randomly assigned people to different types of alcohol treatment, found that the AA model was equally effective to other types of treatment (e.g., cognitive-behavioral treatment) (Policy, 1997), and these effects were maintained over a 3-year follow-up period with almost a third of the participants remaining fully abstinent after 3 years (Kadden et al., 1998). However, this study only compared different types of treatment, so it was difficult to know if AA was better than no treatment at all—perhaps people just reduce their alcohol abuse over time regardless of receiving treatment or not. To answer this question, a 2006 study found that people who attended AA meetings for 27 weeks or more during their first year of treatment were better off 16 years later than people who received no treatment (Moos & Moos, 2006). While these results suggest that the AA model can be an effective treatment model, there have also been some contradictory findings. One examination of eight different treatment trials involving more than 3,000 participants found inadequate evidence for the effectiveness of the AA model as compared to other alcohol treatments (Ferri et al., 2006).

An excellent review of the evidence concluded that while there are some mixed findings about the specific effects of AA treatment, there is significant evidence in support of the effectiveness of the AA treatment model in terms of increased abstinence rates and the association between AA attendance and abstinence rates (Kaskutas, 2009).

Alcoholics Anonymous is one of the most widely-known self-help groups.

couples therapy

a treatment option for people involved in relationships who are experiencing distress

support groups

a form of group therapy which does not necessarily include a professionally trained therapist as the group leader

Culture and Stigma

LO 16.10 **Explain the impact of culture on the stigma of mental illness.**

In the past, doctors often did not tell cancer patients their diagnoses. There was such fear surrounding the disease that those who had cancer and were treated for it were stigmatized and discriminated against. Can you imagine if your friends and family looked down on you because you were undergoing cancer treatment or treatment for another disease? While it may seem outrageous to think of someone being stigmatized because of a medical condition, when considering psychological conditions, we quickly realize how common such stigmatization is in our society. People receiving psychotherapy for depression and other mental illnesses are often viewed as "crazy" or weak or have something inherently wrong with them.

The stigma of mental illness has widespread negative consequences, impacting how the individuals with mental illness are perceived by themselves and others and influencing how resources are allocated for research and treatment. One recent study showed that people with serious mental illness who felt highly stigmatized were seven to nine times more likely to have low self-esteem than people who perceived low levels of stigmatization (Link et al., 2014). Therefore, the perception of stigma by mentally ill individuals may make it even harder for them to recover because of the negative emotional consequences of feeling stigmatized. This study examined whether people believed they were being stigmatized, but what's the reality about people's attitudes toward mental illness? As the following table demonstrates, people often perceive mental illness with more negative attitudes than physical illness, and stigma exists for mental illness in both adults and children (Martin et al., 2000; Martin et al., 2007; Pescosolido, 2013).

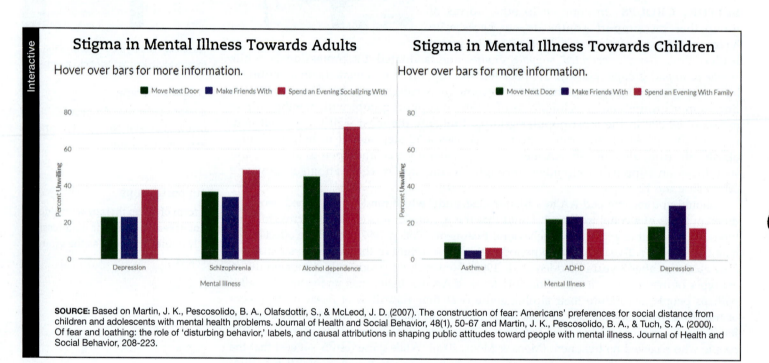

SOURCE: Based on Martin, J. K., Pescosolido, B. A., Olafsdottir, S., & McLeod, J. D. (2007). The construction of fear: Americans' preferences for social distance from children and adolescents with mental health problems. Journal of Health and Social Behavior, 48(1), 50-67 and Martin, J. K., Pescosolido, B. A., & Tuch, S. A. (2000). Of fear and loathing: the role of 'disturbing behavior,' labels, and causal attributions in shaping public attitudes toward people with mental illness. Journal of Health and Social Behavior, 208-223.

To examine changes in attitudes toward people with mental illness and acceptance of mental health treatment over time, a 2011 review of studies looked at attitudes and beliefs about mental illness. The results demonstrated both good and bad news. On the bright side, there was an increase in knowledge about the biological mechanisms associated with mental illness and a greater acceptance of *treatment* for mental illness. The discouraging news was that attitudes toward *people* with mental illness did not improve and may have even worsened in some cases (Schomerus et al., 2012). There have been some promising results showing that anti-stigma campaigns that focus on increasing the level of contact with mentally ill individuals can be effective at reducing stigma (Corrigan et al., 2012). While knowledge-based campaigns were also effective to a degree, the contact-focused programs were the most successful. Overall, it appears that knowledge about the causes of mental illness has been increasing, but increased knowledge has not translated to reduced stigma as much as we might have hoped (Pescosolido et al., 2013).

Ethnic and cultural background appear to be influential factors in how mental illness is viewed and the degree of stigma associated with experiencing mental illness or seeking treatment for a mental health concern. According to the National Alliance on Mental Illness, "One's racial or ethnic background bears upon whether people even seek help in the first place, what types of help they seek, what coping styles and social supports they have, and how much stigma they attach to mental illness" (NAMI Multicultural Action Center). In the United States, minority populations are less likely to seek mental health treatment, in part due to stigma (Hatzenbuehler et al., 2013; Nadeem et al., 2007). Listen to this National Public Radio (NPR) interview with Harvard psychiatry professor, Dr. Alvin Poussaint, as he discusses stigma and mental health treatment in the African American community with an African American woman who experienced the death of her mother by suicide and has herself suffered with depression.

Stigma and Mental Health in the African American Community

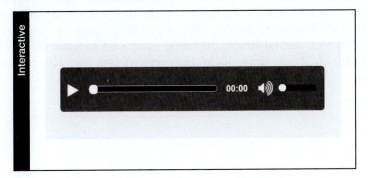

Journal Prompt: Stigma of Mental Illness

In the interview, Dr. Poussaint discusses how the history of racism and discrimination impact the stigma of mental illness in the African American community. This has sometimes been called the "double-stigma" (e.g., Gary, 2005). How do you think minority status and mental health stigma are related?

A patient's cultural background can also influence many aspects of psychotherapy from whether or not the person seeks help to begin with, what type of treatment is viewed as acceptable, whether or not the person drops out of treatment, and whether or not the person responds positively to the treatment. The use of mental health services is lowest among minority groups (de Girolamo et al., 2012; Desai et al., 2014; Garland et al., 2014), and minorities are much more likely to drop out of treatment prematurely (de Haan et al., 2013; Gearing et al., 2014; Swift & Greenberg, 2012). One reason for the utilization discrepancy may lie in cultural differences between the individual seeking care and the therapist or type of therapy provided. These findings have led to a focus in developing cultural competence among therapists by increasing the knowledge, awareness, and skills of therapists for culturally diverse patients. In addition, attempts have been made to adjust treatments to better serve individuals from different cultural backgrounds. At a basic level, treatment can be provided in the native language of the individual. A further step includes the provision of *culturally adapted interventions* whereby the values of the individual's culture are incorporated into the treatment (Dadlani & Scherer, 2009). While attempts have been made to match the therapist and patient on variables such as ethnicity, the results have been mixed (Cabral & Smith, 2011; Maramba & Nagayama, 2002; Sue et al., 1991; Wintersteen et al., 2005; Ziguras et al., 2014), suggesting that this is not the key to improving service delivery. On the other hand, a meta-analysis (a statistical technique that allows the findings from multiple studies to be combined to determine the overall impact of a particular variable) of culturally adapted treatments showed that interventions provided in the patients' native language led to improvements at twice the rate of those provided in English, and interventions targeted or adapted to specific cultural groups led to improvements that were four times more effective than those delivered to groups of mixed cultural backgrounds (Griner & Smith, 2006). Therefore, it does not appear to be important for the therapist and patient to *look* alike in terms of ethnic or cultural background. Instead, it is more important for the therapist to understand the patient's cultural background and adapt the treatment accordingly.

Across the globe, the stigma associated with mental illness differs drastically. The Stigma in Global Context–Mental Health Study (SGC–MHS) is an ongoing 16-country study examining stigma related to major depression and schizophrenia around the world. As Figure 16.5 demonstrates, people living in certain countries reported high levels of concern about having a neighbor with schizophrenia (Pescosolido, 2013). For example, in Bangladesh, more than 75 percent of the individuals surveyed reported that they would be unwilling to live next to someone with schizophrenia. Mental illness in Asian cultures is often viewed as shameful and caused by evil spirits or wrongdoings in the person's past (Kramer et al., 2002; Lauber & Rossler, 2007; Ng, 1997). Likewise, Asian Americans are the least likely to seek mental health treatment compared to other ethnic/racial groups (American Psychiatric Association, 2015). However, stigma was also high in other non-Asian countries, including Cypress and Belgium.

Figure 16.5 Global Stigma

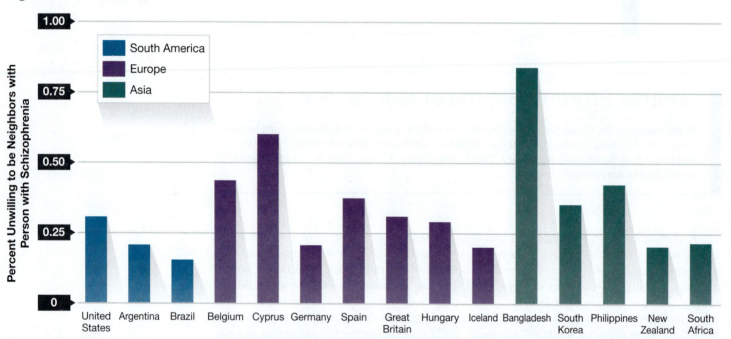

Additional data recently published from the SGC–MHS study shows that stigma is generally higher for schizophrenia than depression in most countries. Furthermore, stigma varies considerably across different countries, but there is a degree of stigma present in all places (Pescosolido et al., 2013).

These findings are particularly important, given the disparity in outcomes for people with serious mental illness who live in different parts of the world. The large-scale International Pilot Study of Schizophrenia conducted by the World Health Organization beginning in 1967 studied the course and outcome of schizophrenia among individuals living in different countries around the globe. One of the most striking findings from this study has been that people with schizophrenia appear to have better recovery rates in countries considered "developing" (primarily African, Asian, and Latin American countries) than countries considered "developed" (primarily European countries and the United States) (Hopper & Wanderling, 2000; Hopper et al., 2007; Mason et al., 1996). Explanations for a finding that has generally been seen as counterintuitive have focused on the role of stigma and culture surrounding mental illness. People with schizophrenia appear to have better outcomes in cultures where the norms, attitudes, and behaviors toward mental illness are less negative. These findings underscore the importance of culture in the stigmatization of mental illness which can in turn have a signifi-cant impact on the likelihood that an individual will seek treatment or that the treatment they receive will be successful.

Quiz for Module 16.9–16.10

1. _____ therapy gives clients the chance to observe others, practice social skills, and change their thinking and behaviors based on other people's influence and input.
   - **a.** Individual
   - **b.** Group
   - **c.** Behavioral
   - **d.** Online

2. Which of the following is a component of successful couples therapy?
   - **a.** Improving communication
   - **b.** Decreasing physical aggression
   - **c.** Resolving issues related to child-rearing
   - **d.** Establishing relationship boundaries

3. Self-help support groups differ from group therapy in that they _____.
   - **a.** are people with similar problems who gather to assist each other through changes

   - **b.** do not have a professionally trained therapist as their leader
   - **c.** offer encouragement and provide a social outlet for those who are experiencing problems
   - **d.** are voluntary in attendance

4. What is one negative consequence of the stigma associated with mental illness?
   - **a.** Decreased attendance at work
   - **b.** Decreased family involvement
   - **c.** Problems with receiving an education
   - **d.** Lowered self-esteem in the individual with the mental illness

5. Which group is most likely to drop out of mental health treatment prematurely?
   - **a.** Children
   - **b.** Minorities
   - **c.** Women
   - **d.** Men

Module 16.11–16.12: Evaluating Therapies

Does talking with a therapist really work? Does it relieve psychological problems and help people achieve happier, healthier lives? And which therapy is best—psychodynamic, humanistic, cognitive, or behavioral? Are certain therapies more useful for certain types of disorders, or for certain types of people? And what about medications—where do they fit in? Finally, if you need to seek treatment for yourself or a loved one in the future, how would you make an informed decision about which type of therapy has the best evidence of effectiveness?

Effectiveness of Therapy

LO 16.11   Describe the research regarding the effectiveness of therapies.

There's plenty of controversy and debate in the world of psychology, and the field of treatment is no exception. Psychologists don't all agree as to whether any type of psychotherapy is effective, and each type of psychotherapy has its champions and skeptics. If you're wondering which type of therapy is "best," however, there's only one safe answer: Each client, each therapist, and each disorder is different. As a result, the usefulness of any therapy depends on the client, the therapist, and the nature of their relationship.

OVERALL EFFECTIVENESS OF PSYCHOTHERAPY   Americans are turning to psychotherapy in increasing numbers, but is this growing confidence in the value of therapy justified? Research indicates that it is. In one classic study, psychologist R. B. Sloane and colleagues (1975) took a group of participants with generalized anxiety and assigned them to one of three groups: a control group that received no psychotherapy, a group that received psychodynamic psychotherapy, and a group that received behavioral psychotherapy. After the participants were double-blindly assessed both before and after treatment (or no treatment in the control group), Sloane found that although all groups improved, the two treatment groups improved significantly more than the control group. Furthermore, although the behavioral group improved slightly more than the psychodynamic group, the difference was insignificant.

Other studies have confirmed these findings: In a meta-analysis of 475 investigations into the efficacy of psychotherapy, Mary Lee Smith and colleagues (1980) concluded that people who receive psychotherapy improve more than about 80 percent of people who do not receive this treatment (see Figure 16.6).

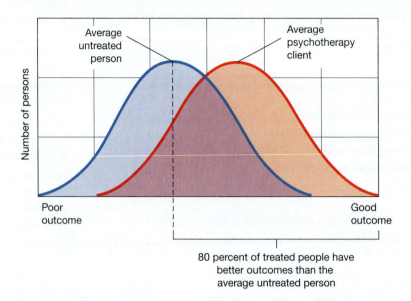

Figure 16.6 Effectiveness of Therapy

It's important to keep a few points in mind in the context of these findings. In general, these experiments are carried out in research institutions with highly experienced, highly trained clinicians who are aware that they are also being assessed. This, in many instances, leads to optimal therapy conditions, which may or may not be available to the average person who seeks psychotherapy (Wells, 2014). In addition, the clients recruited to participate in these experiments may be a slightly biased group; their willingness to seek help may indicate an already existing belief that it can, and will, work.

Recent studies have yielded similar results, showing that in general, most people who receive psychotherapy report improvement and that some therapy appears to be better than no therapy at all (Beutler, 2009; Henggeler & Schaeffer, 2010; Koelen et al., 2014; Kopta et al., 1999; Lemmens et al., 2015; Nathan & Gorman, 2002; Shadish et al., 2000; Shedler, 2010; Thomas & Zimmer-Gembeck, 2007). Additionally, a 1995 study of 7,000 *Consumer Reports* subscribers found that the longer people participated in therapy, the more they improved (Seligman, 1995). Therapy is also a cost-effective treatment option, and patients who received psychological interventions reduced their medical costs by 17 percent compared to a 12.3 percent increase in costs for people who were untreated (Chiles et al., 2002).

COMMON FACTORS OF EFFECTIVE PSYCHOTHERAPY Decades of research demonstrating that psychotherapy is generally effective regardless of the specific type of therapy begs the question "what are the common ingredients of effective therapy?" This question has also been pondered and evaluated by leading experts for many years. Some of the most widely supported common factors of effective therapy include:

allegiance effects

the fact that researchers frequently find that the most effective form of treatment is the one that matches their own theoretical orientation

therapeutic alliance

the quality of the relationship between a therapist and patient

Allegiance Effects: The impact of the therapist's belief in the effectiveness of the treatment he or she is providing (Wampold, 2001) has been associated with treatment outcomes. This has been used to explain why empirical investigations of the effectiveness of specific types of therapy tend to find in favor of the researcher's own preferred therapeutic method (Luborsky et al., 1999).

Therapeutic Alliance: Studies have shown a strong relationship between patients' ratings of the therapeutic relationship and treatment outcome (Horvath & Bedi, 2002;

Horvath et al., 2011). The therapeutic alliance consists of the following three components (Bordin, 1979; Laska et al., 2013):

1. *Bond between therapist and patient.* This bond can be established and strengthened through the characteristics emphasized by Rogers' humanistic model, including genuineness and positive regard.

2. *Goal consensus.* Having agreed-upon goals for treatment has been shown to be positively related to positive outcomes (Tryon & Winograd, 2002). After all, in any endeavor in life, having a partner who shares your same goals and your vision can create a positive and motivating environment.

3. *Agreement about the tasks of therapy.* This requires the therapist and patient to not only agree on the goals, but to also agree on how to achieve them.

Empathy: Therapist empathy, or the ability of the therapist to understand the patient's point of view, is a particularly powerful ingredient of a successful therapeutic relationship (Bohart et al., 2002).

empathy

the ability of the therapist to understand the patient's point of view

COMPARING THE EFFECTIVENESS OF DIFFERENT PSYCHOTHERAPY TECHNIQUES It has been repeatedly shown that psychotherapy is effective for treating most conditions. Additionally, evidence supports the notion that common factors underlie successful therapy. Interestingly, however, research on the effectiveness of different therapeutic techniques has not discovered a single therapeutic strategy that is uniquely effective in treating all people with any disorder. In a recent review of the role of common factors of successful treatment versus the role of specific therapeutic techniques or models, Laska and colleagues (2013) estimated that only 1 percent of variability in recovery rates is due to specific psychotherapy techniques, whereas the majority of improvement was attributed to common factors. As Figure 16.7 shows, this study found that most of the variability in whether or not treatment is successful is related to common factors such as agreement about the goals of treatment between therapist and patient and the therapist's level of empathy. Specific differences between treatment strategies was not found associated with better or worse treatment outcomes.

Figure 16.7 Common Factors vs Specific Ingredients of Different Therapies

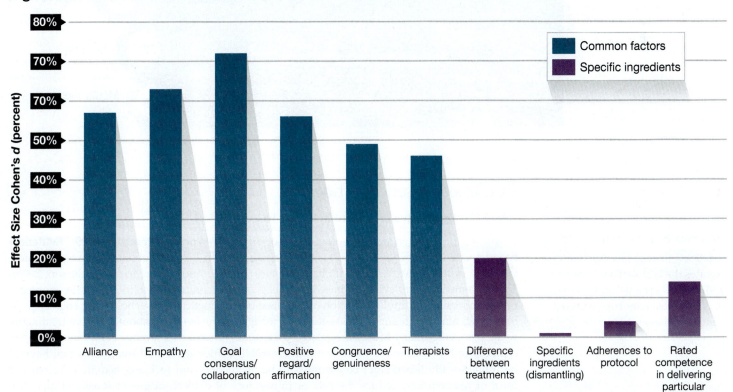

This view is not universally accepted, however, and other experts have argued that there is substantial evidence that some therapeutic techniques are more effective than others for particular conditions (Hofmann & Barlow, 2014). For example, exposure-based treatments for some anxiety disorders (e.g., specific phobias, panic disorder, social phobia) that are the core of behavioral and CBT treatments appear to be the most effective strategies for these conditions (Hofmann & Smits, 2008; Leichsenring et al., 2014). For depression, a variety of psychotherapy models have demonstrated effectiveness, including CBT, psychodynamic, interpersonal, and behavioral strategies (Barth, 2013; Braun, 2013; Cuijpers et al., 2008). For those struggling with bulimia nervosa, CBT is perhaps the best option (Chambless et al., 1998; Hofmann et al., 2012; Norcross, 2002; Poulsen et al., 2014; Spielmans et al., 2013), while family therapy appears to be the most effective in cases of adolescent anorexia nervosa (Dalle Grave et al., 2013; Eisler et al., 2007; Eisler et al., 2000; Le Grange et al., 2012).

EFFECTIVENESS OF MEDICATIONS VERSUS PSYCHOTHERAPY   The question of which is the most effective treatment for psychological problems—psychotherapy or medications—can stir impassioned debate from both sides. Some conditions, such as schizophrenia and bipolar disorder, call for medication as a first line of treatment. For other conditions, such as depression and anxiety, the most effective treatment may be psychotherapy, medications, or a combination of both. Some patients with depression respond immediately and enduringly to SSRIs; some don't. Some benefit greatly from a combination of SSRIs and humanistic therapy; some don't. Some can use what they learn in CBT to overcome their problems; some can't. Each person, each situation, and each treatment is different. As inexact as it may sound, it's the truth: When it comes to treatment of psychopathology, it just depends.

For individuals considering medications versus psychotherapy, there are other factors than overall effectiveness to consider. The financial costs, potential side effects, and relapse rates are also important considerations for many. A 2010 Consumer Reports survey of individuals who had received either psychotherapy, medications, or a combination of both demonstrated that outcomes were generally similar across all groups (see Figure 16.8).

Figure 16.8 Comparing Treatments

76% Talk plus meds

72% Talk only

71% Mostly meds

Evidence-Based Practice

LO 16.12   **Explain the concept of evidence-based practice.**

evidence-based practice (EBP)

practicing therapy in a way that integrates the best available research with clinical expertise in the context of patient characteristics, culture, and preferences

According to the American Psychological Association (APA) policy adopted in 2005, "**Evidence-based practice** in psychology (EBP) is the integration of the best available research with clinical expertise in the context of patient characteristics, culture, and preferences" (Anderson, 2006). The movement toward evidence-based practice has been significant and in 2005, APA adopted a policy endorsing the implementation of evidence-based practice for psychologists. This seems to be a "no-brainer" to many—why would anyone ignore the evidence about effective treatments while practicing in any healthcare-related profession? Intuitive as it may seem, there has been criticism of how this model has been implemented. Critics argue that treatments that haven't been empirically tested can't be assumed to be ineffective, and focusing heavily on a narrow form of research may reduce the role or importance of clinical judgment (Laska et al., 2013; Milton, 2004). In a summary of these objections, Lilienfeld et al. (2013) point out that the APA's

Evidence-Based Practice

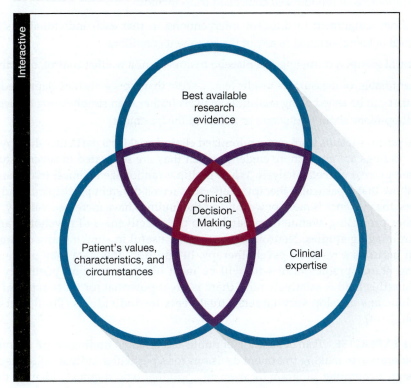

policy on evidence-based practice has three components, each of which have an important role to play in evaluating and implementing psychological treatments.

BEST AVAILABLE RESEARCH EVIDENCE When trying to evaluate which treatments have the best current research evidence, what kinds of research designs are the "best" and what kind of evidence is the most convincing? After all, why can't a therapist treat an individual using a type of therapy and then determine if the treatment was successful based on whether the person's symptoms are improved at the end of treatment? There are several reasons why it's impossible to determine the effectiveness of a particular treatment in this situation. Concerns about *placebo effects* and *spontaneous remission* are the most problematic. For example, remember from Chapter 1 that a placebo effect occurs when a person receives a "fake or inactive" treatment but improves simply because of their belief or expectation that the treatment will be helpful. One of the earliest examples of a placebo treatment comes from the 1780s when Franz Mesmer developed a treatment based on the notion that illness was caused by disturbances in the body's electromagnetic field. He began treating people with a range of illnesses by moving mineral magnets around their bodies. The people he treated often began to have involuntary movements and even convulsions, and many people reported having significant improvement in their symptoms or being cured outright. When his treatment was investigated by King Louis XVI of France, it was discovered that his treatment effects could be replicated by having people hug a magnetized tree. These people indeed experienced convulsions, but the trees were never actually magnetized—demonstrating that Mesmer's treatment was actually based entirely on the placebo effect (Harrington, 2008). Therefore, to demonstrate that a treatment is actually effective, it is important to show that the effect of the treatment is better than that of a placebo.

Spontaneous remission, or recovery without any treatment, must also be ruled out when determining the effectiveness of a particular therapy. For example, among people suffering from depression, more than 50 percent of untreated people will recover within a year (Whiteford et al., 2013). Therefore, demonstrating that a particular therapy is effective for 50 percent of people over a year of treatment is not particularly impressive, given that the same percentage of people would have recovered without any treatment.

The gold standard for research designs in the area of establishing evidence-based treatments is the **randomized controlled trial**. This is a specific and very rigorous research design that

spontaneous remission
recovery without any treatment

randomized controlled trial
a specific and rigorous research design including random assignment, a control group, and quantifiable results that allows for evaluation of the placebo effect and issues related to spontaneous recovery

allows for evaluation of the placebo effect and issues related to spontaneous recovery. Some of the key components of randomized controlled trials include:

- Random assignment to different interventions so that each individual has an equal chance of being assigned to any of the treatment conditions

- Control group(s) consisting of a placebo treatment, or a waitlist control, or both

- Quantifiable, or measurable results (e.g., a score that represents how depressed a person is) that can be tested using statistical analysis (rather than simply using clinician or patient opinions about the success or failure of the treatment)

While positive results from one randomized clinical trial for a particular therapy is promising, the findings are given more credence when they are replicated in several studies and through the process of meta-analysis. When multiple randomized clinical trials can be combined to show that a particular therapy is effective across different participants and different researchers, the evidence is more powerful and the findings have increased validity.

Another promising avenue of research into the effectiveness of psychotherapy comes from neuroimaging studies. Neuroimaging may be useful in showing any changes in the brain that occur as a result of psychotherapy. In addition, this data may prove useful in identifying neural predictors of who will be most likely to respond positively to treatment. While this field is relatively new, there is great potential for these types of findings to help clinicians develop very targeted treatments for individuals (Phillips et al., 2015; Yang et al., 2014).

CLINICAL EXPERTISE If an evaluation of published research findings were the only necessary consideration in making treatment decisions for a particular individual, someone could easily design a computer program (or even an app!) that would quickly identify the appropriate therapy approach for an individual based on key variables such as the diagnosis or primary symptoms. However, a clinician typically conducts the assessment to determine the appropriate diagnosis, if any, and the clinician knows about any specific client characteristics that may make certain research findings applicable or not. For example, if an individual has two co-occurring disorders, the clinician must make a decision about which condition to address first or if there is a treatment that would work equally well for both conditions. There are very few studies examining these types of questions as most randomized clinical trials explicitly exclude participants with multiple diagnoses in order to provide a more "pure" test of the effectiveness of a treatment with a specific diagnostic group. In addition, clinical expertise is required to implement a treatment effectively. Regardless of how much research evidence there is in support of a specific treatment, if it is not implemented effectively, the results will not be the same for a particular individual. Therefore, while some people have argued that the emphasis on evidence-based practice has undermined the role of clinical judgment and expertise, it can be argued that the opposite is actually true. In an evidence-based model, clinical expertise is critical to conduct thorough and valid assessments, evaluate the research literature and apply the findings to a particular individual, and effectively implement the selected treatment.

PATIENT CHARACTERISTICS AND PREFERENCES Just as the therapist brings certain characteristics and skills to the table, so does the patient seeking care. Thus, the evidence-based practice approach also emphasizes the importance of the patient's individual characteristics and preferences.

Individual characteristics:

- *Functional Status.* Defined as an individual's ability to perform normal daily activities required to meet basic needs, fulfill usual roles, and maintain health and well-being (Leidy, 1994; Wilson & Cleary, 1995), functional status is a characteristic that has been related to treatment outcome (American Psychological Association, 2002; Institute of Medicine, 2001; Sackett et al., 2000; Stewart et al., 1989). Two individuals with similar scores on a measure of depression symptoms may respond quite differently to treatment based on whether or not one of them is able to perform daily functioning tasks (e.g., personal care, maintain employment, household responsibilities) at a different level than the other.

- *Readiness to change.* This characteristic refers to the concept of motivation levels. People arrive in treatment at various stages of motivation, depending on the circumstances that brought them there. For example, an adolescent with anorexia nervosa who was forced into treatment by her parents may have a low readiness for change. On the other hand, an adult with a flying phobia who wants to accept a promotion at work that requires travel may have a much higher readiness for change.

- *Level of social support.* There is an abundance of research demonstrating that people who have higher levels of social support when they enter treatment tend to have better results (DiMatteo, 2004; Lindfors et al., 2014; Ogrodniczuk et al., 2002; Thrasher et al., 2010).

Preferences:

Finally, therapists must always recognize that patients have the ultimate authority in making decisions about their care. *Informed consent* is equally as important in psychotherapy as it is in research such that the patient must be made aware of the proposed treatment's procedures and any potential risks associated with the treatment.

Adaptive Pathway 16.3: Treatment Effectiveness

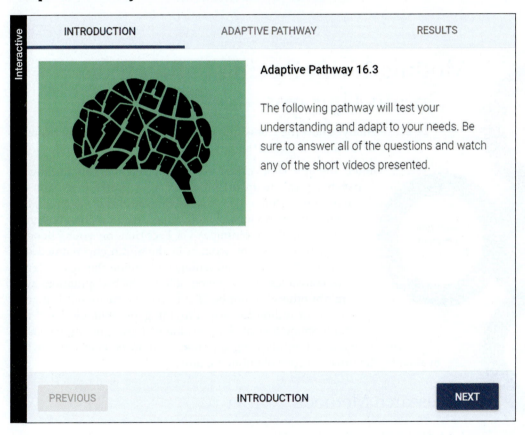

Quiz for Module 16.11–16.12

1. The three "common ingredients" of effective psychotherapy are _____.

    a. empathy, affordability, and accessibility

    b. allegiance effects, therapeutic alliance, and empathy

    c. therapeutic alliance, accessibility, and empathy

    d. affordability, empathy, and allegiance effects

2. Research on the effectiveness of different therapeutic techniques suggests that _____.

    a. there is no single therapeutic strategy uniquely effective in treating all people with any disorder

    b. cognitive-behavioral therapy is superior to other forms of psychotherapy

c. family therapy is superior to individual therapy in most cases

d. psychotherapy is generally ineffective across most cases

3. There is a debate about whether psychotherapy or medication is the most effective form of treatment. What do surveys suggest?

   a. Medication is superior to psychotherapy.

   b. Outcomes are generally similar among all groups.

   c. Psychotherapy is superior to medication.

   d. None of the answers are correct.

4. _____ is the integration of the best available research with clinical expertise in the context of patient characteristics, culture, and preferences.

   a. Research-integrated practice

   b. Clinical-based practice

   c. Evidence-based practice

   d. Evidence-based psychotherapy

5. Trenton has been experiencing depression for several months. He felt hopeful when he discovered a research study that was testing the effectiveness of a new type of drug. Unbeknownst to Trenton, he was assigned to the control group. If the drug manufacturer wanted to show that the medication was better than a placebo, what should the control group receive?

   a. Nothing

   b. A different, established antidepressant

   c. A different, but untested antidepressant

   d. A sugar pill

6. Alicia suffered from anxiety for months before she sought treatment. She was put on a waitlist at a clinic, but by the time she attended her first appointment, her anxiety was already significantly reduced. This is called _____.

   a. spontaneous recovery

   b. double-blind study

   c. placebo effect

   d. longitudinal designed trial

Module 16.13: Piecing It Together: Online Therapy

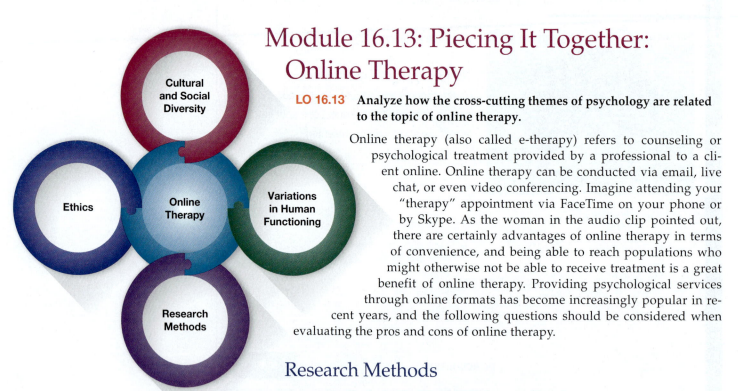

LO 16.13 **Analyze how the cross-cutting themes of psychology are related to the topic of online therapy.**

Online therapy (also called e-therapy) refers to counseling or psychological treatment provided by a professional to a client online. Online therapy can be conducted via email, live chat, or even video conferencing. Imagine attending your "therapy" appointment via FaceTime on your phone or by Skype. As the woman in the audio clip pointed out, there are certainly advantages of online therapy in terms of convenience, and being able to reach populations who might otherwise not be able to receive treatment is a great benefit of online therapy. Providing psychological services through online formats has become increasingly popular in recent years, and the following questions should be considered when evaluating the pros and cons of online therapy.

Research Methods

- How effective is online therapy?
- Does it work as well (or even better) than traditional face-to-face therapy?

When discussing the effectiveness of any type of therapy, remember that the gold standard is a **randomized controlled trial**, which includes random assignment to groups, control group comparisons, and quantifiable results. One of the most important questions about online therapy is whether or not this type of treatment is equally effective to a face-to-face form of therapy. Using a randomized controlled trial to evaluate the effectiveness of online therapy versus face-to-face therapy would look like the following:

1. Random assignment to either receive online therapy, face-to-face therapy, or some sort of placebo treatment (e.g., a patient meets individually with someone, but no active psychological treatment is conducted).

2. Measurement of some outcome variable (e.g., reduced symptoms of anxiety) would be taken before, during, and after each type of treatment and then compared between groups.

Randomized Controlled Trials

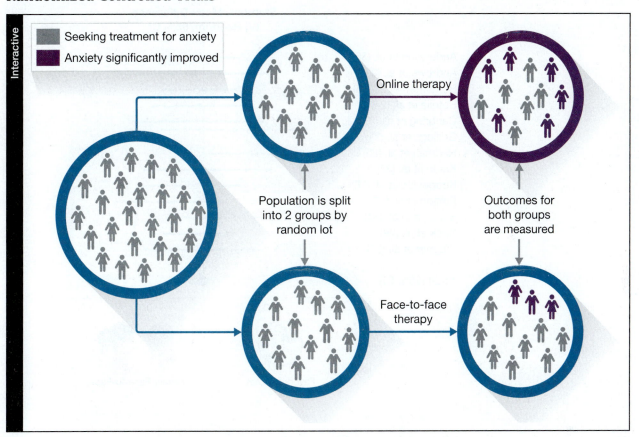

In reality, randomized controlled trials are somewhat rare because of the cost and time associated with this type of research. In addition, when comparing online therapy to face-to-fact therapy, random assignment can also be challenging. Someone may seek out online therapy because he or she can't physically get to an office to see a therapist face-to-face for a variety of reasons. This person would not be able to be "randomly" assigned to the face-to-face group. However, without random assignment, it's difficult to know if any differences between the groups at the end of treatment are due to the treatment itself or pre-existing differences. For example, if people who don't have transportation are placed in the online therapy group while people who do have access to transportation are placed in the face-to-face group, there may be other differences between the groups (e.g., income, social support) that would impact how well the treatment works.

A review of the current literature demonstrates that there have been a limited number of randomized controlled trials comparing online therapy to face-to-face therapy. Although several studies have shown that online therapy can be effective (Andersson & Cuijpers, 2009; Kessler et al., 2009; Ruwaard, 2012), fewer studies directly compare online therapy to face-to-face therapy. The most notable study published by Andersson and colleagues in 2014 included a meta-analysis of 13 studies examining the effectiveness of Internet-delivered cognitive behavior therapy (ICBT) compared to face-to-face cognitive behavior therapy (CBT) among patients with social anxiety disorder, panic disorder, depression, body dissatisfaction, male sexual dysfunction, spider phobias, and tinnitus (or ringing in the ears). The combined data showed that

ICBT and CBT were equally effective across all different patient groups (see Figure 16.9). These findings suggest that people may get just as much benefit from participating in online therapy as they get from seeing a therapist face-to-face.

Figure 16.9 Online vs Face-To-Face Therapy

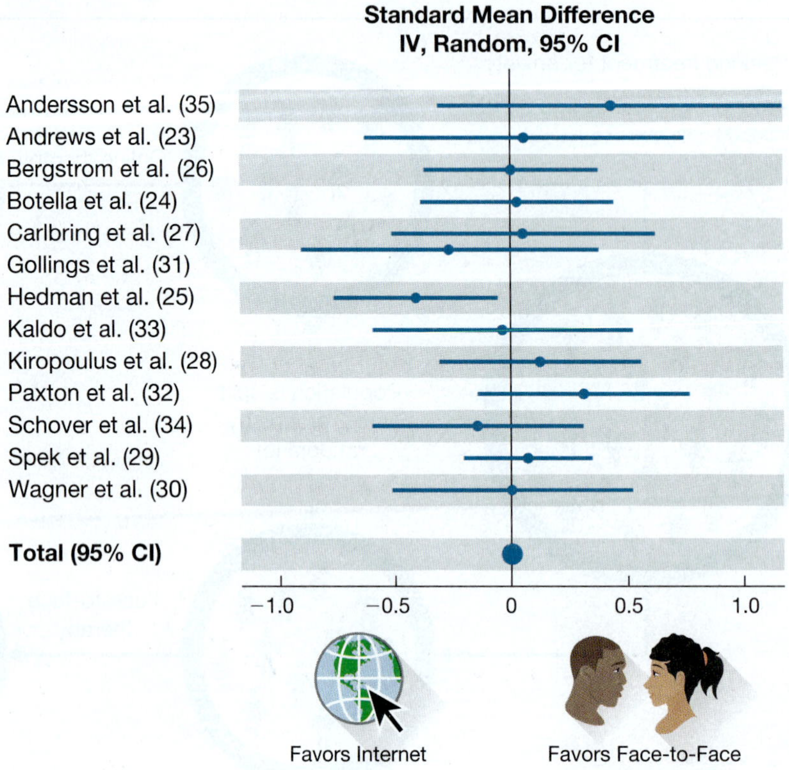

Standard Mean Difference
IV, Random, 95% CI

Andersson et al. (35)
Andrews et al. (23)
Bergstrom et al. (26)
Botella et al. (24)
Carlbring et al. (27)
Gollings et al. (31)
Hedman et al. (25)
Kaldo et al. (33)
Kiropoulus et al. (28)
Paxton et al. (32)
Schover et al. (34)
Spek et al. (29)
Wagner et al. (30)

Total (95% CI)

−1.0   −0.5   0   0.5   1.0

Favors Internet   Favors Face-to-Face

Cultural and Social Diversity

- Can online therapy provide a way to provide treatment to underserved populations?

Some groups of people are considered "underserved" by mental health treatment. Financial limitations are one of the main reasons that many people have limited access to mental health care.

Journal Prompt: How Can Finances Limit Access?

Financial limitations make it difficult for some people to pay for mental health services. What are some other ways that financial limitations make it difficult for some people to receive mental health care?

People who are uninsured often find it impossible to pay out-of-pocket for mental health services. In addition, many people who are living in or near poverty find it very difficult to access transportation to attend appointments, or they may find it difficult to take time off from work and attend appointments during regular working hours when most mental health services are provided. Lack of available childcare is also a barrier to accessing mental health care. In addition, people who live in rural areas or who are physically disabled have increased difficulty in accessing appropriate mental health care.

In addition, as discussed in this chapter, the use of mental health services is lowest among minority groups (de Girolamo et al., 2012; Desai et al., 2014; Garland et al., 2014) (see Figure 16.10). Cultural differences between providers and patients, stigma, and language barriers contribute to the low rate of mental health care among minority groups. Research has shown that providing culturally adapted treatments in a person's native language leads to improvements at 2–4 times the rate of other treatments (Griner & Smith, 2006). However, finding enough therapists who are trained to provide culturally adapted treatments in multiple languages is very difficult.

Figure 16.10 Mental Health Needs Among the African American Population

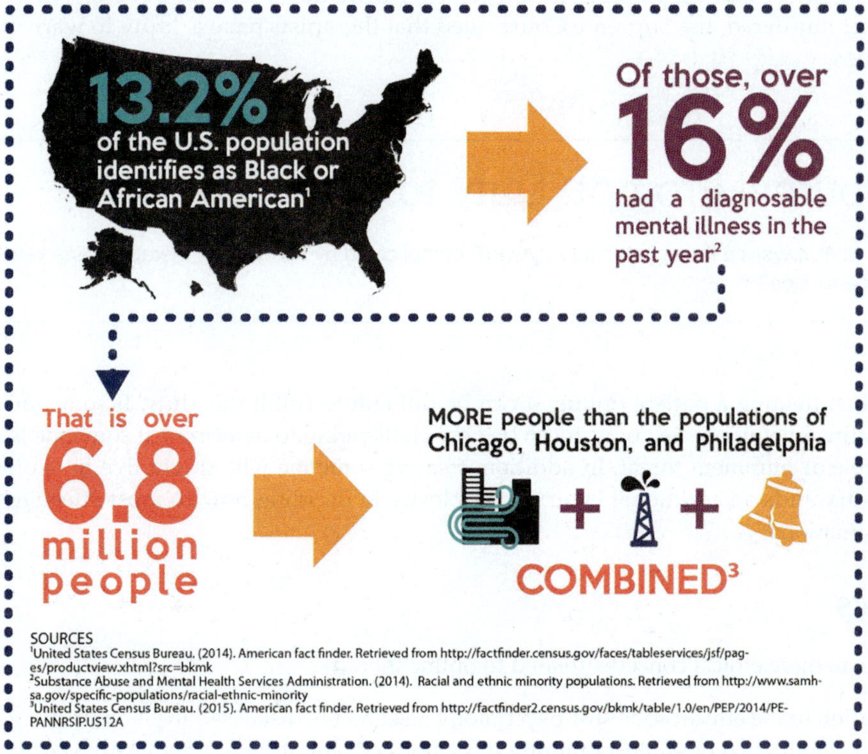

13.2% of the U.S. population identifies as Black or African American[1]

Of those, over **16%** had a diagnosable mental illness in the past year[2]

That is over **6.8 million people**

MORE people than the populations of Chicago, Houston, and Philadelphia **COMBINED**[3]

SOURCES
[1]United States Census Bureau. (2014). American fact finder. Retrieved from http://factfinder.census.gov/faces/tableservices/jsf/pages/productview.xhtml?src=bkmk
[2]Substance Abuse and Mental Health Services Administration. (2014). Racial and ethnic minority populations. Retrieved from http://www.samhsa.gov/specific-populations/racial-ethnic-minority
[3]United States Census Bureau. (2015). American fact finder. Retrieved from http://factfinder2.census.gov/bkmk/table/1.0/en/PEP/2014/PE-PANNRSIP.US12A

When considering all of the factors that impact access to mental health care, online therapy may provide a potential means to provide services to people who would not have been served traditionally due to financial, regional, or cultural challenges. For example, being able to receive treatment in your own home outside of regular working hours would help those people who struggle with transportation problems and difficulty managing work schedules and child care issues. Rather than focusing exclusively on training more therapists to provide culturally adapted therapy, working to provide online access to those therapists who are already proficient or who are bilingual might lead to increased utilization of mental health care by minority groups.

While the potential benefits of online therapy to increase access to mental health care have been discussed in the literature (Aboujaoude et al., 2015; Triplett, 2016; Yuen et al., 2012), there have not been any studies yet to examine whether or not online therapy leads to increased utilization of mental health treatment among minorities or other underserved populations. One meta-analysis showed that online therapy was effective in the short term across eight studies of approximately 500 Asian, African American, and Spanish individuals in improving depression and anxiety (Dorstyn et al., 2013). However, more research is needed to answer questions about online therapy and improved access to care among underserved populations.

Variations in Human Functioning

- Are certain people or problems not suited to receiving treatment online?

What kinds of individuals or problems might be best-suited for online therapy? Much of the research shows that this type of therapy can be effective for a wide range of people and problems. However, it is important to note that online therapy might not be the best option for patients who are feeling suicidal or even homicidal.

Therapists have a legal "duty to warn and protect." This means that mental health providers are ethically and legally required to inform third parties or authorities if a patient poses an imminent risk to himself or herself or to another person. This means that a therapist must take action if a patient is suicidal or homicidal, even if it means violating the patient's confidentiality. In *Tarasoff v. Regents of the University of California* (1976), a patient told a therapist that he planned to kill his ex-girlfriend. When the patient's ex-girlfriend was later murdered, the Supreme Court ruled that therapists have a "duty to warn" in these situations.

Journal Prompt: Duty to Warn

In what ways is a therapist's "duty to warn" complicated by conducting therapy online versus face-to-face?

When treating a patient online, it can be difficult to fulfill this duty. If someone is communicating by voice or text only, it can be very challenging to determine if someone is making a credible or imminent threat. In addition, treating someone who might live in another state or country adds an additional layer of complexity in deciding how to most effectively act in these situations.

Ethics

- Are there ethical concerns related to online therapy?

In addition to the ethical codes for psychology researchers discussed in Chapter 1 (e.g., avoiding deception when possible, obtaining informed consent, minimizing harm), specific ethical issues concern clinical psychologists or other providers of therapy. Table 16.1 includes some examples of ethical guidelines published by the American Psychological Association (APA):

Table 16.1 APA Ethical Principles for Therapists

Ethical Principle	Description
Therapy Involving Couples or Families	When psychologists agree to provide services to several persons who have a relationship, they take reasonable steps to clarify at the outset (1) which of the individuals are clients/patients and (2) the relationship the psychologist will have with each person. If it becomes apparent that psychologists may be called on to perform potentially conflicting roles (such as family therapist and then witness for one party in divorce proceedings), psychologists take reasonable steps to clarify and modify, or withdraw from, roles appropriately.
Sexual Intimacies with Current Patients, Relatives of Patients, or Former Patients	Psychologists do not engage in sexual intimacies with current therapy clients/patients, nor do they engage in sexual intimacies with individuals they know to be close relatives, guardians, or significant others of current clients/patients. Psychologists do not engage in sexual intimacies with former clients/patients for at least two years after cessation or termination of therapy.
Terminating Therapy	(a) Psychologists terminate therapy when it becomes reasonably clear that the client/patient no longer needs the service, is not likely to benefit, or is being harmed by continued service. (b) Psychologists may terminate therapy when threatened or otherwise endangered by the client/patient or another person with whom the client/patient has a relationship. (c) Except where precluded by the actions of clients/patients or third-party payors, prior to termination psychologists provide pretermination counseling and suggest alternative service providers as appropriate.

SOURCE: American Psychological Association. (2002). "Ethical Principles of Psychologists and Code of Conduct." *American Psychologist,* 57(12), 1060-1073.

When it comes to online therapy, some specific ethical issues must be considered:

1. *Privacy:* Therapists must maintain confidentiality and privacy for patients. This poses unique challenges in an online environment. For example, email is not always a secure form of communication, and other people may gain access to confidential information shared via email. In addition, online live chats can potentially be hacked. Online therapists must be aware of the potential threats to privacy and confidentiality and make special efforts to avoid breaches for their patients by using technology that minimizes these risks.

2. *Informed Consent:* Treatment may not be provided to minors without parental or guardian knowledge and consent. When interacting online, it can be challenging to verify the age of the individual, making it difficult to ensure that minors are not being treated without their parents' knowledge or consent.

3. *State Licensure Laws:* To practice as psychologist or counselor, each state requires people to undergo a credentialing process called licensure. This ensures that people who use a certain title (e.g., "psychologist") have demonstrated they have the appropriate education and background to practice as therapist. So, if you are looking for a therapist in the state of Ohio, and you see someone who is called a "psychologist," you can be assured that individual has been approved by the state licensing board to practice as a psychologist. As Figure 16.11 shows, the steps to becoming licensed to practice as a psychologist are quite lengthy. The same process occurs with physicians and many other health providers. After all, it would be very scary if people were allowed to call themselves a neurologist, psychologist, or optometrist without any training or education.

Figure 16.11 Steps to Licensing

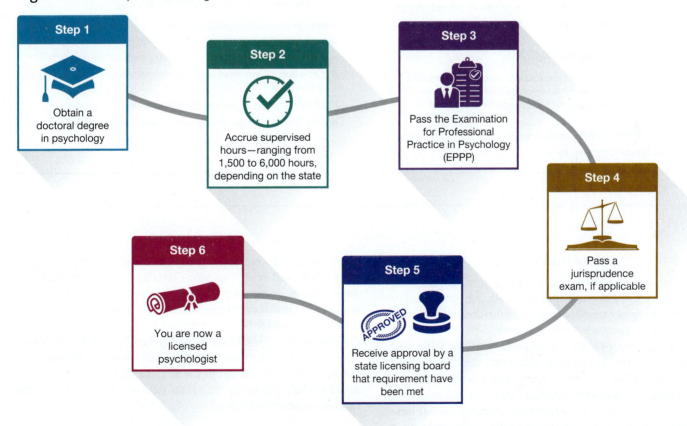

The tricky part when it comes to providing online therapy is that licensure for psychologists and counselors is at the state level. You receive a license to practice in a specific state, and you are not allowed to practice in other states unless you also go through the licensure requirements of that state (and requirements vary from state to state). However, if a patient who lives in Colorado is being treated online by someone who is licensed to practice in Kansas as a psychologist, how do the licensure laws of Colorado apply? To circumvent the need to become licensed in multiple states (which is an expensive and arduous process), some therapists have changed their own titles (e.g., "life coach") to something unregulated by the states. As a consumer, however, this causes further confusion. How can you know the difference between a "life coach" who is actually trained and educated as a competent therapist and a "life coach" who has no proper education or training? As online therapy becomes increasingly popular, licensing boards will need to develop better solutions to these issues.

Quiz for Module 16.13

1. What is one benefit to online therapy?
   a. No licensure is required by the therapist to practice online therapy.
   b. It is less expensive and more effective.
   c. It can reach an underserved population who has limited access to therapy.
   d. There are fewer ethical concerns.

2. The most notable study comparing internet-based cognitive behavioral therapy (ICBT) with face-to-face cognitive behavioral therapy (CBT) showed that _____.
   a. patients in both groups showed an increase in symptoms after the treatment
   b. both treatments were equally effective across all patient groups
   c. both treatments were equally ineffective across all patient groups
   d. face-to face CBT was superior to ICBT

3. If members of an underserved population could receive mental health treatment in their own homes outside of regular working hours, which barriers to treatment might be eliminated or reduced?
   a. Language barriers, work schedule issues, and child care issues
   b. Financial issues, language issues, and cultural issues

   c. Transportation problems, child care issues, and work schedule issues
   d. Cultural issues, transportation issues, and language barriers

4. How would conducting online therapy make it difficult for a therapist to fulfill their "duty to warn" rule?
   a. The therapist may not be informed on each state's rules about "duty to warn."
   b. The therapist has a duty of confidentiality, so they cannot break confidentiality.
   c. Therapists practicing out of state may not be obligated to the same rules.
   d. If someone is communicating via voice or text only, it is difficult to assess imminent or credible threat.

5. What have some therapists done to circumvent the need to be licensed in multiple states for online therapy?
   a. Changed their job title to something such as "life coach"
   b. Only take clients who are from the state in which the therapist is licensed
   c. Only advertise in their state of licensure
   d. Apply for licensure in any state where clients will be recruited

Summary

Module 16.1–16.2: Mental Health Treatment: Then and Now

Treatment for mental health conditions has a sordid past with periods of reform during the 19th and 20th centuries. Today many different types of mental health professions require differing levels of education/licensure with different areas of expertise, which are practiced in diverse settings. **Inpatient treatment,** or services performed while an individual is hospitalized, is necessary when the safety of the individual is at risk. **Residential treatment** includes intense and structured treatment but occurs in a more home-like setting. **Partial hospitalization** occurs when an individual still resides in his/her own home but spends most of the day in a treatment center. The most common level of care for mental health treatment occurs on an **outpatient** basis. **Intensive outpatient treatment**

allows people to maintain their work and/or school obligations while still receiving more intensive treatment multiple days a week. A recent shift has occurred toward **preventive care,** which involves taking measures to prevent people from developing mental health problems in the first place. Despite passage of the **mental health parity law** (which forces insurance companies to make coverage equivalent for physical and mental health), treatment in the current mental health system remains challenging for many, particularly for those who are uninsured or underinsured.

Module 16.3–16.6: Psychological Therapies

Psychotherapy refers to an interaction between a therapist and someone suffering from a psychological problem, the goal of which is to provide support or relief from the problem. **Eclectic psychotherapy** draws ideas and techniques from a variety of therapeutic approaches. **Psychodynamic therapies** like **psychoanalysis** is a type of psychotherapy that aims to help clients bring unconscious conflicts into conscious awareness through the use of **free association** (client reports any image or idea that enters awareness), **dream analysis** (interpreting the **manifest content**—the way the dream is experienced and remembered by the dreamer—to uncover the **latent content,** or the unconscious meaning of the dream), **resistance** (a client's attempts to avoid doing therapeutic work) and **transference** (when a client's unconscious feelings about a significant person in his or her life are instead directed toward the therapist) in their clients. Considered a neo-Freudian approach, **interpersonal psychotherapy** focuses on helping clients improve their relationships as a means to resolving their psychological problems.

Carl Rogers developed the humanistic therapy approach called **person-centered,** or **client-centered therapy,** which focuses on the client's abilities and insights rather than the therapist's thoughts and skills. Key components of person-centered therapy include **active listening** (when the therapist conveys an interest in understanding what the patient says) and therapist interactions based on (1) **genuineness** (therapist must be genuine and willing to express their true feelings), (2) **unconditional positive regard** (therapist must show complete acceptance and support of the client "as is"), and (3) **accurate empathy (**therapist must be able to accurately understand the client's experiences and viewpoint).

Developed by Aaron Beck, **cognitive therapy** is based on the theory that people's psychological problems can be traced to their own illogical or dysfunctional beliefs and thoughts. According to this theory, depression arises from negative **automatic thoughts** and illogical or distorted thinking patterns. Examples of cognitive distortions include **all-or-nothing thinking** (seeing things as black or white, all or none), **overgeneralization** (drawing broad negative conclusions on the basis of a single event), and **mental filter** (focusing only on the negative aspects of a situation and ignoring or "filtering" out any positive aspects). **Cognitive restructuring** focuses on teaching clients to (1) identify their automatic thoughts, (2) evaluate or test the accuracy of their thoughts, and (3) replace their negative automatic thoughts with more realistic thoughts.

Behavior therapy attempts to change behaviors associated with psychological distress using the principles of learning. In **exposure treatment,** people are repeatedly exposed to what they fear until they become accustomed to the stimulus. In **systematic desensitization** people learn to learn to pair states of deep relaxation while being exposed to anxiety-provoking situations using a **fear hierarchy** (a list of increasingly anxiety-inducing situations). **Flooding** habituates clients by exposing them to very intense stimuli first. The goal of **aversive conditioning** is to replace a positive response to a harmful stimulus, such as alcohol, with a punishing response, such as nausea. In reality, many therapists combine both cognitive and behavioral strategies and use what is called **cognitive–behavior therapy (CBT).** The CBT model focuses on the interrelated nature of our thoughts, feelings, and behaviors.

Module 16.7–16.8: Biomedical Therapies

For some, **biomedical therapies** (physiological treatments designed to reduce psychological symptoms) are an important part of an effective treatment plan. **Psychopharmacology,** the study of how drugs affect the mind and behavior, has led to the development of a wide array drugs used to treat psychological disorders. **Antipsychotic drugs** are a class of psychoactive medications used to treat disorders with psychotic symptoms. The **typical antipsychotics** (e.g., Haldol) work primarily on the positive symptoms of schizophrenia by blocking receptors in the brain's dopamine pathways, but they have some serious negative side effects with long-term use. The **atypical antipsychotics** (e.g., Zyprexa) have fewer side effects and can also alleviate negative symptoms by altering the activity of serotonin, in addition to dopamine. **Antidepressants,** which work to alleviate symptoms of depression, have become the third most common prescription drug in the United States. **Tricyclics** work by blocking the reuptake of serotonin and norepinephrine, but have a number of unpleasant and dangerous side effects. **Selective serotonin reuptake inhibitors,** selectively block the reuptake of serotonin in the brain and have relatively few side effects. **Monoamine oxidase (MAO) inhibitors,** which work by inhibiting MAO (an enzyme that metabolizes norepinephrine), also have negative side effects and are often used as a last resort. The newest types of antidepressants, **atypical antidepressants**, affect neurotransmitters in specific combinations. Some research on the effectiveness of antidepressants questions their use in mild to moderate depression cases, although other studies have shown them to be effective across all severity levels. **Anti-anxiety medications** reduce the symptoms associated with many anxiety disorders by slowing down the central nervous system's activity. **Mood-stabilizing medications** such as lithium are used in patients with bipolar disorder. Exactly how lithium works is not clear, but it is generally believed to involve multiple mechanisms of action.

Electroconvulsive therapy (ECT), which involves sending electric shocks to patients' brains, is a very effective treatment for severe treatment-resistant depression. **Lobotomies** are a type of psychosurgery that disconnects the frontal lobe from the rest of the brain and results in a near vegetative state. However, current versions of psychosurgery (e.g., **bilateral anterior capsulotomy** for OCD) are highly localized and targeted to specific areas of the brain. In addition, in a newer treatment called **deep brain stimulation,** surgeons implant a thin wire electrode in the patient's brain; when activated, this electrode can stimulate (not destroy) neurons lying near it which has shown to be effective in patients with severe OCD.

Module 16.9–16.10: Sociocultural Influences on Treatment

Group therapy is a form of psychotherapy in which one or more therapists treat a small number of people in a group setting. **Family therapy** is one specific form of group therapy that focuses on the unique interactions of the family unit. For people involved in relationships who are experiencing distress, **couples therapy** is one treatment option. Another form of group therapy, **support groups,** include *professionally operated* *support groups* (facilitated by professionals) and *self-help support groups* (peer-led and are usually organized by members on a voluntary basis). Alcoholics Anonymous (AA) has significant evidence in support of its effectiveness in terms of increased abstinence rates and the association between AA attendance and abstinence rates.

Stigma of mental illness has widespread negative consequences. Ethnic and cultural background appear to be influential factors in how mental illness is viewed. Stigma varies considerably across different countries but there is a degree of stigma present across all countries. People with schizophrenia appear to have better outcomes in cultures where the norms, attitudes, and behaviors toward mental illness are less negative.

Module 16.11–16.12: Evaluating Therapies

Recent studies have shown that in general, most people who receive psychotherapy report improvement and that some therapy appears to be better than no therapy at all. Some of the most widely supported common factors of effective therapy include (1) **allegiance effects** (the impact of the therapist's belief in the effectiveness of the treatment he or she is providing), (2) the **therapeutic alliance** (consisting of the bond between therapist and patient, goal consensus, and agreement about the tasks of therapy), and (3) **empathy** (the ability of the therapist to understand the patient's point of view). No single therapeutic strategy is uniquely effective in treating all people with any disorder. However, there is evidence that some therapeutic techniques are more effective than others for particular conditions. There is no consensus about the relative effectiveness of psychotherapy versus medication as the results depend heavily on the individual and the specific condition.

According to the APA, **evidence-based practice** in psychology (EBP) is the integration of the best available research with clinical expertise in the context of patient characteristics, culture, and preferences. The importance of establishing that a treatment is superior to placebo effect and rates of **spontaneous remission** (recovery without any treatment) are key. The gold standard for research designs is the **randomized controlled trial,** which includes random assignment, control group comparisons, and quantifiable results. Clinical expertise is also a necessary ingredient of evidence-based practice. Finally, patient characteristics (e.g., functional status, readiness to change, level of social support), culture, and patient personal preferences are also important.

Chapter 16 Quiz

1. SSRIs work by _____ the _____ of serotonin in the brain.

   a. blocking; reuptake
   b. accelerating; reuptake
   c. increasing; breakdown
   d. blocking; production

2. A written agreement between the therapist and the client that specifies the goals for behavioral change is called _____.

   a. contingency management
   b. token economy
   c. behavior chart
   d. goal planning

3. What is an important component to successfully treating people with culturally diverse backgrounds?

   a. Teach the patient English so they can understand the therapist.
   b. Train therapists with the same ethnic or cultural backgrounds.
   c. The therapist needs to understand the patient's cultural background and adapt the treatment accordingly.
   d. Involve the family of the patient in the treatment.

4. What is one of the challenges people face when seeking mental health treatment under the current mental health parity law?

   a. An overabundance of mental health professionals has led to confusion for patients seeking treatment.
   b. A decline in the number of mentally ill people has reduced the need for treatment.
   c. Insurance will not cover mental health treatment.
   d. There is a shortage of qualified mental health professionals.

5. Suki has been attending weekly sessions with her therapist who believes that Suki's childhood experiences have led to her avoidance of relationships. Once the therapist asks questions about Suki's relationship with her mother, Suki begins to miss appointments. In the psychodynamic theory, missing appointments would be considered a sign of _____.

   a. resistance
   b. transference
   c. free association
   d. ego defense

6. Paul had an abusive coach for many years as a child. Later in therapy, he began to direct his unresolved anger for his coach toward his therapist in a process known as _____.

   a. transference
   b. resistance
   c. Oedipal rage
   d. free association

7. According to psychodynamic dream analysis, the actual remembered event in a dream is called the _____ while the symbolic unconscious meaning of dreams is called the _____.

   a. transference; countertransference
   b. manifest content; latent content
   c. latent content; manifest content
   d. countertransference; transference

8. Daryn was struggling with motivation to complete homework and attend classes. She met with a therapist and expressed her frustration with herself and her lack of drive. Daryn asked for tips on how to solve the problem, but the therapist responded with, "It sounds like you are really frustrated with yourself and can't figure out what to do." The therapist has expressed _____.

   a. conditions of worth
   b. unconditional positive regard
   c. accurate empathy
   d. self-actualization

9. Kiley received treatment for depression from someone she thought was a psychologist. She later found out that the person had faked their degree and credentials and had no training in mental health treatment. However, she was puzzled because she felt that her depression was improved significantly during the treatment. This is most likely an example of a(n) _____.

   a. placebo effect
   b. spontaneous remission
   c. unintentional therapeutic effect
   d. randomized controlled trial

10. Ethan has watched his brother receive praise and attention for his running achievements. Ethan has decided that he also would like to receive that type of praise and attention, so he has started to work out and run with his brother. Ethan has learned through _____.

   a. observational learning
   b. exposure therapy
   c. extinction therapy
   d. token economy

11. What was the unintended consequence of the deinstitutionalization movement of the 20th century?

   a. A decrease in the number of people on medications
   b. An increase in the population of prisons and jails
   c. A decrease in the homeless population
   d. A decrease in transitional care for support of the mentally ill

12. Cognitive restructuring helps clients _____, evaluate the accuracy of their thoughts, and _____.

   a. identify their maladaptive behaviors; replace their behaviors with more productive behaviors
   b. identify their automatic thoughts; replace negative automatic thoughts with more realistic thoughts
   c. identify their past thoughts; replace with more current positive thoughts
   d. identify their negative relationships; replace with more positive relationships

13. Richard overate during one meal and thought, "I'm going to end up overweight for the rest of my life." This is an example of which cognitive distortion?

   a. Negative thought pattern
   b. Mental filter
   c. Overgeneralization
   d. All-or-nothing thinking

14. The gold standard for research designs in the area of establishing evidence-based treatments is the _____.

   a. randomized controlled trial
   b. double-blind controlled trial
   c. quasi-experimental research design
   d. correlational research design

15. _____ were established during the 18th century to treat mental illness but ended up leading to _____ of the mentally ill.

   a. Asylums; mistreatment
   b. Asylums; over-medicating
   c. Group homes; overcrowding and abuse
   d. Group homes; over-medicating

16. Rainey worries constantly, has trouble sleeping, and complains of racing and panicky thoughts at times. Louis has experienced depressed mood, low appetite, and insomnia for months. Rainey is prescribed a(n) _____ medication, while Louis is prescribed a(n) _____ medication.

   a. antianxiety; antidepressant
   b. antidepressant; antianxiety
   c. antianxiety; mood stabilizer
   d. mood stabilizer; antianxiety

17. How is ECT administered differently now than it was in the past?

   a. The electrodes are placed inside the brain.
   b. Doctors use muscle relaxers to prevent strong convulsions.
   c. A patient is forced into ECT by their doctor.
   d. It is the first treatment used for depression.

18. The procedure in which surgeons implant a thin wire electrode into the brain to stimulate neurons is called _____.

   a. lobotomy
   b. ECT
   c. deep brain stimulation
   d. psychosurgery

19. According to Irvin Yalom, two of the reasons group therapy is effective include _____ and _____.

    a. socialization; decrease in depression
    b. installation of hope; decrease in depression
    c. universality; increase in repetitive behaviors
    d. installation of hope; socialization techniques

20. Family therapy has been shown to be particularly effective for which groups of people?

    a. Substance abusers and adolescents with anorexia nervosa
    b. Individuals with bipolar disorder and depression
    c. Substance abusers and individuals with schizophrenia
    d. Adolescents with eating disorders and individuals with bipolar disorder

21. What does research suggest about the effectiveness of Alcoholics Anonymous as treatment for substance abuse?

    a. Attendance at AA meetings increases abstinence rates.
    b. AA has no effect on abstinence rates.
    c. Humanistic therapy has better evidence for effectiveness.
    d. The findings are inconsistent.

22. What is an effective way to reduce the stigma against mental illness?

    a. Provide educational campaigns to raise awareness.
    b. Increase contact with people who are mentally ill.
    c. Keep people with mental illness in group homes, separate from others.
    d. Increase awareness of what causes mental illness.

23. _____ care is the most common form of treatment for mental illness.

    a. Intensive outpatient
    b. Partial hospitalization
    c. Outpatient
    d. Inpatient

24. How is mental illness viewed among some Asian cultures?

    a. Mental illness can be cured by having a strong mind and stronger willpower.
    b. Mental illness is genetic and must be avoided by marrying the correct person.
    c. Mental illness is treatable and just needs the correct diagnosis.
    d. Mental illness is shameful and caused by evil spirits.

25. The effectiveness of therapy has been extensively studied. What conclusion can be reached?

    a. Psychotherapy is more effective for the treatment of mental illness than no treatment at all.
    b. Behavioral therapy is better than any other form of therapy.
    c. Cognitive therapy is better than any other form of therapy.
    d. No therapy and psychotherapy have the same effectiveness rates.

26. What is the most effective treatment for phobias?

    a. Exposure-based treatments
    b. Medications
    c. Psychodynamic therapy
    d. Cognitive therapy

27. A person with schizophrenia or bipolar disorder is going to be treated with which type of treatment first?

    a. Cognitive behavioral therapy
    b. Medications
    c. Humanistic therapy
    d. Interpersonal therapy

28. _____ must be ruled out when determining the effectiveness of a particular therapy.

    a. Gender differences
    b. Medication-induced effects
    c. Spontaneous remission
    d. Random effects

29. What is the benefit of atypical antipsychotic medications?

    a. They are covered by insurance, and the typical ones are not covered by insurance.
    b. They have a lower cost.
    c. They have no side effects.
    d. They target the negative symptoms of schizophrenia as well as the positive symptoms.

30. Which type of therapy was developed by Carl Rogers?

    a. Gestalt
    b. Cognitive-behavioral
    c. Psychodynamic
    d. Client-centered

References

Preface

Ackerman, R., & Goldsmith, M. (2011). Metacognitive regulation of text learning: On screen versus on paper. *Journal of Experimental Psychology: Applied, 17*(1), 18–32.

Chen, G., Cheng, W., Chang, T. W., Zheng, X., & Huang, R. (2014). A comparison of reading comprehension across paper, computer screens, and tablets: Does tablet familiarity matter? *Journal of Computers in Education, 1*(2–3), 213–225.

Gurung, R. A., Hackathorn, J., Enns, C., Frantz, S., Cacioppo, J. T., Loop, T., & Freeman, J. E. (2016). Strengthening introductory psychology: A new model for teaching the introductory course. *American Psychologist, 71*(2), 112–124.

Mangen, A., Walgermo, B. R., & Brønnick, K. (2013). Reading linear texts on paper versus computer screen: Effects on reading comprehension. *International Journal of Educational Research, 58*, 61–68.

Singer, L. M., & Alexander, P. A. (2017). Reading on Paper and Digitally: What the Past Decades of Empirical Research Reveal. *Review of Educational Research, 87*(6), 1007–1041.

Chapter 00

American Psychological Association. (2014). Strengthening the common core of the introductory psychology course. Washington, DC: American Psychological Association, Board of Educational Affairs. Retrieved from http://www.apa.org/ed/governance/bea/intro-psych-report.pdf

Baier, K., Hendricks, C., Warren Gorden, K., Hendricks, J. E., & Cochran, L. (2011). College students' textbook reading, or not. In *American Reading Forum Annual Yearbook* (Vol. 31).

Baron, N. S. (2015). *Words onscreen: The fate of reading in a digital world*. Oxford University Press.

Bell, K. E., & Limber, J. E. (2009). Reading skill, textbook marking, and course performance. *Literacy Research and Instruction, 49*(1), 56–67.

Birnbaum, M. S., Kornell, N., Bjork, E. L., & Bjork, R. A. (2013). Why interleaving enhances inductive learning: The roles of discrimination and retrieval. *Memory & Cognition, 41*(3), 392–402.

Callender, A. A., & McDaniel, M. A. (2009). The limited benefits of rereading educational texts. *Contemporary Educational Psychology, 34*(1), 30–41.

Chew, S. L. (2010). Improving classroom performance by challenging student misconceptions about learning. *APS Observer, 23* (4), 51–54.

Clump, M. A., Bauer, H., & Bradley, C. (2004). The extent to which psychology students read textbooks: A multiple class analysis of reading across the psychology curriculum. *Journal of Instructional Psychology, 31*(3), 227–232.

Dunlosky, J., Rawson, K. A., Marsh, E. J., Nathan, M. J., & Willingham, D. T. (2013). Improving students' learning with effective learning techniques promising directions from cognitive and educational psychology. *Psychological Science in the Public Interest, 14*(1), 4–58.

Dunlosky, J., & Rawson, K. A. (2012). Overconfidence produces underachievement: Inaccurate self evaluations undermine students' learning and retention. *Learning and Instruction, 22*(4), 271–280.

Dweck, C. (2006). *Mindset: The new psychology of success.* New York, NY: Random House.

Eisenkraemer, R. E., Jaeger, A., & Stein, L. M. (2013). A systematic review of the testing effect in learning. *Paidéia (Ribeirão Preto), 23*(56), 397–406.

Foster, N. L., Was, C. A., Dunlosky, J., & Isaacson, R. M. (2017). Even after thirteen class exams, students are still overconfident: The role of memory for past exam performance in student predictions. *Metacognition and Learning, 12*(1), 1–19.

Gurung, R. A. (2005). How do students really study (and does it matter)? *Education, 39*, 323–340.

Gurung, R. A., & Martin, R. C. (2011). Predicting Textbook Reading: The Textbook Assessment and Usage Scale. *Teaching of Psychology, 38*(1), 22–28.

Karpicke, J. D., Butler, A. C., & Roediger III, H. L. (2009). Metacognitive strategies in student learning: Do students practise retrieval when they study on their own? *Memory, 17*(4), 471–479.

Kornell, N., & Bjork, R. A. (2008). Learning concepts and categories: Is spacing the "enemy of induction"? *Psychological Science, 19*(6), 585–592.

Lilienfeld, S. O., Lynn, S. J., Ruscio, J., & Beyerstein, B. L. (2010). *50 great myths of popular psychology: Shattering widespread misconceptions about human behavior*. John Wiley & Sons.

Lin, C. H. J., Chiang, M. C., Knowlton, B. J., Iacoboni, M., Udompholkul, P., & Wu, A. D. (2013). Interleaved practice enhances skill learning and the functional connectivity of fronto-parietal networks. *Human Brain Mapping, 34*(7), 1542–1558.

Metcalfe, J. (2009). Metacognitive judgments and control of study. *Current Directions in Psychological Science, 18*(3), 159–163.

Metcalfe, J., & Finn, B. (2008). Evidence that judgments of learning are causally related to study choice. *Psychonomic Bulletin & Review, 15*(1), 174–179.

Miller, T. M., & Geraci, L. (2011). Training metacognition in the classroom: The influence of incentives and feedback on exam predictions. *Metacognition and Learning, 6*(3), 303–314.

Morse, K. O. (2014). Assessing the efficacy of experiential learning in a multicultural environment. *Developments in Business Simulation and Experiential Learning, 28*.

Murtiana, R. (2012). Enhancing students' vocabulary acquisition through deep word processing strategy. *LIA CAR Journal, 5*, 220–229.

Pashler, H., McDaniel, M., Rohrer, D., & Bjork, R. (2008). Learning styles concepts and evidence. *Psychological Science in the Public Interest, 9*(3), 105–119.

Riener, C., & Willingham, D. (2010). The myth of learning styles. *Change: The Magazine of Higher Learning, 42*(5), 32–35.

Roediger, H. L., & Karpicke, J. D. (2006a). Test-enhanced learning taking memory tests improves long-term retention. *Psychological Science, 17*(3), 249–255.

Roediger, H. L., & Karpicke, J. D. (2006b). The power of testing memory: Basic research and implications for educational practice. *Perspectives on Psychological Science, 1*(3), 181–210.

Rohrer, D. (2012). Interleaving helps students distinguish among similar concepts. *Educational Psychology Review, 24*(3), 355–367.

Rohrer, D., & Pashler, H. (2012). Learning styles: Where's the evidence? *Medical Education, 46*(7), 634–635.

Rohrer, D., Dedrick, R. F., & Stershic, S. (2015). Interleaved practice improves mathematics learning, *Journal of Educational Psychology, 107*(3), 900–908.

Strayer, D. L., Drews, F. A., & Crouch, D. J. (2006). A comparison of the cell phone driver and the drunk driver. *Human Factors: Journal of the Human Factors and Ergonomics Society, 48*(2), 381–391.

Subrahmanyam, K., Michikyan, M., Clemmons, C., Carrillo, R., Uhls, Y. T., & Greenfield, P. M. (2013). Learning from paper, learning from screens: Impact of screen reading and multitasking conditions on reading and writing among college students. *International Journal of Cyber Behavior, Psychology and Learning (IJCBPL), 3*(4), 1–27.

van der Schuur, W. A., Baumgartner, S. E., Sumter, S. R., & Valkenburg, P. M. (2015). The consequences of media multitasking for youth: A review. *Computers in Human Behavior, 53*, 204–215.

Chapter 1

Alford, J. R., Hatemi, P. K., Hibbing, J. R., Martin, N. G., Eaves, L. J. (2011). The politics of mate choice. *The Journal of Politics, 73*, 362–379.

American Psychological Association. (2002). Ethical principles of psychologists and code of conduct. *American Psychologist, 57*(12), 1060–1073.

American Psychological Association (2011). *Careers in Psychology*. Retrieved from *Careers in Psychology*. Retrieved from http://www.apa.org/careers/resources/guides/careers.aspx

Assefi, S. L., & Garry, M. (2003). Absolut® memory distortions alcohol placebos influence the misinformation effect. *Psychological Science, 14*(1), 77–80.

Basham, K., Byers, D. S., Heller, N. R., Hertz, M., Kumaria, S., Mattei, L., ... & Shilkret, C. J. (2016). *Inside out and outside in: Psychodynamic clinical theory and psychopathology in contemporary multicultural contexts.* Rowman & Littlefield.

Bechara, A., Damasio, A. R., Damasio, H., & Anderson, S. W. (1994). Insensitivity to future consequences following damage to human prefrontal cortex. *Cognition, 50*(1), 7–15.

Brown, J. (2010). Microgenetic theory of the unconscious 2. Categories and the unconscious. In J. Brown (Ed.) *Neuropsychological Foundations of Conscious Experience* (231–262). Belgium: Les Editions Chromatika.

Bureau of Labor Statistics, U.S. Department of Labor (2015). *Occupational outlook handbook: Psychologists.* Retrieved from http://www.bls.gov/ooh/life-physical-and-social-science/psychologists.htm

Byrne, D. E. (1971). *The attraction paradigm* (Vol. 11). Academic Press.

Confer, J. C., Easton, J. A., Fleischman, D. S., Goetz, C. D., Lewis, D. M., Perilloux, C., & Buss, D. M. (2010). Evolutionary psychology: Controversies, questions, prospects, and limitations. *American Psychologist, 65*(2), 110–126.

Cook, K. (2014). *Kitty Genovese: The Murder, the Bystanders, the Crime That Changed America*. W. W. Norton & Company.

DeStefano, F., Bhasin, T. K., Thompson, W. W., Yeargin-Allsopp, M., & Boyle, C. (2004). Age at first measles-mumps-rubella vaccination in children with autism and school-matched control subjects: A population-based study in metropolitan Atlanta. *Pediatrics, 113*(2), 259–266.

Eckman, P., Friesen, W. V., O'Sullivan, M., Chan, A., Diacoyanni-Tarlatzis, I., Heider, K., ... Tzavaras, A. (1987). Universal and cultural differences in the judgments of facial expressions of emotion. *Journal of Personality and Social Psychology, 53*, 712–717.

Freund, A. M. & Ritter, J. O. (2009). Midlife crisis: A debate. *Gerontology, 55*, 582–591.

Godlee, F., Smith, J., Marcovitch, H. (2011). Wakefield's article linking MMR vaccine and autism was fraudulent. *BMJ, 342*, 64–66.

Hilgard, E. R. (1987). *Psychology in America: A historical survey*. Harcourt Brace Jovanovich.

Immunization Safety Review Committee (2004). *Immunization safety review: Vaccines and autism*. Washington, D.C.: The National Academies Press.

Jack, R. E., Blais, C., Scheepers, C., Schyns, P. G., & Caldara, R. (2009). Cultural confusions show that facial expressions are not universal. *Current Biology, 19*, 1543–1548.

Jack, R. E., Garrod, O. G. B., Yu, H., Caldara, R., & Schyns, P. G. (2012). Facial expressions of emotion are not culturally universal. *National Academy of Sciences of the United States of America, 109*, 7241–7244.

Jain, A., Marshall, J., Buikema, A., Bancroft, T., Kelly, J. P., & Newschaffer, C. J. (2015). Autism occurrence by MMR vaccine status among U.S. children with older siblings with and without autism. *JAMA, 313*(15), 1534–1540.

Latane, B., & Rodin, J. (1969). A lady in distress: Inhibiting effects of friends and strangers on bystander intervention. *Journal of Experimental Social Psychology, 5*, 189–202.

Lachman, M. E., Teshale, S., & Agrigoroaei, S. (2015). Midlife as a pivotal period in the life course: Balancing growth and decline at the crossroads of youth and old age. *International Journal of Behavioral Development, 39*(1), 20–31.

Maglione, M. A., Das, L., Raaen, L., Smith, A., Chari, R., Newberry, S., Shanman, R., Perry, T., Goetz, M. B., & Gidengil, C. (2014). Safety of vaccines used for routine immunization of U.S. children: A systematic review. *Pediatrics, 134*(2), 325–337.

Mahowald, M. W., & Ettinger, M. G. (1990). Things that go bump in the night: The parasomnias revisited. *Journal of Clinical Neurophysiology, 7*, 119–143.

Manning, R., Levine, M., & Collins, A. (2007). The Kitty Genovese murder and the social psychology of helping: The parable of the 38 witnesses. *American Psychologist, 62*(6), 555–562.

Mineka, S., & Öhman, A. (2002). Phobias and preparedness: The selective, automatic, and encapsulated nature of fear. *Biological psychiatry, 52*(10), 927–937.

Montoya, R. M., & Horton, R. S. (2013). A meta-analytic investigation of the processes underlying the similarity-attraction effect. *Journal of Social and Personal Relationships, 30*(1), 64–94.

Mrozek-Budzyn, D., Kieltyka, A., & Majewska, R. (2010). Lack of association between measles-mumps-rubella vaccination and autism in children: A case-control study. *The Pediatric Infectious Disease Journal, 29*, 397–400.

Öhman, A., & Mineka, S. (2003). The malicious serpent snakes as a prototypical stimulus for an evolved module of fear. *Current Directions in Psychological Science, 12*(1), 5–9.

Open Science Collaboration. (2015). Estimating the reproducibility of psychological science. *Science, 349*(6251), aac4716.

Pew Research Center. (2013). Health fact sheet: Highlights of the Pew Internet Project's research related to health and health care. Washington, D.C. http://www.pewinternet.org/fact-sheets/health-fact-sheet/. Accessed November 21, 2015.

Rosenbaum, M. E. (1986). Comment on a proposed two-stage theory of relationship formation: First, repulsion; then, attraction. *Journal of Personality and Social Psychology, 51*, 1171–1172.

Rosenberg, T. (2011, November 24). An electronic eye on hospital hand-washing. *New York Times*. Retrieved from http://opinionator.blogs.nytimes.com/2011/11/24/an-electronic-eye-on-hospital-hand-washing/?_php=true&_type=blogs&_r=2.

Ross, L., Greene, D., & House, P. (1977). The "false consensus effect": An egocentric bias in social perception and attribution processes. *Journal of Experimental Social Psychology, 13*, 279–301.

Shroyer, J. F., & Weimar, W. H. (2010). Comparative analysis of human gait while wearing thong-style flip-flops versus sneakers. *Journal of the American Podiatric Medical Association, 100*(4), 251–257.

Smith, M. J., Ellenberg, S. S., Bell, L. M., Rubin, D. M. (2008). Media coverage of the measles-mumps-rubella vaccine and autism controversy and its relationship to MMR immunization rates in the United States. *Pediatrics, 121*, 836–843.

Soares, S. C., Lindström, B., Esteves, F., & Öhman, A. (2014). The hidden snake in the grass: Superior detection of snakes in challenging attentional conditions. *PLoS one, 9*(12): e114724. https://doi.org/10.1371/journal.pone.0114724

University College London. (2015). Our brain's response to others' good news depends on empathy. *ScienceDaily*, 7 October 2015. www.sciencedaily.com/releases/2015/10/151007111005.htm.

Wakefield, A. J., Murch, S. H., Anthony, A., Linnell, J., Casson, D. M., Malik, M., Berelowitz, M., Dhillon, A. P., Thomson, M. A., Harvey, P., Valentine, A., Davies, S. E., … & Walker-Smith, J. A. (1998). RETRACTED: Ileal-lymphoid-nodular hyperplasia, non-specific colitis, and pervasive developmental disorder in children. *The Lancet, 351*(9103), 637–641.

Watson, J. B., & Rayner, R. (1920). Conditioned emotional reactions. *Journal of Experimental Psychology, 31*, 1–14.

Floy Washburn, M. (1908). Scientific books: The animal mind. *Science, 28*, 275–276.

Chapter 2

Alamri, A., Ughratdar, I., Samuel, M., & Ashkan, K. (2015). Deep brain stimulation of the subthalamic nucleus in Parkinson's disease 2003–2013: Where are we another 10 years on? *British Journal of Neurosurgery, 29*(3), 319–328. doi: 10.3109/02688697.2014.997669

Allen, J. S. (2009). *The lives of the brain: Human evolution and the organ of mind*: Harvard University Press.

Bang Henriksen, M., Johnsen, E., Sunde, N., Vase, A., Gjelstrup, M., & Østergaard, K. (2016). Surviving 10 years with deep brain stimulation for Parkinson's disease–a follow-up of 79 patients. *European Journal of Neurology, 23*(1), 53–61.

Becker, B., Wagner, D., Koester, P., Bender, K., Kabbasch, C., Gouzoulis-Mayfrank, E., & Daumann, J. (2012). Memory-related hippocampal functioning in ecstasy and amphetamine users. *Psychopharmacology, 225*(4), 923–934.

Bumaschny, V. F., Yamashita, M., Casas-Cordero, R., Otero-Corchón, V., de Souza, F. S. J., Rubinstein, M., & Low, M. J. (2012). Obesity-programmed mice are rescued by early genetic intervention. *The Journal of Clinical Investigation, 122*(11), 4203–4212. doi: 10.1172/JCI62543

Bunge, S. A., & Kahn, I. (2009). Cognition: An overview of neuroimaging techniques. *Encyclopedia of Neuroscience, 2*, 1063–1067.

Burle, B., Spieser, L., Roger, C., Casini, L., Hasbroucq, T., & Vidal, F. (2015). Spatial and temporal resolutions of EEG: Is it really black and white? A scalp current density view. *International Journal of Psychophysiology, 97*(3), 210–220. doi: http://dx.doi.org/10.1016/j.ijpsycho.2015.05.004

Cachofeiro, V., & Lahera, V. (2014). The endocrine and cardiovascular systems: A close liaison. *Hormone Molecular Biology and Clinical Investigation, 18*(1–3), 1–2.

Carlson, J. M., Reinke, K. S., & Habib, R. (2009). A left amygdala mediated network for rapid orienting to masked fearful faces. *Neuropsychologia, 47*(5), 1386–1389.

Caroni, P., Donato, F., & Muller, D. (2012). Structural plasticity upon learning: Regulation and functions. *Nature Reviews Neuroscience, 13*(7), 478–490.

Chan, A. K., McGovern, R. A., Brown, L. T., & et al. (2014). Disparities in access to deep brain stimulation surgery for Parkinson's disease: Interaction between African American race and Medicaid use. *JAMA Neurology, 71*(3), 291–299. doi: 10.1001/jamaneurol.2013.5798

Chandran, S., Krishnan, S., Rao, R. M., Sarma, S. G., Sarma, P. S., & Kishore, A. (2014). Gender influence on selection and outcome of deep brain stimulation for Parkinson's disease. *Annals of Indian Academy of Neurology, 17*(1), 66–70. doi: 10.4103/0972-2327.128557

Citri, A., & Malenka, R. C. (2007). Synaptic plasticity: Multiple forms, functions, and mechanisms. *Neuropsychopharmacology, 33*(1), 18–41.

Cleary, D. R., Ozpinar, A., Raslan, A. M., & Ko, A. L. (2015). Deep brain stimulation for psychiatric disorders: Where we are now. *Neurosurgical Focus, 38*(6), 1–24.

Cohen, S., Janicki-Deverts, D., Doyle, W. J., Miller, G. E., Frank, E., Rabin, B. S., & Turner, R. B. (2012). Chronic stress, glucocorticoid receptor resistance, inflammation, and disease risk. *Proceedings of the National Academy of Sciences, 109*(16), 5995–5999.

Davis, M. (1992). The role of the amygdala in fear and anxiety. *Annual Review of Neuroscience, 15*(1), 353–375.

Dazzan, P., Soulsby, B., Mechelli, A., Wood, S. J., Velakoulis, D., Phillips, L. J., … Murray, R. M. (2012). Volumetric abnormalities predating the onset of schizophrenia and affective psychoses: An MRI study in subjects at ultrahigh risk of psychosis. *Schizophrenia Bulletin, 38*(5), 1083–1091.

den Hollander, B., Schouw, M., Groot, P., Huisman, H., Caan, M., Barkhof, F., & Reneman, L. (2012). Preliminary evidence of hippocampal damage in chronic users of ecstasy. *Journal of Neurology, Neurosurgery & Psychiatry, 83*(1), 83–85.

Denys, D., Mantione, M., Figee, M., & et al. (2010). Deep brain stimulation of the nucleus accumbens for treatment-refractory obsessive-compulsive disorder. *Archives of General Psychiatry, 67*(10), 1061–1068. doi: 10.1001/archgenpsychiatry.2010.122

Dietz, M. J., Friston, K. J., Mattingley, J. B., Roepstorff, A., & Garrido, M. I. (2014). Effective connectivity reveals right-hemisphere dominance in audiospatial perception: implications for models of spatial neglect. *The Journal of Neuroscience, 34*(14), 5003–5011.

Eisch, A. J., & Petrik, D. (2012). Depression and hippocampal neurogenesis: A road to remission? *Science, 338*(6103), 72–75.

Elisevich, K., Shukla, N., Moran, J. E., Smith, B., Schultz, L., Mason, K., … Bowyer, S. M. (2011). An assessment of MEG coherence imaging in the study of temporal lobe epilepsy. *Epilepsia, 52*(6), 1110–1119.

Epel, E., Lapidus, R., McEwen, B., & Brownell, K. (2001). Stress may add bite to appetite in women: A laboratory study of stress-induced cortisol and eating behavior. *Psychoneuroendocrinology, 26*(1), 37–49.

Eriksson, P. S., Perfilieva, E., Björk-Eriksson, T., Alborn, A.-M., Nordborg, C., Peterson, D. A., & Gage, F. H. (1998). Neurogenesis in the adult human hippocampus. *Nature Medicine, 4*(11), 1313–1317.

Euston, D. R., Gruber, A. J., & McNaughton, B. L. (2012). The role of medial prefrontal cortex in memory and decision making. *Neuron, 76*(6), 1057–1070.

Farmaki, C., Sakkalis, V., Gjini, K., Boutros, N. N., & Zouridakis, G. (2015). Assessment of sensory gating deficit in schizophrenia using a wavelet transform methodology on auditory paired-click evoked potentials. *Modern Electroencephalographic Assessment Techniques* (pp. 205–229): Springer.

Feil, R., & Fraga, M. F. (2012). Epigenetics and the environment: Emerging patterns and implications. *Nature Reviews Genetics, 13*(2), 97–109.

Fenoy, A. J., Schulz, P., Selvaraj, S., Burrows, C., Spiker, D., Cao, B., … Soares, J. (2016). Deep brain stimulation of the medial forebrain bundle: Distinctive responses in resistant depression. *Journal of Affective Disorders, 203*, 143–151. doi: http://dx.doi.org/10.1016/j.jad.2016.05.064

Fitzpatrick, L. E., & Crowe, S. F. (2013). Cognitive and emotional deficits in chronic alcoholics: A role for the cerebellum? *The Cerebellum, 12*(4), 520–533.

Foss, B., Sæterdal, L. R., Nordgård, O., & Dyrstad, S. M. (2014). Exercise can alter cortisol responses in obese. *Journal of Exercise Physiologyonline, 17*(1), 67–77.

Fothergill, E., Guo, J., Howard, L., Kerns, J. C., Knuth, N. D., Brychta, R., … Hall, K. D. (2016). Persistent metabolic adaptation 6 years after "The Biggest Loser" competition. *Obesity, 24*(8), 1612–1619.

Galic, S., Oakhill, J. S., & Steinberg, G. R. (2010). Adipose tissue as an endocrine organ. *Molecular and Cellular Endocrinology, 316*(2), 129–139.

Gazzaniga, M. S. (2005). Forty-five years of split-brain research and still going strong. *Nature Reviews Neuroscience, 6*(8), 653–659.

Glasser, M. F., Coalson, T. S., Robinson, E. C., Hacker, C. D., Harwell, J., Yacoub, E., … Van Essen, D. C. (2016). A multi-modal parcellation of human cerebral cortex. *Nature, advance online publication*. doi: 10.1038/nature18933

Grant, J. E., Odlaug, B. L., & Chamberlain, S. R. (2016). Long-term deep-brain stimulation treatment for obsessive-compulsive disorder. *The Journal of Clinical Psychiatry, 77*(1), 132–133.

Grill, H. J., & Hayes, M. R. (2012). Hindbrain neurons as an essential hub in the neuroanatomically distributed control of energy balance. *Cell Metabolism, 16*(3), 296–309.

Halpern, C. H., Wolf, J. A., Bale, T. L., Stunkard, A. J., Danish, S. F., Grossman, M., … Baltuch, G. H. (2008).

Deep brain stimulation in the treatment of obesity. *Journal of Neurosurgery, 109*(4), 625–634.

Hamberg, K., & Hariz, G.M. (2014). The decision-making process leading to deep brain stimulation in men and women with Parkinson's disease—An interview study. *BMC Neurology, 14*(1), 1–10. doi: 10.1186/1471-2377-14-89

Heppner, F. L., Ransohoff, R. M., & Becher, B. (2015). Immune attack: The role of inflammation in Alzheimer disease. *Nature Reviews Neuroscience, 16*(6), 358–372.

Hickey, P., & Stacy, M. (2016). Deep brain stimulation: A paradigm shifting approach to treat Parkinson's disease. *Frontiers in Neuroscience, 10*(173), 1–11. doi: 10.3389/fnins.2016.00173

Hoebel, B. G., & Teitelbaum, P. (1962). Hypothalamic control of feeding and self-stimulation. *Science, 135*(3501), 375–377.

Holland, P. C., & Gallagher, M. (2004). Amygdala–frontal interactions and reward expectancy. *Current Opinion in Neurobiology, 14*(2), 148–155.

Holtzheimer, P. E., Kelley, M. E., Gross, R. E., Filkowski, M. M., Garlow, S. J., Barrocas, A., … Chismar, R. (2012). Subcallosal cingulate deep brain stimulation for treatment-resistant unipolar and bipolar depression. *Archives of General Psychiatry, 69*(2), 150–158.

Indersmitten, T., & Gur, R. C. (2003). Emotion processing in chimeric faces: Hemispheric asymmetries in expression and recognition of emotions. *The Journal of Neuroscience, 23*(9), 3820–3825.

Jin, Y., & Phillips, B. (2014). A pilot study of the use of EEG-based synchronized Transcranial Magnetic Stimulation (TMS) for treatment of major depression. *BMC Psychiatry, 14*(1), 1–13.

Kadis, D. S., Pang, E. W., Mills, T., Taylor, M. J., McAndrews, M. P., & Smith, M. L. (2011). Characterizing the normal developmental trajectory of expressive language lateralization using magnetoencephalography. *Journal of the International Neuropsychological Society, 17*(05), 896–904.

Kato, Y., Muramatsu, T., Kato, M., Shibukawa, Y., Shintani, M., & Mimura, M. (2011). Magnetoencephalography study of right parietal lobe dysfunction of the evoked mirror neuron system in antipsychotic-free schizophrenia. *PLoS One, 6*(11), e28087.

Kendler, K., Ohlsson, H., Sundquist, K., & Sundquist, J. (2015). The causes of parent–offspring transmission of drug abuse: A Swedish population-based study. *Psychological Medicine, 45*(1), 87–95.

Kennedy, S. H., Giacobbe, P., Rizvi, S. J., Placenza, F. M., Nishikawa, Y., Mayberg, H. S., & Lozano, A. M. (2011). Deep brain stimulation for treatment-resistant depression: Follow-up after 3 to 6 years. *American Journal of Psychiatry, 168*, 502–510.

Knecht, S., Dräger, B., Deppe, M., Bobe, L., Lohmann, H., Flöel, A., … Henningsen, H. (2000). Handedness and hemispheric language dominance in healthy humans. *Brain, 123*(12), 2512–2518.

Kocher, K. E., Meurer, W. J., Fazel, R., Scott, P. A., Krumholz, H. M., & Nallamothu, B. K. (2011). National trends in use of computed tomography in the emergency department. *Annals of Emergency Medicine, 58*(5), 452–462. e453.

Kotz, S. A., Kalberlah, C., Bahlmann, J., Friederici, A. D., & Haynes, J. D. (2012). Predicting vocal emotion expressions from the human brain. *Human Brain Mapping, 34*(8), 1971–1981.

Kuhn, J., Möller, M., Treppmann, J., Bartsch, C., Lenartz, D., Gruendler, T., … Klosterkötter, J. (2014). Deep brain stimulation of the nucleus accumbens and its usefulness in severe opioid addiction. *Molecular Psychiatry, 19*(2), 145–152.

LeDoux, J. (2007). The amygdala. *Current Biology, 17*(20), R868–R874.

Lemke, M. R., Brecht, H. M., Koester, J., Kraus, P. H., & Reichmann, H. (2005). Anhedonia, depression, and motor functioning in Parkinson's disease during treatment with pramipexole. *The Journal of Neuropsychiatry and Clinical Neurosciences, 17*(2), 214–220.

Light, G. A., Geyer, M. A., Clementz, B. A., Cadenhead, K. S., & Braff, D. L. (2000). Normal P50 suppression in schizophrenia patients treated with atypical antipsychotic medications. *American Journal of Psychiatry, 157*(5), 767–771. doi:10.1176/appi.ajp.157.5.767

Light, G. A., Swerdlow, N. R., Thomas, M. L., Calkins, M. E., Green, M. F., Greenwood, T. A., … Nuechterlein, K. H. (2015). Validation of mismatch negativity and P3a for use in multi-site studies of schizophrenia: Characterization of demographic, clinical, cognitive, and functional correlates in COGS-2. *Schizophrenia Research, 163*(0), 63–72.

Lipton, M. L., Kim, N., Zimmerman, M. E., Kim, M., Stewart, W. F., Branch, C. A., & Lipton, R. B. (2013). Soccer heading is associated with white matter microstructural and cognitive abnormalities. *Radiology, 268*(3), 850–857.

Loos, R. J. (2012). Genetic determinants of common obesity and their value in prediction. *Best Practice & Research Clinical Endocrinology & Metabolism, 26*(2), 211–226.

Lord, S., Lei, W., Craft, P., Cawson, J., Morris, I., Walleser, S., … Houssami, N. (2007). A systematic review of the effectiveness of magnetic resonance imaging (MRI) as an addition to mammography and ultrasound in screening young women at high risk of breast cancer. *European Journal of Cancer, 43*(13), 1905–1917.

MacLean, P. S., Bergouignan, A., Cornier, M.A., & Jackman, M. R. (2011). Biology's response to dieting: the impetus for weight regain. *American Journal of Physiology: Regulatory, Integrative and Comparative Physiology, 301*(3), R581–R600.

Macmillan, M. (2000). Restoring Phineas Gage: A 150th retrospective. *Journal of the History of the Neurosciences, 9*(1), 46–66.

Maguire, E. A., Gadian, D. G., Johnsrude, I. S., Good, C. D., Ashburner, J., Frackowiak, R. S., & Frith, C. D. (2000). Navigation-related structural change in the hippocampi of taxi drivers. *Proceedings of the National Academy of Sciences, 97*(8), 4398–4403.

Maguire, E. A., Woollett, K., & Spiers, H. J. (2006). London taxi drivers and bus drivers: A structural MRI and neuropsychological analysis. *Hippocampus, 16*(12), 1091–1101.

Mahar, I., Bambico, F. R., Mechawar, N., & Nobrega, J. N. (2014). Stress, serotonin, and hippocampal neurogenesis in relation to depression and antidepressant effects. *Neuroscience & Biobehavioral Reviews, 38*, 173–192.

Maher, M. E., Hutchison, M., Cusimano, M., Comper, P., & Schweizer, T. A. (2014). Concussions and heading in soccer: A review of the evidence of incidence, mechanisms, biomarkers and neurocognitive outcomes. *Brain Injury, 28*(3), 271–285.

Manzhulo, I., Ogurtsova, O., Dyuizen, I., & Lamash, N. (2013). The specific response of neurons and glial cells of the ventromedial reticular formation in the rat brainstem to acute pain. *Neurochemical Journal, 7*(1), 62–68.

Mayberg, H. S., Riva-Posse, P., & Crowell, A. L. (2016). Deep brain stimulation for depression: Keeping an eye on a moving target. *JAMA Psychiatry, 73*(5), 439–440. doi: 10.1001/jamapsychiatry.2016.0173

Mazzio, E. A., & Soliman, K. F. (2012). Basic concepts of epigenetics: Impact of environmental signals on gene expression. *Epigenetics, 7*(2), 119–130.

McGown, C., Birerdinc, A., & Younossi, Z. M. (2014). Adipose tissue as an endocrine organ. *Clinics in Liver Disease, 18*(1), 41–58.

Megreya, A. M., & Havard, C. (2011). Left face matching bias: Right hemisphere dominance or scanning habits? *Laterality, 16*(1), 75–92.

Mendez, I., Viñuela, A., Astradsson, A., Mukhida, K., Hallett, P., Robertson, H., … Trojanowski, J. Q. (2008). Dopamine neurons implanted into people with Parkinson's disease survive without pathology for 14 years. *Nature Medicine, 14*(5), 507–509.

Miller, E. K., & Cohen, J. D. (2001). An integrative theory of prefrontal cortex function. *Annual Review of Neuroscience, 24*(1), 167–202.

Moon, Hyo Y., Becke, A., Berron, D., Becker, B., Sah, N., Benoni, G., … van Praag, H. (2016). Running-induced systemic cathepsin B secretion is associated with memory function. *Cell Metabolism, 24*(2), 332–340. doi: 10.1016/j.cmet.2016.05.025

Moreines, J. L., McClintock, S. M., Kelley, M. E., Holtzheimer, P. E., & Mayberg, H. S. (2014). Neuropsychological function before and after subcallosal cingulate deep brain stimulation in patients with treatment-resistant depression. *Depression and Anxiety, 31*(8), 690–698. doi: 10.1002/da.22263

National Spinal Cord Injury Center. (2012). Fact Sheet: Recent Trends in Causes of SCI. Retrieved February 22, 2015, from https://www.nscisc.uab.edu/PublicDocuments/fact_sheets/Recent%20trends%20in%20causes%20of%20SCI.pdf

National Spinal Cord Injury Statistical Center. (2016). *Spinal cord injury facts and figures at a glance.* Birmingham, AL: University of Albama at Birminham.

Norman, A. W. (2008). From vitamin D to hormone D: Fundamentals of the vitamin D endocrine system essential for good health. *The American Journal of Clinical Nutrition, 88*(2), 491S–499S.

Nuthall, G. (2007). *The hidden lives of learners.* Wellington: New Zealand Council for Educational Research Press.

O'Driscoll, K., & Leach, J. P. (1998). "No longer Gage": An iron bar through the head. *BMJ, 317*(7174), 1673–1674.

Öhman, A. (2005). The role of the amygdala in human fear: Automatic detection of threat. *Psychoneuroendocrinology, 30*(10), 953–958.

Olds, J., & Milner, P. (1954). Positive reinforcement produced by electrical stimulation of septal area and other regions of rat brain. *Journal of Comparative and Physiological Psychology, 47*(6), 419–427.

Patuzzo, S., & Manganotti, P. (2014). Deep brain stimulation in persistent vegetative states: Ethical issues governing decision making. *Behavioural Neurology, 2014*, 1–6.

Paulin, M. G. (1993). The role of the cerebellum in motor control and perception. *Brain Behavior and Evolution, 41*, 39–39.

Pedersen, N. L., Plomin, R., McClearn, G. E., & Friberg, L. (1988). Neuroticism, extraversion, and related traits in adult twins reared apart and reared together. *Journal of Personality and Social Psychology, 55*(6), 950–957. doi: 10.1037/0022-3514.55.6.950

Pennington, B. F. (2009). How neuropsychology informs our understanding of developmental disorders. *Journal of Child Psychology and Psychiatry, 50*(1–2), 72–78.

Perry, R., Rosen, H., Kramer, J., Beer, J., Levenson, R., & Miller, B. (2001). Hemispheric dominance for emotions, empathy and social behaviour: Evidence from right and left handers with frontotemporal dementia. *Neurocase, 7*(2), 145–160.

Petrik, D., Lagace, D. C., & Eisch, A. J. (2012). The neurogenesis hypothesis of affective and anxiety disorders: Are we mistaking the scaffolding for the building? *Neuropharmacology, 62*(1), 21–34.

Puigdemont, D., Portella, M. J., Pérez-Egea, R., Molet, J., Gironell, A., de Diego-Adeliño, J., … Pérez, V. (2015). A randomized double-blind crossover trial of deep brain stimulation of the subcallosal cingulate gyrus in patients with treatment-resistant depression: A pilot study of relapse prevention. *Journal of Psychiatry and Neuroscience 40*(4), 224–231. doi: 10.1503/jpn.130295

Raine, A. (2001). Psychopathy, violence, and brain imaging. *Violence and Psychopathy* (pp. 35–55): Springer.

Roberts, C. J., Campbell, I. C., & Troop, N. (2014). Increases in weight during chronic stress are partially associated with a switch in food choice towards increased carbohydrate and saturated fat intake. *European Eating Disorders Review, 22*(1), 77–82.

Roser, M. E., Fiser, J., Aslin, R. N., & Gazzaniga, M. S. (2011). Right hemisphere dominance in visual statistical learning. *Journal of Cognitive Neuroscience, 23*(5), 1088–1099.

Ross, E. D., & Monnot, M. (2008). Neurology of affective prosody and its functional–anatomic organization in right hemisphere. *Brain and Language, 104*(1), 51–74.

Rourke, B. P. (2008). Is neuropsychology a psychosocial science? *Journal of Clinical and Experimental Neuropsychology, 30*(6), 691–699.

Rubenzer, S. J. (2008). The Standardized Field Sobriety Tests: A review of scientific and legal issues. *Law and Human Behavior, 32*(4), 293–313.

Sabelström, H., Stenudd, M., & Frisén, J. (2013). Neural stem cells in the adult spinal cord. *Experimental Neurology, 260*, 44–49.

Sahay, A., Scobie, K. N., Hill, A. S., O'Carroll, C. M., Kheirbek, M. A., Burghardt, N. S., ... Hen, R. (2011). Increasing adult hippocampal neurogenesis is sufficient to improve pattern separation. *Nature, 472*(7344), 466–470.

Sangal, R. B., & Sangal, J. M. (2014). Use of EEG Beta-1 power and theta/beta ratio over Broca's Area to confirm diagnosis of attention deficit/hyperactivity disorder in children. *Clinical EEG and Neuroscience*, 1550059414527284.

Sato, W., & Aoki, S. (2006). Right hemispheric dominance in processing of unconscious negative emotion. *Brain and Cognition, 62*(3), 261–266.

Shen, H. (2014). Neuroscience: Tuning the brain. *Nature, 507*(7492), 290–292. doi:10.1038/507290a

Sironi, V. A. (2011). Origin and evolution of deep brain stimulation. *Frontiers in Integrative Neuroscience, 5*(42), 1–5. doi: 10.3389/fnint.2011.00042

Strick, P. L., Dum, R. P., & Fiez, J. A. (2009). Cerebellum and nonmotor function. *Annual Review of Neuroscience, 32*, 413–434.

Szaflarski, J. P., Binder, J. R., Possing, E. T., McKiernan, K. A., Ward, B. D., & Hammeke, T. A. (2002). Language lateralization in left-handed and ambidextrous people fMRI data. *Neurology, 59*(2), 238–244.

Szaflarski, J. P., Rajagopal, A., Altaye, M., Byars, A. W., Jacola, L., Schmithorst, V. J., ... Holland, S. K. (2012). Left-handedness and language lateralization in children. *Brain Research, 1433*, 85–97.

Takeuchi, T., Duszkiewicz, A. J., & Morris, R. G. (2013). The synaptic plasticity and memory hypothesis: Encoding, storage and persistence. *Philosophical Transactions of the Royal Society B: Biological Sciences, 369*(1633), 1–14.

Tremblay, A., & Chaput, J.-P. (2009). Adaptive reduction in thermogenesis and resistance to lose fat in obese men. *British Journal of Nutrition, 102*(04), 488–492. doi:10.1017/S0007114508207245

van Praag, H., Christie, B. R., Sejnowski, T. J., & Gage, F. H. (1999). Running enhances neurogenesis, learning, and long-term potentiation in mice. *Proceedings of the National Academy of Sciences, 96*(23), 13427–13431.

van Praag, H., Schinder, A. F., Christie, B. R., Toni, N., Palmer, T. D., & Gage, F. H. (2002). Functional neurogenesis in the adult hippocampus. *Nature, 415*(6875), 1030–1034.

Verhulst, B., Neale, M., & Kendler, K. (2015). The heritability of alcohol use disorders: A meta-analysis of twin and adoption studies. *Psychological Medicine, 45*(5), 1061–1072.

Verkhratsky, A., Zorec, R., Rodríguez, J. J., & Parpura, V. (2016). Astroglia dynamics in ageing and Alzheimer's disease. *Current Opinion in Pharmacology, 26*, 74–79.

Walsh, F. (2014). Paralyzed man walks again after cell transplant. Retrieved March 4, 2015, from http://www.bbc.com/news/health-29645760

Wan, C. Y., & Schlaug, G. (2010). Music making as a tool for promoting brain plasticity across the life span. *The Neuroscientist: A Review Journal Bringing Neurobiology, Neurology and Psychiatry, 16*(5), 566–577. doi: 10.1177/1073858410377805

Wildgruber, D., Hertrich, I., Riecker, A., Erb, M., Anders, S., Grodd, W., & Ackermann, H. (2004). Distinct frontal regions subserve evaluation of linguistic and emotional aspects of speech intonation. *Cerebral Cortex, 14*(12), 1384–1389.

Willis, A. W., Schootman, M., Kung, N., Wang, X.-Y., Perlmutter, J. S., & Racette, B. A. (2014). Disparities in deep brain stimulation surgery among insured elders with Parkinson's disease. *Neurology, 82*(2), 163–171.

Wolff, E. (2007). Dual lives of twins separated at birth. Retrieved March 30, 2015, from http://nypost.com/2007/09/23/dual-lives-of-twins-separated-at-birth/

Woodman, G. F. (2010). A brief introduction to the use of event-related potentials (ERPs) in studies of perception and attention. *Attention, Perception and Psychophysics, 72*(8), 2031–2046. doi: 10.3758/APP.72.8.2031

Xia, Q., & Grant, S. F. (2013). The genetics of human obesity. *Annals of the New York Academy of Sciences, 1281*(1), 178–190.

Yazdani, S. O., Pedram, M., Hafizi, M., Kabiri, M., Soleimani, M., Dehghan, M.-M., ... Hashemi, S. M. (2012). A comparison between neurally induced bone marrow derived mesenchymal stem cells and olfactory ensheathing glial cells to repair spinal cord injuries in rats. *Tissue and Cell, 44*(4), 205–213.

Young, W. (2014). Spinal cord regeneration. *Cell Transplantation, 23*(4–5), 573–611.

Yuan, Y., Chang, K., Taylor, J. N., & Mostow, J. (2014). *Toward unobtrusive measurement of reading comprehension using low-cost EEG.* Paper presented at the Proceedings of the Fourth International Conference on Learning Analytics and Knowledge.

Chapter 3

Allison, R. R. (2013). The electromagnetic spectrum: Current and future applications in oncology. *Future Oncology, 9*(5), 657–667.

Ardiel, E. L., & Rankin, C. H. (2010). The importance of touch in development. *Paediatrics & Child Health, 15*(3), 153–156.

Bartoshuk, L. M., & Snyder, D. J. (2013). *Taste: Neuroscience in the 21st Century* (pp. 781–813): Springer.

Basson, M. D., Bartoshuk, L. M., DiChello, S. Z., Panzini, L., Weiffenbach, J. M., & Duffy, V. B. (2005). Association between 6-n-propylthiouracil (PROP) bitterness and colonic neoplasms. *Digestive Diseases and Sciences, 50*(3), 483–489.

Bernat, E., Shevrin, H., & Snodgrass, M. (2001). Subliminal visual oddball stimuli evoke a P300 component. *Clinical Neurophysiology, 112*(1), 159–171.

Besnard, P. (2016). Lipids and obesity: Also a matter of taste? *Reviews in Endocrine and Metabolic Disorders, 17*(2) 1–12.

Boundy, E. O., Dastjerdi, R., Spiegelman, D., Fawzi, W. W., Missmer, S. A., Lieberman, E., ... Chan, G. J. (2016). Kangaroo mother care and neonatal outcomes: A meta-analysis. *Pediatrics, 137*(1), e20152238. doi: 10.1542/peds.2015-2238

Brand, G. (2006). Olfactory/trigeminal interactions in nasal chemoreception. *Neuroscience & Biobehavioral Reviews, 30*(7), 908–917.

Brown, P. K., & Wald, G. (1964). Visual pigments in single rods and cones of the human retina. *Science, 144*(3614), 45–52.

Bruner, J. S., & Minturn, A. L. (1955). Perceptual identification and perceptual organization. *The Journal of General Psychology, 53*(1), 21–28.

Burns, J. W., Nielson, W. R., Jensen, M. P., Heapy, A., Czlapinski, R., & Kerns, R. D. (2015). Specific and general therapeutic mechanisms in cognitive behavioral treatment of chronic pain. *Journal of Consulting and Clinical Psychology, 83*(1), 1–11.

Bushdid, C., Magnasco, M. O., Vosshall, L. B., & Keller, A. (2014). Humans can discriminate more than 1 trillion olfactory stimuli. *Science, 343*(6177), 1370–1372.

Busigny, T., Van Belle, G., Jemel, B., Hosein, A., Joubert, S., & Rossion, B. (2014). Face-specific impairment in holistic perception following focal lesion of the right anterior temporal lobe. *Neuropsychologia, 56*, 312–333.

Choi, M., Lee, W. M., & Yun, S. H. (2015). Intravital microscopic interrogation of peripheral taste sensation. *Scientific Reports, 5*(8661), 1–6.

Choo, A., Tong, X., Gromala, D., & Hollander, A. (2014). Virtual reality and mobius floe: Cognitive distraction as non-pharmacological analgesic for pain management *Games for Health 2014* (pp. 8–12): Springer.

Colletti, L., Mandalà, M., & Colletti, V. (2012). Cochlear implants in children younger than 6 months. *Otolaryngology—Head and Neck Surgery*. doi: 0194599812441572

Colletti, L., Mandalà, M., Zoccante, L., Shannon, R. V., & Colletti, V. (2011). Infants versus older children fitted with cochlear implants: Performance over 10 years. *International Journal of Pediatric Otorhinolaryngology, 75*(4), 504–509.

Collins, J. A., & Olson, I. R. (2014). Beyond the FFA: The role of the ventral anterior temporal lobes in face processing. *Neuropsychologia, 61*, 65–79.

Compton, W. M., Jones, C. M., & Baldwin, G. T. (2016). Relationship between nonmedical prescription-opioid use and heroin use. *New England Journal of Medicine, 374*(2), 154–163. doi: 10.1056/NEJMra1508490

Cone, B., Dorn, P., Konrad-Martin, D., Lister, J., Ortiz, C., & Schairer, K. (2015). Ototoxic medications. Retrieved April 23, 2015, from http://www.asha.org/public/hearing/Ototoxic-Medications/

Daniel, E. (2007). Noise and hearing loss: A review. *Journal of School Health, 77*(5), 225–231.

Dart, R. C., Surratt, H. L., Cicero, T. J., Parrino, M. W., Severtson, S. G., Bucher-Bartelson, B., & Green, J. L. (2015). Trends in opioid analgesic abuse and mortality in the United States. *New England Journal of Medicine, 372*(3), 241–248. doi:10.1056/NEJMsa1406143

Dawood, H., Dawood, H., & Guo, P. (2014). Removal of high-intensity impulse noise by Weber's Law noise identifier. *Pattern Recognition Letters, 49*, 121–130.

de Lange, C. (2013). Hidden talent: What's your superpower? *New Scientist, 218*(2915), 40–45.

De Valois, R. L. (1960). Color vision mechanisms in the monkey. *The Journal of General Physiology, 43*(6), 115–128.

De Valois, R. L., Cottaris, N. P., Elfar, S. D., Mahon, L. E., & Wilson, J. A. (2000). Some transformations of color information from lateral geniculate nucleus to striate cortex. *Proceedings of the National Academy of Sciences, 97*(9), 4997–5002.

Deeb, S. S., & Motulsky, A. G. (2011). Red-green color vision defects. In R. A. Pagon, T. Bird, D, C. R. Dolan, K. Stephens, & M. P. Adam (Eds.), GeneReviews. Seattle, WA: University of Washington.

Deregowski, J. B. (1969). Perception of the two-pronged trident by two-and three-dimensional perceivers. *Journal of Experimental Psychology, 82*(1), 9–13.

Dinehart, M., Hayes, J., Bartoshuk, L., Lanier, S., & Duffy, V. (2006). Bitter taste markers explain variability in vegetable sweetness, bitterness, and intake. *Physiology and Behavior, 87*(2), 304–313.

Doty, R. L., & Kamath, V. (2014). The influences of age on olfaction: A review. *Frontiers in Psychology, 5*(20). doi: 10.3389/fpsyg.2014.00020

Dowell, D., Haegerich, T. M., & Chou, R. (2016). CDC guideline for prescribing opioids for chronic pain—United States, 2016. *JAMA, 315*(15), 1624–1645. doi: 10.1001/jama.2016.1464

Dubin, A. E., & Patapoutian, A. (2010). Nociceptors: The sensors of the pain pathway. *The Journal of Clinical Investigation, 120*(11), 3760–3772. doi: 10.1172/JCI42843

Duffy, V. B., & Bartoshuk, L. M. (2000). Food acceptance and genetic variation in taste. *Journal of the American Dietetic Association, 100*(6), 647–655.

Duffy, V. B., Peterson, J. M., Dinehart, M. E., & Bartoshuk, L. M. (2003). Genetic and environmental variation in taste: Associations with sweet intensity, preference, and intake. *Topics in Clinical Nutrition, 18*(4), 209–220.

Eagleman, D. M. (2001). Visual illusions and neurobiology. *Nature Reviews Neuroscience, 2*(12), 920–926.

Ehde, D. M., Dillworth, T. M., & Turner, J. A. (2014). Cognitive-behavioral therapy for individuals with chronic pain: Efficacy, innovations, and directions for research. *American Psychologist, 69*(2), 153–166.

Field, T. (2015). Smell and taste dysfunction as early markers for neurodegenerative and neuropsychiatric diseases. *Journal of Alzheimers Disorders and Parkinsonism, 5*(186). doi: 10.4172/2161-0460.1000186

Fox, K. (2009). The smell report. *Social Issues Research Centre*, 1–33.

Galanter, E. (1962). *Contemporary Psychophysics*: Holt, Rinehart, Winston.

García-Garibay, O. B., & de Lafuente, V. (2015). The Müller-Lyer illusion as seen by an artificial neural network. *Frontiers in Computational Neuroscience, 9*, 21. doi: 10.3389/fncom.2015.00021

Garrett, B., Taverner, T., Masinde, W., Gromala, D., Shaw, C., & Negraeff, M. (2014). A rapid evidence assessment of immersive virtual reality as an adjunct therapy in acute pain management in clinical practice. *The Clinical Journal of Pain, 30*(12), 1089–1098.

Gatchel, R. J., Peng, Y. B., Peters, M. L., Fuchs, P. N., & Turk, D. C. (2007). The biopsychosocial approach to chronic pain: Scientific advances and future directions. *Psychological Bulletin, 133*(4), 581–624.

Gibson, E. J., & Walk, R. D. (1960). *The "visual cliff":* WH Freeman Company.

Goodale, M. A. (2013). Separate visual systems for perception and action: A framework for understanding cortical visual impairment. *Developmental Medicine and Child Neurology, 55*(s4), 9–12.

Gould, H. J. (2007). *Understanding pain: What it is, why it happens, and how it's managed.* St. Paul, MN: Demos Medical Publishing.

Goyal, M. K., Kuppermann, N., Cleary, S. D., Teach, S. J., & Chamberlain, J. M. (2015). Racial disparities in pain management of children with appendicitis in emergency departments. *JAMA Pediatrics, 169*(11), 996–1002. doi: 10.1001/jamapediatrics.2015.1915

Gregory, R. L. (1968). Perceptual illusions and brain models. *Proceedings of the Royal Society of London. Series B, Biological Sciences, 171*(1024), 279–296.

Gregory, R. L. (1997). Knowledge in perception and illusion. *Philosophical Transactions of the Royal Society of London. Series B: Biological Sciences, 352*(1358), 1121–1127.

Griffin, S. C., & Tsao, J. W. (2014). A mechanism-based classification of phantom limb pain. *Pain, 155*(11), 2236–2242.

Gustafsson, E., Levréro, F., Reby, D., & Mathevon, N. (2013). Fathers are just as good as mothers at recognizing the cries of their baby. *Nature Communications, 4,* 1–5.

Hannibal, K. E., & Bishop, M. D. (2014). Chronic stress, cortisol dysfunction, and pain: A psychoneuroendocrine rationale for stress management in pain rehabilitation. *Physical Therapy, 94*(12), 1816–1825.

Hardie, R. C., & Stavenga, D. G. (1989). *Facets of vision:* Springer-Verlag.

Harris, T. (2001). How hearing works. Retrieved April 22, 2015, from http://health.howstuffworks.com/mental-health/human-nature/perception/hearing.htm

He, M., Abdou, A., Ellwein, L. B., Naidoo, K. S., Sapkota, Y. D., Thulasiraj, R. D., … Congdon, N. G. (2014). Age-related prevalence and met need for correctable and uncorrectable near vision impairment in a multicountry study. *Ophthalmology, 121*(1), 417–422. doi: http://dx.doi.org/10.1016/j.ophtha.2013.06.051

Hearing Loss Association of America. (n.d.). Cochlear implants. Retrieved September 2, 2017, from http://www.hearingloss.org/content/cochlear-implants

Heath, M., Mulla, A., Holmes, S. A., & Smuskowitz, L. R. (2011). The visual coding of grip aperture shows an early but not late adherence to Weber's Law. *Neuroscience Letters, 490*(3), 200–204.

Hering, E. (1964). *Outlines of a theory of the light sense.* Cambridge, MA: Harvard University Press.

Herz, R. S. (2001). Ah sweet skunk! Why we like or dislike what we smell. *Cerebrum, 3*(4), 31–47.

Hoffman, H. G., Chambers, G. T., Meyer III, W. J., Arceneaux, L. L., Russell, W. J., Seibel, E. J., … Patterson, D. R. (2011). Virtual reality as an adjunctive non-pharmacologic analgesic for acute burn pain during medical procedures. *Annals of Behavioral Medicine, 41*(2), 183–191.

Honda, N., Ohgi, S., Wada, N., Loo, K. K., Higashimoto, Y., & Fukuda, K. (2013). Effect of therapeutic touch on brain activation of preterm infants in response to sensory punctate stimulus: A near-infrared spectroscopy-based study. *Archives of Disease in Childhood-Fetal and Neonatal Edition, 98,* F244–F248.

Howe, C. Q., & Purves, D. (2005). The Müller-Lyer illusion explained by the statistics of image–source relationships. *Proceedings of the National Academy of Sciences of the United States of America, 102*(4), 1234–1239.

Hurvich, L. M., & Jameson, D. (1957). An opponent-process theory of color vision. *Psychological Review,* (64, Part 1), 384–404.

Kamper, S. J., Apeldoorn, A. T., Chiarotto, A., Smeets, R. J. E. M., Ostelo, R. W. J. G., Guzman, J., & van Tulder, M. W. (2015). Multidisciplinary biopsychosocial rehabilitation for chronic low back pain: Cochrane systematic review and meta-analysis. *British Medical Journal, 350.* doi: 10.1136/bmj.h444

Kang, N. N., & Koo, J. (2012). Olfactory receptors in non-chemosensory tissues. *Biochemistry and Molecular Biology Reports, 45*(11), 612–622.

Karremans, J. C., Stroebe, W., & Claus, J. (2006). Beyond Vicary's fantasies: The impact of subliminal priming and brand choice. *Journal of Experimental Social Psychology, 42*(6), 792–798. doi: http://dx.doi.org/10.1016/j.jesp.2005.12.002

Kavšek, M., & Granrud, C. E. (2012). Children's and adults' size estimates at near and far distances: A test of the perceptual learning theory of size constancy development. *i-Perception, 3*(7), 459–466.

Kret, M. E., Roelofs, K., Stekelenburg, J. J., & de Gelder, B. (2013). Emotional signals from faces, bodies and scenes influence observers' face expressions, fixations and pupil-size. *Frontiers in Human Neuroscience, 7*(810). doi: 10.3389/fnhum.2013.00810

Ku, S.P., Tolias, A. S., Logothetis, N. K., & Goense, J. (2011). fMRI of the face-processing network in the ventral temporal lobe of awake and anesthetized macaques. *Neuron, 70*(2), 352–362.

Kujawa, S. G., & Liberman, M. C. (2015). Synaptopathy in the noise-exposed and aging cochlea: Primary neural degeneration in acquired sensorineural hearing loss. *Hearing Research, 330,* 1–9.

la Cour, P., & Petersen, M. (2015). Effects of mindfulness meditation on chronic pain: A randomized controlled trial. *Pain Medicine, 16*(4), 641–652.

Lan, G., Sartori, P., Neumann, S., Sourjik, V., & Tu, Y. (2012). The energy-speed-accuracy trade-off in sensory adaptation. *Nature Physics, 8*(5), 422–428.

Légal, J.B., Chappé, J., Coiffard, V., & Villard-Forest, A. (2012). Don't you know that you want to trust me? Subliminal goal priming and persuasion. *Journal of Experimental Social Psychology, 48*(1), 358–360.

Leopold, D. A. (2012). Primary visual cortex, awareness and blindsight. *Annual Review of Neuroscience, 35,* 91–109.

Lin, F. R., Niparko, J. K., & Ferrucci, L. (2011). Hearing loss prevalence in the United States. *Archives of Internal Medicine, 171*(20), 1851–1853.

Livingstone, M., & Hubel, D. (1988). Segregation of form, color, movement, and depth: Anatomy, physiology, and perception. *Science, 240*(4853), 740–749.

Luers, J. C., Hüttenbrink, K.B., Zahnert, T., Bornitz, M., & Beutner, D. (2013). Vibroplasty for mixed and conductive hearing loss. *Otology and Neurotology, 34*(6), 1005–1012.

Macmillan, N. A. (2002). Signal detection theory. In H. Pashler (Ed.), *Stevens' handbook of experimental psychology* (3rd ed., Vol. 4, pp. 43–90). New York, NY: John Wiley & Sons, Inc.

Mao, J. J., Palmer, C., Healy, K., Desai, K., & Amsterdam, J. (2011). Complementary and alternative medicine use among cancer survivors: A population-based study. *Journal of Cancer Survivorship: Research and Practice, 5*(1), 8–17. doi: 10.1007/s11764-010-0153-7

Masaoka, Y., Sugiyama, H., Katayama, A., Kashiwagi, M., & Homma, I. (2012). Slow breathing and emotions associated with odor-induced autobiographical memories. *Chemical Senses.* doi: 10.1093/chemse/bjr120

Masterson, E. A., Tak, S., Themann, C. L., Wall, D. K., Groenewold, M. R., Deddens, J. A., & Calvert, G. M. (2013). Prevalence of hearing loss in the United States by industry. *American Journal of Industrial Medicine, 56*(6), 670–681.

Meghani, S. H., Byun, E., & Gallagher, R. M. (2012). Time to take stock: A meta-analysis and systematic review of analgesic treatment disparities for pain in the United States. *Pain Medicine, 13*(2), 150–174. doi: 10.1111/j.1526-4637.2011.01310.x

Melzack, R. (1992). Phantom limbs. *Scientific American, 266*(4), 120–125.

Mendola, J. D., Dale, A. M., Fischl, B., Liu, A. K., & Tootell, R. B. (1999). The representation of illusory and real contours in human cortical visual areas revealed by functional magnetic resonance imaging. *The Journal of Neuroscience, 19*(19), 8560–8572.

Mennella, J. A., Spector, A. C., Reed, D. R., & Coldwell, S. E. (2013). The bad taste of medicines: Overview of basic research on bitter taste. *Clinical Therapeutics, 35*(8), 1225–1246.

Milner, A. D., & Goodale, M. A. (1995). *The visual brain in action* (Vol. 27): Oxford: Oxford University Press..

Moayedi, M., & Davis, K. D. (2013). Theories of pain: From specificity to gate control. *Journal of Neurophysiology, 109*(1), 5–12.

Möhring, W., Libertus, M. E., & Bertin, E. (2012). Speed discrimination in 6- and 10-month-old infants follows Weber's Law. *Journal of Experimental Child Psychology, 111*(3), 405–418.

Moore, B. C. (2012). *An introduction to the psychology of hearing.* United Kingdom: Emerald Group Publishing Limited.

Mulak, K. E., Best, C. T., Tyler, M. D., Kitamura, C., & Irwin, J. R. (2013). Development of phonological constancy: 19-month-olds, but not 15-month-olds, identify words in a non-native regional accent. *Child Development, 84*(6), 2064–2078.

Naik, K., & Pai, S. (2014). High frequency hearing loss in students used to ear phone music: A randomized trial of 1,000 students. *Indian Journal of Otology, 20*(1), 29–32.

Nasr, S., & Tootell, R. B. (2012). Role of fusiform and anterior temporal cortical areas in facial recognition. *Neuroimage, 63*(3), 1743–1753.

Neitz, J., & Neitz, M. (2008). Colour vision: The wonder of hue. *Current Biology, 18*(16), R700–R702.

Olsen, Y. (2016). The CDC guideline on opioid prescribing: Rising to the challenge. *JAMA, 315*(15), 1577–1579. doi: 10.1001/jama.2016.1910

Pienkowski, M., & Eggermont, J. J. (2012). Reversible long-term changes in auditory processing in mature auditory cortex in the absence of hearing loss induced by passive, moderate-level sound exposure. *Ear and Hearing, 33*(3), 305–314.

Rabinowitz, P. M. (2000). Noise-induced hearing loss. *American Family Physician, 61*(9), 2759–2760.

Racine, M., Tousignant-Laflamme, Y., Kloda, L. A., Dion, D., Dupuis, G., & Choinière, M. (2012a). A systematic literature review of 10 years of research on sex/gender and experimental pain perception–Part 1: Are there really differences between women and men? *Pain, 153*(3), 602–618.

Racine, M., Tousignant-Laflamme, Y., Kloda, L. A., Dion, D., Dupuis, G., & Choinière, M. (2012b). A systematic literature review of 10 years of research on sex/gender and pain perception–Part 2: Do biopsychosocial factors alter pain sensitivity differently in women and men? *Pain, 153*(3), 619–635.

Riley, J. L., Wade, J. B., Myers, C. D., Sheffield, D., Papas, R. K., & Price, D. D. (2002). Racial/ethnic differences in the experience of chronic pain. *Pain, 100*(3), 291–298.

Rosenstein, D., & Oster, H. (1988). Differential facial responses to four basic tastes in newborns. *Child Development, 59,* 1555–1568.

Roth, M. (2006). Some women may see 100 million colors, thanks to their genes. Retrieved May 5, 2015, from http://www.post-gazette.com/news/health/2006/09/13/Some-women-may-see-100-million-colors-thanks-to-their-genes/stories/200609130255

Running, C. A., Craig, B. A., & Mattes, R. D. (2015). Oleogustus: The unique taste of fat. *Chemical Senses, 40*(7), 507–516.

Running, C. A., & Mattes, R. D. (2016). A review of the evidence supporting the taste of non-esterified fatty acids in humans. *Journal of the American Oil Chemists' Society, 93,* 1–12.

Rutherford, W. (1886). A new theory of hearing. *Journal of Anatomy and Physiology, 21*(Pt 1), 166–168.

Schmid, M. C., & Maier, A. (2015). To see or not to see—Thalamo-cortical networks during blindsight and perceptual suppression. *Progress in Neurobiology, 126,* 36–48.

Segall, L., & Fink, E. (2011). Iris scans are the new school IDs. Retrieved April 17, 2015, from http://money.cnn.

com/2013/07/11/technology/security/iris-scanning-school/

Segall, M. H., Campbell, D. T., & Herskovits, M. J. (1963). Cultural differences in the perception of geometric illusions. *Science, 139*(3556), 769–771.

Sehgal, N., Manchikanti, L., & Smith, H. S. (2012). Prescription opioid abuse in chronic pain: A review of opioid abuse predictors and strategies to curb opioid abuse. *Pain Physician, 15,* ES67–ES92.

Sekiyama, K., Miyauchi, S., Imaruoka, T., Egusa, H., & Tashiro, T. (2000). Body image as a visuomotor transformation device revealed in adaptation to reversed vision. *Nature, 407*(6802), 374–377.

Sheffield, D., Biles, P. L., Orom, H., Maixner, W., & Sheps, D. S. (2000). Race and sex differences in cutaneous pain perception. *Psychosomatic Medicine, 62*(4), 517–523.

Sheth, B. R., Sharma, J., Rao, S. C., & Sur, M. (1996). Orientation maps of subjective contours in visual cortex. *Science, 274*(5295), 2110–2115.

Shimizu, M., Sperry, J. J., & Pelham, B. W. (2013). The effect of subliminal priming on sleep duration. *Journal of Applied Social Psychology, 43*(9), 1777–1783.

Shrestha, S., Schofield, P., & Devkota, R. (2013). A critical literature review on non-pharmacological approaches used by older people in chronic pain management. *Indian Journal of Gerontology, 27*(1), 135–161.

Singhal, A., Tien, Y.Y., & Hsia, R. Y. (2016). Racial-ethnic disparities in opioid prescriptions at emergency department visits for conditions commonly associated with prescription drug abuse. *PLoS ONE, 11*(8), e0159224. doi: 10.1371/journal.pone.0159224

Smarandescu, L., & Shimp, T. A. (2014). Drink Coca-Cola, eat popcorn, and choose powerade: testing the limits of subliminal persuasion. *Marketing Letters, 1*–12. doi: 10.1007/s11002-014-9294-1

Smith, P. K., & McCulloch, K. (2012). Subliminal perception. *Encyclopedia of Human Behavior, 5,* 551–557.

Solomon, J. H., & Hartmann, M. J. (2011). Radial distance determination in the rat vibrissal system and the effects of Weber's Law. *Philosophical Transactions of the Royal Society B: Biological Sciences, 366*(1581), 3049–3057.

Sovrano, V. A., da Pos, O., & Albertazzi, L. (2016). The Müller-Lyer illusion in the teleost fish Xenotoca eiseni. *Animal Cognition, 19*(1), 123–132. doi: 10.1007/s10071-015-0917-6

Sperdin, H. F., Spierer, L., Becker, R., Michel, C. M., & Landis, T. (2015). Submillisecond unmasked subliminal visual stimuli evoke electrical brain responses. *Human Brain Mapping, 36*(4), 1470–1483. doi: 10.1002/hbm.22716

Stoughton, C. M., & Conway, B. R. (2008). Neural basis for unique hues. *Current Biology, 18*(16), R698–R699. doi: http://dx.doi.org/10.1016/j.cub.2008.06.018

Sturgeon, J. A. (2014). Psychological therapies for the management of chronic pain. *Psychology Research and Behavior Management, 7,* 115–124.

Sullivan, R. M., Wilson, D. A., Ravel, N., & Mouly, A.-M. (2015). Olfactory memory networks: From emotional learning to social behaviors. *Frontiers in Behavioral Neuroscience, 9*(36), 1–4.

Szagun, G., & Stumper, B. (2012). Age or experience? The influence of age at implantation and social and linguistic environment on language development in children with cochlear implants. *Journal of Speech, Language, and Hearing Research, 55*(6), 1640–1654.

Tait, R. C., & Chibnall, J. T. (2014). Racial/ethnic disparities in the assessment and treatment of pain: Psychosocial perspectives. *American Psychologist, 69*(2), 131–141.

Terry, R., Perry, R., & Ernst, E. (2012). An overview of systematic reviews of complementary and alternative medicine for fibromyalgia. *Clinical Rheumatology, 31*(1), 55–66. doi: 10.1007/s10067-011-1783-5

Tobey, E. A., Thal, D., Niparko, J. K., Eisenberg, L. S., Quittner, A. L., & Wang, N. Y. (2013). Influence of implantation age on school-age language performance in pediatric cochlear implant users. *International Journal of Audiology, 52*(4), 219–229.

Trawalter, S., Hoffman, K. M., & Waytz, A. (2012). Racial bias in perceptions of others' pain. *PLoS ONE, 7*(11), e48546. doi: 10.1371/journal.pone.0048546

Van Wanrooij, M. M., & Van Opstal, A. J. (2004). Contribution of head shadow and pinna cues to chronic monaural sound localization. *The Journal of Neuroscience, 24*(17), 4163–4171.

Verhaert, N., Desloovere, C., & Wouters, J. (2013). Acoustic hearing implants for mixed hearing loss: A systematic review. *Otology and Neurotology, 34*(7), 1201–1209.

Verwijmeren, T., Karremans, J. C., Bernritter, S. F., Stroebe, W., & Wigboldus, D. H. (2013). Warning: You are being primed! The effect of a warning on the impact of subliminal ads. *Journal of Experimental Social Psychology, 49*(6), 1124–1129.

Verwijmeren, T., Karremans, J. C., Stroebe, W., & Wigboldus, D. H. (2011). The workings and limits of subliminal advertising: The role of habits. *Journal of Consumer Psychology, 21*(2), 206–213.

Vokey, J. R., & Read, J. D. (1985). Subliminal messages: Between the devil and the media. *American Psychologist, 40*(11), 1231.

Von Békésy, G. (1963). Hearing theories and complex sounds. *The Journal of the Acoustical Society of America, 35*(4), 588–601.

Von Békésy, G., & Wever, E. G. (1960). *Experiments in hearing* (Vol. 8): McGraw-Hill New York.

Von der Heydt, R., Peterhans, E., & Baumgartner, G. (1984). Illusory contours and cortical neuron responses. *Science, 224*(4654), 1260–1262.

Wandner, L. D., Scipio, C. D., Hirsh, A. T., Torres, C. A., & Robinson, M. E. (2012). The perception of pain in others: How gender, race, and age influence pain perceptions. *The Journal of Pain, 13*(3), 220–227. doi: 10.1016/j.jpain.2011.10.014

Wark, B., Lundstrom, B. N., & Fairhall, A. (2007). Sensory adaptation. *Current Opinion in Neurobiology, 17*(4), 423–429.

Wever, E. G. (1949). Theory of hearing. Oxford, England: Wiley.

WHO. (2015). Hearing loss due to recreational exposure to loud sounds: A review. World Health Organization.

Wiens, S. (2006). Subliminal emotion perception in brain imaging: Findings, issues, and recommendations. *Progress in Brain Research, 156,* 105–121.

Yang, H., He, B. R., & Hao, D. J. (2015). Biological roles of olfactory ensheathing cells in facilitating neural regeneration: A systematic review. *Molecular Neurobiology, 51,* 1–12.

Zeman, A., Obst, O., Brooks, K. R., & Rich, A. N. (2013). The Müller-Lyer illusion in a computational model of biological object recognition. *PLoS ONE, 8*(2), e56126. doi: 10.1371/journal.pone.0056126

Chapter 4

Agarwal, D. P., & Goedde, H. W. (1990). *Alcohol metabolism, alcohol intolerance, and alcoholism: Biochemical and pharmacogenetic approaches.* Berlin, Germany: Springer Science & Business Media.

Alavian, S. M., Mirahmadizadeh, A., Javanbakht, M., Keshtkaran, A., Heidari, A., Mashayekhi, A., ... Hadian, M. (2013). Effectiveness of methadone maintenance treatment in prevention of hepatitis C virus transmission among injecting drug users. *Hepatitis Monthly, 13*(8), E12411.

Alladin, A. (2012). Cognitive hypnotherapy for major depressive disorder. *American Journal of Clinical Hypnosis, 54*(4), 275–293. doi: 10.1080/00029157.2012.654527

Alladin, A., & Alibhai, A. (2007). Cognitive hypnotherapy for depression: An empirical investigation. *International Journal of Clinical and Experimental Hypnosis, 55*(2), 147–166. doi: 10.1080/00207140601177897

American Psychiatric Association. (2013). *Diagnostic and statistical manual of mental disorders, (DSM-5®).* Washington, DC: American Psychiatric Pub.

Arnsten, A. F. (2006). Stimulants: Therapeutic actions in ADHD. *Neuropsychopharmacology, 31*(11), 2376–2383.

Aron, A. R., Robbins, T. W., & Poldrack, R. A. (2014). Inhibition and the right inferior frontal cortex: One decade on. *Trends in Cognitive Sciences, 18*(4), 177–185.

Arons, B. (1992). A review of the cocktail party effect. *Journal of the American Voice I/O Society, 12*(7), 35–50.

Aserinsky, E., & Kleitman, N. (1953). Regularly occurring periods of eye motility, and concomitant phenomena, during sleep. *Science, 118*(3062), 273–274.

Baylor, G. W., & Cavallero, C. (2001). Memory sources associated with REM and NREM dream reports throughout the night: A new look at the data. *Sleep: Journal of Sleep Research & Sleep Medicine, 24,* 165–170.

Becklen, R., & Cervone, D. (1983). Selective looking and the noticing of unexpected events. *Memory & Cognition, 11*(6), 601–608.

Beevi, Z., Low, W. Y., & Hassan, J. (2016). Impact of hypnosis intervention in alleviating psychological and physical symptoms during pregnancy. *American Journal of Clinical Hypnosis, 58*(4), 368–382.

Behar, K. L., Rothman, D. L., Petersen, K. F., Hooten, M., Delaney, R., Petroff, O. A., ... Charney, D. S. (1999). Preliminary evidence of low cortical GABA levels in localized 1H-MR spectra of alcohol-dependent and hepatic encephalopathy patients. *American Journal of Psychiatry 156,* 952–954.

Behnaz, F., & Solhpour, A. (2016). To compare efficacy of hypnosis and intravenous sedation in controlling of important variables of vital signs and evaluate the patient anxiety before and after topical anesthesia in ophthalmic surgery. *Novelty in Biomedicine, 4*(3), 93–99.

Bergin, J. E., & Kendler, K. S. (2012). Common psychiatric disorders and caffeine use, tolerance, and withdrawal: an examination of shared genetic and environmental effects. *Twin Research and Human Genetics: The Official Journal of the International Society for Twin Studies, 15*(4), 473–482.

Besedovsky, L., Lange, T., & Born, J. (2012). Sleep and immune function. *Pflügers Archiv-European Journal of Physiology, 463*(1), 121–137.

Blum, K., Chen, A. L., Giordano, J., Borsten, J., Chen, T. J., Hauser, M., ... Barh, D. (2012). The addictive brain: All roads lead to dopamine. *Journal of Psychoactive Drugs, 44*(2), 134–143.

Bozarth, M. A., & Wise, R. A. (1985). Toxicity associated with long-term intravenous heroin and cocaine self-administration in the rat. *Jama, 254*(1), 81–83.

Bradberry, T. (2012). Caffeine: The silent killer of success. Retrieved June 23, 2015, from http://www.forbes.com/sites/travisbradberry/2012/08/21/caffeine-the-silent-killer-of-emotional-intelligence/

Brandt, S. A., Taverna, E. C., & Hallock, R. M. (2014). A survey of nonmedical use of tranquilizers, stimulants, and pain relievers among college students: Patterns of use among users and factors related to abstinence in non-users. *Drug and Alcohol Dependence, 143,* 272–276.

Bronkhorst, A. W. (2015). The cocktail-party problem revisited: Early processing and selection of multi-talker speech. *Attention, Perception, & Psychophysics, 77,* 1465–1487.

Brooks, P. L., & Peever, J. H. (2012). Identification of the transmitter and receptor mechanisms responsible for REM sleep paralysis. *The Journal of Neuroscience, 32*(29), 9785–9795.

Burkeman, O. (2015). Why can't the world's greatest minds solve the mystery of consciousness? Retrieved June 15, 2015, from http://www.theguardian.com/science/2015/jan/21/-sp-why-cant-worlds-greatest-minds-solve-mystery-consciousness

Cain, N., & Gradisar, M. (2010). Electronic media use and sleep in school-aged children and adolescents: A review. *Sleep Medicine, 11*(8), 735–742.

Cain, S. W., Silva, E. J., Chang, A.-M., Ronda, J. M., & Duffy, J. F. (2011). One night of sleep deprivation affects reaction time, but not interference or facilitation in a Stroop task. *Brain and Cognition, 76*(1), 37–42.

Caporro, M., Haneef, Z., Yeh, H. J., Lenartowicz, A., Buttinelli, C., Parvizi, J., & Stern, J. M. (2012). Functional MRI of sleep spindles and K-complexes. *Clinical Neurophysiology, 123*(2), 303–309.

Cappuccio, F. P., Cooper, D., D'Elia, L., Strazzullo, P., & Miller, M. A. (2011). Sleep duration predicts cardiovascular outcomes: A systematic review and meta-analysis of prospective studies. *European Heart Journal, 32*(12), 1484–1492.

Cardeña, E., Svensson, C., & Hejdström, F. (2013). Hypnotic tape intervention ameliorates stress: A randomized, control study. *International Journal of Clinical and Experimental Hypnosis, 61*(2), 125–145. doi: 10.1080/00207144.2013.753820

Cardeña, E., & Terhune, D. B. (2014). Hypnotizability, personality traits, and the propensity to experience alterations of consciousness. *Psychology of Consciousness: Theory, Research, and Practice, 1*(3), 292–307.

Carrier, L. M., Rosen, L. D., Cheever, N. A., & Lim, A. F. (2015). Causes, effects, and practicalities of everyday multitasking. *Developmental Review, 35*, 64–78.

Centers for Disease Control and Prevention (CDC). (2017). Health effects of cigarette smoking. (2017, May 15). Retrieved September 25, 2017, from https://www.cdc.gov/tobacco/data_statistics/fact_sheets/health_effects/effects_cig_smoking/

Cerdá, M., Wall, M., Keyes, K. M., Galea, S., & Hasin, D. (2012). Medical marijuana laws in 50 states: Investigating the relationship between state legalization of medical marijuana and marijuana use, abuse and dependence. *Drug and Alcohol Dependence, 120*(1), 22–27.

Chalmers, D. J. (1995). Facing up to the problem of consciousness. *Journal of Consciousness Studies, 2*(3), 200–219.

Chang, A.-M., Aeschbach, D., Duffy, J. F., & Czeisler, C. A. (2015). Evening use of light-emitting eReaders negatively affects sleep, circadian timing, and next-morning alertness. *Proceedings of the National Academy of Sciences, 112*(4), 1232–1237.

Chen, T.-T., Ko, C.-H., Chen, S.-T., Yen, C.-N., Su, P.-W., Hwang, T.-J., … Yen, C.-F. (2014). Severity of alprazolam dependence and associated features among long-term alprazolam users from psychiatric outpatient clinics in Taiwan. *Journal of the Formosan Medical Association, 114*, 1–8.

Cheng, G., Zeng, H., Leung, M., Zhang, H., Lau, B., Liu, Y., … So, K. (2013). Heroin abuse accelerates biological aging: A novel insight from telomerase and brain imaging interaction. *Translational Psychiatry, 3*(5), e260.

Chinchanachokchai, S., Duff, B. R., & Sar, S. (2015). The effect of multitasking on time perception, enjoyment, and ad evaluation. *Computers in Human Behavior, 45*, 185–191.

Cobb, N. K., & Abrams, D. B. (2014). The FDA, E-Cigarettes, and the demise of combusted tobacco. *New England Journal of Medicine, 371*(16), 1469–1471. doi:10.1056/NEJMp1408448

Cohen, M. A., Cavanagh, P., Chun, M. M., & Nakayama, K. (2012). The attentional requirements of consciousness. *Trends in Cognitive Sciences, 16*(8), 411–417.

Cohen, R. A., & Albers, E. H. (1991). Disruption of human circadian and cognitive regulation following a discrete hypothalamic lesion: A case study. *Neurology, 41*(5), 726–729.

Cojan, Y., Piguet, C., & Vuilleumier, P. (2015). What makes your brain suggestible? Hypnotizability is associated with differential brain activity during attention outside hypnosis. *Neuroimage, 117*, 367–374.

Coren, S. (1996). Daylight savings time and traffic accidents. *New England Journal of Medicine, 334*(14), 924–925.

Dauvilliers, Y., Arnulf, I., & Mignot, E. (2007). Narcolepsy with cataplexy. *The Lancet, 369*(9560), 499–511.

Daviaux, Y., Mignardot, J.-B., Cornu, C., & Deschamps, T. (2014). Effects of total sleep deprivation on the perception of action capabilities. *Experimental Brain Research, 232*(7), 2243–2253.

de Castro, J. M. (2002). The influence of heredity on self-reported sleep patterns in free-living humans. *Physiology & Behavior, 76*(4), 479–486.

De Coursey, P. J. (1960). Daily light sensitivity rhythm in a rodent. *Science, 131*(3392), 33–35.

De Gennaro, L., & Ferrara, M. (2003). Sleep spindles: An overview. *Sleep Medicine Reviews, 7*(5), 423–440.

DelRosso, L. M., Hoque, R., James, S., Gonzalez-Toledo, E., & Chesson Jr, A. L. (2014). Sleep-wake pattern following gunshot suprachiasmatic damage. *Journal of Clinical Sleep Medicine: JCSM: Official Publication of the American Academy of Sleep Medicine, 10*(4), 443–445.

Dement, W., & Wolpert, E. A. (1958). The relation of eye movements, body motility, and external stimuli to dream content. *Journal of Experimental Psychology, 55*(6), 543–553.

Deneau, G., Yanagita, T., & Seevers, M. (1969). Self-administration of psychoactive substances by the monkey. *Psychopharmacologia, 16*(1), 30–48.

Dettoni, J. L., Consolim-Colombo, F. M., Drager, L. F., Rubira, M. C., de Souza, S. B. P. C., Irigoyen, M. C., … Moreno, H. (2012). Cardiovascular effects of partial sleep deprivation in healthy volunteers. *Journal of Applied Physiology, 113*(2), 232–236.

Dillon, H. R., Lichstein, K. L., Dautovich, N. D., Taylor, D. J., Riedel, B. W., & Bush, A. J. (2014). Variability in self-reported normal sleep across the adult age span. *The Journals of Gerontology Series B: Psychological Sciences and Social Sciences, 70*, 46–56.

Domhoff, G. W. (2005a). The content of dreams: Methodologic and theoretical implications. *Principles and Practices of Sleep Medicine* (4th Ed., pp. 522–534). Philadelphia: WB Saunders Commentary.

Domhoff, G. W. (2005b). Refocusing the neurocognitive approach to dreams: A critique of the Hobson versus Solms debate. *Dreaming, 15*(1), 3–20.

Domhoff, G. W. (2007). Realistic simulation and bizarreness in dream content: Past findings and suggestions for future research. *The New Science of Dreaming: Content, Recall, and Personality Characteristics, 2*, 1–27.

Domhoff, G. W., & Fox, K. C. (2015). Dreaming and the default network: A review, synthesis, and counterintuitive research proposal. *Consciousness and Cognition, 33*, 342–353.

Drew, T., Võ, M. L.-H., & Wolfe, J. M. (2013). The invisible gorilla strikes again: Sustained inattentional blindness in expert observers. *Psychological Science, 24*(9), 1848–1853.

Droppa, M., Boyer, J., Finneran, J., Smith, M., & Bernius, A. (2014). Appreciative inquiry: An innovative new strategy to decrease prescription drug abuse on a college campus. *Journal of Addiction Research and Therapy, 5*, 1–6.

Drummond, M. B., & Upson, D. (2014). Electronic cigarettes: Potential harms and benefits. *Annals of the American Thoracic Society, 11*(2), 236–242.

Drummond, S. P., Anderson, D. E., Straus, L. D., Vogel, E. K., & Perez, V. B. (2012). The effects of two types of sleep deprivation on visual working memory capacity and filtering efficiency. *PloS One, 7*(4), e35653.

Dupuis, L. L., Roscoe, J. A., Olver, I., Aapro, M., & Molassiotis, A. (2017). 2016 updated MASCC/ESMO consensus recommendations: Anticipatory nausea and vomiting in children and adults receiving chemotherapy. *Supportive Care in Cancer, 25*(1), 317–321. doi: 10.1007/s00520-016-3330-z

Edinger, J. D., & Carney, C. E. (2008). *Overcoming insomnia: A cognitive-behavioral therapy approach, therapist guide.* New York, NY: Oxford University Press.

Eimer, M., & Grubert, A. (2015). A dissociation between selective attention and conscious awareness in the representation of temporal order information. *Consciousness and Cognition, 35*, 274–281.

Elkins, G. R., Barabasz, A. F., Council, J. R., & Spiegel, D. (2015). Advancing research and practice: The revised APA Division 30 definition of hypnosis. *American Journal of Clinical Hypnosis, 57*(4), 378–385.

Enck, P., Klosterhalfen, S., Weimer, K., Horing, B., & Zipfel, S. (2011). The placebo response in clinical trials: More questions than answers. *Philosophical Transactions of the Royal Society B: Biological Sciences, 366*(1572), 1889–1895. doi: 10.1098/rstb.2010.0384

Enea, V., & Dafinoiu, I. (2011). Ethical principles and standards in the practice of hypnosis. *Revista Romana de Bioetica, 9*(3), 110–116.

Fabbri, M., Mencarelli, C., Adan, A., & Natale, V. (2013). Time-of-day and circadian typology on memory retrieval. *Biological Rhythm Research, 44*(1), 125–142.

Facco, E., Testoni, I., Ronconi, L., Casiglia, E., Zanette, G., & Spiegel, D. (2017). Psychological features of hypnotizability: A first step towards its empirical definition. *International Journal of Clinical and Experimental Hypnosis, 65*(1), 98–119. doi: 10.1080/00207144.2017.1246881

Farsalinos, K. E., & Polosa, R. (2014). Safety evaluation and risk assessment of electronic cigarettes as tobacco cigarette substitutes: A systematic review. *Therapeutic Advances in Drug Safety, 5*(2), 67–86. doi: 10.1177/2042098614524430

Fisher, S., & Greenberg, R. P. (1985). *The scientific credibility of Freud's theories and therapy.* New York, NY: Columbia University Press.

Fitch, G. M., Soccolich, S. A., Guo, F., McClafferty, J., Fang, Y., Olson, R. L., … Dingus, T. A. (2013). The impact of hand-held and hands-free cell phone use on driving performance and safety-critical event risk. Washington, DC: National Highway Traffic Safety Administration.

Ford, E. S., Cunningham, T. J., & Croft, J. B. (2015). Trends in self-reported sleep duration among US adults from 1985 to 2012. *Sleep, 38*(5), 829–832.

Fortier-Brochu, É., Beaulieu-Bonneau, S., Ivers, H., & Morin, C. M. (2012). Insomnia and daytime cognitive performance: A meta-analysis. *Sleep Medicine Reviews, 16*(1), 83–94.

Fox, T. P., Oliver, G., & Ellis, S. M. (2013). The destructive capacity of drug abuse: An overview exploring the harmful potential of drug abuse both to the individual and to society. *ISRN Addiction, 2013*, 1–6.

Fraigne, J. J., Grace, K. P., Horner, R. L., & Peever, J. (2014). Mechanisms of REM sleep in health and disease. *Current Opinion in Pulmonary Medicine, 20*(6), 527–532.

Friedman, T. W., Robinson, S. R., & Yelland, G. W. (2011). Impaired perceptual judgment at low blood alcohol concentrations. *Alcohol, 45*(7), 711–718.

Gackenbach, J. I., & Kuruvilla, B. (2008). Video game play effects on dreams: Self-evaluation and content analysis. *Eludamos. Journal for Computer Game Culture, 2*(2), 169–186.

Gangwisch, J. E. (2014). A review of evidence for the link between sleep duration and hypertension. *American Journal of Hypertension, 27*(10), 1235–1242.

Gellis, L. A., Park, A., Stotsky, M. T., & Taylor, D. J. (2014). Associations between sleep hygiene and insomnia severity in college students: Cross-sectional and prospective analyses. *Behavior Therapy, 45*(6), 806–816.

Gibbs, R., Davies, G., & Chou, S. (2016). A systematic review on factors affecting the likelihood of change blindness. *Crime Psychology Review, 2*(1), 1–21.

Gilbert, S. P., & Weaver, C. C. (2010). Sleep quality and academic performance in university students: A wake-up call for college psychologists. *Journal of College Student Psychotherapy, 24*(4), 295–306.

Golden, W. L. (2012). Cognitive hypnotherapy for anxiety disorders. *American Journal of Clinical Hypnosis, 54*(4), 263–274. doi: 10.1080/00029157.2011.650333

Gomes, A. A., Tavares, J., & de Azevedo, M. H. P. (2011). Sleep and academic performance in undergraduates: A multi-measure, multi-predictor approach. *Chronobiology International, 28*(9), 786–801.

Gradisar, M., Gardner, G., & Dohnt, H. (2011). Recent worldwide sleep patterns and problems during adolescence: A review and meta-analysis of age, region, and sleep. *Sleep Medicine, 12*(2), 110–118.

Grana, R., Benowitz, N., & Glantz, S. A. (2014). E-cigarettes a scientific review. *Circulation, 129*(19), 1972–1986.

Green, J. P., Page, R. A., Rasekhy, R., Johnson, L. K., & Bernhardt, S. E. (2006). Cultural views and attitudes about hypnosis: A survey of college students across four countries. *International Journal of Clinical and Experimental Hypnosis, 54*(3), 263–280.

Green, J. P., Smith, R. J., & Kromer, M. (2015). Diurnal variations in hypnotic responsiveness: Is there an optimal time to be hypnotized? *International Journal of Clinical and Experimental Hypnosis, 63*(2), 171–181. doi: 10.1080/00207144.2015.1002675

Grinols, A. B., & Rajesh, R. (2014). Multitasking with smartphones in the college classroom. *Business and Professional Communication Quarterly, 77*(1), 89–95.

Grünbaum, A. (1992). Two major difficulties for Freud's theory of dreams. In T. Gelfand & J. Kerr (Eds.), *Freud and the history of psychoanalysis* (pp. 193–214). Hillside, NJ: The Analytic Press, Inc.

Häuser, W., Hagl, M., Schmierer, A., & Hansen, E. (2016). The efficacy, safety and applications of medical hypnosis: A systematic review of meta-analyses. *Deutsches Ärzteblatt International, 113*(17), 289–296. doi: 10.3238/arztebl.2016.0289

Havekes, R., Bruinenberg, V. M., Tudor, J. C., Ferri, S. L., Baumann, A., Meerlo, P., & Abel, T. (2014). Transiently increasing cAMP levels selectively in hippocampal excitatory neurons during sleep deprivation prevents memory deficits caused by sleep loss. *The Journal of Neuroscience, 34*(47), 15715–15721.

Hembrooke, H., & Gay, G. (2003). The laptop and the lecture: The effects of multitasking in learning environments. *Journal of Computing in Higher Education, 15*(1), 46–64.

Hirshkowitz, M., Whiton, K., Albert, S. M., Alessi, C., Bruni, O., DonCarlos, L., ... Kheirandish-Gozal, L. (2015). National Sleep Foundation's sleep time duration recommendations: Methodology and results summary. *Sleep Health, 1*(1), 40–43.

Hobson, J. A., & McCarley, R. (1977). The brain as a dream state generator: An activation-synthesis hypothesis of the dream process. *American Journal of Psychiatry, 134*(12), 1335–1348. doi:10.1176/ajp.134.12.1335

Hobson, R. M., & Maughan, R. J. (2010). Hydration status and the diuretic action of a small dose of alcohol. *Alcohol and Alcoholism, 45*, 1–8.

Howat, P., Sleet, D., & Smith, I. (1991). Alcohol and driving: Is the 0.05% blood alcohol concentration limit justified? *Drug and Alcohol Review, 10*(2), 151–166.

Howell, M. J. (2012). Parasomnias: An updated review. *Neurotherapeutics, 9*(4), 753–775.

Ingravallo, F., Poli, F., Gilmore, E. V., Pizza, F., Vignatelli, L., Schenck, C. H., & Plazzi, G. (2014). Sleep-related violence and sexual behavior in sleep: A systematic review of medical-legal case reports. *Journal of Clinical Sleep Medicine: Official Publication of the American Academy of Sleep Medicine, 10*(8), 927–935.

Inner IDEA. (2014). Meditation 101: Techniques, benefits, & beginner's how-to. Retrieved July 18, 2015, from http://life.gaiam.com/article/meditation-101-techniques-benefits-beginner-s-how

Jacquith, L., Rhue, J. W., Lynn, S. J., & Seevaratnam, J. (1996). Cross-cultural aspects of hypnotizability and imagination. *Contemporary Hypnosis, 13*(2), 94–99.

Jiang, H., White, M. P., Greicius, M. D., Waelde, L. C., & Spiegel, D. (2016). Brain activity and functional connectivity associated with hypnosis. *Cerebral Cortex, 1–11.* doi: 10.1093/cercor/bhw220

Jones, T. M., Durrant, J., Michaelides, E. B., & Green, M. P. (2015). Melatonin: A possible link between the presence of artificial light at night and reductions in biological fitness. *Philosophical Transactions of the Royal Society of London B: Biological Sciences, 370*(1667), 1–10.

Junco, R. (2012). In-class multitasking and academic performance. *Computers in Human Behavior, 28*(6), 2236–2243.

Junco, R., & Cotten, S. R. (2012). No A 4 U: The relationship between multitasking and academic performance. *Computers & Education, 59*(2), 505–514.

Kabat-Zinn, J. (2005). Meditation—It's not what you think. *Mindfulness, 6*(2), 393–395.

Karpinski, A. C., Kirschner, P. A., Ozer, I., Mellott, J. A., & Ochwo, P. (2012). An exploration of social networking site use, multitasking, and academic performance among United States and European university students. *Computers in Human Behavior, 29*(3), 1182–1192.

Kaufmann, C., Wehrle, R., Wetter, T., Holsboer, F., Auer, D., Pollmächer, T., & Czisch, M. (2006). Brain activation and hypothalamic functional connectivity during human non-rapid eye movement sleep: An EEG/fMRI study. *Brain, 129*(3), 655–667.

Keenan, S., & Hirshkowitz, M. (2011). Monitoring and staging human sleep. In M. H. Kryger, T. Roth, & W. C. Dement (Eds.), *Principles and practice of sleep medicine.* (5th ed., pp. 1602–1609). St. Louis: Elsevier Saunders.

Keyes, K. M., Maslowsky, J., Hamilton, A., & Schulenberg, J. (2015). The great sleep recession: Changes in sleep duration among U.S. adolescents, 1991–2012. *Pediatrics, 135*(3), 460–468.

Klauer, S. G., Guo, F., Simons-Morton, B. G., Ouimet, M. C., Lee, S. E., & Dingus, T. A. (2014). Distracted driving and risk of road crashes among novice and experienced drivers. *New England Journal of Medicine, 370*(1), 54–59.

Knight, M., & Mather, M. (2013). Look out—it's your off-peak time of day! Time of day matters more for alerting than for orienting or executive attention. *Experimental Aging Research, 39*(3), 305–321.

Koch, C., & Tsuchiya, N. (2012). Attention and consciousness: Related yet different. *Trends in Cognitive Sciences, 16*(2), 103–105.

Kurina, L. M., McClintock, M. K., Chen, J.-H., Waite, L. J., Thisted, R. A., & Lauderdale, D. S. (2013). Sleep duration and all-cause mortality: A critical review of measurement and associations. *Annals of Epidemiology, 23*(6), 361–370.

Lee, H.-M., & Roth, B. L. (2012). Hallucinogen actions on human brain revealed. *Proceedings of the National Academy of Sciences, 109*(6), 1820–1821.

Lemola, S., Perkinson-Gloor, N., Brand, S., Dewald-Kaufmann, J. F., & Grob, A. (2015). Adolescents' electronic media use at night, sleep disturbance, and depressive symptoms in the smartphone age. *Journal of Youth and Adolescence, 44*(2), 405–418.

Lifshitz, M., Sheiner, E. O., Olson, J. A., Thériault, R., & Raz, A. (2017). On suggestibility and placebo: A follow-up study. *American Journal of Clinical Hypnosis, 59*(4), 385–392.

Llerena, L. E., Aronow, K. V., Macleod, J., Bard, M., Salzman, S., Greene, W., ... Schupper, A. (2014). An evidence-based review: Distracted driver. *Journal of Trauma and Acute Care Surgery, 78*(1), 147–152.

Loflin, M., & Earleywine, M. (2014). A new method of cannabis ingestion: The dangers of dabs? *Addictive Behaviors, 39*(10), 1430–1433.

Lugoboni, F., & Quaglio, G. (2014). Exploring the dark side of the moon: The treatment of benzodiazepine tolerance. *British Journal of Clinical Pharmacology, 77*(2), 239–241.

Magee, C. A., Holliday, E. G., Attia, J., Kritharides, L., & Banks, E. (2013). Investigation of the relationship between sleep duration, all-cause mortality, and preexisting disease. *Sleep Medicine, 14*(7), 591–596.

Maquet, P., Péters, J.-M., Aerts, J., Delfiore, G., Degueldre, C., Luxen, A., & Franck, G. (1996). Functional neuroanatomy of human rapid-eye-movement sleep and dreaming. *Nature, 383*(6596), 163–166.

Martin, T. L., Solbeck, P. A., Mayers, D. J., Langille, R. M., Buczek, Y., & Pelletier, M. R. (2013). A review of alcohol-impaired driving: The role of blood alcohol concentration and complexity of the driving task. *Journal of Forensic Sciences, 58*(5), 1238–1250.

Martinez, D., Saccone, P. A., Liu, F., Slifstein, M., Orlowska, D., Grassetti, A., ... Comer, S. D. (2012). Deficits in dopamine D 2 receptors and presynaptic dopamine in heroin dependence: Commonalities and differences with other types of addiction. *Biological Psychiatry, 71*(3), 192–198.

Maslowsky, J., & Ozer, E. J. (2014). Developmental trends in sleep duration in adolescence and young adulthood: Evidence from a national United States sample. *Journal of Adolescent Health, 54*(6), 691–697.

Maudens, K. E., Patteet, L., van Nuijs, A. L., Van Broekhoven, C., Covaci, A., & Neels, H. (2014). The influence of the body mass index (BMI) on the volume of distribution of ethanol. *Forensic Science International, 243*, 74–78.

May, C. P., & Hasher, L. (1998). Synchrony effects in inhibitory control over thought and action. *Journal of Experimental Psychology: Human Perception and Performance, 24*(2), 363–379.

McNally, R. J., & Clancy, S. A. (2005). Sleep paralysis, sexual abuse, and space alien abduction. *Transcultural Psychiatry, 42*(1), 113–122.

Medeiros-Ward, N., Watson, J. M., & Strayer, D. L. (2014). On supertaskers and the neural basis of efficient multitasking. *Psychonomic Bulletin & Review, 22*(3), 876–883.

Meltzer, L. J., & McLaughlin Crabtree, V. (2015). Confusional arousals, sleep terrors, and sleepwalking. *Pediatric sleep problems: A clinician's guide to behavioral interventions* (pp. 175–182). Washington, DC: American Psychological Association.

Memmert, D. (2006). The effects of eye movements, age, and expertise on inattentional blindness. *Consciousness and Cognition, 15*(3), 620–627.

Meredith, S. E., Juliano, L. M., Hughes, J. R., & Griffiths, R. R. (2013). Caffeine use disorder: A comprehensive review and research agenda. *Journal of Caffeine Research, 3*(3), 114–130.

Mets, M. A., Alford, C., & Verster, J. C. (2012). Sleep specialists' opinion on sleep disorders and fitness to drive a car: The necessity of continued education. *Industrial Health, 50*(6), 499–508.

Meyerson, J. (2014). The myth of hypnosis: The need for remythification. *International Journal of Clinical and Experimental Hypnosis, 62*(3), 378–393.

Minozzi, S., Amato, L., & Davoli, M. (2012). Development of dependence following treatment with opioid analgesics for pain relief: A systematic review. *Addiction, 108*(4), 688–698.

Mitchell, J. A., Rodriguez, D., Schmitz, K. H., & Audrain-McGovern, J. (2013). Sleep duration and adolescent obesity. *Pediatrics, 131*(5), e1428–e1434.

Mole, C. (2008). Attention and consciousness. *Journal of Consciousness Studies, 15*(4), 86–104.

Morin, C. M., & Benca, R. (2012). Chronic insomnia. *The Lancet, 379*(9821), 1129–1141.

Mumenthaler, M. S., Taylor, J. L., O'Hara, R., & Yesavage, J. A. (1999). Gender differences in moderate drinking effects. *Alcohol Research and Health, 23*(1), 55–64.

Muntean, M.-L., Trenkwalder, C., Walters, A. S., Mollenhauer, B., & Sixel-Döring, F. (2015). REM sleep behavioral events and dreaming. *Journal of Clinical Sleep Medicine: JCSM: Official Publication of the American Academy of Sleep Medicine, 11*(4), 537–541.

National Health Sleep Awareness Project. (2014). Rising prevalence of sleep apnea in U.S. threatens public health. Retrieved August 8, 2015, from http://sleepeducation.com/docs/default-document-library/rising-prevalence-of-sleep-apnea-in-u-s-threatens-public-health.pdf

National Institute on Drug Abuse, National Institutes of Health. (2017, April). Trends and statistics. Retrieved September 25, 2017, from https://www.drugabuse.gov/related-topics/trends-statistics

National Institute on Drug Abuse, National Institutes of Health. (2016, January). What are hallucinogens? Retrieved September 25, 2017, from https://www.drugabuse.gov/publications/drugfacts/hallucinogens

National Institute on Drug Abuse, National Institutes of Health. (2013, February). Challenging marijuana myths. Retrieved September 25, 2017, from https://www.drugabuse.gov/about-nida/directors-page/messages-director/2013/02/challenging-marijuana-myths

National Institute of Neurological Disorders and Stroke, National Institutes of Health. (n.d.). Brain basics: Understanding sleep. Retrieved September 24, 2017, from https://www.ninds.nih.gov/Disorders/Patient-Caregiver-Education/Understanding-Sleep#sleep_disorders

Neisser, U. (1979). The control of information pickup in selective looking. *Perception and Its Development: A Tribute to Eleanor J. Gibson*, 201–219. Hillsdale, NJ: L. Erlbaum Associates.

Neisser, U., & Becklen, R. (1975). Selective looking: Attending to visually specified events. *Cognitive Psychology, 7*(4), 480–494.

Nordahl, T. E., Salo, R., & Leamon, M. (2003). Neuropsychological effects of chronic methamphetamine use on neurotransmitters and cognition: A review. *The Journal of Neuropsychiatry and Clinical Neurosciences, 15*(3), 317–325.

Norman, L. J., Heywood, C. A., & Kentridge, R. W. (2013). Object-based attention without awareness. *Psychological Science, 24*(6), 836–843.

Oren, D. A., & Terman, M. (1998). Enhanced: Tweaking the human circadian clock with light. *Science, 279*(5349), 333–334.

Oyemade, A. (2012). New uncontrolled benzodiazepine, phenazepam, emerging drug of abuse. *Innovations in Clinical Neuroscience, 9*(9), 10.

Ozaki, A., Inoue, Y., Hayashida, K., Nakajima, T., Honda, M., Usui, A., ... Takahashi, K. (2012). Quality of life in patients with narcolepsy with cataplexy, narcolepsy without cataplexy, and idiopathic hypersomnia without long sleep time: Comparison between patients on psychostimulants, drug-naive patients and the general Japanese population. *Sleep Medicine, 13*(2), 200–206.

Palagini, L., Maria Bruno, R., Gemignani, A., Baglioni, C., Ghiadoni, L., & Riemann, D. (2013). Sleep loss and hypertension: A systematic review. *Current Pharmaceutical Design, 19*(13), 2409–2419.

Petit, D., Pennestri, M.-H., Paquet, J., Desautels, A., Zadra, A., Vitaro, F., ... Montplaisir, J. (2015). Childhood sleepwalking and sleep terrors: A longitudinal study of prevalence and familial aggregation. *JAMA Pediatrics, 169*(7), 653–658.

Petri, G., Expert, P., Turkheimer, F., Carhart-Harris, R., Nutt, D., Hellyer, P. J., & Vaccarino, F. (2014). Homological scaffolds of brain functional networks. *Journal of the Royal Society Interface, 11*(101), 1–10. doi: 10.1098/rsif.2014.0873

Pigeon, W. R. (2010). Diagnosis, prevalence, pathways, consequences & treatment of insomnia. *The Indian Journal of Medical Research, 131*, 321–332.

Proctor, S. L., Copeland, A. L., Kopak, A. M., Herschman, P. L., & Polukhina, N. (2014). A naturalistic comparison of the effectiveness of methadone and two sublingual formulations of buprenorphine on maintenance treatment outcomes: Findings from a retrospective multisite study. *Experimental and Clinical Psychopharmacology, 22*(5), 424–433.

Remington, A., Cartwright-Finch, U., & Lavie, N. (2014). I can see clearly now: The effects of age and perceptual load on inattentional blindness. *Frontiers in Human Neuroscience, 8*, 1–11.

Rideout, V. J., Foehr, U. G., & Roberts, D. F. (2010). Generation M: Media in the lives of 8- to 18-year-olds. *Henry J. Kaiser Family Foundation.* https://kaiserfamilyfoundation.files.wordpress.com/2013/04/8010.pdf

Roberts, C. J., Campbell, I. C., & Troop, N. (2014). Increases in weight during chronic stress are partially associated with a switch in food choice towards increased carbohydrate and saturated fat intake. *European Eating Disorders Review, 22*(1), 77–82.

Rom, O., Pecorelli, A., Valacchi, G., & Reznick, A. Z. (2015). Are E-cigarettes a safe and good alternative to cigarette smoking? *Annals of the New York Academy of Sciences, 1340*(1), 65–74.

Ruiz, F. S., Andersen, M. L., Martins, R. C., Zager, A., Lopes, J. D., & Tufik, S. (2012). Immune alterations after selective rapid eye movement or total sleep deprivation in healthy male volunteers. *Innate Immunity, 18*(1), 44–54.

Santarcangelo, E. L. (2014). New views of hypnotizability. *Frontiers in Behavioral Neuroscience, 8*, 1–5. doi: 10.3389/fnbeh.2014.00224

Schaefert, R., Klose, P., Moser, G., & Häuser, W. (2014). Efficacy, tolerability, and safety of hypnosis in adult irritable bowel syndrome: Systematic review and meta-analysis. *Psychosomatic Medicine, 76*(5), 389–398.

Schmidt, A., Borgwardt, S., Gerber, H., Wiesbeck, G. A., Schmid, O., Riecher-Rössler, A., ... Walter, M. (2013). Acute effects of heroin on negative emotional processing: Relation of amygdala activity and stress-related responses. *Biological Psychiatry, 76*(4), 289–296.

Schraufnagel, D. E. (2015). Electronic cigarettes: Vulnerability of youth. *Pediatric Allergy, Immunology, and Pulmonology, 28*(1), 2–6. doi: 10.1089/ped.2015.0490

Schredl, M., Atanasova, D., Hörmann, K., Maurer, J. T., Hummel, T., & Stuck, B. A. (2009). Information processing during sleep: The effect of olfactory stimuli on dream content and dream emotions. *Journal of Sleep Research, 18*(3), 285–290.

Schredl, M., & Hofmann, F. (2003). Continuity between waking activities and dream activities. *Consciousness and Cognition, 12*(2), 298–308.

Sees, K. L., Delucchi, K. L., Masson, C., Rosen, A., Clark, H. W., Robillard, H., ... Hall, S. M. (2000). Methadone maintenance versus 180-day psychosocially enriched detoxification for treatment of opioid dependence: A randomized controlled trial. *JAMA, 283*(10), 1303–1310.

Sheiner, E. O., Lifshitz, M., & Raz, A. (2016). Placebo response correlates with hypnotic suggestibility. *Psychology of Consciousness: Theory, Research, and Practice, 3*(2), 146–153.

Shih, M., Yang, Y.-H., & Koo, M. (2009). A meta-analysis of hypnosis in the treatment of depressive symptoms: A brief communication. *International Journal of Clinical and Experimental Hypnosis, 57*(4), 431–442.

Shor, R. E., & Orne, E. C. (1962). *Harvard group scale of hypnotic susceptibility.* Palo Alto, CA: Consulting Psychologists Press.

Short, M. A., Gradisar, M., Lack, L. C., & Wright, H. R. (2013). The impact of sleep on adolescent depressed mood, alertness and academic performance. *Journal of Adolescence, 36*(6), 1025–1033.

Simons, D. J., & Chabris, C. F. (1999). Gorillas in our midst: Sustained inattentional blindness for dynamic events. *Perception-London, 28*(9), 1059–1074.

Simons, D. J., & Levin, D. T. (1997). Change blindness. *Trends in Cognitive Sciences, 1*(7), 261–267.

Sletten, T. L., Rajaratnam, S. M., Wright, M. J., Zhu, G., Naismith, S., Martin, N. G., & Hickie, I. (2013). Genetic and environmental contributions to sleep-wake behavior in 12-year-old twins. *Sleep, 36*(11), 1715–1722.

Smith, M. R., Antrobus, J. S., Gordon, E., Tucker, M. A., Hirota, Y., Wamsley, E. J., ... Emery, R. N. (2004). Motivation and affect in REM sleep and the mentation reporting process. *Consciousness and Cognition, 13*(3), 501–511.

Sperry, S. D., Scully, I. D., Gramzow, R. H., & Jorgensen, R. S. (2015). Sleep duration and waist circumference in adults: A meta-analysis. *Sleep, 38*(8), 1269–76. doi: 10.5665/sleep.4906

Srinivasan, T. (2015). Healing altered states of consciousness. *International Journal of Yoga, 8*(2), 87–88.

Stavrinos, D., Jones, J. L., Garner, A. A., Griffin, R., Franklin, C. A., Ball, D., ... Fine, P. R. (2013). Impact of distracted driving on safety and traffic flow. *Accident Analysis & Prevention, 61*, 63–70.

Stickgold, R., Hobson, J. A., Fosse, R., & Fosse, M. (2001). Sleep, learning, and dreams: Off-line memory reprocessing. *Science, 294*(5544), 1052–1057.

Stogner, J. M., & Miller, B. L. (2015). Assessing the dangers of "dabbing": Mere marijuana or harmful new trend? *Pediatrics, 136*(1), 1–3.

Substance Abuse and Mental Health Services Administration. (2014). Results from the 2013 national survey on drug use and health: Summary of national findings, NSDUH series H-48, HHS publication No.(SMA) 14–4863. Rockville, MD.

Swift, R., & Davidson, D. (1998). Alcohol hangover. *Alcohol Health & Research World, 22*, 54–60.

Tan, G., Rintala, D. H., Jensen, M. P., Fukui, T., Smith, D., & Williams, W. (2015). A randomized controlled trial of hypnosis compared with biofeedback for adults with chronic low back pain. *European Journal of Pain, 19*(2), 271–280. doi: 10.1002/ejp.545

Tefikow, S., Barth, J., Maichrowitz, S., Beelmann, A., Strauss, B., & Rosendahl, J. (2013). Efficacy of hypnosis in adults undergoing surgery or medical procedures: A meta-analysis of randomized controlled trials. *Clinical Psychology Review, 33*(5), 623–636.

Tellegen, A., & Atkinson, G. (1974). Openness to absorbing and self-altering experiences ("absorption"), a trait related to hypnotic susceptibility. *Journal of Abnormal Psychology, 83*(3), 268–277.

Thomas, J. W., & Cohen, M. (2014). A methodological review of meditation research. *Frontiers in Psychiatry, 5*, 1–12.

Trolian, T. L., An, B. P., & Pascarella, E. T. (2016). Are there cognitive consequences of binge drinking during college? *Journal of College Student Development, 57*(8), 1009–1026.

Tsujii, T., Sakatani, K., Nakashima, E., Igarashi, T., & Katayama, Y. (2011). Characterization of the acute effects of alcohol on asymmetry of inferior frontal cortex activity during a go/no-go task using functional near-infrared spectroscopy. *Psychopharmacology, 217*(4), 595–603.

Valli, K., Revonsuo, A., Pälkäs, O., & Punamäki, R.-L. (2006). The effect of trauma on dream content—A field study of Palestinian children. *Dreaming, 16*(2), 63–87.

Valrie, C. R., Bond, K., Lutes, L. D., Carraway, M., & Collier, D. N. (2015). Relationship of sleep quality, baseline weight status, and weight-loss responsiveness in obese adolescents in an immersion treatment program. *Sleep Medicine, 16*(3), 432–434.

van den Pol, A. N. (2000). Narcolepsy: A neurodegenerative disease of the hypocretin system? *Neuron, 27*(3), 415–418. doi: http://dx.doi.org/10.1016/S0896-6273(0000050-7)

van Heugten–van der Kloet, D., Giesbrecht, T., & Merckelbach, H. (2015). Sleep loss increases dissociation and affects memory for emotional stimuli. *Journal of Behavior Therapy and Experimental Psychiatry, 47*, 9–17.

Varga, A. W., Kang, M., Ramesh, P. V., & Klann, E. (2014). Effects of acute sleep deprivation on motor and reversal learning in mice. *Neurobiology of Learning and Memory, 114*, 217–222.

Voit, R., & DeLaney, M. (2005). *Hypnosis in clinical practice: Steps for mastering hypnotherapy.* New York, NY: Routledge.

Wamsley, E. J. (2014). Dreaming and offline memory consolidation. *Current Neurology and Neuroscience Reports, 14*(3), 1–7.

Wamsley, E. J., & Stickgold, R. (2011). Memory, sleep, and dreaming: Experiencing consolidation. *Sleep Medicine Clinics, 6*(1), 97–108.

Ward, E. J., & Scholl, B. J. (2015). Inattentional blindness reflects limitations on perception, not memory: Evidence from repeated failures of awareness. *Psychonomic Bulletin & Review, 22*(3), 722–727.

Watson, N. F., Harden, K. P., Buchwald, D., Vitiello, M. V., Pack, A. I., Weigle, D. S., & Goldberg, J. (2012). Sleep duration and body mass index in twins: A gene-environment interaction. *Sleep, 35*(5), 597–603.

Weathermon, R., & Crabb, D. W. (1999). Alcohol and medication interactions. *Alcohol Research and Health, 23*(1), 40–54.

Weitzenhoffer, A. M., & Hilgard, E. R. (1962). *Stanford hypnotic susceptibility scale, form C* (Vol. 27). Palo Alto, CA: Consulting Psychologists Press.

Werner, A., Uldbjerg, N., Zachariae, R., Wu, C. S., & Nohr, E. A. (2013). Antenatal hypnosis training and childbirth experience: A randomized controlled trial. *Birth, 40*(4), 272–280. doi: 10.1111/birt.12071

Wilder-Smith, A., Mustafa, F., Earnest, A., Gen, L., & MacAry, P. (2013). Impact of partial sleep deprivation on immune markers. *Sleep Medicine, 14*(10), 1031–1034.

Wise, R. A., & Bozarth, M. A. (1987). A psychomotor stimulant theory of addiction. *Psychological Review, 94*(4), 469–492.

Wise, R. A., & Koob, G. F. (2014). The development and maintenance of drug addiction. *Neuropsychopharmacology, 39*(2), 254–262. doi: 10.1038/npp.2013.261

Woodard, F. J. (2005). Perceptually oriented hypnosis: Cross-cultural perspectives. *Psychological Reports, 97*(1), 141–157.

Wright Jr., K. P., McHill, A. W., Birks, B. R., Griffin, B. R., Rusterholz, T., & Chinoy, E. D. (2013). Entrainment of the human circadian clock to the natural light-dark cycle. *Current Biology, 23*(16), 1554–1558. doi: http://dx.doi.org/10.1016/j.cub.2013.06.039

Wright, K. P., Drake, A. L., Frey, D. J., Fleshner, M., Desouza, C. A., Gronfier, C., & Czeisler, C. A. (2015). Influence of sleep deprivation and circadian misalignment on cortisol, inflammatory markers, and cytokine balance. *Brain, Behavior, and Immunity, 47*, 24–34.

Xiao, Q., Keadle, S. K., Hollenbeck, A. R., & Matthews, C. E. (2014). Sleep duration and total and cause-specific mortality in a large U.S. cohort: Interrelationships with physical activity, sedentary behavior, and body mass index. *American Journal of Epidemiology, 180*(10), 997–1006.

Yu, C. K.-C. (2014). Toward 100% dream retrieval by rapid-eye-movement sleep awakening: A high-density electroencephalographic study. *Dreaming, 24*(1), 1–17.

Chapter 5

Abernathy, W. B. (2013). Behavioral approaches to business and industrial problems: Organizational behavior management. In G. J. Madden, W. V. Dube, T. D. Hackenberg, G. P. Hanley, K. A. Lattal (Eds.), *APA Handbook of Behavior Analysis, Vol 2: Translating Principles into Practice* (pp. 501–521). Washington, DC: American Psychological Association.

Anderson, C. A., Sakamoto, A., Gentile, D. A., Ihori, N., Shibuya, A., Yukawa, S., & Kobayashi, K. (2008). Longitudinal effects of violent video games on aggression in Japan and the United States. *Pediatrics, 122*(5), e1067–e1072.

Anderson, C. A., Suzuki, K., Swing, E. L., Groves, C. L., Gentile, D. A., Prot, S., … & Jelic, M. (2017). Media violence and other aggression risk factors in seven nations. *Personality and Social Psychology Bulletin, 43*(7), 986–998.

Anderson, C. A., Shibuya, A., Ihori, N., Swing, E. L., Bushman, B. J., Sakamoto, A., … & Saleem, M. (2010). Violent video game effects on aggression, empathy, and prosocial behavior in eastern and western countries: A meta-analytic review. *Psychological Bulletin, 136*(2), 151–173.

Atthowe Jr., J. M., & Krasner, L. (1968). Preliminary report on the application of contingent reinforcement procedures (token economy) on a "chronic" psychiatric ward. *Journal of Abnormal Psychology, 73*(1), 37.

Avenanti, A., Bueti, D., Galati, G., & Aglioti, S. M. (2005) C. Transcranial magnetic stimulation highlights the sensorimotor side of empathy for pain. *Nature Neuroscience, 8*(7), 955–960. doi:10.1038/nn1481

Baer, D. M., Wolf, M. M., & Risley, T. R. (1968). Some current dimensions of applied behavior analysis. *Journal of Applied Behavior Analysis, 1*(1), 91–97.

Bandura, A., Ross, D., & Ross, S.AA. (1961). Transmission of Aggression through Imitation of Aggressive Models. *Journal of Abnormal & Social Psychology, 63*, 575–582.

Bandura, A. (1986). *Social foundations of thought and action: A social cognitive theory.* Prentice-Hall, Inc.

Baumrind, D. (1996). A blanket injunction against disciplinary use of spanking is not warranted by the data. *Pediatrics, 98*(4), 828–831.

Beck, H. P., Levinson, S., & Irons, G. (2009). Finding little Albert: A journey to John B. Watson's infant laboratory. *American Psychologist, 64*(7), 605–614.

Beecher, M. D. (2008). Function and mechanisms of song learning in song sparrows. *Advances in the Study of Behavior, 38*, 167–225.

Beecher, M. D., Campbell, S. E., & Stoddard, P. K. (1994). Correlation of song learning and territory establishment strategies in the song sparrow. *Proceedings of the National Academy of Sciences, 91*(4), 1450–1454.

Bennett, A. T. (1996). Do animals have cognitive maps? *The Journal of Experimental Biology, 199*(1), 219–224.

Call, J., Carpenter, M., & Tomasello, M. (2005). Copying results and copying actions in the process of social learning: Chimpanzees (Pan troglodytes) and human children (Homo sapiens). *Animal Cognition, 8*(3), 151–163.

Cook, J. (2012). *How Google motivates their employees with rewards and perks.* Retrieved from http://thinkingleader.hubpages.com/hub/How-Google-Motivates-their-Employees-with-Rewards-and-Perks

Cooper, J. O. (1982). Applied behavior analysis in education. *Theory into Practice, 21*(2), 114–118.

Developmental, D. M. N. S. Y., & 2010 Principal Investigators. (2014). Prevalence of autism spectrum disorder among children aged 8 years—Autism and developmental disabilities monitoring network, 11 sites, United States, 2010. *Morbidity and Mortality Weekly Report. Surveillance Summaries 63*(2), 1. Washington, DC.

Di Pellegrino, G., Fadiga, L., Fogassi, L., Gallese, V., & Rizzolatti, G. (1992). Understanding motor events: A neurophysiological study. *Experimental Brain Research, 91*(1), 176–180.

Desimone, R., & Duncan, J. (1995). Neural mechanisms of selective visual attention. *Annual Review of Neuroscience, 18*(1), 193–222.

Digdon, N., Powell, R. A., & Harris, B. (2014). Little Albert's alleged neurological impairment: Watson, Rayner, and historical revision. *History of Psychology, 17*(4), 312.

Doll, C., McLaughlin, T. F., & Barretto, A. (2013). The token economy: A recent review and evaluation. *International Journal of Basic and Applied Science, 2*(1), 131–149.

Eaton, R. L. (1970). Hunting behavior of the cheetah. *The Journal of Wildlife Management, 34*(1) 56–67.

Eikeseth, S., Klintwall, L., Jahr, E., & Karlsson, P. (2012). Outcome for children with autism receiving early and intensive behavioral intervention in mainstream preschool and kindergarten settings. *Research in Autism Spectrum Disorders, 6*(2), 829–835.

Ferguson, C. J. (2007). The good, the bad and the ugly: A meta-analytic review of positive and negative effects of violent video games. *Psychiatric Quarterly, 78*(4), 309–316.

Ferster, C. B., & Skinner, B. F. (1957). *Schedules of reinforcement.* East Norwalk, CT: Appleton-Century-Crofts.

Fielding, C., Lowdermilk, J., Lanier, L. L., Fannin, A. G., Schkade, J. L., Rose, C. A., & Simpson, C. G. (2013). Applied behavior analysis: Current myths in public education. *Journal of the American Academy of Special Education Professionals, Sp/Su*, 83–97.

Frum, L. (2013, November). Emerging technology heightens video-game realism. Retrieved from http://www.cnn.com/2013/11/14/tech/gaming-gadgets/realism-video-games

Gallese, V., Fadiga, L., Fogassi, L., & Rizzolatti, G. (1996). Action recognition in the premotor cortex. *Brain, 119*(2), 593–609.

Garcia, J., & Koelling, R. A. (1966). Relation of cue to consequence in avoidance learning. *Psychonomic Science, 4*(1), 123–124.

Gentile, D. A., Li, D., Khoo, A., Prot, S., & Anderson, C. A. (2014). Mediators and moderators of long-term effects of violent video games on aggressive behavior: practice, thinking, and action. *JAMA Pediatrics, 168*(5), 450–457.

Gentile, D. A., Lynch, P. J., Linder, J. R., & Walsh, D. A. (2004). The effects of violent video game habits on adolescent hostility, aggressive behaviors, and school performance. *Journal of Adolescence, 27*(1), 5–22.

Gershoff, E. T., & Grogan-Kaylor, A. (2016, April 7). Spanking and child outcomes: Old controversies and new meta-analyses. *Journal of Family Psychology.* Advance online publication. http://dx.doi.org/10.1037/fam0000191

GITEACPOC (2014). States with full abolition. Retrieved 5/30/12 from http://www.endcorporalpunishment.org/pages/progress/prohib_states.html

Hahn, C. (2013). *The differences and similarities between classical and operant conditioning.* GRIN Verlag.

Hackenberg, T. D. (2009). Token reinforcement: A review and analysis. *Journal of the Experimental Analysis of Behavior, 91*(2), 257–286.

Hall, P. S. (2013). A new definition of punishment. *Reclaiming Children and Youth, 21*(4), 22–26.

Hickok, G. (2014). *The myth of mirror neurons: The real neuroscience of communication and cognition.* New York, NY: W.W. Norton & Company.

Holden, G. W., Williamson, P. A., & Holland, G. W. (2014). Eavesdropping on the family: A pilot investigation of corporal punishment in the home. *Journal of Family Psychology, 28*(3), 401.

Hulac, D. M., & Briesch, A. M. (2017). *Evidence-Based Strategies for Effective Classroom Management.* New York, NY: Guilford Publications.

Jensen, R. (2006). Behaviorism, latent learning, and cognitive maps: Needed revisions in introductory psychology textbooks. *The Behavior Analyst, 29*(2), 187.

Johnson, R. A., Danis, M., & Hafner-Eaton, C. (2014). U.S. state variation in autism insurance mandates: Balancing access and fairness. *Autism*, doi: 1362361314529191.

Kamenetz, A. (2013). Why video games succeed where the movie and music industries fail. Retrieved from https://www.fastcompany.com/3021008/why-video-games-succeed-where-the-movie-and-music-industries-fail

Kandel, E. R. (2001). The molecular biology of memory storage: A dialogue between genes and synapses. *Science, 294*(5544), 1030–1038.

Kazdin, A. E. (2012). *Behavior modification in applied settings* (7th ed.). Long Grove, IL: Waveland Press.

Kazdin, A. E. (1982). The token economy: A decade later. *Journal of Applied Behavior Analysis, 15*(3), 431–445.

Kodaira, S. I. (1998). A review of research on media violence in Japan. *Children and Media Violence*, 81–105.

Köhler, W. (1927). *The mentality of apes* (2nd ed.). New York, NY: Vintage Books.

Kokaridas, D., Maggouritsa, G., Stoforos, P., Patsiaouras, A., Theodorakis, Y., & Diggelidis, N. (2013). The effect of a token economy system program and physical activity on improving quality of life of patients with schizophrenia: A pilot study. *American Journal of Applied Psychology, 2*(6), 80–88.

Larzelere, R. E. (2000). Child outcomes of nonabusive and customary physical punishment by parents: An updated literature review. *Clinical Child and Family Psychology Review, 3*(4), 199–221.

Larzelere, R. E., & Kuhn, B. R. (2005). Comparing child outcomes of physical punishment and alternative disciplinary tactics: A meta-analysis. *Clinical Child and Family Psychology Review, 8*(1), 1–37.

Lee, S. J., Taylor, C. A., Altschul, I., & Rice, J. C. (2013). Parental spanking and subsequent risk for child aggression in father-involved families of young children. *Children and Youth Services Review, 35*(9), 1476–1485.

Lerman, D. C., & Iwata, B. A. (1995). Prevalence of the extinction burst and its attenuation during treatment. *Journal of Applied Behavior Analysis, 28*(1), 93–94.

Lerman, D. C., & Iwata, B. A. (1996). Developing a technology for the use of operant extinction in clinical settings: An examination of basic and applied research. *Journal of Applied Behavior Analysis, 29*(3), 345–382.

Mandell, D., & Lecavalier, L. (2014). Should we believe the Centers for Disease Control and Prevention's autism spectrum disorder prevalence estimates? *Autism, 18*(5), 482–484.

McIlvaine, A. (2013). Google tackles incentives and rewards. HRE Daily. Retrieved from http://blog.hreonline.com/2013/04/29/google-tackles-incentives-and-rewards/

Mischel, W., Ebbesen, E. B., & Raskoff Zeiss, A. (1972). Cognitive and attentional mechanisms in delay of gratification. *Journal of Personality and Social Psychology, 21*(2), 204.

Molenberghs, P., Cunnington, R., & Mattingley, J. B. (2012). Brain regions with mirror properties: A meta-analysis of 125 human fMRI studies. *Neuroscience & Biobehavioral Reviews, 36*(1), 341–349.

Neggers, Y. H. (2014). Increasing prevalence, changes in diagnostic criteria, and nutritional risk factors for autism spectrum disorders. *International Scholarly Research Notices, 2014.* Retrieved from https://www.hindawi.com/journals/isrn/2014/514026/

Nelson, K. G. (2010). Exploration of classroom participation in the presence of a token economy. *Journal of Instructional Psychology, 37*(1), 49–57.

Nielsen, M., Subiaul, F., Galef, B., Zentall, T., & Whiten, A. (2012). Social learning in humans and nonhuman animals: Theoretical and empirical dissections. *Journal of Comparative Psychology, 126*(2), 109–113.

Nithiananatharajah, J., & Hannan, A. J. (2013). Dysregulation of synaptic proteins, dendritic spine abnormalities and pathological plasticity of synapses as experience-dependent mediators of cognitive and psychiatric symptoms in Huntington's disease. *Neuroscience, 251*, 66–74.

Pavlov, I. P. (1928). *Lectures on conditioned reflexes.* New York, NY: Liveright.

Powell, R. A., Digdon, N., Harris, B., & Smithson, C. (2014). Correcting the record on Watson, Rayner, and Little Albert: Albert Barger as "psychology's lost boy." *American Psychologist, 69*(6), 600–611.

Premack, D. (1959). Toward empirical behavior laws: I. Positive reinforcement. *Psychological Review, 66*(4), 219–233.

Reichow, B. (2012). Overview of meta-analyses on early intensive behavioral intervention for young children with autism spectrum disorders. *Journal of Autism and Developmental Disorders, 42*(4), 512–520.

Rizzolatti, G., & Sinigaglia, C. (2016). The mirror mechanism: A basic principle of brain function. *Nature Reviews Neuroscience, 17*(12), 757–765.

Rizzolatti, G., & Craighero, L. (2004). The mirror-neuron system. *Annual Review of Neuroscience, 27*, 169–192.

Rosqvist, J. (2012). *Exposure treatments for anxiety disorders: A practitioner's guide to concepts, methods, and evidence-based practice.* London: Routledge.

Seligman, M. E. (1971). Phobias and preparedness. *Behavior Therapy, 2*(3), 307–32.

Simons, L. G., Simons, R. L., & Su, X. (2013). Consequences of corporal punishment among African Americans: The importance of context and outcome. *Journal of Youth and Adolescence, 42*(8), 1273–1285.

Simons, D. A., & Wurtele, S. K. (2010). Relationships between parents' use of corporal punishment and their children's endorsement of spanking and hitting other children. *Child Abuse & Neglect, 34*(9), 639–646.

Skinner, B. F. (1938). *The behavior of organisms: An experimental analysis.* Oxford, England: Appleton-Century.

Skinner, B. F. (1953). *Science and human behavior.* New York, NY: Simon and Schuster.

Skinner, B. F. (1961). Teaching machines. *Science, 128*, 969–977.

Skinner, B. F. (1974). *About behaviorism.* New York, NY: Knopf Doubleday Publishing Group.

Subiaul, F., & Schilder, B. (2014). Working memory constraints on imitation and emulation. *Journal of Experimental Child Psychology, 128*, 190–200.

Thorndike, E. L. (1898). Animal intelligence. *Psychological Review Monograph, 2* (4, Whole No. 8).

Tolman, E. C., & Honzik, C. H. (1930). Introduction and removal of reward, and maze performance in rats. *University of California Publications in Psychology, 4, 257–275.*

Tolman, E. C. (1948). Cognitive maps in rats and men. *Psychological Review, 55*(4), 189–208.

Watson, J. B., & Rayner, R. (1920). Conditioned emotional reactions. *Journal of Experimental Psychology, 3*(1), 1–14.

Weissman, A. (1960). The behavioral effects of repeated exposure to three mixed extinction schedules. *Journal of the Experimental Analysis of Behavior, 3*(2), 115–122.

Whiten, A. (2017). Social learning and culture in child and chimpanzee. *Annual Review of Psychology, 68*, 129–154.

Whiten, A., Custance, D. M., Gomez, J. C., Teixidor, P., & Bard, K. A. (1996). Imitative learning of artificial fruit processing in children (Homo sapiens) and chimpanzees (Pan troglodytes). *Journal of Comparative Psychology, 110*(1), 3–14.

Whiten, A., McGuigan, N., Marshall-Pescini, S., & Hopper, L. M. (2009). Emulation, imitation, over-imitation and the scope of culture for child and chimpanzee. *Philosophical Transactions of the Royal Society B: Biological Sciences, 364*(1528), 2417–2428.

Chapter 6

Abel, M., & Bäuml, K.-H. T. (2014). Sleep can reduce proactive interference. *Memory, 22*(4), 332–339.

Altmann, E. M., & Gray, W. D. (2002). Forgetting to remember: The functional relationship of decay and interference. *Psychological Science, 13*(1), 27–33.

American Psychological Association. (2017). *Memories of childhood abuse.* Retrieved from http://www.apa.org/topics/trauma/memories.aspx

Anderson, M. C., & Hanslmayr, S. (2014). Neural mechanisms of motivated forgetting. *Trends in Cognitive Sciences, 18*(6), 279–292.

Annese, J., Schenker-Ahmed, N. M., Bartsch, H., Maechler, P., Sheh, C., Thomas, N., … Corkin, S. (2014). Postmortem examination of patient H.M.'s brain based on histological sectioning and digital 3D reconstruc-

tion. *Nature Communications, 5*, 1–9. doi: 10.1038/ncomms4122

Atherton, K. E., Nobre, A. C., Zeman, A. Z., & Butler, C. R. (2014). Sleep-dependent memory consolidation and accelerated forgetting. *Cortex, 54*, 92–105.

Atkinson, R. C., & Shiffrin, R. M. (1968). *Human memory: A proposed system and its control processes* (Vol. 2). New York, NY: Academic Press.

Atkinson, R. C., & Shiffrin, R. M. (1971). *The control processes of short-term memory*: Stanford University: Citeseer.

Baddeley, A. (2012). Working memory: Theories, models, and controversies. *Annual Review of Psychology, 63*, 1–29.

Baddeley, A., & Hitch, G. J. (1974). Working memory. *The Psychology of Learning and Motivation, 8*, 47–89.

Baddeley, A., & Scott, D. (1971). Short term forgetting in the absence of proactive interference. *The Quarterly Journal of Experimental Psychology, 23*(3), 275–283.

Bargh, J. A. (2006). What have we been priming all these years? On the development, mechanisms, and ecology of nonconscious social behavior. *European Journal of Social Psychology, 36*(2), 147–168.

Bargh, J. A. (2011). Unconscious thought theory and its discontents: A critique of the critiques. *Social Cognition, 29*(6), 629–647.

Barrouillet, P., De Paepe, A., & Langerock, N. (2012). Time causes forgetting from working memory. *Psychonomic Bulletin & Review, 19*(1), 87–92.

Baxendale, S. (2004). Memories aren't made of this: Amnesia at the movies. *BMJ, 329*(7480), 1480–1483.

Berk, M., & Parker, G. (2009). The elephant on the couch: Side-effects of psychotherapy. *Australian and New Zealand Journal of Psychiatry, 43*(787–794).

Bernstein, D. M., & Loftus, E. F. (2009a). The consequences of false memories for food preferences and choices. *Perspectives on Psychological Science, 4*(2), 135–139.

Bernstein, D. M., & Loftus, E. F. (2009b). How to tell if a particular memory is true or false. *Perspectives on Psychological Science, 4*(4), 370–374.

Bernstein, D. M., Scoboria, A., & Arnold, R. (2015). The consequences of suggesting false childhood food events. *Acta Psychologica, 156*, 1–7.

Binder, S., Baier, P. C., Mölle, M., Inostroza, M., Born, J., & Marshall, L. (2012). Sleep enhances memory consolidation in the hippocampus-dependent object-place recognition task in rats. *Neurobiology of Learning and Memory, 97*(2), 213–219.

Bjork, E. L., & Bjork, R. A. (2011). Making things hard on yourself, but in a good way: Creating desirable difficulties to enhance learning. *Psychology and the Real World: Essays Illustrating Fundamental Contributions to Society*, 56–64.

Bliss, T. V., & Collingridge, G. L. (1993). A synaptic model of memory: Long-term potentiation in the hippocampus. *Nature, 361*(6407), 31–39.

Bornstein, B. H., Deffenbacher, K. A., Penrod, S. D., & McGorty, E. K. (2012). Effects of exposure time and cognitive operations on facial identification accuracy: A meta-analysis of two variables associated with initial memory strength. *Psychology, Crime & Law, 18*(5), 473–490.

Bradley, C., & Pearson, J. (2012). The sensory components of high-capacity iconic memory and visual working memory. *Frontiers in Psychology, 3*, 1–8.

Brady, T. F., Konkle, T., Alvarez, G. A., & Oliva, A. (2008). Visual long-term memory has a massive storage capacity for object details. *Proceedings of the National Academy of Sciences, 105*(38), 14325–14329.

Brewer, W. F. (1977). Memory for the pragmatic implications of sentences. *Memory & Cognition, 5*(6), 673–678.

Brewin, C. R. (2012). A theoretical framework for understanding recovered memory experiences. *True and False Recovered Memories*, (pp. 149–173). Springer.

Brewin, C. R., & Andrews, B. (2017). Creating memories for false autobiographical events in childhood: A systematic review. *Applied Cognitive Psychology, 31*(1), 2–23. doi: 10.1002/acp.3220

Brown, J. (1958). Some tests of the decay theory of immediate memory. *Quarterly Journal of Experimental Psychology, 10*(1), 12–21.

Brown, R., & Kulik, J. (1977). Flashbulb memories. *Cognition, 5*(1), 73–99.

Brown, S. C., & Craik, F. I. (2000). Encoding and retrieval of information. In E. Tulving & F. I. M. Craik (Eds.), *The Oxford handbook of memory* (pp. 93–107). New York, NY: Oxford University Press.

Burkard, C., Rochat, L., Emmenegger, J., Juillerat Van der Linden, A. C., Gold, G., & Van der Linden, M. (2014). Implementation intentions improve prospective memory and inhibition performances in older adults: The role of visualization. *Applied Cognitive Psychology, 28*(5), 640–652.

Cai, D., Pearce, K., Chen, S., & Glanzman, D. L. (2012). Reconsolidation of long-term memory in Aplysia. *Current Biology, 22*(19), 1783–1788.

Carpenter, S. K. (2012). Testing enhances the transfer of learning. *Current Directions in Psychological Science, 21*(5), 279–283.

Carvalho, P. F., & Goldstone, R. L. (2017). The sequence of study changes what information is attended to, encoded, and remembered during category learning. *Journal of Experimental Psychology.* doi: http://dx.doi.org/10.1037/slm0000406

Clark, I. A., & Maguire, E. A. (2015). Remembering preservation in hippocampal amnesia. *Annual Review of Psychology, 67*(1), 51–82.

Cowan, N. (2001). The magical number 4 in short-term memory: A reconsideration of mental storage capacity. *Behavioral and Brain Sciences, 24*(1), 87–114.

Cowan, N. (2008). What are the differences between long-term, short-term, and working memory? *Progress in Brain Research, 169*, 323–338. doi: 10.1016/S0079-6123(07)00020-9

Cowan, N. (2010). The magical mystery four: How is working memory capacity limited, and why? *Current Directions in Psychological Science, 19*(1), 51–57. doi: 10.1177/0963721409359277

Craik, F. I., & Tulving, E. (1975). Depth of processing and the retention of words in episodic memory. *Journal of Experimental Psychology: General, 104*(3), 268–294.

D'Ardenne, K., Eshel, N., Luka, J., Lenartowicz, A., Nystrom, L. E., & Cohen, J. D. (2012). Role of prefrontal cortex and the midbrain dopamine system in working memory updating. *Proceedings of the National Academy of Sciences, 109*(49), 19900–19909.

D'Esposito, M., & Postle, B. R. (2015). The cognitive neuroscience of working memory. *Annual Review of Psychology, 66*, 115–142.

Davidson, P. S., Cook, S. P., Glisky, E. L., Verfaellie, M., & Rapcsak, S. Z. (2005). Source memory in the real world: A neuropsychological study of flashbulb memory. *Journal of Clinical and Experimental Neuropsychology, 27*(7), 915–929.

Dede, A. J., Wixted, J. T., Hopkins, R. O., & Squire, L. R. (2013). Hippocampal damage impairs recognition memory broadly, affecting both parameters in two prominent models of memory. *Proceedings of the National Academy of Sciences, 110*(16), 6577–6582.

Deliens, G., Leproult, R., Neu, D., & Peigneux, P. (2013). Rapid eye movement and non-rapid eye movement sleep contributions in memory consolidation and resistance to retroactive interference for verbal material. *Sleep, 36*(12), 1875–1883.

DePrince, A. P., Brown, L. S., Cheit, R. E., Freyd, J. J., Gold, S. N., Pezdek, K., & Quina, K. (2012). Motivated forgetting and misremembering: Perspectives from betrayal trauma theory. *True and False Recovered Memories* (pp. 193–242). New York, NY: Springer.

Dewar, M. T., Cowan, N., & Della Sala, S. (2007). Forgetting due to retroactive interference: A fusion of Müller and Pilzecker's (1900) early insights into everyday forgetting and recent research on anterograde amnesia. *Cortex, 43*(5), 616–634.

Dijksterhuis, A., Bos, M. W., Nordgren, L. F., & Van Baaren, R. B. (2006). On making the right choice: The deliberation-without-attention effect. *Science, 311*(5763), 1005–1007.

Doyon, J., Bellec, P., Amsel, R., Penhune, V., Monchi, O., Carrier, J., … Benali, H. (2009). Contributions of the basal ganglia and functionally related brain structures to motor learning. *Behavioural Brain Research, 199*(1), 61–75.

Eakin, D. K., & Smith, R. (2012). Retroactive interference effects in implicit memory. *Journal of Experimental Psychology: Learning, Memory, and Cognition, 38*(5), 1419–1424.

Faulkner, Z. E., & Leaver, E. E. (2016). Memories: True or false? Physiological measures may answer the question. *Imagination, Cognition and Personality, 36*(2), 92–115.

Feng, W., Wu, Y., Jan, C., Yu, H., Jiang, X., & Zhou, X. (2017). Effects of contextual relevance on pragmatic inference during conversation: An fMRI study. *Brain and Language, 171*, 52–61.

Frenda, S. J., Knowles, E. D., Saletan, W., & Loftus, E. F. (2013). False memories of fabricated political events. *Journal of Experimental Social Psychology, 49*(2), 280–286.

Gabrieli, J. D. (1998). Cognitive neuroscience of human memory. *Annual Review of Psychology, 49*(1), 87–115.

Geraerts, E., Schooler, J. W., Merckelbach, H., Jelicic, M., Hauer, B. J., & Ambadar, Z. (2007). The reality of recovered memories corroborating continuous and discontinuous memories of childhood sexual abuse. *Psychological Science, 18*(7), 564–568.

Glanzer, M., & Cunitz, A. R. (1966). Two storage mechanisms in free recall. *Journal of Verbal Learning and Verbal Behavior, 5*(4), 351–360.

Gobet, F., Lane, P. C., Croker, S., Cheng, P. C., Jones, G., Oliver, I., & Pine, J. M. (2001). Chunking mechanisms in human learning. *Trends in Cognitive Sciences, 5*(6), 236–243.

Godden, D. R., & Baddeley, A. D. (1975). Context-dependent memory in two natural environments: On land and underwater. *British Journal of Psychology, 66*(3), 325–331.

Graf, P., & Schacter, D. L. (1985). Implicit and explicit memory for new associations in normal and amnesic subjects. *Journal of Experimental Psychology: Learning, Memory, and Cognition, 11*(3), 501–518.

Hampstead, B. M., Sathian, K., Phillips, P. A., Amaraneni, A., Delaune, W. R., & Stringer, A. Y. (2012). Mnemonic strategy training improves memory for object location associations in both healthy elderly and patients with amnestic mild cognitive impairment: A randomized, single-blind study. *Neuropsychology, 26*(3), 385–399.

Hardt, O., Nader, K., & Nadel, L. (2013). Decay happens: The role of active forgetting in memory. *Trends in Cognitive Sciences, 17*(3), 111–120.

Heikkilä, J., Alho, K., Hyvönen, H., & Tiippana, K. (2014). Audiovisual semantic congruency during encoding enhances memory performance. *Experimental Psychology, 10*, 1–8.

Herdegen, S., Holmes, G., Cyriac, A., Calin-Jageman, I. E., & Calin-Jageman, R. J. (2014). Characterization of the rapid transcriptional response to long-term sensitization training in Aplysia californica. *Neurobiology of Learning and Memory, 116*, 27–35.

Hirst, W., Phelps, E. A., Meksin, R., Vaidya, C. J., Johnson, M. K., Mitchell, K. J., ... Lustig, C. (2015). A ten-year follow-up of a study of memory for the attack of September 11, 2001: Flashbulb memories and memories for flashbulb events. *Journal of Experimental Psychology: General, 144*(3), 604–623.

Hsu, S. (2013). Police chiefs lead effort to prevent wrongful convictions by altering investigative practices. Retrieved September 26, 2015, from https://www.washingtonpost.com/local/crime/police-chiefs-urge-changes-to-photo-lineups-other-tools-to-prevent-wrongful-convictions/2013/12/02/5d8e9af2-5b69-11e3-bf7e-f567ee61ae21_story.html

Hyman, I. E., & Billings, F. J. (1998). Individual differences and the creation of false childhood memories. *Memory, 6*(1), 1–20.

Hyman, I. E., Husband, T. H., & Billings, F. J. (1995). False memories of childhood experiences. *Applied Cognitive Psychology, 9*(3), 181–197.

Jacoby, L. L., Kelley, C., Brown, J., & Jasechko, J. (1989). Becoming famous overnight: Limits on the ability to avoid unconscious influences of the past. *Journal of Personality and Social Psychology, 56*(3), 326–338.

James, L. E., & Burke, D. M. (2000). Phonological priming effects on word retrieval and tip-of-the-tongue experiences in young and older adults. *Journal of Experimental Psychology: Learning, Memory, and Cognition, 26*(6), 1378–1391.

Jenkins, J. G., & Dallenbach, K. M. (1924). Obliviscence during sleep and waking. *American Journal of Psychology, 35*, 605–612.

Johnson, M. K., Hashtroudi, S., & Lindsay, D. S. (1993). Source monitoring. *Psychological Bulletin, 114*(1), 3–28.

Jonides, J., & Nee, D. E. (2006). Brain mechanisms of proactive interference in working memory. *Neuroscience, 139*(1), 181–193.

Kandel, E. R. (2001). The molecular biology of memory storage: A dialogue between genes and synapses. *Science, 294*(5544), 1030–1038.

Karpicke, J. D., & Aue, W. R. (2015). The testing effect is alive and well with complex materials. *Educational Psychology Review, 27*(2), 317–326.

Kelemen, W. L., & Creeley, C. E. (2003). State-dependent memory effects using caffeine and placebo do not extend to metamemory. *Journal of General Psychology, 130*(1), 70–86.

Kitamura, T., Ogawa, S. K., Roy, D. S., Okuyama, T., Morrissey, M. D., Smith, L. M., ... Tonegawa, S. (2017). Engrams and circuits crucial for systems consolidation of a memory. *Science, 356*(6333), 73–78.

Kolodner, J. L. (1983). Reconstructive memory: A computer model. *Cognitive Science, 7*(4), 281–328.

Lashley, K. S. (1950). *In search of the engram.* Oxford, England: Academic Press.

Lindsay, D. S. (2014). Memory source monitoring applied. In T. J. Perfect & D. S. Lindsay (Eds.), *The sage handbook of applied memory* (pp. 59–75). London, England: Sage Publications.

Lindsay, D. S., & Briere, J. (1997). The controversy regarding recovered memories of childhood sexual abuse pitfalls, bridges, and future directions. *Journal of Interpersonal Violence, 12*(5), 631–647.

Liu, A., Ying, X., & Luo, J. (2012). The flashbulb memory of the positive and negative events: Wenchuan earthquake and acceptance to college. *World Academy of Science, Engineering and Technology, International Journal of Social, Behavioral, Educational, Economic, Business and Industrial Engineering, 6*(5), 738–743.

Loftus, E. F. (1993). The reality of repressed memories. *American Psychologist, 48*(5), 518–537.

Loftus, E. F. (1997). Creating false memories. *Scientific American, 277*(3), 70–75.

Loftus, E. F., & Loftus, G. R. (1980). On the permanence of stored information in the human brain. *American Psychologist, 35*(5), 409–420.

Loftus, E. F., & Palmer, J. C. (1974). Reconstruction of automobile destruction: An example of the interaction between language and memory. *Journal of Verbal Learning and Verbal Behavior, 13*(5), 585–589.

Loney, D. M., & Cutler, B. L. (2016). Coercive interrogation of eyewitnesses can produce false accusations. *Journal of Police and Criminal Psychology, 31*(1), 29–36.

Loosli, S. V., Rahm, B., Unterrainer, J. M., Weiller, C., & Kaller, C. P. (2014). Developmental change in proactive interference across the life span: Evidence from two working memory tasks. *Developmental Psychology, 50*(4), 1060–1072.

Lu, X. (2013). The cerebellum and cerebello-thalamo-cortical channels contribute to new learning and long-term memory of motor skill. *Brain Disorders & Therapy 2*, e106.

Lum, J. A., & Conti-Ramsden, G. (2013). Long-term memory: A review and meta-analysis of studies of declarative and procedural memory in Specific Language Impairment. *Topics in Language Disorders, 33*(4), 282–297.

Luna, K., & Martín-Luengo, B. (2013). Monitoring the source monitoring. *Cognitive Processing, 14*(4), 347–356.

Mantonakis, A., Wudarzewski, A., Bernstein, D. M., Clifasefi, S. L., & Loftus, E. F. (2013a). False beliefs can shape current consumption. *Psychology, 4*(3A), 302–308.

Mantonakis, A., Wudarzewski, A., Bernstein, D. M., Clifasefi, S. L., & Loftus, E. F. (2013b). False beliefs can shape current consumption. *Psychology 4*(3A), 302–308.

Mathy, F., & Feldman, J. (2012). What's magic about magic numbers? Chunking and data compression in short-term memory. *Cognition, 122*(3), 346–362. doi: http://dx.doi.org/10.1016/j.cognition.2011.11.003

McCabe, J. A. (2015). Learning the brain in introductory psychology examining the generation effect for mnemonics and examples. *Teaching of Psychology, 42*(3), 203–210.

McClelland, J. L. (1995). Constructive memory and memory distortions: A parallel-distributed processing approach. In D. L. Schacter (Ed.), *Memory distortion: How minds, brains, and societies reconstruct the past* (pp. 69–90). Boston, MA: President and Fellows of Harvard College.

McClelland, J. L. (2000). Connectionist models of memory. In E. Tulving & F. I. M. Craik (Eds.), *The Oxford handbook of memory* (pp. 583–596). New York, NY: Oxford.

McClelland, J. L. (2011). Memory as a constructive process: The parallel-distributed processing approach. In S. Nalbantian, P. Matthews, & J. McClelland (Eds.), *The memory process: Neuroscientific and humanistic perspectives.* Cambridge, MA: MIT Press.

McClelland, J. L., & Rumelhart, D. E. (1985). Distributed memory and the representation of general and specific information. *Journal of Experimental Psychology: General, 114*(2), 159–188.

McDaniel, M., & Pressley, M. (2012). *Imagery and related mnemonic processes: Theories, individual differences, and applications.* New York, NY: Springer Science & Business Media.

McDermott, K. B., & Chan, J. C. (2006). Effects of repetition on memory for pragmatic inferences. *Memory & Cognition, 34*(6), 1273–1284.

McDevitt, E. A., Duggan, K. A., & Mednick, S. C. (2015). REM sleep rescues learning from interference. *Neurobiology of Learning and Memory, 122*, 51–62.

McNally, R. J. (2017). False memories in the laboratory and in life: Commentary on Brewin and Andrews (2016). *Applied Cognitive Psychology, 31*(1), 40–41. doi: 10.1002/acp.3268

Mensink, G.-J., & Raaijmakers, J. G. (1988). A model for interference and forgetting. *Psychological Review, 95*(4), 434–455.

Meyer, A. N., & Logan, J. M. (2013). Taking the testing effect beyond the college freshman: Benefits for lifelong learning. *Psychology and Aging, 28*(1), 142–147.

Mickes, L., Flowe, H. D., & Wixted, J. T. (2012). Receiver operating characteristic analysis of eyewitness memory: Comparing the diagnostic accuracy of simultaneous versus sequential lineups. *Journal of Experimental Psychology: Applied, 18*(4), 361–376.

Mickley-Steinmetz, K. R., Waring, J. D., & Kensinger, E. A. (2014). The effect of divided attention on emotion-induced memory narrowing. *Cognition & Emotion, 28*(5), 881–892.

Miller, G. A. (1956). The magical number seven, plus or minus two: Some limits on our capacity for processing information. *Psychological Review, 63*(2), 81–97.

Miller, K. J., Siddarth, P., Gaines, J. M., Parrish, J. M., Ercoli, L. M., Marx, K., ... Barczak, N. (2012). The memory fitness program: Cognitive effects of a healthy aging intervention. *American Journal of Geriatric Psychiatry, 20*(6), 514–523.

Mitchell, K. J., & Johnson, M. K. (2009). Source monitoring 15 years later: What have we learned from fMRI about the neural mechanisms of source memory? *Psychological Bulletin, 135*(4), 638–677. doi: 10.1037/a0015849

Mizrahi, M. (2013). Breaking news: Students prefer multiple-choice exams (and they hate writing papers). Retrieved October 4, 2015, from http://philosopherscocoon.typepad.com/blog/2013/01/breaking-news-students-prefer-multiple-choice-exams-and-they-hate-writing-papers.html

Moscovitch, M., & Craik, F. I. (1976). Depth of processing, retrieval cues, and uniqueness of encoding as factors in recall. *Journal of Verbal Learning and Verbal Behavior, 15*(4), 447–458.

Murdock Jr, B. B. (1962). The serial position effect of free recall. *Journal of Experimental Psychology, 64*(5), 482–488.

Nairne, J. S. (2015). *Remembering: Attributions, processes, and control in human memory* (D. S. Lindsay, C. M. Kelley, A. P. Yonelinas, & H. L. Roediger III, Eds.). New York, NY: Psychology Press.

Nash, R. A., Berkowitz, S. R., & Roche, S. (2016). Public attitudes on the ethics of deceptively planting false memories to motivate healthy behavior. *Applied Cognitive Psychology, 30*(6), 885–897. doi: 10.1002/acp.3274

Nash, R. A., Wade, K. A., Garry, M., Loftus, E. F., & Ost, J. (2017). Misrepresentations and flawed logic about the prevalence of false memories. *Applied Cognitive Psychology, 31*(1), 31–33. doi: 10.1002/acp.3265

Ost, J., Wright, D. B., Easton, S., Hope, L., & French, C. C. (2013). Recovered memories, satanic abuse, dissociative identity disorder and false memories in the UK: A survey of clinical psychologists and hypnotherapists. *Psychology, Crime & Law, 19*(1), 1–19.

Otgaar, H., Merckelbach, H., Jelicic, M., & Smeets, T. (2017). The potential for false memories is bigger than what Brewin and Andrews suggest. *Applied Cognitive Psychology, 31*(1), 24–25.

Packard, M. G., & Knowlton, B. J. (2002). Learning and memory functions of the basal ganglia. *Annual Review of Neuroscience, 25*(1), 563–593.

Patihis, L., Frenda, S. J., LePort, A. K., Petersen, N., Nichols, R. M., Stark, C. E., … Loftus, E. F. (2013). False memories in highly superior autobiographical memory individuals. *Proceedings of the National Academy of Sciences, 110*(52), 20947–20952.

Patihis, L., & Loftus, E. F. (2016). Crashing memory 2.0: False memories in adults for an upsetting childhood event. *Applied Cognitive Psychology, 30*, 41–50. doi: 10.1002/acp.3165

Persuh, M., Genzer, B., & Melara, R. D. (2012). Iconic memory requires attention. *Frontiers in Human Neuroscience, 6*, 1–8.

Phelps, E. A., & Sharot, T. (2008). How (and why) emotion enhances the subjective sense of recollection. *Current Directions in Psychological Science, 17*(2), 147–152. doi: 10.1111/j.1467-8721.2008.00565.x

Pinsker, H. M., Hening, W. A., Carew, T. J., & Kandel, E. R. (1973). Long-term sensitization of a defensive withdrawal reflex in Aplysia. *Science, 182*(4116), 1039–1042.

Pope, K. S. (1996). Memory, abuse, and science: Questioning claims about the false memory syndrome epidemic. *American Psychologist, 51*(9), 957–974.

Porter, S., Birt, A. R., Yuille, J. C., & Lehman, D. R. (2000). Negotiating false memories: Interviewer and rememberer characteristics relate to memory distortion. *Psychological Science, 11*(6), 507–510.

Porter, S., Yuille, J. C., & Lehman, D. R. (1999). The nature of real, implanted, and fabricated memories for emotional childhood events: implications for the recovered memory debate. *Law and Human Behavior, 23*(5), 517–537.

Porter, S. B., & Baker, A. T. (2015). CSI (crime scene induction): Creating false memories of committing crime. *Trends in Cognitive Sciences, 19*(12), 716–718.

Raaijmakers, J. G., & Jakab, E. (2012). Rethinking inhibition theory: On the problematic status of the inhibition theory for forgetting. *Journal of Memory and Language, 68*(2), 98–122.

Raaijmakers, J. G., & Shiffrin, R. M. (2003). Models versus descriptions: Real differences and language differences. *Behavioral and Brain Sciences, 26*(6), 753–754.

Ratcliff, R. (2014). Parallel-processing mechanisms and processing of organized information in human memory. In G. E. Hinton & J. A. Anderson (Eds.), *Parallel models of associative memory: Updated edition* (pp. 309–327). New York, NY: Psychology Press.

Rensink, R. A. (2014). Limits to the usability of iconic memory. *Frontiers in Psychology, 5*, 1–9.

Ricker, T. J., Vergauwe, E., & Cowan, N. (2016). Decay theory of immediate memory: From Brown (1958) to today (2014). *Quarterly Journal of Experimental Psychology 69*, 1969–1995.

Roberts, G., Scammacca, N., Osman, D. J., Hall, C., Mohammed, S. S., & Vaughn, S. (2014). Team-based learning: Moderating effects of metacognitive elaborative rehearsal and middle school history content recall. *Educational Psychology Review, 26*(3), 451–468.

Robillard, J. M., & Illes, J. (2016). Manipulating memories: The ethics of yesterday's science fiction and today's reality. *AMA Journal of Ethics, 18*(12), 1225–1231.

Roediger, H. L., & DeSoto, K. A. (2015). Reconstructive memory, psychology of. In J. D. Wright (Ed.), *International encyclopedia of the social & behavioral sciences (second edition)* (pp. 50–55). Oxford: Elsevier.

Roediger, H. L., & Karpicke, J. D. (2006). Test-enhanced learning taking memory tests improves long-term retention. *Psychological Science, 17*(3), 249–255.

Rose, N. S., Craik, F. I., & Buchsbaum, B. R. (2015). Levels of processing in working memory: Differential involvement of frontotemporal networks. *Journal of Cognitive Neuroscience, 27*(3), 522–532.

Rosenbaum, R. S., Gilboa, A., & Moscovitch, M. (2014). Case studies continue to illuminate the cognitive neuroscience of memory. *Annals of the New York Academy of Sciences, 1316*(1), 105–133.

Rundus, D. (1971). Analysis of rehearsal processes in free recall. *Journal of Experimental Psychology, 89*(1), 63–77.

Sana, F., Yan, V. X., & Kim, J. A. (2017). Study sequence matters for the inductive learning of cognitive concepts. *Journal of Educational Psychology, 109*(1), 84–98.

Sanday, L., Zanin, K. A., Patti, C. L., Fernandes-Santos, L., Oliveira, L. C., Longo, B. M., … Frussa-Filho, R. (2013). Role of state-dependent learning in the cognitive effects of caffeine in mice. *International Journal of Neuropsychopharmacology, 16*(7), 1547–1557.

Schacter, D. L., & Loftus, E. F. (2013). Memory and law: What can cognitive neuroscience contribute? *Nature Neuroscience, 16*(2), 119–123.

Schott, B. H., Wüstenberg, T., Wimber, M., Fenker, D. B., Zierhut, K. C., Seidenbecher, C. I., … Richardson-Klavehn, A. (2013). The relationship between level of processing and hippocampal–cortical functional connectivity during episodic memory formation in humans. *Human Brain Mapping, 34*(2), 407–424.

Schwartz, B. L., & Metcalfe, J. (2011). Tip-of-the-tongue (TOT) states: Retrieval, behavior, and experience. *Memory & Cognition, 39*(5), 737–749.

Scoboria, A., Wade, K. A., Lindsay, D. S., Azad, T., Strange, D., Ost, J., & Hyman, I. E. (2017). A mega-analysis of memory reports from eight peer-reviewed false memory implantation studies. *Memory, 25*(2), 146–163.

Shaw, J., & Porter, S. (2015). Constructing rich false memories of committing crime. *Psychological Science, 26*(3), 291–301.

Sherry, D. F., & Vaccarino, A. L. (1989). Hippocampus and memory for food caches in black-capped chickadees. *Behavioral Neuroscience, 103*(2), 308–318.

Sheth, B. R., Varghese, R., & Truong, T. (2012). Sleep shelters verbal memory from different kinds of interference. *Sleep, 35*(7), 985–996.

Sperling, G. (1960). The information available in brief visual presentations. *Psychological Monographs: General and Applied, 74*(11), 1–29.

Staniland, J., Colombo, M., & Scarf, D. (2015). The generation effect or simply generating an effect? *Journal of Comparative Psychology, 129*(4), 329–333. doi: http://dx.doi.org/10.1037/a0039450

Stickgold, R., & Walker, M. P. (2007). Sleep-dependent memory consolidation and reconsolidation. *Sleep Medicine, 8*(4), 331–343. doi: 10.1016/j.sleep.2007.03.011

Talarico, J. M., & Rubin, D. C. (2007). Flashbulb memories are special after all; in phenomenology, not accuracy. *Applied Cognitive Psychology, 21*(5), 557–578.

Tanaka, K. Z., Pevzner, A., Hamidi, A. B., Nakazawa, Y., Graham, J., & Wiltgen, B. J. (2014). Cortical representations are reinstated by the hippocampus during memory retrieval. *Neuron, 84*(2), 347–354.

Thomas, A. K., & Loftus, E. F. (2002). Creating bizarre false memories through imagination. *Memory & Cognition, 30*(3), 423–431.

Townsend, J. T., & Fifić, M. (2004). Parallel versus serial processing and individual differences in high-speed search in human memory. *Perception & Psychophysics, 66*(6), 953–962.

Tullis, J. G., & Benjamin, A. S. (2015). Cue generation: How learners flexibly support future retrieval. *Memory & Cognition, 43*(6), 922–938.

Tulving, E., & Osler, S. (1968). Effectiveness of retrieval cues in memory for words. *Journal of Experimental Psychology, 77*(4), 593–601.

Tulving, E., & Thomson, D. M. (1973). Encoding specificity and retrieval processes in episodic memory. *Psychological Review, 80*(5), 352–373.

Turk, D. J., Brady-van den Bos, M., Collard, P., Gillespie-Smith, K., Conway, M. A., & Cunningham, S. J. (2013). Divided attention selectively impairs memory for self-relevant information. *Memory & Cognition, 41*(4), 503–510.

Underwood, B. J., & Postman, L. (1960). Extraexperimental sources of interference in forgetting. *Psychological Review, 67*(2), 73–95.

Wade, K. A., Garry, M., & Pezdek, K. (2018). Deconstructing rich false memories of committing crime: Commentary on Shaw and Porter (2015). *Psychological Science.* https://doi.org/10.1177/0956797617703667

Wagenmakers, E. J., Beek, T., Dijkhoff, L., Gronau, Q. F., Acosta, A., Adams Jr, R. B., … Bulnes, L. C. (2016). Registered Replication Report: Strack, Martin, & Stepper (1988). *Perspectives on Psychological Science, 11*(6), 917–928.

Ward, P. J., & Walker, J. J. (2008). The influence of study methods and knowledge processing on academic success and long-term recall of anatomy learning by first-year veterinary students. *Anatomical Sciences Education, 1*(2), 68–74.

Weinstein, Y., McDermott, K. B., & Roediger III, H. L. (2010). A comparison of study strategies for passages: re-reading, answering questions, and generating questions. *Journal of Experimental Psychology: Applied, 16*(3), 308–316.

Wells, G. L., & Quinlivan, D. S. (2009). Suggestive eyewitness identification procedures and the Supreme Court's reliability test in light of eyewitness science: 30 years later. *Law and Human Behavior, 33*(1), 1–24.

Wells, G. L., Small, M., Penrod, S., Malpass, R. S., Fulero, S. M., & Brimacombe, C. E. (1998). Eyewitness identification procedures: Recommendations for lineups and photospreads. *Law and Human Behavior, 22*(6), 1–39.

Wenner, M. (2007). Forgetting to remember. *Scientific American Mind, 18*(5), 13.

Wiemers, U. S., Sauvage, M. M., & Wolf, O. T. (2013). Odors as effective retrieval cues for stressful episodes. *Neurobiology of Learning and Memory, 112*, 230–236.

Winocur, G., Sekeres, M. J., Binns, M. A., & Moscovitch, M. (2013). Hippocampal lesions produce both non-graded and temporally graded retrograde amnesia in the same rat. *Hippocampus, 23*(5), 330–341.

Wixted, J. T. (2004). The psychology and neuroscience of forgetting. *Annual Review of Psychology, 55*, 235–269.

Wixted, J. T., Mickes, L., Clark, S. E., Gronlund, S. D., & Roediger III, H. L. (2015). Initial eyewitness confidence reliably predicts eyewitness identification accuracy. *American Psychologist, 70*(6), 515–526.

Yoon, T., Okada, J., Jung, M. W., & Kim, J. J. (2008). Prefrontal cortex and hippocampus subserve different components of working memory in rats. *Learning & Memory, 15*(3), 97–105. doi: 10.1101/lm.850808

Chapter 7

Abutalebi, J. (2008). Neural aspects of second language representation and language control. *Acta Psychologica, 128*(3), 466–478.

Amabile, T. (2012). Componential theory of creativity. *Harvard Business School Working Papers.*

American Psychological Association. (2012). Research with animals in psychology. Retrieved December 5, 2016, from https://www.apa.org/research/responsible/research-animals.pdf

Anderson, J. R. (1993). Problem solving and learning. *American Psychologist, 48*(1), 35–44.

Anderson, J. R., & Bower, G. H. (2014). *Human associative memory.* New York, NY: Psychology Press.

Anderson, J. R., & Matessa, M. (2014). A rational analysis of categorization. In *Proceedings of the Second*

International Conference on Machine Learning (pp. 76–84). Austin, TX.

Ashby, F. G., & Maddox, W. T. (1992). Complex decision rules in categorization: Contrasting novice and experienced performance. *Journal of Experimental Psychology: Human Perception of Performance, 18*(1), 50–71.

Ashby, F. G., & Ell, S. W. (2001). The neurobiology of human category learning. *Trends in Cognitive Sciences, 5*(5), 204–210.

Babb, S. J., & Crystal, J. D. (2006). Episodic-like memory in the rat. *Current Biology, 16*(13), 1317–1321.

Barberis, N. C. (2012). Thirty years of prospect theory in economics: A review and assessment. *Journal of Economic Perspectives, 27*(1), 173–195.

Baron, J. (2000). *Thinking and deciding.* London, UK: Cambridge University Press.

Beran, M. J., Parrish, A. E., Perdue, B. M., & Washburn, D. A. (2014). Comparative cognition: Past, present, and future. *International Journal of Comparative Psychology/ ISCP; sponsored by the International Society for Comparative Psychology and the University of Calabria, 27*(1), 3–30.

Blais, A. (2000). *To vote or not to vote? The merits and limits of rational choice theory.* Pittsburgh, PA: University of Pittsburgh Press.

Boroditsky, L. (2011). How language shapes thought. *Scientific American, 304*(2), 62–65.

British Council. (2014). English as a medium of instruction: A global challenge for the 2010s. Retrieved April 30, 2014, from http://www.britishcouncil.org/education/ihe/knowledge-centre/english-language-higher-education/going-global-emi

Broca, P. (1861). Remarks on the seat of the faculty of articulated language, following an observation of aphemia (loss of speech). *Bulletin de la Société Anatomique, 6*(1861), 330–357.

Camerer, C. F. (2004). Prospect theory in the wild: Evidence from the field. In C. F. Camerer, G. Loewenstein, and M. Rabin (Eds.), *Advances in Behavioral Economics* (148–161). Princeton, NJ: Princeton University Press.

Carey, S., & Bartlett, E. (1978). Acquiring a single new word. *Institute of Education Sciences: Papers and Reports on Child Development, 15,* 17–29.

Chamorro-Premuzic, T., & Reichenbacher, L. (2008). Effects of personality and threat of evaluation on divergent and convergent thinking. *Journal of Research in Personality, 42*(4), 1095–1101.

Cho, S. H., Nijenhuis, J. T., Vianen, A. E., Kim, H. B., & Lee, K. H. (2010). The relationship between diverse components of intelligence and creativity. *Journal of Creative Behavior, 44*(2), 125–137.

Chomsky, N. (1959). A review of B.F. Skinner's verbal behavior. *Language, 35*(1), 26–58.

Chomsky, N. (1965). *Aspects of the theory of syntax.* Cambridge, MA: Multilingual Matters: MIT Press.

Chu, Y., & MacGregor, J. N. (2011). Human performance on insight problem solving: A review. *Journal of Problem Solving, 3*(2), 119–150.

Coleman, J. S., & Fararo, T. J. (1992). *Rational choice theory.* Newbury Park, NY: Sage Publications.

Crystal, J. D., Alford, W. T., Zhou, W., & Hohmann, A. G. (2013). Source memory in the rat. *Current Biology, 23*(5), 387–391.

Dalley, J. W., & Roiser, J. P. (2012). Dopamine, serotonin and impulsivity. *Neuroscience, 215,* 42–58.

Darwin, C. (1871). *The descent of man, and selection in relation to sex.* London: John Murray, Albemarle Street.

Davidson, J. E., & Sternberg, R. J. (2003). *The psychology of problem solving.* Cambridge, MA: Cambridge University Press.

Deák, G.O. (2014). Slow mapping in lexical development. *Encyclopedia of language development* (pp. 544–547). P. Brooks & V. Kampe, Eds. Thousand Oaks, CA: Sage.

Dekker, S. W. (2017). Rasmussen's legacy and the long arm of rational choice. *Applied Ergonomics, 59,* 554–557.

Devine, P. G., Hirt, E. R., & Gehrke, E. M. (1990). Diagnostic and confirmation strategies in trait hypothesis testing. *Journal of Personality and Social Psychology, 58*(6), 952–963.

De Waal, F. (2016). *Are we smart enough to know how smart animals are?* New York, NY: W. W. Norton & Company.

Duffau, H., Moritz-Gasser, S., & Mandonnet, E. (2014). A re-examination of neural basis of language processing: Proposal of a dynamic hodotopical model from data provided by brain stimulation mapping during picture naming. *Brain and Language, 131,* 1–10.

Durkin, H. E. (1937). Trial and error, gradual analysis, and sudden reorganization: An experimental study of problem solving. *Archives of Psychology (Columbia University), 210,* 1–85.

Emery, N. J., & Clayton, N. S. (2004). The mentality of crows: convergent evolution of intelligence in corvids and apes. *Science, 306*(5703), 1903–1907.

Epstein, R., Schmidt, S. M., & Warfel, R. (2008). Measuring and training creativity competencies: Validation of a new test. *Creativity Research Journal, 20*(1), 7–12.

Ferdowsian, H. R., & Beck, N. (2011). Ethical and scientific considerations regarding animal testing and research. *PloS One, 6*(9), e24059.

Fisher, C., Gertner, Y., Scott, R. M., & Yuan, S. (2010). Syntactic bootstrapping. *Wiley Interdisciplinary Reviews: Cognitive Science, 1*(2), 143–149.

Fredrickson, B. L. (2000). Why positive emotions matter in organizations: Lessons from the broaden-and-build theory. *The Psychologist-Manager Journal, 4*(2), 131–142.

Friederici, A. D. (2011). The brain basis of language processing: From structure to function. *Physiological Reviews, 91*(4), 1357–1392.

Friederici, A. D. (2012). The cortical language circuit: From auditory perception to sentence comprehension. *Trends in Cognitive Sciences, 16*(5), 262–268.

Friederici, A. D., & Gierhan, S. M. (2013). The language network. *Current Opinion in Neurobiology, 23*(2), 250–254.

Frimer, J. A., Skitka, L. J., & Motyl, M. (2017). Liberals and conservatives are similarly motivated to avoid exposure to one another's opinions. *Journal of Experimental Social Psychology, 72,* 1–12.

Fuchs-Beauchamp, K. D., Karnes, M. B., & Johnson, L. J. (1993). Creativity and intelligence in preschoolers. *Gifted Child Quarterly, 37*(3), 113–117.

Gerlach, K. D., Spreng, R. N., Gilmore, A. W., & Schacter, D. L. (2011). Solving future problems: Default network and executive activity associated with goal-directed mental simulations. *Neuroimage, 55*(4), 1816–1824.

Gick, M. L. (1986). Problem-solving strategies. *Educational Psychologist, 21*(1–2), 99–120.

Gläscher, J., Adolphs, R., Damasio, H., Bechara, A., Rudrauf, D., Calamia, M., … & Tranel, D. (2012). Lesion mapping of cognitive control and value-based decision making in the prefrontal cortex. *Proceedings of the National Academy of Sciences, 109*(36), 14681–14686.

Gordon, R. G. (2005). *Ethnologue: Languages of the world* (Vol. 15). Dallas, TX: Sil International.

Greenwald, A. G. (1980). The totalitarian ego: Fabrication and revision of personal history. *American Psychologist, 35*(7), 603–618.

Gregory, N. G. (2004). *Physiology and behavior of animal suffering.* Oxford, UK: Blackwell Science.

Grimshaw, G. M., Adelstein, A., Bryden, M. P., & MacKinnon, G. E. (1998). First-language acquisition in adolescence: Evidence for a critical period for verbal language development. *Brain and Language, 63*(2), 237–255.

Guenther, C. L., & Alicke, M. D. (2008). Self-enhancement and belief perseverance. *Journal of Experimental Social Psychology, 44*(3), 706–712.

Guilford, J. P. (1967). *The nature of human intelligence.* New York, NY: McGraw-Hill.

Hackam, D. G., & Redelmeier, D. A. (2006). Translation of research evidence from animals to humans. *JAMA, 296*(14), 1727–1732.

Hardisty, D. J., Johnson, E. J., & Weber, E. U. (2010). A dirty word or a dirty world? Attribute framing, political affiliation, and query theory. *Psychological Science, 21*(1), 86–92.

Harel, A., Kravitz, D., & Baker, C. I. (2013). Beyond perceptual expertise: Revisiting the neural substrates of expert object recognition. *Frontiers in Human Neuroscience, 7,* 885. http://doi.org/10.3389/fnhum.2013.00885.

Harlow, H. F. & Zimmermann, R. R. (1958). The development of affective responsiveness in infant monkeys. *Proceedings of the American Philosophical Society, 102,* 501–509.

Hodgson, G. (2012). On the limits of rational choice theory. *Economic Thought, 1*(1), 94–108.

Inoue, S., & Matsuzawa, T. (2007). Working memory of numerals in chimpanzees. *Current Biology, 17*(23), R1004–R1005.

Jauk, E., Benedek, M., Dunst, B., & Neubauer, A. C. (2013). The relationship between intelligence and creativity: New support for the threshold hypothesis by means of empirical breakpoint detection. *Intelligence, 41*(4), 212–221.

Jenni, N. L., Larkin, J. D., & Floresco, S. B. (2017). Prefrontal dopamine D 1 and D 2 receptors regulate dissociable aspects of decision making via distinct ventral striatal and amygdalar circuits. *Journal of Neuroscience, 37*(26), 6200–6213.

Jennings, W. G., & Beaudry-Cyr, M. (2014). Rational choice theory. *The Encyclopedia of Theoretical Criminology,* 1–3.

Johnson, K. E., & Mervis, C. B. (1997). Effects of varying levels of expertise on the basic level of categorization. *Journal of Experimental Psychology: General, 126*(3), 248–277.

Johnson, J. S, & Newport, E. L. (1991). Critical period effects on universal properties of language: The status of subjacency in the acquisition of a second language. *Cognition, 39*(3), 215–258.

Jung-Beeman, M., Bowden, E. M., Haberman, J., Frymiare, J. L., Arambel-Liu, S., Greenblatt, R., & … Kounios, J. (2004). Neural activity when people solve verbal problems with insight. Plos Biology, 2(4), 500–510.

Kahneman, D. (2011). *Thinking, fast and slow.* New York, NY: Macmillan.

Kahneman, D., & Tversky, A. (1973). On the psychology of prediction. *Psychological Review, 80*(4), 237–251.

Kahneman, D., & Tversky, A. (1979). Prospect theory: An analysis of decision under risk. *Econometrica: Journal of the Econometric Society, 47*(2), 263–292.

Kay, P., & Kempton, W. (1984). What is the Sapir-Whorf hypothesis? *American Anthropologist, 86*(1), 65–79.

Kida, T. E. (2006). *Don't believe everything you think: The 6 basic mistakes we make in thinking.* Amherst, NY: Prometheus Books.

Kim, K. H. (2005). Can only intelligent people be creative? A meta-analysis. *Prufrock Journal, 16*(2–3), 57–66.

Klayman, J., & Ha, Y. W. (1987). Confirmation, disconfirmation, and information in hypothesis testing. *Psychological Review, 94*(2), 211–228.

Kline, M. E., Snedeker, J., & Schulz, L. E. (2011). Children's comprehension and production of transitive sentences is sensitive to the causal structure of events. In *Proceedings of the 33rd Annual Conference of the Cognitive Science Society* (pp. 2538–2543).

Koppel, R. H., & Storm, B. C. (2014). Escaping mental fixation: Incubation and inhibition in creative problem solving. *Memory, 22*(4), 340–348.

Kovács, Á. M., Kühn, S., Gergely, G., Csibra, G., & Brass, M. (2014). Are all beliefs equal? Implicit belief attributions recruiting core brain regions of theory of mind. *Public Library of Science One, 9*(9), https://doi.org/10.1371/journal.pone.0106558.

Kunda, Z. (1999). *Social cognition: Making sense of people.* Cambridge, MA: MIT Press.

Lee, Y. T. (2000). What is missing in Chinese-Western dialectical reasoning. *American Psychologist, 55*(9), 1065–1067.

Legg, S., & Hutter, M. (2007). Universal intelligence: A definition of machine intelligence. *Minds and Machines, 17*(4), 391–444.

Lenneberg, E. H. (1967). *Biological Foundations of Language.* New York, NY: Wiley.

Leonard, M. K., Brown, T. T., Travis, K. E., Gharapetian, L., Hagler, D. J., Dale, A. M., Elman, J. L., & Halgren, E. (2010). Spatiotemporal dynamics of bilingual word processing. *Neuroimage, 49*(4), 3286–3294.

Leslie, I. (2014). How mistakes can save lives: One man's mission to revolutionise the NHS. *New Statesman.*

Retrieved June 4, 2014, from http://www.newstatesman.com/2014/05/how-mistakes-can-save-lives

Levin, I. P., & Gaeth, G. J. (1988). Framing of attribute information before and after consuming the product. *Journal of Consumer Research, 15*(3), 374–378.

Lewis, M. P., Simons, G. F., & Fennig, C. D. (2015). *Ethnologue: Languages of the World* (18th ed.). Dallas, Texas: SIL International.

Lilienfeld, S. O. (2015). The mother of all biases: Confirmation bias in science, practice, and everyday life. Presented at the Annual Convention of the National Institute on the Teaching of Psychology, St. Pete Beach, FL.

Lilienfeld, S. O., Ammirati, R., & Landfield, K. (2009). Giving debiasing away: Can psychological research on correcting cognitive errors promote human welfare? *Perspectives on Psychological Science, 4*(4), 390–398.

Lin, S., & Kernighan, B. W. (1973). An effective heuristic algorithm for the traveling-salesman problem. *Operations Research, 21*(2), 498–516.

Long, M. H. (1993). Second language acquisition as a function of age: Research findings and methodological issues. In K. Hyltenstam & A. Viberg (Eds.) *Progression and regression in language: Sociocultural, neuropsychological, & linguistic perspectives* (196–221). New York, NY: Cambridge University Press.

Maier, N. R. (1931). Reasoning and learning. *Psychological Review, 38*(4), 332–346.

Marian, V., Shildkrot, Y., Blumenfeld, H. K., Kaushanskaya, M., Faroqi-Shah, Y., & Hirsch, J. (2007). Cortical activation during word processing in late bilinguals: Similarities and differences as revealed by fMRI. *Journal of Clinical and Experimental Neuropsychology, 29*(3), 247–265.

Meier, R. P. (1991). Language acquisition by deaf children. *American Scientist, 79*(1), 60–70.

Mercier, H., Zhang, J., Qu, Y., Lu, P., & Van der Henst, J. B. (2015). Do Easterners and Westerners treat contradiction differently? *Journal of Cognition and Culture, 15*(1–2), 45–63.

Miller, G. A. (2003). The cognitive revolution: A historical perspective. *Trends in Cognitive Sciences, 7*(3), 141–144.

Mitchell, A., Gottfried, J., Kiley, J., & Matsa, K. E. (2014). Political polarization and media habits. Pew Research Center. Retrieved October 21, 2014, from: http://www.journalism.org/2014/10/21/political-polarization-media-habits

Mitchell, R., & Mark Hamm. (1997). The interpretation of animal psychology: Anthropomorphism or behavior reading? *Behaviour, 134*(3/4), 173–204. Retrieved from http://www.jstor.org/stable/4535437

Miyamoto, Y. (2013). Culture and analytic versus holistic cognition: Toward multilevel analyses of cultural influences. *Advances in Experimental Social Psychology, 47*, 131–188.

Montuori, A. (2011) Social psychology. In M. A. Runco & S. R. Pritzker (Eds.), *Encyclopedia of Creativity*, (2nd ed., 345–351). San Diego, CA: Academic Press.

Murphy, G. L., & Lassaline, M. E. (1997). Hierarchical structure in concepts and the basic level of categorization. In K. Lamberts & D. Shanks (Eds.), *Knowledge, concepts, and categories* (93–131). East Sussex, UK: Psychology Press.

National Association of Colleges and Employers. (2014). *The skills/qualities employers want in new college graduate hires.* Retrieved November 8, 2014, from https://www.naceweb.org/about-us/press/class-2015-skills-qualities-employers-want.aspx

National Institute on Deafness and Other Communication Disorders. (2010). *NIDCD fact sheet: Speech and language developmental milestones.* (NIH Publication No. 10-4781). Bethesda, MD: NIDCD Information Clearinghouse.

Newell, A., & Simon, H. A. (1972). *Human problem solving.* Englewood Cliffs, NJ: Prentice-Hall.

Nickerson, R. S. (1998). Confirmation bias: A ubiquitous phenomenon in many guises. *Review of General Psychology, 2*(2), 175–220.

Nisbett, R. (2010). *The geography of thought: How Asians and Westerners think differently ... and why.* New York, NY: Simon and Schuster.

Nisbett, R. E., & Norenzayan, A. (2002). Culture and cognition. In H. Pashler & D. Medin (Eds.), *Steven's handbook of experimental psychology.* (3rd ed., 561–597). New York, NY: John Wiley & Sons.

Nisbett, R. E., Peng, K., Choi, I., & Norenzayan, A. (2001). Culture and systems of thought: Holistic versus analytic cognition. *Psychological Review, 108*(2), 291–310.

Ogunnaike, O., Dunham, Y., & Banaji, M. R. (2010). The language of implicit preferences. *Journal of Experimental Social Psychology, 46*(6), 999–1003.

Ohlsson, S. (2012). The problems with problem solving: Reflections on the rise, current status, and possible future of a cognitive research paradigm. *Journal of Problem Solving, 5*(1), 101–128.

Ortega, L. (2014). *Understanding second language acquisition.* London, UK: Routledge.

Owens, K. (2015). *Visuospatial reasoning.* New York, NY: Springer International Publishing

Pariser, E. (2011). *The filter bubble: How the new personalized web is changing what we read and how we think.* New York, NY: Penguin Press.

Paul, R., & Norbury, C. (2012). *Language disorders from infancy through adolescence: Listening, speaking, reading, writing, and communicating.* Amsterdam, Netherlands: Elsevier Health Science.

Peng, K., & Nisbett, R. E. (1999). Culture, dialectics, and reasoning about contradiction. *American Psychologist, 54*(9), 741–754.

Pepperberg, I. M. (1994). Numerical competence in an African gray parrot (Psittacus erithacus). *Journal of Comparative Psychology, 108*(1), 36.

Phillips, W., & Boroditsky, L. (2003). Can quirks of grammar affect the way you think? Grammatical gender and object concepts. In *Proceedings of the 25th annual meeting of the Cognitive Science Society* (pp. 928–933). Mahwah, NJ: Lawrence Erlbaum Associates.

Preckel, F., Holling, H., & Wiese, M. (2006). Relationship of intelligence and creativity in gifted and non-gifted students: An investigation of threshold theory. *Personality and Individual Differences, 40*(1), 159–170.

Regier, T., & Kay, P. (2009). Language, thought, and color: Whorf was half right. *Trends in Cognitive Sciences, 13*(10), 439–446.

Reznikova, Z. R. (2007). Animal intelligence. From individual to social cognition. Cambridge, MA: Cambridge University Press.

Ricks, T. R., Turley-Ames, K. J., & Wiley, J. (2007). Effects of working memory capacity on mental set due to domain knowledge. *Memory & Cognition, 35*(6), 1456–1462.

Rogers, T. T., & McClelland, J. L. (2004). *Semantic cognition: A parallel distributed processing approach.* Cambridge, MA: MIT Press.

Rosch, E. (1978). Principles of categorization. In E. Rosch & B. L. Lloyd (Eds.), *Cognition and categorization.* Hillsdale, NJ: Earlbaum.

Rosch, E., & Mervis, C. B. (1975). Family resemblances: Studies in the internal structure of categories. *Cognitive Psychology, 7*(4), 573–605.

Rosch, E., Mervis, C. B., Gray, W. D., Johnson, D. M., & Boyes-Braem, P. (1976). Basic objects in natural categories. *Cognitive Psychology, 8*(3), 382–439.

Rugg, D. (1941). Experiments in wording questions: II. *Public Opinion Quarterly, 5*(1), 91–92.

Russell, S. J., Norvig, P., Canny, J. F., Malik, J. M., & Edwards, D. D. (2003). *Artificial intelligence: A modern approach* (Vol. 2). Upper Saddle River, NJ: Prentice Hall.

Salamatov, Y. (1999). *TRIZ: The right solution at the right time: A guide to innovative problem solving.* V. Souchkov (Ed.). Hattem: Insytec.

Sanford, A. J., Fray, N., Stewart, A., & Moxley, L. (2002). Perspective in statements of quality, with implications for consumer psychology. *Psychological Science, 13*(2), 130–134.

Savage-Rumbaugh, S., Shanker, S. G., & Taylor, T. J. (1998). *Apes, language, and the human mind.* Oxford University Press.

Schaafsma, S. M., Pfaff, D. W., Spunt, R. P., & Adolphs, R. (2015). Deconstructing and reconstructing theory of mind. *Trends in Cognitive Sciences, 19*(2), 65–72.

Scherer, A. M., Windschitl, P. D., & Smith, A. R. (2013). Hope to be right: Biased information seeking following arbitrary and informed predictions. *Journal of Experimental Social Psychology, 49*(1), 106–112.

Schwanenflugel, P. J., & Rey, M. (1986). The relationship between category typicality and concept familiarity: Evidence from Spanish- and English-speaking monolinguals. *Memory & Cognition, 14*(2), 150–163.

Schwartzstein, J. (2014). Selective attention and learning. *Journal of the European Economic Association, 12*(6), 1423–1452.

Scott, J. (2000). Rational choice theory. In G. Browning, A. Halcli, & F. Webster (Eds.), *Understanding contemporary society: Theories of the present* (126–138). London, UK: Sage Publications.

Shen, W., Yuan, Y., Liu, C., & Luo, J. (2017). The roles of the temporal lobe in creative insight: An integrated review. *Thinking & Reasoning, 23*(4), 321–375.

Siniscalchi, M., Lusito, R., Vallortigara, G., & Quaranta, A. (2013). Seeing left- or right-asymmetric tail wagging produces different emotional responses in dogs. *Current Biology, 23*(22), 2279–2282.

Skinner, B. F. (1957). *Verbal behavior.* Acton, MA: Copley Publishing Group.

Smith, J. D. (2009). The study of animal metacognition. *Trends in Cognitive Sciences, 13*(9), 389–396.

Snyder, M., & Cantor, N. (1979). Testing hypotheses about other people: The use of historical knowledge. *Journal of Experimental Social Psychology, 15*(4), 330–342.

Sternberg, R. J. (2006). The nature of creativity. *Creativity Research Journal, 18*(1), 87–98.

Sternberg, R. J., & Lubart, T. I. (1991). An investment theory of creativity and its development. *Human Development, 34*(1), 1–31.

Sternberg, R. J., & Lubart, T. I. (1992). Buy low and sell high: An investment approach to creativity. *Current Directions in Psychological Science, 1*(1), 1–5.

Sternberg, R. J., & Lubart, T. I. (1995). *Defying the crowd: Cultivating creativity in a culture of conformity.* New York, NY: Free Press.

St Onge, J. R., & Floresco, S. B. (2009). Dopaminergic modulation of risk-based decision making. *Neuropsychopharmacology, 34*(3), 681–697.

Stone, C. A., Silliman, E. R., Ehren, B. J., Apel, K. (2005). *Handbook of language and literacy: Development and disorders.* New York, NY: Guilford Press.

Strong, M., & Prinz, P. M. (1997). A study of the relationship between American sign language and English literacy. *Journal of Deaf Studies and Deaf Education, 2*(1), 37–46.

Svenson, O. (1981). Are we all less risky and more skillful than our fellow drivers? *Acta Psychologica, 47*(2), 143–148.

Swingley, D. (2010). Fast mapping and slow mapping in children's word learning. *Language Learning and Development, 6*(3), 179–183.

Thibaut, F. (2016). Basal ganglia play a crucial role in decision making. *Dialogues in Clinical Neuroscience, 18*(1), 3.

Trask, R. L., & Stockwell, P. (2007). *Language and linguistics: The key concepts.* Taylor & Francis.

Treadway, M. T., Buckholtz, J. W., Cowan, R. L., Woodward, N. D., Li, R., Ansari, M. S., Baldwin, R.M., Schwartzman, A.N., Kessler, R.M., & Zald, D. H. (2012). Dopaminergic mechanisms of individual differences in human effort-based decision-making. *The Journal of Neuroscience, 32*(18), 6170–6176.

Turki, J. (2012). Thinking styles "In Light of Sternberg's Theory" prevailing among the students of Tafila Technical University and its relationship with some variables. *American International Journal of Contemporary Research, 2*(3), 140–152.

Tversky, A., & Kahneman, D. (1973). Availability: A heuristic for judging frequency and probability. *Cognitive Psychology, 5*(2), 207–232.

Vacharkulksemsuk, T., & Fredrickson, B. L. (2013). Looking back and glimpsing forward: The broaden-and-build theory of positive emotions as applied to organizations. In A. B. Bakker (Ed.), *Advances in positive organizational psychology, Volume 1* (45–60). Bingley, UK: Emerald Group Publishing Limited.

Vogeley, K., Bussfeld, P., Newen, A., Herrmann, S., Happe, F., Falkai, P., Maier, W., Shah, N. J., Fink, G. R., & Zilles, K. (2001). Mind reading: Neural mechanisms of theory of mind and self-perspective. *Neuroimage, 14*(1), 170–181.

Vogelgesang, G., Clapp-Smith, R., & Osland, J. (2014). The relationship between positive psychological capital and global mindset in the context of global leadership. *Journal of Leadership & Organizational Studies, 21*(2), 165–178.

Washburn, M. Floy. (1909). *The animal mind: A text-book of comparative psychology.* New York, NY: Macmillan.

Wassmann, J., & Dasen, P. R. (1994). "Hot" and "cold": Classification and sorting among the Yupno of Papua New Guinea. *International Journal of Psychology, 29*(1), 19–38.

Welter, M. M., Jaarsveld, S., van Leeuwen, C., & Lachmann, T. (2016). Intelligence and creativity: Over the threshold together? *Creativity Research Journal, 28*(2), 212–218.

Whorf, B. L. (1956). Science and linguistics. In J. B. Carroll (Ed.). *Language, thought, and reality: Selected writings of Benjamin Lee Whorf.* (265–280) Cambridge, MA: MIT Press.

Wiley, J., & Jarosz, A. F. (2012). Working memory capacity, attentional focus, and problem solving. *Current Directions in Psychological Science, 21*(4), 258–262.

Wunderlich, K., Rangel, A., & O'Doherty, J. P. (2009). Neural computations underlying action-based decision making in the human brain. *Proceedings of the National Academy of Sciences, 106*(40), 17199–17204.

Zuckerman, M., Knee, C. R., Hodgins, H. S., & Miyake, K. (1995). Hypothesis confirmation: The joint effect of positive test strategy and acquiescence response set. *Journal of Personality and Social Psychology, 68*(1), 52–60.

Chapter 8

Ackerman, P. L., & Beier, M. E. (2005). Knowledge and intelligence. In O. Wilhelm & R. W. Engle (Eds.), *Handbook of understanding and measuring intelligence.* Thousand Oaks, CA: Sage.

Alfonso, V. C., Flanagan, D. P., & Radwan, S. (2005). The impact of the Cattell-Horn-Carroll theory on test development and interpretation of cognitive and academic abilities. In D. P. Flanagan & P. L. Harrison (Eds.), *Contemporary intellectual assessment: Theories, tests, and issues* (2nd) (pp. 185–202). New York, NY: Guilford Press.

American Psychiatric Association. (2013). *Diagnostic and statistical manual of mental disorders,* (5th ed.). Arlington, VA: American Psychiatric Publishing.

Aronson, J., Fried, C. B., & Good, C. (2002). Reducing the effects of stereotype threat on African American college students by shaping theories of intelligence. *Journal of Experimental Social Psychology, 38*(2), 113–125.

Barajas, R. J., Philipsen, N., & Brooks-Gunn, J. (2007). Cognitive and emotional outcomes for children in poverty. In D. R. Crane & T. B. Heaton (Eds.), *Handbook of Families and Poverty* (pp. 311–333). Thousand Oaks, CA: Sage.

Barbey, A. K., Colom, R., Solomon, J., Krueger, F., Forbes, C., & Grafman, J. (2012). An integrative architecture for general intelligence and executive function revealed by lesion mapping. *Brain, 135*(4), 1154–1164.

Bar-On, R., Tranel, D., Denburg, N. L., & Bechara, A. (2003). Exploring the neurological substrate of emotional and social intelligence. *Brain, 126*(8), 1790–1800.

Barnett, S. M., & Williams, W. (2004). National intelligence and the emperor's new clothes. *Contemporary Psychology, 49*(4), 389–396.

Barseghian, T. (2012, January 18). *Explosive growth in education apps.* Retrieved from https://ww2.kqed.org/mindshift/2012/01/18/explosive-growth-in-education-apps/.

Benson, E. (2003). Intelligence across cultures: Research in Africa, Asia and Latin America is showing how culture and intelligence interact. *American Psychological Association Monitor, 34*(2), 56.

Benson, N., Hulac, D. M., & Kranzler, J. H. (2010). Independent examination of the Wechsler Adult Intelligence Scale—Fourth Edition (WAIS-IV): What does the WAIS-IV measure? *Psychological Assessment, 22*(1), 121–130.

Benyamin, B., Pourcain, B., Davis, O. S., Davies, G., Hansell, N. K., Brion, M. J., ... & Visscher, P. M. (2014). Childhood intelligence is heritable, highly polygenic and associated with FNBP1L. *Molecular Psychiatry, 19*(2), 253–258.

Binet, A., & Simon, T. (1916). *The development of intelligence in children: The Binet-Simon Scale* (No. 11). Baltimore, MD: Williams & Wilkins Company.

Blair, C., Gamson, D., Thorne, S., & Baker, D. (2005). Rising mean IQ: Cognitive demand of mathematics education for young children, population exposure to formal schooling, and the neurobiology of the prefrontal cortex. *Intelligence, 33*(1), 93–106.

Block, N. J., & Dworkin, G. E. (1976). *The IQ controversy: Critical readings.* Oxford, England: Pantheon.

Boake, C. (2002). From the Binet–Simon to the Wechsler–Bellevue: Tracing the history of intelligence testing. *Journal of Clinical and Experimental Neuropsychology, 24*(3), 383–405.

Botwin, M. D., Buss, D. M., & Shackelford, T. K. (1997). Personality and mate preferences: Five factors in mate selection and marital satisfaction. *Journal of Personality, 65*(1), 107–136.

Bouchard Jr, T. J. (1998). Genetic and environmental influences on adult intelligence and special mental abilities. *Human Biology, 70*(2), 257–279.

Bouchard, T. J., & McGue, M. (1981). Familial studies of intelligence: A review. *Science, 212*(4498), 1055–1059.

Boyatzis, R. E., Good, D., & Massa, R. (2012). Emotional, social, and cognitive intelligence and personality as predictors of sales leadership performance. *Journal of Leadership & Organizational Studies, 19*(2), 191–201.

Brim Jr, O. G., Glass, D. C., Neulinger, J., & Firestone, I. J. (1969). *American beliefs about intelligence.* Hartford, CT: Russell Sage Foundation.

Buj, V. (1981). Average IQ values in various European countries. *Personality and Individual Differences, 2*(2), 168–169.

Burchard, E. G., Ziv, E., Coyle, N., Gomez, S. L., Tang, H., Karter, A. J., ... & Risch, N. (2003). The importance of race and ethnic background in biomedical research and clinical practice. *New England Journal of Medicine, 348*(12), 1170–1175.

Burks, B. S., & Jensen, D. W. (1930). *The promise of youth: Follow-up studies of a thousand gifted children* (Vol. 3). Stanford, CA: Stanford University Press.

Butcher, L. M., Davis, O. S., Craig, I. W., & Plomin, R. (2008). Genome-wide quantitative trait locus association scan of general cognitive ability using pooled DNA and 500K single nucleotide polymorphism microarrays. *Genes, Brain and Behavior, 7*(4), 435–446.

Cadaret, M. C., Hartung, P. J., Subich, L. M., & Weigold, I. K. (2017). Stereotype threat as a barrier to women entering engineering careers. *Journal of Vocational Behavior, 99*, 40–51.

Carroll, J. B. (2003). The higher-stratum structure of cognitive abilities: Current evidence supports g and about ten broad factors. In H. Nyborg (Ed.), *The scientific study of general intelligence: Tribute to Arthur R. Jensen* (pp. 5–21). Amsterdam, Netherlands: Pergamon.

Cantor, N., & Kihlstrom, J. F. (1987). *Personality and social intelligence.* London, UK: Pearson College Division.

Cattell, R. B. (1963). Theory of fluid and crystallized intelligence: A critical experiment. *Journal of Educational Psychology, 54*(1), 1–22.

Chabris, C. F., Hebert, B. M., Benjamin, D. J., Beauchamp, J., Cesarini, D., van der Loos, M., ... & Laibson, D. (2012). Most reported genetic associations with general intelligence are probably false positives. *Psychological Science, 23*(11), 1314–1323.

Chapman, P. D. (1988). *Schools as sorters: Lewis M. Terman, applied psychology, and the intelligence testing movement, 1890–1930.* New York, NY: New York University Press.

Chipuer, H. M., Rovine, M. J., & Plomin, R. (1990). LISREL modeling: Genetic and environmental influences on IQ revisited. *Intelligence, 14*(1), 11–29.

Ciarrochi, J., Deane, F. P., & Anderson, S. (2002). Emotional intelligence moderates the relationship between stress and mental health. *Personality and Individual Differences, 32*(2), 197–209.

Cianciolo, A. T., & Sternberg, R. J. (2008). *Intelligence: A brief history.* Hoboken, NJ: John Wiley & Sons.

Conte, J. M. (2005). A review and critique of emotional intelligence measures. *Journal of Organizational Behavior, 26*(4), 433–440.

Conway, A. R., Getz, S. J., Macnamara, B., & Engel de Abreu, P. M. J. (2011). Working memory and intelligence. In R. J. Sternberg & S. B. Kaufman (Eds.), *The Cambridge handbook of intelligence,* (pp. 394–418). New York, NY: Cambridge University Press.

Daily, D. K., Ardinger, H. H., & Holmes, G. E. (2000). Identification and evaluation of mental retardation. *American Family Physician, 61*(4), 1059–1067.

Daley, T. C., Whaley, S. E., Sigman, M. D., Espinosa, M. P., & Neumann, C. (2003). IQ on the rise the Flynn effect in rural Kenyan children. *Psychological Science, 14*(3), 215–219.

Daniele, V., & Ostuni, N. (2013). The burden of disease and the IQ of nations. *Learning and Individual Differences, 28*, 109–118.

Davies, G., Tenesa, A., Payton, A., Yang, J., Harris, S. E., Liewald, D., ... & Deary, I. J. (2011). Genome-wide association studies establish that human intelligence is highly heritable and polygenic. *Molecular Psychiatry, 16*(10), 996–1005.

Deary, I. J. (2001). Human intelligence differences: A recent history. *Trends in Cognitive Sciences, 5*(3), 127-130.

Deary, I. J., Whalley, L. J., Lemmon, H., Crawford, J. R., & Starr, J. M. (2000). The stability of individual differences in mental ability from childhood to old age: Follow-up of the 1932 Scottish Mental Survey. *Intelligence, 28*(1), 49–55.

Deary, I. J., Whiteman, M. C., Starr, J. M., Whalley, L. J., & Fox, H. C. (2004). The impact of childhood intelligence on later life: Following up the Scottish mental surveys of 1932 and 1947. *Journal of Personality and Social Psychology, 86*(1), 130–147.

Deary, I. J., Yang, J., Davies, G., Harris, S. E., Tenesa, A., Liewald, D., ... & Visscher, P. M. (2012). Genetic contributions to stability and change in intelligence from childhood to old age. *Nature, 482*(7384), 212–215.

Deary, I. J., Pattie, A., & Starr, J. M. (2013). The stability of intelligence from age 11 to age 90 years: The Lothian birth cohort of 1921. *Psychological Science.*

Devlin, B., Daniels, M., & Roeder, K. (1997). The heritability of IQ. *Nature, 388*(6641), 468–471.

Duckworth, A. L., & Seligman, M. E. (2005). Self-discipline outdoes IQ in predicting academic performance of adolescents. *Psychological Science, 16*(12), 939–944.

Duckworth, A. L., Quinn, P. D., Lynam, D. R., Loeber, R., & Stouthamer-Loeber, M. (2011). Role of test motivation in intelligence testing. *Proceedings of the National Academy of Sciences, 108*(19), 7716–7720.

Duncan, G. J., Brooks-Gunn, J., & Klebanov, P. K. (1994). Economic deprivation and early childhood development. *Child Development, 65*(2), 296–318.

Duncan, J., & Owen, A. M. (2000). Common regions of the human frontal lobe recruited by diverse cognitive demands. *Trends in Neurosciences, 23*(10), 475–483.

Dweck, C. S. (2000). *Self-theories: Their role in motivation, personality, and development.* Philadelphia, PA: Psychology Press.

Eysenck, H. (1984). Recent advances in the theory and measurement of intelligence. *Early Child Development and Care, 15*(2–3), 97–115.

Fischer, C. S., Hout, M., Sanchez Jankowski, M., Lucas, S. R., Swidler, A., Voss, K., & Bobo, L. (1996). *Inequality by design: Cracking the bell curve myth.* Princeton, NJ: Princeton University Press.

Flynn, J. R. (1984). The mean IQ of Americans: Massive gains, 1932 to 1978. *Psychological Bulletin, 95*(1), 29–51.

Flynn, J. R. (1987). Massive IQ gains in 14 nations: What IQ tests really measure. *Psychological Bulletin, 101*(2), 171–191.

Flynn, J. R., & Flynn, J. R. (2012). *Are we getting smarter? Rising IQ in the twenty-first century*. New York, NY: Cambridge University Press.

Ford, D. Y. (2005). Intelligence testing and cultural diversity: Pitfalls and promises. *Newsletter of the National Research Center on the Gifted and Talented*. Based on the monograph by Ford (2004) entitled Intelligence Testing and Cultural Diversity: Concerns, Cautions and Considerations. Storrs, CT: The National Research Center on the Gifted and Talented, University of Connecticut.

Frederickson, N., Petrides, K. V., & Simmonds, E. (2012). Trait emotional intelligence as a predictor of socioemotional outcomes in early adolescence. *Personality and Individual Differences, 52*(3), 323–328.

Frey, M. C., & Detterman, D. K. (2004). Scholastic assessment org? The relationship between the scholastic assessment test and general cognitive ability. *Psychological Science, 15*(6), 373–378.

Fujimura, J. H., Bolnick, D. A., Rajagopalan, R., Kaufman, J. S., Lewontin, R. C., Duster, … & Marks, J. (2014). Clines without classes: How to make sense of human variation. *Sociological Theory, 32*(3), 208–227.

Gardner, H. (1983). *Frames of mind: Multiple intelligences*. New York, NY: Basic Books.

Gardner, H. (2004). Audiences for the theory of multiple intelligences. *The Teachers College Record, 106*(1), 212–220.

Georgas, J., Weiss, L. G., Van de Vijver, F. J., & Saklofske, D. H. (Eds.). (2003). *Culture and children's intelligence: Cross-cultural analysis of the WISC-III*. Academic Press.

Goleman, D., (1995) *Emotional intelligence*. New York, NY, England: Bantam Books, Inc.

Gottfredson, L. S. (1997). Why "g" matters: The complexity of everyday life. *Intelligence, 24*(1), 79–132.

Gottfredson, L. S. (1998). The general intelligence factor. *Scientific American, Incorporated 9*(4), 24–29.

Gottfredson, L. S. (2003). Dissecting practical intelligence theory: Its claims and evidence. *Intelligence, 31*(4), 343–397.

Gottfredson, L. S. (2004). Schools and the "g" factor. *The Wilson Quarterly*, 35–45.

Gottfredson, L. S., & Deary, I. J. (2004). Intelligence predicts health and longevity, but why? *Current Directions in Psychological Science, 13*(1), 1–4.

Gow, A. J., Johnson, W., Pattie, A., Brett, C. E., Roberts, B., Starr, J. M., & Deary, I. J. (2011). Stability and change in intelligence from age 11 to ages 70, 79, and 87: The Lothian birth cohorts of 1921 and 1936. *Psychology and Aging, 26*(1), 232–240.

Gregory, R. J. (2004). *Psychological testing: History, principles, and applications*. Boston, MA: Allyn & Bacon.

Grubb, J. (2015, August 18). Kids' gaming makes up nearly 8% of mobile game spending worldwide. Retrieved from http://venturebeat.com/2015/08/18/kids-gaming-makes-up-nearly-8-of-mobile-game-spending-worldwide/

Hanson, J. L., Hair, N., Shen, D. G., Shi, F., Gilmore, J. H., Wolfe, B. L., & Pollak, S. D. (2013). Family poverty affects the rate of human infant brain growth. *PloS One, 8*(12), https://doi.org/10.1371/journal.pone.0080954.

Hathaway, S., & McKinley, J. (1943). Manual for administering and scoring the MMPI.

Haworth, C. M. A., Wright, M. J., Luciano, M., Martin, N. G., De Geus, E. J. C., Van Beijsterveldt, C. E. M., … & Plomin, R. (2010). The heritability of general cognitive ability increases linearly from childhood to young adulthood. *Molecular Psychiatry, 15*(11), 1112–1120.

Heaven, P. C., & Ciarrochi, J. (2012). When IQ is not everything: Intelligence, personality and academic performance at school. *Personality and Individual Differences, 53*(4), 518–522.

Herrnstein, R., & Murray, C. (1994). The bell curve. New York, NY: Simon and Shuster.

Herrnstein, R. J., & Murray, C. (2010). *Bell curve: Intelligence and class structure in American life*. New York, NY: Simon and Schuster.

Horn, J. L. (1982). The aging of human abilities. In J. Wolman (Ed.), *Handbook of developmental psychology* (p. 128). Englewood Cliffs, NJ: Prentice-Hall.

Horton, S., Baker, J., Pearce, W., & Deakin, J. M. (2010). Immunity to popular stereotypes of aging? Seniors and stereotype threat. *Educational Gerontology, 36*(5), 353–371.

Hupp, S., & Jewell, J. (2015). *Great myths of child development*. Hoboken, NJ: John Wiley & Sons.

Hupp, S., Stary, A., & Jewell, J. (2017). Science vs. Silliness for Parents: Debunking the Myths of Child Psychology. *Skeptical Inquirer, 41*(1), 44–47.

Husen, T., & Tuijnman, A. (1991). The contribution of formal schooling to the increase in intellectual capital. *Educational Researcher, 20*(7), 17–25.

Inzlicht, M., & Ben-Zeev, T. (2000). A threatening intellectual environment: Why females are susceptible to experiencing problem-solving deficits in the presence of males. *Psychological Science, 11*(5), 365–371.

Jensen, A. R. (1998). *The "g" factor: The science of mental ability*. Westport, CT: Praeger.

Jensen, A. (2011). *Educational differences* (Vol. 182). London, UK: Routledge.

Jerison, H. (2012). *Evolution of the brain and intelligence*. Amsterdam, Netherlands: Elsevier.

Johns, M., Schmader, T., & Martens, A. (2005). Knowing is half the battle teaching stereotype threat as a means of improving women's math performance. *Psychological Science, 16*(3), 175–179.

Kaufman, A. S. (2009). *IQ testing 101*. New York, NY: Springer Publishing Co.

Kaufman, S. B., Reynolds, M. R., Liu, X., Kaufman, A. S., & McGrew, K. S. (2012). Are cognitive "g" and academic achievement "g" one and the same "g"? An exploration on the Woodcock–Johnson and Kaufman tests. *Intelligence, 40*(2), 123–138.

Kaufman, A. S., & Lichtenberger, E. O. (2005). *Assessing adolescent and adult intelligence*. Hoboken, NJ: John Wiley & Sons.

Keith, T. Z., & Reynolds, M. R. (2010). Cattell–Horn–Carroll abilities and cognitive tests: What we've learned from 20 years of research. *Psychology in the Schools, 47*(7), 635–650.

Kim, K. H. (2005). Can only intelligent people be creative? A meta-analysis. *Journal of Advanced Academics, 16*(2–3), 57–66.

Kincheloe, J. L., Steinberg, S. R., & Gresson III, A. D. (1997). *Measured lies: The bell curve examined*. New York, NY: St. Martin's Press.

Kuncel, N. R., Ones, D. S., & Sackett, P. R. (2010). Individual differences as predictors of work, educational, and broad life outcomes. *Personality and Individual Differences, 49*(4), 331–336.

Kyllonen, P. C., & Christal, R. E. (1990). Reasoning ability is (little more than) working-memory capacity?! *Intelligence, 14*(4), 389-433.

Lagoy, R. (2012). Psychophysical genius: A theory, a controversy, a refinement (Doctoral dissertation). Worcester, MA: Worcester Polytechnic Institute.

Lamont, R. A., Swift, H. J., & Abrams, D. (2015). A review and meta-analysis of age-based stereotype threat: Negative stereotypes, not facts, do the damage. *Psychology and Aging, 30*(1), 180–193.

Landy, F. J. (2005). Some historical and scientific issues related to research on emotional intelligence. *Journal of Organizational Behavior, 26*(4), 411–424.

Lawson, G. M., Hook, C. J., Hackman, D. A., Farah, M. J., Griffin, J. A., Freund, L. S., & McCardle, P. (2014). Socioeconomic status and neurocognitive development: Executive function. In J.A. Griffin, L.S. Freund, & P. McCardle (Eds.), *Executive function in preschool children: Integrating measurement, neurodevelopment, and translational research*. Washington, DC: American Psychological Association.

Legg, S., & Hutter, M. (2007). A collection of definitions of intelligence. In B. Goertzel & P. Wang (Eds.), *Frontiers in artificial intelligence and applications*. Amsterdam, Netherlands: IOS Press.

Leslie, M. (2000). *The vexing legacy of Lewis Terman*. Retrieved from https://alumni.stanford.edu/get/page/magazine/article/?article_id=40678

Li, N. P., Bailey, J. M., Kenrick, D. T., & Linsenmeier, J. A. (2002). The necessities and luxuries of mate preferences: Testing the tradeoffs. *Journal of Personality and Social Psychology, 82*(6), 947–955.

Lichtenberger, E. O., & Kaufman, A. S. (2009). *Essentials of WAIS-IV assessment* (Vol. 50). Hoboken, NJ: John Wiley & Sons.

Locke, E. A. (2005). Why emotional intelligence is an invalid concept. *Journal of Organizational Behavior, 26*(4), 425–431.

Loehlin, J. C., Horn, J. M., & Willerman, L. (1989). Modeling IQ change: Evidence from the Texas adoption project. *Child Development, 60*(4), 993–1004.

Lopez, I. F. H. (1994). The social construction of race: Some observations on illusion, fabrication, and choice. *HeinOnline, 29*(1).

Lubinski, D. (2004). Introduction to the special section on cognitive abilities: 100 years after Spearman's (1904) "general intelligence" objectively determined and measured. *Journal of Personality and Social Psychology, 86*(1), 96–111.

Lynn, R. (2009). What has caused the Flynn effect? Secular increases in the development quotients of infants. *Intelligence, 37*(1), 16–24.

Lynn, R., & Vanhanen, T. (2002). *IQ and the wealth of nations*. Westport, CT: Greenwood Publishing Group.

Lynn, R., & Vanhanen, T. (2006). *IQ and global inequality*. Whitefish, MT: Washington Summit Publishers.

Lynn, R., & Vanhanen, T. (2012). *Intelligence: A unifying construct for the social sciences* (p. 530). London, UK: Ulster Institute for Social Research.

Mandelman, S. D., Barbot, B., & Grigorenko, E. L. (2016). Predicting academic performance and trajectories from a measure of successful intelligence. *Learning and Individual Differences, 51*, 387–393.

Mayer, J. D., Roberts, R. D., & Barsade, S. G. (2008). Human abilities: Emotional intelligence. *Annual Review of Psychology, 59*, 507–536.

Mayer, J. D., & Salovey, P. (1993). The intelligence of emotional intelligence. *Intelligence, 17*(4), 433–442.

Mayer, J. D., Salovey, P., Caruso, D. R., & Sitarenios, G. (2001). Emotional intelligence as a standard intelligence. *Emotion, 1*(3), 232–242.

Mayer, J. D., Salovey, P., & Caruso, D. R. (2004). Emotional intelligence: Theory, findings, and implications. *Psychological Inquiry, 15*(3), 197–215.

McClelland, D. C. (1973). Testing for competence rather than for "intelligence." *American Psychologist, 28*(1), 1–14.

McCleskey, J. (2014). Emotional intelligence and leadership: A review of the progress, controversy, and criticism. *International Journal of Organizational Analysis, 22*(1), 76–93.

McGrew, K. S. (2009). CHC theory and the human cognitive abilities project: Standing on the shoulders of the giants of psychometric intelligence research. *Intelligence, 37*(1), 1–10.

McGrew, K. S. (2005). The Cattell-Horn-Carroll theory of cognitive abilities: Past, present, and future. In D. P. Flanagan & P. L. Harrison (Eds.), *Contemporary intellectual assessment: Theories, tests, and issues* (pp. 136–181). New York, NY: Guilford Press.

McGue, M., Bouchard Jr, T. J., Iacono, W. G., & Lykken, D. T. (1993). Behavioral genetics of cognitive ability: A lifespan perspective. In R. Plomin & G. E. McClearn (Eds.), *Nature, nurture & psychology* (pp. 59–76). Washington, DC: American Psychological Association.

Minton, H. L. (1988). *Lewis M. Terman: Pioneer in psychological testing*. New York, NY: New York University Press.

Mukhopadhyay, C. C., & Henze, R. (2013). *How real is race? A sourcebook on race, culture, and biology*. Lanham, MD: Rowman & Littlefield.

Murphy, K. R. (2014). *A critique of emotional intelligence: What are the problems and how can they be fixed?* Psychology Press.

Naroll, R. (1961). Two solutions to Galton's problem. *Philosophy of Science, 28*(1), 15–39.

Neisser, U. E. (1998). *The rising curve: Long-term gains in IQ and related measures*. Washington, DC: American Psychological Association.

Neisser, U., Boodoo, G., Bouchard Jr, T. J., Boykin, A. W., Brody, N., Ceci, S. J., … & Urbina, S. (1996). Intelligence:

Knowns and unknowns. *American Psychologist, 51*(2), 77–101.

Nelson, C. A., Zeanah, C. H., Fox, N. A., Marshall, P. J., Smyke, A. T., & Guthrie, D. (2007). Cognitive recovery in socially deprived young children: The Bucharest Early Intervention Project. *Science, 318*(5858), 1937–1940.

Newton, J. H., & McGrew, K. S. (2010). Introduction to the special issue: Current research in Cattell–Horn–Carroll–based assessment. *Psychology in the Schools, 47*(7), 621–634.

Niileksela, C. R., Reynolds, M. R., & Kaufman, A. S. (2013). An alternative Cattell–Horn–Carroll (CHC) factor structure of the WAIS-IV: Age invariance of an alternative model for ages 70–90. *Psychological Assessment, 25*(2), 391–404.

Nisbett, R. E., Aronson, J., Blair, C., Dickens, W., Flynn, J., Halpern, D. F., & Turkheimer, E. (2012a). Intelligence: New findings and theoretical developments. *American Psychologist, 67*(2), 130–159.

Nisbett, R. E., Aronson, J., Blair, C., Dickens, W., Flynn, J., Halpern, D. F., & Turkheimer, E. (2012b). Group differences in IQ are best understood as environmental in origin. *American Psychologist, 67*(6), 503–504.

O'Boyle, E. H., Humphrey, R. H., Pollack, J. M., Hawver, T. H., & Story, P. A. (2011). The relation between emotional intelligence and job performance: A meta-analysis. *Journal of Organizational Behavior, 32*(5), 788–818.

Oden, M. H. (1968). *The fulfillment of promise: 40 year follow up of the Terman gifted group*. Stanford, CA: Stanford University Press.

Omi, M., & Winant, H. (2014). *Racial formation in the United States*. London, UK: Routledge.

Passingham, R. E. (1979). Brain size and intelligence in man. *Brain, Behavior and Evolution, 16*(4), 253–270.

Palmer, B., Donaldson, C., & Stough, C. (2002). Emotional intelligence and life satisfaction. *Personality and Individual Differences, 33*(7), 1091–1100.

Payton, A. (2009). The impact of genetic research on our understanding of normal cognitive ageing: 1995 to 2009. *Neuropsychology Review, 19*(4), 451–477.

Petrill, S. A., Lipton, P. A., Hewitt, J. K., Plomin, R., Cherny, S. S., Corley, R., & DeFries, J. C. (2004). Genetic and environmental contributions to general cognitive ability through the first 16 years of life. *Developmental Psychology, 40*(5), 805–812.

Plomin, R., & Deary, I. J. (2015). Genetics and intelligence differences: Five special findings. *Molecular Psychiatry, 20*(1), 98–108.

Plomin, R., DeFries, J. C., & Loehlin, J. C. (1977). Genotype-environment interaction and correlation in the analysis of human behavior. *Psychological Bulletin, 84*(2), 309–322.

Ree, M. J., & Earles, J. A. (1992). Intelligence is the best predictor of job performance. *Current Directions in Psychological Science, 1*(3), 86–89.

Reynolds, C. R., & Ramsay, M. C. (2003). Bias in psychological assessment: An empirical review and recommendations. *Handbook of Psychology*, John Wiley and Sons, Inc.

Risch, N., Burchard, E., Ziv, E., & Tang, H. (2002). Categorization of humans in biomedical research: Genes, race and disease. *Genome Biology, 3*(7), 1–12.

Ritchie, S. J., Booth, T., Hernández, M. D. C. V., Corley, J., Maniega, S. M., Gow, A. J., … & Bastin, M. E. (2015). Beyond a bigger brain: Multivariable structural brain imaging and intelligence. *Intelligence, 51*, 47–56.

Robitaille, A., Piccinin, A. M., Muniz-Terrera, G., Hoffman, L., Johansson, B., Deeg, D. J., … & Hofer, S. M. (2013). Longitudinal mediation of processing speed on age-related change in memory and fluid intelligence. *Psychology and Aging, 28*(4), 887–901.

Roth, P. L., Bevier, C. A., Bobko, P., Switzer, F. S., & Tyler, P. (2001). Ethnic group differences in cognitive ability in employment and educational settings: A meta-analysis. *Personnel Psychology, 54*(2), 297–330.

Royall, D. R., & Palmer, R. F. (2014). "Executive functions" cannot be distinguished from general intelligence: Two variations on a single theme within a symphony of latent variance. *Frontiers in Behavioral Neuroscience, 8*.

Rushton, J. P., & Jensen, A. R. (2005). Thirty years of research on race differences in cognitive ability. *Psychology, Public Policy, and Law, 11*(2), 235–294.

Salguero, J. M., Palomera, R., & Fernández-Berrocal, P. (2012). Perceived emotional intelligence as predictor of psychological adjustment in adolescents: A 1-year prospective study. *European Journal of Psychology of Education, 27*(1), 21–34.

Salovey, P., & Mayer, J. D. (1989). Emotional intelligence. *Imagination, Cognition and Personality, 9*(3), 185–211.

Sattler, J. M. (1992). *Assessment of children—Revised and updated third edition*. San Diego, CA: Jerome M. Sattler, Publisher.

Scheiber, C., & Kaufman, A. S. (2015). Which of the three KABC-II global scores is the least biased? *Journal of Pediatric Neuropsychology, 1*(1–4), 21–35.

Schipolowski, S., Wilhelm, O., & Schroeders, U. (2014). On the nature of crystallized intelligence: The relationship between verbal ability and factual knowledge. *Intelligence, 46*, 156–168.

Schmader, T., Johns, M., & Forbes, C. (2008). An integrated process model of stereotype threat effects on performance. *Psychological Review, 115*(2), 336–356.

Schmidt, F. L., Shaffer, J. A., & Oh, I. S. (2008). Increased accuracy for range restriction corrections: Implications for the role of personality and general mental ability in job and training performance. *Personnel Psychology, 61*(4), 827-868.

Schnack, H. G., van Haren, N. E., Brouwer, R. M., Evans, A., Durston, S., Boomsma, D. I., … & Pol, H. E. H. (2014). Changes in thickness and surface area of the human cortex and their relationship with intelligence. *Cerebral Cortex, 25*(6), 1608–1617.

Schneider, W. J., & McGrew, K. S. (2012). The Cattell-Horn-Carroll model of intelligence. In D. P. Flanagan & P. L. Harrison (Eds.), *Contemporary intellectual assessment: Theories, tests, and issues* (3rd ed.) (pp. 99–144). New York, NY: Guilford Press.

Schneider, W., Niklas, F., & Schmiedeler, S. (2014). Intellectual development from early childhood to early adulthood: The impact of early IQ differences on stability and change over time. *Learning and Individual Differences, 32*, 156–162.

Schroeders, U., Schipolowski, S., & Wilhelm, O. (2015). Age-related changes in the mean and covariance structure of fluid and crystallized intelligence in childhood and adolescence. *Intelligence, 48*, 15–29.

Sears, R. R. (1977). Sources of life satisfactions of the Terman gifted men. *American Psychologist, 32*(2), 119–128.

Shampo, M. A., & Kyle, R. A. (2011, April). J. Craig Venter—The Human Genome Project. *Mayo Clinic Proceedings, 86*(4), 26–27.

Shapiro, J. R., & Williams, A. M. (2012). The role of stereotype threats in undermining girls' and women's performance and interest in STEM fields. *Sex Roles, 66*(3–4), 175–183.

Shaw, P., Greenstein, D., Lerch, J., Clasen, L., Lenroot, R., Gogtay, N., … & Giedd, J. (2006). Intellectual ability and cortical development in children and adolescents. *Nature, 440*(7084), 676–679.

Shim, J. K., Ackerman, S. L., Darling, K. W., Hiatt, R. A., & Lee, S. S. J. (2014). Race and ancestry in the age of inclusion technique and meaning in post-genomic science. *Journal of Health and Social Behavior, 55*(4), 504–518.

Shuttleworth-Edwards, A. B., Kemp, R. D., Rust, A. L., Muirhead, J. G., Hartman, N. P., & Radloff, S. E. (2004). Cross-cultural effects on IQ test performance: A review and preliminary normative indications on WAIS-III test performance. *Journal of Clinical and Experimental Neuropsychology, 26*(7), 903–920.

Simpson, N., Mizen, L., & Cooper, S. A. (2016). Intellectual disabilities. *Medicine, 44*(11), 679–682.

Smedley, A., & Smedley, B. D. (2005). Race as biology is fiction, racism as a social problem is real: Anthropological and historical perspectives on the social construction of race. *American Psychologist, 60*(1), 16–26.

Spearman, C. (1904). "General intelligence," objectively determined and measured. *American Journal of Psychology, 15*(2), 201–292.

Steele, C. M., & Aronson, J. (1995). Stereotype threat and the intellectual test performance of African Americans. *Journal of Personality and Social Psychology, 69*(5), 797–811.

Sternberg, R. J. (1985). *Beyond IQ: A triarchic theory of human intelligence*. Cambridge, Cambridgeshire: Cambridge University Press.

Sternberg, R. J. (2004). Culture and intelligence. *American Psychologist, 59*(5), 325–338.

Sternberg, R. J. (2012). Intelligence. *Wiley Interdisciplinary Reviews: Cognitive Science, 3*(5), 501–511.

Stone, E. A., Shackelford, T. K., & Buss, D. M. (2012). Is variability in mate choice similar for intelligence and personality traits? Testing a hypothesis about the evolutionary genetics of personality. *Intelligence, 40*(1), 33–37.

Stroessner, S., & Good, C. (2011). Stereotype threat: An overview. *Biologie, 8*, 78–92.

Terman, L. M. (1916). The Binet scale and the diagnosis of feeble-mindedness. *Journal of the American Institute of Criminal Law and Criminology, 7*(4), 530–543.

Terman, L. M. (1925). *Mental and physical traits of a thousand gifted children (I)*. Stanford, CA: Stanford University Press.

Terman, L. M & Oden, M. H. (1947). *The gifted child grows up: Twenty-five years' follow-up of a superior group* (Vol. 4). Stanford, CA: Stanford University Press.

Terman, L. M. & Oden, M. H. (1959). *The gifted group at mid-life: Thirty-five years' follow-up of the superior child* (Vol. 5). Stanford, CA: Stanford University Press.

Thaler, N. S., Thames, A. D., Cagigas, X. E., & Norman, M. A. (2015). IQ testing and the African American client. In *Guide to psychological assessment with African Americans* (pp. 63–77). Springer: New York.

Thorsen, C., Gustafsson, J. E., & Cliffordson, C. (2014). The influence of fluid and crystallized intelligence on the development of knowledge and skills. *British Journal of Educational Psychology, 84*(4), 556–570.

Tourva, A., Spanoudis, G., & Demetriou, A. (2016). Cognitive correlates of developing intelligence: The contribution of working memory, processing speed and attention. *Intelligence, 54*, 136–146.

Trahan, L. H., Stuebing, K. K., Fletcher, J. M., & Hiscock, M. (2014). The Flynn effect: A meta-analysis. *Psychological Bulletin, 140*(5), 1332–1360.

Turkheimer, E., Haley, A., Waldron, M., d'Onofrio, B., & Gottesman, I. I. (2003). Socioeconomic status modifies heritability of IQ in young children. *Psychological Science, 14*(6), 623–628.

U.S. Department of Education. (2002). *No child left behind act (20 USC 7801 P.L. 107–110)*. Washington, DC: U.S. Government Printing Office.

Van Rooy, D. L., & Viswesvaran, C. (2004). Emotional intelligence: A meta-analytic investigation of predictive validity and nomological net. *Journal of Vocational Behavior, 65*(1), 71–95.

Visser, B. A., Ashton, M. C., & Vernon, P. A. (2006a). G and the measurement of multiple intelligences: A response to Gardner. *Intelligence, 34*(5), 507–510.

Visser, B. A., Ashton, M. C., & Vernon, P. A. (2006b). Beyond "g": Putting multiple intelligences theory to the test. *Intelligence, 34*(5), 487–502.

von Stumm, S., & Plomin, R. (2015). Socioeconomic status and the growth of intelligence from infancy through adolescence. *Intelligence, 48*, 30–36.

Waterhouse, L. (2006a). Inadequate evidence for multiple intelligences, Mozart effect, and emotional intelligence theories. *Educational Psychologist, 41*(4), 247–255.

Waterhouse, L. (2006b). Multiple intelligences, the Mozart effect, and emotional intelligence: A critical review. *Educational Psychologist, 41*(4), 207–225.

Wechsler, D. (1939). *The measurement of adult intelligence*. Baltimore, MD: Williams & Wilkins Company.

Wechsler, D. (2008). *Wechsler adult intelligence scale–Fourth Edition (WAIS–IV)*. San Antonio, TX: NCS Pearson.

Weiss, L. G., Keith, T. Z., Zhu, J., & Chen, H. (2013a). WAIS-IV and clinical validation of the four-and five-factor interpretative approaches. *Journal of Psycho-educational Assessment, 31(2)*, 94–113.

Weiss, L. G., Keith, T. Z., Zhu, J., & Chen, H. (2013b). WISC-IV and clinical validation of the four-and five-factor interpretative approaches. *Journal of Psychoeducational Assessment, 31(2)*, 114–131.

Whiting, G., & Ford, D. (2009). Cultural bias in testing. Retrieved from http://www.education.com/reference/article/cultural-bias-in-testing

Wicherts, J. M., Dolan, C. V., & van der Maas, H. L. (2010). A systematic literature review of the average IQ of sub-Saharan Africans. *Intelligence, 38(1)*, 1–20.

Winner, E. (2000). The origins and ends of giftedness. *American Psychologist, 55(1)*, 159–169.

Woodley, M. A. (2012). The social and scientific temporal correlates of genotypic intelligence and the Flynn effect. *Intelligence, 40(2)*, 189–204.

Woodley, M. A., te Nijenhuis, J., Must, O., & Must, A. (2014). Controlling for increased guessing enhances the independence of the Flynn effect from "g": The return of the brand effect. *Intelligence, 43*, 27–34.

Yerkes, R. M. (1921). *Psychological examining in the United States Army:* Edited by Robert M. Yerkes (Vol. 15). Washington, DC: U.S. Government Printing Office.

Chapter 9

Ainsworth, M. S. (1979). Infant–mother attachment. *American Psychologist, 34(10)*, 932–937.

Alzheimer's Association. (2013). 2013 Alzheimer's disease facts and figures. *Alzheimer's & Dementia, 9(2)*, 208–245.

Arnett, J. J. (2000). Emerging adulthood: A theory of development from the late teens through the twenties. *American Psychologist, 55(5)*, 469–480.

Arnett, J. J. (2001). Conceptions of the transition to adulthood: Perspectives from adolescence through midlife. *Journal of Adult Development, 8(2)*, 133–143.

Arnett, J. J. (2007). Emerging adulthood: What is it, and what is it good for? *Child Development Perspectives, 1(2)*, 68–73.

Baillargeon, R. (1995). A model of physical reasoning in infancy. *Advances in Infancy Research, 9*, 305–371.

Baillargeon, R. (1996). Infants' understanding of the physical world. *Journal of the Neurological Sciences, 143(1–2)*, 503–529.

Baillargeon, R. (2004). Infants' physical world. *Current Directions in Psychological Science, 13(3)*, 89–94.

Baird, A. A., & Fugelsang, J. A. (2004). The emergence of consequential thought: Evidence from neuroscience. *Philosophical Transactions of the Royal Society of London. Series B, Biological Sciences, 359(1451)*, 1797–1804.

Barkhorn, E. (2013, March 15). Getting married later is great for college-educated women. *Atlantic*. Retrieved from http://www.theatlantic.com/sexes/archive/2013/03/getting-married-later-is-great-for-college-educated-women/274040//

Baumrind, D. (1966). Effects of authoritative parental control on child behavior. *Child Development, 37(4)* 887–907.

Baumrind, D. (1967). Child care practices anteceding three patterns of preschool behavior. *Genetic Psychology Monographs, 75(1)*, 126–132.

Baumrind, D. (1991). Effective parenting during the early adolescent transition. *Family Transitions, 2*, 111–163.

Behnke, M., & Smith, V. C. (2013). Prenatal substance abuse: Short- and long-term effects on the exposed fetus. *Pediatrics, 131*, 1009–1024.

Bennett, C. M., & Baird, A. A. (2006). Anatomical changes in the emerging adult brain: A voxel-based morphometry study. *Human Brain Mapping, 27(9)*, 766–777.

Bherer, L., Erickson, K. I., & Liu-Ambrose, T. (2013). A review of the effects of physical activity and exercise on cognitive and brain functions in older adults. *Journal of Aging Research, 2013*.

Bjorklund, D. F., & Causey, K. B. (2017). *Children's thinking: Cognitive development and individual differences*. SAGE Publications.

Black, K. A., & Schutte, E. D. (2006). Recollections of being loved: Implications of childhood experiences

with parents for young adults' romantic relationships. *Journal of Family Issues, 27(10)*, 1459–1480.

Blakemore, S. J., & Frith, U. (2005). *The learning brain: Lessons for education*. Hoboken, NJ: Blackwell Publishing.

Bloch, F., Thibaud, M., Dugué, B., Breque, C., Rigaud, A. S., & Kemoun, G. (2010). Episodes of falling among elderly people: A systematic review and meta-analysis of social and demographic pre-disposing characteristics. *Clinics, 65(9)*, 895–903.

Bornstein, M. H. (2013). Parenting and child mental health: A cross-cultural perspective. *World Psychiatry, 12(3)*, 258–265.

Bouchard Jr, T. J., Lykken, D. T., McGue, M., Segal, N. L., & Tellegen, A. (1990). Sources of human psychological differences: The Minnesota study of twins reared apart. *Science, 250(4978)*, 223–228.

Bowlby, J. (1969). *Attachment and loss* (Vol. 1). New York, NY: Random House.

Bramlett, M. D., Mosher, W. D. (2002). Cohabitation, marriage, divorce, and remarriage in the United States. *Vital and Health Statistic. Series 23, Data from the National Survey of Family Growth*, 1–32.

Brim, G. (1992). *Ambition: How we manage success and failure throughout our lives*. New York, NY: Basic Books.

Brim, O. G., Ryff, C. D., & Kessler, R. C. (2004). *How healthy are we? A national study of well-being at midlife*. Chicago, IL: University of Chicago Press.

Brown, A. M., & Whiteside, S. P. (2008). Relations among perceived parental rearing behaviors, attachment style, and worry in anxious children. *Journal of Anxiety Disorders, 22*, 263–272.

Brown, F. L., & Slaughter, V. (2011). Normal body, beautiful body: Discrepant perceptions reveal a pervasive 'thin ideal' from childhood to adulthood. *Body Image, 8(2)*, 119–125.

Budday, S., Steinmann, P., & Kuhl, E. (2015). Physical biology of human brain development. *Frontiers in Cellular Neuroscience, 9*, 257.

Bumpass, L., & Raley, K. (2007). Measuring separation and divorce. *Handbook of Measurement Issues in Family Research*, 125–143.

Burke, D., & MacKay, D. (1994). *The handbook of aging and cognition* (3rd ed.). Craik, F. I. M., & Salthouse, T. A. (Eds.). Psychology Press.

Cabeza, R., Nyberg, L., & Park, D. C. (Eds.). (2016). *Cognitive neuroscience of aging: Linking cognitive and cerebral aging*. Oxford University Press.

Cachelin, F. M., Phinney, J. S., Schug, R. A., & Striegel-Moore, R. H. (2006). Acculturation and eating disorders in a Mexican American community sample. *Psychology of Women Quarterly, 30(4)*, 340–347.

Calzo, J. P., Sonneville, K. R., Haines, J., Blood, E. A., Field, A. E., & Austin, S. B. (2012). The development of associations among body mass index, body dissatisfaction, and weight and shape concern in adolescent boys and girls. *Journal of Adolescent Health, 51(5)*, 517–523.

Cargin, J. W., Collie, A., Masters, C., & Maruff, P. (2008). The nature of cognitive complaints in healthy older adults with and without objective memory decline. *Journal of Clinical and Experimental Neuropsychology, 30*, 245–257.

Carruthers, M. (2001). A multifactorial approach to understanding andropause. *Journal of Sexual and Reproductive Medicine, 1(2)*, 69–74.

Carstensen, L. (1991). Selectivity theory: Social activity in life-span context. *Annual Review of Gerontology and Geriatrics, Volume 11, 1991: Behavioral Science & Aging, 11*, 195–217.

Carstensen, L. L. (2006). The influence of a sense of time on human development. *Science, 312*, 1913–1915.

Casey, B. J. (2015). Beyond simple models of self-control to circuit-based accounts of adolescent behavior. *Annual Review of Psychology, 66*, 295–319.

Centers for Disease Control and Prevention (2015a, April 16). *Facts about FASDs*. Accessed 6/16/2016. Retrieved from http://www.cdc.gov/ncbddd/fasd/facts.html

Centers for Disease Control and Prevention. (2015b). Births: Final data for 2014. *National Vital Statistics Reports, 64*, 1–64.

Centers for Disease Control and Prevention (2016a). *Life expectancy*. Accessed 6/16/2016. Retrieved from http://www.cdc.gov/nchs/fastats/life-expectancy.htm

Centers for Disease Control and Prevention. (2016b). *Zika and pregnancy*. Accessed 6/16/2016. Retrieved from: http://www.cdc.gov/zika/index. html

Cho, S., Ryali, S., Geary, D. C., & Menon, V. (2011). How does a child solve 7+8? Decoding brain activity patterns associated with counting and retrieval strategies. *Developmental Science, 14(5)*, 989–1001.

Copen, C. E., Daniels, K., Vespa, J., Mosher, W. D. (2012). First marriages in the United States: Data from the 2006–2010 national survey of family growth. *National Health Statistics Report, 49*. Hyattsville, MD: National Center for Health Statistics.

Cotman, C. W., Berchtold, N. C., Christie, L. A. (2007). Exercise builds brain health: Key roles of growth factor cascades and inflammation. *Trends in Neurosciences, 30*, 464–472.

Craik, F. I., & Rose, N. S. (2012). Memory encoding and aging: A neurocognitive perspective. *Neuroscience & Biobehavioral Reviews, 36(7)*, 1729–1739.

Crews, F., He, J., & Hodge, C. (2007). Adolescent cortical development: A critical period of vulnerability for addiction. *Pharmacology Biochemistry and Behavior, 86*, 189–199.

Cumming, E., Henry, W. E., & Damianopoulos, E. (1961). *Growing old: The process of disengagement*. New York: Basic Books, 210–218.

Cummins, L. H., & Lehman, J. (2007). Eating disorders and body image concerns in Asian American women: Assessment and treatment from a multicultural and feminist perspective. *Eating Disorders, 15(3)*, 217–230.

Danckert, S. L., & Craik, F. I. (2013). Does aging affect recall more than recognition memory? *Psychology and Aging, 28(4)*, 902–909.

Davis, C. L., Tomporowski, P. D., McDowell J. E., Austin, B. P., Miller, P. H., Yanasak, N. E., Allison, J. D., Naglieri, J. A. (2011). Exercise improves executive function and achievement and alters brain activation in overweight children: A randomized controlled trial. *Health Psychology, 30*, 91–98.

DeLamater, J., & Moorman, S. M. (2007). Sexual behavior in later life. *Journal of Aging and Health, 19(6)*, 921–945.

Denison, S., Reed, C., Xu F. (2013). The emergence of probabilistic reasoning in very young infants: Evidence from 4.5- and 6-month olds. *Developmental Psychology, 49*, 243–249.

Duell, N., Icenogle, G., & Steinberg, L. (2016). Adolescent decision making and risk taking. *Child Psychology: A Handbook of Contemporary Issues*, 263–284.

Dunphy, D. C. (1963). The social structure of urban adolescent peer groups. *Sociometry, 26(2)*, 230–246.

Dunson, D. B., Colombo, B., & Baird, D. D. (2002). Changes with age in the level and duration of fertility in the menstrual cycle. *Human Reproduction, 17(5)*, 1399–1403.

Durston, S., Hulshoff Pol, H. E., Casey, B. J., Giedd, J. N., Buitelaar, J. K., & Van Engeland, H. (2001). Anatomical MRI of the developing human brain: What have we learned? *Journal of the American Academy of Child and Adolescent Psychiatry, 40(9)*, 1012–1020.

Eaves, L. J., & Hatemi, P. K. (2008). Transmission of attitudes toward abortion and gay rights: Parental socialization or parental mate selection. *Behavior Genetics, 38(3)*, 247–256.

Egorov, A. V., & Draguhn, A. (2013). Development of coherent neuronal activity patterns in mammalian cortical networks: Common principles and local heterogeneity. *Mechanisms of Development, 130(6)*, 412–423.

Elias, C. L., & Berk, L. E. (2002). Self-regulation in young children: Is there a role for sociodramatic play? *Early Childhood Research Quarterly, 17(2)*, 216–238.

Elliott, M. (1996). Impact of work, family, and welfare receipt on women's self-esteem in young adulthood. *Social Psychology Quarterly, 59(1)*, 80–95.

Elwert, F., & Christakis, N. A. (2008). The effect of widowhood on mortality by the causes of death of both spouses. *American Journal of Public Health, 98(11)*, 2092–2098.

Erikson, E. H. (1993). *Childhood and society*. W. W. Norton & Company.

Etaugh, C. (2008). Women in the middle and later years. In F. L. Denmark & M. Paludi (Eds). Psychology of women: Handbook of issues and theories (2nd ed.) (p. 271–302). Westport, CT: Praeger Publishers.

Everett, D. L. (2009). *Don't sleep, there are snakes: Life and language in the Amazonian jungle*. Profile Books.

Fisher, L. L. (2010). *Sex, romance, and relationships: AARP survey of midlife and older adults*. AARP, Knowledge Management.

Fjell, A. M., McEvoy, L., Holland, D., Dale, A. M., Walhovd, K. B., & Alzheimer's Disease Neuroimaging Initiative. (2014). What is normal in normal aging? Effects of aging, amyloid and Alzheimer's disease on the cerebral cortex and the hippocampus. *Progress in Neurobiology, 117,* 20-40.

Franzoni, E., Gualandi, S., Caretti, V., Schimmenti, A., Di Pietro, E., Pellegrini, G., Craparo, G., Franchi, A., Verrotti, A., & Pellicciari, A. (2013). The relationship between alexithymia, shame, trauma, and body image disorders: Investigation over a large clinical sample. *Neuropsychiatric Disease and Treatment, 9,* 185–193.

Fu, A. Fu, A. S., & Markus, H. R. (2014). My mother and me: Why tiger mothers motivate Asian Americans but not European Americans. *Personality and Social Psychology Bulletin, 40*(6), 739–749.

Gagne, D. A., Von Holle, A., Brownley, K. A., Runfola, C. D., Hofmeier, S., Branch, K. E., & Bulik, C. M. (2012). Eating disorder symptoms and weight and shape concerns in a large web-based convenience sample of women ages 50 and above: Results of the gender and body image (GABI) study. *International Journal of Eating Disorders, 45*(7), 832–844.

Galland, B. C., & Elder, D. E. (2014). Sudden unexpected death in infancy: Biological mechanisms. *Paediatric Respiratory Reviews, 15*(4), 287–292.

Giorgio, A., Santelli, L., Tomassini, V., Bosnell, R., Smith, S., De Stefano, N., & Johansen-Berg, H. (2010). Age-related changes in grey and white matter structure throughout adulthood. *Neuroimage, 51*(3), 943–951.

Goode, E. (1999, February 16). New study finds middle age is prime of life. *New York Times,* 17.

Gordon, S. K., & Clark, W. C. (1974). Application of signal detection theory to prose recall and recognition in elderly and young adults. *Journal of Gerontology, 29*(1), 64–72.

Gow, A. Gow, A. J., Johnson, W., Pattie, A., Brett, C. E., Roberts, B., Starr, J. M., & Deary, I. J. (2011). Stability and change in intelligence from age 11 to ages 70, 79, and 87: The Lothian birth cohorts of 1921 and 1936. *Psychology and Aging, 26*(1), 232–240.

Grabe, S., & Hyde, J. S. (2006). Ethnicity and body dissatisfaction among women in the United States: A meta-analysis. *Psychological Bulletin, 132*(4), 622–640.

Gray, P. (2013). *Free to learn: Why unleashing the instinct to play will make our children happier, more self-reliant, and better students for life*. New York, NY: Basic Books.

Grossbard, J. R., Neighbors, C., & Larimer, M. E. (2011). Perceived norms for thinness and muscularity among college students: What do men and women really want? *Eating Behaviors, 12*(3), 192–199.

Hackshaw, A., Rodeck, C., & Boniface, S. (2011). Maternal smoking in pregnancy and birth defects: A systematic review based on 173,687 malformed cases and 11.7 million controls. *Human Reproduction Update, 17*(5), 589–604.

Haidt, J. (2001). The emotional dog and its rational tail: A social intuitionist approach to moral judgment. *Psychological Review, 108*(4), 814–834.

Haidt, J. (2013). Moral psychology for the twenty-first century. *Journal of Moral Education, 42*(3), 281–297.

Harlow, H. F. (1958). The nature of love. *American Psychologist, 13*(12), 673–685.

Hart, D., & Fegley, S. (1995). Prosocial behavior and caring in adolescence: Relations to self-understanding and social judgment. *Child Development, 66*(5), 1346–1359.

Havighurst, R. J. (1957). The leisure activities of the middle-aged. *American Journal of Sociology, 63,* 152–162.

Helfrich, Y. R., Sachs, D. L., Voorhees, J. J. (2008). Overview of skin aging and photoaging. *Dermatology Nursing, 20,* 177–183.

Hildyard, K. L., & Wolfe, D. A. (2002). Child neglect: Developmental issues and outcomes. *Child Abuse and Neglect, 26,* 679–695.

Hoffman, S. D., & Maynard, R. A. (Eds.). (2008). *Kids having kids: Economic costs & social consequences of teen pregnancy*. Washington, DC: Urban Institute.

Hopkins, J. R. (2011). The enduring influence of Jean Piaget. *Observer: Association for Psychological Science,* 24(10) 154–159.

Huang, H., Shu, N., Mishra, V., Jeon, T., Chalak, L., Wang, Z. J., Rollins, N., Gong, G., Cheng, H., Peng, Y., Dong, Q., & He, Y. (2015). Development of human brain structural networks through infancy and childhood. *Cerebral Cortex, 25*(5), 1389–1404.

Hyman, B. T., Phelps, C. H., Beach, T. G., Bigio, E. H., Cairns, N. J., Carrillo, M. C., Dickson, D. W., Duychkaerts, C., Fosch, M. P., Masliah, W., Mirra, S. S., Nelson, P. T., Schneider, J. A., Rudolf Thal, D., Thies, B. Trojanowski, J. Q., Vinters, H. V., & Montine, T. J. (2012). National Institute on Aging–Alzheimer's Association guidelines for the neuropathologic assessment of Alzheimer's disease. *Alzheimer's and Dementia, 8*(1), 1–13.

Ikonomidou, C., Bittigau, P., Ishimaru, M. J., Wozniak, D. F., Koch, C., Genz, K., Price, M.T., Stefovska, V., Horster, F., Tenkova, T., Dikranian, K., & Olney, J. W. (2000). Ethanol-induced apoptotic neurodegeneration and fetal alcohol syndrome. *Science, 287*(5455), 1056–1060.

James, L. E., Fogler, K. A., & Tauber, S. K. (2008). Recognition memory measures yield disproportionate effects of aging on learning face-name associations. *Psychological Aging, 23,* 657–664.

Jansen, E. C., Marín, C., Mora-Plazas, M., & Villamor, E. (2016). Higher childhood red meat intake frequency is associated with earlier age at menarche. *Journal of Nutrition, 146*(4), 792–798.

Jennings, M. K., Stoker, L., & Bowers, J. (2009). Politics across generations: Family transmission reexamined. *Journal of Politics, 71,* 782–799.

Johnson, K. J., & Mutchler, J. E. (2014). The emergence of a positive gerontology: From disengagement to social involvement. *The Gerontologist, 54,* 93–100.

Johnson, L., Radesky, J., & Zuckerman, B. (2013). Cross-cultural parenting: Reflections on autonomy and interdependence. *Pediatrics, 131*(4), 631–633.

Judge, T. A., Piccolo, R. F., Podsakoff, N. P., Shaw, J. C., & Rich, B. L. (2010). The relationship between pay and job satisfaction: A meta-analysis of the literature. *Journal of Vocational Behavior, 77*(2), 157–167.

Kaufman, A. S., Reynolds, C. R., & McLean, J. E. (1989). Age and WAIS-R intelligence in a national sample of adults in the 20- to 74-year age range: A cross-sectional analysis with educational level controlled. *Intelligence, 13*(3), 235–253.

Keller, H. (2013). Attachment and culture. *Journal of Cross-Cultural Psychology, 44*(2), 175–194.

Kenney, W. L., Craighead, D. H., & Alexander, L. M. (2014). Heat waves, aging, and human cardiovascular health. *Medicine and Science in Sports and Exercise, 46*(10), 1891–1899.

Kim, J., & Cicchetti, D. (2010). Longitudinal pathways linking child maltreatment, emotion regulation, peer relations, and psychopathology. *Journal of Child Psychology and Psychiatry, 51,* 706–716.

Klahr, D. (1992). Information-processing approaches to cognitive development. In M. H. Bornstein & M. E. Lamb (Eds.) Developmental psychology: An advanced textbook (3rd ed., pp. 273–336). Hillsdale, NJ: Erlbaum.

Klein, H., & Shiffman, K. S. (2006). Messages about physical attractiveness in animated cartoons. *Body Image, 3*(4), 353–363.

Kohlberg, L. (1969). *Stage and sequence: The cognitive-developmental approach to socialization* (pp. 347–480). New York, NY: Rand McNally.

Kohlberg, L. (1981). *The philosophy of moral development: Moral stages and the idea of justice* (essays on moral development, Vol. 1). San Francisco, CA: Harper & Row.

Kohlberg, L. (1984). Essays on moral development. *The psychology of moral development: the nature and validity of moral stages*. Vol. 2. New York, NY: Harper & Row.

Kotch, J. B., Lewis, T., Hussey, J. M., English, D., Thompson, R., Litrownik, A. J., Runyan, D. K., Bangdiwala, S. I., Margolis, B., & Dubowitz, H. (2008). Importance of early neglect for childhood aggression. *Pediatrics, 121,* 725–731.

Kroger, J., Martinussen, M., & Marcia, J. E. (2010). Identity status change during adolescence and young adulthood: A meta-analysis. *Journal of Adolescence, 33*(5), 683–698.

Kronenfeld, L. W., Reba-Harrelson, L., Von Holle, A., Reyes, M. L., & Bulik, C. M. (2010). Ethnic and racial differences in body size perception and satisfaction. *Body Image, 7*(2), 131–136.

Kuperberg, A. (2014). Age at coresidence, premarital cohabitation, and marriage dissolution: 1985–2009. *Journal of Marriage and Family, 76*(2), 352–369.

Lamborn, S. D., Mants, N. S., Steinberg, L., and Dornbusch, S. M. (1991). Patterns of competence and adjustment among adolescents from authoritative, authoritarian, indulgent, and neglectful families. *Child Development, 62,* 1049–1065.

Levy, B. R., Pilver, C., Chung, P. H., & Slade, M. D. (2014). Subliminal strengthening improving older individuals' physical function over time with an implicit-age-stereotype intervention. *Psychological Science, 25*(12), 2127–2135.

Liu, C. H., & Matthews, R. (2005). Vygotsky's philosophy: Constructivism and its criticisms examined. *International Education Journal, 6*(3), 386–399.

Löckenhoff, C. E., De Fruyt, F., Terracciano, A., McCrae, R. R., De Bolle, M., Costa, P. T., … & Allik, J. (2009). Perceptions of aging across 26 cultures and their culture-level associates. *Psychology and aging, 24*(4), 941.

Löckenhoff, C. E., Lee, D. S., Buckner, K. M., Moreira, R. O., Martinez, S. J., & Sun, M. Q. (2014). Cross-cultural differences in attitudes about aging: Moving beyond the East-West dichotomy. In *Successful Aging* (pp. 321–337). The Netherlands: Springer.

Lyles, L. (2013, December 20). 50 years later: Women, work, and the work ahead. (Work in Progress): *The Official Blog of the U.S. Department of Labor.* Retrieved from http://social.dol.gov/blog/50-years-later-women-work-and-the-work-ahead//

Macan, T., Gibson, J. M., & Cunningham, J. (2010). Will you remember to read this article later when you have time? The relationship between prospective memory and time management. *Personality and Individual Differences, 48,* 725–730.

Maccoby, E. E., & Martin, J. A. (1983). Socialization in the context of the family: Parent-child interaction. *Handbook of child psychology: Formerly Carmichael's manual of child psychology,* Paul H. Mussen, ed.

Mahy, C. E. V., Moses, L. J., Kliegel, M. (2014). The development of prospective memory in children: An executive framework. *Developmental Review, 34,* 305–326.

Main, M., Hesse, E., Greenberg, Mark T. (Ed.), Cicchetti, D. (Ed.), Cummings, E. Mark (Ed.), (1990). *Attachment in the preschool years: Theory, research, and intervention.* The John D. and Catherine T. MacArthur Foundation series on mental health and development (pp. 161–182). Chicago, IL: University of Chicago Press.

Marcia, J. E. (1966). Development and validation of ego-identity status. *Journal of Personality and Social Psychology, 3*(5), 551–558.

Marcia, J. E. (1980). Identity in adolescence. *Handbook of Adolescent Psychology, 9*(11), 159–187.

Marcia, J. E. (1993). The ego identity status approach to ego identity. In *Ego Identity* (pp. 3–21). New York, NY: Springer.

Marcia, J. E., Waterman, A. S., Matteson, D. R., Archer, S. L., & Orlofsky, J. L. (1993). *Ego identity: A handbook for psychosocial research.* Springer Science & Business Media.

Marrs, C., Olson, G., Saade, G., Hankins, G., Wen, T., Patel, J., & Weaver, S. (2016). Zika virus and pregnancy: A review of the literature and clinical considerations. *American Journal of Perinatology, 33*(07), 625–639.

Martin, E., & Rodriguez, C. (Eds.). (2012). *After Piaget* (Vol. 1). Piscataway, NJ: Transaction Publishers.

Martin, J. A., Hamilton, B. E., Ventura, S. J., Osterman, M. J., Wilson, E. C., & Mathews, T. J. (2013). National vital statistics reports. *National Vital Statistics Reports, 61*(1).

Martin, J. A., Hamilton, B. E., Ventura, S. J., Osterman, M. J., & Mathews, T. J. (2013). Births: Final data for 2011. *National Vital Statistics Report, 62*(1), 1–90.

Martinez, G., Copen, C. E., & Abma, J. C. (2011). Teenagers in the United States: Sexual activity, contraceptive use, and childbearing, 2006–2010. National Survey of Family Growth. *Vital and Health Statistics. Series 23. Data from the National Survey of Family Growth*, (31), 1–35.

Mather, M., Canli, T., English, T., Whitfield, S., Wais, P., Ochsner, K., John, D. E. G., & Carstensen, L. L. (2004). Amygdala responses to emotionally valenced stimuli in older and younger adults. *Psychological Science, 15*(4), 259–263.

Mather, M., & Carstensen, L. L. (2005). Aging and motivated cognition: The positivity effect in attention and memory. *Trends in Cognitive Sciences, 9*(10), 496–502.

Mayyasi, A. (2013, November 2). *At what age do people get married around the world?* Retrieved from: http://priceonomics.com/at-what-age-do-people-get-married-around-the-world

McDonnell-Naughton, M., McGarvey, C., O'Regan, M., & Matthews, T. (2012). Maternal smoking and alcohol consumption during pregnancy as risk factors for sudden infant death. *Irish Medical Journal, 105*(4), 105–108.

Menon, V. (2010). Developmental cognitive neuroscience of arithmetic: Implications for learning and education. *ZDM, 42*(6), 515–525.

Merrill, G. F. (2015). *Our aging bodies.* New Brunswick, NJ: Rutgers University Press.

Mills, M., Rindfuss, R. R., McDonald, P., Te Velde, E. (2011). Why do people postpone parenthood? Reasons and social policy incentives. *Human Reproduction Update, 17*, 848–860.

Miner, J. J., Cao, B., Govero, J., Smith, A. M., Fernandez, E., Cabrera, O. H., Gaarber, C., Noll, M., Klein, R. S., Noguchi, K. K., Mysorekar, I. U., & Diamond, M. S. (2016). Zika virus infection during pregnancy in mice causes placental damage and fetal demise. *Cell, 165*(5), 1081–1091.

Miyake, K., Chen, S. J., & Campos, J. J. (1985). Infant temperament, mother's mode of interaction, and attachment in Japan: An interim report. *Monographs of the Society for Research in Child Development, 50*(209), 276–297.

Morita, A. (2007). Tobacco smoke causes premature skin aging. *Journal of Dermatological Science, 48*, 169–175.

Morrison, M. A., Morrison, T. G., & Sager, C. L. (2004). Does body satisfaction differ between gay men and lesbian women and heterosexual men and women? A meta-analytic review. *Body Image, 1*(2), 127–138.

Morrison, T. G., & McCutcheon, J. M. (2011). Gay and lesbian body images. In T. F. Cash and T. Pruzinsky (Eds.) *Body Image: A handbook of science, practice, and prevention*, (258–265). New York, NJ: The Guilford Press.

Mroczek, D. K. (2001). Age and emotion in adulthood. *Current Directions in Psychological Science, 10*(3), 87–90.

Myers, S. M. (2000). Moving into adulthood: Family residential mobility and first-union transitions. *Social Science Quarterly, 81*(3), 782–797.

Newcombe, N. S. (2013). Cognitive development: Changing views of cognitive change. *Wiley Interdisciplinary Reviews: Cognitive Science, 4*(5), 479–491.

Nykjaer, C., Alwan, N. A., Greenwood, D. C., Simpson, N. A., Hay, A. W., White, K. L., & Cade, J. E. (2014). Maternal alcohol intake prior to and during pregnancy and risk of adverse birth outcomes: Evidence from a British cohort. *Journal of Epidemiology and Community Health, 68*(6) 542–549.

OECD (2016). Mean age of mothers at first childbirth. *OECD Family Database,* Social Policy Division, Paris.

Ornoy, A., & Ergaz, Z. (2010). Alcohol abuse in pregnant women: Effects on the fetus and newborn, mode of action and maternal treatment. *International Journal of Environmental Research and Public Health, 7*, 364–379.

O'Shea, R. S., Dasarathy, S., & McCullough, A. J. (2010). Alcoholic liver disease. *Hepatology, 51*, 307–328.

Palincsar, A. S. (2012). Reciprocal teaching. In J. Hattie & E. M. Anderman (Eds.) *International Guide to Student Achievement* (369–371). New York, NY: Routledge.

Pascual-Sagastizabal, E., Azurmendi, A., Braza, F., Vergara, A. I., Cardas, J., & Sánchez-Martín, J. R. (2014). Parenting styles and hormone levels as predictors of physical and indirect aggression in boys and girls. *Aggressive Behavior, 40*(5), 465–473.

Payne, V. G., & Isaacs, L. D. (1987). Human motor development. New York, NY: McGraw-Hill.

Peplau, L. A., Frederick, D. A., Yee, C., Maisel, N., Lever, J., & Ghavami, N. (2009). Body image satisfaction in heterosexual, gay, and lesbian adults. *Archives of Sexual Behavior, 38*(5), 713–725.

Phillips, D. A., & Shonkoff, J. P. (Eds.). (2000). *From neurons to neighborhoods: The science of early childhood development.* Washington, DC: National Academies Press.

Pineles, B. L., Park, E., & Samet, J. M. (2014). Systematic review and meta-analysis of miscarriage and maternal exposure to tobacco smoke during pregnancy. *American Journal of Epidemiology, 179*(7), 807–823.

Pinquart, M. (2017). Associations of parenting dimensions and styles with externalizing problems of children and adolescents: An updated meta-analysis. *Developmental Psychology 53*(5): 873–932. doi: 10.1037/dev0000295

Piotrowski, J. T., Lapierre, M. A., & Linebarger, D. L. (2013). Investigating correlates of self-regulation in early childhood with a representative sample of English-speaking American families. *Journal of Child and Family Studies, 22*(3), 423–436.

Price, G. R., Mazzocco, M. M., & Ansari, D. (2013). Why mental arithmetic counts: Brain activation during single digit arithmetic predicts high school math scores. *Journal of Neuroscience, 33*(1), 156–163.

Proctor, R. W., & Vu, K. P. L. (2006). The cognitive revolution at age 50: Has the promise of the human information-processing approach been fulfilled? *International Journal of Human-Computer Interaction, 21*(3), 253–284.

Qu, Y., Galvan, A., Fuligni, A. J., Lieberman, M. D., & Telzer, E. H. (2015). Longitudinal changes in prefrontal cortex activation underlie declines in adolescent risk taking. *Journal of Neuroscience, 35*(32), 11308–11314.

Rabbitt, P. (2014). *The Aging Mind: An Owner's Manual.* New York, NY: Routledge.

Rakic, P. (2006). No more cortical neurons for you. *Science, 313*(5789), 928–929.

Resnick, S. M., Pham, D. L., Kraut, M. A., Zonderman, A. B., & Davatzikos, C. (2003). Longitudinal magnetic resonance imaging studies of older adults: A shrinking brain. *Journal of Neuroscience, 23*(8), 3295–3301.

Richardson, J. T., & Vecchi, T. (2002). A jigsaw-puzzle imagery task for assessing active visuospatial processes in old and young people. *Behavior Research Methods, Instruments, & Computers, 34*(1), 69–82.

Richman, S. B., & Mandara, J. (2013). Do socialization goals explain differences in parental control between black and white parents? *Family Relations, 62*(4), 625–636.

Rose, J. E., Behm, F. M., Westman, E. C., & Coleman, R. E. (1999). Arterial nicotine kinetics during cigarette smoking and intravenous nicotine administration: Implications for addiction. *Drug and Alcohol Dependence, 56*(2), 99–107.

Salthouse, T. A. (2009). When does age-related cognitive decline begin? *Neurobiology of Aging, 30*(4), 507–514.

Samaras, N., Frangos, E., Forster, A., Lang, P. O., Samaras, D. (2012). Andropause: A review of the definition and treatment. *European Geriatric Medicine, 3*, 368–373.

Santelli, J. S., Lindberg, L. D., Finer, L. B., & Singh, S. (2007). Explaining recent declines in adolescent pregnancy in the United States: The contribution of abstinence and improved contraceptive use. *American Journal of Public Health, 97*(1), 150–156.

Schneider, J. A., Arvanitakis, Z., Leurgans, S. E., & Bennett, D. A. (2009). The neuropathology of probable Alzheimer disease and mild cognitive impairment. *Annals of Neurology, 66*(2), 200–208.

Schwartz, S. H. (1994). Are there universal aspects in the structure and contents of human values? *Journal of Social Issues, 50*(4), 19–45.

Segal, N. L. (2017). Reared-Apart Chinese Twins: Chance Discovery/Twin-Based Research: Twin Study of Media Use; Twin Relations Over the Life Span; Breast-Feeding Opposite-Sex Twins/Print and Online Media: Twins in Fashion; Second Twin Pair Born to Tennis Star; Twin Primes; Twin Pandas. *Twin Research and Human Genetics, 20*(2), 180–185.

Segal, N. L., & Cortez, F. A. (2014). Born in Korea-adopted apart: Behavioral development of monozygotic twins raised in the United States and France. *Personality and Individual Differences, 70*, 97–104.

Segal, N. L., Tan, T. X., & Graham, J. L. (2015). Twins and virtual twins: Do genetic (as well as experiential) factors affect developmental risks? *Journal of Experimental Child Psychology, 136*, 55–69.

Shipman, K., Edwards, A., Brown, A., Swisher, L., & Jennings, E. (2005). Managing emotion in a maltreating context: A pilot study examining child neglect. *Child Abuse and Neglect, 29*, 1015–1029.

Siegler, R. S., & Braithwaite, D. W. (2017). Numerical development. *Annual Review of Psychology, 68*, 187–213.

Simons-Morton, B. G., & Farhat, T. (2010). Recent findings on peer group influences on adolescent smoking. *Journal of Primary Prevention, 31*, 191–208.

Slater, A. M., Bremner, J. G., Johnson, S. P., & Hayes, R. (2011). The role of perceptual processes in infant addition/subtraction experiments. In L. M. Oakes, C. H. Cashon, M. Casasola, & D. H. Rakison (Eds.) *Infant perception and cognition: Recent advances, emerging theories, and future directions,* (85–110). New York, NY: Oxford Press.

Smolak, L. (2011). Body image development in childhood. Cash, T. F. & Smolak, L. (Eds.), *Body image: A handbook of science, practice, and prevention* (67–75). Guilford Press.

Spiel, E. C., Paxton, S. J., & Yager, Z. (2012). Weight attitudes in 3- to 5-year-old children: Age differences and cross-sectional predictors. *Body Image, 9*(4), 524–527.

Steinberg, L. (2001). We know some things: Parent–adolescent relationships in retrospect and prospect. *Journal of Research on Adolescence, 11*(1), 1–19.

Sternberg, D. A., Ballard, K., Hardy, J. L., Katz, B., Doraiswamy, P. M., & Scanlon, M. (2013). The largest human cognitive performance dataset reveals insights into the effects of lifestyle factors and aging. *Frontiers in Human Neuroscience, 7*, 292.

Streissguth, A. P., Aase, J. M., Clarren, S. K., Randels, S. P., LaDue, R. A., & Smith, D. F. (1991). Fetal alcohol syndrome in adolescents and adults. *JAMA, 265*(15), 1961–1967.

Sullivan, P. M., Dervan, L. A., Reiger, S., Buddhe, S., & Schwartz, S. M. (2015). Risk of congenital heart defects in the offspring of smoking mothers: A population-based study. *Journal of Pediatrics, 166*(4), 978–984.

Surprenant, A. M. (2007). Effects of noise on identification and serial recall of nonsense syllables in older and younger adults. *Aging, Neuropsychology, and Cognition: A Journal on Normal and Dysfunctional Development, 14*, 126–143.

Sütterlin, S., Paap, M., Babic, S., Kübler, A., & Vögele, C. (2012). Rumination and age: Some things get better. *Journal of Aging Research, 2012*.

Suttie, M., Foroud, T., Wetherill, L., Jacobson, J. L., Molteno, C. D., Meintjes, E. M., Hoyme, H. E., Khaole, N., Robinson, L. K., Riley, E. P., Jacobson, S. W., & Hammond, P. (2013). Facial dysmorphism across the fetal alcohol spectrum. *Pediatrics, 131*(113), e779–e788.

Swami, V., Frederick, D. A., Aavik, T., Alcalay, L., Allik, J., Anderson, D., … & Zivcic-Becirevic, I. (2010). The attractive female body weight and female body dissatisfaction in 26 countries across 10 world regions: Results of the International Body Project I. *Personality and Social Psychology Bulletin, 36*(3), 309–325.

Sweeney, M. M. (2010). Remarriage and stepfamilies: Strategic sites for family scholarship in the 21st century. *Journal of Marriage and Family, 72*, 667–684.

Sydell, L. (2014, October 17). Silicon Valley companies add new benefit for women: Egg-freezing. National Public Radio. Retrieved from http://www.npr.org/blogs/alltechconsidered/2014/10/17/356765423/silicon-valley-companies-add-new-benefit-for-women-egg-freezing

Taylor, A., Wilson, C., Slater, A., & Mohr, P. (2012). Self-esteem and body dissatisfaction in young children: Associations with weight and perceived parenting style. *Clinical Psychologist, 16*(1), 25–35.

Thomas, A., & Chess, S. (1977). *Temperament and development.* Oxford England: Brunner/Mazel.

Tremblay, L., Lovsin, T., Zecevic, C., & Larivière, M. (2011). Perceptions of self in 3- to 5-year-old children: A preliminary investigation into the early emergence of body dissatisfaction. *Body Image, 8*(3), 287–292.

Tseng, V. (2004). Family interdependence and academic adjustment in college: Youth from immigrant and U.S.-born families. *Child Development, 75*(3), 966–983.

Tuan, R. S. (2016). Prenatal substance use and developmental disorders: Overview and highlights. *Birth Defects Research Part C: Embryo Today: Reviews, 108*(2), 106–107.

Tun, P. A., & Lachman, M. E. (2008). Age differences in reaction time and attention in a national telephone sample of adults: Education, sex, and task complexity matter. *Developmental Psychology, 45*, 1421–1429.

U.S. Department of Labor, Bureau of Labor Statistics. (2016). *Women in the labor force: A databook.* Retrieved from: http://www.bls.gov/cps/wlf-databook-2016.pdf

U.S. Department of Health and Human Services, Office of Adolescent Health. (2014). *Trends in teen pregnancy and childbearing.* Retrieved from http://www.hhs.gov/ash/oah/adolescent-health-topics/reproductive-health/teen-pregnancy/trends.html

U.S. Census Bureau (2014). *United States census fertility data.* Retrieved from http://www.census.gov/hhes/fertility/data/cps/historical.html

Van den Broeck, A., Vansteenkiste, M., & De Witte, H. (2008). Self-determination theory: A theoretical and empirical overview in occupational health psychology. *Occupational Health Psychology: European Perspectives on Research, Education, and Practice, 1*(3), 63–88.

Van Praag, H. (2009). Exercise and the brain: Something to chew on. *Trends in Neuroscience, 32*, 283–290.

Waxman, O. B. (2013, September 16). Poll: 50 is the "perfect" age. *Time Magazine.* Retrieved from http://newsfeed.time.com/2013/09/16/poll-50-is-the-perfect-age//

Wayment, H. A., & Peplau, L. A. (1995). Social support and well-being among lesbian and heterosexual women: A structural modeling approach. *Personality and Social Psychology Bulletin, 21*(11), 1189–1199.

Wellman, H. M., & Gelman, S. A. (1992). Cognitive development: Foundational theories of core domains. *Annual Review of Psychology, 43*(1), 337–375.

Wertheim, E. H., & Paxton, S. J. (2011). Body image development in adolescent girls. In T. F. Cash and T. Pruzinsky (Eds.) *Body Image: A handbook of science, practice, and prevention,* (76–84). New York, NY: The Guilford Press.

Wienke, C., & Hill, G. J. (2008). Does the "marriage benefit" extend to partners in gay and lesbian relationships? Evidence from a random sample of sexually active adults. *Journal of Family Issues, 30,* 259–289.

Wolfe, B., & Rivers, E. M. (2008). Children's health and health care. In S. D. Hoffman, & R. A. Maynard, (Eds.), *Kids having kids: Economic costs and social consequences of teen pregnancy* (pp. 221–256). Washington, DC: Urban Institute Press.

World Health Organization. (2014). Ageing and life course. *World Health Organization.* Retrieved from http://www.who.int/ageing/en/

Wright, A. M., & Holliday, R. E. (2007). Enhancing the recall of young, young–old and old–old adults with cognitive interviews. *Applied Cognitive Psychology, 21*(1), 19–43.

Wynn, K. (1992). Addition and subtraction by human infants. *Nature, 358*(6389), 749–750.

Wynn, K. (2000). Findings of addition and subtraction in infants are robust and consistent: Reply to Wakeley, Rivera, and Langer. *Child Development, 71*(6), 1535–1536.

Chapter 10

Albuquerque, D., Stice, E., Rodríguez-López, R., Manco, L., & Nóbrega, C. (2015). Current review of genetics of human obesity: from molecular mechanisms to an evolutionary perspective. *Molecular Genetics and Genomics, 290*(4), 1191–1221.

Amabile, T. M., DeJong, W., & Lepper, M. (1976). Effects of externally imposed deadlines on intrinsic motivation. *Journal of Personality and Social Psychology, 34,* 92–98.

Amabile, T. M. (1993). Motivational synergy: Toward new conceptualizations of intrinsic and extrinsic motivation in the workplace. *Human Resource Management Review, 3*(3), 185–201.

American Psychological Association. (2004). The truth about lie detectors (aka polygraph tests). Retrieved from http://www.apa.org/research/action/polygraph.aspx

Aronne, L., Shanahan, W., Fain, R., Glicklich, A., Soliman, W., Li, Y., & Smith, S. (2014). Safety and efficacy of lorcaserin: A combined analysis of the BLOOM and BLOSSOM trials. *Postgraduate Medicine, 126*(6), 7–18.

Avey, J. B., Wernsing, T. S., & Mhatre, K. H. (2011). A longitudinal analysis of positive psychological constructs and emotions on stress, anxiety, and well-being. *Journal of Leadership & Organizational Studies, 18*(2), 216–228.

Bakos, J., Zatkova, M., Bacova, Z., & Ostatnikova, D. (2016). The role of hypothalamic neuropeptides in neurogenesis and neuritogenesis. *Neural Plasticity.* Retrieved from https://www.hindawi.com/journals/np/2016/3276383/

Bandura, A. (1993). Perceived self-efficacy in cognitive development and functioning. *Educational Psychologist, 28*(2), 117–148.

Bartlett, M. S., Littlewort, G. C., Frank, M. G., & Lee, K. (2014). Automatic decoding of facial movements reveals deceptive pain expressions. *Current Biology, 24*(7), 738–743.

Becker, D. V., Kenrick, D. T., Neuberg, S. L., Blackwell, K. C., & Smith, D. M. (2007). The confounded nature of angry men and happy women. *Journal of Personality and Social Psychology, 92*(2), 179.

Björklund, A., & Dunnett, S. B. (2007). Dopamine neuron systems in the brain: An update. *Trends in Neuroscience, 30*(5), 194–202.

Blatt, S. J. (2008). *Polarities of experience: Relatedness and self-definition in personality development, psychopathology, and the therapeutic process.* American Psychological Association.

Böhm, A., & Heitmann, B. L. (2013). The use of bioelectrical impedance analysis for body composition in epidemiological studies. *European Journal of Clinical Nutrition, 67,* S79–S85.

Bolger, N., DeLongis, A., Kessler, R. C., & Schilling, E. A. (1989). Effects of daily stress on negative mood. *Journal of Personality and Social Psychology, 57*(5), 808–818.

Bouret, S., Levin, B. E., & Ozanne, S. E. (2015). Gene-environment interactions controlling energy and glucose homeostasis and the developmental origins of obesity. *Physiological Review, 95*(1), 47–82.

Breslin, P. A. (2013). An evolutionary perspective on food and human taste. *Current Biology, 23*(9), R409–R418.

Brickman, P., Coates, D., & Janoff-Bulman, R. (1978). Lottery winners and accident victims: Is happiness relative? *Journal of Personality and Social Psychology, 36*(8), 917–927.

Broeck, A., Vansteenkiste, M., Witte, H., Soenens, B., & Lens, W. (2010). Capturing autonomy, competence, and relatedness at work: Construction and initial validation of the work-related basic need satisfaction scale. *Journal of Occupational and Organizational Psychology, 83*(4), 981–1002.

Brownell, K. D., & Campos, P. (2007, September 21). Culture matters in the obesity debate. *Los Angeles Times.* Retrieved from http://www.latimes.com/la-op-dustup21sep21-story.html

Burgess, A. M., & Nakamura, B. J. (2014). An evaluation of the two-factor model of emotion: Clinical moderators

within a large, multi-ethnic sample of youth. *Journal of Psychopathology and Behavioral Assessment, 36*(1), 124–135.

C. S. Mott Children's Hospital National Poll on Children's Health (2011). Bariatric surgery for adolescents: How young is too young? Retrieved from http://mottnpch.org/reports-surveys/bariatric-surgery-adolescents-how-young-too-young

Cacioppo, J. T., Berntson, G. G., Larsen, J. T., Poehlmann, K. M., & Ito, T. A. (2000). The psychophysiology of emotion. *Handbook of Emotions, 2,* 173–191.

Cannon, W. B., & Washburn, A. L. (1912). An explanation of hunger. *American Journal of Physiology—Legacy Content, 29*(5), 441–454.

Cannon, W. B. (1927). The James-Lange theory of emotions: A critical examination and an alternative theory. *American Journal of Psychology,* 106–124.

Cawley, J., & Meyerhoefer, C. (2009). The medical care costs of obesity: An instrumental variables approach. *Journal of Health Economics, 31*(1): 219–230, 2012; and Finkelstein, Trogdon, Cohen, et al. Annual medical spending attributable to obesity. *Health Affairs.*

Calvo, M. G., Marrero, H., & Beltrán, D. (2013). When does the brain distinguish between genuine and ambiguous smiles? An ERP study. *Brain and Cognition, 81*(2), 237–246.

Carabelea, C., Boissier, O., & Florea, A. (2004). Autonomy in multi-agent systems: A classification attempt. In *Agents and Computational Autonomy* (pp. 103–113). Springer Berlin Heidelberg.

Cenci, M. A., Kalén, P., Mandel, R. J., & Björklund, A. (1992). Regional differences in the regulation of dopamine and noradrenaline release in medial frontal cortex, nucleus accumbens and caudate-putamen: A microdialysis study in the rat. *Brain Research, 581*(2), 217–228.

Centers for Disease Control and Prevention. (2004). Trends in intake of energy and macronutrients—United States, 1971–2000. *Morbidity and Mortality Weekly Report, 53*(4), 80–82.

Centers for Disease Control and Prevention (2016). Adult obesity facts. Retrieved from https://www.cdc.gov/obesity/data/adult.html

Childerhose, J. E., & Tarini, B. A. (2015). Understanding outcomes in adolescent bariatric surgery. *Pediatrics, 136*(2), e312–e314.

Cho, Y. J., & Perry, J. L. (2012). Intrinsic motivation and employee attitudes role of managerial trustworthiness, goal directedness, and extrinsic reward expectancy. *Review of Public Personnel Administration, 32*(4), 382–406.

Church, A. T., Katigbak, M. S., Locke, K. D., Zhang, H., Shen, J., de Jesús Vargas-Flores, J., ... & Ching, C.M. (2013). Need satisfaction and well-being testing self-determination theory in eight cultures. *Journal of Cross-Cultural Psychology, 44*(4), 507–534.

Clark, M. S. (2014, January). A role for arousal in the link between feeling states, judgments, and behavior. In *Affect and Cognition: 17th Annual Carnegie Mellon Symposium on Cognition* (p. 263). New York, NY: Psychology Press.

Clément, K., Vaisse, C., Lahlou, N., Cabrol, S., Pelloux, V., Cassuto, D., ... & Basdevant, A. (1998). A mutation in the human leptin receptor gene causes obesity and pituitary dysfunction. *Nature, 392*(6674), 398–401.

Cobos, P., Sánchez, M., Garcıa, C., Vera, M. N., & Vila, J. (2002). Revisiting the James versus Cannon debate on emotion: Startle and autonomic modulation in patients with spinal cord injuries. *Biological Psychology, 61*(3), 251–269.

Conner, T., Lilley, S., & Winter, T. (2012, December 19). 'Light amidst the darkness': Heroic teacher Victoria Soto remembered. *NBC News.* Retrieved from http://usnews.nbcnews.com/_news/2012/12/19/16001132-light-amidst-the-darkness-heroic-teacher-victoria-soto-remembered?lite

Council, P. A. (2012). Participation report: The Physical Activity Council's annual study tracking sports, fitness and recreation participation in the USA. Retrieved from http://www.physicalactivitycouncil.com/pdfs/current.pdf

Critchley, H. D. (2005). Neural mechanisms of autonomic, affective, and cognitive integration. *Journal of Comparative Neurology, 493*(1), 154–166.

Dalgleish, T. (2004). The emotional brain. *Nature Reviews Neuroscience, 5*(7), 583–589.

Darwin, C. (1974). M notebook, In H.E. Gruber & P.H. Barrett (Eds.), *Darwin on man* (pp. 266–305). New York, NY: Dutton. (Original work published in 1938).

Darwin, C., & Beer, G. (1951). *The origin of species* (p. 1872). Oxford, England: Oxford University Press.

Davis, M. (2007). Measuring adiposity in health research. *Handbook of Physiological Research Methods in Health Psychology,* 259–275.

Deci, E. L. (1971). Effects of externally mediated rewards on intrinsic motivation. *Journal of Personality and Social Psychology, 18*(1), 105–115.

Deci, E. L., Connell, J. P., & Ryan, R. M. (1989). Self-determination in a work organization. *Journal of Applied Psychology, 74*(4), 580–590.

Deci, E. L., Koestner, R., & Ryan, R. M. (1999). A meta-analytic review of experiments examining the effects of extrinsic rewards on intrinsic motivation. *Psychological Bulletin, 125,* 627–668.

Deci, E. L., & Ryan, R. M. (2000). The "what" and "why" of goal pursuits: Human needs and the self-determination of behavior. *Psychological Inquiry, 11*(4), 227–268.

Deci, E. L., Ryan, R. M., Gagné, M., Leone, D. R., Usunov, J., & Kornazheva, B. P. (2001). Need satisfaction, motivation, and well-being in the work organizations of a former eastern bloc country: A cross-cultural study of self-determination. *Personality and Social Psychology Bulletin, 27*(8), 930–942.

Demment, M. M., Haas, J. D., & Olson, C. M. (2014). Changes in family income status and the development of overweight and obesity from 2 to 15 years: A longitudinal study. *BMC Public Health, 14*(1), 417–425.

Diamond, D. M., Campbell, A. M., Park, C. R., Halonen, J., & Zoladz, P. R. (2007). The temporal dynamics model of emotional memory processing: A synthesis on the neurobiological basis of stress-induced amnesia, flashbulb and traumatic memories, and the Yerkes-Dodson law. *Neural Plasticity.*

Diener, C. I., & Dweck, C. S. (1978). An analysis of learned helplessness: Continuous changes in performance, strategy, and achievement cognitions following failure. *Journal of Personality and Social Psychology, 36*(5), 451–462.

Diener, C. I., & Dweck, C. S. (1980). An analysis of learned helplessness: II. The processing of success. *Journal of Personality and Social Psychology, 39*(5), 940–952.

Diener, E., Oishi, S., & Lucas, R. E. (2003). Personality, culture, and subjective well-being: Emotional and cognitive evaluations of life. *Annual Review of Psychology, 54*(1), 403–425.

Drewnowski, A. (1997). Taste preferences and food intake. *Annual Review of Nutrition, 17*(1), 237–253.

Dror, O. E. (2014). The Cannon–Bard thalamic theory of emotions: A brief genealogy and reappraisal. *Emotion Review, 6*(1), 13–20.

Dutton, D. G., & Aron, A. P. (1974). Some evidence for heightened sexual attraction under conditions of high anxiety. *Journal of Personality and Social Psychology, 30*(4), 510–517.

Dweck, C. S. (2000). *Self-theories: Their role in motivation, personality, and development.* Psychology Press.

Dvoskin, R. (2008). Sweeter than cocaine. *Scientific American Mind, 19*(2), 16.

Early Growth Genetics (EGG) Consortium. (2012). A genome-wide association meta-analysis identifies new childhood obesity loci. *Nature Genetics, 44*(5), 526–531.

Eisenberg, N., & Lennon, R. (1983). Sex differences in empathy and related capacities. *Psychological Bulletin, 94*(1), 100–131.

Ekelund, U., Ward, H. A., Norat, T., Luan, J. A., May, A. M., Weiderpass, E., ... & Johnsen, N. F. (2015). Physical activity and all-cause mortality across levels of overall and abdominal adiposity in European men and women: The European Prospective Investigation into Cancer and Nutrition Study (EPIC). *American Journal of Clinical Nutrition, 101*(3), 613–621.

Ekman, P., & Friesen, W. V. (1971). Constants across cultures in the face and emotion. *Journal of Personality and Social Psychology, 17*(2), 124–129.

Ekman, P., & Friesen, W. V. (1975). *Pictures of facial affect.* Palo Alto, CA: Consulting Psychologists Press.

Ekman, P., Levenson, R. W., & Friesen, W. V. (1983). Autonomic nervous system activity distinguishes among emotions. *Science, 221*(4616), 1208–1210.

Ekman, J. (1987). Exposure and time use in willow tit flocks: The cost of subordination. *Animal Behaviour, 35*(2), 445–452.

Ekman, P. (1994). Strong evidence for universals in facial expressions: A reply to Russell's mistaken critique. *Psychological Bulletin, 115*(2), 268–287.

Ekman, P. (1999). Basic emotions in T. Dalgleish and T. Power (Eds.), *The handbook of cognition and emotion,* 45–60. Hoboken, NJ: John Wiley and Sons.

Elliott, R., & Dolan, R. J. (1998). Activation of different anterior cingulate foci in association with hypothesis testing and response selection. *Neuroimage, 8*(1), 17–29.

Elliott, R., Rubinsztein, J. S., Sahakian, B. J., & Dolan, R. J. (2002). The neural basis of mood-congruent processing biases in depression. *Archives of General Psychiatry, 59*(7), 597–604.

Erickson, K., Drevets, W., Clark, L., Cannon, D. M., Bain, E. E., Zarate, C. A., ... & Sahakian, B. J. (2005). Affective go/no-go performance: mood congruent bias in unmedicated patients with major depressive disorder. *American Journal of Psychiatry, 162,* 2171–2173.

Farias, M. M., Cuevas, A. M., & Rodriguez, F. (2011). Set-point theory and obesity. *Metabolic Syndrome and Related Disorders, 9*(2), 85–89.

Farooqi, I. S., & O'Rahilly, S. (2014). 20 years of leptin: Human disorders of leptin action. *Journal of Endocrinology, 223*(1), T63-T70.

Fernandez, N., Dory, V., Ste-Marie, L. G., Chaput, M., Charlin, B., & Boucher, A. (2012). Varying conceptions of competence: An analysis of how health sciences educators define competence. *Medical Education, 46*(4), 357–365.

Fernet, C., Austin, S., Trépanier, S. G., & Dussault, M. (2013). How do job characteristics contribute to burnout? Exploring the distinct mediating roles of perceived autonomy, competence, and relatedness. *European Journal of Work and Organizational Psychology, 22*(2), 123–137.

Fields, D. A., Goran, M. I., & McCrory, M. A. (2002). Body-composition assessment via air-displacement plethysmography in adults and children: A review. *American Journal of Clinical Nutrition, 75*(3), 453–467.

Franck, C., Grandi, S. M., & Eisenberg, M. J. (2013). Taxing junk food to counter obesity. *American Journal of Public Health, 103*(11), 1949–1953.

Frank, M. G., Ekman, P., & Friesen, W. V. (1993). Behavioral markers and recognizability of the smile of enjoyment. *Journal of Personality and Social Psychology, 64*(1), 83–93.

Frequently asked questions about lobotomies (2005, November 16). NPR. Retrieved from http://www.npr.org/templates/story/story.php?storyId=5014565

Friedman, J. M., & Halaas, J. L. (1998). Leptin and the regulation of body weight in mammals. *Nature, 395*(6704), 763–770.

Gendron, M., Roberson, D., van der Vyver, J. M., & Barrett, L. F. (2014). Perceptions of emotion from facial expressions are not culturally universal: Evidence from a remote culture. *Emotion, 14*(2), 251–262.

Gloy, V. L., Briel, M., Bhatt, D. L., Kashyap, S. R., Schauer, P. R., Mingrone, G., ... & Nordmann, A. J. (2013). Bariatric surgery versus non-surgical treatment for obesity: a systematic review and meta-analysis of randomised controlled trials. *BMJ, 347,* f5934.

Goodman, M., Carpenter, D., Tang, C. Y., Goldstein, K. E., Avedon, J., Fernandez, ... & Hazlett, E. A. (2014). Dialectical behavior therapy alters emotion regulation and amygdala activity in patients with borderline personality disorder. *Journal of Psychiatric Research, 57,* 108–116.

Hagerty, M. R. (1999). Testing Maslow's hierarchy of needs: National quality-of-life across time. *Social Indicators Research, 46*(3), 249–271.

Harris, R. B. (1990). Role of set-point theory in regulation of body weight. *The FASEB Journal, 4*(15), 3310–3318.

Hall, J. A. (1984). Nonverbal sex differences: Communication accuracy and expressive style. Baltimore: Johns Hopkins University Press.

Hall, J. A. (1987). On explaining gender differences: The case of nonverbal communication. In P. Shaver & C. Hencrick (Eds.), *Review of Personality and Social Psychology, 7,* 177–200.

Hart, P. (2003). *Teachers' thinking in environmental education: Consciousness and responsibility.* New York, NY: Peter Lang.

Hazlett, E. A., Zhang, J., New, A. S., Zelmanova, Y., Goldstein, K. E., Haznedar, M. M., ... & Chu, K. W. (2012). Potentiated amygdala response to repeated emotional pictures in borderline personality disorder. *Biological Psychiatry, 72*(6), 448–456.

Henderlong, J., & Lepper, M. R. (2002). The effects of praise on children's intrinsic motivation: a review and synthesis. *Psychological Bulletin, 128*(5), 774–795.

Heo, M., Wylie-Rosett, J., Pietrobelli, A., Kabat, G. C., Rohan, T. E., & Faith, M. S. (2014). U.S. pediatric population-level associations of DXA-measured percentage of body fat with four BMI metrics with cutoffs. *International Journal of Obesity, 38*(1), 60–68.

Herman, C. P. (2015). The social facilitation of eating: A review. *Appetite, 86,* 61–73.

Hinney, A., Bettecken, T., Tarnow, P., Brumm, H., Reichwald, K., Lichtner, P., ... & Hebebrand, J. (2006). Prevalence, spectrum, and functional characterization of melanocortin-4 receptor gene mutations in a representative population-based sample and obese adults from Germany. *Journal of Clinical Endocrinology & Metabolism, 91*(5), 1761–1769.

Hinney, A., Vogel, C. I., & Hebebrand, J. (2010). From monogenic to polygenic obesity: Recent advances. *European Child & Adolescent Psychiatry, 19*(3), 297–310.

Hossein, M., Asadzadeh, H., Shabani, H., Ahghar, G., Ahadi, H., & Shamir, A. S. (2011). The role of invitational education and intelligence beliefs in academic performance. *Journal of Invitational Theory and Practice, 17,* 3–10.

Huang Cao, Z. F. (2015). *Neuronal circuits and reinforcement mechanisms underlying feeding behavior.* Doctoral dissertation, University of Cambridge.

Hull, C. L. (1943). *Principles of behavior: An introduction to behavior theory.* New York, London: D. Appleton-Century Company, Incorporated.

Hull, C. L. (1952). A behavior system; an introduction to behavior theory concerning the individual organism. New Haven, CT: Yale University Press.

Hussain, S., Richardson, E., Ma, Y., Holton, C., De Backer, I., Buckley, N., Dhillo, W., Bewixk, G., Zhang, S., Carling, D., Bloom, S. & Gardiner, J. (2015). Glucokinase activity in the arcuate nucleus regulates glucose intake. *Journal of Clinical Investigation, 125*(1), 337–349.

Inge, T. H., Jenkins, T. M., Xanthakos, S. A., Dixon, J. B., Daniels, S. R., Zeller, M. H., & Helmrath, M. A. (2017). Long-term outcomes of bariatric surgery in adolescents with severe obesity (FABS-5+): A prospective follow-up analysis. *The Lancet Diabetes & Endocrinology, 5*(3), 165–173.

Iyengar, S. S., & Lepper, M. R. (1999). Rethinking the value of choice: A cultural perspective on intrinsic motivation. *Journal of Personality and Social Psychology, 76*(3), 349.

James, W. (1890). The consciousness of self. *The Principles of Psychology, 8.*

James, W. (1890/1950). *The principles of psychology.* New York, NY: Dover Publications.

Joormann, J., & Arditte, K. A. (2013). The relational theory of attention: Implications for the processing of emotional stimuli in psychological disorders. *Australian Psychologist, 48*(6), 399–401.

Kim, D. D., Krishnarajah, J., Lillioja, S., de Looze, F., Marjason, J., Proietto, J., ... & Hughes, T. E. (2015). Efficacy and safety of beloranib for weight loss in obese adults: A randomized controlled trial. *Diabetes, Obesity and Metabolism, 17*(6), 566–572.

Klüver, H., & Bucy, P. C. (1937). "Psychic blindness" and other symptoms following bilateral temporal lobectomy in Rhesus monkeys. *American Journal of Physiology 119*, 352–353.

Koenigsberg, H. W., Denny, B. T., Fan, J., Liu, X., Guerreri, S., Mayson, S. J., ... & Siever, L. J. (2014). The neural correlates of anomalous habituation to negative emotional pictures in borderline and avoidant personality disorder patients. *American Journal of Psychiatry, 171*(1), 82–90.

Koltko-Rivera, M. E. (2006). Rediscovering the later version of Maslow's hierarchy of needs: Self-transcendence and opportunities for theory, research, and unification. *Review of General Psychology, 10*(4), 302–317.

Krashes, M. J., Shah, B. P., Madara, J. C., Olson, D. P., Strochlic, D. E., Garfield, A. ... & Lowell, B. B. (2014). An excitatory paraventricular nucleus to AgRP neuron circuit that drives hunger. *Nature, 507*(7491), 238–242.

Lange, C. G. (1885). The mechanism of the emotions. *The Emotions.* Williams & Wilkins, Baltimore, MD, 33–92.

Lazarus, R. S. (1991). Cognition and motivation in emotion. *American Psychologist, 46*(4), 352–367.

Lazarus, R. S. (1995). Vexing research problems inherent in cognitive-mediational theories of emotion and some solutions. *Psychological Inquiry, 6*(3), 183–196.

Larsen, R. J., Kasimatis, M., & Frey, K. (1992). Facilitating the furrowed brow: An unobtrusive test of the facial feedback hypothesis applied to unpleasant affect. *Cognition & Emotion, 6*(5), 321–338.

Lee, H., Andrew, M., Gebremariam, A., Lumeng, J. C., & Lee, J. M. (2014). Longitudinal associations between poverty and obesity from birth through adolescence. *American Journal of Public Health, 104*(5), e70–e76.

LeDoux, J. E. (1994). Emotion, memory and the brain. *Scientific American, 270*(6), 50–57.

Lepper, M. R., Greene, D., & Nisbett, R. E. (1973). Undermining children's intrinsic interest with extrinsic rewards: A test of the "overjustification" hypothesis. *Journal of Personality and Social Psychology, 28*, 129–137.

Levenson, R. W. (2014). Emotion and the autonomic nervous system: Introduction to the special section. *Emotion Review, 6*(2), 91–92.

Levine, J. A. (2011). Poverty and obesity in the U.S. *Diabetes, 60*(11), 2667–2668.

LoBue, V., Matthews, K., Harvey, T., & Thrasher, C. (2014). Pick on someone your own size: The detection of threatening facial expressions posed by both child and adult models. *Journal of Experimental Child Psychology, 118*, 134–142.

Locke, A. E., Kahali, B., Berndt, S. I., Justice, A. E., Pers, T. H., Day, F. R., ... & Croteau-Chonka, D. C. (2015). Genetic studies of body mass index yield new insights for obesity biology. *Nature, 518*(7538), 197–206.

Lonsdale, C., & Hodge, K. (2011). Temporal ordering of motivational quality and athlete burnout in elite sport. *Medicine and Science in Sports and Exercise, 43*(5), 913–921.

Look AHEAD Research Group. (2014). Eight-year weight losses with an intensive lifestyle intervention: The look AHEAD study. *Obesity 22*(1), 5–13.

Lumeng, J. C., & Hillman, K. H. (2007). Eating in larger groups increases food consumption. *Archives of Disease in Childhood, 92*(5), 384–387.

Lutes, L. D., Damschroder, L. J., Masheb, R., Kim, H. M., Gillon, L., Holleman, R. G., ... & Richardson, C. R. (2017). Behavioral treatment for veterans with obesity: 24-month weight outcomes from the ASPIRE-VA small changes randomized trial. *Journal of General Internal Medicine, 32*(1), 40–47.

Mandler, G. (2003). Emotion. *Handbook of Psychology.* Hoboken, NJ: John Wiley & Sons, Inc.

Maslow, A. H. (1943). A theory of human motivation. *Psychological Review, 50*(4), 370–396.

Maslow, A. H. (1969). Various meanings of transcendence. *The Journal of Transpersonal Psychology, 1*(1), 56–66.

Maslow, A. H., (1970). *Motivation and Personality* (Vol. 2). J. Fadiman & C. McReynolds (Eds.). New York, NY: Harper & Row.

Matsumoto, D. (2009). 15 culture and emotional expressions. *Understanding culture: Theory, research, and application*, 271–287.

Matsumoto, D., & Hwang, H. S. (2013). Cultural influences on nonverbal behavior. *Nonverbal Communication: Science and Applications: Science and Applications*, 97–120.

McClure, E. B. (2000). A meta-analytic review of sex differences in facial expression processing and their development in infants, children, and adolescents. *Psychological Bulletin, 126*(3), 424–453.

McDougall, W. (1926)."The principal instincts and the primary emotions." Chapter 3 in *An introduction to social psychology* (revised edition). Boston, MA: John W. Luce & Co., 47–92.

Michalska, K. J., Kinzler, K. D., & Decety, J. (2013). Age-related sex differences in explicit measures of empathy do not predict brain responses across childhood and adolescence. *Developmental Cognitive Neuroscience, 3*, 22–32.

Murphy, P. K., & Alexander, P. A. (2002). What counts? The predictive powers of subject-matter knowledge, strategic processing, and interest in domain-specific performance. *Journal of Experimental Education, 70*(3), 197–214.

Neal, D. T., & Chartrand, T. L. (2011). Embodied emotion perception amplifying and dampening facial feedback modulates emotion perception accuracy. *Social Psychological and Personality Science, 2*(6), 673–678.

Nie, Y., Chua, B. L., Yeung, A. S., Ryan, R. M., & Chan, W. Y. (2015). The importance of autonomy support and the mediating role of work motivation for well-being: Testing self-determination theory in a Chinese work organisation. *International Journal of Psychology, 50*(4), 245–255.

Ng, M., Fleming, T., Robinson, M., Thomson, B., Graetz, N., Margono, C., ... & Ammar, W. (2014). Global, regional, and national prevalence of overweight and obesity in children and adults during 1980–2013: A systematic analysis for the Global Burden of Disease Study 2013. *The Lancet, 384*(9945), 766–781.

O'Brien, P. E., MacDonald, L., Anderson, M., Brennan, L., & Brown, W. A. (2013). Long-term outcomes after bariatric surgery: Fifteen-year follow-up of adjustable gastric banding and a systematic review of the bariatric surgical literature. *Annals of Surgery, 257*(1), 87–94.

Ogden, C. L., Carroll, M. D., Lawman, H. G., Fryar, C. D., Kruszon-Moran, D., Kit, B. K., & Flegal, K. M. (2016). Trends in obesity prevalence among children and adolescents in the United States, 1988–1994 through 2013–2014. *JAMA, 315*(21), 2292–2299.

Phillips, A. G., Ahn, S., & Howland, J. G. (2003). Amygdalar control of the mesocorticolimbic dopamine system: Parallel pathways to motivated behavior. *Neuroscience & Biobehavioral Reviews, 27*(6), 543–554.

Pollak, S. D., Cicchetti, D., Hornung, K., & Reed, A. (2000). Recognizing emotion in faces: Developmental effects of child abuse and neglect. *Developmental Psychology, 36*(5), 679–688.

Porter, S., & Ten Brinke, L. (2008). Reading between the lies identifying concealed and falsified emotions in universal facial expressions. *Psychological Science, 19*(5), 508–514.

Poti, J., Mendez, M., Ng, S. W., & Popkin, B. (2015). Are food processing and convenience linked with the nutritional quality of foods purchased by U.S. households? *The FASEB Journal, 29*(1 Supplement), 587–589.

Poverty USA: A CCHD Initiative (2014). Poverty map. Retrieved from http://www.povertyusa.org/the-state-of-poverty/poverty-map-state/

Puzziferri, N., Roshek, T. B., Mayo, H. G., Gallagher, R., Belle, S. H., & Livingston, E. H. (2014). Long-term follow-up after bariatric surgery: A systematic review. *JAMA, 312*(9), 934–942.

Quested, E., Bosch, J., Burns, V. E., Cumming, J., Ntoumanis, N., & Duda, J. L. (2011). Basic psychological need satisfaction, stress-related appraisals, and dancers' cortisol and anxiety responses. *Journal of Sport and Exercise Psychology, 2011*(33), 828–846.

Rolls, B. J., Morris, E. L., & Roe, L. S. (2002). Portion size of food affects energy intake in normal-weight and overweight men and women. *American Journal of Clinical Nutrition, 76*(6), 1207–1213.

Ryan, R. M., Deci, E. L., & Grolnick, W. S. (1995). Autonomy, relatedness, and the self: Their relation to development and psychopathology. *Ariel, 128*(151.189), 155.

Ryan, R. M., & Deci, E. L. (2000). Self-determination theory and the facilitation of intrinsic motivation, social development, and well-being. *American Psychologist, 55*(1), 68–78.

Ryan, R. M., & Deci, E. L. (2016). Facilitating and hindering motivation, learning, and well-being in schools: Research and observations from self-determination theory. *Handbook of Motivation at School*, 96.

Safdar, S., Friedlmeier, W., Matsumoto, D., Yoo, S. H., Kwantes, C. T., Kakai, H., & Shigemasu, E. (2009). Variations of emotional display rules within and across cultures: A comparison between Canada, USA, and Japan. *Canadian Journal of Behavioural Science, 41*(1), 1–10.

Sakurai, T., Amemiya, A., Ishii, M., Matsuzaki, I., Chemelli, R. M., Tanaka, H., ... & Yanagisawa, M. (1998). Orexins and orexin receptors: A family of hypothalamic neuropeptides and G protein-coupled receptors that regulate feeding behavior. *Cell, 92*(4), 573–585.

Salehi, B., Cordero, M. I., & Sandi, C. (2010). Learning under stress: The inverted-U-shape function revisited. *Learning & Memory, 17*(10), 522–530.

Salonia, A., Fabbri, F., Zanni, G., Scavini, M., Fantini, G. V., Briganti, A., Naspro, R., Parazzini, F. Gori, E., Rigatti, P. & Montorsi, F. (2006). Chocolate and women's sexual health: An intriguing correlation. *Journal of Sexual Medicine, 3*(3), 476–482.

Schachter, S., & Singer, J. (1962). Cognitive, social, and physiological determinants of emotional state. *Psychological Review, 69*(5), 379–399.

Schachter, S. (1964). The interaction of cognitive and physiological determinants of emotional state. *Advances in Experimental Social Psychology, 1*, 49–80.

Schiefele, U. (1991). Interest, learning, and motivation. *Educational Psychologist, 26*(3–4), 299–323.

Schwartz, M. B., Schneider, G. E., Choi, Y. Y., Li, X., Harris, J., Andreyeva, T., ... & Appel, L. J. (2017). Association of a community campaign for better beverage choices with beverage purchases from supermarkets. *JAMA Internal Medicine, 177*(5), 666–674.

Secher, A., Jelsing, J., Baquero, A. F., Hecksher-Sørensen, J., Cowley, M. A., Dalbøge, L. S., ... & Knudson, L. B. (2014). The arcuate nucleus mediates GLP-1 receptor agonist liraglutide-dependent weight loss. *Journal of Clinical Investigation, 124*(10), 4473–4488.

Sellers, M. (2013). Toward a comprehensive theory of emotion for biological and artificial agents. *Biologically Inspired Cognitive Architectures, 4*, 3–26.

Silventoinen, K., Rokholm, B., Kaprio, J., & Sørensen, T. I. A. (2010). The genetic and environmental influences on childhood obesity: A systematic review of twin and adoption studies. *International Journal of Obesity, 34*(1), 29–40.

Simpson, K. A., Martin, N. M., & Bloom, S. R. (2008). Hypothalamic regulation of appetite. *Expert Review of Endocrinology & Metabolism, 3*(5), 577–592.

Snoep, L. (2008). Religiousness and happiness in three nations: A research note. *Journal of Happiness Studies, 9*(2), 207–211.

Soenens, B., Luyckx, K., Vansteenkiste, M., Luyten, P., Duriez, B., & Goossens, L. (2008). Maladaptive perfectionism as an intervening variable between psychological control and adolescent depressive symptoms: A three-wave longitudinal study. *Journal of Family Psychology, 22*(3), 465–474.

Soenens, B., Vansteenkiste, M., Vandereycken, W., Luyten, P., Sierens, E., & Goossens, L. (2008). Perceived parental psychological control and eating-disordered symptoms: Maladaptive perfectionism as a possible intervening variable. *Journal of Nervous and Mental Disease, 196*(2), 144–152.

Soper, B., Milford, G. E., & Rosenthal, G. T. (1995). Belief when evidence does not support theory. *Psychology & Marketing, 12*(5), 415–422.

Soussignan, R. (2002). Duchenne smile, emotional experience, and autonomic reactivity: A test of the facial feedback hypothesis. *Emotion, 2*(1), 52–74.

Stanley, B. G., & Leibowitz, S. F. (1985). Neuropeptide Y injected in the paraventricular hypothalamus: A powerful stimulant of feeding behavior. *Proceedings of the National Academy of Sciences, 82*(11), 3940–3943.

Sternson, S. M., Betley, J. N., & Cao, Z. F. H. (2013). Neural circuits and motivational processes for hunger. *Current Opinion in Neurobiology, 23*(3), 353–360.

Sternson, S. M., & Atasoy, D. (2014). Agouti-related protein neuron circuits that regulate appetite. *Neuroendocrinology, 100*(2–3), 95–102.

Strack, F., Martin, L. L., & Stepper, S. (1988). Inhibiting and facilitating conditions of the human smile: a non-obtrusive test of the facial feedback hypothesis. *Journal of Personality and Social Psychology, 54*(5), 768–777.

Stockdale, S. L., & Williams, R. L. (2004). Cooperative learning groups at the college level: Differential effects on high, average, and low exam performers. *Journal of Behavioral Education, 13*(1), 37–50.

Stone, A. A., & Neale, J. M. (1984). Effects of severe daily events on mood. *Journal of Personality and Social Psychology, 46*(1), 137–144.

Talma, H., Chinapaw, M. J. M., Bakker, B., HiraSing, R. A., Terwee, C. B., & Altenburg, T. M. (2013). Bioelectrical impedance analysis to estimate body composition in children and adolescents: A systematic review and evidence appraisal of validity, responsiveness, reliability and measurement error. *Obesity Reviews, 14*(11), 895–905.

Talwar, V., & Lee, K. (2011). A punitive environment fosters children's dishonesty: A natural experiment. *Child Development, 82*(6), 1751–1758.

Tartaglia, L. A., Dembski, M., Weng, X., Deng, N., Culpepper, J., Devos, R., … & Muir, C. (1995). Identification and expression cloning of a leptin receptor, OB-R. *Cell, 83*(7), 1263–1271.

Teixeira, P. J., Silva, M. N., Coutinho, S. R., Palmeira, A. L., Mata, J., Vieira, P. N., … & Sardinha, L. B. (2010). Mediators of weight loss and weight loss maintenance in middle-aged women. *Obesity, 18*(4), 725–735.

Teixeira, P. J., Carraça, E. V., Markland, D., Silva, M. N., & Ryan, R. M. (2012). Exercise, physical activity, and self-determination theory: A systematic review. *International Journal of Behavioral Nutrition and Physical Activity, 9*(1), 78.

The State of Obesity (2016). *Adult Obesity in the United States*. Retrieved from http://stateofobesity.org/adult-obesity/

Thomas, J. G., Bond, D. S., Phelan, S., Hill, J. O., & Wing, R. R. (2014). Weight-loss maintenance for 10 years in the National Weight Control Registry. *American Journal of Preventive Medicine, 46*(1), 17–23.

Toombs, R. J., Ducher, G., Shepherd, J. A., & Souza, M. J. (2012). The impact of recent technological advances on the trueness and precision of DXA to assess body composition. *Obesity, 20*(1), 30–39.

Uchida, Y., Norasakkunkit, V., & Kitayama, S. (2013). Cultural constructions of happiness: Theory and empirical evidence. In *The Exploration of Happiness* (pp. 269–280). Springer Netherlands.

Ulijaszek, S. J. (2002). Human eating behaviour in an evolutionary ecological context. *Proceedings of the Nutrition Society, 61*(04), 517–526.

Van den Broeck, A., Vansteenkiste, M., Lens, W., & De Witte, H. (2010). Unemployed individuals' work values and job flexibility: An explanation from expectancy-value theory and self-determination theory. *Applied Psychology, 59*(2), 296–317.

Vander Elst, T., Van den Broeck, A., De Witte, H., & De Cuyper, N. (2012). The mediating role of frustration of psychological needs in the relationship between job insecurity and work-related well-being. *Work & Stress, 26*(3), 252–271.

Vansteenkiste, M., & Ryan, R. M. (2013). On psychological growth and vulnerability: Basic psychological need satisfaction and need frustration as a unifying principle. *Journal of Psychotherapy Integration, 23*(3), 263.

Vartanian, L. R., Spanos, S., Herman, C. P., & Polivy, J. (2015). Modeling of food intake: A meta-analytic review. *Social Influence, 10*(3), 119–136.

Vlachopoulos, S. P., Katartzi, E. S., & Kontou, M. G. (2011). The basic psychological needs in physical education scale. *Journal of Teaching in Physical Education, 30*(3), 263–280.

Wagenmakers, E. J., Beek, T., Dijkhoff, L., Gronau, Q. F., Acosta, A., Adams Jr, R. B., … & Bulnes, L. C. (2016). Registered Replication Report: Strack, Martin, & Stepper (1988). *Perspectives on Psychological Science, 11*(6), 917-928.

Weinstein, N., DeHaan, C. R., & Ryan, R. M. (2010). Attributing autonomous versus introjected motivation to helpers and the recipient experience: Effects on gratitude, attitudes, and well-being. *Motivation and Emotion, 34*(4), 418–431.

Wickham, R. J., Solecki, W., Rathbun, L. R., Neugebauer, N. M., Wightman, R. M., & Addy, N. A. (2013). Advances in studying phasic dopamine signaling in brain reward mechanisms. *Frontiers in Bioscience* (Elite edition), 982.

Williams, M. A., & Mattingley, J. B. (2006). Do angry men get noticed? *Current Biology, 16*(11), R402–R404.

Wise, R. A. (1978). Catecholamine theories of reward: A critical review. *Brain Research, 152*(2), 215–247.

Wise, R. A., & Rompré, P. P. (1989). Brain dopamine and reward. *Annual Review of Psychology, 40*(1), 191–225.

Yach, D., Stuckler, D., & Brownell, K. D. (2006). Epidemiologic and economic consequences of the global epidemics of obesity and diabetes. *Nature Medicine, 12*(1), 62–66.

Yanovski, S. Z., & Yanovski, J. A. (2014). Long-term drug treatment for obesity: A systematic and clinical review. *JAMA, 311*(1), 74–86.

Yawson, D. O., Armah, F. A., & Pappoe, A. N. (2009). Enabling sustainability: Hierarchical need-based framework for promoting sustainable data infrastructure in developing countries. *Sustainability, 1*(4), 946–959.

Yerkes, R. M., & Dodson, J. D. (1908). The relation of strength of stimulus to rapidity of habit-formation. *Journal of Comparative Neurology and Psychology, 18*(5), 459–482.

Zajonc, R. B. (1968). Attitudinal effects of mere exposure. *Journal of Personality and Social Psychology, 9*(2p2), 1–27.

Zentall, S. R., & Morris, B. J. (2010). "Good job, you're so smart": The effects of inconsistency of praise type on young children's motivation. *Journal of Experimental Child Psychology, 107*(2), 155–163.

Zentall, S. R., & Morris, B. J. (2012). A critical eye: Praise directed toward traits increases children's eye fixations on errors and decreases motivation. *Psychonomic Bulletin & Review, 19*(6), 1073–1077.

Zhang, Y. X., Wang, Z. X., Zhao, J. S., & Chu, Z. H. (2016). Trends in overweight and obesity among rural children and adolescents from 1985 to 2014 in Shandong, China. *European Journal of Preventive Cardiology, (23)*12:1314–1320.

Zuckerman, M., Porac, J., Lathin, D., Smith, R., & Deci, E. L. (1978). On the importance of self-determination for intrinsically motivated behaviour. *Personality and Social Psychology Bulletin, 4*, 443–446.

Zwintscher, N. P., Azarow, K. S., Horton, J. D., Newton, C. R., & Martin, M. J. (2013). The increasing incidence of adolescent bariatric surgery. *Journal of Pediatric Surgery, 48*(12), 2401–2407.

Chapter 11

Aboud, F. E., & Spears Brown, C. (2013). Positive and negative intergroup contact among children and its effect on attitudes. In G. Hodson & M. Hewstone (Eds.), *Advances in Intergroup Contact*, (176–199). New York, NY: Psychology Press.

Alanko, K., Santtila, P., Harlaar, N., Witting, K., Varjonen, M., Jern, P., … & Sandnabba, N. K. (2010). Common genetic effects of gender atypical behavior in childhood and sexual orientation in adulthood: A study of Finnish twins. *Archives of Sexual Behavior, 39*(1), 81–92.

Alexander, G. M., & Hines, M. (2002). Sex differences in response to children's toys in nonhuman primates (Cercopithecus aethiops sabaeus). *Evolution and Human Behavior, 23*(6), 467–479.

Allen, L. S., & Gorski, R. A. (1992). Sexual orientation and the size of the anterior commissure in the human brain. *Proceedings of the National Academy of Sciences of the United States of America, 89*(15), 7199–7202.

American Bar Association. (2012). *Enrollment and degrees awarded 1963–2012 academic years*. Chicago, IL: Section of Legal Education and Admissions to the Bar.

American Psychological Association. (2009). *Report of the American Psychological Association's Task Force on Appropriate Therapeutic Responses to Sexual Orientation*. Washington, DC: American Psychological Association. Retrieved from http://www.apa.org/pi/lgbt/resources/therapeutic-response.pdf

American Psychiatric Association. (2011). *Sexual orientation*. Washington, DC: American Psychiatric Association. Retrieved from http://web.archive.org/web/20110722080052/http:/www.healthyminds.org/More-Info-For/GayLesbianBisexuals.aspx

American Psychiatric Association. (2013). *Diagnostic and statistical manual of mental disorders, (DSM-5®)*. American Psychiatric Publisher.

Archer, J. (2004). Sex differences in aggression in real-world settings: A meta-analytic review. *Review of General Psychology, 8*(4), 291–322.

Aries, E. (1987). Gender and communication. In P. Shaver & C. Hendrick (Eds.), *Sex and gender: Review of personality and social psychology*, Vol. 7., 149–176. Thousand Oaks, CA, US: Sage Publications, Inc.

Aubrey, J. S., & Gerding, A. (2015). The cognitive tax of self-objectification. *Journal of Media Psychology, (27)*, 22–32.

Bailey, J. M., & Bell, A. P. (1993). Familiality of female and male homosexuality. *Behavior Genetics, 23*(4), 313–322.

Bailey, J. M., Bobrow, D., Wolfe, M., & Mikach, S. (1995). Sexual orientation of adult sons of gay fathers. *Developmental Psychology, 31*(1), 124–129.

Bailey, J. M., Dunne, M. P., & Martin, N. G. (2000). Genetic and environmental influences on sexual orientation and its correlates in an Australian twin sample. *Journal of Personality and Social Psychology, 78*(3), 524–536.

Bailey, J. M., & Zucker, K. J. (1995). Childhood sex-typed behavior and sexual orientation: A conceptual analysis and quantitative review. *Developmental Psychology, 31*(1), 43–55.

Baumeister, R. F. (2000). Gender differences in erotic plasticity: The female sex drive as socially flexible and responsive. *Psychological Bulletin, 126*, 347–374.

Baumeister, R. F. (2013). Gender differences in motivation shape social interaction patterns, sexual relationships, social inequality, and cultural history. In M. K. Ryan & N. R. Branscombe (Eds.), *The SAGE handbook of gender and Psychology*, (270–285). London, UK: Sage Publications Ltd.

Baumeister, R. F., Catanese, K. R., & Vohs, K. D. (2001). Is there a gender difference in strength of sex drive? Theoretical views, conceptual distinctions, and a review of relevant evidence. *Personality and Social Psychology Review, 5*(3), 242–273.

Becker, J. C., & Swim, J. K. (2012). Reducing endorsement of benevolent and modern sexist beliefs: Differential effects of addressing harm versus pervasiveness of benevolent sexism. *Social Psychology, 43*(3), 127–137.

Beede, D. N., Julian, T. A., Langdon, D., McKittrick, G., Khan, B., & Doms, M. E. (2011). Women in STEM: A gender gap to innovation. *Economics and Statistics Administration Issue Brief, 4*(11).

Bem, S. L. (1975). Sex role adaptability: One consequence of psychological androgyny. *Journal of Personality and Social Psychology, 31*(4), 634–643.

Bem, S. L. (1981). Gender schema theory: A cognitive account of sex typing. *Psychological Review, 88*(4), 354–364.

Bem, S. L. (1993). *The lenses of gender: Transforming the debate on sexual inequality*. New Haven, CT: Yale University Press.

Berenbaum, S. A., & Resnick, S. M. (1997). Early androgen effects on aggression in children and adults with congenital adrenal hyperplasia. *Psychoneuroendocrinology, 22*(7), 505–515.

Berkowitz, L. (1993). *Aggression: Its causes, consequences, and control*. New York, NY: Mcgraw-Hill Book Company.

Bettencourt, B., & Kernahan, C. (1997). A meta-analysis of aggression in the presence of violent cues: Effects of gender differences and aversive provocation. *Aggressive Behavior, 23*(6), 447–456.

Biblarz, T. J., & Savci, E. (2010). Lesbian, gay, bisexual, and transgender families. *Journal of Marriage and Family, 72*(3), 480–497.

Biddulph, S. (2013). *Raising boys: Why boys are different—and how to help them become happy and well-balanced men.* New York, NY: Celestial Arts.

Binns, C. (2006). *What makes a lefty: Myths and mysteries persist.* Live Science. Retrieved from http://www.livescience.com/655-lefty-myths-mysteries-persist.html

Björkqvist, K., Österman, K., & Kaukiainen, A. (1992). The development of direct and indirect aggressive strategies in males and females. In K. Björkqvist & P. Niemelä (Eds.), *Of mice and women: Aspects of female aggression* (pp. 51–64).

Blanchard, R. (1997). Birth order and sibling sex ration in homosexual versus heterosexual males and females. *Annual Review of Sex Research, 8,* 27–67.

Blanchard, R. (2001). Fraternal birth order and the maternal immune hypothesis of male homosexuality. *Hormones and Behavior, 40*(2), 105–114.

Blanchard, R., Zucker, K. J., Siegelman, M., Dickey, R., & Klassen, P. (1998). The relation of birth order to sexual orientation in men and women. *Journal of Biosocial Science, 30,* 511–519.

Bogaert, A. F., & Skorska, M. (2011). Sexual orientation, fraternal birth order, and the maternal immune hypothesis: A review. *Frontiers in Neuroendocrinology, 32*(2), 247–254.

Bramen, J. E., Hranilovich, J. A., Dahl, R. E., Chen, J., Rosso, C., Forbes, E. E., ... & Sowell, E. R. (2012). Sex matters during adolescence: Testosterone-related cortical thickness maturation differs between boys and girls. *PloS one, 7*(3), 1–9.

Brennan, P. (2012) Sexual Selection. *Nature Education Knowledge, 3*(10): 79–84.

Brody, J. E. (1981, March 7). Male hormone ties to aggressive acts. *New York Times.* Retrieved from http://www.nytimes.com

Brody, L., & Brody, L. (2009). *Gender, emotion, and the family.* Cambridge, MA: Harvard University Press.

Brown, L. M., & Gilligan, C. (1993). Meeting at the crossroads: Women's psychology and girls' development. *Feminism & Psychology, 3*(1), 11–35.

Burri, A., & Spector, T. (2011). Recent and lifelong sexual dysfunction in a female UK population sample: Prevalence and risk factors. *Journal of Sexual Medicine, 8*(9), 2420–2430.

Burton, L.A., Rabin, L., Vardy, S.B., Frohlich, J., Wyatt, G., Dimitri, D., ... & Guterman, E. (2004). Gender differences in implicit and explicit memory for affective passages. *Brain and Cognition 54*(3): 218–224.

Buss, D. M., & Duntley, J. D. (2006). The evolution of aggression. In M. Schaller, J. A. Simpson, & D. T. Kenrick (Eds.), *Evolution and social psychology* (263–286). New York, NY: Psychology Press.

Bussey, K., & Bandura, A. (1999). Social cognitive theory of gender development and differentiation. *Psychological Review, 106*(4), 676–713.

Caldera, Y. M., Huston, A. C., & O'Brien, M. (1989). Social interactions and play patterns of parents and toddlers with feminine, masculine, and neutral toys. *Child Development,* 70–76.

Calzo, J. P., Antonucci, T. C., Mays, V. M., & Cochran, S. D. (2011). Retrospective recall of sexual orientation identity development among gay, lesbian, and bisexual adults. *Developmental Psychology, 47*(6), 1658–1673.

Camperio-Ciani, A., Corna, F., & Capiluppi, C. (2004). Evidence for maternally inherited factors favouring male homosexuality and promoting female fecundity. *Proceedings of the Royal Society: Biological Sciences, 271*(1554), 2217–2221.

Card, N. A., Stucky, B. D., Sawalani, G. M., & Little, T. D. (2008). Direct and indirect aggression during childhood and adolescence: A meta-analytic review of gender differences, intercorrelations, and relations to maladjustment. *Child Development, 79*(5), 1185–1229.

Carroll, J. (2007, July 20). Do Americans want to be surprised by the sex of their baby? Retrieved from http://www.gallup.com/poll/28180/americans-want-surprised-sex-their-baby.aspx

Carvalho, J., Gomes, A. Q., Laja, P., Oliveira, C., Vilarinho, S., Janssen, E., & Nobre, P. (2013). Gender differences in sexual arousal and affective responses to erotica: The effects of type of film and fantasy instructions. *Archives of Sexual Behavior, 42*(6), 1011–1019.

Centers for Disease Control and Prevention. (2015a). *STDs in adolescents and young adults.* [Data file]. Retrieved from https://www.cdc.gov/std/stats14/adol.htm

Centers for Disease Control and Prevention. (2015b). *STDs and HIV—CDC fact sheet.* [Data file]. Retrieved from http://www.cdc.gov/std/hiv/stdfact-std-hiv-detailed.htm

Centers for Disease Control and Prevention. (2016). *Oral sex and HIV Risk.* [Data file]. Retrieved from https://www.cdc.gov/hiv/risk/oralsex.html

Chandra, A., Copen, C. E., & Mosher, W. D. (2013). Sexual behavior, sexual attraction, and sexual identity in the United States: Data from the 2006–2010 national survey of family growth. In A. K. Baumle (Ed.) *International handbook on the demography of sexuality* (pp. 45–66). Netherlands: Springer.

Chaplin, T. M. (2015). Gender and emotion expression: A developmental contextual perspective. *Emotion Review, 7*(1), 14–21.

Cheryan, S. (2012). Understanding the paradox in math-related fields: Why do some gender gaps remain while others do not? *Sex roles, 66*(3), 184–190.

Chivers, M. (2010). A brief update on the specificity of sexual arousal. *Sexual & Relationship Therapy, 25*(4), 407–414.

Christensen, B. S., Grønbæk, M., Osler, M., Pedersen, B. V., Graugaard, C., & Frisch, M. (2011). Sexual dysfunctions and difficulties in Denmark: Prevalence and associated sociodemographic factors. *Archives of Sexual Behavior, 40*(1), 121–132.

Cheng, M. Y., & Lin, Y. Y. (2012). The effect of gender differences in supervisors' emotional expression and leadership style on leadership effectiveness. *African Journal of Business Management, 6*(9), 3234–3245.

Chung, W. S., Lim, S. M., Yoo, J. H., & Yoon, H. (2013). Gender difference in brain activation to audio-visual sexual stimulation: Do women and men experience the same level of arousal in response to the same video clip? *International Journal of Impotence Research, 25*(4), 138–142.

Cloud, J. (2007). Yep, they're gay. *Time.* Retrieved from http://www.time.com/time/magazine/article/0,9171,1582336,00.html

Colapinto, J. (1997, December 11). The true story of John Joan. *Rolling Stone,* 54–97.

Colapinto, J. (2000). *As nature made him: The boy who was raised as a girl.* New York, NY: HarperCollins Publishers.

Colarelli, S. M., Spranger, J. L., & Hechanova, M. (2006). Women, power, and sex composition in small groups: An evolutionary perspective. *Journal of Organizational Behavior, 27*(2), 163–184.

COMPANY NEWS: Mattel says it erred: Teen talk Barbie turns silent on math. (1992, October 21). *New York Times.* Retrieved from http://www.nytimes.com/1992/10/21/business/company-news-mattel-says-it-erred-teen-talk-barbie-turns-silent-on-math.html

Confer, J. C., Easton, J. A., Fleischman, D. S., Goetz, C. D., Lewis, D. M., Perilloux, C., & Buss, D. M. (2010). Evolutionary psychology: Controversies, questions, prospects, and limitations. *American Psychologist, 65*(2), 110–126.

Copen, C. E., Chandra, A., & Febo-Vazquez, I. (2016). Sexual behavior, sexual attraction, and sexual orientation among adults aged 18–44 in the United States: Data from the 2011–2013 National Survey of Family Growth. *National Health Statistics Reports,* (88), 1–14.

Dabbs, J. M., Chang, E. L., Strong, R. A., & Milun, R. (1998). Spatial ability, navigation strategy, and geographic knowledge among men and women. *Evolution and Human Behavior, 19*(2), 89–98.

Darwin, C. (1871). *The descent of man, and selection in relation to sex* (Vol. 1). London, UK: Murray.

Davis, P. J. (1999). Gender differences in autobiographical memory for childhood emotional experiences. *Journal of Personality and Social Psychology, 76*(3), 498–510.

Dawood, K., Pillard, R. C., Horvath, C., Revelle, W., & Bailey, J. M. (2000). Familial aspects of male homosexuality. *Archives of Sexual Behavior, 29*(2), 155–163.

Dean, C. (2006, July 18). Dismissing 'sexist opinions' about women's place in science: A conversation with Ben A. Barres. *New York Times.* Retrieved from http://www.nytimes.com/2006/07/18/science/18conv.html

Diamond, L. M. (2007). A dynamical systems approach to the development and expression of female same-sex sexuality. *Perspectives on Psychological Science, 2*(2), 142–161.

Diamond, L. M. (2008). *Sexual fluidity.* Cambridge, MA: Harvard University Press.

Dixson, B. J., & Brooks, R. C. (2013). The role of facial hair in women's perceptions of men's attractiveness, health, masculinity and parenting abilities. *Evolution and Human Behavior, 34*(3), 236–241.

Downs, E., & Smith, S. L. (2010). Keeping abreast of hypersexuality: A video game character content analysis. *Sex Roles, 62*(11–12), 721–733.

Driscoll, E.V. (2008). Bisexual species: Unorthodox sex in the animal kingdom. *Scientific American. 19,* 68–73.

Dunn, K. M., Jordan, K., Croft, P. R., & Assendelft, W. J. J. (2002). Systematic review of sexual problems: Epidemiology and methodology. *Journal of Sex & Marital Therapy, 28*(5), 399–422.

Eagly, A. H. (1987). *Sex differences in social behavior: A social-role interpretation.* Hillsdale, NJ: Lawrence Erlbaum Associates.

Eagly, A. H., & Steffen, V. J. (1986). Gender and aggressive behavior: a meta-analytic review of the social psychological literature. *Psychological Bulletin, 100*(3), 309–330.

Eagly, A. H. (2013). *Sex differences in social behavior: A social-role interpretation.* Hillsdale: NJ: Lawrence Erlbaum Associates.

Eagly, A. H., & Johnson, B. T. (1990). Gender and leadership style: A meta-analysis. *Psychological Bulletin, 108*(2), 233–256.

Eichenberg, R. C. (2016). Gender difference in American public opinion on the use of military force, 1982–2013. *International Studies Quarterly, 60*(1), 138–148.

Ellis, L., & Blanchard, R. (2001). Birth order, sibling sex ratio, and maternal miscarriages in homosexual and heterosexual men and women. *Personality and Individual Differences, 30*(4), 543–552.

Even the Score. (2015). *Women's sexual health equity.* Retrieved from http://eventhescore.org/get-the-facts/

Farr, R. H., Diamond, L. M., & Boker, S. M. (2014). Female same-sex sexuality from a dynamical systems perspective: Sexual desire, motivation, and behavior. *Archives of Sexual Behavior, 43*(8), 1477–1490.

Federal Bureau of Investigation (2014). *Hate crime statistics.* Retrieved from http://www.fbi.gov/news/stories/2014/december/latest-hate-crime-statistics-report-released/latest-hate-crime-statistics-report-released

Feldman, H. A., Goldstein, I., Hatzichristou, D. G., Krane, R. J., & McKinlay, J. B. (1994). Impotence and its medical and psychosocial correlates: Results of the Massachusetts Male Aging Study. *Journal of Urology, 151*(1), 54–61.

Fox, J., Bailenson, J. N., & Tricase, L. (2013). The embodiment of sexualized virtual selves: The Proteus effect and experiences of self-objectification via avatars. *Computers in Human Behavior, 29*(3), 930–938.

Frances, A. J. (2013, February 15). *The power of sexual selection: How psychology influences evolution and vice versa.* Retrieved from https://www.psychologytoday.com/blog/dsm5-in-distress/201302/the-power-sexual-selection

Fredrickson, B. L., & Roberts, T. A. (1997). Objectification theory. *Psychology of Women Quarterly, 21*(2), 173–206.

Fredriksen-Goldsen, K. I., Kim, H. J., Barkan, S. E., Muraco, A., & Hoy-Ellis, C. P. (2013). Health disparities among lesbian, gay, and bisexual older adults: Results from a population-based study. *American Journal of Public Health, 103*(10), 1802–1809.

Freud, S. (1920). The psychogenesis of a case of female homosexuality. *International Journal of Psycho-Analysis, 1*(2), 129–130.

Freud, S. (1922). Some Neurotic Mechanisms in Jealousy, Paranoia and Homosexuality. In: J. Strachey (Ed. & Trans.) The Standard Edition of the Complete Psychological Works of Sigmund Freud (Vol. 18). London: Hogarth Press, pp 221–224.

Frisen, L., Nordenstrom, A., Falhammar, H., Filipsson, H., Holmdahl, G., Janson, P. O., … & Nordenskjold, A. (2009). Gender role behavior, sexuality, and psychosocial adaptation in women with congenital adrenal hyperplasia due to CYP21A2 deficiency. *Journal of Clinical Endocrinology & Metabolism, 94*(9), 3432–3439.

Galinsky, E., Aumann, K., & Bond, J. T. (2009). *Times are changing: Gender and generation at work and at home.* Families and Work Institute.

Garde, K., & Lunde, I. (1980). Female sexual behaviour. A study in a random sample of 40-year-old women. *Maturitas, 2*(3), 225–240.

Garnets, L., & Kimmel, D. C. (Eds.). (2013). *Psychological perspectives on lesbian, gay, and bisexual experiences.* New York, NY: Columbia University Press.

Gartrell, N., & Bos, H. (2010). U.S. national longitudinal lesbian family study: Psychological adjustment of 17-year-old adolescents. *Pediatrics, 126*(1), 28–36.

Gartrell, N. K., Bos, H. M., & Goldberg, N. G. (2011). Adolescents of the U.S. national longitudinal lesbian family study: Sexual orientation, sexual behavior, and sexual risk exposure. *Archives of Sexual Behavior, 40*(6), 1199–1209.

Gartrell, N., Deck, A., Rodas, C., Peyser, H., & Banks, A. (2005). The national lesbian family study: 4 interviews with 10-year-old children. *American Journal of Orthopsychiatry, 75* (4), 518–524.

Gartzia, L., & van Engen, M. (2012). Are (male) leaders "feminine" enough? Gendered traits of identity as mediators of sex differences in leadership styles. *Gender in Management: An International Journal, 27*(5), 296–314.

Gat, A. (2010). Why war? Motivations for fighting in the human state of nature. In P. M. Kappeler & J. Silk (Eds.) *Mind the gap* (pp. 197–220). Berlin, Germany: Springer Berlin Heidelberg.

Gilligan, C. (1982). *In a different voice: Psychological theory and women's development.* Cambridge, MA: Harvard University Press.

Gilligan, C., Lyons, N. P., & Hammer, T. J. (1990). (Eds). *Making connections: The relational worlds of adolescent girls at Emma Willard School.* Cambridge, MA: Harvard University Press.

Giuliano, F., Jackson, G., Montorsi, F., Martin-Morales, A., & Raillard, P. (2010). Safety of sildenafil citrate: Review of 67 double-blind placebo-controlled trials and the postmarketing safety database. *International Journal of Clinical Practice, 64*(2), 240–255.

Glater, J. D. (2001, March 26). Women are close to being majority of law students. *New York Times.* Retrieved from http://www.nytimes.com/2001/03/26/business/women-are-close-to-being-majority-of-law-students.html?pagewanted=all

Glick, P., & Fiske, S. T. (2001). An ambivalent alliance: Hostile and benevolent sexism as complementary justifications for gender inequality. *American Psychologist, 56*(2), 109–118.

Glicksman, E. (2013). Transgender today. *Monitor on Psychology, 44*(4), 36–38.

Goble, P., Martin, C. L., Hanish, L. D., & Fabes, R. A. (2012). Children's gender-typed activity choices across preschool social contexts. *Sex Roles, 67*(7–8), 435–451.

Golombok, S., & Tasker, F. (1996). Do parents influence the sexual orientation of their children? Findings from a longitudinal study of lesbian families. *Developmental Psychology, 32*(1), 3–11.

Gonsiorek, J.C. (1991). The empirical basis for the demise of the illness model of homosexuality. In J. C. Gon-siorek & J. D. Weinrich (Eds.), *Homosexuality: Research implications for public policy.* (115–136). Thousand Oaks, CA: Sage Publications.

Goodin, S. M., Van Denburg, A., Murnen, S. K., & Smolak, L. (2011). "Putting on" sexiness: A content analysis of the presence of sexualizing characteristics in girls' clothing. *Sex Roles, 65*(1–2), 1–12.

Graff, K. A., Murnen, S. K., & Krause, A. K. (2013). Low-cut shirts and high-heeled shoes: Increased sexualization across time in magazine depictions of girls. *Sex Roles, 69*(11–12), 571–582.

Gunderson, E. A., Ramirez, G., Levine, S. C., & Beilock, S. L. (2012). The role of parents and teachers in the development of gender-related math attitudes. *Sex Roles, 66*(3–4), 153–166.

Gur, R. C., Turetsky, B. I., Matsui, M., Yan, M., Bilker, W., Hughett, P., & Gur, R. E. (1999). Sex differences in brain gray and white matter in healthy young adults: Correlations with cognitive performance. *Journal of Neuroscience, 19*(10), 4065–4072.

Hagstad, A., & Janson, P. O. (1984). Sexuality among Swedish women around forty: An epidemiological survey. *Journal of Psychosomatic Obstetrics & Gynecology, 3*(3–4), 191–203.

Hains, R. (2015, August 13). *Target will stop labeling toys for boys or for girls. Good.* Retrieved from https://www.washingtonpost.com/posteverything/wp/2015/08/13/target-will-stop-selling-toys-for-boys-or-for-girls-good/

Hald, G. M. (2006). Gender differences in pornography consumption among young heterosexual Danish adults. *Archives of Sexual Behavior, 35*(5), 577–585.

Hall, J. A. (1984). *Nonverbal sex differences: Communication accuracy and expressive style.* Baltimore, MD: Johns Hopkins University Press.

Hall, J. A. (1987). On explaining gender differences: The case of nonverbal communication. In P. Shaver & C. Hendrick (Eds.), *Sex and gender: Review of personality and social psychology,* Vol. 7, (177–200). Thousand Oaks, CA: Sage Publications.

Hamann, S., Herman, R. A., Nolan, C. L., & Wallen, K. (2004). Men and women differ in amygdala response to visual sexual stimuli. *Nature Neuroscience, 7*(4), 411–416.

Hamer, D. H., Hu, S., Magnuson, V. L., Hu, N., & Pattatucci, A. M. (1993). A linkage between DNA markers on the X chromosome and male sexual orientation. *Science, 261*(5119), 321–327.

Harris, J. M., Cherkas, L. F., Kato, B. S., Heiman, J. R., & Spector, T. D. (2008). Normal variations in personality are associated with coital orgasmic infrequency in heterosexual women: A population-based study. *Journal of Sexual Medicine, 5*(5), 1177–1183.

Hartley, R. E., Frank, L. K., Goldenson, R., & Hartley, R. E. (2013). *Understanding children's play.* Abingdon, Oxon: Routledge.

Harvey, S. M. (1987). Female sexual behavior: Fluctuations during the menstrual cycle. *Journal of Psychosomatic Research, 31,* 100–110.

Hatton, E., & Trautner, M. N. (2011). Equal opportunity objectification? The sexualization of men and women on the cover of *Rolling Stone. Sexuality & Culture, 15*(3), 256–278.

Heiman, J. R. (1977). A psychophysiological exploration of sexual arousal patterns in females and males. *Psychophysiology, 14*(3), 266–274.

Hepp, U., Kraemer, B., Schnyder, U., Miller, N., & Delsignore, A. (2005). Psychiatric comorbidity in gender identity disorder. *Journal of Psychosomatic Research, 58,* 259–261.

Herbenick, D., Reece, M., Schick, V., Sanders, S. A., Dodge, B., & Fortenberry, J. D. (2010). Sexual behavior in the United States: Results from a national probability sample of men and women ages 14–94. *Journal of Sexual Medicine, 7*(s5), 255–265.

Herlitz, A., Nilsson, L. G., & Bäckman, L. (1997). Gender differences in episodic memory. *Memory & Cognition, 25*(6), 801–811.

Hines, M. (2006). Prenatal testosterone and gender-related behaviour. *European Journal of Endocrinology, 155*(suppl 1), S115–S121.

Hines, M., Ahmed, S. F., & Hughes, I. A. (2003). Psychological outcomes and gender-related development in complete androgen insensitivity syndrome. *Archives of Sexual Behavior, 32*(2), 93–101.

Hines, M., Brook, C., & Conway, G. S. (2004). Androgen and psychosexual development: Core gender identity, sexual orientation, and recalled childhood gender role behavior in women and men with congenital adrenal hyperplasia (CAH). *Journal of Sex Research, 41*(1), 75–81.

Hines, M., Constantinescu, M., & Spencer, D. (2015). Early androgen exposure and human gender development. *Biology of Sex Differences, 6* (1), 1–5.

Hogenboom, M. (2015). *Are there any homosexual animals?* BBC. Retrieved from http://www.bbc.com/earth/story/20150206-are-there-any-homosexual-animals

Hooker, E. (1957). The adjustment of the male overt homosexual. *Journal of Projective Techniques, 21*(1), 18–31.

Hönekopp, J., & Watson, S. (2011). Meta-analysis of the relationship between digit-ratio 2D: 4D and aggression. *Personality and Individual Differences, 51*(4), 381–386.

Hu, S., Pattatucci, A. M. L., Patterson, C., Li, L., Fulker, D. W., Cherny, S. S., et al. (1995). Linkage between sexual orientation and chromosome Xq28 in males but not in females. *Nature Genetics, 11,* 248–256.

Hughes, G. (2007). Diversity, identity and belonging in e-learning communities: Some theories and paradoxes. *Teaching in Higher Education, 12*(5–6), 709–720.

Hughes, I. A. (2008). Disorders of sex development: A new definition and classification. *Best Practice & Research Clinical Endocrinology & Metabolism, 22*(1), 119–134.

Hyde, J. S., & Linn, M. C. (1988). Gender differences in verbal ability: A meta-analysis. *Psychological Bulletin, 104*(1), 53–69.

Hyde, J. S., Fennema, E., & Lamon, S. J. (1990). Gender differences in mathematics performance: A meta-analysis. *Psychological Bulletin, 107*(2), 139–155.

Hyde, J. S., Lindberg, S. M., Linn, M. C., Ellis, A. B., & Williams, C. C. (2008). Gender similarities characterize math performance. *Science, 321*(5888), 494–495.

Hyde, J. S. (2014). Gender similarities and differences. *Annual Review of Psychology, 65,* 373–398.

Imperato-McGinley, J., Peterson, R. E., Gautier, T., & Sturla, E. (1979). Androgens and the evolution of male-gender identity among male pseudohermaphrodites with 5α-reductase deficiency. *New England Journal of Medicine, 300*(22), 1233–1237.

Impett, E. A., Schooler, D., & Tolman, D. L. (2006). To be seen and not heard: Femininity ideology and adolescent girls' sexual health. *Archives of Sexual Behavior, 35*(2), 129–142.

Inter-Parliamentary Union (2015). *Proportion of seats held by women in national parliaments.* [Data file]. Retrieved from http://data.worldbank.org/indicator/SG.GEN.PARL.ZS

IsHak, W. W., & Tobia, G. (2013). DSM-5 changes in diagnostic criteria of sexual dysfunctions. *Reproductive System & Sexual Disorders, 2*(122). doi:10.4172/2161-038X.1000122

Italie, L. (2013, July 26). Birth day surprise: Couples now waiting until baby is born to learn its gender. Retrieved from http://www.columbian.com/news/2013/jul/26/birth-day-surprise-couples-now-waiting-until-baby/

James, S. E., Herman, J. L., Rankin, S., Keisling, M., Mottet, L., & Anafi, M. (2016). The report of the 2015 U.S. transgender survey. Washington, DC: National Center for Transgender Equality.

Johansson, A., Sundbom, E., Höjerback, T., & Bodlund, O. (2010). A five-year follow-up study of Swedish adults with gender identity disorder. *Archives of Sexual Behavior, 39*(6), 1429–1437.

Jones, B. A., & Griffiths, K. M. (2015). Self-objectification and depression: An integrative systematic review. *Journal of Affective Disorders, 171,* 22–32.

Jones, C. M., Braithwaite, V. A., & Healy, S. D. (2003). The evolution of sex differences in spatial ability. *Behavioral Neuroscience, 117*(3), 403–411.

Jongenelis, M. I., Byrne, S. M., & Pettigrew, S. (2014). Self-objectification, body image disturbance, and eating disorder symptoms in young Australian children. *Body Image, 11*(3), 290–302.

Jordan-Young, R. M. (2012). Hormones, context, and "brain gender": A review of evidence from congenital adrenal hyperplasia. *Social Science & Medicine, 74*(11), 1738–1744.

Kahneman, D., Diener, E., & Schwarz, N. (Eds.). (1999). *Well-being: Foundations of hedonic psychology.* New York, NY: Russell Sage Foundation.

Kark, R., Waismel-Manor, R., & Shamir, B. (2012). Does valuing androgyny and femininity lead to a female advantage? The relationship between gender-role, transformational leadership and identification. *The Leadership Quarterly, 23*(3), 620–640.

Kendler, K. S., Thornton, L. M., Gilman, S. E., & Kessler, R. C. (2000). Sexual orientation in a U.S. national sample of twin and nontwin sibling pairs. *American Journal of Psychiatry, 157*(11), 1843–1846.

Kushner, H. I. (2011). Cesare Lombroso and the pathology of left-handedness. *The Lancet, 377*(9760), 118–119.

Lamminmäki, A., Hines, M., Kuiri-Hänninen, T., Kilpeläinen, L., Dunkel, L., & Sankilampi, U. (2012). Testosterone measured in infancy predicts subsequent sex-typed behavior in boys and in girls. *Hormones and Behavior, 61*(4), 611–616.

Laumann, E. O., Paik, A., & Rosen, R. C. (1999). Sexual dysfunction in the United States: Prevalence and predictors. *Journal of the American Medical Association, 281*(6), 537–544.

Lawrence, A. A. (2010). Sexual orientation versus age of onset as bases for typologies (subtypes) for gender identity disorder in adolescents and adults. *Archives of Sexual Behavior, 39*, 514–545.

LeVay, S. (1991). A difference in hypothalamic structure between heterosexual and homosexual men. *Science, 253*(5023), 1034–1037.

Lindberg, S. M., Hyde, J. S., Petersen, J. L., & Linn, M. C. (2010). New trends in gender and mathematics performance: A meta-analysis. *Psychological Bulletin, 136*(6), 1123–1135.

Lindsey, L. L. (2015). *Gender roles: A sociological perspective.* New York, NY: Routledge.

Lowe, P. A., Mayfield, J. W., & Reynolds, C. R. (2003). Gender differences in memory test performance among children and adolescents. *Archives of Clinical Neuropsychology, 18*(8), 865–878.

Maccoby, E. E. (1998). *The two sexes: The implications of childhood divergence for adult relationships.* Cambridge, MA: Harvard University Press.

Major, B., Schmidlin, A. M., & Williams, L. (1990). Gender patterns in social touch: The impact of setting and age. *Journal of Personality and Social Psychology Bulletin, 10*, 634–643.

Maloney, E. A., Waechter, S., Risko, E. F., & Fugelsang, J. A. (2012). Reducing the sex difference in math anxiety: The role of spatial processing ability. *Learning and Individual Differences, 22*(3), 380–384.

Mark, K. P., & Murray, S. H. (2012). Gender differences in desire discrepancy as a predictor of sexual and relationship satisfaction in a college sample of heterosexual romantic relationships. *Journal of Sex & Marital Therapy, 38*(2), 198–215.

Martel, L. D., Hawk, S., & Hatfield, E. (2004). Sexual behavior and culture. *Encyclopedia of Applied Psychology, 3*, 385–392.

Martin, M. (2012, January 18). *Gender controversy stacks up against 'Lego Friends.'* Tell Me More @ National Public Radio Podcast. Retrieved from http://www.npr.org/2012/01/18/145397007/gender-controversy-stacks-up-against-lego-friends

Martin, C. L., Ruble, D. N., & Szkrybalo, J. (2002). Cognitive theories of early gender development. *Psychological Bulletin, 128*(6), 903–933.

Masters, W. H., & Johnson, V. E. (1966). *Human sexual response.* Boston, MA: Little, Brown & Co.

Meston, C. M., & Frohlich, P. F. (2000). The neurobiology of sexual function. *Archives of General Psychiatry, 57*(11), 1012–1030.

Meston, C. M., & Buss, D. M. (2007). Why humans have sex. *Archives of Sexual Behavior, 36*(4), 477–507.

Meuwissen, I., & Over, R. (1992). Sexual arousal across phases of the human menstrual cycle. *Archives of Sexual Behavior, 21*(2), 101–119.

Meyer, D. E., & Schvaneveldt, R. W. (1971). Facilitation in recognizing pairs of words: Evidence of a dependence between retrieval operations. *Journal of Experimental Psychology, 90*, 227–234.

Meyer III, W., Bockting, W. O., Cohen-Kettenis, P., Coleman, E., DiCeglie, D., Devor, H., … & Wheeler, C. (2001). The Harry Benjamin International Gender Dysphoria Association's standards of care for gender identity disorders, sixth version. *Journal of Psychology & Human Sexuality, 13*(1), 1–30.

Meyer-Bahlburg, H. F., Dolezal, C., Baker, S. W., & New, M. I. (2008). Sexual orientation in women with classical or non-classical congenital adrenal hyperplasia as a function of degree of prenatal androgen excess. *Archives of Sexual Behavior, 37*(1), 85–99.

Miller, D., Fernandez, C. A., & Lee, D. J. (2013). National Health Interview Survey. *Encyclopedia of Behavioral Medicine*, 1286–1288.

Mitchell, A. D., & Allen, L. (2011). Androgyny. *Encyclopedia of child behavior and development*, 94–95.

Money, J., & Mathews, D. (1982). Prenatal exposure to virilizing progestins: An adult follow-up study of twelve women. *Archives of Sexual Behavior, 11*(1), 73–83.

Money, J., & Norman, B. F. (1987). Gender identity and gender transposition: Longitudinal outcome study of 24 male hermaphrodites assigned as boys. *Journal of Sex & Marital Therapy, 13*(2), 75–92.

Myers, D. G. (2014). Most are straight, some are gay, and why it is that way: The science of sexual orientation. *Modern Believing, 55*(2), 127–139.

Nesbitt, M. N., & Penn, N. E. (2000). Gender stereotypes after thirty years: A replication of Rosenkrantz, et al. (1968). *Psychological Reports, 87*(2), 493–511.

Newport, F. (2015, May 21). *Americans greatly overestimate percent gay, lesbian in U.S.* Retrieved from http://www.gallup.com/poll/183383/americans-greatly-overestimate-percent-gay-lesbian.aspx

Pacilli, M. G., Tomasetto, C., & Cadinu, M. (2016). Exposure to sexualized advertisements disrupts children's math performance by reducing working memory. *Sex Roles, 74*(9–10), 389–398.

Pangelinan, M. M., Zhang, G., VanMeter, J. W., Clark, J. E., Hatfield, B. D., & Haufler, A. J. (2011). Beyond age and gender: Relationships between cortical and subcortical brain volume and cognitive-motor abilities in school-age children. *Neuroimage, 54*(4), 3093–3100.

Paul, B., & Linz, D. G. (2008). The effects of exposure to virtual child pornography on viewer cognitions and attitudes toward deviant sexual behavior. *Communication Research, 35*(1), 3–38.

Prins, J., Blanker, M. H., Bohnen, A. M., Thomas, S., & Bosch, J. L. (2002). Prevalence of erectile dysfunction: A systematic review of population-based studies. *International Journal of Impotence Research, 14*(6), 422–432.

Ramirez, M. C., Luque, G. M., Ornstein, A. M., & Becu-Villalobos, D. (2010). Differential neonatal testosterone imprinting of GH-dependent liver proteins and genes in female mice. *Journal of Endocrinology, 207*(3), 301–308.

Rath, S., & Mishra, A. (2013). Self-efficacy of androgynous and sex-typed employed and unemployed women. *Journal of Social Sciences, 2*(3), 139–145.

Reichman, J. (1998). *I'm not in the mood: What every woman should know about improving her libido.* New York, NY: Quill/William Morrow.

Reilly, D., Neumann, D. L., & Andrews, G. (2015). Sex differences in mathematics and science achievement: A meta-analysis of national assessment of educational progress assessments. *Journal of Educational Psychology, 107*(3), 645–662.

Reiner, W. G., & Gearhart, J. P. (2004). Discordant sexual identity in some genetic males with cloacal exstrophy assigned to female sex at birth. *New England Journal of Medicine, 350*(4), 333–341.

Roselli, C. E., Larkin, K., Resko, J. A., Stellflug, J. N., & Stormshak, F. (2004). The volume of a sexually dimorphic nucleus in the ovine medial preoptic area/anterior hypothalamus varies with sexual partner preference. *Endocrinology, 145*(2), 478–483.

Rosenkrantz, P., Vogel, S., Bee, H., Broverman, I., & Broverman, D. M. (1968). Sex-role stereotypes and self-concepts in college students. *Journal of Consulting and Clinical Psychology, 32*(3), 287–295.

Rubin, K. H., Bukowski, W. M., & Parker, J. G. (2007). Peer interactions, relationships, and groups. *Handbook of Child Psychology.* III:10.

Rudman, L. A., & Glick, P. (2012). *Social psychology of gender: How power and intimacy shape gender relations.* New York, NY: Guilford Press.

Rupp, H. A., & Wallen, K. (2008). Sex differences in response to visual sexual stimuli: A review. *Archives of Sexual Behavior, 37*(2), 206–218.

Saad, L. (2012, September 7). In U.S., half of women prefer a job outside the home. Retrieved from http://www.gallup.com/poll/157313/half-women-prefer-job-outside-home.aspx

Sadker, D. (1999). Gender equity: Still knocking at the classroom door. *Educational Leadership, 56*, 22–27.

Saewyc, E. M. (2011). Research on adolescent sexual orientation: Development, health disparities, stigma, and resilience. *Journal of Research on Adolescence, 21*(1), 256–272.

Sanders, A. R., Martin, E. R., Beecham, G. W., Guo, S., Dawood, K., Rieger, G., … & Bailey, J. M. (2015). Genome-wide scan demonstrates significant linkage for male sexual orientation. *Psychological Medicine, 45*(7), 1379–1388.

Sapadin, L. A. (1988). Friendship and gender: Perspectives of professional men and women. *Journal of Social and Personal Relationships, 5*(4), 387–403.

Savic, I., Berglund, H., & Lindström, P. (2005). Brain response to putative pheromones in homosexual men. *Proceedings of the National Academy of Sciences of the United States of America, 102*(20), 7356–7361.

Savin-Williams, R. C., Joyner, K., & Rieger, G. (2012). Prevalence and stability of self-reported sexual orientation identity during young adulthood. *Archives of Sexual Behavior, 41*(1), 103–110.

Schmitt, D. P., Jonason, P. K., Byerley, G. J., Flores, S. D., Illbeck, B. E., O'Leary, K. N., & Qudrat, A. (2012). A reexamination of sex differences in sexuality new studies reveal old truths. *Current Directions in Psychological Science, 21*(2), 135–139.

Schulze, S., & Naidu, N. (2014). Exploring gender differences in the connectedness of South African adolescents. *Journal of Social Sciences, 40*(2), 193–202.

Seavey, C. A., Katz, P. A., & Zalk, S. R. (1975). Baby X. *Sex Roles, 1*(2), 103–109.

Simons, J. S., & Carey, M. P. (2001). Prevalence of sexual dysfunctions: Results from a decade of research. *Archives of Sexual Behavior, 30*(2), 177–219.

Slater, A., & Tiggemann, M. (2015). Media exposure, extracurricular activities, and appearance-related comments as predictors of female adolescents' self-objectification. *Psychology of Women Quarterly, 39*(3), 375–389.

Slater, A., & Tiggemann, M. (2016). Little girls in a grown up world: Exposure to sexualized media, internalization of sexualization messages, and body image in 6- to 9-year-old girls. *Body Image, 18*, 19–22.

Smith, S. L., Choueiti, M., Prescott, A., & Pieper, K. (2012). Gender roles & occupations: A look at character attributes and job-related aspirations in film and television. *Geena David Institute on Gender in Media.*

Smolak, L., & Murnen, S. K. (2011). The sexualization of girls and women as a primary antecedent of self-objectification. In Calogero, Rachel M., Tantleff-Dunn, Stacey, & Thompson, J. Kevin (Eds.), *Self-objectification in women: Causes, consequences, and counteractions.* (pp. 53–75). Washington, DC: American Psychological Association.

Starr, C. R., & Ferguson, G. M. (2012). Sexy dolls, sexy grade-schoolers? Media & maternal influences on young girls' self-sexualization. *Sex Roles, 67*(7–8), 463–476.

Statistics Canada. (2003). *Rates of victims of police-reported violent crime by age group.* [Data file]. Retrieved from Canadian Centre for Justice Statistics.

Statistics Canada. (2008). *Rates of victims of police-reported violent crime by age group.* [Data file]. Retrieved from Canadian Centre for Justice Statistics.

Statistics Canada. (2015). *Rates of victims of police-reported violent crime by age group.* [Data file]. Retrieved from Canadian Centre for Justice Statistics.

Summers, C. J. (Ed.). (2004). *The queer encyclopedia of music, dance, & musical theater.* San Francisco, CA: Cleis Press.

Tamres, L. K., Janicki, D., & Helgeson, V. S. (2002). Sex differences in coping behavior: A meta-analytic review and an examination of relative coping. *Personality and Social Psychology Review, 6*(1), 2–30.

Tannen, D. (1990). *You just don't understand: Women and men in conversation.* London, UK: Virago.

Taylor, S. E. (2002). *The tending instinct: Women, men, and the biology of our relationships.* New York, NY: Times Books.

Tiggemann, M., & Slater, A. (2015). The role of self-objectification in the mental health of early adolescent girls: Predictors and consequences. *Journal of Pediatric Psychology, 40*(7), 704–711.

Tilson, E. C., Sanchez, V., Ford, C. L., Smurzynski, M., Leone, P. A., Fox, K. K., ... & Miller, W. C. (2004). Barriers to asymptomatic screening and other STD services for adolescents and young adults: Focus group discussions. *BMC Public Health, 4*(1).

Tolman, D. L., & McClelland, S. I. (2011). Normative sexuality development in adolescence: A decade in review, 2000–2009. *Journal of Research on Adolescence, 21*(1), 242–255.

Turner, W. J. (1995). Homosexuality, type 1: An Xq28 phenomenon. *Archives of Sexual Behavior, 24*(2), 109–134.

United States Department of Justice (2015). *Crime in the United States, 2014.* [Data file]. Retrieved from https://ucr.fbi.gov/crime-in-the-u.s/2014/crime-in-the-u.s.-2014/persons-arrested/main

United States Department of Labor: Bureau of Labor Statistics. (2015). *Household data annual average* [Data file]. Retrieved from http://www.bls.gov/cps/cpsaat11.pdf

VanderLaan, D. P., & Vasey, P. L. (2011). Male sexual orientation in Independent Samoa: Evidence for fraternal birth order and maternal fecundity effects. *Archives of Sexual Behavior, 40*(3), 495–503.

van Engen, M. L., & Willemsen, T. M. (2004). Sex and leadership styles: A meta-analysis of research published in the 1990s. *Psychological Reports, 94*(1), 3–18.

Van Hulle, C. A., Goldsmith, H. H., & Lemery, K. S. (2004). Genetic, environmental, and gender effects on individual differences in toddler expressive language. *Journal of Speech, Language, and Hearing Research, 47*(4), 904–912.

Voyer, D., Voyer, S., & Bryden, M. P. (1995). Magnitude of sex differences in spatial abilities: A meta-analysis and consideration of critical variables. *Psychological Bulletin, 117*(2), 250–270.

Voyer, D., Postma, A., Brake, B., & Imperato-McGinley, J. (2007). Gender differences in object location memory: A meta-analysis. *Psychonomic Bulletin & Review, 14*(1), 23–38.

Wallien, M. S. C., & Cohen-Kettenis, P. T. (2008). Psychosexual outcome of gender-dyphoric children. *Journal of the American Academy of Child & Adolescent Psychiatry, 47,* 1413–1423.

Walker, J. (2004, May 24). *The death of David Reimer.* Retrieved from http://reason.com/archives/2004/05/24/the-death-of-david-reimer

Wierckx, K., Van Caenegem, E., Elaut, E., Dedecker, D., Van de Peer, F., Toye, K., ... & T'Sjoen, G. (2011). Quality of life and sexual health after sex reassignment surgery in transsexual men. *Journal of Sexual Medicine, 8*(12), 3379–3388.

Williams, L. M., Mathersul, D., Palmer, D. M., Gur, R. C., Gur, R. E., & Gordon, E. (2009). Explicit identification and implicit recognition of facial emotions: I. Age effects in males and females across 10 decades. *Journal of Clinical and Experimental Neuropsychology 31*(3): 257–277.

Wood, W. (1987). Meta-analytic review of sex differences in group performance. *Psychological Bulletin, 102*, 53–71.

Wong, W. I., & Hines, M. (2015). Effects of gender color-coding on toddlers' gender-typical toy play. *Archives of Sexual Behavior, 44*(5), 1233–1242.

World Health Organization. (2006). *Defining sexual health: Report of a technical consultation on sexual health, 28–31 January 2002, Geneva.* World Health Organization.

Yang, J. H., Baskin, L. S., & DiSandro, M. (2010). Gender identity in disorders of sex development. *Urology, 75*(1), 153–159.

Zack, N. (2009). Transsexuality and Daseia Y. Cavers-Huff. In L.J. Shrage (Ed.). *You've changed,* (66–80). New York, NY: Oxford University Press.

Zaidi, Z. F. (2010). Gender differences in human brain: A review. *Open Anatomy Journal, 2*(1), 37–55.

Zell, E., Krizan, Z., & Teeter, S. R. (2015). Evaluating gender similarities and differences using metasynthesis. *American Psychologist, 70*(1), 10–20.

Zucker, K. J. (2010). The DSM diagnostic criteria for gender identity disorder in children. *Archives of Sexual Behavior, 39*(2), 477–498.

Zucker, K. J., Bradley, S. J., Owen-Anderson, A., Kibblewhite, S. J., Wood, H., Singh, D., & Choi, K. (2012). Demographics, behavior problems, and psychosexual characteristics of adolescents with gender identity disorder or transvestic fetishism. *Journal of Sex & Marital Therapy, 38*(2), 151–189.

Zurbriggen, E. L., Collins, R. L., Lamb, S., Roberts, T. A., Tolman, D. L., Ward, L. M., & Blake, J. (2007). Report of the APA task force on the sexualization of girls. American Psychological Association: Washington, DC. Retrieved from http://www. apa. org/pi/wpo/sexualizationrep.pdf

Chapter 12

Abu-Ras, W., & Abu-Bader, S. H. (2008). The impact of the September 11, 2001, attacks on the well-being of Arab Americans in New York City. *Journal of Muslim Mental Health, 3*(2), 217–239.

Adams, S. K., & Kisler, T. S. (2013). Sleep quality as a mediator between technology-related sleep quality, depression, and anxiety. *Cyberpsychology, Behavior, and Social Networking, 16*(1), 25–30.

Ader, R., & Cohen, N. (1993). Psychoneuroimmunology: Conditioning and stress. *Annual Review of Psychology, 44*(1), 53–85.

Aizer, A. A., Chen, M.-H., McCarthy, E. P., Mendu, M. L., Koo, S., Wilhite, T. J., ... & Martin, N. E. (2013). Marital status and survival in patients with cancer. *Journal of Clinical Oncology, 31*(31), 3869–3876.

Al-Barashdi, H. S., Bouazza, A., & Jabur, N. H. (2015). Smartphone addiction among university undergraduates: A literature review. *Journal of Scientific Research & Reports, 4*(3), 210–225.

Allan, R. (2014). John Hunter: Early association of type A behavior with cardiac mortality. *American Journal of Cardiology, 114*(1), 148–150.

American Psychological Association. (2013). Stress and exercise. Retrieved October 23, 2017, from http://www.apa.org/news/press/releases/stress/2013/exercise.aspx

Anderson, M. (2015). *The demographics of device ownership.* Pew Research Center. Retrieved from http://www.pewinternet.org/2015/10/29/the-demographics-of-device-ownership/

Anderson, M., & Perrin, A. (2017). *Tech adoption climbs among older adults.* Retrieved July 5, 2017, from http://www.pewinternet.org/2017/05/17/tech-adoption-climbs-among-older-adults/

Antoni, M. H. (2013). Psychosocial intervention effects on adaptation, disease course and biobehavioral processes in cancer. *Brain, Behavior, and Immunity, 30*, S88–S98.

Antoni, M. H., Cruess, D. G., Klimas, N., Maher, K., Cruess, S., Kumar, M., ... & Fletcher, M. A. (2002). Stress management and immune system reconstitution in symptomatic HIV-infected gay men over time: Effects on transitional naïve T cells (CD4+ CD45RA+ CD29+). *American Journal of Psychiatry, 159*, 143–145.

Archer, S., Buxton, S., & Sheffield, D. (2014). The effect of creative psychological interventions on psychological outcomes for adult cancer patients: A systematic review of randomised controlled trials. *Psycho-Oncology, 24*(1), 1–10.

Arns, M., Heinrich, H., & Strehl, U. (2013). Evaluation of neurofeedback in ADHD: The long and winding road. *Biological Psychology, 95*, 108–115.

Aschbrenner, K. A., Mueser, K. T., Bartels, S. J., & Pratt, S. I. (2013). Perceived social support for diet and exercise among persons with serious mental illness enrolled in a healthy lifestyle intervention. *Psychiatric Rehabilitation Journal, 36*(2), 65–71.

Bakker, D., Kazantzis, N., Rickwood, D., & Rickard, N. (2016). Mental health smartphone apps: Review and evidence-based recommendations for future developments. *JMIR Mental Health, 3*(1), 1–7. doi: 10.2196/mental.4984

Bartley, C. A., Hay, M., & Bloch, M. H. (2013). Meta-analysis: Aerobic exercise for the treatment of anxiety disorders. *Progress in Neuro-Psychopharmacology Biological Psychiatry, 45*, 34–39. doi: 10.1016/j.pnpbp.2013.04.016

Bender, J. L., Jimenez-Marroquin, M.-C., & Jadad, A. R. (2011). Seeking support on Facebook: A content analysis of breast cancer groups. *Journal of Medical Internet Research, 13*(1), e16. doi: 10.2196/jmir.1560

Berry, J. W. (1997). Immigration, acculturation, and adaptation. *Applied Psychology, 46*(1), 5–34.

Bishop, S. R., Lau, M., Shapiro, S., Carlson, L., Anderson, N. D., Carmody, J., ... & Velting, D. (2004). Mindfulness: A proposed operational definition. *Clinical Psychology: Science and Practice, 11*(3), 230–241.

Bloss, C. S., Wineinger, N. E., Peters, M., Boeldt, D. L., Ariniello, L., Kim, J. Y., ... & Topol, E. J. (2016). A prospective randomized trial examining health care utilization in individuals using multiple smartphone-enabled biosensors. *PeerJ, 4*(e1554), 1–16.

Blumenthal, J. A., Sherwood, A., Babyak, M. A., Watkins, L. L., Waugh, R., Georgiades, A., ... & Hinderliter, A. (2005). Effects of exercise and stress management training on markers of cardiovascular risk in patients with ischemic heart disease: A randomized controlled trial. *JAMA 293*(13), 1626–1634.

Bohlmeijer, E., Prenger, R., Taal, E., & Cuijpers, P. (2010). The effects of mindfulness-based stress reduction therapy on mental health of adults with a chronic medical disease: A meta-analysis. *Journal of Psychosomatic Research, 68*(6), 539–544.

Bomyea, J., Ramsawh, H., Ball, T., Taylor, C., Paulus, M., Lang, A., & Stein, M. (2015). Intolerance of uncertainty as a mediator of reductions in worry in a cognitive behavioral treatment program for generalized anxiety disorder. *Journal of Anxiety Disorders, 33*, 90–94.

Bouchard, S., Bernier, F., Boivin, É., Morin, B., & Robillard, G. (2012). Using biofeedback while immersed in a stressful videogame increases the effectiveness of stress management skills in soldiers. *PloS One, 7*(4), e36169. doi: https://doi.org/10.1371/journal.pone.0036169

Bowler, R. M., Harris, M., Li, J., Gocheva, V., Stellman, S. D., Wilson, K., ... Cone, J. E. (2012). Longitudinal mental health impact among police responders to the 9/11 terrorist attack. *American Journal of Industrial Medicine, 55*(4), 297–312.

Brady, K. T., & Sinha, R. (2005). Co-occurring mental and substance use disorders: The neurobiological effects of chronic stress. *American Journal of Psychiatry, 162*(8), 1483–1493.

Cannon, W. B. (1915). *Bodily changes in pain, hunger, fear, and rage: An account of recent researches into the function of emotional excitement.* New York, NY: D. Appleton and Company.

Cardoso, C., Ellenbogen, M. A., Serravalle, L., & Linnen, A.-M. (2013). Stress-induced negative mood moderates the relation between oxytocin administration and trust: Evidence for the tend-and-befriend response to stress? *Psychoneuroendocrinology, 38*(11), 2800–2804.

Cheever, N. A., Rosen, L. D., Carrier, L. M., & Chavez, A. (2014). Out of sight is not out of mind: The impact of restricting wireless mobile device use on anxiety levels among low, moderate and high users. *Computers in Human Behavior, 37*, 290–297.

Chen, J., Bauman, A., & Allman-Farinelli, M. (2016). A study to determine the most popular lifestyle smartphone applications and willingness of the public to share their personal data for health research. *Telemedicine and e-Health, 22*(8), 655–665.

Chida, Y., & Steptoe, A. (2009). The association of anger and hostility with future coronary heart disease: A meta-analytic review of prospective evidence. *Journal of the American College of Cardiology, 53*(11), 936–946. doi: http://dx.doi.org/10.1016/j.jacc.2008.11.044

Choi, S.-W., Kim, D.-J., Choi, J.-S., Ahn, H., Choi, E.-J., Song, W.-Y., … & Youn, H. (2015). Comparison of risk and protective factors associated with smartphone addiction and Internet addiction. *Journal of Behavioral Addictions, 4*(4), 308–314.

Cohen, S., & Janicki-Deverts, D. (2012). Who's stressed? Distributions of psychological stress in the United States in probability samples from 1983, 2006, and 2009. *Journal of Applied Social Psychology, 42*(6), 1320–1334.

Cohen, S., Janicki-Deverts, D., & Doyle, W. J. (2015). Self-rated health in healthy adults and susceptibility to the common cold. *Psychosomatic Medicine, 77*(9), 959–968. doi: 10.1097/psy.0000000000000232

Cohen, S., Janicki-Deverts, D., Doyle, W. J., Miller, G. E., Frank, E., Rabin, B. S., & Turner, R. B. (2012). Chronic stress, glucocorticoid receptor resistance, inflammation, and disease risk. *Proceedings of the National Academy of Sciences, 109*(16), 5995–5999. doi: 10.1073/pnas.1118355109

Compare, A., Bigi, R., Orrego, P. S., Proietti, R., Grossi, E., & Steptoe, A. (2013). Type D personality is associated with the development of stress cardiomyopathy following emotional triggers. *Annals of Behavioral Medicine, 45*(3), 299–307.

Costenbader, K. H., Gay, S., Alarcón-Riquelme, M. E., Iaccarino, L., & Doria, A. (2012). Genes, epigenetic regulation and environmental factors: Which is the most relevant in developing autoimmune diseases? *Autoimmunity Reviews, 11*(8), 604–609.

Crossley, K. (2012, June 19). *Why you get sick after exams.* Survive Law. Retrieved from https://www.survivelaw.com/single-post/769-why-you-get-sick-after-exams

Deaton, A., & Stone, A. A. (2013). Two happiness puzzles. *American Economic Review, 103*(3), 591–597.

Dembroski, T. M., MacDougall, J. M., Herd, J. A., & Shields, J. L. (1979). Effect of level of challenge on pressor and heart rate responses in type A and B subjects. *Journal of Applied Social Psychology, 9*(3), 209–228.

Dhabhar, F. S. (2014). Effects of stress on immune function: The good, the bad, and the beautiful. *Immunologic Research, 58*(2–3), 193–210.

Dickson, K. S., Ciesla, J. A., & Reilly, L. C. (2012). Rumination, worry, cognitive avoidance, and behavioral avoidance: Examination of temporal effects. *Behavior Therapy, 43*(3), 629–640.

Dimsdale, J. E. (2008). Psychological stress and cardiovascular disease. *Journal of the American College of Cardiology, 51*(13), 1237–1246. doi: http://dx.doi.org/10.1016/j.jacc.2007.12.024

Dubay, L. C., & Lebrun, L. A. (2012). Health, behavior, and health care disparities: Disentangling the effects of income and race in the United States. *International Journal of Health Services, 42*(4), 607–625.

Eberth, J., & Sedlmeier, P. (2012). The effects of mindfulness meditation: A meta-analysis. *Mindfulness, 3*(3), 174–189. doi: 10.1007/s12671-012-0101-x

Effros, R. B. (2011). Telomere/telomerase dynamics within the human immune system: Effect of chronic infection and stress. *Experimental Gerontology, 46*(2), 135–140.

Elani, H. W., Allison, P. J., Kumar, R. A., Mancini, L., Lambrou, A., & Bedos, C. (2014). A systematic review of stress in dental students. *Journal of Dental Education, 78*(2), 226–242.

Elhai, J. D., Dvorak, R. D., Levine, J. C., & Hall, B. J. (2017). Problematic smartphone use: A conceptual overview and systematic review of relations with anxiety and depression psychopathology. *Journal of Affective Disorders, 207*, 251–259. doi: 10.1016/j.jad.2016.08.030

Elhai, J. D., Levine, J. C., Dvorak, R. D., & Hall, B. J. (2016). Fear of missing out, need for touch, anxiety and depression are related to problematic smartphone use. *Computers in Human Behavior, 63*, 509–516.

Enez Darcin, A., Kose, S., Noyan, C. O., Nurmedov, S., Yılmaz, O., & Dilbaz, N. (2016). Smartphone addiction and its relationship with social anxiety and loneliness. *Behaviour & Information Technology, 35*(7), 520–525.

Engel, G. L. (1977). The need for a new medical model: A challenge for biomedicine. *Science, 196*(4286), 129–136.

Epel, E. S., & Lithgow, G. J. (2014). Stress biology and aging mechanisms: Toward understanding the deep connection between adaptation to stress and longevity. *The Journals of Gerontology Series A: Biological Sciences and Medical Sciences, 69* (Suppl 1), S10–S16.

Esch, T., Fricchione, G. L., & Stefano, G. B. (2003). The therapeutic use of the relaxation response in stress-related diseases. *Medical Science Monitor, 9*(2), RA23–RA34.

Evans, G. W., & Kim, P. (2013). Childhood poverty, chronic stress, self-regulation, and coping. *Child Development Perspectives, 7*(1), 43–48.

Fetzner, M. G., & Asmundson, G. J. (2015). Aerobic exercise reduces symptoms of posttraumatic stress disorder: A randomized controlled trial. *Cognitive Behaviour Therapy, 44*(4), 301–313.

Firth, J., Torous, J., Nicholas, J., Carney, R., Rosenbaum, S., & Sarris, J. (2017). Can smartphone mental health interventions reduce symptoms of anxiety? A meta-analysis of randomized controlled trials. *Journal of Affective Disorders, 218*, 15–22.

Flor, H., Haag, G., & Turk, D. C. (1986). Long-term efficacy of EMG biofeedback for chronic rheumatic back pain. *Pain, 27*(2), 195–202.

Folkman, S., Lazarus, R. S., Gruen, R. J., & DeLongis, A. (1986). Appraisal, coping, health status, and psychological symptoms. *Journal of Personality and Social Psychology, 50*(3), 571–579.

Friedman, M., Byers, S. O., Diamant, J., & Rosenman, R. H. (1975). Plasma catecholamine response of coronary-prone subjects (Type A) to a specific challenge. *Metabolism, 24*(2), 205–210.

Friedman, M., Rosenman, R. H., Carroll, V., & Tat, R. J. (1958). Changes in the serum cholesterol and blood clotting time in men subjected to cyclic variation of occupational stress. *Circulation, 17*(5), 852–861.

Frisch, M., & Brønnum-Hansen, H. (2009). Mortality among men and women in same-sex marriage: A national cohort study of 8333 Danes. *American Journal of Public Health, 99*(1), 133–137.

Fumaz, C. R., Gonzalez-Garcia, M., Borras, X., Ferrer, M. J., Muñoz-Moreno, J. A., Peña, R., … & Fernandez-Castro, J. (2009). Increased peripheral proinflammatory cytokines in HIV-1–infected patients with prolonged viral suppression suffering from high psychological stress. *JAIDS Journal of Acquired Immune Deficiency Syndromes, 52*(3), 427–428.

Gaab, J., Rohleder, N., Nater, U., & Ehlert, U. (2005). Psychological determinants of the cortisol stress response: The role of anticipatory cognitive appraisal. *Psychoneuroendocrinology, 30*(6), 599–610.

Garland, E. L., Boettiger, C. A., & Howard, M. O. (2011). Targeting cognitive-affective risk mechanisms in stress-precipitated alcohol dependence: An integrated,

biopsychosocial model of automaticity, allostasis, and addiction. *Medical Hypotheses, 76*(5), 745–754.

Gerin, W., Chaplin, W., Schwartz, J. E., Holland, J., Alter, R., Wheeler, R., … & Pickering, T. G. (2005). Sustained blood pressure increases after an acute stressor: The effects of the 11 September 2001 attack on the New York City World Trade Center. *Journal of Hypertension, 23*(2), 279–284.

Gevensleben, H., Kleemeyer, M., Rothenberger, L. G., Studer, P., Flaig-Rohr, A., Moll, G. H., … & Heinrich, H. (2013). Neurofeedback in ADHD: Further pieces of the puzzle. *Brain Topography, 27*(1), 20–32. doi: 10.1007/s10548-013-0285-y

Gleeson, M., Bishop, N. C., Stensel, D. J., Lindley, M. R., Mastana, S. S., & Nimmo, M. A. (2011). The anti-inflammatory effects of exercise: Mechanisms and implications for the prevention and treatment of disease. *Nature Reviews Immunology, 11*(9), 607–615.

Goforth, A. N., Oka, E. R., Leong, F. T., & Denis, D. J. (2014). Acculturation, acculturative stress, religiosity and psychological adjustment among Muslim Arab American adolescents. *Journal of Muslim Mental Health, 8*(2), 3–19.

Gomes, A. R., Faria, S., & Gonçalves, A. M. (2013). Cognitive appraisal as a mediator in the relationship between stress and burnout. *Work & Stress, 27*(4), 351–367.

González-Castro, P., Cueli, M., Rodríguez, C., García, T., & Álvarez, L. (2016). Efficacy of neurofeedback versus pharmacological support in subjects with ADHD. *Applied Psychophysiology and Biofeedback, 41*(1), 17–25. doi: 10.1007/s10484-015-9299-4

Gouin, J.-P., & Kiecolt-Glaser, J. K. (2011). The impact of psychological stress on wound healing: Methods and mechanisms. *Immunology and Allergy Clinics of North America, 31*(1), 81–93. doi: 10.1016/j.iac.2010.09.010

Grande, G., Romppel, M., & Barth, J. (2012). Association between type D personality and prognosis in patients with cardiovascular diseases: A systematic review and meta-analysis. *Annals of Behavioral Medicine, 43*(3), 299–310.

Groesz, L. M., McCoy, S., Carl, J., Saslow, L., Stewart, J., Adler, N., … Epel, E. (2012). What is eating you? Stress and the drive to eat. *Appetite, 58*(2), 717–721.

Gurung, R. (2013). *Health psychology: A cultural approach*: Cengage Learning.

Hargrove, M. B., Becker, W. S., & Hargrove, D. F. (2015). The HRD eustress model: Generating positive stress with challenging work. *Human Resource Development Review, 14*(3), 279–298.

Hassan, S., Karpova, Y., Baiz, D., Yancey, D., Pullikuth, A., Flores, A., … & Danial, N. (2013). Behavioral stress accelerates prostate cancer development in mice. *Journal of Clinical Investigation, 123*(2), 874–886.

Hawi, N. S., & Samaha, M. (2016). To excel or not to excel: Strong evidence on the adverse effect of smartphone addiction on academic performance. *Computers & Education, 98*, 81–89.

Helms, H. M. & Demo, D. H. (2005). Everyday hassles and family stress. In P. C. McKenry & S. J. Price (Eds.), *Families and Change: Coping with Stressful Events and Transitions*, (pp. 355–378). London, England: Sage Publishers.

Hidajat, M., Zimmer, Z., Saito, Y., & Lin, H.-S. (2013). Religious activity, life expectancy, and disability-free life expectancy in Taiwan. *European Journal of Ageing, 10*(3), 229–236.

Higgins, J. P. (2016). Smartphone applications for patients' health and fitness. *American Journal of Medicine, 129*(1), 11–19. doi: http://dx.doi.org/10.1016/j.amjmed.2015.05.038

Hiscock, R., Bauld, L., Amos, A., Fidler, J. A., & Munafo, M. (2012). Socioeconomic status and smoking: A review. *Annals of the New York Academy of Sciences, 1248*(1), 107–123.

Holmes, T. H., & Rahe, R. H. (1967). The social readjustment rating scale. *Journal of Psychosomatic Research, 11*(2), 213–218.

Holtmann, M., Sonuga-Barke, E., Cortese, S., & Brandeis, D. (2014). Neurofeedback for ADHD: A review of current evidence. *Child and Adolescent Psychiatric Clinics of North America, 23*(4), 789–806.

Hopwood, T. L., & Schutte, N. S. (2017). Psychological outcomes in reaction to media exposure to disasters and large-scale violence: A meta-analysis. *Psychology of Violence, 7*(2), 316–327. doi: 10.1037/vio0000056

Huang, Q., & Chen, G. (2014). Does marriage affect survival among the elderly in China? *Gerontechnology, 13*(2), 214.

Huffman, J. C., Beale, E. E., Celano, C. M., Beach, S. R., Belcher, A. M., Moore, S. V., ... & Gaggin, H. K. (2016). Effects of optimism and gratitude on physical activity, biomarkers, and readmissions after an acute coronary syndrome. *Circulation: Cardiovascular Quality and Outcomes, 9*(1), 55–63.

Jackson, L. A., & Wang, J.-L. (2013). Cultural differences in social networking site use: A comparative study of China and the United States. *Computers in Human Behavior, 29*(3), 910–921.

Jacob, R., Arnold, L. D., Hunleth, J., Greiner, K. A., & James, A. S. (2014). Daily hassles' role in health seeking behavior among low-income populations. *American Journal of Health Behavior, 38*(2), 297–306.

Jazaieri, H., Goldin, P. R., Werner, K., Ziv, M., & Gross, J. J. (2012). A randomized trial of MBSR versus aerobic exercise for social anxiety disorder. *Journal of Clinical Psychology, 68*(7), 715–731. doi: 10.1002/jclp.21863

Jiya, T. (2016). A realisation of ethical concerns with smartphone personal health monitoring apps. *ACM SIGCAS Computers and Society, 45*(3), 313–317.

Johnson, N. (2015). Soma crisis. *Journal of Traditional and Complementary Medicine, 5*(4), 179–181.

Josefsson, T., Lindwall, M., & Archer, T. (2014). Physical exercise intervention in depressive disorders: Meta-analysis and systematic review. *Scandinavian Journal of Medicine & Science in Sports, 24*(2), 259–272.

Jukes, S. (2016). News in the digital age: What does it mean for media literacy? *Media Education Research Journal, 7*(1), 5–17.

Kabat-Zinn, J. (1982). An outpatient program in behavioral medicine for chronic pain patients based on the practice of mindfulness meditation: Theoretical considerations and preliminary results. *General Hospital Psychiatry, 4*(1), 33–47.

Kannangara, T. S., Lucero, M. J., Gil-Mohapel, J., Drapala, R. J., Simpson, J. M., Christie, B. R., & van Praag, H. (2011). Running reduces stress and enhances cell genesis in aged mice. *Neurobiology of Aging, 32*(12), 2279–2286.

Kanner, A. D., Coyne, J. C., Schaefer, C., & Lazarus, R. S. (1981). Comparison of two modes of stress measurement: Daily hassles and uplifts versus major life events. *Journal of Behavioral Medicine, 4*(1), 1–39.

Kanner, A. D., Feldman, S. S., Weinberger, D. A., & Ford, M. E. (1987). Uplifts, hassles, and adaptational outcomes in early adolescents. *Journal of Early Adolescence, 7*(4), 371–394.

Karam, A., Clague, J., Marshall, K., & Olivier, J. (2015). The view from above: Faith and health. *The Lancet, 386*, e22–e24.

Khansari, N., Shakiba, Y., & Mahmoudi, M. (2009). Chronic inflammation and oxidative stress as a major cause of age-related diseases and cancer. *Recent Patents on Inflammation & Allergy Drug Discovery, 3*(1), 73–80.

Kim, H. S., Sherman, D. K., & Taylor, S. E. (2008). Culture and social support. *American Psychologist, 63*(6), 518–526.

Kim, I. O., & Shin, S. H. (2016). Effects of academic stress in middle school students on smartphone addiction: Moderating effect of self-esteem and self-control. *Journal of Korean Academy of Psychiatric and Mental Health Nursing, 25*(3), 262–271.

Kim, J., & Lee, J.-E. R. (2011). The Facebook paths to happiness: Effects of the number of Facebook friends and self-presentation on subjective well-being. *Cyberpsychology, Behavior, and Social Networking, 14*(6), 359–364.

Kim, Y., Sohn, D., & Choi, S. M. (2011). Cultural difference in motivations for using social network sites: A comparative study of American and Korean college students. *Computers in Human Behavior, 27*(1), 365–372.

Kober, S. E., Witte, M., Ninaus, M., Neuper, C., & Wood, G. (2013). Learning to modulate one's own brain activity: The effect of spontaneous mental strategies. *Frontiers in Human Neuroscience, 7*, 1–12. doi: 10.3389/fnhum.2013.00695

Koenders, P. G., & van Strien, T. (2011). Emotional eating, rather than lifestyle behavior, drives weight gain in a prospective study in 1,562 employees. *Journal of Occupational and Environmental Medicine, 53*(11), 1287–1293.

Koenig, H. G. (2012). Religion, spirituality, and health: The research and clinical implications. *ISRN Psychiatry, 2012*, 1–33.

Koolhaas, J., Bartolomucci, A., Buwalda, B., De Boer, S., Flügge, G., Korte, S., ... & Palanza, P. (2011). Stress revisited: A critical evaluation of the stress concept. *Neuroscience & Biobehavioral Reviews, 35*(5), 1291–1301.

Kotozaki, Y., Takeuchi, H., Sekiguchi, A., Yamamoto, Y., Shinada, T., Araki, T., ... Kiguchi, M. (2014). Biofeedback-based training for stress management in daily hassles: An intervention study. *Brain and Behavior, 4*(4), 566–579.

Kristeller, J., Wolever, R. Q., & Sheets, V. (2013). Mindfulness-based eating awareness training (MB-EAT) for binge eating: A randomized clinical trial. *Mindfulness, 5*(3), 282–297.

Kroemeke, A. (2016). Depressive symptom trajectories over a 6-year period following myocardial infarction: Predictive function of cognitive appraisal and coping. *Journal of Behavioral Medicine, 39*(2), 181–191.

Kudo, N., Shinohara, H., & Kodama, H. (2014). Heart rate variability biofeedback intervention for reduction of psychological stress during the early postpartum period. *Applied Psychophysiology and Biofeedback, 39*(3–4), 203–211.

Lakey, B., & Orehek, E. (2011). Relational regulation theory: A new approach to explain the link between perceived social support and mental health. *Psychological Review, 118*(3), 482–495.

Lamkin, D. M., Sung, H. Y., Yang, G. S., David, J. M., Ma, J. C., Cole, S. W., & Sloan, E. K. (2015). α 2-Adrenergic blockade mimics the enhancing effect of chronic stress on breast cancer progression. *Psychoneuroendocrinology, 51*, 262–270.

Lange, A., Yeh, J., Messerlian, C., Hauser, R., Chavarro, J., Gaskins, A., & Toth, T. (2016). Smartphone fertility app use among couples of reproductive age: Potential use of big data to improve fertility care and advance reproductive health research. *Fertility and Sterility, 106*(3), e111.

Lazar, S. W., Bush, G., Gollub, R. L., Fricchione, G. L., Khalsa, G., & Benson, H. (2000). Functional brain mapping of the relaxation response and meditation. *Neuroreport, 11*(7), 1581–1585.

Lemola, S., Perkinson-Gloor, N., Brand, S., Dewald-Kaufmann, J. F., & Grob, A. (2015). Adolescents' electronic media use at night, sleep disturbance, and depressive symptoms in the smartphone age. *Journal of Youth and Adolescence, 44*(2), 405–418.

Leserman, J., Petitto, J. M., Golden, R. N., Gaynes, B. N., Gu, H., Perkins, D. O., ... & Evans, D. L. (2000). Impact of stressful life events, depression, social support, coping, and cortisol on progression to AIDS. *American Journal of Psychiatry, 157*, 1221–1228.

Levy, B. R., Slade, M. D., Kunkel, S. R., & Kasl, S. V. (2002). Longevity increased by positive self-perceptions of aging. *Journal of Personality and Social Psychology, 83*(2), 261–270.

Lewis, G. F., Hourani, L., Tueller, S., Kizakevich, P., Bryant, S., Weimer, B., & Strange, L. (2015). Relaxation training assisted by heart rate variability biofeedback: Implication for a military predeployment stress inoculation protocol. *Psychophysiology, 52*(9), 1167–1174.

Li, J., Brackbill, R. M., Stellman, S. D., Farfel, M. R., Miller-Archie, S. A., Friedman, S., ... Cone, J. (2011). Gastroesophageal reflux symptoms and comorbid asthma and posttraumatic stress disorder following the 9/11 terrorist attacks on World Trade Center in New York City. *American Journal of Gastroenterology, 106*(11), 1933–1941.

Linden, D. E. J. (2014). Neurofeedback and networks of depression. *Dialogues in Clinical Neuroscience, 16*(1), 103–112.

Liu, C.-H., Lin, S.-H., Pan, Y.-C., & Lin, Y.-H. (2016). Smartphone gaming and frequent use pattern associated with smartphone addiction. *Medicine, 95*(28), 1–4.

López-Rocha, S. Y. (2014). Stress and acculturation. In W. C. Cockerham, R. Dingwall, & S. R. Quah (Eds.), *The Wiley Blackwell Encyclopedia of Health, Illness, Behavior, and Society.* Hoboken, NY: Wiley-Blackwell.

Lovallo, W. R. (2005). Cardiovascular reactivity: Mechanisms and pathways to cardiovascular disease. *International Journal of Psychophysiology, 58*(2), 119–132.

Lupien, S. J., McEwen, B. S., Gunnar, M. R., & Heim, C. (2009). Effects of stress throughout the lifespan on the brain, behaviour and cognition. *Nature Reviews Neuroscience, 10*(6), 434–445.

Maier, C., Laumer, S., Eckhardt, A., & Weitzel, T. (2015). Giving too much social support: Social overload on social networking sites. *European Journal of Information Systems, 24*(5), 447–464. doi: 10.1057/ejis.2014.3

Manenschijn, L., Schaap, L., Van Schoor, N., Van der Pas, S., Peeters, G., Lips, P., ... & Van Rossum, E. (2013). High long-term cortisol levels, measured in scalp hair, are associated with a history of cardiovascular disease. *Journal of Clinical Endocrinology & Metabolism, 98*(5), 2078–2083.

Marchand, W. R. (2012). Mindfulness-based stress reduction, mindfulness-based cognitive therapy, and Zen meditation for depression, anxiety, pain, and psychological distress. *Journal of Psychiatric Practice, 18*(4), 233–252.

Marques, A. H., Bjørke-Monsen, A.-L., Teixeira, A. L., & Silverman, M. N. (2014). Maternal stress, nutrition and physical activity: Impact on immune function, CNS development and psychopathology. *Brain Research, 1617*, 28–46.

Martin, C. K., Correa, J. B., Han, H., Allen, H. R., Rood, J. C., Champagne, C. M., ... & Bray, G. A. (2012). Validity of the Remote Food Photography Method (RFPM) for estimating energy and nutrient intake in near real-time. *Obesity (Silver Spring), 20*(4), 891–899. doi: 10.1038/oby.2011.344

Martin, C. K., Nicklas, T., Gunturk, B., Correa, J. B., Allen, H. R., & Champagne, C. (2014). Measuring food intake with digital photography. *Journal of Human Nutrition and Dietetics: The Official Journal of the British Dietetic Association, 27*(0 1), 72–81. doi: 10.1111/jhn.12014

Matés, J. M., Segura, J. A., Alonso, F. J., & Márquez, J. (2012). Oxidative stress in apoptosis and cancer: An update. *Archives of Toxicology, 86*(11), 1649–1665.

Mathur, C., Erickson, D. J., Stigler, M. H., Forster, J. L., & Finnegan Jr, J. R. (2013). Individual and neighborhood socioeconomic status effects on adolescent smoking: A multilevel cohort-sequential latent growth analysis. *American Journal of Public Health, 103*(3), 543–548.

Matthews, K. A., Gump, B. B., Harris, K. F., Haney, T. L., & Barefoot, J. C. (2004). Hostile behaviors predict cardiovascular mortality among men enrolled in the Multiple Risk Factor Intervention Trial. *Circulation, 109*(1), 66–70.

McCallie, M. S., Blum, C. M., & Hood, C. J. (2006). Progressive muscle relaxation. *Journal of Human Behavior in the Social Environment, 13*(3), 51–66.

Meek, A. (2016). Media traumatization, symbolic wounds and digital culture. *CM: Communication and Media, 11*(38), 91–110.

Menzies, J. R., Skibicka, K. P., Dickson, S. L., & Leng, G. (2012). Neural substrates underlying interactions between appetite stress and reward. *Obesity Facts, 5*(2), 208–220.

Michels, N., Sioen, I., Braet, C., Eiben, G., Hebestreit, A., Huybrechts, I., ... & De Henauw, S. (2012). Stress, emotional eating behaviour and dietary patterns in children. *Appetite, 59*(3), 762–769.

Miller, G. E., Chen, E., & Parker, K. J. (2011). Psychological stress in childhood and susceptibility to the chronic diseases of aging: Moving toward a model of behavioral and biological mechanisms. *Psychological Bulletin, 137*(6), 959–997.

Montgomery, P. S., & Ehrisman, W. J. (1976). Biofeedback alleviated headaches: A follow-up. *Headache: The Journal of Head and Face Pain, 16*(2), 64–65.

Myers, D. G. (2000). The funds, friends, and faith of happy people. *American Psychologist, 55*(1), 56–67.

Myrtek, M. (2001). Meta-analyses of prospective studies on coronary heart disease, type A personality, and hostility. *International Journal of Cardiology, 79*(2), 245–251.

Nabi, R. L., Prestin, A., & So, J. (2013). Facebook friends with (health) benefits? Exploring social network site use and perceptions of social support, stress, and well-being. *Cyberpsychology, Behavior, and Social Networking, 16*(10), 721–727.

Nagaraja, A. S., Armaiz-Pena, G. N., Lutgendorf, S. K., & Sood, A. K. (2013). Why stress is BAD for cancer patients. *Journal of Clinical Investigation, 123*(2), 558–560. doi: 10.1172/JCI67887

National Center for Health. (2012). *Health, United States, 2011: With special feature on socioeconomic status and health.* Hyattsville, MD: National Center for Health Statistics.

National Center for Health. (2014). *Health, United States, 2013: With special feature on prescription drugs.* Hyattsville, MD: National Center for Health Statistics.

Nunan, D., & Di Domenico, M. (2013). Market research and the ethics of big data. *International Journal of Market Research, 55*(4), 505–520.

Oertelt-Prigione, S. (2012). The influence of sex and gender on the immune response. *Autoimmunity Reviews, 11*(6), A479–A485.

Oh, H. J., Ozkaya, E., & LaRose, R. (2014). How does online social networking enhance life satisfaction? The relationships among online supportive interaction, affect, perceived social support, sense of community, and life satisfaction. *Computers in Human Behavior, 30*, 69–78.

Olmstead, K., & Atkinson, M. (2015). *Apps permissions in the Google play store.* Pew Research Center. Retrieved from http://www.pewinternet.org/2015/11/10/apps-permissions-in-the-google-play-store/

Padela, A. I., & Heisler, M. (2010). The association of perceived abuse and discrimination after September 11, 2001, with psychological distress, level of happiness, and health status among Arab Americans. *American Journal of Public Health, 100*(2), 284–291.

Peacock, E. J., & Wong, P. T. (1990). The Stress Appraisal Measure (SAM): A multidimensional approach to cognitive appraisal. *Stress Medicine, 6*(3), 227–236.

Pearson, C., & Hussain, Z. (2016). Smartphone addiction and associated psychological factors. *Addicta: The Turkish Journal of Addictions, 3*(2), 1–15.

Pedersen, S. S., & Denollet, J. (2006). Is Type D personality here to stay? Emerging evidence across cardiovascular disease patient groups. *Current Cardiology Reviews, 2*(3), 205–213.

Peters, R. D., Le Berre, M., & Pomeau, Y. (2012). Prediction of catastrophes: An experimental model. *Physical Review E, 86*(2), 1–21. https://doi.org/10.1103/PhysRevE.86.026207

Ponce, A. N., Lorber, W., Paul, J. J., Esterlis, I., Barzvi, A., Allen, G. J., & Pescatello, L. S. (2008). Comparisons of varying dosages of relaxation in a corporate setting: Effects on stress reduction. *International Journal of Stress Management, 15*(4), 396–407.

Quaresma, A., Palmeira, A., Martins, S., Minderico, C., & Sardinha, L. (2014). Effect of a school-based intervention on physical activity and quality of life through

serial mediation of social support and exercise motivation: The PESSOA program. *Health Education Research, 29*(6), 906–917.

Quintero, O. L., Amador-Patarroyo, M. J., Montoya-Ortiz, G., Rojas-Villarraga, A., & Anaya, J.-M. (2012). Autoimmune disease and gender: Plausible mechanisms for the female predominance of autoimmunity. *Journal of Autoimmunity, 38*(2), J109–J119.

Rasmussen, H. N., Scheier, M. F., & Greenhouse, J. B. (2009). Optimism and physical health: A meta-analytic review. *Annals of Behavioral Medicine, 37*(3), 239–256.

Ratanasiripong, P., Ratanasiripong, N., & Kathalae, D. (2012). Biofeedback intervention for stress and anxiety among nursing students: A randomized controlled trial. *Journal of Nursing Education, 54*(9), 520–524.

Reuter, S., Gupta, S. C., Chaturvedi, M. M., & Aggarwal, B. B. (2010). Oxidative stress, inflammation, and cancer: How are they linked? *Free Radical Biology & Medicine, 49*(11), 1603–1616. doi: 10.1016/j.freeradbiomed.2010.09.006

Riley, K. E., & Kalichman, S. (2015). Mindfulness-based stress reduction for people living with HIV/AIDS: Preliminary review of intervention trial methodologies and findings. *Health Psychology Review, 9*(2), 224–243.

Rodin, J. (2014). Health, control, and aging. In M. M. Baltes & P. B. Baltes (Eds.), *Psychology Revivals: The Psychology of Control and Aging* (pp. 139–165). New York, NY: Psychology Press.

Rogers-Sirin, L., Ryce, P., & Sirin, S. R. (2014). Acculturation, acculturative stress, and cultural mismatch and their influences on immigrant children and adolescents' well-being. In R. Dimitrova, M. Bender, & F. van de Vijver (Eds.), *Global perspectives on well-being in immigrant families* (pp. 11–30). New York, NY: Springer.

Romero-Sanchiz, P., Nogueira-Arjona, R., Godoy-Ávila, A., Gavino-Lázaro, A., & Freeston, M. H. (2015). Narrow specificity of responsibility and intolerance of uncertainty in obsessive-compulsive behavior and generalized anxiety symptoms. *International Journal of Cognitive Therapy, 8*(3), 239–257.

Rosch, P. J. (1979). Stress and cancer: A disease of adaptation? *Cancer, Stress, and Death* (pp. 187–212): Springer.

Rosenman, R. H., Brand, R. J., Jenkins, C. D., Friedman, M., Straus, R., & Wurm, M. (1975). Coronary heart disease in the Western Collaborative Group Study: Final follow-up experience of 8 1/2 years. *JAMA, 233*(8), 872–877.

Rutters, F., Nieuwenhuizen, A. G., Lemmens, S. G., Born, J. M., & Westerterp-Plantenga, M. S. (2009). Acute stress-related changes in eating in the absence of hunger. *Obesity, 17*(1), 72–77.

Samaha, M., & Hawi, N. S. (2016). Relationships among smartphone addiction, stress, academic performance, and satisfaction with life. *Computers in Human Behavior, 57*, 321–325.

Sarafino, E. P., & Ewing, M. (1999). The hassles assessment scale for students in college: Measuring the frequency and unpleasantness of and dwelling on stressful events. *Journal of American College Health, 48*(2), 75–83. doi: 10.1080/07448489909595677

Sarafino, E. P., & Smith, T. W. (2014). *Health psychology: Biopsychosocial interactions*: Hoboken, NJ: Wiley & Sons.

Sarason, I. G., Johnson, J. H., & Siegel, J. M. (1978). Assessing the impact of life changes: Development of the Life Experiences Survey. *Journal of Consulting and Clinical Psychology, 46*(5), 932–946.

Scheier, M. F., & Carver, C. S. (1985). Optimism, coping, and health: Assessment and implications of generalized outcome expectancies. *Health Psychology, 4*(3), 219–247.

Schmitt, M. T., Branscombe, N. R., Postmes, T., & Garcia, A. (2014). The consequences of perceived discrimination for psychological well-being: A meta-analytic review. *Psychological Bulletin, 140*(4), 1–28.

Schneider, R. H., Grim, C. E., Rainforth, M. V., Kotchen, T., Nidich, S. I., Gaylord-King, C., ... & Alexander, C. N. (2012). Stress reduction in the secondary prevention of cardiovascular disease randomized, controlled trial of transcendental meditation and health education in

Blacks. *Circulation: Cardiovascular Quality and Outcomes, 5*(6), 750–758.

Schneiderman, N., Ironson, G., & Siegel, S. D. (2005). Stress and health: Psychological, behavioral, and biological determinants. *Annual Review of Clinical Psychology, 1*, 607–628. doi: 10.1146/annurev.clinpsy.1.102803.144141

Schwabe, L., Dickinson, A., & Wolf, O. T. (2011). Stress, habits, and drug addiction: A psychoneuroendocrinological perspective. *Experimental and Clinical Psychopharmacology, 19*(1), 53–63.

Schweizer, A., Berchtold, A., Barrense-Dias, Y., Akre, C., & Suris, J.-C. (2017). Adolescents with a smartphone sleep less than their peers. *European Journal of Pediatrics, 176*(1), 131–136. doi: 10.1007/s00431-016-2823-6

Selye, H. (1973). The evolution of the stress concept: The originator of the concept traces its development from the discovery in 1936 of the alarm reaction to modern therapeutic applications of syntoxic and catatoxic hormones. *American Scientist, 61*(6), 692–699.

Selye, H. (1975). Confusion and controversy in the stress field. *Journal of Human Stress, 1*(2), 37–44.

Selye, H. (1986). Stress, cancer, and the mind. In S. B. Day (Ed.), *Cancer, stress, and death* (pp. 11–19) New York, NY: Springer.

Shanmugasegaram, S., Flett, G. L., Madan, M., Oh, P., Marzolini, S., Reitav, J., ... & Sturman, E. D. (2014). Perfectionism, type D personality, and illness-related coping styles in cardiac rehabilitation patients. *Journal of Health Psychology, 19*(3), 417–426.

Shennan, C., Payne, S., & Fenlon, D. (2011). What is the evidence for the use of mindfulness-based interventions in cancer care? A review. *Psycho-Oncology, 20*(7), 681–697.

Siegler, I. C., Brummett, B. H., Martin, P., & Helms, M. J. (2013). Consistency and timing of marital transitions and survival during midlife: The role of personality and health risk behaviors. *Annals of Behavioral Medicine: A Publication of the Society of Behavioral Medicine, 45*(3), 338–347. doi: 10.1007/s12160-012-9457-3

Signorello, L. B., Cohen, S. S., Williams, D. R., Munro, H. M., Hargreaves, M. K., & Blot, W. J. (2014). Socioeconomic status, race, and mortality: A prospective cohort study. *American Journal of Public Health, 104*(12), e98–e107.

Singh, G. K., & Siahpush, M. (2006). Widening socioeconomic inequalities in US life expectancy, 1980–2000. *International Journal of Epidemiology, 35*(4), 969–979.

Singh, G. K., & Siahpush, M. (2014). Widening rural–urban disparities in life expectancy, U.S., 1969–2009. *American Journal of Preventive Medicine, 46*(2), e19–e29.

Slattery, M. J., Grieve, A. J., Ames, M. E., Armstrong, J. M., & Essex, M. J. (2013). Neurocognitive function and state cognitive stress appraisal predict cortisol reactivity to an acute psychosocial stressor in adolescents. *Psychoneuroendocrinology, 38*(8), 1318–1327.

Smart, J. F., & Smart, D. W. (1995). Acculturative stress the experience of the Hispanic immigrant. *The Counseling Psychologist, 23*(1), 25–42.

Smith, S. M., & Vale, W. W. (2006). The role of the hypothalamic-pituitary-adrenal axis in neuroendocrine responses to stress. *Dialogues in Clinical Neuroscience, 8*(4), 383–395.

Sonnenberg, C., Deeg, D., Van Tilburg, T., Vink, D., Stek, M., & Beekman, A. (2013). Gender differences in the relation between depression and social support in later life. *International Psychogeriatrics, 25*(1), 61–70.

Stagl, J. M., Lechner, S. C., Carver, C. S., Bouchard, L. C., Gudenkauf, L. M., Jutagir, D. R., ... & Antoni, M. H. (2015). A randomized controlled trial of cognitive-behavioral stress management in breast cancer: Survival and recurrence at 11-year follow-up. *Breast Cancer Research and Treatment, 154*(2), 319–328. doi: 10.1007/s10549-015-3626-6

Stapleton, A. (2012). Coaching clients through the quarter-life crisis: What works. *International Journal of Evidence Based Coaching and Mentoring, Special Issue, 6*, 130–145.

Starr, L. R., Stroud, C. B., & Li, Y. I. (2016). Predicting the transition from anxiety to depressive symptoms in early adolescence: Negative anxiety response style as a moderator of sequential comorbidity. *Journal of Affective Disorders, 190*, 757–763.

Straub, R. O. (2014). *Health psychology*. New York, NY: Worth Publishers.

Street, M., Smerieri, A., Petraroli, A., Cesari, S., Viani, I., Garrubba, M., … & Bernasconi, S. (2011). Placental cortisol and cord serum IGFBP-2 concentrations are important determinants of postnatal weight gain. *Journal of Biological Regulators and Homeostatic Agents, 26*(4), 721–731.

Su, D., Stimpson, J. P., & Wilson, F. A. (2014). Racial disparities in mortality among middle-aged and older men: Does marriage matter? *American Journal of Men's Health, 9*(4), 289–300. doi: 10.1177/1557988314540199

Suls, J., Krantz, D. S., & Williams, G. C. (2013). Three strategies for bridging different levels of analysis and embracing the biopsychosocial model. *Health Psychology, 32*(5), 597–601.

Suls, J., & Rothman, A. (2004). Evolution of the biopsychosocial model: prospects and challenges for health psychology. *Health Psychology, 23*(2), 119–125.

Svansdottir, E., Denollet, J., Thorsson, B., Gudnason, T., Halldorsdottir, S., Gudnason, V., … & Karlsson, H. D. (2012). Association of type D personality with unhealthy lifestyle, and estimated risk of coronary events in the general Icelandic population. *European Journal of Preventive Cardiology, 20*(2), 322–330.

Tamers, S. L., Beresford, S. A., Cheadle, A. D., Zheng, Y., Bishop, S. K., & Thompson, B. (2011). The association between worksite social support, diet, physical activity and body mass index. *Preventive Medicine, 53*(1), 53–56.

Tandon, P. S., Zhou, C., Sallis, J. F., Cain, K. L., Frank, L. D., & Saelens, B. E. (2012). Home environment relationships with children's physical activity, sedentary time, and screen time by socioeconomic status. *International Journal of Behavioral Nutrition and Physical Activity, 9*(88), 1–9.

Tatomir, A., Micu, C., & Crivii, C. (2014). The impact of stress and glucocorticoids on memory. *Clujul Medical, 87*(1), 3–6. doi: 10.15386/cjm.2014.8872.871.at1cm2

Taylor, S. E. (2006). Tend and befriend biobehavioral bases of affiliation under stress. *Current Directions in Psychological Science, 15*(6), 273–277.

Taylor, S. E. (2011). Social support: A review. *The Handbook of Health Psychology,* 189–214.

Taylor, S. E., Klein, L. C., Lewis, B. P., Gruenewald, T. L., Gurung, R. A., & Updegraff, J. A. (2000). Biobehavioral responses to stress in females: Tend-and-befriend, not fight-or-flight. *Psychological Review, 107*(3), 411–429.

Todd, B. L., Moskowitz, M. C., Ottati, A., & Feuerstein, M. (2013). Stressors, stress response, and cancer recurrence: A systematic review. *Cancer Nursing, 37*(2), 114–125.

Topham, N. J., & Hewitt, E. W. (2009). Natural killer cell cytotoxicity: how do they pull the trigger? *Immunology, 128*(1), 7–15. doi: 10.1111/j.1365-2567.2009.03123.x

Torres, L., Driscoll, M. W., & Voell, M. (2012). Discrimination, acculturation, acculturative stress, and Latino psychological distress: A moderated mediational model. *Cultural Diversity and Ethnic Minority Psychology, 18*(1), 17–25.

Ullman, T. A., & Itzkowitz, S. H. (2011). Intestinal inflammation and cancer. *Gastroenterology, 140*(6), 1807–1816. doi: 10.1053/j.gastro.2011.01.057

van der Waerden, J. E., Hoefnagels, C., Hosman, C. M., Souren, P. M., & Jansen, M. W. (2013). A randomized controlled trial of combined exercise and psycho-education for low-SES women: Short-and long-term outcomes in the reduction of stress and depressive symptoms. *Social Science & Medicine, 91*, 84–93.

van der Zwan, J. E., de Vente, W., Huizink, A. C., Bögels, S. M., & de Bruin, E. I. (2015). Physical activity, mindfulness meditation, or heart rate variability biofeedback for stress reduction: A randomized controlled trial. *Applied Psychophysiology and Biofeedback, 40*(4), 257–268.

Van Deursen, A. J., Bolle, C. L., Hegner, S. M., & Kommers, P. A. (2015). Modeling habitual and addictive smartphone behavior: The role of smartphone usage types, emotional intelligence, social stress, self-regulation, age, and gender. *Computers in Human Behavior, 45*, 411–420.

Venkatesh, B., & Ram, N. (2015). Eustress: A unique dimension to stress management. *Voice of Research, 4*(2), 26–29.

Versteeg, H., Spek, V., Pedersen, S. S., & Denollet, J. (2012). Type D personality and health status in cardiovascular disease populations: A meta-analysis of prospective studies. *European Journal of Preventive Cardiology, 19*(6), 1373–1380.

Vitlic, A., Lord, J. M., & Phillips, A. C. (2014). Stress, ageing and their influence on functional, cellular and molecular aspects of the immune system. *Age, 36*(3), 1169–1185.

Volkow, N. D., Wang, G.-J., & Baler, R. D. (2011). Reward, dopamine and the control of food intake: Implications for obesity. *Trends in Cognitive Sciences, 15*(1), 37–46. doi: 10.1016/j.tics.2010.11.001

Volkow, N. D., Wang, G.-J., Tomasi, D., & Baler, R. D. (2013a). The addictive dimensionality of obesity. *Biological Psychiatry, 73*(9), 811–818.

Volkow, N. D., Wang, G. J., Tomasi, D., & Baler, R. D. (2013b). Obesity and addiction: Neurobiological overlaps. *Obesity Reviews, 14*(1), 2–18.

von Haaren, B., Haertel, S., Stumpp, J., Hey, S., & Ebner-Priemer, U. (2015). Reduced emotional stress reactivity to a real-life academic examination stressor in students participating in a 20-week aerobic exercise training: A randomised controlled trial using Ambulatory Assessment. *Psychology of Sport and Exercise, 20*, 67–75.

Walburn, J., Vedhara, K., Hankins, M., Rixon, L., & Weinman, J. (2009). Psychological stress and wound healing in humans: A systematic review and meta-analysis. *Journal of Psychosomatic Research, 67*(3), 253–271.

Ward, A. F., Duke, K., Gneezy, A., & Bos, M. W. (2017). Brain drain: The mere presence of one's own smartphone reduces available cognitive capacity. *Journal of the Association for Consumer Research, 2*(2), 140–154. doi: 10.1086/691462

Wen, C. P., Wai, J. P. M., Tsai, M. K., & Chen, C. H. (2014). Minimal amount of exercise to prolong life to walk, to run, or just mix it up? *Journal of the American College of Cardiology, 64*(5), 482–484. doi: 10.1016/j.jacc.2014.05.026

Wen, C. P., Wai, J. P. M., Tsai, M. K., Yang, Y. C., Cheng, T. Y. D., Lee, M.-C., … & Wu, X. (2011). Minimum amount of physical activity for reduced mortality and extended life expectancy: A prospective cohort study. *The Lancet, 378*(9798), 1244–1253. doi: http://dx.doi.org/10.1016/S0140-6736(11)60749-6

Wethington, E., Glanz, K., & Schwartz, M. D. (2015). *Stress, coping, and health behavior*. San Fransciso, CA: Jossey-Bass.

Wiederhold, B. K., Boyd, C., Sulea, C., Gaggioli, A., & Riva, G. (2014). *Marketing analysis of a positive technology app for the self-management of psychological stress* (pp. 83–87): IOS Press.

Wisniewski, P. J., Joseph, L., Composto, G., & Campbell, S. C. (2015). *Exercise reduces DNA damage, inflammation and apoptotic markers in the brain of high fat fed animals*. Paper presented at the International Journal of Exercise Science: Conference Proceedings.

Wright, M., Creed, P., & Zimmer-Gembeck, M. J. (2010). The development and initial validation of a brief daily hassles scale suitable for use with adolescents. *European Journal of Psychological Assessment, 26*(3), 217–223.

Wyer, R. S., & Srull, T. K. (2014). *Perspectives on anger and emotion: Advances in social cognition* (Vol. VI). New York, NY: Psychology Press.

Wyon, D. P. (2000). Individual control at each workplace: The means and potential benefits. In D. Clements-Croome (Ed.), *Creating the productive workplace,* (pp. 192–206). London, England: E & FN SPON.

Yen, C.-F., Ko, C.-H., Yen, J.-Y., Chang, Y.-P., & Cheng, C.-P. (2009). Multi-dimensional discriminative factors for Internet addiction among adolescents regarding gender and age. *Psychiatry and Clinical Neurosciences, 63*(3), 357–364. doi: 10.1111/j.1440-1819.2009.01969.x

Yoon, E., Chang, C.-T., Kim, S., Clawson, A., Cleary, S. E., Hansen, M., … & Gomes, A. M. (2013). A meta-analysis of acculturation/enculturation and mental health. *Journal of Counseling Psychology, 60*(1), 15–30.

Young, K. D., Zotev, V., Phillips, R., Misaki, M., Yuan, H., Drevets, W. C., & Bodurka, J. (2014). Real-time fMRI neurofeedback training of amygdala activity in patients with major depressive disorder. *PLoS ONE, 9*(2), e88785. doi: 10.1371/journal.pone.0088785

Zhao, L., Xu, J., Liang, F., Li, A., Zhang, Y., & Sun, J. (2015). Effect of chronic psychological stress on liver metastasis of colon cancer in mice. *PLoS One, 10*(10), e0139978. https://doi.org/10.1371/journal.pone.0139978

Zotev, V., Phillips, R., Yuan, H., Misaki, M., & Bodurka, J. (2014). Self-regulation of human brain activity using simultaneous real-time fMRI and EEG neurofeedback. *NeuroImage, 85*, 985–995.

Chapter 13

Abramsky, T., Watts, C. H., Garcia-Moreno, C., Devries, K., Kiss, L., Ellsberg, M., Jansen, H. & Heise, L. (2011). What factors are associated with recent intimate partner violence? Findings from the WHO multi-country study on women's health and domestic violence. *BMC Public Health, 11*(1), 109–126.

Adams, D. C., & Salois, M. J. (2010). Local verses organic: A turn in consumer preferences and willingness-to-pay. *Renewable Agriculture and Food Systems, 25*(4), 331–341.

Adolphs, R. (1999). Social cognition and the human brain. *Trends in Cognitive Sciences, 3*(12), 469–479.

Agerstrom, J., & Rooth, D. O. (2011). The role of automatic obesity stereotypes in real hiring discrimination. *Journal of Applied Psychology, 96*(4), 790–805.

Ajzen, I. (1991). The theory of planned behavior. *Organizational Behavior and Human Decision Processes, 50*(2), 179–211.

Ajzen, I., & Fishbein, M. (2000). Attitudes and the attitude-behavior relation: Reasoned and automatic processes. *European Review of Social Psychology, 11*(1), 1–33.

Alibeli, M. A., & Yaghi, A. (2012). Theories of prejudice and attitudes toward Muslims in the United States. *International Journal of Humanities and Social Science, 2*(1), 21–29.

Allen, M. (1991). Meta-analysis comparing the persuasiveness of one-sided and two-sided messages. *Western Journal of Speech Communication, 55*(4), 390–404.

Allport, G. W. (1954). *The nature of prejudice*. Cambridge, MA: Addison-Wesley.

American Psychological Association. (2010). Ethical principles of psychologists and code of conduct. Retrieved from http://www.apa.org/ethics/code/principles.pdf

Anderson, C. A., & Anderson, D. C. (1984). Ambient temperature and violent crime: Tests of the linear and curvilinear hypothesis. *Journal of Personality and Social Psychology, 46*, 91–97.

Andersen, S. M., & Przybylinski, E. (2014). Cognitive distortion in interpersonal relations: Clinical implications of social cognitive research on person perception. *Journal of Psychotherapy Integration, 24*(1), 13–24.

Archer, J. (2004). Sex differences in aggression in real-world settings: A meta-analytic review. *Review of General Psychology, 8*(4), 291–322.

Aronson, E., & Gonzalez, A. (1988). Desegregation, jigsaw, and the Mexican-American experience. In P. A. Katz & D. A. Taylor, (Eds.), *Eliminating Racism: Profiles in Controversy*. New York, NY: Plenum Press.

Aronson, E., Wilson, T. D., & Akert, R. M. (2013). *Social Psychology: Eighth edition*. Boston, MA: Pearson.

Asch, S. E. (1955). Opinions and social pressure. *Readings about the Social Animal, 193*, 17–26.

Asch, S.E. (1956). Studies of independence and conformity: A minority of one against a unanimous majority. *Psychological Monographs, 70*(9, Whole no. 416).

Baddeley, M., & Parkinson, S. (2012). Group decision-making: An economic analysis of social influence and individual difference in experimental juries. *The Journal of Socio-Economics, 41*, 558–573.

Bair-Merritt, M. H. (2010). Intimate partner violence. *Pediatrics in Review, 31*(4), 145–150.

Banaji, M.R., & Greenwald, A.G. (1995). Implicit gender stereotyping in judgments of fame. *Journal of Personality and Social Psychology, 68,* 181–198.

Banuazizi, A., & Movahedi, S. (1975). Interpersonal dynamics in a simulated prison: A methodological analysis. *American Psychologist, 30*(2), 152–160.

Bar, M. & Neta, M. (2006). Humans prefer curved visual objects. *Psychological Science, 17*(8), 645–648.

Barasch, A., Levine, E. E., Berman, J. Z., & Small, D. A. (2014). Selfish or selfless? On the signal value of emotion in altruistic behavior. *Journal of Personality and Social Psychology, 107*(3), 393–413.

Barlett, C. P. (2013). Anonymously hurting others online: The effect of anonymity on cyberbullying frequency. *Psychology of Popular Media Culture.* Advance online publication. doi: 10.1037/a0034335

Barlett, C. P., Gentile, D. A., Anderson, C. A., Suzuki, K., Sakamoto, A., Yamaoka, A., & Katsura, R. (2014). Cross-cultural differences in cyberbullying behavior: A short-term longitudinal study. *Journal of Cross-Cultural Psychology, 45*(2), 300–313.

Bartels, J. M. (2015). The Stanford prison experiment in introductory psychology textbooks: A content analysis. *Psychology Learning & Teaching, 14*(1), 36–50.

Batool, S., & Najma, I. M. (2010). Role of attitude similarity and proximity in interpersonal attraction among friends (C 310). *Journal of Innovation Management and Technology, 1*(2), 142–146.

Batson, C. D. (1990). How social an animal? The human capacity for caring. *American Psychologist, 45,* 336–346. doi: 10.1037/0003-066X.45.3.336

Bem, D. J. (1967). Self-perception: An alternative interpretation of cognitive dissonance phenomena. *Psychological Review, 74*(3), 183–200.

Bem, D. J. (1972). Self-perception theory. In L. Berkowitz (Ed.), *Advances in experimental social psychology* (Vol. 6, pp. 1–62). New York, NY: Academic Press.

Berkowitz, L. (1983). Aversively stimulated aggression: Some parallels and differences in research with animals and humans. *American Psychologist, 38,* 1135–1144.

Berkowitz, L. (1989). Frustration-aggression hypothesis: Examination and reformulation. *Psychological Bulletin, 106,* 59–73.

Berscheid, E. (2010). Love in the fourth dimension. *Annual Review of Psychology, 61,* 1–25.

Black, M. C., Basile, K. C., Breiding, M. J., Smith, S. G., Walters, M. L., Merrick, M. T., Chen, J., & Stevens, M. R. (2011). *The National Intimate Partner and Sexual Violence Survey (NISVS): 2010 summary report.* Atlanta, GA: National Center for Injury Prevention and Control, Centers for Disease Control and Prevention.

Bodenhausen, G. V., Kang, S. K., & Peery, D. (2012). Social categorization and the perception of social groups. *The Sage handbook of social cognition,* 318–336.

Bond, C. F., & Titus, L. J. (1983). Social facilitation: A meta-analysis of 241 studies. *Psychological Bulletin, 94*(2), 265–292.

Borchers, T. (2012). *Persuasion in the media age.* Long Grove, IL: Waveland Press.

Bramlett, M., & Mosher W. (2001). First marriage dissolution, divorce, and remarriage: United States. *Advance Data From Vital and Health Statistics. No.323.* Hyattsville, MD: National Center for Health Statistics.

Brochu, P. M., & Esses, V. M. (2011). What's in a name? The effects of the labels "fat" versus "overweight" on weight bias. *Journal of Applied Social Psychology, 41,* 1981–2008.

Brochu, P. M., & Dovidio, J. F. (2014). Would you like fries (380 calories) with that? Menu labeling mitigates the impact of weight-based stereotype threat on food choice. *Social Psychological and Personality Science, 5*(4), 414–421.

Burger, J. M. (2009). Replicating Milgram: Would people still obey today? *American Psychologist, 64*(1), 1–11.

Buss, D. M. (1989). Conflict between the sexes: Strategic interference and the evocation of anger and upset. *Journal of Personality and Social Psychology, 56*(5), 735–747.

Buss, D. M., & Shackelford, T. K. (1997). Human aggression in evolutionary psychological perspective. *Clinical Psychology Review, 17*(6), 605–619.

Butke, P., & Sheridan, S.C. (2010). An analysis of the relationship between weather andaggressive crime in Cleveland, Ohio. *Weather, Climate, and Society, 2,* 127–139.

Byrne, D. (1961). Interpersonal attraction and attitude similarity. *Journal of Abnormal and Social Psychology, 62*(3), 713–715.

Campbell, W. K., & Sedikides, C. (1999). Self-threat magnifies the self-serving bias: A meta-analytic integration. *Review of General Psychology, 3*(1), 23–43.

Cann, A., Sherman, S. J., & Elkes, R. (1975). Effects of initial request size and timing of a second request on compliance: The foot in the door and the door in the face. *Journal of Personality and Social Psychology, 32*(5), 774–782.

Carnahan, T., & McFarland, S. (2007). Revisiting the Stanford Prison Experiment: Could participant self-selection have led to the cruelty? *Personality and Social Psychology Bulletin, 33*(5), 603–614.

Chaiken, S. (1979). Communicator physical attractiveness and persuasion. *Journal of Personality and Social Psychology, 37*(8), 1387.

Chaiken, S. (1980). Heuristic versus systematic information processing and the use of source versus message cues in persuasion. *Journal of Personality and Social Psychology, 39*(5), 752–766.

Choi, I., & Nisbett, R. E. (1998). Situational salience and cultural differences in the correspondence bias and actor-observer bias. *Personality and Social Psychology Bulletin, 24*(9), 949–960.

Cialdini, R. B., Cacioppo, J. T., Bassett, R., & Miller, J. A. (1978). Low-ball procedure for producing compliance: Commitment then cost. *Journal of Personality and Social Psychology, 36*(5), 463–476.

Cohen, D., Nisbett, R.E., Bowdle, B.R., & Schwarz, N. (1996). Insult, aggression, and the southern culture of honor: "An experimental ethnography." *Journal of Personality and Social Psychology, 70,* 945–960.

Clark, K.B. & Clark, M. K. (1947). Racial identification and preference in Negro children. In T. Newcomb & E. Hartley (Eds.), *Readings in social psychology,* (169–178). New York, NY: Holt, Rinehart & Winston.

Clark, J. K., & Wegener, D. T. (2013). Message position, information processing, and persuasion: The Discrepancy Motives Model. *Advances in Experimental Social Psychology, 47,* 189–232.

Conner, M., Godin, G., Sheeran, P., & Germain, M. (2013). Some feelings are more important: Cognitive attitudes, affective attitudes, anticipated affect, and blood donation. *Health Psychology, 32*(3), 264–272.

Craig, I. W., & Halton, K. E. (2009). Genetics of human aggressive behaviour. *Human Genetics, 126,* 101–113.

Cuddy, A. J., Glick P., & Beninger, A. (2011). The dynamics of warmth and competence judgments, and their outcomes in organizations. *Research in Organizational Behavior, 31,* 73–98.

D'Angelo, J., & Van Der Heide, B. (2013). The formation of physician impressions in online communities: Negativity, positivity, and nonnormativity effects. *Communication Research, 43*(1), 49–72.

Dabbs Jr, J. M., Jurkovic, G. J., & Frady, R. L. (1991). Salivary testosterone and cortisol among late adolescent male offenders. *Journal of Abnormal Child Psychology, 19*(4), 469–478.

Darley, J. M., & Latané, B. (1968). Bystander intervention in emergencies: Diffusion of responsibility. *Journal of Personality and Social Psychology, 8,* 377–383.

Dasgupta, N. & Rivera, L.M. (2008). When social context matters: The influence of long-term contact and short-term exposure to admired outgroup members on implicit attitudes and behavioral intentions. *Social Cognition, 26*(1), 112–123.

De Koker, P., Mathews, C., Zuch, M., Bastien, S., & Mason-Jones, A. J. (2014). A systematic review of interventions for preventing adolescent intimate partner violence. *Journal of Adolescent Health, 54*(1), 3–13.

Desmet, A., Bastiaensens, S., Van Cleemput, K., Poels, K., Vandebosch, H., & De Bourdeaudhuij, I. (2012). Mobilizing bystanders of cyberbullying: an exploratory study into behavioural determinants of defending the victim. In Wiederhold, B. K. & Riva, G. (Eds.) *Annual review of cybertherapy and telemedicine,* pp. 58–63.

Deutsch, M. & Gerard, H. B. (1955). A study of normative and informational social influences upon individual judgment. *Journal of Abnormal and Social Psychology, 51*(3), 629–636.

Dollard, J., Doob, L. W., Miller, N. E., Mowrer, O. H., & Sears, R. R. (1939). *Frustration and Aggression.* New Haven, CT: Yale University Press.

Dovidio, J. F., Gaertner, S. L., & Kawakami, K. (2003). Intergroup contact: The past, present and the future. *Group Processes & Intergroup Relations, 6,* 5–21.

DeWall, C. N., & Way, B. M. (2014). A new piece to understanding the intimate partner violence puzzle: What role do genetics play? *Violence Against Women, 20*(4), 414–419.

Eaves, L., Heath, A., Martin, N., Maes, H., Neale, M., Kendler, K., & Corey, L. (1999). Comparing the biological and cultural inheritance of personality and social attitudes in the Virginia 30,000 study of twins and their relatives. *Twin Research, 2*(02), 62–80.

Echebarria-Echabe, A., & Guede, E. F. (2003). Extending the theory of realistic conflict to competition in institutional settings: Intergroup status and outcome. *Journal of Social Psychology, 143*(6), 763–782.

Eerland, A., Guadalupe, T. M., & Zwaan, R. A. (2011). Leaning to the left makes the Eiffel Tower seem smaller: Posture-modulated estimation. *Psychological Science, 22*(12), 1511–1514.

Esses, V. M., Jackson, L. M., & Armstrong, T. L. (1998). Intergroup competition and attitudes toward immigrants and immigration: An experimental model of intergroup conflict. *Journal of Social Issues, 54,* 699–724.

Fazio, R. H., Jackson, J. R., Dunton, B. C., & Williams, C. J. (1995). Variability in automatic activation as an unobtrusive measure of racial attitudes: A *bona fide* pipeline? *Journal of Personality and Social Psychology, 69,* 1013–1027.

Feigin, S., Owens, G., & Goodyear-Smith, F. (2014). Theories of human altruism: A systematic review. *Annals of Neuroscience and Psychology, 1*(1), 1–9. Retrieved from http://www.vipoa.org/neuropsychol

Festinger, L., & Carlsmith, J.M. (1959). Cognitive consequences of forced compliance. *Journal of Abnormal and Social Psychology, 58,* 203–210.

Festinger, L., & Maccoby, N. (1964). On resistance to persuasive communications. *Journal of Abnormal and Social Psychology, 68*(4), 359–366.

Fischer, P., Krueger, J. I., Greitemeyer, T., Vogrincic, C., Kastenmüller, A., Frey, D., … & Kainbacher, M. (2011). The bystander-effect: A meta-analytic review on bystander intervention in dangerous and non-dangerous emergencies. *Psychological Bulletin, 137*(4), 517–537.

Fischer, P., & Greitemeyer, T. (2013). The positive bystander effect: Passive bystanders increase helping in situations with high expected negative consequences for the helper. *Journal of Social Psychology, 153*(1), 1–5.

Fiske, S. T., Cuddy, A. J., & Glick, P. (2007). Universal dimensions of social cognition: Warmth and competence. *Trends in Cognitive Sciences, 11*(2), 77–83.

Fiske, S. T., & Taylor, S. E. (2013). *Social cognition: From brains to culture.* Thousand Oaks, CA: Sage.

Flynn, B. S., Worden, J. K., Bunn, J. Y., Connolly, S. W., & Dorwaldt, A. L. (2011). Evaluation of smoking prevention television messages based on the elaboration likelihood model. *Health Education Research, 26*(6) 976–987.

Francis, A. M. & Mialon, H. M. (2014). 'A diamond is forever' and other fairy tales: The relationship between wedding expenses and marriage duration. Social Science Research Network. Retrieved from http://papers.ssrn.com/sol3/Papers.cfm?abstract_id=2501480

Freedman, J. L., & Fraser, S. C. (1966). Compliance without pressure: The foot-in-the-door technique. *Journal of Personality and Social Psychology, 4*(2), 195–202.

Freeman, J. B., & Ambady, N. (2011). Hand movements reveal the time-course of shape and pigmentation processing in face categorization. *Psychonomic Bulletin & Review, 18*(4), 705–712.

Freeman, J. B., Ma, Y., Han, S., & Ambady, N. (2013). Influences of culture and visual context on real-time social categorization. *Journal of Experimental Social Psychology, 49*(2), 206–210.

Gawronski, B., & Bodenhausen, G.V. (2011). The associative-propositional evaluation model: Theory, evidence, and open questions. In M. P. Zanna & J. M. Olsen (Eds.), *Advances in experimental social psychology,* Volume 44 (59–127). San Diego, CA: Elsevier.

George, J. F. (2004). The theory of planned behavior and Internet purchasing. *Internet Research, 14*(3), 198–212.

Gamble, J. L., & Hess, J. J. (2012). Temperature and violent crime in Dallas, Texas: Relationships and implications of climate change. *Western Journal of Emergency Medicine, 13*(3), 239– 246.

Gigerenzer, G., & Gaissmaier, W. (2011). Heuristic decision making. *Annual Review of Psychology, 62,* 451–482.

Gini, G., & Espelage, D. L. (2014). Peer victimization, cyberbullying, and suicide risk in children and adolescents. *JAMA, 312*(5), 545–546.

Gotlieb, M. R., Scholl, R. M., Ridout, T. N., Goldstein, K. M., & Shah, D. V. (2017). Cumulative and long-term campaign advertising effects on trust and talk. *International Journal of Public Opinion Research, 29*(1), 1–22. doi: 10.1093/ijpor/edv047

Gottman, J. M. & Silver, N. (1999). *The seven principles for making marriage work: A practical guide from the country's foremost relationship expert.* New York, NY: Three Rivers Press.

Greenfeld, L.A. (1998). *Alcohol and crime: An analysis of national data on the prevalence of alcohol involvement in crime.* Washington, DC: Document NCJ-168632, Bureau of Justice Statistics. Retrieved August 20, 2008, from http://www.ojp.usdoj.gov/bjs

Greenwald, A. G., Banaji, M. R., Rudman, L. A., Farnham, S. D., Nosek, B. A., & Mellott, D. S. (2002). A unified theory of implicit attitudes, stereotypes, self-esteem, and self-concept. *Psychological Review, 109,* 3–25.

Greenwald, A. G., McGhee, D. E., & Schwartz, J. K. L. (1998). Measuring individual differences in implicit cognition: The Implicit Association Test. *Journal of Personality and Social Psychology, 74,* 1464–1480.

Guéguen, N. (2002). Foot-in-the-door technique and computer-mediated communication. *Computers in Human Behavior, 18*(1), 11–15.

Guéguen, N., Jacob, C., & Meineri, S. (2011). Effects of the door-in-the-face technique on restaurant customers' behavior. *International Journal of Hospitality Management, 30*(3), 759–761.

Guéguen, N., Pascual, A., & Dagot, L. (2002). Low-ball and compliance to a request: An application in a field setting. *Psychological Reports, 91*(1), 81–84.

Guerin, B. (1986). Mere presence effects in humans: A review. *Journal of Personality and Social Psychology, 22,* 38–77.

Hahn, A., Judd, C. M., Hirsh, H. K., & Blair, I. V. (2014). Awareness of implicit attitudes. *Journal of Experimental Psychology, 143*(3), 1369–1392.

Hanson, K. L., Medina, K. L., Padula, C. B., Tapert, S. F., & Brown, S. A. (2011). Impact of adolescent alcohol and drug use on neuropsychological functioning in young adulthood: 10-year outcomes. *Journal of Child & Adolescent Substance Abuse, 20,* 135–154.

Harkins, S. G. & Szymanski, K. (1989). Social loafing and group evaluation. *Journal of Personality and Social Psychology, 56,* 934–941.

Hatemi, P. K., Gillespie, N. A., Eaves, L. J., Maher, B. S., Webb, B. T., Heath, A. C., … & Martin, N. G. (2011). A genome-wide analysis of liberal and conservative political attitudes. *Journal of Politics, 73*(1), 271–285.

Hatfield, E., & Sprecher, S. (1986). Measuring passionate love in intimate relationships. *Journal of Adolescence, 9*(4), 383–410.

Heider, F. (1958). *The psychology of interpersonal relations.* New York, NY: Wiley.

Hein, S., Grumm, M., & Fingerle, M. (2011). Is contact with people with disabilities a guarantee for positive implicit and explicit attitudes? *European Journal of Special Needs Education, 26*(4), 509–522.

Herman, C. P. (2015). The social facilitation of eating: A review. *Appetite, 86,* 61–73.

Hines, D. A., & Douglas, E. M. (2010a). Intimate terrorism by women towards men: Does it exist? *Journal of Aggression, Conflict, and Peace Research, 2*(3), 36–56.

Hines, D. A., & Douglas, E. M. (2010b). A closer look at men who sustain intimate terrorism by women. *Partner Abuse,* 1(3), 286–313. doi: 10.1891/1946-6560.1.3.286

Hite, D. M., Voelker, T., & Robertson, A. (2014). Measuring perceived anonymity: The development of a context independent instrument. *Journal of Methods and Measurement in the Social Sciences, 5*(1), 22–39.

Hovland, C. I., Janis, I. L., & Kelley, H. H. (1953). *Communication and persuasion; psychological studies of opinion change.* New Haven, CT: Yale University Press.

Hurley, D. (2005, April 19). Divorce rate: It's not as high as you think. *New York Times.* Retrieved from http://www.nytimes.com/2005/04/19/health/divorce-rate-its-not-as-high-as-you-think.html

Jackson, J. M. & Williams, K. D. (1988). Social loafing: A review and theoretical analysis. Unpublished manuscript. Fordham University.

Janis, I. L. (1972). Victims of groupthink: A psychological study of foreign-policy decisions and fiascoes. Oxford, England: Houghton-Mifflin.

Jennings, W. G., Okeem, C., Piquero, A. R., Sellers, C. S., Theobald, D., & Farrington, D. P. (2017). Dating and intimate partner violence among young persons ages 15–30: Evidence from a systematic review. *Aggression and Violent Behavior, 33,* 107–125.

Jensen-Campbell, L., Graziano W. G., & West, S. G. (1995). Dominance, prosocial orientation, and female preferences: Do nice guys really finish last? *Journal of Personality & Social Psychology, 68,* 427–440.

Jeong, S. H., & Hwang, Y. (2015). Multitasking and persuasion: The role of structural interference. *Media Psychology, 18*(4), 451-474. doi: 10.1080/15213269.2014.933114.

Jones, E. E. & Nisbett, R. (1971). The actor and the observer: Divergent perceptions of the causes of behavior. In E. E. Jones et al. (Eds.), *Attribution: Perceiving the causes of behavior,* (79–94). Morristown, NJ: General Learning Press.

Jones, E. E. (1998). Major developments in five decades of social psychology. In D. T. Gilbert, S. T. Fiske, & G. Lindzey (Eds.), *The Handbook of Social Psychology* (4th ed., Vol. 1, pp. 3). Boston, MA: McGraw-Hill.

Katsikopoulos, K. V. (2011). Psychological heuristics for making inferences: Definition, performance, and the emerging theory and practice. *Decision Analysis, 8*(1), 10–29.

Kennedy, S., & Ruggles, S. (2014). Breaking up is hard to count: The rise of divorce in the United States, 1980–2010. *Demography, 51*(2), 587–598.

Kerr, N. L., & Brunn, S. E. (1983). Dispensability of member effort and group motivation losses: Free-rider effects. *Journal of Personality and Social Psychology, 44,* 7–94.

Kervyn, N. Yzerbyt, V., & Judd, C. M. (2010). Compensation between warmth and competence: Antecedents and consequences of a negative relation between the two fundamental dimensions of social perception. *European Review of Social Psychology, 21,* 155–187.

Khan, R. F., & Sutcliffe, A. (2014). Attractive agents are more persuasive. *International Journal of Human-Computer Interaction, 30*(2), 142–150.

Kim, M., & Lennon, S. (2008). The effects of visual and verbal information on attitudes and purchase intentions in internet shopping. *Psychology and Marketing, 25*(2), 146–178.

Kitayama, S., & Park, J. (2010). Cultural neuroscience of the self: Understanding the social grounding of the brain. *Social Cognitive and Affective Neuroscience, 5*(2–3), 111–129.

Kowalski, R. M., Limber, S. P., Limber, S., & Agatston, P. W. (2012). Cyberbullying: Bullying in the digital age. John Wiley & Sons.

Kowalski, R. M., Giumetti, G. W., Schroeder, A. N., & Lattanner, M. R. (2014). Bullying in the digital age: A critical review and meta-analysis of cyberbullying research among youth. *Psychological Bulletin, 140*(4), 1073-1137.

Labarre, M., Bourassa, C., Holden, G. W., Turcotte, P., & Letourneau, N. (2016). Intervening with fathers in the context of intimate partner violence: An analysis of ten programs and suggestions for a research agenda. *Journal of Child Custody, 13*(1), 1–29.

Latané, B. (1981). The psychology of social impact. *American Psychologist, 36,* 343–356.

Latané, B., & Darley, J. M. (1970). The unresponsive bystander: Why doesn't he help? New York, NY: Appleton–Century–Crofts.

Lau, R. R., Andersen, D. J., Ditonto, T. M., Kleinberg, M. S., & Redlawsk, D. P. (2017). Effect of media environment diversity and advertising tone on information search, selective exposure, and affective polarization. *Political Behavior, 39*(1), 231–255. doi: 10.1007/s11109-016-9354-8

Lenhart, A., Madden, M., Smith, A., Purcell, K., Zickuhr, K., & Rainie, L. (2011, November 8). *Teens, kindness and cruelty on social network sites.* Retrieved August 25, 2017, from http://www.pewinternet.org/2011/11/09/teens-kindness-and-cruelty-on-social-network-sites/

Lewis, D. O., Pincus, J. H., Feldman, M., Jackson, L., & Bard, B. (1986). Psychiatric, neurological, and psychoeducational characteristics of 15 death row inmates in the United States. *American Journal of Psychiatry, 143,* 838–845.

Lieber, C. (2014, January). *Why is CrossFit so popular right now?* Racked. Retrieved from https://www.racked.com/2014/1/6/7626799/why-crossfit-is-all-the-rage-these-days

Lieberman, M. D. (2010). *Social cognitive neuroscience.* Hoboken, NJ: John Wiley & Sons.

Lovibond, S., & Adams, W. (1979). The effects of three experimental prison environments on the behaviour of non-convict volunteer subjects. *Australian Psychologist, 14*(3), 273–287.

Lozada, M., D'Adamo, P., & Fuentes, M. A. (2011). Beneficial effects of human altruism. *Journal of Theoretical Biology, 289,* 12–16.

Lumsdaine, A. A., & Janis, I. L. (1953). Resistance to "counterpropaganda" produced by one-sided and two-sided "propaganda" presentations. *Public Opinion Quarterly, 17*(3), 311–318.

Lu, A. S. (2013). An experimental test of the persuasive effect of source similarity in narrative and nonnarrative health blogs. *Journal of Medical Internet Research, 15*(7), e142. doi: 10.2196/jmir.2386

Madden, M., Lenhart, A., Cortesi, S., Gasser, U., Duggan, M., Smith, A., & Beaton, M. (2013, May 21). Part 1: Teens and Social Media Use. Retrieved August 25, 2017, from http://www.pewinternet.org/2013/05/21/part-1-teens-and-social-media-use/

Magee, R. G. (2013). Can a print publication be equally effective online? Testing the effect of medium type on marketing communications. *Marketing Letters, 24*(1), 85–95.

Manning, R., Levine, M., & Collins, A. (2007). The Kitty Genovese murder and the social psychology of helping: The parable of the 38 witnesses. *American Psychologist, 62*(6), 555–562.

Masten, C. L., Morelli, S. A., & Eisenberger, N. I. (2011). An fMRI investigation of empathy for 'social pain' and subsequent prosocial behavior. *Neuroimage, 55*(1), 381–388.

Masuda, T., & Nisbett, R. E. (2001). Attending holistically versus analytically: Comparing the context sensitivity of Japanese and Americans. *Journal of Personality and Social Psychology, 81*(5), 922–934.

Miles, D. R., & Carey, G. (1997). Genetic and environmental architecture of human aggression. *Journal of Personality and Social Psychology, 72,* 207–217.

Milgram, S. (1963). Behavioral study of obedience: An experimental view. *The Journal of Abnormal and Social Psychology, 67*(4), 371-378.

Milgram, S. (1965). Some conditions of obedience and disobedience to authority. *Human Relations, 18*(1), 57–76.

Milgram, S. (1974). Obedience to authority: An experimental view. New York: Harper and Row.

Montoya, R. M., & Horton, R. S. (2013). A meta-analytic investigation of the processes underlying the similarity-attraction effect. *Journal of Social and Personal Relationships, 30*(1), 64–94.

Montoya, E. R., Terburg, D., Bos, P. A., & Van Honk, J. (2012). Testosterone, cortisol, and serotonin as key regulators of social aggression: A review and theoretical perspective. *Motivation and Emotion, 36*(1), 65–73.

Moreland, R. L., & Beach, S. R. (1992). Exposure effects in the classroom: The development of affinity among students. *Journal of Experimental Social Psychology, 28*(3), 255–276.

Morris, M. W., Nisbett, R. E., & Peng, K. (1995). Causal attribution across domains and cultures. In D. Sperber, D. Premack, & A. J. Premack (Eds.), *Symposia of the Fyssen Foundation. Causal cognition: A multidisciplinary debate* (pp. 577-614). New York: Clarendon Press/Oxford University Press.

Moskowitz, G. B. (2005). *Social cognition: Understanding self and others.* Guilford Press.

Myers, D. (2016, July 18). Still fearing the wrong things. The Psychology Community blog post. Retrieved August 29, 2017, from https://community.macmillan.com/community/the-psychology-community/blog/2016/07/18/still-fearing-the-wrong-things

Napolitan, D. A., & Goethals, G. R. (1979). The attribution of friendliness. *Journal of Experimental Social Psychology, 15,* 105–113.

Neff, K. D. (2011). Self-compassion, self-esteem, and well-being. *Social and Personality Psychology Compass, 5*(1), 1–12.

Newcomb, T. M. (1956). The prediction of interpersonal attraction. *American Psychologist, 11*(11), 575–586.

Newheiser, A. K. & Olsen, K. R. (2012). White and black American children's implicit intergroup bias. *Journal of Experimental Social Psychology, 48*(1), 264–270.

Nisbett, R. E., & Cohen, D. (1996). *Culture of honor: The psychology of violence in the South.* Boulder, CO: Westview Press.

NoBullying.com (2014). *Cyberbullying and bullying statistics 2014, finally!* Retrieved from http://nobullying.com/cyberbullying-bullying-statistics-2014-finally/

NoBullying.com (2015, December 22). *Cyber bullying girls, are they more common?* Retrieved from http://nobullying.com/is-cyber-bullying-more-common-with-girls/

Nosek, B. A., Banaji, M. R., & Greenwald, A. G. (2002). Harvesting implicit group attitudes and beliefs from a demonstration web site. *Group Dynamics: Theory, Research, and Practice, 6*(1), 101–115.

Oltmanns, T. F., & Turkheimer, E. (2009). Person perception and personality pathology. *Current Directions in Psychological Science, 18*(1), 32–36.

Ortigue, S., Bianchi-Demicheli, F., Patel, N., Frum, C., & Lewis, J. W. (2010). Neuroimaging of love: fMRI meta-analysis evidence toward new perspectives in sexual medicine. *Journal of Sexual Medicine, 7*(11), 3541–3552.

Olsen, R. (2014, November 07). What makes for a stable marriage? Retrieved from http://www.randalolson.com/2014/10/10/what-makes-for-a-stable-marriage/

Olson, R. (2014, October 10). *What makes for a stable marriage?* Blog post. Retrieved from http://www.randalolson.com/2014/10/10/what-makes-for-a-stable-marriage/

Oyserman, D., Coon, H. M., & Kemmelmeier, M. (2002). Rethinking individualism and collectivism: Evaluation of theoretical assumptions and meta-analyses. *Psychological Bulletin, 128*(1), 3–72.

Park, H., Xiang, Z., Josiam, B., & Kim, H. (2014). Personal profile information as cues of credibility in online travel reviews. *Anatolia, 25*(1), 13–23.

Patchin, Justin W. (2016) Summary of cyberbullying research. Retrieved from https://cyberbullying.org/summary-of-our-cyberbullying-research

Patzer, G. L. (1983). Source credibility as a function of communicator physical attractiveness. *Journal of Business Research, 11*(2), 229–241.

Pavlov, K. A., Chistiakov, D. A., & Chekhonin, V. P. (2012). Genetic determinants of aggression and impulsivity in humans. *Journal of Applied Genetics, 53*(1), 61–82.

Pearce, N., Cross, D., Monks, H., Waters, S., & Falconer, S. (2011). Current evidence of best practice in whole-school bullying intervention and its potential to inform cyberbullying interventions. *Australian Journal of Guidance and Counselling, 21*(01), 1–21.

Penner, L. A., Dovidio, J. F., Piliavin, J. A., & Schroeder, D. A. (2005). Prosocial behavior: Multilevel perspectives. *Annual Review of Psychology, 56,* 365–392.

Pettigrew, T. F., & Meertens, R. W. (1995). Subtle and blatant prejudice in Western Europe. *European Journal of Social Psychology, 25*(1), 57–75.

Pettigrew, T. F., & Tropp, L. R. (2006). A meta-analytic test of intergroup contact theory. *Journal of Personality and Social Psychology, 90,* 751–783.

Pettigrew, T. F., & Tropp, L. R. (2008). How does intergroup contact reduce prejudice? Meta-analytic tests of three mediators. *European Journal of Social Psychology, 38*(6), 922–934.

Petty, R. E. & Cacioppo, J. T. (1986). The elaboration likelihood model of persuasion. In L. Berkowitz (Ed.), *Advances in Experimental Social Psychology, 19,* 123–205. New York, NY: Academic Press.

Petty, R. E., & Wegener, D. T. (2014). Thought systems, argument quality, and persuasion. In R. S. Wyer, Jr. & T. K. Srull (Eds.), *The content, structure, and operation of thought systems* (147–162). Hillsdale, NJ: Lawrence Erlbaum Associates.

Petty, R. E., Wheeler, S. C., & Tormala, Z. L. (2003). Persuasion and attitude change. *Handbook of psychology.* Pew Internet Research Project (2011).

Pornpitakpan, C. (2004). The persuasiveness of source credibility: A critical review of five decades' evidence. *Journal of Applied Social Psychology, 34*(2), 243–281.

Post, J. M. & Panis, L. K. (2011). Crimes of obedience: "Groupthink" at Abu Ghraib. *International Journal of Group Psychotherapy, 61*(1), 49–66.

Postmes, T., & Spears, R. (1998). Deindividuation and antinormative behavior: A meta-analysis. *Psychological Bulletin, 123*(3), 238–259.

Powers, J., & Comstock, G. (2012). The rumors of television's demise have been greatly exaggerated: What the data say about the future of television content in a child's digital world. *Journal of Mass Communication Journalism, 2*(111), 1–8.

Pruitt, D. G., & Teger, A. I. (1969). The risky shift in group betting. *Journal of Experimental Social Psychology, 5*(2), 115–126.

Puckett, J. M., Petty, R. E., Cacioppo, J. T., & Fischer, D. L. (1983). The relative impact of age and attractiveness stereotypes on persuasion. *Journal of Gerontology, 38*(3), 340–343.

Ratner, K. G. & Amodio, D. M. (2013). Seeing "us vs. them": Minimal group effects on the neural encoding of faces. *Journal of Experimental Social Psychology, 49,* 298–301.

Reagans, R. (2011). Close encounters: Analyzing how social similarity and propinquity contribute to strong network connections. *Organization Science, 22*(4), 835–849.

Reichelt, J., Sievert, J., & Jacob, F. (2014). How credibility affects eWOM reading: The influences of expertise, trustworthiness, and similarity on utilitarian and social functions. *Journal of Marketing Communications, 20*(1–2), 65–81.

Reicher, S., & Haslam, S. A. (2006). Rethinking the psychology of tyranny: The BBC prison study. *The British Journal of Social Psychology, 45,* 1–40.

Reis, H. T., Maniaci, M. R., Caprariello, P. A., Eastwick, P. W., & Finkel, E. J. (2011). Familiarity does indeed promote attraction in live interaction. *Journal of Personality and Social Psychology, 101*(3), 557–570.

Rhee, S. H., & Waldman, I. D. (2002). Genetic and environmental influences on antisocial behavior: A meta-analysis of twin and adoption studies. *Psychological Bulletin, 128*(3), 490–529.

Rhodes, N., & Wood, W. (1992). Self-esteem and intelligence affect influenceability: The mediating role of message reception. *Psychological Bulletin, 111*(1), 156–171.

Ross, L. (1977). The intuitive psychologist and his shortcomings. In L. Berkowitz (Ed.), *Advances in experimental social psychology.* (Vol. 10, pp. 173–220). New York, NY: Academic Press.

Rosenberg, S., Nelson, C., & Vivekananthan, P. S. (1968). A multidimensional approach to the structure of personality impressions. *Journal of Personality and Social Psychology, 9*(4), 283–294.

Rosenblatt, P. C. (1966). Persuasion as a function of varying amounts of distraction. *Psychonomic Science, 5*(2), 85–86.

Rowe, D. C., Almeida, D. M., & Jacobson, K. C. (1999). School context and genetic influences on aggression in adolescence. *Psychological Science, 10,* 277–280.

Royne, M. B., Levy, M. & Martinez, J. (2011). The public health implications of consumers' environmental concern and their willingness to pay for an eco-friendly product. *Journal of Consumer Affairs, 45*(2), 329–343.

Ruggieri, S., & Boca, S. (2013). At the roots of product placement: The mere exposure effect. *Europe's Journal of Psychology, 9*(2), 246–258.

Schneider, D. J. (1973). Implicit personality theory: A review. *Psychological Bulletin, 79*(5), 294–309.

Schneider, S. K., O'Donnell, L., Stueve, A., & Coulter, R. W. (2012). Cyberbullying, school bullying, and psychological distress: A regional census of high school students. *American Journal of Public Health, 102*(1), 171–177.

Schwab, N., Harton, H.C., Cullum, J.G. (2014). The effects of emergent norms and attitudes on recycling behavior. *Environment and Behavior, 46,* 403–422.

Sherif, M. (1966). *In common predicament: Social psychology of intergroup conflict and cooperation.* Boston, MA: Houghton Mifflin.

Simms, A., & Nichols, T. (2014). Social loafing: A review of the literature. *Journal of Management Policy and Practice, 15*(1), 58–67.

Slepian, M., Weisbuch, M., Rule, N.O. & Ambady, N. (2011). Tough and tender: Embodied categorization of gender. *Psychological Science, 22*(1), 26–28.

Smith, C. T., & De Houwer, J. (2014). The impact of persuasive messages on IAT performance is moderated by source attractiveness and likeability. *Social Psychology, 45,* 437–448.

Smith, A., & Duggan, M. (2013). *Online dating and relationships.* Pew Research Center. Retrieved from http://www.pewinternet.org/2013/10/21/online-dating-relationships/

Sourander, A., Klomek, A. B., Ikonen, M., Lindroos, J., Luntamo, T., Koskelainen, M., … & Helenius, H. (2010). Psychosocial risk factors associated with cyberbullying among adolescents: A population-based study. *Archives of General Psychiatry, 67*(7), 720–728.

Sprecher, S. (2013). Correlates of couples' perceived similarity at the initiation stage and currently. *Interpersona: An International Journal on Personal Relationships, 7*(2), 180–195.

Sprecher, S., & Regan, P. C. (1998). Passionate and companionate love in courting and young married couples. *Sociological Inquiry, 68*(2), 163–185.

Statistic Brain Research Institute. (2017, May 12). Online dating statistics. Retrieved from https://www.statisticbrain.com/online-dating-statistics/

Steele, C. M. & Aronson, J. (1995). Stereotype threat and the intellectual test performance of African-Americans. *Journal of Personality and Social Psychology, 69,* 797–811.

Sternberg, R. J. (1995). Love as a story. *Journal of Social and Personal Relationships, 12,* 541–546.

Sternberg, R. J. (2013). Searching for love. *Sociological Review, 27,* 295–303.

Stiles-Shields, C., & Carroll, R. A. (2015). Same-sex domestic violence: Prevalence, unique aspects, and clinical implications. *Journal of Sex & Marital Therapy, 41*(6), 636–648. doi: 10.1080/0092623X.2014.958792

Stopfer, J. M., Egloff, B., Nestler, S., & Back, M. D. (2014). Personality expression and impression formation in online social networks: An integrative approach to understanding the processes of accuracy, impression management and meta-accuracy. *European Journal of Personality, 28*(1), 73–94.

Sullivan, B. (2006, Aug 9). *Cyberbullying newest threat to kids.* Retrieved from http://www.nbcnews.com/id/14272228/ns/technology_and_science-security/t/cyberbullying-newest-threat-kids/

Sullivan, B. (2016). NBCNews.com. 2006. "Cyberbullying newest threat to kids." http://www.nbcnews.com/id/14272228/ns/technology_and_science-security/t/cyberbullying-newest-threat-kids/

Tajfel, H. (Ed.). (1982). *Social identity and intergroup relations.* New York, NY: Cambridge University Press.

Todorov, A., Pakrashi, M., & Oosterhof, N. N. (2009). Evaluating faces on trustworthiness after minimal time exposure. *Social Cognition, 27*(6), 813–833.

Todorov, A., & Porter, J. M. (2014). Misleading first impressions different for different facial images of the same person. *Psychological Science, 25*(7), 1404–1417.

Tokunaga, R. S. (2010). Following you home from school: A critical review and synthesis of research on cyberbullying victimization. *Computers in Human Behavior, 26*(3), 277–287.

Tol, W. A., Greene, M. C., Likindikoki, S., Misinzo, L., Ventevogel, P., Bonz, A. G., … & Mbwambo, J. K. K. (2017). An integrated intervention to reduce intimate partner violence and psychological distress with refugees in low-resource settings: Study protocol for the Nguvu cluster randomized trial. *BMC Psychiatry, 17*(186), 1–13. doi: 10.1186/s12888-017-1338-7

Toomey, T. L., Erickson, D. J., Carlin, B. P., Lenk, K. M., Quick, H. S., Jones, A. M., & Harwood, E.M. (2012). The association between density of alcohol establishments and violent crime within urban neighborhoods. *Alcohol: Clinical & Experimental Research, 36*(8), 1468–1473.

Trivers, R. L. (1971). The evolution of reciprocal altruism. *Quarterly Review of Biology, 46,* 35–57.

Tsikerdekis, M. (2013). The effects of perceived anonymity and anonymity states on conformity and groupthink in online communities: A Wikipedia study. *Journal of the American Society for Information Science and Technology, 64*(5), 1001–1015.

Tsintsadze-Maass, E. & Maass, R. W. (2014). Groupthink and terrorist radicalization. *Terrorism and Political Violence, 0,* 1–24.

Turner, M., & Hunt, N. (2014). What does your profile picture say about you? The accuracy of thin-slice personality judgments from social networking sites made at zero-acquaintance. In *Social Computing and Social Media* (pp. 506–516). Springer International Publishing.

Vandello, J. A., Cohen, D., & Ransom, S. (2008). U.S. southern and northern differences in perceptions of norms about aggression mechanisms for the perpetuation of a culture of honor. *Journal of Cross-Cultural Psychology, 39*(2), 162–177.

von Dawans, B., Fischbacher, U., Kirschbaum, C., Fehr, E., & Heinrichs, M. (2012). The social dimension of stress reactivity acute stress increases prosocial behavior in humans. *Psychological Science, 23*(6), 651–660.

Voyles, E. C., Bailey, S. F., & Durik, A. M. (2015). New pieces of the jigsaw classroom: Increasing accountability to reduce social loafing in student group projects. *The New School Psychology Bulletin, 13*(1), 11–20.

Wang, C. C., & Yeh, W. J. (2013). Avatars with sex appeal as pedagogical agents: Attractiveness, trustworthiness, expertise, and gender differences. *Journal of Educational Computing Research, 48*(4), 403–429.

Ward, B. W., Clarke, T. C., Nugent, C. N., Schiller, J. S. (2016). Early release of selected estimates based on data from the 2015 National Health Interview Survey. National Center for Health Statistics. Available from: http://www.cdc.gov/nchs/nhis.htm

Waytz, A., Zaki, J., & Mitchell, J. P. (2012). Response of dorsomedial prefrontal cortex predicts altruistic behavior. *Journal of Neuroscience, 32*(22), 7646–7650.

Webber, J. (2013). Character, attitude, and disposition. *European Journal of Philosophy, 23 (4),* 1082–1096.

Wells, S., Graham, K., Tremblay, P. F., & Magyarody, N. (2011). Not just the booze talking: Trait aggression and hypermasculinity distinguish perpetrators from victims of male barroom aggression. *Alcoholism: Clinical & Experimental Research, 35*(4), 613–620.

Weng, H. Y., Fox, A. S., Shackman, A. J., Stodola, D. E., Caldwell, J. Z., Olson, M. C., Roger, G. M. & Davidson, R. J. (2013). Compassion training alters altruism and neuralresponses to suffering. *Psychological Science, 24*(7), 1171–1180.

White, H. R., Brick, J., Hansell, S. (1993). A longitudinal investigation of alcohol use and aggression in adolescence. *Journal of Studies on Alcohol,* Supplement no. 11, 62–77.

Wilder, D. A. (1981). Perceiving persons as a group: Categorization and intergroup relations. In D. L. Hamilton (Ed.), *Cognitive processes in stereotyping and intergroup behavior.* Hillsdale, NJ: Erlbaum.

Willis, J., & Todorov, A. (2006). First impressions making up your mind after a 100-ms exposure to a face. *Psychological Science, 17*(7), 592–598.

World Health Organization. (2013). *Global and regional estimates of violence against women: Prevalence and health effects of intimate partner violence and non-partner sexual violence.* Retrieved from http://apps.who.int/iris/bitstream/10665/85239/1/9789241564625_eng.pdf?ua=1

Wunsch, G., Russo, F., & Mouchart, M. (2010). Do we necessarily need longitudinal data to infer causal relations? *Bulletin of Sociological Methodology, 106*(1), 5–18. doi:10.1177/0759106309360114

Yardi, S., & Boyd, D. (2010). Dynamic debates: An analysis of group polarization over time on twitter. *Bulletin of Science, Technology, & Society, 30*(5), 316–327.

Ying, X., Li, H., Jiang, S., Peng, F., & Lin, Z. (2014). Group laziness: The effect of socialloafing on group performance. *Social Behavior and Personality: An International Journal, 42*(3), 465–471.

Zahn-Waxler, C., Friedman, R. J., Cole, P. M., Mizuta, I., & Hiruma, N. (1996). Japanese and United States preschool children's responses to conflict and distress. *Child Development, 67,* 2462–2477.

Zajonc, R. B. (1965). Social facilitation. *Science, 149,* 269–274.

Zajonc, R. B. (1968). Attitudinal effects of mere exposure. *Journal of Personality and Social Psychology, 9*(2p2), 1–27.

Zarate, M. A., Garcia, B., Garza, A. A., & Hitlan, R. T. (2004). Cultural threat and perceived realistic group conflict as dual predictors of prejudice. *Journal of Experimental Social Psychology, 40*(1), 99–105.

Zimbardo, P. G. (1969). The human choice: Individuation, reason, and order versus deindividuation, impulse, and chaos. *Nebraska Symposium on Motivation, 17,* 237–307.

Zimbardo, (1971). The pathology of imprisonment. *Society, 9*(6), 4–8.

Chapter 14

Adelstein, J. S., Shehzad, Z., Mennes, M., DeYoung, C. G., Zuo, X.-N., Kelly, C., … & Castellanos, F. X. (2011). Personality is reflected in the brain's intrinsic functional architecture. *PloS one, 6*(11), e27633.

Alderfer, C. P. (1969). An empirical test of a new theory of human needs. *Organizational Behavior and Human Performance, 4*(2), 142–175. Doi: http://dx.doi.org/10.1016/0030-5073(69)90004-X

Aldridge, J., Kilgo, J. L., & Jepkemboi, G. (2014). Four hidden matriarchs of psychoanalysis: The relationship of Lou von Salome, Karen Horney, Sabina Spielrein and Anna Freud to Sigmund Freud. *International Journal of Psychology and Counselling, 6*(4), 32–39.

Alegria, A. A., Blanco, C., Petry, N. M., Skodol, A. E., Liu, S.-M., Grant, B., & Hasin, D. (2013). Sex differences in antisocial personality disorder: Results from the national epidemiological survey on alcohol and related conditions. *Personality Disorders: Theory, Research, and Treatment, 4*(3), 214–222.

Allik, J., & McCrae, R. R. (2004). Toward a geography of personality traits patterns of profiles across 36 cultures. *Journal of Cross-Cultural Psychology, 35*(1), 13–28.

Allport, G. W., & Odbert, H. S. (1936). *Trait-names: A psycho-lexical study.* Princeton, NJ: Psychological Review.

American Psychiatric Association. (2013). *Diagnostic and statistical manual of mental disorders, (DSM-5®).* Washington, DC: American Psychiatric Pub.

Amodio, D. M., Master, S. L., Yee, C. M., & Taylor, S. E. (2008). Neurocognitive components of the behavioral inhibition and activation systems: Implications for theories of self-regulation. *Psychophysiology, 45*(1), 11–19.

Anderson, M. L. (2012). How not to do personality neuroscience: Brain structure and the Big Five. Retrieved February 21, 2016, from http://www.psychologytoday.com/blog/after-phrenology/201202/how-not-do-personality-neuroscience-brain-structure-and-the-big-five

April, K. A., Dharani, B., & Peters, K. (2012). Impact of locus of control expectancy on level of well-being. *Review of European Studies, 4*(2), 124–137.

Archer, R. P., Buffington-Vollum, J. K., Stredny, R. V., & Handel, R. W. (2006). A survey of psychological test use patterns among forensic psychologists. *Journal of Personality Assessment, 87*(1), 84–94.

Armstrong, S. J., Cools, E., & Sadler-Smith, E. (2012). Role of cognitive styles in business and management: Reviewing 40 years of research. *International Journal of Management Reviews, 14*(3), 238–262.

Arslan, C., Dilmaç, B., & Hamarta, E. (2009). Coping with stress and trait anxiety in terms of locus of control: A study with Turkish university students. *Social Behavior and Personality: An International Journal, 37*(6), 791–800.

Bandura, A. (1977). Self-efficacy: Toward a unifying theory of behavioral change. *Psychological Review, 84*(2), 191–215.

Bandura, A. (1989). Human agency in social cognitive theory. *American Psychologist, 44*(9), 1175–1184.

Bandura, A., & Locke, E. A. (2003). Negative self-efficacy and goal effects revisited. *Journal of Applied Psychology, 88*(1), 87–99.

Bandura, A., O'Leary, A., Taylor, C. B., Gauthier, J., & Gossard, D. (1987). Perceived self-efficacy and pain control: Opioid and nonopioid mechanisms. *Journal of Personality and Social Psychology, 53*(3), 563–571.

Barrett, P. T., Petrides, K., Eysenck, S. B., & Eysenck, H. J. (1998). The Eysenck Personality Questionnaire: An examination of the factorial similarity of P, E, N, and L across 34 countries. *Personality and Individual Differences, 25*(5), 805–819.

Bayne, E. (2011). *Womb envy: The cause of misogyny and even male achievement?* Paper presented at the Women's Studies International Forum.

Ben-Porath, Y. S., & Tellegen, A. (2008). *MMPI-2-RF: Manual for administration, scoring and interpretation.* Minneapolis, MN: University of Minnesota Press.

Block, J. (1977). P scale and psychosis: Continued concerns. *Journal of Abnormal Psychology, 85,* 431–434.

Block, J., & Robins, R. W. (1993). A longitudinal study of consistency and change in self-esteem from early adolescence to early adulthood. *Child Development, 64*(3), 909–923.

Bouchard Jr, T. J., & Loehlin, J. C. (2001). Genes, evolution, and personality. *Behavior Genetics, 31*(3), 243–273.

Bouchard, T. J. (2004). Genetic influence on human psychological traits a survey. *Current Directions in Psychological Science, 13*(4), 148–151.

Brenner, C. (2007). Freud's great voyage of discovery. *Psychoanalytic Quarterly, 76*(1), 9–25.

Burke, L., & Witt, L. (2002). Moderators of the openness to experience-performance relationship. *Journal of Managerial Psychology, 17*(8), 712–721.

Cairney, J., Hay, J. A., Faught, B. E., Leger, L., & Mathers, B. (2008). Generalized self-efficacy and performance on the 20-metre shuttle run in children. *American Journal of Human Biology, 20,* 132–138.

Cale, E. M., & Lilienfeld, S. O. (2002). Sex differences in psychopathy and antisocial personality disorder:

A review and integration. *Clinical Psychology Review*, 22(8), 1179–1207.

Camara, W. J., Nathan, J. S., & Puente, A. E. (2000). Psychological test usage: Implications in professional psychology. *Professional Psychology: Research and Practice*, 31(2), 141–154.

Carver, C. S., & White, T. L. (1994). Behavioral inhibition, behavioral activation, and affective responses to impending reward and punishment: The BIS/BAS scales. *Journal of Personality and Social Psychology*, 67(2), 319–333.

Cascio, M. I., Magnano, P., Elastico, S., Costantino, V., Zapparrata, V., & Battiato, A. (2014). The relationship among self-efficacy beliefs, external locus of control and work stress in public setting schoolteachers. *Open Journal of Social Sciences*, 2(11), 149–156.

Cattell, H. E. P., & Mead, A. D. (2008). The sixteen personality factor questionnaire (16PF). *The SAGE Handbook of Personality Theory and Assessment*, 2, 135–159.

Cattell, R. B. (1945). The principal trait clusters for describing personality. *Psychological Bulletin*, 42(3), 129–161.

Cervera, S., Lahortiga, F., Angel Martínez-González, M., Gual, P., Irala-Estévez, J. D., & Alonso, Y. (2003). Neuroticism and low self-esteem as risk factors for incident eating disorders in a prospective cohort study. *International Journal of Eating Disorders*, 33(3), 271–280.

Cervone, D., Shadel, W. G., & Jencius, S. (2001). Social-cognitive theory of personality assessment. *Personality and Social Psychology Review*, 5(1), 33–51.

Chapman, B. P., Weiss, A., Barrett, P., & Duberstein, P. (2013). Hierarchical structure of the Eysenck Personality Inventory in a large population sample: Goldberg's trait-tier mapping procedure. *Personality and Individual Differences*, 54(4), 479–484.

Compton, W. M., Conway, K. P., Stinson, F. S., Colliver, J. D., & Grant, B. F. (2005). Prevalence, correlates, and comorbidity of DSM-IV antisocial personality syndromes and alcohol and specific drug use disorders in the United States: Results from the national epidemiologic survey on alcohol and related conditions. *Journal of Clinical Psychiatry*, 66(6), 677–685.

Coolidge, F. L., Moor, C. J., Yamazaki, T. G., Stewart, S. E., & Segal, D. L. (2001). On the relationship between Karen Horney's tripartite neurotic type theory and personality disorder features. *Personality and Individual Differences*, 30(8), 1387–1400.

Corr, P. J., & Cooper, A. J. (2016). The reinforcement sensitivity theory of personality questionnaire (RST-PQ): Development and validation. *Psychological Assessment*, 28(11), 1427–1440.

Costa, P., Terracciano, A., & McCrae, R. R. (2001). Gender differences in personality traits across cultures: Robust and surprising findings. *Journal of Personality and Social Psychology*, 81(2), 322–331.

Costa, P. T., & McCrae, R. R. (1992). *Revised NEO Personality Inventory (NEO-PI-R) and NEO Five-Factor Inventory (NEOFFI) professional manual*. Odessa, FL: Psychological Assessment Resources

Cramer, P. (2000). Defense mechanisms in psychology today: Further processes for adaptation. *American Psychologist*, 55(6), 637–646.

De Brito, S. A., Viding, E., Kumari, V., Blackwood, N., & Hodgins, S. (2013). Cool and hot executive function impairments in violent offenders with antisocial personality disorder with and without psychopathy. *PloS one*, 8(6), e65566.

DeYoung, C. G., & Gray, J. R. (2009). Personality neuroscience: Explaining individual differences in affect, behavior, and cognition. *The Cambridge Handbook of Personality Psychology*, 323–346.

DeYoung, C. G., Hirsh, J. B., Shane, M. S., Papademetris, X., Rajeevan, N., & Gray, J. R. (2010). Testing predictions from personality neuroscience brain structure and the Big Five. *Psychological Science*, 21(6), 820–828.

DeYoung, C. G., Quilty, L. C., Peterson, J. B., & Gray, J. R. (2014). Openness to experience, intellect, and cognitive ability. *Journal of Personality Assessment*, 96(1), 46–52.

Dolan, M., & Völlm, B. (2009). Antisocial personality disorder and psychopathy in women: A literature review on the reliability and validity of assessment instruments. *International Journal of Law and Psychiatry*, 32(1), 2–9.

Eckstein, D., Aycock, K. J., Sperber, M. A., McDonald, J., Van Wiesner, V., Watts, R. E., & Ginsburg, P. (2010). A review of 200 birth-order studies: Lifestyle characteristics. *Journal of Individual Psychology*, 66(4), 408–434.

Egorova, M., Parshikova, O., & Pyankova, S. (2014). Sensation seeking and personality dimensions. *Personality and Individual Differences*, 60, S69.

Elliot, A. J., & Thrash, T. M. (2002). Approach-avoidance motivation in personality: Approach and avoidance temperaments and goals. *Journal of Personality and Social Psychology*, 82(5), 804–818.

Erickson, S. K., Lilienfeld, S. O., & Vitacco, M. J. (2007). A critical examination of the suitability and limitations of psychological tests in family court. *Family Court Review*, 45(2), 157–174.

Eysenck, H. J. (1967). *The biological basis of personality* (Vol. 689): Transaction Publishers.

Eysenck, S., & Zuckerman, M. (1978). The relationship between sensation-seeking and Eysenck's dimensions of personality. *British Journal of Psychology*, 69(4), 483–487.

Eysenck, S. B., & Eysenck, H. J. (1964). An improved short questionnaire for the measurement of extraversion and neuroticism. *Life Sciences*, 3(10), 1103–1109.

Eysenck, S. B., & Eysenck, H. J. (1967). Salivary response to lemon juice as a measure of introversion. *Perceptual and Motor Skills*, 24(3c), 1047–1053.

Eysenck, S. B., Eysenck, H. J., & Barrett, P. (1985). A revised version of the psychoticism scale. *Personality and Individual Differences*, 6(1), 21–29.

Fazel, S., & Danesh, J. (2002). Serious mental disorder in 23,000 prisoners: A systematic review of 62 surveys. *The Lancet*, 359(9306), 545–550.

Ferguson, C. J. (2010). Genetic contributions to antisocial personality and behavior: A meta-analytic review from an evolutionary perspective. *Journal of Social Psychology*, 150(2), 160–180.

Flynn, F. J. (2005). Having an open mind: The impact of openness to experience on interracial attitudes and impression formation. *Journal of Personality and Social Psychology*, 88(5), 816–826.

Freud, A. (1992). *The ego and the mechanisms of defence*: London, England: Karnac Books.

Freud, S. (1920). *A general introduction to psychoanalysis*. New York: Boni and Liveright.

Freud, S. (1961). *New introductory lectures on psycho-analysis* (Vol. 2). New York, NY: W. W. Norton & Company.

Freud, S. (1978). *Basic works of Sigmund Freud* (J. Strachey, Ed.). Franklin Library.

Furnham, A., Richards, S. C., & Paulhus, D. L. (2013). The dark triad of personality: A 10-year review. *Social and Personality Psychology Compass*, 7(3), 199–216.

Gable, P. A., & Harmon-Jones, E. (2013). Trait behavioral approach sensitivity (BAS) relates to early (< 150 ms) electrocortical responses to appetitive stimuli. *Social Cognitive and Affective Neuroscience*, 8(7), 795-798.

Gable, S. L., Reis, H. T., & Elliot, A. J. (2000). Behavioral activation and inhibition in everyday life. *Journal of Personality and Social Psychology*, 78(6), 1135–1149.

Gale, C. R., Batty, G. D., & Deary, I. J. (2008). Locus of control at age 10 years and health outcomes and behaviors at age 30 years: The 1970 British Cohort Study. *Psychosomatic Medicine*, 70(4), 397–403.

Gay, P. (1998). *Freud: A life for our time*. New York, NY: W. W. Norton & Company.

George, J. M., & Zhou, J. (2001). When openness to experience and conscientiousness are related to creative behavior: An interactional approach. *Journal of Applied Psychology*, 86(3), 513–524.

Glenn, A. L., Johnson, A. K., & Raine, A. (2013). Antisocial personality disorder: A current review. *Current Psychiatry Reports*, 15(12), 1–8.

Gray, J. A. (1970). The psychophysiological basis of introversion-extraversion. *Behaviour Research and Therapy*, 8(3), 249–266.

Greening, T. (2006). Five basic postulates of humanistic psychology. *Journal of Humanistic Psychology*, 46(3), 236–239.

Greenwald, A. G., McGhee, D. E., & Schwartz, J. L. (1998). Measuring individual differences in implicit cognition: The implicit association test. *Journal of Personality and Social Psychology*, 74(6), 1464–1480.

Greenwald, A. G., Poehlman, T. A., Uhlmann, E. L., & Banaji, M. R. (2009). Understanding and using the Implicit Association Test: III. Meta-analysis of predictive validity. *Journal of Personality and Social Psychology*, 97(1), 17–41.

Griffith, J. W., Zinbarg, R. E., Craske, M. G., Mineka, S., Rose, R. D., Waters, A. M., & Sutton, J. M. (2010). Neuroticism as a common dimension in the internalizing disorders. *Psychological Medicine*, 40(7), 1125–1136. doi: 10.1017/S0033291709991449

Hall, C., & Lindzey, G. (1978). *Theories of personality*. New York, NY: John Wiley and Sons, Inc.

Hampson, S. E., & Goldberg, L. R. (2006). A first large-cohort study of personality-trait stability over the 40 years between elementary school and midlife. *Journal of Personality and Social Psychology*, 91(4), 763–779. doi: 10.1037/0022-3514.91.4.763

Hansen, J. T. (2000). Psychoanalysis and humanism: A review and critical examination of integrationist efforts with some proposed resolutions. *Journal of Counseling & Development*, 78(1), 21–28.

Harakeh, Z., Scholte, R. H., de Vries, H., & Engels, R. C. (2006). Association between personality and adolescent smoking. *Addictive Behaviors*, 31(2), 232–245.

Harrington, R., & Loffredo, D. A. (2010). MBTI personality type and other factors that relate to preference for online versus face-to-face instruction. *The Internet and Higher Education*, 13(1), 89–95.

Heath, A., & Martin, N. (1990). Psychoticism as a dimension of personality: A multivariate genetic test of Eysenck and Eysenck's psychoticism construct. *Journal of Personality and Social Psychology*, 58(1), 111–121.

Helle, A. C., Trull, T. J., Widiger, T. A., & Mullins-Sweatt, S. N. (2017). Utilizing interview and self-report assessment of the Five-Factor Model to examine convergence with the alternative model for personality disorders. *Personality Disorders: Theory, Research, and Treatment*, 8(3), 247–254.

Heylighen, F. (1992). A cognitive-systemic reconstruction of Maslow's theory of self-actualization. *Behavioral Science*, 37(1), 39–58.

Hirsh, J. B. (2015). Extraverted populations have lower savings rates. *Personality and Individual Differences*, 81, 162–168.

Hirsh, J. B., DeYoung, C. G., Xu, X., & Peterson, J. B. (2010). Compassionate liberals and polite conservatives: Associations of agreeableness with political ideology and moral values. *Personality and Social Psychology Bulletin*, 36(5), 655–664.

Hsieh, P., Sullivan, J. R., & Guerra, N. S. (2007). A closer look at college students: Self-efficacy and goal orientation. *Journal of Advanced Academics*, 18(3), 454–476.

Hunsley, J., Lee, C. M., & Wood, J. M. (2003). Controversial and questionable assessment techniques. In S. O. Lilienfeld, S. J. Lynn, & J. M. Lohr (Eds.), *Science and Pseudoscience in Clinical Psychology* (pp. 39–76). New York, NY: Guilford Press.

Jacobi, J. (1999). *Complex/archetype/symbol in the psychology of CG Jung* (Vol. 21). New York, NY: Routledge.

Jensen-Campbell, L. A., & Graziano, W. G. (2001). Agreeableness as a moderator of interpersonal conflict. *Journal of Personality*, 69(2), 323–362.

Judge, T. A., Higgins, C. A., Thoresen, C. J., & Barrick, M. R. (1999). The Big Five personality traits, general mental ability, and career success across the life span. *Personnel Psychology*, 52(3), 621–652.

Jung, C. G. (1959). *The archetypes and the collective unconscious*. New York, NY: Bollingen Foundation Inc.

Kadden, R. M., & Litt, M. D. (2011). The role of self-efficacy in the treatment of substance use disorders. *Addictive Behaviors*, 36(12), 1120–1126.

Kennedy, R. B., & Kennedy, D. A. (2004). Using the Myers-Briggs type indicator in career counseling. *Journal of Employment Counseling, 41*(1), 38–43.

Kenrick, D. T., & Funder, D. C. (1988). Profiting from controversy: Lessons from the person-situation debate. *American Psychologist, 43*(1), 23–34.

Kirkpatrick, M. A., Stant, K., Downes, S., & Gaither, L. (2008). Perceived locus of control and academic performance: Broadening the construct's applicability. *Journal of College Student Development, 49*(5), 486–496.

Kline, P. (2014). *Fact and fantasy in Freudian theory* (2nd ed.). New York, NY: Routledge.

Komarraju, M., Karau, S. J., & Schmeck, R. R. (2009). Role of the Big Five personality traits in predicting college students' academic motivation and achievement. *Learning and Individual Differences, 19*(1), 47–52.

Kramer, U., de Roten, Y., Perry, J. C., & Despland, J.-N. (2013). Beyond splitting: Observer-rated defense mechanisms in borderline personality disorder. *Psychoanalytic Psychology, 30*(1), 3–15.

Krueger, R. F., & Johnson, W. (2008). Behavioral genetics and personality. *Handbook of Personality: Theory and Research, 287–310.*

Lahey, B. B. (2009). Public health significance of neuroticism. *American Psychologist, 64*(4), 241–256. doi: 10.1037/a0015309

Lajunen, T. (2001). Personality and accident liability: Are extraversion, neuroticism and psychoticism related to traffic and occupational fatalities? *Personality and Individual Differences, 31*(8), 1365–1373. doi: http://dx.doi.org/10.1016/S0191-8869(00)00230-0

Lilienfeld, S. O., Wood, J. M., & Garb, H. N. (2000). The scientific status of projective techniques. *Psychological Science in the Public Interest, 1*(2), 27–66.

Lilienfeld, S. O., Wood, J. M., & Garb, H. N. (2001, May). What's wrong with this picture? (critique of projective tests). *Scientific American, 284,* 80–87.

Litt, M. D., Kadden, R. M., & Petry, N. M. (2013). Behavioral treatment for marijuana dependence: Randomized trial of contingency management and self-efficacy enhancement. *Addictive Behaviors, 38*(3), 1764–1775.

Little, B. R. (2014). *Me, myself, and us: The science of personality and the art of well-being.* New York, NY: PublicAffairs.

Maclean, J. C., Xu, H., French, M. T., & Ettner, S. L. (2014). Mental health and high-cost health care utilization: New evidence from axis II disorders. *Health Services Research, 49*(2), 683–704.

Major, D. A., Turner, J. E., & Fletcher, T. D. (2006). Linking proactive personality and the Big Five to motivation to learn and development activity. *Journal of Applied Psychology, 91*(4), 927–935.

Maslow, A. H. (1961). Lessons from the peak-experiences. *Journal of Humanistic Psychology, 2*(9), 9–18.

McCrae, R. R. (1987). Creativity, divergent thinking, and openness to experience. *Journal of Personality and Social Psychology, 52*(6), 1258–1265.

McCrae, R. R., Costa, J., Paul T, & Martin, T. A. (2005). The NEO–PI–3: A more readable revised NEO personality inventory. *Journal of Personality Assessment, 84*(3), 261–270.

McCrae, R. R., & Costa Jr, P. T. (2007). Brief versions of the NEO-PI-3. *Journal of Individual Differences, 28*(3), 116–128.

McCrae, R. R., & Terracciano, A. (2005). Universal features of personality traits from the observer's perspective: Data from 50 cultures. *Journal of Personality and Social Psychology, 88*(3), 547–561.

Meijers, J., Harte, J. M., Jonker, F. A., & Meynen, G. (2015). Prison brain? Executive dysfunction in prisoners. *Frontiers in Psychology, 6.*

Michael, J. (2003). Using the Myers-Briggs type indicator as a tool for leadership development? Apply with caution. *Journal of Leadership & Organizational Studies, 10*(1), 68–81.

Mihura, J. L., Meyer, G. J., Dumitrascu, N., & Bombel, G. (2013). The validity of individual Rorschach variables: Systematic reviews and meta-analyses of the comprehensive system. *Psychological Bulletin, 139*(3), 548–605.

Millon, T. (2012). On the history and future study of personality and its disorders. *Annual Review of Clinical Psychology, 8,* 1–19.

Mischel, W. (1973). Toward a cognitive social learning reconceptualization of personality. *Psychological Review, 80*(4), 252–283.

Mischel, W., & Shoda, Y. (1995). A cognitive-affective system theory of personality: Reconceptualizing situations, dispositions, dynamics, and invariance in personality structure. *Psychological Review, 102*(2), 246–268.

Morgan, A. B., & Lilienfeld, S. O. (2000). A meta-analytic review of the relation between antisocial behavior and neuropsychological measures of executive function. *Clinical Psychology Review, 20*(1), 113–136.

Morgan, J. H. (2011). On becoming a person (1961) Carl Rogers' celebrated classic in memoriam. *Journal of Psychological Issues in Organizational Culture, 2,* 95–105.

Moutafi, J., Furnham, A., & Crump, J. (2007). Is managerial level related to personality? *British Journal of Management, 18*(3), 272–280.

National Collaborating Center for Mental Health. (2010). *Antisocial personality disorder: Treatment, management and prevention.* Leicester: The British Psychological Society.

Norcross, J. C., & Rogan, J. D. (2013). Psychologists conducting psychotherapy in 2012: Current practices and historical trends among division 29 members. *Psychotherapy, 50*(4), 490–495.

Ockene, J. K., Mermelstein, R. J., Bonollo, D. S., Emmons, K. M., Perkins, K. A., Voorhees, C. C., & Hollis, J. F. (2000). Relapse and maintenance issues for smoking cessation. *Health Psychology, 19*(1S), 17–31.

Olson, K. R., & Weber, D. A. (2004). Relations between big five traits and fundamental motives. *Psychological Reports, 95*(3), 795–802.

Patterson, T. G., & Joseph, S. (2007). Person-centered personality theory: Support from self-determination theory and positive psychology. *Journal of Humanistic Psychology, 47*(1), 117–139.

Pemment, J. (2013). The neurobiology of antisocial personality disorder: The quest for rehabilitation and treatment. *Aggression and Violent Behavior, 18*(1), 79–82.

Perkins, K. A., Parzynski, C., Mercincavage, M., Conklin, C. A., & Fonte, C. A. (2012). Is self-efficacy for smoking abstinence a cause of, or a reflection on, smoking behavior change? *Experimental and Clinical Psychopharmacology, 20*(1), 56–62.

Perry, J. C., & Bond, M. (2012). Change in defense mechanisms during long-term dynamic psychotherapy and five-year outcome. *American Journal of Psychiatry, 169*(9), 916–925.

Perry, J. C., & Cooper, S. H. (1989). An empirical study of defense mechanisms: I. Clinical interview and life vignette ratings. *Archives of General Psychiatry, 46*(5), 444–452.

Petras, H., Kellam, S. G., Brown, C. H., Muthén, B. O., Ialongo, N. S., & Poduska, J. M. (2008). Developmental epidemiological courses leading to antisocial personality disorder and violent and criminal behavior: Effects by young adulthood of a universal preventive intervention in first-and second-grade classrooms. *Drug and Alcohol Dependence, 95,* S45–S59.

Pittenger, D. J. (2005). Cautionary comments regarding the Myers-Briggs type indicator. *Consulting Psychology Journal: Practice and Research, 57*(3), 210–221.

Rammstedt, B., Goldberg, L. R., & Borg, I. (2010). The measurement equivalence of Big-Five factor markers for persons with different levels of education. *Journal of Research in Personality, 44*(1), 53–61.

Raine, A., Lencz, T., Bihrle, S., LaCasse, L., & Colletti, P. (2000). Reduced prefrontal gray matter volume and reduced autonomic activity in antisocial personality disorder. *Archives of General Psychiatry, 57*(2), 119–127.

Rotter, J. B. (1954). *Social learning and clinical psychology.* Englewood Cliffs, NJ: Prentice-Hall.

Rotter, J. B. (1966). Generalized expectancies for internal versus external control of reinforcement. *Psychological Monographs: General and Applied, 80*(1), 1–28.

Rotter, J. B., Seeman, M., & Liverant, S. (1962). Internal versus external control of reinforcement: A major variable in behavior theory. *Decisions, Values, and Groups, 2,* 473–516.

Ryman, S. G., Gasparovic, C., Bedrick, E. J., Flores, R. A., Marshall, A. N., & Jung, R. E. (2011). Brain biochemistry and personality: A magnetic resonance spectroscopy study. *PloS One, 6*(11), e26758.

Samuels, J. (2011). Personality disorders: Epidemiology and public health issues. *International Review of Psychiatry, 23*(3), 223–233.

Schiffer, B., Müller, B. W., Scherbaum, N., Hodgins, S., Forsting, M., Wiltfang, J., … & Leygraf, N. (2011). Disentangling structural brain alterations associated with violent behavior from those associated with substance use disorders. *Archives of General Psychiatry, 68*(10), 1039–1049.

Schmitt, D. P., Allik, J., McCrae, R. R., & Benet-Martínez, V. (2007). The geographic distribution of Big Five personality traits patterns and profiles of human self-description across 56 nations. *Journal of Cross-Cultural Psychology, 38*(2), 173–212.

Sefcik, D. J., Prerost, F. J., & Arbet, S. E. (2009). Personality types and performance on aptitude and achievement tests: Implications for osteopathic medical education. *Journal of the American Osteopathic Association, 109*(6), 296–301.

Segal, N. L. (2013). Personality similarity in unrelated look-alike pairs: Addressing a twin study challenge. *Personality and Individual Differences, 54*(1), 23–28.

Segal, N. L., Graham, J. L., & Ettinger, U. (2013). Unrelated look-alikes: Replicated study of personality similarity and qualitative findings on social relatedness. *Personality and Individual Differences, 55*(2), 169–174.

Shoda, Y., Wilson, N. L., Chen, J., Gilmore, A. K., & Smith, R. E. (2013). Cognitive-affective processing system analysis of intra-individual dynamics in collaborative therapeutic assessment: Translating basic theory and research into clinical applications. *Journal of Personality, 81*(6), 554–568.

Solms, M. (2006). Freud returns. *Scientific American Mind, 17*(2), 28–35.

Soper, B., Milford, G. E., & Rosenthal, G. T. (1995). Belief when evidence does not support theory. *Psychology & Marketing, 12*(5), 415–422.

Spokas, M., & Heimberg, R. G. (2009). Overprotective parenting, social anxiety, and external locus of control: Cross-sectional and longitudinal relationships. *Cognitive Therapy and Research, 33*(6), 543–551.

Steiger, A. E., Allemand, M., Robins, R. W., & Fend, H. A. (2014). Low and decreasing self-esteem during adolescence predict adult depression two decades later. *Journal of Personality and Social Psychology, 106*(2), 325–338.

Stevens, A. (1982). *Archetype: A natural history of the self.* New York, NY: Routledge.

Taki, Y., Thyreau, B., Kinomura, S., Sato, K., Goto, R., Wu, K., … & Fukuda, H. (2012). A longitudinal study of the relationship between personality traits and the annual rate of volume changes in regional gray matter in healthy adults. *Human Brain Mapping, 34*(12), 3347–3353.

Tellegen, A., Lykken, D. T., Bouchard, T. J., Wilcox, K. J., Segal, N. L., & Rich, S. (1988). Personality similarity in twins reared apart and together. *Journal of Personality and Social Psychology, 54*(6), 1031–1039.

Triandis, H. C. (2001). Individualism-collectivism and personality. *Journal of Personality, 69*(6), 907–924.

Triandis, H. C., & Suh, E. M. (2002). Cultural influences on personality. *Annual Review of Psychology, 53*(1), 133–160.

Turkheimer, E., Pettersson, E., & Horn, E. E. (2014). A phenotypic null hypothesis for the genetics of personality. *Annual Review of Psychology, 65,* 515–540. doi: 10.1146/annurev-psych-113011-143752

Vazire, S., & Carlson, E. N. (2011). Others sometimes know us better than we know ourselves. *Current Directions in Psychological Science, 20*(2), 104–108.

Verme, P. (2009). Happiness, freedom and control. *Journal of Economic Behavior & Organization, 71*(2), 146–161.

Visscher, P. M., Hill, W. G., & Wray, N. R. (2008). Heritability in the genomics era—concepts and misconceptions. *Nature Reviews Genetics, 9*(4), 255–266.

Wahba, M. A., & Bridwell, L. G. (1976). Maslow reconsidered: A review of research on the need hierarchy theory. *Organizational Behavior and Human Performance, 15*(2), 212–240. doi: http://dx.doi.org/10.1016/0030-5073(76)90038-6

Watson, D., Clark, L. A., & Carey, G. (1988). Positive and negative affectivity and their relation to anxiety and depressive disorders. *Journal of Abnormal Psychology, 97*(3), 346–353.

Westen, D. (1998). The scientific legacy of Sigmund Freud: Toward a psychodynamically informed psychological science. *Psychological Bulletin, 124*(3), 333–371.

Williams, P. G., Rau, H. K., Cribbet, M. R., & Gunn, H. E. (2009). Openness to experience and stress regulation. *Journal of Research in Personality, 43*(5), 777–784.

Williams, T., & Williams, K. (2010). Self-efficacy and performance in mathematics: Reciprocal determinism in 33 nations. *Journal of Educational Psychology, 102*(2), 453–466.

Zimring, F. (2000). Empathic understanding grows the person. *The Person-Centered Journal, 7*(2), 101–113.

Chapter 15

Abbott, J. D., Cumming, G., Fidler, F., & Lindell, A. K. (2013). The perception of positive and negative facial expressions in unilateral brain-damaged patients: A meta-analysis. *Laterality: Asymmetries of Body, Brain and Cognition, 18*(4), 437–459.

Almeida, O. P., Draper, B., Pirkis, J., Snowdon, J., Lautenschlager, N. T., Byrne, G., … & Flicker, L. (2012). Anxiety, depression, and comorbid anxiety and depression: Risk factors and outcome over two years. *International Psychogeriatrics, 24*(10), 1622–1632.

American Foundation for Suicide Prevention. (2015). *Facts and figures.* Retrieved May 25, 2015, from www.afsp.org/understanding-suicide/facts-and-figures

American Psychiatric Association. (2013). *Diagnostic and statistical manual of mental disorders, (DSM-5®).* Washington, DC: American Psychiatric Pub.

Anestis, M. D., Khazem, L. R., Law, K. C., Houtsma, C., LeTard, R., Moberg, F., & Martin, R. (2015). The association between state laws regulating handgun ownership and statewide suicide rates. *American Journal of Public Health* (0), e1–e9.

Arcelus, J., Haslam, M., Farrow, C., & Meyer, C. (2013). The role of interpersonal functioning in the maintenance of eating psychopathology: A systematic review and testable model. *Clinical Psychology Review, 33*(1), 156–167.

Axelson, D., Goldstein, B., Goldstein, T., Monk, K., Yu, H., Hickey, M. B., … & Birmaher, B. (2015). Diagnostic precursors to bipolar disorder among offspring of parents with bipolar disorder: A longitudinal study. *American Journal of Psychiatry, 172*(7), 638–646. doi: 10.1176/appi.ajp.2014.14010035

Axelson, D. A., Birmaher, B., Findling, R. L., Fristad, M. A., Kowatch, R. A., Youngstrom, E. A., … & Diler, R. S. (2011). Concerns regarding the inclusion of temper dysregulation disorder with dysphoria in the *Diagnostic and Statistical Manual of Mental Disorders,* 5th edition. *Journal of Clinical Psychiatry, 72*(9), 1257–1262. doi: 10.4088/JCP.10com06220

Baek, J. H., Park, D. Y., Choi, J., Kim, J. S., Choi, J. S., Ha, K., … Hong, K. S. (2011). Differences between bipolar I and bipolar II disorders in clinical features, comorbidity, and family history. *Journal of Affective Disorders, 131*(1), 59–67.

Bandura, A. (1969). *Principles of behavior modification.* Oxford, England: Holt, Rinehart, & Winston.

Bandura, A., Ross, D., & Ross, S. A. (1961). Transmission of aggression through imitation of aggressive models. *Journal of Abnormal and Social Psychology, 63*(3), 575–582.

Beck, A. T. (1964). Thinking and depression: II. Theory and therapy. *Archives of General Psychiatry, 10*(6), 561–571.

Beck, A. T. (1991). Cognitive therapy: A 30-year retrospective. *American Psychologist, 46*(4), 368–375.

Beck, A. T. (2002). Cognitive models of depression. *Clinical Advances in Cognitive Psychotherapy: Theory and Application, 14*, 29–61.

Beck, A. T. (2005). The current state of cognitive therapy: A 40-year retrospective. *Archives of General Psychiatry, 62*(9), 953–959.

Beck, A. T., Brown, G., Steer, R. A., Eidelson, J. I., & Riskind, J. H. (1987). Differentiating anxiety and depression: A test of the cognitive content-specificity hypothesis. *Journal of Abnormal Psychology, 96*(3), 179–183.

Beck, J. S. (1995). *Cognitive therapy:* Wiley Online Library.

Beckham, E. E., Leber, W. R., Watkins, J. T., Boyer, J. L., & Cook, J. B. (1986). Development of an instrument to measure Beck's cognitive triad: The Cognitive Triad Inventory. *Journal of Consulting and Clinical Psychology, 54*(4), 566–567.

Bellivier, F., Etain, B., Malafosse, A., Henry, C., Kahn, J.-P., Elgrabli-Wajsbrot, O., … Scott, J. (2011). Age at onset in bipolar I affective disorder in the USA and Europe. *World Journal of Biological Psychiatry,* 1–8. doi: 10.3109/15622975.2011.639801

Belsky, D. W., Caspi, A., Arseneault, L., Bleidorn, W., Fonagy, P., Goodman, M., … Moffitt, T. E. (2012). Etiological features of borderline personality related characteristics in a birth cohort of 12-year-old children. *Development and Psychopathology, 24*(1), 251–265. doi: 10.1017/S0954579411000812

Benowitz-Fredericks, C. A., Garcia, K., Massey, M., Vasagar, B., & Borzekowski, D. L. (2012). Body image, eating disorders, and the relationship to adolescent media use. *Pediatric Clinics of North America, 59*(3), 693–704.

Berge, J. M., Loth, K., Hanson, C., Croll-Lampert, J., & Neumark-Sztainer, D. (2012). Family life cycle transitions and the onset of eating disorders: A retrospective grounded theory approach. *Journal of Clinical Nursing, 21*(9–10), 1355–1363.

Bhugra, D. (2005). The global prevalence of schizophrenia. *PLoS Medicine, 2*(5), 372.

Biederman, J., Faraone, S. V., Wozniak, J., Mick, E., Kwon, A., & Aleardi, M. (2004). Further evidence of unique developmental phenotypic correlates of pediatric bipolar disorder: Findings from a large sample of clinically referred preadolescent children assessed over the last 7 years. *Journal of Affective Disorders, 82* Suppl 1, S45–58. doi: 10.1016/j.jad.2004.05.021

Blader, J. C., & Carlson, G. A. (2007). Increased rates of bipolar disorder diagnoses among U.S. child, adolescent, and adult inpatients, 1996–2004. *Biological Psychiatry, 62*(2), 107–114. doi: 10.1016/j.biopsych.2006.11.006

Blatt, S. J., & Levy, K. N. (1998). A psychodynamic approach to the diagnosis of psychopathology. *Making diagnosis meaningful: Enhancing evaluation and treatment of psychological disorders,* 73–110.

Bora, E., & Pantelis, C. (2015). Meta-analysis of cognitive impairment in first-episode bipolar disorder: Comparison with first-episode schizophrenia and healthy controls. *Schizophrenia Bulletin, 41*(5), 1095–1104.

Borkovec, T., Hazlett-Stevens, H., & Diaz, M. (1999). The role of positive beliefs about worry in generalized anxiety disorder and its treatment. *Clinical Psychology & Psychotherapy, 6*(2), 126–138.

Bornovalova, M. A., Huibregtse, B. M., Hicks, B. M., Keyes, M., McGue, M., & Iacono, W. (2013). Tests of a direct effect of childhood abuse on adult borderline personality disorder traits: A longitudinal discordant twin design. *Journal of Abnormal Psychology, 122*(1), 180–194.

Boysen, G. A., & VanBergen, A. (2013). A review of published research on adult dissociative identity disorder: 2000–2010. *Journal of Nervous and Mental Disease, 201*(1), 5–11.

Brady, K. T., & Sinha, R. (2014). Co-occurring mental and substance use disorders: The neurobiological effects of chronic stress. *American Journal of Psychiatry, 162*(8), 1483–1493.

Bratland-Sanda, S., & Sundgot-Borgen, J. (2013). Eating disorders in athletes: Overview of prevalence, risk factors and recommendations for prevention and treatment. *European Journal of Sport Science, 13*(5), 499–508.

Breslau, N., Chilcoat, H. D., Kessler, R. C., Peterson, E. L., & Lucia, V. C. (1999). Vulnerability to assaultive violence: Further specification of the sex difference in post-traumatic stress disorder. *Psychological Medicine, 29*(04), 813–821.

Breslau, N., Davis, G. C., Andreski, P., Peterson, E. L., & Schultz, L. R. (1997). Sex differences in posttraumatic stress disorder. *Archives of General Psychiatry, 54*(11), 1044–1048.

Brock, R. L., & Kochanska, G. (2015). Interparental conflict, children's security with parents, and long-term risk of internalizing problems: A longitudinal study from ages 2 to 10. *Development and Psychopathology, FirstView,* 1–10. doi:10.1017/S0954579415000279

Brown, A. S., Schaefer, C. A., Wyatt, R. J., Goetz, R., Begg, M. D., Gorman, J. M., & Susser, E. S. (2000). Maternal exposure to respiratory infections and adult schizophrenia spectrum disorders: A prospective birth cohort study. *Schizophrenia Bulletin, 26*(2), 287–295.

Bruce, S. E., Buchholz, K. R., Brown, W. J., Yan, L., Durbin, A., & Sheline, Y. I. (2013). Altered emotional interference processing in the amygdala and insula in women with post-traumatic stress disorder. *Neuroimage: Clinical, 2*, 43–49.

Bruch, H. (1962). Perceptual and conceptual disturbances in anorexia nervosa. *Psychosomatic Medicine, 24*(2), 187–194.

Buchanan, R. W., Breier, A., Kirkpatrick, B., Ball, P., & Carpenter Jr, W. T. (2014). Positive and negative symptom response to clozapine in schizophrenic patients with and without the deficit syndrome. *American Journal of Psychiatry, 155*(6), 751–760.

Buchsbaum, M. S., & Haier, R. J. (1983). Psychopathology: Biological approaches. *Annual Review of Psychology, 34*(1), 401–430.

Campbell, R. D., & Long, L. A. (2014). Culture as a social determinant of mental and behavioral health: A look at culturally shaped beliefs and their impact on help-seeking behaviors and service use patterns of black Americans with depression. *Best Practices in Mental Health, 10*(2), 48–62.

Carleton, R. N., Mulvogue, M. K., Thibodeau, M. A., McCabe, R. E., Antony, M. M., & Asmundson, G. J. (2012). Increasingly certain about uncertainty: Intolerance of uncertainty across anxiety and depression. *Journal of Anxiety Disorders, 26*(3), 468–479.

Carlsson, A., & Carlsson, M. L. (2006). A dopaminergic deficit hypothesis of schizophrenia: The path to discovery. *Dialogues in Clinical Neuroscience, 8*(1), 137–142.

Carpenter, R. W., Tomko, R. L., Trull, T. J., & Boomsma, D. I. (2013). Gene-environment studies and borderline personality disorder: A review. *Current Psychiatry Reports, 15*(1), 336–336. doi: 10.1007/s11920-012-0336-1

Carpenter, R. W., & Trull, T. J. (2013). Components of emotion dysregulation in borderline personality disorder: A review. *Current Psychiatry Reports, 15*(1), 335–335. doi: 10.1007/s11920-012-0335-2

Cash, T. F., & Brown, T. A. (1987). Body image in anorexia nervosa and bulimia nervosa: A review of the literature. *Behavior Modification, 11*(4), 487–521.

Cavanagh, M., Quinn, D., Duncan, D., Graham, T., & Balbuena, L. (2014). Oppositional defiant disorder is better conceptualized as a disorder of emotional regulation. *Journal of Attention Disorders.* doi: 10.1177/1087054713520221

Chiang, H. (2015). Translating culture and psychiatry across the Pacific: How koro became culture-bound. *History of Science, 53*(1), 102–119.

Clark, D. M., Salkovskis, P. M., Öst, L.-G., Breitholtz, E., Koehler, K. A., Westling, B. E., … Gelder, M. (1997). Misinterpretation of body sensations in panic disorder. *Journal of Consulting and Clinical Psychology, 65*(2), 203–213.

Cohen, D., Bonnot, O., Bodeau, N., Consoli, A., & Laurent, C. (2012). Adverse effects of second-generation antipsychotics in children and adolescents: A Bayesian meta-analysis. *Journal of Clinical Psychopharmacology, 32*(3), 309–316.

Corrigan, P. W., Morris, S. B., Michaels, P. J., Rafacz, J. D., & Rüsch, N. (2012). Challenging the public stigma of mental illness: A meta-analysis of outcome studies. *Psychiatric Services, 63*(10), 963–973. doi:10.1176/appi.ps.201100529

Craddock, N., & Sklar, P. (2013). Genetics of bipolar disorder. *The Lancet, 381*(9878), 1654–1662.

Crowell, S. E., Beauchaine, T. P., & Linehan, M. M. (2009). A biosocial developmental model of borderline personality: Elaborating and extending Linehan's theory. *Psychological Bulletin, 135*(3), 495–510. doi: 10.1037/a0015616

Cummings, C. M., Caporino, N. E., & Kendall, P. C. (2014). Comorbidity of anxiety and depression in children and adolescents: 20 years after. *Psychological Bulletin, 140*(3), 816–845.

Daskalakis, N. P., & Binder, E. B. (2015). Schizophrenia in the spectrum of gene–stress interactions: The FKBP5 example. *Schizophrenia Bulletin, 41*, 323–329 .

Davey, G. C. (2007). Psychopathology and treatment of specific phobias. *Psychiatry, 6*(6), 247–253.

Davidson, J. R. T., Stein, D. J., Shalev, A. Y., & Yehuda, R. (2014). Posttraumatic stress disorder: Acquisition, recognition, course, and treatment. *Journal of Neuropsychiatry and Clinical Neurosciences, 16*(2), 135–147. doi:10.1176/jnp.16.2.135

Dervic, K., Oquendo, M. A., Grunebaum, M. F., Ellis, S., Burke, A. K., & Mann, J. J. (2004). Religious affiliation and suicide attempt. *American Journal of Psychiatry, 161*, 2303–2308.

Deveney, C. M., Connolly, M. E., Haring, C. T., Bones, B. L., Reynolds, R. C., Kim, P., … Leibenluft, E. (2013). Neural mechanisms of frustration in chronically irritable children. *American Journal of Psychiatry, 170*(10), 1186–1194. doi: 10.1176/appi.ajp.2013.12070917

Diederen, K. M., Neggers, S. F., Daalman, K., Blom, J. D., Goekoop, R., Kahn, R. S., & Sommer, I. E. (2010). Deactivation of the parahippocampal gyrus preceding auditory hallucinations in schizophrenia. *American Journal of Psychiatry, 167*, 427–435.

Dimsdale, J. E., Creed, F., Escobar, J., Sharpe, M., Wulsin, L., Barsky, A., … Levenson, J. (2013). Somatic symptom disorder: An important change in DSM. *Journal of Psychosomatic Research, 75*(3), 223–228.

Dingemans, A. E., & van Furth, E. F. (2012). Binge eating disorder psychopathology in normal weight and obese individuals. *International Journal of Eating Disorders, 45*(1), 135–138.

Domschke, K., & Reif, A. (2012). Behavioral genetics of affective and anxiety disorders. *Behavioral Neurogenetics* (pp. 463–502): Springer.

Dorahy, M. J., Brand, B. L., Şar, V., Krüger, C., Stavropoulos, P., Martínez-Taboas, A., … Middleton, W. (2014). Dissociative identity disorder: An empirical overview. *Australian and New Zealand Journal of Psychiatry, 48*(5), 402–417.

Dow, M. G. (1993). Affective disorders. In A. S. Bellack & M. Hersen (Eds.), *Handbook of behavior therapy in the psychiatric setting* (p. 258). Boston, MA: Springer.

Dutta, A. K., Santra, S., Sharma, H., Voshavar, C., Xu, L., Mabrouk, O., … & Reith, M. E. (2014). Pharmacological and behavioral characterization of D-473, an orally active triple reuptake inhibitor targeting dopamine, serotonin and norepinephrine transporters. *PLoS One, 9*(11), e113420. doi: 10.1371/journal.pone.0113420

Erlangsen, A., Eaton, W. W., Mortensen, P. B., & Conwell, Y. (2012). Schizophrenia—A predictor of suicide during the second half of life? *Schizophrenia Research, 134*(2), 111–117.

Fairburn, C. G., Cooper, Z., Doll, H. A., & Davies, B. A. (2005). Identifying dieters who will develop an eating disorder: A prospective, population-based study. *American Journal of Psychiatry, 162*(12), 2249–2255.

Fairburn, C. G., & Harrison, P. J. (2003). Eating disorders. *The Lancet, 361*(9355), 407–416.

Fatemi, S. H., Folsom, T. D., Rooney, R. J., Mori, S., Kornfield, T. E., Reutiman, T. J., … Hsu, J. (2012). The viral theory of schizophrenia revisited: Abnormal placental gene expression and structural changes with lack of evidence for H1N1 viral presence in placentae of infected mice or brains of exposed offspring. *Neuropharmacology, 62*(3), 1290–1298.

Fedoroff, I. C., & McFarlane, T. (1998). Cultural aspects of eating disorders. In S. S. Kazarian & D. R. Evans (Eds.), *Cultural Clinical Psychology: Theory Research and Practice* (pp. 152–176). New York, NY: Oxford University Press.

Findling, R. L., Correll, C. U., Nyilas, M., Forbes, R. A., McQuade, R. D., Jin, N., … & Carlson, G. A. (2013). Aripiprazole for the treatment of pediatric bipolar I disorder: A 30-week, randomized, placebo-controlled study. *Bipolar Disorders, 15*(2), 138–149. doi: 10.1111/bdi.12042

Fisak Jr., B., & Grills-Taquechel, A. E. (2007). Parental modeling, reinforcement, and information transfer: Risk factors in the development of child anxiety? *Clinical Child and Family Psychology Review, 10*(3), 213–231.

Fish, J. M. (1996). *Culture and therapy: An integrative approach.* Lanham, MD: Jason Aronson, Inc.

Flament, M. F., Henderson, K., Buchholz, A., Obeid, N., Nguyen, H. N., Birmingham, M., & Goldfield, G. (2015). Weight status and DSM-5 diagnoses of eating disorders in adolescents from the community. *Journal of the American Academy of Child & Adolescent Psychiatry, 54*(5), 403–411. e402.

Ford, M. R., & Widiger, T. A. (1989). Sex bias in the diagnosis of histrionic and antisocial personality disorders. *Journal of Consulting and Clinical Psychology, 57*(2), 301–305.

Fornito, A., Zalesky, A., Pantelis, C., & Bullmore, E. T. (2012). Schizophrenia, neuroimaging and connectomics. *Neuroimage, 62*(4), 2296–2314.

Fowles, D. C. (2002). Biological variables in psychopathology: A psychobiological perspective. *Comprehensive Handbook of Psychopathology* (pp. 85–104): Springer.

Frances, A. (2013a). The new crisis of confidence in psychiatric diagnosis. *Annals of Internal Medicine, 159*(3), 221–222. doi: 10.7326/0003-4819-159-3-201308060-00655

Frances, A. (2013b). The new somatic symptom disorder in DSM-5 risks mislabeling many people as mentally ill. *BMJ, 346.* doi: http://dx.doi.org/10.1136/bmj.f1580

Frances, A., & Batstra, L. (2013). Why so many epidemics of childhood mental disorder? *Journal of Developmental & Behavioral Pediatrics, 34*(4), 291–292.

Frankel, R. M., Quill, T. E., & McDaniel, S. H. (2003). *The biopsychosocial approach: Past, present, and future.* Rochester, NY: University Rochester Press.

Fredrikson, M., Annas, P., Fischer, H., & Wik, G. (1996). Gender and age differences in the prevalence of specific fears and phobias. *Behaviour Research and Therapy, 34*(1), 33–39.

Freud, S. (1920). *A general introduction to psychoanalysis.* New York, NY: Boni and Liveright.

Fusar-Poli, P., & Meyer-Lindenberg, A. (2013a). Striatal presynaptic dopamine in schizophrenia, part I: Meta-analysis of dopamine active transporter (DAT) density. *Schizophrenia Bulletin, 39*(1), 22–32.

Fusar-Poli, P., & Meyer-Lindenberg, A. (2013b). Striatal presynaptic dopamine in schizophrenia, part II: Meta-analysis of [18F/11C]-DOPA PET studies. *Schizophrenia Bulletin, 39*(1), 33–42. doi: 10.1093/schbul/sbr180

Garner, D. M., Garfinkel, P. E., Stancer, H. C., & Moldofsky, H. (1976). Body image disturbances in anorexia nervosa and obesity. *Psychosomatic Medicine, 38*(5), 327–336.

Gaser, C., Nenadic, I., Buchsbaum, B. R., Hazlett, E. A., & Buchsbaum, M. S. (2004). Ventricular enlargement in schizophrenia related to volume reduction of the thalamus, striatum, and superior temporal cortex. *American Journal of Psychiatry, 161,* 154–156.

Gejman, P. V., Sanders, A. R., & Duan, J. (2010). The role of genetics in the etiology of schizophrenia. *Psychiatric Clinics of North America, 33*(1), 35–66.

Gentes, E. L., & Ruscio, A. M. (2011). A meta-analysis of the relation of intolerance of uncertainty to symptoms of generalized anxiety disorder, major depressive disorder, and obsessive–compulsive disorder. *Clinical Psychology Review, 31*(6), 923–933.

Gilbert, P. (1995). Biopsychosocial approaches and evolutionary theory as aids to integration in clinical psychology and psychotherapy. *Clinical Psychology & Psychotherapy, 2*(3), 135–156.

Gilbert, P. (2013). Depression: The challenges of an integrative, biopsychosocial evolutionary approach. *The Wiley-Blackwell Handbook of Mood Disorders, 2nd ed.,* 229–288.

Goodwin, R. D., & Gorman, J. M. (2002). Psychopharmacologic treatment of generalized anxiety disorder and the risk of major depression. *American Journal of Psychiatry, 159,* 1935–1937.

Gottesman, I. I. (2001). Psychopathology through a life span-genetic prism. *American Psychologist, 56*(11), 867–878.

Grilo, C., White, M., Gueorguieva, R., Wilson, G., & Masheb, R. (2013). Predictive significance of the overvaluation of shape/weight in obese patients with binge eating disorder: findings from a randomized controlled trial with 12-month follow-up. *Psychological Medicine, 43*(06), 1335–1344.

Grimmer, Y., Hohmann, S., & Poustka, L. (2014). Is bipolar always bipolar? Understanding the controversy on bipolar disorder in children. *F1000Prime Reports, 6*(111), 1–8. doi: 10.12703/P6-111

Gunderson, J. G. (2011). Borderline personality disorder. *New England Journal of Medicine, 364*(21), 2037–2042.

Gupta, D. K., & Mundra, K. (2005). Suicide bombing as a strategic weapon: An empirical investigation of Hamas and Islamic Jihad. *Terrorism and Political Violence, 17*(4), 573–598.

Haastrup, E., Bukh, J. D., Bock, C., Vinberg, M., Thørner, L. W., Hansen, T., … & Ullum, H. (2012). Promoter variants in IL18 are associated with onset of depression in patients previously exposed to stressful-life events. *Journal of Affective Disorders, 136*(1), 134–138.

Haenisch, B., & Bönisch, H. (2011). Depression and antidepressants: insights from knockout of dopamine, serotonin or noradrenaline re-uptake transporters. *Pharmacology & Therapeutics, 129*(3), 352–368.

Hagman, J., Gardner, R. M., Brown, D. L., Gralla, J., Fier, J. M., & Frank, G. K. (2015). Body size overestimation and its association with body mass index, body dissatisfaction, and drive for thinness in anorexia nervosa. *Eating and Weight Disorders-Studies on Anorexia, Bulimia and Obesity, 20*(4), 449–455.

Halmi, K. A., Sunday, S. R., Strober, M., Kaplan, A., Woodside, D. B., Fichter, M., … Kaye, W. H. (2000). Perfectionism in anorexia nervosa: Variation by clinical subtype, obsessionality, and pathological eating behavior. *American Journal of Psychiatry, 157,* 1799–1805.

Hanrahan, F., Field, A. P., Jones, F. W., & Davey, G. C. (2013). A meta-analysis of cognitive therapy for worry in generalized anxiety disorder. *Clinical Psychology Review, 33*(1), 120–132.

Hansen, J. T. (2000). Psychoanalysis and humanism: A review and critical examination of integrationist efforts with some proposed resolutions. *Journal of Counseling & Development, 78*(1), 21–28.

Hausenblas, H. A., Campbell, A., Menzel, J. E., Doughty, J., Levine, M., & Thompson, J. K. (2013). Media effects of experimental presentation of the ideal physique on eating disorder symptoms: A meta-analysis of laboratory studies. *Clinical Psychology Review, 33*(1), 168–181.

Havassy, B. E., Alvidrez, J., & Owen, K. K. (2004). Comparisons of patients with comorbid psychiatric and substance use disorders: Implications for treatment and service delivery. *American Journal of Psychiatry, 161,* 139–145.

Higgins, E. T. (1987). Self-discrepancy: A theory relating self and affect. *Psychological Review, 94*(3), 319–340.

Hirsch, C. R., Mathews, A., Lequertier, B., Perman, G., & Hayes, S. (2013). Characteristics of worry in generalized anxiety disorder. *Journal of Behavior Therapy and Experimental Psychiatry, 44*(4), 388–395.

Ho, B.-C., Nopoulos, P., Flaum, M., Arndt, S., & Andreasen, N. C. (2014). Two-year outcome in first-episode schizophrenia: Predictive value of symptoms for quality of life. *FOCUS 2,* 131–137.

Hollon, S. D., & Beck, A. T. (1994). *Cognitive and cognitive-behavioral therapies* (4th ed.). Oxford, England: John Wiley & Sons.

Hor, K., & Taylor, M. (2010). Review: Suicide and schizophrenia: A systematic review of rates and risk factors. *Journal of Psychopharmacology, 24*(4 suppl), 81–90.

Hudson, J. L. (2014). Parent-child relationships in early childhood and development of anxiety & depression. In R. E. Tremblay (Ed.), *Encyclopedia of early childhood development*. Centre for Excellence for Early Childhood Development.

Insel, T. (2010). Diagnosis: Pediatric bipolar disorder? Retrieved November 01, 2017, from https://www.nimh.nih.gov/about/directors/thomas-insel/blog/2010/diagnosis-pediatric-bipolar-disorder.shtml

Jacobi, C., Hayward, C., de Zwaan, M., Kraemer, H. C., & Agras, W. S. (2004). Coming to terms with risk factors for eating disorders: application of risk terminology and suggestions for a general taxonomy. *Psychological Bulletin, 130*(1), 19–65.

James, A., Hoang, U., Seagroatt, V., Clacey, J., Goldacre, M., & Leibenluft, E. (2014). A comparison of American and English hospital discharge rates for pediatric bipolar disorder, 2000 to 2010. *Journal of the American Academy of Child and Adolescent Psychiatry, 53*(6), 614–624. doi: 10.1016/j.jaac.2014.02.008

Jardri, R., Pouchet, A., Pins, D., & Thomas, P. (2011). Cortical activations during auditory verbal hallucinations in schizophrenia: a coordinate-based meta-analysis. *American Journal of Psychiatry, 168*(1), 73–81.

Javidi, H., & Yadollahie, M. (2012). Post-traumatic stress disorder. *International Journal of Occupational and Environmental Medicine, 3*(1), 1–9.

Jones, S. R., & Fernyhough, C. (2007). A new look at the neural diathesis–stress model of schizophrenia: the primacy of social-evaluative and uncontrollable situations. *Schizophrenia Bulletin, 33*(5), 1171–1177.

Jordan, J., McIntosh, V. V., Carter, J. D., Rowe, S., Taylor, K., Frampton, C., … Joyce, P. R. (2014). Bulimia nervosa-nonpurging subtype: Closer to the bulimia nervosa-purging subtype or to binge eating disorder? *International Journal of Eating Disorders, 47*(3), 231–238.

Kalibatseva, Z., & Leong, F. T. (2011). Depression among Asian Americans: Review and recommendations. *Depression Research and Treatment, 2011,* 1–9.

Kaye, W. H., Bulik, C. M., Thornton, L., Barbarich, N., Masters, K., & Group, P. F. C. (2004). Comorbidity of anxiety disorders with anorexia and bulimia nervosa. *American Journal of Psychiatry,161,* 2215–2221.

Keizer, A., Smeets, M. A., Dijkerman, H. C., Uzunbajakau, S. A., van Elburg, A., & Postma, A. (2013). Too fat to fit through the door: First evidence for disturbed body-scaled action in anorexia nervosa during locomotion. *PLoS One, 8*(5), e64602.

Kemp, J. J., Lickel, J. J., & Deacon, B. J. (2014). Effects of a chemical imbalance causal explanation on individuals' perceptions of their depressive symptoms. *Behaviour Research and Therapy, 56,* 47–52.

Keshavan, M. S., Nasrallah, H. A., & Tandon, R. (2011). Schizophrenia,"Just the Facts" 6. Moving ahead with the schizophrenia concept: from the elephant to the mouse. *Schizophrenia Research, 127*(1), 3–13.

Kessler, R. C., Berglund, P. A., Chiu, W. T., Deitz, A. C., Hudson, J. I., Shahly, V., … Benjet, C. (2013). The prevalence and correlates of binge eating disorder in the World Health Organization World Mental Health Surveys. *Biological Psychiatry, 73*(9), 904–914.

Kessler, R. C., Ruscio, A. M., Shear, K., & Wittchen, H.-U. (2010). Epidemiology of anxiety disorders *Behavioral Neurobiology of Anxiety and Its Treatment* (pp. 21–35): Springer.

Kieseppä, T., Partonen, T., Haukka, J., Kaprio, J., & Lönnqvist, J. (2004). High concordance of bipolar I disorder in a nationwide sample of twins. *American Journal of Psychiatry, 161,* 1814–1821.

Kirkpatrick, B. (2013). Understanding the physiology of schizophrenia. *Journal of Clinical Psychiatry, 74*(3), e05.

Klenk, M. M., Strauman, T. J., & Higgins, E. T. (2011). Regulatory focus and anxiety: A self-regulatory model of GAD-depression comorbidity. *Personality and Individual Differences, 50*(7), 935–943.

Klonsky, E. D., & May, A. M. (2014). Differentiating suicide attempters from suicide ideators: A critical frontier for suicidology research. *Suicide and Life-Threatening Behavior, 44*(1), 1–5.

Klumpp, H., Angstadt, M., & Phan, K. L. (2012). Insula reactivity and connectivity to anterior cingulate cortex

when processing threat in generalized social anxiety disorder. *Biological Psychology, 89*(1), 273–276.

Kreider, A. R., Matone, M., Bellonci, C., dosReis, S., Feudtner, C., Huang, Y.-S., … Rubin, D. M. (2014). Growth in the concurrent use of antipsychotics with other psychotropic medications in Medicaid-enrolled children. *Journal of the American Academy of Child & Adolescent Psychiatry, 53*(9), 960–970. doi: 10.1016/j.jaac.2014.05.010

Kuo, J. R., Khoury, J. E., Metcalfe, R., Fitzpatrick, S., & Goodwill, A. (2015). An examination of the relationship between childhood emotional abuse and borderline personality disorder features: The role of difficulties with emotion regulation. *Child Abuse & Neglect, 39,* 147–155.

Kuo, J. R., & Linehan, M. M. (2009). Disentangling emotion processes in borderline personality disorder: Physiological and self-reported assessment of biological vulnerability, baseline intensity, and reactivity to emotionally-evocative stimuli. *Journal of Abnormal Psychology, 118*(3), 531–544. doi: 10.1037/a0016392

Landreau, F., Galeano, P., Caltana, L. R., Masciotra, L., Chertcoff, A., Pontoriero, A., … Tous, M. I. (2012). Effects of two commonly found strains of influenza A virus on developing dopaminergic neurons, in relation to the pathophysiology of schizophrenia. *PLoS One, 7*(12), e51068.

Law, K. C., Khazem, L. R., & Anestis, M. D. (2015). The role of emotion dysregulation in suicide as considered through the ideation to action framework. *Current Opinion in Psychology, 3,* 30–35.

Lee, S., Lam, I. M., Kwok, K. P., & Leung, C. M. (2014). A community-based epidemiological study of health anxiety and generalized anxiety disorder. *Journal of Anxiety Disorders, 28*(2), 187–194.

Leibenluft, E. (2011). Severe mood dysregulation, irritability, and the diagnostic boundaries of bipolar disorder in youths. *American Journal of Psychiatry, 168*(2), 129–142. doi: 10.1176/appi.ajp.2010.10050766

Leichsenring, F., Leibing, E., Kruse, J., New, A. S., & Leweke, F. (2011). Borderline personality disorder. *The Lancet, 377*(9759), 74–84.

Leichsenring, F., & Salzer, S. (2014). A unified protocol for the transdiagnostic psychodynamic treatment of anxiety disorders: An evidence-based approach. *Psychotherapy, 51*(2), 224–245.

Levitan, R. D., Rector, N. A., & Bagby, R. M. (1998). Negative attributional style in seasonal and nonseasonal depression. *American Journal of Psychiatriy, 155,* 428–430.

Lewis, D. A., & Gonzalez-Burgos, G. (2006). Pathophysiologically based treatment interventions in schizophrenia. *Nature Medicine, 12*(9), 1016–1022.

Lewis, D. O., Yeager, C. A., Swica, Y., Pincus, J. H., & Lewis, M. (1997). Objective documentation of child abuse and dissociation in 12 murderers with dissociative identity disorder. *American Journal of Psychiatry, 154*(12), 1703–1710.

Lichtenstein, P., Yip, B. H., Björk, C., Pawitan, Y., Cannon, T. D., Sullivan, P. F., & Hultman, C. M. (2009). Common genetic determinants of schizophrenia and bipolar disorder in Swedish families: A population-based study. *The Lancet, 373*(9659), 234–239.

Likhtik, E., Stujenske, J. M., Topiwala, M. A., Harris, A. Z., & Gordon, J. A. (2014). Prefrontal entrainment of amygdala activity signals safety in learned fear and innate anxiety. *Nature Neuroscience, 17*(1), 106–113.

Lilienfeld, S. O., & Arkowitz, H. (2012). *Diagnosis of borderline personality disorder is often flawed.* Scientific American. Retrieved June 4, 2015, from http://www.scientificamerican.com/article/the-truth-about-borderline/

Lilienfeld, S. O., Kirsch, I., Sarbin, T. R., Lynn, S. J., Chaves, J. F., Ganaway, G. K., & Powell, R. A. (1999). Dissociative identity disorder and the sociocognitive model: Recalling the lessons of the past. *Psychological Bulletin, 125,* 507–523.

Lindfors, O., Knekt, P., Virtala, E., Laaksonen, M. A., & Group, H. P. S. (2012). The effectiveness of solution-focused therapy and short-and long-term psychodynamic psychotherapy on self-concept during a 3-year follow-up. *Journal of Nervous and Mental Disease, 200*(11), 946–953.

Lochman, J. E., Evans, S. C., Burke, J. D., Roberts, M. C., Fite, P. J., Reed, G. M., … Elena Garralda, M. (2015). An empirically based alternative to DSM-5's disruptive mood dysregulation disorder for ICD-11. *World Psychiatry, 14*(1), 30–33. doi: 10.1002/wps.20176

Loeb, K. L., Lock, J., Greif, R., & le Grange, D. (2012). Transdiagnostic theory and application of family-based treatment for youth with eating disorders. *Cognitive and Behavioral Practice, 19*(1), 17–30.

Lopez, S. R., & Guarnaccia, P. J. (2000). Cultural psychopathology: Uncovering the social world of mental illness. *Annual Review of Psychology, 51*(1), 571–598.

Lyubomirsky, S., Layous, K., Chancellor, J., & Nelson, S. K. (2015). Thinking about rumination: The scholarly contributions and intellectual legacy of Susan Nolen-Hoeksema. *Annual Review of Clinical Psychology, 11,* 1–22.

Machado, B. C., Gonçalves, S. F., Martins, C., Hoek, H. W., & Machado, P. P. (2014). Risk factors and antecedent life events in the development of anorexia nervosa: A Portuguese case-control study. *European Eating Disorders Review, 22*(4), 243–251.

MacQueen, G. M., & Young, L. T. (2001). Bipolar II disorder: Symptoms, course, and response to treatment. *Psychiatric Services, 52*(3), 358–361. doi:10.1176/appi.ps.52.3.358

Marsman, A., van den Heuvel, M. P., Klomp, D. W., Kahn, R. S., Luijten, P. R., & Pol, H. E. H. (2013). Glutamate in schizophrenia: A focused review and meta-analysis of 1H-MRS studies. *Schizophrenia Bulletin, 39*(1), 120–129.

Masheb, R., & White, M. A. (2012). Bulimia nervosa in overweight and normal-weight women. *Comprehensive Psychiatry, 53*(2), 181–186.

Mayes, S. D., Waxmonsky, J. D., Calhoun, S. L., & Bixler, E. O. (2016). Disruptive mood dysregulation disorder symptoms and association with oppositional defiant and other disorders in a general population child sample. *Journal of Child and Adolescent Psychopharmacology, 26*(2), 101–106.

McEvoy, P. M., & Mahoney, A. E. (2012). To be sure, to be sure: Intolerance of uncertainty mediates symptoms of various anxiety disorders and depression. *Behavior Therapy, 43*(3), 533–545.

McEvoy, P. M., Watson, H., Watkins, E. R., & Nathan, P. (2013). The relationship between worry, rumination, and comorbidity: Evidence for repetitive negative thinking as a transdiagnostic construct. *Journal of Affective Disorders, 151*(1), 313–320.

McGurk, S. R., Moriarty, P. J., Harvey, P. D., Parrella, M., White, L., Friedman, J., & Davis, K. L. (2000). Relationship of cognitive functioning, adaptive life skills, and negative symptom severity in poor-outcome geriatric schizophrenia patients. *Journal of Neuropsychiatry and Clinical Neurosciences, 12,* 257–264.

McLean, C. P., Asnaani, A., Litz, B. T., & Hofmann, S. G. (2011). Gender differences in anxiety disorders: prevalence, course of illness, comorbidity and burden of illness. *Journal of Psychiatric Research, 45*(8), 1027–1035.

Michl, L. C., McLaughlin, K. A., Shepherd, K., & Nolen-Hoeksema, S. (2013). Rumination as a mechanism linking stressful life events to symptoms of depression and anxiety: Longitudinal evidence in early adolescents and adults. *Journal of Abnormal Psychology, 122*(2), 339–352. doi: 10.1037/a0031994

Midgley, N., Cregeen, S., Hughes, C., & Rustin, M. (2013). Psychodynamic psychotherapy as treatment for depression in adolescence. *Child and Adolescent Psychiatric Clinics of North America, 22*(1), 67–82.

Miltenberger, R. (2012). *Behavior modification: Principles and procedures.* Belmont, CA: Wadsworth Cengage Learning.

Moghadam, A. (2009). Motives for martyrdom: Al-Qaida, Salafi Jihad, and the spread of suicide attacks. *International Security, 33*(3), 46–78.

Moncrieff, J. (2014). The medicalisation of "ups and downs": The marketing of the new bipolar disorder. *Transcultural Psychiatry, 51*(4), 581–598.

Moreno, C., Laje, G., Blanco, C., Jiang, H., Schmidt, A. B., & Olfson, M. (2007). National trends in the outpatient diagnosis and treatment of bipolar disorder in youth. *Archives of General Psychiatry, 64*(9), 1032–1039.

Müller-Oerlinghausen, B., Berghöfer, A., & Bauer, M. (2002). Bipolar disorder. *The Lancet, 359*(9302), 241–247.

Nolen-Hoeksema, S. (1991). Responses to depression and their effects on the duration of depressive episodes. *Journal of Abnormal Psychology, 100*(4), 569–582.

Nugent, N. R., Tyrka, A. R., Carpenter, L. L., & Price, L. H. (2011). Gene–environment interactions: Early life stress and risk for depressive and anxiety disorders. *Psychopharmacology, 214*(1), 175–196. doi: 10.1007/s00213-010-2151-x

Nurnberger, J. I., McInnis, M., Reich, W., Kastelic, E., Wilcox, H. C., Glowinski, A., … & Gershon, E. S. (2011). A high-risk study of bipolar disorder: Childhood clinical phenotypes as precursors of major mood disorders. *Archives of General Psychiatry, 68*(10), 1012–1020.

Olfson, M., Blanco, C., Liu, S., Wang, S., & Correll, C. U. (2012). National trends in the office-based treatment of children, adolescents, and adults with antipsychotics. *Archives of General Psychiatry, 69*(12), 1247–1256. doi: 10.1001/archgenpsychiatry.2012.647

Ormel, J., Oldehinkel, A. J., & Brilman, E. I. (2001). The interplay and etiological continuity of neuroticism, difficulties, and life events in the etiology of major and subsyndromal, first and recurrent depressive episodes in later life. *American Journal of Psychiatry, 158,* 885–891.

Overmier, J. B. (2014). Learned helplessness: State or stasis of the art. *Advances in Psychological Science, Biological and Cognitive Aspects, 2,* 301–316.

Pantelis, C., Yücel, M., Wood, S. J., Velakoulis, D., Sun, D., Berger, G., … & McGorry, P. D. (2005). Structural brain imaging evidence for multiple pathological processes at different stages of brain development in schizophrenia. *Schizophrenia Bulletin, 31*(3), 672–696.

Parcesepe, A. M., & Cabassa, L. J. (2013). Public stigma of mental illness in the United States: A systematic literature review. *Administration and Policy in Mental Health, 40*(5), 384–399. doi: 10.1007/s10488-012-0430-z

Parens, E., & Johnston, J. (2010). Controversies concerning the diagnosis and treatment of bipolar disorder in children. *Child and Adolescent Psychiatry and Mental Health, 4*(9), 1–14.

Paris, J. (2002). Chronic suicidality among patients with borderline personality disorder. *Psychiatric Services, 53*(6), 738–742. doi:10.1176/appi.ps.53.6.738

Paris, J. (2012). The rise and fall of dissociative identity disorder. *Journal of Nervous and Mental Disease, 200*(12), 1076–1079.

Park, S. (2011). Defence of cultural relativism. *Cultura International Journal of Philosophy of Culture and Axiology, 8*(1), 159–170.

Park, Y. C., & Park, S.-C. (2012). Why do suicide and depression occur? *Journal of the Korean Medical Association, 55*(4), 329–334.

Perry, S., Cooper, A. M., & Michels, R. (1987). The psychodynamic formulation: Its purpose, structure, and clinical application. *American Journal of Psychiatry, 144,* 543–550.

Petersen, L., & Sørensen, T. I. (2011). Studies based on the Danish Adoption Register: Schizophrenia, BMI, smoking, and mortality in perspective. *Scandinavian Journal of Public Health, 39*(7 suppl), 191–195.

Peterson, A., Thome, J., Frewen, P., & Lanius, R. A. (2014). Resting-state neuroimaging studies: A new way of identifying differences and similarities among the anxiety disorders? *Canadian Journal of Psychiatry. Revue Canadienne de Psychiatrie, 59*(6), 294–300.

Peterson, C., & Seligman, M. E. (1983). Learned helplessness and victimization. *Journal of Social Issues, 39*(2), 103–116.

Pettegrew, J. W., Keshavan, M. S., & Minshew, N. J. (1993). Nuclear magnetic resonance spectroscopy: Neurodevelopment and schizophrenia. *Schizophrenia Bulletin, 19*(1), 35–53.

Polivy, J., & Herman, C. P. (2002). Causes of eating disorders. *Annual Review of Psychology, 53*(1), 187–213.

Rachman, S. (1997). A cognitive theory of obsessions. *Behaviour Research and Therapy, 35*(9), 793–802.

Rachman, S. (2002). A cognitive theory of compulsive checking. *Behaviour Research and Therapy, 40*(6), 625–639.

Rachman, S., Levitt, K., & Lopatka, C. (1987). Panic: The links between cognitions and bodily symptoms—I. *Behaviour Research and Therapy, 25*(5), 411–423.

Rachman, S., & Seligman, M. (1976). Unprepared phobias: "Be prepared." *Behaviour Research and Therapy, 14*(5), 333–338.

Rand Corporation. (2008). *One in five Iraq and Afghanistan veterans suffer from PTSD or major depression.* Retrieved June 6, 2015, from http://www.rand.org/news/press/2008/04/17.html

Rapee, R. M. (2012). Family factors in the development and management of anxiety disorders. *Clinical Child and Family Psychology Review, 15*(1), 69–80.

Reichborn-Kjennerud, T., Ystrom, E., Neale, M. C., Aggen, S. H., Mazzeo, S. E., Knudsen, G. P., … & Kendler, K. S. (2013). Structure of genetic and environmental risk factors for symptoms of DSM-IV borderline personality disorder. *JAMA Psychiatry, 70*(11), 1206–1214. doi: 10.1001/jamapsychiatry.2013.1944

Reitz, S., Krause-Utz, A., Pogatzki-Zahn, E. M., Ebner-Priemer, U., Bohus, M., & Schmahl, C. (2012). Stress regulation and incision in borderline personality disorder—A pilot study modeling cutting behavior. *Journal of Personality Disorders, 26*(4), 605–615.

Rhoades, G., & Şar, V. (2005). *Trauma and dissociation in a cross-cultural perspective.* Binghamton, NY: Haworth Press.

Ritchey, M., Dolcos, F., Eddington, K. M., Strauman, T. J., & Cabeza, R. (2011). Neural correlates of emotional processing in depression: Changes with cognitive behavioral therapy and predictors of treatment response. *Journal of Psychiatric Research, 45*(5), 577–587.

Robinson, J., Sareen, J., Cox, B. J., & Bolton, J. M. (2011). Role of self-medication in the development of comorbid anxiety and substance use disorders: A longitudinal investigation. *Archives of General Psychiatry, 68*(8), 800–807.

Roelofs, K., Spinhoven, P., Sandijck, P., Moene, F. C., & Hoogduin, K. A. (2005). The impact of early trauma and recent life-events on symptom severity in patients with conversion disorder. *Journal of Nervous and Mental Disease, 193*(8), 508–514.

Rosenfield, S., & Mouzon, D. (2013). Gender and mental health. *Handbook of the Sociology of Mental Health* (pp. 277–296): Springer.

Rosenhan, D. L. (1973). On being sane in insane places. *Science, 179*(4070), 250–258.

Rowa, K., & Antony, M. M. (2008). Generalized anxiety disorder. In W. E. Craighead, D. J. Miklowitz, & L. W. Craighead (Eds.), *Psychopathology: History, Diagnosis, and Empirical Foundations,* (pp. 78–115). Hoboken, NJ: Wiley.

Rozée, P. D., & Van Boemel, G. (1990). The psychological effects of war trauma and abuse on older Cambodian refugee women. *Women & Therapy, 8*(4), 23–50.

Ruscio, A., Stein, D., Chiu, W., & Kessler, R. (2010). The epidemiology of obsessive-compulsive disorder in the National Comorbidity Survey Replication. *Molecular Psychiatry, 15*(1), 53–63.

Rush, A. J., Khatami, M., & Beck, A. T. (1975). Cognitive and behavior therapy in chronic depression. *Behavior Therapy, 6*(3), 398–404.

Ryan, N. D. (2013). Severe irritability in youths: Disruptive mood dysregulation disorder and associated brain circuit changes. *American Journal of Psychiatry, 170*(10), 1093–1096. doi:10.1176/appi.ajp.2013.13070934

Sam, D. L., & Moreira, V. (2012). Revisiting the mutual embeddedness of culture and mental illness. *Online Readings in Psychology and Culture, 10*(2), doi.org/10.9707/2307-0919.1078

Sar, V. (2011). Epidemiology of dissociative disorders: An overview. *Epidemiology Research International, 2011,* 1–8. doi: 10.1155/2011/404538

Sar, V., Akyüz, G., Kundakçi, T., Kiziltan, E., & Dogan, O. (2004). Childhood trauma, dissociation, and psychiatric comorbidity in patients with conversion disorder. *American Journal of Psychiatry, 161*(12), 2271–2276.

Saveanu, R. V., & Nemeroff, C. B. (2012). Etiology of depression: Genetic and environmental factors. *Psychiatric Clinics of North America, 35*(1), 51–71.

Savoy, R., Frederick, B., Keuroghlian, A., & Wolk, P. (2012). Voluntary switching between identities in dissociative identity disorder: A functional MRI case study. *Cognitive Neuroscience, 3*(2), 112–119.

Sayo, A., Jennings, R. G., & Van Horn, J. D. (2012). Study factors influencing ventricular enlargement in schizophrenia: A 20-year follow-up meta-analysis. *Neuroimage, 59*(1), 154–167.

Schlumpf, Y. R., Nijenhuis, E. R., Chalavi, S., Weder, E. V., Zimmermann, E., Luechinger, R., … Jäncke, L. (2013). Dissociative part-dependent biopsychosocial reactions to backward masked angry and neutral faces: An fMRI study of dissociative identity disorder. *Neuroimage: Clinical, 3,* 54–64.

Schudlich, T. D. R., Youngstrom, E. A., Martinez, M., KogosYoungstrom, J., Scovil, K., Ross, J., … Findling, R. L. (2015). Physical and sexual abuse and early-onset bipolar disorder in youths receiving outpatient services: Frequent, but not specific. *Journal of Abnormal Child Psychology, 43*(3), 453–463.

Seeman, M. V., & Seeman, P. (2014). Is schizophrenia a dopamine supersensitivity psychotic reaction? *Progress in Neuro-Psychopharmacology and Biological Psychiatry, 48,* 155–160.

Seeman, P. (2013). Schizophrenia and dopamine receptors. *European Neuropsychopharmacology, 23*(9), 999–1009.

Seeman, P., Guan, H.-C., & Van Tol, H. H. (1993). Dopamine D4 receptors elevated in schizophrenia. *Nature, 365,* 441–445.

Seim, R. W., & Spates, C. R. (2009). The prevalence and comorbidity of specific phobias in college students and their interest in receiving treatment. *Journal of College Student Psychotherapy, 24*(1), 49–58.

Seligman, M. E. (1971). Phobias and preparedness. *Behavior Therapy, 2*(3), 307–320.

Serpell, L., Treasure, J., Teasdale, J., & Sullivan, V. (1999). Anorexia nervosa: Friend or foe? *International Journal of Eating Disorders, 25*(2), 177–186.

Shobe, E. R. (2014). Independent and collaborative contributions of the cerebral hemispheres to emotional processing. *Frontiers in Human Neuroscience, 8,* 1–19.

Smolak, L., Murnen, S. K., & Ruble, A. E. (2000). Female athletes and eating problems: A meta-analysis. *International Journal of Eating Disorders*(27), 371–380.

Spiegel, D., Loewenstein, R. J., Lewis-Fernández, R., Sar, V., Simeon, D., Vermetten, E., … Dell, P. F. (2011). Dissociative disorders in DSM-5. *Depression and Anxiety, 28*(12), E17–E45.

Staebler, K., Helbing, E., Rosenbach, C., & Renneberg, B. (2011). Rejection sensitivity and borderline personality disorder. *Clinical Psychology & Psychotherapy, 18*(4), 275–283.

Stein, M. B., Jang, K. L., Taylor, S., Vernon, P. A., & Livesley, W. J. (2002). Genetic and environmental influences on trauma exposure and posttraumatic stress disorder symptoms: A twin study. *American Journal of Psychiatry, 159,* 1675–1681.

Stice, E., Marti, C. N., & Rohde, P. (2013). Prevalence, incidence, impairment, and course of the proposed DSM-5 eating disorder diagnoses in an 8-year prospective community study of young women. *Journal of Abnormal Psychology, 122*(2), 445–457.

Substance Abuse and Mental Health Services Administration. (2013). *Results from the 2012 National Survey on Drug Use and Health: Mental health findings.* Rockville, MD.

Sullivan, E. M., Annest, J. L., Simon, T. R., Luo, F., & Dahlberg, L. L. (2015). Suicide trends among persons aged 10–24 years—United States, 1994–2012. *MMWR: Morbidity and Mortality Weekly Report, 64,* 201–205.

Sullivan, P. F., Magnusson, C., Reichenberg, A., Boman, M., Dalman, C., Davidson, M., … & Långström, N. (2012). Family history of schizophrenia and bipolar disorder as risk factors for autism. *Archives of General Psychiatry, 69*(11), 1099–1103.

Sullivan, P. F., Neale, M. C., & Kendler, K. S. (2000). Genetic epidemiology of major depression: Review and meta-analysis. *Genetic Epidemiology, 157*(10), 1552–1562.

Suvisaari, J. M., Haukka, J. K., & Lönnqvist, J. K. (2001). Season of birth among patients with schizophrenia and their siblings: Evidence for the procreational habits hypothesis. *American Journal of Psychiatry, 158*, 754–757.

Sylvester, C., Corbetta, M., Raichle, M., Rodebaugh, T., Schlaggar, B., Sheline, Y., … Lenze, E. (2012). Functional network dysfunction in anxiety and anxiety disorders. *Trends in Neurosciences, 35*(9), 527–535.

Thomas-Antérion, C., Dubas, F., Decousus, M., Jean-guillaume, C., & Guedj, E. (2014). Clinical characteristics and brain PET findings in 3 cases of dissociative amnesia: Disproportionate retrograde deficit and posterior middle temporal gyrus hypometabolism. *Neurophysiologie Clinique/Clinical Neurophysiology, 44*(4), 355–362.

Torrey, E. F., Miller, J., Rawlings, R., & Yolken, R. H. (1997). Seasonality of births in schizophrenia and bipolar disorder: A review of the literature. *Schizophrenia Research, 28*(1), 1–38.

Trace, S. E., Baker, J. H., Peñas-Lledó, E., & Bulik, C. M. (2013). The genetics of eating disorders. *Annual Review of Clinical Psychology, 9*, 589–620.

Tye, K. M., Mirzabekov, J. J., Warden, M. R., Ferenczi, E. A., Tsai, H.-C., Finkelstein, J., … Andalman, A. S. (2013). Dopamine neurons modulate neural encoding and expression of depression-related behaviour. *Nature, 493*(7433), 537–541.

Valenstein, E. (1988). *Blaming the brain: The truth about drugs and mental health.* New York, NY: Simon and Schuster.

Van Der Hart, O., & Nijenhuis, E. (2001). Generalized dissociative amnesia: Episodic, semantic and procedural memories lost and found. *Australian and New Zealand Journal of Psychiatry, 35*(5), 589–600.

van der Heiden, C., Muris, P., & van der Molen, H. T. (2012). Randomized controlled trial on the effectiveness of metacognitive therapy and intolerance-of-uncertainty therapy for generalized anxiety disorder. *Behaviour Research and Therapy, 50*(2), 100–109.

Voigt, K., Wollburg, E., Weimann, N., Herzog, A., Meyer, B., Langs, G., & Löwe, B. (2012). Predictive validity and clinical utility of DSM-5 Somatic Symptom Disorder—Comparison with DSM-IV somatoform disorders and additional criteria for consideration. *Journal of Psychosomatic Research, 73*(5), 345–350.

Walder, D. J., Faraone, S. V., Glatt, S. J., Tsuang, M. T., & Seidman, L. J. (2014). Genetic liability, prenatal health, stress and family environment: Risk factors in the Harvard Adolescent Family High Risk for Schizophrenia Study. *Schizophrenia Research, 157*(1), 142–148.

Woody, S. R., Whittal, M. L., & McLean, P. D. (2011). Mechanisms of symptom reduction in treatment for obsessions. *Journal of Consulting and Clinical Psychology, 79*(5), 653–664.

World Health Organization, (2000). Cross-national comparisons of the prevalences and correlates of mental disorders. *Bulletin of the World Health Organization, 78*, 413–426.

World Health Organization. (2015). *Gender disparities in mental health.* Geneva: World Health Organization.

Woud, M. L., Zhang, X. C., Becker, E. S., McNally, R. J., & Margraf, J. (2014). Don't panic: Interpretation bias is predictive of new onsets of panic disorder. *Journal of Anxiety Disorders, 28*(1), 83–87.

Wright, I. C., Rabe-Hesketh, S., Woodruff, P. W., David, A. S., Murray, R. M., & Bullmore, E. T. (2000). Meta-analysis of regional brain volumes in schizophrenia. *American Journal of Psychiatry, 157*(1), 16–25.

Young, S. L., Taylor, M., & Lawrie, S. M. (2015). "First do no harm." A systematic review of the prevalence and management of antipsychotic adverse effects. *Journal of Psychopharmacology, 29*(4), 353–362.

Zhou, B., Lacroix, F., Sasaki, J., Peng, Y., Wang, X., & Ryder, A. G. (2014). Unpacking cultural variations in social anxiety and the offensive-type of Taijin Kyofusho

through the indirect effects of intolerance of uncertainty and self-construals. *Journal of Cross-Cultural Psychology, 45*(10), 1561–1578.

Zimmermann, J., Löffler-Stastka, H., Huber, D., Klug, G., Alhabbo, S., Bock, A., & Benecke, C. (2015). Is it all about the higher dose? Why psychoanalytic therapy is an effective treatment for major depression. *Clinical Psychology and Psychotherapy, 22*, 469–487.

Chapter 16

Aboujaoude, E., Salame, W., & Naim, L. (2015). Telemental health: A status update. *World Psychiatry, 14*(2), 223–230.

Albee, G. W. (1986). Toward a just society: Lessons from observations on the primary prevention of psychopathology. *American Psychologist, 41*(8), 891–898.

American Psychiatric Association (2015). Asian American-Pacific Islanders. *Let's Talk About Brochures.* Retrieved from http://www.psychiatry.org/asian-americans

American Psychological Association. (2002). Criteria for evaluating treatment guidelines. *American Psychologist, 57,*1052–1059.

Anderson, I. M. (2000). Selective serotonin reuptake inhibitors versus tricyclic antidepressants: A meta-analysis of efficacy and tolerability. *Journal of Affective Disorders, 58,* 19–36.

Anderson, N. B. (2006). Evidence-based practice in psychology. *American Psychologist, 61*(4), 271–285.

Anderson, H. D., Pace, W. D., Libby, A. M., West, D. R., & Valuck, R. J. (2012). Rates of 5 common antidepressant side effects among new adult and adolescent cases of depression: A retrospective U.S. claims study. *Clinical Therapeutics, 34*(1), 113–123.

Anderson, R. J., Frye, M. A., Abulseoud, O. A., Lee, K. H., McGillivray, J. A., Berk, M., & Tye, S. J. (2012). Deep brain stimulation for treatment-resistant depression: Efficacy, safety and mechanisms of action. *Neuroscience & Biobehavioral Reviews, 36*(8), 1920–1933.

Andersson, G., & Cuijpers, P. (2009). Internet-based and other computerized psychological treatments for adult depression: A meta-analysis. *Cognitive Behaviour Therapy, 38*(4), 196–205.

Andersson, G., Cuijpers, P., Carlbring, P., Riper, H., & Hedman, E. (2014). Guided Internet-based vs. face-to-face cognitive behavior therapy for psychiatric and somatic disorders: A systematic review and meta-analysis. *World Psychiatry, 13*(3), 288–295.

Andrade, L., Caraveo-Anduaga, J. J., Berglund, P., Bijl, R., Kessler, R. C., Demler, O., … & Wittchen, H. U. (2014). Cross-national comparisons of the prevalences and correlates of mental disorders. *Bulletin of the World Health Organization, 78*(4), 413–426.

Andrews, J., Briggs, A., Porter, R., Tucker, P., & Waddington, K. (2013). *The history of Bethlem.* New York, NY: Routledge.

Asylum [Def. 2]. (n.d.). *Oxford Dictionaries Online.* In Oxford Dictionaries. Retrieved May 7, 2015, from http://www.oxforddictionaries.com/us/definition/american_english/asylum

Augustyn, M., Brent, D., & Hermann, R. (2013). *Overview of fears and specific phobias in children.* Retrieved from: http://www.uptodate.com/contents/overview-of-fears-and-phobias-in-children-and-adolescents

Barbui, C., Cipriani, A., Patel, V., Ayuso-Mateos, J. L., & van Ommeren, M. (2011). Efficacy of antidepressants and benzodiazepines in minor depression: Systematic review and meta-analysis. *British Journal of Psychiatry, 198*(1), 11–16.

Barth, J., Munder, T., Gerger, H., Nüesch, E., Trelle, S., Znoj, H., … & Cuijpers, P. (2016). Comparative efficacy of seven psychotherapeutic interventions for patients with depression: a network meta-analysis. *Focus, 14*(2), 229–243.

Beck, A. T. (1979). *Cognitive therapy and the emotional disorders.* Penguin: London, UK.

Bedlam [Def. 3]. (n.d.). *Merriam Webster Online.* In Merriam Webster. Retrieved May 7, 2015, from http://www.merriam-webster.com/dictionary/bedlam

Benson, L. A., McGinn, M. M., & Christensen, A. (2012). Common principles of couple therapy. *Behavior Therapy, 43*(1), 25–35.

Bergsholm, P., Larsen, J. L., Rosendahl, K., & Holsten, F. (1989). Electroconvulsive therapy and cerebral computed tomography. *Acta Psychiatrica Scandinavia, 80*(6), 566–572.

Berlim, M. T., Tovar-Perdomo, S., & Fleck, M. P. (2015). Treatment-resistant major depressive disorder: Current definitions, epidemiology, and assessment. In A.F. Carvalho & R.S. McIntyre (Eds.), *Treatment-Resistant Mood Disorders.* (1–13). Oxford, UK: Oxford University Press.

Beutler, L.E. (2009). Making science matter in clinical practice: Redefining psychotherapy. *Clinical Psychology: Science and Practice, 16*(3), 301–317. doi: 10.1111/j.1468-2850.2009.01168.x.

Bohart, A., Elliott, R., Greenberg, L., & Watson, J. (2002). *Empathy.* In J. Norcross et al. (Ed.), *Psychotherapy relationships that work.* New York, NY: Oxford University Press.

Bond, G. R., Drake, R. E., Mueser, K. T., & Latimer, E. (2001). Assertive community treatment for people with severe mental illness. *Disease Management and Health Outcomes, 9*(3), 141–159.

Bordin, E. S. (1979). The generalizability of the psychoanalytic concept of the working alliance. *Psychotherapy: Theory, Research & Practice, 16*(3), 252–260.

Bostwick, J. R., Casher, M. I., & Yasugi, S. (2012). Benzodiazepines: A versatile clinical tool; evidence supports their use for alcohol withdrawal, insomnia, anxiety disorders, and other conditions. *Current Psychiatry, 11*(4), 54–64

Bowden, C. L., Mosolov, S., Hranov, L., Chen, E., Habil, H., Kongsakon, R., Manfredi, R. & Lin, H. N. (2010). Efficacy of valproate versus lithium in mania or mixed mania: A randomized, open 12-week trial. *International Clinical Psychopharmacology, 25*(2), 60–67.

Bozarth, J. (2007). Unconditional positive regard. In M. Cooper, M. O'Hara, P. F. Schmid, & A. Bohart (Eds.), *The handbook of person-centered psychotherapy and counselling,* (182–193), Basingstoke, UK: Palgrave Macmillan.

Braun, S. R., Gregor, B., & Tran, U. S. (2013). Comparing bona fide psychotherapies of depression in adults with two meta-analytical approaches. *PloS one, 8*(6), doi: 10.1371/journal.pone.0068135

Bridge, J.A., Iyengar, S., Salary, C.B., Barbe, R.P., Birmaher, B., Pincus, H.A., Ren, L., Brent, D.A., MD. (2007). Clinical response and risk for reported suicidal ideation and suicide attempts in pediatric antidepressant treatment: A meta-analysis of randomized controlled trials. *Journal of the American Medical Association, 297*(15): 1683–1696.

Burns, D. D. (1999). *The feeling good handbook.* New York, NY: Plume/Penguin Books.

Cabral, R. R., & Smith, T. B. (2011). Racial/ethnic matching of clients and therapists in mental health services: a meta-analytic review of preferences, perceptions, and outcomes. *Journal of Counseling Psychology, 58*(4), 537–554.

Cahill, S. P., Carrigan, M. H., & Christopher, F. (1999). Does EMDR work? And if so, why? A critical review of controlled outcome and dismantling research. *Journal of Anxiety Disorders, 13*(1–2), 5–33.

Cahill K., Stevens, S., Perera, R., Lancaster, T. (2012). Pharmacological interventions for smoking cessation: An overview and network meta-analysis. *Cochrane Database of Systematic Reviews 2013,* (5). doi: 10.1002/14651858.CD009329.pub2

Chabardès, S., Polosan, M., Krack, P., Bastin, J., Krainik, A., David, O., Bougerol, T., & Benabid, A. L. (2013). Deep brain stimulation for obsessive-compulsive disorder: Subthalamic nucleus target. *World Neurosurgery, 80*(3–4), S31-e1-S31.e8.

Chambless, D. L., Baker, M. J., Baucom, D. H., Beutler, L. E., Calhoun, K. S., Crits-Christoph, P., … & Woody, S.

R. (1998). Update on empirically validated therapies, II. *Clinical Psychologist, 51*(1), 3–16.

Chiles, J. A., Lambert, M. J., & Hatch, A. L. (2002). Medical cost offset: A review of the impact of psychological interventions on medical utilization over the past three decades. In N. A. Cummings, W. T. O'Donohue, & K. E. Ferguson (Eds.), *The impact of medical cost offset on practice and research: Making it work for you.* Reno, NV: Context Press.

Cipriani, A., Geddes, J. R., Furukawa, T. A., & Barbui, C. (2007). Metareview on short-term effectiveness and safety of antidepressants for depression: An evidence-based approach to inform clinical practice. *Canadian Journal of Psychiatry, 52*(9), 553–562.

Coffey, C. E. (Ed.). (1993). *Clinical science of electroconvulsive therapy.* Washington, DC: American Psychiatric Press.

Consensus Conference. (1985). Electroconvulsive therapy. *Journal of the American Medical Association, 254,* 2103–2108.

Corrigan, P. W., Morris, S. B., Michaels, P. J., Rafacz, J. D., & Rüsch, N. (2012). Challenging the public stigma of mental illness: A meta-analysis of outcome studies. *Psychiatric Services, 63*(10), 963–973.

Cuijpers, P., van Straten, A., Andersson, G., & van Oppen, P. (2008). Psychotherapy for depression in adults: A meta-analysis of comparative outcome studies. *Journal of Consulting and Clinical Psychology, 76*(6), 909–922.

Cuijpers, P., Geraedts, A. S., van Oppen, P., Andersson, G., Markowitz, J. C., & van Straten, A. (2011). Interpersonal psychotherapy for depression: A meta-analysis. *American Journal of Psychiatry, 168*(6), 581–592.

D'Astous, M., Cottin, S., Roy, M., Picard, C., & Cantin, L. (2013). Bilateral stereotactic anterior capsulotomy for obsessive-compulsive disorder: Long-term follow-up. *Journal of Neurology, Neurosurgery & Psychiatry, 84*(11), 1208–1213.

Dadlani, M., & Scherer, D. (2009). *Culture in psychotherapy practice and research: Awareness, knowledge, and skills.* Retrieved from http://www.divisionofpsychotherapy.org/dadlani-and-scherer-2009

Dalle Grave, R., Calugi, S., Doll, H. A., & Fairburn, C. G. (2013). Enhanced cognitive behaviour therapy for adolescents with anorexia nervosa: An alternative to family therapy? *Behaviour Research and Therapy, 51*(1), R9–R12.

Davis III, T. E., Reuther, E. T., May, A. C., Rudy, B. M., Munson, M. S., Jenkins, W. S., & Whiting, S. E. (2013). The Behavioral Avoidance Task Using Imaginal Exposure (BATIE): A paper-and-pencil version of traditional in vivo behavioral avoidance tasks. *Psychological Assessment, 25*(4), 1111–1119.

Dear, M. J., & Wolch, J. R. (2014). *Landscapes of despair: From deinstitutionalization to homelessness.* Princeton, NJ: Princeton University Press.

Decker, S. L. (2013). Two-thirds of primary care physicians accepted new Medicaid patients in 2011–12: A baseline to measure future acceptance rates. *Health Affairs, 32*(7), 1183–1187.

de Girolamo, G., Dagani, J., Purcell, R., Cocchi, A., & McGorry, P. D. (2012). Age of onset of mental disorders and use of mental health services: Needs, opportunities and obstacles. *Epidemiology and Psychiatric Sciences, 21*(01), 47–57.

de Haan, A. M., Boon, A. E., de Jong, J. T., Hoeve, M., & Vermeiren, R. R. (2013). A meta-analytic review on treatment dropout in child and adolescent outpatient mental health care. *Clinical Psychology Review, 33*(5), 698–711.

DeNavas-Walt, C., Proctor, B. D., & Smith, J. C. (2013). Income, poverty, and health insurance coverage in the United States: 2006. *Current Population Reports: Consumer Income. U.S. Department of Commerce, Economics and Statistics Administration, U.S. Census Bureau,* 1.

Desai, R. A., Dausey, D. J., & Rosenheck, R. A. (2014). Mental health service delivery and suicide risk: The role of individual patient and facility factors. *American Journal of Psychiatry, 162*(2), 311–318.

Dharmshaktu, P., Tayal, V., & Kalra, B. S. (2012). Efficacy of antidepressants as analgesics: A review. *Journal of Clinical Pharmacology, 52*(1), 6–17.

DiMatteo, M. R. (2004). Social support and patient adherence to medical treatment: A meta-analysis. *Health Psychology, 23*(2), 207–218.

Diniz, B. S., Machado-Vieira, R., & Forlenza, O. V. (2013). Lithium and neuroprotection: Translational evidence and implications for the treatment of neuropsychiatric disorders. *Neuropsychiatric Disease and Treatment, 9,* 493–500.

Dixon, J. F., & Hokin, L. E. (1998). Lithium acutely inhibits and chronically up-regulates and stabilizes glutamate uptake by presynaptic nerve endings in mouse cerebral cortex. *Proceedings of the National Academy of Sciences, 95*(14), 8363–8368.

Dorstyn, D. S., Saniotis, A., & Sobhanian, F. (2013). A systematic review of telecounselling and its effectiveness in managing depression amongst minority ethnic communities. *Journal of Telemedicine and Telecare, 19*(6), 338–346.

Dubicka, B., Hadley, S., & Roberts, C. (2006). Suicidal behaviour in youths with depression treated with new-generation antidepressants. *British Journal of Psychiatry, 189*(5), 393–398.

Eisler, I., Simic, M., Russell, G. F., & Dare, C. (2007). A randomised controlled treatment trial of two forms of family therapy in adolescent anorexia nervosa: A five-year follow-up. *Journal of Child Psychology and Psychiatry, 48*(6), 552–560.

Eisler, I., Dare, C., Hodes, M., Russell, G., Dodge, E., & Le Grange, D. (2000). Family therapy for adolescent anorexia nervosa: The results of a controlled comparison of two family interventions. *Journal of Child Psychology and Psychiatry and Allied Disciplines, 41*(6), 727–736.

Eranti, S., Psych, M. R. C., Mogg, A., Pluck, G., Landau, S., … & Psych, M. R. C. (2007). A randomized, controlled trial with 6-month follow-up of repetitive transcranial magnetic stimulation and electroconvulsive therapy for severe depression. *American Journal of Psychiatry, 164*(1), 73–81.

Eysenck, H. J. (2013). *Experiments in behaviour therapy: Readings in modern methods of treatment of mental disorders derived from learning theory,* London, UK: Pergamon Press.

Ferri, M., Amato, L., & Davoli, M. (2006). Alcoholics Anonymous and other 12-step programmes for alcohol dependence. *The Cochrane Library, 3.*

Food and Drug Administration. (2004, March 22). *FDA public health advisory: Worsening depression and suicidality in patients being treated with antidepressant.* Retrieved from http://www.fda.gov/cder/drug/antidepressants/AntidepressantPHA.htm

Food and Drug Administration. (2007, May 2). *FDA public health advisory: FDA proposes new warnings about suicidal thinking, behavior in young adults who take antidepressant medications.* Retrieved from http://www.fda.gov/NewsEvents/Newsroom/PressAnnouncements/2007/ucm108905.htm

Foulds, J., Burke, M., Steinberg, M., Williams, J. M., & Ziedonis, D. M. (2004). Advances in pharmacotherapy for tobacco dependence. *Expert Opinion on Emerging Drugs, 9*(1), 39–53.

Furmark, T., Tillfsfors, M., Marteinsbottir, I., Pissiota, A., Långström, B., & Fredrikson, M. (2002). Common changes in cerebral blood flow in patients with social phobia treated with citalopram or cognitive-behavioral therapy. *Archives of General Psychiatry, 59,* 425–433.

Furukawa, T. A., McGuire, H., & Barbui, C. (2002). Meta-analysis of effects and side effects of low dosage tricyclic antidepressants in depression: Systematic review. *British Medical Journal, 325*: 991.

Garland, A. F., Lau, A. S., Yeh, M., McCabe, K. M., Hough, R. L., & Landsverk, J. A. (2014). Racial and ethnic differences in utilization of mental health services among high-risk youths. *American Journal of Psychiatry, 162*(7), 1336–1343.

Garnaat, S. L., & Greenberg, B. D. (2014). *Deep brain stimulation for severe and intractable obsessive–compulsive disorder.* Retrieved from http://www.futuremedicine.com/doi/abs/10.2217/ebo.13.466

Gary, F. A. (2005). Stigma: Barrier to mental health care among ethnic minorities. *Issues in Mental Health Nursing, 26*(10), 979–999.

Geddes, J. R., Carney, S. M., Davies, C., Furukawa, T. A., Kupfer, D. J., Frank, E., & Goodwin, G. M. (2003). Relapse prevention with antidepressant drug treatment in depressive disorders: A systematic review. *The Lancet, 361*(9358), 653–661.

Gearing, R. E., Townsend, L., Elkins, J., El-Bassel, N., & Osterberg, L. (2014). Strategies to predict, measure, and improve psychosocial treatment adherence. *Harvard Review of Psychiatry, 22*(1), 31–45.

Gibbons, R. D., Hur, K., Brown, C. H., Davis, J. M., & Mann, J. J. (2012). Benefits from antidepressants: Synthesis of 6-week patient-level outcomes from double-blind placebo-controlled randomized trials of fluoxetine and venlafaxine. *Archives of General Psychiatry, 69*(6), 572–579.

Gibbons, R. D., Coca Perraillon, M., Hur, K., Conti, R. M., Valuck, R. J., & Brent, D. A. (2015). Antidepressant treatment and suicide attempts and self-inflicted injury in children and adolescents. *Pharmacoepidemiology and Drug Safety, 24*(2), 208–214.

Gibbons, R. D., & Mann, J. J. (2014). The Relationship Between Antidepressant Initiation and Suicide Risk. *Psychiatric Times,* December 31, 2014.

Glass, R. M. (2001). Electroconvulsive therapy: Time to bring it out of the shadows. *Journal of the American Medical Association, 285*(10), 1346–1348.

Gold, P. W., Machado-Vieira, R., & Pavlatou, M. G. (2015). Clinical and biochemical manifestations of depression: Relation to the neurobiology of stress. *Neural Plasticity, 2015,* 1–11.

Goode, E. (2003, January 28). Even in the age of Prozac, some still prefer the couch. *New York Times.* Retrieved September 23, 2008, from http://www.nytimes.com

Greenberg, B. D., Malone, D. A., Friehs, G. M., Rezai, A. R., Kubu, C. S., Malloy, P. F., Salloway, S.P., Okun, M.S., Goodman, W.K., & Rasmussen, S. A. (2006). Three-year outcomes in deep brain stimulation for highly resistant obsessive–compulsive disorder. *Neuropsychopharmacology, 31*(11), 2384–2393.

Griner, D., & Smith, T. B. (2006). Culturally adapted mental health intervention: A meta-analytic review. *Psychotherapy: Theory, Research, Practice, Training, 43*(4), 531–548.

Gueorguieva, R., Mallinckrodt, C., & Krystal, J. H. (2011). Trajectories of depression severity in clinical trials of duloxetine: Insights into antidepressant and placebo responses. *Archives of General Psychiatry, 68*(12), 1227–1237.

Hallahan, B., Newell, J., Soares, J. C., Brambilla, P., Strakowski, S. M., Fleck, D. E., … & McDonald, C. (2011). Structural magnetic resonance imaging in bipolar disorder: An international collaborative mega-analysis of individual adult patient data. *Biological Psychiatry, 69*(4), 326–335.

Hammad, T. A., Laughren, T., & Racoosin, J. (2006). Suicidality in pediatric patients treated with antidepressant drugs. *Archives of General Psychiatry,63*(3), 332–339.

Harrington, A. (2008). *The cure within: A history of mind-body medicine.* New York, NY: W. W. Norton & Company.

Hatzenbuehler, M. L., Phelan, J. C., & Link, B. G. (2013). Stigma as a fundamental cause of population health inequalities. *American Journal of Public Health, 103*(5), 813–821.

Hazel, M. T. (2005). Visualization and systematic desensitization: Intervention for habituating and sensitizing patters of public speaking anxiety. *Dissertation Abstracts International Section A: Humanities and Social Sciences, 66*(1–a), 30.

Henggeler, S. W., & Schaeffer, C. M. (2010). Treating serious emotional and behavioural problems using multisystemic therapy. *Australian and New Zealand Journal of Family Therapy, 31*(2), 149–164. doi: 10.1375/anft.31.2.149

Hill, C. E., & Nakayama, E. Y. (2000). Client-centered therapy: Where has it been and where is it going? A comment on Hathaway. *Journal of Clinical Psychology, 56*(7), 875–961.

Hofmann, S. G., & Smits, J. A. (2008). Cognitive–behavioral therapy for adult anxiety disorders: A meta-analysis of randomized placebo-controlled trials. *Journal of Clinical Psychiatry, 69*(4), 621–632.

Hofmann, S. G., Asnaani, A., Vonk, I. J., Sawyer, A. T., & Fang, A. (2012). The efficacy of cognitive behavioral therapy: A review of meta-analyses. *Cognitive Therapy and Research, 36*(5), 427–440.

Hofmann, S. G., & Barlow, D. H. (2014). Evidence-based psychological interventions and the common factors approach: The beginnings of a rapprochement? *Psychotherapy, 51*(4), 510–513.

Hoge, E. A., Ivkovic, A., & Fricchione, G. L. (2012). Generalized anxiety disorder: Diagnosis and treatment. *BMJ, 345*(e7500), 37–42.

Honberg, R., Diehl, S., Kimball, A., Gruttadaro, D., & Fitzpatrick, M. (2011). *State mental health cuts: A national crisis.* National Alliance on Mental Illness: Arlington, VA.

Hopper, K., & Wanderling, J. (2000). Revisiting the developed versus developing country distinction in course and outcome in schizophrenia: Results from ISoS, the WHO collaborative follow-up project. *Schizophrenia Bulletin, 26*(4), 835–846.

Hopper, K., Harrison, G., Janca, A., & Norman Sartorius, M. D. (Eds.). (2007). *Recovery from schizophrenia: An international perspective: A report from the WHO Collaborative Project, the international study of schizophrenia.* Oxford University Press.

Horvath, A. O., & Bedi, R. P. (2002). *The alliance.* In J. C. Norcross (Ed.), *Psychotherapy relationships that work: Therapist contributions and responsiveness to patients* (pp. 37–69). New York, NY: Oxford University Press.

Horvath, A. O., Del Re, A. C., Flückiger, C., & Symonds, D. (2011). Alliance in individual psychotherapy. *Psychotherapy, 48*(1), 9–16.

Huh, J., Goebert, D., Takeshita, J., Lu, B. Y., & Kang, M. (2011). Treatment of generalized anxiety disorder: A comprehensive review of the literature for psychopharmacologic alternatives to newer antidepressants and benzodiazepines. *The Primary Care Companion to CNS Disorders, 13*(2), doi: 10.4088/PCC.08r00709blu

Institute of Medicine. (2001). *Crossing the quality chasm: A new health system for the 21st century.* Washington, DC: National Academy Press.

James, D. J. & Glaze, L. E. (2006). *Special report: Mental health and treatment of inmates and probationers.* Washington, DC: U.S. Department of Justice, Bureau of Justice Statistics.

Jope, R. S. (1999). Anti-bipolar therapy: Mechanism of action of lithium. *Molecular Psychiatry, 4*(2), 117–128.

Kadden, R., Carbonari, J., Litt, M., Tonigan, S., & Zweben, A. (1998). Matching alcoholism treatments to client heterogeneity: Project MATCH three-year drinking outcomes. *Alcoholism, Clinical and Experimental Research, 22*, 1300–1311.

Kaplan, H. I., & Saddock, B. J. (Eds.). (1989). *Comprehensive textbook of psychiatry, V.* Baltimore, MD: Williams and Wilkins.

Kapur, S., & Seeman, P. (2014). Does fast dissociation from the dopamine D2 receptor explain the action of atypical antipsychotics? A new hypothesis. *American Journal of Psychiatry, 158*(3), 360–369.

Kaskutas, L. A. (2009). Alcoholics Anonymous effectiveness: Faith meets science. *Journal of Addictive Diseases, 28*(2), 145–157.

Kesey, K. (2002). *One flew over the cuckoo's nest.* London, UK: Penguin.

Kessing, L. V., Hellmund, G., Geddes, J. R., Goodwin, G. M., & Andersen, P. K. (2011). Valproate v. lithium in the treatment of bipolar disorder in clinical practice: observational nationwide register-based cohort study. *British Journal of Psychiatry, 199*(1), 57–63.

Kessler, D., Lewis, G., Kaur, S., Wiles, N., King, M., Weich, S., … & Peters, T. J. (2009). Therapist-delivered internet psychotherapy for depression in primary care: A randomised controlled trial. *The Lancet, 374*(9690), 628–634.

Kessler, R. C., Berglund, P., Demler, O., Jin, R., Merikangas, K. R., & Walters, E. E. (2005). Lifetime prevalence and age-of-onset distributions of DSM-IV disorders in the National Comorbidity Survey Replication. *Archives of General Psychiatry, 62*(6), 593–602.

Khalatbari, J., Samkhaniyani, E., & Ghorbanshirodi, S. (2012). Comparison of effectiveness between thought stasis, flooding, and regular desensitization techniques on OCD patients' washing obsession. *Life Science Journal, 9*(3), 2619–2624.

Khalid, N., Atkins, M., Tredget, J., Giles, M., Champney-Smith, K., & Kirov, G. (2008). The effectiveness of electroconvulsive therapy in treatment-resistant depression: A naturalistic study. *Journal of ECT, 24*(2), 141–145.

Kirsch, I., Deacon, B. J., Huedo-Medina, T. B., Scoboria, A., Moore, T. J., & Johnson, B. T. (2008). Initial severity and antidepressant benefits: A meta-analysis of data submitted to the Food and Drug Administration. *PLoS Med, 5*(2), doi: 10.1371/journal.pmed.0050045

Klein, M. H., Michels, J. L., Kolden, G. G., & Chisolm-Stockard, S. (2001). Congruence or genuineness. *Psychotherapy: Theory, Research, Practice, Training, 38*(4), 396–400.

Klerman, G. L., & Weissman, M. M. (1994). *Interpersonal psychotherapy of depression: A brief, focused, specific strategy.* Lanham, MD: Rowman & Littlefield Publisher.

Koelen, J. A., Houtveen, J. H., Abbass, A., Luyten, P., Eurelings-Bontekoe, E. H., Van Broeckhuysen-Kloth, S. A., … & Geenen, R. (2014). Effectiveness of psychotherapy for severe somatoform disorder: meta-analysis. *British Journal of Psychiatry, 204*(1), 12–19.

Kopta, S. M., Lueger, R. J., Saunders, S. M., & Howard, K. I. (1999). Individual psychotherapy outcome and process research: Challenges leading to greater turmoil or positive transition? *Annual Review of Psychology, 50*, 441–469.

Kramer, E. J., Kwong, K., Lee, E., & Chung, H. (2002). Cultural factors influencing the mental health of Asian Americans. *Western Journal of Medicine, 176*(4), 227–231.

Laska, K. M., Gurman, A. S., & Wampold, B. E. (2013). Expanding the lens of evidence-based practice in psychotherapy: A common factors perspective. *Psychotherapy, 51*(4), 467–481.

Lauber, C., & Rössler, W. (2007). Stigma towards people with mental illness in developing countries in Asia. *International Review of Psychiatry, 19*(2), 157–178.

Le Grange, D., Lock, J., Agras, W. S., Moye, A., Bryson, S. W., Jo, B., & Kraemer, H. C. (2012). Moderators and mediators of remission in family-based treatment and adolescent focused therapy for anorexia nervosa. *Behaviour Research and Therapy, 50*(2), 85–92.

Lehman, A. F., Steinwachs, D. M., Dixon, L. B., Goldman, H. H., Osher, F., Postrado, L., … & Zito, J. (1998). Translating research into practice: The schizophrenic patient outcomes research team (PORT) treatment recommendations. *Schizophrenia Bulletin, 24*, 1–10.

Leichsenring, F., Salzer, S., Beutel, M. E., Herpertz, S., Hiller, W., Hoyer, J., … & Leibing, E. (2014). Psychodynamic therapy and cognitive-behavioral therapy in social anxiety disorder: A multicenter randomized controlled trial. *American Journal of Psychiatry, 170*(7), 759–767.

Leidy, N. K. (1994). Functional status and the forward progress of merry-go-rounds: Toward a coherent analytical framework. *Nursing Research, 43*(4), 196–202.

Lemmens, L. H. J. M., Arntz, A., Peeters, F., Hollon, S. D., Roefs, A., & Huibers, M. J. H. (2015). Clinical effectiveness of cognitive therapy v. interpersonal psychotherapy for depression: Results of a randomized controlled trial. *Psychological Medicine, 45*(10), 2095–2110.

Lenzenweger, M. F., Dworkin, R. H., & Wethington, E. (1989). Models of positive and negative symptoms in schizophrenia: An empirical evaluation of latent structures. *Journal of Abnormal Psychology, 98*(1), 62–70.

Levis, D. J., & Hare, N. (2013). A review of the theoretical rationale and empirical support for the extinction approach of implosive (flooding) therapy. *Progress in Behavior Modification, 4*, 299.

Lilienfeld, S. O., Ritschel, L. A., Lynn, S. J., Cautin, R. L., & Latzman, R. D. (2013). Why many clinical psychologists are resistant to evidence-based practice: Root causes and constructive remedies. *Clinical Psychology Review, 33*(7), 883–900.

Linde, K., Kriston, L., Rücker, G., Jamil, S., Schumann, I., Meissner, K., … & Schneider, A. (2015). Efficacy and acceptability of pharmacological treatments for depressive disorders in primary care: Systematic review and network meta-analysis. *Annals of Family Medicine, 13*(1), 69–79.

Link, B. G., Struening, E. L., Neese-Todd, S., Asmussen, S., & Phelan, J. C. (2014). Stigma as a barrier to recovery: The consequences of stigma for the self-esteem of people with mental illnesses. *Psychiatric Services, 52*(12), 1621–1626.

Lindfors, O., Ojanen, S., Jääskeläinen, T., & Knekt, P. (2014). Social support as a predictor of the outcome of depressive and anxiety disorder in short-term and long-term psychotherapy. *Psychiatry Research, 216*(1), 44–51.

Lock, J., & Le Grange, D. (2012). *Treatment manual for anorexia nervosa: A family-based approach.* New York, NY: Guilford Press.

Luborsky, L., Diguer, L., Seligman, D. A., Rosenthal, R., Krause, E. D., Johnson, S., Halperin, G., Bishop, M., Berman, J.S., & Schweizer, E. (1999). The researcher's own therapy allegiances: A "wild card" in comparisons of treatment efficacy. *Clinical Psychology: Science and Practice, 6*(1), 95–106.

Malhi, G. S., Tanious, M., Das, P., Coulston, C. M., & Berk, M. (2013). Potential mechanisms of action of lithium in bipolar disorder. *CNS Drugs, 27*(2), 135–153.

Mancini, A. D., Moser, L. L., Whitley, R., McHugo, G. J., Bond, G. R., Finnerty, M. T., & Burns, B. J. (2015). Assertive community treatment: Facilitators and barriers to implementation in routine mental health settings. *Psychiatric Services, 60*(2), 189–195.

Maramba, G. G., & Nagayama Hall, G. C. (2002). Meta-analyses of ethnic match as a predictor of dropout, utilization, and level of functioning. *Cultural Diversity and Ethnic Minority Psychology, 8*(3), 290–297.

Marcus, M., Yasamy, M. T., Van Ommeren, M., Chisholm, D., & Saxena, S. (2012). Depression: A global public health concern. *WHO Department of Mental Health and Substance Abuse, 1*, 6–8.

Martin, J. K., Pescosolido, B. A., & Tuch, S. A. (2000). Of fear and loathing: The role of "disturbing behavior," labels, and causal attributions in shaping public attitudes toward people with mental illness. *Journal of Health and Social Behavior, 41*(2), 208–223.

Martin, J. K., Pescosolido, B. A., Olafsdottir, S., & McLeod, J. D. (2007). The construction of fear: Americans' preferences for social distance from children and adolescents with mental health problems. *Journal of Health and Social Behavior, 48*(1), 50–67.

Mason, P., Harrison, G., Glazebrook, C., Medley, I., & Croudace, T. (1996). The course of schizophrenia over 13 years: A report from the International Study on Schizophrenia (ISoS) coordinated by the World Health Organization. *British Journal of Psychiatry, 169*(5), 580–586.

McIntosh, V. V., Jordan, J., Carter, F. A., Luty, S. E., McKenzie, J. M., Bulik, C. M., Frampton, C.M.A., & Joyce, P. R. (2014). Three psychotherapies for anorexia nervosa: A randomized, controlled trial. *American Journal of Psychiatry, 162*(4), 741–747.

McNeil, D. W., & Zvolensky, M. J. (2000). Systematic desensitization. In A. E. Kazdin (Ed.), *Encyclopedia of psychology* (Vol. 7, pp. 533–535). Washington, DC: American Psychological Association.

Medicaid: Centers for Medicare and Medicaid Services. *Behavioral health services.* Retrieved from https://www.medicaid.gov/medicaid-chip-program-information/by-topics/benefits/mental-health-services.html

Meltzer, H. Y. (2013). Update on typical and atypical antipsychotic drugs. *Annual Review of Medicine, 64*, 393–406.

Milton, M. (2004). The ethics (or not) of evidence-based practice. In R. Tribe & J. Morrissey, (Eds.), *The Handbook of Professional and Ethical Practice for Psychologists, Counsellors and Psychotherapists* (263–276). New York, NY: Routledge.

Moos, R. H., & Moos, B. S. (2006). Participation in treatment and Alcoholics Anonymous: A 16-year follow-up of initially untreated individuals. *Journal of Clinical Psychology, 62*(6), 735–750.

Moreland, C. S., Bonin, L., Middleman, A. B., Augustyn, M., Brent, D., & Solomon, D. (2013). *Effect of antidepressants on suicide risk in children and adolescents.* Retrieved from http://www.uptodate.com/contents/effect-of-antidepressants-on-suicide-risk-in-children-and-adolescents

Mulrow, C. D. (1999, March). Treatment of depression—newer pharmacotherapies, summary. *Evidence Report/Technology Assessment, 7.* Agency for health care policy and research, Rockville, MD. Retrieved September 23, 2008, from http://www.ahrq.gov/clinic/epcsums/deprsumm.htm

Murphy, R., Straebler, S., Basden, S., Cooper, Z., & Fairburn, C. G. (2012). Interpersonal psychotherapy for eating disorders. *Clinical Psychology & Psychotherapy, 19*(2), 150–158.

Nadeem, E., Lange, J. M., Edge, D., Fongwa, M., Belin, T., & Miranda, J. (2007). Does stigma keep poor young immigrant and U.S.-born black and Latina women from seeking mental health care? *Psychiatric Services, 58*(12), 1547–1554.

Nami Multicultural Action Center. Facts about Stigma and Mental Illness in Diverse Communities. Home Page. National Alliance on Mental Illness, n.d. Web. 5 June 2015.

Nathan, P. E., & Gorman, J. M. (2002). Efficacy, effectiveness and the clinical utility of psychotherapy research. In P. E. Nathan and J. M. Gorman (Eds.), *A guide to treatments that work* (2nd ed.). New York, NY: Oxford University Press.

Nathan, P. E., & Gorman, J. M. (Eds.). (2015). *A guide to treatments that work.* Oxford, UK: Oxford University Press.

National Center for Health Statistics (US). Health, United States 2010: With Special Feature on Death and Dying 2011. Hyattsville, MD.

Newman, B., & Newman, P. (2014). *Development through life: A psychosocial approach.* Boston, MA: Cengage Learning.

News24. (2001, August 6). *Rosie O'Donnell breaks silence on her depression.* Retrieved from http://www.news24.com/xArchive/Archive/Rosie-ODonnell-breaks-silence-on-her-depression-20010805

Ng, C. H. (1997). The stigma of mental illness in Asian cultures. *Australian and New Zealand Journal of Psychiatry, 31*(3), 382–390.

Norcross, J. C. (2002). *Psychotherapeutic relationships that work.* New York, NY: Oxford University Press.

Ogrodniczuk, J. S., Piper, W. E., Joyce, A. S., McCallum, M., & Rosie, J. S. (2002). Social support as a predictor of response to group therapy for complicated grief. *Psychiatry, 65*(4), 346–357.

Olfson, M., Marcus S. C., & Shaffer, D. (2006). Antidepressant drug therapy and suicide in severely depressed children and adults. *Archives of General Psychiatry, 63*(8), 865–872.

Oliver, B. E., Gascón, J., Aparicio, A., Ayats, E., Rodriguez, R., Maestro, D. L. J., Garcia-Bach, M., & Soler, P. A. (2002). Bilateral anterior capsulotomy for refractory obsessive-compulsive disorders. *Stereotactic and Functional Neurosurgery, 81*(1–4), 90–95.

Ottosson, J. O., & Odeberg, H. (2012). Evidence-based electroconvulsive therapy. *Acta Psychiatrica Scandinavica, 125*(3), 177–184.

Pan, D. (2013, April 29). *MAP: Which states have cut treatment for the mentally ill the most? Mother Jones.* Retrieved from http://www.motherjones.com/mojo/2013/04/map-states-cut-treatment-for-mentally-ill

Parker, G., Roy, K., Hadzi, P. D., & Pedic, F. (1992). Psychotic (delusional) depression: A meta-analysis of physical treatments. *Journal of Affective Disorders, 24*(1), 17–24.

Payne, N. A., & Prudic, J. (2009). Electroconvulsive therapy Part I: A perspective on the evolution and current practice of ECT. *Journal of Psychiatric Practice, 15*(5), 346–368.

Pescosolido, B. A., Medina, T. R., Martin, J. K., & Long, J. S. (2013). The "backbone" of stigma: Identifying the global core of public prejudice associated with mental illness. *American Journal of Public Health, 103*(5), 853–860.

Phillips, M. L., Chase, H. W., Sheline, Y. I., Etkin, A., Almeida, J. R., Deckersbach, T., & Trivedi, M. H. (2015). Identifying predictors, moderators, and mediators of antidepressant response in major depressive disorder: Neuroimaging approaches. *American Journal of Psychiatry, 172*(2), 124–138.

Pickar, D., Labarca, R., Linnoila, M., Roy, A., Hommer, D., Everett, D., & Payl, S. M. (1984). Neuroleptic-induced decrease in plasma homovanillic acid and antipsychotic activity in schizophrenic patients. *Science, 225*(4665), 954–957.

Policy, R. (1997). Matching alcoholism treatments to client heterogeneity: Project MATCH posttreatment drinking outcomes. *Journal of Studies on Alcohol, 58*(1), 7–29.

Poulsen, S., Lunn, S., Daniel, S. I., Folke, S., Mathiesen, B. B., Katznelson, H., & Fairburn, C. G. (2014). A randomized controlled trial of psychoanalytic psychotherapy or cognitive-behavioral therapy for bulimia nervosa. *American Journal of Psychiatry, 171*(1), 109–116.

Pratt, L. A., Brody, D. J., & Gu, Q. (2011). Antidepressant use in persons aged 12 and over: United States, U.S. Department of Health and Human Services. *NCHS Data Brief, 76,* 2005–2008.

Price, M., Mehta, N., Tone, E. B., & Anderson, P. L. (2011). Does engagement with exposure yield better outcomes? Components of presence as a predictor of treatment response for virtual reality exposure therapy for social phobia. *Journal of Anxiety Disorders, 25*(6), 763–770.

Rogers, C. R. (1961). *On becoming a person: A therapist's view of psychotherapy.* Boston, MA: Houghton Mifflin.

Rogers, C. R. (1966). *Client-centered therapy.* American Psychological Association.

Rogers, C. R. (1980). *A way of being.* Boston, MA: Houghton Mifflin.

Rosa, A. R., Fountoulakis, K., Siamouli, M., Gonda, X., & Vieta, E. (2011). Is anticonvulsant treatment of mania a class effect? Data from randomized clinical trials. *CNS Neuroscience & Therapeutics, 17*(3), 167–177.

Rowe, C. L. (2012). Family therapy for drug abuse: Review and updates 2003–2010. *Journal of Marital and Family Therapy, 38*(1), 59–81.

Rück, C., Karlsson, A., Steele, J. D., Edman, G., Meyerson, B. A., Ericson, K., Nyman, H., Asberg, M., & Svanborg, P. (2008). Capsulotomy for obsessive-compulsive disorder: Long-term follow-up of 25 patients. *Archives of General Psychiatry, 65*(8), 914–921.

Rummel-Kluge, C., Komossa, K., Schwarz, S., Hunger, H., Schmid, F., Kissling, W., Davis, J.M., & Leucht, S. (2012). Second-generation antipsychotic drugs and extrapyramidal side effects: A systematic review and meta-analysis of head-to-head comparisons. *Schizophrenia Bulletin, 38*(1), 167–177.

Ruwaard, J., Lange, A., Schrieken, B., Dolan, C. V., & Emmelkamp, P. (2012). The effectiveness of online cognitive behavioral treatment in routine clinical practice. *PLoS One, 7*(7), doi: 10.1371/journal.pone.0040089

Sachs, G. S., Nierenberg, A. A., Calabrese, J. R., Marangell, L. B., Wisniewski, S. R., Gyulai, L., ... & Thase, M,E. (2007). Effectiveness of adjunctive antidepressant treatment for bipolar depression. *New England Journal of Medicine, 356*(17), 1711–1722.

Sackett, D. L., Straus, S. E., Richardson, W. S., Rosenberg, W., & Haynes, R. B. (2000). *Evidence-based medicine: How to practice and teach EBM* (2nd ed.). London, UK: Churchill Livingstone.

Santos Jr., A. D., Oliveira, M. C., Andrade, T. D. S., Freitas, R. R. D., Banzato, C. E. M., Azevedo, R. C. S. D., & Botega, N. J. (2013). Twenty years of electroconvulsive therapy in a psychiatric unit at a university general hospital. *Trends in Psychiatry and Psychotherapy, 35*(3), 229–233.

Sartorius, N. (1998). Stigma: What can psychiatrists do about it? *The Lancet, 352*(9133), 1058–1059.

Schomerus, G., Schwahn, C., Holzinger, A., Corrigan, P. W., Grabe, H. J., Carta, M. G., & Angermeyer, M. C. (2012). Evolution of public attitudes about mental illness: A systematic review and meta-analysis. *Acta Psychiatrica Scandinavica, 125*(6), 440–452.

Seabrook, J. A., & Avison, W. R. (2012). Socioeconomic status and cumulative disadvantage processes across the life course: Implications for health outcomes. *Canadian Review of Sociology/Revue canadienne de sociologie, 49*(1), 50–68.

Seawell, A. H., Cutrona, C. E., & Russell, D. W. (2014). The effects of general social support and social support for racial discrimination on African American women's well-being. *Journal of Black Psychology, 40*(1), 3–26.

Seeman, P. (2002). Atypical antipsychotics: Mechanism of action. *Canadian Journal of Psychiatry. Revue canadienne de psychiatrie, 47*(1), 27–38.

Seligman, M. E. P. (1995). The effectiveness of psychotherapy: The *Consumer Reports* study. *American Psychologist, 50*(12), 965–974.

Shadish, W. R., Matt, G. E., Navarro, A. M., & Phillips, G. (2000). The effects of psychological therapies under clinically representative conditions: A meta-analysis. *Psychological Bulletin, 126*(4), 512–529.

Shedler, J. (2010). The efficacy of psychodynamic psychotherapy. *American Psychologist, 65,* 98–109. doi: 10.1037/a0018378

Shedler, J. (2012). The efficacy of psychodynamic psychotherapy. In R. A. Levy, S. Ablon, & H. Kachele (Eds.), *Psychodynamic Psychotherapy Research: Evidence-Based Practice and Practice-Based Evidence,* (9–25). New York, NY: Springer Publishing.

Sloane, R. B., Staples, F. R., Cristol, A. H., & Yorkston, N. J. (1975). Short-term analytically oriented psychotherapy versus behavior therapy. *American Journal of Psychiatry, 132*(4), 373–377.

Smith, M. L., Glass, G. V., & Miller, T. I. (1980). *The benefits of psychotherapy.* Baltimore, MD: Johns Hopkins University Press.

Smith, L. A., Cornelius, V. R., Azorin, J. M., Perugi, G., Vieta, E., Young, A. H., & Bowden, C. L. (2010). Valproate for the treatment of acute bipolar depression: Systematic review and meta-analysis. *Journal of Affective Disorders, 122*(1), 1–9.

Spielmans, G. I., Benish, S. G., Marin, C., Bowman, W. M., Menster, M., & Wheeler, A. J. (2013). Specificity of psychological treatments for bulimia nervosa and binge eating disorder: A meta-analysis of direct comparisons. *Clinical Psychology Review, 33*(3), 460–469.

Solomon, D. A., Keitner, G. I., Miller, I. W., Shea, M. T., & Keller, M. B. (1995). Course of illness and maintenance treatments for patients with bipolar disorder. *Journal of Clinical Psychiatry, 56*(1), 5–13.

Stanton, M. D., & Shadish, W. R. (1997). Outcome, attrition, and family–couples treatment for drug abuse: A meta-analysis and review of the controlled, comparative studies. *Psychological Bulletin, 122*(2), 170–191.

Stewart, A. L., Greenfield, S., Hays, R. D., Wells, K., Rogers, W. H., Berry, S. D., McGlynn, E.A., & Ware, J. E. (1989). Functional status and well-being of patients with chronic conditions: Results from the Medical Outcomes Study. *Journal of the American Medical Association, 262*(7), 907–913.

Sue, S., Fujino, D. C., Hu, L. T., Takeuchi, D. T., & Zane, N. W. (1991). Community mental health services for ethnic minority groups: A test of the cultural responsiveness hypothesis. *Journal of Consulting and Clinical Psychology, 59*(4), 533–540.

Sullivan, H. S. (1938). Psychiatry: Introduction to the study of interpersonal relations. *Psychiatry, 1*(1), 121–134.

Sullivan, H. S. (1954). *The psychiatric interview* (No. 506). New York, NY: W. W. Norton & Company.

Sullivan, H. S. (Ed.). (2013). *The interpersonal theory of psychiatry.* New York, NY: Routledge.

Swift, J. K., & Greenberg, R. P. (2012). Premature discontinuation in adult psychotherapy: A meta-analysis. *Journal of Consulting and Clinical Psychology, 80*(4), 547–559.

Taubes, G. (1994). Will new dopamine receptors offer a key to schizophrenia? *Science, 265*(5175), 1034–1035.

The, U. K. (2003). Efficacy and safety of electroconvulsive therapy in depressive disorders: A systematic review and meta-analysis. *The Lancet, 361*(9360), 799–808.

Thomas, R., & Zimmer-Gembeck, M.J. (2007). Behavioural outcomes of Parent-Child Interaction Therapy and Trip P-Positive Parenting Program: A review and meta-analysis. *Journal of Abnormal Child Psychology, 35*(3), 475–495.

Thrasher, S., Power, M., Morant, N., Marks, I., & Dalgleish, T. (2010). Social support moderates outcome in a randomized controlled trial of exposure therapy and (or) cognitive restructuring for chronic posttraumatic stress disorder. *Canadian Journal of Psychiatry. Revue canadienne de psychiatrie, 55*(3), 187–190.

Titmarsh, S. (2013). Is dopamine still the key to treating schizophrenia? *Progress in Neurology and Psychiatry, 17*(4), 21–22.

Triplett, N. S. (2016). Addressing the gaps in mental health care for Spanish-speaking individuals in Durham, NC: A needs assessment and compilation of relevant empirical literature. *Yale Review of Undergraduate Research in Psychology*, 60–70.

Truax, C. B., & Wittmer, J. (2012). The effect of the therapist's degree of focus on defense and his level of accurate empathy on therapeutic outcome. *Canadian Journal of Counselling and Psychotherapy/ Revue canadienne de counseling et de psychothérapie, 4*(3), 199–203.

Tryon, G. S., & Winograd, G. (2002). Goal consensus and collaboration. In J. C. Norcross (Ed.), *Psychotherapy relationships that work* (pp. 106–122). New York, NY: Oxford University Press.

Turner, E. H., Matthews, A. M., Linardatos, E., Tell, R. A., & Rosenthal, R. (2008). Selective publication of antidepressant trials and its influence on apparent efficacy. *New England Journal of Medicine, 358*(3), 252–260.

United States Department of Labor. (2010, January 29). *Fact Sheet: The Mental Health Parity and Addiction Equity Act of 2008 (MHPAEA)*. Washington, DC: U.S. Government Printing Office.

Wampold, B. E. (2001). *The great psychology debate: Models, methods, and findings*. Mahwah, NJ: Erlbaum.

Wang, C., & Chen, W. (2000). The efficacy of behavior therapy in 9 patients with phobia. *Chinese Mental Health Journal, 14*, 351–352.

Weissman, M. M. (1999). Interpersonal psychotherapy and the health care scene. In D. S. Janowsky (Ed.), *Psychotherapy indications and outcomes*. Washington, DC: American Psychiatric Press.

Wells, K. B. (2014). Treatment research at the crossroads: The scientific interface of clinical trials and effectiveness research. *American Journal of Psychiatry, 156*(1), 5–10.

Wersebe, H., Sijbrandij, M., & Cuijpers, P. (2013). Psychological group treatments of social anxiety disorder: A meta-analysis. *PloS one, 8*(11), doi: 10.1371/journal. pone.0079034

Whiteford, H. A., Harris, M. G., McKeon, G., Baxter, A., Pennell, C., Barendregt, J. J., & Wang, J. (2013). Estimating remission from untreated major depression: A systematic review and meta-analysis. *Psychological Medicine, 43*(8), 1569–1585.

Whitfield, G. (2010). Group cognitive–behavioural therapy for anxiety and depression. *Advances in Psychiatric Treatment, 16*(3), 219–227.

Wiens, A. N., & Menustik, C. E. (1983). Treatment outcome and patient characteristics in an aversion therapy program for alcoholism. *American Psychologist, 38*(10), 1089–1096.

Wilson, I. B., & Cleary, P. D. (1995). Linking clinical variables with health-related quality of life: A conceptual model of patient outcomes. *Journal of the American Medical Association, 273*(1), 59–65.

Wintersteen, M. B., Mensinger, J. L., & Diamond, G. S. (2005). Do gender and racial differences between patient and therapist affect therapeutic alliance and treatment retention in adolescents? *Professional Psychology: Research and Practice, 36*(4), 400–408.

Wolpe, J. (1958). *Psychotherapy by reciprocal inhibition*. Stanford, CA: Stanford University Press.

Wolpe, J., & Plaud, J. J. (1997). Pavlov's contributions to behavior therapy: The obvious and the not so obvious. *American Psychologist, 52*(9), 966–972.

Yalom, I. D. (1995). *The theory and practice of group psychotherapy*. New York, NY: Basic Books.

Yang, Y., Kircher, T., & Straube, B. (2014). The neural correlates of cognitive behavioral therapy: Recent progress in the investigation of patients with panic disorder. *Behaviour Research and Therapy, 62*, 88–96.

Yuen, E. K., Goetter, E. M., Herbert, J. D., & Forman, E. M. (2012). Challenges and opportunities in internet-mediated telemental health. *Professional Psychology: Research and Practice, 43*(1), 1–8.

Zhan, S., Liu, W., Li, D., Pan, S., Pan, Y., Li, Y., Lin, G., & Sun, B. (2014). Long-term follow-up of bilateral anterior capsulotomy in patients with refractory obsessive-compulsive disorder. *Clinical Neurology and Neurosurgery, 119*, 91–95.

Ziguras, S., Klimidis, S., Lewis, J., & Stuart, G. (2014). Ethnic matching of clients and clinicians and use of mental health services by ethnic minority clients. *Psychiatric Services, 54*(4), 535–541.

Zuo, C., Ma, Y., Sun, B., Peng, S., Zhang, H., Eidelberg, D., & Guan, Y. (2013). Metabolic imaging of bilateral anterior capsulotomy in refractory obsessive compulsive disorder: An FDG PET study. *Journal of Cerebral Blood Flow & Metabolism, 33*(6), 880–887.

Glossary

abnormal psychology   the study of mental disorders and other abnormal thoughts and behaviors

absolute threshold   the smallest amount of energy needed to detect a stimulus (light, sound, pressure, taste, or odor) at least 50 percent of the time

academic psychologists   psychologists who usually divide their time between supervising and teaching students, completing administrative tasks, and carrying out psychological research

accommodation   the process through which we adjust and refine our schemas to incorporate new information

acculturation   the extent to which a member of one cultural group adopts the beliefs and behaviors of another group

acculturative stress   the stress and psychological toll resulting from living in a new culture

accurate empathy   a key component of person-centered therapy in which a therapist is able to accurately infer the thoughts and feelings of the patient

achievement   a person's level of knowledge in a particular area

acquisition phase   the period of time during classical conditioning when the neutral stimulus comes to evoke the conditioned response

action potential   a brief electrical charge that travels down the neuron; a neural impulse

activation-synthesis hypothesis   theory of dreaming that dreams are the result of the brain's attempt to make sense of random neural activity

active listening   a key component of person-centered therapy in which a therapist echoes, restates, and seeks clarification of patients' statements to convey an interest in understanding what the patient is saying

activity theory of aging   suggests that elderly people are happiest when they stay active and involved in the community

actor-observer bias   an attributional bias in which a person attributes their own actions to situational causes, whereas as an observer they make a dispositional attribution for the same events

acute stress disorder   development of fear, anxiety, and other re-experiencing symptoms in response to a traumatic experience; symptoms last between three days and one month after the trauma

additive color mixture   a process involving the mixing of light, where additional wavelengths are added together and reflected, eventually creating white light

adolescence   the period of transition from childhood to adulthood that usually occurs around age 10–12 and continues until age 18–21

adrenal androgen   the hormone that increases during puberty and plays an important role in the development of sexual interest

adrenal glands   glands located at the top of each kidney that play an important role in the stress response by secreting predominantly epinephrine and some norepinephrine

aerobic exercise   sustained exercise that increases heart and lung fitness

affective forecasting   predictions about one's future emotional state

afterimage   an image that remains in the visual field once the stimulus has been removed

ageism   prejudice against people based upon their age

aggression   any purposeful behavior intended to cause physical or psychological harm to others

aggression   any purposeful behavior intended to cause physical or psychological harm others

agonist   a neurotransmitter or drug that binds to cell receptors and produces a biological response

agoraphobia   intense fear of being in a situation from which escape is difficult or impossible

algorithms   step-by-step problem-solving procedure that guarantees the ability to discover a solution to a particular problem

allegiance effects   the fact that researchers frequently find that the most effective form of treatment is the one that matches their own theoretical orientation

alleles   genes located in the same position on a pair of chromosomes

all-or-none law   a principle regrading action potentials; states if the electrical impulse reaches its threshold, the neuron will fire and, if the impulse does not reach its threshold, the neuron will not fire

all-or-nothing thinking   a type of cognitive distortion in which a person sees things in absolute, black or white, terms that leave little room for middle ground

alpha waves   high frequency, low amplitude brain waves characteristic of a relaxed or drowsy state

altruism   behavior carried out with the goal of helping others without concern for one's own safety or self-interest

Alzheimer's disease   the most common form of dementia characterized by progressive and irreversible declines in memory, thinking, and language

amygdala   part of the limbic system; a structure involved in fear detection, aggression, and reward

amyloid plaques   the accumulation of protein fragments between nerve cells which is often found in people with Alzheimer's disease

analytic intelligence   one of Sternberg's three types of intelligence that includes the ability to analyze and evaluate ideas, solve problems, and make decisions

analytic thinking   breaking down a problem into multiple parts to find a solution

androgens   male sex hormones

androgynous   people who have both masculine and feminine traits

andropause   gradual sexual changes that occur in aging males; includes decline in sperm count, testosterone level, and speed of erection and ejaculation

angular gyrus   area of the brain associated with language that lies between Wernicke's area and the visual cortex of the occipital lobe that is particularly important in tasks of reading and writing

anorexia nervosa   eating disorder where an individual purposely loses weight to a point below which is considered healthy

antagonist   a neurotransmitter or drug that binds to cells receptors and blocks the effects of another substance

anterograde amnesia   type of amnesia characterized by the inability to form new memories; people with anterograde amnesia can remember events from their past, but have difficulty creating new long-term memories

anti-anxiety medications   medications that can provide relief for some people suffering from anxiety disorders, often by targeting the physiological symptoms associated with anxiety

antibodies   large, Y-shaped proteins used by the immune system to chemically suppress the damaging effects of antigens

antidepressants   medications that work alleviate symptoms of depression

antigens   a toxin or other foreign substance that induces an immune response in the body, especially the production of antibodies.

antipsychotic drugs   medications used to treat disorders in which psychotic symptoms, such as hallucinations, paranoia, and delusions, predominate

anxiety disorder   group of psychological disorders characterized by prolonged, uncontrollable, and sometimes vague feelings of worry or anxiety

anxious-ambivalent/resistant attachment   infants who are insecure and overly emotional in their relationship with their caregiver so that they are extremely distressed when their mothers leave the room and difficult to soothe, even when their mothers return

anxious-avoidant attachment   infants who do not seek contact with a caregiver when distressed so that they do not appear to be particularly distressed when their mothers leave the room and actively ignore their mothers upon their return

applied behavior analysis (ABA) or behavior modification   using the principles of operant psychology to address problems and issues of social importance to people

applied psychology   refers to the use of psychological theory and practice to tackle real-world problems

aptitude   a person's capacity to learn

archetypes   prototypical images from the collective unconscious that can be seen repeatedly in various forms of art, literature, dreams, and religions

arcuate fasciculus   tract of nerves connecting Broca's and Wernicke's areas that when damaged leads to conduction aphasia

assimilation   the process through which we incorporate new experiences in terms of existing schemas

attachment   the emotional bond newborns share with their caregivers

attention   the act of directing cognitive resources in a particular direction

attitude   an evaluative belief or opinion about people, objects, or ideas

attribution   an explanation about the cause of our own or others' behavior

attribution theory   theory that we understand a behavior by attributing it either to an internal disposition or an external situation

atypical antidepressants   these include newer medication that affect neurotransmitters (including serotonin, norepinephrine, and dopamine) in specific combinations to reduce symptoms of depression

atypical antipsychotics medications that reduce symptoms of psychosis that are newer and have fewer negative side effects compared to the typical antipsychotics

auditory coding a type of processing used by the brain based on sounds

authoritarian a style of parenting in which parents exert high levels of control over their children, expect unquestioning obedience, and are very punitive

authoritative a style of parenting in which parents are warm and affectionate but also sensitive and responsive to their children's behavior and needs

automatic thoughts thoughts that automatically come to mind and can be negative and/or biased which can lead to depressed mood according to the cognitive model of therapy

autonomic nervous system part of the peripheral nervous system responsible for the involuntary functions of the internal organs of our bodies

autonomy the need to be causal agents of one's own life without being controlled by others

availability heuristic a mental shortcut that relies on information that is easily recalled or readily available

availability heuristic a mental shortcut that tells us that if we can bring examples of an event to mind easily, that event must be common

aversive conditioning a type of conditioning in which the goal is to replace a positive response to a harmful stimulus, such as alcohol, with a negative response

axon part of a neuron; a long, thin fiber responsible for carrying information to the end of the neuron

basal ganglia a set of interconnected structures next to the thalamus that are an essential participant in motor control, cognition, different forms of learning (particularly motor learning), and emotional processing

basal metabolic rate (BMR) an estimate of how many calories the body burns when at rest

basic concepts this level of concept provides significantly more specific information than superordinate concepts

basilar membrane a stiff, structural component of the cochlea, which is lined with thousands of hair cells

bystander effect occurs in situations requiring help where the greater the number of bystanders present, the less likely any individual bystander is to help the person in need

behavior therapy a type of psychotherapy which attempts to change behaviors associated with psychological distress using the principles of learning

behavioral activation system (BAS) brain system that activates approach behavior in response to the anticipation of a reward

behavioral approach an approach to psychology that concentrates on observable behavior that can be directly measured and recorded

behavioral explanation theoretical orientation that views psychological disorders resulting from environmental factors and learned behavior

behavioral genetics field of study recognizing the interaction of genes and environment and how they influence each other to produce behavior

behavioral inhibition system (BIS) brain system that inhibits approach behavior in response to the anticipation of punishment

behavioral medicine an interdisciplinary approach to medical treatment that integrates medical, psychological, and sociocultural knowledge to increase life expectancy and enhance quality of life

behavioral observations method of assessment that involves observing behaviors (often in a natural environment) to make judgments about an individual's personality

belief bias the effect that occurs when our own beliefs distort or bias our ability to reason logically

belief perseverance a tendency to hold on to beliefs, even when we are presented with evidence that refutes our beliefs

belongingness level three of Maslow's hierarchy of needs that focuses on the need for affection, love, friendship, and intimacy

benevolent sexism the acceptance of positive stereotypes that propagates unfairness and inequalities based on gender

beta waves low-amplitude, high frequency, and irregular brain waves present during active wakefulness

bilateral anterior capsulotomy a surgery that serves to disconnect the circuitry in the orbitofrontal cortex which has been implicated as playing a role in OCD

Binet-Simon scales the first widely used intelligence test developed by French psychologist Alfred Binet and psychiatrist Theodore Simon to help teachers identify students with special needs

binge-eating disorder eating disorder that involves recurrent episodes of binge eating without subsequent compensatory behaviors

binocular cue a depth perception cue that involves the use of both eyes

biofeedback a form of stress-management therapy that requires participants to monitor and adjust their own physiological states

biological approach perspective in psychology that includes the study of biological bases of behavior and focuses on the structure of the nervous system as well as the function of the nervous system

biological preparedness an organism's predisposition to develop associations between certain types of stimuli and responses based on evolutionary survival

biological psychology a specific field within neuroscience that focuses on the scientific study of the biological basis of behavior and mental processes

biomedical therapies physiological treatments designed to reduce psychological symptoms

biopsychosocial approach theoretical orientation that considers biological, psychological, and sociocultural factors when explaining causes for psychological disorders

biopsychosocial perspective a perspective in understanding stress and health that includes biological, psychological, and social factors

bipolar I disorder psychological disorder where individuals experience at least one manic episode; most individuals have recurring mood episodes, alternating between periods of mania and major depression

bipolar II disorder psychological disorder where individuals experience at least one hypomanic episode and one major depressive episode

blind observers observers who do not know what the research is about and are thus not subject to observer bias

blind spot receptorless area at the back of the eye where the optic nerve exits; images focused on this part of the retina are not seen in the visual field

blindsight blindness in part of the visual field due to damage to the primary visual cortex; despite not being able to consciously see, individuals are often still aware of the characteristics of objects in the blind spot

borderline personality disorder personality disorder that involves dramatic and erratic emotions and behaviors that often include self-harming behavior

bottom-up processing method of perception that involves processing information from the raw data, or environmental stimuli, up to the brain

brain damage the destruction or degeneration of brain cells

brainstem the "stem" or core of the brain that extends from the spinal cord through the brain and plays an important role in consciousness, pain, and other life-sustaining functions

brightness a characteristic of color derived from the amplitude, or height, of wavelengths

Broca's area the area of the brain in the left frontal lobe associated with the production of speech

bulimia nervosa eating disorder characterized by recurrent episodes of binge eating and purging behaviors

bystander effect when the presence of other people hinders a particular individual from helping a victim

Cannon-Bard theory proposes that the cognitive and physiological components of emotions happen simultaneously

case study an in-depth study of one individual or a few individuals

catastrophes unpredictable, large-scale, stressful events, such as natural disasters or terrorist attacks.

catatonia symptom of schizophrenia involving abnormal motor (movement) behavior

catatonic stupor extreme form of catatonia that involves paralysis

Cattell-Horn-Carroll (CHC) model of intelligence a hierarchical model of intelligence that includes nine different broad ability areas broken down into more than 70 narrow abilities

central executive functioning a set of mental processes that involves mental control and self-regulation

central nervous system (CNS) the largest part of the nervous system, which includes the brain and spinal cord

central route persuasive technique that focuses on strong, well-presented arguments are personally relevant and that appeal to reason

cephalocaudal rule the tendency for motor skills and physical growth to emerge in sequence from top to bottom

cerebellum a structure in the hindbrain located behind the pons and medulla, which works to control and process perceptions and motor movements

chaining a method of shaping complex behavior by rewarding a combination or series of responses performed in a particular order

change blindness a form of selective inattention where large changes in the environment are overlooked resulting from a break in the visual field or lack of attention

chronological age the amount of time someone has been alive

chunking strategy of combining individual small chunks of information into larger meaningful units

cilia hair cell receptors in the ear that send messages through the auditory nerve to the auditory cortex in the brain

circadian rhythm biological clock that regulates various bodily functions on approximately a 24-hour cycle

classical conditioning an automatic or reflexive type of learning that occurs by making associations between different events and stimuli

client-centered therapy/person-centered therapy a form of humanistic psychotherapy in which the therapeutic process focuses on the patient's abilities and insights while the therapist takes a nondirective and supportive role

clinical psychology a field of psychology that deals with the diagnosis and treatment of people with specific mental or behavioral problems

clinical social workers professionals who apply social work theory and methods to help individuals deal with a variety of mental health and daily living problems

cliques small, same-sex groups of three to nine members who share intimate secrets and see themselves as best friends

closure Gestalt principle of perception involving the tendency to perceive images as complete objects

cochlea a fluid-filled structure in the inner ear that receives vibrations from the small bones of the middle ear (hammer, anvil, and stirrup)

cochlear implant a hearing device that takes sounds from the external environment and converts them to electrical signals to be interpreted by the brain

cocktail party phenomenon ability to selectively tune into particular messages while filtering out others in a crowded, noisy, or chaotic environment

cognition mental processes, including thinking, knowing, judging, problem solving, and remembering

cognition the mental activities associated with sensation and perception, thinking, knowing, remembering, and communicating, to find answers

cognition the mental activities associated with thinking, knowing, remembering, and communicating

cognitive affective processing system (CAPS) theory stating an individual's response to a given situation depends on the psychological features present in that situation

cognitive appraisal cognitive interpretation and evaluation of a stressor

cognitive dissonance a state of psychological tension that develops when a person is faced with two conflicting attitudes or a conflicting attitude and behavior.

cognitive illusions type of visual illusion that involves higher-order thinking, such as an individual's knowledge and assumptions about the world; examples include ambiguous or impossible pictures

cognitive psychology a field of psychology concerned with mental processes such as perception, thinking, learning, and memory that seeks to understand how people process information they collect from their environment

cognitive restructuring an important part of most cognitive therapies in which therapists teach patients to identify their negative automatic thoughts, evaluate or test the accuracy of their thoughts, and replace them with more realistic thoughts

cognitive therapy a form of psychotherapy developed by Aaron Beck based on the theory that people's psychological problems can be traced to their own illogical or dysfunctional beliefs and thoughts

cognitive triad explanation for mood disorders that includes negative thinking about themselves, the world, and the future

cognitive–behavior therapy (CBT) a type of psychotherapy which focuses on the interrelated nature of our thoughts, feelings, and behaviors

cognitive-mediational theory the theory of emotion proposed by Lazarus that the cognitive interpretation of an event or stimulus mediates, or comes before the physiological arousal or emotional experience

cohorts a group of people who share a common temporal life experience

collective unconscious Jungian concept reflecting a shared pool of memories and images common to all humans

color constancy recognizing that the color of an object doesn't change even though the reflected wavelengths of light change in different environments; for example, knowing a red apple is red regardless of whether or not it is seen during the day or at dusk

comorbidity condition where a person is diagnosed with two or more psychology disorders

companionate love one type of love; feelings of affection and intimacy for another person

comparative psychology the scientific study of nonhuman animal mental processes and behavior

competence the need to feel effective when interacting in the environment

complete androgen insensitivity syndrome (CAIH) a condition that causes a genetic male fetus to develop external female genitalia because the receptors for androgens fail to function

compliance a change in a person's behavior that occurs in response to a direct request

computed tomography (CT scan) a machine that takes a series of x-rays from many different perspectives, which is sent to a computer that interprets the data and displays a two-dimensional image of the structure

concepts mental groupings of similar objects, events, and people

concordance rate the probability that one twin develops a condition if the other twin has it

conditioned response (CR) occurs when a previously neutral stimulus leads to the response originally associated with the unconditioned stimulus

conditioned stimulus during classical conditioning, when a previously neutral stimulus comes to produce the conditioned response because of an association with the unconditioned stimulus

conditions of worth internalizing message suggesting conditions that one must meet before they are accepted by another person. Develops when someone does not experience unconditional positive regard

conduction aphasia when individuals can understand and produce speech but are unable to repeat words or sentences spoken by other people

conductive hearing loss a type of hearing impairment where sound is not conducted properly through the outer or middle ear

cones visual receptors specializing in the perception of color; found primarily in the fovea

confederate a person who takes part in an experiment who is seemingly a subject but is really working with the researcher

confidence intervals provides a range of scores that most likely encompass the "true" score to take into account the error associated with a measure

confirmation bias the belief that something is already true and the tendency to therefore look for evidence that proves our beliefs while failing to notice evidence that disproves those beliefs

conformity adjusting one's behavior or thinking to align or conform to a group standard

confounding variable a variable other than the independent variable that could have an impact on the dependent variable

connectionist models of memory an approach in cognitive science that describes memory as interconnected networks in the brain

consciousness awareness of the internal and external environment

construct validity the degree to which a test measures the construct it claims to measure

contingency management a behavior change strategy that typically involves a written agreement between the therapist and patient that specifies the goals for behavioral change, the details regarding the reinforcements that can be earned, and any negative consequences for failing to meet the goal

continuity Gestalt principle of perception involving the tendency to view intersecting lines as part of a continuous pattern, rather than as a series of separate lines

continuous model model of development suggesting that human development occurs as a gradual but consistent process over time

continuous positive airway pressure (CPAP) treatment for sleep apnea, which involves wearing a mask that uses air pressure to keep the airway open during sleep

continuous reinforcement when a desired response is reinforced every time it occurs; this schedule results in rapid learning, but if the reinforcement stops, extinction also occurs rapidly

contralateral a neurological principle stating that each side of the brain controls the opposite side of the body

control group a group of participants in an experiment who are either given no treatment or who are given treatment that should have no effect

conventional morality Kohlberg's second level of moral development in which morality is defined by convention—caring for others and conforming to social laws is right simply because they are the rules within society

convergence monocular cue of depth perception; the inward movement of the eyes that occurs when looking at something close-up

convergent thinking thinking that occurs when we are confronted with a well-defined, straightforward problem that has a single right/wrong answer

conversion disorder (functional neurological symptom disorder) psychological disorder characterized by the sudden, temporary loss of a sensory or motor function; symptoms can include blindness, paralysis, deafness, or numbness of particular body parts

coping strategies psychological methods used to reduce or minimize stress

cornea the protective cover over the eye; refracts light to focus on objects

coronary heart disease a condition characterized by the clogging of the vessels that nourish the heart muscle; a leading cause of death in North America

corpus callosum band of axons that enables communication between the right and left hemispheres of the brain

correlation coefficient describes the strength and direction of the relationship between two variables

correlational studies a type of study that allows researchers to measure the degree to which two variables are related

counseling psychologists professionals who focus on how people function both personally and in their relationships across the lifespan

couples therapy a treatment option for people involved in relationships who are experiencing distress

creative intelligence one of Sternberg's three types of intelligence that includes a person's ability to adapt to new situations, come up with unique ideas, and think of novel solutions to problems

creativity the ability to come up with new ideas that can lead to a particular outcome

critical period hypothesis (CPH) suggests a limited window of opportunity for children to effectively learn language

critical thinking a way of processing information in which a person examines assumptions, evaluates evidence, looks for hidden agendas, and assesses conclusions

cross-sectional studies studies that observe different individuals of different ages at one point in time to track differences related to age

cross-sequential study a type of study which includes a combination of both cross-sectional and longitudinal designs by examining several different cohorts over time

crowds larger, mixed-sex groups who tend to get together socially on weekends

crystallized intelligence the ability to use learned skills, knowledge, and experience

cued recall information from long-term memory becomes available after a retrieval cue is presented

cultural relativism understanding that any individual's behavior or psychological symptom must be evaluated in the context of their own culture

culture-bound syndromes disorders that only exist in specific cultural groups

culture-bound valid only within a particular culture

daily hassles frequent and common stressors experienced in daily life, such as traffic jams, busy schedules, and unexpected delays.

debrief to provide participants with a verbal description of the true nature and purpose of a study after the study occurs

decay short-term memory loss due to information disappearing over time

decision aversion the state of attempting to avoid making any decision at all

decision making the process of selecting and rejecting a course of action from several available options

deep brain stimulation (DBS) a treatment for medical and psychological disorders that involves direct electrical stimulation of the brain

deep brain stimulation a form of medical therapy in which surgeons implant a thin wire electrode in the patient's brain that when activated can stimulate neurons lying near it

defense mechanisms originate from the ego; mental processes of self-deception that help alleviate worry and anxiety often produced by the id

deindividuation a loss of individual identity and personal responsibility that can occur when an individual is part of a group experience

delayed ejaculation requiring a prolonged period of sexual stimulation before being able to ejaculate

delayed reinforcement a significant delay in time between the desired response of an organism and the delivery of a reinforcer

delta waves higher amplitude, lower frequency brain waves that appear when sleep deepens; characteristic of stage N3 of sleep

delusions positive symptom of schizophrenia involving fixed and rigid, false beliefs

dementia a progressive loss of cognitive functioning in areas such as memory, reasoning, planning, decision making, and social functioning

dendrites the bushy end of the neuron responsible for receiving the incoming signal from the previous neuron

dependent variable the variable that is being measured in an experiment to determine the impact of changes in the independent variable

depressants class of drugs that depress or slow down the central nervous system and other bodily functions

depth perception the ability to judge distances of objects and to see them in three dimensions

descriptive study a study that enables researchers to observe and describe behaviors without investigating the relationship between specific variables

developmental age a measure of a child's development using age norms

developmental psychologists psychologists who study the physical, cognitive, and social changes that humans experience throughout the lifespans

developmental psychology branch of psychology that studies the physical, cognitive, and social changes of humans throughout the lifespan

diathesis-stress model model for explaining schizophrenia that suggests that the disorder develops from a genetic predisposition that interacts with emotional or environmental stress

difference threshold just noticeable difference (jnd) the minimum difference between two stimuli needed to detect the difference at least 50 percent of the time

difficult temperament infants with irregular eating/sleeping patterns who are slow to adapt to change and respond negatively to frustration

diffusion of responsibility theory suggesting the more people there are witnessing the same event, the more likely each person is to *diffuse the responsibility*, or assume that somebody else is going to take action

direct aggression aggressive acts that directly target an individual

discontinuous model a model of developmental suggesting that development occurs in distinct steps or stages

discrimination negative behavior toward members of a group solely as a result of their membership in that group

disengagement theory of aging theory that elderly people gradually and willingly withdraw themselves from the world around them in preparation for death

disorganized thinking and speech group of symptoms of schizophrenia where individuals may think or speak in ways that are jumbled, illogical, or incoherent

disorganized-disoriented attachment infants who do not have a consistent response to their mother's absence or return, appearing to be confused or hesitant and display contradictory behaviors

dispositional attribution attributing our own, or another person's behavior to personality or personal characteristics

dissociative amnesia psychological disorder that causes sudden, selective memory loss, which is usually precipitated by a traumatic event

dissociative disorders group of psychological disorders where the normal cognitive processes are fragmented, causing a sudden loss of memory or change in personality

dissociative identity disorder (DID) psychological disorder where a person experiences two or more, sometimes vastly different, personalities

distress the negative effects experienced when confronted with stress

divergent thinking thought processes used to generate many different possible solutions to a problem

dizygotic twins fraternal twins that develop when two eggs are released and are both fertilized by two different sperm

DNA (deoxyribonucleic acid) molecules that constitute the building blocks of chromosomes; genes are contained within DNA

dominant genes genes that will always be expressed, even when paired with a recessive gene

door-in-the-face technique compliance technique that involves making a large request first and then, when that request is refused, making a smaller request that seems reasonable in comparison

double-blind experiment an experiment in which neither the participants nor the experimenters know who is receiving a particular treatment

dream analysis a psychodynamic therapy technique which focuses on discovering repressed conflicts or memories that often surface symbolically in dreams

dreams the sequences of images, feelings, ideas, and impressions that occur during sleep

drive-reduction theory Clark Hull's theory that we act when a physiological need creates an aroused state that drives us to reduce the need. Based on the premise that humans are motivated to maintain a state of homeostasis.

DSM-5 Diagnostic and Statistical Manual for Mental Disorders (fifth edition) is the American Psychiatric Association's official guide for diagnosing mental, or psychological disorders

dualism the belief that the mind does not cease to exist when the body dies and that thoughts and ideas can exist separately from the body

ear drum part of the outer ear that vibrates in response to sounds in the environment

easy temperament infants with regular eating/sleeping patterns who adapt easily to change and can tolerate frustration

echoic memory part of sensory memory that involves the ability to briefly and accurately remember sounds

eclectic approach an approach in which psychologists draw on multiple different perspectives and theories to gain an understanding of human behavior or mental processes

eclectic psychotherapy a form of psychotherapy which draws ideas and techniques from a variety of therapeutic approaches.

efficacy expectancy belief an individual has in themselves that they can perform the behavior required to produce a particular outcome

effortful processing using time and energy to processing information deeply to aid understanding and memory; opposite of maintenance rehearsal

ego psychodynamic component of personality that represents the rational part of the mind. Operates according to the reality principle

elaboration likelihood model a theory of persuasion that suggests the most effective persuasive technique depends on the motivation of the listener

elaborative rehearsal an effortful processing strategy that focuses on elaborating on the information and making it personally meaningful

electroconvulsive therapy (ECT) electric currents are passed through the brain, intentionally triggering a brief seizure in an attempt to reduce psychiatric symptoms such as severe depression

electroencephalogram (EEG) noninvasive technique to studying brain activity that measures electrical activity of the brain

embodied cognition a field of study that examines how bodily sensations influence person perception

embryonic stage stage of prenatal development that occurs after implantation into the female uterus around two weeks after conception and continues until eight weeks of gestation

emerging adulthood a period of time between adolescence and adulthood in primarily Western cultures during which emotional ties with parents loosen, but dependence on parents for financial and emotional support remains

emotion a subjective reaction to an object, event, person, or memory that includes physiological arousal, expressive behavior, and cognitive experiences

emotion regulation the use of cognitive strategies to control and influence our own emotional responses

emotional intelligence a person's ability to perceive, understand, manage, and utilize his or her emotions

emotion-focused coping influencing one's own emotional response to a stressful situation as a method of coping

empathy the ability of the therapist to understand the patient's point of view

empiricism the view that knowledge originates through experience

encoding process used to consolidate information from working memory to long-term memory

encoding specificity information is encoded along with its context; memory recall is best when the retrieval context matches the encoding context

endocrine system secondary and slower communication system in the body that involves hormones, which control most major bodily functions (e.g., immune system, growth, fertility, metabolism)

epigenetics the study of heritable changes in gene function that cannot be explained by any changes in the DNA but likely involve environmental effects

episodic memories a type of explicit memory involving entire sequences of events; memories tend to be autobiographical

episodic memory memory of specific events or experiences

erectile disorder a recurrent inability to achieve or maintain an adequate erection during partnered sexual activities

erotic plasticity the degree to which sexual attraction tends to be fluid

esteem level four in Maslow's hierarchy of needs that focuses on the need for self-esteem, achievement, independence, and prestige

ethics refers to the moral principles that guide a person's or group's behavior

eustress positive effects that can result from stress; often in relation to positive, yet stressful, situations

evidence-based practice (EBP) practicing therapy in a way that integrates the best available research with clinical expertise in the context of patient characteristics, culture, and preferences

evolutionary approach an approach to psychology that explores ways in which patterns of human behavior may be beneficial to people's survival

evolutionary cognition field of study focused on the fact that cognitive abilities develop across different species over time based on what skills/abilities help a species adapt to a particular environment and provide a survival advantage

excitement phase the first phase of the sexual response cycle when arousal occurs

executive function the ability to plan and assess complex tasks, make decisions, engage in socially appropriate behavior, and create and work toward goals; associated with the prefrontal cortex

exemplar a specific remembered instance used in the formation of new concepts when a new stimulus is encountered

experimental group a group of participants in an experiment who receive the variable being tested

experiments a type of study that enables researchers to determine causality by manipulation of one or more independent variables and observing the effect on some outcome

explanatory style an approach people use to explain why or how events occurred; style can be optimistic or pessimistic

explicit attitudes beliefs or opinions that are held consciously and can be reported to others

explicit memories conscious memories of facts or experiences

explicit stereotype a consciously held set of beliefs about a group of people

exposure effect when the familiarity of a stimulus primes us to react with a certain emotion

exposure therapy a type of behavioral therapy in which people are repeatedly exposed to what they fear until they become so accustomed to it that they no longer experience the same level of fear or anxiety

expressive language skills the ability to communicate with others using language

expressive traits traditionally feminine traits and behaviors

external genitalia the penis and scrotum in males and the labia, clitoris, and external vagina in females

external locus of control belief that the situation, rewards, and fate are controlled by outside forces

extinction burst a burst of responding following the removal of previous reinforcement

extinction the disappearance of a learned behavior when the behavior is no longer reinforced or no longer associated with the unconditioned stimulus

extrinsic motivation when people are motivated to engage in a particular behavior to gain a reward or to avoid a negative outcome

facial feedback hypothesis theory that facial expressions can influence emotional experiences

factor analysis statistical technique designed to identify patterns of correlations based on responses to numerous questions

false consensus effect a person's tendency to overestimate the extent to which others share his or her beliefs and behaviors

family therapy a form of group therapy that focuses on the unique interactions of the family unit

fast mapping the ability to acquire and retain new words or concepts with minimal exposure

fear hierarchy a list of increasingly anxiety-inducing situations associated with the patient's specific fear that is used in exposure therapy

feature detector neurons that respond to specific types of features in the visual field

female orgasmic disorder a significant delay, reduction of intensity, or cessation of ability to achieve orgasm in females

fetal alcohol spectrum disorders (FASD) physical and cognitive abnormalities in children resulting from a pregnant mother's alcohol intake

fetal stage stage of prenatal development that occurs from around eight weeks of gestation until birth

fight-or-flight response a physiological response to stress trigged by the release of hormones from the adrenal glands; prepares the body to fight back or flee to safety

figure ground Gestalt principle that involves the ability to distinguish the object we are focusing on—the figure—from its surroundings—the ground

five-factor model trait theory of personality suggesting five underlying factors (traits) of personality: openness to experience, conscientiousness, extraversion, agreeableness, and neuroticism

fixation the tendency to become entrenched in thinking a certain way, which leads to the inability to see a problem from a fresh perspective

fixation unhealthy focus on one particular psychosexual stage that continues into adulthood. May be the result of an inability to resolve psychosexual conflicts associated with a particular stage

fixed mindset the belief that our abilities are inborn and unchangeable

fixed-interval schedules when a behavior is reinforced after a fixed time period; fixed-interval schedules produce rapid responses at the expected time of reward and slower responses outside of those times

fixed-ratio schedules when a behavior is reinforced after a set number of responses; fixed-rate schedules produce high rates of responding with only a brief pause following reinforcement

flashbulb memories vivid, long-lasting memories about the circumstances surrounding the discovery of an extremely emotional event

flooding form of exposure therapy that habituates patients by immediately exposing them to their most feared situation (i.e., the top step of their fear hierarchy)

fluid intelligence the ability to think and reason abstractly and solve problems

Flynn effect the phenomenon in which there is a significant increase in average IQ scores over time

focused attention meditation type of meditation that involves directing attention toward an object for the entire meditation session

foot-in-the-door technique a compliance technique that involves asking people to comply with a small request first and then, after they agree, making a larger request

formal concepts concepts that have a rigid set of rules or parameters for membership

fovea a depressed spot in the retina that occupies the center of the visual field

framing the way a decision or problem is presented

fraternal birth-order effect a finding related to sexual orientation showing that each additional older brother that a male has increases the odds that the male will be gay by 33 percent

free association a psychodynamic therapy technique in which the therapist encourages the patient to relax his or her mind and begin reporting every image or idea that enters their conscious awareness

free recall retrieval of information from long-term memory without the help of any kind of retrieval cues

frequency the rate of a sound wave measured in cycles per second, or hertz (Hz); determines the pitch of a sound

frequency theory theory stating the pitch of a sound is perceived by the brain based on the rate (i.e., the frequency) of neural firing; best explains low pitched sounds

frontal lobes part of that brain that lies behind the forehead that performs a variety of integration and management functions

frustration-aggression hypothesis theory suggesting that aggression can occur when people feel frustrated as a result of being blocked from obtaining their goals

functional fixedness a bias that limits the ability to think about objects in unconventional ways

functional magnetic resonance imaging (fMRI) a procedure that uses MRI technology to capture a picture of the brain in addition to measurement of brain activity

functionalism a school of psychology focused on how organisms use their learning and perceptual abilities to function in their environment

fundamental attribution error the tendency to attribute others' behavior to dispositional (internal) rather than situational (external) factors

gate control theory of pain theory suggesting information about pain is conveyed through two different nerve fibers (a thin fiber for pain and a thicker fiber relaying touch, pressure, and vibration); pain can be inhibited by activating larger nerve fibers, which closes the smaller pain gates

gender dysphoria persistent feelings of identification with the opposite gender and discomfort with the sex assigned at birth

gender identity our self-identification as male or female, a blend of both, or neither

gender roles expectations about the way women and men behave based on their gender

gender schema theory a theory of gender development stating that children develop schemas for what is "male" and what is "female" through the process of social and cognitive learning

gender stereotypes widely held concepts about a person or group of people that are based only on gender

gender the set of behaviors and characteristics that define the degree to which someone is masculine or feminine

gender typed boys and men who show traditionally masculine traits and behaviors and girls and women who show traditionally feminine traits and behaviors

general adaptation syndrome (GAS) theory proposed by Hans Selye that describes how the body adaptively responds to stress over prolonged periods of time.

general intelligence (or _g_) represents a broad mental capacity that influences performance on mental tasks

generalized anxiety disorder (GAD) psychological disorder involving uncontrollable worry and other cognitive and physiological symptoms

genes sections of DNA that contain specific instructions to make thousands of different proteins in the body

genitopelvic pain/penetration disorder when females experience an involuntary contraction of the pelvic floor muscles around the vagina resulting in an inability to penetrate

genome complete set of "instructions" or genetic material for an organism

genotype the entire genetic makeup of an organism

genuineness a key component of person-centered therapy in which the therapist must be genuine and willing to express their true feelings

germinal stage stage of development that the zygote enters after fertilization that lasts two weeks culminates with the implantation into the female's uterus

gerontology an interdisciplinary field that studies the process of aging and the aging population

Gestalt psychology a perspective in psychology that focuses on the study of how people integrate and organize perceptual information into meaningful wholes

glial cells (glia) abundant and versatile cells in the central nervous system that play an important role in supporting neurons; also thought to be potentially related to the development of Alzheimer's disease

glucose level of blood sugar that helps determine hunger and satiety

goal state the state one is working toward when engaged in problem solving

gonads glands involved in sexual development, which include the _ovaries_ in females and the _testes_ in males

grammar combines syntax and semantics to provide a system of rules that governs the way people compose and use language

group polarization the tendency for like-minded groups to become more extreme in their opinions and positions as a result of being part of the group

group therapy a form of therapy in which one or more therapists treat a small number of people in a group setting

groupthink occurs when group members' opinions become so uniform that any dissent becomes impossible

growth mindset the belief that one's abilties can be developed through effort and dedication

gustatory sense sense of taste

hallucinations positive symptoms of schizophrenia that involves false sensory perceptions

hallucinogens class of drugs that can produce unusual sensations, distortions in the perception of reality, and intense emotional mood swings

health psychology the psychological aspect of behavioral medicine that focuses on the development of strategies to eliminate or reduce the risk of illness and disease

heritability estimates an estimation of how much variability in a trait is due to genetics

heritability the degree to which genetics (genotype) explains the individual variations in observable traits (phenotypes)

heroin a narcotic that activates specific opioid receptors that stimulate dopamine in the reward centers of the brain, causing feelings of intense pleasure

heterozygous nonidentical pairs of alleles (genes located in the same position on the pair of chromosomes)

heuristics informal rules or mental shortcuts that make solving problems or decision making quicker and simpler

hierarchies of concepts a method of classifying concepts that progresses from broad to narrow

hierarchy of needs a model proposed by Maslow focusing on the fact that some needs must be fulfilled before we will be motivated to achieve other higher goals

higher-order conditioning when a conditioned stimulus eventually acts as an unconditioned stimulus in a second round of conditioning

hindbrain the evolutionarily oldest part of the brain located at the top of the spinal cord; responsible for the majority of the basic functions required for survival

hindsight bias a person's erroneous belief that he or she knew something all along after an event has occurred

hindsight bias our tendency to overestimate our previous knowledge of situations

hippocampus part of the limbic system; a structure essential for creating and consolidating information to make new memories

holistic thinking a focus on the "whole" or interconnectedness of systems and objects

homeostasis a state of balance or equilibrium

homozygous identical pairs of alleles (genes located in the same position on the pair of chromosomes)

hormones chemical messengers secreted by the glands into the bloodstream that regulate the activity of cells or organs

hue color, which is derived from the wavelength of light that hits the eye

humanistic approach an approach to psychology based on the belief that people are innately good and that mental and social problems result from deviations from this natural tendency

humanistic approach approach to therapy that addresses psychological problems through a lens of positivity and optimism

humanistic theories theories of personality emphasizing the need for conscious understanding and the ability to attain self-fulfillment/self-actualization

hyperthyroidism condition resulting from an _overactive_ thyroid; can produce symptoms of heart palpitations, sweating, diarrhea, increased appetite with weight loss, heat sensitivity, and bulging eyes

hypnosis a state consciousness involving focused attention and reduced awareness of surroundings, accompanied by an enhanced state of suggestibility

hypomania milder form of mania that causes less severe mood elevations and does not interfere with normal daily functioning

hypothalamic-pituitary-adrenal (HPA) axis the neuroendocrine system responsible for the reacting to stress; produces cortisol

hypothalamus part of the limbic system; a structure that links the nervous system to the endocrine system and plays an important role in the regulation of biological drives

hypothesis a testable prediction about new facts, based on existing theories

hypothyroidism   a condition that results from an *underactive* thyroid; can produce symptoms of tiredness, weight gain, cold intolerance, and slowed heart rate

iconic memory   part of sensory memory that involves the ability to briefly and accurately remember visual images

id   Freudian component of personality that is present at birth and tries to satisfy basic drives and survival instincts

identity   our sense of self

illness anxiety disorder   psychological disorder formerly known as hypochondriasis, which involves significant health anxiety and anxiety-related checking and avoidance behaviors

illusory contour   a visual illusion where lines or contours are perceived but do not exist

immediate reinforcement   when the desired behavior and the delivery of a reinforcer occur very close in time

implicit attitudes   beliefs and opinions that are unconscious (involuntary or uncontrollable) and can automatically influence behaviors

implicit memories   memories that exist below the level of conscious awareness

implicit personality theory   a heuristic in person perception that involves assuming a person with a particular personality characteristic will think and behave in other ways that are typically associated with that central personality characteristic.

implicit stereotypes   unconscious beliefs or opinions about a group of people that influence the individual's attitudes and behaviors

independent variable   a variable that a researcher manipulates or changes in an experiment

indirect aggression   includes acts that do not directly involve the target of the aggression but are used to harm a person's relationships or social standing

individual psychology   theory of personality (Adler) that suggests there is a universal motivation to achieve superiority, while emphasizing that each person's unique struggle with feelings of inferiority is the key to understanding their personality

industrial and organizational (I/O) psychology   an area of applied psychology in which psychologists scientifically study human behavior in organizations and the workplace

information processing approach   general theory of memory stating memories are encoded, stored, and retrieved later when needed

informational social influence   an explanation for conformity that results from the perceived knowledge of others brought to the group situation

Informed consent   when a study participant has agreed to participate after being provided with full knowledge of the potential benefits and risks of participating in the research

ingroup   the tendency for people to favor their own group positions and members. An explanation for how prejudice can develop

initial state   state during problem solving in which there is incomplete or unsatisfactory information

inpatient treatment   services performed while an individual is hospitalized

insight learning   sudden realization of how to solve a problem that does not occur as a result of trial-and-error

insight   when a solution to a problem presents itself suddenly

insomnia   a sleep disorder characterized by dissatisfaction with the duration or quality of sleep

instincts   unlearned complex behaviors with a fixed pattern throughout a species

Institutional Review Board (IRB)   an ethics review panel established by a publicly funded research institution to evaluate all proposed research by that institution

instrumental traits   traditionally masculine traits and behaviors

insulin   a hormone released by the pancreas that tells the body to convert glucose to fat

intellectual disability   includes deficits in intellectual functioning with accompanied deficits in adaptive functioning

intellectual giftedness   intellectual abilities that are significantly higher than average

intelligence quotient (IQ)   a number representing a person's overall intellectual ability that used to be based on the relationship between an individual's actual age and his/her mental age but is now based on a standard score with a mean of 100 and a standard deviation of 15

intelligence   the ability to learn and adapt from experience, solve problems, and apply knowledge in new situations

intensive outpatient treatment   treatment which allows people to maintain their work and/or school obligations while still receiving more intensive treatment multiple days a week

interference   explanation for short-term memory loss whereby new information interferes with the information currently in short-term memory

internal consistency   a measure of how well the items on the test measure the same construct

internal locus of control   belief that an individual controls the situation, their own rewards and, therefore, their own fate

interneurons   neurons that send information between sensory neurons and motor neurons

interpersonal psychotherapy   a type of psychotherapy which focuses on helping patients improve their relationships as a means to resolving their psychological problems

interposition   a depth perception cue; when an object or person blocks another, the one in the back is perceived to be further away

interrater reliability   a measure of the degree of consistency between two different observers of the same behavior

intersex   when someone is born with ambiguous genitalia

interview   a form of data collection in which people provide oral descriptions of themselves that can either be strictly structured, with a set list of questions, or loosely structured and more conversational

intrinsic motivation   engaging in a behavior for the sake of enjoyment

introspection   an examination of one's own conscious thoughts and feelings

investment theory of creativity   theory that creative people are able to take ideas that are new or not highly valued and transform them through the process of creativity to become valuable

iris   a colored muscle that dilates (gets bigger) or constricts (gets smaller) the pupil in response to light

James-Lange theory of emotion   theory that emotions are the result of physiological arousal

judgment   a skill that allows people to form opinions, reach conclusions, and evaluate situations objectively and critically

just-world phenomenon   the belief that the world is a fair place in which good people are rewarded and bad people are punished

laboratory study   a study conducted in a location specifically set up to facilitate collection of data and allow control over environmental conditions

language acquisition device (LAD)   the innate ability to learn the rules of grammar in any language

language   the system of symbols that enables us to communicate our ideas, thoughts, and feelings

latent content   the unconscious or symbolic meaning of a dream

latent content   the underlying meaning of a dream where the unconscious, repressed wishes, and drives of the dreamer are expressed

latent learning   learning that is not immediately expressed and occurs without any obvious reinforcement

lateral hypothalamus   area of the hypothalamus that controls the experience of hunger

law of effect   if a response produces a *satisfying effect*, the response is likely to occur again

learned helplessness   tendency to remain in a punishing situation because of a history of repeated failures to escape in the past

learning   a relatively permanent change in behavior due to experience

lens   a flexible structure in the eye that changes shape to refract and focus light on the retina

limbic system   a set of brain structures responsible for a number of survival-related and emotionally-driven behavior; includes the thalamus, hypothalamus, basal ganglia, amygdala, and hippocampus

linear perspective   a depth perception cue where converging parallel lines suggest distance

linguistic relativity hypothesis   hypothesis that the way people think is strongly affected by their native language

literal visual illusions   illusions that create images different from the objects or situations that make them (e.g., a rainbow)

lobotomies   a procedure that disconnects the frontal lobe from the rest of the brain

locus of control   perception or belief about the amount of control one has over situations

longitudinal study   a type of study in which the same individuals are observed over a period of time to track changes over time

long-term memory   according to the 3-stage model of memory, the structure where information is stored for long periods of time

long-term potentiation (LTP)   biological explanation for the development of long-term memories; memories are formed as a result of strengthened neural connections

lowball technique   a compliance technique that involves offering an attractive deal and then changing the terms of the deal later (thus increasing the overall cost of the deal)

lymphocytes   white blood cells that attempt to attack foreign invaders (i.e., atigens) in the body; B cells, T cells and NK cells are all types of lymphocytes

magnetic resonance imaging (MRI)   an imaging procedure that utilizes a large magnet to examine the structural aspects of the brain, an organ, or tissue

magnetoencephalography (MEG) procedure that measures faint *magnetic fields* generated by brain activity and provides precise information about brain activation and spatial localization

maintenance rehearsal memory strategy that involves repeating or rehearsing information to maintain it in short-term memory

major depressive disorder (MDD) psychological disorder involving either depressed mood or loss of interest in most activities, accompanied by four other symptoms that last for more than two weeks

male hypoactive sexual desire disorder when males experience either a complete lack of or significant reduction in sexual interest/arousal

mania periods of euphoria (feelings of excessive happiness) often accompanied by elevated self-esteem, increased talkativeness, enhanced energy, and a decreased need for sleep

manifest content the actual, remembered content of a dream, including the storyline, characters, and specific details

manifest content the way a dream is experienced and remembered by the dreamer

marijuana a drug containing tetrahydrocannabinol (THC); can produce altered sensations, feelings of well-being, and changes in cognition

masking when you express one emotion outwardly while experiencing a different emotion internally

means-end analysis examining the difference between the initial state and the goal state in problem solving and then forming subgoals that will ultimately lead to the goal state

medical model perspective that suggests that physical and psychological disorders develop, and should be treated, in the same way

meditation an alerted state of consciousness that may involve focused and regulated breathing, specific body positions, minimization of external distractions, mental imagery, and/or mental clarity

meditation stress management strategy that involves training the mind to become present, aware, and open to experiences

medulla structure in the hindbrain where the spinal cord and brain meet; responsible for several autonomic life-sustaining responses (i.e. breathing, heartbeat, and reflexes such as vomiting, coughing, and swallowing)

memory a collection of information and experiences stored in the brain for retrieval at a later time

menarche the onset of menstruation in girls

menopause the end of the menstrual cycle and ability to bear children in women

mental age a measure of an individual's intellectual level based on the age at which it takes an average individual to reach the same level of attainment

mental disorder clinically significant disturbance in a person's thoughts, emotions, or behavior that reflects dysfunction in mental functioning

mental filter a type of cognitive distortion that occurs when someone focuses only on the negative aspects of a situation and ignores or "filters" out any positive aspects

mental set a preexisting state of mind used to solve problems because it helped solve similar problems in the past

mental-health parity law law passed in October 2008 that forces insurance companies who provide mental health benefits to make the coverage equivalent to coverage for other medical problems

mere exposure effect theory explaining interpersonal attraction that states the repeated exposure to other people leads to feelings of attraction

microsaccades small, jerky movements of the eye, which allow neurons to rest, therefore preventing exhaustion

midbrain part of the brain between the hindbrain and the forebrain, which serves as a relay station for visual and auditory information and is the center of the auditory and visual reflexes

mindfulness-based stress reduction (MBSR) a structured stress-reduction program based on the principles of meditation and mindfulness

mirror neurons neurons that fire not only when an animal engages in a particular action, but also if the animal observes another animal engaging in the same action

misinformation effect when an event or situation occurring after the initial memory modifies that memory and affects the accuracy of recall

mixed hearing loss hearing impairment that involves a combination of both sensorineural and conductive hearing loss

mnemonics memory strategies that connect information to be learned to something else that then serves as a trigger for retrieval

modeling the act of observing behavior exhibited by someone else in order to imitate the behavior

monoamine oxidase (MAO) inhibitors the earliest antidepressants, which work by inhibiting MAO (an enzyme that metabolizes norepinephrine), also have negative side effects and are often used as a last resort

monocular cues cues that indicate depth or distance that can be seen with just one eye

monozygotic twins identical twins that develop when one egg is fertilized by one sperm and then the egg splits into half and two fetuses develop with identical genetic makeup

mood-congruent processing the tendency to selectively perceive stimuli congruent with one's emotional state

mood-stabilizing medications medications such as lithium that are prescribed when people experience the drastic mood changes typical of bipolar disorder

morphemes the smallest units in a language that have meaning

motion parallax a depth perception cue; the sense that objects further away are moving more slowly

motivated forgetting the active forgetting of experiences, typically in response to a stressful or traumatic situation

motivation a need or desire that energizes and directs behavior

motor (efferent) neurons neurons that carry information *away from* the central nervous system to the muscles and glands

motor cortex structure at the back of the frontal lobes responsible for generating the neural impulses that control the execution of movements

motor development the emergent ability to execute physical actions

müllerian system a female reproductive system

Müller-Lyer illusion a geometric illusion where the length of lines appears shorter or longer, depending on whether the arrowheads are pointing in or out

multitasking attention divided among two or more stimuli or activities

myelin sheath fatty layer that covers the axon; serves as protection and speeds up the transmission of information down the axon

N1 the first stage of sleep where alpha wave activity decreases and larger, slower theta wave activity increases

N2 the second stage of sleep characterized by increased relaxation and a period of light sleep

N3 the third stage of sleep consisting of deep sleep characterized by higher amplitude delta waves

narcolepsy a sleep disorder characterized by excessive daytime sleepiness and periodic, uncontrollable sleep attacks

narcotics a category of drugs used medically in the management of pain

natural concepts concepts that develop through our own experiences in the world

natural selection a theory that organisms best adapted to their environment tend to survive and transmit their genetic characteristics to succeeding generations

naturalistic observation the study of people or animals in their own environment

nature inherited characteristics that influence personality, physical growth, intellectual growth, and social interactions

negative afterimage an afterimage where the colors seen are the opposite of those originally presented

negative correlations a relationship between two variables signifying that as one variable increases, the other variable decreases

negative punishment removing something desirable or enjoyable after a behavior with the intention of decreasing the likelihood of that behavior occurring again in the future

negative reinforcers strengthening or increasing a response by removing an unpleasant consequence

negative symptoms symptoms of schizophrenia that represent a pathological deficit, or the absence of emotions or behaviors that are typically present in a psychologically healthy individual

neglectful/uninvolved a style of parenting in which parents make few demands on their children and they are also unresponsive to their children's needs or behavior

neurofeedback a stress management technique that focuses on specifically training individuals to control their own brain activity; similar to biofeedback

neurofibrillary tangles twisted strands of protein within neurons often seen in individuals with Alzheimer's disease

neurogenesis the birth of new neurons

neuron a tiny, excitable cell that receives stimulation and transmits information to other neurons throughout the body

neuropsychology a specialty in psychology that focuses on understanding brain-behavior relationships and the application of such knowledge to human problems

neuropsychology specialty within the field of psychology that focuses on how the structure and function of the brain impacts psychological processes and behavior

neuroscience multidisciplinary field devoted to the study of the nervous system and the brain

neurotransmitters chemical messengers of the nervous system

neutral stimulus a stimulus that doesn't naturally elicit the reflexive/desired response in classical conditioning

nightmares scary dreams, which almost always occur during REM sleep

normal distribution a bell-shaped frequency distribution showing that most scores cluster in the middle of the graph and the rest taper off symmetrically toward either end

normative investigations research studies performed with healthy ("normative") participants to establish normal behavior or average performance in a population

normative social influence an explanation for conformity that results from people's desire for others' approval and longing to be part of a group

nurture environmental influences such as parental styles, physical surroundings, and economic issues

obedience complying with direct requests that come from a person perceived to be in a position of authority

observational learning learning by observing and imitating others

observer bias a situation in which an observer expects to see a particular behavior and notices only actions that support that expectation

obsessive-compulsive disorder (OCD) psychological disorder involving repeated and uncontrollable thoughts, images, or urges (obsessions) that are often followed by repetitive and ritualistic behaviors (compulsions) in an effort to reduce the anxiety brought about by the obsessions

occipital lobes structures located at the rearmost part of the skull and known for their visual processing abilities

oculomotor cues depth perception cues involving the activity within the eyes

olfaction the sense of smell

open monitoring meditation type of meditation that involves nonjudgmental observation of all aspects of experience (e.g., thoughts, emotions, sounds)

operant conditioning learning related to voluntary behavior that occurs through the application of consequences after a particular behavior is performed

operational definition a precise definition of each variable, including a specification of how the variables will be measured in the context of research

opponent-process theory theory of color vision stating there are three special visual receptors that work in pairs and in an opposing manner

optic chiasm an area in the brain where a portion of both optic nerves cross over and continue to the visual cortex

optic nerve nerve that carries the neural messages from the eye to the brain to be processed

optimal arousal theory the theory that people are motivated to achieve an ideal level of arousal

orexin a hormone secreted by the lateral hypothalamus that produces feelings of hunger

orgasm phase the third stage of the sexual response cycle when climax occurs

outcome expectancies assumptions about the consequences of behavior that influence the degree to which an individual may exhibit an internal or external locus of control

outgroup the tendency for people to dislike people who are viewed as outside of their own group; an explanation for how prejudice can develop

outpatient treatment mental health treatment which occurs in a variety of outpatient settings (e.g., hospital-based clinics, counseling centers, private practice offices) and are most appropriate for people who are medically stable and able to function independently between appointments

ova immature eggs contained in the ovaries

ovaries the female reproductive organ where ova are produced and released

overconfidence the tendency to think we are more knowledgeable or accurate in our judgments than we really are

overgeneralization a type of cognitive distortion that occurs when a person draws broad negative conclusions on the basis of a single event

overjustification effect when an external incentive is added to behaviors that are already driven by intrinsic motivation, thereby decreasing internal motivation

pancreas organ of the endocrine and digestive systems that produces hormones, including *insulin* and *glucagon,* which are important for regulating the concentration of glucose in the bloodstream

panic attack sudden episode of intense fear accompanied with physiological symptoms, such as tightening of the chest and shortness of breath, which often occurs unexpectedly

panic disorder psychological disorder where an individual experiences recurrent panic attacks, some of which are unexpected, followed by feelings of worry or dread about the potential of future panic attacks

parallel distributed processing model of memory example of a connectionist memory model that states memories are distributed throughout the brain and represented in the pattern of activation between neurons

parallel processing the ability of the brain to simultaneously perceive many aspects of an object at one time

paraphilic disorders a class of disorders related to atypical sexual behavior that causes distress to the person, and/or makes the person a serious threat to the mental health or physical well-being of others

parasomnias abnormal behavioral, experiential, or physiological events that occur in conjunction with sleep

parasympathetic division division of the autonomic nervous system that brings the body back to its resting rate following the fight-or-flight response

parasympathetic nervous system a division of the autonomic nervous system responsible for returning the body to its natural resting state

parietal lobes structures located in front of the occipital lobes, just above the temporal lobes, responsible for processing and integrating sensory information related to taste, temperature, and touch

partial (intermittent) reinforcement when responses are only occasionally reinforced; this produces slower initial learning, but the learning is more resistant to extinction

partial hospitalization treatment which occurs when an individual still resides in his/her own home but spends up to seven days a week in treatment at a mental health center or hospital

passionate love a type of love that involves intense longing and desire for another person that has physiological, cognitive, emotional, and behavioral components

perceived control the extent to which an individual believes they are in control of a situation

perception process in which the brain selects, organizes, and interprets sensory information

perceptual constancy the perception of a stimulus remains the same even though some of its characteristics may have changed

perceptual illusions an experience where the perception of a stimulus is different than the actual evoking stimulus

perceptual set the tendency for previous experiences and expectations to influence how situations or objects are perceived

perceptual speed the ability to quickly and accurately compare letters, numbers, objects, pictures, or patterns

peripheral nervous system (PNS) branch of the nervous system outside of the central nervous system (CNS) responsible for carrying information from the CNS to various organs and parts of the body

peripheral route persuasive technique that involves evaluating an argument based on tangential cues rather than on the argument's merits

permissive a style of parenting in which parents are warm and very involved in the lives of their children but they place very few limits on behavior

perpetuating causes factor in explaining the development of psychological disorders that focuses on the consequences of a disorder that helps maintain psychological symptoms

persistent depressive disorder chronically depressed condition that lasts for at least two years for adults and one year for children

person perception refers to the different mental processes used to perceive the personality characteristics of others

personal control sense of having control over one's environment

personality disorders long-standing, rigid, and maladaptive patterns of behavior that make it difficult for individuals to sustain healthy social relationships

personality neuroscience field of personality development that utilizes brain imaging techniques to examine the brain's structure and function and how they relate to personality

personality psychology a subfield of psychology that focuses on the study of patterns of thoughts, feelings, and behaviors that make a person unique

person-situation controversy controversy within the social-cognitive perspective surrounding the extent to which the situation influences an individual's behavior. Developed as a reaction to trait theories of personality suggesting only stable personality traits predicted behavior

persuasion a deliberate effort to change an attitude, belief, or feeling about a particular issue or topic

persuasive communication actively attempting to change an attitude or belief by delivering a message that advocates a specific side of an issue through a particular medium such as a speech or an advertisement

phenotype the observable characteristics that come from the genetic makeup of the organism

phonemes the smallest units of sound that are possible in a language

physical aggression includes any behavior that threatens or causes physical harm to another person.

physiological dependence process in which the body becomes physically dependent, or reliant, on the drug; typically involves tolerance and/or withdrawal

physiological illusions illusions that result from excessive stimulation to the eyes or brain

pictorial cues monocular cues that provide information about depth communicated through two-dimensional pictures

pineal gland a gland located deep in the center of the brain; plays an important role in the sleep-wake cycle

pituitary gland referred to as the *master gland*; releases hormones to influence all other glands and hormones in the body

place theory theory of hearing; states that different pitches activate different sets of hair cells along the cochlea's basilar membrane

placebo effect phenomenon in which participants taking a placebo react as if they were receiving treatment simply because they believe they are actually receiving treatment

plateau phase the second phase of the sexual response cycle which includes the period of sexual excitement prior to orgasm

pleasure principle process by which the id seeks immediate gratification and pays no attention to societal expectations or constraints

polygraph tests machines designed to measure physiological characteristics including heart rate/blood pressure, skin conductivity, and respiration in order to make inferences about the truthfulness of a person's statement

pons structure in the hindbrain, above the medulla; connects the lower and upper parts of the brain

positive correlation a relationship between two variables signifying that as one variable increases, the other variable also increases

positive punishment adding something undesirable after a behavior with the intention of decreasing the likelihood of that behavior occurring again in the future

positive reinforcers something that strengthens or increases a response by adding a pleasurable consequence

positive symptoms symptoms of schizophrenia that reflect a pathological excess or additions to normal functions, such as delusions, hallucinations, and disorganized thinking and speech

positron emission tomography (PET) brain imaging technique that produces a three-dimensional image of the functioning of the brain

postconventional morality Kohlberg's highest level of moral reasoning in which moral reasoning is based on abstract principles such as justice, liberty, and equality

posttraumatic stress disorder (PTSD) psychological disorder that develops in response to a traumatic event; symptoms must be present for more than one month and include the development of fear, anxiety, and other re-experiencing symptoms in response to the traumatic experience

practical intelligence one of Sternberg's three types of intelligence that includes a person's ability to find solutions to problems and use those solutions in practical, everyday situations

pragmatic inference the effects real-world knowledge and experience can have on the accuracy of memories

precipitating cause factor in explaining the development of psychological disorders that focuses on the events and experiences in daily life that may initiate the onset of a particular disorder

preconventional morality Kohlberg's lowest level of moral reasoning in which behavior that is rewarded is viewed as right, while behavior that is punished is viewed as wrong

predictive validity the degree to which a specific test predicts future behavior

predisposing cause factor in explaining the development of psychological disorders that focuses on the existing, underlying factors that increase the susceptibility of developing a particular disorder

prefrontal cortex a small area of the brain located in the foremost portion of the frontal lobe responsible for the complex processes referred to as executive function (e.g., planning, decision making, expression of personality)

prefrontal lobotomies psychosurgery in which the connection between the frontal lobes and the parts of the brain that control emotions is severed

prejudice a negative, learned attitude toward individuals or groups of people

Premack principle high probability (or preferred) behaviors can be used to reinforce low probability (or nonpreferred) behaviors

premature ejaculation ejaculation with minimal sexual stimulation before or shortly after penetration and before the person wishes it

premenstrual dysphoric disorder (PMDD) psychological disorder involving significant mood symptoms (e.g., mood swings, irritability, sadness, anxiety) during the week leading up to the onset of menstruation in women

presbyopia a hardening of the lens of the eye that leads to blurred near vision; typically occurs between the ages of 35 and 60

preventive care taking measures to prevent people from developing mental health problems in the first place by addressing the conditions thought to cause or contribute to them

primacy effect the tendency to remember words at the beginning of a list

primary appraisal initial evaluation of the seriousness of the stressor and the demands it will require; part of a cognitive appraisal of stress

primary drives drives based on innate biological needs such as hunger and thirst

primary reinforcer naturally reinforcing stimuli because they satisfy a basic biological need such as hunger or thirst

primary sex characteristics reproductive organs and external genitalia

primary sex characteristics sex-specific reproductive organs

priming aspect of implicit memory involving presenting a stimulus that activates unconscious associations that then lead to a predictable response

proactive interference forgetting occurs when previously learned information interferes with the ability to recall new information

problem solving the act of combining current information with information stored in your memory to find a solution to a task

problem-focused coping an attempt to alleviate stress directly, by eliminating the source of a stressor or by changing behaviors that occur during the stressful situations

procedural memory type of memory consisting of habits and skills

projective tests type of personality assessment that claims to access an individual's unconscious thoughts/wishes. The test typically involves ambiguous stimuli (e.g., picture, drawing, fill in the blank sentence) and the client is asked to talk or write about the stimuli, which is then interpreted by the therapist

proprioceptors sensory receptors that provide information about body position and movement

prosocial behavior behavior carried out with the goal of helping others

prospect theory the tendency to avoid risk in situations where we stand to gain but to become more risk seeking when facing a potential loss

prospective memory remembering to perform a specific action such as calling someone back or bringing lunch to the office

prototype a mental image or a typical example that exhibits all of the features associated with a certain category

proximity tendency to perceive objects close to one another as part of the same group

proximity the physical distance between people

proximodistal rule the tendency for motor skills to emerge in sequence from inside to outside

psychiatric nurses a branch of nursing concerned with assessing mental health needs or treating people with mental disorders within a medical setting

psychic determinism belief, typical in the psychoanalytic/psychodynamic perspective, that unconscious processes underlie all conscious thoughts and actions

psychoactive drug a chemical substance that alters brain function, resulting in changes in consciousness, perception, and/or mood

psychoanalysis a type of psychotherapy that utilizes Freudian concepts with an emphasis on the influence of the unconscious

psychoanalysis a type of therapy that utilizes Freudian concepts with an emphasis on the influence of the unconscious

psychoanalysis theory and treatment of personality, originally developed by Sigmund Freud, that relies heavily on therapist interpretation of a client's unconscious desires

psychodynamic approach an approach to psychology based on the belief that behaviors are motivated by internal factors unavailable to the conscious mind

psychodynamic explanation theoretical orientation that views unconscious, repressed thoughts, and memories from childhood as the cause of psychological disorders

psychodynamic therapy a form of psychotherapy which views the symptoms of a disorder as side effects of a deeper, underlying problem that needs to be resolved

psychological dependence the emotional or motivational symptoms associated with repeated drug use, such as intense cravings, inability to concentrate on other nondrug-related activities, and/or feeling restless when not taking the drug

psychology the scientific study of behavior and mental processes

psychoneuroimmunology an interdisciplinary field of study that emphasizes the interaction of psychological, neurological/endocrine, and immunological processes in stress and illness

psychopathology scientific study of mental/psychological disorders

psychopharmacology   the study of how drugs affect the mind and behavior

psychophysics   the study of the relationship between physical characteristics of stimuli and the sensory experiences that accompany them

psychosexual stages   component of psychoanalytic theory focusing on developmental stages during which the id's desire for pleasure focuses on many of the body's erogenous zones

psychotherapy   when a trained therapist interacts with someone suffering from a psychological problem with the goal of providing support or relief from the problem

puberty   period of physical development when the physical changes that lead to sexual maturation occur

punishment   consequences for behavior that decrease the probability of that behavior occurring again

pupil   small hole in the middle of the eye that allows light to enter

random assignment   the process by which participants in an experiment are randomly placed into experimental and control groups

random sampling   a technique in which the participants in a survey are chosen randomly in an attempt to get an accurate representation of a population

randomized controlled trial   a specific and rigorous research design including random assignment, a control group, and quantifiable results that allows for evaluation of the placebo effect and issues related to spontaneous recovery

rapid eye movement (REM)/stage R   a deep stage of sleep consisting of rapid eye movement (REM) typically associated with dreaming; sometimes referred to as paradoxical sleep

rapid subcortical pathway   the "low road" where messages are sent directly from the thalamus to the amygdala without going to the cortex, enabling quick behavioral responses without first making a cognitive interpretation

rational choice theory   the theory that decisions are made logically by determining how likely each outcome of that decision is as well as the positive or negative value of each outcome

reactivity   a phenomenon that occurs in situations where a research participant's behavior is different than normal because the participant is being observed

realistic conflict theory   theory explaining prejudice stating that the degree of hostility and prejudice between groups is proportional to the scarcity of resources in the environment

reality principle   process by which the ego attempts to achieve the id's goals through actions that will be pleasurable rather than painful

reason   the ability to organize information and beliefs into a series of steps leading to a conclusion

recency effect   tendency to easily recall words at the end of the list

receptive language skills   the ability to understand language

receptor cell   a cell in a sensory organ stimulated by energy, leading to sensation

recessive   genes that will not present themselves when paired with another gene that is dominant

reciprocal altruism   explanation of altruism that suggests people may only carry out altruistic acts because of the expectation of being the recipient of altruism at some point in the future or because they have been helped by altruism in the past

reciprocal determinism   social-cognitive concept that highlights the bidirectional relationship between the environment, behavior, and personality

recognition   retrieval of information that occurs after seeing the correct answer provided among a group of possible answers

reconstructive memory   the act of remembering requires a reconstruction of previous events

reflexes   involuntary responses

reflexes   rapid and automatic neuromuscular actions generated in response to a specific stimulus

refractory period   short period of time after an action potential where the neuron is not able to fire again

relatedness   the need to feel connected to other people in meaningful ways

relative height   a pictorial cue based on the principle of size constancy, suggesting that taller objects are further away

relative size   a pictorial cue based on size constancy, suggesting that smaller objects are further away

relaxation therapy   a group of techniques aimed at helping relax the body and the mind

reliability   consistency of an assessment measure

reliability   the consistency of a measure

replication   the process of repeating a study using the same methods with different participants

representative sample   a sample that has demographics and characteristics that match those of the population as a whole

representativeness heuristic   solving problems or making decisions about the probability of an event under uncertainty by comparing it to our existing prototype of the event

residential treatment   treatment provided through a live-in facility where patients receive intense and structured treatment

resistance   a psychodynamic term that refers to a patient's attempts to avoid engaging in the therapeutic process

resolution phase   the fourth phase of the sexual response cycle during which there is a return to normal functioning

resting potential   state of tension between the negative charge inside the cell relative to the outside of the cell; prepares the neuron for an action potential

reticular formation   collection of neurons, primarily in the midbrain, involved in consciousness and arousal; also related to motor control and perception and blockage of pain

retina   multilayered tissue at the back of the eye responsible for visual transduction, or the conversion of the light stimuli into neural communication leading to vision

retinal disparity   referring to the slightly different images seen by the right and left eye (due to the distance between the two retinas); a primary binocular cue for depth perception

retrieval cues   bits of information that trigger the memory to become available

retrieval   the ability to access information from long-term memory when needed

retroactive interference   forgetting occurs when new information interferes with the ability to recall older memories

retrograde amnesia   type of amnesia characterized by the loss of past memories

reuptake   a process that transports many of the released neurotransmitters back into the presynaptic neuron

reversible figure   an illusion where it is difficult to distinguish the figure from the ground (e.g., the Rubin vase)

risky shift   decisions made in groups become riskier than they would be if made by individuals alone

rods   retinal receptors that respond to varying degrees of light and dark; work best in dimly lit conditions

rorschach test   projective personality assessment that presents a series of 10 inkblots to clients, who are instructed to say whatever comes to mind upon viewing them. The responses are interpreted by a therapist and thought to be a window into the client's unconscious

safety   level two in Maslow's hierarchy of needs that focuses on the need to feel safe and secure

saturation   refers to the richness of a color

scaffolding   the process of providing appropriate assistance to a learner which is removed gradually as the learner becomes more independent

scapegoat theory   a concept suggesting that prejudice results from the need to find someone to blame for negative circumstances; scapegoats are typically individuals associated with an outgroup

scatterplot   a graph with two axes where each dot represents an individual data point

schemas   concepts or frameworks around which we organize and interpret information

schizophrenia   severe psychological disorder involving psychosis, which is characterized by delusions, hallucinations, disorganized thinking, abnormal movements, and lack of motivation and emotional expression

school psychologists   professionals who engage in the science and practice of psychology within the context of schools

scientific method   a process for conducting an objective inquiry through data collection and analysis

secondary appraisal   reassessment of a stressful situation that focuses on the resources and actions needed to help overcome the stressor

secondary drives   drives learned though conditioning such as money

secondary reinforcer   something that becomes satisfying or pleasurable through its association with a primary reinforcer

secondary sex characteristics   nonreproductive traits that develop during puberty such as breasts and hips in girls, facial hair and deeper voices in boys, and pubic and underarm hair for both boys and girls

secondary sex characteristics   the sexual organs and traits that develop at puberty and are not directly involved in reproduction

secure attachment   children who are upset when their mother leaves but are soon comforted by parental contact upon their mother's return

selective attention   a conscious focus on one stimulus or perception at a given time

selective inattention/inattentional blindness   environmental stimuli that are screened out or ignored while attention is selectively focused on something else

selective serotonin reuptake inhibitors (SSRIs)   antidepressant medications that selectively block the reuptake of serotonin in the brain and have fewer side effects than tricyclics

self-actualization an individual's experience of becoming their real self (rather than striving for their ideal self) and realizing their fullest potential as a human being

self-actualization level five in Maslow's hierarchy of needs that focuses on realizing one's potential as a person by seeking personal growth

self-actualization the achievement of one's full potential

self-concept a person's understanding of who he or she is; this is reflected in the way an individual thinks of themselves

self-determination theory (SDT) theory that all humans have three universal psychological needs including autonomy, relatedness, and competence that must be satisfied in order to facilitate a natural tendency toward human growth

self-efficacy an individual's expectations and beliefs about their own abilities to perform certain tasks

Self-objectification occurs when a person focuses more on how his/her body is perceived by others than his/her own internal perception of his/her body

self-perception theory people infer (or develop) their attitudes about various topics by observing their own behaviors

self-report inventories objective personality assessments that require the person to read and answer a number of questions; responses to those questions are interpreted by comparing them to standardized norms from a large group of people

self-report questionnaire a form of data collection in which people are asked to rate or describe their own behavior or mental state

self-serving bias an attributional bias that involves people taking personal credit for their own successes but blaming their failures on external events beyond their control

self-transcendence level six in Maslow's hierarchy of needs that focuses on the need to go beyond the self and experience oneness with the greater whole or higher truth

semantic coding a type of processing that is based on meaning

semantic memories type of explicit memories that contain factual and conceptual information

semantics the meaning of words and sentences in a given language

sensation process where physical energy from the environment is converted into neural signals to be interpreted by the brain

sensorineural hearing loss hearing loss that results from damage to the cochlea in the inner ear or from damage to the nerve pathways from the inner ear to the brain

sensory (afferent) neurons neurons that carry information toward the central nervous system from the sensory organs (eyes, ears, nose, tongue, and skin)

sensory adaptation occurs when a sense is exposed to an unchanging stimulus and eventually stops registering the existence of that stimulus

sensory memory according to the 3-stage model of memory, the first memory store that retains sensory stimulation for a short time; an extension of perception

serial position effect when recalling a list of words/items most people can remember words from the beginning and the end of the list

set of operations the steps you need to take in problem solving to reach the goal state from the initial state

set point theory a theory that suggests that our body is biologically programmed to defend a certain body weight

sex our biological classification as male or female based on the sex chromosomes contained in our DNA, our reproductive organs, and our anatomical features

sexism prejudice and discrimination based on gender

sexual dysfunctions ongoing problems with sexual functioning that cause distress and impairment for individuals and relationships

sexual interest/arousal disorder when females experience either a complete lack of or significant reduction in sexual interest/arousal

sexual objectification being viewed primarily as an object of sexual desire

sexual orientation refers to the pattern of a person's sexual attractions.

sexual selection a type of natural selection in which the preference by one sex for certain characteristics of the other sex or a competitive advantage of certain traits leads the sexes to evolve in different forms

sexually transmitted infections (STIs) infections that are spread primarily through person-to-person sexual contact

shape constancy objects are perceived as the same shape even though the retinal image may change as a result of different viewpoints

shaping the use of reinforcement of successive approximations of a desired end behavior

short-term memory the structural component of memory that is responsible for storing relatively small amounts of information for a short time

signal detection theory theory explaining differences in people's responses to stimuli based on varying circumstances

significant life changes stressful common life events, such as moving out of a childhood home, getting married or divorced, losing a loved one, or changing career paths.

similarity principle of interpersonal attraction that the more two people have in common, the more likely they are to experience increased attraction to that person

similarity the tendency to perceive objects that are the same shape, size, or color as part of a pattern

single-blind experiments an experiment in which research participants do not know whether they have been assigned to the experimental or control group

situational attribution attributing our own, or another person's behavior to external factors such as the situation or environment

size constancy the perception of an object's size doesn't change, regardless of changes in distance

sleep apnea a sleep disorder involving regular interruptions of breathing during sleep

sleep terrors a parasomnia characterized by scary dreams and increased autonomic nervous system activity; typically occurs during NREM sleep and therefore can be accompanied by movement

sleep the daily, natural loss of consciousness controlled by the brain

sleepwalking a parasomnia that occurs during NREM sleep in response to an abnormal transition from deep sleep (e.g. Stage N3) to REM or a lighter stage of sleep

Slow mapping when a new word is acquired through a gradual process that requires repeated exposures

slower cortical pathway the "high road" where messages are sent from the thalamus to the visual cortex and then back to the amygdala, allowing your perceptions (or interpretations) to affect your emotions

slow-to-warm temperament infants with generally regular eating/sleeping patterns who can adapt to change with repeated exposure and have mildly negative responses to frustration

social anxiety disorder psychological disorder involving marked and persistent fears of being scrutinized by others or embarrassed/humiliated in a public setting

social categorization grouping people or things according to certain characteristics such as age, race, and gender

social cognition an area within social psychology that focuses on the role of cognitive processes in terms of how people think about others

social connectedness the quality and number of meaningful relationships an individual may have among friends, family, and the community

social facilitation the tendency to perform easy or well-learned tasks better when observed by others

social identity model of deindividuating effects an explanation for behavior that takes into account the shared social identity of a group and the situational group norms

social intuitionist Haidt's theory that we have an instant gut reaction to moral situations, which precedes moral reasoning

social learning theory a theory of gender development stating that children learn gendered behavior by observing and imitating adults and responding to rewards and punishments

social loafing the tendency for people to put less effort into a task when they are part of a group because they believe their individual efforts don't matter or that they will not be held personally responsible for the outcome

social norms the spoken and unspoken rules about what behavior is considered appropriate in a given society

social psychology a field of psychology involving the scientific attempt to explain how the thoughts, feelings, and behaviors of individuals are influenced by the actual, imagined, or implied presence of other human beings

social psychology the scientific study of how people's thoughts, feelings, and behaviors are influenced by the actual, imagined, or implied presence of others

social role theory of gender theory proposed by Alice Eagly stating that inherent physical differences between men and women lead to the formation of gender roles in the division of labor in the home and at work

social support the comfort, caring, and help available to an individual experiencing stress, from a network of supportive friends and family members

social-cognitive theories theories of personality that places emphasis on beliefs and expectations, both conscious and unconscious, that individuals form through their interactions with the environment

sociocultural perspective an approach in which psychologists examine the influence of social and cultural factors on human behavior and mental processes

socioemotional selectivity theory of aging theory that suggests that as people grow older and realize that the time they have left is limited, they focus on enjoying the present rather than looking to the future

soma cell body of the neuron; contains the nucleus, which houses the cell's genetic information

somatic nervous system part of the peripheral nervous system; receives stimuli from the outside world, coordinates movements, and performs other tasks under conscious control

somatic symptom disorder psychological disorder involving the combination of the presence of a physical symptom(s) plus abnormal thoughts, feelings, or behaviors in response to the symptom(s)

somatosensory cortex structure located at the front of the parietal lobe that receives and interprets information about bodily sensations

sound shadow the absorption of sound by the head; sound waves hit one ear first, then are dampened by the head, which aids in the location of sound

sound wave a change in air pressure caused by molecules of air or fluid colliding and moving apart

source monitoring error memory error that involves attributing it to the wrong source

source traits underlying factor or origin of surface traits

specific intelligence (or "s") represents abilities related to a specific single mental activity

specific phobia persistent, irrational fear of a specific object or situation

sperm male sex cells

spontaneous recovery the brief reappearance of a previously extinguished response

spontaneous remission recovery without any treatment

sports psychologists professionals who use psychological knowledge and skills to address optimal performance and well-being of athletes and sports organizations

stability versus change the degree to which traits remain stable and unchanging versus malleable over years of growth and maturation

stage R/rapid eye movement (REM) a deep stage of sleep consisting of rapid eye movement (REM) typically associated with dreaming; sometimes referred to as paradoxical sleep

standard deviation a measure of the typical distance between the scores of a distribution and the mean, which indicates how widely individual scores in a group vary

standardization the process of establishing test norms and the guidelines for uniform administration and scoring

Stanford-Binet Intelligence Scale a standardized intelligence test measuring cognitive abilities in children and adults that was originally an English adaptation of the Binet-Simon scales in French

stem cells unspecified cells with the capability to evolve into other types of specialized cells in the body (e.g., brain cells, red blood cells)

stereotype a type of heuristic or mental shortcut involving general attitudes and beliefs about a group of people

stereotype threat an experience where a person has the knowledge that they must work against an existing stereotype; often includes an awareness of the risk of confirming the negative stereotype as a result of the outcome of the situation

stereotype threat when worry about confirming a negative stereotype leads to underperformance on a test by a member of a stereotyped group

stimulants a drug that excites or increases the functioning of the central nervous system

stimulus discrimination responding to the original stimulus only without responding to other stimuli

stimulus generalization responding to stimuli similar to but distinct from the original stimulus

stranger anxiety a fear of strangers that is a survival strategy that enables babies to perceive unfamiliar faces as potentially threatening

stress the perceived discrepancy between the physical or psychological demands of a situation and the individual's biological, psychological, or social resources to cope with the demands.

stressors the experiences we encounter in life that cause stress; events we perceive as threatening or challenging

structuralism a school of psychology concerned with studying the individual elements of consciousness

structured interviews standardized interviews that have a specific list of questions, which are administered exactly as written

subliminal perception when sensation falls below the absolute threshold

subliminal persuasion using subliminal techniques to influence people's behaviors

subordinate concepts the most specific type of concepts that includes the narrowest categories

substance use disorder a psychological disorder characterized by a pattern of drug use leading to distress or significant impairment in functioning

subtractive color mixture when adding additional colors removes (subtracts) wavelengths of light, eventually resulting in black (e.g., mixing paints)

sudden infant death syndrome (SIDS) the unexplained death of a seemingly healthy infant

suggestibility a person's level of susceptibility to the opinions and influence of others

suicide intentional, self-inflicted behavior resulting in death

superego psychoanalytic component of personality that considers societal constraints and acceptable forms of behavior

superordinate concepts the categories that are the broadest or include the most concepts

support groups a form of group therapy which does not necessarily include a professionally trained therapist as the group leader.

suprachiasmatic nucleus (SCN) small part of the hypothalamus that controls the circadian clock

surface traits personality traits that are easily visible to others (e.g., warm, gregarious, outspoken) and originate from source traits

survey a series of questions about people's behavior or opinions, in the form of a questionnaire or interview

sympathetic nervous system branch of the autonomic nervous system responsible for the involuntary functions of the body's internal organs; particularly active during times of stress

synapse small space between the presynaptic neuron and the postsynaptic neuron; filled with the neurotransmitter after an action potential

synaptic plasticity the ability of the brain to adapt and change over time

synaptic pruning a process in which excess synapses are gradually reduced during childhood

syntax the rules about how words are to be arranged to form sentences in a given language

systematic desensitization a type of exposure therapy in which people learn to pair states of deep relaxation while being exposed to anxiety-provoking situations using a fear hierarchy

taste aversion classically conditioned dislike and avoidance of a certain food following illness

taste buds taste receptor cells located in the fungiform papillae on the tongue

telegraphic speech the two-word stage of language development in early childhood when speech resembles an old-fashioned telegram

temperament aspects of personality considered innate and not learned

temporal lobes section of the brain located in front of the occipital lobes and above the ears, involved primarily in auditory processing, including understanding language

tend-and-befriend response where women faced with stress seek affiliation-related behaviors (e.g., nurturing, seeking care) that appear to be motivated, in part, by the hormone, oxytocin; alternative to the traditional "fight-or-flight" response

teratogens agents that can negatively impact the development of an embryo or fetus

terminal button located at the end of each neuron; contains vesicles holding the neurotransmitter, which is released into the synapse during an action potential

test norms a way to compare an individual's score relative to the performance of others

testes male gonads

testosterone the principal male sex hormone

test-retest reliability evaluating the consistency of test scores over time

texture gradient a pictorial cue that assumes that objects with visible texture appear closer than those with little or no texture

thalamus structure located just above the brainstem that processes incoming sensory information and directs the messages to the appropriate areas of the cerebral cortex

thematic apperception test (TAT) projective personality assessment that presents clients with a series of ambiguous images/scenes and asks them to tell a story about what is happening in each picture

theory of multiple intelligences theory of intelligence that proposes nine specific modalities of intelligence rather than a single general ability

therapeutic alliance the quality of the relationship between a therapist and patient

theta waves brain waves associated with the transition to sleep; may be present in N1 and N2 stages of sleep

threshold theory of creativity states that above average intelligence is a necessary condition for someone to be able to engage in the thinking processes that lead to creativity

thyroid gland one of the largest endocrine glands located at the base of the neck that plays an important role in metabolism and controls how sensitive the body is to the effects of other hormones

timbre referring to sound; the purity and complexity of tone

token economy providing tokens (e.g., stickers, coins, points) for desired behaviors that can be exchanged for something rewarding

tolerance a form of physiological dependence where the body becomes used to a drug, resulting in an increased need for the drug to achieve the same effects

top-down processing perception that relies heavily on previous knowledge and experience; also known as knowledge-based processing

trait relatively stable disposition to behave in a particular way

trait theories theories of personality that suggest there are sets of meaningful and distinct personality dimensions that can be used to describe how people differ from one another

transduction the process through which physical energy, such as light or sound, is converted into an electrical (neural) charge

transference a psychodynamic term referring to a patient's unconscious feelings about a significant person in his or her life that are instead directed toward the therapist

transgender umbrella term used to describe a person whose gender identity is different from that which was assigned at birth

traumatic brain injury (TBI) physical trauma or a head injury from an outside source

trial and error type of problem solving that involves trying a potential solution and discarding that option if it fails while moving on to the next potential solution

triangular theory of love a theory developed by Robert Sternberg describing interpersonal relationships using three components of love: intimacy, passion, and commitment

trichromatic theory of color vision a theory that there are three different types of retinal receptors that are each sensitive to varying wavelengths of light; also called Young-Helmholtz theory of color vision

tricyclics antidepressant medications that work by blocking the reuptake of serotonin and norepinephrine that have been associated with worse side effects than newer medications such as SSRIs

two-factor theory theory developed by Schachter and Singer that the cognitive evaluation following physiological arousal leads to the experience of emotion

Type A personality type described as more competitive, impatient, verbally aggressive, ambitious, and outgoing; more likely to experience a heart attack.

Type B personality type described as easygoing and relaxed.

Type D "distressed" personality type; people who experience increased negative emotions and avoid self-expression in social interactions; negative prognostic factor for those who have experienced a heart attack

typical antipsychotics antipsychotic drugs discovered in the 1950s that work by blocking receptors in the brain's dopamine pathways which are not particularly effective in treating the negative symptoms of schizophrenia and are associated with negative side effects

unconditional positive regard a key component of person-centered therapy in which therapists must accept and support the patient regardless of what the person says or does

unconditional positive regard ability to accept and value another person despite their problems or weaknesses

unconditioned response (UCR) the naturally occurring or reflexive response to an unconditioned stimulus

unconditioned stimulus (UCS) stimuli that elicit a natural or reflexive response without prior experience

universality hypothesis Darwin's hypothesis that facial expressions are understood across all cultures

unstructured interviews unstandardized interviews that allow the clinician to ask a variety of self-determined questions

valence a positive or negative value along a continuum assigned to an emotion

validity a test's ability to accurately measure the construct it is designed to measure

validity accuracy of an assessment measure

variable a characteristic that can vary, such as age, weight, or height

variable-interval schedules reinforcing behavior after variable periods of time; generally produce slow and steady behavioral responses

variable-ratio schedules reinforcing behavior after varying and unpredictable numbers of responses; have high response rates and produce behavior that is difficult to extinguish

ventromedial hypothalamus part of the hypothalamus that controls the experience satiety center

verbal aggression includes verbal communication that is intended to cause psychological harm rather than physical harm

vesicles small, fluid-filled sacs located in the terminal buttons; typically hold the neurotransmitter

virtual reality exposure exposure therapy conducted using computer simulations that help patients learn to be increasingly desensitized to anxiety-inducing situations

visual accommodation a process that involves the lens of the eye changing shape to best refract and focus light on the retina

visual coding a type of processing that is based on visual images

volley principle theory of hearing, suggesting neurons take turns firing thereby combining forces to create more a more complicated neural signal

wavelengths the distance between the peak of each wave of energy; measured in nanometers

Weber's Law law in psychophysics; the difference between two objects (i.e., difference threshold) varies proportionally to the initial size of the stimulus

Wernicke's area the area of the brain in the left temporal lobe focused on language comprehension

withdrawal symptoms physiological symptoms produced by the body when a drug is absent from the system

Wolffian system a male reproductive system

womb envy neo-Freudian concept proposed by Horney stating that men experience jealousy due to the woman's role in nurturing and sustaining life (through pregnancy, birthing, and lactation)

working backward when you start at the goal state and then work your way backward to determine a solution to a problem

working memory structural component of memory that allows for the manipulation of information for cognitively complex tasks and for the limited and temporary storage of that information

X chromosomes A sex chromosome, two of which are normally present in female cells (designated XX) and only one in male cells (designated XY)

Y chromosome a sex chromosome that is normally present only in male cells, which are designated XY

Yerkes-Dodson law law that states performance generally peaks with a moderate level of arousal

zone of proximal development a key component of Vygotsky's theory of cognitive development that highlights the difference between what a child can do alone versus what a child can do together with a more competent person

zygote a single fertilized cell

Credits

Text Credits

Chapter Prologue

Graphic by Nigel Holmes; Based on the work of Professor Carol Dweck; Roediger, H. L., & Karpicke, J. D. (2006b). The power of testing memory: Basic research and implications for educational practice. Perspectives on Psychological Science, 1(3), 181–210; Based on Wilson, R. (2014) "Growth vs Fixed Mindset For Elementary Students," Wayfaring Path. Retrieved from https://wayfaringpath.coetail.com/2014/12/02/growth-vs-fixed-mindset-for-elementary-students; Based on Roediger, H. L., & Karpicke, J. D. (2006a). Test enhanced learning taking memory tests improves long term retention. Psychological science, 17(3), 249–255. Retrieved from http://psych.wustl.edu/memory/Roddy%20article%20PDF%27s/Roediger%20&%20Karpicke%20(2006)_PsychSci.pdf; Danae Hudson and Brooke Wisenhunt

Chapter 1

Hilgard, E. R. (1987). Psychology in America: A historical survey. Harcourt Brace Jovanovich; Watson, John B. "Behaviorism Chicago." IL: Phoenix (1930); U.S. Bureau of labor Statistics; U.S. Bureau of labor Statistics, Occupational Employment Satistics(2016); Based on Birnbaum, M. S., Kornell, N., Bjork, E. L., & Bjork, R. A. (2013). Why interleaving enhances inductive learning: The roles of discrimination and retrieval. Memory & -cognition, 41(3), 392–402. See also Kornell, N., & Bjork, R. A. (2008). Learning concepts and categories is spacing the "enemy of induction". Psychological science, 19(6), 585–592; Murtiana, R. (2012). Enhancing students' vocabulary acquisition through deep word processing strategy. LIA CAR journal, 5, 220–229; Lowell Lindsay Bennion (1959). Religion and the Pursuit of Truth. Utah: Deseret Book Company; Hartwig, M. K., Was, C. A., Isaacson, R. M., & Dunlosky, J. (2012). General knowledge monitoring as a predictor of in-class exam performance. British Journal of Educational Psychology, 82(3), 456–468; Metcalfe, J. (2009). Metacognitive judgments and control of study. Current Directions in Psychological Science, 18(3), 159–163; Based on Kandpal, M., & Kandpal, A. (2014), "Establishing Correlation between Size Estimation Metrics and Effort: A Statistical Approach," International Journal of Computer Applications, vol. 95, no. 21; Cook, K. (2014). Kitty Genovese: The Murder, the Bystanders, the Crime That Changed America. W.W. Norton & Company; Immunization Safety Review Committee. Immunization safety review: vaccines and autism. National Academies Press, 2004; The Science Facts about Autism and Vaccines. An Infographic developed by Nowsourcing; The Science Facts about Autism and Vaccines. An Infographic developed by Nowsourcing.

Chapter 2

Macmillan, M. (2000) An Odd Kind of Fame: Stories of Phineas Gage. Cambridge, Mass.: MIT Press; Based on Conditions. The tech Museum of Innovation. Accessed from http://genetics.thetech.org/ask a geneticist/als genetics snp; http://www.genome.gov/10001772. All About The Human Genome Project (HGP); Michael Okun (2016). How to control the brain by Michael Okun and Kelly Foote at TEDxUF; Helen Shen, "Neuroscience: Tuning the brain," Nature Magazine, March 19, 2014; Based on Steve Smith. "Racial Disparity In Health Care: High Costs Of Insurance, Lack Of Access Keep Minorities From Getting Help They Need". Medical Daily. Jan 29, 2016. Accessed from http://www.medicaldaily.com/ racial disparity health care high costs insurance lack access keep minorities 371452.

Chapter 3

Based on Retrieved from http://becuo.com/electromagnetic spectrum in nanometers; Based on Episode 5 Sensation and Perception, My Psych lab. Retrieved from http://visual.pearsoncmg.com/mypsychlab/index.php?clipId=168; Based on https://faculty.washington.edu/chudler/chvision.html; Based on Kenneth R. Spring and Michael W. Davidson. "Introduction to the Primary Colors." Olympus. Retrieved from https://www.olympuslifescience.com/en/microscoperesource/primer/lightandcolor/primarycolorsintro/; Based on Ari Siletz (July 2014). "A Brief Look at the Theory of Color Perception." 20/20. Retrieved from https://www.2020mag.com/article/a brief look at the theory of color perception; Based on http://imgbuddy.com/shape%20constancy%20example.asp; Based on Abigail A. Baird (2010). "Think Psychology". Harlow, Essex: Pearson Education; Gaetano Kanizsa (1976), "Illusionary contours", published in Scientific American; Rock's Primal Scream. Dir. Gary Greenwald. 1983. VHS; Based on Abigail A. Baird (2010). "Think Psychology". Harlow, Essex: Pearson Education; Based on Necker, L. A. (1832) "Observations on some remarkable optical phænomena seen in Switzerland; and on an optical phænomenon which occurs on viewing a figure of a crystal or geometrical solid," The London, Edinburgh, and Dublin Philosophical Magazine and Journal of Science, vol. 1, no. 5, 329–337; Hill, W. E. (William Ely), 1887–1962, "My wife and my mother-in-law. They are both in this picture - find them," Illus. in: Puck, v. 78, no. 2018 (1915 Nov. 6), p. 11.; Gregory, R. L. (1997). "Knowledge in perception and illusion." Philosophical Transactions of the Royal Society of London. Series B: Biological Sciences, 352(1358), 1121–1127; Data from U.S. State Prescribing Rates, 2016. Center for Disease Control. https://www.cdc.gov/drugoverdose/maps/rxstate2016.html; Based on Raymond C Tait and John T Chibnall (2014). "Racial/Ethnic Disparities in the Assessment and Treatment of Pain Psychosocial Perspectives," American Psychologist, vol. 69, no. 2, 131–141. Retrieved from https://www.researchgate.net/profile/Raymond_Tait/publication/260250917_RacialEthnic_Disparities_in_the_Assessment_and_Treatment_of_Pain_Psychosocial_Perspectives/links/542afac90cf277d58e8a0f68.pdf.

Chapter 4

Chalmers, D. J. (1995). Facing up to the problem of consciousness. Journal of Consciousness Studies, 2(3), 200 219; René Descartes (1916). A Discourse on Method. London: J.M. Dent & sons, Ltd; Based on National Sleep Foundation. http://sleepfoundation.org/how sleep works/how much sleep do we really need; Based on National Sleep Foundation. http://sleepfoundation.org/how sleep works/how much sleep do we really need; Based on A fictional EEG showing a sleep spindle and K complex in stage 2 sleep, Neocadre (2 December 2008); Petri, G., et. al. "Homological scaffolds of brain functional networks," Journal of the Royal Society Interface, vol. 11, no. 101, (29 October 2014). Article published under CC4.0; Petri, G., et. al. "Homological scaffolds of brain functional networks," Journal of the Royal Society Interface, vol. 11, no. 101, (6 December 2014). Article published under CC4.0; American Psychiatric Association. (2013). Diagnostic and statistical manual of mental disorders, (DSM-5®). Washington, DC: American Psychiatric Pub; Petri, G., et. al. "Homological scaffolds of brain functional networks," Journal of the Royal Society Interface, vol. 11, no. 101, (29 October 2014). Article published under CC4.0; Based on National Institute on Drug Abuse, National Institutes of Health, U.S. Department of Health and Human Services. Retrieved from http://www.drugabuse.gov/ related topics/trends statistics/infographics/marijuana use educational outcomes; 17: Elkins, G. R., Barabasz, A. F., Council, J. R., & Spiegel, D. (2015). Advancing research and practice: The revised APA Division 30 definition of hypnosis. American Journal of Clinical Hypnosis, 57(4), 378–385.

Chapter 5

Pavlov, Ivan Petrovich (1928). Lectures on conditioned re?exes. New York: Liveright, 414; Based on Thorndike's Puzzle Box by Jacob Sussman; Based on Schedules of Reinforcement. Retrieved from http://www.rhsmpsychology.com/Handouts/schedules_of_reinforcement.htm; Skinner, B. F. (1961). "Teaching machines." Science, vol. 128, 969–977; Cook, J. (May 27, 2012). How Google motivates their employees with rewards and perks. Hub Pages. Retrieved from http://thinkingleader.hubpages.com/hub/How Google Motivates their Employees with Rewards and Perks; Based on Sasha Long, "Behavior Week Surprise Addition: The Dos and Don'ts of a Token Economy," The Autism Helper, 15 Sptember 2012; Frum, L. (November 14, 2013). Emerging technology heightens video game realism. CNN. Retrieved from http://www.cnn.com/2013/11/14/tech/gaming gadgets/realism video games; Data from Gentile, Douglas A., et. al. "Mediators and Moderators of Long Term Effects of Violent Video Games on Aggressive Behavior," JAMA Pediatrics, vol. 168, no. 5, 450–457, (May 2014). http://jamanetwork.com/journals/jamapediatrics/fullarticle/1850198.

Chapter 6

Based on Atkinson, R. C., & Shiffrin, R. M. (1968). Human memory: A proposed system and its control processes (Vol. 2). New York: Academic Press; Based on Atkinson, R. C., & Shiffrin, R. M. (1968). Human memory: A proposed system and its control processes (Vol. 2). New York: Academic Press; Based on Declarative Memory, Photoreading. Taken From http://www.readfast.co.uk/declarative memory/; Based on Declarative Memory, Photoreading. Taken From http://www.readfast.co.uk/declarative memory; Based on Figure1 Serial position effect. Serial Position Effect and Rehearsal. Retrieved from http://www.indiana.edu/~p1013447/dictionary/serpos.htm; Data from Godden, D.R., Baddeley, A.D., (1975), Context Dependent Memory in Two Natural Environments: On Land and Underwater, British Journal of Psychology, Blackwell Publishing Ltd., Vol. 66, Issue 3. Pages 325–331; Based on Myers, D. G., DeWall, N. C., (2014), Psychology in everyday life, New York: Worth Publishers; Based on http://kasperspiro.com/; Based on Danae Hudson and Brooke Wisenhunt; Dennis Coon (2005). Psychology: A Modular Approach to Mind and Behavior. Belmont, CA: Wadsworth/Thomson Learning; Baxendale, S. (2004). Memories aren't made of this: Amnesia at the movies. BMJ, 329(7480), 1480 1483; American Psychological Association. http://www.apa.org/topics/trauma/memories.aspx; Nash, R. A., Berkowitz, S. R., & Roche, S. (2016). Public attitudes on the ethics of deceptively planting false memories to motivate healthy behavior. Applied Cognitive Psychology, 30(6), 885–897. doi: 10.1002/acp.3.

Chapter 7

Adapted from Rosch, E., & Mervis, C. B. (1975). Family resemblances: Studies in the internal structure of categories. Cognitive psychology, 7(4), 573–605; Craig A. Giffi, C. A. et.al. "Help wanted: American manufacturing competitiveness and the looming skills gap." Deloitte Review Issue 16 (Jan. 26, 2015); Based on Daniel Kahneman (2011). Thinking, Fast and Slow. New York: Farrar, Straus and Giroux; Nickerson, R. S. (1998). Confirmation bias: A ubiquitous phenomenon in many guises. Review of general psychology, 2(2), 175–220; Based on Amy Mitchell, et.al. Political Polarization & Media Habits. Journalism & Media, PEW Research Center. October 21, 2014; Based on Robert Epstein, Steven M. Schmidt, and Regina Warfel. Measuring and Training Creativity Competencies: Validation of a New Test. Creativity Research Journal, vol. 20, no. 1, 7–12. http://www.researchgate.net/profile/Robert_Epstein4/publication/233027638_Measuring_and_Training_Creativity_Competencies_Validation_of_a_New_Test/links/54f748960cf2ccffe9db0815.pdf; Chomsly, N. (1957) Syntactic structures. New York, N.Y.: Mouton de Gruyter.

Chapter 8

Deary, I. J., Whiteman, M. C., Starr, J. M., Whalley, L. J., & Fox, H. C. (2004). The Impact of Childhood Intelligence on Later Life: Following Up the Scottish Mental Surveys of 1932 and 1947. Journal of Personality and Social Psychology, 86(1), 130 147; Alfonso, V.C., Flanagan, D.P., Radwan, S. (2005). ""The Impact of the Cattell–Horn–Carroll Theory on Test Development and Interpretation of Cognitive and Academic Abilities"", Contemporary Intellectual Assessment, Second Edition: Theories, Tests, and Issues, Edited by Dawn P. Flanagan and Patti L. Harrison."; Based on Hughes, J. (2014). Enhancing Virtues: Intelligence (Part 1), Ethical Technology; Based on Jacobs, K., Watt, D., Roodenburg, J., (2013). Why can't Jonny read? Bringing theory into cognitive assessment, InPsych 2013, Australian Psychological Society; Sternberg, Robert. (2004). Culture and Intelligence. The American psychologist. 59. 325–38; Based on Gardner, H., (1983). Frames of Mind: The Theory of Multiple Intelligences, Basic Books, 1983; National Park Service. Statue of Liberty National Monument; Based on Jacobs, K., Watt, D., Roodenburg, J., (2013). Why can't Jonny read? Bringing theory into cognitive assessment, InPsych 2013, Australian Psychological Society; 3; 346; Angier, N., (2000). Study Finds Region of Brain May Be Key Problem Solver. Stated by Dr. John Duncan; Based on US Census (2010); Based on Dr. Eowyn, "How smart or stupid is your country?" Fellowship of the Minds, 11 October 2014; Hupp, S., Jewell, J., (2015). Great Myths of Child Development Great Myths of Psychology. John Wiley and Son, 2015; Stated by Vincent Lombardi and published in Business week no.2490-2498 (1977), original from University of Minnesota; Based on Nature versus Nurture. (2017). In ScienceAid. Retrieved Oct 7, 2017, from https://scienceaid.net/psychology/approaches/naturenurture.html; Haworth C, Wright M, Luciano M, et al. The heritability of general cognitive ability increases linearly from childhood to young adulthood. Molecular psychiatry. 2010;15(11):1112–1120; Data from Nelson CA, Zeanah CH, Fox NA, Marshall PJ, Smyke AT, Guthrie D. Cognitive recovery in socially deprived young children: the Bucharest Early Intervention Project. Science. 2007 Dec 21; 318(5858):1937–40; Woodley, M. A., te Nijenhuis, J., Must, O., & Must, A. (2014). Controlling for increased guessing enhances the independence of the Flynn effect from g: The return of the Brand effect. Intelligence, 43, 27 34; Kremer, W., (2015). Are humans getting cleverer?, BBC. Adapted from What Is Intelligence?: Beyond the Flynn Effect, Flynn J. R., (2007), Figure 1, p.8; Based on David Wechsler (2008). WAIS IV technical and interpretive manual. San Antonio, Tex.: Pearson; Buj. V. (1981). Average IQ values in various European countries. Personality and Individual Differences, 2: 168–169; Schmader, T., Johns, M., & Forbes, C. (2008). An integrated process model of stereotype threat effects on performance. Psychological Review, 115(2), 336–356; Based on Steele, Claude & Aronson, Joshua. (1995). Stereotype Threat and The Intellectual Test-Performance of African-Americans. Journal of Personality and Social Psychology; Title IX — General Provisions (2000), US Department of Education; American Psychiatric Association (2013). Diagnostic and Statistical Manual of Mental Disorders (DSM-5®) 5e, American Psychiatric Pub.

Chapter 9

THE POSTNATAL DEVELOPMENT OF THE HUMAN CEREBRAL CORTEX, VOLUMES IVIII, by Jesse LeRoy Conel, Cambridge, Mass.: Harvard University Press, Copyright © 1939, 1941, 1947, 1951, 1955, 1959, 1963, 1967 by the President and Fellows of Harvard College. Copyright © renewed 1967, 1969, 1975, 1979, 1983, 1987, 1991; Erikson, E. H. (1993). Childhood and society. WW Norton & Company; Bellis, M. A., Drowning, J. & Ashton, J. R. (2006) "Adults at 12? Trends in puberty and their public health consequences," Journal of Epidemiology & Community Health, vol. 60, no, 11; Based on Trends in Teen Pregnancy and Childbearing Teen Births. Office of Adoloescent Health. Retrived from https://www.hhs.gov/ash/oah/adolescent development/reproductive health and teen pregnancy/teen pregnancy and childbearing/trends/index.html; Kohlberg, L. (1969). Stage and sequence: The cognitive developmental approach to socialization. New York: Rand McNally. pp. 347–480; Based on Marcia, J. E. (1980) Identity in adolescence. Chapter 5 in In J. Adelson (Ed.) Handbook of Adolescent Psychology. New York: Wiley; Arnett, J. J. (2001). Conceptions of the transition to adulthood: Perspectives from adolescence through midlife. Journal of adult development, 8(2), 133–143; Based on CDC/NCHS, National Vital Statistics System; Fergus I.M.Craik and Nathan S.Rose (2012). "Memory encoding and aging: A neurocognitive perspective." Neuroscience and Behavioral Reviews, vol. 36, no. 7, p. 1729–1739; Woolfolk, Ann, "Toshiko Takaezu," Princeton Alumni Weekly, Vol. 83(5), 6 October 1982, p. 32; Based on Arielle Kuperberg (March 4, 2014). "Age at Coresidence, Premarital Cohabitation, and Marriage Dissolution: 1985–2009," Journal of Marriage and Family, vol. 76, no. 2, p. 352–369; Mark Twain (1835–1910), America author and Humorist; Grossbard, Joel R., Neighbors, Clayton and Larimer, Mary E. (August 2011). "Perceived Norms for Thinness and Muscularity among College Students: What Do Men and Women Really Want?," Eating Behaviors, vol. 12, no. 3, p. 192–199. Retrieved from https://www.ncbi.nlm.nih.gov/pmc/articles/PMC3134786/figure/F1/; 2012 Cosmetic Surgery Age Distribution Age 13–19, 2012 Plastic Surgery Statistics. Retrieved from https://www.plasticsurgery.org/documents/News/Statistics/2012/plastic-surgery-statistics-full-report-2012.pdf; 2012 Plastic Surgery Statistics. American Society of Plastic Surgeons. Accessed from https://www.plasticsurgery.org/documents/News/Statistics/2012/plastic surgery statistics full report 2012.pdf.

Chapter 10

Defining Adult Overweight and Obesity, Overweight & Obesity. Retrieved from https://www.cdc.gov/obesity/adult/defining.html; Based on 2017 Participation Report. The Physical Activity Council's annual study tracking sports, fitness, and recreation participation in the US, retrieved from http://www.physicalactivitycouncil.com/pdfs/current.pdf; Maslow, A.H. (1943), "A Theory of Human Motivation", Psychological Review, 50, 370–396; Maslow, A. H., Frager, R., & Cox, R. (1970). Motivation and personality (Vol. 2). J. Fadiman, & C. McReynolds (Eds.). New York: Harper & Row; Ryan, R. M., & Deci, E. L. (2000). Self determination theory and the facilitation of intrinsic motivation, social development, and well being. American Psychologist, 55(1), 68–78; Based on Self DeterminationTheory by Christina Donelly, Jtneill – Own work. Licensed under CC BY 3.0 via Wikimedia Commons; Dweck, S., (2000), "Self theories: Their Role in Motivation, Personality, and Development", Essays in social psychology, Philadelphia, PA: Psychology Press; Maslow, A.H. (1943), "A Theory of Human Motivation", Psychological Review, 50, 370–396; Maslow, A. H., Frager, R., & Cox, R. (1970). Motivation and personality (Vol. 2). J. Fadiman, & C. McReynolds (Eds.). New York: Harper & Row; Ryan, R. M., & Deci, E. L. (2000). Self-determination theory and the facilitation of intrinsic motivation, social development, and well-being. American Psychologist, 55(1), 68–78; ased on Self DeterminationTheory by Christina Donelly, Jtneill – Own work. Licensed under CC BY 3.0 via Wikimedia Commons; based on Self DeterminationTheory by Christina Donelly, Jtneill – Own work. Licensed under CC BY 3.0 via Wikimedia Commons; Based on Stangor, C., "Introduction to Psychology", Flat World Knowledge, L.L.C., 2010; Based on Dutton, D. G., & Aron, A. P. (1974). Some evidence for heightened sexual attraction under conditions of high anxiety. Journal of personality and social psychology, 30(4), Darwin, C.R., (1872), Expression of the Emotions in Man and Animals, London: John Murray; Figure taken from http://keywordsuggest.org/gallery/738961.html; Based on Adult Obesity Facts, Overweight & Obesity. Retrieved from https://www.cdc.gov/obesity/data/adult.html; Based on Poverty Map, The State of Poverty, Poverty USA. Copyright © 2012 United States Conference of Catholic Bishops, Washington, D.C. Used with permission. All rights reserved. Please visit our website at www.povertyusa.org. Retrieved from http://www.povertyusa.org/the-state-of-poverty/poverty-map-state/#; Brownell, K. D. & Campos, P. (2007, September 21). Culture Matters in the Obesity Debate. Los Angeles Times. Retrieved from: http://www.latimes.com/la%20op%20dustup21sep21%20story.html; Jones, D. P., "Sugary Drink Sales Drop After Community Campaign," UConn Today, 6 March 2017. Copyright (2017). Robert Wood Johnson Foundation. Used with permission from the Robert Wood Johnson Foundation; Rudd Center for Food Policy and Obesity; Gina Kolata, "After 'The Biggest Loser,' Their Bodies Fought to Regain Weight," The New York Times, May 2, 2015; Dweck, C. S. (2000). Self theories: Their role in motivation, personality, and development. Psychology Press.

Chapter 11

Data from http://www.norc.org/PDFs/sexmoralfinal_06%2021_FINAL.PDF; Based on Kristoffer Magnusson (2014). Interpreting Cohen's d effect size: an interactive visualization. Psychologist. Retrieved from http://rpsychologist.com/d3/cohend; Based on Types of Human Memory: Diagram by Luke Mastin; Barriers and Bias: The Status of Women in Leadership. What Is the Gender Leadership Gap? http://www.aauw.org/research/barriers and bias; Kushner, H. I. (2011). Cesare Lombroso and the pathology of left-handedness. The Lancet, 377(9760), 118–119; American Psychological Association, 2009; Driscoll, E.V. (2008). Bisexual Species: Unorthodox Sex in the Animal Kingdom. Scientific American. 19, 68–73; Data from The Global Divide on Homosexuality: Greater Acceptance in More Secular and Affluent Countries, Global Attitudes & Trends, PEW Research Center. Retrieved from http://www.pewglobal.org/2013/06/04/the global divide on homosexuality; Based on Lydia Saad, "U.S. Acceptance of Gay/Lesbian Relations Is the New Normal," Gallup News, May 14, 2012; Based on The Lowdown on How to Prevent STDs. Centers for Disease Control and Prevention. Retrieved from https://www.cdc.gov/std/prevention/lowdown/lowdown text only.htm; Reprinted from World Health Organization. (2006). Defining sexual health: report of a technical consultation on sexual health, 28–31 January 2002, Geneva. World Health Organization; Based on Lydia Saad, "U.S. Acceptance of Gay/Lesbian Relations Is the New Normal," Gallup News, May 14, 2012; Based on Sexually Transmitted Diseases, ACT for Youth Center of Excellence. Retrieved from http://www.actforyouth.net/sexual_health/behaviors/std.cfm; Zurbriggen, E. L. et al. (2010) Report of the APA Task Force on the Sexualization of Girls. American Psychological Association; Based on Meyer, D. E., & Schvaneveldt, R. W. (1971). Facilitation in recognizing pairs of words: Evidence of a dependence between retrieval operations. Journal of Experimental Psychology, 90, 227–234; Based on Mary Nell Trautner and Erin Hatton, "Gender, Sexualization, and Rolling Stone," Sociological Images, December 30, 2011.

Chapter 12

Based on Healthy Body, Healthy Mind TV series. Information Television Network; Selye, H. (1973). The Evolution of the Stress Concept: The originator of the concept traces its development from the discovery in 1936 of the alarm reaction to modern therapeutic applications of syntoxic and catatoxic hormones. American Scientist, 692–699; Based on Hargrove, M. Blake, Wendy S Becker & Debra F. Hargrove (2015), "The HRD Eustress Model: Generating Positive Stress with Challenging Work," Human Resource Development Review, vol. 14, no. 46, 279–298; Based on Smaith, S. L., Choueiti, M., Prescott, A., & Pieper, K. (2013), "Gender roles & occupations: A look at character attributes and job-related aspirations in film and television," Geena Davis Institute on Gender and Media. Retrieved from https://seejane.org/wp-content/uploads/full-study-gender-roles-and-occupations-v2.pdf; Data from Woolf, S. H. et al, "How are income and wealth linked to health and longevity?." The Urban Institute, 13 April 2015; Based on Koch, M. W., Bjerregaard, P., & Curtis, C. (2004). Acculturation and mental health empirical verification of JW Berry's model of acculturative stress. International journal of circumpolar health, 63, 371–376; Based on Stressed spelled backwards is desserts! – via chibird.tumblr.com; Based on Stressed spelled backwards is desserts! – via chibird.tumblr.com; Based on © 2000 Shannon Burns. www.shannonburns.com; Based on American Psychological Association. (2013). Stress and exercise. Retrieved October 23, 2017, from http://www.apa.org/news/press/releases/stress/2013/exercise.aspx; Based on http://www.savvyrealestateinvestor.com/glass half empty half full spending time/; Based on Koenig, H. G. (2012). Religion, spirituality, and health: The research and clinical implications. ISRN Psychiatry, 2012, 1–33; Data from Monica Anderson, "The Demographics of Device Ownership," Technology Device Ownership, Pew Research Center, 29 October 2015.

Chapter 13

Jones, E. E. (1998). Major Developments in Five Decades of Social Psychology. In D. T. Gilbert, S. T. Fiske, & G. Lindzey (Eds.), The Handbook of Social Psychology (4th ed., Vol. 1, pp. 3). Boston, MA: McGraw Hill; Rosenberg, S. et al. (1968) A multidimensional approach to the structure of personality impressions. J. Pers. Soc. Psychol. 9, 283–294; Jones, E.E. & Nisbett, R. (1971). The actor and the observer: Divergent perceptions of the causes of behavior. In E.E. Jones et al. (Eds.) Attribution: Perceiving the causes of behavior, (79 94). Morristown, NJ: General Learning Press; Gawronski, B. & Bodenhausen, G.V. (2011). The associative propositional evaluation model: Theory, evidence, and open questions. In M.P. Zanna & J.M. Olsen (Eds.), Advances in experimental social psychology, Volume 44 (59–127). San Diego, CA: Elsevier; Hahn, A., Judd, C.M., Hirsh, H.K., & Blair, I.V. (2014). Awareness of implicit attitudes. Journal of Experimental Psychology, 143(3), 136–1392; Lieber, C. (January 6, 2014) Why is CrossFit So Popular Right Now?. Fitness week 2014, Racked; Brochu, P. M., & Esses, V. M. (2011). "What's in a name? The effects of the labels "fat" versus "overweight" on weight bias." Journal of Applied Social Psychology, 41, 1981–2008; Lewis, D.O., Pincus, J.H., Feldman, M., Jackson, L., & Bard, B. (1986). Psychiatric, neurological, and psychoeducational characteristics of 15 death row inmates in the United States. American Journal of Psychiatry, 143, 838–845.; Pavlov et al., 2011; Cohen, D., Nisbett, R.E., Bowdle, B.R., Schwarz, N. (1996). "Insult, aggression, and the southern culture of honor: "An experimental ethnography." Journal of Personality and Social Psychology, 70, 945–960; Data from Online Dating Statistics. http://www.statisticbrain.com/online dating statistics; 71: Bair Merritt, M. H. (2010). "Intimate partner violence." Pediatrics in review, 31(4), 145–150; Bob Sullivan, "Cyberbullying Newest Threat to Kids". NBC News. August 9, 2006.

Chapter 14

Freud, S. (1961). New introductory lectures on psychoanalysis (Vol. 2). New York: WW Norton & Company; istock. Inc.; Based on Cattell, R. B. (1945). The principal trait clusters for describing personality. Psychological Bulletin, 42(3), 129–161; 641: Based on Cattell, H. E. P., & Mead, A. D. (2008). The sixteen personality factor questionnaire (16PF). The SAGE Handbook of Personality Theory and Assessment, 2, 135–159; Based on Eysenck, S. B., & Eysenck, H. J. (1964). An improved short questionnaire for the measurement of extraversion and neuroticism. Life Sciences, 3(10), 1103–1109; Information from Costa, P. T., & McCrae, R. R. (1992). Revised NEO Personality Inventory (NEO PI R) and NEO Five Factor Inventory (NEOFFI) professional manual. Odessa, FL: Psychological Assessment Resources; T urkheimer, E., Pettersson, E., & Horn, E. E. (2014). A phenotypic null hypothesis for the genetics of personality. Annual Review of Psychology, 65, 515–540. doi: 10.1146/annurev-psych-113011-143752; Based on Schiffer, B., Müller, B. W., Scherbaum, N., Hodgins, S., Forsting, M., Wiltfang, J., Leygraf, N. (2011). Disentangling structural brain alterations associated with violent behavior from those associated with substance use disorders. Archives of General Psychiatry, 68(10), 1039–1049.

Chapter 15

Joyce Beaulieu D., Sulkowski M.L. (2016) The Diagnostic and Statistical Manual of Mental Disorders: Fifth Edition (DSM 5) Model of Impairment. In: Goldstein S., Naglieri J. (eds) Assessing Impairment. Springer, Boston, MA; Campbell, R. D., & Long, L. A. (2014). Culture as a social determinant of mental and behavioral health: A look at culturally shaped beliefs and their impact on help seeking behaviors and service use patterns of black Americans with depression. Best Practices in Mental Health: An International Journal, 10(2), 48–62; Dickens, Charles. (1873) Works of Charles Dickens: Dombey and son, Volume 10 of Works of Charles Dickens; American Psychiatric Association (2013). Diagnostic and Statistical Manual of Mental Disorders (DSM 5®), 5th Edition. Washington, Londres: American Psychiatric Association; Gallo JJ, Rabins PV. (1999). Depression Without Sadness: Alternative Presentations of Depression in Late Life. American Family of Physician, 60(3):820–826; Based on https://www.afsp.org/understanding suicide/facts and figures; United States. Public Health Service (1999). The Surgeon General's call to action to prevent suicide. Washington, DC: Dept. of Health and Human Services, U.S Public Health Service; Seligman, M.E.P., et.al. (1993). Learned Helplessness: A Theory for the Age of Personal Control. New York: Oxford University Press; Dingemans, Alexandra & J Bruna, M & Van Furth, Eric. (2002). Binge eating disorder: A review. International journal of obesity and related metabolic disorders: journal of the International. Association for the Study of Obesity, 26. 299 307. 10.1038/sj.ijo.0801949; American Psychiatric Association (2013). Diagnostic and Statistical Manual of Mental Disorders (DSM 5®), 5th Edition. Washington, Londres: American Psychiatric Association; MJ Dorahy, et al. (2014). Dissociative identity disorder: An empirical overview. Australian & New Zealand Journal of Psychiatry, 48(5): 402–417; Top 10 Pharmaceutical Companies 2017, IgeaHub. Retrieved from https://igeahub.com/2017/03/14/top 10 pharmaceutical companies 2017.

Chapter 16

Andrews, J., Briggs, A., Porter, R., Tucker, P., & Waddington, K. (2013). The history of Bethlem. New York, NY: Routledge; Data from Statisticians, B. J. S. (2006). Mental Health Problems of Prison and Jail Inmates. Mental Health, 101, 1. Washington, DC: U.S. Dept. of Justice, Office of Justice Programs, Bureau of Justice Statistics. Table 1; Based on Brown, H. (2013). Looking for Evidence That Therapy Works. The New York Times. Image by Lars Leetaru; Shedler, J. (2012). The efficacy of psychodynamic psychotherapy. In R.A. Levy, S. Ablon, & H. Kachele (Eds.), Psychodynamic Psychotherapy Research: Evidence Based Practice and Practice Based Evidence, (9 25). New York, NY: Springer Publishing; Rogers, C. R. (1961). On becoming a person: A therapist's view of psychotherapy. Boston, MA: Houghton Mifflin; Danae Hudson and Brooke Wisenhunt; Based on Behavior Contract: Tweens and Teens. Behavior Contracts, Kid Pointz; Based on Beck, A.T. (1979). Cognitive Therapy of Depression Guilford clinical psychology and psychotherapy series. New York: The Guilford Press; Beck, A. T., "Depression: Clinical, Experimental, and Theoretical Aspects," University of Pennsylvania Press, 1967; Based on Homa, J. (2013). What is CBT?. Adult Psychology. Balance Psychology. Retrieved from http://balancepsychology.com.au/what is cbt/; Based on The Art of Medicine (2015). Basics of Pharmacology I – Characteristics of Drugs. PHARMACOLOGY Introduction to Pharmacology I – Characteristics of Drugs. The Art of Medicine. Retrieved from https://theartofmed.wordpress.com/2015/05/28/introduction to pharmacology i characteristics of drugs/; Based on Lattimore, K. et.al. (2005). Selective Serotonin Reuptake Inhibitor (SSRI) Use during Pregnancy and Effects on the Fetus and Newborn: A Meta-Analysis. Journal of Perinatology 25, 595–604.; News24. (2001, August 6). Rosie O'Donnell breaks silence on her depression. News24. Retrieved from http://www.news24.com/xArchive/Archive/Rosie ODonnell breaks silence on her depression 20010805; Based on dos Santos, A. jr.et.al. (2013). Twenty years of electroconvulsive therapy in a psychiatric unit at a university general hospital. Trends in Psychiatry and Psychotherapy, 35(3). ISSN 2237 6089; Yalom, I. D. (1995). The theory and practice of group psychotherapy. New York, NY: Basic Books; Benson, L. A., McGinn, M. M., & Christensen, A. (2012). Common principles of couple therapy. Behavior therapy, 43(1), 25–35; Nami Multicultural Action Center. "Facts about Stigma and Mental Illness in Diverse Communities." Home Page. National Alliance on Mental Illness, n.d. Web. 5 June 2015; Based on Pescosolido, B. A. (2013). The Public Stigma of Mental Illness What Do We Think; What Do We Know; What Can We Prove?. Journal of health and social behavior, 54(1), 1–21; Data from Laska, K. M., et.al. (2014). Expanding the lens of evidence-based practice in psychotherapy: a common factors perspective. Psychotherapy, 51(4): 467–81; APA Presidential Task Force on Evidence-Based Practice. (2006). Evidence-based practice in psychology. American Psychologist, 61, 271–285; Based on Best antidepressant for anxiety according to our readers (2010). Readers reveal the therapists and drugs that helped. Consumer Reports; Based on Haynes, L., et.al. (2012). Test, Learn, Adapt: Developing Public Policy with Randomised Controlled Trials| Cabinet Office; Based on Andersson, G. et.al.(2014). Guided Internet-based vs. face-to-face cognitive behavior therapy for psychiatric and somatic disorders: a systematic review and meta-analysis. World Psychiatry, 13(3): 288–295; Black & African American Communities and Mental Health. Mental Health America. Retrieved from http://www.mental-healthamerica.net/african-american-mental-health; Based on Dittman, M. (2004). What you need to know to get licensed. American Psychological Association. Retrieved from http://www.apa.org/gradpsych/2004/01/get-licensed.aspx.

Mental Illness What Do We Think; What Do We Know; What Can We Prove?. Journal of health and social behavior, 54(1), 1–21; Data from Laska, K. M., et.al. (2014). Expanding the lens of evidence based practice in psychotherapy: a common factors perspective. Psychotherapy, 51(4): 467–81; APA Presidential Task Force on Evidence Based Practice. (2006). Evidence based practice in psychology. American Psychologist, 61, 271–285; Based on Best antidepressant for anxiety according to our readers (2010). Readers reveal the therapists and drugs that helped. Consumer Reports; Danae Hudson and Brooke Wisenhunt; Based on Haynes, L., et.al. (2012). Test, Learn, Adapt: Developing Public Policy with Randomised Controlled Trials| Cabinet Office; Based on Andersson, G. et.al.(2014). Guided Internet based vs. face to face cognitive behavior therapy for psychiatric and somatic disorders: a systematic review and meta analysis. World

Psychiatry, 13(3): 288–295; Black & African American Communities and Mental Health. Mental Health America. Retrieved from http://www.mentalhealthamerica.net/african american mental health; Ethical Principles of Psychologists and Code of Conduct (2010). American Psychological Association; Based on Dittman, M. (2004). What you need to know to get licensed. American Psychological Association. Retrieved from http://www.apa.org/gradpsych/2004/01/get-licensed.aspx; State Mental Health Cuts: The Continuing Crisis. National Alliance on Mental Illness, November, 2011.

Chapter AIE

Hiramatsu, L., and T. Garland, Jr. 2016. Nature or nurture? Heritability in the classroom. Physiological and Biochemical Zoology 89: 457–461.

Photo Credits

Chapter 1

007: INTERFOTO/Alamy Stock Photo; 009: Everett Collection Historical/Alamy Stock Photo; 009: Bettmann/Getty Images; 010: George Rinhart/Getty Images; 010: Michael Rougier/Getty Image; 020: Biosphoto/Superstock; 021: ibreakstock/Shutterstock; 022: Kayte Deioma/PhotoEdit; 022: Hero Images Inc./Alamy Stock Photo; 022: mrfiza/Shutterstock; 027: Thompson Geoff/Cartoonstock; 029: New York Daily News/Getty Images; 031: Mike Baldwin/CartoonStock; 035: RETRACTED: Ileal-lymphoid-nodular hyperplasia, non-specific colitis, and pervasive developmental disorder in children Wakefield, AJ et al. The Lancet, Volume 351, Issue 9103, 637–641; 037: National Archives.

Chapter 2

044: agsandrew/Shutterstock; 044: MELBA PHOTO AGENCY/Alamy Stock Photo; 046: ryzhov/123RF; 052: Vladimir; salman/Shutterstock; 060: Danae Hudson; 061: BSIP SA/Alamy Stock Photo; 061: Science Source; 062: Hank Morgan/Science Source; 062: James King-Holmes/Henry Luckhoo/Science Source; 062: Henry Westheim Photography/Alamy Stock Photo: 062: Science Source; 062: Hong xia/Shutterstock; 062: Science Source; 065: 4X5 Collection/SuperStock; 067: pathdoc/Shutterstock; 072: SPL/Science Source; 072: Andrey Popov/Shutterstock; 072: Image Source Plus/Alamy Stock Photo; 076: molekuul.be/Shutterstock; 076: DGL Images/Shutterstock; 079: Myrleen Pearson/Alamy Stock Photo; 079: DreamPictures/Getty Images; 083: Living Art Enterprises/Science Source.

Chapter 3

092: Xavier ROSSI/Gamma-Rapho/Getty Images); 093: Mark Parisi/Off the mark cartoons' 094: Science Library/Alamy Stock Photo; 108: Newscom; 108: diskoVisnja/Shutterstock; 110: S. Ishihara; 111: Paul Fearn/Alamy Stock Photo; 115: Brian A Jackson/Shutterstock; 115: Andreas Altenburger/Alamy Stock Photo; 118: inewfoto/Shutterstock; 121: CartoonStock; 123: LightField Studios/Alamy Stock Photo; 125: Mattias Lindberg/Shutterstock; 125: Mattias Lindberg/Shutterstock; 126: Chris Madden/Alamy Stock Photo; 129: Danita Delimont/Getty Images; 131: Mark Richard/PhotoEdit; 132: Anton Petrus/Getty Images; 138: Allegra Boverman/Associated Press.

Chapter 4

144: Bloomicon/Shutterstock; 145: Pool/Getty Images; 146: vgajic/Getty Images; 149: NCBI (National Center for Biotechnology Information); 149: Trafton Drew, Melissa L. H. Vo, and Jeremy M. Wolfe; 151: BSIP SA/Alamy Stock Photo; 161: Mike Baldwin/Cartoonstock; 169: Universal History Archive/Getty Images; 171: PHOVOIR/Alamy Stock Photo; 172: Center for Disease Control and Prevention; 173: Vaclav Volrab/Shutterstock; 174: Chanus/Shutterstock; 178: GARO/PHANIE/Getty Images; 178: ZUMA Press Inc/Alamy Stock Photo; 180: John Mitchell/Alamy Stock Photo.

Chapter 5

187: Bloomicon/Shutterstock; 189: Andrey_Popov/Shutterstock; 191: John B. Watson; 199: Radius Images/Alamy Stock Photo; 207: brackish_nz/Shutterstock; 208: BSIP SA/Alamy Stock Photo; 211: Rosanne Tackaberry/Alamy Stock Photo; 211: Noam Armonn/Shutterstock; 214: 3LH/SuperStock; 214: 3LH/SuperStock; 217: David Grossman/Alamy Stock Photo; 219: Greenland/Shutterstock; 220: PhotoAlto/Alamy Stock Photo.

Chapter 6

228: Christopher Lane/Getty Images; 232: ktsdesign/Shutterstock; 234: Westend61 GmbH/Alamy Stock Photo; 234: Mike Gruhn/Cartoonstock; 247: Marc Tielemans/Alamy Stock Photo; 252: NASA Archive/Alamy Stock Photo; 266: National Institutes of Health; 269: imageBROKER/Alamy Stock Photo; 272: Stock-Asso/Shutterstock; 272: Kong Hon Loh/Alamy Stock Photo; 274: Mikael Karlsson/Alamy Stock Photo.

Chapter 7

281: Bloomicon/Shutterstock; 286: Barry Morgan/Alamy Stock Photo; 288: Scanrail1/Shutterstock; 293: Tetra Images/Alamy Stock Photo; 293: Blend Images/Alamy Stock Photo; 293: Andriy Popov/Alamy Stock Photo; 300: PA Images/Alamy Stock Photo; 304: Cartoonstock; 306: Gasbergen Cartoons; 310: Tim Cordel/Cartoonstock; 311: Everett Collection Historical/Alamy Stock Photo; 311: |Dpa picture alliance/Alamy Stock Photo; 313: Grizelda/Cartoonstock; 315: Paul Kingsley/Alamy Stock Photo; 320: Darwin, Charles. (1871). The Descent of Man. London: Charles Murray; 320: Washburn,M.F/MacMillan; 320: Frans Lanting Studio/Alamy Stock Photo; 320: Rick Friedman/Getty Images; 320: Irina No/Shutterstock; 320:Jonathan Crystal; 320: ragnarocks/123RF; 323: Magic Mine/Shutterstock; 323: imageBROKER/Alamy Stock Photo; 323: Redmond Durrell/Alamy Stock Photo; 323: WILDLIFE GmbH/Alamy Stock Photo; 323: Elsevier.

Chapter 8

332: Cartoonstock; 341: Everett Collection Historical/Alamy Stock Photo; 342: National Park Service. Statue of Liberty National Monument; 343: Bettmann/Contributo/Getty Images; 344: Shutterstock; 349: Jerome M. Sattler; 356: Mike Abrahams/Alamy Stock Photo; 367: Serhii Kucher/123rf.

Chapter 9

377: Bloomicon/Shutterstock; 380: naf/Cartoonstock; 384: Jiang Dao Hua/Shutterstock; 385: Cartoon Stock; 385: ANDRZEJ WOJCICKI/Getty Images; 385: Dr G. Moscoso/Science Source; 385: Arno Massee/Science Source; 386: David Wall/Alamy Stock Photo; 386: Dmitry Polonskiy/Shutterstock; 392: Nina Leen/Getty Images; 407: National Institute on Aging; 412: Monkey Business Images. Shutterstock; 417: Cathy Wilcox.

Chapter 10

428: Bloomicon/Shutterstock; 430: Marcio Jose Bastos Silva/Shutterstock; 434: Oak Ridge National Laboratory; 438: Rawpixel.com/Shutterstock; 448: Laura Hall/Global Integration; 451: Dpa Picture Alliance/Alamy Stock Photo; 451: US Air Force Photo/Alamy Stock Photo; 451: NMUIM/Alamy Stock Photo; 452: Science History Images/Alamy Stock Photo; 455: USDA; 456: Phanie/Alamy Stock Photo; 456Ursu Florina/Alamy Stock Photo.

Chapter 11

468: Bloomicon/Shutterstock; 469: Thomson Reuters; 470: Everett Collection Historical/Alamy Stock Photo; 474: MediaFuzeBox/Shutterstock; 474: Dixson, Barnaby & Brooks, Robert. (2013). The role of facial hair in women's perceptions of men's attractiveness, health, masculinity and parenting abilities. Evolution and Human Behavior. 34. 236–241. 10.1016/j.evolhumbehav.2013.02.003; 475: Maciej Dakowicz/Alamy Stock Photo; 476: Losevsky Pavel/Alamy Stock Photo; 476: D. Hurst/Stockimo/Alamy Stock Photo; 476: UrbanZone/Alamy Stock Photo; 476: Sam Dao/Alamy Stock Photo; 477: Zero Creatives/Getty Images; 499: Hemis/Alamy Stock Photo; 507: DreamPictures/GettyImages; 508: travelstock.ca/Alamy Stock Photo; 512: Starr, C. R., & Ferguson, G. M. (2012). Sexy dolls, sexy grade-schoolers? Media & maternal influences on young girls' self-sexualization. Sex Roles, 67(7–8), 463–476.

Chapter 12

520: Bloomicon/Shutterstock; 521: Westend61/GettyImages; 521: JBphotoeditorial/Alamy Stock Photo; 522: MARK RALSTON/AFP/Getty Images; 529: Cultura Creative (RF)/Alamy Stock Photo; 535: Marekuliasz/Shutterstock; 546: javi_indy/Shutterstock; 550: Phanie/Alamy Stock Photo; 550: vsop/Shutterstock; 550: Dave Crombeen/Alamy Stock Photo; 550: guruXOX/Shutterstock; 554: antoniodiaz/Shutterstock.

Chapter 13

561: Bloomicon/Shutterstock; 562: FEMA/Alamy Stock Photo; 562: Mario Tama/Getty Images; 565: Emilio Ereza/Alamy Stock Photo; 569: ZUMA Press, Inc./Alamy Stock Photo; 569: ZUMA Press, Inc./Alamy Stock Photo572: Randy Glasbergen; 575: Matej Kastelic/Shutterstock; 575: Art Directors & TRIP/Alamy Stock Photo; 575: brackish_nz/Shutterstock; 576: Barry Diomede/Alamy Stock Photo; 577: DigitalVision/Getty Photo; 579: Gado Images/Alamy Stock Photo; 579: Alexandra Milgram; 581: Dan Dalton/Getty Images; 582: Foap AB/Alamy Stock Photo; 583: Robert Davis/Alamy Stock Photo; 583: David Goldman/AP Images; 583: Lonely Planet Image/Getty Images; 584: Philip G. Zimbardo, Inc.; 585: PACIFIC PRESS/Alamy Stock Photo; 587: Richard Lautens/Contributor; 588: Stephen Barnes/Northern Ireland Loyalists/Alamy Stock Photo; 589: Kane513/Shutterstock; 595: Paul Pickard/Alamy Stock Photo; 596: Wartenberg/Picture Press/Getty Images

Chapter 14

623: Bloomicon/Shutterstock; 625: Shutterstock; 626: Based on Freud, S. (1978). Basic works of Sigmund Freud (J. Strachey Ed.): Franklin Library; 631: GL Archive/Alamy Stock Photo; 639: Shutterstock; 658: Kovalchuk Oleksandr/Shutterstock; 659: PhotoEdit; 666: 3D_Creations/Shutterstock.

Chapter 15

676: MELBA PHOTO AGENCY/Alamy Stock Photo; 683: Lewis Williams/Alamy Stock Photo; 683: 123RF; 688: Danae Hudson; 688: AF archive/Alamy Stock Photo; 702: United Archives GmbH/Alamy Stock Photo; 707: National Library of Medicine; 707: National Library of Medicine.

Chapter 16

721: Bloomicon/Shutterstock; 723: Photo by Daily Mirror/Mirrorpix/Mirrorpix via Getty Images; 739: MIGUEL MEDINA/AFP/Getty Images; 750: Monkey Business Images/Shutterstock; 751: Steve Skjold/Alamy Stock Photo.

Name Index

Subject Index